Dedicated to My Guru
Dr. J.D. Varma
with Reverence and Affection

Based Mainly on UGC Model Curriculum

MACROECONOMICS

THEORY AND POLICY

(For Students of Economics, Commerce, Business Management and Competitive Examinations)

ADVANCED ANALYSIS OF

- Income and Employment Determination
- Theories of Consumption Function and Investment
- Monetary Demand & Supply
- Money, Prices and Inflation
- Theories of Business Cycles and Stabilisation Policies
- New Classical Macroeconomics based on Rational Expectations
- New Keynesian Economics
- Government Budget Constraint, Fiscal Policy and Fiscal Deficit
- Open Economy Macroeconomics : Balance of Payments Foreign Exchange Rate and International Economic Linkages
- Nature of Unemployment and Development Strategies for Labour-Surplus Developing Countries.
- Theories of Economic Growth : Harrod-Domar Model; Neoclassical Growth Theory; New Theory of Growth, and Lewis' Model of a Labour-Surplus Economy

Dr. H.L. AHUJA
M.A. Ph.D. (DSE)
Formerly, Senior Reader
Department of Economics
Zakir Husain Delhi College
University of Delhi
Delhi

THOROUGHLY REVISED NINETEENTH EDITION

S. CHAND & COMPANY PVT. LTD.
(AN ISO 9001: 2008 COMPANY)
RAM NAGAR, NEW DELHI-110055

S. CHAND & COMPANY PVT. LTD.
(An ISO 9001 : 2008 Company)
Head Office: 7361, RAM NAGAR, NEW DELHI - 110 055
Phone: 23672080-81-82, 9899107446, 9911310888
Fax: 91-11-23677446
Shop at: **schandgroup.com**; e-mail: **info@schandgroup.com**

Branches :

AHMEDABAD : 1st Floor, Heritage, Near Gujarat Vidhyapeeth, Ashram Road, **Ahmedabad** - 380 014, Ph: 27541965, 27542369, ahmedabad@schandgroup.com

BENGALURU : No. 6, Ahuja Chambers, 1st Cross, Kumara Krupa Road, **Bengaluru** - 560 001, Ph: 22268048, 22354008, bangalore@schandgroup.com

BHOPAL : Bajaj Tower, Plot No. 2&3, Lala Lajpat Rai Colony, Raisen Road, **Bhopal** - 462 011, Ph: 4274723, 4209587. bhopal@schandgroup.com

CHANDIGARH : S.C.O. 2419-20, First Floor, Sector - 22-C (Near Aroma Hotel), **Chandigarh** -160 022, Ph: 2725443, 2725446, chandigarh@schandgroup.com

CHENNAI : No.1, Whites Road, Opposite Express Avenue, Royapettah, **Chennai** - 600014 Ph. 28410027, 28410058, chennai@schandgroup.com

COIMBATORE : 1790, Trichy Road, LGB Colony, Ramanathapuram, **Coimbatore** -6410045, Ph: 2323620, 4217136 coimbatore@schandgroup.com **(Marketing Office)**

CUTTACK : 1st Floor, Bhartia Tower, Badambadi, **Cuttack** - 753 009, Ph: 2332580; 2332581, cuttack@schandgroup.com

DEHRADUN : 1st Floor, 20, New Road, Near Dwarka Store, **Dehradun** - 248 001, Ph: 2711101, 2710861, dehradun@schandgroup.com

GUWAHATI : Dilip Commercial (Ist floor), M.N. Road, Pan Bazar, **Guwahati** - 781 001, Ph: 2738811, 2735640 guwahati@schandgroup.com

HALDWANI : Bhatt Colony, Talli Bamori, Mukhani, **Haldwani** -263139 **(Marketing Office)** Mob. 09452294584

HYDERABAD : Padma Plaza, H.No. 3-4-630, Opp. Ratna College, Narayanaguda, **Hyderabad** - 500 029, Ph: 27550194, 27550195, hyderabad@schandgroup.com

JAIPUR : 1st Floor, Nand Plaza, Hawa Sadak, Ajmer Road, **Jaipur** - 302 006, Ph: 2219175, 2219176, jaipur@schandgroup.com

JALANDHAR : Mai Hiran Gate, **Jalandhar** - 144 008, Ph: 2401630, 5000630, jalandhar@schandgroup.com

KOCHI : Kachapilly Square, Mullassery Canal Road, Ernakulam, **Kochi** - 682 011, Ph: 2378740, 2378207-08, cochin@schandgroup.com

KOLKATA : 285/J, Bipin Bihari Ganguli Street, **Kolkata** - 700 012, Ph: 22367459, 22373914, kolkata@schandgroup.com

LUCKNOW : Mahabeer Market, 25 Gwynne Road, Aminabad, **Lucknow** - 226 018, Ph: 4076971, 4026791, 4065646, 4027188, lucknow@schandgroup.com

MUMBAI : Blackie House, IInd Floor, 103/5, Walchand Hirachand Marg, Opp. G.P.O., **Mumbai** - 400 001, Ph: 22690881, 22610885, mumbai@schandgroup.com

NAGPUR : Karnal Bagh, Near Model Mill Chowk, **Nagpur** - 440 032, Ph: 2720523, 2777666 nagpur@schandgroup.com

PATNA : 104, Citicentre Ashok, Mahima Palace , Govind Mitra Road, **Patna** - 800 004, Ph: 2300489, 2302100, patna@schandgroup.com

PUNE : Sadguru Enclave, Ground floor, Survey No. 114/3, Plot no. 8 Alandi Road , Vishrantwadi **Pune** – 411015 Ph: 64017298 pune@schandgroup.com

RAIPUR : Kailash Residency, Plot No. 4B, Bottle House Road, Shankar Nagar, **Raipur** - 492 007, Ph: 2443142,Mb. : 09981200834, raipur@schandgroup.com **(Marketing Office)**

RANCHI : Shanti Deep Tower, Opp.Hotel Maharaja, Radium Road, **Ranchi**-834001 Mob. 09430246440 ranchi@schandgroup.com

SILIGURI : 122, Raja Ram Mohan Roy Road, East Vivekanandapally, P.O., Siliguri, **Siliguri**-734001, Dist., Jalpaiguri, (W.B.) Ph. 0353-2520750 **(Marketing Office)** siliguri@schandgroup.com

VISAKHAPATNAM: No. 49-54-15/53/8, Plot No. 7, 1st Floor, Opp. Radhakrishna Towers, Seethammadhara North Extn., **Visakhapatnam** - 530 013, Ph-2782609 (M) 09440100555, visakhapatnam@schandgroup.com **(Marketing Office)**

First Edition 1986
Subsequent Editions and Reprint 1988, 90, 94, 96, 98, 99, 2001, 2002, 2004 (Twice), 2006, 2007, 2008 (Twice), 2009, 2010, 2011, 2012; Nineteenth Revised Edition 2013
Reprint 2014

ISBN : 81-219-0433-1 Code : 08F 135

PRINTED IN INDIA

By Nirja Publishers & Printers Pvt. Ltd., 54/3/2, Jindal Paddy Compound, Kashipur Road, Rudrapur-263153, Uttarakhand and published by S. Chand & Company Pvt. Ltd., 7361, Ram Nagar, New Delhi -110 055.

PREFACE TO THE NINETEENTH EDITION

It is a matter of great pleasure for me to bring out the nineteenth edition of the book after one year of the publication of 18th edition. The book has been further revised in the light of UGC model Curriculum for M.A., M.Com. and B.A. (Hons.) and B.Com. (Hons.) classes of Indian Universities. In the present new edition we have made the following changes.

1. **Chapter 6 concerning consumption function has been thoroughly revised and the concept of Keynes's psychological law of consumption has been made clear and non-proportionate relationship between increases in consumption and income (i.e. falling of APC) has been explained.**
2. **Chapter 8 dealing with investment demand Tobin's Theory of investment has been critically examined.**
3. **Chapter 10 relating to AD-AS model with flexible prices, Friedman's Natural Rate Hypothesis has been discussed.**
4. **In Chapter 11 with regard to issue of wage cut to remove unemployment Keynes's effect and real balance effect (Pigou effect) has been discussed. Besides, *Insider-outsider Model* has been explained in this context.**
5. **In Chapter 13 Friedman's analysis of short-run Phillips Curve with adaptive expectations and further his view that there is trade off between inflation and unemployment only in the short run has been examined .**
6. **In Chapter 17 concerning money and its function, we have explained how the function of money as a *store of value* is adversely affected by inflation. Besides, we have clearly brought out that to describe money as a *veil* is not .correct as it plays an important role in influencing economic activity.**
7. **In Chapter 19A RBI's easy monetary policy in 2008-09 to overcome recession and economic slowdown and tightening of monetary policy by it in 2010-11, 2011-12 and 2012-13 to fight inflation has been critically examined.**
8. **Chapter 34 and its appendix dealing with balance of payments has been extensively revised and the role of capital flows to meet the current account deficit (CAD) has been explained.**
9. **In appendix to Chapter 26 on inflation we have explained how price indices of WPI and CPI are prepared for measuring the rate of inflation.**
10. **In Chapter 33A which is concerned with Fiscal Deficit and Economic Growth we explained what is the safe limit for fiscal deficit. Besides, we have explained the role of fiscal multiplier and tax buoyancy for economic growth in developing countries. Further we have explained how fiscal consolidation can be achieved by cutting unproductive Government expenditure and raising tax-GDP ratio.**
11. **We have extensively revised appendix to Chapter 39 concerning "*Saving, Investment and India's Growth Performance*' and explained why there has been a setback to India's growth story in the last two to three years.**
12. **Finally, we have made significant changes in our last chapter on Global Financial Crisis and Eurozone Debt Crisis, especially we have added the explanation of recent *Crisis in Cyprus* and its bailout by EU and IMF.**

It is worth noting that we have not only confined ourselves to mere Keynesian Macroeconomics but have also critically examined the **post-Keynesian developments in macroeconomics** such as monetarism, concepts of aggregate demand and supply with flexible prices (i.e. AD-AS model), synthesis of Classical and Keynesian theories in terms of IS-LM model, cost-push and structurallist theories of inflation, **Phillips curve** concept visualising trade-off between inflation and unemployment, post-Keynesian theories of consumption, investment and demand for money, supply-side economics, problem of stagflation, ***Lucas' New Classical Rational Expectations Theory*** and ***New Keynesian Macroeconomic Theory***. In fact, an attempt has been made to incroporate the *latest trends and tendencies* in macroeconomic analysis and policy. For this purpose some chapters have been re-written and the study of new topics has been included.

The new chapters have been added to cover new topics of macroeconomic theory. Since many universities have prescribed the study of the **theories of economic growth** in their revised syllabi, we have added the new Part VIII in this book which deals with the critical examination of **Harrod-Domar Model of Growth, Neoclassical Theory of Growth, New Growth Theory i.e., Endogenous Growth Model. Lewis Model of Development with Surplus Labour.** We have also discussed the relevance of these growth theories for the developing countries like India. Besides, a comprehensive new chapter 38 analysing **International Economic Linkages and Mundell-Fleming Model of an Open Economy with Perfect Capital Mobility** have been added. The inclusion of this chapter will enhance the understanding of the students of the impact of globalisation of the Indian economy that is currently taking place.

An important feature of this book is that it has kept in view the macroeconomic environment of the developing economies, especially the Emerging Indian economy while analysing and discussing various theories and policies of macroeconomics. It has been amazing for me to note that some authors of Textbooks of Macroeconomics, following Dr. V.K.R.V. Rao's article written in early nineteen fifties of the last century are still writing that Keynesian macroeconomic theory, especially the principles of investment multiplier and demand deficiency, are inapplicable to the developing countries like India. This is quite incorrect in the present-day context of the Indian macroeconomic environment. In the last over sixty years of economic development and structural transformation of the Indian economy, many of the concepts and theories of Keynesian macroeconomics have become relevant. Therefore, in this book we have discussed how the Keynesian theories of investment multiplier, demand constraint, investment behaviour of business class, consumption function, demand-pull inflation and Keynes' rationale for the intervention of Government through adoption of fiscal and monetary policies to revive and stabilise the economy are relevant for developing countries like India. Besides, in the eighteenth edition we added a chapter 45 in which we analysed the ***nature of unemployment and development strategies for labour-surplus developing countries***.

In view of the above changes made, the book will be useful not only for the **Honours and Postgraduate Classes of Economics and Commerce** but also of professional courses such as **MBA, CA, ICWA, Honours in Journalism and Business Economics, Engineering, Banking and of Competitive Examinations such as IAS and Allied Services, IES (Indian Economic Service).** I hope the present edition of the book will be of immense use for the students. Suggestions for further improvement of the book from the fellow teachers and students will be heartily welcomed. The author can be approached through e-Mail: drhlahuja@gmail.com.

69, Vaishali
Pitampura
Delhi—110 088

Dr. H.L. AHUJA

CONTENTS

PART I
MACROECONOMICS

PART II
POST-KEYNESIAN DEVELOPMENTS IN MACROECONOMICS

PART III

MONETARY DEMAND AND SUPPLY

PART IV
MONEY, PRICES AND INFLATION

PART V
BUSINESS CYCLES AND MACROECONOMIC POLICY

PART VI

GOVERNMENT AND THE MACROECONOMY : GOVERNMENT'S BUDGET CONSTRAINT AND FISCAL POLICY

PART VII
OPEN ECONOMY MACROECONOMICS

PART VIII
THEORIES OF ECONOMIC GROWTH

PART I

MACROECONOMICS : THEORY OF INCOME AND EMPLOYMENT

- Nature and Scope of Macroeconomics
- Circular Flow of Income and National Income Accounting
- Classical Theory of Income and Employment
- Keynes's Theory of Employment : An Outline
- Determination of National Income : Basic Two Sector Keynesian Model
- Consumption Function
- Theory of Multiplier
- Investment Demand
- Aggregate Demand - Aggregate Supply Model (with Variable Prices)
- Unemployment, Full Employment And Wage-Price Flexibility

CHAPTER 1
Nature and Scope of Macroeconomics

In the first volume of this book we have studied microeconomics which is concerned with the behaviour of individual consumers, factor owners, firms and individual industries and markets. It is through their interaction that microeconomic theory explains how prices of products and factors are determined and how resources are allocated between various products. In microeconomic theory it is assumed that full employment of resources such as labour and capital prevails and analyses how they are allocated among different products. Further, it explains whether resource allocation achieved is economically efficient. In this second volume we will study macroeconomic theory and its applications to the formulation of economic policies. In this chapter we shall briefly explain what macroeconomics is about and why the English economist J.M. Keynes laid stress on macroeconomic analysis as a separate study from microeconomic analysis. Besides, we shall explain the various issues that are studied in macroeconomics. In the end we shall briefly explain the various post-keynesian developments in macroeconomics. We shall also discuss the importance of the study of macroeconomics.

What is Macroeconomics?

Whereas microeconomics deals with the analysis of small individual units of an economy such as individual consumers, individual firms, individual industries and markets and explains how prices of products and factors are determined. On the basis of these prices microeconomics explains how resources are allocated among various products and how income distribution among factors is determined. On the other hand, *macroeconomics is concerned with the analysis of the behaviour of the economic system in totality. Thus, macroeconomics studies how the large aggregates such as total employment, national product or national income of an economy and the general price level are determined. Macroeconomics is therefore a study of aggregates. Besides, macroeconomics explains how the productive capacity and national income of the country increase over time in the long run.*

Professor Gardner Ackley makes the distinction between macroeconomics and microeconomics more clearly when he says, "macroeconomics concerns itself with such variables as the aggregate volume of the output of an economy, with the extent to which its resources are employed, with the size of the national income, with the 'general price level'. Microeconomics, on the other hand, deals with the division of total output among industries, products and firms and the allocation of resources among competing uses. It considers problem of income distribution. Its interest is in relative prices of particular goods and services."[1]

It is evident from above that the subject matter of macroeconomics is to explain what *determines the level of total economic activity* (that is, the size of the national income and employment) and fluctuations (*i.e.*, ups and downs) in it in the short run. It also explains what causes the general price level to rise and determines the rate of inflation in the economy. Besides, modern macroeconomics analyses those factors which determine the increase in productive capacity and national income in the long run. The problem of increasing productive capacity and national income over time in the long run is called the problem of *economic growth*. Thus, what determines rate of growth of an economy is also the concern of macroeconomics.

1. Gardner Ackley, *Macroeconomic Theory*, 1961, p. 4

Thus, why is national income higher today than it was in 1950? Why does rate of unemployment in a free market economy go up in a period and falls in another period? Why do some countries have high rates of inflation, while others maintain price stability? What causes alternating periods of depression and boom (generally described as business cycles)? Why should government intervene in the economy and what policy it should adopt to check inflation, control business cycles, raise level of national income, reduce unemployment and restore equilibrium in the balance of payments are some of the important questions which macroeconomics attempts to answer.

The Origin and Roots of Macroeconomics

The Great Depression. Beginning in late 1929, capitalist economies of the world experienced a severe depression which created a lot of involuntary unemployment and also a sharp fall in their GDP. This depression was caused by drastic decline in private investment. For example, in the United States in 1929, 1.5 million workers were unemployed. After four years in 1933 this unemployment of labour rose to 13 million people out of labour force of 51 million, that is, around 25 per cent of labour force became unemployed. The similar situation prevailed in Britain and other capitalist countries. This depression spurred a great deal of controversy among economists about the causes of this depression and the policies to overcome it and restore full employment. It was at this time that a noted British economist J.M. Keynes (1883-1946) challenged the view of classical economists who applied microeconomic models to explain depression and involuntary unemployment. By emphasising that the prevailing depression and large-scale involuntary unemployment was due to lack of aggregate effective demand resulting from a fall in private investment he laid the foundation of modern macroeconomics. In his theory he showed that economy was not-self-correcting and therefore there was a need for the government to intervene and take appropriate fiscal measures to restore full employment in the economy.

Classical and neoclassical economists[2] assumed that full-employment of labour and other resources always prevailed in the economy and concentrated mainly upon explaining how the resources were allocated to the production of various goods and services and how the relative prices of products and factors were determined. It is mainly because of their full-employment assumption that they concentrated on the problem of determination of prices, outputs and resource employment in the individual industries. They believed that if there were departures from full employment, a free market economy would automatically work in way that would restore full employment of resources. They argued that involuntary unemployment and underutilisation of the productive capacity could not occur in capitalist economies if market mechanism were allowed to work freely without any interference by the trade unions. Thus, according to them, even when deficiency of aggregate demand arises as it happens during the times of recession or depression, prices and wages would change in such a way that employment, output and national income would not decline. The belief of classical economists that full-employment of labour and capital stock will always exist was based on *Say's Law of Markets*. According to Say's Law, *supply creates its own demand* and therefore, the problem of lack of demand for supply of goods and services does not arise. Factors which produce goods and services for supply in the market get rewards (wages, interest and rent) for their contributions to the production of goods and services produced. Thus, incomes earned become expenditure made on goods and services. Therefore, the problem of deficiency of demand does not arise. They thus could not provide adequate explanation of the occurrence of huge unemployment that prevailed during depression of 1930s in the capitalist economies. What is worse, the classical economists, particularly A.C. Pigou tried to apply the economic laws that hold good in the case of an individual industry to the case of the behaviour of the whole economic system and macroeconomic variables.

However, the classical model was not found to be true as the depression appeared to be not self-

2. Note that Keynes called all those economists who preceded him as classical economists. Thus, neoclassical economists are included in the term classical economists as used by Keynes.

correcting. During the Great Depression of 1930s unemployed remained at a high level for nearly 10 years. At that time, an eminent British economist A.C. Pigou asserted that involuntary unemployment existing at the time of depression in the 1930s was due to the obstacles put up by trade unions and government and further that this involuntary unemployment could be eliminated and employment expanded by cutting down the wages. A noted British economist J.M. Keynes challenged this classical viewpoint during the early nineteen thirties when severe depression took place in the capitalist countries such as Britain and the U.S.A. While the cut in wages may expand employment in an individual industry, the reduction in wages throughout the economy will result in fall in incomes of the working classes and is ikely to cause decrease in the level of aggregate demand. The fall in aggregate demand will tend to lower the level of employment rather than expand it.

Though there were pre-Keynesian theories of business cycles and the general price level that were "macro" in nature, but it was J.M. Keynes, an eminent British economist, who laid stress on macroeconomic analysis and put forward a general theory of income and employment in his revolutionary book, "*A General Theory of Employment, Interest and Money*" published in 1936. Keynes' theory made a genuine break from the classical and neo-classical economics and produced such a fundamental and drastic change in economic thinking that his macroeconomic analysis has earned the names '*Keynesian Revolution*' and '*New Economics*'. Keynes in his analysis made a frontal attack on the classical '*Say's Law of Markets*' which was the basis of full-employment assumption of classical view that involuntary unemployment could not prevail in a free private enterprise economy. He showed how the equilibrium level of national income and employment was determined by aggregate demand and aggregate supply and further that due to lack of aggregate effective demand equilibrium level of income and employment might well be established at far less than full-employment level in a free-market capitalist economy. This causes involuntary unemployment of labour on the one hand and excess productive capacity (*i.e.* under-utilisation of the existing capital stock) on the other. His macroeconomic model reveals how consumption function, investment function, liquidity preference function, conceived in aggregate terms, interact to determine the level of national income and employment.

Further, the fall in employment in the Great Depression of 1930s and emergence of huge unemployment of labour which in some countries went up to 25 per cent of labour force gives unmistakable evidence that aggregate demand is not always large enough to ensure full-employment of labour and full use of productive capacity.

After Keynes, there has been significant developments in macroeconomics. Apart from what determines the level of employment of labour and use of productive capacity, modern macroeconomics is concerned with many more issues such as the problems of inflation, economic growth, business cycles, stagflation and the balance of payments and the exchange rate. The analysis of these six major issues describes the scope of macroeconomics. We shall be explaining all these six issues of macroeconomics in detail in later chapters. Here we shall explain only briefly what these problems are.

THE MAJOR ISSUES AND CONCERNS OF MACROECONOMICS

As explained above, Keynes in his book '*Theory of Employment, Interest and Money*' explained how levels of income and employment were determined in a free market economy. During the Second World War period, he extended his macro-theory to explain inflation. However, after Keynes, economists have further developed and extended macroeconomics. We briefly explain below tha main issues of macroeconomics.

Employment and Unemployment. The first major issue in macroeconomics is to explain what determines the level of employment and national income in an economy and therefore what causes involuntary unemployment. Why is level of national income and employment very low in times of depression as in 1930s in various capitalist countries of the world. This will explain the cause of huge unemployment that emerged in these countries. As mentioned above, classical economists denied that there could be involuntary unemployment of labour and other resources for a long time. They thought that with changes in wages and prices, unemployment would be automatically removed and full employment established. But this did not appear to be so at the time of depression in the thirties and after. Keynes explained that level of employment and national income is determined by aggregate demand and aggregate supply. With aggregate supply curve remaining unchanged in the short run, it is the deficiency of aggregate demand that cause underemployment equilibrium with the appearance of involuntary unemployment. According to him, it is the changes in private investment that causes fluctuations in aggregate demand and is therefore, responsible for the problems of cyclical unemployment. We will explain Keynes's theory of employment and income and its various aspects in detail in the subsequent chapters.

Determination of National Income (or GNP). National income is the value of all final goods and services produced in a country in a year. Level of national income or what is called Gross National Product (GNP) shows the performance of the economy in a year and determines the *overall living standards of the people* of a country. The higher the per capita national income, the greater the amounts of goods and services available for consumption per individual on an average. Given the technology used for production, the magnitude of employment goes hand-in-hand with the change in size of national income. The fluctuations in economic activity primarily manifest themselves in changes in national income and employment. When all resources in an economy are being employed for production, the size of national income generated is called *potential GNP* or full-employment level of income. In a free market economy, the changes in aggregate demand cause divergence of national income from the level of potential GNP in the short run.

It is important to note that in a developing country such as India it is not a mere level of aggregate demand that determines national income. In it the *supply-side* factors such as availability of physical capital, human capital (skills and education of people), material resources, the technology used for production in agricultures and industries play a more important role in the determination of national income.

General Price Level and Inflation. Another macroeconomic issue is to explain the problem of inflation. Inflation has been a major problem faced by both the developed and developing countries in the last fifty years. Classical economists thought that it was the quantity of money in the economy that determined the general price level in the economy and, according to them, rate of inflation depended on the growth of money supply in the economy. Keynes criticised the `*Quantity Theory of Money*' and showed that expansion in money supply did not always lead to inflation or rise in price level. Keynes who before the Second World War explained that involuntary unemployment and depression were due to the deficiency of aggregate demand, during the war period when prices rose very high he explained in a booklet '*How to Pay for War*' that just as unemployment and depression were caused by the deficiency of aggregate demand, inflation was due to the excessive aggregate demand. Thus, Keynes put forward what is now called *demand-pull theory of inflation*. After Keynes, theory of inflation has been further developed and many theories of inflation depending upon various causes have been put forward. *Cost-push* and *structuralist* theories of inflation have been put forward. To analyse the problem of inflation is an important issue of macroeconomics.

Business Cycles. Throughout history market economies have experienced what are called business cycles. Business cycles refer to fluctuations in output and employment with alternating periods of boom and recession. In boom periods both output and employment are at high levels, whereas in recession periods both output and employment fall and as a consequence large unemployment come to exist in the economy. When these recessions are extremely severe, they are called depressions.

What are the causes of these business cycles or ups and downs in market economies is an important macroeconomic issue which has been highly controversial. The objective of macroeconomic policy is to achieve economic stability with equilibrium at full employment level of output and income. We shall discuss various theories of business cycles and also monetary and fiscal policies to control business cycles and achieve economic stability.

Stagflation. How to control business cycles and achieve economic stability has been a very difficult problem for the economies to solve ? But during the decade of 1970s and in some later times in the subsequent decades market economies have experienced a still more intricate problem which has been described as stagflation. While in business cycles, recession or depression is accompanied by high unemployment and falling prices, *in the seventies recession or stagnation was accompanied by not only high unemployment but also rapid inflation.* Since in that period high unemployment and recession (or stagnation) co-existed with high inflation, this problem was given the name stagflation. This stagflation could not be explained with the Keynesian theory which focuses on the demand side. Therefore, a new economic thought which is called *Supply-side Economics* emerged which explained stagflation by laying stress on the supply-side of economic activity. Stagflation is an important issue of modern macroeconomics. Stagflation along with supply-side economics will be explained at length in a separate chapter.

Economic Growth. Another important issue in macroeconomics is to explain what determines economic growth in a country. Economic growth means *sustained* increase in national income (GNP) or per capita income over a sufficiently long period of time. Given the availability of natural resources, economic growth of a country depends on the growth of physical capital, human capital and progress in technology. The growth of all these factors requires saving and investment. The growth rate can therefore the stepped up by raising the rates of saving and investment. However, the expansion in these factors determines the increase in productive capacity. To ensure full use of the rising productive capacity aggregate to demand for output must be increasing sufficiently.

Theory of economic growth or what is simply called *growth economics* which has been recently developed a good deal is an important branch of macroeconomics. The problem of growth is a long-run problem and Keynes did not deal with it. In fact, Keynes is said to have once remarked that "in the long run we are all dead". From this remark of Keynes it should not be understood that he thought long run to be quite unimportant. By this remark he simply emphasized the importance of short-run problem of fluctuations in the level of economic acitivity (involuntary cyclical unemployment, depression). It was Harrod[3] and Domar[4] who extended the Keynesian analysis to the long-run problem of growth with stability. They laid stress on the dual role of investment—one of *income-generating*, which Keynes considered, and the second of *capacity-creating* which Keynes ignored because of his preoccupation with the short run. In view of the fact that an investment adds to the productive capacity (*i.e.*, capital stock), then if growth with stability (*i.e.*, without stagnation or inflation) is to be achieved, income or demand must be increasing at a rate large enough to ensure the full utilisation of the increasing capacity. Thus, macroeconomic models of Harrod and Domar have explained the rate of growth of income that must take place if the steady growth of the economy is to be achieved. These days growth economics has been further developed and extended a good deal and new theories of growth have been put forward by Solow, Meade, Kaldor and Joan Robinson.

It is important to note that in the context of developing countries, *economic growth* has been distinguished from *economic development*. Economic development is a more inclusive concept than economic growth. Economic development is generally understood to mean that apart from increase in national income or per capita income poverty, unemployment and inequality must also

3. R.F. Harrod, *Towards a Dynamic Economics*, (1948).
4. E.D. Domar, Expansion and Employment, *American Economic Review* (March 1947).

be declining in the growth process. Besides, according to Amartya Sen, winner of Nobel Price in economics freedom to improve the quality of life of the poor, their freedom from undernourishment, freedom from illiteracy, freedom from illness are essential requirements of economic development. *It is the building up capabilities of the poor and enlargement of the opportunities to gain freedom in these respects* that Amartya Sen calls development[5]. The macroeconomics for developing countries must therefore concern itself with not only economic growth but also econnomic developemnt.

Since the above growth theories apply particularly to the present-day developed economies, special theories which explain the causes of underdevelopment and poverty in less developed countries (LDCs) and which also suggest strategies for initiating and accelerating growth in them have also been propounded. These special growth theories relating to less developed countries (LDCs) are generally known as *Economics of Development*. We shall discuss some theories of development such as *balanced growth theory* of Nurkse, *unbalanced growth theory* of Hirschman, *'theory of economic development with unlimited supplies of labour'* of Arthur Lewis in this book.

Balance of Payments and Exchange Rate. Balance of payments is the record of economic transactions of the residents of a country with the rest of the world during a period. The aim to prepare such a record is to present an account of all receipts on account of goods exported, services rendered and capital received by the residents of a country and the payments made for goods imported, services received and capital transferred to other countries by residents of a country. There may be deficit or surplus in balance of payments. Both create problems for an economy. An important effect is that the transactions in balance of payment are influenced by the exchange rate. The exchange rate is the rate at which a country's currency is exchanged for foreign currencies. The instability in exchange rate has been a major problem in recent years which has given rise to serious balance of payments problems. During the 12 years period (1901-2002), Indian rupee depreciated to a large extent in terms of US dollar giving rise to serious problems. In the year 2003, the Indian rupee started appreciating against the US dollar. During the two years 1997 and 1998, currencies of many South-East Asian Countries and Japan rapidly depreciated in terms of US dollar. This creates the situation of economic crisis which needs to be overcome. Both interrelated problems of balance of payments and instability of foreign exchange rate will be analysed in a separate part of this book.

THE ROLE OF GOVERNMENT IN THE MACROECONOMY

In modern macroeconomics, the intervention by the government to influence economic activity is well recognised. It is now widely believed that instability is inherent in a free-market economy and further that there is no any self-correcting mechanism to ensure stability at full employment level and sustained economic growth. There are three types of economic policy that are used by the government to influence the working of macroeconomy.

1. Fiscal Policy
2. Monetary Policy
3. Growth Policies

We will discuss these three policy instruments in detail in the subsequent chapters. However, we briefly explain them below and indicate what they are concerned with.

Fiscal Policy. An important way the government affects the economy is through the adoption of appropriate fiscal policy. The fiscal policy refers to taxation and expenditure decisions of the government. Before Keynes it was believed that the government budget should preferabily be balanced, that is, revenue collected through taxes should be equal to the expenditure made by the government. Keynes showed that balanced budget is not good under all circumstances. He advocated that at times of depression, *deficit budget* should be made to get the economy out of it and to

5. Amartya Sen, *Developmetn as Freedom*, Oxford University Press, 2000.

eliminate involuntary unemployment. In case of deficit budget the government expenditure exceeds revenue collected through taxes. The budget deficit arises when the government increases its expenditure without raising taxes or it arises when taxes are reduced without cutting back an expenditure. Therefore, the policy of budget deficit represents expansionary fiscal policy. The budget deficit raises aggregate demand and leads to the increase in national income and employment.

To meet the budget deficit, the government borrows from the banks and the public and pays interest to them. This raises debt burden of the government. The borrowing by the government increases the demand for loanable funds and leads to rise in rate of interest. The higher interest rate discourages private investment. It is therefore claimed that government borrowing to finance budget deficit *crowds out* some private investment so that net effect of budget deficit on expansion in output and employment is small. We will explain in detail in a subsequent chapters how far this crowding-out effect is significant.

However, to avoid borrowing and rise in public debt, the alternative way to finance the budget deficit is printing of money by the government. The danger of financing budget deficit through printing of money is that it may lead to inflation in the economy. The implications of different ways of financing budget deficit will be discussed in detail in a later chapter.

On the contrary, when there is high inflation in the economy the government can check it by reducing its expenditure or raising taxes and in this way make a surplus budget. This will tend to reduce aggregate demand which will help in controlling inflation. Thus fiscal policy is an important instrument used by the government to change the level of of aggregate demand and thereby affect income, employment and prices.

Monetary Policy

Monetary policy is another important instrument which the government (or Central Bank of the country) uses to achieve the objectives of price stability, full-employment and economic growth. Monetary policy refers to the policies regarding growth of money supply, availability of credit and interest or cost of credit. Monetary policy is an important tool of controlling inflation in the economy. It is generally believed that large expansion in money supply causes rise in price level. To check inflation *tight monetary policy is* adopted wherein rate of interest is raised and availability of credit is reduced. When interest rate rises, businessmen and households find it more costly to borrow. This discourages demand for credit and leads to the contraction of money supply in the economy. Besides, to discourage the creation of excess credit by the banks for investment and consumption purposes, cash reserve ratio is raised or Government bonds and securities are sold to the banks and the public. The decrease in credit for investment and consumption will cause decline in aggregate demand which will exert downward pressure on prices.

On the contrary to get the economy out of recession expansionary monetary policy is adopted. The increase in money supply lowers the rate of interest. The credit from banks becomes cheaper which encourages investment. At lower interest rate households also tend to borrow more for consumption. As a result, aggregate demand in the economy increases which raises levels of output and employment. However, it may be noted that Keynes was not optimistic about the efficacy of monetary policy to tackle the problem of depression and unemployment. He argued that demand for money at the time of depression is highly interest-elastic and therefore expansion in money supply will not lead to lowering of interest rate significantly. Besides, according to him, investment demand is not much interest-elastic so that even smaller interest rate will not stimulate investment.

In a developing country such as India the right monetary policy can play a useful role for achieving the objectives of higher economic growth with price stability. For example, in India the Reserve Bank of India ensures that while genuine demand for credit for investment by firms must be met, the excessive growth in money supply and credit be avoided. The Reserve Bank of India has been often adjusting its monetary policy to suit the changing economic situation.

Growth Policies

Money economists doubt the efficacy of fiscal and monetary policies to eliminate the fluctuations in the economic activity through *demand management* (that is, influencing the level of aggregate demand). A school of economic thought known as *supply-side economics* argues that focus of government policy should shift from demand management to stimulation of aggregate supply of output. For example, in the seventies when the USA and Britain experienced the problem of *stagflation*, some economists suggested that instead of demand management the government should reduce taxes to increase the incentives to work, save and invest more. More labour supply and more investment will increase the supply of goods and services. As a result, price level will fall and at the same time output will rise. The policies to reduce inflation through expansion in supply of output are generally described as *supply-side policies.*

Besides, for promotion of growth, especially in developing countries, the government adopts appropriate fiscal and monetary policies. It is generally bilieved that higher economic growth in the developing countries will lead to the reduction in a poverty and unemployment. To raise the rate of saving and investment the government must take appropriate fiscal and monetary measures. Recently, it has been found that policy of moderate taxes generate more revenue through greater tax complianice and at the same time it provides incentives to save and invest more. In developing countries in order to speed up economic growth the government should increase its expenditure on infrastructure such as irrigation projects, roads and highways, power, telecommunication, ports etc. Besides, as has been emphasised by Amartya Sen, for accelerating growth and removal of poverty the government must invest more in social sector consisting of education, health, literacy. It is important to note that a developing country cannot rely on private sector investment alone which is governed and guided by profit motive. Therefore, to supplement the prive sector investment the government itself should directly undertake investment to promote and accelerate economic growth.

POST-KEYNESIAN DEVELOPMENTS IN MACROECONOMICS

There have been significant developments of macroeconomic ideas in the post-Keynesian era. These developments came about as a critique of Keynesian macroeconomics. We briefly explain below the following three main developments in macroeconomics after Keynes:

(1) Monetarism
(2) Supply-side Economics
(3) Rational Expectations Theory

Monetarism

American economist Milton Friedman, a Nobel Laureate in economics, criticised Keynes' macroeconomics and put forward a new view or idea. Milton Friedman along with Anna Schwartz published an important work "*A Monetary History of the United States*" in which they argued that monetary policy is the prime engine in causing fluctuations in economic activity by bringing about changes in aggregate demand. Milton Friedman made a sharp criticism of Keynes's view that monetary policy was quite ineffective instrument in bringing about economic stability. In fact, he asserted that monetary policy caused or contributed to almost all recessions he studied. He stressed that even the Great Depression of 1930s was primarily caused by the tight monetary policy adopted at that time. He further argued that the Great Depression of the 1930s did not show the failure of free-market system, but the failure of Government's interventionist policy, especially monetary policy of the Central Bank which landed the U.S. economy into depression. According to Friedman, it is the excessive contraction of money supply by the Federal Reserve Bank System (which is the

Central Bank of the U.S.A.) that caused depression in the U.S. economy. There are differences between the monetarists and Keynesians in respect of two important issues. First issue relates to the relationship between money supply and inflation. The second relates to the role of Government in the economy.

Monetarists led by Friedman believe that *inflation is always and everywhere a monetary phenomenon.* According to them, inflation is caused by the rapid expansion of money supply in the economy. Friedman and his followers restated the classical quantity theory of money and made improvements in it but retained its essence that it is the greater increase in money supply relative to growth of output that causes inflation. In order to control inflation, they suggest a constant growth rate of money supply in the economy.

An important feature of monetarism is that to achieve economic stabilisation it is opposed to the adoption of *activist role* by the Government. As against this, Keynesian economists emphasise that active role should be played by the Government to control business cycles and achieve economic stability. Like classical economists, monetarists also believe that a free-market economy is inherently stable and if the economy departs from the state of full-employment, full-employment equilibrium is restored through automatic adjustments in it. Therefore, they even argue that Government or its central bank should not adopt *active* discretionary monetary policy, rather it *should pursue a policy of stable rate of growth of money supply.*

In sharp contrast to the monetarists' view, Keynes and his followers advocate the adoption of activist role by the Government. In this respect Keynesian lays stress on the adoption of discretionary fiscal and monetary policies.[6] Besides, Keynesian economists believe that expansion in money supply does not always cause inflation in the economy. According to them, whether or not increase in money supply will lead to inflation depends on the possibility of expansion in output. When the economy is in the grip of depression, the increase in money supply is likely to lead to the large expansion in output of goods which will prevent the rise in prices. Similarly, monetarists are opposed to the fiscal policy of budget deficits and public debt. They argue for reducing taxes and lowering public expenditure so that the role of Government in the economy is restricted.

Supply-Side Economics

In the 1970s and early eighties the problem of stagflation appeared in which high inflation was accompanied by high rate of unemployment. This problem of stagflation demonstrated that Keynes's theory which focused on fluctuations in aggregate demand as responsible for either high unemployment or high inflation could not explain the problem of stagflation in which both high unemployment and high inflation occurred together. The failure of Keynesian economics to deal with stagflation led some economists to believe that problem was on the supply side of economic activity. The problem looked quite strange and Keynesian policies were incapable of solving it. Following Keynesian policy, if expansionary fiscal and monetary measures were taken to raise aggregate demand to remove stagnation or high unemployment, it accelerated inflation further. On the other hand, if steps were taken to lower aggregate demand to lower the inflation rate, it would have further increased the already high unemployment rate. Supply-side economists pointed out that it was *supply-shocks*, delivered among others by reduction in oil supplies and *increase in oil prices* that caused the problem of stagflation. As a result of contraction in supply due to the adverse supply shocks, given the aggregate demand curve, price level and inflation rate could rise on the one hand and aggregate output could fall giving rise to more unemployment on the other.

Advocates of supply-side economics argued that for the expansion in aggregate supply and thereby increase in employment opportunities, incentives to work, save and invest more were

6. Keynes himself advocated for the adoption of only discretionary fiscal policy to cure depression and control inflation but his followers generally called *'New Keynesians'* emphasise both fiscal and monetary policies to attain economic stability.

required to be promoted. According to them, more work or labour, and higher investment will lead to the increase in aggregate supply. The increase in aggregate supply, given the aggregate demand curve, will lead to the increase in employment on the one hand and reduction of inflation on the other. According to them, high rates of income tax serve as disincentives to work, save and invest more. Therefore, to encourage more saving, work and investment, they advocated for the reduction in the then prevailing high rates of income tax. As a result of more work and investment, aggregate supply will increase which will not only cause employment to rise and unemployment to decrease but also lower the rate of inflation.

Besides, in the opinion of the supply-side economists the reduction in tax rates will increase income and output to such an extent that even with lower rates of taxes, the Government revenue will increase which would tend to reduce Government's budget deficit. In this respect, the concept of *Laffer curve* has been put forward, according to which when rate of a tax is increased from zero upward, , Government's revenue from it initially rises, but after a point further hike in the rate of a tax brings about decrease in revenue for the Government. Therefore, they are of the view that higher rates of personal taxes are responsible for low tax-revenue. Therefore, they assert that with lowering of tax rates, not only national income and employment will increase through greater labour supply and investment but this will also reduce Government's budget deficit by increasing tax revenue. We will critically examine in detail the supply-side economics in a separate chapter.

New Classical Macroeconomics : Rational Expectations Theory

Recently, a new macroeconomic theory has been put forward which is also opposed to Keynesian macroeconomic theory and policy which focused on aggregate demand for goods and services. According to this new classical macroeconomic theory, consumers, workers and producers behave rationally to promote their interests and welfare. On the basis of their *rational expectations*, based on all the available information, they make quick adjustments in their behaviour. Therefore, according to the supporters of rational expectations theory, involuntary unemployment cannot prevail. They argue that producers and consumers collect all the necessary information about economic situation and policies and determine their behaviour according to the rational expectations formed on the basis of all information collected. According to them, people do not make any mistakes in establishing correct relationship between economic events and Government's policies on the one hand, and the results that follow from them on the other. In other words, they always make correct predictions from the Government's policies and changes in the economic environment. For example, when Government makes a deficit budget they will expect that rates of interest will rise. Therefore, they will attempt to take loans now when the rates of interest are lower so as to save themselves from paying higher interest rates in the future. Unfortunately, because of this behaviour the interests rates rise immediately rather than in future.

A significant difference between the Keynesian theory and rational expectation theory may be noted here. In the Keynesian theory deficit in Government budget leads to increase in aggregate demand and will therefore promote private investment. On the other hand, according to rational expectations theory, budget deficit will cause rate of interest to rise which will discourage private investment. Thus, according to rational expectations theory, increase in aggregate demand as a result of budget deficit is offset by decrease in private investment so that national output, income and employment remain unaffected.

Similarly, according to rational expectations theory, if central bank of a country increases the money supply, consumers, producers and workers will expect rationally that price level will rise. On the basis of these rational expectations, workers would get their wages raised, landlords will raise their rent, lenders and bankers will increase the rate of interest, and producers will raise their profit margins. As a result of these adjustments by various persons, the effect of expansion in money supply on these persons will get cancelled. According to the rational expectations theorists, since the consumers, workers and producers themselves make adjustments to save them from the adverse effects of economic events and policies there is no need for the Government to intervene in the economy through adoption of proper macroeconomic policy. Thus, like the Friedman and other monetarists, supporters of rational expectations theory are opposed to the activist role by the Government. According to them, it is very difficult to implement an activist policy successfully. They are of the view that market is usually in full-employment equilibrium and people make self-adjustments in their behaviour to protect and promote their interests. The Government cannot achieve any success in improving economic situation through its activist policy. As compared to the Government individuals themselves are in a better position to take corrective measures to safeguard their interests.

WHY A SEPARATE STUDY OF MACROECONOMICS

Now an important question which arises is why a separate study of the economic system as a whole or its large aggregates is necessary. Can't we generalise about the behaviour of the economic system as a whole or about the behaviour of large aggregates such as aggregate consumption, aggregate saving, aggregate investment from the economic laws governing the behaviour patterns of the individual units found by microeconomics. In other words, can't we obtain the laws governing the macroeconomic variables such as total national product, total employment and total income, general price level, etc by simply adding up, multiplying or averaging the results obtained from the behaviour of the individual firms and industries. The answer to this question is the behaviour of the economics system as a whole or the macroeconomic aggregates is not merely a matter of addition or multiplication or averaging of what happens in the various individual parts of the whole. As a matter of fact, in the economic system what is true of parts is not necessary true of the whole. Therefore, the application of micro-approach to generalise about the behaviour of the economic system as a whole or macroeconomic aggregates is incorrect and may lead to misleading conclusions. Therefore, a separate macro-analysis is needed to study the behaviour of the economic system as a whole in respect of various macroeconomic aggregates. When laws or generalisations are true of constituent individual parts but untrue and invalid in case of the whole economy, paradoxes seem to exist. Boulding has called these paradoxes as *macro-economic paradoxes*. It is because of the existence of these macro-economic paradoxes that there is a justification for making macro-analysis of the behaviour of the whole economic system or its large economic aggregates. Thus Professor Boulding rightly remarks, "*It is these paradoxes more than any other factor, which justify the separate study of the system as whole, not merely as an inventory or list of particular items, but as a complex of aggregates.*[7]

Professor Boulding further elaborates his point by liking the economic system with a forest and the individual firms or industries with the trees in the forest. Forest, he says, is the aggregation of trees but it does not reveal the same properties and behaviour pattern as those of the individual trees. It will be misleading to apply the rules governing the individual trees to generalise about the behaviour of the forest.

Various examples of macro-paradoxes (that is, what is true of parts is not true of the whole) can be given from the economic field. We shall give two such examples of savings and wages, on the basis of which Keynes laid stress on evolving and applying macroeconomic analysis as separate and distinct approach from microeconomic analysis.

Paradox of Thrift. Savings are generally good for individuals. People save for some motives in view. They save for meeting their needs in old age, for education of their children, for purchasing durable goods such as houses and cars and thereby raise their standards of living. Further, they save for making investment or deposits in banks which raise their income in future years. But an interesting paradox of thrift arises which shows importance of macroeconomic analysis as distinct from microeconomic analysis. The paradox of thrift arises because it so happens that when *all people* in

7. K.E. Boulding, *A Reconstruction of Economics* (1952), p. 173

a society try to save more but they are actually unable to do so. Not only that, the attempt to save more by *all people* cause their income or standard of living to decline. Keynes's macroeconomic analysis helps to explain this paradox, Keynes's pointed out that efforts to save more, especially at times of depression, will lower the consumption demand of the people and will therefore adversely affect aggregate demand in the economy. *The decline in aggregate demand will cause national output and income to fall and unemployment to increase*. At the lower level of national income, savings will fall to the original level but the consumption of the people will be less than before which implies that people would become worse off as a result of their decision of saving more. Thus decision to save more will deepen the economic depression. It goes to the credit of Keynses's theory of effective demand as determinant of national income and his multiplier theory (which shows that income and employment fall more than the original rise in saving) that paradox of thrift has been resolved. It clearly shows at times of depression, more savings deepen the economic crisis.

Wage-Employment Paradox. Another common example to prove that what is true for the individual may not be true for the society as a whole is the wage-employment relationship. As pointed out above, classical and neo-classical economists, especially A.C. Pigou, contended that the cut in money wages at times of depression and unemployment would lead to the increase in employment and thereby eliminate unemployment and depression. Now, it is true that a cut in money wages in an individual industry will lead to more employment in that industry. It is quite commonplace conclusion of microeconomic theory that, given the demand curve for labour, at a lower wage more men will be employed. But for the society or economy as a whole this is highly misleading. If the wages are cut all round in the economy, as was suggested by Pigou and others on the basis of wage-employment relationship in an individual industry, the aggregate demand for goods and services in the society will decline, since wages are incomes of the workers which constitute majority in the society. The decline in aggregate demand will mean the decrease in demand for goods of many industries. Because the demand for labour is a derived demand, *i.e*., derived from the demand for goods, the fall in aggregate demand for goods will result in the decline in demand for labour which will create more unemployment rather than reduce it.

Fallacy of Composition

We thus see that the laws or generalisations which hold good for the behaviour of an individual consumer, firm or industry may be quite invalid and misleading when applied to the behaviour of the economic system as a whole. There is thus *a fallacy of composition*. This is so because what is true of individual components is not true of the collective whole. As mentioned above, these are called macroeconomic paradoxes and it is because of these paradoxes that a separate study of the economic system as a whole is essential.

Macroeconomic analysis takes account of many relationships which are not applicable to individual parts at all. For instance, an individual may save more than that he invests or he may invest more than he saves, but for economy as a whole it is one of the important principles of Keynesian macroeconomics that actual savings are always equal to actual investment. Likewise, for an individual or a group of individuals, expenditure may be more or less than the income but the national expenditure of the economy must be equal to the national income. In fact, the national expenditure and national income are two identical things. Similarly, in the case of full employment, an individual industry may increase its output and employment by bidding away the workers from other industries, but the economy cannot increase its output and employment in this way. Thus what applies to an individual industry, does not do so in case of the economic system as a whole.

We therefore conclude that a separate and distinct macroeconomic analysis is essential if we want to understand the true working of the economic system as a whole. From this it should not be understood that microeconomic theory is worthless and should be abandoned. As a matter of fact, microeconomics and macroeconomics are complementary to each other rather than being competitive. The two types of theories deal with different subjects, one deals mainly with the explanation of relative prices of goods and factors and the other mainly with the short-run determination of income and employment of the society and its long-run economic growth. The study of both micro and macro-economics is therefore necessary. Professor Samuelson rightly says, "There is really no opposition between micro and macro-economics. Both are absolutely vital. And you are only half-educated if you understand the one while being ignorant of the other."[8]

IMPORTANCE OF MACROECONOMICS

To Understand the Working of Macroeconomy : Macroeconomic Paradoxes. The study of macroeconomics is important in its own sake, as it tells us how the economy as a whole works. We cannot obtain and derive the laws governing macroeconomic variables such as national income, total employment, general price level by studying the microeconomic decisions of individual consumers, firms and industries. This is because what is true and valid in case of an individual firm or industry may not be valid for the economy as a whole. Boulding has pointed out several *macroeconomic paradoxes* which reveal that results obtained from the study of the behaviour of individual firms or industries may lead us to *misleading conclusions about the working of the macroeconomy*. Boulding compared it to the case of a forest and its trees. According to him, it will be misleading to apply the rules governing the individual trees to generalise about the behaviour of the forest.

Two examples of macroeconomic paradoxes will make it clear why the study of macroeconomic analysis separate from microeconomics is important. Take the case of wages. A neoclassical economist A.C. Pigou suggested all-round cut in wage rates to promote employment and thereby to solve the problem of unemployment that prevailed in times of Great Depression. We know from the marginal productivity theory of distribution of microeconomics that in the case of an individual firm or industry, it is quite valid that at a lower wage rate, an individual firm or industry will employ more labour. But this does not apply to the whole economy. This is because wages are not only cost for a firm or industry, they represent incomes of the workers who constitute a majority in a society. Fall in wages means decline in their incomes which would lead to a fall in aggregate demand for goods and services. This fall in aggregate demand will cause national output and employment to decline. Thus, from the viewpoint of the economy as a whole cut in wages will increase unemployment of labour rather than reducing it.

The second important example of a macroeconomic paradox relates to saving. When an individual saves more he is able to invest more and the higher investment yields more income for him in the future. But this result does not necessarily apply to the case when a society saves more. Suppose the economy is in the grip of recession and a society as a whole decides to save more. This may not only fail to increase national income but ultimately even saving may not rise as well. This is called *paradox of thrift*. This happens because more saving than before leads to the decrease in aggregate demand for goods and services. The fall in aggregate demand will cause the level of national income to decline and at the lower level of national income, less saving will be done. Thus, the initial increase in saving will not only lead to lower national income and output but eventually even saving of the society may not rise.

The above two examples of macroeconomic paradoxes clearly reveal that a *separate macroeconomic analysis is important to understand the working of the economy as a whole.*

Important Nature of Macroeconomic Issues. Macroeconomics is concerned with the study of issues and problems which are of vital importance for determining well-being of the people.

8. Paul A. Samuelson, *Economics*, 10th edition, 1976.

Macroeconomic problems such as unemployment, inflation, instability of foreign exchange rate cause a lot of human suffering. Unemployment creates a lot of misery for the unemployed workers and gives rise to many social evils. Unemployment involves waste of economic resources and loss of potential output. Inflation erodes real incomes or purchasing power of the people. It redistributes national income in favour of rich and thus creates more income inequalities. Inflation sends more people under the poverty line and thus accentuates the problem of poverty. Similarly, depreciation of domestic currency encourages flight of capital from an economy and increases the prices of imports and thereby adds to the inflationary pressures in the economy. Macroeconomics explains the causes of such important problems and help in formulating economic policies to tackle them.

Importance of Macroeconomics for Accelerating Economic Growth. Macroeconomics explains the factors which determines economic growth and brings out what causes slowdown in productivity growth. Every community wants to grow economically because economic growth helps to raise the standards of living of the people. Moreover, higher rate of economic growth helps in solving the problems of poverty and unemployment in the developing countries like India. Macroeconomic models of Harrod-Domar and Solow reveal that increase in the rate of saving and investment (or capital formation) and improvement in technology are the important factors determining economic growth. Macroeconomic theories also reveal that lack of growth in aggregate effective demand may serve as constraint to the growth process of an economy. Thus, macroeconomic provides us knowledge as to how to achieve self-sustained economic growth.

Understanding Business Cycles. Business cycles have been the biggest ailment of market economies. Though there is no unanimity in macroeconomic theory about the proper explanation of business cycles, significant advances have been made in bringing out the causes which lead to them. Fluctuations in aggregate demand due to volatile nature of investment demand, as explained by Keynes, together with the interaction of multiplier and accelerator provides an adequate explanation of business cycles. It is because of this understanding about business cycles that has helped to adopt proper fiscal and monetary policies to check business cycles and also due to these policies that severity of business cycles in recent years has greatly reduced. This shows that important contribution made by macroeconomics in controlling business cycles.

Formulating Government's Macroeconomic Policies. Understanding how the economy works which is obtained from macroeconomics has a practical value in formulation of government's fiscal and monetary policies. With the knowledge of the causes of recession and inflation brought out by macroeconomics governments formulate proper fiscal and monetary policies to tackle them. During recession, expansionary fiscal and monetary policies are adopted to lift the economy out of recession. On the other hand, inflation has been checked quite successfully by tight monetary policy and contractionary fiscal policy. Besides, the understanding about the factors which determine economic growth, fiscal and monetary policies have been so designed as to raise saving and investment and also to promote technological improvement of the production process. Further, with the knowledge furnished by macroeconomics about fluctuations in market economies, central bank often intervenes to achieve foreign exchange rate stability.

Individual Decision-Making. The understanding about the working of the economy as a whole helps the individuals to take better decisions. For example, the knowledge about macroeconomics helps them to assess the impact of government's economic policies. If on the basis of certain Government's economic policy they predict that inflation rate will increase, they may decide to act in the present in a way to ward off the adverse effects of inflation. The knowledge of macroeconomics tells them that inflation will erode their real incomes, will lower the real rate of interest, will make exports dearer than before. Keeping in view these impacts of inflation arising out of government's policy they will make decisions so as to save themselves from the undesirable consequencies of inflation. Similarly, people's decisions about whether or not to buy a house, or a new car, give loans to others at present would be governed by their predictions about the likely state of the economy. These predictions, it may be noted, are based by the individuals on their understanding of macroeconomics.

Importance in Business Decisions. The understanding of macroeconomics also helps a good deal to businesses or their managers who are faced with various decision-making problems. Business firms do not work in vacuum. The level of overall economic activity (*i.e.*, national income and employment), aggregate demand conditions, government's policies (both fiscal and monetary) the rate of inflation affect business firms. These aggregates of the economy make up overall *business environment* which affects decisions of managers. Forecasts of future demand and investment decisions by managers are especially based on the state of the economy and its growth process.

QUESTIONS FOR REVIEW

1. What is macroeconomics ? How will you distinguish it from microeconomics ?
2. What are the important problems that constitute the subject matter of macroeconomics ? Briefly explain them.
3. What are macro-economic paradoxes ? Explain any two of them. Explain how these paradoxes limit the applicability of microeconomic theories to explain the behaviour of the economy as a whole.
4. In what sense did Keynes bring about revolution in economics ?
5. Macro-economics has been described as a study of aggregates. Name some important 'aggregates' or variables whose behaviour is analysed in macroeconomics. Explain them briefly.
6. Why is there a need for a separate theory of macroeconomics ? Explain.
7. What is involuntary unemployment ? Why did classical economists believe that involuntary unemployment cannot exist in a free market economy ?
8. Explain briefly the following models of macroeconomics. In what fundamental ways do they differ from the Keynesian model ?
   1. Monetarism
   2. Supply-side economics
   3. Rational expectations theory
9. Keynesian macroeconomics is said to be irrelevant for developing countries like India. Do you agree ? Explain briefly ?
10. Name which of the following problems fall within the purview of macro-economics ?
    1. How is general price level determined ?
    2. Determination of output of a cotton textile industry.
    3. How is wage rate of computer engineer determined ?
    4. The problem of unemployment in the eonomy.
    5. On what factors does economic growth of a country depend ?
    6. How is level of national income determined ?
    7. Deficit in the balance of payments of a country ?
11. Explain the importance of the study of macroeconomics ?
12. What policy instruments are available with the government to achieve full employment, price stability and economic growth ? Explain them briefly.

CHAPTER 2

Circular Flow of Income and National Income Accounting

MEANING OF NATIONAL INCOME

The labour and capital of a country acting on its natural resources produce annually a certain amount of goods and services. This is called national income of the country. *National income of a country can be defined as the total market value of all final goods and services produced in the economy in a year.* Two things must be noted in regard to this meaning of national income. First, it measures the market value of annual output. In other words, national income is a *monetary measure.* This is because there is no other way of adding up the different sorts of goods and services except with their money prices. But in order to know accurately the changes in physical output, the figure for national income is adjusted for price changes. Secondly, for calculating national income accurately all goods and services produced in any given year must be counted only once, and not more than once. Most of the goods go through a series of production stages before reaching a market. As a result, parts or components of many goods are bought and sold many times. Hence, in order to avoid counting several times the parts of goods that are sold and resold, national income only includes the market value of all *final goods* and ignores the transactions involving *intermediate goods.*

The above way of explaining national income is only one way of interpreting it. In fact, the concept of national income has three interpretations. It represents a total value of production (as explained above), it represents a receipts total, and it represents an expenditure total. It is an obvious fact that every expenditure is at the same time a receipt. In other words, amount spent is equal to amount received. But if goods and services are valued at their market prices, we have three-fold identity, namely, that the value received equals the value paid equals the value of goods and services produced and sold.

To explain the above idea let us take an economy where there are only two agents: households and firms. Firms are required to produce goods. To produce them, they require services of factors of production. Factors of production are paid the rewards for their contribution to the production of goods. Thus incomes of these factors arise in the course of production. The sales value of net production must equal the sum total of payments made by the firms to the factors of production in the course of production. The sales value of net production must equal the sum total of payments made by the firms to the factors of production in the form of wages, rents, interest and profits. These incomes in turn become the sources of expenditure. Thus income flows from the firms to the households in exchange for productive services. This income again returns to the firms when expenditure is made by the households on the goods produced by the firms.

From above it follows that: *National Income = National Product = National Expenditure.* In other words, there are three measures of national income of a country.

(*a*) the sum of values of all final goods and services produced.

(*b*) the sum of all incomes, in cash and kind, accruing to factors of production in a year; and

(*c*) the sum of consumers' expenditure, net investment expenditure and government expenditure on goods and services.

Sum of all income, sum of values of all final production, and sum of all expenditures will be the same, but the significance of each arises from the fact that they reflect the three basic activities of the nation's economy, viz., production, distribution and expenditure.

CIRCULAR FLOW OF INCOME

The modern economy is a monetary economy. In the modern economy, money is used in the process of exchange. Money has facilitated the process of exchange and has removed the difficulties of the barter system. Thus money acts as a medium of exchange. The households supply the economic resources or factors to the productive firms and receive in return the payments in terms of money. In is thus clear that, in the monetary economy, there will be flows of money corresponding to the flows of economic resources and the flows of goods and services. But each money flow is in opposite direction to the real flow.

Circular Income Flow in a Two Sectors Economy

Real flows of resources, goods and services have been shown in Fig. 2.1. In the upper loop of this figure, the resources such as land, capital and entrepreneurial ability flow from households to business firms as indicated by the arrow mark. In opposite direction to this, money flows from business firms to the households as factor payments such as wages, rent, interest and profits. In the lower part of the figure, money flows from households to firms as consumption expenditure made by the households on the goods and services services produced by the firms, while the flow of goods and services is in

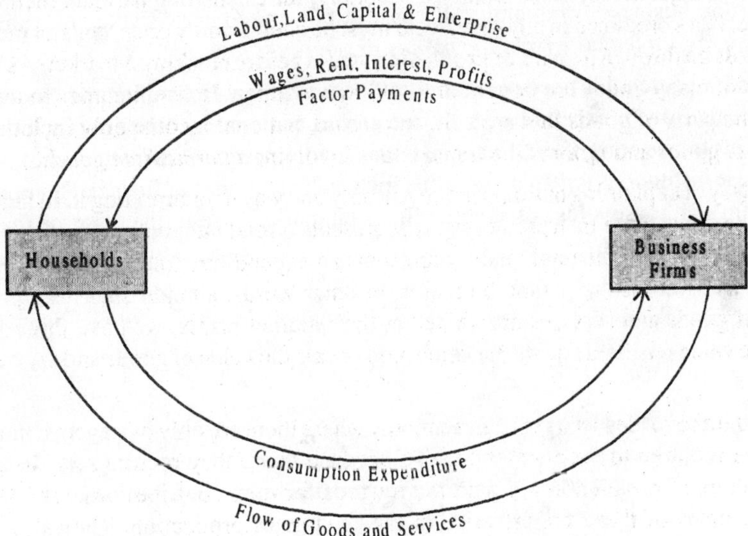

Fig. 2.1. *Circular Flow of Income in a simple two sector Economy*

opposite direction from business firms to households. Thus we see that money flows from business firms to households as factor payments and then it flows from households to firms. Thus there is, in fact, *a circular flow of money or income*. This circular flow of money will continue indefinitely week by week and year by year. This is how the economy functions. It may, however, be pointed out that this flow of money income will not always remain the same in volume. In other words, the flow of money income will not always continue at a constant level. In year of depression, the circular flow of money income will contract, *i.e.*, will become lesser in volume, and in years of prosperity it will expand, *i.e.*, will become greater in volume. This is so because the flow of money is a measure of national income and will, therefore, change with changes in the national income. In year of depression, when national income is low, the volume of the flow of money will be small and in years of prosperity when the level of national income is quite high, the flow of money will be large.

In order to make our analysis simple and to explain the central issues involved, we take many assumptions. In the first place, we assume that neither the households save from their incomes, nor the firms save from their profits. We further assume that the government does not play any part in the national economy. In other words, the government does not receive any money from the people by way of taxes, nor does the government spend any money on the goods and services produced by the firms or on the resources and services supplied by the households. Thirdly, we assume that the economy neither imports goods and services, nor exports anything. In other words, in our above analysis we have not taken into account the role of foreign trade. In fact we have explained above the flow of money that occurs in the functioning of a closed economy with no savings and no role of government.

Circular Money Flow with Saving and Investment

In our above analysis of the circular flow of money we have assumed that all income which the households receive, they spend it on consumer goods and services. A result, circular flow of money speeding and income remains undiminished. We will now explain if households save a part of their income, how their savings will affect money flows in the economy. When households save, their expenditure on goods and services will decline to that extent and as a result money flow to the business firms will contract. With reduced money receipts, firms will hire fewer workers (or lay off some workers) or reduce the factor payments they make to the suppliers of factors such as workers. This will lead to the fall in total incomes of the households. Thus, savings reduce the flow of money expenditure to the business firms and will cause a fall in economy's total income. *Economists therefore call savings a leakage from the money expenditure flow.*

But savings by households need not lead to reduced aggregate spending and income if they find their way back into flow of expenditure. In free market economies there exists a set of institutions such as banks, insurance companies, financial houses, stock markets where households deposit their savings. All these institutions together are called financial institutions or financial market. We assume that all the savings of households come in the financial market. We further assume that there are no inter-households borrowings.

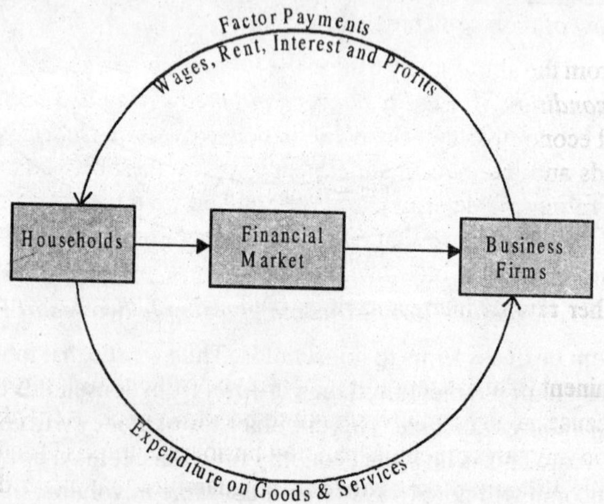

Fig. 2.2. *Circular Money Flow with Saving and Investment*

It is business firms who borrow from the financial market for investment in capital goods such as machines, factories, tools and instruments, trucks. Firms spend on investment in order to expand their productive capacity in future. Thus, through investment expenditure by borrowing the savings of the households deposited in financial market, are again brought into the expenditure stream and as a result total flow of spending does not decrease. Circular money flow with saving and investment is illustrated in Fig. 2.2 where in the middle part a box representing financial market is drawn. Money flow of savings is shown from the households towards the financial market. Then flow of investment expenditure is shown as borrowing by business firms from the financial market[1].

Condition for the Constancy of Circular Money Flow

Now the question arises what is the condition for the flow of money income to continue at a steady level so that it makes possible the production and subsequent flow of a given volume of goods and services at constant prices. To explain this we have to introduce saving and investment in the analysis of circular flow of income. As mentioned above, saving a part of income means it is not spent on consumer goods and services. In other words, saving *is withdrawal of some money from the income flow.* On the other hand, investment means some money is spent on buying new capital goods to expand production capacity. In other words, *investment is injection of some money in circular flow of income.* For the circular flow of income to continue unabated, the withdrawal of money from the income stream by way of saving must equal injection of money by way of investment expenditure. Therefore, planned savings must be equal to planned investment if the constant money income flow in an economy is to be obtained. Now, what will happen if planned investment expenditure falls short of the planned savings? As a result of fall in planned investment expenditure, income, output and employment will fall and therefore the flow of money will contract. If the equality between planned savings and planned investment is disturbed by increase in savings, then the immediate effect will be that the stocks of goods lying in the shelves of the shops will increase (as some of the goods will not be sold due to the fall in consumption *i.e.,* increase in savings). Owing to the deficiency of demand for goods and the accumulation of stocks, retailers will place small orders with the wholesalers. Consequently, smaller amount of goods will be produced and therefore fewer capital goods like machinery will be indeed with the result that fixed investment will tend to fall. Thus the ultimate effect of either the fall in planned investment or the increase in planned savings is the same, namely, the fall in income, output, employment and prices with the result that the flow of money will contract.

On the other hand, if the equality between planned savings and planned investment is disturbed by the increase in investment demand, the result will be increase in income, output and employment. Consequently, the flow of money income will expant.

It is thus clear from the above analysis that the *flow of money income will continue at a constant level only when the condition of equality between planned saving and investment is satisfied.* It was believed by classical economists that financial market provides a mechanism which coordinates the savings of households and the investment expenditure, by the firms. Rate of interest, which is the price for the use of savings, is determined by saving and investment. If savings exceed investment expenditure, rate of interest falls so that, at a lower rate of interest, investment increases and both become equal. On the contrary, if investment expenditure is greater than savings, rate of interest will rise so that at a higher rate of interest savings increase and become equal to planned investment expenditure.

However, an eminent British economist J.M. Keynes refuted the above argument that changes in rate of interest will cause saving and investment to become equal. According to him, since in a free market capitalist economy, investment is made by business enterprises and savings are mostly done by households and for different reasons, there is no guarantee that planned investment will be equal to planned savings and thus fluctuations in income, output and employment are inevitable. As a

1. It may be noted that business firms also save when they do not distribute among shareholders all the profits made by them and keep the undistributed profits as reserves. We are ignoring them in our money flow analysis as firms themselves use their savings for buying machinery and making other investment expenditure.

result, circular flow of income does not continue at a steady level in a free-enterprise capitalist economy unless certain corrective and preventive steps are taken by the government to maintain stability in the economy.

Saving-Investment Identity in National Income Accounts

Despite the fact that people who save are different from the business firms which primarily invest, in national income accounts savings are identical or always equal to investment in a simple two sector economy having no roles of Government and foreign trade. This is a basic identity in national income accounts which needs to be carefully understood. Of course, in our above analysis of circular flow of income, we explained that planned investment by business firms can differ from savings by household. But in that analysis we referred to *planned or intended* investment and savings which often differ and affect the flow of national income. However, in national income accounts we are concerned with *actual saving* and *actual investment*. It is these actual or realised saving and investment that are identical in national income accounts. We can prove their identity in the following way.

In a simple economy which has neither government, nor foreign trade, the value of *output produced* which we denote by Y is equal to the value of *output sold*. Since the value of output sold in a simple two sector economy is equal to the sum of consumption expenditure and investment expenditure we have

$$Y \equiv C + I \qquad \ldots (i)$$

where Y = Value of aggregate output, C = Consumption expenditure and I = Investment expenditure.

A pertinent question which arises here is what happens to the unsold output. The unsold output leads to the *increase in the inventories of goods* and in national income accounting increase in inventories of goods is treated as a part of actual investment. This may be considered as the firms selling the goods to themselves to add to their inventories. Thus, gross national product (GNP) produced is used either for consumption or for investment.

Now, look at the gross national product or income in the simple economy from the viewpoint of its allocation between consumption and saving. Since national income (which is equal to GNP) can be either consumed or saved,[1]. We have

$$Y \equiv C + S \qquad \ldots (ii)$$

From the identities (*i*) and (*ii*) we get

$$C + I \equiv Y \equiv C + S \qquad \ldots (iii)$$

The left hand side of the identity (*iii*), namely $C + I = Y$ shows the components of aggregate demand (that is, aggregate expenditure on goods and services produced) and the right-hand side of the identitiy (*iii*) namely $Y = C + S$ shows the allocation of national income to either consumption or saving. Thus, the identity (*iii*) shows that the value of output produced or sold is equal to the total income received. It is income received that is spent on goods and services produced.

Now subtracting the consumption (C) from both sides of the identity (*iii*) we have

$$I = S$$

Thus, in ***our two sector simple economy with neither government, nor foreign trade, investment is identically equal to saving.***

---

1. Note that decisions about saving are made both by households and business firms. In national income accounts they are generally put together and referred to as private sector savings.

Circulr Income Flows in three Sector Economy with Government Sector

In our above analysis of money flow, we have ignored the existence of government for the sake of making our circular flow model simple. This is quite unrealistic because government absorbs a good part of the incomes earned by households. Government affects the economy in a number of ways. Here we will concentrate on its taxing, spending and borrowing roles. Government purchases goods and services just as households and firms do. Government expenditure takes many forms including spending on capital goods and infrastructure (highways, power, communication), on defence goods, and on education and public health and so on. These add to the money flows which are shown in Fig. 2.3 where a box representing Government has been drawn. It will be seen that government purchases of goods and services from firms and households are shown as flow of money spending on goods and services.

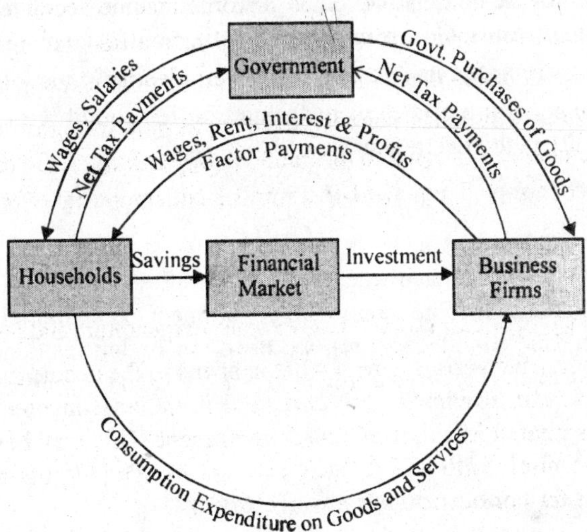

Fig. 2.3. *Circular Money Flow Model with Government*

Government expenditure may be financed through taxes, out of assets or by borrowing. The money flow from households and business firms to the government is labelled as tax payments in Fig. 2.3 This money flow includes all the tax payments made by households less transfer payments received from the Government. Transfer payments are treated as negative tax payments.

Another method of financing Government expenditure is borrowing from the financial market. This can be represented by the money flow from the financial market to the Government and is labelled as Government borrowing (To avoid confusion we have not drawn this money flow from financial market to the Government). Government borrowing increases the demand for credit which causes rate of interest to rise. The government borrowing through its effect on the rate of interest affects the behaviour of firms and households. Business firms consider the interest rate as cost of borrowing and the rise in the interest rate as a result of borrowing by the Government lowers private investment. However, households who view the rate of interest as return on savings feel encouraged to save more.

It follows from above that the inclusion of the Government sector significantly affects the overall economic situation. Total expenditure flow in the economy is now the sum of consumption expenditure (denoted by C), investment expenditure (I) and Government expenditure (denoted by G). Thus

$$\text{Total expenditure } (E) = C + I + G \qquad \ldots(i)$$

Total income (Y) received is allocated to consumption (C), savings (S) and taxes (T). Thus

$$Y = C + S + T \qquad \ldots(ii)$$

Since expenditure(E) made must be equal to the income received (Y), from equations (i) and (ii) above we have

$$C + I + G = C + S + T \qquad \ldots (iii)$$

Since C occurs on both sides of the equation (*iii*) and will therefore be cancelled out, we have

$$I + G = S + T \qquad \ldots (iv)$$

By rearranging we obtain

$$G - T = S - I \qquad \ldots (v)$$

Equation (*v*) is very significant as it depicts what would be the consequences if government budget is not balanced. If Government expenditure (G) is greater than the tax revenue (T), that is, $G > T$, the government will have a budget deficit. To finance the budget deficit, the Government will borrow from the financial market. For this purpose, then private investment (I) by business firms must be less than the savings(S) of the households. Thus Government borrowing reduces private investment in the economy. In other words, Government borrowing *crowds out* private investment.

Another important conclusion that can be drawn from national income account identity incorporating Government expenditure relates to the condition for equilibrium in the financial market. National income identity with government expenditure is

$$Y = C + I + G$$

or

$$Y - C - G = I \qquad \ldots (vi)$$

In the expression (*vi*), the left hand side ($Y - C - G$) represents national saving or simply saving (S). Note that in this National Income Identity all government expenditure is treated as consumption expenditure. To understand the identity (*vi*), we break up its left hand side representing national saving into two parts, namely, (1) *private saving* ($Y - T - C$) and (2) *public saving* (i.e. saving of the government ($T - G$). Thus

$$S = (Y - T - C) + (T - G) = Y - C - G$$

(Note that $Y - T$ is disposable income)

If the economy is to remain in a steady state, the *flows into* the financial market (i.e. private saving and public saving) must balance the *flows out of* the financial market. Thus, for the economy to remain in a steady state

$$Y - T - C + (T - G) = I$$

That is, for the economy to remain in a steady state, the sum of private saving and public saving must equal investment.

Money Flows in the Four Sector Open Economy : Adding Foreign Sector

We now turn to explain the money flows that are generated in an open economy, that is, economy which have trade relations with foreign countries. Thus, the inclusion of the foreign sector will reveal to us the interaction of the domestic economy with foreign countries. Foreigners interact with the domestic firms and households through exports and imports of goods and services as well as through borrowing and lending operations through financial market. Goods and services produced within the domestic territory which are sold to the foreigners are called exports.

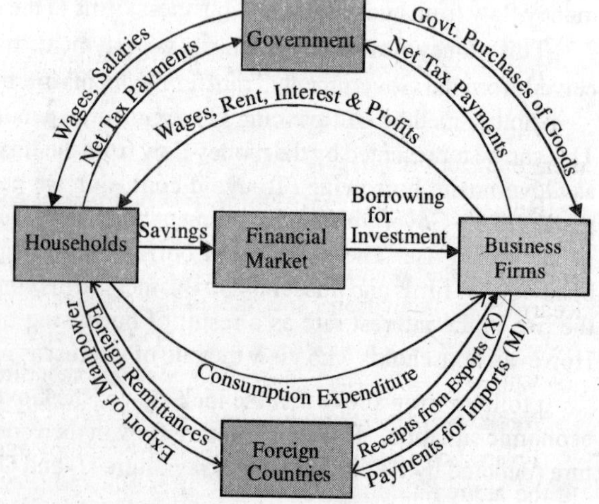

Fig. 2.4. *Circular Flow of Income in an Open Economy with Government and Foreign Sector*

On the other hand, purchases of foreign-made goods and services by domestic households are called imports. Figure 2.4 illustrates additional money flows that occur in the open economy when exports and imports also exist in the economy. In our analysis, we assume it is only the business firms of the domestic economy that interact with foreign countries and therefore export and import goods and services. A flow of money spending on imports have been shown to be occurring from the domestic business firms to the foreign countries (*i.e.*, rest of the world). On the contrary, flow of money expenditure on exports of a domestic economy has been shown to be taking place from foreign countries to the business firms of the domestic economy. If exports are equal to the imports, then there exists a balance of trade. Generally, exports and imports are not equal to each other. If value of exports exceeds the value of imports, *trade surplus* occurs. On the other hand if value of imports exceeds value of exports of a country, *trade deficit* occurs.

In the open economy there is interaction between countries not only through exports and imports of goods and services but also through borrowing and lending funds or what is also called financial market. These days financial markets around the world have become well integrated. When there is a trade surplus in the economy, that is, when exports (X) exceed imports (M), *net capital outflow* will take place. By net capital outflow we mean foreigners will borrow from domestic savers to finance their purchases of our exports. In this way as a result of net capital outflow domestic savers will lend to foreigners, that is, acquire foreign financial assets.

On the contrary, in case of import surplus, that is, when imports are greater than exports, trade deficit will occur. Therefore, in case of trade deficit, domestic consumer households and business firms will borrow from abroad to finance their excess of imports over exports. This means there will be capital inflow in our economy. As a result, foreigners will acquire domestic financial assets.

Saving-Investment Identity in the Open Economy

From the circular flows that occur in the open economy the national income must be measured by aggregate expenditure that includes net of exports, that is, $X–M$ where X represents exports and M represents imports. Imports must be subtracted from the total expenditure made by foreigners on our domestically produced goods and services exported to them to get the value of net exports. Thus, in the open economy

$$\text{National Income} = C + I + G + NX$$

where NX represents net exports, $X–M$.

Since national income can be either consumed, saved or paid as taxes to the Government we have

$$C + I + G + NX = C + S + T$$

Since C is common on both sides of the above equation we have

$$I + G + NX = S + T \qquad \ldots (vi)$$

The above equation (*vi*) shows that in the open economy sum of private investment (I), Government expenditure (G) and net exports (NX) is equal to the sum of savings and tax revenue.

Relation of Aggregate Domestic Output and Expenditure with Trade Balance. The national income account identity of the open economy can be used further to show how aggregate domestic output (Y) and aggregate expenditure ($C + I + G$) and net exports (*i.e.* trade balance) are related. Rearranging the national income of the open economy ($Y = C + I + G + NX$) we have

$$NX = Y – (C + I + G)$$

Where $C + I + G$ is aggregate domestic expenditure. Thus

Net Exports = National Domestic Product (Y) – *Aggregate Domestic Expenditure*

From above it follows that in an open economy aggregate domestic expenditure need not be equal to the aggregate domestic output of goods and services (*i.e.* Y). If aggregate domestic output (Y) exceeds aggregate domestic expenditure ($C + I + G$), we export the excess of domestic output, that is, net exports (NX) are positive ($NX > 0$). On the other hand, if domestic output is less than domestic expenditure we import this shortfall (i.e. $NX < 0$).

Foreign Capital Flows and Trade Balance. As in the case of a closed economy goods market are intimately related to the financial market in the open economy. To show this, let us rearrange the national income accounts identity ($Y = C + I + G + NX$) of the open economy.

$$Y - C - G = I + NX \quad \ldots (vii)$$

The left hand side of the above equation (*i.e.* $Y - C - G$) represents national saving (S). Note that all Government expenditure is here treated as consumption expenditure. Thus, it follows from above that

$$S = I + NX$$

or

$$S - I = NX \quad \ldots (viii)$$

The national income identity of expression (*viii*) shows that the *economy's net exports (NX) must always be equal to the difference between saving and investment. The net exports are also called trade balance because it, shows the difference between exports and imports of an economy*. The trade balance (NX) may be positive or negative. If exports exceed imports, trade balance (NX) is positive and if exports fall short of imports, the trade balance (NX) is negative.

But the important result that follows from national income identity of the open economy relates to the link between *international capital flows* and the *goods market*. If $S - I$ in (*viii*) is positive, that is, if the economy's national saving exceeds domestic investment it will be lending the excess funds to foreigners, that is, there will be *net capital outflow* from the economy. On the other hand, if $S - I$ is negative, that is, if domestic investment exceeds domestic saving, the economy will be borrowing from abroad to finance the excess investment. That is, there will be *net capital inflow* into the economy to finance higher capital formation in the economy.

It follows from above that net capital flows ($S - I$) always equal the trade balance or to current account balance which is the broader term that includes *invisibiles* also.

NATIONAL INCOME AND NATIONAL PRODUCT

The sum of all incomes of the people of a country is called national income. This national income is greatly related to the national product. In fact in a two sector economy without the Government and its imposition of indirect taxes and grant of subsidies and also assuming no depreciation national income and national product are one and the same thing. The incomes which different people of the society get are obtained by them for their contribution of labour, land, capital and entrepreneurial services to the national production. Hence the income which the labourers get are wages for the productive services which labourers lend to the various firms which undertake the work of production. Similarly, the owners of land get income as rent because of their contribution of land to the productive firms; the capitalists get interest for lending their money capital to the entrepreneurs for undertaking any work of production or business. The entrepreneurs get profits for starting and organising the work of production and bearing risk and uncertainty involved in it. It is thus clear that the different individuals of a country obtain their income either as wages of their labour, or as interest on their money capital, or as rent for their land, or as profits for their enterprise. The sum of incomes obtained as wages, rent, interest and profits is the national income of the country.

Various households obtain their income from the productive firms or businesses which utilise their labour, land, capital and other services for the production of goods and services. The incomes earned by the various households and individuals from the work of production are in fact costs of production of the goods produced. The total value of all final goods and services produced by various productive firms or businesses in a year is known as national product. Therefore, the national product of a country can be estimated by multiplying the total output of final goods and services with their market prices.

Hence the total national product in terms of rupees or value which is produced by various productive firms in a year, will be distributed among the various productive factors which have contributed to its production. Therefore, out of this national production (in value terms) wages will be paid to those households which have sold their labour to the productive firms. Out of this total value of the national product, land owners would get rent for the contribution of the services of land and capitalists would get interest for lending money capital to the productive firms. After the payment of wages, rent, interest, what is left is the profits of the entrepreneurs who set up productive firms, organise their work and bear risk and uncertainty and because of these services they get profits. It is thus clear the national product (value of total output of final goods and services in a year of a country) is distributed among wages, rents, interests and profits. As we have stated above, the sum of total wages, total interest, total rents and total profits is national income. Hence national product will be equal to he national income. The above conclusion that in a two-sector economy without Government and foreign trade national inocme equals national product can be expressed in the form of the following equation.

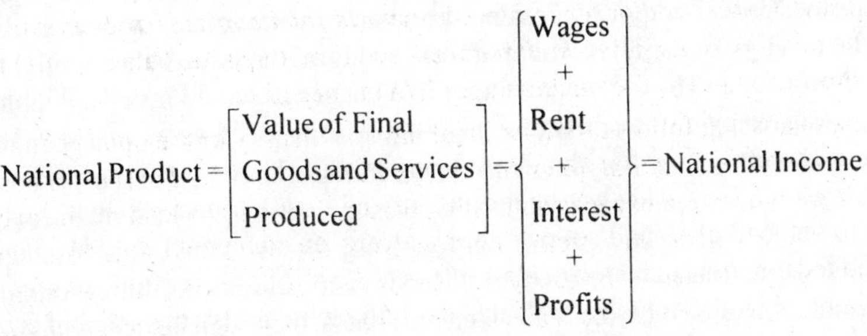

$$\text{National Product} = \begin{bmatrix} \text{Value of Final} \\ \text{Goods and Services} \\ \text{Produced} \end{bmatrix} = \begin{Bmatrix} \text{Wages} \\ + \\ \text{Rent} \\ + \\ \text{Interest} \\ + \\ \text{Profits} \end{Bmatrix} = \text{National Income}$$

From the above analysis it is evident that national income and national product are one and the same thing. Professor J.R. Hicks rightly writes, "*The value of the net social product of the community and the sum of the incomes of its members are exactly equal. The net social product and the social income are one and the same thing.*"[1]

It needs to be emphasised that the above conclusion regarding equality of national product and national income is valid only in our simple two sector eocnomy where we have assumed no depreciation funds are kept and also no role of Government (and therefore no indirect taxes collected by it and no subsidies granted by it). In case of a real economy, firms keep a part of some value created as depreciation allowance which therefore do not become a part of the income of the factors. When role of Government is brought into our analysis, a part of the value of output is taken away by the Government as indirect taxes and therefore the incomes of factor owners are reduced to that extent. Thus, only in the absence of depreciation funds and net indirect taxes, national product will be equal to national income. In our simple economy we assume away these depreciation funds and net indiret taxes levied by the Government on business firms to emphasise the point that national income does not come out of thin air, it is in fact generated by the production of goods and services. Therefore, growth in national income can be achieved by the increase in production of goods and services.

CONCEPTS OF NATIONAL INCOME

There are various concepts of national income which we study below one by one.

Gross National Product (GNP)

This is the basic national accounting measure of the total output or aggregate supply of goods and services. *Gross National Product is defined as the total market value of all final goods and services produced in a year in a country.* Two things must be noted in regard to gross national product. First, it measures the market value of annual output. In other words, GNP is a *monetary measure*. There is no other way of adding up the different sorts of goods and services produced in a year except in terms of their money prices. But in order to know accurately the changes in physical output, the figure for gross national product is adjusted for price changes.

1. J.R. Hicks, *The Social Framework*

Secondly, for calculating gross national product accurately, all goods and services produced in any given year must be counted once, and not more than once. Most of the goods go through a series of production stages before reaching a market. As a result, parts or components of many goods are bought and sold many times. Hence to avoid counting several times the parts of goods that are sold and resold, gross national product includes the market value of only final goods and ignores transactions involving intermediate goods.

Final Goods and Intermediate Goods

What do we mean by *final goods*? Final goods are those goods which are purchased for final use and not for resale or further processing. Intermediate goods, on the other hand, are those goods which are purchased for further processing or for resale. The sale of intermediate goods is excluded from gross national product. Why? Because the value of final goods includes the value of all intermediate goods used in their production. The inclusion of intermediate goods would involve double counting and will therefore give an exaggerated estimate of gross national product. An example will clarify this point. Suppose in our economy only two things are being produced, raw cotton worth Rs. 1000 and cotton cloth worth Rs. 2000. Now what will be the measure of gross national product? For finding it, if we add up the sales value of cloth and cotton, there is clearly an element of *double counting* in the sense that we have added the value of cotton *twice*—one as the sales value of cotton and secondly when we added to it the value of cloth. Actually, the value of cloth includes also the value of cotton which having been accounted for already should not be added second time.

Further, it is worth noting that Gross National Product (GNP) includes only *currently produced* goods and services in a year. It is a *flow measure* of output of goods and services per time period, say in a year. In it are only goods and services produced in a particular year are included. Market transactions involving goods produced in previous periods such as old houses, cars, factories built earlier are not included in GNP of the current year. Similarly, purchase and sale of assets such as stock and bonds do not involve current production of goods and are therefore excluded from GNP of the year.

Lastly, Gross National Product (GNP) refers to the value of goods and services currently produced by *normal residents of a country*. These residents may be national or non-national companies. Thus, many foreign companies have set up plants in India. They are owned by non-nationals but work to produce goods and services within the domestic territory of India and generate incomes for the Indian people employed in them. These foreign companies can only send back to their own countries profits earned by them.

Gross national product has the following components :

1. Value of *final consumer goods and services* produced in a year and consumed by two households which is denoted by to *consumption* (*C*) by households.
2. Value of *new capital goods produced and additiôn to the inventories of goods* such as raw materials, unfinished goods and consumer goods produced but not sold during a year. This is called *Gross Private Investment* (*I*).
3. Value of output of General Government which is taken to be equal to the value of *purchases of goods and services by the Government* which we denote by *G*.
4. Net Exports (*NX*) which is equal to value of goods *exported* minus the value of goods *imported* (*M*).
5. Net Factor Income from Abroad which we will explain below

Net Factor Income From Absoad

Now, what does net factor income from abroad stand for? The sum of factor incomes such as wages and salaries (*i.e.*, compensation of employees), rent, interest and profits generated within the domestic territory of a country in a year is called domestic factor income. It includes factor incomes generated both by residents and non-residents working in the domestic territory of a country. For example, non-residents (*i.e.*, foreigners) work in the domestic territory of India and earn wages and salary. Thus, foreign individuals and companies from the USA, Great Britain and other countries have acquired property such as factories, offices, buildings, places and have also acquired financial assets such as bonds and shares of Indian companies. This generates incomes in the form of rent and interest to them. In addition to this, foreign residents—individuals and companies—have set up industrial plants and factories producing goods and services from which they earn profits.

On the other hand, Indians go abroad and work in the territories of other countries and earn wages and salaries. Likewise, some Indian individuals and corporate companies have acquired assets such as buildings, factories, commercial space, and have also invested in bonds, bank deposits of foreign countries and thus receive rent and interest. Some Indian companies have set up factories abroad and earn profits.

Now, the *net factor income from abroad is the difference between factor income received from abroad by normal residents of India for rendering factor services in other countries on the one hand and the factor incomes paid to the foreign residents for factor services rendered by them in the domestic territory of India on the other.*

Net factor income earned from abroad have therofore the following three components:

1. *Net* compensation of employees.
2. *Net* income from property *i.e.*, rent, interest and income from entrepreneurship (that is, profits and dividends).
3. *Net* retained earnings of the resident companies working in foreign countries.

(Note that '*Net*' in the above means the difference between the relevant income of normal residents earned from abroad and the same type of incomes paid to non-residents working in the domestic territory of a country)

Gross Domestic Product (GDP)

Another important concept of national income is gross domestic product (GDP). Gross domestic product is the money value of all final goods and services produced by normal *residents as well as non-residents in the domestic territory of a country but does not include net factor income earned from abroad.* Thus difference between gross domestic product (GDP) and gross national product (GNP) at market prices arises due to the existence of '*net factor income from abroad*'. Gross domestic product does not include net factor income from abroad, whereas gross national product includes it. Therefore,

Gross Domestic Product (at market prices) or

$$GDP_{MP} = GNP_{MP} - \text{net factor income from abroad}$$

or $$GNP_{MP} = GDP_{MP} + \text{net factor income from abroad}$$

It should however be noted that net factor income from abroad should not be confused with income from *net exports* which are a part of both gross national product (GNP) and gross domestic product (GDP). Net exports equal total exports minus imports. Gross exports are the total value of domestically produced goods and services sold to foriegn buyers in a year and are therefore a part of Gross Domestic Product (GDP) and not a factor income from abroad. On the other hand, imports are the value of imported goods and services pruchased by the domestic buyers. Therefore, imports do not form a part of GDP or GNP. In national income accounting, we subtract the value of imports from the value of exports to arrive at net exports which are a part of GDP and therefore also of GNP. Thus, earnings from net exports are quite distinct from net factor income from abroad.

Thus, we can obtain Gross Domestic Product (GDP) by adding up the first four items of Gross National Product listed above. Thus

$$GDP = C + I + G + X_n$$

$$\text{where } X_n = (X - M)$$

We have graphically depicted GDP by second bar in Figure 2.

GNP	GDP	NDP_{MP}	NDP_{FC}
Net factor income from abroad			
Gross Private Investment	Gross Private Investment	Less Depreciation	
		Net Private Investment	Less Net Indirect Taxes
Net Exports (Xn)	Net Exports	Net Exports	Wages + Profits + Interest + Rent
Government Purchases (G)	Government Purchases	Government Purchases	
Consumption Expenditure (C)	Consumption Expenditure	Consumption Expenditure	

Fig. 2.5. *Various Concepts of National Product*

(Note: By adding Factor Income from Abroad to NDP_{MP} and NDP_{FC} we get NNP_{MP} and NNP_{FC} (respectively).

Net National Product (NNP) or National Income at Market Prices

The second important concept of national income is that of net national product (NNP). In the production of gross national product of a year, we consume or use up some fixed capital *i.e.*, equipment, machinery, etc. The capital goods, like machinery, wear out or fall in value as a result of its consumption or use in the production process. This consumption of fixed capital or fall in the value of fixed capital due to wear and tear is called depreciation. When charges for depreciation are deducted from the gross national product we get net national product. Clearly, it means the *market value of all final goods and services* after providing for depreciation. Therefore, it is also called '*national income at market prices*'. Therefore,

Net National Product or National Income at Market Prices } = Gross National Product – Depreciation

National Income (NI) or National Income at Factor Cost (NNP_{FC})

National Income at factor cost which is also simply called *national income* means the sum of all incomes earned by resource suppliers for their contribution of land, labour, capital and entrepreneurial ability which go into the year's net production. In other words, national income (or national income at factor cost) shows how much it costs society in terms of economic resources to produce net output. It is really the national income at factor cost for which we use the term National Income. The difference between national income (or national income at factor cost) and net national product (national income at market prices) arises from the fact that *indirect taxes* and *subsidies* cause market prices of output to be different from the factor incomes resulting from it. Suppose for instance, a metre of mill cloth sold for Rs. 200 includes Rs. 25 on account of the excise and the sales tax. In this case while the market price of the cloth is Rs. 200 a metre, the factors engaged in its production and distribution would receive Rs. 175 a metre. The value of cloth at factor cost would thus be equal to its value at market price less the indirect taxes on it. On the other hand, a subsidy causes the market price to be less than the factor cost. Suppose handloom cloth is subsidised at the rate of Rs. 10 per metre and it sells at Rs. 90 per metre. Then while the consumer pays Rs. 90 per metre, the factors engaged in the production and distribution of such cloth will receive Rs. 100 per metre (Rs. 90 + 10 = Rs. 100). The value of handloom cloth at factor cost would thus be equal to its market price plus the subsidies paid on it. It follows, therefore, that the national income (or national income at factor cost) is equal to net national product minus indirect taxes plus subsidies.

$$\left.\begin{array}{l}\text{National Income}\\ \text{or}\\ \text{National Income at}\\ \text{Factor Cost}\end{array}\right\} = \text{Net National Product (National Income at Market Prices)} - \text{Indirect Taxes} + \text{Subsidies}$$

Net of indirect taxes and subsidies is called Net Indirect Taxes. Therefore,
National Income = Net National Product – Net Indirect Taxes

Personal Income (PI)

Personal Income is the sum of all incomes actually received by all individuals or households during a given year. National income, that is, total incomes earned and personal income, that is, total incomes received must be different because some incomes which are earned such as social security contributions, corporate income taxes and undistributed corporate profits are not actually received by households, and conversely, some incomes which are received like transfer payments are not currently earned (examples of transfer payments are old-age pensions, unemployment compensation, relief payments, interest payments on the public debt, etc.). Obviously, in moving from national income as an indicator of income earned to personal income as an indicator of income actually received, we must subtract from national income those three types of income which are earned but not received and add those incomes which are received but currently not earned. Therefore,

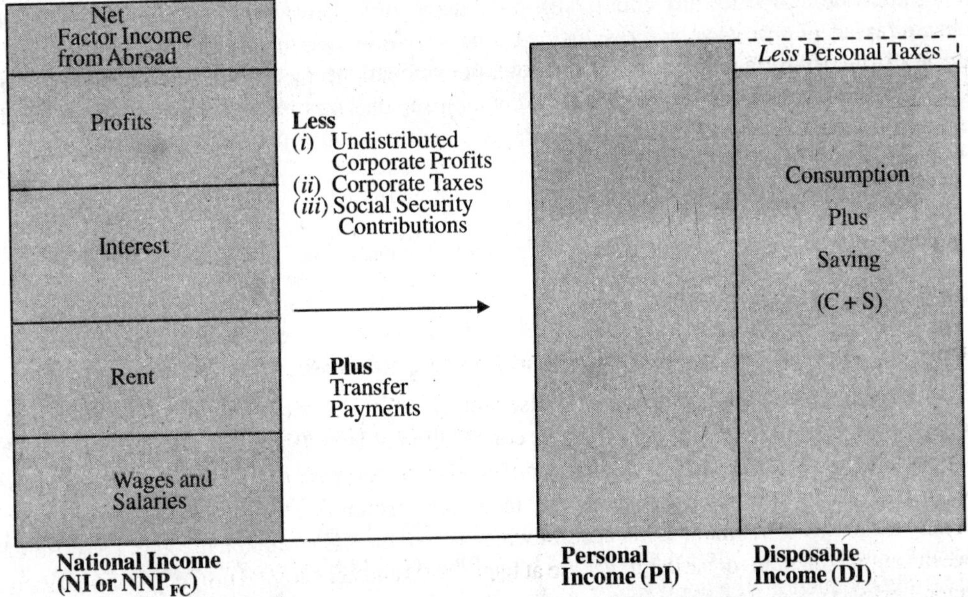

Fig. 2.6. *From National Income to Disposable Income*

Personal Income = National Income — Social Security Contributions — Corporate Income Taxes —Undistributed Corporate Profits + Transfer Payments.

Disposable Income (DI)

Even whole of the incomes which are actually received by the people are not available to them for consumption. This is because governments levy some personal taxes such as income tax, personal property taxes. Therefore, after a part of personal income is paid to government in the form of *personal taxes* like income tax, personal property taxes, etc., what remains of personal income is called *disposable income*. Therefore,

Disposable Income = Personal Income – Personal Taxes.

Disposable Income can either be either consumed or saved. Hence,

Disposable Income = Consumption + Saving.

How do we get personal income and disposable income from national income is illustrated in Figure 2.6.

MEASUREMENT OF NATIONAL INCOME

Since factor *incomes* arise from the production of goods and services, and since incomes are spent on goods and services produced, three alternative methods of measuring national income are possible.

1. Value Added Method.

This is also called *output method or production method.* In this method the contribution of each enterprise to the generation of flow of goods and services is measured. Under this method, the economy is divided into different industrial sectors such as agriculture, fishing, mining, construction, manufacturing, trade and commerce, transport, communication and other services. Then, the net value added at factor cost (NVA_{FC}) by each productive enterprise as well as by each industry or sector is estimated. Measuring net value added at factor cost (NVA_{FC}) by each industry requires first to find out the value of output.

Let us explain how we arrive at net value added at factor cost (NVA_{FC}) from value of output step by step. An important estimate which we have to make in this method is to find out the value of various goods and services produced by enterprises in the domestic territory of a country. *The quantity of goods and services produced by a particular enterprise multiplied by their market prices is called value of output.* By summing up the value of output of all producing enterprises in a given industry or a sector we can obtain the value of output of that industry or sector. A major part of output of a firm or enterprise is sold in the market and termed as *sales*. The remaining part of output which is *not sold* in the accounting year is added to the stock of goods or inventories. Thus.

Value of output of an enterprise = Sales + Change in Stocks

Gross Value Added at Market Prices (GVA_{MP}). Gross value added measures the contribution to the value of output of a product produced during a year. As mentioned above, value of output is estimated by multiplying the quantity of output with the market prices. Therefore, gross value added at market prices by a production unit is obtained by deducting the value of intermediate consumption (that is, the value of intermediate goods such as raw materials used from the value of output (at market prices) produced. Thus.

Gross value added at market prices (GVA_{MP}) = *Value of Output – Intermediate Consumption*

A firm disposes of its value added at market prices (GVA_{MP}) among the three items : (1) making depreciation provision for consumption of fixed capital during the year, (2) making payments of indirect taxes such as excise duties, sales tax, import duty to the government, and (3) making factor payments suhc as wages, interest and profits to the factors of production whose services have been used for the production of a good.

Net Value Added at Market Prices (NVA_{MP}). When from gross value added at market prices we deduct depreciation on account of consumption of fixed capital during the production process of a good during the year, we get Net Value Added at market prices (NVA_{MP}). Thus

$NVA_{MP} = GVA_{MP}$ – Consumption of Fixed Capital i.e. Depreciation

Thus net value added is net of depreciation or consumption of fixed capital.

Net Value Added at Factor Cost (NVA_{FC}). When adjustment is made in net value added at market prices (NVA_{MP}) for the payment of net indirect taxes, (that is, indirect taxes such as sales tax, excise duty, customs duties to the government minus subsidies received from the government) we get Net Value Added at Factor Cost (NVA_{FC}) This is because after the subtraction of depreciation amount and net indirect taxes what remains is used for making payments to factors of production such as wages to labour, interest on capital borrowed, rent for land and building hired from others and profits and dividends to entrepreneur. In other words, NVA_{FC} measures the value of factor cost a firm has to incur.

Summing up the net values added at factor cost (NVA_{FC}) by all productive enterprises of an industry or sector gives us the net value added at factor cost of each industry or sector. We then add up net values added at factor cost by all industries or sectors to get *net domestic product at factor cost* (NDP_{FC}). Lastly, to the net domestic product we add the *net factor income from abroad* to get *net national product at factor cost* (NNP_{FC}) which is also called national income. Thus,

NI or $NNP_{FC} = NDP_{FC}$ + Net factor income from abroad

This method of calculating national income can be used where there exists a census of production for the year. In many countries, the data of production of only important industries are known. Hence this method is employed along with other methods to arrive at the national income. The one great advantage of this method is that it reveals the relative importance of the different sectors of the economy by showing their respective contributions to the national income.

Precautions. The following precautions should be taken while measuring national income of a country through value added method:

1. *Imputed rent values* of self-occupied houses should be included in the value of output. Though these payments are not made to others, their values can be easily estimated from prevailing values in the market.
2. Sale and purchase of *second-hand goods* should not be included in measuring value of output of a year because their values were counted in the year of output of the year of their production. Of course, commission or brokerage earned in their sale and purchase has to be included because this is a new service rendered in the current year.
3. *Value of production for self-consumption* arc be counted while measuring national income. In this method, the production for self-consumption should be valued at the prevailing market prices.
4. *Value of services of housewives* are not included because it is not easy to find out correctly the value of their services.
5. Value of intermediate goods *must not* be counted while measuring value added because this will amount to double counting.

2. Income Method

This method approaches national income from distribution side. In other words, this method measures national income at the phase of distribution and appears as income paid and or received by individuals of the country. Thus, under this method, *national income is obtained by summing up of the incomes of all individuals of a country.* Individuals earn incomes by contributing their own services and the services of their property such as land and capital to the national production. Therefore, national income is calculated by adding up the rent of land, wages and salaries of employees, interest on capital, profits of entrepreneurs (including undistributed corporate profits) and incomes of self-employed people. This method of estimating national income has the great advantage of indicating the distribution of national income among different income groups such as landlords, owners of capital, workers, entrepreneurs. Measurement of national income through income method involves the following main steps:

1. Like the value added method, the first step in income method is also to *identify* the productive enterprises and then *classify* them into various industrial sectors such as agriculture, fishing, forestry, manufacturing, transport, trade and commerce, banking, etc.

2. The second step is to classify *the factor payments*. The factor payments are classified into the following groups:

1. *Compensation of employees* which includes wages and salaries, employers' contribution to social security schemes.
2. *Rent and also royalty*, if any.
3. *Interest*.
4. *Profits*: Profits are divided into three sub-groups:
   (*i*) Dividends
   (*ii*) Undistributed profits
   (*iii*) Corporate income tax

5. *Mixed income of the self-employed*: In India as in other developing countries there is fifth category of factor income which is termed as *mixed income of self-employed*. In India a good number of people are engaged in household industries, in family farms and other unorganised enterprises. Because of self-employment nature of the business it is difficult to separate wages for the work done by the self-employed from the surplus or profits made by them. Therefore, the incomes earned by them are mix of wages, rent, interest and profit and are, therefore, called *mixed income of the self-employed*.

3. The third step is to *measure factor payments*. Income paid out by each enterprise can be estimated by gathering information about the number of units of each factor employed and the income paid out to each unit of every factor. Price paid out to each factor multiplied by the number of units of each factor employed would give us the factor's income.

4. The *adding up of factor payments* by all enterprises belonging to an industrial sector would give us the incomes paid out to various factors by a *particular* industrial sector.

5. By summing up the incomes paid out by *all industrial sectors* we will obtain domestic factor income which is also called net domestic product at factor cost (NDP_{FC}).

			Net Indirect Taxes
	Net Factor Income from abroad	Consumption of Fixed Capital	Consumption of Fixed capital
Dividends	Profits	Dividends	Profits
Undistributed Profits		Undistributed Profits	
Corporate Income Tax		Corporate Income Tax	
Interest	Interest	Interest	Interest
Rent	Rent	Rent	Rent
Mixed Income of Self-employed	Mixed Income of Self-employed	Mixed income of Self-employed	Mixed Income of Self-employed
Compensation of Employees	Compensation of Employees	Compensation of Employees	Compensation of Employees
NDP_{FC}	**NNP_{FC}**	**GDP_{FC}**	**GDP_{MP}**

Figure 2.7. Income Approach to National Income

6. Finally, by adding net factor income earned from abroad to domestic factor income or NDP_{FC} we get net national product at factor cost (NNP_{FC}) which is also called *national income.*

Income approach to measurement of national income is shown through bar diagrams in Figure 2.7

Compensation of Employees

From the above items of income categories compensation of employees require further explanation. Compensation of employees by the producers is the sum of wages and salaries, paid both in cash and kind, and contribution to social security schemes of the employees made by the employers. Thus, it has the following components:

Wages and Salaries: These include all payments made by the employers to their employees, both in cash and kind, for the services they render to their employers.

Wages and Salaries Payable in Cash. They include the following:

(1) Wages and salaries received in cash by the employees from their employers.
(2) Payments received by the employees for overtime work done by them.
(3) Travelling allowance received by the employees for going to and coming home from their work-places.
(4) Bonuses, if any, receivable by the workers.
(5) Dearness allowance paid to the employees to neutralise the rise in cost of living.
(6) Vacation allowance and sick leave allowance.
(7) Leave travelling allowance (LTC).
(8) Commission provided, if any, to the sales staff on the sales.

Wages and Salaries in kind. These are the remuneration in kind received in the form of goods and services by the employees for their use by themselves or by the members of their households. The following are some important types of remuneration received in kind.

(1) Housing accommodation provided free of cost.
(2) Free meals and drinks (such as tea, coffee, cold drinks) provided free to the employees when they are on duty.
(3) Uniforms and special clothing, if any, received free of cost by the employer.
(4) The free services of vehicles (cars, scooters, vans etc.) provided by the employers to their employees.
(5) Free provision of goods and services which are produced by the enterprises themselves. Free travelling by the staff of railways or airlines, free coal to the workers working in coal mines fall in this category.
(6) Creches provided by the employers for the children of their employees.
(7) Value of interest on the free-interest loans given by the employers to their employees or value of concessions in interest on loans given on concessional rates of interest by the employers to their employees.
(8) Value of recreation and sport facilities provided by the employers to their employees and the members of their households.

Employers' contributions to social security schemes. Employers' contribution relating to the social security schemes of their employees such as life insurance, casualty insurance, contributory provident fund (CPF), pension schemes are also a part of the compensation of employees.

In addition to the above, in India's national income accounting, salaries and allowances paid to members of Parliament and State Legislatures, pay and allowances to the President of India, State Governors, ministers of Central and State Cabinets are also treated as compensation of employees.

Precautions. While estimating national income through income method the following precautions should be taken:

1. *Transfer payments* are not included in estimating national income through this method.

1. *Transfer payments* are not included in estimating national income through this method.

2. *Imputed rent* of self-occupied houses are included in national income as these houses provide services to those who occupy them and its value can be easily estimated from the market value data.

3. *Illegal money* such as *hawala money, money earned through smuggling* etc. are not included as they cannot be easily estimated.

4. *Windfall gains* such as prizes won, lotteries are also not included.

5. Corporate profit tax (that is, tax on income of the companies) should not be separately included as it has already been included as a part of profits.

6. *Death duties, gift tax, wealth tax, tax on lotteries*, etc., are paid from past savings or wealth and not from current income. Therefore, they should not be treated as a part of national income of a year.

7. The receipts from the *sale of second-hand goods* should not be treated as a part of national income. This is because the sale of second-hand goods does not create new flows goods and services in the current year.

8. Income equal to the *value of production used for self-consumption* should be estimated and included in the measure of national income.

Expenditure Method

Expenditure method arrives at national income by adding up all expenditures made on goods and services during a year. Income can be spent either on consumer goods or capital goods. Again, expenditure can be made by private individuals and households or by government and business enterprises. Further, people of foreign countries spend on the goods and services which a country exports to them. Similarly, people of a country spend on imports of goods and services from other countries. We add up the following types of expenditure by households, government and by productive enterprises to obtain national income.

1. Expenditure on consumer goods and services by individuals and households. This is called *final private consumption expenditure*, and is denoted by C.
2. Government's expenditure on goods and services to satisfy collective wants. This is called *government's final consumption expenditure*, and is denoted by G.
3. The expenditure by productive enterprises on capital goods and inventories or stocks. This is called *gross domestic capital formation*, or gross domestic investment and is denoted by I or GDCF. Gross domestic capital formation is divided into two parts:
   (*i*) Gross fixed capital formation
   (*ii*) Addition to the stocks or inventories of goods
4. The expenditure made by foreigners on goods and services of a country exported to other countries which are called exports and are denoted by *X*. We deduct from exports (*X*) the expenditure by people, enterprises and government of a country on imports (*M*) of goods and services from other countries. That is, we have to estimate net exports (that is, exports – imports) or (*X*—*M*).

Thus, we add up the above four types of expenditure to get final expenditure on gross domestic product at market prices (GDP_{MP}). Thus,

GDP_{MP} = Private final consumption expenditure + Government's final consumption expenditure + Gross domestic capital formation + Exports — Imports or

$$GDP_{MP} = C + G + I + (X - M)$$
$$= C + G + I + Xn$$

On deducting consumption of fixed capital (*i.e.*, depreciation) from gross domestic product at market prices (GDP_{MP}) we get net domestic product at market prices (NDP_{MP}).

In this method, we then subtract net indirect taxes (that is, indirect taxes – subsidies) to arrive at net domestic product at factor cost (NDP_{FC}).

Gross Domestic Capital Formation	Less Depreciation		Net Factor Income from abroad
	Net Domestic Capital Formation	Less Net Indirect Tax	Net Domestic Capital Formation
Govt. Final Consumption Expenditure	Govt. Final Consumption Expenditure		Govt.Final Consumption Expenditure
Private Final Consumption Expenditure	Private Final Consumption Expenditure		Private Final Consumption Expenditure
Net Exports (X–M)	Net Exports (X–M)		Net Exports (X–M)

$\mathbf{GDP_{MP}} \longrightarrow \mathbf{NDP_{MP}} \longrightarrow \mathbf{NDP_{FC}} \longrightarrow \mathbf{NNP_{MP}}$

Fig. 2.5. *Expenditure Approach to National Income Concepts*

Lastly, we add 'net factor income from abroad' to obtain net national product at factor cost (NNP_{FC}), which is called national income. Thus,

$NNP_{FC} = GDP_{MP}$ – Consumption of Fixed capital - Net Indirect taxes + Net Factor Income from Abroad.

Expenditure approach to national income is shown through bar diagram in Table 2.2.

(**Note:** To any concept of the domestic product, if we add '*Net Income from Abroad*' we will get corresponding National Product)

Government's expenditure on goods and services need explanation in some detail.

Government's Final Consumption Expenditure on Goods and Services

The general government provides services such as defence, law and order, public health, education, cultural services, etc., to satisfy collective wants of its citizens. The government purchases various goods and services from others for providing its services to the people and incurs cost on them. This cost of goods and services purchased by the government to provide its services to the people to satisfy collective wants is called intermediate consumption. Further, the government employs several persons, such as soldiers, policemen, other official clerks, secretaries in various departments and pays them wages and salaries. Thus, compensation to employees (that is wages, salaries, etc.), both in cash and in kind, is another type of cost incurred by the Government. Since government generally *does not sell* its services and instead provides them free of cost or sells them at a price much lower than production cost, the value of services provided by the government are valued at their cost to the government. The cost is the sum of (1) expenditure on intermediate consumption incurred by Government and (2) compensation to employees (wages and salaries etc.).

However, the government also sells some goods and services, though at nominal prices, such as hospital fees, tuition fees charged from the students in Government institutions. In order to find out the cost of government services, proceeds from sales of some goods and services, if any, by the government must be deducted.

Thus, the Government's final consumption expenditure on goods and services includes the following items.

1. Compensation of employees
2. Intermediate consumption expenditure by the General Government which refers to purchases of goods and services by the Government *less* sales of some goods by it.
3. Consumption of fixed capital.

Transfer Payments by the Government. Government expenditure on goods and services needs to be distinguished from transfer payments by the government. A good amount of Government expenditure is undertaken on making transfer payments which is not included in gross national product. Main examples of transfer payments are social security benefits, unemployment allowance, old age pensions, interest on public debt. The reason for excluding them in estimation of national income is that in sharp contrast to Government purchases of goods and services, they are not paid in exchange for the *contribution to the current production of goods* or rendering of any service by the recipients to the Government in the current year. In making transfer payments the Government just transfers a part of its revenue to specific individuals without any contribution by them to the current production of goods and services. To include these transfer payments in national income would amount to overestimate current year's production. Therefore, they are not included in national income of a year.

Precautions. While estimating Gross Domestic Product through expenditure method or measuring final expenditure on Gross National Product, the following precautions should be taken:

1. *Second-hand goods*: The expenditure made on second-hand goods should not be included because this does not contribute to the current year production of goods and services.

2. *Purchase of shares and bonds.* Expenditure on purchase of old shares and bonds from other people and from business enterprises should not be included while estimating Gross Domestic Product through expenditure method. This is because bonds and shares are mere financial claims and do not represent expenditure on currently produced goods and services.

3. *Expenditure on transfer payments* by government such as unemployment benefits, old-age pension should also not be included because no goods or productive services are produced in exchange by the recipients of these payments.

4. *Expenditure on intermediate goods* such as fertilisers and seeds by the farmers and wool, cotton and yarn by manufacturers of garments should also be excluded. This is because we have to avoid double counting. Therefore, for estimating Gross Domestic Product we have to include only *expenditure on final goods* and services.

Difficulties in the Measurement of National Income

There are many difficulties in measuring national income of a country accurately. The difficulties involved are both conceptual and statistical in nature. Some of these difficulties or problems involved in the measurement of national income are enumerated below.

1. **Treatment of non-monetary transactions.** The first problem relates to the *treatment of non-monetary transactions* such as the services of housewives to the members of their families and farm output consumed at home. On this point, the general agreement is *to exclude the services of housewives while to include the value of farm output consumed at home in the estimate of national income.* This, however, gives rise to certain anomalies. For example, if a man employs a maid-servant for household work, payment to her will appear as a positive item in national income. If the next day the man were to marry the maid-servant, she would be performing the same services as before but without payments. In this event the value of national income would go down though the real amount of goods and services performed remains the same as before.

2. **Treatment of Government activities in national income accounts.** The second difficulty arises with regard to the treatment of the government in national income accounts. On this point the general viewpoint is that as regards the administrative functions of the government like justice, administration and defence are concerned they should be treated as giving rise to final consumption of such services by the community as a whole so that contribution of general government activities will be equal to the amount of wages and salaries paid by the government. As regards capital formation by the government, this is treated as par with capital formation by private enterprises.

3. **Treatment of income generated by foreign firms.** The third major problem arises with regard to the treatment of income arising out of activities of the foreign firms in a country. Should their income form a part of the national income of the country in which they are located or should it belong to the national income of the country owning the firms? On this point, the IMF viewpoint which is generally accepted is that production and income arising from a foreign enterprise should be ascribed to the country in which production takes place. However, profits earned by foreign companies are credited to the parent country.

Difficulties of Measuring National Income in Developing Countries

In developing countries like India, we face some special difficulties in estimating national income. Some of these difficulties are given below:

1. A great difficulty in estimating national income in the developing countries like India arises because of the *prevalence of non-monetised transactions in such countries* so that a considerable part of the output does not come into the market at all. Agriculture still being largely in the nature of subsistence farming in these countries, a major part of output is consumed at the farm itself. The national statistician, therefore, has to face the problem of finding a suitable measure of value for this part of national output.

2. Because of illiteracy in the developing countries most producers have no idea of the quantity and value of their output and do not follow the practice of keeping regular accounts. This makes the task of getting reliable information from a large number of petty producers all the more difficult."

3. Because of underdevelopment, *occupational specialisation is still incomplete*, so that there is a lack of differentiation in economic functioning. An individual may receive income partly from farm ownership, partly from manual work in industry in the slack season, etc. This makes the task of estimating national income very difficult.

4. Another difficulty in measuring national income in the developing countries arises because *production, both agricultural and industrial, is unorganised* and scattered in these countries. This does not admit of easy calculation. In India, agriculture, cottage industries and indigenous banking are some of the production sectors which are unorganised and scattered. An assessment of output produced by self-employed agriculturists, small producers and owners of household enterprises in the unorganised sectors requires an element of guess work which makes the figure for national income unreliable.

5. The greatest difficulty in the measurement of national income in the developing countries is general *lack of adequate statistical data.* Inadequacy, non-availability and unreliability of statistics is a great handicap in measuring national income in these countries. As stated above, statistical information regarding agriculture and allied occupations, and household enterprises is not available. Even the statistical information regarding the enterprises in the organised sector is sketchy and unreliable. There is no accurate information available regarding consumption, investment expenditure and savings of either rural or urban population.

NOMINAL GNP AND REAL GNP

Nominal GNP, as explained above, is the money value of all final goods and services produced in a year. This money value is obtained using current year market prices of final goods and services produced. However, Nominal GNP does not truly indicate the real performance or economic growth of a country over time if prices are changing. While nominal GNP may be increasing due to rise in price level, the quantity of goods and services produced may remain constant. Therefore, in order to estimate to what extent the amount of final goods and services produced has increased we have to eliminate the effect of change in prices on the nominal value of GNP in the current year. To do so the economists evaluate the output of final goods and services produced in a year using the market prices that prevaited in a certain chosen year, called as the *base year*. Estimates of India's real GNP which were made using

1993-94 as the base year has now been changed to the year 1999-2000. Thus, in India now market prices of the year 1999-2000 are used to estimate the real GNP which is also called *national income at constant prices*.

How this valuation is done using the market prices of a base year can be illustrated through a simple numerical example. Suppose an imaginary economy produces only four final goods, namely, wheat, standard cloth, milk and computers whose prices in the current year 2006-07 and the base year (i.e., 1999-2000) are given in column 3 and 5 of Table–1. The amounts of final goods, wheat, cloth, milk and computers in the current year 2006-07 are given in column 2.

Tabel–1. Estimation of Real GNP

Final Goods	*Quantities produced in 2006-07*	*Market Prices in 2006-07*	*Value of Final Goods at Current market Prices of 2006-07 (Rs.)*	*Market Price in base year (1999-2000)*	*Value of Final Goods at base year (1999-200) prices*
1	2	3	4	5	6
Wheat (quintals)	650	700 per quintal	4,55,000	550	3,57,500
Standard cloth (metres)	345	120 per metre	41,400	100	34,500
Milk (litres)	520	15 per litre	7,800	12	6,240
Computers (Nos.)	200	2500 per unit	50,00,000	18000	3,66,0000
			5504200		3998240

In order to obtain the *nominal GNP* for the current year 2006-07 we multiply the quantities of four final commodities by the market prices of the current year 2006-07 and the results are given in column 4. By adding up the market values of all the final goods at current prices we get the total value equal to Rs. 5504200 for the year 2006-07. Rs. 5504200 is the nominal GNP for the current year 2006-07.

For obtaining the value of *real GNP* for the current year 2006-07 we multiply the outputs of final goods produced in the current year 2006-07 by the prices of the base year (1999-2000), and record the estimates in column 6. Summing up the values of four final goods evaluated at base-year prices we get the total estimate of Rs. 3998240 which is the real GNP (or gross national income at constant prices) for the current year 2006-07.

It may be noted that real GNP and nominal GNP for the base year will be the same.

It will noticed from Table–1 that for the current year 2006-07, whereas the value of nominal GNP is equal to Rs. 5504200, the real GNP is only Rs. 3998240. This is because market prices have risen between the base year (1999-2000) and the current year 2006-07.

The calculation of real GNP helps us to know whether the availability of real goods and services in the economy has increased over time. *Besides, by calculating the percentge change of real GNP in a year enables us to measure rate of economic growth in a year*. Further, it is real GNP that is often used for making comparisons of international standards of living and rates of economic growth of various countries.

Finally, with the help of nominal GNP and real GNP we can measure rate of inflation that has taken place over time. This measure of rate of inflation is known as **GNP deflator**. This is calculated as follows :

$$\text{GNP Deflator} = \frac{\text{Nominal GNP of a year}}{\text{Real GNP of the year}} \times 100$$

LIMITATIONS OF GDP CONCEPT AS A MEASURE OF SOCIAL WELFARE

National income, or GNP, as explained in the last chapter, measures the value of aggregate output of goods and services produced in a year. Since goods and services satisfy the wants of the people, national income or GNP has often been used as a measure of satisfaction or economic welfare of the people. The greater the magnitude of national income, the greater the level of economic welfare. Besides, economic progress or what is now generally called economic growth has been measured in terms of increase in national income (that is, increase in GNP or NNP) in terms of total or per capita income. In recent years doubts have been expressed about the validity of national income or gross national product (GNP) as a measure and index of economic welfare.

It has been asserted by several modern economists that national income as it is usually defined is not a satisfactory measure of economic welfare. According to them, in order to obtain a true measure of economic welfare, some adjustments both in the form of additions and subtractions have to be made in the aggregate of national income. National income, as it is usually conceived and measured, includes some things that do not increase welfare of the people. Therefore, such things ought to be excluded in order to get a true measure of economic welfare. This true measure of economic welfare is now often called "*Net Economic Welfare*" or simply *NEW*. On the other hand, the usual concept of national income excludes some goods and services which increase satisfaction of the people and therefore ought to be included in any good index of Net Economic Welfare.

As regards the things that ought to be added to obtain the index of Net Economic Welfare (NEW), the first important thing is the *value of satisfaction that people derive from leisure*. The usual concept of national income (or GNP) does not attach any significance to the amount of leisure people enjoy. However, the individuals derive satisfaction not only from the consumption of goods and services but also from leisure they have. Therefore, for constructing any index of net economic welfare, the value of leisure which the people enjoy must also be included. For example, if the average working hours are reduced, this is likely to reduce national production or national income but may raise welfare of the people by enabling them to enjoy more leisure.

The other important items that ought to be added to obtain a true measure of welfare are the *non-marketed personal services* (that is, the personal services which are not sold and purchased in the market) which also greatly raise the satisfaction and welfare of the people. For instance, services rendered by the housewives to the family members greatly add to their welfare but they are not recorded in national income accounting. Likewise, personal services rendered by the individuals to themselves such as gardening, painting one's own house significantly raise their welfare but do not get registered in the national income or GNP. Hence in order to get any true index of economic welfare, the value of non-market activities such as personal services which increase welfare ought to be incorporated.

As regards the items that have to be deducted from the national income, mention may be made of those harmful effects which result from increase in output. As is well known, the production of modern industries pollutes the environment such as polluting air, water and calmness which significantly reduce welfare of the people. Though modern industrialization has greatly increased national income of the countries but by causing *air pollution, water pollution and noise* has tended to reduce the welfare of the people. Therefore, for preparing a measure of net welfare, negative values ought to be assigned to the *environment pollution* that results from the production of goods and services. The various forms of pollution of environment have often been referred to as *costs of economic growth,* which like other costs, have to be deducted to obtain the index of net economic welfare.

Apart from environment pollution, certain other deductions on account of wasteful and non-productive expenditure such as Government expenditure on police and law courts so as to maintain law and order and on defence to protect the country from external aggression. These have been called "*regrettable costs*", because economists consider them regrettable necessities expenditure on which does not lead to increase in welfare of the people. Hence expenditure on them should be excluded from GNP to arrive at the measure of net economic welfare.

To sum up, the relation between national income (GNP) and Net Economic Welfare (NEW) can be represented as follows:

Real GNP
– Depreciation
+ Value of leisure
+ Value of non-market activities (*i.e.*, services of housewives and personal services)
– Environment pollution
– Regrettable costs
= Net Economic Welfare

But it is worth-mentioning that even the measure of Net Economic Welfare (NEW) as defined above does not truly indicate the welfare enjoyed by the people. There are other things which play a significant role in determining welfare of a nation and which do not get registered in national income or in Net Economic Welfare. Thus, *composition of national output* as between wage goods and luxuries and also the *distribution of goods between individuals* determine welfare to a great extent. If with the increase in total national income and per capita income, the rich are getting richer and the poor getting poorer, then this growth in national income and per capita income cannot be said to promote welfare. Professor Hicks rightly remarks, "*the national income only measure the total volume of goods and services at the disposal of the community during the year; it can tell us nothing, for example, about the way in which the national income is divided up between rich and poor.*"[2]

Further national income and per capita income are also not true measures of welfare because they do not consider the composition of output. A country's national income and per capita income may be very high but the well-being of the people may be very low because the national output consist of a larger quantity of war material. This is a very important factor because it is well known fact that various countries are spending quite a large part of national budgets on the manufacture of war materials and the greater the expenditure on the defence forces, the smaller will be the actual well-being of the people, given the size of national and per capita income.

Similarly, the well-being of the people also depends upon the relative proportions of wage-goods (necessities) and luxuries in the composition of national product. It may be noted that in a country if luxuries are being produced in relatively greater quantities than the wage-goods, then in that case while the few rich will be rolling in luxuries, the poor will be deprived of even sufficient quantities of necessities of life. Likewise, national and per capita income do not accurately reflect improvements in the quality of products. This is a shortcoming because improvements in the quality of products affect the economic welfare of the people as much as the increase in quantities of goods.

Lastly, the increase in national income does not truly indicate the increase in welfare of the people because it does not take into account *how the national income is being produced and how the increase in it has been brought about*. If increase is national income has been brought about by making workers work longer hours which impair their health and efficiency, then this increase in national income will not promote welfare but will adversely affect it. Similarly, if the increase in national income has been obtained by introducing labour-saving machinery throwing out a large number of workers out of employment, this growth in national income which increases unemployment and therefore cannot lead to the increase in social welfare.

SOME EXAMPLES OF NATIONAL INCOME CALCULATION

We solve below some numerical problems of calculation of national income by three methods, namely, expenditure method, income method and value added method.

Problem 1. *Calculate (1) GDP at market prices and (2) national income from the following information.*

	Rs.
Personal consumption expenditure	*6,500*
Indirect taxes less subsidies	*150*
State government consumption and investment expenditure	*500*
Central government consumption and investment expenditure	*2,000*
Change in business inventories	*100*
Gross private domestic fixed investment	*1,200*
Exports	*900*
Net factor payments to rest of the world	*– 100*
Imports	*1,200*
Depreciation	*200*

DU BA(Hons.) 2006

Solution.

(*i*) GDP_{MP} = (Private Consumption Expenditure + Gross private investment (both fixed and inventories) + Gov. Expenditure (both State and Central) + Net exports (X–M))

= 6500 + (1200 + 100) + (500 + 2000) + (900 – 1200)

= 6500 + 1300 + 2500 – 300

= 10,000

(*ii*) *National Income.* National income is net national product at factor cost (NNP_{FC}). Therefore, to find out *net* domestic product at factor cost we have to deduct depreciation and net indirect taxes from GDP_{MP} and to get *national* income we have to deduct net factor payments to the rest of the world. Thus

NI or NNP_{FC} = GDP_{MP} – Depreciation – net Indirect taxes (*i.e.* indirect taxes less subsidies) – net factor payments to the rest of the world.

NI = 10,000 – 200 – 150 – 100

= 9550

Problem 2. *Calculate the national income and personal disposable income from the following information :*

GDP_{MP}	*6,000*
Receipts of factor income from the rest of the world	*150*
Payments of factor income to the rest of the world	*225*
Depreciation	*800*
Indirect taxes minus subsidies	*700*
Corporate Profits	*1,200*
Dividend	*600*
Transfer payments to persons	*1,300*
Personal Taxes	*1,500*

D.U. BA (Hons.) 2007

Solution.

(*i*) National Income is Net National Product at factor cost

NI or NNP_{FC} = GDP_{MP} – Depreciation – Net Indirect taxes + Net Factor income from abroad

= 6000 – 800 – 700 + (150 – 225)

= 6000 –1500 – 75

= 6000 – 1575

= 4425

(*ii*) Personal Disposable income = National Income – Retained Corporate Profits + Transfer Payments to Persons – Personal taxes

PDI = 4425 – (1200 – 600) + 1300 – 1500
= 4425 – 600 + 1300 – 1500
= 3625

(Note: Retained corporate profits equals corporate profits minus dividends paid to shareholders)

Problem 3. *Calculate (1) Net Domestic Product at market Prices and (2) National Income from the following date of all the enterprises in an economy.*

		Rs. in Crore
(i)	***Subsidies***	***10***
(ii)	***Sales***	***1000***
(iii)	***Closing stock***	***100***
(iv)	***Indirect taxes***	***50***
(v)	***Intermediate Consumption***	***300***
(vi)	***Opening stock***	***200***
(vii)	***Consumption of fixed capital***	***150***
(viii)	***Net factor income from abroad***	***10***

Solution.

NDP_{MP} and National Income be obtained through *value added method.* Net Domestic Product at Market Prices is the sum of net value added by all enterprises in the economy.

Value of output = Sales + Change in stock
= 1000 + (Closing Stock – Opening Stock)
= 1000 + (100 – 200)
= 900 crore

Net value added (NVA) at market prices (NDP_{MP}) = Value of output–Intermediate Consumption – Consumption of fixed capital
= 900 – 300 – 150
= 450 crore

National Income (NNP_{FC}) = NDP_{FC} Net Indirect taxes + Net factor income from abroad
= 450 – (50 – 10) + 10
= 450 – 40 + 10
= 420 crore

QUESTIONS FOR REVIEW

1. Explain the circular flow of income in an economy. What does it measure ?

2. Describe the circular flow of income in a two-sector economy with households and business firms. What determines the magnitude of circular flow of income and expenditure ?

3. What is meant by saving and investment ? How do they affect circular flow of income in a free market economy ?

4. Despite the fact that motives to save are different from the motives of business men to invest, in national income accounts savings are always equal to investment.

5. How does the addition of Government in a two sector economy affect circular flow of income? If Government's budget is deficit, how will it affect circular flow of income ?

6. Show with a circular income flow model of a two sector economy that national product equals national income.
7. In a three sector economy with firms, households and Government show with a circular income flow model that the sum of private investment and Government expenditure equals the sum of saving and taxes.
8. What is meant by withdrawals and injections ? How do they affect the size of circular flow of income and expenditure in an economy ?
9. If investment by business firms falls short of savings, how will it affect the circular flow of income ?
10. How will circular income flow in an economy be affected if a country has foreign trade transactions?
11. In an open economy, explain with a circular income flow model that the sum of investment, Government expenditure and net exports must equal the sum of savings and taxes.
12. Explain the following :
    (*i*) Net Value added
    (*ii*) Net factor Income from Abroad
    (*iii*) Compensation of Employees
    (*iv*) Transfer Payments by the Government
13. Distinguish between the following :
    1. Net National Product at Market Prices (NNP_{MP}) and National Income.
    2. Government Expenditure on goods and services and Transfer Payments.
    3. Nominal National Income and Real National Income.
14. How are Aggregate domestic output and expenditure related to trade balance ?
15. Explain saving – investment identify in an open economy.
16. Show that the difference between saving and investment of an economy always equals trade balance ?
17. Explain how foreign capital flows are related to domestic saving and investment.

CHAPTER 3
Classical Theory of Income and Employment : Full Employment Model

Economy in the Long Run : The Classical Full-Employment Model

Before explaining the Keynesian macro-theory of income and employment, it will be in the fitness of things to explain classical theory regarding income and employment determination. The study of classical theory of income and employment is essential because some of the aspects of classical theory are more relevant to the conditions prevailing in the developing countries and this theory highlights those factors which govern income and employment in these countries. While the Keynesian theory emphasises the role of effective demand in the determination of income and employment, classical economists believed that in a free-market economy there was always a tendency toward the establishment of full employment of labour and there was sufficient demand for the output produced. Note that Keynes called all economists who preceded him (including Marshall and Pigou) as classical economists.

CLASSICAL THEORY OF EMPLOYMENT : AN INTRODUCTORY ANALYSIS

Classical theory of employment and output is based on the following two basic notions:

1. Say's Law
2. Wage-price flexibility

We explain below these two notions of classical theory

Say's Law and Classical Theory

According to the classical theory propounded by Ricardo and Adam Smith, levels of income and employment are governed by fixed capital stock on the one hand and wage-goods fund on the other. It may be noted in the beginning that the classical theory believes in full employment or near full employment prevailing in the economy. This belief of classical theory regarding the existence of full employment in the economy is based on Say's Law put forward by a French economist J.B. Say. According to J.B. Say's law, *"Supply creates its own demand"*. This implies that every increase in production made possible by the increase in the productive capacity or the stock of fixed capital will be sold in the market and there will be no problem of lack of demand. Thus, classical economists rule out the possibility of overproduction; there being no problem in selling the output produced. According to Say's Law, greater production automatically leads to a greater money income which creates the market for the greater flow of goods produced. Thus, deficiency in demand being no problem, the process of capital accumulation and expansion of productive capacity will continue till all people are employed and there is no reason why the productive capacity created remains unutilized or underutilized. According to this theory, the income which is not spent on consumer goods and thus saved will become investment expenditure. Therefore, investment equals saving. Thus, the leakage caused by the saving in the income flow is made up by the investment expenditure. In this way, a given productive capacity continues to be fully utilized and no problem of deficiency of demand arises.

Classical economists thought that if price mechanism in a capitalist economy is allowed to work freely without any interference by the Government, there is always a tendency towards full-employment in it. Of course, they admitted that in advanced capitalist economies often certain circumstances arise due to which they are is not in full-employment equilibrium. But they firmly believed that there was always a tendency towards full-employment in the economy and certain economic forces automatically operate so as to move the economy towards full employment. Therefore, according to the classical economists, whenever there are lapses from full-employment level, these are removed automatically by the working of free price mechanism. The modern economists do not regard this aspect of classical theory of employment as valid and correct description of the real world. J.M. Keynes bitterly criticised the classical theory of automatic full-employment.

The classical theory of employment was based upon two basic assumptions. The first assumption is that there is always enough expenditure or aggregate demand to purchase the total production at full-employment level of resources. In other words, in this theory the classical economists disregarded the problem of deficiency of demand for purchasing goods produced at full-employment level of resources. The second assumption is that even when deficiency of aggregate expenditure or demand arises, the ***prices, wages and interest would adjust quickly*** so that equilbrium is restored at full-employment level of output.

The classical view that there was no problem of deficiency of expenditure and demand was based upon Say's law of markets. J.B. Say has been a famous French economist of the 19th century. Say's law is based upon the fact that every production of goods also creates incomes equal to the value of goods produced and these incomes are spent on purchasing these goods. In other words, production of goods itself creates its own purchasing power, that is, demand for buying them. Therefore, Say's law is expressed as "***supply creates its own demand***", that is, the supply of goods produced creates demand for it equal to its own value with the result that the problem of general overproduction does not arise. In this way in Say's law, the possibility of lack of aggregate demand has not been visualised.

Say's law expresses an important fact about the working of a free-enterprise economy. The fact is that the source of demand for goods is the incomes earned by various factors of production employed for their production. All unemployed and idle labourers and other resources when employed for production, create their own demand because the total incomes which they earn create equal market demand for the goods produced by their employment. When a new entrepreneur employs some factors of production and pays them their monetary rewards, he not only increases the supply of goods but also at the same time creates the demand for them. Therefore, it is the production which creates market or demand for goods. Production is the only source of demand. Dillard rightly writes that "*Say's Law of Markets*" is the denial of the possibility of deficiency of aggregate demand. Therefore, employment of more resources will always be profitable and will take place to the point of full-employment, subject to the limitation that the contributors of the resources are willing to accept rewards no greater than their physical productivity justifies. There could be no general unemployment, according to this view, if workers will account what they are worth."[1]

We thus see that according to Say's law aggregate expenditure or demand will always be such that all resources are fully employed. The factors which participate in productive activity and earn incomes from it, they spend a good part of their incomes on consumer goods and some part they save. But, according to classical economists, the savings by the individuals are actually spent on investment or capital goods. Since saving when invested also becomes expenditure or demand, in classical theory the whole income is spent, partly on consumption and partly on investment. There is thus no reason for any leakage in the income stream and hence supply creates its own demand. Now, a question arises as to how in classical theory saving becomes equal to investment expenditure. According to the classical theory, it is the rate of interest which makes investment equal to saving. When savings of the people increase, the rate of interest declines. As a result of fall in the rate of interest, demand for

1. D. Dillard, *Economics of J.M. Keynes*.

investment rises and in this way investment becomes equal to the increased savings. Hence, according to the classical economists, it is the interest rate changes that bring about equality between saving and investment and, therefore, Say's law applies in spite of saving by the people. This guarantees full employment in the economy. In other words, it is changes in the rate of interest due to which the withdrawal of some money from the income stream as a result of savings automatically comes back to it in the form of investment expenditure and therefore income flow continues unchanged and supply goes on creating its own demand.

Wage-Price Flexibility and Full-Employment

The classical economists also proved the validity of the assumption of full-employment with an other fundamental logic. According to them, the amount of production which the business firms can supply does not depend only on aggregate demand or expenditure but also on the prices of products. When aggregate demand for goods and services decline due to the fall in investment, the economy will still remain at full-employment level of output. According to them, this happens because product prices fall quickly so that quantity demanded increases to restore equilibrium at full-employment level of output. In this way, they expressed the view that in spite of the decline in aggregate demand caused by the decline in investment, the real output, income and employment will not fall provided the fall in prices of products brings about balance between demand and supply at full-employment level of output.

Classical economists thought that a free-market capitalist economy is self-correcting. Owing to the intense competition between the sellers of products as a consequence of the fall in demand, the prices will decline. This is because when aggregate expenditure on goods or demand for them declines, the various sellers and producers reduce the prices of their products so as to avoid the excessive accumulation of stocks of goods with them. Hence, according to the classical logic, decline in demand will bring down the prices of products and not the amount of production and employment. But now a question arises to what extent the sellers or producers will tolerate the decline in prices. However, to make their business profitable they will have to reduce the prices of the factors of production such as labour. When due to decrease in demand for output, demand for labour declines, this will cause a fall in wages quickly so that labour-demanded increases to restore labour-market equilibrium at full-employment. Thus, a fall in wages of labour ensures that all workers will get employment. If some workers do not want to work at reduced wages, they will not get any job or employment and therefore will remain unemployed. But, according to classical economists, those workers who do not want to work at lower wages and thus remain unemployed are only *voluntarily unemployed.* This voluntary unemployment is not real unemployment. According to the classical thought, it is ***involuntary unemployment*** which is not possible in a free-market capitalist economy. All those workers who want to work at the going wage rate determined by market forces will get employment. That is, full employment of labour continous to prevail due to quick adjustment of wages.

During the period 1929-33 when there was a great depression in capitalist economies, a renowned neoclassical economist Pigou suggested a cut in wage rates in order to remove huge and widespread unemployment prevailing at that time. According to him, the cause of depression or unemployment was that the Government and trade unions of workers were preventing the free working of the capitalist economies and were artificially keeping the wage rates at high levels. He expressed the view that if the wage rates were cut down, demand for labour would increase so that all would get employment. It was at this time that J.M. Keynes challenged the classical theory and put forward a new theory of income and employment. He brought about a fundamental change in economic thought regarding the determination of income and employment in a developed capitalist economy. Therefore, it is often said that *Keynes brought about a revolution in our economic theory and laid the foundation of macroeconomic theory.*

THE CLASSICAL THEORY OF EMPLOYMENT AND OUTPUT (INCOME) : A FORMAL FULL-EMPLOYMENT MODEL

Classical economists such as Adam Smith and Ricardo maintained that the growth of income and employment depends on the growth of the stock of fixed capital and inventories of wage goods. But, in the short run, the stock of fixed capital and wage goods inventories are given and constant. According to them, even in the short run full-employment of labour force would tend to prevail as the economy would not experience any problem of deficiency of demand. On the basis of their theory they denied the possibility of the existence of *involuntary unemployment* in the economy. The short-run classical theory of income and employment can be explained through the following three stages:

1. *Determination of income and employment when there is no saving and* investment;
2. *Determination of income and employment in an economy with saving and investment; and*
3. *Determination of income and employment : Role of money and prices.*

Determination of Income and Employment in the Short Run Without Saving and Investment

According to the classical theory, the magnitude of national income and employment depends on the aggregate production function and the supply and demand for labour. To show this let us assume that the economy produces one homogeneous and divisible good, say corn. Let symbol Y stand for output of this good. To produce this good we require two factors of production : (1) labour which we denote by N and (2) capital which we denote by K. Thus we have the following aggregate prodcution function

$$Y = F(N, K, T) \quad ...(i)$$

In the short run the stock of capital (i.e. plant and equipment) is assumed to be fixed. The state of technology is also assumed to be constant in the short run. Thus, rewritting the aggregate production function we have

$$Y = F(N, \bar{K}, \bar{T}) \quad ...(ii)$$

The bar over the symbol K and T for capital and technology indicates that stock of capital and technology is fixed. It is worth noting that changes in capital stock and technology will cause a shift in the production function.

Therefore, with a fixed capital stock and a given and constant technology, the output Y (or what is also the real income) would increase only when employment of labour N increases. That is, employment of labour and output (income) rise or fall together. Now, according to classical theory, with a fixed capital stock and given technology as employment of labour increases, marginal product of labour would diminish. This is the famous law of diminishing returns of the classical economics.

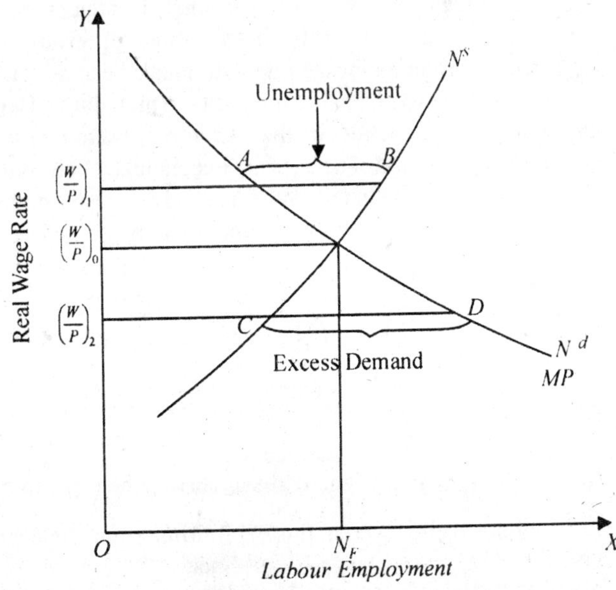

Fig. 3.1. *Labour-Market Equilibrium : Determination of Employment and Wages*

Labour Market Equilibrium

The demand for labour is derived from this short-run production function, that is, diminishing marginal product of labour. The classical theory assumes perfect competition in both the factor and product markets . Further, assuming that the firms which undertake the task of production attempt to maximise profits, they will employ labour until the marginal product of labour is equal to the given real wage rate. It may be noted that real wage rate is given by nominal wage rate divided by the general price, level, that is, real wage rate $= \frac{W}{P}$ where W is the nominal or money wage rate and P is the average price level. Thus, a firm will employ so much labour at which

$$\frac{W}{P} = MP_N$$

where MP_N stands for marginal product of labour

At a lower real wage rate, more labour will be demanded or employed by the firms and *vice versa.* Thus, the demand curve for labour is derived from the marginal product curve of labour. In fact, the former coincides with the latter. Thus demand function for labour can be written as

$$N^d = f\left(\frac{W}{P}\right) \qquad \ldots (iii)$$

Consider Fig. 3.1 where *MP* curve depicts the diminishing marginal product of labour with a given stock of fixed capital and a given state of technology. As explained just above, marginal prouct (*MP*) curve of labour also represents the demand curve of labour (N^d).

On the other hand, the *supply of labour by the households in the economy depends on their pattern of preference between income and leisure.* The classical theory assumes that in the short run when population does not vary, supply curve of labour slopes upward. Now, what is the rational behind the upward-sloping supply curve of labour. This is based on the assumption that households or individual workers maximise their utility or satisfaction in their choice of work (which yields them income) and leisure. When real wage rate rises, two effects work in opposite direction. It may be noted that real wage is the opportunity cost or relative price of lesiure. When real wage rate rises leisure becomes relatively more expensive, that is, opportunity cost or price of leisure in terms of income forgone by not working goes up. This induces the individual to work more (i.e. supply more labour hours) and thereby substitutes income for leisure. This is the substitution effect. On the other hand, with a rise in real wage rate individuals become relatively richer than before, and this induces them to consume more of all commodities (including leisure which is regarded as a normal commodity). This is income effect of the rise in real wage rate which tends to increase leisure and reduce labour-hours supplied. The classical economists believed that substitution effect is larger than income effect of the rise in real wage rate and as a result supply of labour increases with the rise in wage rate. Thus the supply function of labour can be written as

$$N^s = g\left(\frac{W}{P}\right) \qquad \ldots (iv)$$

This implies that at a higher wage rate, more labour would be supplied and *vice versa.* It will be seen from Fig. 3.1 that supply and demand for labour are in equilibrium at the real wage rate $\left(\frac{W}{P}\right)_0$.

Hence, given the supply and demand curves, the wage rate $\left(\frac{W}{P}\right)_0$ is determined. It will be seen that ON_F labour is employed in this equilibrium situation. Thus, *in classical theory level of employment is determined by labour market equilibrium.* This *equilibrium between supply and demand for labour at the real wage rate* $\left(\frac{W}{P}\right)_0$ *implies that all those who offer their labour services at this wage rate are in fact employed.* There is neither excess supply of labour, nor excess demand for labour. In other words, there is no involuntary unemployment of labour in this equilibrium situation and full employment of labour prevails. If somehow real wage rate in the labour market is higher than this equilibrium wage rate $\left(\frac{W}{P}\right)_0$, say it is equal to $\left(\frac{W}{P}\right)_1$, then it will be observed from Fig. 3.1 that excess supply of labour equal to *AB* would emerge. In other words, at real wage rate $\left(\frac{W}{P}\right)_1$, *AB* workers will be unemployed.

But given the competition among workers, the excess supply of labour at wage rate $\left(\frac{W}{P}\right)_1$ would cause the wage rate to fall to the equilibrium level $\left(\frac{W}{P}\right)_0$ at which the labour market is cleared. On the contrary, if somehow real wage rate in the labour market is $\left(\frac{W}{P}\right)_2$, the firms would demand more labour than is offered at this real wage rate. As a result of the competition among the firms to hire labour desired by them, the wage rate would go up to the equilibrium level $\left(\frac{W}{P}\right)_0$. At $\left(\frac{W}{P}\right)_0$ to repeat, all those who offer their labour services are in fact demanded and employed. *It therefore follows that at the real wage* $\left(\frac{W}{P}\right)_0$*, there is no involuntary unemployment, or, in other words, full-employment of labour prevails. Further, it is the wage flexibility (i.e., quick adjustment in wage rate) which brings about this full-employment situation.*

To clarify further the restoration of full employment of labour due to quick adjustment of real wage rate let us consider the decrease in demand for labour following the fall in aggregate demand for output as it happens when depression or recession occurs in the economy. Consider Fig. 3.1(A) where following the decrease in aggregate demand for output labour demand curve shifts to the left so that at the initial wage rate $\frac{W_0}{P_0}$ fewer workers will be demanded than the number of workers who are will-

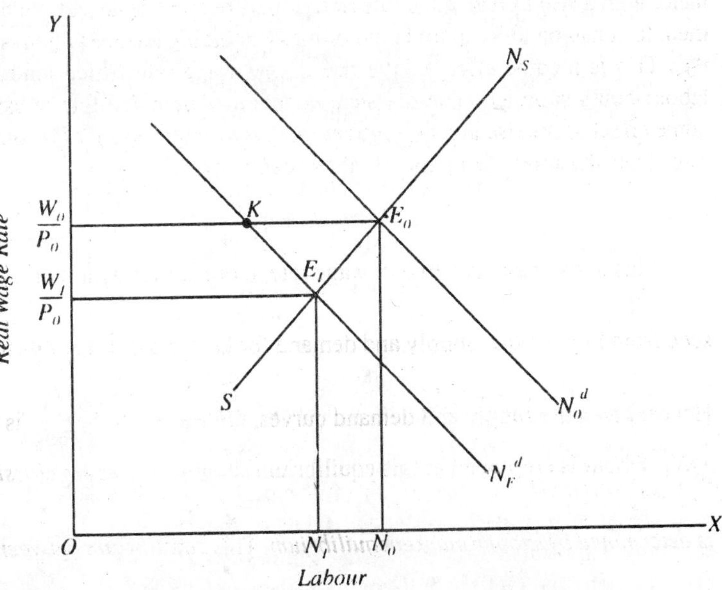

Fig. 3.1A. *Adjustment of real wage rate*

ing to supply their labour at this wage rate. As a result (as is seen from Fig. 3.1A) the excess supply of labour equal to KE_0 will emerge at this initial real wage rate $\frac{W_0}{P_0}$. However, in the classical full employment model this excess supply of labour (i.e. unemployment of workers) will cause real wage rate to fall to $\frac{W_1}{P_0}$ (where $W_1 < W_0$) at which new equilibrium between demand for and supply of labour is again established at point E_1. Note that even in this new labour market equilibrium at lower real wage rate $\frac{W_0}{P_0}$ full employment of labour prevails as all those who are willing to work at this real wage rate find employment. Of course, N_0N_1 workers have voluntarily withdrawn themselves from labour force and therefore no one remains involuntarily unemployed.

Determination of Output

How much output will be produced in this full employment situation can be readily known from the short run aggregate production function. *OY* which is drawn in the lower part of Fig. 3.2, shows the relationship between employment of labour (*N*) and total output (*Y*), given the stock of fixed capital (i.e., a set of machines, equipment and buildings) and given the technology. This short-run production function *OY* shows that as more workers are employed, output increases but at a diminishing rate, that is, there are *diminishing returns to labour*. It will be seen from the lower panel of Fig. 3.2 that, *given the stock of fixed capital and the state of technology*, full employment of labour ON_F produces OY_F output. This output OY_F of output will constitute the income of the society and will be distributed between wages and profits. Thus sum of wages as reward for labour and total profits as reward for capital would constitute the total income of the society and would be equal to the national output OY_F produced.

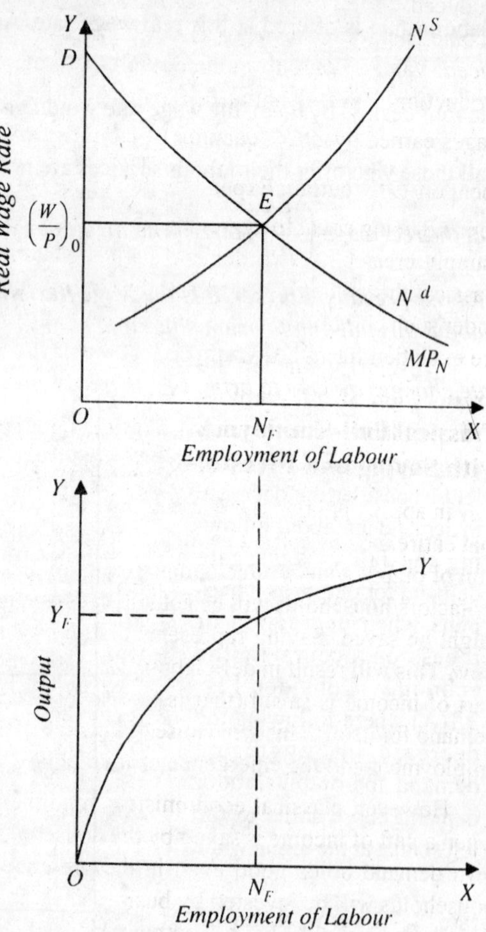

Fig. 3.2. *Classical Theory : Determination of Employment and Output*

It follows from above that the quick changes in the real wage rate upward or downward ensures that neither excess supply of labour, nor excess demand for labour will persist and thus equilibrium will be reached with full employment of labour in the economy. Further, given the stock of capital and the state of technology with this full employment of labour, total output or income of the economy equal to OY_F is determined. The level of output OY_F is referred to as **full-employment level of output or potential GDP** of the economy. This is also often called **aggregate supply.** The potential GDP or full-employment level of output is the amount of goods and services that producers are willing to produce, given their stock of fixed capital (machines, equipment and buildings) and given technology, when labour market is in equilibrium and all workers who want the work at the going wage rate find employment. It will be seen from Fig. 3.2 that full employment of labour as determined by labour market equilibrium is N_F and given the short-run production function OY, potential GDP or full employment output is Y_F (See lower part of Fig. 3.2). To conclude, *potential GDP or full-employment output* is the level of output when with adjustment of wages labour market is in equilibrium and all workers who want to work at the going wage rate find employment and firms are using their plant and equipment at normal rates of their utilisation.

Now, an important question to enquire is what guarantees that output produced by the full employment level of labour and capital (assumed as fixed in the short run) will be actually demanded. If this does not happen, then the problem of insufficient demand for the output will emerge which will ultimately lead to reduction in output and employment and hence to the emergence of involuntary unemployment.

Say's Law and the Absence of Deficiency of Demand. In the absence of saving and investment which we are assuming here, classical economists ruled out the possibility of deficiency of aggregate demand on the basis of Say's law. Say's law, as mentioned above, states that *supply creates its own demand*, that is, acts of production of goods create demand equal to the value of output of goods produced. Factors of production earn their incomes during the process of production. If no part of income is saved as is being assumed here the *entire income will be spent on consumer goods produced.* Value of output produced will therefore be equal to the income generated in the process of production. Thus, quantity demanded will be equal to the supply of output produced. In Fig. 3.2, wages earned by ON_F quantity of labour employed and profits earned by the entrepreneurs will be spent on OY_F output. Expenditure so made will be equal to the value of output produced. Aggregate demand being equal to aggregate supply, there is no problem of deficiency of demand. Say's law that "supply creates its own demand" holds and full employment of labour is guaranteed. In this way classical theory denies the possibility of involuntary unemployment. It needs to be emphasised that under such conditions, two things ensure full employment. First, it is because saving and investment are excluded from the system so that entire income is spent on consumer goods. Second, *real wage rate changes quickly to bring about equilibrium between demand for and supply of labour.*

Classical Full-Employment Model: Determination of Income (output) and Employment with Saving and Investment

In applying Say's law that supply creates its own demand an invalid assumption was made above that entire income earned by the households will be actually spent. Although it is correct that production of output generates an equal amount of income but what is the guarantee that all income earned by factors/households will be actually spent on goods and services produced. In fact, a part of income might be saved. Saving represents a *withdrawal or leakage* of some income from the expenditure flow. This will result in deficiency of demand or expenditure on output of goods produced. Thus, if a part of income is saved (that is, not spent), supply of output produced would not create sufficient demand for itself. This will cause deficiency of aggregate demand which will cause fall in output and employment and the emergence of involuntary unemployment.

However, classical economists denied the possibility of deficiency of aggregate demand even when a part of income is saved by the households. They showed that Say's law that supply creates its own demand holds good even in the presence of saving. They argued that every rupee saved by households will be invested by businessmen, that is, investment expenditure will be equal to savings done by households. In fact, output produced consists of consumer goods and capital goods. Income earned from production will be partly spent on consumer goods and partly on investment in capital goods. When at full employment level of output what is not spent on consumer goods is saved and investment expenditure on capital goods made by businessmen equals this saving. Therefore, there is no deficiency of demand or expenditure and circular flow of income goes on undisturbed. Thus, when investment equals saving at full employment level of output supply goes on creating its own demand to maintain full employment. Now in bringing about equality between saving and investment, capital market plays a crucial role.

Capital - Market Equilibrium : Determination of Interest

Now, the pertinent question is what is the guarantee that investment expenditure will be equal to savings of the households. *According to classical economists, it is the changes in the rate of interest that brings about equality between saving and investment.* Further, according to them, rate of interest is determined in the capital market by supply of savings and demand for investment. The investment demand is stipulated to be decreasing function of the rate of interest. At the lower rate of interest, more would be borrowed for investment. On the other hand, the savings of the people are taken to be the increasing function of the rate of interest, that is,the higher the rate of interest, the larger the savings and *vice versa*. The capital market will be in equilibrium at the rate of interest at which the demand for investment is equal to the supply of savings. The changes in rate of interest would cause investment and supply of saving to become equal. This is illustrated in Fig. 3.3. It will be seen that intersection of investment demand cuve *II* and the supply of savings curve *SS* determines the rate of interest i_0. At a higher rate of interest i_2, the investment demand is less than the intended supply of savings. Due to the excess supply of savings, rate of interest would fall to i_0. On the contrary, at a lower rate of interest, say i_1, the demand for investment exceeds the supply of savings. Now, due to the excess demand for investment in the capital market rate of interest would go up. Thus, it is at rate of interest i_0 that capital market is in equilibrium, *i.e.*, investment is equal to savings ($I = S$).

Now an important thing to know about classical theory is when due to decline in profit expectations of business firms investment falls as it happens in times of recession or depression how it then explains that demand deficiency problem would not arise and equilibrium will continue to remain at full employment level. This is illustrated in Figure 3.4, where initially saving and investment are in equilibrium at rate of interest i_0. Now suppose that due to fall in profit expectations investment by

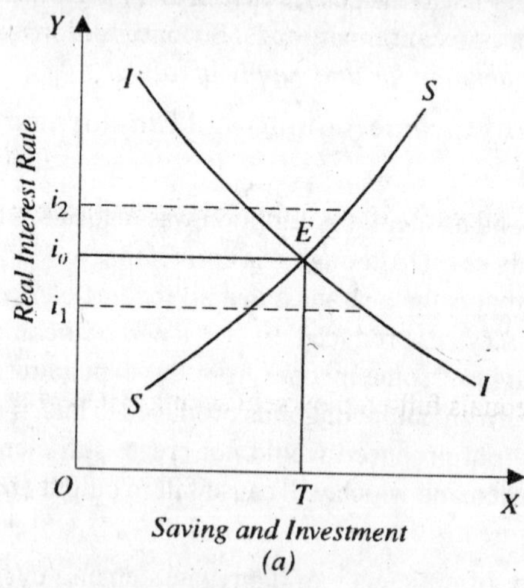

Fig. 3.3. *Capital Market Equilibrium*

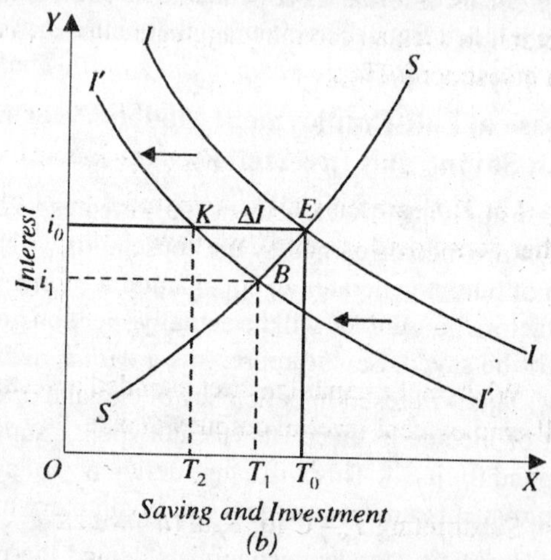

Fig. 3.4. *Decrease in investment demand does not disturb full-employment equilibrium.*

business firms decreases by ΔI or *EK* causing a shift in the investment curve to the left to the new position $I'I'$. With this at the initial rate of interest i_0, supply of savings exceeds investment by *KE*. This excess supply of savings will put downward pressure on rate of interest and as result interest will fall to i_1, at which saving and investment are again equal. According to classical theory, the lower interest induces more investment and therefore as a result of fall in interest to i_1, investment increases from OT_2 to OT_1. Besides, with the fall in interest rate from i_0 to i_1, savings decline by T_0T_1, which implies consumption demand will increase by T_0T_1. Thus, *shift in investment demand curve to the left results in lowering of rate of interest which leads to more investment and consumption demand so that aggregate demand is not affected.* It is thus clear that due to adjustment in interest rate even decline in investment does not give rise to demand deficiency problem and full-employment continues to prevail.

It follows from above that the equality between investment and saving brought about by changes in the rate of interest would guarantee that aggregate demand for output would be equal to aggregate supply of output. Thus, the problem of deficiency of aggregate demand would not be faced and full employment of labour will prevail.

Now an important thing to explain is how capital market equilibrium ensures equality between saving and investment at full-employment level of output. It is easy to understand how equilibrium between saving and investment in the capital market ensures equilibrium at full-employment output with the help of circular flow of income. *Savings by households are lekages of money from the income flow, while investment expenditure is injection of money into it.* Given the full employment level of output as determined by labour market equilibrium and short-run aggregate production function, if the *leakage* (i.e. saving) from income flow that measures full-employment output (income) is equal to *injection* (investment) into it the aggregate expenditure (i.e., aggregate demand for goods and services) would equal full employment level of output (income). Thus, the product market will continue to be in equilibrium and money flow will continue undisturbed at full employment level of income.

National Income Accounts Relationship and Saving – Investment Equilibrium

We can also use national income accounts relationship to show when investment is equal to saving at the full employment level of output, aggregate demand equals aggregate supply of output at the full employment level. This is explained below.

Let us take the case of a simple two sector economy with no government and foreign trade sectors. In such an economy aggregate demand is the sum of two components : (*i*) Consumption and (2) investment. Thus,

$$\text{Aggregate demand} = C + I \quad \ldots(i)$$

Let Y_F represents full employment level of output (income). Since full-employment income is either consumerd or saved, we have

$$Y_F = C + S_F$$

or

$$S_F = Y_F - C \quad \ldots(ii)$$

When in the capital market intended investment (*I*) equals full-employment saving (*i.e.* saving at full-employment level of output we have

$$I = S_F \quad \ldots(iii)$$

Substituting $Y_F - C$ for S_F in (*iii*) we have

$$I = S_F = Y_F - C \quad \ldots(iv)$$

Substituting (*iv*) into aggregate demand equation (*i*) we get

Aggregate demand $= C + I = C + (Y_F - C) = Y_F$

Thus it is proved that aggregate demand equals full-employment level of output (income). That is, even in case of saving, product market is in equilibrium at full-employment level of output.

Classical Theory of Income and Employment : Money, Prices and Inflation

Now, we shall examine how full employement of labour is assured in the classical theory even when money is introduced in the system. The introduction of money does not affect the result of the classical theory that problem of deficiency of aggregate demand would not be experienced by the free-market system and therefore full employment of labour is guaranteed. *The quantity of money, according to the classical theory, determines only the price level of output and in no way affects the real magnitudes of saving and investment. Further, since quantity of money determines the price level of output, it also affects real wage rate*, that is, the ratio of money wages and the price level, or $\frac{W}{P}$. But with increase in money supply, money wages and price level change in such a way that real wage rate in the equilibrium situation remains constant and equilibrium in the labour market is automatically restored. Besides, with the increase in money supply and consequent change in the price level, saving-investment equilibrium will not be disturbed and therefore deficiency of aggregate demand will not arise.

Quantity Theory of Money : Determination of Price Level. Let us first explain how in classical theory price level in the economy is determined. Classical economists believed in the *Quantity Theory of Money* according to which it is the supply of money that determines price level in an economy. Quantity theory of money is generally expressed by Fisher's equation of exchange[2], income version of which is stated as under:

$$MV = PY \quad ...(i)$$

or $$P = \frac{MV}{Y} \quad ...(ii)$$

where M = Quantity of money
V = Income velocity of circulation of money
Y = Level of aggregate output (or real income)
P = Price level of goods and services

Income velocity of money is defined as the number of times a unit of money is used for purchase of final goods and services in a period, say during a year. In classzical theory velocity is assumed to be constant. Besides, in classical theory level of aggregate output is determined by the supply of productive resources, (*i.e.*, capital stock, availability of labour, land etc.) and the state of technology which do not change in the short run. Further, due to operation of Say's law and wage-price flexibility full employment of resources occurs in the economy. Thus, with a given amount of productive resources such as labour and capital stock and constant technology and with further assumption that they are fully utilised and employed, the aggregate output (Y) is held constant at full-employment level of output in the short run.

Now, with velocity of money (V) and aggregate output (Y) remaining constant, price level is determined by the money supply (M) and increases in money supply brings about rise in price level in the same proportion. The supply of money is fixed by the monetary policy of the Government or its Central Bank (e.g. Reserve Bank of India). The important question is what determines the demand for money. In the classical theory the function of money is to serve as medium of exchange and therefore demand for money is determined by the *money value of transactions* occuring in the economy. The aggregate output (Y) multiplied by the price level (i.e. PY) indicates the total money value of goods and services transacted (i.e. sold and purchased). Now, since a unit of money is used to make transactions of goods and services more than once in a year as measured by the velocity of money (V), a given amount of money can be used to make transactions of a larger amount

2. Quantity theory of money and Fisher's Equation of Exchange will be explained and critically examined in detail in a separate chapter.

of goods and services constituting GDP transacted during a period. PY is the nominal value of GDP and $\frac{1}{V}$ in equation (ii) above is the inverse of velocity of money. $\frac{1}{V}$ has another name k used by Cambridge economists. In this Cambridge version of Quantity of Theory, $M^d = kPY$ where k is the *proportion of national income* (*i.e.* GDP or PY) which is held (*i.e.* demanded) by the people to make transactions of goods and services during a period.

As stated above, price level as determined by the interaction of supply of money and demand for money in equilbrium. Thus in equilibrium :

$$M = M^d \text{ where } M \text{ stands for money supply, } M^d \text{ for demand for money}$$

$$\text{or} \quad M = \frac{PY}{V}$$

$$P = \frac{MV}{Y}$$

Monetary equilibrium in the classical theory is shown in Fig. 3.5 where demand for money $\left(\frac{PY}{V}\right)$ is shown by a rising straight line $\left(\frac{PY}{V}\right)$ which indicates that with V and Y being held constant demand for money increases proportionately to the rise in price level. As price level rises people demand more money for transaction purposes.

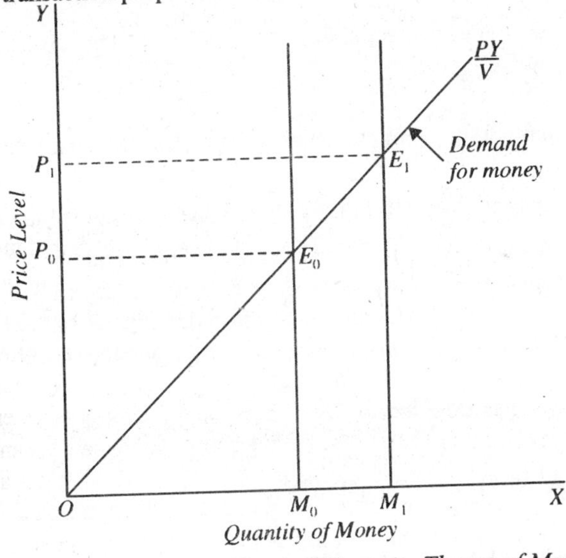

Fig. 3.5. *Determination of Price Level : Classical Quantity Theory of Money*

Now, if supply of money fixed by the Government (or the Central Bank) is equal to M_0, the demand for money $\left(\frac{PY}{V}\right)$ equals the supply of money, M_0 at price level P_0. Thus, with supply of money equal to M_0 equilibrium price level P_0 is determined. If money supply is increased, how the monetary equilibrium will change? Suppose money suply is increased to M_1, at the initial price level P_0 the people will be holding more money than they demand at it. Therefore, they would want to reduce their money holding. In order to reduce their money holding they would increase their spending on goods and services. In response to the increase in money spending by the households the firms will increase prices of their goods and services. As prices rise, the households will need and demand more money to hold for transaction purposes (*i.e.* for buying goods and services). It will be seen from Fig. 3.5 that with the increase in money suply to M_1 new equilibrium between demand for money and suply of money is attained at point E_1 on the demand for money curve $\frac{PY}{V}$ and price level has risen to P_1.

CLASSICAL AGGREGATE SUPPLY CURVE

Aggregate supply curve describes the relationship between aggregate supply of output with price level. Classical theory regards aggregate supply curve to be perfectly inelastic. Now, an important question is why in classical model, aggregate supply curve is perfectly inelastic. As explained above, aggregate output Y_F is determined by the equilibrium level of employment N_F, given the aggregate production function, Equilibrium level of employment along with real wage rate is determined by labour market equilibrium, that is, equilibrium between demand for the supply of labour. Thus, in classical theory aggregate supply curve is determined by supply-side factors, namely, preferences of households or individuals regarding work and leisure, the stock of capital (and other factor endowments), the state of technology. Supply of labour, as seen above, is determined by indvidual preferences between work and leisure and demand curve for labour is determined by marginal product of labour.

Thus in classical model aggregate supply curve reflects supply-determined nature of output and does not depend on the aggregate demand and price level. The classical aggregate supply curve is shown in Fig. 3.6. The pertinent question is how with changes in price level, which in the classical theory depends on the quantity of money, leaves levels of employment and output unaffected. The reason for this is that *changes in price level causes equal proportionate changes in money wage rate* with the result that the equilibrium real wage rate which is given by $\frac{W}{P}$ remains constant and therefore equilibrium level of employment does not get affected. The adjustment process works in the following way.

If due to the increase in supply of money price level rises, with a given money wage rate (W), real wage rate, which is equal to $\frac{W}{P}$, will fall. At a real wage rate lower than the equilibrium real wage rate, the quantity demanded of labour will exceed the supply of labour. This disequilibrium between labour demand and supply will cause money wage rate to rise to the level so that original real wage rate determined by labour market equilibrium is restored. Suppose that in labour-market equilibrium money wage rate is W_1 and given the price level equal to P_1, and the equilibrium real wage rate will be $\frac{W_1}{P_1}$. Now, if price level is doubled to $2P_1$ money wage rate rises to $2W_1$, then the equilibrium real wage rate will become equal to $\frac{2W_1}{2P_1} = \frac{W_1}{P_1}$. Thus, with equal proportionate increase in money wage rate as a result of rise in price level, equilibrium real wage rate and level of employment will remain unaffected. Thus, with rise in price level, level of employment remains unchanged and, given the aggregate production function, level of output will remain constant. This implies that aggregate supply curve of output is perfectly inelastic. Thus whatever the price level, money wage rate changes in such a way that equilibrium real wage rate, level of employment and therefore output remain constant. Thus in classical theory aggregate supply of output is determined by supply-side real variables such as labour supply, stock of

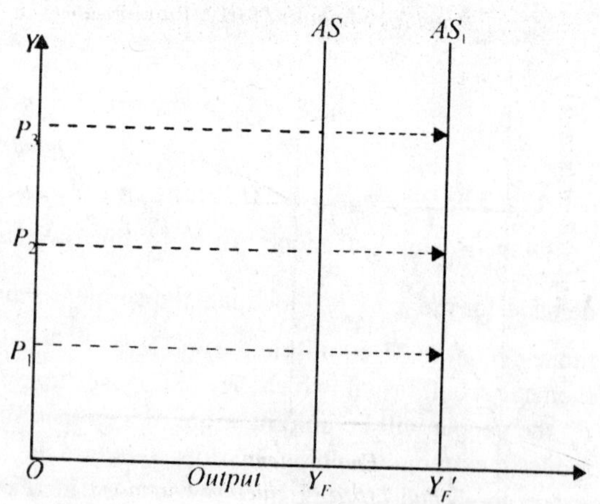

Fig. 3.6. *Classical Aggregate Supply Curve*

fixed capital and state of technology and does not depend on money and prices.

Now, what causes shift in aggregate supply curve. It is changes in real supply-side factors such as supply of labour, change in capital stock through investment and change in technology that cause a shift in aggregate supply curve. For example, if supply of labour increases, the full-employment level of labour will increase. Given the aggregate production function, increase in full-employment labour will bring about rise in potential GDP which is another name for aggregate supply. This will cause shift in aggregate supply curve to the right as shown in Fig. 3.6. Further, if as a result of investment capital stock (K) increases, short-run aggregate production function will shift upward and therefore with a given supply of labour, potential GDP or aggregate supply will increase leading to the right-ward shift in aggregate supply curve. Similarly, introduction of new technology that raises productivity of workers will cause an upward shift in the short-run aggregate production function and with a given supply of labour will raise potential GDP or aggregate supply.

CLASSICAL THEORY OF OUTPUT AND EMPLOYMENT : COMPLETE CLASSICAL MODEL*

We now illustrate the complete classical model of income and employment determination in an economy in Fig. 3.7. In panel (a) of this figure labour market equilibrium is shown wherein it will be seen that the intersection of demand for and supply of labour determines the real wage rate $\left(\frac{W_0}{P_0}\right)$. At

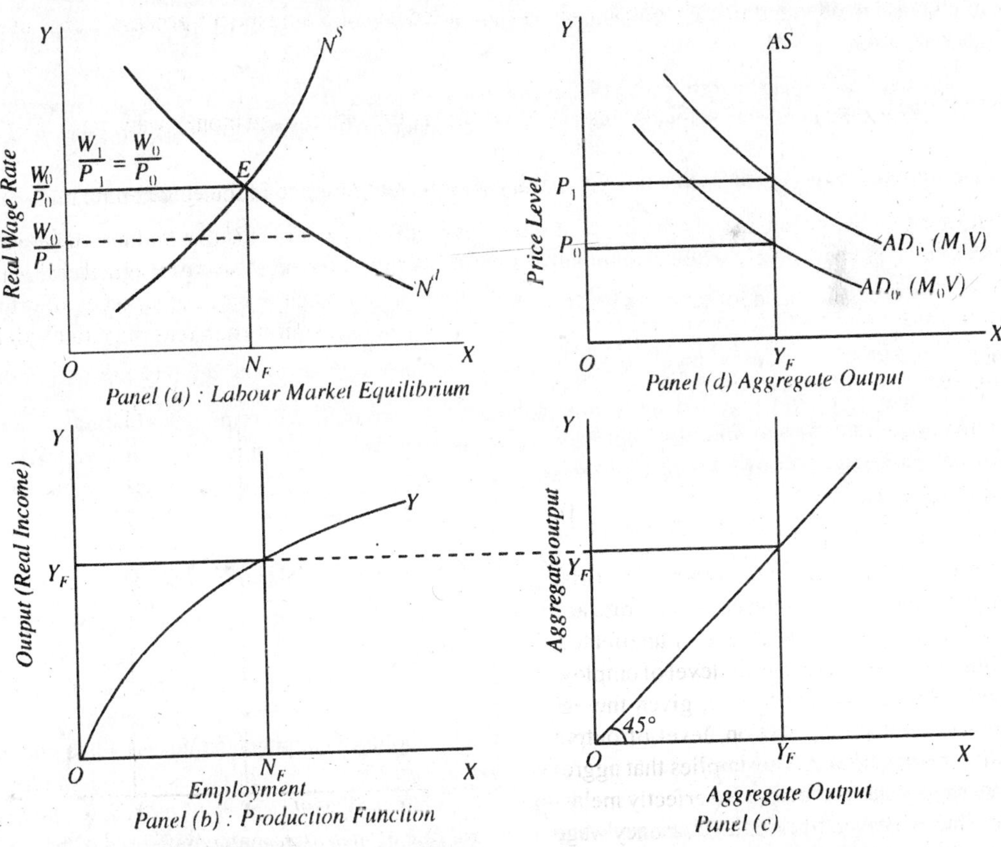

Fig. 3.7. *Determination of Income and Employemnt : Complete Classial Model*

* This section is meant for higher level courses in macroeconomics.

this equilibrium real wage rate the amount of labour employed is N_F and, as explained above, this is full employment level. As depicted in panel (*b*) of the figure this full employment level of labour N_F produces Y_F level of output (or income). In panel (*c*) of Figure 3.7 we have drawn 45° line that is used to transfer the level of output on the vertical axis in panel (*b*) to the horizontal axis of panel (*c*). In panel (*d*) we have shown the determination of price level through intersection of the curves of aggregate demand for goods and services and aggregate supply of output, as conceived by the quantity theory of money. In the classical theory, aggregate supply curve *AS* is a vertical straight line at full-employment level of output Y_F. Thus, given the constant velocity of money V, the quantity of money M_0 will determine the *expenditure or aggregate demand for goods and services* equal to M_0V according to which aggregate demand curve for goods and services (with flexible prices) is AD_0 as shown in panel(d) of Fig. 3.7. It will be seen from panel (*d*) of Fig. 3.7 that intersection of vertical aggregate supply curve *AS* at full-employment level of output Y_F and aggregate demand curve AD_0 determines the price level P_0. With price level at P_0, the money wage rate is W_0 so that $\left(\frac{W_0}{P_0}\right)$ is the real wage rate as determined by the intersection of demand for and supply of labour [see panel (*a*) of Fig. 3.7].

Now, a relevant question is how this equilibrium level of real wage rate, prices, employment and output (income) will change following the increase in the quantity of money. Suppose the quantity of money increases from M_0 to M_1. With the given capital stock (as we are considering the short-run case) and the labour force being already fully employed, the output cannot increase. Therefore, as depicted in panel (*d*) following the increase in money supply to M_1 aggregate demand or expenditure will increase to M_1V and thereby causing aggregate demand curve to shift to AD_1. As a result, price level rises from P_0 to P_1.

However, as explained above, with the given money wage rate W_0, the rise in price level from P_0 to P_1 will cause a fall in real wage rate. As will be seen from panel (*a*), with the rise in price level to P_1, real wage rate falls to $\frac{W_0}{P_1}$. This will cause temporary disequilibrium in the labour market. At the lower real wage rate $\frac{W_0}{P_1}$, more labour is demanded than is supplied. Given the competition among the firms, this excess demand for labour will cause the money wage rate to rise to W_1 level so that the real wage is bid up to the original level $\frac{W_1}{P_1}=\frac{W_0}{P_0}$. With the real wage rate being quickly restored to the original level, employment of labour N_F and total output or income Y_F will remain unaffected. To sum up, *the result of increase in money supply is to raise money wages and prices in equal proportion, leaving real wages, employment and output unaffected.* The results of decrease in money supply can be similarly worked out.

NEUTRALITY OF MONEY AND CLASSICAL DICHOTOMY

An important conclusion which follows from the classical theory of output and employment is that *changes in the quantity of money affect only nominal variables (i.e. money wages, nominal interest rate, nominal GNP, money balances), and have no influence whatsoever on the real variables of the economy* such as real GNP (*i.e.* output of goods and services produced), level of employment (*i.e.* number of labour - hours or number of workers employed), real wage rate (*i.e.* wage rate in terms of its purchasing power). Actually, as seen above in Fig. 3.7 according to classical full-employment model, the nominal variables move in proportion to changes in the quantity of money, while real variables such as GNP, employment, real wage rate, real rate of interest remain unaffected. Classical economists explained that real variables such as GNP, employment, real wage rate are determined by real factors such as stock of capital, the state of technology, marginal physical product of labour, households' preferences regarding work and leisure. In the classical model based on flexibility of prices and wages, changes in money supply only affect the price level and *nominal* magnitudes (i.e. money wages, nominal interest rate), while the real variabiles such as levels of labour employment and output, saving and investment, real wages, real rate of interest remain unaffected. That is, money is neutral in its effect on the real variables of the economy. **In the classical theory real variables such as levels of output and employment, real wages, real rate of interest, as mentioned above, depend on the stock of capital (*K*), supply of labour (*N*) and the state of technology (*T*).** Thus the *nominal* variables and the *real* variables are determined by two different sets of factors. *The independence of real variables from changes in money supply and nominal variables is called classical dichotomy.*

The neutrality of money can be graphically illustrated from Fig. 3.7. Suppose to begin with, the stock of money in the economy is equal to M_0. With this, as will be seen from panel (*d*) of Figure 3.7, aggregate demand curve for output is AD_0 which with interaction with aggregate supply curve *AS* determines price level P_0. Given the price level P_0, labour-market equilibrium determines money wage rate W_0 (*i.e.* real wage rate $\frac{W_0}{P_0}$) and level of employment N_F (see panel (*a*) of Fig. 3.7). The level of employment N_F, given the production function, determines aggregate output Y_F in panel (*b*) of Figure 3.7.

Now suppose there is expansion in money supply from M_0 to M_1 which causes an upward shift in the aggregate demand curve AD_0 to AD_1 [see panel (*d*) of Fig. 3.7]. As a result of this upward shift in the aggregate demand curve from AD_0 to AD_1, price level rises from P_0 to P_1. Now, as will be seen from panel (*a*) of Fig. 3.7, with money wage rate W_0 and the higher price level equal to P_1, real wage rate falls to $\frac{W_0}{P_1}$ at which demand for labour exceeds supply of labour. This will cause, according to classical theory, money wage rate to rise to W_1 *in equal proportion to the rise in price level* so that real wage is restored to the original level $\left(\frac{W_1}{P_1}=\frac{W_0}{P_0}\right)$ and labour-market equilibrium determines the original level of employment N_F. With the same level of labour employment aggregate output (*i.e.* GNP) will not be affected. Thus, we see that with the expansion in money supply, nominal wage rate and price level have risen, but real wage rate, level of employment and output remain constant. Hence it shows that money is neutral in its effect on real variables.

Neutrality of Money : Changes in Money Supply and Saving-Investment Equilibrium. According to the classical theory, money performs the function of merely a medium of exchange of goods and services and is therefore demanded only for transaction purposes. This means alternative to holding money is the purchase of goods and services. Therefore, demand for and supply of money in the classical system does not determine the rate of interest. When the quantity of money increases, it will leave the *real rate of interest* unchanged and hence the amount of output saved and allocated to investment (*i.e.*, *real savings and investment*) will remain the same as shown in Fig. 3.8. This means the increase in money supply does not disturb the capital market saving-investment equality and consequently the continuation of full-employment equilibrium. However, it may be noted that

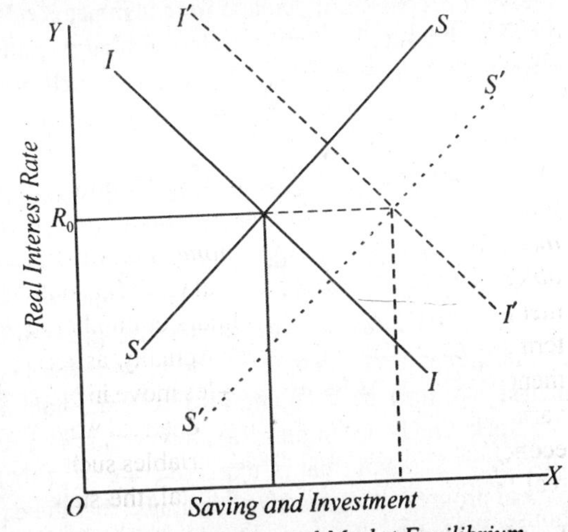

Fig. 3.8. *Capital Market Equilibrium*

the higher level of prices of commodities would mean that investment expenditure in money terms will increase in the same proportion as the rise in prices even though the output of commodities allocated for investment purposes remains the same. But this increase in *monetary expenditure* for investment is matched by the increase in *monetary savings* brought about by the rise in prices. The higher prices of commodities also mean a proportionate increase in the amount of money received from the sale of commodities so that savers are willing to provide proportionately larger amount of savings at a given rate of interest. Thus, with the increase in quantity of money, the supply curve of nominal savings and investment curves will shift to the right as shown by dotted $S'S'$ and $I'I'$ curves by the same proportion so that the same real rate of interest is maintained and the same amounts of real savings and investment in terms of commodities are made at the higher price level.

A serious limitation of the classical concept of neutrality of money may be noted. As seen above, *the neutrality of money is a basic result reached in the classical full-employment model based on flexibility of prices and wages*. If increase in money supply and consequent rise in prices has no real effects, then inflation would not be a matter of concern. However, we know that inflation is a matter of serious concern as it lowers standards of living of the people and also adversely affects economic growth. Inflation affects the distribution of income in a society. It hurts the poor most. Therefore, efforts are made to control inflation and achieve price stability in the economy.

KEYNES'S CRITIQUE OF CLASSICAL THEORY

Keynes in his renowned book "*General Theory*" severely criticised the classical theory of employment. We explain below various criticisms of classical theory made by Keynes.

Keynes challenged Say's Law. Keynes criticised Say's Law and proved that it was quite invalid. As we have said above, according to Say's Law, every supply or production creates its own demand and therefore problems of over-production and unemployment do not arise. It is, of course, true that supply creates demand for goods because the various factors which are employed in a productive activity earn incomes from it, which in turn are spent on goods. For example, when factors of production are employed in producing cloth, then the incomes in the form of wages, rent, interest and profits accrue to them which they spend on various goods. But from this it does not follow that the supply of production will create its own entire demand. The incomes earned by the various factors of production are equal to the value of output produced, but this does not mean that the whole income received by the factors of production will be spent on goods and services. A part of the income is saved and the saved part does not necessarily create demand for goods and services. If entrepreneurs do not invest equal to the desired savings, then aggregate demand which, without government intervation, consists of demand for consumer goods and capital goods, will not be enough to purchase the available supply of output. Hence, if aggregate demand is not sufficient to purchase the available supply, the producers would be unable to sell their whole output due to which their profits would decline and as a result they would reduce their level of production giving rise to involuntary unemployment in the economy.

In a given period, consumers spend a part of their income on consumption and the rest they save. Likewise, in a period, the entrepreneurs plan to spend on factories and machines, that is, they plan to invest. Aggregate demand is the sum of consumption demand and investment demand. But in a free market capitalist economy, the persons who save are often different from those who invest and further that the factors that determine savings are different from the factors which determine investment by the entrepreneurs. People save to provide for their old age, to accumulate money for education and marriage of their children and also save and hold money balances for speculative motive, that is, to buy stocks and bonds in future to earn profits. But investment by entrepreneurs depends upon marginal efficiency of capital (that is, expected rate of profit), rate of interest, population growth and technological progress. Keynes also explained that the equality between saving and investment cannot be brought about by changes in interest rate as saving mainly depends on income and it is changes in income that bring about equality between saving and investment rather than changes in rate of interest. But classical economists ignored the changes in level of income because of their assumption of full-employment.

To conclude, savers and investors are different people with different motives. Much of the economy's saving is done by households while investment is mostly done by business firms on the basis of profit expectations and the amount of investment they want to make fluctuates widely from year to year and is unlikely to be equal to savings which households want to do. This affects aggregate demand and causes fluctuations in income, output and employment in capitalist economies. We thus see that there is no any mechanism in a free market economy which guarantees that investments made by the entrepreneurs are equal to the saving by the people. If the desired investment by entrepreneurs falls short of the amount of saving at full-employment level of income, the equilibrium of the economy will be at less than full employment level and as a result involuntary unemployment will emerge in the economy. In this way, according to Keynes, there is no reason that sum of consumption expenditure and investment expenditure is necessarily equal to the value of output produced. In other words, there is no guarantee that aggregate demand will be equal to aggregate forthcoming at full-employment level of resources. Hence, it is not necessary that the economy will be in equilibrium at the level of full employment. This invalidates Say's law, since according to it over-production and unemployment cannot occur.

Keynes proved Pigou's view that cut in money wages will restore full-employment as fallacious. Keynes also criticised Pigou's view that a general fall in wages and prices in times of depression will remove unemployment and automatically restore full empooyment in the economy if market mechanism is allowed to work freely without any obstruction by trade unions and Government. According to Keynes, a general fall in wages will not bring about increase in employment because the reduction in wages will reduce aggregate demand for goods. Keynes put forward the view that *wages are not only the cost of production, they are also incomes of the workers* which constitute the majority of the population of a country. As a result of a *general fall* in wages, the incomes of the workers will fall due to which aggregate demand will decline. As a result of decline in aggregate demand, level of production will have to be reduced and less labour will be employed than before. This will create more unemployment rather than reducing it. No doubt, as a result of a general cut in wages, cost of production of industries will fall but with the fall in costs, the demand for the products will not increase because due to the *all-round cut in wages,* purchasing power of the working class will decrease. Hence all-round cut in wages will reduce the level of employment by reducing aggregate demand and will thus deepen the depression.

There is a fundamental difference between Keynes and Pigou in respect of the relationship between wages and employment. Pigou thought that level of employment in an economy depends upon the level of money wages and therefore reduction in money wages will promote employment. On the other hand, Keynes thought that the level of employment depends upon the aggregate demand and aggregate demand declines as a result of an all-round cut in money wages.

Classical economists thought that a general cut in wages would reduce the cost of production of various industries but they ignored the fact that a general cut in wages will also reduce the incomes of the workers. In view of the fall in incomes and aggregate demand, how will manufacturers be able to sell their whole output? It is the sales of output that makes the wheel of trade, output and employment going. However, note that the classical theory is valid in case of an individual industry. With the decline in wages, the cost of the industry decreases and as a result the price of its product falls. The industry will be able to sell a larger amount of output at a lower price because it is not necessary that the goods produced by the industry are to be purchased by the workers employed in that industry whose wages have been reduced. But in the case of the economy as a whole, this is not valid because a general cut in wages will reduce the incomes of the working class and as a result enough demand will not be there for the output produced by the whole economy. This deficiency in demand will reduce demand for workers as a result of which unemployment will spread among them. Although it is true that a reduction in real wages (i.e. money wages relative to the general price level, $\frac{W}{P}$) in a single firm or industry is not likely to affect the *overall demand* for that product, it is quite wrong to assume that a *general economy-wide reduction in wages* of *all workers* have no effect on aggregate demand. Pigou and other classical economists *committed a logical falacy* in their thinking by applying the analysis which is true for a particular firm or industry to the economy as a whole. Thus, the fundamental flaw in Pigou and other classical economists is that they applied partial equilibrium analysis, which is valid in the case of an individual industry, to the determination of income and employment in the whole economy. The determination of the level of aggregate income and employment in the economy should be explained with the aid of general equilibrium analysis rather than with partial or particular equilibrium analysis of microeconomics.

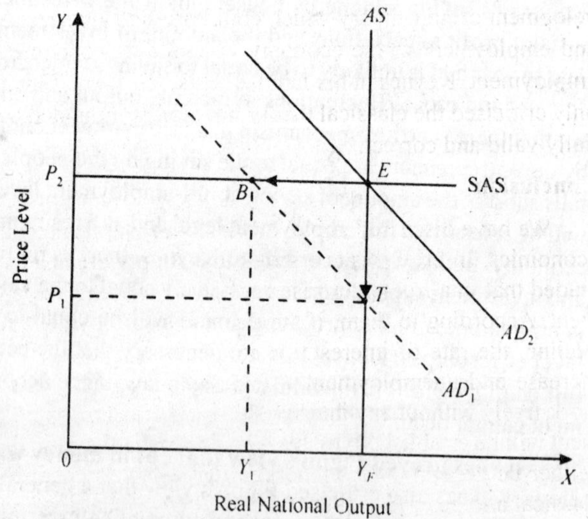

Fig. 3.9. *Wage-Price Flexibility : Keynes vs. Classics*

Sticky Wages and Unemployment : A basic idea of classical economists is that in a free market economy full employment is the normal state of affairs and any deviation from it will be automatically corrected through quick adjustment in prices and wages. As explained above, when during the period of great repression, 25 per cent of labour force in the USA was unemployed A.C. Pigeon wrote, "With perfectly free competition, there will always be a strong tendency toward full employment. Such *unemployment as exists at any time is due wholly to the frictional resistances that prevent the appropriate wage and price adjustments being made instantaneously.*"[3]

On the contrary, Keignes explained that unemployment that prevailed during depression was due to fall in aggregate demand and argued that prices and wages were inflexible downward (i.e. sticky) and fall in aggregate demand causes decline in real output and employment. As a result, involuntary unemployment emerges.

The Classical and Keynessian viewpoints are illustrated in figure 3.9 through *AS-AD* model. According to classical economists, aggregate supply curve is vertical at full employment output Y_F and is represented by *AS*. Keynes's short run aggregate supply curve is given by the horizontal line *SAS*. Suppose, to begin with, aggregate demand curve is AD_2 which intersects aggregate supply curve *AS* at point *E* with price level equal to P_2. Now suppose that aggregate demand declines due to the fall in investment demand or due to the contraction in money supply and as a result aggregate demand curve shifts leftward to the new position AD_1 (dotted). *According to the classical economists, prices and wages would adjust quickly so that equilibrium will be achieved at point T at the lower price level P_1, level of national output remaining unchanged at full-employment output level Y_F.* Thus, in the classical framework, if market system is allowed to work freely, even with the fall in aggregate demand, full employment tends to prevail and no involuntary unemployment can exist.

On the other hand, according to Keynes, *prices and wages are sticky* and therefore Keynes's short-run aggregate supply curve is flat as is represented by *SAS* in Figure 3.9. Therefore, when there is leftward shift in aggregate demand due to decline in desired investment, the real national output will fall by *EB* or Y_FY_1, price level and money wages remaining incharged.[4] We shall discuss in detail

3. A.C. Pigou, *The Theory of Unemployment*, 1933 (Italics added)

in a later chapter the Keynesian and Classical theories regarding wage-price flexibility and employment.

Because of the above-mentioned shortcomings of the classical theory, there was a need for development of new theory which could provide a correct explanation of the determination of income and employment in the economy. A capitalist economy cannot automatically attain a state of full employment. Keynes in his famous work "*General Theory of Employment, Interest and Money*" not only criticised the classical theory but also propounded a new one which is still regarded as substantially valid and correct.

Conclusion

We have discussed above Say's law of classical economics. This is a basic law of the classical economics. In brief this law states that supply creates its own demand. From this, it has been concluded that in a free-enterprise capitalist economy, there is always a tendency towards full employment. According to them, if sometimes unemployment appears in the economy, then wages would decline, the rate of interest and prices would also fall. As a result, employment of labour would increase and unemployment will be automatically removed, provided the economy is allowed to work freely without any interference by Government and trade unions. Hence a state of full employment will be established. In this way due to the *flexibility of wages, prices and interest rate*, there can neither be general overproduction, nor unemployment in the economy for a long time. Therefore, classical and neoclassical economists thought that there was always a tendency toward full-employment provided no restrictions were placed in the working of free and perfect competition. Thus, according to them, the Government need not interfere in the working of the economy and should follow a *laissez fair policy*. But Keynes proved this as invalid not only theoretically but also practically. Keynes put forward a new theory of income and employment which is the correct explanation of the phenomenon in a developed capitalist economy. For this purpose, Keynes invented new concepts such as propensity to consume, marginal efficiency of capital, liquidity preference which affect the level of income and employment in the economy. Keynes also proved that a cut in wages would not cure depression and unemployment, but would worsen them. Following Keynesian revolution in economic theory and the recognition of the fact that economic fluctuations or lapses from full-employment will not be automatically corrected, it is now believed by many economists that Government should play an active and important role to promote economic stability at the level of full-employment by taking appropriate fiscal and monetary measures. *Laissez faire* policy should not, therefore, be followed by the Government in the modern world.

QUESTIONS FOR REVIEW

1. What is Say's Law ? How did classical economists use this law to show that there could not be involuntary unemployment in the economy ?
2. "The supply creates its own demand" How did classical economists justify this argument ? How did Keynes challenge its validity ?
3. Explain briefly classical theory of income and employment. How does this theory show that a free market economy *automatically* adjusts to full employment level ?
4. What is meant by wage-price flexibility ? How does classical full-employment model show that in a free enterprise competitive economic system flexibility of wages and prices always ensures full employment.
5. Explain how Keynes showed that money wage cut would fail to increase employment.
6. What is aggregate demand ? How classical economists showed that there would always be sufficient aggregate demand even when there is saving by the households ?
7. What is meant by *neutrality of money* ? How did classical economists explain that money had

4. Note that modern Keynesians consider the short-run aggregate supply curve to be gently sloping upward. Therefore, when aggregate demand falls, there is a small fall in price but a large fall in real national output and employment.

no effect on real income, output and employment.

OR

Why are only the price level and money wages affected by a change in the money supply in the classical full employment model ? *DU BA (Hons.) 2009*

8. How is the level of output determined in a classical full employment model ? What will happen to output if investment demand falls due to the decline in profit expectations of business firms ?

9. How are saving and investment balanced ? Why will demand and supply in the product market be equal if saving and investment are equal ?

10. What are the main factors according to Keynes that may prevent the attainment of full-employment when wages and prices are flexible.

11. Explain briefly Keynes's critique of classical theory of income and employment

12. What mechanism in classical theory of output and employment ensures equality between saving and investment at full employment ? How did Keynes prove it as fallacious ?

13. What is meant by neutrality of money. Show that why money is neutral under the classical model of output and employment .

14. What determines the economy's productive capacity or potential GDP. (i.e. long-run aggregate supply). How does it change when (a) labour supply increases, (b) capital stock increases as a result of net investment, (c) technology improves ?

15. In a full employment model where all prices are flexible, explain how the financial capital market reaches its equilibrium. When investment falls, how in a free market economy in this model equilibrium at full employment level of output is restored ? *DU BA (Hons.) 2007*

16. Show when saving and investment are equal at full-employment output there is equilibrium in the product market at full employment. *DU BA (Hons.) 2008*

17. How are leakages and injections balanced in a free market economy ? Why will demand and supply in the product market be equal if leakages and injections are equal ?

18. In classical full employment model, how is price level determined ? Explain diagramatically. How is the rate of inflation related to the rate of growth of the money supply ?

19. Why is long-run classical aggregate supply a vertical straight line ? What determines the aggregate demand for goods in the classical theory of output and employment ? How does interaction between the two determine the general price level ?

20. Show the effects of introduction of a new technology on labour market, product market capital market in the classical full employment model with perfect wage price flexibility. *DU BA(Hons.) 2006*

21. Show with the classical full employment model how the increase in labour supply through increase in labour participation rate will affect labour market, product market ?

APPENDIX TO CHAPTER 3

Using Classical Full Employment Model to Explain the Impact of Changes in Technology and Labour Supply*

Introduction

Though the classical full employment model does not explain fluctuations in economic activity as it assumes quick adjustment of wages and prices to equate demand and supply, it is useful for explaining the effects of changes in various real factors such as a change in technology, increase in labour supply on labour, product and capital markets, especially in the long run. In *the long run wages and prices adjust to balance demand and supply and thereby clear the markets.* Besides, the full employment model explains how changes that originate in one market affect other markets in the economy. As shall be explained below, changes in labour market equilibrium affect product and capital market equilibrium. Thus, full employment model makes *general equilibrium analysis* of the economy. In this appendix we will use the full employment model to explain below the effects of

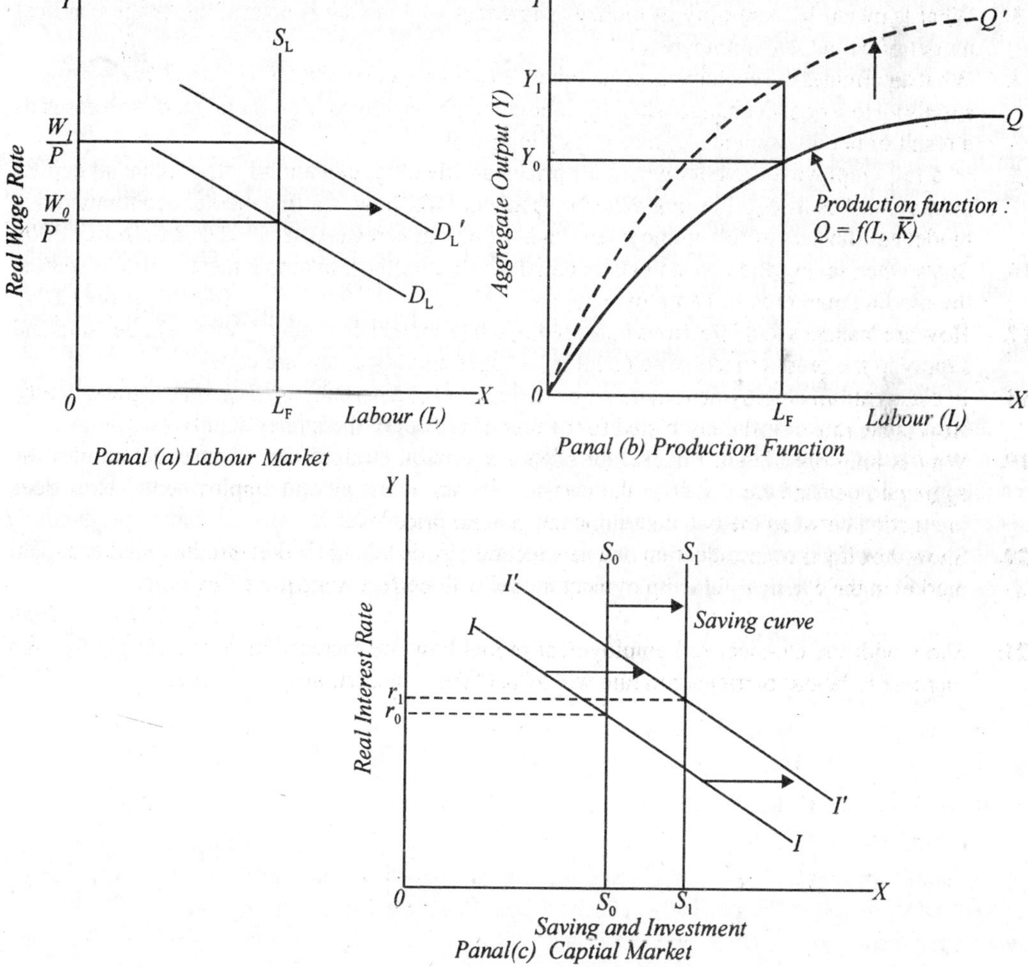

Fig. 3A.1. *Effects of Changes in Technolgoy*

* This analysis of Classical Full-Employment Model is based on analysis of Joseph E Stiglitz, a Nobel laureate, in his book, *Economics*, third edition, 2002, published by W.W Norton and Co.

changes in two things : (1) the effect of change in technology (*e.g.* the introduction of computers in providing various services in the economy), (2) the effect of increase in supply of labour,

EFFECT OF CHANGES IN TECHNOLOGY

Impact on Real Wages. The use of new improved technology, for example, the introduction of use of computers makes the workers more productive and therefore results in increase in their marginal products. This will cause increase in quantity demanded of workers at each real wage rate and bring about a shift in the labour demand curve to the right as shown in Panel (*a*) of Fig. 3A.1. For simplifying the analysis we have taken labour supply curve S_L in Panel (*a*) of Figure 3.1 as a vertical straight line which shows that labour supply curve is completely insensitive to changes in real wage rate. It will be seen firm Panel (*a*) that with change in technology (*e.g.* introduction of personal computers) and resultant increase in worker's productivity, demand curve of labour shifts from D_L to D'_L and as a result real wage rate rises from $\frac{W_0}{P}$ to $\frac{W_1}{P}$.

Impact on Output. With the introduction of new technology as the productivity of workers increases the short-run production function shifts upward from OQ to QQ' as shown in Panel (*b*) of Fig. 3A.1 As a result potential GDP (or full-employment level of output) increases from OY_0 to OY_1. However, the product market equilibrium can be maintained at full employment level if aggregate demand increases sufficiently so that the firms are able to sell this new higher level of output. This can happen only if the real interest rate adjusts to equate saving and investment in the capital market. With this adjustment in real interest rate both investment and saving will increase to reach new equilibrium at full-employment level of output. *At each real rate of interest, investment will increase as the introduction of new technology will open up new profitable opportunities for investment.* Besides, as full-employment income and real wage rate increase, they will cause rise in both consumption and saving depending upon marginal propensity to consume . As a result, saving curve will shift to the right as shown in Panel (*c*) of Fig. 3A.1 and in the new equilibrium real interest can either rise, remain the same or fall depending upon the extent of shifts in the investment and saving curves. However, whatever be the effect on the real interest rate investment will certainly increase.

In our above analysis we have explained the *current or short-sun effects of new technology and investment induced by it.* There will be more future effects in the long run of introduction of new technology and as a result of increase in investment. As more plant and equipment come into existence as a result of enhanced investment, this will lead to the increase in future productive capacity which will generate higher economic growth.

EFFECT OF INCREASE IN LABOUR SUPPLY

Labour supply can increase as a result of (*i*) natural rate of population growth, (*ii*) increase in labour force participation rate, and (*iii*) immigration of labour to a country. Let us assume that labour force increases due to rise in labour force participation rate. Labour force participation rate is proportion of workers who are in the labour force (either employed or seeking employment). Labour force participation rate has generally increased due to rise in participation of women in labour force.

Impact on Labour Market and Real Wage

The effect of increase in labour supply due to rise in labour force participation rate or growth of population is shown in Figure. 3A.2. For simplifying our analysis we have taken labour supply curve as a vertical straight line (*i.e.* perfectly inelastic to real wage rate) . In Panel (*a*) of Fig. 3A.2 with the given demand curve of labour D_L and initial labour force equal to L_0 labour market is in equilibrium at real wage rate $\frac{W_0}{P}$ at full-employment level of labour L_0. Now, if labour supply increases to L_1 due to rise in labour force participation rate, labour supply curve shifts to right to SL_1. It will be observed from Panel (*a*) that with the increase in labour supply to L_1, real wage rate falls to $\frac{W_1}{P}$

while equilibrium employment increases to L_1. It may be noted that at the lower real wage rate $\left(\frac{W_1}{P}\right)$, it becomes profitable for the firms to increase the demand for labour so as to become equal to the new labour supply.

Impact on Aggregate Output

Now, in Panel (*b*) of Fig. 3A.2 where short-run production function OQ is shown, at the initial full employment level L_0, potential GDP (*i.e.* aggregate output) is Y_0. When due to increase in labour force participation rate full-employment level of labour increases to L_1 (in Panel (*a*)), the potential GDP (or aggregate output) in Panel (2) increases to Y_1.

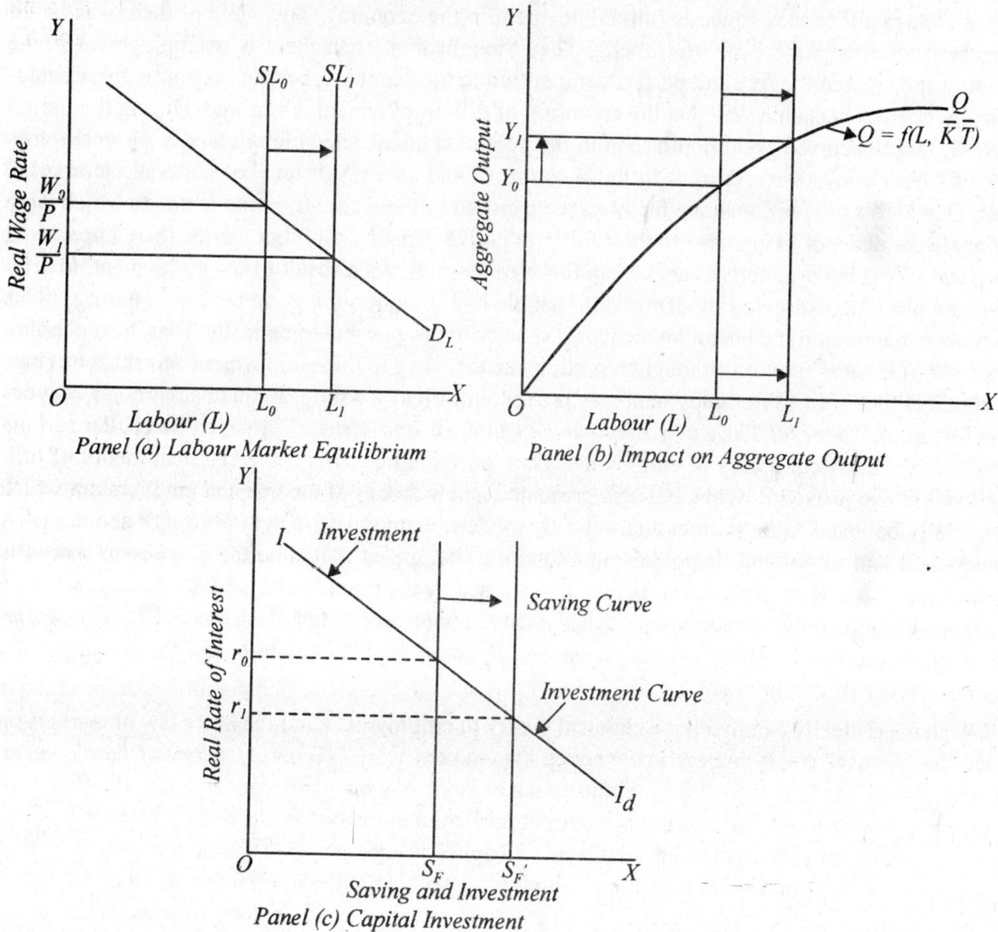

Fig. 3A.2. *Impact of Increase in Labour Supply on Real Wage Rate, Potential GDP and Real Rate of Interest.*

Impact on Capital Market

Now, with the increase in output as a result of increase in labour supply incomes of the people will increase leading to the increase in both consumption and saving at each level of real rate of interest. As this will cause the saving curve to shift to the right, it will affect the capital market equilibrium shown in Panel (*c*) of Fig. 3A.2. Initially, with investment demand curve I_d and full employment saving S_F, capital market is in equilibrium at real rate of interest r_0. Now, with increase in labour supply and resultant increase in full employment output (or potential GDP) to Y_1 saving, curve shift to the right to S'_F, capital market will now be in equilibrium at lower real rate of interest r_1. At lower real rate of interest more investment projects become profitable and therefore investment demand increase to become equal to S'_F.

Chapter 4
Keynes's Theory of Employment : An Outline

Introduction : Keynesian Revolution

Classical economists were of the view that there is always full employment in the economy or there is always a tendency towards full-employment in the economy. This view of them was based upon their belief in *Say's Law of Markets*. They thought that when there is unemployment in the economy, then, given the free and perfect competition in the economy, certain economic forces automatically operate in such a way that the condition of full-employment is restored. During the period 1929-33, there occurred great depression in the capitalist countries which caused huge unemployment of labour and other resources in those countries and as a result level of national income fell down. Due to this depression many factories were closed in these countries and factories which were working were also not being used to their full productive capacity. In other words, there appeared a good deal of excess productive capacity in these economies. As a result of unemployment, low income and production created by depression, people had to undergo a good deal of sufferings. This condition of depression and unemployment did not seem to disappear automatically. Therefore, people's belief in the classical economic thought regarding the tendency to full-employment was shaken. Thus, the classical theory of full employment was proved empirically wrong. In this background, Keynes wrote his book "*General Theory of Employment. Interest and Money*" in which he challenged the validity of the classical theory of employment. Not only did he criticise the classical theory of full-employment and proved it wrong but also presented a new theory of income and employment which is generally believed to be correct and valid by modern economists. Keynes brought about such a fundamental and important change in our economic thought at that time the Keynesian theory is generally known as *new economics*. By being impressed by the fundamental and revolutionary nature of change in our economic theory by Keynes, many economists called his "*General Theory of Employment, Interest and Money*" as the *Keynesian Revolution*. We explain below the outline of the Keynes's theory of employment.

We have critically examined the classical theory of employment and the Say's law of markets on which the classical theory is based. Keynes in his eminent work "*General Theory of Employment, Interest and Money*" not only criticised the classical Say's law but also propounded a new theory of income and employment. Keynes in his work put forward a more systematic and realistic analysis of the determinants of employment in an advanced capitalist economy and the factors which lead to unemployment. Keynes tried to prove that full-employment is not the normal feature of an advanced capitalist economy and that underemployment equilibrium is its normal feature. Keynes also invented new tools and concepts of economic analysis in terms of which he propounded his theory of income and employment. These new tools and concepts are propensity to consume, multiplier, marginal efficiency of capital and liquidity preference. We will explain these concepts in detail in later chapters. Here we will explain only the outline of the Keynesian theory of income and employment.

It is important to note that Keynesian theory of income and employment is a short run theory because Keynes assumes that the amount of capital, the size of population and labour force, technology, efficiency of labourers, etc., do not change. That is why in Keynesian theory, the amount of employment depends upon the level of national income and production. This is because, given the amount of capital, technology and labour efficiency, increase in income and output can be obtained by employment of more labour. Therefore, in the Keynesian short run, the higher the level of national income, the greater the amount of employment, and lower the level of national income, the lower the amount of employment. Hence the Keynes' theory of employment determination is also the Keynes' theory of income determination. But, for the simplicity, in this chapter we shall explain the Keynesian theory in terms of employment and all the diagrams we will draw will show explicitly the determination of employment. In the next chapter, we will explain Keynesian theory in terms of national income through *income expenditure analysis* and the diagrams which we will draw there will explicitly show the income determination. But it is important to note that the factors that determine the level of income are the same as those that determine the level of employment; only the diagrams used to show their determination are different.It is important to note that Keynes thought that prices and wages do not adjust quickly to balance demand and supply. Therefore, in his theory of income and employment he *assumes that prices remain constant.*

KEYNES'S THEORY OF EMPLOYMENT: PRINCIPLE OF EFFECTIVE DEMAND

At the outset, it may be noted that in Keynesian theory of income and employment determination, principle of effective demand occupies a significant place. In an advanced capitalist economy, the level of employment depends upon the level of aggregate effective demand, the greater the level of effective demand, the greater the amount of employment in the economy. How many men will be employed by an individual firm depends upon the number of persons employed which will make maximum profits. Likewise, in the whole economy, how many men will be employed by firms or entrepreneurs in the economy depends upon the fact that they make their individual profits. In the whole economy, the amount of employment is determined by aggregate supply and aggregate demand. We will now discuss below these concepts of aggregate supply and aggregate demand function and will show how they determine the equilibrium level of employment.

Aggregate Supply Function

When entrepreneurs employ some people they incur some cost of production. If the proceeds obtained from the sale of output produced by a certain number of people employed is greater than the cost of production incurred, it will be wrothwhile to employ them. The cost of production incurred on the employment of a certain number of labourers must be received by the entrepreneur, otherwise they will not produce and provide employment to labour. At any given level of employment of labour, *aggregate supply price is the total amount of money which all the entrepreneurs in the economy taken together must expect to receive from the sale of the output produced* by the given number of labourers employed. In other words, *aggregate supply price is the total cost of production* incurred by employing a contain given number of labourers. It is obvious that if the cost of production incurred by the entrepreneur in employing a certain number of labourers is not covered, they will reduce the amount of employment offered. As the amount of employment of labour increases, the total cost of production will also increase. Therefore, aggregate supply price will rise as more labour is employed to produce goods and services. *Keynes's aggregate supply function (curve) shows the relationship between the number of workers employed and the receipts which all firms in the economy must get if it is just worth employing them prices remaining constant.* In other words, Keynes's aggregate supply function (curve) shows the relationship between the number of workers employed and the aggregate supply price. Thus we can construct a schedule or *curve of aggregate supply showing aggregate supply price at different levels of employment.*

Let us now explain in detail the factors on which aggregate supply curve depends. *The aggregate supply curve depends ultimately on the physical and technical conditions of production* (that is, capital stock, the state of technology and the nature of production function). However, physical and technical conditions remain constant in the short-run. Hence, given these technical conditions, the level of output can be increased only by increasing employment of labour. But, when output and employment are increased, more cost of production is incurred. Whether production is subject to the law of increasing, diminishing or constant returns, when more workers are employed to increase production, more cost has to be incurred since additional workers are to be paid wages. Hence, more workers will be employed only if the entrepreneurs *must expect to receive* greater revenue so as to cover the rise in cost incurred. Therefore, the aggregate supply curve slopes upward to the right.

The *slope* of the aggregate supply curve (function) depends on the physical or technical conditions of production. If the technical conditions are such that with the increase in output, marginal cost of production does not rise, the aggregate supply curve will be a straight line. On the other hand, if technical conditions are such that diminishing returns occur with the increase in employment of labour, marginal cost of production will rise with the increase in the level of output. This will make the slope of aggregate supply curve to increase with the increase in employment of labour. Besides, if with the increase in employment of labour, wage rate of labour rises, the slope of aggregate supply curve will increase with the employment of more labour. It is however worth noting that Keynes thought in conditions of depression/recession when huge unemployment of labour prevailed in the economy, with the increase in employment of labour to produce more, wage rate will remain constant. Assuming that marginal cost of production rises with the increase in employment of labour, upward rising aggregate supply curve *AS* with increasing slope as more labour is employed is shown in Fig. 4.1. This aggregate supply curve (function) depicts rising aggregate supply price at various levels of labour employment.

We have said that the aggregate supply is determined by the physical and technical conditions prevailing in the economy, that is, the quantity and quality of labour, stock of capital and raw materials available in the economy and the state of technology. As these changes, or as production technology is improved, *AS* curve will also change. But in the analysis of the determination of employment in the advanced capitalist economies in the short run aggregate supply curve can be assumed to be given and constant. This is for the simple reason that in times of depression the main problem of advanced capitalist economies is how to employ idle manpower and capital resources to increase production by raising demand and not that how the productive capacity be raised by augmenting the stock of capital or by improving the techniques of production. That is why Keynes assumed the *AS* curve to be constant and paid greater attention to the factors determining aggregate demand. The need of the moment in times of recession is to increase aggregate demand so that the equilibrium be achieved at full-employment level. When aggregate demand is increased, the aggregate demand curve will shift upward and it will intersect the *AS* curve more on the right, *i.e.*, the number of men employed will increase.

When the full-employment level has been reached, then, given the stock of fixed capital and the prevailing technology, output and employment cannot be further increased by increasing aggregate demand. Under such conditions increase in aggregate demand will only result in inflation. In such a situation, it becomes necessary to cause a rightward shift in the aggregate supply curve by making addition to the stock of capital and effecting improvements in production technology. This will contain the inflationary pressures. In other words, efforts should be made to increase aggregate supply when full-employment level has already been achieved and the economy is in the grip of inflation.

The curve of aggregate supply price *AS* starts from the point of origin and slopes upward to the right. In the beginning aggregate supply price curve *AS* rises slowly, afterwards it rises rapidly. This curve *AS* shows that as the number of men employed is increased, the aggregate supply price rises slowly in the beginning and rapidly afterwards. This is because cost of production rises as more people are employed and further due to the operations of law of diminishing returns total cost of production increases at an increasing rate. Once all the men willing to get employment are employed, then we have a state of full employment. When the state of full employment is reached further increases in aggregate demand or expenditure will be unable to increase employment further since output of goods and services cannot be increased further as no more labour is available for production after full-employment level is reached. Therefore, aggregate supply curve assumes a vertical shape after full-employment is reached. In Fig. 4.1, ON_F is the level of full-employment at which aggregate supply curve assumes a vertical shape.

Aggregate Demand Function

It is aggregate demand function which plays a more important role in the determination of employment. Aggregate demand function (curve) shows for each possible level of employment the total sum of money (proceeds) which all the firms or entrepreneurs in the economy *actually expect* to receive from the sale of output produced by those workers employed in the economy. *The amount of expenditure actually expected by when a given number of workers are employed to produce goods and services is called aggregate demand price.* Like the aggregate supply price, aggregate demand

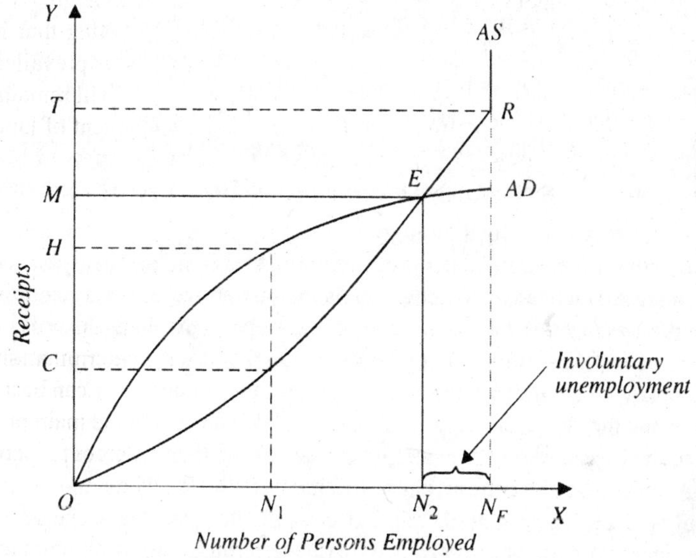

Fig. 4.1. *Determination of Employment*

price also varies at different levels of employment. This is because at different levels of employment different income levels would be generated and at different income levels, expenditure, especially consumption expenditure, would be different. Aggregate demand has the following four components : (1) *Consumption demand,* (2) *Investment demand,* (3) *Government expenditure, and* (4) *Net Exports (that is, exports – imports).* In this introduction to the theory of employment, we confine ourselves to the consumption demand and investment demand and will introduce Government expenditure and net exports in a later chapter of this book.

Thus the factors which determine aggregate demand are the factors which determine consumption demand and investment demand. Consumption demand depends on disposable income on the one hand and propensity to consume on the other. Propensity to consume depends on some subjective factors such as willingness to save, desire to imitate others' higher levels of living and objective factors such as price level, taxation policy of the Government, rate of interest. Given these factors, changes in which cause a shift in the entire consumption function, the higher the level of disposable income, the greater the amount of consumption demand. As regards investment demand, according to Keynes, it is determined by rate of interest on the one hand and marginal efficiency of capital on the other. While rate of interest is more or less sticky, it is changes in *marginal efficiency of capital* (*i.e., expected rate of return*) that cause frequent changes in inducement to invest. Marginal efficiency of capital means expected rate of profit by the entrepreneurs from the investment they propose to undertake. When prospects for profit making in future are bright, there will be more investment. If investors become pessimistic about profit earning in future, they will undertake less new investment.

But what are the factor on which business expectations about opportunities of making profits depend. The expected rate of profits (which Keynes calls marginal efficiency of capital) of business men depends on their estimates of consumer demand for goods, taxation policy of the Government, expectations regarding changes in technology. It is worth noting that it is due to the frequent changes in business expectations that investment demand is volatile. When business men become pessimistic about profit earning, investment declines which lowers aggregate demand. On the other hand, when entrepreneurs become bullish or optimistic, they undertake new investment on a large scale which raises the level of aggregate demand of the economy. On the other hand, *consumption function*, according to Keynes, remains stable in the short run. However, *amount of consumption demand* increases as the income rises in the short run. Therefore, we can construct a schedule or curve of aggregate demand showing different aggregate demand prices at different levels of employment. The curve of aggregate demand is shown by the curve *AD* in Fig. 4.1. The aggregate demand price curve also rises from left to right. It will be seen in Fig. 4.1 that when ON_1 number of men are employed, the aggregate demand price is *OH* and when ON_2 men are employed, aggregate demand price is *OM*.

Determination of the Equilibrium Level of Employment by Effective Demand

In Fig. 4.1 we have shown together aggregate supply curve and aggregate demand curve. The amount of employment is measured along the *X*-axis and the receipts or proceeds obtained at various levels of employment are measured along the *Y*-axis. As said above, aggregate supply curve shows the revenue or receipts *which must be received* by the entrepreneurs so as to provide employment to different numbers of workers, whereas aggregate demand curve shows proceeds or receipts which entrepreneurs *actually do expect* to receive at different levels of employment and production. These aggregate demand and the aggregate supply curves determine the level of employment in the economy. Given that the perfect competition prevails in the economy, then so long as opportunities to earn profits or make money exist, the entrepreneurs will increase the level of employment. The opportunities to make profits exist if aggregate demand price is greater than the aggregate supply price for a given number of employment. This analysis explains determination of national income by relating income (output) to aggregate expenditure on goods and services. Thus, aggregate expenditure shows aggregate demand for goods and services. For example, in Figure 4.1 at ON_1 number of persons employed aggregate demand price *OH* exceeds aggregate supply price *OC*. Therefore, it is profitable to offer employment to ON_1 workers. Therefore, so long as aggregate demand price exceeds aggregate supply price, the entrepreneurs will go on employing extra workers. When at a level of employment aggregate demand price becomes equal to aggregate supply price, then after this it will be no more profitable to employ workers. Since beyond this point aggregate supply price will exceed aggregate demand price, the cost of production incurred on employing a certain number of people will not be covered. Therefore, when aggregate demand price falls short of aggregate supply price, employment of labour will fall.

Equilibrium level of employment is determined by the intersection of aggregate demand curve and the aggregate supply curve, where the amount of money which the entrepreneurs actually expect to receive from employing a certain number of workers is equal to the amount of money which they must receive. In other words, *the employment of labour will be in equilibrium at the level at which aggregate demand price equals aggregate supply price*. It will be seen from Fig. 4.1 that aggregate supply curve and aggregate demand curve intersect at point *E* and therefore ON_2 level of employment is determined. It will be noticed that *at less than* ON_2 level of employment, aggregate demand curve *AD* lies above the aggregate supply curve *AS* showing that it is profitable to expand the amount of employment. However, beyond ON_2 amount of employment, the aggregate demand curve *AD* lies below aggregate supply curve *AS*, which shows that it is no more profitable to employ extra workers beyond ON_2. We, therefore, conclude that ON_2 is the equilibrium level of employment which will be determined by aggregate demand curve *AD* and aggregate supply curve *AS*.

Effective Demand : Further Clarification

We are now in a position to explain more clearly what effective demand means and how it is important for determination of employment and output in the economy. We have seen that the magnitude of employment in the economy is determined by the equilibrium between aggregate demand and aggregate supply. There is an aggregate demand function for an economy which shows aggregate demand price at varying levels of employment.

But of these varying levels of employment the *aggregate demand at which a level of employment is also equal to the aggregate supply is called effective demand.* In other words, effective demand is that aggregate demand price which becomes '*effective*' because it is equal to aggregate supply price and thus represents a position of short-run equilibrium. There are several other points on the aggregate demand curve but what distinguishes effective demand from all these points is that at this point the aggregate demand price is equal to aggregate supply price. On all other points, aggregate demand price is either more or less than aggregate supply price.

It is thus clear that employment in the economy in the short run is determined by effective demand. The higher the level of effective demand, the greater is the volume of employment, and *vice versa*. Unemployment is due to the deficiency of effective demand and the basic remedy to remove this unemployment is to raise the level of the effective demand. The classical economists believed that effective demand was always large enough to ensure full employment. But Keynes proved that it was not so and that is why the phenomenon of unemployment is common in free-market capitalist economies.

Under-employment Equilibrium : The Problem of Demand Deficiency

It is not necessary that the equilibrium level of employment is always at full employment. Equality between aggregate demand and aggregate supply does not necessarily indicate the full employment level. The economy can be in equilibrium at less than full employment or, in other words, an

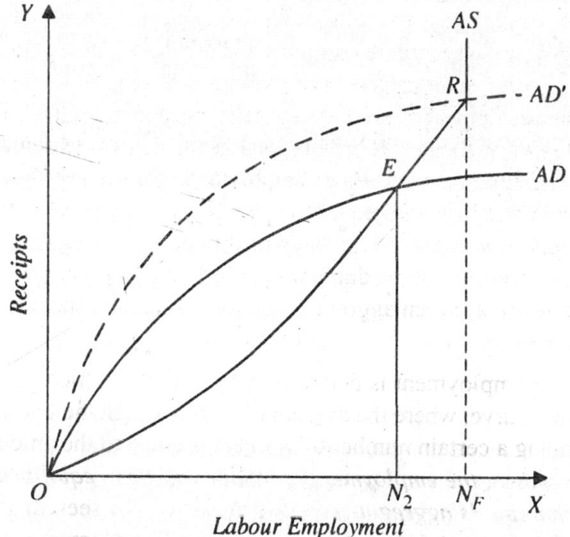

Fig. 4.2. *Raising aggregate demand curve to achieve full-employment*

under-employment equilibrium can exist. The classical economists denied that there could be an equilibrium at less than full employment, because they believed that supply would always create its own demand and therefore no problem of deficiency of aggregate effective demand would be experienced. Keynes demolished the classical thesis of full employment both on theoretical grounds and on the basis of illustrations from real life.

It will be seen from Fig. 4.2 that in the situation of equilibrium at the employment level ON_2, the N_2N_F persons remain unemployed. Thus equilibrium at E represents an under-employment equilibrium (or, in other words, less than full-employment equilibrium). It is important to note that N_2N_F persons are *involuntarily unemployed*: they are willing to work at the existing wage rates but are unable to find jobs. It is important to remember that, according to Keynes, this *unemployment is due to deficiency of aggregate demand.*

This unemployment will be removed and full-employment equilibrium will be reached if through increase in investment demand or increase in consumption, or increase in both, aggregate demand curve shifts upward so that it intersects the aggregate supply curve at point *R* as depicted in Fig. 4.2. It will be seen that with the intersection of aggregate demand and aggregate supply curves at point *R*, equilibrium is established at full-employment level ON_F.

According to Keynes, *aggregate demand price and aggregate supply price will be equal at full-employment only if investment demand is sufficient to cover the gap between the aggregate supply price corresponding to full-employment level and the consumption expenditure out of income at the full-employment level.* The view of Keynes is that when investment demand falls short of this gap between full-employment income and consumption recession occurs resulting in the emergence of involuntary unemployment. According to him, when inducement to invest in capitalist countries declines due to the fall in marginal efficiency of capital (*i.e.*, expected rate of profit), aggregate demand falls so that equilibrium is established at less than full-employment level. As a result, output and income of the community also fall.

SUMMARY OF KEYNES'S THEORY OF EMPLOYMENT

After explaining Keynes's theory of employment at some length, we are now in a position to describe it in a summary form bringing out relationship between various elements or factors that go to determine the equilibrium level of employment.

1. Level of output or income of a country depends on the level of employment. Given the capital stock and technology, greater the employment of labour, the higher the level of aggregate output or national income.
2. The level of employment depends on the magnitude of effective demand which is the sum of consumption demand and investment demand at the point where aggregate supply curve intersects the aggregate demand curve.
3. Aggregate supply of an economy depends on physical and technical conditions of production. Since these factors do not change much in the short run, aggregate supply curve remains constant in the short run. Aggregate supply curve slopes upward to the right as level of employment increases. This is because with the increase in labour employment, the greater cost has to be incurred.
4. Aggregate demand in a simple Keynesian model consists of consumption demand and investment demand. Since the consumption demand increases with the increase in labour employment, aggregate demand curve also slopes upward to the right. In the Keynes's model, *investment demand is regarded as autonomous of changes in income or employment.*
5. Consumption demand depends on propensity to consume on the one hand and disposable income on the other. Propensity to consume of a community does not change much in the short run. Therefore, consumption function which relates consumption demand with the level of income remains stable in the short run.

6. Investment demand depends on the rate of interest and marginal efficiency of capital. According to Keynes, rate of interest is determined by supply of money and the state of liquidity preference. Marginal efficiency of capital (*i.e.*, expected rate of profit) depends on the expected future yields or *profit expectations* of entrepreneurs on the one hand and *replacement cost of capital* on the other.
7. According to Keynes, while rate of interest is more or less sticky it is frequent changes in profit expectations of the entrepreneurs, that is, changes in marginal efficiency of capital that cause a great deal of fluctuations in investment by entrepreneurs. Investment demand is thus highly volatile and causes recession or depression when it falls, and boom and prosperity when it increases significantly.

We summarise below the various determinants of employment and income (output) in a tabular form.

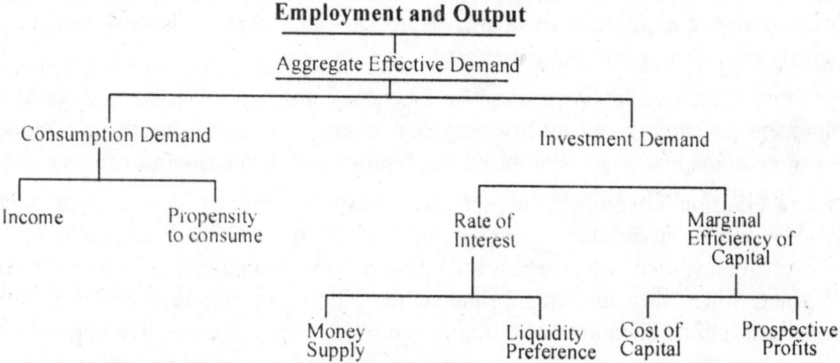

INVOLUNTARY UNEMPLOYMENT : KEYNES'S MONEY-WAGE RIGIDITY MODEL

According to Keynes, due to money wage rigidity, that is, downward inflexibility of money wages results in involuntary unemployment of labour. The workers are rendered unemployed because at a given wage rate supply of labour exceeds demand for labour. Keynes believed that money wage would not change sufficiently in the short run to keep the economy at full employment. Classical economists believed that money wage rate is perfectly flexible and adjusts to bring demand for and supply of labour in equilibrium and keep the economy at full employment level. To understand money wage-rigidity which results in unemployment we have to examine why labour market does not clear through reduction in money wages, Keynes gave three reasons for the stickiness of money wage rate. It may be noted that stickiness or rigidity of money wage implies that money wage rate will not quickly change, especially in the downward direction to keep equilibrium at full employment level.

Causes of Money Wage Rigidity

1. **Money Illusion.** The first reason why firms fail to cut wages despite an excess supply of labour is that workers will resist any move for cut in money wages though they might accept fall in real wages brought about by rise in prices of commodities. Keynes attributed this to money illusion on the part of the workers. *By money illusion it is meant that workers fail to realise that value of money, that is, its purchasing power in terms of commodities, changes when prices rise.* They regard money such as a rupee as something which has a stable value or purchasing power, that a rupee is a rupee and a dollar is a dollar with fixed real purchasing power. Therefore, while they would strongly oppose and resist any cut in money wages, they would not resist much if their real wages are reduced through rise in prices of commodities with money wages remaining constant. Thus Keynes wrote, "*Whilest workers will usually resist a reduction of money wages, it is not their practice to withdraw their labour whenever there is a rise in the price of wage goods*"

There are two reasons for existence of money illusion.

(*i*). First reason for the existence of money illusion is that workers of a firm or industry think that though rise in prices reduce their real wages, but that this rise in prices equally affect workers in other industries so that their relative wages as compared to those employed in other industries remain the same. Therefore, workers who are more concerned with their relative position with other workers will strongly resist the cut in their money wages, while they will not oppose so strongly their cut in real wages through rise in the general price level.

(*ii*). The second reason for strong resistance to cut in money wages is that the workers blame their own employers for this, whereas they think that a cut in real wages through rise in prices in general is the outcome of the working of general economic forces over which strikes in an industry would have little effect. However, it does not necessarily mean that trade unions remain silent spectators if they feel that changes in Government policy adversely affects their economic interests.

From the above two reasons given for money illusion it follows that if additional employment can be created by lowering real wages, it is more practical to do so *through bringing about rise in general price level rather than by cutting money wages*.

2. **Wage Fixation Through Contracts.** In most of the free market economies such as those of USA and Great Britain, wages are fixed by the firms through contracts made with the workers for a year or two. There is little possibility of changing money wages fixed through contracts when the situation of either labour surplus or shortage emerges. For workers organised into trade unions wages are even rigid. Through collective bargaining by trade unions with the employers wage scales are fixed for 3 to 4 years by contract. Money wages cannot be changed when either surplus or shortage of labour emerges during the period of the contract. Trade unions of workers never accept wage cuts even if some of union workers remain unemployed. Thus the sticky or rigid money wages lead to the existence of involuntary unemployment. This means that labour market does not clear in the short run.

3. **Minimum Wage Laws.** Another reason for money wage rigidity or, what is also called money-wage stickiness, is the intervention by the Government in fixing minimum wages below which employers are not permitted to pay wages to the workers.

4. **Efficiency Wages.** Another factor which accounts for money-wage rigidity is that employers themselves are not interested in lowering wages as high wages make workers more efficient and productive. The adverse effect of lower wages on workers' efficiency may explain the unwillingness on the part of employers to cut money wages despite the excess supply of or unemployment of workers at higher money wages.

We have explained above the practical difficulties pointed out by Keynes and his followers which are faced by firms in reducing wages and which therefore explain money-wage rigidity or stickiness. The sticky or rigid money wages above the equilibrium level cause unemployment of labour.

Price Flexibility and Rigid Money Wage : Keynes's View of Involuntary Unemployment

In Keynes' contractual view of labour market, it is assumed that whereas prices are free to vary, the money wage is fixed. It is important to note that Keynesians do not believe that money wage rate is completely fixed or sticky. What do they actually mean by sticky wages is that money wages do not fall quickly to bring demand for and supply of labour in equilibrium at full employment. In their view money wages are very slow to adjust sufficiently to ensure full employment of labour when there is a decline in aggregate demand resulting in lowering of prices of products. As a consequence, involuntarily unemployment comes into existence. It may be further noted that Keynes was particularly concerned with downward rigidity of money wages at which the demand for labour exceeds the supply of labour and consequently unemployment or excess supply of labour emerges. It is important to note that Keynes accepted the classical theory of labour demand according to which firms demand labour up to the point at which real wage rate (that is, money wage rate divided by the price level or,

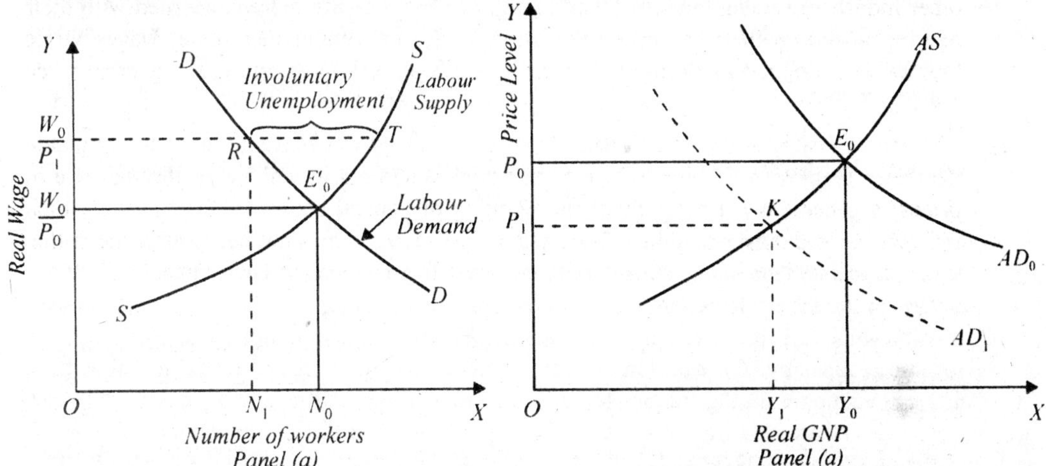

Fig. 4.3. *Keynes's Rigid Money Wage and Flexible Price Model : The Emergence of Involuntary Unemployment*

W/P) is equal to the marginal product of labour. At a higher real wage rate, less amount of labour will be demanded and, at a lower real wage rate, more labour will be demanded or employed. In other words, demand curve of labour is downward sloping. Keynes' theory of involuntary unemployment based on price flexibility and money wage rigidity is deplicted in Figure 4.3

In panel (b) of Fig. 4.3 short-run aggregate supply curve *AS* and aggregate demand curve AD_0 have been drawn and through their interaction determine price level P_0 and the level of real *GNP* equal to Y_0.* It is important to note that short-run aggregate supply curve *AS* has been drawn with a given fixed money wage rate, say W_0. In panel (*a*) of Figure 4.3 the level of labour employment N_0 shows the number of jobs when the economy is producing Y_0 level of national output in panel (b) corresponding to the equilibrium between aggregate supply *AS* and aggregate demand AD_0 at price level P_0, with a fixed money wage and the level of *GNP* equal to Y_0. The labour market must be in equilibrium at point E_0 or real image rate W_0/P_0 at which N_0 workers are demanded and employed. All those who are willing to get jobs at the real wage rate W_0/P_0 are in fact demanded and employed. Thus, equilibrium at E_0' or at level of employment N_0 represents full-employment equilibrium.

Now consider again panel (*b*) of Fig. 4.3 suppose due to fall in marginal efficiency of capital there is reduction in investment demand which along with its multiplier effect causes a leftward shift in the aggregate demand curve *AD*. Since Keynes believed that with a fixed money wage rate aggregate supply curve *AS* is given and remains unchanged, it will be seen from panel (*b*) of Fig. 4.3 that new aggregate demand curve AD_1 and the fixed aggregate supply curve *AS* interesect at point *K* determining new equilibrium lower price P_1 and smaller real *GNP* equal to Y_1. Keynes asserted that the economy would remain stuck at point *K* with less than full-employment level of output Y_1 and lower price level P_1. Now, a glance at panel (*a*) of Fig. 4.3 shows that with fixed money image W_0 and

* Students should note that concepts of aggregate demand curve (*AD*) and aggregate supply curve (*AS*) used in this Figure 4.3 are different from those used earlier in this chapter. Aggregate demand curve drawn in this Figure 4.3, means the *total quantity of goods and services households, firms and Government are willing to buy at various price levels*. Similarly, aggregate supply curve (*AS*) here means the total output of goods and services that all firms in the economy are willing to produce and supply at different price levels. These concepts of aggregate demand and aggregate supply curves will be explained in a separate chapter.

lower price level P_1 ($P_1 < P_0$), the real wage rate rises to W_0/P_1. It will be seen from panel (*a*) of Fig. 4.3 that at this higher real wage rate W_0/P_1, the smaller amount of labour N_1 will be demanded and employed by all firms in the economy. However, at this higher wage rate W_0/P_1 (with money wage rate fixed at W_0), *RT* number of workers are rendered unemployed. It is in this way that Keynes explained that with money wage rate remaining fixed at the level W_0 and with flexible prices, the fall in aggregate demand results in persistent involuntary unemployment. Thus, by explaining the emergence of persistent involuntary unemployment Keynes made a fundamental departure from the classical view of a free market economy which denied the existence of involuntary unemployment except for a short time.

WHAT CAUSES DEPRESSION AND INVOLUNTARY UNEMPLOYMENT: KENYES'S VIEW

During 1929-33, capitalist economies found themselves in the grip of depression. Such was the severity of this depression that in the USA the rate of unemployment which was 3.2 per cent in 1929 shot up to 25% of the labour force in 1933. Besides, there was a drastic decline in Gross National Product (GNP) which fell from 315 billion dollars in 1929 to 222 billion dollars in 1933, that is, national income declined by 30 per cent during these four years period. This reflects a dismal picture of the American economy during the period of Great Depression. In England as well as in other European countries also such a grave situation of severe recession and huge unemployment prevailed during this period. Before 1929-33 and even after it, recessions have occurred in these economies but they have not been as severe as that took place during 1929-33.

Classical economists had no valid explanation of such a severe depression and large-scale cyclical unemployment of labour. A.C. Pigou and other economists of his view attributed this situation to the high wage rates kept by trade unions and Government. Pigou, therefore, suggested all-round cut in wages to increase employment and to remove depression and unemployment. However, this solution of the problem was neither logically sound nor practical to be implemented. Keynes challenged this view of the classical economists and put forward a different explanation of depression and cyclical unemployment which was accepted by many as logical and correct. He explained his viewpoint in

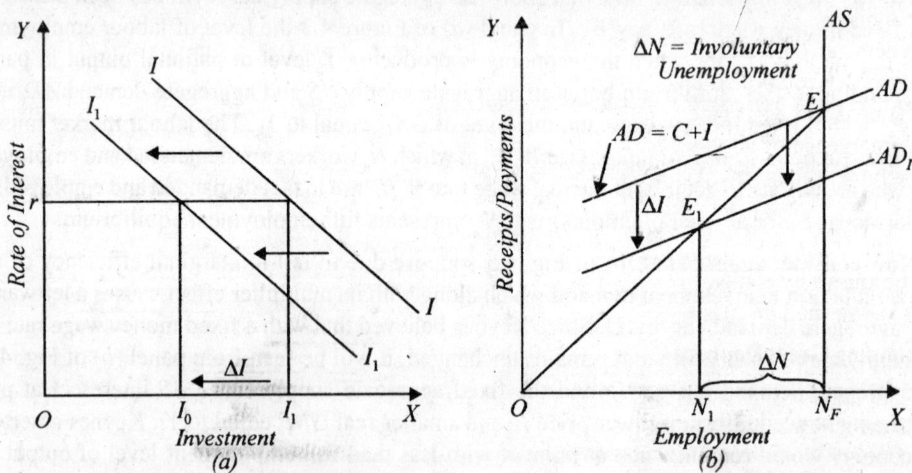

Fig. 4.4. *What Causes Depression and Cyclical Unemployment : Keynes' Explanation.*

his now noted work, '*General Theory of Employment, Interest, and Money*'. He not only gave a sound and valid explanation of depression and its associated problem of cyclical unemployment but also suggested effective policy measures to cure them.

According to Keynes, the cause of depression and cyclical unemployment in the industrialised capitalist countries was sharp decline in private investment due to the adverse business expectations about profit making. There was a wave of pessimism prevailing among investors. The decline in private investment due to fall in marginal efficiency of capital (that is, expected rate of return) caused a fall in aggregate demand and resulted in less than full-employment equilibrium. Consequently, level of output and employment fell drastically and involuntary unemployment came to prevail on a large scale. The involuntary unemployment that prevails in times of recession/depression is called cyclical unemployment and, as we have seen above, according to Keynes, it is due to deficiency of aggregate demand.

Large fluctuations in investment, according to Keynes, is due to the uncertain basis of profit expectations on which investment decisions are made. To quote him, "*We have to admit that our basis of knowledge for estimating the yield ten years hence of a railway, a copper mine, a textile factory, the goodwill of a patent medicine ... amounts to little and sometimes to nothing.*"[1] In view of this uncertainty of future. Keynes stressed that investment decisions were greatly influenced by how optimistic or pessimistic investors feel. He used the term ***animal spirits*** to describe these pessimistic or optimistic expectations of the investors about profit earning from investment projects. The term animal spirits implies that there may be no good or intelligent basis for expectations on which investors base their decisions. Thus involuntary unemployment emerges due to fall in aggregate demand brought about by decline in investment. Therefore, the cause of depression or cyclical involuntary unemployment is the deficiency of aggregate demand.

It will be useful to explain through a diagram how a fall in investment causes a decline in level of output and employment and results in cyclical unemployment. This is illustrated in Fig. 4.4. It will be seen from Figure 4.4 (*a*) that due to adverse profit expectations or pessimism of investors, investment demand curve shifts to the left from II to $I'I'$. With this it will be seen that investment falls from I_1 to I_0 at a given rate of interest. This fall in investment demand by I_1I_0 causes a downward shift in the aggregate demand curve from AD to AD_1 (See Fig. 4.4 (*b*). As a result, the equilibrium between aggregated demand and aggregate supply which was initially at full employment level N_F (which corresponds to point E where the two curves intersect) falls to the new equilibrium level of employment)ON_1. Thus involuntary unemployment equal to N_FN_1 or ΔN emerges due to fall in aggregate demand. Therefore, the *cause of Keynesian cyclical unemployment is deficiency of aggregate demand.* It should also be noted, that the decline in the level of employment following the fall in investment and aggregate demand also results in decrease in GNP or national income of a country. The emergence of large-scale unemployment and drastic decline in level of output and national income represents a situation of depression.

It is also important to note that with the help of his theory of multiplier Keynes showed that the fall in the level of employment and income was much greater than that of decline in investment. This can be known by comparing decline in investment demand ΔI) and fall in employment (ΔN) in Figure 4.4 (*b*). We shall discuss Keynes' theory of income multiplier at length in a later chapter.

Explaining Great Depression (1929-33) : Monetarist View

We have explained above Keynes' view that great depression of 1929-33 was caused by fall in investment caused by the drastic fall in the profit expectations of business class. The decline in investment, according to him, caused aggregate demand to fall which along with the reverse working of multiplier caused conditions of depression (*i.e.* high rate of unemployment, substantial decrease in GNP and fall in prices) Keynes and his followers emphasise the role of fiscal policy (increase in Government expenditure and cut in taxation) to stimulate investment. They downplayed the role of monetary policy and in fact pointed out that monetary policy in the thirties during the depression period proved to be unimportant and ineffective. As a matter of fact, they asserted that monetary

1. J.M. Kenyes, *op. cit.*, pp 149-150

policy was tried during the depression period to revive the economy but miserably failed. At times of depression, according to them, businessmen are in the grip of pessimism about future profitability of investment and more money made available through easy and liberal monetary policy would not be effective in reviving the economy. It was in this context that some Keynesian economists remarked that '*money does not matter*' and also referred to the policy of making more credit available for investment by businesses 'you can bring horse to water but cannot make it drink'. Thus Keynesian view prevailed during the forties and fifties almost unchallenged. Keynes' view was attacked by Milton Friedman, a Nobel Laureate in economics, in the middle of fifties. Friedman and Schwartz in their important work '*A Monetary History of the United States*' written in 1963 Quoted statistical evidence from the United States, and argued that "a re-examination of of the Great Depression of the 1930s demonstrated that, contrary to general belief, it had been a tragic testament to the great power of monetary policy, not to its impotence'[2] They pointed out drastic decline in the quantity of money was made by Federal Reserve System (the Central Banks of the USA) from 1929 to 1933 which was responsible for severe depression in the American economy. They argued that the failure of the federal Reserve system to prevent bank failures and the drastic decrease in money supply during 1930-1933 increased the intensity of depression. To quote them, "The US Federal Reserve System, could have prevented the *decline of one-third* in the quantity of money that occurred from 1929 to 1933. Had it done so, the evidence indicated, the depression would have been far milder and briefer"[3].

We thus see that Freidman and other monetarists emphasise monetary policy in causing depression. In fact, they go to the other extreme view '*money alone matters*'. However, in our view in recent recession during 2000-2003.the Fed Reserve System made successive cuts in rate of interest more than 7 times to revive the American economy without any success. For stimulating investment and growth, it cut the rate of interest even below 1 per cent, the lowest in the last 50 years but failed in its objective to overcome recession. Even in India Reserve Bank also lowered the bank rate, several times during 1998 – 2003 and reduced it to 6 per cent - the lowest in forty years to bring about industrial recovery but seems to have been failed. In the case of the USA, the signs of recovery in the first quarter of 2003-04 seems to have been the result of drastic reduction in taxation to the extent of 3.5 billion dollars and huge increase in defence expenditure for war in Iraq. Both of these are fiscal policies suggested by Keynesians that seems to have worked to start a recovery in the American economy.

To conclude, in the view of present author the truth lies in between the two extreme views of Keynes and Friedman. Therefore, modern economists give importance to both fiscal and monetary policies for influencing investment and growth in GNP. Both can be complements to each other Furthermore, profit expectations of entrepreneurs and cost and availability of credit play a significant role in determining national income, employment and price level in the economy.

POLICY IMPLICATIONS OF KEYNES'S THEORY OF EMPLOYMENT AND INCOME

Keynes's theory has important policy implications for raising the level of employment and income in the economy. When the equilibrium of the economy is at less than full-employment level and as a consequence there is depression or recession in the economy and with it huge unemployment of labour prevails. According to Keynes, this occurs due to lack of aggregate effective demand. There are two types of policies which may be adopted to overcome this situation of recession and unemployment. They are (1) monetary policy and (2) fiscal policy. Under monetary policy, through expansion in money supply rate of interest can be lowered which will encourage private investment. With the increase in private investment, aggregate demand will increase (that is, aggregate demand curve

---

2. *Op. cit.*, p. 300
3. Freidman and Schwartaz, *Monetary History of the United States*, 1963, p. 300.

will shift upward) which will raise the equilibrium level of employment. As a result, the economy will be lifted out of recessionary conditions and unemployment will be removed.

However, Keynes had serious doubts about the effectiveness of monetary policy. He was of the view that in times of depression rate of interest is already very low and at this liquidity preference curve of the community (that is, the curve of demand for money to hold) is *absolutely elastic, that is, it is of horizontal shape.* Therefore, in this situation when money supply is increased, rate of interest will not fall. Thus, with no fall in the rate of interest, private investment will not pick up further.

Importance of Fiscal Policy

In view of ineffectiveness of monetary policy, Keynes laid stress on the role of fiscal policy in curing recession/depression and removing involuntary unemployment. Under the fiscal policy, a major measure is the *increase in expenditure by the Government on several types of public works* in times of depression. The increase in Government expenditure will cause an upward shift in the aggregate demand curve. This increase in aggregate demand will bring about increase in employment and output. If the increase in Government expenditure and as a result rise in aggregate demand is sufficient, it will help in achieving equilibrium at full-employment level. As a result, depression and involuntary unemployment will be eliminated. It is worth noting that in this regard Keynes put forward a theory of multiplier which strengthened the case for raising Government expenditure on public works in times of depression or when large-scale unemployment prevailed in the economy. We shall discuss the theory of multiplier at length in later chapter. Briefly, theory of multiplier implies that increase in Government expenditure will raise aggregate demand and therefore output and employment not by the amount of increase in Government expenditure but by a multiple of it.

Another important measure of fiscal policy to raise employment and output is the *reduction in taxes.* When rates of personal taxes such as income tax are reduced, disposable income of the people increases which brings about rise in their demand for consumption. The rise in consumption demand pushes up aggregate demand curve and helps in removing recession and unemployment. It may be noted that on the recommendations of Keynesian economists American President John Kennedy made a drastic cut in income taxes in 1964. This had a great success as output and employment in the USA increased significantly and, as a result, recession and unemployment were removed. Cut in personal taxes to boost aggregate demand has also been applied in later years in the USA as well as in Great Britain. Recently in 2003, the President of the USA Geoge W. Bush has made a 3.5 billion cut in taxes to revive the American economy. .

In the end, it is important to note that modern economists though agree with Keynes' view about the effectiveness of fiscal policy in curing recession, they do not share Keynes' view about the ineffectiveness of monetary policy. It may however be noted that, according to the modern Keynesians and others, liquidity preference curve of the community is fairly elastic even in times of recession which implies that expansion in money supply will cause a decline in interest rate and will therefore stimulate private investment. Further, according to them, investment demand curve is also fairly elastic which implies that fall in interest rate will have significant impact on private investment. Thus, according to modern economists, both monetary and fiscal policies are important instruments whereby aggregate demand of the economy can be changed. We shall discuss in detail the roles of monetary and fiscal policies for attaining economic stabilisation in later chapters.

That the free market system does not guarantee economic stability and full employment has been proved by the recent ***global financial crisis*** (2007-09) which started in the US as a result of collapse of financial system following bursting of housing bubble and spread to other countries (including India) through global linkages of free trade and capital flows and caused global slowdown. The market system which was believed by the classical economists monetarists, led by Milton Friedman and new classical economists led by Robert Lucas to correct itself automatically and recover from the crisis failed to deliver. As a result, there were loud protests about the failure of the free market system to ensure economic stability and full employment.

Again it were Keynesian policies which came to the rescue of the US, India and other countries which were gripped by severe recession. These countries adopted Keynesian expansionary fiscal and monetary policies which to provide stimulus to the economies by raising aggregate demand so as to get out of recessionary conditions. These counter cyclical Keynesian policies worked and in the recession-ridden economies of the US, European countries, Australia, Japan, China and India, economic recovery started and by the early 2010 they seem to have returned to the path growth.

QUESTIONS FOR REVIEW

1. Explain Keynes' theory of employment. How does it differ from classical theory ?
2. In what respects do the Classical and Keynesian theories of employment differ ? Spell out the reasons for under-employment equilibrium in the Keynesian model.
3. Explain how, according to Keynes, *involuntary unemployment* is caused by lack of effective demand. How is the money wage-rigidity responsible for the emergence of involuntary unemployment ?
4. The logical starting point of Keynes' theory of employment is the principle of effective demand. Explain.
5. What do you understand by the term 'money illusion' in the Keynesian theory of employment ? Is wage-price rigidity a conseuence of money illusion.
6. What are the policy implications of Keynesian theory of income and employment ? Have they been successfully used to overcome recession ?
7. Define effective demand. How does it determine level of empooyment in a country ?

CHAPTER 5

Determination of National Income : Keynes's Basic Two Sector Model

Keynes's Income-Expenditure Approach

We have explained in the previous chapter how the level of employment is determined in an advanced c .pitalist economy. We explained there Keynesian theory with special reference to the determir tion of employment. It is worth noting here that the Keynesian theory is relevant in the context of the short run only since the stock of capital, techniques of production, efficiency of labour, the size of population, forms of business organisation have been assumed to remain constant in this theory. Further in his model of income determination *Keynes assumed that price level in the economy remains unchanged.* Therefore, in the Keynesian theory which deals with the short run, the level of income of the country will change as a result of changes in the level of labour employment. Thus, in free market economy in the short run, when capital stock and technology remain unchanged, income is a function of labour employment. In fact, both income and employment go together. The higher the level of employment, the higher the level of income. As level of employment is determined by aggregate demand and aggregate supply, the level of income is also determined by aggregate demand and aggregate supply. In this chapter, we shall explain how the equilibrium level of national income is determined through *Keynes's income-expenditure analysis.* This analysis explains determination of national income by relating income (output) to aggregate expenditure on goods and services. The, aggregate expenditure shows aggregate demand for goods and services. Keynesian theory of income determination can be explained by assuming two sectors in the economy, namely, households and business firms. Keynes focussed on this simple two sector model of determination of national income and derived conclusions regarding policy formulation from this basic model. Analysis of determination of national income can be extended to incorporate Government and foreign trade. We start with the analysis of determination of national income by *taking a simple two-sector economy with a fixed price level.*

Aggregate Expenditure (with a Fixed Price Level)

Aggregate expenditure is the total expenditure which at given fixed prices all households and business firms want to make on goods and services in a period at various levels of national income. Though J.M. Keynes used the term *aggregate demand*, in modern macroeconomics, the term *aggregate expenditure* is generally used. The terms of aggregate demand and aggregate supply are now generally used in the model with variable price level. In this chapter however we use the term aggregate demand and aggregate expenditure interchangeably but assume that price level remains constant. In a two-sector closed economy, aggregate expenditure or aggregate demand consists of two components: First, there is consumption demand, and secondly, there is a demand for capital goods, which is called investment demand. Thus, by aggregate expenditure we mean how much expenditure the households and the entrepreneurs are willing to undertaking on consumption and investment. Therefore,

Aggregate Demand = Consumption Demand + Investment Demand

$$AE = AD = C + I$$

where AE stands for aggregate expenditure, C for consumption demand and I for investment demand.

Using the term aggregate expenditure instead of aggregate demand we have

Aggregate Expenditure = Consumption expenditure + Investment expenditure

or $$AE = C + I$$

Consumption Demand. As for consumption demand, it depends upon the propensity to consume of the community and the level of national income. Given the propensity to consume, as income increases, consumption demand will also increase. In other words, given the propensity to consume, consumption demand is a function of income. Consumption function can take several forms. The most common form of short-run consumption function is

$$C = a + bY$$

where a is the intercept term of the function and represents *autonomous consumption* whereas *b* represents the slope of the consumption function. According to Keynes's theory current consumption expenditure depends primarily on current income. Further, according to Keynes, the chief factor that determines consumption expenditure is disposable income, that is, income available after taxes. Increase in personal taxes reduces personal disposable income and therefore consumption expenditure.

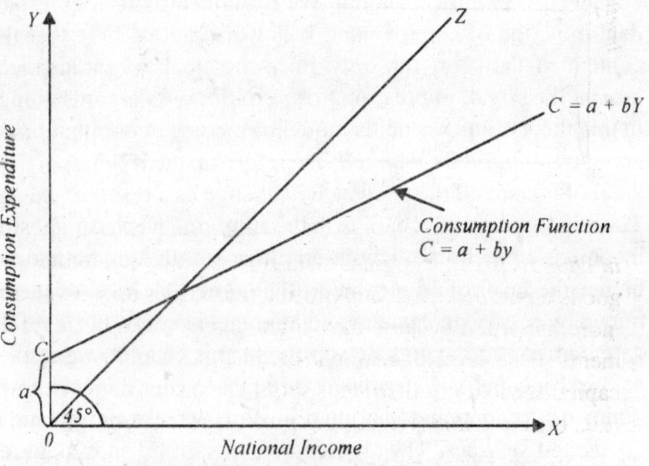

Fig. 5.1. *Consumption Function*

Consider Fig. 5.1 in which national income is measured along the *X*-axis and consumption demand (*C*) is shown on the Y-axis. In this figure, a straight line *OZ* which makes 45° angle with the *X*-axis has been drawn. This straight line *OZ* with 45° angle with the *X*-axis represents the *reference income line* to measure the difference between consumption and level of income. This is also often called *income line.* This 45° line represents national income in money terms. In fact, national product and income are the same things. In this figure a curve *C* has also been drawn which represents consumption function, $C = a + by$ of the community. This curve of consumption function slopes upward from left to right, which shows that as income increases the amount of consumption demand also increases. As income line *OZ* makes 45° angle with the *X*-axis, the *gap between the consumption function curve C and the income line OZ represents the saving of the community.* The reason for this is that a part of the income is consumed and a part is saved, *i.e.*, National Income = Consumption + Saving. This is also written as $Y = C + S$, where *y* represents income, *C* consumption and *S* saving. It will be seen from Fig. 5.1 that the gap between the consumption function curve *C* and the income line *OZ* goes on increasing as income increases. In other words, the amount of saving or saving gap increases as income increases.

It is worth mentioning that in the short-run consumption function does not change. This is because the propensity to consume, that is, the whole consumption function curve *C* depends upon the tastes, perferences, the income distribution in the soceity, the population level, wealth of the people etc., which do not undergo much change in the short run. The implication of the stability of consumption function is that the consumption demand is primarely determined by the level of current national income.

However, through changes in monetary policy and fiscal policy by the Government the consumption function can be shifted. For example, when rate of interest, an instrument of monetary policy, is reduced, the people borrow more for durable consumer goods such as cars, airconditioners, houses and with this at a given level of income consumption demand increases causing upward shift in the consumption function curve. Similarly, when income tax, an instrument of fiscal policy, is reduced disposable income of the households increases and as a result at a given level of national income (GDP), consumption demand increases leading to the upward shift in consumption function.

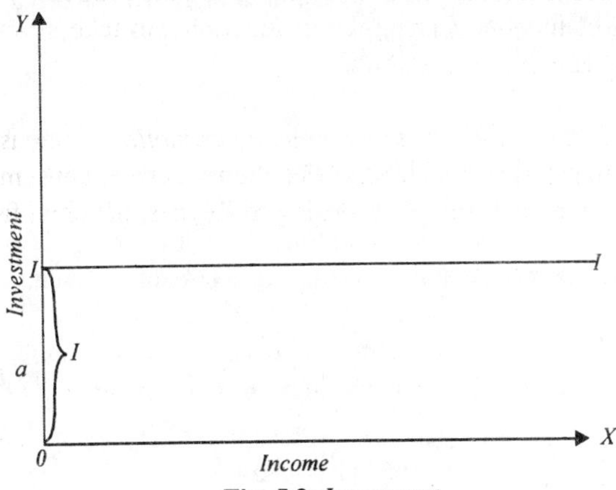

Fig. 5.2. *Investment*

Investment Demand. The other component of the aggregate demand is investment which is a crucial factor in the determination of equilibrium level of national income. Investment demand depends upon two factors; (1) marginal efficiency of capital and (2) rate of interest. Of these two factors, rate of interest is comparatively stable and does not frequently change in the short run. Therefore, the fluctuations in the level of investment demand chiefly depend upon the changes in the marginal efficiency of capital. *The marginal efficiency of capital means the expeted rate of profit which the business community hopes to get from the investment in capital assets.* Marginal efficiency of capital depends upon the replacement cost of the capital goods on the one hand, and profit expectations of enterpreneurs on the other. Profit expectations are more important because they often change even in the short run and cause fluctuations in investment. If the level of national income and employment is desired to be raised in a free market capitalist economy, then steps should be taken which will raise the expectations of the enterpreneurs (i.e., business firms) regarding profit-earning from investment.

In any particular year, there will be a given level of investment demand which, as seen above, is determined by marginal efficiency of capital and a given rate of interest. However, in Keynes's theory investment being determined by marginal efficiency of capital and rate of interest does not depend on the level of income. Thus, in Keynesian theory of income determination, investment does not vary with change in income. In other words, in *Keynes' income-expenditure analysis investment is treated as autonomous of income, that is, investment does not change with a change in the level of income.* This type of investment is shown in Figure 5,2. This is the assumption which Keynes made and in this chapter we will also do likewise. In actual practice when the level of income rises, the demand for goods will also rise and this will favourably affect the expectations of the entrepreneurs regarding making of profits. Rise in the profit expectations will raise the marginal efficiency of capital which in turn will increase the level of investment. But it is quite clear that investment demand does not directly depend upon income; it is only affected indirectly by changes in income. Therefore, in our Figure 5.3 we have taken a given amount of investment demand independent of the level of income and added it to upward sloping consumption function curve to get aggregate expenditure curve $C + I$. The distance between the C curve and the $C + I$ curve is parallel to the C curve throughout

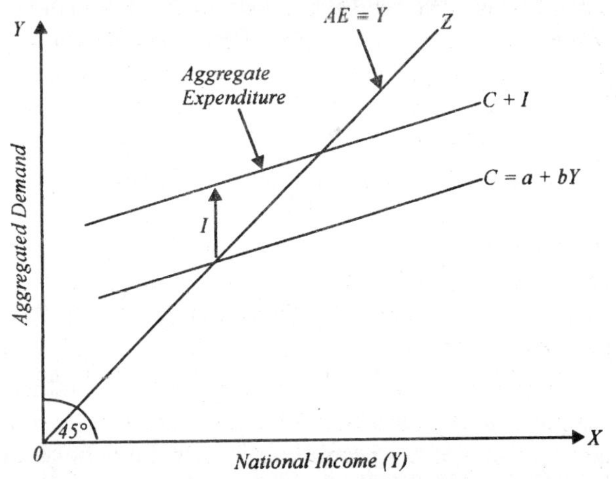

Fig. 5.3. *Aggregate Expenditure Curve of a Two-Sector Economy*

which indicates that the level of investment is constant and does not change with the change in income. It may however be noted that with either a change in the rate of interest or in marginal efficiency of capital investment will change. Therefore, in income-expenditure diagram as shown in Fig. 5.3, *a different new amount of investment* of will have to be taken.

Aggregate Output

As mentioned above, in the short run the level of national income and employment in a free-market economy depends upon the equilibrium between aggregate expenditure and aggregate output. We have also explained above the various components of aggregate expenditure on goods and services. We now run to explain the aggregate supply and factors on which it depends. It is important to note again that Keynes in his analysis assumed that prices and wages remain constant in the short run.

In an economy with out any role of Government, national income *means the total money value of goods and services produced in an economy in a year*. There are two important constituents of aggregate output.

1. the supply or output of final consumer goods and services in a year; and
2. the output of capital goods which are also called producer goods because they help in producing further goods.

National income is the same thing as national product as both represents the value of output of final goods and services produced. In fact, aggregate supply or money value of national product of goods and services is distributed among the various factors of production as wages, rent, interest and profits as rewards them for their contribution to the national product.

The aggregate output which is also sometimes referred to as aggregate supply of goods of an economy depends upon the stock of capital, the amount of labour used and the state of technology. In the short run, stock of capital remains constant and therefore output can be increased by increasing the amount of labour employed. Like the classical economists Keynes also thought that aggregate output or national income depend the short-run production function with a given capital stock and constant technology. Thus, we have the following production function in the short run.

$$Y = (N, \bar{K}, \bar{T})$$

where Y is national output, $\bar{K}$ is the constant amount of capital stock, $\bar{T}$ is the constant state of technology and N is the labour employed which is a variable factor.

It may be noted that the amount of production which a given amount of labour can produce depends upon the given stock of capital and state of technology. The higher the level of technology, more can be produced with the help of given resources. Since J.M. Keynes in the nineteen thirties and we at present are concerned with the determination of income and employment *in the short run*, the stock of capital and the state of technology are assumed to be constant. For similar reasons, size of population is also assumed to be constant. However, the amount of labour employed out of this given size of population can vary depending upon the demand for labour.

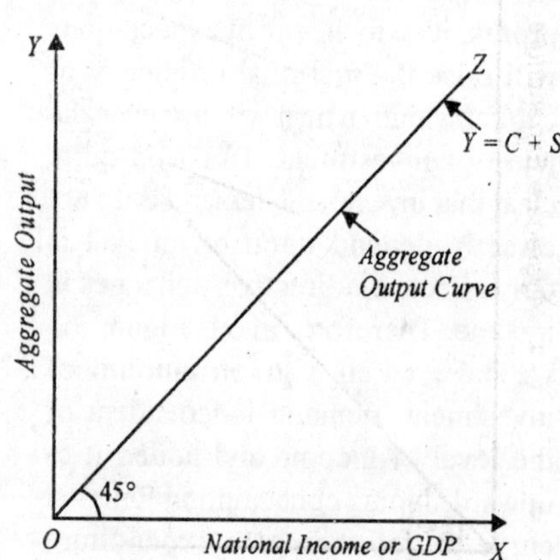

Fig. 5.4. *45° Line Showing Aggregate Output.*

45° Line as Aggregate Output Curve (With Fixed Prices)

In the income-expenditure analysis with which we are presently concerned we need to compare Gross Domestic Product (or National Income) with aggregate expenditure (*AE*), also called aggregate demand (*AD*), which is represented on the vertical axis. For this purpose we draw a 45° line from the origin which helps us to *transfer* Gross Domestic Product or real National Income (i.e. gross supply of output at constant prices) from the horizontal axis to the vertical axis for comparing it with total expenditure on goods and services. At every point of this 45° line from the origin, the vertical distance equals horizontal distance which measures real national income or GDP which is generally denoted by *Y*. This 45° line is also called income line along which $Y = C + S$ because income can either be consumed or saved.

The essential feature which emerges from all this is that more output will be produced and supplied at the given price level in response to increase in aggregate demand or expenditure. In other words, whatever the aggregate demand, more output of goods will be produced and supplied at the same price before full-employment of resources is reached. This type of aggregate supply curve has been shown by 45° *OZ* line drawn against the *X* and *Y* axes in Fig. 5.4 where along the *X*-axis real national income (GDP) and along the *Y*-axis aggregate supply of output are measured. However, as noted above, aggregate output and real national income (GDP) are identical.

It follows from above that 45° line shows two things. First, it shows *varying* levels of aggregate production or the supply of goods (both consumer and capital goods) that will be offered for sale at the given price level at various levels of aggregate expenditure. This shows that up to the level of full-employment of resources *any amount* of aggregate supply of output will be forthcoming at the given price level depending on the aggregate demand or expenditures. The greater the aggregate demand or expenditure, the greater the aggregate supply of output at the given price level. Secondly, it represents national income. In fact, as you would have read in national income accounting, national product and national income are the same things.

Equilibrium Level of National Income

Now, we shall explain how through the intersection of aggregate demand and aggregate supply curves the equilibrium level of national income is determined in Keynes's two sector model. $C + I$ curve represents the aggregate expenditure and 45° *OZ* line represents aggregate supply of output.

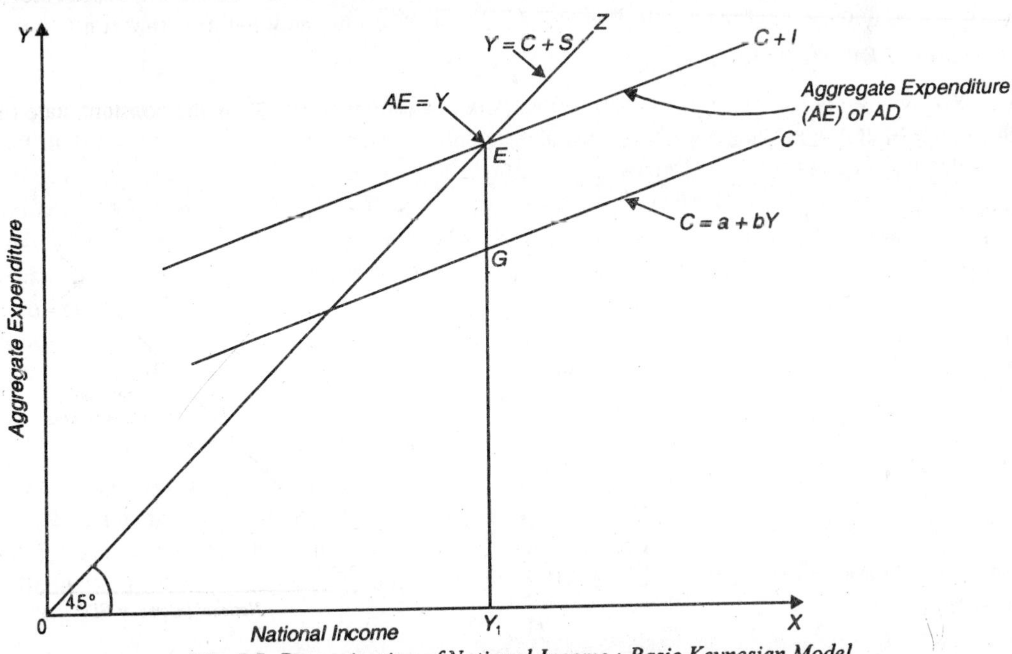

Fig. 5.5. *Determination of National Income : Basic Keynesian Model*

Normally the goods and services are produced by firms when they think they can sell them in the market. There will be equilibrium in the goods market when total output of goods and services produced will be equal to the total demand for output. Aggregate demand for them is represented by aggregate expenditure. In equilbrium aggregate expenditure (which is denoted by *AE*) must equal aggregate output (GDP). Since aggregate output or GDP equals national income (*Y*) we have the following condition for equilibrium.

$$AE = GDP = Y$$

It will be seen in Fig. 5.5 that aggregate expenditure curve (*AE*) or $C + I$ curve intersects 45° line at point *E* which satisfies the equilibrium condition. That is, a point *E* which corresponds to the income level OY_1, aggregate expenditure is equal to aggregate output. Therefore, *E* is the equilibrium point and OY_1 represents the equilibrium level of national income. Now, income cannot be in equilibrium at levels smaller than OY_1, since aggregate expenditure exceeds aggregate supply of output as $C+I$ curve which depicts aggregate expenditure of output lies above 45° line. This excess demand will be met by the firms selling goods from their stocks or inventories of goods kept by them. This leads to the decline in inventoires of goods below the desired levels. This unintended fall in inventories will induce the firms to expand their output of goods and services to meet the extra demand for them and keep their inventories of goods at the desired levels. Thus when at a given level of national income, aggregate expenditure (*i.e.*, aggregate demand) exceeds aggregate output, national income will increase. With this increase in national income or output, employment of labour will also rise to produce the increment in output. This process of expansion in output under the pressure of excess demand will continue till national income OY_1 is reached.

On the countrary, the equilibrium level of national income cannot be greater than OY_1 because at any level greater than OY_1 aggregate expenditure or demand ($C + I$) falls short of aggregate output. This will cause the increase in inventoires of goods with the firms beyond the desired levels. To this situation of the unintended increase in inventories of goods, the firms will respond by cutting down production to keep their inventories at the desired levels. Thus, deficiency in aggregate demand relative to the aggregate supply of output will lead to the fall in national income and output until the level OY_1 is reached where aggregate expenditure ($C + I$) is equal to the value of aggregate output. Thus, OY_1 is the equilibrium level of national income.

Principle of Effective Demand

We have seen above that the equilibrium level of national income is determined by aggregate demand and aggregate supply of output. Consider Fig. 5.5 where it will be seen that, the prices remaining constant, aggregate expenditure (*AE*) curve $C + I$ *shows varying levels of aggregate demand at various levels of national income. The particular aggregate demand which is equal to aggregate output and therefore determines the equilibrium national income is called effective demand.* In other words, effective demand is that level of aggregate demand (aggregate expenditure) which becomes effective in determining equilibrium level of income because it is equal to aggregate supply of output. This is called *Keynesian principle of effective demand.* In Fig. 5.5, the effective demand is equal to Y_1E. Note that the level of national income OY_1 which has been determined, equals the effective demand Y_1E ($OY_1 = Y_1E$).

There are several other points on the aggregate demand (expenditure) curve but what distinguishes effective demand from all these points is that at this point aggregate demand is equal to aggregate output. On all other points aggregate demand is either more or less than aggregate output. Thus, the level of national income is determined by and equal to effective demand. In a two sectors Keynesian model, we can express the principle of effective demand in symbolic terms as under :

$$Y = AE^* \text{ or } AD^*$$

$$AD^* = AE^* = C + I$$

$$Y = AD^* = C + I$$

where Y = National Income
AD^* = Effective demand
C = Consumption demand
I = Investment

Note that *star mark* on AE or AD shows the aggregate demand which becomes effective.

Importance. It is thus clear that national income and employment in the short run are determined by effective demand (or, in other words, effective aggregate expenditure). The higher the level of effective demand, the greater the levels of national income and employment and vice-versa. *Unemployment is due to deficiency of effective demand and the basic remedy to remove this unemployment is to raise the level of effective demand.* Due to their belief in Say's law and in quick adjustment of wages and prices to balance between demand and supply the classical economists believed that effective demand was always large enough to ensure full-employment. But Keynes proved that it was not so and that is why the problem of involuntary unemployment was common in the free-market capitalist economies.

Equilibrium is not Necessarily Established at Full-Employment Level

The most important contention of J.M. Keynes in his now famous work "General Theory of Employment, Interest and Money" was that in a capitalist economy it is not necessary that the equilibrium level of income is established at the level of full-employment. This view of Keynes was quite contrary to the views of the classical economists who believed that the economy always tended towards full-employment. Keynes refuted this important idea of the classical economics. To understand the Keynesian viewpoint consider Fig. 5.6. Suppose the full-employment level of labour corresponds to the level of national income equal to OY_F. Thus OY_F represents the level of income at which there is full-employment in the economy. But, as seen above, the equilibrium level of income is not established at OY_F but at OY_1 at which some number of labour will be unemployed. Thus equilibrium at OY_1 is known as ***under-employment equilibrium***. It is worth noting that in the situation depicted in Fig. 5.6 the equilibrium level of national income will be established at full-employment level only when investment demand is sufficiently large to fill the saving gap be

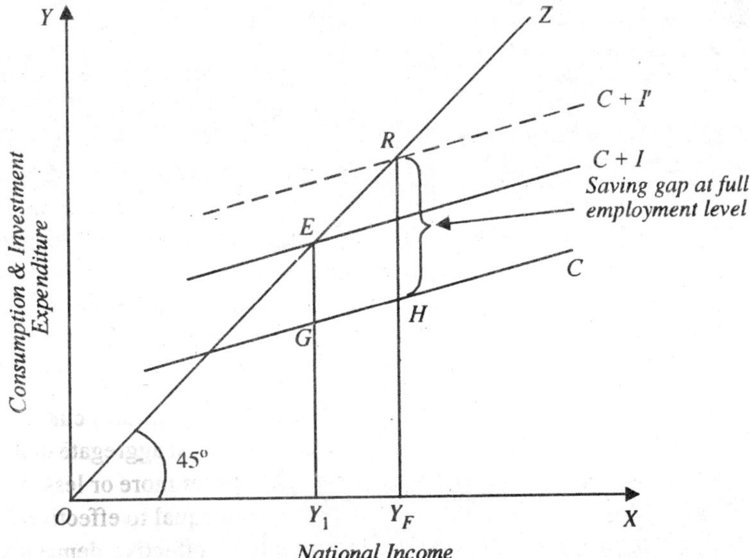

Fig. 5.6. *Under-employment Equilibrium due to Insufficiency of Investment Expenditure*

tween income and consumption at the full-employment level of income OY_F. It will be seen from Fig. 5.6, that corresponding to the full-employment level of income OY_F, RH is the saving of the community. Therefore, if the equilibrium is to be established at OY_F level, then investment demand must be equal to level of saving *RH* at full employment level of income Y_F. But the prevailing investment demand is only equal to *EG* which is less than *RH*. With *RH* as the level of investment and the *C* curve as the level of propensity to consume, $C + I$ curve intersects the 45° aggregate output curve *OZ* at point *R* and therefore determines equilibrium level of income equal to OY_F at which labour will be fully employed.

But there is not guarantee that the investment demand will be equal to the saving gap corresponding to full-employment level of income. There are various reasons for this. First, the people who save are not necessary those who make investment; while it is the general public which save but only few people constituting the entrepreneurial class undertakes investment. Secondly, the factors which determine saving are quite different from those which determine investment. While the people save for providing for the education, marriages of their children and also for contingency purposes such as diseases and unemployment periods. They also save in order to acquire durable goods such as houses, gold and jewellery. They also save to accumulate sufficient funds for their old age. But the level of investment depends upon marginal efficiency of capital and rate of interest in the short run and on the level of population, technological progress in the long run. Therefore, it is not essential that investment should be equal to the amount of savings by the people at full-employment level. If due to the adverse changes in the profit expectations of the entrepreneurs, level of investment falls, the equilibrium level of national income will also decline.

It is also worth noting that if aggregate expenditure increases beyond the $C + I'$ in Fig. 5.6 it will mean that the economy is spending and demanding more than it can produce. The result of this will be rise in prices of the commodities. In other words, if the investment demand in any year is higher than *HR*, in Fig. 5.6, then the inflationary process will start. In this situation, national income will rise beyond OY_F only in money terms but not in real terms.

DETERMINATION OF EQUILIBRIUM LEVEL OF NATIONAL INCOME: ALGEBRAIC ANALYSIS

A study of how the level of national income is determined will become more clear by using simple mathematics. As has been explained above, the level of national income is in equilibrium at which aggregate demand equals aggregate supply of output. In a simple model of income determination in which we do not consider the impact of Government expenditure and taxation and also exports and imports, the national income is the sum of consumption demand (*C*) and investment demand (I), that is,

$$Y = C + I$$

where *Y* stands for the level of national income.

Suppose the consumption function is of the following form :

$$C = a + bY$$

a is the intercept term in the consumption function and therefore represents the autonomous consumption expenditure which does not very with income. b is a constant which represents the marginal propensity to consume (mpc $\Delta C/\Delta Y$). Thus total consumption demand is equal to the sum of autonomous consumption expenditure (*a*) and the induced consumption expenditure (*bY*).

Now suppose that investment demand equals I_a. This investment I_a is autonomous because this does not depend on income. Thus, we get the following three equations for the determination of the equilibrium level of national income.

$$Y = C + I \qquad ...(i)$$

$$C = a + bY \qquad ...(ii)$$

$$I = I_a \qquad ...(iii)$$

Substituting the values of C and I in equation (i) we have

$$Y = a + bY + Ia \quad ...(iv)$$

$$Y - bY = a + Ia$$

$$Y(1-b) = a + Ia$$

$$Y = \frac{1}{1-b}(a + I_a) \quad ...(v)$$

The equation (v) shows the equilibrium level of national income when aggregated expenditure equals aggregate supply of output. *The equation (v) reveals that autonomous consumption and autonomous investment (a + I_a) generates so much expenditure or aggregate demand which is equal to the income generated by the production of goods and services.* From the equation (v) it also follows that the equilibrium level of national income can be known from multiplying the elements of autonomous expenditure (that is, $a + I_a$) by the term $\frac{1}{1-b}$ which is equal to the value of multiplier.

Further, it also follows that equilibrium level of income is higher, the greater the marginal propensity to consume (*i.e.*, b), autonomous consumption (a) and autonomous investment (I_a).

The multiplier tells us how much increase in income occurs when *autonomous investment* (*or consumption*) increases by Re. 1, that is, multiplier is $\frac{\Delta Y}{\Delta I}$ and its value is equal to $\frac{1}{1-b}$ where b stands for marginal propensity to consume (MPC). Thus, multiplier $= \frac{\Delta Y}{\Delta I} = \frac{1}{1-b}$. Further, it also follows that equilibrium level of income is higher, the greater the marginal propensity to consume (*i.e.* b) and autonomous investment (I).

Now, higher the marginal propensity to consume (b), the greater the value of multiplier. For example, if marginal propensity to consume (b) is 0.8, investment multiplier is

$$\frac{\Delta Y}{\Delta I} = \frac{1}{1-08} = \frac{1}{0.2} = 1 \times \frac{10}{2} = 5$$

If *MPC* or $b = 0.75$, multiplier is

$$= \frac{\Delta Y}{\Delta I} = \frac{1}{1-0.75} = \frac{1}{0.25} = \frac{100}{25} = 4$$

We can find out the increase in income (ΔY) resulting from a certain increase in investment (ΔI) by using this multiplier relationship. Thus

$$\frac{\Delta Y}{\Delta I} = \frac{I}{1-b}$$

$$\Delta Y = \Delta I . \frac{1}{1-b}$$

If marginal propensity to consume is equal to 0.8, with the increase in investment by ₹ 100 crore the increase in income will be :

$$\frac{\Delta Y}{\Delta I} = \frac{1}{1-b}$$

$$\Delta Y = \Delta I \times \frac{1}{1-b} = 100 \times \frac{1}{1-0.8}$$

$$100 \times \frac{1}{0.2} = 100 \times 5 = 500 \text{ crore}$$

Illustrations of Equilibrium Level of Income with Numerical Examples

A few numerical examples will make it clear how the equilibrium level of national income is determined.

Problem 1. Suppose in an economy, autonomous investment (I) is ₹ 600 crores and the following consumption function is given :

$$C = 200 + 0.8Y$$

Given the above, find out the equilibrium level of income.

Solution. The equilibrium level of income is

$$Y = C + I$$

$$C = 200 + 0.8Y \quad \ldots (i)$$

$$I = 600$$

Putting the values of C and I in the equilibrium (i) we have

$$Y = 200 + 0.8Y + 600$$

$$(Y - 0.8Y) = 200 + 600$$

$$Y(1 - 0.8) = 800$$

or

$$Y = \frac{800}{0.2} = \frac{800}{\frac{2}{10}} = \text{₹ } \mathbf{4000.}$$

Alternative Method. We can directly use equation (V) above in our general algebraic analysis using multiplier and autonomous items (i.e., autonomous consumption and investment) to obtain equilibrium national income. The multiplier is given by $\frac{1}{1-b}$ where $b = MPC$ which is equal to 0.8 in the present problem. Autonomous consumption in the present problem is 200 crore and autonomous investment is 600 crore. Thus

$$Y = \frac{1}{1-b}(a + I_a)$$

$$= \frac{1}{1-0.8}(200+600) = 5(800)$$

$$= 4000 \text{ crore}$$

Problem 2. *Suppose the consumption function of an economy is C = 0.8 Y. Planned investment by entrepreneurs for a year is ₹ 500 crores. Find out what will be the equilibrium level of income.*

Solution.

$$Y = C + I$$

$$C = 0.8Y$$

$$I = \text{₹ } 500 \text{ crore}$$

Substituting the values of C and I in (i) we have

$$Y = 0.8Y + 500$$

$$Y - 0.8Y = 500$$

$$Y(1 - 0.8) = 500$$

$$0.2 = 500$$

$$y = 500 \times \frac{10}{2} = \text{₹ } 2500 \text{ crore.}$$

Using Alternative Method.

$$Y = \frac{1}{1-b}(a + I_a) = 5(0 + 500) = \text{₹ } 2500 \text{ Crore}$$

Problem 3. *Suppose the consumption of an economy is given by*

$$C = 20 + 0.6Y$$

The following investment function is given :

$$I = 10 + 02\ Y$$

What will be the equilibrium level of national income ?

Solution. Note that in this problem, investment varies with income. However, this will not hange our method of determining equilibrium level of income.

$$Y = C + I$$

$$C = 20 + 0.6Y \qquad \ldots (i)$$

$$I = 10 + 0.2Y$$

Substituting the values of C and I in (i) we have

$$Y = 20 + 0.6Y + 10 + 0.2Y$$

$$Y = 30 + 0.8Y$$

$$Y - 0.8Y = 30$$

$$Y(1 - 0.8Y) = 30$$

$$0.2Y = 30$$

$$Y = 30 \times \frac{10}{2} = 150$$

Thus, we find that the equilibrium level of income to be equal to 150.

National Income and Employment

In the previous chapter we have explained the determination of level of employment and in the present chapter we have discussed the determination of national income. In fact, the levels of national income and employment are determined jointly. It is only for the better understanding of macroeconomic theory that we have presented their analysis separately. It will now be appropriate if we now explain their determination jointly by aggregate demand and supply. It is worth nothing that, in Keynesian theory, employment is a function of income. Relation between income and labour employment is given by short-run production function showing diminishing returns to labour. This short-run production function can be stated as under :

$$Y = f(N, \bar{K}, \bar{T})$$

According to above function, given the capital stock and technology, the greater the level of national output (*i.e.* income or Y), the greater will be the number of workers (N) employed. As ex-

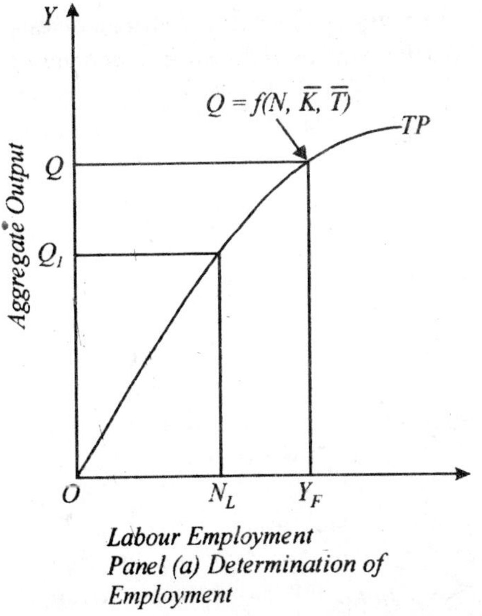

Panel (a) Determination of Employment

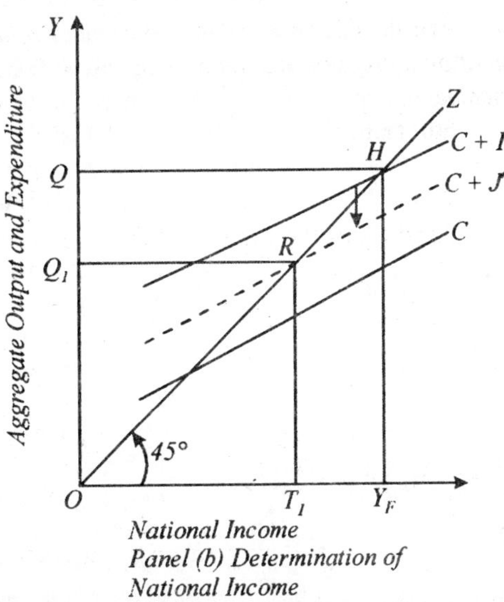

Panel (b) Determination of National Income

Fig. 5.7. *The Emergence of Involuntary Unemployment.*

plained above in detail that, according to Keynesian theory, levels of national income and employment are determined by aggregate effective demand. In a closed economy with no intervention by the government, aggregate demand consists of consumption demand and investment demand. According to Keynes, consumption function is stable in the short run and it is investment demand which is highly volatile in the short run as it depends on profit expectations of business men. Equilibrium at full employment level of income is determined when investment expenditure fills the saving gap at full employment level of national income. Consider Fig. 5.7 where in panel (*b*) determination of national income is shown through intersection of aggregate demand and aggregate supply curves. According to Keynes, equilibrium at full-employment level of income OY_F will be determined if planned investment expenditure by entrepreneurs is equal to saving *HT* at full-employment level of national income OY_F Total expenditure (*i.e.*, aggregate demand) and output produced are both equal to *OQ* corresponding to equilibrium point *H*, ($OQ = OY_F$). In the left-side panel (*a*) where production function curve *TP* has been drawn , we have measured employment of labour on the *X*-axis and aggregate output on the *Y*-axis. It will be seen from this left-side panel (*a*) that output *OQ* is produced by employing ON_F amount of labour. We assume that ON_F represents full employment of labour, that is, all workers who want to work at the prevailing wage rate are getting employment. With this full employment of labour, national income equal to OY_F is being generated ($OY_F = OQ$).

Now, Keynes argued that if somehow or the other profit expectations of entrepreneurs become dim, this would cause a fall in the expected rate of return resulting in reduction in investment expenditure. With the fall in investment expenditure, aggregate demand curve shifts downward to the dotted position $C + I'$ which intersects 45° line *OZ* at point *R*. As a result, new equilibrium level of national income OY_1 is determined ($OY_1 = OQ_1$).

It will be seen from left side panel (*a*) that aggregate output (*i.e.*, national product) OQ_1 is produced by employing ON_1 amount of labour. Thus, as a result of fall in aggregate demand, N_1N_F number of workers are rendered unemployed. N_1N_F workers will be involuntarily unemployed. According to Keynes, there is no any mechanism which should ensure that this involuntary unemployment will be automatically eliminated.

Anti-Recessionary Economic Policy : Shifting Aggregate Expenditure Curve Upward

Now, an important question is what measures can be adopted to overcome recession or involuntary unemployment which comes into existence as a result of deficiency of aggregate demand brought about by a fall in investment.

From our above analysis of determination of income and employment it is clear that increase in equilibrium level of national income can be brought about by increases in any components of aggregate demand, namely, consumption demand (*C*), private investment demand (*I*), Government expenditure (*G*), and net exports (X_n). In order to increase national income through upward shift in the consumption function, *the Government can reduce personal income taxes*. In 1964, the reduction in income tax by John Kennedy Government in USA was quite successful in boosting consumption demand and thereby raising aggregate output. As a result, more income and employment were generated. The rate of unemployment sharply declined and the American economy was lifted out of depression. Recently, in 2002 and again in early 2008, the President George W. Bush made a significant cut of 3.5 billion dollars in income tax to revive the American economy. He refunded a good amount of income tax collected from the people in these years. The cut in direct taxes increases the disposable income of the people which tends to raise their consumption demand. However, there is a limitation of cut in direct taxes for raising aggregate demand because a part of the increases in disposbale income can be saved rather than being spent on goods and services. This happened in the United States in the year 2008. To boost aggregate demand, indirect tax can also be also be reduced. In India also in December 2008, to correct the sagging demand for industrial products under the fiscal stimulus package 4 per cent across the board cut in central excise duty was made by the Government. This too has a limitation because benefit of this cut in excise duty may not be fully passed on to the consumers by reducing prices.

Secondly, the equilibrium level of national income (GNP) and employment can be increased by *raising the rate of private investment* (I). Through monetary policy measures businessmen can be induced to invest more by lowering the rate of interest and increasing the availability of credit. We know that the lower the rate of interest, the higher will be the level of private investment. Alternatively, the Government may encourage private investment by reducing tax on profits or corporate income so that post-tax rate of profit will be higher than before. The higher level of investment will shift the aggregate demand or expenditure curve ($C + I + G$) upward and determine a higher level of national income and employment.

Thirdly, the recession can be overcome and national income (GNP) and employment can more efficiently be increased by *increasing Government expenditure* (G). It was the increase in Government expenditure on Public Works Programme which was the main recommendation of Keynes to raise the level of national output and income to restore equilibrium at full-employment level. Recently in 1993-94, President Clinton stepped up public expenditure on public works in the USA to overcome recession in the American economy and reduce unemployment. Again, in 2009 president Obama gave a fiscal stimulus of over $ 800 billion the major part of which was the increase in Government expenditure to raise aggregate demand to overcome recession in the American Economy. In India also fiscal stimulus packages were announced in 2008-09 under which government expenditure, especially on infrastruture, was increased to revive the slowing Indian economy. It may be noted that increase in Government expenditure not only directly raises national but also, like the increase in private investment has the multiplier effect on levels of income and employment.

Lastly, the *expansion in positive net exports* (X_n) will also cause an increase in equilibrium level of national income and employment. Exports can be promoted through tax concession on profits earned through exports as well as making credit available on lower interest rate for purpose of exporting goods. Another common measure adopted to promote exports is the depreciation of national currency. Depreciation makes the exports cheaper and imports costlier which raise net exports (X_n). However, when there is global recession depreciation of its currency by each country will offset the effect of others.

It follows from above that a mix of fiscal and monetary policy measures can be adopted to increase aggregate demand and thereby to lift the economy out of recession.

DETERMINATION OF NATIONAL INCOME: SAVING-INVESTMENT APPROACH

We have seen how equilibrium level of national income is determined by the interaction of aggregate demand and aggregate supply. The equilibrium level of national income is established at the point where aggregate demand equals aggregate supply. But there is an alternative method for the explanation of the determination of national income. This alternative method explains the determination of national income directly by intended saving and investment.

Look at the Fig. 5.5 again. In this figure, at the equilibrium level of national income OY_1, saving and investment are equal to GE. Given the aggregate demand curve $C + I$, the amount of saving at income greater than OY_1 exceeds investment and for income less than OY_1 investment exceeds saving. It is obvious that intended saving and investment are equal only at the equilibrium level of national income and when intended saving and investment are not equal, national income will not be in equilibrium. Let us see why it is so and how national income is determined by intended saving and investment.

When at a certain level of national income, intended investment by the entrepreneurs is more than intended saving by the people, this would mean that aggregate expenditure is greater than aggregate supply of output. This will lead to the decline in inventories below the desired level. This would induce the firms to increase production, raising the level of income and employment. The result will be that national output will be increased on account of which national income will go up. Further, when at any level of income, investment is less than saving. It means that aggregate demand is less than aggregate supply. As a result, the entrepreneurs will not be able to sell their entire output at given prices. The result will be that output will be reduced which will result in the reduction of national income.

Thus, when, at any level of national income, investment demand of the entrepreneurs is less than the intended savings of the people, the national income will decrease. It will come down to the level at which investment spending is just equal to the planned savings by the community. But, when at any level of national income, intended investment demand on the part of the enterpreneurs is equal to intended savings of the people, it means that aggregate demand is equal to the total output or aggregate supply and therefore the national income will be equilibrium. Hence, equilibrium level of national income will be determined at the level at which the amount of intended investment by the enterpreneurs is equal to the amount of intended savings by the people.

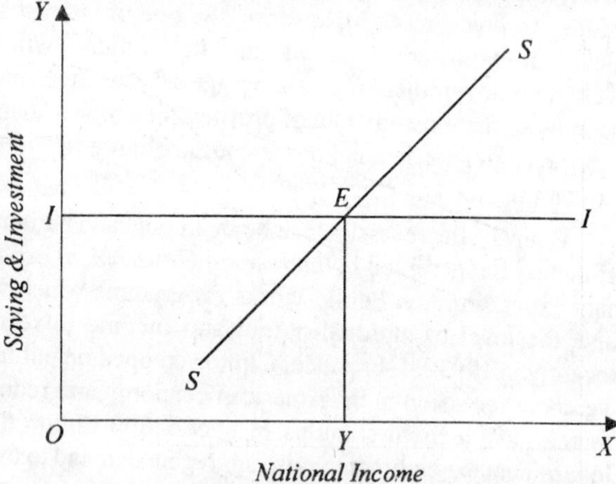

Fig. 5.9. Determination of National Income : Saving-Investment Approach

We can explain the determination of national income through saving and investment in another way. *Saving represents withdrawal of some money from the income stream. On the other hand, investment represents injection of money into the income stream.* Now, if intended investment is greater than intended saving, it means that more money has been put into the income stream than has been taken out of it. As a result, income stream, *i.e.*, flow of national income would expand. On the contrary, if investment is less than intended saving, it means that less amount of money has been put into the income stream than has been taken out of it. The result would be that national income would decrease. But when investment is just equal to saving, it would mean that as much money has been put into the income stream as has been taken out of it. The result will be that the national income will neither increase nor decrease, *i.e.*, it will be in equilibrium. It is thus clear that the equilibrium level of national income will be determined at the level at which the intended investment is equal to intended saving.

The determination of national income by investment and saving is illustrated in Fig. 5.9. In this figure, national income is shown along the *X*-axis. *SS* is the saving curve which shows intended saving at different levels of income, *II* curve shows investment demand *i.e.*, intended investment. The *II* investment curve has been drawn parallel to the *X*-axis. This is done on the assumption that in any year the enterpreneurs intend to invest a certain amount of money. This implies that we assume that investment is independent of change in income, that is, investment does not change with income.

The saving curve *SS* and the investment curve *II* intersect each other at *E*. That is, the intended investment and intended saving are equal at the *OY* level of income. Hence, *OY* is the equilibrium level of income. It will be seen from the Fig. 5.9 that at the level of income less than *OY*, the amount of intended investment is more than intended savings. As a result, income will increase. On the contrary, at the level of income a greater than *OY*, the amount of intended investment is less than the intended savings with the result that income will decrease. The decrease in income will continue until it becomes equal to *OY*. At the level of *OY* income, intended investment and intended saving are equal, so that there is neither the tendency for income to increase, nor to decrease. Hence, national income *OY* is determined. It is thus clear that national income is determined by the investment and saving.

Synthesis between the Two Approaches

The determination of national income has been explained above by two methods. The equilibrium level of national income is determined where two conditions are fulfilled :

(*i*) *Aggregate Expenditure or Demand = Aggregate Supply of output*, and

(*ii*) *Intended Investment = Intended Savings.*

As has been explained above, the equality between aggregate demand (expenditure) and aggregate supply (output) and equality between intended investment and intended saving in reality mean the same thing. This is illustrated in Fig. 5.10. It will be seen in this figure that aggregate demand curve $C + I$ intersects aggregate supply curve OZ at point Q and thereby determines national income equal to OY. In the lower part of this diagram we have draw intended savings curve SS and intended investment curve II. It is worthwhile to note that saving curve SS has been derived from the consumption function curve C and measures the gap between income and consumption at various levels of income. Further, investment curve II drawn in the lower part of the figure represents the difference between consumption function curve C and aggregate demand curve $C + I$. This difference is the amount of intended investment assumed in this figure. We thus see that both saving and investment curves drawn in the lower part are embedded in the upper part showing aggregate demand and aggregate supply. It is because of this that intended saving and intended investment curves also determine the same level of national income OY which is determined through the equality of aggregate demand $(C + I)$ and aggregate supply.

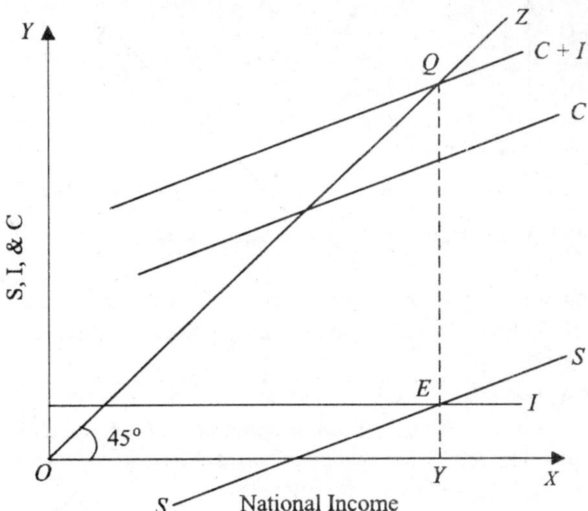

Fig. 5.10. *Synthesis between Aggregate income-Expenditure Approach and Saving-Investment Approach*

Saving-Investment Approach : Algebraic Analysis

That the level of national income is determined by the equality of planned saving and planned investment can be derived from the equilibrium condition explained above that level of income is equal to effective demand.

That is,

$$Y = AD^* \qquad \ldots (i)$$

Where AD^* represents effective aggregate demand or expenditure

Now in our simple economy, effective aggregate demand (AD^*) is equal to the sum of consumption expenditure and investment expenditure. Thus

$$AD^* = C + I$$

or

$$Y = C + I \qquad \ldots (ii)$$

Now

$$C = Y - S$$

Substituting $Y - S$ for C in equation (ii) we have

$$Y = Y - S + I$$

$$Y - Y + S = I$$

or

$$S = I \qquad \ldots (iii)$$

Thus, we reach at the alternative condition of equlibrium of national income, namely, planned (intended) saving be equal to planned (intended) investment.

We can further extend saving – investment approach to show the determination of national income as a multiple of autonomous factors. Since investment is treated as autonomous of national income, its amount is taken to be a fixed amount determined *exogenously*. Therefore we have

$$I = \bar{I}$$

Saving function as derived from the consumption function ($C = a + by$) can be written as**

$$S = -a + (1-b)Y$$

In equilibrium

$$\bar{I} = -a + (1-b)Y$$

$$(1-b)Y = \bar{I} + a$$

$$Y = \frac{1}{1-b}(\bar{I} + a) \quad \text{... } (iv)$$

where $\frac{1}{1-b}$ is the value of multiplier and b = marginal propensity to consume and therefore $1 - b$ = marginal propensity to save. The equation (*iv*) describes the same condition which we at derived earlier. Note that a in equation (*iv*) is autonomous consumption which is intercept term in the consumption function.

Numerical Problem on Saving-Investment Approach

Problem 4. *Suppose the level of autonomous investment in an economy is 200 crores. The following saving function is given :*

$S = -80 + 0.25Y$

Find the equilibrium level of income.

Solution. According to the saving-investment approach, the level of income is in equilibrium at which

$$S = I \quad \text{... } (i)$$

Given, $S = -80 + 0.25Y$, and

I = Rs. 200 crores

Substituting the values of S and I in the equilibrium equation we have

$$-80 + 0.25Y = 200$$

$$0.25Y = 200 + 80 = 280$$

$$Y = 280 \times \frac{100}{25} = 1120 \text{ crores}$$

Note that we can also use the equation (iv) derived above to obtain the equilibrium level of national income. Thus $Y = \frac{1}{1-b} = (I + a)$

Now, $b = 1 - 0.25 = 0.75$, $a = 80$ and $I = 200$

$$\text{Thus } Y = \frac{1}{1-0.75} = (200 + 80)$$

$$= \frac{1}{0.25} \times 280 = 1120 \text{ crores.}$$

RELATIONSHIP BETWEEN SAVING AND INVESTMENT

An important controversy in macroeconomics relates to the relationship between saving and investment. Many economists before J.M. Keynes were generally of the view that saving and investment are generally not equal; they are equal only under condition of equilibrium. Besides, they thought that equality between saving and investment is brought about by changes in the rate of interest. Keynes

** This can be derived as follows

Since $C = Y - S$, consumption function can be written as

$Y - S = a + bY$

$S = -a - bY + Y$ or $S = -a + (1-b)Y$

in his famous work "**General Theory of Employment, Interest and Money**" put forward the view that saving and investment are always equal. This gave rise to a severe controversy in economics as to whether saving and investment are always equal or they are generally unequal. This controversy has now been resolved, and there is general agreement among economists about the correct relationship between saving and investment. Modern economists use the concepts of saving and investment in two different senses. In one sense, saving and investment are always equal, equilibrium or no equilibrium. In the second sense, saving and investment are equal only in equilibrium; they are unequal under conditions of disequilibrium. We shall explain below in detail the relationship between saving and investment in these two different senses.

It will be useful to recall here the meaning of saving and investment. In the beginning of this chapter we mentioned that investment is the addition made to the stock of capital during a period. In the stock of capital are included new machines, raw materials, buildings, tools and implements and addition to the inventories of raw materials, goods in process, finished consumer goods. When in a certain year there is net addition to the stock of capital, investment is said to have taken place. It is worth mentioning here that by investment we do not mean the stock of capital but the net addition to the stock of capital *i.e., investment is a flow concept.* Of course, addition to the stock of capital is made through the flow of investment. In every year stock of capital expands through net investment.

On the other hand, by saving we mean the part of the income which has not been spent on consumer goods and services. In other words, saving is the difference between income and consumption expenditure. It is worth noting that in consumption expenditure all types of expenditure are not included. If an individual spends a part of his income on providing irrigation facilities, for buying tools and machinery, then that expenditure is not the consumption expenditure; it is in fact an investment expenditure. In order to obtain the saving, we have only to deduct the consumption expenditure from income and not the investment expenditure. When an individual makes investment expenditure he is deemed to spend his saved income on investment. For instance, if a farmer's annual income is Rs. 10,000 and he spends Rs. 6,000 on consumer goods and services and spends Rs. 1,000 on the construction of a well for his fields, and another Rs. 1,000 on building a drainage system for his fields and providing fencing, then his saving would be 10 – 6 = Rs. 4 thousands. The expenditure of Rs. 2,000 on the well, drainage and fencing will be included in the saving and will not constitute the consumption expenditure. If Y represents the national income of a country and C the total consumption, then the saving of the country will be equal to $Y - C$. Thus,

$$S = Y - C$$

Ex-post Savings and Ex-post Investment are always Equal

Pre-Keynesian economists were of the view that savings and investment are generally not equal. This is firstly because saving and investment are made by two different classes of people. While investment is undertaken by entrepreneurial class of the society, saving is done by the general public. Secondly, saving and investment depend upon different factors and are made for different purposes and motives. Therefore, it is not inevitable that savings and investment of a society must always be equal. Besides, some pre-Keynesian economists pointed out that investment expenditure is also undertaken by borrowing money from the banks which create new credit for this purpose. It was thus pointed out that more amount of investment than savings is possible because excess of investment over savings is financed by new bank credit. But Keynes expressed a totally opposite view that saving and investment are always equal. The sense in which savings and investment are always equal refers to the *actual* savings and *actual* investment made in the economy during a year. They are *also called ex-post saving and ex-post investment.* If we have to calculate that during the year 2004-05, how much actual savings and investment have been made in India, we will have to deduct the total consumption expenditure made by the citizens of India during that year from the national income. Likewise, the real investment during the year 2004-05 of the Indian economy will be obtained by summing up the investments actually made by the Indian people during that year. In fact, in national income accounting, estimates of savings and investment are made in this actual or ex-post sense.

The second sense in which saving and investment terms are used is that in a certain year how much saving or how much investment people of the country *desire or intend* to do. Therefore, saving and investment in this sense are known as *desired, intended or planned savings and investment.* They are also called *ex-ante saving and ex-ante investment.*

Keynes in his book, "***General Theory of Employment, Interest and Money***" showed that in spite of the fact that saving and investment are done by two different classes of people and also for different purposes and motives ex-post (actual) saving and ex-post (actual) investment are always equal. Thus, he used the word saving and investment in the ex-post or actual sense and proved the equality between saving and investment in the following way :

Income of a country is earned in two ways: (1) by producing and selling consumer goods and services, and (2) by producing and selling capital goods. That is, national income of a country is composed of the value of consumer goods and services and the value of capital goods. This can be expressed in the form of the following equation:

$$\text{National Income} = \text{Consumption} + \text{Investment}$$

$$\text{or} \quad Y = C + I \qquad ...(i)$$

where Y stands for national income, C for consumption and I for investment.

The above equation represents the production or earning side of the national income. The second aspect of national income is the expenditure side. The total national income can be fully consumed but generally it does not happen so. In actual practice, a part of the total income is spent on consumption and the remaining part is saved. From this we get the following equation:

$$\text{National Income} = \text{Consumption} + \text{Saving}$$

$$\text{or} \quad Y = C + S \qquad ...(ii)$$

where Y stands for national income, C for consumption and S for saving.

In the above two equations (*i*) and (*ii*) it is clear that national income is equal to the sum of consumption and investment and also equal to the sum of consumption and saving. From this it follows that :

$$\text{Consumption} + \text{Saving} = \text{Consumption} + \text{Investment}$$

$$C + S = C + I \qquad ...(iii)$$

In equation (*iii*) above, since C occurs on both sides of the equation, we get:

$$\text{Saving} = \text{Investment}$$

$$\text{or} \quad S = I$$

From the foregoing analysis, it follows that saving and investment are defined in such a way that they are necessarily equal to each other. In equation (*i*), investment is that part of national income which is obtained from the production of goods other than those consumed and in equation (*ii*) saving is that part of national income which is not spent on consumption. Hence in the actual or ex-post sense, saving and investment by definition are equal.

It is worth mentioning that in macroeconomics, saving and investment do not refer to the saving and investment by an individual; they refer to the saving and investment of the whole community or economy. Saving and investment by an individual can differ but *in the ex-post sense, saving of the whole economy must always be equal to investment.*

Now the question arises why ex-post saving and ex-post investment are always equal. For instance, when less investment is planned by the entrepreneurs then how actual (ex-post) investment becomes equal to actual (ex-post) saving. On the other hand, if planned (or intended) investment exceeds intended saving, then how actual (ex-post) investment and saving are made equal. In this connection it is worth mentioning that following Keynes modern economists include inventories of goods in investment. It is changes in these unplanned or unintended inventory investment that make the actual investment and saving equal to each other in any period of time.

For example, when at a level of national income intended (ex-ante) savings exceed planned (ex-ante) investment, aggregate expenditure ($C + I$) will not be sufficient to buy all the goods produced at that level of income. As a result, there will be unplanned or unintended increase in inventories of goods with businessmen. It is unintended because it results from the shortage of aggregate demand to buy the total output of goods produced, prices remaining fixed. Thus *actual (ex-post) investment which equals planned investment plus unplanned or unintended increase in inventory investment becomes equal to actual (ex-post) saving.* Note that since businessmen will not be interested in holding on to these unwanted extra inventories, they will cut back production in the next period.

On the other hand, if in a period planned investment exceeds planned (ex-ante) savings, aggregate expenditure ($C + I$) and therefore sales would exceed planned output of goods. This will lead to the *unintended or unplanned decline in inventories* of goods. As a result, actual (ex-post) investment (that is, planned investment minus unintended decline in inventory investment) will turn out to be equal to actual saving in that period of time. Of course, unintended decline in inventories of goods would induce business men to expand production of goods in the next period and thereby causes increase in level of national income. We thus see that in the ex-post or realised sense, saving and investment are always equal.

Ex-ante Saving and Ex-ante Investment are Equal only in Equilibrium

As said above, in the desired, planned or ex-ante sense, saving and investment can differ. In fact planned or ex-ante saving and investment are generally not equal to each other. This is due to the fact that the persons or classes who save are different from those who invest. Savings are done by general public for various objectives and purposes. On the other hand, investment is made by the entrepreneurial class in the community and is generally governed by marginal efficiency of capital on the one hand and rate of interest on the other hand. Therefore, savings and investment in planned or ex-ante sense generally differ from each other. But through the mechanism of change in the income level, there is tendency for ex-ante saving and ex-ante investment to become equal. When in a year planned investment is larger than planned saving, the level of income rises. At a higher level of income, more is saved and therefore intended saving becomes equal to intended investment. On the other hand, when planned saving is greater than planned investment in a period, the level of income will fall. At a lower level of income, less will be saved and therefore planned saving will become equal to planned investment. We thus see that *planned or ex-ante saving and planned or ex-ante investment are brought to equality through changes in the level of income.* When ex-ante saving and ex-ante investment are equal, level of income is in equilibrium i.e., it has no tendency to rise or fall. It is thus clear that whereas realised or ex-post saving is always equal to realised or ex-post investment, intended, planned or ex-ante saving and investment may differ; intended or ex-ante saving and investment have only a tendency to be equal and are equal only at the equilibrium level of income.

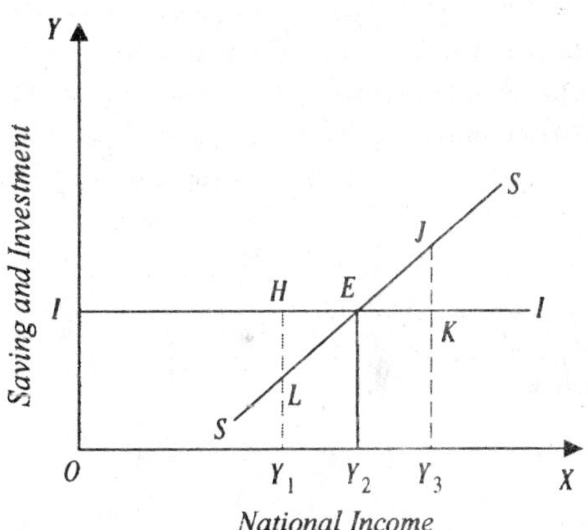

Fig. 5.11. *Equality between Saving and Investment in the Ex-ante Sense*

That the planned or intended saving is equal to intended investment only at the equilibrium level of income can be easily understood from Fig. 5.11. In this figure, national income is measured along the X-axis while saving and investment are measured along the Y-axis. SS is the saving curve which slopes upward indicating thereby that with the rise in income, saving also increases. II is the investment curve. Investment curve II is drawn as horizontal straight line because, following Keynes, it has been assumed that investment is independent of the level of income i.e., it depends upon factors other than the current level of income. It will be seen from the Fig. 5.11 that saving and investment curves intersect at point *E*. Therefore, *OY* is the equilibrium level of income. If the level of income is OY_1, the intended investment is Y_1H whereas the intended saving is Y_1L. It is thus clear that at OY_1 level of income, intended investment is greater than intended saving. As a result of this, level of income will rise and at higher levels of income more will be saved. It will be seen that with the rise in income to OY_2, saving rises and becomes equal to investment. On the other hand, if in any period, level of income is OY_3 intended investment is Y_3K and intended saving is Y_3J. As a result of this, level of national income will fall to OY_2 at which ex-ante saving and ex-ante investment are once again equal and thus level of national income is in equilibrium. To sum up, whereas ex-post savings and ex-post investment are always equal, ex-ante saving and ex-ante investment are equal only in equilibrium.

CONCEPTS OF INFLATIONARY AND DEFLATIONARY GAPS

Inflationary Gap

It is useful and important to understand the concept of inflationary gap because with it we are able to know the main cause of the rise in general level of prices. The equilibrium of an economy is established at the level of full-employment when aggregate demand or total expenditure is equal to the level of income corresponding to full-employment. This happens when the amount of investment is equal to the saving gap corresponding to full-employment level of income. Consider Fig. 5.12 where OY_F is national income corresponding to the level of full-employment. Equilibrium at na-tional income OY_F would be established only when aggregate demand or total expenditure ($C + I + G$) is equal to YF_E (YF_E is equal to OY_F). Real national income cannot increase beyond OY_F because when all means of production including labour are fully employed, there is no possibility of further rise in production or real national income. Thus when aggregate demand is greater than the aggregate demand YF_E which is required to establish the equilibrium at OY_F level of national income, the equilibrium would not be established at OY_F.

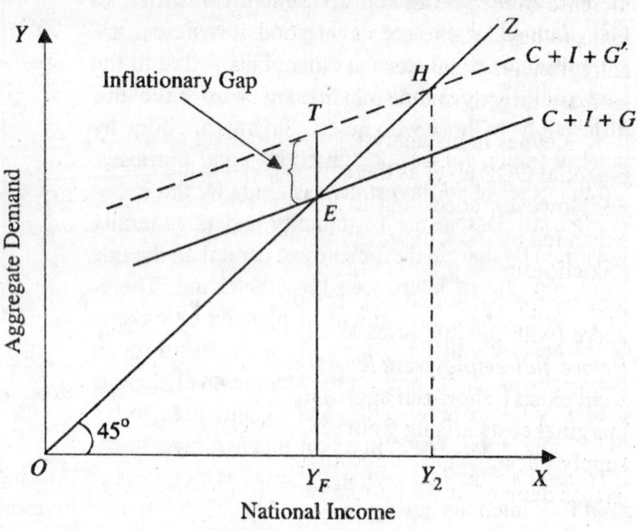

Fig. 5.12. *Inflation Gap*

It would be seen from Fig. 5.12 that aggregate demand Y_FT is greater than aggregate demand YFE which is required to maintain the equilibrium at OY_F. Thus with the level of aggregate demand ($C + I + G'$), which is obtained by adding expenditure *ET* to the aggregate demand curve $C + I + G$, equilibrium would not be established at OY_F which corresponds to full-employment level of income. The actual aggregate demand being greater than YF_E by the amount *ET* the level of nation income would be greater than OY_F. Since OY_F is full-employment level of national income, actual production cannot increase beyond that but there would be rise in prices which would raise the money value of OY_F production. The amount by which the actual aggregate demand exceeds the level of national income corresponding to full employment is known as inflationary gap because this excess of aggregate demand causes inflation or rise in prices in the country. In Fig. 5.12 this excess of aggregate demand or inflationary gap is equal to *ET*. It would be seen from Fig. 5.12 that the aggregate demand curve $C + I + G'$ intersects 45° line (*OZ* line) at H so that equilibrium level of national income would be OY_2. It should be carefully understood that there is no difference between OY_F and OY_2 in terms of real income or actual production; only as a result of rise in price level, national income has increased from OY_F to OY_2 in money terms. Inflationary gap represents excess demand in relation to aggregate production or supply of output which brings about demand-pull inflation. J.M. Keynes in his revolutionary book "*General Theory of Employment, Interest and Money*" did not discuss the concept of inflationary gap because he was then preoccupied with the analysis of the state of depression and deflation. During the Second World War when the problem of inflation cropped up, then Keynes applied his macroeconomic analysis to explain inflation as well and in this connection he put forward the concept of inflationary gap.

The analysis of inflationary gap brings out an important cause of inflation in the economy. This analysis shows that it is the *emergence of excess aggregate demand over aggregate supply of output* that causes inflation or general rise in price level in the economy, especially when due to capacity constraint aggregate output cannot by increased to match the increase in aggregate demand. Therefore, this Keynesian inflation has been called *demand pull-inflation*. The excess aggregate demand may arise due to the increase in consumption demand or investment demand directly as well as indirectly through the multiplier effect. Consumption demand mainly increases when there is increase in income and wealth of the people or reduction in rate of interest inducing people to get loans to buy durable consumer goods. Similarly, when there is increase in investment by the private entrepreneurs or increase in Government expenditure, incomes and therefore demands of the people increase directly and also indirectly through the multiplier effect.

Keynes in his analysis explained that true inflation would occur only after full-employment or potential GDP level as thereafter due to capacity constraint, aggregate supply cannot be increased at all. However, according to the present-day thinking, short-run aggregate supply of output can be expanded by inducing people to work over-time or arranging more shifts in the work place or by the reduction in the frictional and structural unemployment through easier or more quickly finding of jobs by the frictionally or strucutrally unemployed workers. Therefore, short-run aggregate supply curve (with flexible price level) slopes upward even after full-employment or potential GDP level. *Before full-employment level* (or what is now generally called level at which only *natural unemployment* exists) short-run aggregate supply curve (with flexible prices) is sloping upward due to rising marginal costs arising from several bottlenecks. Now, given the upward sloping short-run aggregate supply curve, when due to increase in aggregate demand, aggregate demand curve shifts upward excess demand at the current price level emerges which leads to the rise in general price level.

It may however be noted that in developing countries such as ours Keynesian concept of full employment (or the present-day concept of natural unemployment rate) is not relevant as there is no any pricise full-employment level due to the existence of disguised unemployment. The nature of unemployment in developing countries is different. Moreover, in developing countries like India agricultural output varies a good deal due to uncertain monsoon. When there is fall in agricultural output due to inadequate monsoon, rising aggregate demand outstrips aggregate supply of output resulting in inflation in the economy.

Deflationary Gap

In the theory of income and employment, the concept of deflationary gap occupies an important place, since in a capitalist economy unemployment and depression occur due to this gap. According to Keynesian theory of income and employment, equilibrium at the level of full- employment is established when aggregate demand consisting of consumption demand plus investment demand plus government demand ($C + I + G$) is equal to the national income at the level of full-employment. This happens when investment and government demand is equal to the saving gap at full-employment level of national income. If aggregate demand is less than the full-employment level of national income, i.e., when investment and government demand is less than the saving gap at full-employment level of income, the deficiency of aggregate demand occurs due to which national income and employment will fall below the full-employment level causing unemployment and depression in the economy. The concept of deflationary gap is illustrated in Fig. 5.13 in which along the X-axis national income is measured and along the Y-axis level of aggregate demand is measured. Suppose national income at the level of full-employment is equal to OY_F. Now the equilibrium level of income and employment would be established at OY_F when aggregate demand (consumption demand plus investment demand) is equal to YF_E (which is equal to national income OY_F). But in the real world if aggregate demand is less than the full-employment level of income OY_F or it is less than YF_E, then the problem of deficiency of aggregate demand will arise. Therefore, EK in Fig. 5.13 represents deflationary gap. Hence, deflationary gap represents the difference between the actual aggregated demand and the aggregate demand which is required to establish the equilibrium at full-employment level of income.

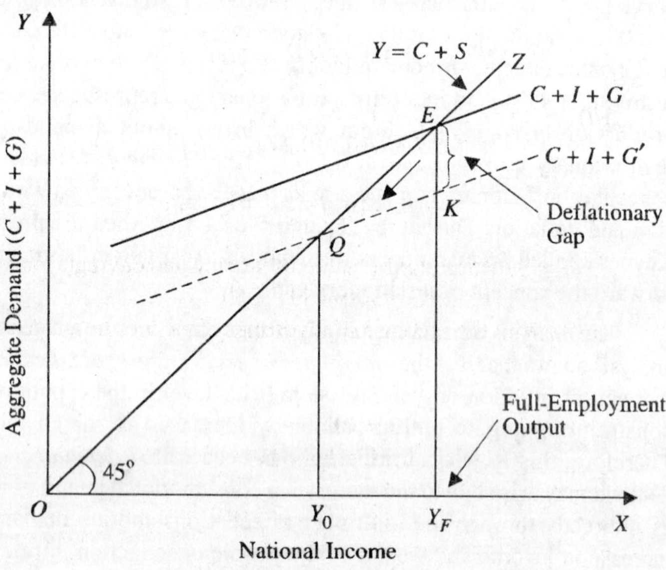

Fig. 5.13. *Deflationary Gap*

It should be carefully understood that due to the deflationary gap EK, the level of national income and employment will decline. The decline in national income and employment will not only be equal to the deflationary gap EK but it will be much greater than this. The decline in national income is determined by the value of the multiplier. In Fig. 5.13 when aggregate demand curve is $C+I+G'$ deflationary gap is equal to EK. The aggregate demand curve $C+I+G'$ (dotted) which cuts the 45° line at point Q asp result of which equilibrium is established at OY_1 level of national income. It will be seen from Fig. 5.13 that OY_1 is less than full-employment level of income OY_F. Deflationary gap represents the situation of deficient demand in the economy. This deficiency in aggregate demand causes fall in national output and level of employment. As a result, unvoluntary unemployment in the economy emerges. The depression of 1929-33 in capitalist countries was caused by the emergence of deflationary gap or by demand deficiency in these economies.

NUMERICAL PROBLEMS

Problem 1. *Given the saving function $S = -10 + 0.2y$ and autonomous investment, I = ₹ 5 crore.*

(*i*) *Find the equilibrium level of income.*

(*ii*) *Find the level of consumption.*

(*iii*) *If investment increases permanently by ₹ 5 crores, what will be the new levels of income and consumption*

Solution : (*i*) According to saving-investment approach, equilibrium level of national income is determined by equality between planned saving and investment. Thus,

$$S = I \qquad \text{...}(i)$$

$$-10 + 0.2Y = 50$$

$$0.2\,Y = 50 + 10 = 60$$

$$Y = 60 \times \frac{10}{2} = 300$$

(*ii*)

$$C = Y - S \qquad \text{...}(ii)$$

$$S = -10 + 0.2Y$$

$$= -10 + \frac{2}{10} \times 300 = 50$$

Substituting the value of income and saving(*s*) in equation (*ii*), we have

$$C = 300 - 50 = 250$$

(*iii*) With the increase in investment by ₹ 5 crores, the new investment will become equal to ₹ 55 crores.

$$S = I$$

$$-10 + 0.2Y = 55$$

$$0.2Y = 55 + 10 = 65$$

$$Y = 65 \times \frac{10}{2} = 325$$

Thus, new level of income = ₹ 325 crores.

Now, saving $= -10 + 0.2Y$

$$= -10 + \frac{2}{10} \times 325$$

$$= -10 + 65 = 55$$

$$\text{consumption } (C) = Y - S$$

$$= 325 - 55$$

$$= 270$$

Problem 2. *The following consumption function of an economy is given :*

40 + 0.8Y where Y is national income

If the planned level of investment in a year equals ₹ 75 crores, what will be the equilibrium level of national income and consumption ?

Solution : Equilibrium level of national income is determined where

$$Y = C + I$$

Now,

$$C = 40 + 0.8\,Y$$

$$I = 75$$

$$Y = 40 + 0.8Y + 75$$

$$Y - 0.8Y = 40 + 785 = 115$$

$$0.2Y = 115$$

$$Y = 115 + \frac{10}{2} = 575$$

$$C = Y - I = 575 - 75 = 500$$

Problem 3. *For an economy following consumption function is given :*

$$C - 60 + 0.75\,Y.$$

(*a*) *If investment in a year is ₹ 35 crores what will be the equilibrium level of income or output ?*

(*b*) *If full-employment level of income (i.e. level of potential output) is ₹ 460 crores what investment is required to be undertaken to ensure equilibrium at full-employment.*

Solution : (*a*)

$$Y = C + I$$
$$Y = 60 + 0.75Y + 35$$
$$Y - 0.75Y = 60 + 35 = 95$$
$$Y(1 - 0.75) = 95$$
$$0.25Y = 95$$
$$Y = 95 \times \frac{100}{25} = 380$$

(*b*) To ensure full-employment equilibrium, investment should be equal to the saving gap at full-employment income. With the given full-employment income equal to ₹ 460,

$$S_F = Y_F - C_F = Y_F - (60 + 0.75Y_F)$$
$$= 460 - 60 - (0.75 \times 460)$$
$$= 400 - 345 = 55$$

Thus, investment required for full-employment equilibrium is 55 crores.

QUESTIONS FOR REVIEW

1. Explain how equilibrium level of national income is determined by level of effective demand in a simple two-sector Keynesian model. Is this equilibrium necessarily established at full employment level ?
2. Explain the equilibrium of national income by consumption and investment. When will the equilibrium be established at full-employment ?
3. (*i*) Saving and Investment are *always equal.*
   (*ii*) Saving and Investment are *equal only in equilibrium.*
   How would you reconcile the above two statments ?
4. Explain Keynes' income-expenditure approach to the determination of national income. Why can this equilibrium be reached below full-employment level of output ?
5. Define planned (desired) saving and planned (desired) investment. Explain how equilibrium level of national income is determined by planned saving and planned investment. Why is this equilibrium not always attained at full-employment level ?
6. What do you understand by the equilibrium level of national income. Explain that both saving–investment approach and aggregate demand–aggregate supply approach yeild the same level of equilibrium.
7. In a three sectors economy with firms, households and Government show that aggregate demand will equal aggregate supply only at the level of output and income at which savings and taxes equal Government expenditure and planned investment.
8. Explain the Keynesian concept of aggregate demand. How is the Keynesian aggregate demand function different from the classical demand function.
9. Explain the concept of deflationary gap. What are the causes and consequences of this gap ?
10. (a) What is meant by under-employment equilibrium ? Explain the factors which cause it.
    (b) Explain the various measures that can be taken to increase the equilibrium level of income and employment. Is it possible to increase the level of income without increasing the level of investment ?
11. Explain the concept of inflationary gap. What are its causes and consequences ?
12. Explain how the Keynesian theory of inflationary gap explains the emergence of inflation in the economy. What steps can be taken to prevent inflation ?
13. What, according to Keynes, is the cause of recession or depression in the economy. What measures can be adopted to overcome recession in the economy ?

APPENDIX TO CHAPTER 5

Keynes's Complete Macroeconomic Model : Integrating Goods Market with Money Market

Linking Goods Market with Money Market

As explained in the previous chapter classical economists thought that supply of money only determines the price level and nominal variables and has no effect on the real variables of the economy such as level of real income (output) and employment. However, in Keynes's theory money plays an important role in determination of real income and employment. In fact *Keynes brought about integration between money market and goods market.* Keynes was able to do so because he explained that rate of interest is determined by demand for money (which he called liquidity preference) and supply of money, that is, through market equilibrium, while classical economists thought that rate interest was determined by saving and investment, that is, through capital market equilibrium. It is the rate of interest which is crucial channel through which money market is linked with goods market Changes in money supply by monetary policy can bring about changes is rate of interest which determines investment. And, according to Keynes, it is investment which plays a crucial real in determining level of real income and employment. For example, increase in the supply of money will lower the rate of interest. Since investment depends on the rate of interest and marginal efficiency of capital, at the lower rate of interest more investment will be undertaken. The higher investment will lead to the greater level of real national income and employment. In fact, Keynesian analysis brings out that monetary policy can play significant role in influencing the real variables and controlling business cycles.

However, Keynes pointed out that *effect of increase in money supply depends on interest elasticity of demand for money (i.e. liquidity preference curve) and interest sensitivity of investment demand.* The greater the elasticity of demand for money, and lower the elasticity of investment demand curve, the smaller will be the effect of changes in money supply on national income and employment. Though during the period of great depression (1929 – 33), Keynes pointed out that demand for money was highly elastic and therefore he argued that effect of monetary policy would not be enough to lift the economy out of depression and therefore he emphasised that along with monetary policy expansionary fiscal policy should be adopted to raise aggregate demand and thereby to increase the levels of real income and employment. However, according to him, in *normal times*, monetary policy is quite effective in determining real income and employment.

Empirical evidence after Keynes has revealed that even during recessions demand for money is not absolutely interest-elastic and also investment demand is fairly interest-elastic. Therefore, the modern Keynesian economists emphasise the roles of both monetary and fiscal policies to achieve economic stability.

Keynes's Complete Macroeconomic Model

In Fig. 5A.1 we have graphically depicted Keynes's complete macroeconomic model that shows how Keynes integrates money market and real goods market. In Panel (c) in Fig. 5A.1 money market equilibrium is shown. Given the money supply equal to M_0 money supply curve MS_0 intersects money demand curve *LP* at rate of interest r_0. It will be seen from panel (*d*) that at rate of interest r_0, investment is I_0. Then in panel (*b*) with the consumption function curve C and investment equal to I_0, aggregate demand curve is $C + I_0$ which intersects the 45° income line *OZ* at point *E* and determines level of real national income equal to Y_0. Panel (*a*) of the figure shows that Y_0 level of national income generates N_0 level of labour employment.

Now suppose that there is increase in money supply from M_0 to M_1 which causes shifts in money supply curve from MS_0 to MS_1. As a result, rate of interest falls from r_0 to r_1 Panal (*d*) Fig. 5A.1 shows that at a lower interest rate r_1 investment increase from I_0 to I_1. With this increase in

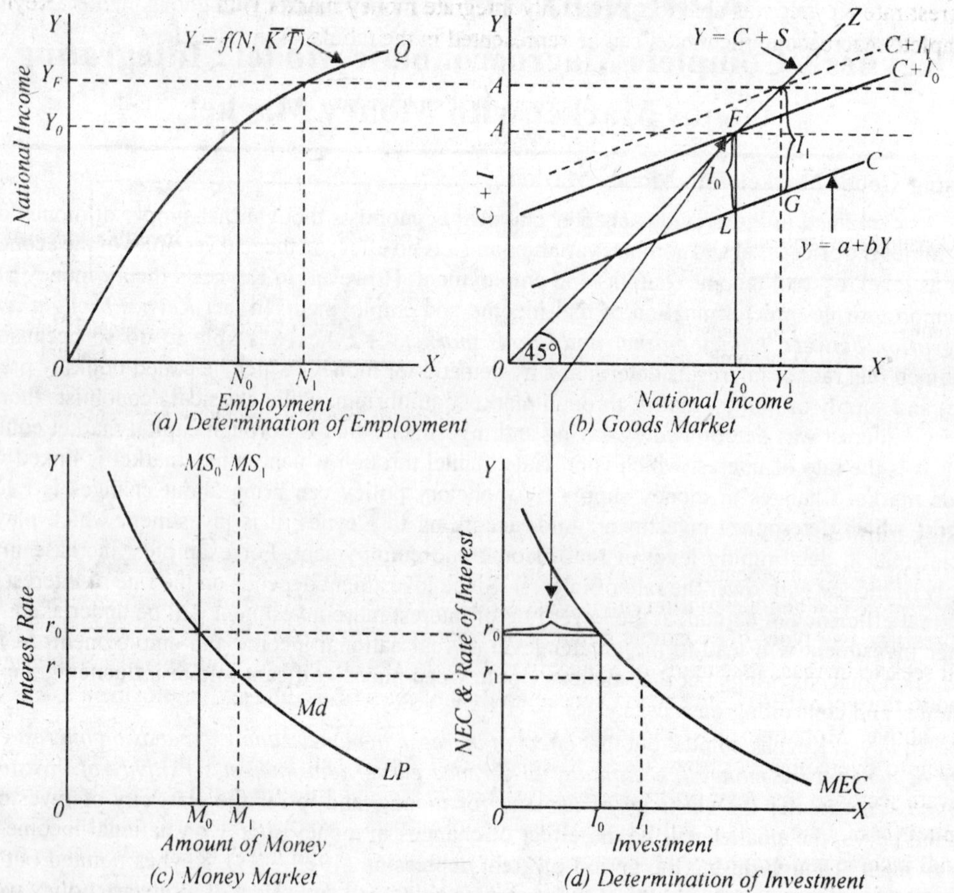

Fig. 5A.1. *The Keynes's Complete Macroeconomic Model : Integrating Money Market with Goods Market*

investment (ΔI), aggregate demand curve shifts above to the position $C + I_1$. With this increase in aggregate demand, level of real national income increases from Y_0 to Y_1. Corresponding to this increase in real national income the level of labour employment in Panel (*a*) rises from ON_0 to ON_1.

It is evident from above that Keynes succeeded in integrating money market with goods market and with this he showed that money supply plays an important role in determining real variables such as real investment (*i.e.* addition to the stock of capital), real national output and employment.

It follows from above that liquidity preference, money supply, rate of interest, consumption function and investment are crucial elements in Keynes's model which determine level of income and employment. Figure 5A.1 also shows how changes in rate of interest through their effect on investment shifts aggregate expenditure (aggregate demand) curve and thereby affect level of income and employment. For example, if money supply is increased from M_0 to M_1, it will be seen from Panel (*c*) that rate of interest falls from r_0 to r_1. In Panel (*d*) at lower rate interest r_1, investment .increases to I_1, Now, it will be seen Panel from (*b*) that with higher investment I_1 aggregate expenditure curve shifts upward to $C + I_1$ (dotted). With this new expenditure curve (+ I, equilibrium level of national income increase to Y_1 which causes labour employment to rise from N_0 to N_1. The increase in money supply has led to the increase in real income and employment. In Chapter 5 in Fig. 5.3 where Keynes's simple model of income determination is shown we have taken investment as *exogenously* fixed amount autonomous of income. However, as seen in Fig. 5A.1, rate of interest is *endogenously* determined in Keynes's complete macroeconomic model and it is through the channel of change in interest rate Keynes was able to successfully integrate money market with goods market Keynes's complete macroeconomic model can be represented in the tabular form as under :

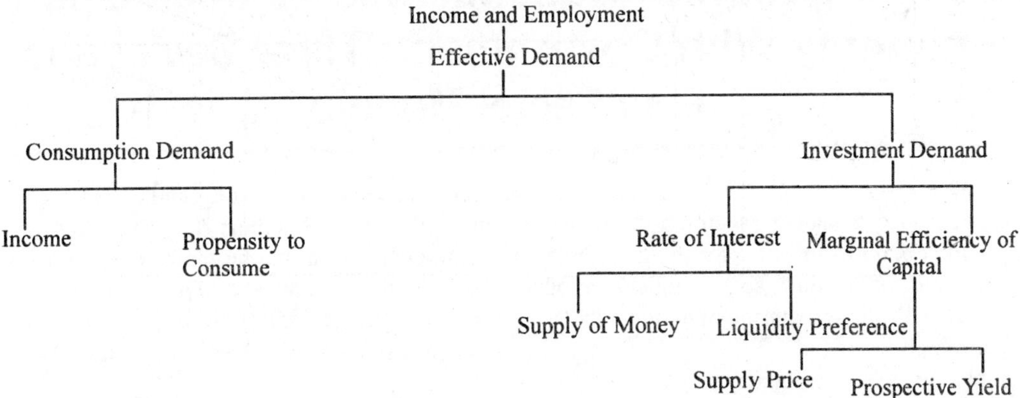

Policy Implications

The policy implication of Keynes's model of the determination of income and employment may be noted. When the equilibrium is at less than full employment and the economy is in a state of depression, two types of economic policies, monetary and fiscal, may be adopted. Monetary policy will seek to increase the supply of money to reduce the rate of interest. This lower interest rate will tend to raise private investment and consequently the levels of income and employment as has been seen above. More than the cheap money policy Keynes strongly advocated for the adoption of *fiscal policy* to overcome recession. Under fiscal policy Government may give tax concessions to the private sector so that their profit may rise resulting in the upward shift in the marginal efficiency of capital (MEC) curve. This will raise the amount of private investment and will help in raising national income and employment. Besides, Keynes emphasized that under fiscal policy Government may itself increase its expenditure on Public Works which will increase income and employment not only directly but also indirectly through the working of multiplier.

EXERCISES

1. Explain how Keynes links money market with goods market. What are its policy implications ? *DU. BA(Hons.)*
2. Show how changes in interest rate affect aggregate demand and level of income and employment. Does lowering of interest rate by the Central Bank of a country always succeed in overcoming recession in the economy ? Discuss.
3. What type of interest rate policy is adopted to check inflation ? Explain the transmission mechanism in this regard.
4. In Keynes's macroeconomic model money is not neutral and affects the magnitudes of real variables. Explain.

CHAPTER 5A*

Determination Of National Income in an Open Economy With Government: Three Sector and Four Sector Models

We carry our analysis of determination of national income further in this chapter. Having explained the Keynesian two sector model of determination of national income in the previous chapter, we will explain in this chapter the determination of national income in the three sector and four sector models. The three sector model incorporates the role of government with its expenditure and taxation in the determination of national income. In the a four sector model we add the foreign trade in our analysis of determination of national income and discuss how exports and imports affect national income of a country.

DETERMINATION OF NATIONAL INCOME WITH GOVERNMENT : THREE SECTOR MODEL

Government Expenditure and National Income

In our analysis of two sector model we have explained how the equilibrium level of national income is determined by the consumption function and autonomous investment demand. In our analysis we did not take into account the role of Government expenditure in the determination of national income. However, in all economies today including the free-market capitalist economies such as those of U.S.A., Britain, Japan, the Government expenditure on goods and services plays an important role in the determination of national income and therefore it should also be included in the analysis of income determination. It is important to note here that the magnitude of Government expenditure on such things as highways, public parks, education, health services is governed by the consideration of promoting social welfare, employment and growth in the economy and does not depend on the level of income of the economy. Therefore, in the simple Keynesian model of income determination, the Government expenditure is treated as *autonomous expenditure*. We further assume for the moment that Government spends on goods and services but imposes no taxes. We denote Government expenditure by G. Thus in the three sector economy when we take into account the income generating effects of Government expenditure, we get the following equation for the equilibrium level of national income.

$$Y = C + I + G \qquad \dots (i)$$

where Y is national income or output and $C + I + G$ represents the level of aggregate demand including Government expenditure, G.

Since consumption function $C = a + bY$ *where b stands for marginal propensity to consume* and a for autonomous consumption expenditure, we can rewrite the equilibrium level of national income as under :

$$\begin{aligned} Y &= a + bY + I + G \\ Y - bY &= a + I + G \\ Y(1 - b) &= a + I + G \end{aligned}$$

$$Y = \frac{1}{1-b}(a + I + G) \qquad \dots (ii)$$

Thus it is clear that the *equilibrium level of income (when impact of Government expenditure is also considered) is equal to the sum of three types of fixed autonomous expenditure*, namely, autono-

*This chapter is meant for higher level courses in macroeconomics mous consumption, autonomous investment and Government expenditure $(a + I + G)$ multiplied by the value of the multiplier $[1/(1 - b)]$.

Graphic Illustration

The impact of Government expenditure on goods and services on the equilibrium level of national income is illustrated in Fig. 5B.1. The $C + I$ is the aggregate expenditure curve which has been obtained by adding autonomous investment equal to I to the consumption functional curve. On top of the consumption curve C, we have added the Government expenditure on goods and services (G) and investment demand (I) to get the aggregate expenditure (or aggregate demand) curve $C + I + G$. With this, the equilibrium national income OY is determined at the level at which the aggregate expenditure curve $(C + I + G)$ interests the 45° line, that is, aggregate demand $(C + I + G)$ equals aggregate supply of output. The reason for the determination of equilibrium level of income at OY when Government expenditure is included in the aggregate demand curve is the same as stated earlier. It will be observed from Fig. 5B.1 that at a level of national income *less* than OY aggregate expenditure $C + I + G$ exceeds aggregate output. This implies unintended decline in the inventories of goods with the firms which will induce them to expand the level of aggregate output to the level OY. On the contrary, at the level of national income *greater* than OY, the aggregate expenditure is less than aggregate output. This deficiency of aggregate demand for goods will cause unintended accumulation of inventories. The firms would respond to this by cutting back production of goods which will lead to the reduction of national income to OY.

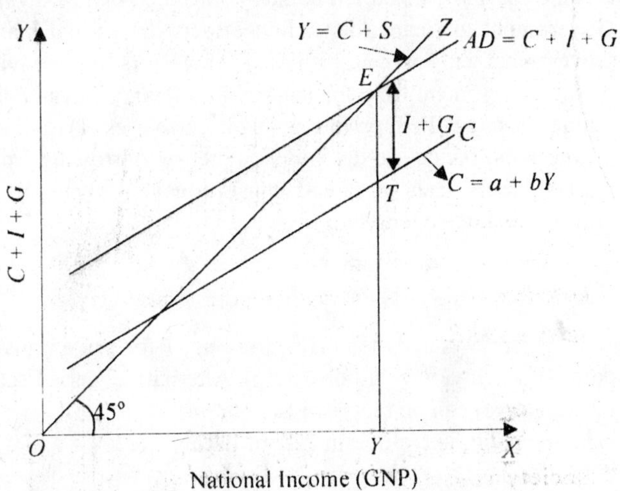

Fig. 5B.1. *Determination of National Income : The Three Sector Model*

It is important to note that *in the presence of Government expenditure, national income is determined at the level at which the saving gap is equal to the sum of private investment and Government expenditure $(I + G)$.*

This can be shown as under :

In equilibrium, $Y = C + I + G$

or $Y - C = I + G$

Since $Y - C = \text{Saving } (S)$

Therefore, in equilibrium $S = I + G$

It may be further noted that just as investment expenditure has a multiplier effect on increase in income *Government expenditure too has a multiplier effect. It will be seen from equation (ii) above Government expenditure (G) multiplier, like that of autonomous consumption (a) and investment (I) multiplier, is equal to* $\frac{1}{1-b}$

Government Expenditure, Budget Deficit and Capital Market

We have explained above how the government expenditure affects the product market by bringing about increase in aggregate demand. Now, an important question is how the Government expenditure is financed. Imposition of taxes is an important way of financing Government expenditure. But taxes reduce aggregate demand in the product market by lowering disposable income of the community and thereby causing a decline in its consumption expenditure. Therefore, if Government expenditure equals tax revenue collected ($G = T$), then Government has a balanced budget and much of the expansionary effect of government expenditure is offset by taxes levied. If Government increases its expenditure without raising taxes, (*i.e.* $G > T$), then it has a *budget deficit* which has a large expansionary effect on the product market and, as seen above, leads to increase in national income (*GDP*). This deficit budget is financed by borrowing from the public. But borrowing by the Government to finance its deficit affects the capital market. This is because borrowing by the Government will compete with private investors for the saving of the public. As a result of borrowing by the Government from the market, less saving is available for private investment. When the Government runs a deficit, private saving has two uses (1) to finance private investment and (2) to finance Government budget deficit which is met by borrowing from the public. Equilibrium in the capital market occurs when private saving is equal to private investment plus budget deficit, $G - T$, (i.e. Government borrowing).

Thus, in equilibrium in the capital market

$$S_p = I + (G - T)$$

where S_p stands for private saving, I for private investment, and $(G - T)$ stands for budget deficit (*i.e.* Government borrowing). Alternatively, the fiscal deficit of the Government ($G - T < 0$, i.e., negative) can be regarded as *government disaving*. Therefore, in case of fiscal deficit or negative *Government savings*, national saving will decrease and national saving curve will shift to the left. How budget deficit or Government borrowing reduces or crowds out private investment is illustrated through Figure 5B.2 where to begin with vertical saving curve S_0 intersects the downward sloping investment curve II at point E_0 and determines real interest rate r_0 at which private investment equal to I_0 takes place. Now as a result of Government borrowing to finance its budget deficit $(G - T)$ national saving available for investment falls and the national saving curve shifts to the left[2] to the new position S_1. Thus when Government borrows to finance budget deficit, Government is said to dissave and therefore in this case Government or public saving is negative ($G - T = - S_g$). Note further that national saving = private saving and Government saving ($S = S_p + S_g$). As a result of fiscal deficit and consequent leftward shift in the national saving curve to S_1, the capital market is now in equilibrium at point E_1 and rate of interest rises to r_1. At this higher interest rate r_1, private investment falls to I_1. Thus, borrowing by the Government to finance its budget deficit has led to crowding out of private investment. As mentional above, a part of private saving is used to finance private investment and a part to finance budget deficit of the Government.

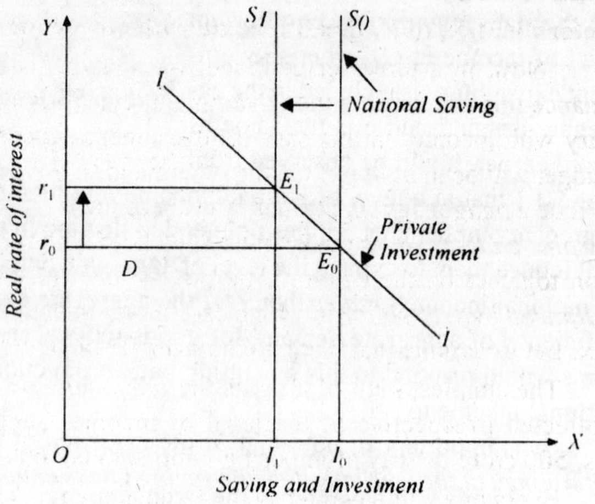

Fig. 5B.2. *Effect of Budget Deficit and Government Borrowing on Capital Market*

It is worth noting that when Government expenditure is fully matched by increase in taxes (*i.e.* $G = T$) we have a balanced budget but it will still have a expansionary effect on national income, though, as shall be explained below, the multiplier effect of a balanced budget is equal to one.

2. Note that all expenditure by the Government is here treated as consumption expenditure

However, since in case of balanced budget increase in Government expenditure is matched by increase in taxes which reduces disposable income $Y_d = Y - T$. And reduction in disposable income (Y_d) leads to decrease in both consumption and saving ($Y_d = C + S$). This decrease in private saving will cause rate of interest to rise and thereby crowds out private investment.

Further, when the Government has a *budget surplus* (i.e. $T > G$), it has a *positive saving* which will lead to the increase in national saving and make more funds available for private sector to borrow. This will cause real rate of interest to fall. As a result, higher private investment will occur in case of surplus budget.

It is worth noting that in our above analysis Government expenditure has been treated as consumption expenditure on goods and services purchased to satisfy collective wants. However, this is strictly true in case of a purely free-market economy such as that of the US where the Government is not a major investor. But in case of India's mixed economy the Government is an important investor and a good part of its borrowing is used for investment purposes, especially for investment in infrastructure projects such as transport, highways, roads, ports etc. Such Government borrowing for investment purposes cannot be considered as consumption expenditure or *dissaving*. Therefore, it has a large expansionary effect on national income with a usual multiplier effect. Viewed as such Government borrowing for investment, especially for infrastructure projects in developing countries, may *crowd in* private investment rather than crowding it out. This is so because lack of adequate infrastructure hinders private investment.

Determination of National Income with Government Expenditure and a Lump Sum Tax

Now, in a three sector model we analyse the impact of Government expenditure when to finance this expenditure the government levies a lump sum tax. Note that a lump-sum tax does not vary with income. In this case if government expenditure equals revenue from lump-sum tax, its budget will be in *balance*. On the other hand, if government expenditure exceeds tax revenue, there will be a *budget deficit*. Further, if tax revenue is more than its expenditure, government will have a *surplus budget*. We are thus concerned here with the impact of government expenditure and taxation together on the determination of national income. Let us assume *the government follows a balanced budget policy* in which case government expenditure equals tax revenue from lump-sum tax. Let us assume that there are no *transfer payments* made by the government.

The simplest kind of a tax is the *lump-sum tax* in which a given fixed amount of revenue is collected irrespective of the level of income. Suppose government has decided to raise extra Rs. 500 crore by way of imposing lump-sum tax on the public.

Every one will have to pay the fixed amount out of his income as his share of lump sum tax. In the aggregate, the disposable income of the economy will be reduced by this fixed amount of lump-sum tax *i.e.*, (500 crore) whatever the level of national income (GNP). Consequently, people will consume less after the levy of lump-sum tax. A lump-sum tax of Rs. 500 crores imposed by the Government will reduce the disposable income by the same amount, that is, by Rs. 500 crores. As a result, the people will consume less (and also save less) at each level of national income (GNP). However, it is worth mentioning that *consumption will not fall by the full amount of the tax* because a part of the reduction in disposable income due to the tax was being consumed and a part of it was being saved prior to taxation. Therefore, reduction in disposable income due to the lump-sum tax will partly cause a decline in consumption and partly a decline in saving. Therefore, the amount by which consumption will fall due to the introduction of lump-sum tax will be equal to the amount of tax multiplied by the marginal propensity to consume. If ΔY_d stand for change in disposable income, T for tax imposed and MPC for marginal propensity to consume, then the decline in consumption ($-\Delta C$) due to the imposition of lump sum tax is given by

$$-\Delta C = T.MPC$$

Since a lump-sum tax causes a change in disposable income (Y_d)

Therefore tax, $T = \Delta Y_d$

$$-\Delta C = \Delta Y_d \,.\, MPC$$

Let us take an example. If the aggregate amount collected by way of lump-sum tax is Rs. 500 crore and *MPC* is 0.75, then the decline in consumption ($-\Delta C$)due to lump-sum tax will be Rs. 500 × 0.75 = Rs. 375 crores.

On the contrary, *if lump-sum tax is reduced*, the consumption will increase by the amount of reduction in the lump-sum tax multiplied by the marginal propensity to consume ($+\Delta C = +\,\Delta Y_d.$ *MPC*).

The impact of imposition of lump-sum tax on consumption function is graphically shown in Figure 5B.3. It will be seen from this figure that introduction of lump-sum tax shifts the consumption function curve *C* downward to the new position *C'* by the amount given by the tax amount multiplied by the *MPC*. Similarly, the reduction in lump-sum income tax shifts the consumption function curve upward to *C''*.

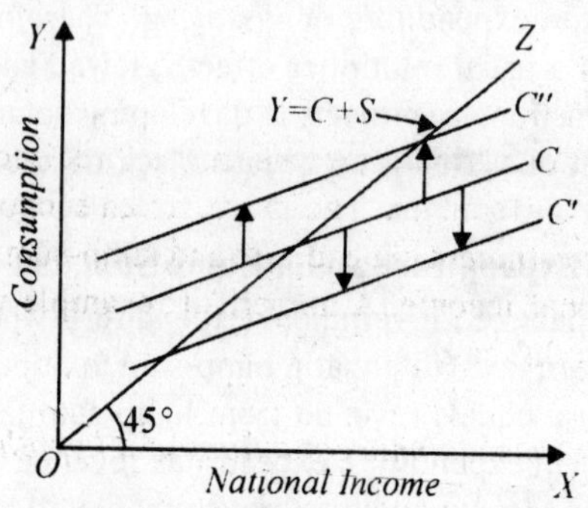

Fig. 5B.3. *Effect of Lump-Sum Tax on Consumption Function*

Fig. 5B.4. *Effect of Lump-Sum Tax on National Income*

Figure 5B.4 shows the effect of imposition of lump-sum tax on the equilibrium level of national income (GNP). It will be observed from Figure 5B.4 that due to lump-sum tax equal to *T*, and consequently downward shift in aggregate expenditure curve to the new dotted position $C'' + I + G$, the equilibrium level of national income falls from OY_0 to OY_1. An important point worth mentioning is that the fall in the level of income ($-\Delta Y$) is not equal to the amount of tax (*T*) collected but by a multiple of it, tax multiplier being equal to $\frac{-b}{1-b}$ where *b* stands for marginal propensity to consume. Thus, $\frac{-b}{1-b}$ or $\frac{-MPC}{1-MPC}$ is **tax multiplier of a lump-sum tax**. We will explain this tax multiplier in detail in a later section. It will be seen that tax multiplier is negative.

It will be seen from Figure 5B.4 that *if Government reduces lump sum income tax*, the consumption function curve shifts upward to the new position C''. From this it follows that *reduction in tax by the government will increase the disposaible income of the society and raise consumption demand. The rise in consumption demand will raise the equilibrium level of income by a multiple amount depending on the marginal propensity to consume.*

Algebraic Analysis

Three sector model with the above specifications can be developed as follows :

$$Y = AD = C + \bar{I} + \bar{G}$$

or

$$Y = C + \bar{I} + \bar{G} \qquad ...(i)$$

Now, consumption function can be stated as :

$$C = a + bY_d$$

Where a is constant autonomous consumption expenditure, Y_d is disposable income. In this three sector model with lump-sum tax and no transfer payments, consumption function can be written as

$$C = a + b(Y - T)$$

where T = lump-sum tax

or $C = a + bY - bT$

Substituting the value of C in income equation (i) we have

$$Y = a + bY - bT + \bar{I} + \bar{G}$$

$$Y - bY = a - bT - \bar{I} + \bar{G}$$

$$Y(1-b) = a - bT + \bar{I} + \bar{G}$$

$$Y = \frac{1}{1-b}\left(a - bT + \bar{I} + \bar{G}\right) \quad ...(ii)$$

The equation (ii) furnishes us the equilibrium level of national income in the three sector economy when there is both government expenditure and lump sum tax. Therefore, for an economy if the data regarding consumption function, investment, Government expenditure and lump-sum tax are given we can compute the equilibrium level of national income. A numerical example will clarify the determination of equilibrium level of income in this case.

Numerical Examples

Problem 1. *The following data characterises the macroeconomic conditions of a hypothetical economy*

$C = 50 + 0.8\, Y_d$

$I = 100$

$G = T = 75$

where C, I, and Y_d are consumption, investment and disposable income respectively. Calculate equilibrium income of the economy. What is the value of multiplier?

Solution: Note that since $G = T$, budget of the Government is balanced.

$Y = C + I + G$

$C = a + bY_d = a + b(Y - T)$

Substituting the values of C, I and G we have :

$$Y = 50 + 0.8\,(Y - 75) + 100 + 75$$

$$= 50 + 0.8Y - 60 + 100 + 75$$

$$Y = 165 + 0.8Y$$

$$Y - 0.8Y = 165$$

$$Y(1 - 0.8) = 165$$

$$0.2\,Y = 165$$

$$Y = 165 \times \frac{10}{2} = 825$$

Thus, equilibrium level of income is 825.

Value of multiplier of autonomous consumption (50) and autonomous investment (100) is

$$\frac{1}{1-b} = \frac{1}{1-mpc}$$

$$= \frac{1}{1-mpc} = \frac{1}{1-0.8} = \frac{1}{0.2}$$

$$= \frac{10}{2} = 5$$

Since in the present case $G = T$, there is a balanced budget, therefore

$$\text{value of balanced budget multiplier} = \frac{1}{1-b} + \frac{-b}{1-b}$$

$$= \frac{1}{1-0.8} + \frac{-0.8}{1-0.8} = \frac{1}{0.2} + \frac{-0.8}{0.2} = 5 - 4 = 1$$

Therefore, due to multiplier (5) of autonomous consumption and investment (50 + 100) income increases by 150 × 5 = 750 and since value of balance budget multiplier is 1, Government expenditure and tax (= 75) causes income to rise by 1 × 75 = 75. Therefore, the equilibrium level of national income = 750 + 75 = 825.

Problem 2. *You are given the following data for an economy*

Consumption $C = 20 + 0.8\,Y_d$
Investment $I = 50$
Government expenditure $G = 20$
Taxes $T = 10$

Find (a) equilibrium level of income (b) If lump sum taxes increase by 10 (i) what is the equilibrium level of income, and (ii) lump sum tax multiplier

(c) If government expenditure decreases by 10, what is (i) equilibrium level of income, (ii) Government expenditure multiplier

(d) Can you explain the difference between in the answer for (b) and (c)

DU. BA(Hons.) 2006

Ans. (*a*) $Y = C + I + G$

$$C = 20 + 0.8\,Y_d = 20 + 0.8\,(Y - T)$$
$$= 20 + 0.8\,(Y - 10)$$
$$I = 50 \text{ and } G = 20, \text{ and } T = 10$$
$$\therefore \quad Y = 20 + 0.8\,(Y - 10) + 50 + 20$$
$$= 20 + 0.8\,Y - 8 + 50 + 20$$
$$Y - 0.8Y = 82$$
$$Y(1 - 0.8) = 82$$
$$Y = \frac{82}{1-0.8} = \frac{82}{0.2} = 82 \times \frac{10}{2} = 410$$

(*b*) (*i*) With increase in lump sum tax by 10, the change in equilibrium level of income will be

$$\Delta Y = \Delta T \times \text{Lump Sum Tax Multiplier}$$
$$= 10 \times \frac{-b}{1-b} \text{ where } b = MPC = 0.8$$
$$= 10 \times \frac{-0.8}{1-0.8} = 10 \times \frac{-0.8}{0.2} = -40$$

Therefore, new equilibrium level of income is 410 – 40 = 370

(*b*) (*i*) Lump Sum Tax Multiplier $= \frac{-b}{1-b} = \frac{-0.8}{1-0.8} = \frac{-0.8}{0.2} = -4$

(*c*) (*i*) With decrease in government expenditure by 10 the change in equilibrium level of income

$$\Delta Y = -\Delta G \times \frac{1}{1-b} = -10 \times \frac{1}{1-0.8} = -10 \times \frac{1}{0.2}$$

$$= -10 \times \frac{10}{2} = -50$$

Therefore, new equilbrium level of income = 410 – 50 = 360

(*ii*) Government expenditure multiplier $= \frac{1}{1-b} = \frac{1}{1-0.8} = \frac{1}{0.2} = 5$

(*d*) *Explaining the difference in the Impact of decrease in Government Expenditure and increase in Lump-sum tax.*

A decrease in Government expenditure causes a decrease in aggregate expenditure by the same amount and will therefore have a greater impact on income. On the other hand, increase in lump-sum tax which will cause reduction in disposable income by the same amount but reduction in expenditure will be smaller because households will cut their consumption expenditure by the amount of tax multiplied by marginal propensity to consume. Thus, in this case decrease in consumption expenditure ($-\Delta C$) will be equal to $-\Delta T \times MPC$, that is, $-\Delta C = \Delta T \times MPC$. Thus, if lump sum tax is increased by Rs. 10, then, given $MPC = 0.8$, the decrease in consumption expenditure will be 10×0.8 = Rs. 8, that is, less than Rs. 10.

Determination of National Income in the Three Sector Economy with Lump-Sum Tax and Transfer Payments

We have explained above the determination of national income in the three sector economy when government expenditure is financed by imposition of lump sum tax. We now extend our model to include transfer payments and see how they affect determination of national income. *Transfer payments are payments to the people by the government for which it receives no service or goods in return from them*. Transfer payments are made by the government to promote social welfare. Unemployment allowance, poverty relief grants, social security contributions, old age pension are some important examples of transfer payments. Transfer payments are antithesis of tax. Whereas tax reduces disposable income of the people, transfer payments increase their disposable income.

Transfer payments may be autonomous of tax or they may be financed by imposition of a lump sum tax. If, like the government expenditure on goods and services, transfer payments are financed through tax, then transfer payments become a part of government expenditure (*G*) and imposition of additional tax to finance transfer payments become a part of total lump sum tax (*T*) which reduces disposable income. Therefore, in this case when transfer payments are financed through additional taxes, the analysis of income determination is similar to the model of income determination with government expenditure and lump sum tax explained above. However, the inclusion of transfer payments which are of autonomous type makes the analysis of income determination somewhat different. We describe it below.

Since transfer payments increase the disposable income of the people, they will increase their consumption expenditure depending on their propensity to consume. Thus

$$C = a + bY_d$$

$$Y_d = Y - T + TR$$

where T is lump sum tax and TR is transfer payments

$$\therefore \quad C = a + b(Y - T + TR)$$

$$Y = C + I + G$$

$$= a + b(Y - T + TR) + I + G$$

$$Y = a + bY - bT + bTR + I + G$$

$$Y - bY = a - bT + bTR + I + G$$

$$Y(1-b) = a - bT + bTR + I + G$$

$$Y = \frac{1}{1-b}(a - bT + bTR + I + G) \qquad \text{... (ii)}$$

Government Expenditure Multiplier and Transfer Payments Multiplier

It is important to note that the multiplier of government expenditure on goods and services is different from transfer payments multiplier. This is because whereas Government expenditure on goods and services raises aggregate demand directly by its full amount, the transfer payments raises consumption demand by bTR, that is, *less than the full amount* depending on the marginal propensity to consume. Let us illustrate it by using income equation (*ii*).Suppose government expenditure increases by ΔG. Then, increased income is

$$Y + \Delta Y = \frac{1}{1-b}(a - bT + bTR + I + G + \Delta G) \qquad \text{...(iii)}$$

Subtracting equation (*ii*) from equation (*iii*) we have

$$\Delta Y = \frac{1}{1-b}(\Delta G)$$

or
$$\frac{\Delta Y}{\Delta G} = \frac{1}{1-b}$$

Thus, **Government expenditure multiplier,** $\frac{\Delta Y}{\Delta G} = \frac{1}{1-b}$.

If instead of increase in government expenditure on goods and services, government increases transfer payments by ΔTR we will get the following income equation

$$Y + \Delta Y = \frac{1}{1-b}\left(a - bT + bTR + b\Delta TR + I + G\right) \qquad \text{... (iv)}$$

Subtracting equation (*ii*) from equation (*iv*) we have

$$\Delta Y = \frac{1}{1-b} b\Delta TR$$

or
$$\frac{\Delta Y}{\Delta TR} = \frac{b}{1-b}$$

Thus, **transfer payments multiplier,** $\frac{\Delta Y}{\Delta TR} = \frac{b}{1-b}$

Taking the difference between the Government expenditure multiplier and transfer payments multiplier we have

$$\frac{1}{1-b} - \frac{b}{1-b} = \frac{1-b}{1-b} = 1$$

Numerical Example

Problem. *Suppose the structural model of an economy is given below :*

$C = 100 + 0.75\, Y_d$

$I = 200$

$G = T = 100$

$TR = 50$

where G is government expenditure on goods and services, T is lump sum tax and TR are transfer payments

(1) *Find the equilibrium level of income*

(2) *Calculate Government expenditure multiplier and transfer payments multiplier. What is the difference between the two ?*

(3) *If full-employment level of income is 1600 crores, how much government expenditure be increased to attain full employment ?*

Solution :

$$Y = C + I + G$$
$$= a + bY_d + I + G$$

Disposable income $Y_d = Y - T + TR$

Therefore, $Y = a + b(Y - T + TR) + I + G$

Substituting the values of various parameters and variables we have

$$Y = 100 + 0.75\,(Y - 100 + 50) + 200 + 100$$
$$= 100 + 0.75Y - 75 + 37.5 + 200 + 100$$
$$Y - 0.75Y = 100 - 75 + 37.5 + 200 + 100$$
$$Y(1 - 0.75) = 362.5$$
$$0.25\,Y = 362.5$$
$$Y = 362.5 \times \frac{100}{25} = 1450$$

Thus, equilibrium income is 1450 crores

(2) Government expenditure multiplier $(G_m) = \frac{1}{1-b} = \frac{1}{1-0.75} = \frac{1}{0.25}$

$$= 4$$

Transfer payments multiplier $(TR_m) = \frac{b}{1-b} = \frac{0.75}{1-0.75} = \frac{0.75}{0.25}$

$$= 3$$

The difference between G_m and TR_m is $4 - 3 = 1$

(3) The equilibrium income of Rs. 1450 crores falls short of full-employment income of 1600 crores by $1600 - 1450 = 150$ crores. ΔG required to achieve full employment income is given by

$$\Delta Y = G_m \times \Delta G$$

or $$\Delta G = \frac{\Delta Y}{G_m}$$ (G_m is government expenditure multiplier)

$$= \frac{150}{4} = 37.5 \text{ crores}$$

Proportional Income Tax and Equilibrium Level of National Income

Now, instead of lump sum tax, if Government levies proportional income tax how it will affect the consumption function curve and the equilibrium level of income. With proportional income tax, a *fixed percentage* of income is collected as tax, irrespective of the level of income. If an income tax at the rate of 25 per cent of income is levied regardless of the level of income, it will be an example of a proportional income tax. As in case of lump-sum tax, the introduction of proportional income tax will reduce the disposable income. This will bring about decline in the amount of consumption and saving at each level of real national income. However, in case of proportional income tax consumptionwill not fall by the same amount at each level of income but instead it will fall by the *same percentage of the level of income.* Therefore, as a result of proportional income tax, the consumption function curve rotates downward (with point *a* as a pivot) to the right, so that the fall in amount of consumption varies but fall as a pecentage of income level remains the same. This is shown in fig. 5B.5 where the vertical distance between the consumption function curve *C* before tax and the consumption function curve *C′* after tax is equal to the fall in consumption due to the proportional income tax. It is however worth noting that in case of proportional income tax at *each level of real national income, consumption falls by the tax revenue multiplied by the marginal propnesity to consume.*

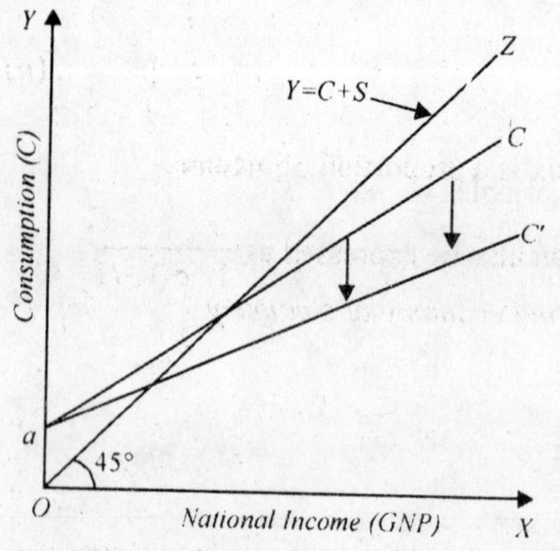

Fig. 5B.5. *Effect of Proportional Income Tax on Consumption Function*

Fig. 5B.6. *Effect of Proportional Income Tax on Aggregate Demand and National Income*

In figure 5B.6 we have shown the effect of proportional income tax on the equilibrium level of national income tax. As a result of imposition of proportional income tax, the aggregate demand curve $C + I + G$ rotates downward due to the downward rotation of consumption function curve. It will be seen from Figure 5A.5 that due to imposition of prooprotional income tax, the equilibrium level of national income falls from OY_0 to OY_1. It may be noted that other things remaining the same, the higher rate of proportional income tax, the greater the fall in consumption and, therefore, the greater the decline in equilibrium level of national income.

THREE SECTOR MODEL FURTHER EXTENDED*
(Incorporating Proportional Income Tax)

So far in our above analysis of determination of equilibrium national income in a three sector economy we have assumed autonomous constant investment, apart from consumption function of households and Government expenditure on goods and services and transfer payments. In the further extension of the model we also include *proportional income tax*, that is, a tax levied as a fixed percentage or proportion of income irrespective the level of income . Mathematically proportional income tax is therefore expressed as tY where t is the rate or proportion of income which is payable as a tax. In a real economy proportional income tax may be imposed along with any lump sum tax. Thus, the total tax (T) can be expressed as

$$T = tY$$

where t = rate or proportion of income tax

Y = Income

Equilibrium income, $Y = C + I + G$ ...(*i*)

where $C = a + bY_d$

$$= a + b(Y - tY + TR)$$

* This section is meant for Honours and Postgraduate Students.

Substituting the consumption function in equation (*i*) for equilibrium income we have

$$Y = a + b(Y - tY + TR) + I + G$$

$$= a + bY - btY + bTR + I + G$$

$$Y - bY + btY = a + bTR + I + G$$

$$Y(1 - b + bt) = a + bTR + I + G$$

$$Y = \frac{1}{1 - b + bt}(a + bTR + I + G) \quad ...(ii)$$

Note that $\frac{1}{1-b+bt}$ represents tax multiplier when tax is a proportion of income.

Tax multiplier with tax as a proportion of income can also be expressed as $\frac{1}{1-b(1-t)}$.

Problem 1. *Given the following information about the economy of a country.*

Consumption function, $C = 85 + 0.5\,Y_d$

Investment function, $I = 85$

Government spending $G = 60$

Net Taxes, $T = 40 + 0.25\,Y$

(*i*) *Solve for equilibrium income and consumption*

(*ii*) *How much does the government collect in net taxes when the economy is in equilibrium*

(*iii*) *What is the government's budget deficit, or surplus.* **DU, B.A (Hons.) 2007**

Solution.(*i*) Equilibrium income (Y) = $C + I + G$

$$C = 85 + 0.5\,Y_d$$

Since $Y_d = Y - T$

$$C = 85 + 0.5[Y - (40 + 0.25Y)]$$

$$= 85 + 0.5Y - 20 - 0.125\,Y$$

$$= 65 + 0.375\,Y$$

$$Y = C + I + G$$

$$= 65 + 0.375\,Y + 85 + 60$$

$$Y - 0.375Y = 210$$

$$Y(1 - 0.375) = 210$$

$$Y = \frac{210}{1-0.375} = \frac{210}{0.625} = 210 \times \frac{1000}{625}$$

$$= 336$$

(*i*) Equilibrium income is 336

and Equilibrium Consumption $= 65 + 0.375\,Y$

$$= 65 + 0.375 \times 336$$

$$= 65 + 126$$

$$= 191$$

(*ii*) Tax money collected by the Government

$$T = 40 + 0.25Y$$

$$= 40 + 0.25 \times 336$$

$$= 40 + 84$$

$$= 124$$

(*iii*)*Government budget deficit or surplus*, Since government expenditure (G) is less than its tax revenue, there will be surplus budget.

Budget surplus $= 124 - 60 = 64$

Numerical Example 2. *For an economy the following data is given :*

Consumption (C) = 100 + 0.8 Y.

Investment (I) = 150

Government Expenditure (G) = 75

Rate of income tax (T) = 0.25Y

(a) Find the equilibrium level of income.

(b) What is the value of multiplier with tax and without tax.

Ans. Reduced form for the equilibrium level of income is

$$Y = \frac{1}{1-b+bt}(a+I+G)$$

Given $b = 0.8$, $t = 0.25$, $a = 100$, $I = 150$ and $G = 75$. Substituting these values in equation for equilibrium income we have

$$Y = \frac{1}{1-0.8+08\times 0.25}(100+150+75)$$

$$= \frac{1}{1-0.8+0.2}(325)$$

$$= \frac{1}{1-0.6}(325) = \frac{1}{0.4}(325)$$

$$Y = 2.5\,(325)$$
$$= 812.5$$

The value of proportional tax multiplier $= \dfrac{1}{1-b+bt}$

$$= \frac{1}{1-0.8+0.8\times 0.25}$$

$$= \frac{1}{1-0.6} = \frac{1}{0.4}$$
$$= 2.5$$

The value of multiplier without tax $= \dfrac{1}{1-b} = \dfrac{1}{1-0.8} = \dfrac{1}{0.2} = 5$

Numerical Problem 3. *For a closed economy, the following data is given*

Consumption, $C = 50 + 0.8Y_d$

Investment, $I = 70$

Government expenditure, $G = 200$

Transfer payments, $TR = 100$

Rate of Income Tax, $t = 0.2Y$

(a) *Write the reduced form of equation for equilibrium income*

(b) *Find out equilibrium income*

(c) *What is the value of multiplier ?*

Solution :

(a) Reduced form of the equation for equilibrium income is

$$Y = \frac{1}{1-b+bt}(a+bTR+I+G)$$

(b) Substituting the values of parameters in the above equation for equilibrium income we have

$$Y = \frac{1}{1-0.8+0.8\times0.2}(50+0.8\times100+70+200)$$

$$= \frac{1}{1-0.64}(50+80+70+200)$$

$$= \frac{1}{0.36}(400)$$

$$= 400\times\frac{100}{36} = 1111$$

Thus, the equilibrium income is 1111

$$\text{Tax Multiplier} = \frac{1}{1-b+bt} = \frac{1}{1-0.8+0.8\times0.2}$$

$$= \frac{1}{1-0.64} = \frac{1}{0.36}$$

$$= \frac{100}{36} = 2.77$$

THE LUMP-SUM-TAX MULTIPLIER

We have explained the multiplier effect of change in Government expenditure on goods and services and of change in transfer payments (*TR*) on the equilibrium level of income. We will now explain the multiplier effect of *change in tax*. Reduction in taxes has often been used by the policy makers to increase aggregate demand of the economy and thereby to lift the economy out of recession. For example, in 1964 John F Kennedy, the president of the United States made a substantial cut in personal and corporate taxes to stimulate expenditure on consumption and investment to bring about expansion in income and employment in the economy. This policy of cut in taxes to revive the American economy had a grand success. There was a large growth in Gross Domestic Product (GDP) of the United States in 1964 and 1965. There was a substantial fall in unemployment as a result of the policy of cut in taxes.

Recently when George Bush was elected president in 2001 the American economy found itself in the grip of recession. He also made a drastic cut in income tax to stimulate aggregate demand so as to overcome recession. Again this policy of tax cut was greatly successful and the American economy recovered in 2003-04.

The change in lump sum income tax and proportional income tax affect equilibrium income differently, but both have a multiplier effect on equilibrium income. We have already explained the effect of lump-sum income tax and proportional income tax on the equilibrium level of income. We are now concerned with analysing the effect of change in lump sum tax and proportional income tax. For the sake of simplicity and convenience we explain the multiplier effect of lump sum income tax.

Note that while a cut in tax will have a positive effect on equilibrium income, increase in tax will reduce equilibrium income.

Suppose the government *increases lump-sum income tax* by ΔT we are interested to know its multiplier effect on income. As found above, in the three sector economy with Government expenditure and lump-sum tax :

$$Y=\frac{1}{1-b}(a-bT+I+G) \quad \text{...(1)}$$

where T is lump sum income tax. Now, a decrease in lump-sum income tax by ΔT will cause a change in income (that is, ΔY). Increase in tax will reduce the disposable income and therefore the consumption demand. As a result of increase in tax, consumption demand will decrease by the change in tax times the marginal propensity consume, that is, $\Delta Y = b\Delta T$. Let us incorporate change in the tax (ΔT) in the three sector equation (1) for equilibrium income and see how much change in income (ΔY) it brings about. Thus

$$Y+\Delta Y=\frac{1}{1-b}[a-b(T+\Delta T)+I+G]$$

$$Y+\Delta Y=\frac{1}{1-b}(a-bT-b\Delta T+I+G) \quad \text{...(2)}$$

Now subtracting equation (1) from equation (2) we have

$$\Delta Y=\frac{1}{1-b}(-b\Delta T)$$

Dividing both sides by ΔT we have

$$\frac{\Delta Y}{\Delta T}=\frac{-b}{1-b} \quad \text{...(3)}$$

$\frac{\Delta Y}{\Delta T}$ is the expression for tax multiplier. It will be seen that tax multiplier is *negative*. It will be seen that increase in tax by ΔT will *reduce* equilibrium income by a multiple. For example, if marginal propensity to consume is 0.75, then the tax multiplier is

$$\frac{\Delta Y}{\Delta T}=\frac{-b}{1-b}=\frac{-0.75}{1-0.75}=\frac{-0.75}{0.25}=-3$$

This means that increase in tax by Re. 1 will cause a decline in equilibrium income by 3.

Note that we can similarly prove that a *cut in tax* will *raise* the equilibrium income through the tax multiplier. Therefore, in case of *reduction in lump sum income tax*, the tax multiplier is

$$\frac{\Delta Y}{\Delta T}=\frac{b}{1-b}$$

With 0.75 as marginal propensity to consume, tax multiplier of cut in tax is,

$$\frac{\Delta Y}{\Delta T}=\frac{0.75}{1-0.75}=\frac{0.75}{0.25}=3.$$

Problem. *The following specifications are given for an economy*
Consumption, $C = 250 + 0.75\,Y_d$ *where* Y_d *is disposable income*
Government expenditure $G = 150$
Investment $I = 80$
Taxes $T = 200$

(i) Find the equilibrium level of income (Y), Consumption (C) and Private Sector Saving (S_P)
(ii) Using the value of tax multiplier how much will income increase if taxes are reduced by 30
DU BA (Hons.) 2009

Ans. Equilibrium

$$Y = C + I + G$$

$$C = 250 + 0.75\, Y_d$$

$$= 250 + 0.75\,(Y - T)$$

$$= 250 + 0.75\,(Y - 200)$$

$$Y = 250 + 0.75\,(Y - 200) + 80 + 150$$

$$= 250 + 0.75Y - 150 + 80 + 150$$

$$(Y - 0.75Y) = 250 - 150 + 80 + 150$$

$$Y(1 - 0.75) = 330$$

$$Y = \frac{330}{1-0.75} = \frac{330}{0.25} = 330 \times \frac{100}{25} = 1320$$

$$\text{Consumption, } C = 250 + 0.75\,(Y - T)$$

$$= 250 + 0.75\,(1320 - 200)$$

$$= 250 + \frac{75}{100} \times 1120$$

$$= 250 + 840$$

$$\text{or } \quad C = 1090$$

$$\text{Private Sector Saving } (S_p) = \text{Disposable income} - \text{Consumption}$$

$$\text{Disposable Income} = Y - T$$

$$\text{Private Saving } S_p = Y - T - C$$

$$= 1320 - 200 - 1090$$

$$= 30$$

(*ii*) The *decrease* in taxes will lead to increase in income by raising consumption expenditure.

$$\text{Tax multiplier when taxes are reduced} = \frac{b}{1-b}$$

$$\text{Decrease in Taxes} \qquad - 30$$

$$\text{Increase in Income} \qquad = \Delta T \times \frac{b}{1-b}$$

$$= 30 \times \frac{0.75}{1-0.75}$$

$$= 30 \times \frac{0.75}{0.25} = 90$$

BALANCED BUDGET MULTIPLIER

We now analyse the impact of balanced budget of the government. In case of a balanced budget, the government's expenditure is equal to its tax revenue, that is, $G = T$ and therefore when the government increases its expenditure by ΔG, then it also raises taxes to get more tax revenue (ΔT) so that $\Delta T = \Delta G$. The effect of a balanced budget on the equilibrium income is described by the *balanced budget multiplier* which is also called *balanced budget theorem*. According to this, the *balanced budget multiplier is always equal to one.* We prove it below by assuming a lump sum tax.

In order to analyse the effect of a balanced budget multiplier, we reproduce below the equation for equilibrium income for a three sector economy.

$$Y = \frac{1}{1-b}\left(a - b\overline{T} + I + G\right) \quad \text{... (1)}$$

where $\overline{T}$ is constant lump sum tax levied by the government.

Let us incorporate increase in government expenditure (ΔG) fully financed by additional lump sum tax (ΔT), that is, $\Delta G = \Delta T$. By doing so we get

$$Y + \Delta Y = \frac{1}{1-b}\left[a - b(\overline{T} + \Delta T) + I + G + \Delta G\right] \quad \text{...(2)}$$

Subtracting equation (1) from equation (2) we have

$$\Delta Y = \frac{1}{1-b}\left(-b\Delta T + \Delta G\right)$$

Since in a balanced budget, $\Delta T = \Delta G$

$$\Delta Y = \frac{1}{1-b}\left(-b\Delta G + \Delta G\right)$$

$$\Delta Y\,(1-b) = \Delta G\,(1-b)$$

or

$$\Delta Y = \Delta G \quad \text{...(3)}$$

Dividing both sides of the above equation by ΔG we have

$$\frac{\Delta Y}{\Delta G} = \frac{\Delta G}{\Delta G} = 1$$

Thus, balanced budget multiplier is equal to one. This implies that when $\Delta G = \Delta T$ and budget is therefore balanced, national income increases by the same amount as the increase in government expenditure.

Alternative Proof

That the balanced budget multiplier is equal to one can be proved in an alternative way. Balance budget multiplier is the sum of government expenditure multiplier and lump-sum tax multiplier.

Government expenditure multiplier (G_m) = $\frac{1}{1-b}$

where b represents marginal propensity to conseve

Lump-sum tax multiplier (T_m) = $\frac{-b}{1-b}$

Balanced budget multiplier = $G_m + T_m$

$$= \frac{1}{1-b} + \frac{-b}{1-b}$$

$$= \frac{1-b}{1-b} = 1$$

Thus, the balanced budget multiplier is equal to one.

NUMERICAL EXAMPLES

Problem. *Suppose we have an economy characterised by the following functions :*

$$C = 100 + 0.8\,Y_d$$

$\bar{I} = 100$

$\bar{G} = 100$

$\bar{T} = 100$

(Figures are in crores)

(*a*) *Find the equilibrium level of income.*

(*b*) *How much increase in income will take place if government expenditure on goods and services increases by Rs. 60 crores.*

(*c*) *Find the tax multiplier and balanced budget multiplier*

(*d*) *Find the equilibrium level of national income if* $T = \bar{T} + tY = 100 + 0.25Y$.

Solution :

(*a*) Equilibrium $Y = C + \bar{I} + \bar{G}$

$$Y = a + bY_d + \bar{I} + \bar{G}$$

Therefore, $Y = a + b(Y - \bar{T}) + \bar{I} + \bar{G}$

Substituting the values of *a*, *b*, $\bar{T}$, $\bar{I}$ and $\bar{G}$ we have

$$Y = 100 + 0.8\,(Y - 100) + 100 + 100$$
$$= 100 + 0.8Y - 80 + 100 + 100$$

$$Y - 0.8Y = 220$$
$$Y(1 - 0.8) = 220$$
$$0.2Y = 220$$
$$Y = 220 \times \frac{10}{2} = 1100$$

(*b*) Government expenditure multiplier (G_m) = $\frac{1}{1-b} = \frac{1}{1-0.8} = 5$

Increase in national income if government expenditure increases by 60 crores.

$$\Delta Y = G_m . \Delta G$$
$$= 5 \times 60 = 300$$

(*c*) Tax multiplier, $T_m = \frac{-b}{1-b} = \frac{-0.8}{1-0.8} = \frac{-0.8}{0.2}$

$$= -4$$

Balanced Budget Multiplier = $G_m + T_m$

$= 5 + (-4)$

$= 1$

(*d*) The equilibrium level of national income when $T = \bar{T} + tY$ $100 + 0.25Y$

Note that $\bar{T}$ (= 100) is a fixed lump sum tax that does not vary with income while tY will vary with income (Y) depending on the value of t.

$$Y = \frac{1}{1-b+bt}\left(a - b\bar{T} + \bar{I} + \bar{G}\right)$$

$$= \frac{1}{1-0.8+0.2}(100 - 0.80 \times 100 + 100 + 100)$$

$$=\frac{1}{1-0.6}(100-80+100+100)$$

$$=\frac{1}{0.4}(220)$$

$$= 2.5\ (220) = 550$$

DETERMINATION OF NATIONAL INCOME IN AN OPEN ECONOMY: THE FOUR SECTOR MODEL

In modern times economies of different countries are integrated with each other though some are more integrated than others. An open economy is one which has not only trade relations with other countries but has financial capital flows between it and other economies of the world. It is because of such openness and integration of the economies of the world that recent financial crisis that occurred in the United States in 2007 has significantly affected other economies (including that of India) causing global meltdown through its affect on trade and capital flows. Under capital flows, funds flow from one country to another. Foreign trade of goods and services affect product market and influences the determination of national income of a country as net exports (*i.e.* exports–imports) is a part of aggregate demand for output produced by an economy. On the other hand, capital flows in an open economy provide funds for financing domestic investment or for financing government budget deficits. or financing current account deficit. If the demand for funds in an economy exceeds domestic national saving, the private sector and Government of an open economy can get them from abroad either through borrowing or direct investment by foreign investors. We start with the analysis of impact of inclusion of foreign trade on the determination of national income of a country.

Foreign Trade and National Income in an Open Economy

In the four sector model of determination of national income, we add the foreign trade sector to the three sectors, namely, households, firms, and Government. Foreign trade, that is, volume of exports and imports of a country also affects the level of national income of a country. We now extend the Keynesian model of determination of national income by including the effect of exports and imports of a country on the generation of income. For example, the exports of India represent the foreign demand and generates income for the Indian people. On the other hand, imports represent the demand for foreign goods by the Indians and generate incomes for the people of other countries. Therefore, imports tend to reduce the domestic aggregate expenditure. It therefore follows that national income will depend on the net exports, that is, exports minus imports $(X-M)$ where X stands for exports and M for imports. The exports and imports of a country depend to a great extent on the level of economic activity (that is, the level of output and income of the country). Thus, when the growth of industrial output in India is rapid, it will generate greater demand for imported materials. On the other hand, the higher industrial growth would also cause our exports to rise provided there is demand for our goods abroad. However, in the Keynesian model of income determination, exports and imports are considered as autonomous, that is, independent of income, being determined outside the model. Further, as mentioned above, the increase or decrease in aggregate expenditure or demand due to exports and imports depends on the *net exports*, that is, $X–M$ which we may write as NX. If the net exports are positive, there will be addition to the aggregate demand or expenditure of a country. On the other hand, if the net exports are negative, there will be decrease in aggregate expenditure.

When we include net exports (NX) in our analysis we get the following equation for the equilibrium level of income.

$$Y = C + I + G + (X - M)$$

where

$$C = a + b\,(Y - T) = a + bY - bT$$

$$Y = a + bY - bT + I + G + NX$$

or
$$Y(1-b) = a - bT + I + G + NX$$
$$Y = \frac{1}{1-b}(a - bT + I + G + NX)$$

Thus, the equilibrium level of income is the sum of all fixed autonomous expenditures (*i.e.*, $a - bT + I + G + NX$) times the value of multiplier $[1/1 - b]$. It is worth noting that in the four sector model, national income is determined at the level at which saving gap between consumption and income is equal to the sum of investment, Government expenditure and net exports. (that is, $I + G + NX$)

Graphic Illustration. In Fig. 5B.7, we have depicted the determination of national income when there are positive net exports (that is, when exports exceed imports, $X - M > 0$. To obtain the aggregate expenditure curve incorporating the positive net exports (NX) we add the $I + G + NX$ to the consumption function curve C to get the higher aggregate expenditure curve $C + I + G + NX$ which intersects the 45° line at point R and determines a level of income OY. If the net exports NX were negative, that is, imports exceed exports, $X - M < 0$, the aggregate demand curve incorporating net exports would lie at a lower level than $C + I + G$ curve and determine a lower level of income.

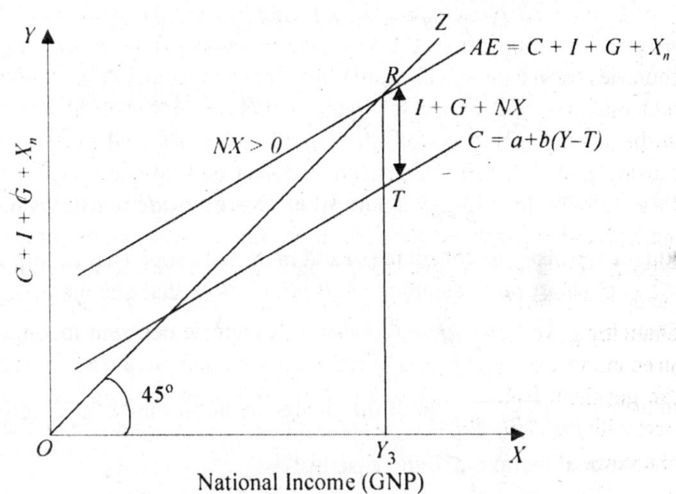

Fig. 5B.7. *Determination of National Income with Foreign Trade : Four Sector Model*

Four Sector Model Further Extended : Foreign Trade Multiplier

So far in our analysis of four sector model of income determination we have assumed that both exports and imports are constant autonomous items, that is, independent of income. In our later chapters concerning the external sector we shall explain in detail what are the factors that determine exports and imports of a country. In the model of income determination while exports are regarded as constant autonomous factor *determined exogenously* (that is, $X = \overline{X}$), imports are treated as function of two variables, namely, (1) autonomous imports (*i.e.* independent of income), and (2) level of income. Thus, import function used in the model can be written as

$$M = \overline{M} + mY$$

where $\overline{M}$ represents autonomous imports, mY represents imports dependent on level of income (Y) and m is marginal propensity to import. Given the marginal propensity to import (m), as income increases, mY will increase.

By incorporating the above import function we can derive the complete four sector model of income determination as follows

$$Y = C + I + G + (X - M) \qquad \ldots(i)$$

where $C = a + b(Y - T)$

and $$M = \overline{M} + mY$$

Substituting the consumption function and import function in the income equation ... (i) we have

$$Y = a + b(Y - T) + I + G + \left[X - \left(\bar{M} + mY\right)\right]$$

$$= a + bY - bT + I + G + X - \bar{M} - mY$$

$$Y - bY + mY = a - bT + I + G + X - \bar{M}$$

$$Y(1 - b + m) = a - bT + I + G + X - \bar{M}$$

$$Y = \frac{1}{1-b+m}(a - bT + I + G + X - \bar{M})$$

where the term $\frac{1}{1-b+m}$ is known as *foreign trade multiplier* whose value is determined by marginal propensity to consume (b) and marginal propensity to import (m). *Foreign trade multiplier is also known as open economy multiplier.* Note that change in any autonomous factor of the model such as X, G, I, a, $\bar{M}$ will cause a change in national income by the value of the foreign trade multiplier $\left(\frac{1}{1-b+m}\right)$ times the change in the amount of the factor. Thus, if exports increase by ΔX, the national income will increase by

$$\Delta Y = \frac{1}{1-b+m} . \Delta X$$

The value of foreign trade multiplier (i.e. open economy multiplier) is less than the closed economy investment or Government expenditure. This is because imports represents the demand for foreign goods and services and generate income for people of *other countries*. Like saving, imports represent leakage from the domestic income stream.

Incorporating Proportional Income Tax in the Four Sector Model

If in the above four sector model of income determination proportional income tax is incorporated, then only the term of foreign trade multiplier will change, the other terms of the model remaining the same. Thus, if income tax is of form $T = \bar{T} + tY$ where T is constant lump-sum, t is the proportion of income that is taken as tax. With incorporation of proporational income tax, the value of foreign trade multiplier becomes :

$$= \frac{1}{1 - b(1-t) + m}$$

or

$$= \frac{1}{1 - b + bt + m}$$

where t is the proportional income tax rate.

With this proportional income tax, the above equilibrium income equation can be written as

$$Y = \frac{1}{1 - b(1-t) + m}\left(a - bT + I + G + X - \bar{M}\right)$$

TRADE BALANCE (NET EXPORTS) AND FOREIGN CAPITAL FLOWS

In an open economy as in the closed economy product markets and capital markets are closely related. To know this relationship let us consider the equilibrium level of national income in an open economy which is :

$$Y = C + I + G + (X - M) \qquad \ldots \text{(i)}$$

where $X - M$ are net exports (N^X)

Therefore, rearranging the above equation and writing NX for $X - M$ we have

$$Y - C - G = I + NX \qquad \ldots (2)$$

Now $Y–C–G$ represents national saving[1] which we represent by S.

Writting S for national saving ($Y–C–G$) is equation (2) we have

$$S = I + NX \qquad \ldots (2)$$

or

$$S - I = NX \qquad \ldots (3)$$

From equation (3) it is evident that difference between domestic saving and domestic investment ($S - I$) equals net exports (NX). *Since difference between domestic saving and investment (S – I) represents capital flows*, equation (3) reveals that capital flows between an economy and the foreign ones are related to net exports (NX) which are also called *trade balance*. If for a country domestic saving exceeds domestic investment ($S > I$) then the country would have *positive* net *capital outflows* which means residents of the country would be lending or investing abroad more than the foreigners would be lending or investing in the country concerned. The equation (3) above shows that these *positive net capital outflows* imply that they will be equal to *positive net exports* (NX), that is, the country will be exporting more than it will be importing. Foreigners will need financial loans to buy that country's more goods and services than they are exporting to it. This has been the relationship with Japan and the US. Japan has a trade surplus (i.e. positive net exports) with the US and to enable the US to buy more Japanese goods than Japan is importing from it, it has been lending to the US which has been running a trade deficit, that is, there has been net capital outflows from Japan to the US.

Now, when domestic saving of a country is less than the domestic investment ($S < I$ or $S - I$ is negative), the equation (3) above reveals that the net exports (NX) will be negative (i.e., the country has a trade deficit) and, therefore, there will *net capital-inflow*. The net capital inflow implies that the country's will be borrowing from abroad or receiving foreign investment. The country having negative net exports or deficit trade balance requires foreign capital funds either through borrowing from foreigners or foreign investment so as to enable it to import more goods and services than it is exporting them. For example, in India we have a *deficit in the current account of balance of payments* (which has the same meaning as the concept of trade balance involving both goods and services) for several years now so that foriegn saving or capital inflow have contributed to the increase in investment in India. Though the share of capital inflows (foriegn savings) as a per cent of its GDP in India are relatively very small.

It follows from above that *international flow of capital to finance investment and international flow of goods and services are two sides of the same coin.*[2]

NUMERICAL PROBLEMS

Problem 1. *An economy is characterised by the following equations:*

C (Consumption)	=	$60 + 0.9Y_d$
I (Investment)	=	10
G (Government expenditure)	=	10
T (Tax)	=	0

1. Note that national saving $Y - C - G$ is the sum of private saving ($Y - T - C$) and Government saving ($T - G$). Thus $Y - T - C + T - G = Y - C - G$
2. See N. Gregory Mankiw, *Macroeconomics*, Worth Publishers, New York 5th edition, 2003, p. 118

X *(Exports)* $= 20$
M *(Imports)* $= 10 + 0.05\,Y$

(a) *What is the equilibrium income?*
(b) *Calculate trade balance.*
(c) *What is the value of foreign trade multiplier ?*

Solution : (*a*) *National Income*

$$Y = C + I + G + Nx$$
$$= (60 + 0.9\,Y_d) + 10 + 10 + 20 - (10 + 0.05Y)$$
$$= 60 + 0.9\,(Y - T) + 10 + 10 + 20 - 10 - 0.05Y$$
$$= 60 + 0.9Y - 0 + 30 - 0.05Y$$
$$Y = 90 + .85Y$$
$$Y - 0.85Y = 90$$
$$0.15Y = 90$$
$$Y = 90 \times \frac{100}{15} = 600$$

(*b*) *Trade Balance* $= X - M$
$$= 20 - (10 + 0.05Y)$$

Substituting the value of Y we have

$$\text{Trade balance} = 20 - \left(10 + \frac{5}{100} \times 600\right)$$
$$= 20 - 10 - 30 = -20$$

Trade balance is in deficit.

(*c*) *Value of foreign trade multiplier* $= \dfrac{1}{1 - b + m}$

Where b is marginal propensity to consume, and m is marginal propensity to import.

$$\text{Foreign trade multiplier} = \frac{1}{1 - 0.9 + 0.05}$$
$$= \frac{1}{1 - 0.85} = \frac{1}{0.15}$$
$$= \frac{100}{15} = 6.66$$

Problem 2. *Behavioural and structural equations of an economy are given below :*

$$C = 100 + b(Y - 50 - tY)$$
$$I = 50$$
$$G = 50$$
$$X = 10$$
$$M = 5 + 0.1Y$$

The marginal propensity to consume (b) *is equal to 0.8 and proportional income tax rate,* $t = 0.25$.

(*a*) *Find the equilibrium national income*
(*b*) *Find foreign trade multiplier*
(*c*) *Find equilibrium value of imports*
(*d*) *If equilibrium national income falls short of full-employment income by Rs. 50, how much government should increase its expenditure to attain full-employment.*

Solution :

(*a*) Reduced form of the equation for equilibrium income is

$$Y = \frac{1}{1-b(1-t)+m}(a - bT + I + G + X - \bar{M})$$

Substituting the values of the variables and parameters we have

$$Y = \frac{1}{1-0.8(1-0.25)+0.1}(100-50\times0.8+50+50+10-5)$$

$$Y = \frac{1}{1-0.8+0.2+0.1}(100-40+50+50+10-5)$$

$$= \frac{1}{0.5}(165)$$

$$= 2(165) = 330$$

(*b*) Foreign trade multiplier $= \dfrac{1}{1-b(1-t)+tm}$

$$= \frac{1}{1-0.8(1-0.25)+0.1}$$

$$= \frac{1}{1-0.8+0.2+0.1}$$

$$= \frac{1}{0.5} = 2$$

(*c*) Equilibrium value of imports can be obtained by substituting the equilibrium income (330) in the import function. Thus

$$M = 5 + 0.1Y$$
$$= 5 + 0.1 \times 330$$
$$= 38$$

(*d*) Required increase in Government expenditure to attain Rs. 50 increase in income can be obtained as under

$$\Delta Y = \text{Foreign Trade multiplier} \times \Delta G$$
$$\Delta Y = 2 \times \Delta G$$

Or $$\Delta G = \frac{\Delta Y}{2} = \frac{50}{2} = 25$$

EXERCISES

1. How does Government expenditure on goods and services affect level of national income ? Has it a multiplier effect ? What is the value of government expenditure multiplier.
2. Show that with Government expenditure in a three sector economy (households, firms and Government) equilibrium of national income is established at the level where sum of investment and Government expenditure ($I + G$) is equal to the amount of saving.
3. Show how the increase in Government expenditure without raising taxes (*i.e.* incurring budget deficit) affects national income, real rate of interest and private investment. Illustrate diagrammatically.
4. It is often asserted that budget deficit crowds out private investment. Do you agree ? Explain.
5. Show what will be the effect of cut in government expenditure without reduction in taxes (creating budget surplus in this way) affect equilibrium national income, real rate of interest and private investment in the economy.

[**Hints.** A cut in government expenditure without reducing taxes leads to increase in public saving (*i.e.* $T - G$ increases). This causes a shift in national saving curve to the right and leads to the fall in rate of interest and increase in private investment.

6. Show how does a cut in taxes without being balanced by cut in government expenditure affect real interest rate and investment.

7. What is effect of a balanced budget (*i.e.* increasing government expenditure matched by increase in equal amount of taxes) on national income, real interest rate and investment

8. Explain how balanced budget has an expansionary effect. What is value of balanced budget multiplier ? Explain.

9. How does cut in direct taxes lead to increase in national income ? What is the size of lump-sum tax multiplier ?

10. Assuming full-employment in an economy balanced budget *increase* in taxes and Government expenditure will reduce consumption and investment and raise the real interest rate ? Explain.

11. Assuming full-employment prevails in an economy, increased government expenditure matched by taxes crowds out private investment.

12. When the government runs a budget deficit, how capital market is affected ?

13. What are the components of aggregate expenditure in an open economy. With Government spending on goods and services show that equilibrium level of national income in an open economy is established at the level at which $I + G + NX$ equals saving.

14. Explain foreign trade multiplier (the open economy multiplier). What is its value ? Why is it smaller than closed economy expenditure multiplier ? ***DU B.A (Hons.) 2007***

15. You are given the following information about an economy.

Consumption function	$C = 80 + 0.8Y$
Investment function	$I = 80$
Government fspending	$G = 60$
Net Taxes	$T = 60$
Exports	$X = 20$
Imports	$M = 0.2Y_d$

(*i*) What is the current account balance for this economy

(*ii*) What is the value of the open economy multiplier ? ***DU. B.A.(Hons.) 2007***

(**Note** : Since in this question no data of '*invisibles*' are given current account balance equals *trade balance*).

16. You are given the following information about an economy –

Consumption function, C = 1000 + 0.5 ($Y - T$)

Investment, I = ₹ 2,000 crores.

Government expenditure = ₹ 1,000 crores

Taxes = ₹ 1,000 crores

(*i*) Find the equilibrium level of GDP without taxes.

(*ii*) Find the equilibrium level of GDP with taxes.

(*iii*) Use your answers in (*i*) and (*ii*) above to calculate the tax multiplier.

(*iv*) Explain the working of the tax multiplier intuitively. ***DU B.A., (Hons.) 2008***

[**Hints.** Find the equilibrium level of GDP (*i.e.* national income Y), first by laking $T = 0$ and then find the equilibrium GDP *i.e.*, (Y) by taking $T = 1000$. Then tax multiplier is $\frac{\Delta Y}{\Delta T}$. Note that $\Delta T = 1000$.)

17. Explain the relationship between the trade deficit and the inflow of foreign capital.

18. International flow of capital to finance investment and international flow of goods and services are two sides of the same coin. Explain.

CHAPTER 6

Consumption Function

Introduction

In the previous chapter we have explained how the level of national income is determined. In the present chapter and the succeeding one we shall study the factors that determine consumption demand and investment demand – the two important components of aggregate demand. As we have seen, given the aggregate supply, the level of income or employment is determined by the level of aggregate demand; the greater the aggregate demand, the greater the level of income and employment and vice versa. Keynes was not interested in the factors determining the aggregate supply since he was concerned with the short run and the existing productive capacity. We will also not explain in detail the factors which determine the aggregate supply and will confine ourselves to explaining the determinants of aggregate demand. In the present chapter we will explain the consumption demand and the factors on which it depends and how it changes over a period of time. The investment demand will be explained in the next chapter. Consumption demand depends upon the level of income and the propensity to consume.

The Concept of Consumption Function

As the demand for a good depends upon its price, similarly consumption of a community depends upon the level of income. In other words, consumption is a function of income. *The consumption function relates the amount of consumption to the level of income.* When the income of a community rises, consumption also rises. How much consumption rises in response to a given increase in income depends upon the marginal propensity to consume. It should be borne in mind that the *consumption function is the whole schedule which describes the amounts of consumption at various levels of income.* We give in Table 6.1 on the next page such a schedule of consumption function.

Consumption function should be carefully distinguished from the *amount of consumption.* By consumption function is meant the whole schedule which shows consumption at various levels of income, whereas *amount of consumption means the amount consumed at a specific level of income.* The schedule given in Table 6.1 reflects the consumption function of a community *i.e.,* it indicates how the amount of consumption changes in response to the changes in income. From the schedule given in Table 6.1 it will be seen that at the level of income equal to ₹ 1200 crore, the amount of consumption is ₹ 1090 crores. As the national income increases to ₹ 1500 crore, the amount of consumption rises to ₹ 1300 crore. Thus, with a given consumption function, amount of consumption is different at different levels of income.

The schedule of consumption function in Table 6.1 reveals an important fact that when income rises, consumption also rises but not as much as the income. This fact about consumption function was emphasised by Keynes who first of all evolved the concept of consumption function. The reason why consumption rises less than income is that a part of the increment in income is saved. Therefore, we see that when income increases from ₹ 1000 crore to ₹ 1100 crore, the amount of consumption rises from ₹ 950 crore to 1020 crore. Thus, with the increase in income by ₹ 100 crore, consumption rises by ₹ 70 crore; the remaining ₹ 30 crore are saved. Similarly, when income rises from ₹ 1100 crore to ₹1200 crore, the amount of consumption increases from ₹ 1020 crore to ₹ 1090 crore.

Table 6.1. Linear Consumption Function

Income (₹ in crores) Y	Consumption (₹ in crores) C	Average Propensity to Consume $\left(\frac{C}{Y}\right)$	Marginal Propensity to Consume $\left(\frac{\Delta C}{\Delta Y}\right)$
1000	950	$\frac{950}{1000} = 0.950$	—
1100	1020	$\frac{1020}{1100} = 0.927$	$\frac{70}{100} = .70$
1200	1090	$\frac{1090}{1200} = 0.908$	$\frac{70}{100} = .70$
1300	1160	$\frac{1160}{1300} = 0.892$	$\frac{70}{100} = .70$
1400	1230	$\frac{1230}{1400} = 0.878$	$\frac{70}{100} = .70$
1500	1300	$\frac{1300}{1500} = 0.867$	$\frac{70}{100} = .70$
1600	1370	$\frac{1370}{1600} = 0.856$	$\frac{70}{100} = .70$

Here also, as a result of increase in income by ₹ 100 crore, the amount of consumption has risen by ₹ 70 crore and the remaining ₹ 30 crore have been saved. The same applies to further increases in income and consumption. We shall see later that Keynes based his theory of multiplier on the proposition that consumption increases less than income and this theory of multiplier occupies an important place in macroeconomics.

In the Keynesian Consumption function given in Table 6.1 while marginal propensity to consume $\left(\frac{\Delta C}{\Delta Y}\right)$ remains constant at ₹ 70 crore, average propensity to consume is $\left(\frac{C}{Y}\right)$ is falling with the increase in income. It should be noted that Keynesian consumption function given in Table 6.1 is linear as marginal propensity to consume which measures the slope $\left(\frac{\Delta C}{\Delta Y}\right)$ of the consumption function curve is constant. It is noteworthy that while marginal propensity to consume $\left(\frac{\Delta C}{\Delta Y}\right)$ in the consumption function given in Table 6.1 is constant, average propensity to consume $\left(\frac{C}{Y}\right)$ falls with increase in national income (Y). *The fall in average propensity to consume with the increase in income has an important implication that increase in consumption is not proportional to increase in income*. Besides, as will be seen from Table 6.1 in Keynesian consumption function, $MPC < APC$ at various levels of income. We shall explain the importance of these two features of Keynesian consumption function later.

Consumption demand depends on income and propensity to consume. Propensity to consume depends on various factors such as price level, interest rate, stock of wealth and several subjective factors. *Since Keynes was concerned with short-run consumption function he assumed price level, interest rate, stock of wealth etc. constant in his theory of consumption*. Thus with these factors being assumed constant in the short run, Keynesian consumption function considers consumption as a function of *current* income. Thus

$$C = f(Y)$$

In a specific form, Keynesian consumption function can be written as:

$$C = a + bY$$

where a and b are constants. While a is intercept term of the consumption function, b stands for slope of the consumption function and therefore represents marginal propensity to consume and Y represents the level of *current income.*

Keynesian consumption function, namely, $C = a + bY$ has been depicted by CC' curve in Fig.6.1 in which along the X-axis national income and along the Y-axis the amount of consumption are measured. In this figure, a line OZ making 45° angle with the X-axis, has been drawn. Because line OZ makes 45° angle with the X-axis every point on it is equidistant from both the X-axis and Y-axis. Therefore, if consumption function curve coincides with 45° line OZ it would imply that the amount of consumption is equal to the income at every level of income. In this case, with the increase in income, consumption would also increase by the same amount. As has been said above, in actual practice consumption increases less than the increase in income. Therefore, in actual practice the curve depicting the consumption function will deviate from the 45° line. If we represent the above consumption schedule by a curve, we would get the propensity to consume curve such as CC' in Fig. 6.1.

It is evident from Fig. 6.1 that the consumption function curve CC' deviates from the 45° line OZ. At lower levels of income, the consumption function curve CC' lies above the OZ line, signifying that at these lower levels of income consumption is greater than the income. It is so because at lower levels of income, a nation may draw upon its accumulated savings to maintain its consumption standard or it may borrow from abroad. As income increases, consumption also increases and at the national income level OY_0, consumption is equal to income. Beyond this, with the increase in income,

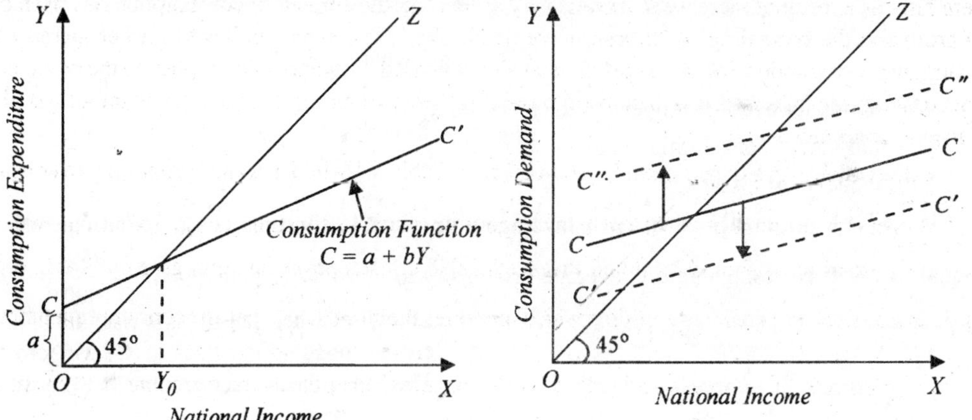

Fig. 6.1. *Keynesian Linear Consumption Function* **Fig. 6.2.** *Shift in Consumption Function*

consumption increases but less than the increase in income and therefore, consumption function curve CC' lies below the 45° line OZ beyond Y_0. An important point to be noted here is that beyond the level of income OY_0, the gap between consumption and income is widening. The difference between consumption and income represents savings. Therefore, *with the increase in income, saving gap widens* and, as we shall see later, this has a significant implication in macroeconomics.

It is useful to point out here that *when the consumption function of a community changes, the whole consumption function curve changes or shifts.* When propensity to consume increases, it means that at any given level of income more is consumed than before. Therefore, as a result of increase in propensity to consume of the community, the whole consumption function curve shifts upward as has been shown by the upper curve $C''C''$ in Fig. 6.2. On the contrary, when the propensity to consume of the community decreases, the whole consumption function curve shifts downward signifying that at any given level of income, less is consumed than before.

Average and Marginal Propensity to Consume

There are two important concepts of propensity to consume, the one being average propensity to consume and the other marginal propensity to consume. They should be carefully distinguished, for they are equal in some cases but different in others. Consider Table 6.1, where we have calculated the average and marginal propensity to consume in columns 3 and 4. As seen above, consumption changes as income changes. Now, how much consumption changes in response to a given change in income depends upon the average and marginal propensity to consume. Thus, propensity to consume of a community can be known by the average and marginal propensity to consume. *Average propensity to consume is the ratio of the amount of consumption to total income*. Therefore, average propensity to consume is calculated by dividing the amount of consumption by the total income. Thus,

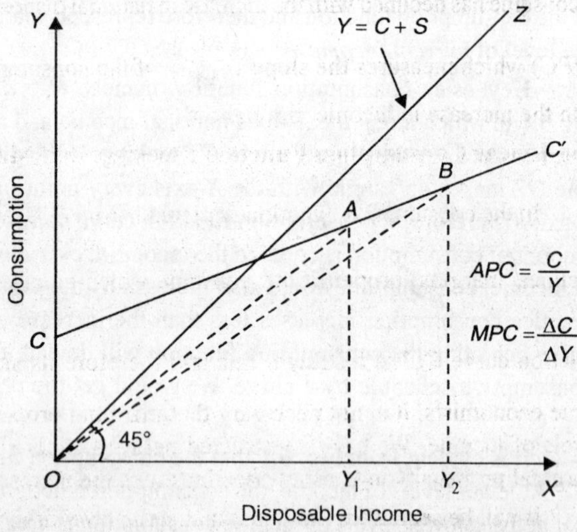

Fig. 6.3. *Consumption Function: Declining Average Propensity to Consume and Constant Marginal Propensity to Consume*

$$APC = \frac{C}{Y}, \text{ where}$$

APC stands for average propensity to consume,

C for amount of consumption, and

Y for the level of income.

In the Table 6.1 it will be seen that at the level of income ₹ 1000 crores, consumption expenditure is equal to ₹ 950 crores. Therefore, average propensity to consume is here equal to $\frac{950}{1000} = 0.95$. Likewise, when the income rises to ₹ 1200 crore, consumption rises to ₹ 1090 crores. Therefore, the average propensity to consume will be $\frac{1090}{1200} = 0.908$. In this schedule of consumption function, the average propensity to consume declines with the increase in income. Keynesian consumption function *CC′* is shown in Figures 6.1 and 6.3. Average propensity to consume at a point on the consumption function curve can be obtained by measuring the slope of the ray from the origin to that point. For example, at income level OY_1, corresponding point on the consumption function curve is *A*. Therefore, at OY_1 income level, average propensity to consume (*APC*) is the slope of the ray *OA*.

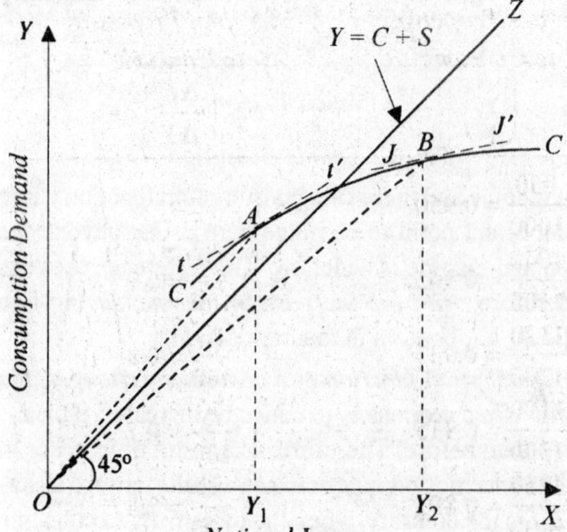

Fig. 6.4. *Non-Linear Consumption Function: Declining both marginal and Average Propensity to Consume*

Similarly, at income level OY_2, average propensity to consume is the slope of the ray *OB*. It will be observed from Fig.6.3 that slope of *OB* is less than that of *OA*. Therefore, average propensity to consume at income level OY_2 is less than that at income level OY_1. In other words, average propensity to consume has declined with the increase in national disposable income. However, marginal to consume (*MPC*) which measures the slope $\left(\frac{\Delta C}{\Delta Y}\right)$ of the consumption function curve *CC′* remains constant with the increase in income throughout

Non-Linear Consumption Function : Average and Marginal Propensity to Consume

In the consumption function depicted in Fig. 6.3, though average propensity to consume $\left(\frac{C}{Y}\right)$ declines, marginal propensity to consume which equals $\frac{\Delta C}{\Delta Y}$ remains constant since consumption function curve *CC′* is a straight line and therefore its slope $\left(\frac{\Delta C}{\Delta Y}\right)$ is constant. But, according to some economists, it is not necessary that marginal propensity to consume should be the same at all levels of income. We have constructed below another schedule of consumption function in which marginal propensity to consume declines with the increase in income.

It will be seen from Table 6.2 that at the level of income of ₹ 100 crores, marginal propensity to consume is 0.9, and when income rises to ₹ 1500 crores, the marginal propensity to consume has declined to 0.5. When with the increase in income both marginal propensity to consume and average propensity to consume decline, then the curve of consumption function is not a straight line but has a concave shape as shown in Fig. 6.4. From any point on the propensity to consume curve *CC* we can find out average propensity to consume by joining that point with the point of origin by a straight line whose slope will measure the average propensity to consume. In Fig. 6.4, if we have to find out average propensity to consume at point *A* on the consumption function curve *CC*, we connect point *A* with the origin by a straight line. Now, the slope of the line *OA i.e.*, AY_1/OY_1 will indicate the average propensity to consume. Similarly, at point *B* of the given consumption function *CC*, the average propensity to consume will be given by the slope of the line *OB* which is equal to BY_2/OY_2.

Table 6.2

Non-Linear Consumption Function : Average and Marginal Propensity to Consume

Income (₹ in crores) Y	*Consumption (₹ in crores)* C	*Average Propensity to Consume* $\left(\frac{C}{Y}\right)$	*Marginal Propensity to Consume* $\left(\frac{\Delta C}{\Delta Y}\right)$
1000	950	$\frac{950}{1000} = 0.950$	–
1100	1040	$\frac{1040}{1100} = 0.945$	$\frac{90}{100} = 0.9$
1200	1120	$\frac{1120}{1200} = 0.933$	$\frac{80}{100} = 0.8$
1300	1190	$\frac{1190}{1300} = 0.915$	$\frac{70}{100} = 0.7$
1400	1250	$\frac{1250}{1400} = 0.893$	$\frac{60}{100} = 0.6$
1500	1300	$\frac{1300}{1500} = 0.866$	$\frac{50}{100} = 0.5$

The glance at the figure will show that the slope of the line OB is smaller than the slope of the line OA. Therefore, average propensity to consume at point B or at income level OY_2 is less than at point A or income level OY_1.

Marginal Propensity to Consume. The concept of marginal propensity to consume is very important because from it we can know how much part of the increment in income is consumed and how much saved. Marginal propensity to consume is the ratio of change in consumption to the change in income. Thus :

$$MPC = \frac{\Delta C}{\Delta Y}$$

where, MPC stands for marginal propensity to consume,

ΔC for change in consumption, and

ΔY for change in income.

Marginal propensity to consume needs to be carefully distinguished from average propensity to consume. Whereas average propensity to consume is the ratio of total consumption to total income, *i.e.*, $\frac{C}{Y}$, the marginal propensity to consume is the ratio of change in consumption to the change in income, *i.e.* $\frac{\Delta C}{\Delta Y}$.

The concept of marginal propensity to consume can be easily understood with the aid of Table 6.2, in column 4 of which we have calculated the marginal propensity to consume at various levels of income. In this schedule when income rises from ₹ 1000 crores to ₹ 1100 crores, the consumption increases from ₹ 950 crores to ₹ 1040 crores. Here the increment in income is ₹ 100 crores and the increment in consumption is ₹ 90 crores. Therefore, marginal propensity to consume which is $\frac{\Delta C}{\Delta Y}$ is here equal to $\frac{90}{100}$ or 0.9. Similarly, when national income rises to ₹ 1200 crores and as a result consumption increases from ₹ 1040 crores to ₹ 1120 crores, the marginal propensity to consume is now equal to $\frac{80}{100}$ or 0.8. In Table 6.2, it will be seen that marginal propensity to consume declines as the income rises. It is worth noting that when with the increase in income average propensity to consume declines, marginal propensity to consume is less than average propensity to consume. This is in accordance with the usual relationship between the average and marginal quantities, $MPC < APC$. This is evident from Table 6.2.

Marginal propensity to consume can be estimated by drawing the tangent at a point on the consumption function curve. Consider Fig. 6.4 where curve CC depicting the consumption function has been drawn. Marginal propensity to consume at point A on this will be equal to the slope of the tangent tt' drawn at this point. Similarly, marginal propensity to consume at point B on it is given by the slope of the tangent JJ' drawn at this point. It will be seen that slope of the tangent JJ' is less than the slope of the tangent tt'. Therefore, marginal propensity to consume at point B on the consumption function CC in Fig. 6.4 is smaller than the marginal propensity to consume at point A on this consumption function. Thus, marginal propensity to consume declines with the increases in income in the non-linear consumption function curve CC in Fig. 6.4. Thus *when marginal propensity to consume declines with the increase in income, consumption function is non-linear whose slope declines as income rises*. Non-linear consumption function is shown in Fig. 6.4 where the slope of the propensity to consume curve CC declines as income increases. In Fig. 6.1 and Fig. 6.3 propensity to consume curve is a straight line *i.e.*, the slope of the consumption function curve remains constant. Therefore, marginal propensity to consume which is given by the slope of the consumption function curve remains constant in Figures 6.1 and 6.3

It is worth noting that marginal propensity to consume is neither zero nor equal to one. It has been found by empirical studies *that marginal propensity to consume varies between zero and unity.* If the marginal propensity to consume was zero, then the whole of the increment in income would have been saved and the consumption function curve would have a horizontal shape. As we have seen before, this is not so realistic. On the other hand, if the marginal propensity to consume was equal to unity, then the whole of the increment in income would be consumed and in that case consumption function curve would have coincided with 45° line.

SAVING FUNCTION

As mentioned above, consumption increases as income increases but less than the rise in income. We will now explain what happens to saving when income increases. Saving is defined as the part of income which is not consumed because disposable income is either consumed or saved.

Thus,

$$Y = C + S$$

$$S = Y - C$$

where Y = Disposable income, C = Consumption, S = Saving

Like consumption, saving is also a function of income. Thus, saving function can be written as

$$S = f(Y)$$

Saving function is a counterpart of a consumption function, Therefore, given a particular consumption, function, we can derive the corresponding saving function. Let us take the Keynesian consumption, namely, $C = a + bY$. We can derive saving function corresponding to it.

$$\text{Since } Y = C + S$$

$$S = Y - C \qquad \text{... } (i)$$

Now, substituting the Keynesian consumption function for C in (i) we have

$$S = Y - (a + bY)$$

$$= Y - a - bY$$

$$= -a + Y - bY$$

$$= -a + (1 - b)\,Y \qquad \text{... } (ii)$$

Note that $(1 - b)$ in the above saving function in *(ii)* is the value of marginal propensity to save where b is the value of marginal propensity to consume. Let us give a numerical example. Suppose the following consumption function is given.

$$C = 150 + 0.80\,Y$$

$$S = Y - C$$

Substituting the given consumption function for C we have

$$S = Y - 150 - 0.80\,Y$$

$$= -150 + Y - 0.80\,Y$$

$$= 150 + (I - 0.80)\,Y$$

$$= -150 + 0.20\,Y$$

Note that 0.20 represents marginal propensity to save. It also follows from above that the sum of marginal propensity to consume and marginal propensity to save is equal to one $(MPC + MPS = 1)$. It is important to distinguish between average propensity to save and marginal propensity to save.

Average Propensity to Save (*APS*). An important relationship between income and saving is described by the concept of average propensity to save. *(APS)*. Average propensity to save is the proportion of disposable income that is saved (*i.e.* not consumed). Mathematically

$$APS = \frac{\text{Savings}}{\text{Disposable Income}} = \frac{S}{Y}$$

Like the average propensity to consume *(APC)* average propensity to save also generally varies as income increases. As seen above, average propensity to consume *(APC)* falls as income increases. This implies that average propensity to save will increase as income rises.

Let us derive an important relationship between average propensity to consume and average propensity to save. Restating below the relation that income is either consumed or saved:

$$C + S = Y$$

Dividing both sides by disposable income Y we have

$$\frac{C}{Y} + \frac{S}{Y} = \frac{Y}{Y} = 1$$

Since $\frac{C}{Y}$ is average propensity to consume and $\frac{S}{Y}$ is average propensity to save, we have

$$APC + APS = 1$$

or $$APS = 1 - APC$$

This means, for example, that if a society consumes 75 per cent of its disposable income, that is, $APC = 0.75$, then it will save 25 per cent of its disposable income or its average propensity to save (*APS*) will be 0.25 $(1 - 0.75 = 0.25)$.

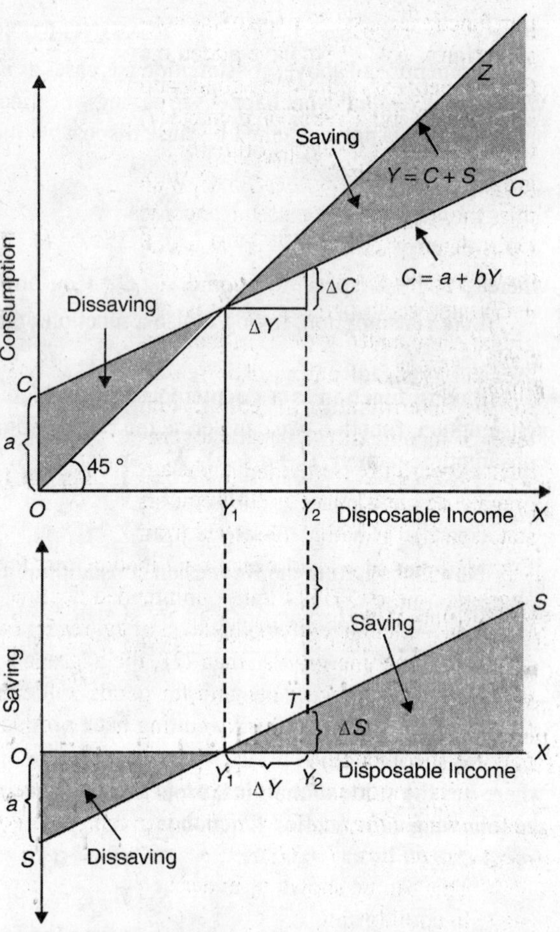

Fig. 6.5. *Saving Function derived from Consumption Function*

In Fig. 6.6 we have drawn the saving curve *SS* in the panel at the bottom. The saving curve *SS* shows the gap between consumption curve *CC* and the income curve *OZ* in the upper panel of Fig. 6.5. It will be seen that upto income level OY_1, consumption exceeds income, that is, there is dissaving. Beyond income level OY_1, there is positive saving. It is worth mentioning that as average propensity to consume *(APC)* falls with the increase in income in the upper panel, average propensity to save rises as income increases. Thus in Fig. 6.6 with the increase in income not only the absolute amount of saving increases, the average propensity to save also increases.

Marginal Propensity to Save (*MPS*). Whereas average propensity to save indicates the proportion of income that is saved, marginal propensity to save represents how much of the *additional* disposable income is devoted to saving. The marginal propensity to save is therefore change in saving induced by a change in the disposable income.

Thus,

$$MPS = \frac{\Delta S}{\Delta Y}$$

For example, if disposable income increases from rupees 10,000 to 12,000 and this causes planned savings to increase by ₹ 500 crores, marginal propensity to save is:

$$MPS = \frac{500}{2000} = \frac{1}{4} = 0.25$$

Since the additional income is either consumed or saved, *the sum of marginal propensity to consume and marginal propensity to save is equal to one.*

$$MPC + MPS = 1$$

This can be mathematically proved as under

From $C + S = Y$, it follows that any change in income (ΔY) must induce either change in consumption (ΔC) or change in saving (ΔS). Thus.

$$\Delta C + \Delta S = \Delta Y$$

Dividing both sides by ΔY we have

$$\frac{\Delta C}{\Delta Y} + \frac{\Delta S}{\Delta Y} = \frac{\Delta Y}{\Delta Y} = 1$$

$$MPC + MPS = 1$$

The concept of marginal propensity to save is graphically shown at the bottom of Fig. 6.6. It will be seen from this figure that when disposable income increases from OY_1 (say ₹ 10,000) to OY_2 (say ₹ 12,000), that is, $\Delta Y =$ ₹ 2000, the saving increases by Y_2T, (₹ 500), that is, ΔS is ₹ 500. Thus marginal propensity to save (*MPS*) is

$$\frac{\Delta S}{\Delta Y} = \frac{Y_2T}{Y_1Y_2} = \frac{500}{2000} = \frac{1}{4} = 0.25$$

KEYNES'S THEORY OF CONSUMPTION

Keynes in his *"General theory"*, published in 1936, laid the foundations of modern macroeconomics. The concept of consumption function plays an important role in Keynes' theory of income and employment. Keynes mentioned several subjective and objective factors which determine consumption of a society. However, according to Keynes, of all the factors it is the *current level of income* that determines the consumption of an individual and also of society. Since Keynes laid stress on the *absolute size of current income* as a determinant of consumption, his theory of consumption is also known as **absolute income theory of consumption.** While Keynes recognized that many subjective and objective factors including interest rate and wealth influenced the level consumption expenditure, he emphasised that it is the **current level of income** on which the consumption spending of an individual and the society depends.

Keynes's Psychological Law of Consumption. Further, Keynes put forward a *psychological law of consumption,* according to which, as income increases consumption increases but not by as much as the increase in income. In other words, marginal propensity to consume is less than one but greater than zero. That is,

$$1 > \frac{\Delta C}{\Delta Y} > 0$$

Thus implies that out of an increment in income a part is consumed and a part saved. To quote Keynes, "*The amount of aggregate consumption depends mainly on the amount of aggregate income. The fundamental psychological law, upon which we are entitled to depend with great confidence both a priori from our knowledge of human nature and from (the detailed facts of experience is that men (and women, too) are disposed, as a rule and on an average to increase their consumption as their income increases, but not by as much as the increase in their income.*"[1]

Keynes's consumption theory has three features. First, he suggests that consumption expenditure depends mainly on absolute income of the current period, that is, consumption is a positive function of the *absolute level of current income*. The more income in a period one has, the more is likely to be his consumption expenditure in that period. In other words, in any period the rich people tend to consume more than the poor people do. Secondly, he propounds a psychlogical law of consumption, according to which marginal propensity to consume is less than one but greater than zero. Thirdly, Keynes points out that *consumption expenditure does not have a proportional relationship with income*. According to him, as income increases, a smaller proportion of income is consumed. The proportion of consumption to income is called average propensity to consume (*APC*). Thus, the third property of Keynes's consumption function is that *average propensity to consume (APC) falls as income increases.*

The Keynes' consumption function can be expressed in the following form

$$C = a + bY_d$$

where C is consumption expenditure and Y_d *is* the real disposable income which equals gross national income minus taxes, a and b are constants, where a is the intercept term, that is, the amount of consumption expenditure at zero level of income. Thus, a is *autonomous consumption.* The parameter b is the marginal propensity to consume (*MPC*) which measures the increase in consumption spending in response to per unit increase in disposable income. Thus, $b = MPC = \frac{\Delta C}{\Delta Y}$

The behaviour of consumption expenditure as perceived by Keynes implies that the marginal propensity to consume is less than average propensity to consume ($MPC < APC$). This is because as income increases consumption does not rise proportionately and as income falls consumption does not fall proportunately. This is because people protect their consumption standards by not reducing their consumption proportionately to the reduction in their income. Implication of the proposition that $MPC < APC$ as income increases is that the ratio of consumption demand to income falls. This can be seen from Figure 6.3 where the slope of consumption function curve is *marginal propensity to consume (MPC) which remains constant* and the slope of the lines such as *OA* and *OB* from the origin to points *A* and *B* on the consumption function line *CC'* measure *APC*, that is, ratio C/Y at these points is falling showing that consumption demand does not increase proportionately to increase in national income. This Keynesion consumption function is shown in figure 6.1 and 6.3.

In Fig. 6.3 we have shown a linear consumption function with an intercept term. In this form of linear consumption function, though marginal propensity to consume ($\Delta C/\Delta Y$) is constant, average propensity to consume is declining with the increase in income as indicated by the slopes of the lines *OA* and *OB* at levels of income Y_1 and Y_2 respectively. The straight line *OB* .drawn from the origin indicating average propensity to consume at higher income level Y_2 has a relatively less slope than the straight line *OA* drawn from the origin to point *A* at lower income level Y_1. The decline in average propensity to consume as the income increases implies that the *proportion of income that is saved increases with the increase in national income of the country.* This result also follows from the studies of family budgets of various families at different income levels. The fraction of income spent on consumption by the rich families is lower than that of the poor families. In other words, the rich families save a higher proportion of their income as compared to the poor families.

The assumption of diminishing average propensity to consume is a significant part of Keynesian theory of income and employment. This implies that as income increases, a progressively larger proportion of national income would be saved. Therefore, to achieve and maintain equilibrium at full-employment level of income, increasing proportion of national income is needed to be invested.

1. J.M. Keynes, *The General Theory of Employment, Interest and Money,* (New York : Harcourt), First Edition, 1936, p. 96.

If sufficient profitable opportunities for investment are not available, the economy would then run into trouble and in that case it would not be possible to maintain full-employment because aggregate demand will fall short of full-employment output. On the basis of this increasing proportion of saving with the increase in income and consequently the emergence of the problem of demand deficiency, some Keynesian economists such as Hanson based the theory of *secular stagnation* on the declining propensity to consume.

Important Features of Keynes's Consumption Function

In macroeconomics, Keynes's consumption function plays a highly important role. Therefore, it is essential to state its important features. The following are the important features of Keynes's consumption function:

1. First, *absolute level of current income is the important factor that determines consumption* of the community. Increase in national income causes an increase in consumption. On the other hand, classical economists thought that it was rate of interest that primarily determined saving and consumption of the community. A rise in rate of interest induces the people to save more and thus to reduce their level of consumption. According to Keynes, though rate of interest is one of the factors that determine consumption of the community, he did not consider it a very important determinant of it. By considering level of *current income* as the most important factor determining consumption and saving, Keynes made a significant contribution to the macroeconomic theory.
2. The second important feature of Keynes' consumption function is that *marginal propensity to consume is less than one* but greater than zero ($0 < MPC < 1$). As has been explained above, the feature of Keynes's consumption function that marginal propensity to consume is less than one is known as Keynes's psychological law of consumption. According to this law, as income increases, consumption increases but not as much as the increase in income. We will explain in a later chapter that Keynes's theory of multiplier is based on the marginal propensity to consume being less than one but greater than zero.
3. In *Keynes consumption function, namely,* $C = a + by$, *as income increases, average propensity to consume (APC) falls.* Keynes was of the view that rich people relatively save a higher proportion of their income so that at higher levels of income average propensity to consume (*APC*), that is, proportion of total consumption to national income falls as national income rises.
4. Another important feature of consumption function as put forward by Keynes is that *it remains stable in the short run.* Consumption function, according to Keynes, depends on various institutional factors such as distribution of income and wealth and psychological factors such as willingness to save. Since there cannot be much changes in these institutional and psychological factors, consumption function remains stable in the short run, that is, it does not shift upward or downward. Therefore, Keynes in his theory explains the determination of income and employment in the short run by considering that the consumption function is stable.

DETERMINANTS OF PROPENSITY TO CONSUME

The important question is on what factors does the consumption demand of a community depend. In other words, what are the factors that determine the level and position of the propensity to consume or the consumption function. Keynes divided the factors determining the propensity to consume into two groups: one group of factors was called by him as objective factors and the second group was named by him as subjective factors. We shall explain below in detail these objective and subjective factors which affect the consumption function of a community.

Objective Factors

The following six types of objective factors influence the consumption function:

(1) Changes in the General Price Level : Real Balance Effect. The general price level is an important factor which influences the consumption of a community. When the general price level increases or, in other words, when inflation occurs, the consumption function shifts downward. This is because the rise in the general price level, real value (that is, purchasing power) of people's money balances and financial assets with fixed monetary values declines. This causes a downward shift in the consumption function. This is called *real balance effect.* Similarly, when the general price level falls, real value of money balances and financial assets increases. This will induce people to consume relatively more out of their current income. This will cause an upward shift in the consumption function.

(2) Fiscal Policy. Fiscal policy of the Government, especially taxation policy affects the propensity to consume of the country. By levying excise duties, sales tax, the Government can cut down the consumption and thereby increase savings of the community. Likewise, when the Government reduces taxes, consumption of the people increases and this raises the propensity to consume. Rationing and price control by the Government also affects the propensity to consume, as was witnessed during the Second World War. In the modern times, pursuing of the welfare state policy by the Government under which progressive taxes have been levied on the rich people and the revenue obtained from them have been spent to provide many social security benefits and amenities to the poor people, has tended to raise the consumption function.

(3) Rate of Interest. Rate of interest also affects the propensity to consume and save. It is generally believed that higher rate of interest induces the people to save more and this results in reducing their propensity to consume. But this is not true in the case of all the people. Some individuals are of such a type who want a certain fixed income in the future. And when the rate of interest rises these individuals consume more and save less because with higher rate of interest they can obtain the given fixed income with lesser savings. Therefore, when the rate of interest rises such individuals save less than before. Thus, it cannot be said with certainty whether with the changes in the rate of interest the propensity to consume of the whole community will change or not.

(4) Stock of Wealth. The stock of wealth owned by the households in the economy is also an important factor that determines propensity to consume. In wealth we include not only *real assets* such as land, houses, automobiles but also *financial assets* such as cash balances, saving and fixed deposits with banks, stocks and bonds possessed by households. The greater the amount of wealth accumulated by households in the economy, the greater is generally the propensity to consume *(i.e.* the greater the amount of consumption out of any level of current income). The important motive of the people to save is to accumulate wealth. Generally speaking, the greater the wealth which people have accumulated, the weaker is the incentive to save further. In other words, the other things remaining the same the increase in wealth generally causes an upward shift in the consumption function and decrease is wealth causes a downward shift in the consumption function.

An important example which is often cited to emphasise the importance of wealth as a determinant of consumption is the stock market crash of 1929 in England (*i.e.* drastic fall in share prices) which substantially reduced the financial wealth of the households overnight resulting in shifting the consumption function downward.

(5) Credit Conditions and Consumer Indebtedness. The availability of easy credit causes an increase in consumption and shifts the consumption function upward. It is now a common experience in India that in recent years lowering of lending interest rates by Indian banks on loans for houses, cars, computers and other durable consumer goods has greatly increased the consumption of the people and shifted consumption function upward. On the other hand, tightening of credit produces an opposite effect, that is, causes a downward shift in the consumption function, Furthermore, the recent increase in facilities of Credit Cards by banks and their acceptance buy sellers of consumer goods have also worked to shift the consumption function upward in India.

Similarly, the level of consumer indebtedness also greatly affects the propensity to consume of the people. If the households are heavily indebted, say 25 to 30 per cent of their current, they are committed to save *(i.e.* consume less) to that extent so that they are able to pay their instalments of previous credit taken. Thus, the greater the degree of indebtedness of households 'in the economy, the higher will be the consumption function curve and *vice versa.*

(6) Income Distribution. Lastly, distribution of income in a society also determines the level of consumption function. If national income is more unequally distributed, the lower will be the propensity to consume. This is because propensity to consume of the rich is relatively less as compared to that of the poor. Therefore, if inequalities in income distribution increase, this reduces the consumption out of any given level of national income and thus causes a downward shift in the consumption function.

(7) Windfall Gains and Losses. Windfall gains and losses also affect the propensity to consume. When the prices of the shares go up, the shareholders begin to think themselves better off and this raises their consumption. On the other hand, when the prices of the shares go down, the shareholders have to suffer sudden losses and they begin to think themselves relatively poorer than before. This induces them to reduce their consumption. We thus see that the windfall gains and losses affect the propensity to consume.

(8) Change in Expectations. Changes in the expectations of the people also influence the propensity to consume. When people expect that war will break out in the near future and they expect prices to go up, then they will try to spend more on goods so as to meet the needs of the immediate future. This raises the consumption function in the current period. On the other hand, when people expect the prices to fall they reduce their current consumption so that they should spend more when the prices actually fall.

Subjective Factors

Among the subjective factors are included those factors which induce and prompt people to save some part of their income. First, people save because they want to provide for unforeseen contingencies, such as illness, unemployment, accidents, etc. Secondly, people are induced to save because they want to provide for the expected future needs such as education of the children, marriages of their children, etc. Thirdly, several people wish to save from their current incomes so that they may be able to use accumulated savings for investment which will increase their future income. Investments will bring them more income in the form of more profits and interest. Fourthly, people are motivated to save so that they can accumulate large wealth which will increase their social status. With increased wealth they would think themselves to be economically more independent and they could buy many things with more wealth. Further, many individuals also save so that they can use them for speculative purposes and other business projects. Besides, several people are prompted to save for the sake of leaving a good fortune for their heirs and children. Lastly, many people save because of their miserly instinct and habits. The accumulation of more wealth gives them a great psychic satisfaction.

The above subjective factors increase the propensity to save and therefore reduce the propensity to consume. These subjective factors play a crucial rule in determining the level and shape of the consumption function. However, Keynes pointed out and rightly so that some subjective factors raise the propensity to consume. The desire for ostentation generally leads to greater consumption expenditure. People have a natural instint to imitate others' consumption habits. As pointed out by Duesenberry, people in lower and middle income ranges imitate the consumption standards of the higher income groups and this increases their propensity to con-sume. This has been called *demonstration effect* which is a great subjective or psychological force that works in raising the propensity to consume.

Subjective factors also lead the business firms to save much or little from their incomes. Many of the subjective factors which influence the savings of the firms are the following ; (1) *Enterprise*—

Many business industrial firms desire to save a part of their current income so that they can make investment in new enterprises and carry out expansion in the future. Business firms generally save a good part of their income for their further expansion. (2) *Liquidity*—Business firms also are induced to save so that they can face contingencies in the future. If they have good amount of liquid wealth in their hands, they would be able to meet the emergent situations more successfully. More cautious and farsighted firms will save more than others on this count. (3) *Successful Management*—Many managers of the business firms are motivated to save more because they want to prove themselves successful managers. With the investment of the saved money, the income of a firm increases and their managers are regarded as successful. (4) *Financial Prudence*—Business firms desire to save for making up the depreciation in plant and machinery. Since after some years business firms have to replace their plant and machinery, if a good part of their current income is not saved, it would not be possible for them to replace plant and machinery. If the firms put aside a greater part of their income for depreciation or replacement purposes, they would pay lower dividends to the shareholders and this will generally lower the propensity to consume of a community. On the other hand, if the firms keep a relatively small amount for depreciation, they will pay larger amounts as dividends to the shareholders and this will generally increase the propensity to consume of the community. Lastly, firms also want to save because they have to repay their debts.

We have explained above various subjective and objective factors which taken together determine the consumption function of a community. It is worth noting that propensity to consume does not generally change in the short run, because it depends more on psychological and institutional factors which change only in the long run. *The institutional factors which determine the distribution of income in the society are important forces determining the consumption function.* And these institutional factors do not change in the short run. Therefore, Keynes was of the view that consumption function remains stable in the short run.

In the next chapter we shall critically examine Keynes's consumption function and compare it with other theories of consumption, function.

Life Cycle and Permanent Consumption Theories of Consumption.

Since Keynes propounded his theory of consumption there have been significant developments in this field and some alternative theories of consumption have been put forward. However, all these post-keynesian theories of consumption *relate consumption to some form of income*. First, J.S. Duesenberry expressed the view that consumption expenditure of individuals depends not on their own absolute incomes but on their *incomes relative to the incomes of others*. Therefore, Duesenberry's theory of consumption is called, *Relative Income Theory of consumption*. Second, Modigliani and Ando put forward a theory known as '*Life Cycle Theory of Consumption* according to which individuals plan their consumption profile for their while life time which depends not so much on their current income but on *their expectations of whole life time income*. Further, a famous American economist Milton Friedman advanced an hypothesis regarding consumers' behaviour called permanent income hypothesis according to which *consumption of individuals depends on their permanent incomes rather their current levels of income*. We will critically examine these post-keynsion theories of consumption in the next chapter. Here we will explain here briefly life cycle theory of consumption and permanent Income Hypothesis.

In Keynes's theory of consumption function, *current* consumption expenditure depends mainly on *current income*. After Keynes some economists such as Franco Modigliani and Miltion Friedman pointed out that individuals while making their consumption decisions take into account not only the current income which was emphasised by Keynes but also the income they expect to receive in the future. Therefore, the consumption theories of Franco Modigliani and Milton Friedman, have been called *Future-Oriented Consumption theories* by Joseph Stiglitz.[2] Consumption theory put forward by Modigliani and Ando is called *Life-Cycle Theory of Consumption* as they lay stress that in

2. See J. Stiglitz, *Economics*, 2002, p. 634

deciding about consumption out of income in the working years of their life individuals attempt to save for the post-retirement period. Their motive for doing so is to smooth their consumption in their entire life span. That is, they save from the current income of working period of their life so that will not have to cut down consumption level after they retire.

Like Modigliani, and Ando, Miltion Friedman also thinks that *expectations about future income affect, consumption* in a current period. He points out that people save in good years so that they have not to curtail consumption in bad years. In other words, in Friedman's view consumption of individuals or households depends on *permanent income* in contrast to *current income* level as emphasised by Keynes. *By permanent income he means average long-run income.* Therefore, Friedman's theory is known as *permanent consumption hypothesis*. According to this view, temporary changes in income such as bonus received in a year, or large capital gains received due to rise in prices of shares or real estate would not have the same effect as the permanent changes in income, that is, changes in long-run average income. According to Friedman, transitory changes in income will have little effect on consumption while permanent changes in income will have large effect on consumption. Thus, according to Friedman's permanent consumption theory, if households could predict their future income level, they will adjust their consumption levels according to their average long-run income.

Milton Friedman emphasises that consumption of individuals is affected by changes in individuals' wealth which is a stock variable in contrast to the current income which is a flow variable. Friedman's permanent consumption theory suggests that individuals' consumption depends on how well-off they are and that is better measured by their wealth. Individuals' wealth change when the value of their assets such as prices of stock shares and real estate change. When their prices rise people enjoy capital gains which make them wealthier and as a result their consumption out of a given income rises. With this consumption function curve shifts above. Commenting on the future-oriented theories of consumption and saving of Modigliani and Friedman Joseph Stiglitz write, "Both Modigliani and Friedman stressed that individuals generally try to stabilise their consumption using savings to smooth consumption so that it does not fluctuate dramatically from year to year. They also stressed that individuals will be forward looking, basing current consumption decisions on their expectations about future income"[3].

Implications. There are three important implications of the above two future-oriented theories of consumption and saving. First important implication is that *changes in expectations about future income* effect the current consumption of individuals even though their current income has not changed. Consider the case when an economy is currently experiening recession as has been the case in 2008-09 afflicted by global financial crisis and global meltdown, people became quite pessimistic about their future income prospects which led them to curtail consumption and save more even though their current income did not change. This causes the consumption function curve to shift downward.

Another implication is that one-time or temporary changes in income will cause only a small change in consumption. Suppose a person has a windfall gain of ₹ 10 lakhs in a year due to his winning a lottery. Given his marginal propensity to consume equal to 0.8, the Keynesian consumption function predicts that his consumption will increase by ₹ 8 lakhs and the remaining ₹ 2 lakhs will be saved by him in that year. On the other hand, the future-oriented theories of Modigliani and Freidman predict that the consumption of extra income gained by the lottery winner during a year will be spread over his life time or over a long-period of time. Similarly, a more important case from the viewpoint of economic policy is the *temporary reduction in the direct tax* at the time of recession by the government to boost consumption demand as had been done even recently by the US government in 2007-08 and 2008-09 to fight recession will have only limited effect on consumption. The above two future-oriented theories predict that contrary to the prediction of the Keynesian model the temporary reduction in direct taxes will be much less effective in boosting consumption demand as due to uncer-

3. Stiglitiz, *op. cit.*, p.634

tain economic prospects much of the income gained through transitory tax reduction will be saved. The evidence from the US shows this has in fact been the case.

The third related implication of the future-oriented theories is that since changes in income that individuals expect to be only temporary will have only small effect on consumption spending, marginal propensily to consume will be lower and the multiplier effect of such changes in taxes will be smaller. To conclude, leaving aside the cases of temporary changes in income and the concern of the forward looking people to ensure same consumption standard in the future, the Keynesian theory of consumption is right in visualising that individuals' consumption spending is more dependent on current income. To quote Stiglitz again, "*The permanent income and life-cycle saving hypothesis contain large elements of truth. Families do save for their retirement and they do smooth their consumption between good years and bad.* Even so, *households spending appear to be more depended on current income than either future-oriented theory would suggest*"[4].

Consumption Function Puzzle: Keynes's Consumption Function and Kuznets Findings

Empirical studies of long-term times series data of the US economy for the period 1869-1938 made by the noted American economist Kuznets estimated a consumption function which contradicts Keynes' consumption function which was found to be correct on the basis of cross-section studies of household budget data and short-term time series data. *This contradiction between Kuznets empirical findings and Keynes' consumption function has been called con-sumption function puzzle.* Efforts have been made by several economists to resolve this puzzle and new theories of consumption function have been put forward to resolve the conflict between Keynes's consumption function and Kuznets's findings. These alternative theories of consumption function will be discussed in the next chapter.

To compare the Keynes' and Kuznets's consumption functions, it will be useful to write them in algebraic form and graphically represent them. Keynes's consumption function can be algebraically written as below:

$$C = a + bY \qquad ...(1)$$

where *a* is a positive intercept term which is also called *autonomous consumption* as it does not vary with income. The constant *a* shows that even when income is zero, a certain consumption is present. This is possible when in any year a community can live either on its past savings or borrow from other communities. Keynes' consumption function is shown in Fig. 6.6

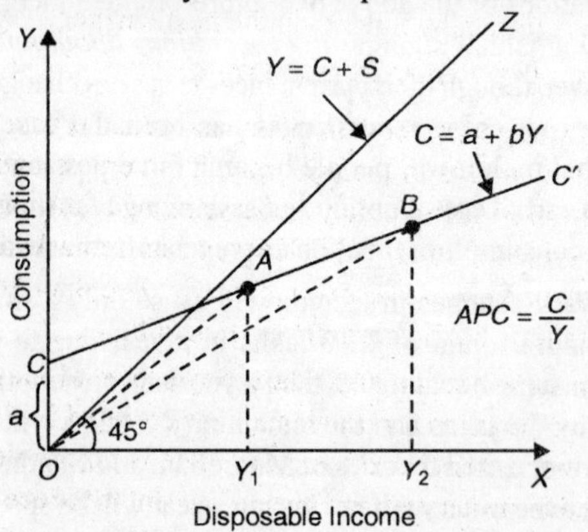

Fig. 6.6. *Keynes Consumption Function: Falling Average Propensity to Consume*

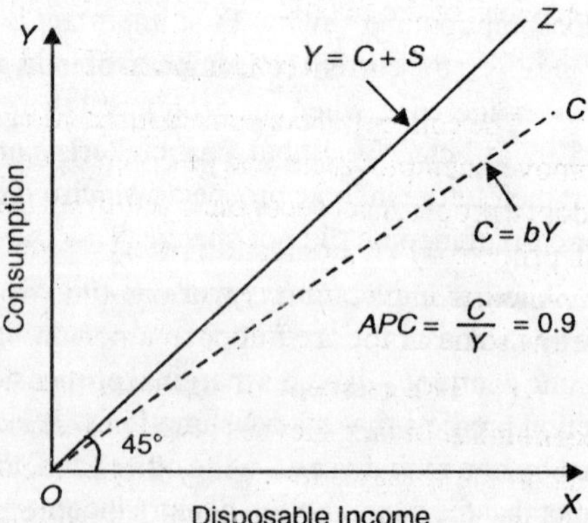

Fig. 6.7. *Kuznets's Consumption Function: Constant APC*

Secondly, *b* in the consumption function represents marginal propensity to consume $\left(\frac{\Delta C}{\Delta Y}\right)$. The above mentioned Keynes's consumption function ($C = a + bY$) shows that average propensity to

4. Stiglitz *op.* cit. p. 635 (italics added)

consume $\left(\frac{C}{Y}\right)$ falls as income increases. This can be known by comparing slopes of the rays *OA* and *OB* at income levels Y_1 and Y_2 respectively in Fig. 6.6.

Kuznets's Consumption Function

On the other hand, Kuznets found that consumption function is of the following form:

$$C = bY \quad ...(2)$$

In Kuznets' consumption function there is no intercept term (that is, autonomous consumption). This is shown in Fig. 6.7 where it will be seen that Kuznets consumption function curve starts from the origin and is very near to 45° line depicting that the propensity to consume *(b)* is very high. From his empirical study Kuznets estimated that average propensity to consume was nearly 0.9. Besides, by dividing the entire period (1869-1933) into three overlaping 30 years sub-periods Kuznets found that the proportion of consumption to income (that is, average propensity to consume) was nearly the same and equal to about 0.87 in all the three sub-periods. Thus Kuznets concluded that there was no tendency for the average propensity to consume to decline as disposable income rises. Thus, rounding off Kuznets estimated propensity to consume is equal to 0.9. His consumption function presented in equation (2) can be rewritten as

$$C = 0.97 \quad ...(3)$$

From the above discussion it follows that implication of Keynes's consumption function ($C = a + bY$) and Kuznets consumption function ($C = bY$) are different. *Whereas in Keynes' consumption function APC falls as income rises, in Kuznets s function it remains constant over a long period.* Further, the value of marginal propensity to consume which is less than one is much higher in Kuznets's function as compared to that of Keynes. The reconciliation between two types of consumption functions has been made by some economists by pointing out that whereas Keynes's function is short-run consumption function *Kuznets s function is concerned with long run and is referred to as long-run consumption function.* In the long run, short run consumption function curve shifts above and therefore in the long run consumption function, propensity to consume is higher as compared to that in the short run. *Further, Friedman's permanent Income Hypothesis and Modigliani's Life Cycle Hypothesis* have also tried to reconcile the two functions by referring to the short-run and long-run consumption behaviour of the people. We will discuss these consumption hypothesis in the next chapter.

IMPORTANCE OF CONSUMPTION FUNCTION

The concept of consumption function is greatly important both in theory and actual practice. To remove unemployment and to control economic fluctuations in the economy, it is very essential to adopt a proper macroeconomic policy. In the formation of such a policy, understanding of the concept of propensity of consume is very essential. Therefore. Prof. A.H. Hansen has remarked that "*consumption function is epoch-making contribution of Keynes to economic theory*". We shall explain below some of the theoretical and practical importance of this consumption function.

(1) **The concept of consumption function helps us to invalidate Say's law of classical economics.** In fact, Keynes relied on his consumption function for proving the invalidity of Say's law. According to Say's law, every supply creates its own demand and therefore there is no problem of deficiency of aggregate demand. Therefore, general overproduction and unemployment in the economy is not possible because adequate amount of aggregate demand is ever present. Now, according to Keynes's psychological law of consumption, when income increases consumption increases but less than the increase in income (that is, *MPC* is less than one) and therefore saving gap emerges between income and consumption. This saving gap implies that all output produced may not be sold in a period and the problem of deficiency of demand will arise unless this saving gap is matched by an equal amount of investment demand. There is no guarantee that the saving done will be automatically invested or, in other words, it is not necessary that investment demand will be equal to the saving gap.

Thus, the contention of the Say's law that every supply creates its equal demand is not valid. No doubt, every supply or production creates income equal to the output produced. But since all income is not consumed and there is no guarantee that investment will be equal to the saving so emerged, Say's law is proved invalid. When investment is less than the saving gap corresponding to full-employment level of income, the aggregate demand is not sufficient to provide full-employment to the people and other resources. Thus, the problem of deficiency of effective demand and hence general unemployment and overproduction arises in a free enterprise capitalist economy.

(2) The concept of propensity to consume is also important because **it brings out crucial significance of investment demand** for determination of the level of income and employment in a capitalist economy. From the concept of propensity to consume we know that consumption increases less than the increase in income and as a result gap emerges between income and consumption. To maintain a certain given level of income and employment, gap between income and consumption at that level must be bridged by investment expenditure otherwise it will not' be possible to maintain that level of income and employment because aggregate demand would not be large enough. This indicates the crucial importance of the investment demand in the determination of income and employment. To prevent the establishment of underemployment equilibrium in the economy or, in other words, for achieving full-employment equilibrium, investment demand must be equal to the saving gap at the level of full-employment. Keynes also showed that consumption function remains stable in the short run and therefore economic fluctuations in a capitalist economy are largely due to the fluctuations in investment demand. Thus from the concept of propensity to consume it follows that investment demand is vitally important in determining the level of income and employment. If it were possible to raise the propensity to consume in the short run, then without raising investment, we could have raised the level of income and employment. Since propensity to consume at a given level of income generally remains stable, we have to increase investment for achieving full employment in the economy.

(3) Another crucial importance of the Keynesian concept of consumption function is that **we derive the theory of multiplier from it which has great practical importance in the formulation of macro-economic policy,** especially of public works in times of depression. As we shall study in the next chapter, the magnitude of multiplier is equal to the reciprocal of one minus marginal propensity to consume $\left(K = \dfrac{1}{1 - MPC}\right)$, where K stands for multiplier and MPC for marginal propensity to consume. According to Keynes's psychological law of consumption marginal propensity to consume is less than one. According to this concept of multiplier, when investment increases, income, output and employment increase by a multiple amount, depending upon the size of the multiplier. Income increases manifold than the original investment because of the nature of consumption function. When some investment in some projects is undertaken, it leads to the increase in income of those employed in the projects but the process does not stop here. The increases in income are further spent on consumption and this leads to further increase in income and so the chain of increases in income and consumption continues and the ultimate increase in income and employment is multiple of the original increment in investment. If the marginal propensity to consume were equal to zero, then all increments in income brought about by additional investment would have been saved and therefore multiplier process would not have worked. Since the marginal propensity to consume is greater than zero, the increase in net investment have a multiplier effect on income, output and employment. Thus, the effect of investment on income depends on the size of the multiplier which depends on the value of the marginal propensity to consume. The greater the marginal propensity to consume, the greater the size of the multiplier.

(4) From the concept of consumption function, we can also explain ***why there is a tendency for the marginal efficiency of capital to decline.*** The declining tendency of the marginal efficiency of

capital is due to the nature of the consumption function. Two features of consumption function are important. First, the marginal propensity to consume is less than one which implies that as income increases, consumption increases less than this. Secondly, consumption function is stable in the short run *i.e.*, it does not shift much in the short run. As we know that the level of investment is a crucial factor in the determination of income and employment, fluctuations in the levels of income and employment depend primarily on the fluctuations in investment. The investment demand in the short run is determined by the rate of interest on the one hand and marginal efficiency of capital on the other. Since the rate of interest is relatively sticky, it is the marginal efficiency of capital which greatly affects the level of investment in the short run. Marginal efficiency of capital is nothing but the expected rate of profit on investment in the future. Thus, the marginal efficiency of capital is determined by the expectations of the entrepreneurs regarding the earning of profits from capital assets in the future.

Now, the most important fact that affects the entrepreneurs' expectations regarding profit prospects and thereby the marginal efficiency of capital is the level of future consumption demand for goods and services. Their estimate of future consumption demand depends on, among others, on the population growth. If population growth of a country is expected to fall as was estimated in the early thirties when Keynes wrote his book (*General Theory of Employment, Interest and Money*), this would adversely affect future consumption demand which in turn would adversely affect investment in the long run, Besides, according to Keynes, average propensity to consume (*APC*) falls as income of a community increases overtime. This also adversely affects inducement to invest. If there does not occur capital-using technological change, this will result in decline in investment opportunities in the long run, causing secular stagnation. Thus we see that in the Keynesian scheme of things level of investment depends upon the level of consumption demand in the long run.

Since marginal propensity to consume is less than one and also the consumption function is stable when income increases, consumption does not increase proportionately. As a result, the aggregate demand becomes deficient and the marginal efficiency of capital declines. The decline in the marginal efficiency of .capital adversely affects investment which stops rising. As a result, the growth process stops and ecpnomic recession occurs. In this way, Keynes himself and later important Keynesian economist, Prof. A.H. Hansen developed the theory of ***secular stagnation*** (i.e., prolonged period of depression of indefinite future) for the mature capitalist economies. This secular stagnation theory is based upon the assertion that investment opportunities in a capitalist economy will be exhausted soon due to the absence of the possibilities of increasing consumption demand. The meagre opportunities of increasing investment in the mature capitalist economies, according to them, were partly due to the constancy of consumption function and declining average propensity to consume which caused the marginal efficiency of capital to decline.

(5) As has been explained above, Keynesian concept of propensity to consume also **helps us in explaining the *turning points of a business cycle.*** The economy swings down from the peak it reaches because with marginal propensity to consume being less than one and average propensity to consume falling with increase in income consumption demand does not increase as much as the increase in income and output. Over time this causes deficiency in aggregate demand causing fall in marginal efficiency of capital which adversely affects investment demand by private business men. Likewise, economy's downward movement stops and it starts recovery because marginal propensity to consume being less than one and average propensity to consume (*APC*) rises as income decreases people do not reduce their consumption as much as the reduction in their income. Even during depression people try to maintain their previous level of consumption. This ultimately induce investment for replacement of capital goods which wear out over a period of business cycle. With the working of Keynesian investment multiplier recovery from recession gathers momentum.

QUESTIONS FOR REVIEW

1. What is consumption function ? Explain the objective and subjective factors which determine consumption expenditure in the economy. What are three forms of consumption function ? How do *APC* and *MPC* behave in these forms of consumption function ? Which form of the consumption function seems to be realistic ?
2. Explain Keynes' psychological law of consumption. Explain its importance in the determination of income and employment in the economy.
3. Explain and graphically represent Keynesian consumption function $C = a + bY$. How do marginal propensity to consume (*MPC*) and average propensity to consume (*APC*) change with increase in income in this consumption function ?
4. What is consumption function ? Explain the factors that cause shift in the consumption function.
5. Distinguish between Keynes' consumption function and Kuznet's consumption function. How have these two consumption functions been reconciled ?
6. What is consumption function puzzle ? How has it been resolved ?
7. What is consumption function ? Explain its importance in the theory of determination of income and employment
8. (*a*) What is a saving function ? Derive a saving function from the consumption function, $C = a + bY$

   (*b*) Show that the sum of *APC* and *APS* is equal to one .
9. "Consumption function is an epoch making contribution to the tools of economic analysis analogous to but even more important than Marshall's discovery of the demand function" (Hansen) Discuss.
10. Why does the *APC* differ from *MPC* ? What factors other than income are likely to be most important in determining consumption ?
11. Giveñ the data of the disposable income (Y_d) and amount of consumption at the initial level of income (₹ 100). Assuming that marginal propensity consume is 50 per cent. Complete the Table and draw the graphs of consumption and saving functions.

Y_d	C	S	APC	MPC	APS	MPS
₹ 100	150					
200						
300						
400						
500						
600						

12. Explain the important features of Keynesian Consumption function.
13. Explain briefly 'Life Cycle theory of consumption' and 'permanent income theory of consumption'. How do they differ from Keynesian theory of consumtion ?

CHAPTER 7*

Post-Keynesian Theories of Consumption

Introduction

In the previous chapter we explained the concept of consumption function which plays an important role in the theory of income and employment. Keynes mentioned several subjective and objective factors which determine consumption of a society. However, according to Keynes, of all the factors it is the *current level of income* that determines the consumption of an individual and also of society. Since Keynes lays stress on the *absolute size of income as a determinant of consumption,* his theory of consumption is also known as *absolute income theory*. Further, Keynes put forward a *psychlological law of consumption, according to which, as income increases consumption increases but not by as much as the increase in income. In other words, marginal propensity to consume is less than one.*

$$1 > \frac{\Delta C}{\Delta Y} > 0$$

Since Keynes propounded his theory of consumption there have been significant developments in this field and several alternative theories of consumer behaviour have been put forward. First, Duesenberry has propounded that consumption expenditure depends on income of an individual relative to incomes of others rather than the absolute size of his own income. His theory is therefore called *Relative Income Theory of Consumption*. Secondly, Modigliani put forward a theory known as *life cycle hypothesis*, according to which an individual plans his even consumption profile in his lifetime which depends not so much on his current income but on his expectations of income in the whole lifetime. Further, a famous American economist Friedman has advanced a hypothesis regarding consumption behaviour, called *permanent income hypothesis*, according to which consumption of an individual depends on permanent income rather than current level of income.

It is important to mention here an important puzzle about consumption function pointed out by Kuznets, a nobel prize-winner in economics. Contrary to Keynes's proposition that proportion of income spent on consumption declines as income increases (that is, average propensity to consume falls with the increase in income), Kuznets found from a statistical empirical study of consumption of the economy of the USA that average propensity to consume had remained constant over a long period despite the substantial increase in income. How the average propensity to consume has remained stable despite the substantial increase in income has been a great puzzle in consumption theory. We shall study below how modern theories of consumption such as Duesenberry's relative income theory of consumption life cycle hypothesis and Friedman's permanent income theory succeed in resolving this puzzle.

RELATIVE INCOME THEORY OF CONSUMPTION

An American economist J.S. Duesenberry put forward the theory of consumer behaviour which lays stress on relative income of an individual rather than his absolute income as a determinant of his consumption. Another important departure made by Duesenberry from Keynes's consumption theory

*This chapter is meant for higher level courses in macroeconomics.

is that, according to him, the consumption of a person does not depend on his current income but on a certain previously reached income level.

According to Duesenberry's relative income hypothesis, consumption of an individual is not the function of his absolute income but of his relative position in the income distribution in a society, that is, his consumption depends on his income relative to the incomes of other individuals in the society. For example, if the incomes of *all individuals* in a society increase by the *same percentage*, then their relative income would remain the same, though their absolute income would have increased. According to Duesenberry, because their relative income of individuals remain the same they will spend the same proportion of their income on consumption as they were doing before the absolute increase in their income. That is, the average propensity to consume (*APC*) will remain the same despite the increase in their absolute income.

As mentioned above, empirical studies based on time-series data made by Kuznets reveal that over a long period the average propensity to consume remains almost constant. Now, Duesenberry's relative income hypothesis suggests that in the long run the community would continue to consume the same proportion of income as its income increases. According to Duesenberry, saving as a proportion of income of the individuals with relatively low incomes would not rise much with the increase in their incomes. That is, their savings would not rise to the same proportion of income as was being done by the individuals who had the same higher income prior to the present increase in income. This is because with the increase in incomes of all individuals by the same proportion, the relative incomes of the individuals would not change and therefore they would consume the same proportion of their income. This applies to all individuals and households. It therefore follows that assuming that relative distribution of income remains the same with the growth of income of a society, its average propensity to consume (APC) would remain constant. Thus, this conclusion of the relative income hypothesis differs from the Keynesian theory of consumption according to which, as seen above, as absolute income of a community increases, it will devote a smaller proportion of its income to consumption expenditure, that is, its APC will decline.

It is important to note that relative income theory implies that with the increase in income of a community, the relative distribution of income remaining the same, it does not move along the same aggregate consumption function, but its consumption function shifts upward. Since as income increases, movement along the same consumption function curve implies a fall in average propensity to consume, *Duesenberry's relative income hypothesis suggests that as income increases consumption function curve shifts above so that average propensity to consume remains constant.*

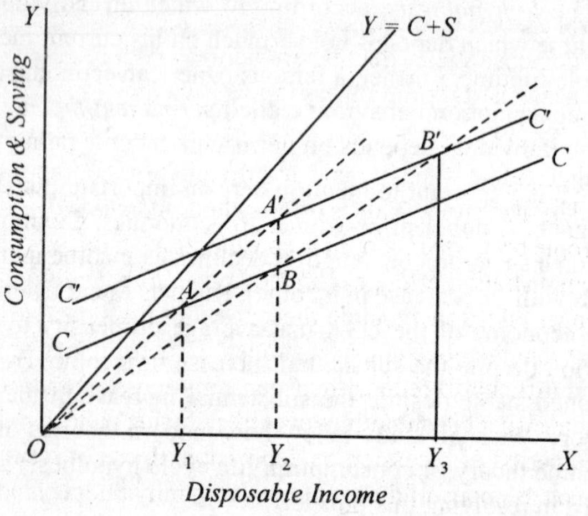

Fig. 7.1. *Duesenberry's Relative Income Theory of Consumption*

This is illustrated in Figure 7.1. Suppose a family A' has Y_1 level of income and is spending Y_1A' on consumption. Suppose its income level rises to Y_2. Now, its consumption would not rise only to Y_2B (*i.e.* equal to the consumption of the family B at Y_2 income level) but to Y_2A' where A' lies on the same ray from the origin as the previous point A of consumption. *This implies that the consumption expenditure of family A has risen in the same proportion as its income with the result that its average propensity to consume remains constant.*

Likewise, if income of family B which is having consumption expendiutre Y_2B at income level

Y_2, rises to Y_3, its consumption expenditure will increase to Y_3B' where B' lies on the same ray from the origin as B. This again means that the proportion of income devoted to consumption by family B (*i.e.* its *APC*) remains constant as there is increase in its absolute income. Thus, *if the proportion of income* devoted to consumption of the average family at each income level remains the same as its income increases, the aggregate consumption of the community as proportion of its income will also remain constant though its absolute consumption and absolute savings will increase with the absolute increse in income.

As income increases and a society moves along the same consumption function curve, its average propensity to consume falls. But Duesenberry's relative income hypothesis suggests that *as income increases consumption function curver shifts above* so that average propensity to consume remains constant. In Figure 7.1 it will be seen that if points A′ and B′ are joined together, we get, a new consuption function curve C′C′.

Demonstration Effect. By emphasising relative income as a determinant of consumption, the relative income hypothesis suggests that individuals or households try to imitate or copy the consumption levels of their neighbours or other families in a particular community. This is called demonstration effect or *Duesenberry effect.* Two things follows from this. First, the average propensity to consume does not fall. This is because *if incomes of all families increase in the same proportion, distribution of relative incomes would remain unchanged and therefore the proportion of consumption expenditure to income which depends on relative income will remain constant.*

Secondly, a family with a given income would devote more of his income to consumption if it is living in a community in which that income is regarded as relatively low because of the working of demonstration effect. On the other hand, a family will spend a lower proportion of its income if it is living in a community in which that income is considered as relatively high because demonstration effect will not be present in this case. For example, the recent studies of household expenditure made in India reveal that the families with a given income, say Rs. 5000 per month spend a larger proportion of their income on consumption if they live in urban areas as compared to their counterparts in rural areas. The higher propensity to consume of families living in urban areas is due to the working of demonstration effect where families with relatively higher income reside whose higher consumption standards tempt others in lower income brackets to consume more.

Ratchet Effect. The other significant part of Duesenberry's relative income hypothesis is that it suggests that when income of individuals or households falls, their consumption expenditure does not fall to that extent. This is often called a *ratchet effect.* This is because, according to Duesenberry, the people try to maintain their consumption at the highest level attained earlier. This is partly due to the demonstration effect explained above. People do not want to show to their neighbours that they no longer afford to maintain their previous high standard of living. Further, this is also partly due to the fact that they become accustomed to their previous higher level of consumption and it is quite hard and difficult to reduce their consumption expenditure when their income has fallen. They maintain their earlier consumption level by reducing their savings. Therefore, the fall in their income, as during the period of recession or depression, does not result in decrease in consumption expenditure very much as one would conclude from family budget studies.

This is illustrated in Figure 7.2 where on the X-axis we measure disposable income and on the *Y*-axis the consumption and savings. Starting with disposable income of zero, we assume that there is steady growth of disposable inocme till it reaches Y_1. The linear consumption function C_{LR} is the long-run consumption function. It will be seen from the figure that at Y_1 level of disposable income, the consumption expenditure equals Y_1C_1. Now suppose with initial income level Y_1, there is recession in the economy with the result that disposable income falls to the level Y_0. According to Duesenberry, consumption would not fall greatly to the level Y_0C_0 as the long-run consumption function curve C_{LR} would suggest. In their bid to maintain their consumption level previously reached people would now save less and reduce their consumption level only slightly to $Y_0C'_0$ whereas point C'_0 is on the short-run consumption function curve C_{SR}. Since $Y_0C'_0 > Y_0C_0$, the average propensity to consume at income level Y_0 is greater at C'_0 than at C_1 at income level Y_1 (A ray drawn from the origin to the point C'_0 will have greater slope than that of OC_1). When the economy recovers from recession and disposable income increases, the economy would move along the short-run consumption function curve C_{SR} till the consumption level C_1 is reached at income level Y_1. Beyond this, with the growth of income the consumption will increase along the long-run consumption function curve CL_R.

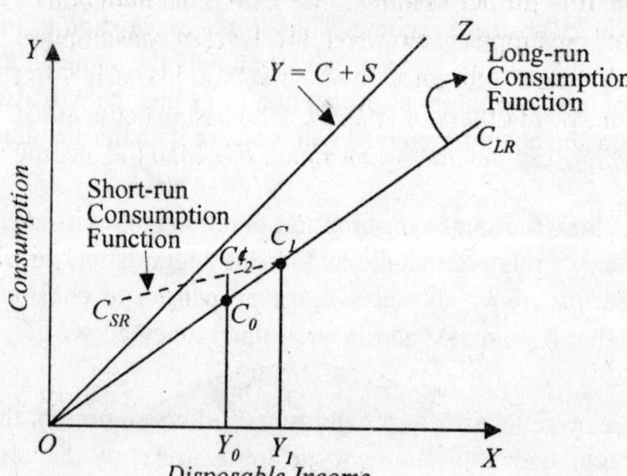

Fig. 7.2. *Duesenberry's Ratchet Effect*

Aggregate consumption function of the community. From the analysis of demonstration and ratchet effects it follows that Duesenberry's relative income hypothesis provides an explanation for why *aggregate consumption function of the community may be flatter than the family budget studies would suggest.* Duesenberry emphasizes that it is relative income rather than absolute income which determines consumption expenditure of households. When income of the community increases, relative income remaining constant, the proportion of consumption expenditure to income will not increase much because relative incomes of the households remain the same (Note that this implies that saving ratio will not rise much). Due to demonstration effect every household will increase its expenditure in the same proportion as the increase in income. On the other hand, if the income of the community decreases, the consumption expenditure would not decline much due to the ratchet effect according to which people try to maintain their previously attained higher level of consumption. This makes the consumption function of the community flatter than suggested by the cross-sectional family budget studies.

Further, it also follows from the Duesenberry relative income hypothesis that *short-run aggregate consumption function of the community is linear rather than curved.* As stated above, if, in the short run, the level of income increases, the proportion of consumption expenditure to income is not likely to increase much due to the operation of demonstration effect and with the fall in income the proportion of consumption to income is not likely to decline much due to the ratchet effect. This makes the short-run aggregate consumption function of the community linear. It is worth noting that Duesenberry's theory assumes that relative distribution of income does not change much. This is in accord with the facts of the real world situation where changes in income distribution do not take place in the short run. Thus Duesenberry's theory provides a convincing explanation in terms of demonstration and ratchet effects why aggregate consumption function is linear rather than non-linear.

LIFE CYCLE THEORY OF CONSUMPTION

An important post-Keynesian theory of consumption has been put forward by Modigliani and Ando[1] which is known as life cycle theory. According to life cycle theory, the *consumption in any period is not the function of current income of that period but of the whole lifetime expected income.*

1. See Ando, A., Modigliani, Franco "The Life Cycle Hypothesis of Saving: Aggregate Implications and Tests," *American Economic Review*, March 1963, pp, 55-84 and Modigliani, "The Life Cycle Hypothesis of Saving and the Demand for Wealth and Supply of Capital," *Social Research*, June 1966, pp. 160-217.

Thus, in life cycle hypothesis the individual is assumed to plan a pattern of consumption expenditure based on expected income in their entire lifetime. It is further assumed that individual maintains a more or less constant or slightly increasing level of consumption. However, this level of consumption is limited by his expectations of lifetime income. A typical individual in this theory in his early years of life spends on consumption either by borrowing from others or spending the assets bequeathed from his parents. It is in his main working years of his lifetime that he consumes less than the income he earns and therefore makes net positive savings. He invests these savings in assets, that is, accumulates wealth which he consumes in the future years. In his lifetime after retirement he again dissaves, that is, consumes more than his income in these later years of his life but is able to maintain or even slightly increase his consumption in the lifetime after retirement.

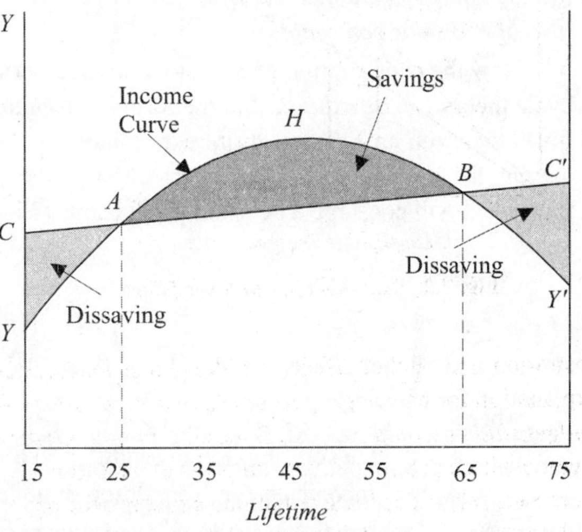

Fig. 7.3. *Life Cycle Theory of Consumption*

Life cycle hypothesis has been depicted in Fig. 7.3. It is assumed that a typical individual knows exactly at what age he will die. In Fig. 7.3 it is taken that the individual would die at the age of 75 years. That is, years 75 is his expected lifetime. If it is further assumed that net savings in the entire lifetime is zero, that is, the savings done by the individual in his working years of his life is equal to the dissavings made by him in his early years of life before he is able to earn income as well as the dissavings which he makes after retirement. It is also assumed for the sake of simplicity that interest paid on his assets is zero. The curve *YY'* shows income pattern of the whole life-time of the individual whereas *CC'* is the curve of consumption which is assumed to be slightly increasing as the individual grows old. It is assumed that our individual enters into labour force (*i.e.*, working life) at the age of 15 years. It will be noticed from Fig. 7.3 that upto the age of 25 years his income, though increasing, is less than his consumption, that is, he will be dissaving during the first 15 years of his working life. To finance his excess consumption over his income, he may be borrowing from others.

Beyond the age of 25 or point A on the income and consumption curves and upto the age of 65 years his income exceeds his consumption, that is, he will be saving during this period of his working life. With these savings he will build up assets or wealth. He may use these savings or wealth to pay off his debt incurred by him in the early stage of his working life. Another important motive of his savings and building up assets or wealth is to provide for his consumption after retirement when his income drops below his level of consumption. It will be observed from the Fig. 7.3 that beyond point B (that is, after retirement at 65 years) his current income falls short of his consumption and therefore he once again dissaves. He would be using his accumulated assets or wealth from his earlier working years to meet the dissavings after retirement at the age of 65. It is important to note that we assume that he does not intend to leave any assets for his children. Given this assumption, his net savings over his lifetime will be zero. Therefore, in Fig. 7.3 his savings during the period when he earns more than his consumption expenditure, that is, the *shaded* area *AHB* will be equal to the two areas of dissavings, *CYA* + *BC'Y'*. Thus he dies leaving behind no assets or wealth. He has planned his consumption expenditure over the years that his net savings at the time of death are zero. However, this assumption can be relaxed if he wishes to leave some assets or wealth for his children as is usually the case in

India. In case he wants to bequeath some assets for his children and wife, he will have to save more in the working period of his life so that his total savings exceed the total dissavings.

Some important conclusions follow from the life cycle theory of consumption. The fundamental idea of the life-cycle hypothesis is that people make their consumption plans for their entire lifetime and further that they make their lifetime consumption plans on the basis of their expectations of lifetime income. Thus in the life cycle model *consumption is not a function of current income but of the expected lifetime income. Besides, in life cycle theory the wealth presently held by individuals also affects their consumption.*

How the consumption of an individual in a period depends on these factors highlighted by life cycle theory can be expressed in the form of an equation. To do so let us consider an individual of a given age with an *additional life* expectancy of T years and intends to retire from working after serving for N years more. Then suppose that in the current period and thereafter in his life span the individual will consume a constant proportion, 1/T of his life-time income in equal instalments per year.

Thus

$$C_t = \frac{1}{T}(Y_{Lt} + (N-1)Y_L^e + W_t)$$

where

C_t = the consumption expenditure in the current period t

Y_{Lt} = Income earned from doing some labour in the current period t

$N-1$ = remaining future years of doing some labour or work

Y_L^e = the average annual income expected to be earned over N–1 years for which individual plans to do some work

W_t = the presently held wealth or assets

It will be observed from the above equation that life cycle hypothesis suggests that consumption in any period does not depend only on current income but also on expected income over his entire working years. Besides, consumption in any period also depends on his presently owned wealth or assets which are built up during the prime working years of one's life when income exceeds savings.

The general consumption behaviour as suggested by Ando-Modigliani life cycle hypothesis can be expressed in the following functional form:

$$C_t = b_1 Y_{Lt} + b_2 Y^e_L + b_3 W_t$$

where

C_t = Consumption expenditure in a period t.

Y_{Lt} = Income earned from doing some labour in the current period t.

Y_L^e = the average annual income expected to be earned from labour during the further years of working life.

W_t = wealth currently owned

b_1 represents marginal propensity to consume out of current income

b_2 is marginal propensity to consume out of expected lifetime income, and

b_3 is the marginal propensity to consume out of wealth.

It is significant to note that consumption would not be much responsive to changes in current income (*i.e.*, Y_{Lt}) unless it also changes expected future lifetime income (Y^e_L). A one time or temporary change in income, say, by ₹ 1000, will affect consumption in the same way as the increase in wealth. The consumption of these ₹ 1000 will be spread over the entire lifetime in a planned consumption flow per period. With 50 years of future life, increase of ₹1000 of transient or temporary income will raise the consumption by 1000/50 = ₹ 20 per period. This implies that consumption function curve will shift above. A permanent increase in income that is expected to persist throughout the working years, which implies that in future expected lifetime income also rises, will produce a large effect on consumption in each of the remaining period of one's lifetime. Further, the increase in wealth will shift the consumption function upward, that is, will increase the intercept term of the consumption function.

To estimate behaviour of the consumer on the basis of life cycle hypothesis, one is required to make some assumptions how people form their expectations regarding labour income over their life time. In the study of consumption function for the United States, Ando and Modigliani made the assumption that the expected future labour income is simply a multiple of current labour income. Thus, according to this assumption,

$$Y_L^e = \beta Y_{LT}$$

where β is a multiple of current labour income. This assumption implies that people revise their expected labour income of future by a certain multiple of the change in current labour income. With this assumption, aggregate consumption function for the community can be expressed as under

$$C_1 = (b_1 + b_2\beta)Y_{LT} + b_3 W_t$$

This function has been estimated taking time-series data for the U.S.A. and the following estimates have been obtained :–

$$C_t = 0.72\ Y_{LT} + 0.06\ W$$

According to these estimates, if current labour income increases by ₹100 along with assumed effect on expected future income, consumption will increase by ₹ 72 per period. Besides, the increase in wealth by ₹ 100 will raise the consumption expenditure by ₹ 6. It therefore follows that according to life cycle hypothesis the relationship between income and consumption is non-proportional, increase in labour income by ₹ 100 crore leads to increase in consumption by ₹ 72. Further, the increase in wealth will shift the consumption function upward, that is, will increase the intercept term of the consumption function.

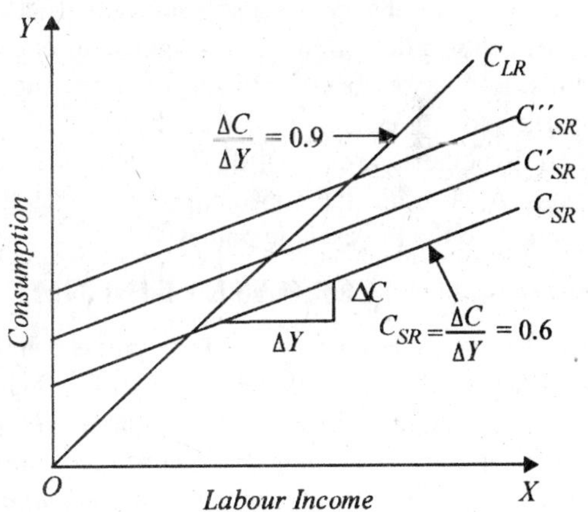

Fig. 7.4. *Life Cycle Consumption and Income : Short Run and Long Run*

The consumption function based on life cycle hypothesis is illustrated in Fig. 7.4 where along the X-axis we measure disposable income and along the *Y*-axis the consumption expenditure. The short-run consumption function is shown by the curve C_{SR} which has a slope of 0.6 which is the marginal propensity to consume out of labour income in the short run. This short-run consumption function is linear and has an intercept term indicating that average propensity to consume declines as labour income increases and *MPC* < *APC*. *The intercept of the short-run consumption function measures the effect of wealth on consumption.* Since wealth increases over a period of time due to savings in the prime working years, the short-run consumption function will be shifting upward, that is, the intercept of the short-run consumption function will be increasing as wealth grows in the long run. Overtime the shift in the short-run consumption function may trace a series of points on a long-run consumption function C_{LR} passing through the origin.

Since the ratios of wealth and labour income to the personal disposable income are constant over time, the life cycle consumption function is in accord with the conclusion arrived at by Kuznets from the long-run time series data that the long-run consumption function is proportional, with average propensity to consume (*APC* or *MPC*) remaining constant and being equal to nearly 0.9. These facts are quite consistent with the long-run consumption function of life cycle hypothesis and thus help in resolving the Kuznets puzzle.

Life cycle hypothesis also explains the non-proportional relationship between consumption and income found in the cross-sectional family budget-studies. It has been found in these studies that high income families consume a smaller proportion of their income, that is, their average propensity to consume (*APC*) is relatively lower than those of the low-income families. This can be easily explained by life-cycle hypothesis. Suppose we choose a random sample of families from the population and rank them according to their incomes. The families with higher incomes are expected to be middle-aged income earners who are in the prime working years of their lifetime and therefore earn more than they consume (*i.e.*, their *APC* will be relatively lower). On the other hand, the families with lower incomes are likely to have relatively high proportion of new entrants into the labour force and the old people who have retired and, as seen above, they consume more than their current income and their *APC* being quite high pushes up the *APC* of the low income families.

Shortcomings. Although life cycle theory has provided an explanation of various puzzles about consumption function, it is not without critics, Gardner Ackley[2] has criticized the assumption of life cycle hypothesis that in making consumption plans, households have "a definite and conscious vision."

According to Ackley, the possession of this vision on the part of households sounds unrealistic. Further, according to him, to assume that a household has complete knowledge of "family's future size, including the life expectancy of each member, entire lifetime profile of income of each member, the extent of credit available in the future, future emergencies, opportunities and social pressure which have a bearing on consumption spending" is quite unrealistic.

Life cycle theory has also been criticized that it fails to recognize the importance of *liquidity constraints* in determining the response of consumption to income. According to critics, even if a household has a concrete vision of future income, the opportunities to borrow from the capital markets for quite a long period on the basis of expected future income, as has been visualised by life cycle hypothesis, are very little. This creates the liquidity constraints for deciding about consumption plans. As a result, the consumption becomes highly responsive to current income which is quite contrary to the life cycle hypothesis.

PERMANENT INCOME THEORY OF CONSUMPTION

Permanent income theory of consumers' behaviour has been put forward by a well-known American economist, Milton Friedman.[3] Though Friedman's permanent income hypothesis differs from life cycle consumption theory in details, it has important common features with the latter. Like the life cycle approach, according to Friedman, consumption is determined by long-term expected income rather than current level of income. *It is this long-term expected income which is called by Friedman as permanent income* on the basis of which people make their consumption plans. To make his point clear, Friedman gives an example which is worth quoting. According to Friedman, an individual who is paid or receives income only once a week, say on Friday, he would not concentrate his consumption on one day with zero consumption on all other days of the week. He argues that an individual would prefer a smooth consumption flow per day rather than plenty of consumption today and little consumption tomorrow. Thus consumption in one day is not determined by income received on that particular day. Instead, it is determined by average daily income received for a period. This is on the line of life cycle hypothesis. Thus, according to him, people plan their consumption on the basis of expected average income over a long period which Friedman calls permanent income.

---

2. Gardner Ackley, "Discussion of a Paper by James Tobin and W. Dolde in Consumer Spending and Monetary Policy, The Linkages, Federal Reserve Bank of Boston, 1971.
3. Milton Friedman, *A Theory of Consumption Function*, Princeton University Press, 1957.

It may be noted that permanent income or expected long-term average income is earned from both "human and non-human wealth". The income earned from human wealth which is also called human capital refers to the return on income derived from selling household's labour services, that is, efforts and abilities of its labour. This is generally referred to as labour income. Non-human wealth consists of tangible assets such as saved money, debentures, equity shares, real estate and consumer durables. It is worth noting that Friedman regards consumer durables such as cars, refrigerators, airconditioners, television sets as part of households' non-human wealth. The imputed value of the flow of services from these consumer durables is considered as consumption by Friedman.

Relationship between Consumption and Permanent Income

Now, what is the precise relationship between consumption and permanent income (that is, the expected long period average income). According to permanent income hypothesis, Friedman thinks that consumption is proportional to permanent income

$$C^p = kY^P$$

where Y^p is the permanent income

C^p is the permanent consumption

k is the proportion of permanent income that is consumed.

The proportion or fraction k of permanent income that is consumed depends upon the following factors:

1. Rate of interest (*i*). At a higher rate of interest the people would tend to save more and their consumption expenditure will decrease. The lowering of rate of interest will have opposite effect on the consumption.

2. The proportion of non-human wealth to human wealth. The relative amounts of income from physical assets (*i.e., non-human wealth*) and income from labour (i.e., *human wealth*) also affects consumption expenditure. This is denoted by the term w in the parmanent consumption function and is measured by the ratio of non-human wealth to income. In his permanent income hypothesis Friedman suggests that consumption expenditure depends a good deal on the wealth or assets possessed by the people. The greater the amount of wealth or assets held by an individual, the greater would be its propensity to consume and vice-versa.

3. Desire to add to one's wealth. Lastly, households' *preference for immediate consumption as against the desire to add to the stock of wealth or assets* also determines the proportion of permanent income to be devoted to consumption. The desire to add to one's wealth rather than to fulfil one's wants of immediate consumption is denoted by *u*.

Thus rewriting the consumption function based on Friedman's permanent income hypothesis we have

$$C^p = k\,(i, w, u)\; Y^p$$

The above function implies that permanent consumption is function of permanent income. The proportion of permanent income devoted to consumption depends on the rate of interest (i), the ratio of non-human wealth to labour income (w) and desire to add to the stock of assets (u).

Permanent and transitory income. In addition to permanent income, the individual's income may contain a transitory component that Friedman calls as a transitory income. *A transitory income is a temporary income that is not going to persist in future periods.* For example, a clerk in an office may get a substantial income from overtime work in a month which he thinks cannot be maintained. Thus, this large overtime income for a month will be transitory component of income. According to Friedman, transitory income is not likely to have much effect on consumption. Thus, income of an individual consists of two parts, permanent and transitory, which we may write as under:

$$Y^m = Y^p + Y^t$$

where Y^m is measured income in a period, Y^p is the permanent income and Y^t is transitory income.

Measuring Permanent Income

To make the permanent income hypothesis operational we need to measure permanent income. Permanent income, as is generally defined is *"the steady rate of consumption a person could maintain for the rest of his or her life, given the present level of wealth and income now and in the future."*[4] However, it is very difficult for a person to know what part of any change in income is likely to persist and is therefore permanent and what part would not persist and is therefore transitory. Friedman has suggested a simple way of measuring permanent income by relating it to the current and past incomes. According to him, permanent income is equal to the last year's income plus a *proportion of change in income* occurred between the last year and the current year. Thus, permanent income can be measured as under:

$$Y^p = Y_{t-1} + a(Y_t - Y_{t-1}) \quad o < a < 1 \qquad \text{----- (1)}$$

$$Y^p = aY_t + (1 - a)\,Y_{t-1} \qquad \text{----- (2)}$$

Let us illustrate this with an example. Suppose, the proportion of change in income in the last year and the current year equals 0.6 and the last year's income (Y_{t-1}) is Rs. 80,000 and the current year's income (Y_t) is Rs. 85,000, then from above equation permanent income can be estimated as under.

$$\begin{aligned} Y^p &= 0.6\,(85{,}000) + (1 - 0.6)\,80{,}000 \\ &= 51{,}000 + 32{,}000 \\ &= 83{,}000 \end{aligned}$$

It is worthwhile to note the two features of the above equations estimating permanent income. First, if $Y_t = Y_{t-1}$, it implies that current year's income is equal to last year. This further means that last year income is being maintained and therefore the individual would expect to earn the same income in the future also. In this case then permanent income is equal to the current or last year's income. Secondly, when income of an individual increases in the current year as compared to the last year, the permanent income will be less than the current year's income. This is because individual is not sure whether the increase in income will persist in the future and therefore does not immediately revise his estimate of permanent income by the full amount of the increase in his income in the current year.

Permanent Income, Long-Run and Short-Run Consumption Functions

Now, having known the meaning of permanent income and permanent consumption we can describe the precise relationship between consumption and income both in the short run and the long run as under.

$$C = kY^p = kaY_t + k\,(1 - a)\,Y_{t-1}$$

In the above consumption function ka is the marginal propensity to consume in the short-run which is obviously less than the long-run marginal propensity to consume which is equal to k. Thus, according to Friedman's permanent income hypothesis, short-run marginal propensity to consume differs from long-run marginal propensity to consume, the latter being greater than the former. Further, $k(1-a)Y_{t-1}$ is the intercept of the short-run consumption function.

Friedman's permanent income hypothesis is illustrated in Figure 7.5. It shall be seen from this figure that *permanent consumption function is represented by the long-run consumption function curve C_{LR}, ($C_{LR} = kY^p$). This long-run consumption function shows the proportional relationship between consumption and income and is a straight line passing through the origin which implies that APC is constant and is equal to MPC.*

In accordance with permanent income hypothesis, *short-run consumption function curves are flatter as compared to the long-run consumption function curve indicating that the short-run*

4. Dornbusch, R. and Fischer, S., *Macroeconomics*, McGraw-Hill, Fifth Edition, 1990, p. 279.

marginal propensity to consume is lower than long-run marginal propensity to consume. The reason for this is that the individual is not sure whether the increase in income will persist over the longer period which determines the consumption plans of individuals. Therefore, the individuals do not fully adjust their consumption expenditure according to their higher current income than would be the case if the current increase in income is expected to be permanent. If the rise in income happens to be permanent, that is, if the next year's income is equal to the higher income of the current year, the individual will fully adjust his consumption expenditure to the higher income level.

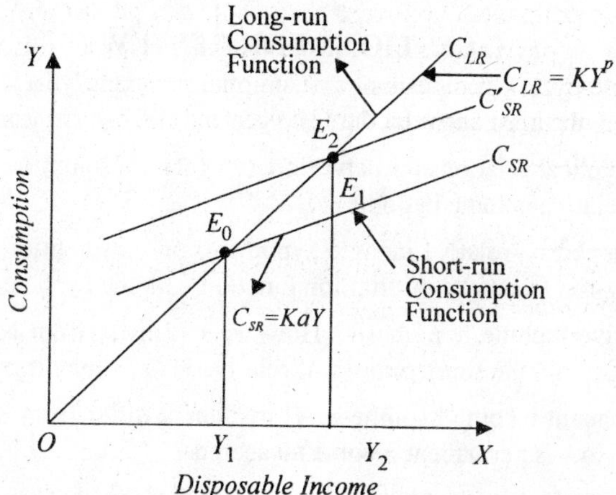

Fig. 7.5. *Permanent Income Hypothesis : Long-Run and Short-Run Consumption Functions*

It is important to note that in our above analysis we have assumed that full adjustment of consumption expenditure to change in income takes place in two years time. In this case permanent income is the average of the two years incomes. However, *in real world permanent income depends on expectations of income for a much longer period depending upon the vision of the individual.* In case of longer vision adjustment of consumption expenditure will take place slowly over a long period. However, if the individual is sure that the increase in income is permanent he will adjust his consumption quickly to higher current income. It, therefore, follows that whereas in the short run average propensity to consume falls as income increases because people are not sure whether the increase in income will persist or not. But when they actually find that the increase in income is permanent, they fully adjust their consumption to their higher permanent income as reflected in the long-run consumption function.

Conclusion

Permanent income hypothesis is similar to life cycle hypothesis and differs only in details. Like the life cycle hypothesis, permanent income hypothesis can explain the puzzle about the relationship between consumption and income, namely, whereas in the long-run time series data, consumption-income ratio (*i.e.*, *APC*) is constant, in the short run it declines with the increase in income as we have seen above. The permanent income hypothesis is quite consistent with the constancy of *APC* in the long run and its variation in the short run.

Permanent income hypothesis is also consistent with the evidence from the cross-sectional budget studies that high income families have low average propensity to consume than that of low-income families. A sample of high income families at a given time is likely to contain a relatively larger number of families who are having positive transitory increase in incomes. Since the consumption depends on permanent income, the average propensity to consume computed as the ratio of consumption to measured income $\left[APC = \frac{C}{Y^m}\right]$ where $Y^m = Y^p + Y^t$ will be relatively low. On the other hand, a sample of families with low income at a given time would contain a relatively larger number of families experiencing negative transitory incomes and therefore in their case the average propensity to consume estimated as $\frac{C}{Y^p + Y^t}$ will be relatively high.

Further, by laying stress on changes in rate of interest and the wealth or assets held by the people and desire to add to one's wealth as important determinants of consumption and savings, Friedman's permanent income hypothesis has made an important contribution to the theory of consumption and saving.

QUESTIONS FOR REVIEW

1. Explain the life cycle hypothesis of consumption, Compare the major differences of this hypothesis with the permanent Income Hypothesis of Consumption.
2. Explain the cyclical relationship between aggregate consumption and national income in terms of the relative income hypothesis.
3. Explain Duesenberry, relative income hypothesis of consumption behaviour. How does it reconcile long-run (sector) consumption function with the cyclical consumption function ?
4. What is relative income hypothesis? How does it differ from Keynes' absolute income hypothesis. Explain the shortcomings of relative income hypothesis.
5. Explain permanent income hypothesis. How does it differ from Keynes' absolute income hypothesis ? How is permanent income measured ?
6. How does permanent income hypothesis explain that the short-run marginal propensity to consume is lower than the long-run marginal propensity to consume ? Do you think that the short-run *MPC* of someone whose income is highly variable will be relatively low ? Why ?
7. Explain the permanent income hypothesis of consumption. Explain its weaknesses.
8. What is money illusion ? How does it affect the consumption of those who suffer from it ?
9. Explain the concepts of demonstration effect and ratchet effect. How do they ensure that proportion of consumption to national income, that is, average propensity to consume remains the same as income increases.
10. How does life cycle hypothesis resolve the apparent contradiction between Keynes's short run consumption which suggests a non-proportional relation between consumption and income and Kuznets finding that relationship between consumption and income is proportional ?

CHAPTER 8

Investment Demand

Introduction

Levels of national income and employment in the short run depend upon the level of aggregate demand. The aggregate demand consists of two constituents—consumption demand and investment demand. In the previous chapter we have studied the consumption function and the various factors which determine it. In the present chapter we shall discuss the factors which determine the investment demand or inducement to invest. Since consumption function is more or less stable in the short run, investment demand is of crucial importance in the determination of income and employment. The greater the level of investment, the greater the level of income and employment. According to Keynes, the equilibrium of a capitalist economy is generally not established at the level of full employment, primarily because investment demand is insufficient to fill up the saving gap corresponding to the level of full employment. Therefore, underemployment equilibrium, on which Keynes laid a great stress, is due to the lack of investment demand as compared to the amount of saving at full-employment level of income, there emerges an *inflationary gap* in the economy which brings about the rise in general price level. We thus see that investment demand plays a vital role in the determination of national income, employment and prices in the country.

Meaning of Investment

It is useful to make the meaning of investment clear. When a person buys shares, bonds or debentures of a public limited company from the market, it is generally said that he has made investment. But this is not the real investment which determines income and employment in the country and with which we are here concerned. Buying of existing shares and bonds by an individual is merely a financial investment. When one individual purchases the shares or bonds, some other one would sell them. Thus, the purchase and sale of the shares merely represents the change in the ownership of assets which already exists rather than the creation of new capital assets. It is the new addition to the stock of physical capital such as plant, machines, trucks, new factories and so on that creates income and employment. Therefore, *by real investment we mean the addition to the stock of physical capital.* Thus, in economics, investment means the new expenditure incurred on addition of capital goods such as machines, buildings, equipment, tools, etc. The addition to the stock of physical capital, i.e., net investment-raises the level of aggregate demand which brings about addition to the level of income and employment in the economy. Keynes and many other economists also include the increase in the *inventories* of consumer goods in the capital of the country and therefore in the investment.

TYPES OF INVESTMENT

Distinction must be drawn between the following three types of investment:

1. Business fixed investment
2. Residential investment
3. Inventory investment

We explain below their meanings and the factors which determine them.

Business Fixed Investment

Business fixed investment means investment in the machines, tools and equipment that businessmen buy for use in further production of goods and services. The stock of these machines or plant equipment etc. represents fixed capital. The term 'fixed' in it implies that expenditure made on the machines, equipment etc. continues to be used for production for a relatively long time. This is in contrast to inventory investment whose components will be either used shortly for production or sold shortly to others for further production.

Business fixed investment is important in two respects. First, business fixed investment is an important component of aggregate demand and therefore plays a significant role in the determination of natural income and employment. Business fixed investment is a volatile component of aggregate demand and, as Keynes emphasized, fluctuation in levels of fixed business investment is responsible for business cycles in a free market economy.

As we shall explain in detail later in this chapter Keynes put forward a theory of investment which states that business fixed investment is determined by *expected rate of profit* (which he calls *marginal efficiency of capital*) and rate of interest. Since rate of interest in the short run is relatively sticky, it is changes in expectations about earning profits in future that cause fluctuations in business fixed investment.

According to the neoclassical theory, business fixed investment is determined by the marginal product of capital the one the hand and user's cost of capital on the other. The user's cost of capital merely depends on the price of capital goods, the interest rate and the depreciation rate. According to the neoclassical model, if marginal product of capital exceeds user's cost of capital, firms will find it profitable to undertake fixed investment. In this model, rate of interest, which is an important component of the user cost of capital, and taxation of profits play an important role in the determination of business fixed investment. The neoclassical theory will be discussed in detail later in this chapter.

Residential Investment

Residential investment refers to the expenditure which people make on constructing or buying new houses or dwelling apartments for the purpose of living or renting out to others. Residential investment varies from 3 per cent to 5 per cent of GDP in various countries. Two important features of residential investment are worth noting. First, since the average life of a housing unit is of 40 to 50 years, the stock of existing housing units at a point of time is very large as compared to the new residential investment in a year (i.e. flow of residential investment). Second, there is well developed resale market for housing units so that people who construct or own them can sell them in this secondary market.

Residential investment depends on price of existing housing units. The higher the price of existing units, the higher will be investment in constructing and buying new housing units. The price of housing units is determined by demand for housing units which slopes downward and the supply of existing units which is a fixed quantity and its supply curve is therefore vertical straight line.

In the long run demand for housing is determined by rate of population and formation of new households. The higher rate of population growth will lead to the increase in demand for housing units. The tendency towards two-member households has led to greater demand for housing units. Income is another important factor determining demand for houses and therefore greater residential investment. Since level of income over time fluctuates a good deal, there is strong cyclical pattern of investment in residential construction.

Finally, interest is another important that determines demand for dwelling units. Most houses, especially in cities, are purchased by borrowing funds from banks for a long time, say 20 to 25 years. Generally, the houses purchased are mortgaged with banks or other financial institutions who provide funds for this purpose. The individuals who purchase houses on mortgage borrowing pay monthly instalment of original sum borrowed plus interest. Therefore demand for housing units is highly sensitive to changes in rate of interest. Therefore, monetary policy has a substantial effect on residential investment.

Inventory Investment

Firms hold inventories of raw materials, semi-finished goods to be processed into final goods. The firms also hold inventories of finished goods to be sold shortly. The *change in the inventories* or stocks of these goods with the firms is called inventory investment. Now, why do firms hold inventories? The first motive of holding inventories is *smoothing of the level of production.* The firms experience temporary booms and busts in sales of their output. Instead of adjusting their production each time to match the changes in sales of the product they find cheaper to produce goods *at a steady rate.* With this steady rate of production when sales are low, the firms will be producing more than they are selling and therefore in these periods they will hold the extra goods produced as inventories. On the other hand, when sales are high with a steady rate of production, they will be producing less than they sell. In such periods to meet the market demand for goods, they will take out goods from inventories to meet the demand.

The second reason for holding inventories is that *it is less costly* for a firm to buy inputs such as raw materials *less frequently in large quantities* to produce goods and therefore it is required to hold inventories of raw materials and other intermediate products. Buying small quantities of the materials more frequently to produce goods is a more costly affair.

The third reason for holding inventories by the firms is to avoid '*running out of stock' possibilities* when their sales of goods are high and therefore it is profitable to sell at that time. This requires them to hold inventories of goods.

Determinants of Inventory Investment

The inventories of raw materials and goods depend on the level of output which a firm plans to produce. An important model that explains the inventories of raw materials and goods is the *accelerator model.* Though the accelerator model applies to all types of investment, it applies best in case of inventory investment. According to the accelerator model, the firms hold the total stock of inventories of raw materials and goods that is proportional to their level of output. When manufacturing firms' level of output is high, they require to keep more inventories of materials and of goods in process of being converted into finished products. When the economy is booming, retail firms would like to hold more inventories so that the goods they are selling may not go out of stock and their customers went away disappointed. Thus, if N stands for the stock of inventories and Y for level of output, then

$$N = \beta Y$$

where β is proportion of output (Y) that the firms want to hold as inventories.

Now, since inventory investment (I) means the change in stock of inventories, it can be written as follows :

$$I_n = \Delta N = \beta \Delta Y$$

The accelerator model predicts that given the parameter β when output of firms increases, inventory investment will increase and when output falls, the inventory investment by firms will decline. In fact, when output of goods falls due to slackening of demand, the firms will allow the inventories to run down which implies negative inventory investment.

The empirical macroeconomic studies made in United States indicated that for every dollar increase in GDP, there is 0.20 of inventory investment. That is, value of β in the accelerator model is 0.2. In quantitative terms, the accelerator model of inventory investment can be written as

$$I_n = 0.2 \ \Delta Y$$

Autonomous Investment and Induced Investment

After Keynes two types of investments have been distinguished. One is *autonomous investment* and the second is *induced investment.* By autonomous investment we mean the investment which does not change with the changes in the income level and is therefore independent of income. Keynes thought that the level of investment depends upon marginal efficiency of capital and the rate of interest. He thought changes in income level will not affect investment. This view of Keynes is based upon his preoccupation with short-run problem. He was of the opinion that changes in income level with affect investment only in the long run. Therefore, considering as he was the short-run problem he treated investment as independent of the changes in the income level. In fact the distinction between autonomous investment and induced investment has been made by post-Keynesian economists. *Autonomous investment refers to the investment which does not depend upon changes in the income level.* This autonomous investment generally takes place in houses, roads, public undertakings and in other types of economic infrastructure such as power, transport and communication. This *autonomous investment depends more on population growth and technical progress than on the level of income.* Most of the investment undertaken by Government is of the autonomous nature. The investment undertaken by Government in various development projects to accelerate economic growth of the country is of autonomous type. The autonomous investment is depicted in Fig. 8.1 where it will be seen that whatever the level of national income, investment remains the same at I_a. Therefore the autonomous investment curve is a horizontal straight line.

On the other hand, induced investment is that investment which is affected by the changes

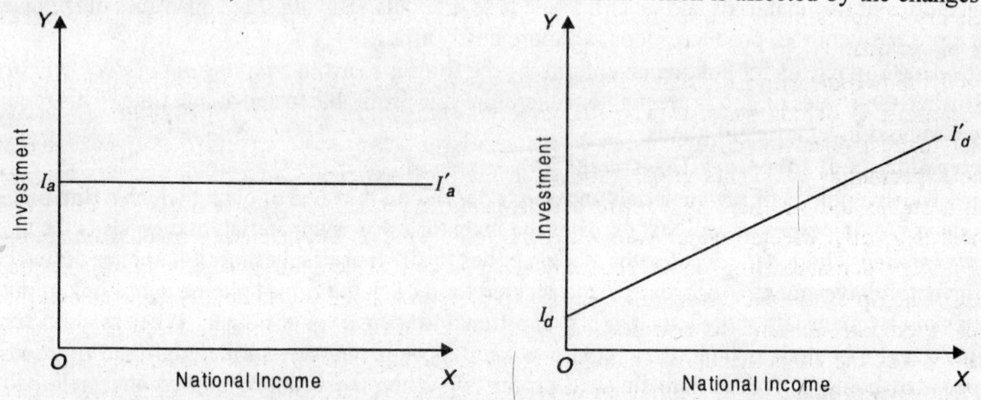

Fig. 8.1. *Autonomous Investment* **Fig. 8.2.** *Induced Investment*

in the level of income. The greater the level of income, the larger will be the consumption of the community. In order to produce more consumer goods, more investment has to be made in capital goods so that greater output of consumer goods becomes possible. Keynes regarded rate of interest as a factor determining induced investment but the empirical evidence gathered so far suggests that induced investment depends more on income than on the rate of interest. Induced investment is shown in Fig. 8.2 where it will be seen that with the increase in national income, induced investment is increasing. Increase in national income implies that demand for output of goods and services increases. To produce greater output, more capital goods are required to produce them. To have more capital goods more investment has to be undertaken. This induced investment is undertaken both in fixed capital assets and in inventories. The essence of induced investment is that greater income and therefore greater aggregate demand affects the level of investment in the economy. The induced investment underlines the concept of the prin-ciple of accelerator, which is highly useful in explaining the occurrence of trade cycles.

KEYNES'S THEORY OF INVESTMENT

According to Keynes investment demand depends upon two factors: (1) expected rate of profits to which Keynes gives the name *Marginal Efficiency of Capital,* and. (2) the rate of interest. It can be easily shown that investment is determined by expected rate of profit and the rate of interest. A person having an amount of savings has two alternatives before him. Either he should invest his savings in machines, factories, etc., or he can lend his savings to others on a certain rate of interest. If investment undertaken in machines or factories is expected to fetch 25% rate of profit, while the current rate of interest is only 15%, then it is obvious that the person would invest his savings in machinery or factory.

It follows from above, if investment is to be profitable then the expected rate of profit must not be less than the current market rate of interest. If the expected rate of profit is greater than the market rate of interest, new investment will take place. If an entrepreneur does not invest his own savings but has to borrow from others, then it becomes much clear that the expected rate of profit from investment in any capital asset must not be less than the rate of interest he has to pay. For instance, if an entrepreneur borrows funds from others at 15% rate of interest, then the investment proposed to be undertaken will actually be undertaken only if the expected rate of profit from it is more than 15 per cent. We thus see that investment depends upon marginal efficiency of capital on the one hand and the rate of interest on the other. Investment will be undertaken in any given form of capital asset so long as expected rate of profit or marginal efficiency of capital falls to the level of the current market rate of interest. The equilibrium of the entrepreneur is established at the level of investment where expected rate of profit or marginal efficiency of capital is equal to the current rate of interest. Therefore, the theory of investment is also based upon the assumption that the entrepreneur tries to maximize his profits.

Of the two determinants of inducement to invest, marginal efficiency of capital or expected rate of profit is of comparatively greater importance than the rate of interest. This is because rate of interest does not change much in the short run; it is more or less sticky. But changes in the expectations of profits greatly affect the marginal efficiency of capital and make it very much unstable and volatile. As a result of changes in marginal efficiency of capital, investment demand is greatly affected which causes aggregate demand to fluctuate very much. The changes in aggregate demand bring about economic fluctuations which are generally known as trade cycles. When profit expectations of businessmen are good, large investment is undertaken which causes aggregate demand to rise and bring about conditions of boom and prosperity in the economy. On the other hand, when expectations regarding profits are adverse, the rate of investment falls which causes decline in aggregate demand and brings about depression, unemployment and excess productive capacity in the economy. Thus, the changes in the marginal efficiency of capital play a crucial role in causing changes in the investment level and economic activity.

We have read in the theory of interest that, according to Keynes, the rate of interest is determined by liquidity preference and the supply of money. The greater the liquidity preference, the greater the rate of interest. Given the liquidity preference curve, the greater the supply of money, the lower will be the rate of interest. We have already studied how the rate of interest is determined. We explain below in detail the concept of marginal efficiency of capital and describe the factors on which it depends.

Marginal Efficiency of Capital

As has been pointed out above, the concept of marginal efficiency of capital refers to the rate of profit expected to be made from investment in certain capital assets. The rate of profit expected from an extra unit of a capital asset is known as marginal efficiency of capital. Now, the question is how the marginal efficiency of capital is measured. Suppose an entrepreneur invests money in a certain machinery, how will he estimate the expected rate of profit from it. To estimate the marginal efficiency of capital, the entrepreneur will first take into consideration how much price he has to pay for the particular capital asset. The price which he has to pay for the particular capital asset is called its *supply price* or *cost of capital*. The second thing which he will consider is that how much yield he expects to obtain from investment from that particular capital asset. A capital asset continues to produce goods and yield income over a long period of time. Therefore, an entrepreneur has to estimate the prospective yield from a capital asset over his whole life period. Thus, the supply price and the prospective yields of a capital asset determine the marginal efficiency of capital. By deducting the supply price from the prospective yield during whole life of a capital asset the entrepreneur can estimate the expected rate of profit or marginal efficiency of capital. Keynes has defined the marginal efficiency of capital in the following words: "I define the marginal efficiency of capital as being equal to that rate of discount which would make the present value of the series of annuities given by the returns expected from the capital asset during its life just equal to its supply price." Thus, according to Keynes, marginal efficiency of capital is the rate of discount which renders the prospective yields from a capital asset over its whole life period equal to the supply price of that asset. Therefore, we can obtain the marginal efficiency of capital in the following way:

$$\text{Supply Price} = \text{Discounted Prospective Yields}$$

$$C = \frac{R_1}{1+r} + \frac{R_2}{(1+r)^2} + \frac{R_3}{(1+r)^3} \ldots\ldots + \frac{R_n}{(1+r)^n}$$

In the above formula, C stands for Supply Price or Replacement Cost and R_1, R_2, R_3, .. R_n etc., represent the annual prospective yields from the capital asset, r is that rate of discount which renders the annual prospective yields equal to the supply price of the capital asset. Thus, r represents the expected rate of profit or marginal efficiency of capital.

The measurement of marginal efficiency of capital can be illustrated by an arithmatical example. Suppose it costs 3000 rupees to invest in a certain machinery and the life of the machinery is two years, that is, after two years it becomes quite useless, having no value. Suppose further that in the first year the machinery is expected to yield income of Rs. 1100 and in the second year Rs. 2420/-. By substituting these values in the above formula, we can calculate the value of r, that is, the marginal efficiency of capital.

$$\text{Supply Price} = \text{Discounted Prospective Yields}$$

$$C = \frac{R_1}{(1+r)} + \frac{R_2}{(1+r)^2}$$

$$3000 = \frac{1{,}100}{1+r} + \frac{2{,}420}{(1+r)^2}$$

On calculating the value of r in the above equation it is found to be equal to 10. In other words, marginal efficiency of capital is here equal to 10 per cent. If we put the value of r, that is, 10 in the above equation, we obtain the following:

$$3{,}000 = \frac{1{,}100}{1.10} + \frac{2{,}420}{(1.10)^2}$$

$$= 1{,}000 + 2{,}000 = 3{,}000$$

Marginal Efficiency of Capital in General. We have explained above the marginal efficiency of a *particular type* of capital asset. But we also require to know the marginal efficiency of capital *in general.* It is the marginal efficiency of capital in general that will indicate the scope for investment opportunities at a particular time in any economy. *At a particular time in an economy the marginal efficiency of that particular capital asset which yields the greatest rate of profit, is called the marginal efficiency of capital in general.* In other words, marginal efficiency of capital in general is the greatest of all the marginal efficiencies of various types of capital assets which could be produced but have not yet been produced. Thus, marginal efficiency of capital in general represents the highest expected rate of return to the community from an extra unit of a capital asset which yields the maximum profit which could be produced.

Keeping in view the existing stock of a capital asset, we can always calculate the marginal efficiency of any particular capital asset. The marginal efficiency of capital will vary when more is invested in a given particular capital asset. In any given period of time marginal efficiency of capital from every type of capital asset will decline as more investment is undertaken in it. In other words, marginal efficiency of a particular type of capital asset will be sloping downward as the stock of capital increases. The main reason for the decline in marginal efficiency of capital with the increase in investment in it is that the prospective yields from capital asset fall as more units are installed and used for production of a good. Prospective yields decline because when more quantity of a good is produced with the greater amount of a capital asset prices of goods decline. The second reason for the decline in the marginal efficiency of capital is that the supply price of the capital asset may rise because the increase in demand for it will bring about increase in its cost of production.

Rate of Interest and Investment Demand Curve

We have explained above how the marginal efficiency of capital is estimated. We can represent diminishing marginal efficiency of capital in general by a curve which will slope downward. This has been done in Fig. 8.3 in which along the *X-axis* investment in capital assets is measured and along the *X*-axis marginal efficiency of capital in general is shown. It will be seen from the figure that when investment in capital asset is equal to 07,, marginal efficiency of capital is i,. When the investment is increased to OI_2, marginal efficiency of capital falls to i_2. Likewise, when investment rises to OI_3, marginal efficiency of capital further diminishes to i_3.

We have seen above that inducement to invest depends upon the marginal efficiency of capital

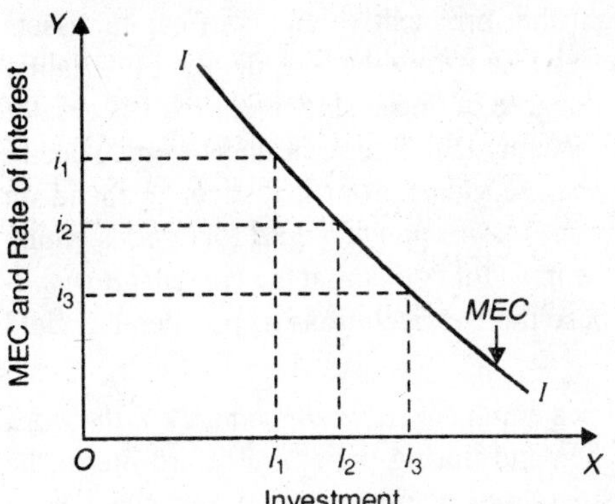

Fig. 8.3. *Investment Demand Curve*

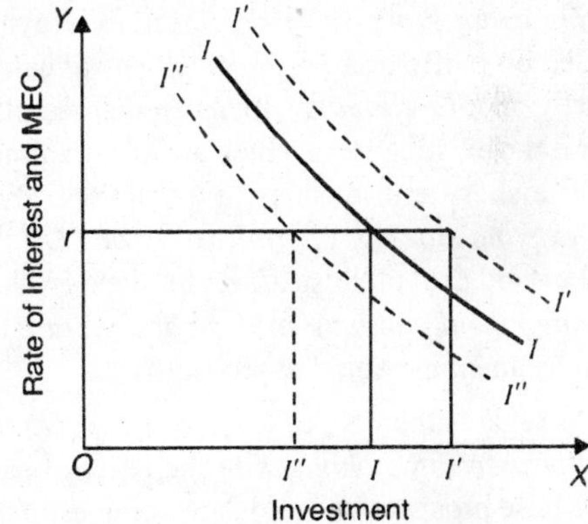

Fig. 8.4. *Shifts in Investment Demand Curve due to Changes Marginal Efficiency of Capital*

and the rate of interest. With the given particular rate of interest and given the curve of marginal efficiency of capital in general we can show what will be the equilibrium level of investment in the economy. If in Fig. 8.3 along the *Y*-axis, rate of interest is also shown, then level of investment can be easily determined. The equilibrium level of investment will be established at the point where marginal efficiency of capital becomes equal to the given current rate of interest. Thus, if the rate of interest is i_1 then I_1 investment will be undertaken. Since at OI_1 level of investment marginal efficiency of capital is equal to the rate of interest i_1. If the rate of interest falls to i_2, investment in the capital assets will rise to OI_2 since at OI_2 level of investment the new rate of interest i_2 is equal to the marginal efficiency of capital. Thus, we see that the curve of marginal efficiency of capital in general shows the demand for investment or inducement to invest at various rates of interest. Hence marginal efficiency of capital curve represents the investment demand curve. This investment demand curve shows how much investment will be undertaken by the entrepreneurs at various rates of interest. If the investment demand curve is less elastic, then investment demand will not increase much with the fall in the rate of interest. But if the investment demand curve or marginal efficiency of capital curve is very much elastic, then the changes in the rate of interest will bring about large changes in investment demand.

Business Expectations and Investment Demand Curve

We have studied above that the marginal efficiency of capital depends upon the supply price of capital on the one hand and prospective yields on the other. It is important to note here that the prospective yields are greatly affected by the expectations of the entrepreneurial class regarding profit making. These expectations generally change very frequently. Indeed, it is the profit expectations of the entrepreneur which determine the level of investment. When the expectations of the entrepreneur regarding profit making become dim, the marginal efficiency of capital declines and as a result demand for investment falls. The occurrence of depression is mainly due to the pessimistic expectations of the entrepreneurial class regarding profit making. On the contrary, when the expectations of the entrepreneurs regarding profit opportunities increase, their inducement to invest rises. As a result of the increase in investment, aggregate demand in the economy increases and levels of income and employment increase. We thus see that profit expectations of entrepreneurs greatly affect investment demand and consequently the level of income and employment.

We have explained above that, according to Keynes, marginal efficiency of capital along with rate of interest determines the level of investment and therefore of the levels of income and employment. A significant contribution of Keynes is that he emphasized the important role that business expectations play in determing the prospective yield from assets on which marginal efficiency of capital and therefore the level of investment depends. He drew distinctions between *short-term expectations and long-term expectations*. Keynes thought that prospective yields of capital assets depended on partly *existing facts* which we can assume to be known with a fair degree of certainty and partly on *future events* which can be predicted with a degree of uncertainty and involves greater risk. It is the existing facts which are known almost with certainty that determine short-term expectations. The short-term business expectations about prospective yields from investment depend on (*i*) the *existing stock of capital assets and* (*ii*) the *strength of consumer demand* for goods which require a good deal of those assets for their production. The investors think that the *current consumption demand will continue in immediate future* too and base their expectations of prospective yield from investment in capital assets on it.

As regards the state of *long term expectations*, Keynes emphasized *future changes in the stock of capital assets* and *changes* in the level of aggregate demand during the entire future life of the assets whose prospective yields are being estimated. Business men acquiring new assets which have long life for production of goods are more concerned with long-run forces on which future earnings from capital assets depend. It is these long-run forces which make long-run expectations about future yields that make them quite uncertain. Changes in these long term expectations make investment quite valatile. Therefore, Keynes gave great importance to the state of confidence for determining investment.

It should be carefully noted that when the expectations regarding prospective yields change, the whole curve of the marginal efficiency of capital will shift. If profit expectations fall, the marginal efficiency of capital curve, that is, investment demand curve will shift downward to left, as shown by the shift of the curve from *II* to *I''I''* in Fig. 8.4. On the other hand, when the profit expectations of the entrepreneurial class become better than before, the marginal efficiency of capital curve will shift upward to the right, as shown by the marginal efficiency of capital curve *I'I'*. Downward shift in the marginal efficiency of capital curve indicates that at the given rate of interest, less investment will be undertaken than before. And upward shift in the marginal efficiency of capital curve indicates that more will be invested at the given rate of interest than before. In Fig. 8.4 when in the beginning, investment demand curve, that is, marginal efficiency of capital curve is represented by *II*, at the rate of interest *r*, demand for investment is *OI*, As a result of downward shift in the marginal efficiency of capital curve to *I''I''*, investment demand at the rate of interest *r* falls to *OI''*. When the marginal efficiency of capital shifts upward to *I'I'*, investment demand at the given rate of interest *r* rises to *OI'*.

It follows, therefore, that the rate of investment also depends on marginal efficiency of capital and the rate of interest. If investment demand is interest-elastic, a reduction in rate of interest tends to stimulate investment. But it may fail to do so, if marginal efficiency of investment is already lower than the rate of interest (as may well happen during a depression). Of the two determinants of the rate

of investment, marginal efficiency of investment is more volatile than the rate of interest.

The rate of interest is usually 'sticky' in the short run, while marginal efficiency of investment can fluctuate from one extreme to another. If there is a divergence between the two, usually the marginal efficiency of investment will adjust to the rate of interest. If, for example, the marginal efficiency of investment is 20 per cent, while the current rate of interest is 12 per cent, forces will be set in motion so as to bring the former to the level of the latter. In such a situation, there will be more investment because marginal efficiency of investment is greater than the rate of interest, and with the increase in investment, marginal efficiency of investment will fall. At the point where it is just reduced to the level of the current rate of interest, further investment will cease.

FACTORS CAUSING SHIFT IN INVESTMENT DEMAND CURVE

Investment is highly volatile and fluctuates greatly. It is fluctuations in investment that is mainly responsible for fluctuations in aggregate demand. We have seen above that investment demand depends on rate of interest and marginal efficiency of capital, that is, expected rate of profit in investment. Now, an important question is what are the factors that determine marginal efficiency of capital which determines investment demand. There are several factors which cause shift in the marginal efficiency of investment curve and brings about change in investment demand. We discuss these factors below :

1. Changes in Marginal Efficiency of Capital due to Changes in Expectations. The Keynesian theory gives importance to profit expectations of business for determining marginal efficiency of capital and therefore investment in the economy. It is worth mentioning here the concept of **animal spirits** of Keynes. Keynes pointed out that it was not possible to make rational calculations about the future profitability of investment. He believed that the swings of optimism and pessimism of the business class were more important driving forces in the stock market that determine investment. It is these swings of optimism and pessimism about future profitability of investment which he referred to as *animal spirits.* According to Keynes, it is these animal spirits rather than economic fundamentals that determine investment by business firms.

We now term to explain **fundamental economic factors** that determine the profitability of investment on which investment demand depends.

2. Expected Demand for Products. Expected net return on investment by a business firm depends to a large extent on the demand for its product it anticipates. For the economy as a whole the marginal efficiency of investment (*i.e.* expected net return on investment) depends significantly on the consumption expenditure of households on the products produced in the economy. As studied in the previous chapter, apart from income, consumption expenditure on goods and services depends on several factors such as propensity, to save of the people, price level, rate of interest, stock of wealth, taxation policy of the government. Changes in these factors would cause a change in consumption of households and demand for the products.

3. Technology and Innovations. In the recent years advances in technology and introduction of new products and processes have been important determinants of investment. The introduction new improved technology and new products makes it necessary to build new plants or install new capital equipment. This stimulates investment in new capital goods. An important recent example of this is the introduction of micro-computers for use in various fields of industries and services. This has spurred new investment in computers and other related equipments. Another important recent example is the introduction of mobile cellular telephones which has boosted investment in telecommunications by business class.

In addition to the above, advances in technology and new inventions *make investment more productive.* Increase in productivity of capital causes the firms to invest more at a given rate of interest. As a result, curve of marginal efficiency of capital shifts to the right.

4. User Cost of Capital. The user cost of capital also greatly influences the rate of return on capital. The user cost of capital depends on the real rate of interest, rate of depreciation, corporate income taxes, investment tax credit, if any. The lower real rate of interest, lower corporate income taxes, higher investment tax credit, the lower will be the user cost of capital which will increase the rate of return on capital and stimulate investment. On the other hand, the higher real rate of interest, the higher corporate income tax will discourage investment and shift the curve of marginal efficiency of capital to the left. It may be noted that real rate of interest is the nominal rate of interest minus expected rate of inflation.

5. Availability of Credit. Besides cost of credit, availability of credit also determines investment in the economy. Investment is financed in three ways : (1) Borrowing from the banks and other financial institutions, (2) raising resources through issue of equity capital that is, selling shares in the stock market and (3) internal savings of the companies (*i.e.* retained earnings of the companies). If the Central Bank of a country follows tight monetary policy [*i.e.,* higher bank rate, the higher cash reserve ratio (CRR)], credit availability for investment will be less which will decourage private investment. If the Central bank adopts expansionary or easy monetary policy credit availability from banks increases which is likely to encourage investment.

6. Fiscal Policy. Fiscal policy of the Government, especially expenditure and taxation policy of it can work in two ways. If Government increases investment and finance it by borrowing from the open market, this will raise the rate of interest which will crowd out private investment. However, if expansionary monetary policy is adopted simultaneously rate of interest will not rise and therefore crowding out effect will not occur. But there are beneficial effects of expansionary fiscal policy of the Government as well. Increase in Government expenditure, say on infrastructure such as power, communication, highways, roads will raise the incomes of the people which will through the multiplier effect cause a significant increase in aggregate demand for goods produced by the private sector and raise the profit expectations of business firms. This will encourage private investment. Many Indian economists believe that increase in Government expenditure, especially if it is made on infrastructure *crowds in* private investment rather than *crowds it out.*

ACCELERATOR THEORY OF INVESTMENT

We have explained in a previous chapter the Keynesian concept of multiplier which states that as the investment increase, income increases by a multiple amount. On the other hand, there is a concept of accelerator which was not taken into account by Keynes has become popular after Keynes, especially in the discussions of theories of trade cycles and economic growth. The acceleration principle describes the effect quite opposite to that of multiplier. According to this, *when income or consumption increases, investment will increase by a multiple amount.* When income and therefore consumption of the people increases, the greater amount of the commodities will have to be produced. This will require more capital to produce them if the already given stock of capital is fully used. Since in this case, investment is induced by changes in income or consumption, this is known as *induced investment.* The accelerator is the numerical value of the relation between the increase in investment resulting from an increase in income. The net induced investment will be positive if national income increases and induced investment may fall to zero if the national income or output remains constant.

To produce a given amount of output, it requires a certain amount of capital. If Y_t output is required to be produced and v is capital-output ratio, the required amount of capital to produce Y_t output will be given by the following equation:

$$K_t = vY_t \qquad \ldots(i)$$

where K_t stands for the stock of capital

Y_t for the level of output or income, and

v for capital-output ratio.

This capital-output ratio v is equal to $\frac{K}{Y}$ and in the theory of accelerator this capital-output ratio is assumed to be constant. Therefore, under the assumption of constant capital-output ratio, changes in output are made possible by changes in the stock of capital. Thus, when income is Y_t then required stock of capital $K_t = vY_t$, when output or income is equal to Y_{t-1}, then required stock of capital will be $K_{t-1} = vY_{t-1}$.

It is clear from above that when income increases from Y_{t-1} in period t–1 to Y_t in period, t, then the stock of capital will increase from K_{t-1} to K_t. As seen above, K_{t-1} is equal to vY_{t-1} and K_t is equal to vY_t. Hence, the increase in the stock of capital in period t is given by the following equation:

$$K_t - K_{t-1} \qquad = vY_t - vY_{t-1}$$

Since increase in the stock of capital in a year $(K_t - K_{t-1})$ represents investment in that year, the above equation (*ii*) can be written as below:

$$I_{t1} = V(y_t - y_{t-1})$$

Equation (*iii*) reveals that as a result of increase in income in any year t from a previous year t – 1, increase in investment will be v times more than the increase in income. Hence, it is v *i.e.*, capital-output ratio which represents the magnitude of the accelerator. If the capital-output ratio is equal to 3, then as a result of a certain increase in income, investment will increase three times more *i.e.*, accelerator here will be equal to 3.

It thus follows that *investment is a function of change in income.* If income or output increases over time, that is, when Y_t is greater than Y_{t-1} then investment will be positive. If income declines, that is, Y_t is less Y_{t-1} then disinvestment will take place. And if the income remains constant, that is, $Y_t = Y_{t-1}$ the investment will be equal to zero.

An arithmetical example will make clear the working of the accelerator. This has been represented in the accompanying table. We have made the following assumptions in making this table:

(*i*) Capital-output ratio remains constant and is equal to 3.

(*ii*) The depreciation that takes place in the stock of capital is equal to one-fifth of the stock existing in the *previous year.* Therefore, one-fifth of the stock of capital is to be replaced every year.

Table 8.1. Explanation of the Accelerator

Period	*Output (income)*	*Required Stock of Capital*	*Investment*		
			Capital Replacement	*Net Investment*	*Gross Investment*
(1)	(2)	(3)	(4)	(5)	(6)
t – 1	500	1,500	300	0	300
t	510	1,530	300	30	330
t + 1	525	1,575	306	45	351
t + 2	550	1,650	315	75	390
t + 3	575	1,725	330	75	405
t + 4	575	1,725	345	0	345
t + 5	560	1,680	345	– 45	300
t + 6	550	1,650	336	– 30	306
t + 7	500	1,500	330	– 150	180
t + 8	400	1,200	300	– 300	0
t + 9	400	1,200	240	0	240

In the table, it is supposed that in period t – 1 and several periods before it, output or income is equal to Rs. 500. Given that the capital-output ratio is equal to 3, then to produce Rs. 500 worth of output, Rs. 1500 worth of capital will be required. [$K = vY$; 1500 = 3(500)] which is written in column (3). Since depreciation of capital occurred in period t – 1, will be one-fifth of the stock of capital existing in the previous period (which is also Rs. 1500). Therefore, replacement investment in period t – 1 will be equal to Rs. 300. Since as compared to the previous period, there is no change in output in period $t-1$, the net investment in period $t-1$ will be equal to zero. As a result, the gross investment in period $t-1$ will be equal to Rs. 300.

Now suppose that production in the period t rises to Rs. 510 crores as a result of increase in Government expenditure or autonomous investment. To produce output worth Rs. 510 crores, total capital worth Rs. 1530 is required [$K_t = vY_t$ 1530 = 3(510)] which is written in column (3). Thus, as a result of increase in output (income) by Rs. 10, net investment has increased by Rs. 30, that is, 1530 – 1500 = 30 which means that accelerator is here equal to 3. In period t the depreciation equation equal to l/5th of the capital stock of period $t-1$ will occur, that is, capital depreciation of Rs. 300, (1/5 × 1500 = 300) will occur in period t. Therefore, capital replacement investment in period t will be equal to Rs. 300. Thus, gross investment in period t will be equal to 30 + 300 = 330. In this way, if output (or income) increases by Rs. 15 in period $t+1$, Rs. 25 in period $t+2$, and also Rs. 25 in period $t+3$, the net investment will increase by three times the increment in output (or income), that is, net investment will increase by Rs. 45 in period $t+1$, Rs. 75 in period $t+2$ and also Rs. 75 in period $t+3$. It will be further observed from Table 6.1 that when output falls in period $t+5$ by Rs. 15, the net, investment will decline by 3 times of it, that is, equal to Rs. 45. Likewise, from changes in output in different periods we can find out net investment that will take place in any period and with the capital replacement investment we can obtain the gross investment that will occur in any period.

A glance at columns 2, 5 and 6 will show that with a change in output, investment will increase by a multiple of it. This shows that acceleration principle is a powerful destabilising force working in the economy. If the accelerator is the only force at work, then we shall have too much of instability in the economy—more than is actually found. In real life, we find that there are limits to instability, both in the upward as well as the downward direction, so that fluctuations in economic activity or what are called business cycles must have a peak as well as a bottom.

Criticism of the Accelerator Theory

The principle of acceleration has come in for a good deal of criticism in recent years. For example, it has been pointed out by Kaldor that we cannot assume a constant value of the accelerator throughout the trade cycle, that is, it is not true that an increase in output or income by an amount must always give rise to a multiple increase in investment. This is because, if already, some machines are lying idle, we shall try to use them before rushing in for new equipment. Also, if expectation of entrepreneurs is that the rise in demand brought about by increase in income or output is only a temporary one, they well try to meet it by overworking the existing machinery rather than installing a new plant. Thus, *in the theory of accelerator it has been assumed that there is no excess capacity existing in consumer goods industries.* In other words, it has been assumed that no machines are lying idle and no extra shift working is possible. If there had been excess capacity and extra shift working was possible, the supply of goods could be increased with the existing equipment and the accelerator would not come into play.

Further, in the principle of acceleration principle it *has also been assumed that in the capital goods industries, there exists surplus productive capacity.* If there is no excess capacity in the machine-making industries, increased demand for machines caused by the requirement for additional output would not lead to increase in the supply of machines. In the absence of supply of machines, investment cannot increase in the short run. It is thus assumed in the accelerator theory that the machine-making industry is capable of increasing its output for the time being at least. The supply can be increased by reducing stocks of finished machines, by working extra shifts, and so on. But stocks cannot be reduced below zero and working double shifts or adoption of other experiments is found to be expensive. Only when the demand has increased permanently, will the entrepreneurs find it worthwhile to increase investment in machine-making industries.

The size of the accelerator does not remain constant over time. Its value will be affected by the businessmen's calculation regarding the profitability of installing new plants to make more machines on the basis of their probable working life. It is also assumed that the demand for machines will remain stable in future, although the increase in demand has suddenly cropped up. However, in spite of the "above limitations of acceleration principle, it points out an important force which causes economic fluctuations in the economy. Economists like Samuelson, Hicks and Dusenberry have shown how accelerator combined with multiplier provides an adequate and satisfactory theory of trade cycles that occur in the capitalist economies.

THE NEOCLASSICAL THEORY OF INVESTMENT

After Keynes a new classical theory of investment has been developed to explain investment behaviour with regard. to fixed business investment. This theory is called neoclassical theory of investment behaviour because it is based on the neoclassical theory of optimal capital accumulation which is determined by relative prices of factors of production. It may be recalled that fixed business investment refers to the purchase of machines, construction of new factories, ware houses, office buildings etc. by businessmen. The neoclassical theory of investment throws new light on the causes of fluctuations in investment which are responsible for occurrence of business cycles in a free market economy. The neo classical theory explains that at a particular time how much capital stock a firm desires to achieve. Further, according to this theory *rate of investment is determined by the speed with which* firms adjust their capital stocks towards the desired level. Because it takes time to build and install new machines, construct new factories warehouses etc. the firms cannot immediately achieve the desired level of capital stock. Therefore, the firms have to decide with what rate or speed per period it makes adjustment in their stock of capital to attain the desired level of capital stock.

Firms use capital along with labour to produce goods and services for sale in the market. In deciding about the amounts of labour and capital to be used for production the firms are guided by not only the prices of these factors but also the contributions they make to the production and revenue of the firms. According to this neoclassical theory, investment, that is, addition to the stock of capital in an economy is determined by *marginal product of capital* (MPK) and *user cost of capital* which is also called *real rental cost of capital* Marginal product of capital (MPK) measures the addition to the production by using an additional unit of capital, labour and technology remaining constant. Due to the operation of the law of diminishing returns, marginal product of capital declines as more units of capital are used for production, the other factories being held constant. The user cost of capital will be explained in detail later, but it essentially stands for the rental for capital a firm owns or gets it on rent basis and measures the opportunity cost of the funds spent on production or purchase of a capital equipment.

The firms try to maximise profits or maximise the present value. Therefore, as long as the value of marginal product of capital (which are in fact marginal receipts or benefits it gets from the use of capital in production) exceeds the rental or user cost capital, it will be profitable for the firm to add to its stock of capital. It will be maximising its profits when it has achieved the stock of capital at which marginal product of capital (MPK) equals user cost of capital. We can derive the desired stock of capital by using the neoclassical production function which is popularly known as Cobb Douglas production function. The Cobb Douglas production function can be written as under :

$$Y = A K^{\alpha} L^{1-\alpha}$$

where Y stands for output, K for capital, L for labour and A is a parameter that measures the level of technology and α is a parameter that measures capital's share of output.

Marginal product of capital can be obtained by differentiating the production function with respect to labour. Thus

$$MPK = \frac{\partial Y}{\partial K} = aAK^{\alpha-1}L^{1-\alpha}$$

$$MPK = \frac{\alpha AK^{\alpha}L^{1-\alpha}}{K} = \frac{\alpha Y}{K}$$

---

1 See D. W. Jorgenson, Theory of Corporate Investment Behaviour, *American Economic Review,* Sept 1968 and D. W. Jorgenson and C.D. Siebert, Optimal Capital Accumulation and Corporate Investment Behaviour, *Theory of Political Economy,* Nov–Dec. 1968.

Thus, $$\text{MPK} = \frac{\alpha Y}{K} \quad \text{... (1)}$$

Let r is the price or user cost of capital and p is the price of output. To maximise profits, a firm will equate the marginal product of capital to the real rental price (*i.e.* user cost) of capital $\left(\frac{r}{p}\right)$. Thus

$$\alpha \frac{Y}{K} = \frac{r}{p}$$

or $$K = \alpha \frac{p}{r} Y$$

Thus, the desired stock of capital can be written as

$$K^* = \alpha \frac{p}{r} Y_t \quad \text{... (2)}$$

The equation (2) shows that the desired stock of capital (K^*) depends on the size of output (Y_t), real cost of capital $\left(\frac{r}{p}\right)$. The equation (2) reveals that the higher the rental cost of capital (r) the lower will be the desired capital stock by the firm and vice versa. The equation (2) further reveals that the greater the expected output (Y_t) the greater the desired capital stock. It may be noted that while in accelerator theory the changes in the stock of capital depends on the changes in output in neoclassical theory, the desired stock of capital depends not only the planned output (Y_t) but also on the ratio of rental price of capital to price of output $\left(\frac{r}{p}\right)$. As shall be explained later in detail, the rentated or user cost of capital is determined by the price of capital goods, rate of interest, rate of depreciation and expected rate of inflation and the various features of tax system such as corporate tax rate, investment tax break etc.

The determination of the desired stock of capital is illustrated in Fig. 8.5 where on the X-axis we measure capital stock and on the Y-axis we measure MPK and rental cost of capital. As long as the marginal product of capital (MPK) is greater than the rental price or user cost of capital, it pays the firm to add to its stock of capital. It will be seen from Fig.8.5 that marginal product of capital is diminishing as there is increase in the stock of capital. Thus the firm will continue adding to the stock of capital (*i.e.* continue making investment) until the marginal product of capital (MPK) is equal to the rental price of capital. If the rental price of capital is r_0, the firm continue investing until the capital stock $K^r{}_0$ is reached. K^*_0 is the desired capital stock, given the rental price of capital equal to r_0 and for the given level of output (*i.e.* GDP) equal to, say Y_1). It will be further seen from Fig.8.5 that at the lower rental price of capital r_1, the firm's desired capital stock will increase to K^*_1.

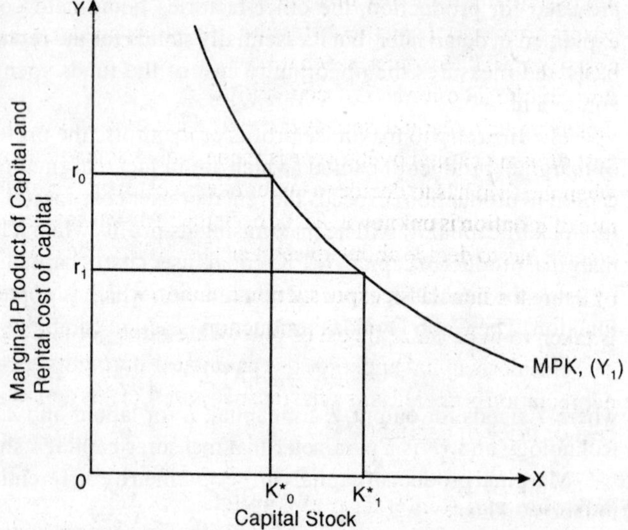

Fig. 8.5. *The Determination of Desired Stock of Capital*

Expected Output and Desired Capital Stock

The equation (2) shows that desired capital stock depends on the level of output (Y_t). But this output level for which determines the desired stock of capital is not the current output level but the expected output level for some future period in which capital stock will be used for production. For some investment projects, future time for which output is planned may be few weeks or months away but for investment projects concerning power and steel future output level, is planned many years ahead. However, current output level affects the expectations of future output level. As the equation (2) above reveals that desired capital stock depends on the level of output, and in case of the economy as a whole, on the level of national income (GDP). When the level of output or national income is expected to increase the whole curve of marginal product of capital (MPK) will shift to the right as in shown in Fig. 8.6. With this increase in the level of national product from Y_0 to Y_1, at the given rental cost of capital r_0, the desired capital stock increases from K_0 to K_1

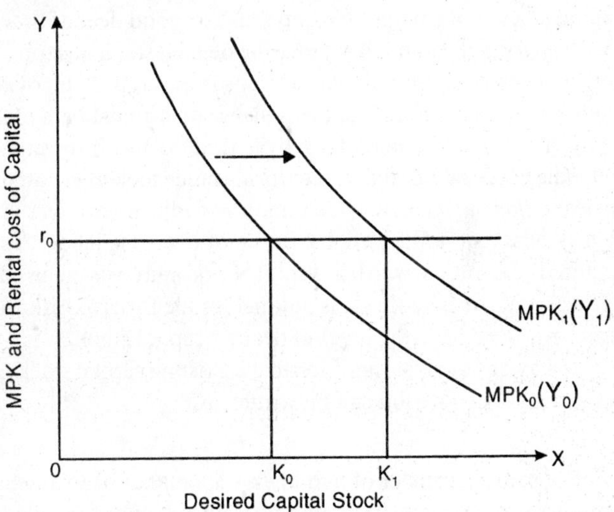

Fig. 8.6. *Desired Capital Stock and the level of National Product*

Rental Cost of Capital. Since the desired capital stock and change in it depends on the rental cost of capital, it is important to know how rental cost of capital is estimated. If a firm finances its investment (that is, purchase of new capital goods) by borrowing, then rate of interest on the funds borrowed for investment purpose is an important element of rental cost of capital. However, when inflation in the economy is occurring money value of capital rises over time, and as a result the firms make capital gain. Therefore, the real cost of using capital over a year is money interest payment minus the nominal capital gain. At a time when the firm has to decide to undertake investment, the nominal rate of interest is known to it but the rate of inflation is unknown. At the best, the firm can have an *expected inflation rate* over the next years when it has to decide about investment. Therefore, the real cost of capital is estimated by nominal rate of interest adjusted for expected rate of inflation (π^e). Thus, expected real interest rate, that is, $i - \pi^e$ is taken to to be the real cost of borrowing funds for adding to the stock of capital.

Besides, capital undergoes wear and tear during its use for production in a year. Conventionally, depreciation is treated is as a flat rate per year. Let this depreciation is d per cent per year. Thus the rental cost or price of capital (r) is

$$r = i - \pi^e + d \qquad \text{... (3)}$$

Taxation and Rental Cost of Capital.

Besides, real rate of interest and depreciation, taxes levied by the government also affect rental cost of capital. The corporation tax which is the tax on profits of the public limited companies and investment tax break or development rebate are the two important tax elements which influence the rental cost of capital. Corporation tax is generally believed as a proportion, say of the profits of the companies. The greater the corporation income tax the higher the rental cost of capital. The tax system of various countries also provide for investment tax credit to promote investment and development. Under investment tax credit scheme, the firms are allowed a certain rebate, say 10 per cent of their investment expenditure, on the tax payable.

Thus investment tax break reduces the rental cost of capital. If t_c represents the percent tax rebate on investment expenditure per year, then real cost of capital can be expressed as under :

$$r = i - \pi + d - t_c.$$

CAPITAL STOCK ADJUSTMENT : FLEXIBLE ACCELERATOR MODEL

The equation for desired capital stock, namely, $K^* = \alpha \frac{P}{r} Y_t$ shows that the desired capital stock depends on real rental cost of capital and the level of output (Y_t). When these variables change, the desired capital stock will change. Then the gap between the existing actual capital stock and the desired capital stock will emerge. It always takes a good deal of time for the firms to make adjustment in the existing stock of capital to achieve the desired stock of capital. In other words, capital stock cannot be adjusted immediately and there are lags in the adjustment of actual capital stock to the level of desired capital stock. Therefore, the firms make some adjustment in the capital stock in each period to finally attain the desired capital stock over time. If the firms attempt to adjust their actual capital stock immediately, in addition to what may be called the *direct cost* of investment projects, the firms will have to bear *adjustment costs*. The examples of adjustment costs are costs of temporary shutdown of plants to make the required additions, hiring of overtime labour, especially skilled labour, to complete the required construction work in a short period and costs incurred due to disruption of production. In view of these adjustment costs, it is optimal for the firms to make adjustment in the capital stock gradually over time to achieve the level of desired capital stock.

It may be noted that addition to the existing capital stock in each period is called investment. Thus, investing (I_t) in a period can be written as

$$I_t = K_t - K_{t-1}$$

There are a number of hypotheses about the speed at which firms attempt to make adjustment in capital stock over time. An important such hypothesis is called **flexible accelerator model**. According to this model, firms plan to invest, that is, add to the stock of capital per period to make only partial adjustment to fill up the gap between the desired capital stock and the existing capital stock. However, according to this flexible accelerator model, *the greater the gap between the current capital stock and the desired capital stock, the larger the firm's rate of investment per period.*

Thus, according to the flexible accelerator model, to make partial adjustment in each period the firms decide to undertake investment is each period, which is a fraction, say λ, of the total gap between the existing capital stock and the desired capital stock in each period. Let the capital stock at the end of the last period be denoted by K_{t-1}, then the gap between the desired capital stock and the existing capital stock is $K^* - K_{t-1}$. Only fraction λ of the gap ($K^* - K_{t-1}$) will be filled in each period to eventually attain the desired capital stock over time. Thus when the firm adds a fraction λ of the gap, $K^* - K_{t-1}$ to the capital stock existing at the end of the last period (K_{t-1}), the capital stock at the end the current period (K_t) will be

$$K_t = K_{t-1} + \lambda (K^* - K_{t-1}) \quad \text{... (3)}$$

Rearranging the equation (3) we have

$$K_t - K_{t-1} = \lambda (K^* - K_{t-1})$$

The addition to the capital stock during a period, that is, $K_t - K_{t-1}$ measures the rate of net investment. Therefore, rewritting the equation (3) we have

$$I_t = K_t - K_{t-1} = \lambda (K^* - K_{t-1}) \quad \text{... (4)}$$

The equation (4) shows the partial and gradual adjustment of capital stock through investment in each period to reach the desired stock of capital over time. Only a part of the desired change in the capital stock is filled in each period by investment. Since in this flexible accelerator model investment in a given period is the result of changes in expected income or output during a number of previous periods, it shows a slower response of investment to changes in current period. This implies that investment will be less volatile in the short run than is the case with the simple accelerator model which visualises the response of investment to changes in current income wholly in one period. Empirical evidence corraborates the results of the flexible accelerator model as investment though volatile is not actually as volatile as simple accelerator model predicts.

The flexible accelerator model can also be modified to allow for changes in the speed with which investment is carried out (that is, the change in fraction λ is in fact the choice variable for the firm which is affected by such factors as the availability of credit, rate of interest, corporate tax rate, investment tax credit etc. For example, if rate of interest is lower, more investment will be undertaken to fill the gap between the desired capital stock and the existing capital stock than would be the case if rate of interest is higher. Thus flexible accelerator model is quite consistent with the Keynesian theory that investment is negatively related to the rate of interest.

Graphic illustration of Capital Stock Adjustment

Capital stock adjustment through investment over time is illustrated in Figure 8.7 where along the horizontal axis we have shown the time and along the vertical axis we measure the capital stock. In the beginning of the period 1, the capital stock is K_1 and suppose the desired capital stock of the firm is K^*. Thus $K^* - K_1$ is the gap between the desired capital stock and the existing capital stock. Suppose the speed of capital stock adjustment is, $\lambda = 0.5$. This implies that in each period one half of the desired capital stock and the existing capital stock is filled. Thus, in period t_1, the existing stock in the beginning of the period of K_1 and given $\lambda = 0.5$, the firm will add to the stock of capital, that is, undertake

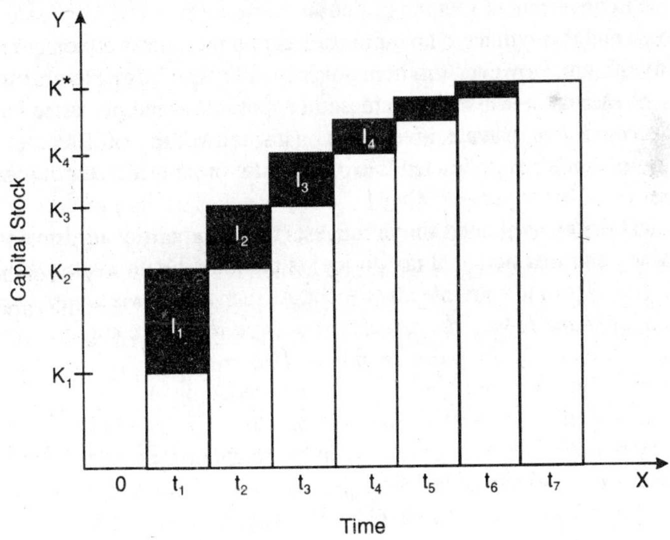

Figure 8.7. *Adjustment of Capital Stock and Investment*

investment equal to $0.5\ (K^* - K_1) = I_1$ in period t_1. Now in period t_2, the existing stock of capital will be K_2 and given $\lambda = 0.5$, the firm will undertake investment of $0.5(K^* - K_2) = I_2$ as shown by the shaded rectangle. It will be seen from Figure 8.7 that investment I_2 in period t_2 is less than investment I_1 in period t_1. This is because as net investment or addition to capital stock is made in period t_1 the gap between desired capital stock and the current capital stock is reduced and therefore the additional adjustment in capital stock in period t_2 becomes less in absolute terms. Similarly, capital stock is adjusted through additional net investments in the next periods, in each period one-half (*i.e.* 0.5) of the remaining gap is filled until period t_7 when almost the whole gap between the desired capital stock and the existing capital stock is completely closed. It may be noted that the higher λ is, the faster the gap is filled.

In equation (4) we have derived an investment function that shows that investment depend on the desired capital stock K^* and the existing capital stock K_{t-1}. Any factor that raises the desired capital stock will increase the rate of investment. Accordingly, increase in expected output and a reduction in rental cost of capital will cause increase in investment. As seen above, rental cost of capital depends on nominal rate of interest, expected rate of inflation, corporate income tax, the investment tax credit which are important variables that determine the rental cost of capital will also affect investment in the economy.

To conclude our discussion of business fixed investment we have derived the neoclassical investment function of the following form :

$$I_{n,t} = F(Y^e, i_t, d, \pi^e, t_c, K_{t-1}) \quad \text{... (5)}$$

This shows net investment depends on expected level of output (Y^e), the various elements of rental or user cost of capital such as nominal interest rate i_t, expected rate of inflation (π^e), corporate income tax including investment tax credit, and the existing stock of capital. Given the existing stock of capital, an increase in expected output (Y^e), expected rate of inflation (π^e) and the investment tax credit will all increase investment. On the other hand, increase in nominal rate of interest (i_t) and the corporate income tax will cause net investment to decline.

Fiscal and Monetary Policies and Investment

Now it is important to explain that the neoclassical theory of investment suggests what types of fiscal and monetary policies can promote investment. In our Keynesian analysis of fiscal policy we found that increase in government spending or cut in personal taxes will increase aggregate demand and national income and this will have favourable effect on marginal efficiency of capital which will tend to increase investment. However, this high government spending and low personal tax policy also adversely affects investment because the increase in aggregate demand caused by it would raise the interest rate and *crowds out* private investment. This crowding out effect of high government expenditure and low personal tax policy tends to offset its favourable effect on investment via, increase in aggregate demand.

The neoclassical theory explained above suggests that if expansionary fiscal policy (that is, high government spending and low personal tax policy) is combined with a tax policy such as a greater investment tax credit will promote private investment. As seen above, *the investment tax credit is a sort of subsidy on investment and lowers the rental cost of capital.* As a result, *the crowding out effect of expansionary fiscal policy via increase in nominal interest can be avoided.* Besides, making adjustment in the rate of investment tax credit, it can be used as an alternative instrument to monetary policy as a means of stabilising investment demand to achieve price stability as both investment tax credit and monetary policy work through change in the rental cost of capital.

In addition to above, the expansionary fiscal policy raises the level of income and expected output of the firms and will therefore raise the level of desired capital stock and hence stimulate investment. (Recall that $K^* = \alpha \frac{P}{r} . Y_t$).

T*his beneficial effect of expansionary fiscal policy, "may be quantitatively more important than any negative effect of a fiscal policy induced increase in interest rates. Which effect dominates depends on the importance of output growth versus the cost of capital as determinants of investment.*"[2]

However, as regards corporation tax is concerned increase in it is likely to adversely affect rental cost of capital and will therefore discourage investment. On the other hand, reduction in corporation

2.Richard T. Froyen *Macroeconomics; Theories and Policy*, 6th ed. Pearson Education, 2001, pp. 299 – 300.

tax will increase profitability of investment through reduction in the rental or user cost of capital.

As regards monetary policy it affects investment demand through its effect on real rate of interest. The neoclassical theory does not suggest any different monetary policy than that visualised in Keynesian and monetarest macroeconomic theories. *In neoclassical theory, expansionary monetary policy lowers interest rate which would reduce rental cost of capital and will increase the desired capital stock. Thus expansionary monetary policy stimulates private investment.*

Tobin's q Theory of Investment

Many economists believe that fluctuations in stock market do not reflect the true state of fundamentals of the firms and the economy. Influenced by exogenous factors, even when the fundamentals of the firms or the economy are quite strong stock market prices fall sharply lowering the market value of the capital installed by the firms which discourage more investment by them. Therefore, many consider stock market movements as poor economic indicators. In India we have seen in recent years stock market is highly volatle and movements in it have been determined not by India's own economic fundamentals but by factors originating abroad such as financial crisis of the US in 2008-09, Eurozone crisis occurring in 2010-2012, who wins the presidential election in the US. Of course global happenings such as US financial crisis and Eurozone debt problem may affect India's exports, but stock market movements in India have been out of all proportions to their effects on Indian firms and give wrong signals about the state of fundamentals of the Indian economy.

However, *in the world today we cannot ignore the link* between the stock market and corporate firms and therefore the economy as a whole as much of investment is made by the corporate firms and this is affected by stock market prices. A noted American economist, James Tobin put forward a view that links fluctuations in stock market with fluctuations in investment. It should be noted that the *stock* refers to the *total market value of share capital* of a corporate firm which is owned by its shareholders. The shareholders of a firm get return in the form of annual dividends as well as capital gains arising from the rise in prices of shares of a firm. The shares of a corporate firm are traded in the stock market. When the prices of shares of a firm rise, the value of the capital installed by the firm will increase. This will induce the firm to add to its stock of capital installed and thus makes more investment. The increase in the market value of capital of firms influences incentive to invest more by the firms. *James Tobin in his q-theory of investment put forward the view that the firms base their investment decision on the estimate of the value the stock market places on the firms assets or capital installed relative to the cost of replacing them.* It may be noted that share prices of firms tend to be high when firms offer good opportunities for profitable investment because profitable opportunities determine the future incomes of the shareholders of the firms. Tobin writes its q-ratio as under:

$$q = \frac{\text{Market Value of Firm's Capital Stock}}{\text{Replacement Cost of the Capital Stock}}$$

The market value of installed capital of firms is determined by the prices of their shares in the stock-market while the replacement cost of the installed capital is the cost that will be incurred if the capital assets of the firms have to be produced and procured if they were produced in the current period.

Tobin argued that investments by the firms depend on whether q is greater or less than one. When q-ratio is greater than one, it implies that the stock market places a higher value on firm's installed capital than its replacement cost. This provides incentive to the firm to add to its installed capital stock. That is, the firm will make more investment. On the other hand, if *q ratio* of a firm is less than one, this implies that the stock market values its stock of capital assets less than its replacement cost. This will discourage managers of a firm to replace its capital assets as they wear out. Thus, according to Tobin, it is q-ratio of a firm as to whether its value is greater or less than one that determines investment by a firm.

Tobin's q-theory of investment has been shown to be closely related to neoclassical theory of investment. *It is noteworthy that Tobin's q depends on both current and future economic profits earned from installed capital.*

According to neoclassical theory of investment, if marginal product of capital (MP_K) is greater than the cost of capital, the firm will be making profits on their installed capital. These profits will induce others to own shares of the firm. As a result, the market value of the stock of installed capital by the firm will rise. This means higher value of q-ratio of the firm which will provide incentive to the firm to invest more by repoducing or buying more capital assets. Likewise, if the marginal product of capital (MP_K) is less than the cost of installed capital of the firms, the firms will be having *loses on* their stock of capital assets. This will reduce the market value of its installed capital and thus lowering the value of q.

Merits of Tobin's q-ratio as a measure of inducement to invest, as mentioned above, is that it reflects both the current and future profitability of capital assets of the firm. For example, if government in its annual budget reduces the corporate income tax beginning next year, this will result in larger expected profits after tax for the firms. These larger expected profits will raise the value of the existing capital of the firm and therefore induce the firms to install more capital, that is, make more investment Mankiw therefore writes, "*Tobins's q-theory of investment emphasies that investment decisions depend not only current policies but also on policies expected to prevail in the near future*"[3].

IMPACT OF INFLATION ON INVESTMENT

Interest represents the cost of funds used for investment Therefore, as explained above, interest representing cost of funds is an important factor that determines investment. It is generally assumed that investment depends on *nominal* rate of interest, that is, rate of interest that is observed in the market. However, *what matters for investment, is the real rate of interest, that is, interest rate after taking into account the effect of inflation.* The inflation, given the nominal interest rate, will lower the real rate of interest. Thus when inflation is expected real rate of interest differs from nominal or market rate of interest. Let i represents *nominal* rate of interest and r real rate of interest and π^e expected inflation rate, then

$$r = i - \pi^e$$

If nominal rate of interest is 11 per cent and expected rate of inflation is 5 per cent, then real rate of interest will be $11 - 5 = 6$ per cent. The real interest rate measures the expected real value in terms of goods and services that has to be paid by the borrower (investor) to the lenders of money. The real rate of interest therefore represents the real cost of borrowing funds (*i.e.* real cost of capital) for investment.

If inflation rates are small and steady, the nominal interest rates are not very misleading as a measure of cost of capital as in this case nominal and real interest rates will differ only by a small and fairly constant margin. It is only when inflation rate is highly variable and the expected inflation by borrowers and lenders is very high that it becomes important to distinguish between nominal interest rate and real interest rate. It is important to note that it is real rate of interest measuring true cost of capital that is relevant for investment decisions by businesses. Given the marginal efficiency of capital (*i.e.* investment demand curve) and *the nominal interest rate,* the higher the inflation rate the lower will be the real interest rate and therefore the investors will be induced to invest more.

However, the beneficial effect of inflation on investment is a highly controversial issue. First, it is essential here to draw distinction between anticipated and unanticipated inflation. In case of unanticipated inflation prices rise faster than money wages and therefore causes a fall in real wages and a rise in profit margins. It is this rise in profit margins that induce businessmen to increase employment and invest more. However when inflation is anticipated or expected, money wages will be quickly adjusted to higher inflation rate and the alleged beneficial effect of inflation on employment and investment will not exist. Further, the alleged beneficial effect of inflation on investment is also based on the view that since wages lag behind rise in prices, inflation causes higher profit margins and redistributes income in favour of the wealthy investor class, it will lead to increase in aggregate savings

3. Mankiw, op. cit. p. 469

which would ensure more investment. However, this argument is based on the classical theory that investment always expands to absorb higher level of saving. If higher profits leads to the increase in share of wealthy investors in national income, it will cause income-share of workers (*i.e.* wage earners) to decline. This may reduce the aggregate demand for goods and services which will adversely affect marginal efficiency (*i.e.* profitability) of investment and lower investment rate in the long run.

That inflation is not conducive to saving and investment in the long run is borne out by the empirical evidence from the United States for the period 1949 – 75 when there was uninterrupted inflation. Referring to the experience of this period, Shapiro writes, "The corporate profits and non-corporate business shares of national income declined substantially over these years of almost uninterrupted inflation. To the extent that rate of long-run economic growth depends on the rate of capital accumulation, a major basis for the conclusion that inflation promotes rapid economic growth is undermined given that wages no longer lag during inflation as they apparently did in time of past."[4]

It follows from above that effect of inflation on investment in the long run should not be judged merely by its effect on *cost of borrowing* (*i.e.* real rate of interest), but also how it affects level of saving, distributive shares of income, demand for goods and therefore its profitability and marginal efficiency of capital .

However, it is now widely recognised especially in developing countries like India that, far from encouraging saving and generating higher rate of investment inflation slows down the rate of capital accumulation. There are several reasons responsible for this. First, as seen above, when due to rapid inflation value of money is declining, people will not like to keep money with themselves and will, therefore, be eager to spend it before its value goes down heavily. This raises their consumption demand and therefore lowers their saving. Besides, people find that the rapid inflation will erode the real value of their savings. This discourages them to save. Thus, *inflation or rapid rise in prices serves as a disincentive to save*. Secondly, *inflation or rising prices leads to unproductive forms of investment in gold, jewellery, real estate, construction of luxury houses* etc. These unproductive forms of wealth do not add to the productive capacity of the economy and are quite useless from the viewpoint of economic growth. Thus, inflation may lead to more investment but much of this is of unproductive type. In this way economic surplus is frittered away in unproductive investment.

While there is no agreement among economists whether or not moderate or mild inflation encourages saving and therefore ensures higher rate of capital accumulation and economic growth, there is however a complete unanimity that a very rapid inflation or what is often called hyperinflation discourages saving and hinders economic growth. Further, barring the special case of hyperinflation, whether or not saving is encouraged by inflation depends on whether *wages lag behind prices*. If wages quickly adjust to rise in prices, especially when inflation is expected or anticipated, beneficial effect of inflation will not be there. Besides, inflation promotes investment by lowering real rate of interest if it is unanticipated. Anticipated inflation will quickly raise the nominal interest rate and as a result real rate of interest will not be affected.

MONETARY AND FISCAL POLICY MEASURES AND INVESTMENT

Both monetary and fiscal policy measures affect investment. In what follows we first analyse the effect of discretionary monetary policy and then of discretionary fiscal policy.

Monetary Policy and Investment

As explained above, interest rate measures the cost of capital and along with marginal efficiency of capital (*i.e.* expected rate of return on investment) determines the level of investment. It is primarily through its *effect on interest rate* that monetary policy affects investment decisions. Besides interest rate, investment also depends on the *availability of funds or credit*, especially from the banks. The easy monetary policy which aims at lowering interest rate and increasing the availability of credit will lead to more investment. It may be noted that under easy monetary policy the Central Bank lowers the bank

4. Edward Shapiro, *Macroeconomic Analysis* (New York, Harcourt) 4th edition, 1978, p. 443

rate and other rates of interest such as *repo rate*. It can also lower the cash reserve ratio. The lowering of bank rate and other rates of interest sends a signal to the banks to reduce their lending rates. The lowering of cash-reserve ratio (CRR) leads to the more liquidity or extra cash reserves with banks. This not only increases the availability of more credit for investment by businessmen lent also puts downward pressure on lending interest rates as a result of increase in the supply of lendable funds with the banks. In India, Reserve Bank of India often lowers a *repo rate* (which is a interest rate charged by RBI for borrowing by commercial banks at times of need for a very short period, even for a day) to ensure lowering of lending rates by banks and thereby to stimulate private investment. At a lower interest rate, given the schedule of marginal efficiency of capital, more investment will be undertaken by business firms. The Central Bank can also undertake open market operations to increase availability of bank credit for investment. For thus purpose it buys government securities from the banks and pays rupee funds to them. This raises money supply in the economy which not only make more funds available for lending to businessmen but also tends to lower interest rates.

Keynes and his early followers believed that monetary policy is not very effective for increasing private investment. This view was based on the assumption that during the period of depression rate of interest was already very low and at this low interest rate there is *liquidity rap* in the demand curve for money. Under these conditions, they thought the expansion in money supply by the banks will not lower interest rate. Besides, they believed that investment demand is relatively inelastic so that even lowering of interest rate will not cause much increase in investment. However, later empirical evidence shows that at relevant rates of interest demand for money is quite elastic (that is , liquidity trap does not exist at the generally prevailing interest rates). As a result, expansionary monetary policy lowers interest rate and thereby stimulates private investment. Besides, later empirical evidence also shows that investment demand schedule is quite elastic and therefore lowering of interest rate and more availability of funds lead to more investment. Therefore, the modern Keynesians have veered round to the view that discretionary monetary policy can be effective in raising private investment to get rid of recession in the economy and to promote economic growth.

One modification in our above analysis of the impact of monetary policy on investment which is required is the incorporation of distinction between *nominal interest rate and real interest rate.* As explained earlier, it is the real interest rate that is relevant for investment decisions. Therefore, monetary policy must affect the real interest rate if it has to stimulate private investment. However, it is worth noting that in both the Keynesian and monetarist theories expected inflation depends primarily on the inflation prevailing in the recent past and further that it changes slowly over time. Under these conditions changes in monetary rate of interest will mean changes in real interest rate for all practical purposes. In view of this, our above analysis of the effect of monetary policy on investment remains unchanged.

Fiscal Policy and Investment

We now turn to explain the effect of fiscal policy on investment. It is generally believed that there is *adverse effect* of expansionary fiscal policy on private investment. According to this view, though increase in government spending financed by borrowing would bring about increases in aggregate demand for goods and services, it would raise interest rate. Borrowing by the government would raise the demand for funds or money in the market which, given the supply of money, would cause interest rate to rise. The higher interest rate would lower private investment. Thus, it is asserted that expansionary fiscal policy *crowds out private investment*. Another route through which adverse effect of expansionary fiscal policy is brought out is that the increase in aggregate demand as a result of expansionary fiscal policy in terms of either increase in government expenditure or cut in taxes would raise aggregate demand and lead to increase in national income. However, the increase in national income would bring about increase in transactions demand for money which, given the supply of money, would cause interest rate to rise and lower private investment. The reduction or crowding out of private investment would offset a part of the initial expansionary effect on aggregate demand brought about by increase in government expenditure or reduction in taxation. If investment demand is highly elastic , the decrease in private investment resulting from the rise in interest rate will be quite substantial.

However, in view of the present author even if there is significant crowding-out effect on private investment of expansionary fiscal policy, it can be avoided if as a part of expansionary fiscal policy tax policy of providing *investment tax credit* to the business firms is adopted. Under investment tax credit policy, a deduction from business income or profits equal to a certain percentage of investment made in machinery and equipment is allowed. As this lowers the tax liability of the firm and reduces the cost of capital, policy of investment tax credit stimulates investment and will offset *adverse effect* on private investment of expansionary fiscal policy. Thus our Finance Minister Mr. P. Chitambaram in 2013-14 budget has announced investment tax credit at the rate of 15 per cent on investment in capital equipment for the corporate firms which make investment of ₹ 100 crore or more in plant and equipment in a year. This is in addition to the annual depreciation allowance on capital already enjoyed by these firms.

Further, in our view, the crowding-out effect of expansionary fiscal policy has been exaggerated by the critics of Keynes. As a matter of fact when government raises its expenditure or cuts personal income tax, aggregate demand for goods and services increases which raises expectations of increased sales and revenue of the business firms. This improves profitability or marginal efficiency of investment. This is more valid at times of depression when private investment declines due lack of demand for goods and services. Thus when expected profitability or marginal efficiency of capital rises due to increase in aggregate demand resulting from expansionary fiscal policy, investment demand curve shifts to the right and businessmen invest more at any given rate of interest. This can more than offset any adverse effect on private investment due to rise in interest.

Further, according to *investment theory based on acceleration principle* investment depends on expected changes in output or national income. Thus, even in the absence of investment tax credit expansionary fiscal policy that increases national output or national income through its beneficial effect on aggregate demand will stimulate private investment through accelerator principle.

In the context of developing country like India the expansionary fiscal policy even when increased government expenditure is financed by borrowing can have beneficial effect on private investment, especially when the economy is experiencing recession or slowdown in economic growth. If in such a situation the government increases its expenditure and spends money on infrastructure projects, it will have a favourable effect on private investment as the latter is often constrained by lack of adequate infrastructure facilities. Besides, when manufacturing industries in developing countries experience recessionary conditions due to sluggish demand, as happened in India during the period 1997 to 2002, increase in public expenditure will lead to increase in aggregate demand through its multiplier effect and thereby improve the demand conditions for increase in private investment.[5]

It follows from above that it is not necessarily true that expansionary fiscal policy crowds out private investment. The expansion in public expenditure can have a beneficial effect on private investment.

NUMERICAL PROBLEM

Problem : *Given the saving function S = – 10 + 0.2Y and autonomous investment I = Rs. 50 cores*

(*i*) *Find the level of consumption*

(*ii*) *If investment decreases permanently by Rs. 5 crore, what is the new level of consumption.*

Solution : (*i*)

$$C = Y - S$$

Given $$S = -10 + 0.2Y \ldots$$

$$C = Y - (-10 + 0.2Y)$$

5. This point is more fully discussed in Chapter 12 concerning '*Relevance of Keynesian Economics to Developing Countries*'.

$$= Y + 10 - 0.2Y \quad \ldots (i)$$

Now, in equilibrium $S = I$

$$I = 50$$

$$-10 + 0.2Y = 50$$

$$0.2Y = 60$$

$$Y = 60 \times \frac{10}{2} = 300$$

Now substituting the value of Y in (*i*) we have

$$C = 300 + 10 - 0.2 \times 300 = 310 - 60 = 250$$

(*ii*) Decrease in investment by Rs. 5 core will cause national income to decline by a multiple of decrease in investment. **Thus** $\Delta Y = \Delta I \times$ multiplier

Now, multiplier $= \dfrac{1}{1 - mp_s} = \dfrac{1}{1 - 0.8} = 5$ Therefore, $\Delta Y = -5 \times 5 = -25$ crores.

New, income = 300 – 25 = 275 crore

The new level of consumption

= 275 × mpc

= 275 × 0.8 = 220

QUESTIONS FOR REVIEW

1. What do you understand by investment function ? Explain the factors that influence the level of investment in the economy.
2. Distinguish between autonomous investment and induced investment. Explain the factors that determine the level of investment in the economy
3. What is meant by marginal efficiency of capital ? How is it calculated ? What are the factors that determine marginal efficiency of capital in the economy ?
4. What is marginal efficiency of investment ? What role do expectations of entrepreneurs play in determining marginal efficiency of investment or capital ?
5. How do changes in the rate of interest influence the decision to invest ? Is investment interest elastic ?
6. What is the accelerator theory of investment ? Is it a good representation of investment behaviour ?
7. Critically examine the view that investment spending depends on the changes in the level of output.
8. "Consumption and investment are complementary during deflation, but competitive at full employment." Discuss.
9. The accelerator principle becomes inoperative during periods of excess capacity. Explain.
10. Discuss the view that investment spending depends on change in the level of income.
11. Define marginal efficiency of capital. How does it determine the volume of investment ?
12. Distinguish between marginal efficiency of captial (MEC) and marginal efficiency of investment (MEI). Given marginal efficiency of capital (MEC), how would the stock of capital get adjusted when there is a fall in the rate of interest ?
13. Explain the factors that lead to the discrepancy between the actual and desired stock of capital?
14. What is meant by a firm's desired capital stock ? Why does the firm adjust gradually towards it ? How does an investment tax credit scheme affect the amount of investment ?
15. What factors, according to neoclassical theory, determine investment in an economy ? Explain.
16. Explain Tobin's q – theory of investment. Is it related to Neoclassical Theory of Investment ?
17. If inflation is conducive to investment.
18. Explain role of cheap monetary policy in promoting private investment. Is it effective in stimulating private investment ?
19. Critically examine the role of expansionary fiscal policy in boosting private investment. How can its adverse effect on private investment be offset ?

CHAPTER 9
Theory of Multiplier

THE CONCEPT OF MULTIPLIER

The theory of multiplier occupies an important place in the modern theory of income and employment. The concept of multiplier was first of all developed by F.A. Kahn in the early 1930s. But Keynes later further refined it. F.A. Kahn developed the concept of multiplier with reference to the increase in employment, direct as well as indirect, as a result of initial increase in investment and employment. Keynes, however, propounded the concept of multiplier with reference to the increase in total income, direct as well as indirect, as a result of original increase in investment and income. Therefore, whereas Kahn's multiplier is known as '*employment multiplier*', Keynes's multiplier is known as *investment* or *income multiplier*. The essence of multiplier is that total increase in income, output or employment is manifold the original increase in investment. For example, if investment equal to Rs. 100 crores is made, then the income will not rise by Rs. 100 crores only but a multiple of it. If as a result of the investment of Rs. 100 crores, the national income increases by Rs. 300 crores, multiplier is equal to 3. If as a result of investment of Rs. 100 crores, total national income increases by Rs. 400 crores, multiplier is 4. The multiplier is, therefore, the ratio of increment in income to the increment in investment. If ΔI stands for increment in investment and ΔY stands for the resultant increase in income, then multiplier is equal to the ratio of increment in income (ΔY) to the increment in investment (ΔI). Therefore $k = \frac{\Delta Y}{\Delta I}$ where k stands for multiplier.

Now, the question is why the increase in income is many times more than the initial increase in investment. It is easy to explain this. Suppose Government undertakes investment expenditure equal to Rs. 100 crores on some public works, say the construction of rural roads. For this Government will pay wages to the labourers engaged, prices for the materials to the suppliers and remunerations to other factors who make contribution to the work of road-building. The total cost will amount to Rs. 100 crores. This will increase incomes of the people equal to Rs. 100 crores. But this is not all. The people who receive Rs. 100 crores will spend a good part of them on consumer goods. Suppose marginal propensity to consume of the people is 4/5 or 80%. Then out of Rs. 100 crores they will spend Rs. 80 crores on consumer goods, which would increase incomes of those people who supply consumer goods equal to Rs. 80 crores. But those who receive these Rs. 80 crores will also in turn spend these incomes, depending upon their marginal propensity to consume. If their marginal propensity to consume is also 4/5, then they will spend Rs. 64 crores on consumer goods. Thus, this will further increase incomes of some other people equal to Rs. 64 crores. In this way, the chain of consumption expenditure would continue and the income of the people will go on increasing. But every additional increase in income will be progressively less since a part of the income received will be saved. Thus, we see that the income will not increase by only Rs. 100 crores, which was initially invested in the construction of roads, but by many time more.

Derivation of Investment Multiplier

How much increase in national income will take place as a result of an initial increase in investment can be expressed in the following mathematical form:

Increase in income Or

$$\Delta Y = 100 + 100 \times 4/5 + 100(4/5)^2 + 100(4/5)^3 + 100(4/5)^4...$$
$$= 100[1 + (4/5) + (4/5)^2 + (4/5)^3 + (4/5)^4...]$$

But the above series is one of geometric progression.Therefore, increase in income (ΔY)

$$= 100 \frac{1}{1-4/5} \quad ...(i)$$
$$= 100 \times \frac{1}{1/5}$$
$$= 100 \times 5$$
$$= 500$$

It is thus clear that if the marginal propensity to consume is 4/5, the investment of Rs. 100 crores leads to the increase in the national income by Rs. 500 crores. Therefore, multiplier here is equal to 5. We can express this in a general formula. If ΔY stands for increase in income, ΔI stands for increase in investment and *MPC* for marginal propensity to consume, we can write the equation (*i*) above as follows:

$$\Delta Y = \Delta I \frac{1}{1-MPC}$$
$$\frac{\Delta Y}{\Delta I} = \frac{1}{1-MPC}$$

$\frac{\Delta Y}{\Delta I}$ measures the size of the multiplier. Therefore,

$$\text{Size of multiplier or } k = \frac{1}{1-MPC} \quad ...(ii)$$

It is clear from above that the size of multiplier depends upon the marginal propensity to consume of the community. The multiplier is the reciprocal of one minus marginal propensity to consume. However, we can express multiplier in a simpler form. As we know that saving is equal to income minus consumption, one minus marginal propensity to consume will be equal to marginal propensity to save, that is, 1 – *MPC* = *MPS*. Therefore, multiplier is equal to $\frac{1}{1-MPC} = \frac{1}{MPS}$.

Algebraic Derivation of Multiplier

The multiplier can be derived algebraically as follows:

Writing the equation for the equilibrium level of income we have

$$Y = C + I \quad ...(1)$$

As in the multiplier analysis we are concerned with changes in income induced by changes in investment, rewriting the equation (1) in terms of changes in the variables we have

$$\Delta Y = \Delta C + \Delta I \quad ...(2)$$

In the simple Keynesian model of income determination, change in investment is considered to be autonomous or independent of changes in income while changes in consumption are function of changes in income.

In the consumption function,

$$C = a + bY$$

where a is a constant term, b is marginal propensity to consume which is also assumed to remain constant. Therefore, change in consumption can occur only if there is change in income. Thus

$$\Delta C = b\Delta Y \qquad ..(3)$$

Substituting (3) into (2) we have

$$\Delta Y = b\Delta Y + \Delta I$$

$$\Delta Y - b\Delta Y = \Delta I$$

$$\Delta Y\,(1-b) = \Delta I$$

$$\Delta Y = \frac{1}{1-b}\Delta I$$

$$\frac{\Delta Y}{\Delta I} = \frac{1}{1-b}$$

As b stands for marginal propensity to consume

$$\frac{\Delta Y}{\Delta I} = \frac{1}{1-MPC} = \frac{1}{MPS}$$

This is the same formula of multiplier as obtained earlier. Note that the value of multiplier $\frac{\Delta Y}{\Delta I}$ will remain constant as long as marginal propensity to consume remains the same.

Calculating the Size or Value of Multiplier

The multiplier tells us how much increase in income occurs when *autonomous investment* increases by ₹ 1, that is, investment multiplier is $\frac{\Delta Y}{\Delta I}$ and its value is equal to $\frac{1}{1-b}$ where b stands for marginal propensity to consume (*MPC*). Thus, multiplier $= \frac{\Delta Y}{\Delta I} = \frac{1}{1-b}$. Further, since $1-b$ equals marginal propensity to save (*MPS*), the value of investment multiplier is equal to $\frac{1}{1-b} = \frac{1}{s}$ where s stands for marginal propensity to save. In other words, the size of multiplier is equal to $\frac{1}{1-MPC} = \frac{1}{MPS}$. Thus, the value of multiplier can be obtained if we know either the value of *MPC* or *MPS*.

Now, higher the marginal propensity to consume (b) (or the lower the value of marginal propensity to save (s), the greater the value of multiplier. For example, if marginal propensity to consume (b) is 0.8, investment multiplier is

$$\frac{\Delta Y}{\Delta I} = \frac{1}{1-08} = \frac{1}{0.2} = 1 \times \frac{10}{2} = 5$$

If *MPC* or $b = 0.75$, multiplier is

$$= \frac{\Delta Y}{\Delta I} = \frac{1}{1-0.75} = \frac{1}{0.25} = \frac{100}{25} = 4$$

As mentioned above, the size or value of multiplier can be calculated using either the value of marginal propensity to consume (*MPC*) or the value of marginal property to save (*MPS* or s). In fact, the value of multiplier is the reciprocal of marginal propensity to save $\left(\frac{\Delta Y}{\Delta I} = \frac{1}{MPS} \text{ or } \frac{1}{s}\right)$. When marginal propensity to consume is 0.8, marginal propensity to save will be $1-0.8 = 0.2$. The multiplier will be $\frac{1}{0.2}$ or $\frac{1}{2/10} = 5$. Likewise if marginal propensity to consume (b) is 0.75, marginal propensity to save will be $1-0.75 = 0.25$ and multiplier will be $\frac{1}{0.25} = \frac{1}{25/100} = 4$.

Given the size of multiplier, we can find out the increase in income (ΔY) resulting from a certain increase in investment (ΔI) by using the multiplier relationship. Thus

$$\frac{\Delta Y}{\Delta I} = \frac{1}{1-b}$$

$$\Delta Y = \Delta I . \frac{1}{1-b}$$

If marginal propensity to consume is equal to 0.8, with the increase in investment by ₹ 100 crore the increase in income will be :

$$\frac{\Delta Y}{\Delta I} = \frac{1}{1-b}$$

$$\Delta Y = \Delta I \times \frac{1}{1-b} = 100 \times \frac{1}{1-0.8}$$

$$100 \times \frac{1}{0.2} = 100 \times 5 = 500$$

Two Limiting Cases of the Value of Multiplier. There are two limiting cases of the multiplier. One limiting case occurs when the marginal propensity to consume is equal to one, that is, when the whole of the increment in income is consumed and nothing is saved. In this case, the size of multiplier will be equal to infinity, that is, a small increase in investment will bring about a very large increase in income and employment so that full employment is reached and even the process goes beyond that. "In such circumstances, the Government would need to employ only one road builder to raise income indefinitely, causing first full employment and then a limitless spiral of inflation."[1] However, this is unlikely to occur since marginal propensity to consume in the real world is less than one. The other limiting case occurs when marginal propensity to consume is equal to zero, that is, when nothing out of the increment in income is consumed, and the whole increment in income is saved. In this case, the value of the multiplier will be equal to one. That is, in this case, the increment in income will be equal to the original increase in investment and not a multiple of it. But in actual practice the marginal propensity to consume is less than one but more than zero $\left(1 > \frac{\Delta C}{\Delta Y} > 0\right)$. Therefore, *the value of the multiplier is greater than one but less than infinity.*

Assumptions of Multiplier Theory

In our above explanation of multiplier, we have made many simplifying assumptions. First, we have assumed that the *marginal propensity to consume remains constant throughout* as the income increases in various rounds of consumption expenditure. However, the marginal propensity to consume may differ in various rounds of consumption expenditure. But this constancy of marginal propensity to consume is a realistic assumption, since all available empirical evidence shows that marginal propensity to consume is very stable in the short run. Secondly, we have assumed that there is a net increase in investment in a period and no further indirect effects on investment in that period occur or if they occur they have been taken into account so that there is a given net increase in investment. Further, we have assumed that *there is no any time-lag* between the increase in investment and the resultant increment in income. That is, increment in income takes place instantaneously as a result of increment in investment. J.M. Keynes ignored the time-lag in the process of income generation and therefore his multiplier is also called *instantaneous multiplier.* In recent years, the importance of time lag has been recognised and concept of dynamic multiplier has been developed on that basis. But in an ele-mentary study as the present one the time lags will be ignored as was done by Keynes.

1. Stonier and Hague, *A Textbook of Economic Theory,* 4th edition, 1972.

Another important assumption in the theory of multiplier is that *excess capacity exists in the consumer goods industries* so that when the demand for them increases, more amounts of consumer goods can be produced to meet this demand. If there is no excess capacity in consumer goods industries, the increase in demand as a result of some original increase in investment will bring about rise in prices rather than increases in real income, output and employment. As we shall see later, Keynes's multiplier was evolved in the context of advanced capitalist economies which were in grip of depression and in times of depression and there did exist excess capacity in the consumer goods industries due to lack of aggregate demand. The Keynesian multiplier effect is very small in developing countries like India since there is not much excess capacity in consumer goods industries.

In our above analysis of the multiplier process we have taken a closed economy, that is, we have not taken into account imports and exports. If ours were an open economy, then a part of the increment in consumption expenditure would have been made on imports of goods from abroad. This would have caused increment in income in foreign countries rather than within the country. This will reduce the value of the multiplier. *Imports are important leakage from the multiplier process* and we have ignored them in our above analysis for the purpose of simplicity.

It is worth noting that multiplier not only works in money terms but also in real terms. In other words, multiple increment in income as a result of a given net increase in investment does not only take place in money terms but also in terms of real output, that is, in terms of goods and services. When incomes increase as a result of investment and these increments in income are spent on consumer goods, the output of consumer goods is increased to meet the extra demand brought about by increased incomes. Therefore, real income or output, increases by the same amount as the increment in money incomes, since *the prices of goods have been assumed to be constant.* Of course, we have assumed, as has been mentioned above, that there exists excess productive capacity in the consumer goods industries so that when the demand for consumer goods increases, their production can be easily increased to meet this demand. However, if due to some bottlenecks output of goods cannot be increased in response to increasing demand, prices will rise and as result the real multiplier effect will be small.

Diagrammatic Representation of Multiplier

We havc already explained that the level of national income is determined by the equilibrium between aggregate demand and aggregate supply. In other words, the level of national income is fixed at the level where $C + I$ curve intersects the 45° income curve. With such a diagram we can explain the multiplier. The multiplier is illustrated in Fig. 9.1. In this figure C represents marginal propensity to consume. Marginal propensity to consume has been here assumed to be equal to $\frac{1}{2}$ *i.e.,* 0.5. Therefore, the slope of the curve C of marginal propensity to consume curve C has been taken to be equal to 0.5. $C + I$ represents aggregate demand or expenditure curve. It will be seen from Fig. 9.1 that the aggregate demand curve $C + I$ which intersects the 45° line at point E so that the level of income equal to OY_1 is determined. If investment increases by the amount EH we can then find out how much increment in income and occur as a result of this. As a consequence of increase in investment

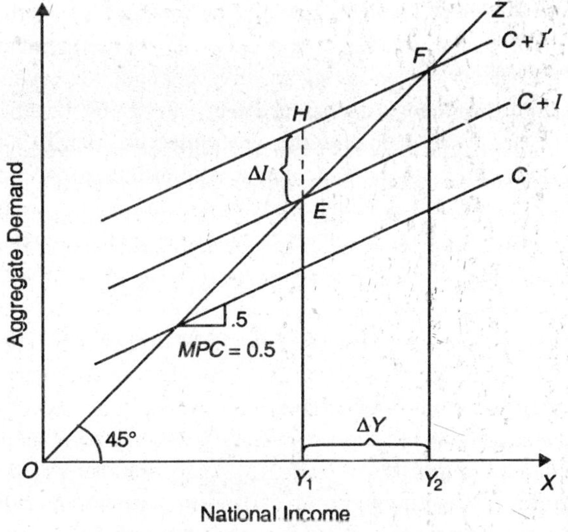

Fig. 9.1. *Keynes's Income Multiplier*

by *EH,* the aggregate expenditure curve shifts upward to the new position $C + I'$. This new aggregate demand curve $C + I'$ intersects income line at point *F* so that the equilibrium level of income increases to *OY*. Thus, as a result of increase in investment equal to *EH,* the income has increased by Y_1Y_2. It will be seen from the figure that Y_1Y_2 is greater than *EH.* On measuring it will be found that Y_1Y_2 is *twice* the length of *EH.* This is as it is expected because the market propensity to consume is here equal to $\frac{1}{2}$ and therefore the size of multiplier will be equal to 2.

The multiplier can be illustrated through saving investment diagram also. In a previous chapter we explained the determination of national income also through saving the investment. Therefore, the multiplier can also be explained with the help of saving investment diagram, as has been shown in Fig. 9.2. In this figure *SS* is the saving curve indicating that as the level of income increases, the community plans to save more. *II* is the investment curve showing the level of investment planned to be undertaken by the investors in the community. The investment has been taken to be a constant amount and autonomous of changes in income. This investment level *OI* has been determined the marginal efficiency of capital and the rate of interest. Investment being autonomous of income means that it does not change with the level of income. Keynes treated investment as autonomous of income and we will here follow him. It will be seen from Fig. 9.2 that saving and investment curves intersect at point *E,* that is, planned saving and planned investment are in equilibrium at the level of income OY_1. Thus, with the given saving and investment curves level of income equal to OY_1 is determined. Now suppose that there is an increase in investment by the amount II'. With this increase in investment, the investment curve shifts to the new dotted position $I'I'$. This new investment curve $I'I$ intersects the saving curve at point *F* and a new equilibrium as reached at the level of income OY_2. A glance at the Fig. 9.2 will reveal that the increase in income Y_1Y_2 is greater than the increase in investment by II''. On measuring these increments in income and investment it will be found that the increment in income $Y_1 Y_2$ is *two times* the increment in investment II'. This is because we have here assumed that propensity

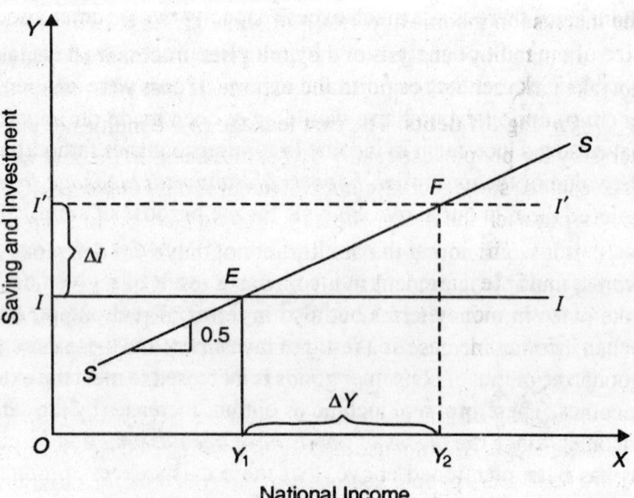

Fig. 9.2. *Multiplier Explained with the Aid of Savings-Investment Diagram*

to save is equal to $\left(\frac{1}{2}\right.$ or marginal propensity of consume is equal to $\left.\frac{1}{2}\right)$. Therefore, the slope of the saving curve has been taken to be equal to $\frac{1}{2}$ or 0.5. Thus in this case multiplier is equal to 2.

$$\text{Multiplier} = \frac{\Delta Y}{\Delta I} = \frac{Y_1Y_2}{II'} = \frac{1}{MPS} = 2$$

Since marginal propensity to save is here equal to $\frac{1}{2}$, the multiplier on the basis of our above formula, namely, $K = \frac{1}{MPS}$ will be equal to 2.

LEAKAGES IN THE MULTIPLIER PROCESS

We have seen above that as a result of increase in investment, the level of income increases by a multiple of it. In our above analysis, saving is a leakage in the multiplier process. Had there been no saving and as a result marginal propensity to consume were equal to 1, the multiplier would have been equal to infinity. In that case as a result of some initial increase in investment, income would go on rising indefinitely. Since marginal propensity to consume is actually less than one, some saving does take place. Therefore, multiplier in actual practice is less than infinity. But besides saving, there are other leakage in the process of income generation which reduces the size of the multiplier. Therefore, the increase in income as a result of some increase in investment will be less than warranted by the size of the multiplier measured by the given marginal propensity to consumer. We explain below the various leakages that occur in the income stream and reduce the size of multiplier in the real world.

Paying off debts. The first leakage in the multiplier process occurs in the form of payment of debts by the people, especially by businessmen. In the real world, all income received by the people as a result of some increase in investment is not consumed. A part of the increment in income is used for paying back the debts which the people have taken from moneylenders, banks or other financial institutions. The incomes used for paying back the debts do not get spent on consumer goods and services and therefore leak away from the income stream. This reduces the size of the multiplier. Of course, when incomes received by the moneylenders, banks or institutions are again lent back to the people, they come back to the income stream and enhance the size of multiplier. But this may or may not happen.

Holding of idle cash balances. If the people hold a part of their increment in income as idle cash balances and do not use it for consumption, they also constitute leakage in the multiplier process. As we have seen, people keep part of their income for satisfying their precautionary and speculative motives, money kept for such purposes is not consumed and therefore does not appear in the successive rounds of consumption expenditure and therefore reduces the increments in total income and output.

Imports. In our above analysis of the working of the multiplier process we have taken the example of a closed economy, that is, an economy with no foreign trade. If it is an open economy as is usually the case, then a part of increment in income will also be spent on the imports of consumer goods. The proportion of increments in income spent on the imports of consumer goods will generate income in other countries and will not help in raising income and output in the domestic economy. Therefore, imports constitute another important leakage in the multiplier process. Suppose marginal propensity to save of an open economy is $\frac{1}{4}$, *i.e.,* marginal propensity to consume is $\frac{3}{4}$. Suppose further that marginal propensity to import is $\frac{1}{4}$, the size of the multiplier without imports will be equal to 4 but the size of the multiplier with the marginal propensity to import equal to $\frac{1}{4}$ and the marginal propensity to consume equal to $\frac{3}{4}$ will be smaller.

$$\text{Multiplier in an Open Economy} = \frac{1}{1-(MPC-MPI)} = \frac{1}{1-MPC+MPI}$$

where *MFC* stands for marginal propensity to consumed and *MPI* for marginal propensity to import.

In our example quoted above, where marginal propensity to consume is equal to $\frac{3}{4}$ and marginal propensity to import is equal to $\frac{1}{4}$, the multiplier is:

$$K = \frac{1}{1-\left(\frac{3}{4}-\frac{1}{4}\right)} = \frac{1}{\frac{1}{2}} = 2$$

We, therefore, see that the size of multiplier instead of being equal to 4, as it would have been in the case of a closed economy, is equal to 2 in the open economy with $\frac{1}{4}$ as the marginal propensity to import.

Taxation. Taxation is another important leakage in the multiplier process. The increments in income which the people receive as a result of increase in investment are also in part used for payment of taxes. Therefore, the money used for payment of taxes does not appear in the successive rounds of consumption expenditure in the multiplier process, and the multiplier is reduced to that extent. However, if the money raised through taxation is spent by the Government, the leakage through taxation will be offset by the increase in Government expenditure. But it is not necessary that all the money raised through taxation is spent by the Government as it happens when Government makes a surplus budget. No doubt, if the Government expenditure increases by an amount equal to the taxation, it would not have any adverse effect on the increases in income and investment and in this way there would be no leakage in the multiplier process.

Increase in Prices. Price inflation constitutes another important leakage in the working of the multiplier process in real terms. As we have noted above, the multiplier works in real terms only when as a result of increase in money income and aggregate demand, output of consumer goods is also increased. When output of consumer goods cannot be easily increased, a part of the increases in the money income and aggregate demand raises prices of the goods rather than their output. Therefore, the multiplier is reduced to the extent of price inflation. In developing countries like India the extra incomes and demand are mostly spent on foodgrains whose output cannot be increased so easily. Therefore, the increments in demand raise the prices of goods to a greater extent than the increase in their output. Besides, in developing countries like India, there is not much excess capacity in many consumer goods industries, especially in agriculture and other wage-goods industries. Therefore, when income and demand increase as a result of increase in investment, it generally raises the prices of these goods rather than their output and therefore weakens the working of the multiplier in real terms. Thus, in 1950s and 1960s it was often asserted, especially by Dr. V.K.R.V. Rao and Dr. A.K. Gupta that Keynesian theory of multiplier was not very much relevant to the conditions of developing countries like India.[2] However, we shall discuss later in this chapter that this old view of the working of Keynesian multiplier in the present-day developing countries is not fully correct.

The above various leakages reduce the multiplier effect of the investment undertaken. If these leakages are plugged, the effect of change in investment on income and employment would be greater.

Importance of the Concept of Multiplier

Multiplier is one of the most important concepts developed by J.M. Keynes to explain the determination of income and employment in an economy. The theory of multiplier has been used to explain the cumulative upward and downward swings of the trade cycles that occur in a free-enterprise capitalist economy. When investment in an economy rises, it has a multiple and cumulative effect on national income, output and employment. As a result, economy experiences rapid upward movement. On the other hand, when due to some reasons, especially due to the adverse change in the expectations of the business class, investment falls, then backward working of the multiplier causes a multiple and cumulative fall in income, output and employment and as a result the economy rapidly moves on downswing of the trade cycle. Thus, Keynesian theory of multiplier helps a good deal in explaining

2. See, V.K.R.V. Rao, Investment, Income and the Multiplier in an Underdeveloped Economy printed in A.N. Agarwala and S.P. Singh (edited). *The Economics of Underdevelopment,* Oxford, 1958.

the movements of trade cycles or fluctuations in the economy.

The theory of multiplier has also a great practical importance in the field of fiscal policy to be pursued by the Government to get out of the depression and achieve the state of full employment. To get rid of depression and remove unemployment, Government investment in public works was recommended even before Keynes. But it was thought that the increase in income will be limited to the amount of investment undertaken in these public works. But the importance of public works is enhanced when it is realisėd that the total effect on income, output and employment as a result of some initial investment has a multiplier effect. Thus, Keynes recommended Government investment in public works to solve the problem of depression and unemployment. The public investment in public works such as road building, construction of hospitals, schools, irrigation facilities will raise aggregate demand by a multiple amount. The multiple increase in income and demand will also encourage the increase in private investment. Thus, the deficiency in private investment which leads to the state of depression and underemployment equilibrium will now be made up and a state of full employment will be restored. If the multiplier had not worked, the income and demand would have risen as a result of some public investment but not as much as they rise with the multiplier effect. Inspired by the Keynesian theory of multiplier. Expansionary fiscal policy of increase in Government expenditure and reduction in income tax was have been adopted by President John Kenedy and press president George W. Bush in the United State of America to remove involuntary unemployment and depreciation. This had a great success in removing unemployment and, depression and therefore, Keynesian theory of multiplier was vindicated and as a result people's belief in it increased.

A Numerical Problem on Multiplier

Problem 1. *Suppose the level of autonomous investment in an economy is Rs. 200 crores and consumption function of the economy is :*

$$C = 80 + 0.75Y$$

(*a*) *What will be the equilibrium level of income?*

(*b*) *What will be the increase in national income if investment increases by Rs. 25 crores.*

Solution. (*a*) For equilibrium level of income,

$$Y = C + I \quad ...(i)$$

where $C = 80 + 0.75$

$I = 200$ crores

Substituting the values of C and I in (1) we have

$$Y = 80 + 0.75\text{K} + 200$$

$$(Y - 0.75Y) = 80 + 200 = 280$$

$$0.25\, Y = 280$$

$$Y = 280 \times \frac{100}{25} = 1120$$

Equilibrium level of income is therefore equal to 1120 crores.

(*b*) How much increase in income will occur as a result of increase in investment by Rs. 25 crores depends on the size of multiplier. The size of multiple is determined by the value of marginal propensely to consume. In the given consumption function ($C = 80 + 0.75Y$) marginal propensity to consume is equal to 0.75 or $\frac{3}{4}$. Thus,

$$\text{multiplier} = \frac{1}{1 - MPC} = \frac{1}{1 - \frac{3}{4}} = 4$$

Thus, with increase in investment by Rs. 25 crores, national income will rise by 25 × 4 = 100 crores.

Problem 2. *Suppose in a country investment increases by Rs. 100 and consumption is given by C = 10 + 0.6Y (where C = consumption and Y = income). How much increase will there take place in income ?*

Solution.

Multiplier, $k = \frac{\Delta Y}{\Delta I}$

or $\Delta Y = k.\Delta I$ ... (i)

Now, multiplier, $k = \frac{1}{1 - MPC}$

In the given consumption function, $MPC = 0.6$

$$K = \frac{1}{1-0.6} = \frac{1}{0.4} = \frac{1}{\frac{4}{10}} = \frac{1}{\frac{2}{5}} = 2.5$$

Substituting the value of $k = 2.5$ and ΔI = Rs. 100 in (1) above, we have

$\Delta Y + 2.5 \times 100 = 250$

Problem 3. *What increase in investment is needed to raise income by Rs. 4,000 crores, if MPC is 0.75 ? How much will there be increase in consumption and saving due to this increase in income ?*

Solution. How much increase in investment is required to raise income by Rs. 4,000 crores depends on the value of multiplier and the size of multiplier (*k*) depends on the marginal propensity to consume (*MPC*). Thus,

Multiplier $(K) = \frac{1}{1 = MPC} = \frac{1}{1-0.75} = \frac{1}{0.25} = 4$

Now, $K = \frac{\Delta Y}{\Delta I}$

or $\Delta I = \frac{\Delta Y}{K}$ ... (*i*)

Substituting the value of ΔY and K in (*i*), we have

$$\Delta I = \frac{4000}{4} = 1000$$

Thus, investment should rise by Rs. 1,000 to achieve Rs. 4,000 increase in income.

THE PARADOX OF THRIFT

An interesting paradox arises when all people in a society try to save more but in fact they are unable to do so. The multiplier theory of Keynes helps a good deal in explaining this paradox. According to this paradox of thrift, the attempt by the people as a whole to save more for hard times such as impending period of recession or unemploy-ment may not materialise and in their bid to save more the society infact may not only end up with the same savings (Or, even lower savings) but also in the process cause their consumption or standard of living to decline. Thrift (*i.e.,* the desire to save more) is considered to be a virtue in most of the societies and it is regarded as an act of prudence on the part of individuals to save for a rainy day. According to a proverb, "a penny saved is a penny earned". Further, according to classical economists, savings determine investment which plays a crucial role in accelerating the rate of economic growth. However, the paradox of thrift shows that the efforts to save more, especially in times of depression, may actually deepen the economic crisis and cause output to fall and unemployment to increase. It goes to the credit of Keynes that with his multiplier theory he was able to resolve the paradox of thrift. Keynesian explanation of paradox of thrift has been shown in Fig. 9.3. According to the Keynesian theory, the saying "penny saved is penny earned" is quite inappropriate for the economy as a whole when it is working at underemployment equilibrium, that is, when there prevails recession or depression. Keynes has showed that if *all* people in a society decide to save more, they may actually fail to do so but nevertheless reduce their consumption. This is because, according to Keynes, the effort to save more by all in a society will lower the aggregate demand for goods and services resulting in a drop in the level of national income. At the lower level of national income, the saving fall to the original level but consumption will be less than before which implies that the people would become worse off.

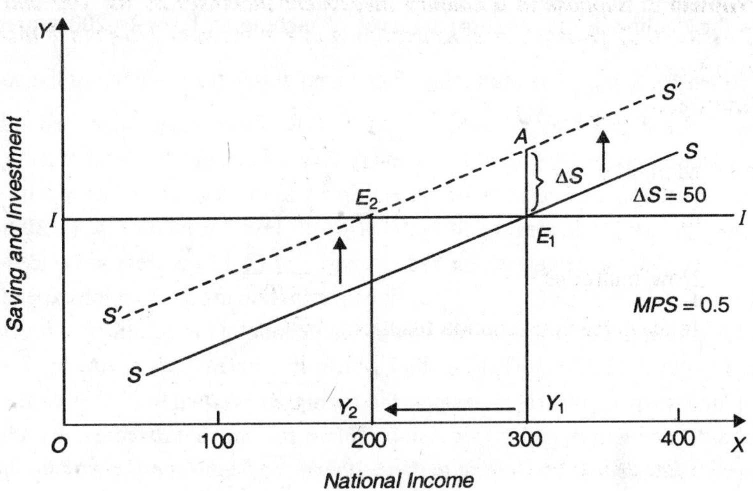

Fig. 9.3. *The Paradox of Thrift*

Consider Fig. 9.3, where *SS* is the saving curve with a slope equal to 0.5, and *II* is the planned investment curve. It will be seen that saving and investment curves intersect at point E_1 and determines level of income equal to Y_1 or ₹ 300 crores. Now suppose that expecting hard times ahead all people try to save more by the amount of ₹ 50 crores which would cause an autonomous downward shift in the consumption function. This downward shift in the consumption function brings about an upward shift by ₹ 50 crores or E_1A in the saving function curve to *S′S′*. This new saving function curve *S′S′* cuts the planned investment curve *II* at point E_2 according to which new equilibrium level of income falls to Y_2 or ₹ 200 crores. It is important to note that level of income does not drop only by the amount (E_1A or ₹ 50 crores), that is, by the extent of reduction in consumption due to more saving but by a multiple of it. With marginal propensity to save (*MPS*) being equal to 0.5 or $\frac{1}{2}$, the value of multiplier would be $1/MPS = 1\frac{1}{2} = 2$. Further, the decline in consumption due to more saving would cause the multiplier to work in reverse, that is, the multiplier would operate to reduce the level of consumption and income by a magnified amount. The decline in consumption expenditure of the people by ₹ 50 crores in the first instance due to more saving by them implies that the producers and sellers of goods and services will find their income to fall by ₹ 50 crores. But the reverse process will not stop here. Given the marginal propensity to consume being equal to 0.5 or $\frac{1}{2}$, the producers sellers of goods and services in turn would spend ₹ 25 crores less when they find their income has fallen by ₹ 50 crores. It will be observed from Fig. 9.3 that this process of reduction on the level of income will continue till the new saving is equal to investment at the lower level of income Y_2 (₹ 200 crores), that is, the level of income has declined by ₹ 100 crores (50 × 2) from its initial equilibrium level of income Y_1 of ₹ 300 crores. Thus the attempt by all people to save more has led to the decline in the equilibrium level of income to Y_2 or ₹ 200 crores at which, with marginal propensity to consume remaining unchanged at 0.5 or $\frac{1}{2}$, saving of the society will fall to the initial level of Y_1E or ₹ 100 crores (200 × 0.5 = 100). This is clearly depicted in Fig. 7.3. With the decrease in planned saving by ₹ 50 crores at every level of income the saving function (*SS*) shifts upward. This sets in motion the operation of the multiplier in the reverse and as will be seen from the Fig. 9.3, the new equilibrium is reached at the new lower level of income Y_2 (₹ 200 crores). It is important to observe that the saving which had risen to Y_1A (₹ 150 crores) has once again fallen to the original level of ₹ 100 crores ($Y_2E_2 = Y_1E_1$) due to reduction in consumption expenditure inducing the working of multiplier in the reverse which causes a decline in the equilibrium level of income from K_t (₹ 300 crores) to Y_2 (₹ 200 crores). In other words, the increases in saving by ₹ 50 crores has led to the fall in income by ₹ 100 crores because the multiplier is equal to 2. This explains the paradoxical feature of an economy gripped by recession. *This is paradoxical because in their attempt to save more the people have caused a decline in their income and consumption with no increase in the saving of the society at all.*

In our analysis we have assumed that the planned investment is fixed, that is, determined outside the model. In other words, the investment has been assumed to be *autonomous of income,* that is, it does not vary with income.

Can We Avert the Paradox of Thrift?

Paradox of thrift holds good when a free market economy is in the grip of recession or depression and investment demand is inadequate due to lack of profit opportunities. However, it has been pointed out by some economists that paradox of thrift can be averted if the extra savings that the people do for a rainy day are somehow channeled into additional investment through financial markets. Indeed, the classical economists argued that the increase in the supply of savings would lead to the fall in the rate of interest which would induce increase in planned investment. If this happens, then in our saving-investment diagram the investment curve *II* would shift up to *I′I′* and as will be seen from Fig. 9.4 the new equilibrium level of income may not fall and therefore the paradox of thrift is averted. In Fig. 9.4, initially the saving curve (S_1S_1) and investment curve (*II*) intersect at point E_1 and determine Y_1 level of income. Now, if the people of the society expecting difficult times ahead, desire to save E_1A more. If these extra savings, for reasons mentioned above, result in more investment, the investment curve will shift to *I′I′*, the new equilibrium will be at point *A* corresponding to the original level of income Y_1. In this way the paradox of thrift has been averted.

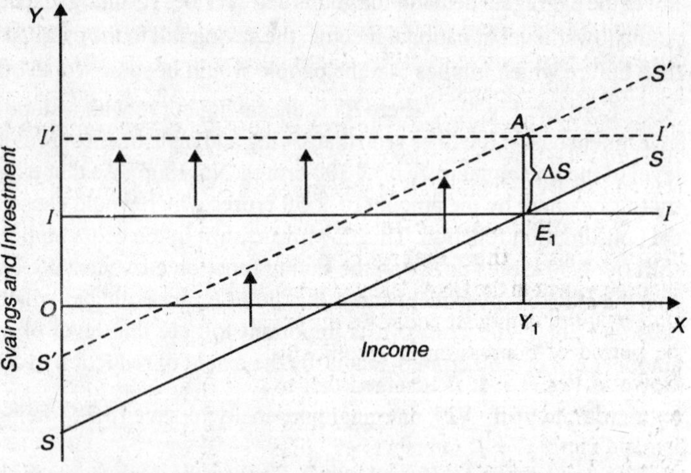

Fig. 9.4. *The Situation when paradox of thrift does not hold*

However, according to the modern economists, especially the followers of Keynes, the empirical evidence does not support the above argument of averting the paradox of thrift. This is because at times of recession or depression, the prospective yields from investment are so small that no possible reduction in the rate of interest will induce sufficient increase in investment. Thus, according to them, in a free-market and private enterprise economy without Government intervention paradox of thrift cannot be averted. Of course, if the Government intervenes as it does even in the present-day predominantly private enterprise economies of the USA and Great Britain, it can mobilise the extra savings of the people and invest them in some worthwhile projects and thus prevent aggregate demand and income from falling. This can happen because undertaking of investment by the Government is not motivated by profit motive but by the considerations of promoting social interest and economic growth. It is because of this that the role of the Government has greatly increased for overcoming recession in the capitalist countries.

THE KEYNESIAN EXPLANATION OF GREAT DEPRESSION: THE IMPACT OF MULTIPLIER

During the 1930s the capitalist economies experienced severe depression which caused widespread involuntary unemployment, substantial loss of output and income and crushing hunger and poverty among the working classes. As explained earlier, the classical economists attributed this unemployment and depression to the higher was rates maintained by the trade unions and the Government. However, this explanation did not prove to be valid. It was English economist J.M. Keynes who radically departed from the classical thought and put forward the view that it was the large decline in investment that caused the depression and substantial increase in involuntary unemployment. According to Keynes, the investment was highly volatile and it was a drastic decline in it due to the pressimistic expectations of the entrepreneurs about the prospective profits from investment that brought about a decline in aggregate demand (expenditure) which through working of the multiplier in the reverse caused a magnified fall income (output) and employment. For example, during the first four years (1929-33) of depression in the USA the unemployment which was only 3.2 per cent in 1929 soared to 25 per cent in 1933, that is, one out of four in the labour force in the United States became unemployed. The level of national income dropped from $ 315 billion in 1929 to $ 222 billion in 1933 at 1972 prices, a decline of $ 93 billion in just four years. According to Keynes, this was caused by a drastic fall in investment from $ 56 billion in 1929 to $ 8.5 billion in 1993.

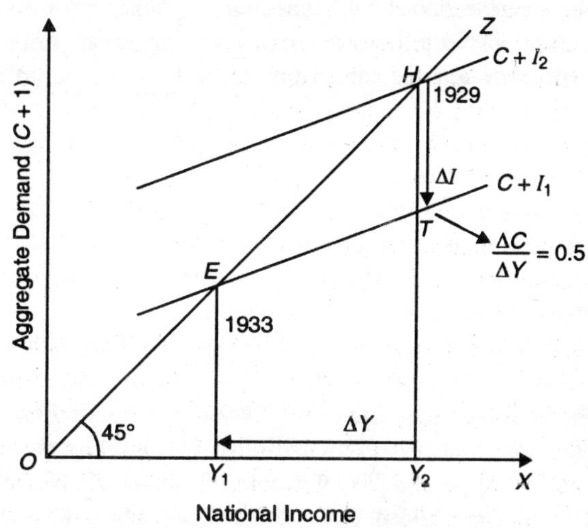

Fig. 9.5. *Depression of 1930s Caused by a Decline in Investment and Reverse Working of Multiplier*

The huge decline in national income and the emergence of unemployment in the USA, UK and other industrialised capitalist countries during the period of depression is graphically shown in Fig. 9.5. It is assumed that to begin with, say in 1929, the aggregate demand curve C + I_2 intersects 45° line at point H and determines equilibrium level of income at full-employment or potential output level OY_1. The sharp decline in investment by the amount *HT* due to the fall in profitability of investment following a crash in stock markets in 1929 and other unfavourable events caused a downward shift in the aggregate demand curve to C + I_1 (where $I_1 < I_2$). This new aggregate demand curve $C + I_1$ intersects the 45° line at point *E* and accordingly determines equilibrium level of income OY_1 which is much lower than full-employment level OY_F and thus represents a state of depression with a large unemployment of workers. *The important point made by Keynes was that income would not fall merely equal to the decline in investment but by a multiple of it.* In fact, during the depression period of 1930s, it actually happened so and is evident from the Table 9.1. It will be seen from the Figure 9.5 that the decline in national income Y_FY_1 is not equal to the fall in investment by *HT* by out by a multiple of it. Y_FY_1 is twice that of *HT*. As explained above, this is due to the working of multiplier in the reverse. Further note that after taking into all leakages in the multiplier process it has been assumed that marginal propensity to consume is equal to 0.5 which yields the value of multiplier 1/1-*MPC* = 1/1-1/2 = 2, This is why fall in income by Y_FY_1 is twice the decline in investment by *HT*.

Now, the historical record of this period about the various components of aggregate demand of the US economy shows that changes in net exports and Government expenditure were quite small and they mostly offset each other during the period 1929-33. The drastic drop in private investment appears to be the basis reason for the huge fall in aggregate demand or spending. The private investment which was $ 56 billion in 1920 fell to only $8.5 billion in 1933 in the U.S.A., the decline

Table 9.1

			(in billion US $)
	1929	**1933**	**Change**
Investment	56	8.5	47.5
National Income	315	222	93
Unemployment (% of labour force)	3.2	25	21.8

of $ 47.5 billion in four years. But, as has been explained by Keynes, the decrease in aggregate expenditure was not merely equal to $ 47.5 billion, but by a multiple amount due to the operation of the multiplier in the reverse. It has been estimated that taking into account all leakages in the multiplier process, the value of the multiplier was around 2 during the period. Therefore, as a result of sharp decline in investment by $ 47.5 billion and consequently operation of the multiplier in the reverse there was a fall in the induced consumption expenditure. Thus, as a result of the sharp drop in private investment and resultant fall in induced consumption due to working of multiplier caused much bigger decrease ($ 93 billion) in the level of aggregate effective demand, income and output. This is in accordance with the value of multiplier being equal to around 2. Multiplier is here equal to

$$\frac{\Delta Y}{\Delta I} = \frac{93}{47.3} = 1.96$$

Thus, the Keynesian theory of income determination provides a fairly accurate explanation of the first four years of the great depression. This looks rather simple but during the early 1930s it was not understood at all. Only after when the Keynesian prescription toward off depression and involuntary unemployment, namely, launching by the Government public works programme financed by the deficit budgets to raise aggregate demand, such as adopted under New Deal Policy in the U.S.A. proved to be a great success that economists and intellectuals were convined about the validity of the Keynes's explanation of depression. An important result of the success of the Keynesian model was that fiscal policy as an instrument for controlling business cycles came into prominence. Further, it now became clear that the Government intervention, though the adoption of appropriate fiscal and monetary policies, can avert the collapse of the economy such as that happened during 1929-33.

LIMITATIONS OF THE WORKING OF KEYNESIAN MULTIPLIER IN THE DEVELOPING COUNTRIES

The Old View

In the early fifties an eminent Indian economist Dr. V.K. R.V. Rao and some others explained that in developing countries like India Keynesian multiplier did not work in real terms, that is, does not operate to increase income and employment by a multiple of the initial increase in investment.[3] He claimed that the concept of investment multiplier was valid in the context of the situation of depression in the industrialised developed economies of the UK and the USA where there existed a lot of access productive capacity and a larger number of open involuntary unemployment. He argued that in such a situation of a depressed economy there was a high elasticity of supply of output to changes in demand for them. Therefore, in the developed capitalist economies ridden with depression increase in investment leading to successive rounds of consumption expenditure raises aggregate demand. Due to the existence of large excess capacity and involuntary unemployment under conditions of depression aggregate supply of outputs highly elastic, increase in aggregate demand brings about increase in real income, output and employment which is a multiple of original increase in investment.

On the other hand, they claimed that in underdeveloped countries there was little excess capacity in consumer goods industries and therefore supply of output was inelastic. Therefore, when there is injection of investment, and as a result through successive rounds of the operation of multiplier, aggregate demand for consumer goods increases, it results mainly in rise in money income brought about through rise in prices and not an increase in real national income.

The second condition, according to Dr. Rao and his followers for the working of multiplier in raising national income and employment was that the supply of raw materials, financial capital must be sufficiently elastic so that when aggregate demand increases as a result of multiplier effect of increase in investment the supply of output could be increased adequately to meet this higher demand for goods and services. They argued that in underdeveloped countries like India due to under-developed nature of their economies, there was acute scarcity of raw materials, other intermediate goods such as steel, cement and financial capital which put great obstacles for the working of multiplier in real terms.

The third condition required for the working of multiplier in real terms was that there should be involuntary open unemployment so that when aggregate demand for goods increases as a consequence of new investment, the adequate supply of workers must be forthcoming to be employed in the production processes of various industries. They argued this condition too was not fulfilled in the under-developed countries where there existed disguised unemployment, especially in the agricultural sector. The disguisedly unemployed workers who are supported by joint family system could not be easily shifted to be employed in the industries for expansion of output to achieve the multiplier effect.

Lastly, it was pointed out that the under-developed countries like India had predominantly agricultural economies and income elasticity of demand for foodgrains was very high in these economies. In view of this when increase in investment leads to the rise in money incomes of the people, a large part is spent on foodgrains. But the supply of agricultural products is inelastic because their production is subject to uncertain natural factors like Monsoon and climate and further there was lack of irrigation facilities, improved seeds, fertilizers etc. Hence it was difficult to increase agricultural production in response to the increase in demand through the multiplier effect of increase in investment.

It follows from above that the Keynesian assumptions for the working of multiplier in real terms, namely (1) the supply of output of goods is elastic due to the existence of large excess capacity, (b) the supply of raw materials and others intermediate goods can be adequately increased, (c) there

3. Dr. V.K.R.V. Rao, Investment, Income and Multiplier in an Under-developed Economy, *Indian Economic Review,* February 1952.

exists involuntarily unemployed workers searching for work and, (d) sufficiently elastic agricultural output. In view of the earlier economists these assumptions for realising the multiplier effect in terms of rise in real income and employment were not valid in case of under-developed countries. Therefore, according to them, Keynesian multiplier did not operate in real terms in under-developed countries and actually leads to the rise in price or inflationary conditions in them.

The Relevance of Multiplier for Developing Countries : The Modern View

We have explained above the views of some eminent Indian economists, such Dr. V.K.R.V. Rao, Dr. A.K. Dass Gupta expressed during the early fifties regarding non-operation of the Keynesian multiplier in the under-developed countries. But the situation in the present day developing countries has substantially changed in the last 60 years. There has been a lot of economic growth and structural transformation in the Indian economy during the last half a centuary so that supply conditions today have become significantly elastic. So in the present state of the Indian economy and also of some other developing economies, it cannot be said that Keynesian multiplier is not applicable in real terms in them. However, it may be noted that even in the fifties and early sixties the view that Keynesian multiplier did not work in the under-developed countries did not go entirely unchallanged. Thus commenting on Dr. Rao's article Dr. K.N. Raj remarked that "Discarding the Keynesian thesis as altogether inoperative in under-developed countries is really throwing the baby away with the bath water".[4] Similarly Dr. D.R. Khatkhate wrote, "In conclusion we may state that the multiplier can operate in an under-developed economy when it is associated with a carefully designed pattern of investment. The theory that the multiplier works in a backward economy only with reference to the money income is based on static assumptions and is, therefore, not correct"[5]. Likewise, Dr. Ashok Mathur write. "Our main objection against the view that Keynesian multiplier does not operate in the under-developed countries is that it views the operation of multiplier process in a completly static setting and as a purely short-period concept, whereas the very rationale of economic development is long run dynamic change. Once we relax these two restrictive assumptions, the essential content of the Keynesian multiplier, that is increase of investment results in an increase in output which is much in excess of the original outlay on investment holds true in case of the developing as much as in the developed economies"[6]

At present, in the beginning of the new millenium as a result of economic growth both in the industrial and agricultural sectors the Indian economy has a widely diversified structure and supply of output has become quite elastic, at least in the industrial sector. Besides, at times there is a lot of excess or unutilised capacity in several industries in India due to the deficieny of aggregate demand. The potential for increasing raw materials and intermediate products such as cement, steel and fertilizers has significantly increased to meet the rising demand for them.

If there is injection of investment it will result in manifold increase in output or real income and employment through the working of the multiplier. If the injection of new investment package is quite diversified and balanced, as is generally planned in our Five Years Plans, the investment and growth in several industries simultaneously will create not only additional demand for each other as was visualised by Nurkse[7] but will also create productive, capacities in them which will ultimately over a period of time will result in multiple increase in output an employment.

---

4. Dr. K.N. Raj, "Dr. Rao on Investment, Income and the Multiplier in an Under-developed Economy -a comment" *Indian Economic Review,* p. 1952.-
5. D.R. Khatkhate "The Multiplier Process in Developing Economies" *Indian Economic Journal,* Oct. 1954.
6. Ashok Mathur, On Throwing the Baby away with the Bath Water, *Indian Economic Journal,* April-June; 1965
7. Ragnar Nurkse, *Problems of Capital Formation in Underdeveloped Countries,*
8. See E. Domar, Capital Expansion, Rate of Growth and Employment, *Economica*, Vol. 14, 1946 and R.E. Harrod, *Towards Dynamic Economics*, Macmillan & Co. London, 1948.

It is worth noting that in India today there is not only a lot of preexisting excess production capacity in the Indian industries but new investment every year also creates additional production capacity which with some time lag will result in increase in real income or output, if adequate aggregate demand is forthcoming for its utilisation. Harrod-Domar in their famous dynamic growth models emphasised that investment not only creates demand but also new productive capacity[8]. Thus, if we look at increment in investment from the viewpoint of dynamics of development and take a longer time horizon, multiplier effect of new investment in the developing countries can become a reality. It is true that increase in money incomes and demand may tend to occur ahead of the increase in real income but subject to some time lag between investment and consequent increase in production capacity, the latter would tend to catch up with the former. The significant point to note is that investment not only creates demand but it also creates production capacity. Ultimately there is no reason as to why multiplier effect of new investment on real income or output may not materialise, though the actual period required for realisation of the multiplier effect depends on various time lags in the process of income generation and capacity creation. The wider the range ot industries over which initial investment is undertaken the greater will be the multiplier effect. This is because monetary demand or expenditure generated by investment in any one industry would be easily met by the increase in production capacity in a variety of industries. In this way increase in demand resulting from investment would not lead to rise in prices but will cause real output to rise.

Agriculture and Multiplier. As mentioned above, the argument for non-operation of multiplier in underdeveloped countries was also partly based on the inelastic nature of supply of agricultural output especially foodgrains as it was pointed out that a large part of monetary demand or money incomes generated by investment would be spent on foodgrains. Inability to meet the rise in demand for foodgrains would cause rise in price level or inflation in the economy rather than increase in real output. It may be pointed out that thanks to the spread of green revolution technology expansion in irrigation facilities in various states of India, foodgrains production can be adequately increased in response to rising demand for foodgrains.

Furthermore, it was asserted by Dr. Rao, the existence of disguised unemployment in underdeveloped countries instead of Keynesian type involuntary open unemployment also prevented the working of multiplier in real terms. In thc Indian economy today there are a large number of involuntarily unemployed workers crying out for employment. So this argument for failure of multiplier to work in real terms no longer hold good in the present economic situation.

To conclude, in the present economic situation of the Indian economy with a lot of excess production capacity in several consumer goods industries and a large potential for expanding agricultural production, increase in investment would produce a real multiplier effect on increasing real income and output without causing inflationary pressures in the economy. Multiplier effect of new investment can be further increased, if investment package is quite diversified covering a large number of industries (including agriculture) so that monetary demand and income generated by any one industry can be adequately met by increase in output capacity in other industries. Further, even when their is no preexisting excess capacity in the industries increase in investment leads to the increase is demand for consumption goods which in turn cause further rise on investment to meet that consumption demand. The effect of increase in consumption demand on expansion in investment is generally referred to as *accelerator.* Indeed, the combined working of multiplier and acceleration, which is called *super-multiplier,* leading to manifold increase in output can take place in the growth process in the developing countries like India[9].

---

9. See V.N. Pandit, Macroeconomic Characteristics of the Indian Economy, in Prabhat Patnaik, ed. *Macro-economics,* Oxford University Press, p. 205.

QUESTIONS FOR REVIEW

1. What is investment multiplier ? How is it related to marginal propensity to Consume ? [**Hints** : Keynes' investment multiplier is also called Income multiplier.]
2. Wht is income multiplier ? Find out the value of multiplier given the following : *(a)* $MPC = 0.80$, *(b)* $MPC = 0.75$, *(c)* $MPS = 0.20$, *(d)* $MPS = 0.50$.
3. Explain the concept of investment multiplier or marginal propensity to same is 0.1, what is the value of multiplier.
4. Explain the Keynesian theory of investment multiplier. What are possible leakages in the multiplier mechanism ?
5. Keynesian investment multiplier does not operate in the developing countries like India." Do you agree ? Discuss.
6. "Multiplier does not work in real terms in developing countries" *(Dr. V.K.R.V Rao)* What prevents the multiplier to work in real terms in India ?
7. Even though marginal propensity to consume is quite high in LDCs, an increase in government expenditure may have little expansionary effect. Discuss

   D.U., B.A. (Hons) 1995.
8. Distinguish between static multiplier and dynamic multiplier Explain them through appropriate graphs.
9. *(a)* Explain the concept of multiplier. How does it work ?
10. What is paradox of thrift ? How would you explain it.
11. "If all people in a society decide to save more, they may actually fail to do so, but nevertheless reduce their consumption.". Expalin.
12. Explain and illustrated diagrammatically the concept of multiplier. Discuss the leakages that may occur in the operation of multiplier in an economy.
13. Explain how Keynes showed that *if all people* in a society decide to save more, they may actually fail to do so. Under what circumstances is it true ?
14. Explain the significance of multiplier in the Keynes's explanation of depression in the economy.
15. Does Keynesion, multiplier work in developing countries ? Discuss.
16. In developing countries Keynesian multiplier works in money terms and not in real terms of increase in output and employment. Discuss.

APPENDIX TO CHAPTER 9*

Static and Dynamic Multiplier

In our foregoing analysis we have explained the operation of multiplier without considering the role of time element in the process of generation of income and employment as a result of initial increase in investment. In fact our analysis of multiplier so far implies that consequent to the initial increase in investment the new equilibrium level of income is reached instantaneously. This, of course, is unrealistic. The process of expansion in income, triggered by an increase in investment always takes time. The successive rounds of spending and respending involves the passage of time. But *our static analysis of multiplier does not consider the time path of change in income and consumption that follows the increase in investment.* Therefore, a realistic model of multiplier requires that due attention is paid to the changes in induced consumption and income over time consequent to a change in investment. In our analysis below we first derive algebraically simple static multiplier and then explain dynamic multiplier.

Derivation of Static Multiplier

As mentioned above, in static multiplier, changes in income and induced consumption consequent to the change in investment, are analysed *without considering the time path of these changes.* Static multiplier can be derived algebraically as follows:

Writing the equation for the equilibrium level of income we have

$$Y = C + I \qquad ...(1)$$

As in the multiplier analysis we are concerned with changes in income induced by changes in investment, rewriting the equation (1) in terms of changes in the variables we have

$$\Delta Y = \Delta C + \Delta I \qquad ...(2)$$

In the simple Keynesian model of income determination, change in investment is considered to be autonomous or independent of changes in income while changes in consumption are function of changes in income.

In the consumption function,

$$C = a + bY$$

where a is a constant term, b is marginal propensity to consume which is also assumed to remain constant. Therefore, change in consumption can occur only if there is change in income. Thus

$$\Delta C = b \, \Delta Y \qquad ...(3)$$

Substituting (3) into (2) we have

$$\Delta Y = b \, \Delta Y + \Delta I$$

$$\Delta Y - b \, \Delta Y = \Delta I$$

$$\Delta Y (1 - b) = \Delta I$$

$$\Delta Y = \frac{1}{1-b} \Delta I$$

*. This appendix is meant for Honours and Postgraduate Courses in Macroeconomics.

or $$\frac{\Delta Y}{\Delta I} = \frac{1}{1-b}$$

As b stands for marginal propensity to consume

$$\frac{\Delta Y}{\Delta I} = \frac{1}{1-MPC} = \frac{1}{MPS}$$

This is the same formula of multiplier as obtained earlier. Note that the value of multiplier $\frac{\Delta Y}{\Delta I}$ will remain constant as long as marginal propensity to consume remains the same.

Dynamic Multiplier : Continuous Injection Model

A dynamic model of multiplier can be formulated by using *period or sequence analysis* which considers time path of the changes in relevant variables and also in which value of a variable in a period depends on its value in the previous period. Let us assume a level of national income is in equilibrium in period 1. Now, the firm decide to increase the amount of investment in period 2. It may be recalled that investment by the firms means their expenditure on new capital goods. When the investment expenditure is increased by the firms in period 2, income of the factors engaged in the production of capital goods will rise in the same period 2. It is also assumed that there exists excess capacity in capital goods industries so that they can increase the production and supply of these goods in response to the increase in aggregate demand in the same period in which investment is increased and consequently factor incomes earned in the capital goods industries rise. It is further assumed that there is a one period lag in response of change in consumption to the change in income. That is, a change in consumption in a period t is a function of change in income of the previous period, that is, $t - 1$.

With the above assumptions we state below the equation of a simple model of dynamic multiplier

$$Y_t = C_t + I_t \quad ...(a)$$

$$C_t = a + bY_{t-1} \quad ... (b)$$

$$I_t = I_t \quad ... (c)$$

From the equation (*c*) it will be observed that consistent with Keynesian multiplier model we have assumed investment as an autonomous variable, that is, it is not dependent on changes in income and is determined by the variables outside the model.

Now substituting equations (*b*) and (*c*) into (*a*) we have

$$Y_t = a + bY_{t-1} + I_t \quad ... (d)$$

Note that *the difference between the dynamic analysis from the static analysis of multiplier made earlier is that we are now considering time lag in the consumption function*. How as a result of change in investment a level of equilibrium income changes over successive periods of time to reach a new equilibrium level of income is explained below.

We assume that no change in investment or any other component of aggregate demand occurs in period 1 and equilibrium level if income is equal to Y_1 in this period. In period 2 the level of investment increases and income also increases in this period by the same amount so that $\Delta Y = \Delta I$ in period 2. We *assume that this change in investment is permanent*, that is, it continues to be made in every subsequent period. In period 3, consumption expenditure increase because of theincrease in income (ΔI or ΔY) in the period 2, assuming one period lag in the consumption function. Therefore, income (Y_2) at the end of period 2

$$= Y_1 + \Delta I$$

In period 3 income will rise firstly because of the induced consumption demand (equal to $\Delta C = b \Delta Y$) brought about by the increase in income in period 2. Since increase in income in period 2 is equal to increase in investment, ($\Delta Y = \Delta I$ in period 2) increase in consumption in period 3 can also be written as $b \Delta I$. Secondly, income in period 3 will also rise because of the continuous change in investment which would also occur in period 3. Thus, at the end of period 3, level of income will rise to:

$$Y_3 = Y_1 + b\Delta I + \Delta I$$

In period 4, income increases again by the amount of new increase in investment (ΔI) in period 4 plus the increase in income due to the induced consumption expenditure resulting from the increase in income or consumption expenditure in period 3 (*i.e.* $b \Delta I$). The increase in consumption expenditure or income on account of this in period 4 will be $b.b\Delta I = b^2 \Delta I$ plus the change in consumption expenditure induced by change in investment (and therefore income) in period 3 by ΔI. Thus at the end of period 4, total change in the income will become :

$$Y_4 = Y_1 + \Delta I + b\Delta I + b^2 \Delta I$$

This process of expansion in income will continue indefinitely and the increase in income or spending in every successive period will become smaller and smaller. The whole of this process of expansion in consumption expenditure and income can be easily understood with the bar diagram shown in figure 9A.1. It has been shown through arrows in this figure 9A.1. how with a continuous change in investment (ΔI), starting from period 2, the income increases and also when income generated by changes in consumption expenditure is represent in successive periods of time. The process continue infinitely.

We can mathematically obtain what the level of income at the end of n periods will be

$$Y_n = Y_1 + \Delta I + b.\Delta I + b^2 . \Delta I + b^3 . \Delta I + ...+... + b^{n-1} \Delta I$$

$$Y_n - Y_1 = \Delta I + b.\Delta I + b^2 . \Delta I + b^3 . \Delta I + ... +... + b^{n-1} \Delta I$$

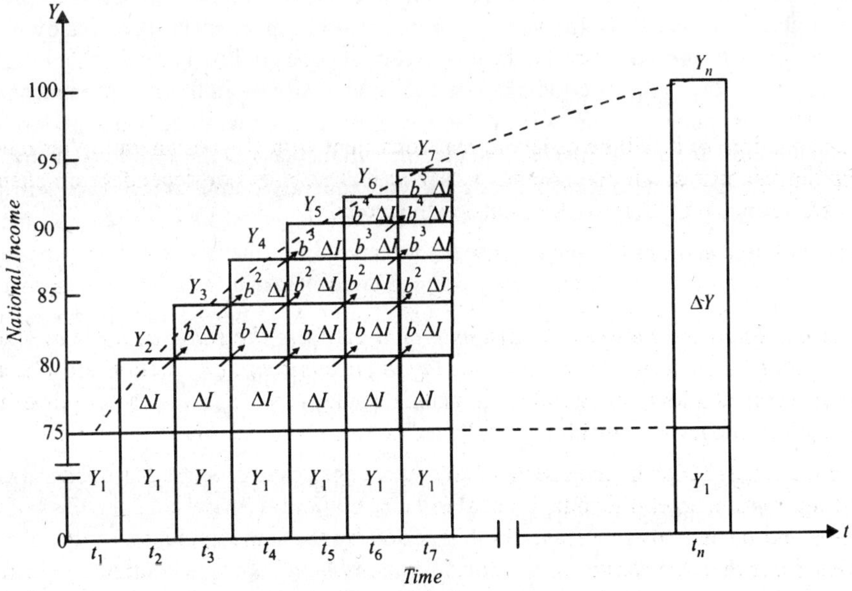

Fig. 8A.1. *Dynamic Multiplier : The Continuous Investment Injection Multiplier*

From the right hand side of the above equation ΔI can be factored out.

$$Y_n - Y_1 = \Delta I\,(1 + b + b^2 + b^3 + ... + b^{n-1})$$

The expression in parentheses in the above equation is a geometric progression where 1 is the first term in the series and b is the common ratio ($b \neq 0$). Using the formula for the sum of the geometric series we have

$$Y_n - Y_1 = \Delta I\left(\frac{1-b^n}{1-b}\right)$$

Where b is the common ratio representing the marginal propensity to consume. If we assume that $0 < b < 1$ (that is, marginal propensity to consume is positive but is less than 1), it can be inferred that b^n becomes very small as n becomes very large so that as $n \to \propto$, the change in the level of income ($\Delta Y = Y_n - Y_1$) tends to become equal to

$$Y_n - Y_1 = \Delta I\left(\frac{1}{1-b}\right)$$

or $$\frac{Y_n - Y_1}{\Delta I} = \frac{1}{1-b}$$

or $$\frac{\Delta Y}{\Delta I} = \frac{1}{1-b}$$

Thus we see how a continuous change of income in investment generates multiple increase in income over time through spending of induced consumption expenditure.

Dynamic Multiplier : Single Injection Model

In another type of dynamic multiplier, instead of continuous injection of investment in every period, there is a *single of once-for-all increase in investment.* In this case, let us assume that in period 1 equilibrium level of income is Y_1. Now, in period 2, investment increases by ΔI. Consequently, *additional income* earned by the factors in capital goods industries will go up by ΔI (that is, in period 2, $\Delta Y = \Delta I$). In the third period, income will not increase by additional investment as we are considering a single injection of investment. However, assuming that there is one period lag in the consumption function, in period 3 the level of income will increase as the additional factor-incomes equal to ΔI will be spent on consumer goods and consequently output and income will increase. Given that b is the marginal propensity to consume, income in period 3 will increase by $b\,\Delta I$ due to the induced consumption expenditure. In period 4, income will further rise when people who receive income equal to $b\,\Delta I$ in period 3 spend it on consumer goods in period 4. Due to this further induced consumption expenditure, income will rise by $b\,.\,b\,\Delta I$ or $b^2\,\Delta I$ in period 4. This process will continue and in period 5, income will rise by $b^3.\Delta I$, in period 6 income will rise by $b^4\,\Delta I$ due to the induced consumption expenditure but in each successive period the increase in income will become smaller and smaller so that in infinity, the equilibrium level of income will return to its initial value in period I. This is depicted in figure 9A.2.

The process of income expansion over n periods through this multiplier process when there is single injection of investment, is given by

$$\Delta Y = \Delta Y^2 + \Delta Y^3 + \Delta Y + ... + \Delta Y_n$$

or $$\Delta Y = \Delta I + b\Delta I + b^2\,\Delta I + ... + b^{n-1}\,\Delta I$$

$$\Delta Y = \Delta I\,(1 + b + b^2 ... + b^{n-1})$$

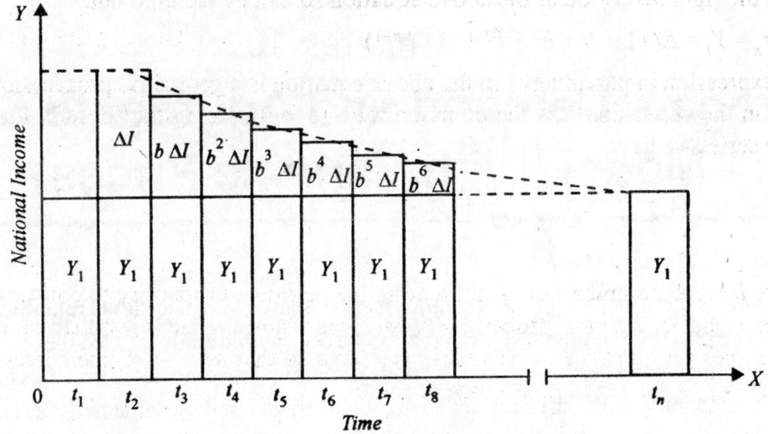

Fig. 9A.2. *Dynamic Multiplier : Single Injection Model*

Figures in parentheses are geometric series whose sum yields

$$\frac{1-b^n}{1-b}$$

Since b^n is a negligible amount and can therefore be ignored we have

$$\Delta Y = \Delta I\left(\frac{1}{1-b}\right)$$

or

$$\frac{\Delta Y}{\Delta I} = \frac{1}{1-b}$$

This value of the multiplier implies that a single increase in investment generates multiple increase in income over time (the value of this multiplier being equal to $\frac{1}{1-b}$), but after generation of this sum of income, equilibrium level of income returns to the initial value Y_1. This is depicted in Figure 9A.2.

QUESTIONS FOR REVIEW

1. What is static multiplier ? Derive its value mathematically.
2. What is dynamic multiplier ? Explain continuous injection and single injection versions of dynamic multiplier.

CHAPTER 10

Aggregate Demand and Aggregate Supply Model (With Variable Prices)

Introduction to AD-AS Model

Keynes in his theory of income and employment assumed that price level remained constant. As explained in the previous chapters Keynes in his macroeconomic analysis used these concepts which related aggregate demand and supply to the levels of national income. Concerned as he was with the problem of an economy under the grip of depression characterised by demand deficiency and excess capacity in the economy he assumed the price level to remain constant.

On the other hand, classical economists thought national output or income was determined by real factors such as capital stock, state of technology, labour supply and in no way affected by the general price level which was determined by the quantity of money. This classical doctrine is generally referred to as **classical dichotomy**. Thus *AD-AS* model with flexible price level highlights the breakdown of **classical dichotomy**. The aggregate demand and aggregates supply model, which is generally referred to as *AD-AS* model is used to explain fluctuations in output, price level and rate of inflation in the economy.

In what follows we explain the concepts of aggregate demand and aggregate supply with flexible price level and analyse how the interaction between the two determines jointly the aggregate output (*i.e.* real GDP) and the general price level.

Aggregate Demand (AD)

Let us first explain aggregate demand. ***Aggregate demand*** *is the total desired quantity of goods and services that are bought by consumer households, private investors, government and foreigners at each possible price level, other things being held constant.* Thus aggregate demand is not any quantity demanded at a particular price level but is a whole schedule of total output demanded at various price levels and is represented by a curve. The aggregate demand has four components: consumption demand, private investment demand, Government purchases of goods and services and net exports. *Thus, aggregate demand curve depicts the total output of goods and services which households, firms, and Government are willing to buy at each possible price level.*

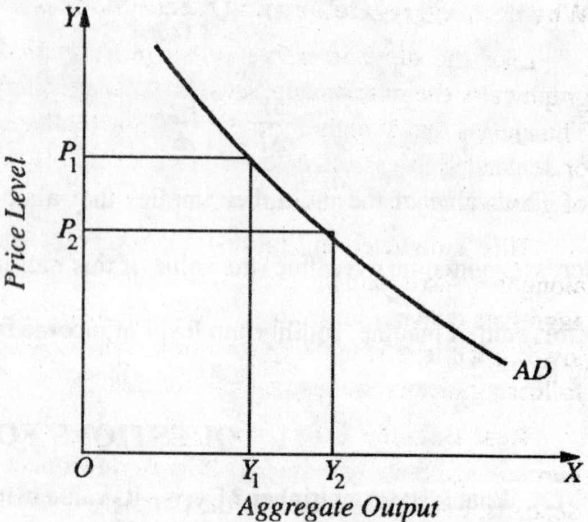

Fig. 10.1. *Aggregate Demand Curve with Varying Price Level*

Thus aggregate demand curve shows the relationship between the total quantity demanded of goods and services and general price level. It is worth noting that aggregate demand curve (*AD*) differs from the ordinary demand curve of an individual commodity with which we are concerned in microeconomics though both slope downward to the light. In case of a demand curve of an individual commodity when price of a commodity rises, it will tend to be substituted by other commodities which are its close substitutes resulting in fall in the quantity demanded of the commodity at a higher price. Thus, the slope of demand curve of an individual commodity depends mainly on the possibility of substitution between the commodities. On the other hand, as we shall see below, the slope of aggregate demand curve depends on factors totally different from those that cause demand curve of an individual commodity to slope downward. We have drawn an *AD* curve in Figure 10.1 where on the horizontal axis we measure level of aggregate output and on the vertical axis we measure the general price level. As will be seen from Figure 10.1 aggregate demand curve *AD* slopes downward to the right.

It is important to note that the *AD-AS* model is unlike that of market demand-supply model of microeconomic theory. When we consider demand and supply in a particular market, say for cotton cloth, rise in its price will cause increase in its quantity supplied but in doing so resources will be withdrawn from other goods. Such reallocation of resources between products and consequently rise in output of one product and fall in that of the other is not considered in macroeconomics where we are concerned with determination of aggregate output, total employment of resources in the economy as a whole. Similarly, in macroecnomic model of aggregate demand and aggregate supply we study the determination of general price level and does not explain the relative prices of various products.

In what follows we will explain in detail the concepts of aggregate demand (*AD*) and aggregate supply (*AS*) curves and their likely shape and factors determining them. We will also explain some important controversial issues of macroeconomics with this *AD-AS* model.

Why does Aggregate Demand Curve Slope Downward ?

Like the demand curve of an individual commodity aggregate demand curve showing graphically the relationship between total spending and price levels slopes downward to the right. This means that at higher price levels, the total spending or quantity of aggregate output purchased or demanded is less and at lower price level the total spending or total purchases of aggregate output of goods is higher.

This is depicted in Figure 10.1. Aggregate output demanded per period of time is measured along the *X*-axis, and the general price level along the *Y*-axis. It should be carefully understood why aggregate demand for output or total spending falls at higher aggregate price level and increases at lower price levels, or, in other words, why aggregate demand (*AD*) curve slopes downward. The following factors are responsible for this.

Real Balance Effect. First, the changes in the general price level affect the real value or *purchasing power of money balances and monetary assets* with fixed nominal values (such as bank deposits, bonds, etc.) held by the people. With the rise in the general price level, the real value of these monetary assets will fall making people feel poorer than before. This induces them to consume less and therefore lead to the decline in quantity of output purchased by them. Conversely, if the price level falls, the real value of their monetary assets increases inducing them to buy more. This is called *real balance effect* of the change in the price level.

Rate of Interest Effect. Secondly, another important reason for the downward sloping nature of aggregate demand curve is *the effect of change in general price level on the rate of interest and through it on investment demand.* At a higher price level, the people will require more money for conducting a given amount of transactions. This will lead to the increase in the demand for money for making transactions. Given the money supply, the increase in demand for money will cause the rate of interest to go up. At a higher rate of interest, demand for investment in new capital goods (*i.e.* plant, machinery and equipment) will decrease. On the contrary, if aggregate price level falls, demand for money for transaction purposes will decline and, the money supply being given, this will lead to the fall in the rate of interest. At the lower rate of interest, investment demand will increase. To conclude, *the investment demand and the general price level are also inversely related.*

Foreign Trade Effect. Thirdly, changes in the price level also causes a change in *foreign demand for goods*. This is called *foreign trade effect of the change in price level*. If a general price level in India falls, its exports will become cheaper leading to their increase. On the other hand, the lower price level in India will induce India people to buy India goods instead of imported ones. Thus, fall in general price level in India will lead to more exports and lesser imports causing expansion in aggregate demand for Indian goods. On the contrary, a rise in price level in India will lead to decline in its exports (*i.e.* foreign demand for Indian goods) and increase in its imports. Thus, rise in price level, that is, inflation will cause a decline in net exports.

To sum up, the quantity of aggregate demand for consumption, investment and net exports increases with a fall in the price level and declines with a rise in the price level. This means that aggregate demand curve showing relationship between aggregate output demanded and the general price level slopes downward to the right as is shown in Figure 10.1.

Derivation of Aggregate Demand Curve

We can now derive the aggregate demand curve using Keynesian income-expenditure framework and incorporating price level into the model. It should be noted that Keynesian aggregate expenditure curve ($C + I + G + X_n$) shows planned aggregate expenditure at various levels of national income (*i.e.* real *GNP*), the aggregate demand curve (*AD*), which we are considering here shows equilibrium aggregate expenditure (*i.e.* equilibrium quantity of aggregate output demanded) at various price levels. In order to derive this aggregate demand curve with flexible prices we ask the question what is the effect of change in the price level on the economy's aggregate expenditure ($C + I + G + X_n$) function.

As has been explained above, a change in the price level causes a change in the quantity demanded through producing three effects, namely, *real balance effect*, *interest rate effect*, and *foreign trade effect*. Let us suppose the price level falls. As explained above, with a lower price level real purchasing power of the money balances or financial assets with fixed nominal values held by the people will increase. As a consequence, the people will start feeling themselves richer. Thus lower price level will induce people to consume more at each level of national income. That is, consumption function curve in the income expenditure model will shift above which in turn will cause upward shift in the aggregate expenditure ($C + I + G + X_n$) curve. This is illustrated in Figure 10.2. In panel (*a*) at the top of this figure, we have shown the determination of equilibrium level of real national income (*i.e.* equilibrium level of aggregate output demanded). Initially, at a price level P_0, the aggregate expenditure function curve (C + I + G + X_n) intersects the 45° line at point E_0 according to which Y_0 is the equilibrium quantity of real *GNP* or aggregate output demanded. At the level Y_0 of GNP, planned aggregate expenditure is equal to the value of aggregate national output. Thus, at the initial price level P_0 the equilibrium quantity of aggregate output demanded is Y_0. Therefore, in the panel (*b*) at the bottom we represent aggregate output Y_0 directly against price level P_0.

Suppose the price level falls from P_0 to P_2. With this real purchasing power of the money balances and financial assets held by the people will increase and they will be induced to consume more than before. As a result, consumption function curve will shift above causing upward shift in the aggregate expenditure curve to the new higher position ($C_2 + I + G + X_n$). It will be seen from Figure 10.2 that this new aggregate expenditure function curve $C_2 + I + G + X_n$ intersects the 45° line at point E_2 yielding greater quantity of aggregate output demanded Y_2. Thus, in panel (*b*) at the bottom we show aggregate output Y_2 against the lower price level P_2. This shows that at a lower

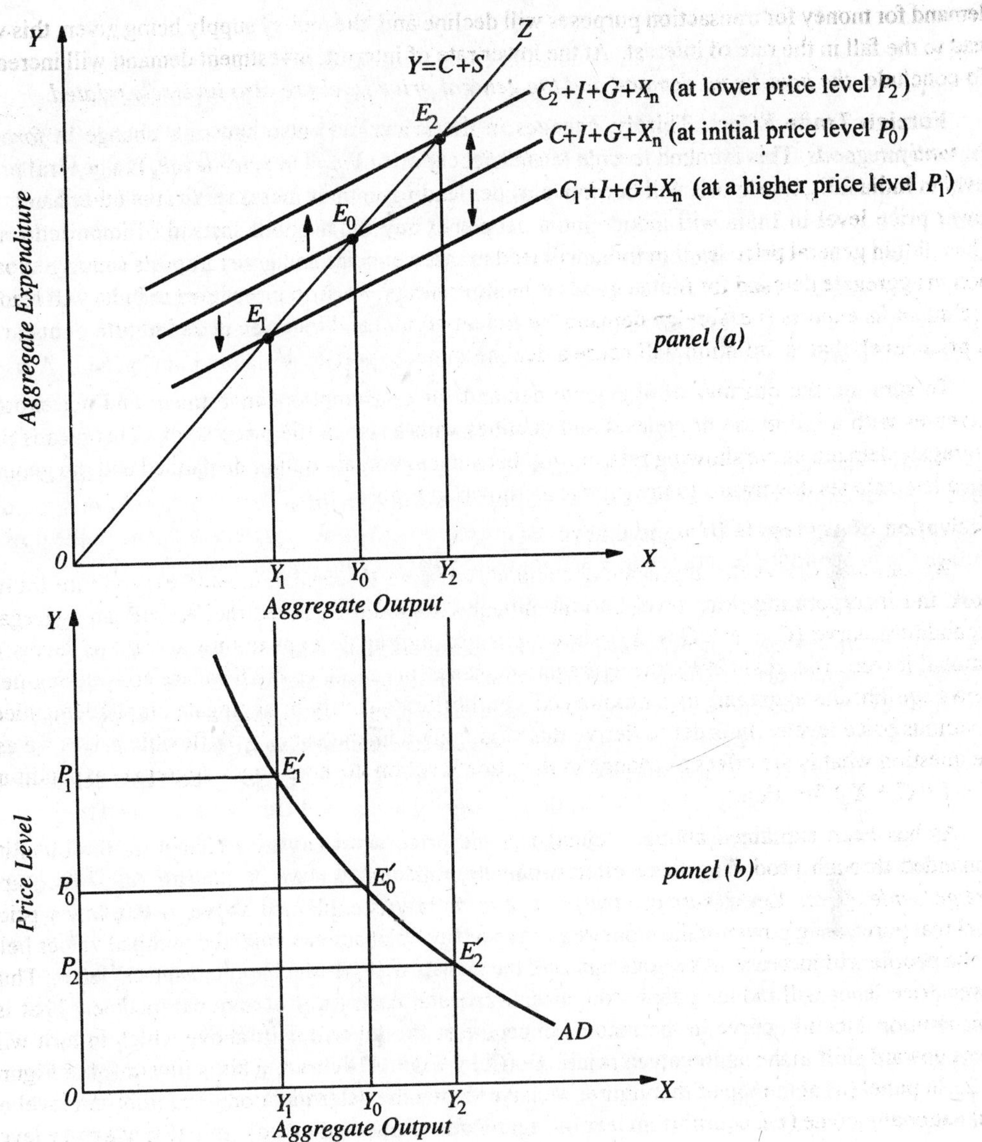

Fig. 10.2. *Derivation of Aggregate Demand Curve*

price level, more aggregate output is demanded.

Now, suppose instead of fall in price level the price level rises from P_0 to P_1. At a higher price level, the real value of money balances and financial assets with fixed nominal value will decrease. As a result, people will feel poorer than before causing them to spend less on consumption than before at each level of national income. This will cause a downward shift in the consumption function causing the whole aggregate expenditure function curve to shift downward to the new lower level $C_1 + I + G + X_n$. It will be seen from the upper panel of Fig. 10.2 that the new aggregate expenditure curve $C_1 + I + G + X_n$ intersects line at point E_1 and determines a lower level equilibrium aggregate output demanded and produced. Accordingly, against a higher price OP_1, we plot a smaller aggregate output Y_1 demanded. It will be seen from the panel (*b*) at the bottom of Fig. 10.2 that aggregate demand curve obtained by plotting various equilibrium quantities of aggregate output demanded at different price levels slope downward to the right.

We have derived above aggregate demand curve with flexible prices by considering the effect of changes in price level on consumption function and through it on aggregate expenditure curve. Similarly, we can consider the effect of changes in price level on two other components of aggregate expenditure, such as investment demand (*I*) and net exports (X_n). Thus, when price falls, less money will be required to meet transaction motive of demand for money. As a result, with a fall in price, demand for money will decrease and, given the money supply, this will cause the rate of interest to fall. At a lower interest rate, investment will increase causing the aggregate expenditure curve to shift above and determine a higher level of equilibrium aggregate output demanded. Conversely, the rise in price level will require more money for transaction purposes and therefore demand for money will increase causing rate of interest to rise, money supply remaining unchanged. A rise in interest rate will thus bring about decrease in investment demand which will shift the aggregate expenditure curve downward and thus lower the aggregate output demanded.

Similarly, changes in the price level affect exports (*X*) and imports (*M*) and will therefore cause change in net exports (*Xn*). For example, a fall in the domestic price level causes exports to go up and imports to decline. This will tend to raise net exports ($X_n = X - M$) and will lead to the upward shift in the expenditure function curve and increase in aggregate output demanded.

Shift in Aggregate Demand Curve and Multiplier Effect

As in micro-economic analysis of demand, it is important to know the factors that cause shift in aggregate demand curve. We have derived above an aggregate demand curve from the shifts in aggregate expenditure curve caused by changes in price level. Now, *when some factors other than the price level change which cause shifts in aggregate expenditure curve*, they will cause a shift in aggregate demand curve, that is, there will be increase or decrease in aggregate output demanded *at every price level.* In our analysis of derivation of aggregate demand curve, we assumed the changes in aggregate expenditure and hence aggregate output demanded resulting from changes in price level. In our above analysis of derivation of aggregate demand curve *we considered Government expenditure (G), taxation (I), investment (I) and money supply (M) constant as they were treated as autonomous of changes in price level* (and induced changes in the rate of interest). *When these non-price factors change, aggregate demand curve will shift.* For example, suppose Government expenditure increases by ΔG, this will raise aggregate expenditure curve upward. As a result, equilibrium level of aggregate output will increase at the given price level. This means shift in aggregate demand curve at the given price. Consider Figure 10.3. In upper panel of this figure, to begin with, aggregate expenditure curve at a given price level, say *P*, is $C + I + X_n + G$ which intersects 45° line at point *E* yielding equilibrium level of national income or output equal to Y_1. In panel at the bottom, the equilibrium output demanded Y_1 is shown against the given price level *P*. Now suppose the Government increases its expenditure by ΔG. As a result, with price level remaining fixed at *P*, aggregate expenditure curve in the upper panel shifts upward to the higher position ($C + I + X_n + G + \Delta G$), which intersects 45° line at point *H* yielding a higher level of equilibrium output Y_2. Since price remains fixed at *P*, the greater quantity Y_2 of equilibrium output demanded is shown on a *higher aggregate demand* curve. This means aggregate demand curve has shifted outward as a result of increase in Government expenditure. We have taken one price level *P* and have shown how increases in Government expenditure causes greater aggregate demand at that given price. Similarly, we can take other price levels and corresponding aggregate expenditure curves in the upper panel and show how increase in Government expenditure will mean greater aggregate demand than before at each price. In this way, we find the entire aggregate demand curve has shifted to the right as a result of increase in Government expenditure, that is, more aggregate output is demanded at each price.

Multiplier effect. It will be recalled that increase in Government expenditure or investment has a multiplier effect on aggregate output depending on the size of multiplier. In our Figure 10.3 increase in Government expenditure by ΔG has caused aggregate output to increase by Y_1Y_2 or RT. Thus the increase of Y_1Y_2 in *GNP* or increase in aggregate output demanded by *RT* is given by

$$\Delta Y = Y_1Y_2 = RT = \Delta G \frac{1}{1-mpc}$$

Where *mpc* is the marginal propensity to consume and $\frac{1}{1-mpc}$ is the value of multiplier. As in case of increase in Government expenditure, *reduction in taxes* will also increase aggregate output demanded at each price level and will therefore cause a shift in aggregate demand curve.

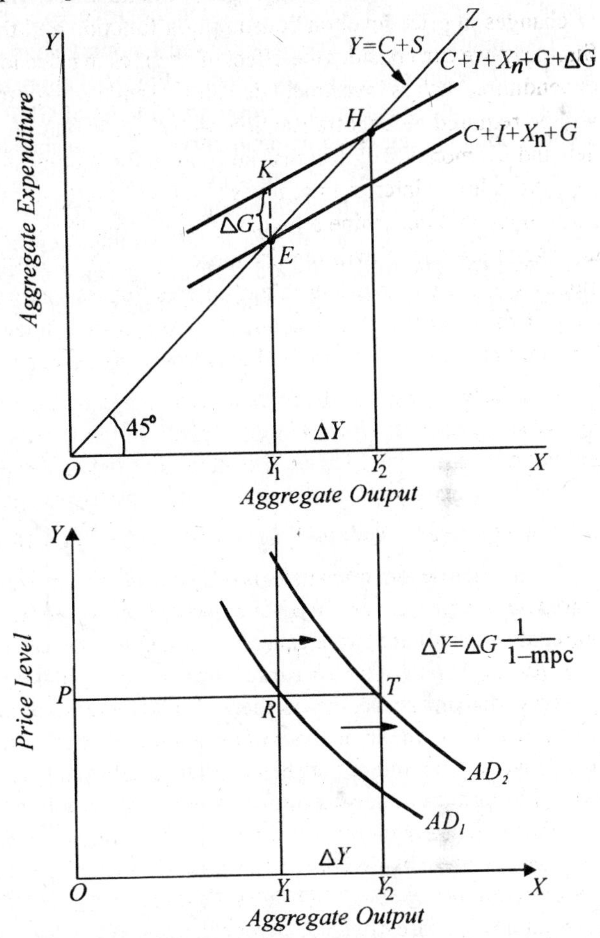

Fig. 10.3. *Shift in Aggregate Demand Curve*

Similarly, *increase in money supply (M)* will cause a rightward shift in aggregate demand curve. In the derivation of a given aggregate demand curve, money supply in the economy is held constant. If at a given price level, money supply is increased, the interest rate will fall. The fall in interest rate will cause investment demand to increase. Aggregate output demanded will thus be greater at the given price level. Thus, expansion in money supply brings about shift in aggregate demand curve to the right.

The same logic applies to the effect of contractionary fiscal and monetary policies. A decrease in Government expenditure or increase in taxes will cause *AD* curve to shift to the left. Similarly, decrease in investment autonomous of any change in the price level will also shift the *AD* curve to the left. Similarly, contraction in money supply (*M*) at a given price level will lead to the leftward shift in the aggregate demand curve.

Multiplier with Changes in Price Level

In our above analysis of multiplier with aggregate demand curve, it is assumed that price level remains constant and the firms are willing to supply more output at a given price. How much national income or GNP increases as a result of any autonomous expenditure such as government expenditure, investment expenditure, net exports is determined by a shift in aggregate demand curve by the size of simple Keynesian multiplier when price level is fixed. This implies a horizontal short-run supply curve. However, as studied above, short-run aggregate supply curve slopes upward as the firms are willing to supply additional output in the short run only at a higher price level. With short-run aggregate supply curve sloping upward, a rightward shift in aggregate demand curve raises new equilibrium GNP level not equal to the horizontal shift in the aggregate demand curve but less than it.

Consequently, the size of multiplier is smaller than that of simple Keynesian multiplier with a given fixed price level. This is because a part of expansionary effect of GNP of the increase in autonomous government expenditure is offset by rise in the price level.

The multiplier effect in case of upward-sloping short-run aggregate supply curve is shown in Fig. 10.4. To begin with, in the top panel of Fig. 10.4 aggregate expenditure curve AE_0 intersects 45° line at point B and determines Y_0 equilibrium level of GNP. In the panel at the bottom of Fig. 10.4 the corresponding aggregate demand curve AD_0 and the short-run aggregate supply curve SAS to intersect at B' at the above determined GNP level Y_0. Now suppose autonomous investment expenditure (which is independent of changes in price level) increases by ΔI. As a result, aggregate expenditure curve AE shifts upward to AE_1 and determines new equilibrium GNP level equal to Y_2. In the lower panel (*b*), due to the upward shift in aggregate expenditure curve, aggregate demand curve shifts rightward from AD to AD_1. The horizontal shift in the aggregate demand curve *at a given price*

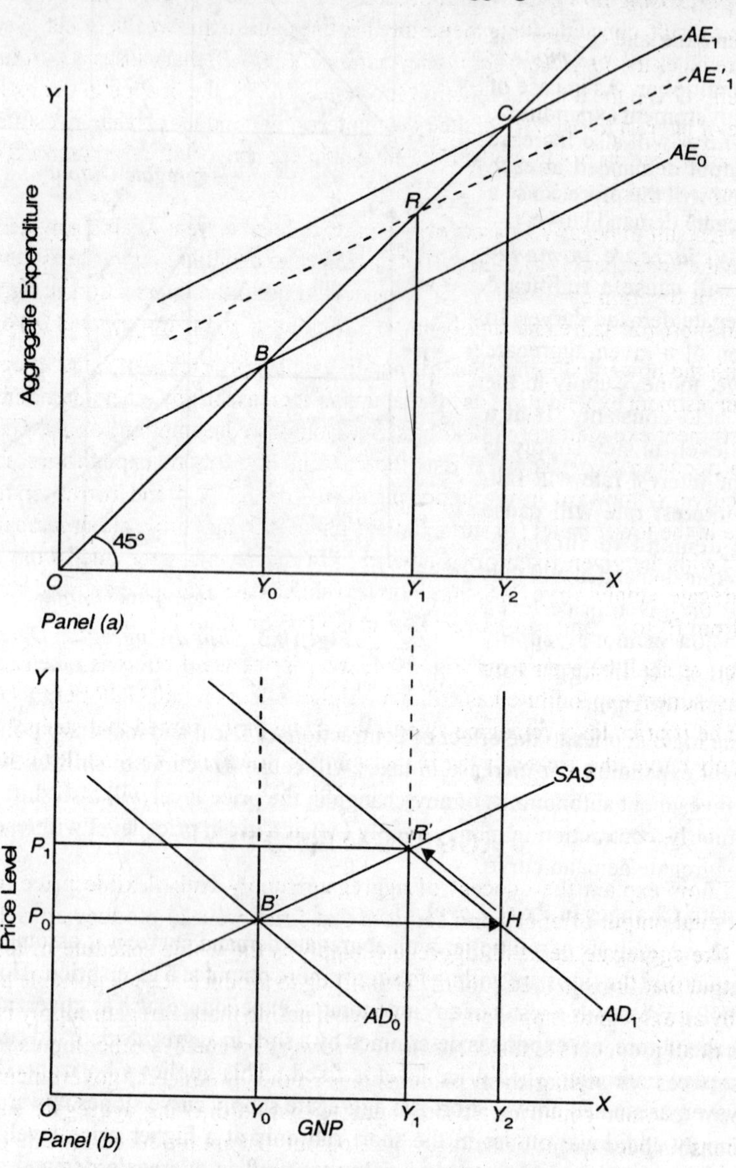

Fig. 10.4. *Multipler Effect with Changes in Price Level*

level is determined by the increase in aggregate expenditure multiplied by the simple Keynesian multiplier at the given fixed price level ($B'H$ or $\Delta Y = \Delta I \dfrac{1}{1-MPC}$)

But given the upward sloping short-un aggregate supply curve SAS with new aggregate demand curve AD_1, price level does not remain fixed. As will be seen from the lower panel (*b*) of Fig. 10.4, the aggregate demand curve AD_1, intersects the short-run aggregate supply curve SAS at point R' and as a result price level rises to P_1.

Now, with this rise in price level to P_1, aggregate expenditure curve in the upper panel (*a*) will not remain unaffected but will shift downward. This fall in aggregate expenditure curve is due to the adverse effects on wealth or real balances, interest rate and net exports. Much of wealth is held in the form of bank deposits, bonds and shares of companies and other assets. With the rise in price level, *real value or purchasing power* of wealth possessed by the people declines. This induces them to spend less. As a result, consumption expenditure declines due to this wealth effect. Secondly, the rise in price level reduces the *supply of real money balances* (M^s / P) that causes a shift in money supply curve to the left. Given the demand function for money (M^d), the decline in the real money supply will cause rate of interest to rise. Now, the rise in interest will induce private investment expenditure to decline. Lastly, rise in price level in the domestic economy will adversely affect exports of a country causing net exports to fall.

Thus, as a result of negative effects of rise in price level on real wealth, private investment and net exports, in the upper panel (*a*) of Fig. 10.4 aggregate expenditure curve shifts downward to AE_1' (dotted) so that it determines GNP level Y_1 corresponding to the intersection of aggregate demand curve AD_1 and short-run aggregate supply curve SAS point R' in the lower panel (*b*) of this Fig. 10.4.

Thus with the upward sloping short-run-aggregate supply curve SAS, the effect of increase in autonomous investment expenditure (or for that matter increase in any other autonomous expenditure such as Government expenditure, net exports, autonomous consumption) on the GNP level can be visualised to occur in two stages. First, increase in investment expenditure shifts aggregate expenditure curve AE upward in the upper panel (*a*) of Fig. 10.4 and correspondingly aggregate demand curve in the lower pancl (*b*) shifts to the right to AD_1 and bring about increase in GNP level from Y_0 to Y_2 with the given fixed price level P_1. In the second stage due to the upward sloping short-run aggregate supply curve SAS, the rightward shift in the aggregate demand curve causes price level to rise from P_0 to P_1 and causes decrease in GNP from Y_2 to Y_1.

However, as shall be seen from Fig. 10.4, when price level effect is taken into account, the increase in investment expenditure has still a multiplier effect on real GDP but this effect is smaller than it would be if price level remained fixed. It may be further noted that steeper the slope of the short-run supply curve, the greater is the increase in the price level and smaller is the effect on real GNP.

AGGREGATE SUPPLY

We will now explain the concept of aggregate supply with flexible price level. Aggregate supply is the total output of goods and services that firms want to produce at each possible price level. Thus, like aggregate demand, aggregate supply is the whole schedule of total quantities of aggregate output that firms in the economy are willing to produce at each possible price level and is represented by an aggregate supply curve. It is worth noting that aggregate supply is the outcome of the decisions of all producers in the economy to hire workers and buy other inputs for production of goods and services for selling them to consumers, other producers, government as well as for exporting them to other countries. It may be noted while drawing aggregate supply curve that depicts relationship been quantities of aggregate output that are produced for sale in the market by the firms in the economy at various price levels, all other factors that affect aggregate supply are held constant.

Short-run Aggregate Supply Curve

In the model of determination of general price level, the concept of aggregate supply curve which relates aggregate supply of output with price level is used. In this sense, *aggregate supply curve shows the various amounts of aggregate output which the producers in the economy are willing to produce and sell in the market at various price levels.* There is a lot of disagreement among economists about the shape of aggregate supply curve. The classical economists assumed that there normally prevailed full employment of resources in the economy. According to them, if at any time there is deviation from this full employment level, the wages, interest and prices quickly and automatically adjust or change to restore equilibrium at the full employment level. Thus, in the classical theory, the aggregate supply curve of output is perfectly inelastic (*i.e.* a vertical straight line) at the output level corresponding to full-employment level of resources. This aggregate supply curve relating aggregate supply with price level of the classical theory of income and employment is shown in Figure 10.5. by *AS* curve.

As mentioned above, Keynes considered the situation of economic depression when the economy was operating before the level of full employment of resources. He further believed that in such a situation money wage rates were sticky *i.e.* remain constant. He further assumed that average and margined products of labour remain constant when more of it is employed following the increase in aggregate demand. With these assumptions, more aggregate output is produced and supplied at the given price level in response to increase in aggregate demand. But when full employment of labour and capital stock is attained and aggregate demand further increases, aggregate supply of output being unable to increase any more, it is the price level that will rise in response to the increase in aggregate demand. The Keynes's aggregate supply curve depicting the relationship between price level and the aggregate production (supply) *during the period of depression and involuntary unemployment* when there is a lot of excess capacity in the economy is shown in Figure 10.6 where it will be seen that aggregate supply is a horizontal straight line (*i.e.* perfectly elastic) up to the level of full employment showing thereby that in response to increase in aggregate demand more is produced and supplied at the same price level *OP*. Since output of goods and services cannot be increased beyond the full-employment level, Keynes's aggregate supply curve becomes vertical at it.

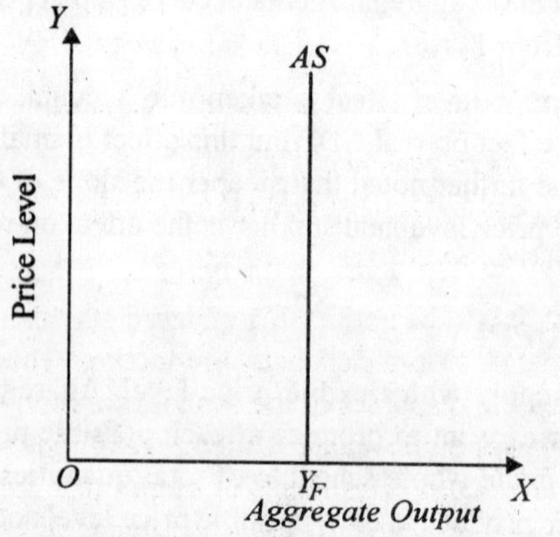

Fig. 10.5. *Aggregate Supply Curve : Classical View*

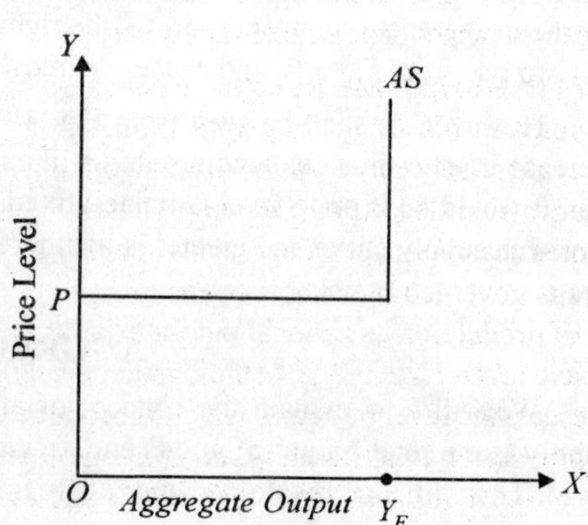

Fig. 10.6. *Keynes's Aggregate Supply Curve*

It may however be noted that Keynes recoganised that as the aggregate supply approaches close to the full-employment level the cost of output per unit tends to rise due to the rise in wage rate and also due to diminishing returns to extra factors employed. But, according to Keynes, the rise in price level before full employment or less than capacity output will not be much.

It is evident from above that shape of aggregate supply curve is a highly controversial issue. As mentioned above, aggregate supply curve indicates the total output which the producers are willing and able to sell at different price levels. It is important to note that as the average price level rises above the current marginal cost of production, producers find it profitable to expand output. When the economy is working substantially below capacity, that is at times of depression or severe recession, the more can be produced without much rise in marginal cost of production and therefore the short-run aggregate supply curve is nearly flat. With the given stock of capital (*i.e.* plant and equipment) when output is expanded the diminishing returns and rising marginal costs occur which ultimately cause the short-run aggregate supply curve to slope upward gently. But as the firms in the economy approach near their capacity output their marginal costs sharply rise which causes sharply rising aggregate supply curve. At *the level of capacity output*, that is, when the given resources of the economy are fully employed, aggregate supply curve (*AS*) becomes a vertical straight line as classical economists assumed.

Three Ranges of Short-run Aggregate Supply Curve

As mentioned above, there is a dispute among economists about the nature and shape of aggregate supply curve. Classical economists thought the aggregate supply curve is a vertical straight line, whereas Keynesian economists are of the view that it is a horizontal straight line or very gently upward sloping. On the other hand, some modern macro-economists draw distinction between the short-run and long-run aggregate supply curve. We will explain these different viewpoints later in this chapter and in some following chapters. For the present purpose, it is useful to think of short-run aggregate supply curve as comprising three segments or ranges-: (1) the horizontal range, (2) the intermediate (or upward sloping) range, and (3) the vertical range. This aggregate supply curve having three distinct segments is shown in Figure 10.7. Let us now give reasons for these three ranges of aggregate supply curve.

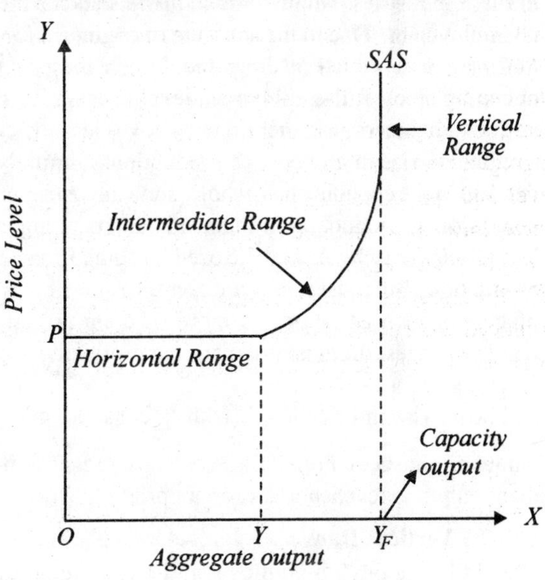

Fig. 10.7. *Short-run Aggregate Supply Curve with Three Ranges*

(1) **Horizontal Range.** Because Keynes and his early followers thought aggregate supply curve was horizontal, this range is also called *Keynesian range*. It may be noted that the shape of aggregate supply curve is governed by what happens to unit cost of production as national output expands or contracts. It will be noticed from Figure 10.7 that we have taken Y_F as the full-employment level of output, that is, Y_F is the capacity production. This represents the level of output which is produced when available resources of the economy are fully employed or used. Therefore, this full-employment or capacity output is also called *potential output*. Now, it will be seen that horizontal or Keynesian range comprises levels of output that are substantially less than the full capacity production Y_F. This implies that during this horizontal range of output upto *Y*, the economy can expand its production without facing rise in unit cost of production. This is in fact the stage when the economy is in the grip of severe recession or depression with a lot of idle capacity in the form of unemployed labour, unutilised machinery and other capital equipment. These idle or unused resources can be put to use without causing any rise in unit cost of production and therefore without any *upward pressure* on the price level. The unemployed labour would be willing to work at the current wage rate (that is, without any need for offering higher wage

rate to them). Since other resources are lying unused, no shortages or bottlenecks will be experienced causing higher cost per unit or rise in the price level, if aggregate output is expanded in this range.

Coversely, this horizontal range also means that when aggregate output contracts in this segment, the product and resource prices do not fall, that is, they are inflexible downward. It is only real output and employment which will fall, wages and prices remaining constant. As Keynes explained the situation of severe depression, he assumed aggregate supply curve to be horizontal. Therefore, in times of depression which he was analysing, while product prices and wages are inflexible downward it is real national output and employment that would fall.

(2) **Intermediate Range.** It will be seen in Figure 10.7 that in this intermediate range between the output levels Y and Y_F, increase in aggregate output brings about rise in price level, that is, aggregate supply curve slopes upward in this range. There are more than one reasons for this upward sloping range of *AS* curve. First, the national economy consists of several industries and resource markets and full-employment is not attained simultaneously in all industries and in respect of all types of workers. For example, as the national production expands in this range some industries, say electronics and computer hardware may experience shortage of skilled engineers engaged in these industries, while some industries such as textile industries may be still facing quite large unemployment. Due to the shortage of engineers for some crucial industries, bottlenecks in production may arise which push up the cost in these industries while the economy as a whole is still operating below full-employment level. Secondly, in order to overcome shortage of skilled workers such as engineers, as mentioned above, less efficient or less skilful workers may be employed resulting in rise in unit cost of production. Similarly, even before full employment of resources, is reached in the economy as a whole, some industries may experience shortage of raw materials due to expansion of production in them encounters rising unit costs of production. Further, the older and less efficient machines may be used by some firms and industries when they reach close to capacity production. But most important factor responsible for rising cost is the decline in marginal products of factors such as labour as more of them are employed in expanding production. Even with constant wages, diminishing marginal productivity of labour implies rise in unit cost of production and hence rise in price level (with W constant, marginal cost $\left(\frac{W}{WP_L}\right)$ will rise if marginal product of labour diminishes). For all these reasons, unit cost of production increases even before full-employment output is reached and product prices must rise if firms have to recover the rising costs.

(3) **Vertical Range.** Aggregate supply curve in this range is perfectly inelastic or vertical straight line at the full-employment level of output, which is designated by Y_F in Figure 10.7 Since classical economists thought the aggregate supply curve was vertical, this range is also called *classical range*. The vertical shape of aggregate supply curve implies that any further rise in the price level will fail to cause any increase in aggregate output because the economy is already using its available resources fully and producing its potential output. With full-employment of resources, some firms may try to expand production by taking away resources from other firms with the offer of higher prices to them. But gain of resources and addition to output in some firms mean the loss of resources and output in other firms, with no net addition to aggregate output. But this process of bidding away resources will cause resource prices to go up resulting in higher product prices, real aggregate output remaining constant. It is important to note that when we talk of full-employment of resources, or full-employment level of output, we consider that workers work for normal hours daily and normal days per week, working of usual number of shifts with normal intensity of using machines. Besides, in determining full-employment or capacity output we allow for the existence of frictional and structural unemployment.

Modern View. The modern view about short-run aggregate supply curve slightly differs from that of Keynes. However, there is now a general consensus among modern economists that when the economy is working substantially below capacity, that is, at times of depression or severe recession, the more can be produced without much rise in marginal cost of production and therefore the aggregate supply curve is *nearly flat* rather than perfectly horizontal. This first range is therefore called *nearly flat range*. With the given stock of capital (*i.e.* plant and equipment) when output is expanded beyond this range the diminishing returns and rising marginal costs occur which ultimately cause the aggregate supply curve to slope upward gently. Thus there is a part of gently rising short-run aggregate supply curve which represents *intermediate range* of short run aggregate supply curve. But as the firms in the economy approach near their capacity output their marginal costs rise sharply which cause sharply rising aggregate supply curve. Beyond the level of capacity-output, that is, when the given resources of the economy are fully employed, short-run aggregate supply curve (*SAS*) becomes a highly steep curve. This is because, unlike the view of Keynes, modern economists think that there is some scope of increasing aggregate ouιput beyond the so called full employment level by reduction in frictional and structural unemployment and by inducing work force to work over time.

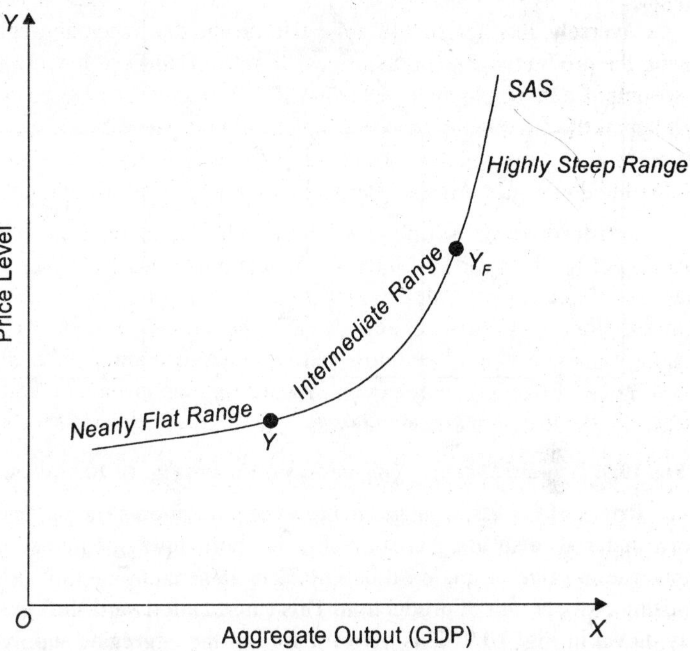

Fig. 10.8 *Short-run Aggregate Supply Curve with Three Ranges*

Thus the short-run aggregate supply curve has there segments or ranges-: (1) the *nearly flat range*, (2) the *intermediate upward-sloping range*, and (3) *the highly steep range*. This aggregate supply curve having three distinct segments is shown in Figure 10.8.

Shifts in Short-run Aggregate Supply Curve

In explaining the upward-sloping nature of short-run aggregate supply we stated that aggregate supply curve depicts the relationship between price level and aggregate output (i.e. real GDP), *other factors* such as wages, input prices, technology and indirect taxes that determine aggregate supply being held constant. Now, it is the *changes* in these other determining factors that cause a *shift* in the aggregate supply curve. We explain below the factors that cause a shift in aggregate supply curve.

Changes in Wage Rate. Change in wage rate of workers is an important factor that causes a shift in short-run aggregate supply curve. For example, when wage rate of workers increases, they cause a leftward shift in short-run aggregate supply curve. This is because increase in wages raises cost per unit of output. With a given price of output, higher wage rate means profit per unit of output will decline. As production becomes less profitable, it is likely that the firms will cut back on production and supply less output. Now when wage rate of workers increases, it causes a leftward shift in short-run aggregate supply curve as shown in Fig. 10.9.

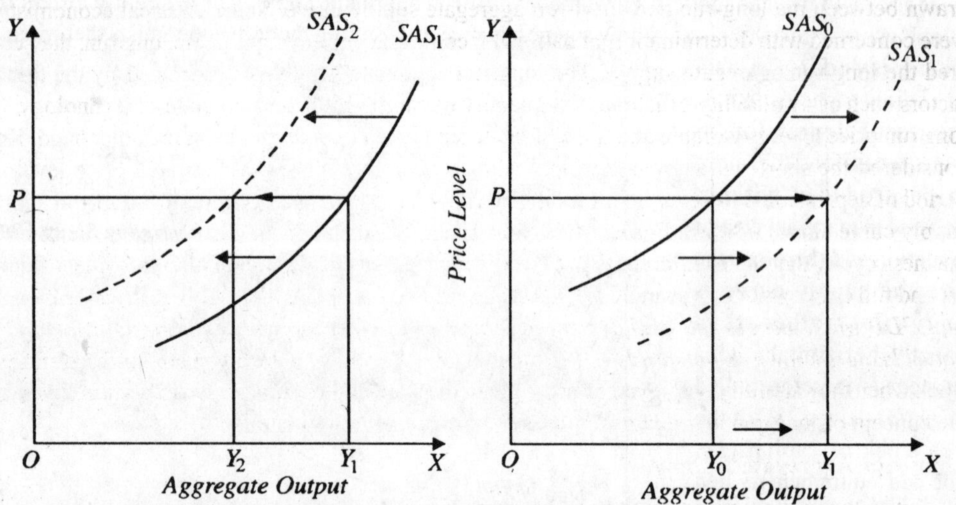

Fig. 10.9. *Leftward Shift in Aggregate Supply Curve* **Fig. 10.10.** *Rightward Shift in Aggregate Supply Curve*

Prices of Inputs. Changes in prices of other inputs such as energy (for example, crude oil) and raw materials also bring about a shift in short-run aggregate supply curve. It is well known that increase in price of crude oil by OPEC in 1973 and again in 1979 affected aggregate supply by raising cost per unit of production. This caused a leftward shift in short-run aggregate supply curve as shown in Fig. 10.9. This *leftward shift* in the aggregate supply curve implies that at any given price level less output is supplied than before.

On the other hand, when price of crude oil falls as has happened at several occasions in the past, aggregate supply curve shifts to the right as is shown Fig. 10.10 indicating that at any given price level more output will be produced and supplied than before.

Change in Technology. The change in technology is another important factor that causes a shift in aggregate supply curve. When there is improvement in technology, productivity of factors rises causing a fall in the unit cost of production. This brings about a rightward shift in aggregate supply curve (as depicted in Fig. 10.10) showing that at any given price level more will be produced and supplied than before.

Business Taxes and Subsidies. Increase in rates of business taxes such as excise duty, sales tax, customs duties raises per unit cost of production just as rise in wage rate. (Note that tax is considered as cost of production as it raises the supply price of output). Thus, by levying business taxes or increasing their rates causes a leftward shift in the aggregate supply curve. On the other hand, lowering of taxes as happened during the recent global slowdown (2007-09), caused by bursting of sub-prime housing loans bubble in the United States, will cause a shift in the aggregate supply curve to the right. Provision of subsidies on products of various industries also causes a shift in the aggregate supply curve to the right.

Available Supply of Resources. Lastly, a very important factor determining the position of aggregate supply curve is the available quantity of resources. When the available supplies of resources such as labour and capital increase, the short-run aggregate supply curve will shift to the right. As labour force grows and supply of capital is increased through investment, the short-run short-run aggregate supply curve will shift to the right implying that more output will be produced for sale at any given price level.

LONG-RUN AGGREGATE SUPPLY CURVE

In our above analysis we did not distinguish between the short-run and long-run aggregate supply curve with a variable price level. In the modern macroeconomic analysis the distinction is drawn between the long-run and short-run aggregate supply curve. Since classical economists who were concerned with determination of national income and employment in the long run, they considered the long-run aggregate supply. The long-run aggregate supply is determined by the three real factors such as availability of labour, the quantity of capital stock and the state of technology. In the long run price level is variable and the aggregate supply curve is vertical. On the other hand, Keynes considered the short-run aggregate supply which is perfectly elastic at the fixed price level in the period of depression. However, in the modern or new Keynsian macroeconomics short-run aggregate supply curve slopes upward. Further, this short-run aggregate supply fluctuates over the course of a business cycle, that is, in different phases of the business cycle. The level of employment fluctuates around full employment level and GDP fluctuates around the potential GDP. Note *that the quantity of real GDP when there is full employment of labour or in other words, when unemployment is at its natural rate is known as potential GDP*. Potential GDP depends on the given labour force and capital stock when they are fully employed or used, given the state of technology. We explain below in detail the concept of long-run aggregate supply and short-run aggregate supply.

Long-run Aggregate Supply

The long-run aggregate supply of output or real GDP depends on three factors (1) the quantity of available labour (2) the stock of capital and (3) the state of technology. The aggregate production function which describes the influence of these three factors is written as :

$$Y = F(L, K, T)$$

Where Y is the quantity of aggregate output or real GDP, L is the quantity of labour, K is the stock of capital and T is the state of technology. At any given time, the stock of capital and state of technology are given and fixed. Though at any time population of a country is fixed but the quantity of labour is variable; it depends on the preferences between work and leisure of the people on the one hand and the decisions of the firms about the demand for labour on the other. People supply labour only if wage rate which is reward for their work effort is sufficient to overcome their preference for leisure. The higher the wage rate, the greater is the quantity of labour supplied. On the other hand, the firms demand labour if it is profitable to use it for production. The lower the wage rate, which is the cost of labour, the greater is the quantity of labour used. The equilibrium wage rate and the quantity of labour employed are determined by labour market equilibrium. The labour market is in equilibrium at the wage rate at which the quantity of labour demanded equals the quantity of labour supplied. *At this equilibrium wage rate, all those who are willing to supply their labour are in fact demanded and employed. Therefore, at this equilibrium wage rate, full employment of labour is said to prevail.*

However, even at full employment, there are always some workers searching for jobs and some firms are looking for workers to offer them employment. This is because of two factors, frictional and structural. Every week some workers leave their old jobs and search for new better jobs more suited to their skills and ability. But due to lack of information, it takes time to find the new jobs even through these are available. This represents what is called *frictional unemployment*. Second, every week or month some industries are declining due to changes in technology or preferences of the people for goods while others are expanding. In this case while some people are laid off from the declining industries but sometime is required before they acquire new skills and training needed for employment in the expanding industries. Therefore, for some time they remain unemployed though job vacancies for them exist. This second type of unemployment is called *structural unemployment*.

Thus, at any time some frictional and structural unemployment inevitably exist in a free market economy. Therefore, in modern macroeconomics, the amount of frictional and structural unemployment is called the *natural rate of unemployment*. Around 4 to 5 per cent of labour force in the developed free-market economies represents the natural rate of unemployment. And full employment is said exist in spite of the existence of frictional and structural unemployment. As mentioned above, the *quantity of real GDP produced and supplied when there is full employment (that is, when there exists only natural rate of unemployment) is called potential GDP*. It may be noted again that potential GDP depends on full employment of labour, the full use of the existing stock of capital and the available technology.

The long-run aggregate supply describes the relationship between the quantity of real GDP and the price level in the long run when real GDP equals potential GDP. The long-run aggregate supply curve is a vertical line (at potential GDP level) as shown by *LAS* in Figure 10.11. *The long-run aggregate supply is vertical because potential GDP does not vary with price level, that is, it is independent of the price level*. For example, when aggregate demand curve is AD_2, price level is at 160 (WPI) and when aggregate demand falls and aggregate demand curve shifts to the left to AD_1 and determines price level equal to 130 (WPI), aggregate output remains unchanged at potential GDP equal to $\overline{Y}$. *The reason for the independence of potential GDP from the price level is that the movement along the long-run aggregate supply curve involves not only the change in price level of goods but also prices of factor inputs such as wages of labour etc*. For example, when there is 5 per cent decrease in the prices of goods and services, this is matched by the same (*i.e.* 5 per cent) decline in wage rate and other factor prices so that relative prices and real wage rate remain unchanged. This explains why it is profitable to produce the same quantity of real GDP at lower price level of goods and services. When price level of goods and services falls, the cost also falls as wage rate and other factor prices fall by the same percentage. Therefore, aggregate supply of output (*i.e.* real GDP) in the long run also remains constant at potential GDP level.

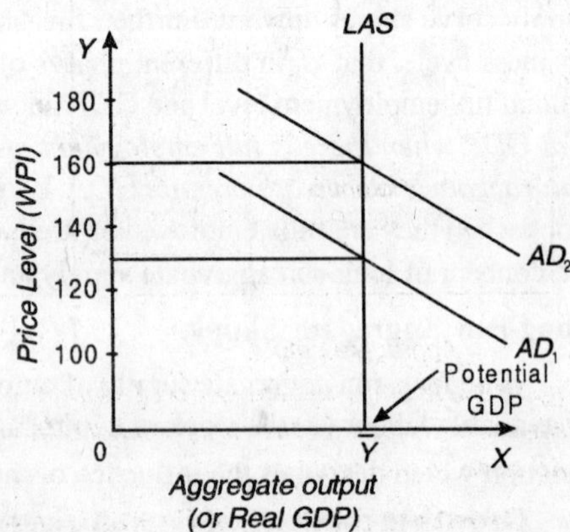

Figure 10.11. *Long-Run Aggregate Supply Curve*

It is evident from above that long-run aggregate supply curve is the same as the classical aggregate supply curve.

Changes or Shifts in Long-run Aggregate Supply Curve

We have seen above that long-run aggregate supply curve is a vertical straight line at the level of potential GDP. Changes in price level bring about a movement along the long-run aggregate supply, but the quantity of aggregate supply remains fixed at the level of potential GDP. *It is changes in potential GDP that causes a shift in the long-run aggregate supply curve*. The following factors cause a change in potential GDP resulting in a shift in the long-run aggregate supply curve.

1. The change in the full-employment quantity of labour.
2. Change in the stock of capital.
3. Progress in technology.

Increase in Labour Force. Labour is an important resource of production. Over time, given the capital stock and the state of technology potential GDP will increase as full-employment quantity of labour force increases. Therefore, the increase in the full-employment quantity of labour force causes a shift in the long-run aggregate supply curve to the right as shown in Figure 10.14. It may be noted that changes in labour employment over the business cycle cause fluctuations in real GDP. But these changes in real GDP that take place over the business cycle are not changes in potential GDP. As mentioned above, changes in potential GDP occur due to changes in labour force and stock of capital, and improvement in technology.

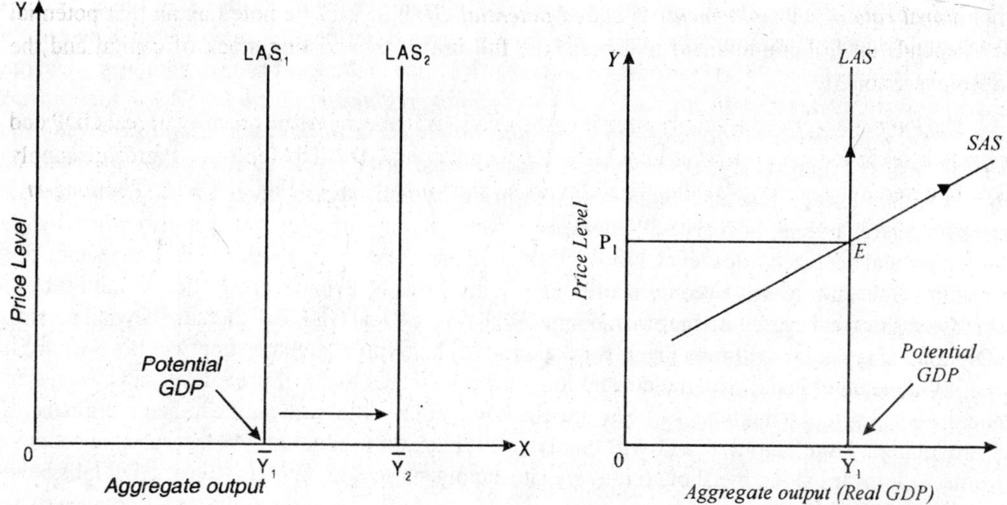

Fig. 10.12. *Increase in Labour Force, Capital Stock and Progress in Technology Increase potential GDP and shifts LAS curve to the right.*

Figure 10.13. *Short-run Aggregate Supply Curve along with Long-run Aggregate Supply Curve*

Growth in the Stock of Capital The stock of capi tal in an economy determines the productive capacity of the economy. The larger the stock of capital in the economy, the more productive is the labour force of the economy and the greater is its potential GDP. The higher per capita output and potential GDP of the American economy as compared to those of the Indian economy are mainly due to the greater stock of capital in the United States. Note that in the capital stock the modern economists include not only physical capital but also human capital. Human capital means the acquired skills, education and training of the workers. Like the increase in labour force, growth in capital stock also brings about increase in potential GDP and causes a shift in the long-run aggregate supply curve (LAS) to the right.

Progress in Technology. Progress in technology enables firms to produce more from the given resources. Empirical research studies have shown that technological progress is by far the most important source of increase in GDP over the past two centuries. It is due to advances in technology that a modern worker, both in industry and agriculture produces many times more output than the worker in the olden times. Thus, even with the fixed quantities of labour and capital, progress in technology raises potential GDP and causes in shift in the long run aggregate supply curve to the right.

Change in Money Wages and Other Resource Prices. It is worthwhile to note that changes in money wages and other factor prices such as *the price of oil affect the short-run aggregates supply curve but do not affect the long-run aggregate supply curve*. This is because along the long-run aggregate supply curve any change in the money wage rate or other resource prices bring about an equal percentage change in the price level so that *relative prices* and *real* wage rate remain constant. Since the relative prices remain the same, the firms do not have any incentive to increase or reduce their production and therefore potential GDP and long-run aggregate supply curve remain constant. However, changes in money wage rate and other resource prices affect firms' cost of production and therefore cause a shift in short-run aggregate supply curve. For example, when money wage rate and other resource prices rise, firms' costs go up and therefore they will be willing to supply smaller quantity of output at each price level. As a result, short-run aggregate supply curve shifts to the left.

Relation of Short-Run Aggregate Supply Curve with Long-Run Aggregate Supply Curve

In macroeconomics short run is defined as the period during which aggregate output has fallen either below potential GDP or has risen above potential GDP. Accordingly, in the short run, the rate of unemployment either increases above the natural rate of unemployment or falls below the natural rate of unemployment. Thus short-run aggregate supply curve describes the relationship between the aggregate output (*i.e.* real GDP) produced and the price level in the short run when money wage rate and other factor prices remain constant. The *short-run aggregate supply curve (SAS) slopes upward to the right and intersects the long-run aggregate supply curve at the current and expected price level.* Consider Figure 10.13. If the current and expected price level is P_1, then on this basis the contracts about wage rate and other resource prices would have been reached. Therefore, the short-run aggregate supply curve will intersect the vertical long-run aggregate supply curve (LAS) at the current and expected price level. Now, if the actual price level rises, wages and other factor prices remaining constant, it will become profitable for the firms to expand production resulting in the increase in short-run aggregate supply of output. With this, the real GDP will increase beyond potential GDP and the economy will move rightward along the short-run aggregate supply curve *SAS* in Fig. 10.13. On the other hand, with the current long-run price equal to P_1, if price level falls, wages and other resource prices remaining the same, the firms will not be able to cover the higher marginal costs of producing a large output $\overline{Y_1}$ and will therefore cut back on production. As a result, the economy will move leftward along the short-run aggregate supply curve *SAS*. With this, real GDP falls below the potential GDP level.

It is evident from above why short-run aggregate supply curve (*SAS*) slopes upward. The firms produce the output that maximises profits, if the price level of goods and services rises while the wage rates and other resource costs per unit remain the same, it pays the firms to expand production. Thus more real GDP is produced and supplied at a higher price level.

Let us briefly distinguish between the movement along the short-run aggregate supply curve (*SAS*) and the movement along the long-run aggregate supply curve (*LAS*). When the price level rises, with money wage rate and other resource prices remaining the same, it is profitable to produce more goods and services which bring about increase in the quantity of real GDP produced and supplied. As a result, there is a movement along the short-run aggregate supply curve (*SAS*) as shown in Figure 10.13 by the upward-sloping arrow. On the other hand, when the price level rises and *also there is the same percentage rise in wage rate and other resource prices*, relative prices of goods and services remaining unchanged it is not profitable to produce more output of goods and services. As a result, real GDP remains equal to the potential GDP and there is a movement along the long-run aggregate supply curve (*LAS*) as shown by vertical arrow mark in Fig. 10.13.

Changes in Short-Run Aggregate Supply

We have seen above that changes in wage rate and other resource prices such as prices of petroleum products do not affect long-run aggregate supply (*LAS*) whose position depends on the quantity of labour force, stock of capital and state of technology. However, changes in wage rate and other resource prices bring about a change in the short-run aggregate supply curve (*SAS*) through their effect on the costs of the firms. It is worth noting that the short-run aggregate supply curve is drawn by assuming that wage rate, other resource prices such as price of oil, rate of interest remain constant. The higher the wage rate or other resource prices, the greater is the cost of the firms and therefore the firms will be willing to supply the smaller quantity

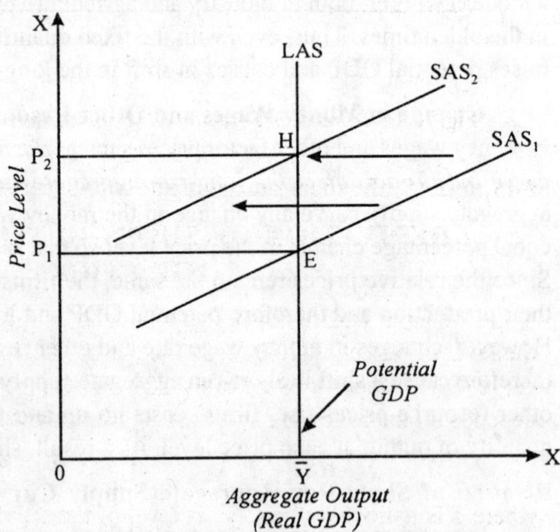

Fig. 10.14. *Shift in Short-Run Aggregate Supply Curve*

of goods at each price level. As a result, the increase in wage rate or in any other resource price will cause a shift in the short-run aggregate supply (*SAS*) curve to the left. This is shown in Fig. 10.14 where initially the short run aggregate supply curve is SAS_1. A rise in the wage rate causes the leftward shift in short-run aggregate supply curve to SAS_2. It is noteworthy that the vertical distance between the two short-run aggregate supply curves *EH* will be equal to the percentage change in the wage rate. It was the rise in prices of oil, generally called ***supply shocks*** that happened in 1973-74 and again in 1979-80 that brought about a leftward shift in short-run aggregate supply curve and caused *stagflation* in a number of developed countries.

On the other hand, if money wage rate or any other resource price falls, short-run aggregate supply curve will shift to the right. Further, it needs to be emphasised that the changes in nominal wage rate or the change in any other resource price does not affect the potential GDP and therefore does not cause a shift in the long-run aggregate supply curve.

Changes in Potential GDP and Aggregate Supply Curve

As explained above, changes in potential GDP are brought about by changes in labour force, capital-stock and state of technology. Any increase in potential GDP increases both the long-run and short run supply curves. This is illustrated in fig. 10.15. To start with, with potential GDP equal to $\overline{Y}_1$ the long run aggregate supply curve is LAS_1.

If due to increase in either labour force or stock of capital or improvement in technology potential GDP rises to $\overline{Y}_2$, the long run aggregate supply increases causing a rightward shift in the long-run aggregate supply curve to LAS_2. Moreover, increase in potential GDP effected by either increase in labour force or capital stock or improvement in technology would also increase the short-run aggregate supply and shift the short-run aggregate supply curve (*SAS*) to the right. This will be observed from Fig. 10.15 where along with the rightward shift in the long-run aggregate supply curve from LAS_1 to LAS_2 the short-run aggregate supply curve also shifts to the right from SAS_1 to SAS_2.

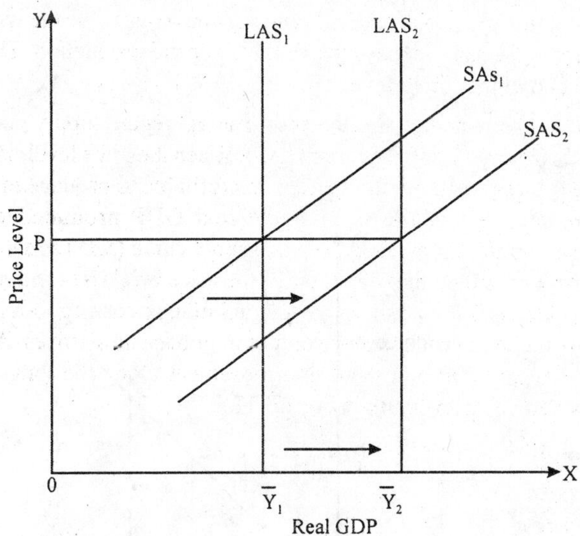

Fig. 10.15. *Increase in Potential GDP affects both the long-run and short-run aggregate supply curves.*

DERIVATION OF SHORT-RUN AGGREGATE SUPPLY CURVE : THE STICKY WAGE MODEL

We have studied above that while the long-run supply curve (LAS) is a vertical straight line at the level of potential GNP (or at the natural rate of unemployment), the short-run aggregate supply curve (SAS) slopes upward to the right. There are three models of aggregate supply but all of them depends on the following short-run aggregate supply equation.

$$Y = \overline{Y} + \alpha (P - P^e), \qquad \alpha > 0$$

where Y is national output, $\overline{Y}$ is level of potential GNP, P is the price level and P^e is the expected price level. The parameter α shows how much output changes in response to the unexpected changes in the price level. $\frac{1}{\alpha}$ will measure the slope of the short-run aggregate supply curve.

An important model of aggregate supply curve assumes that nominal (*i.e.* money) wages are sticky in the short run and emphasise that nominal wages are *slow in adjustment to the unexpected changes in the price level.* The sticky nature of nominal wages is due to the following reasons :

1. The nominal wages are fixed by long-term contracts. Therefore, nominal wages cannot adjust quickly when there is unexpected change in the price level.
2. In the industries where formal labour contracts do not prevail, there are implicit agreements between workers and employers about nominal wages. These prevent the quick adjustment in nominal wages when economic conditions warrant.
3. Wages also depend on social norms and notions of equity. These also prevent changes in wages in the short run.

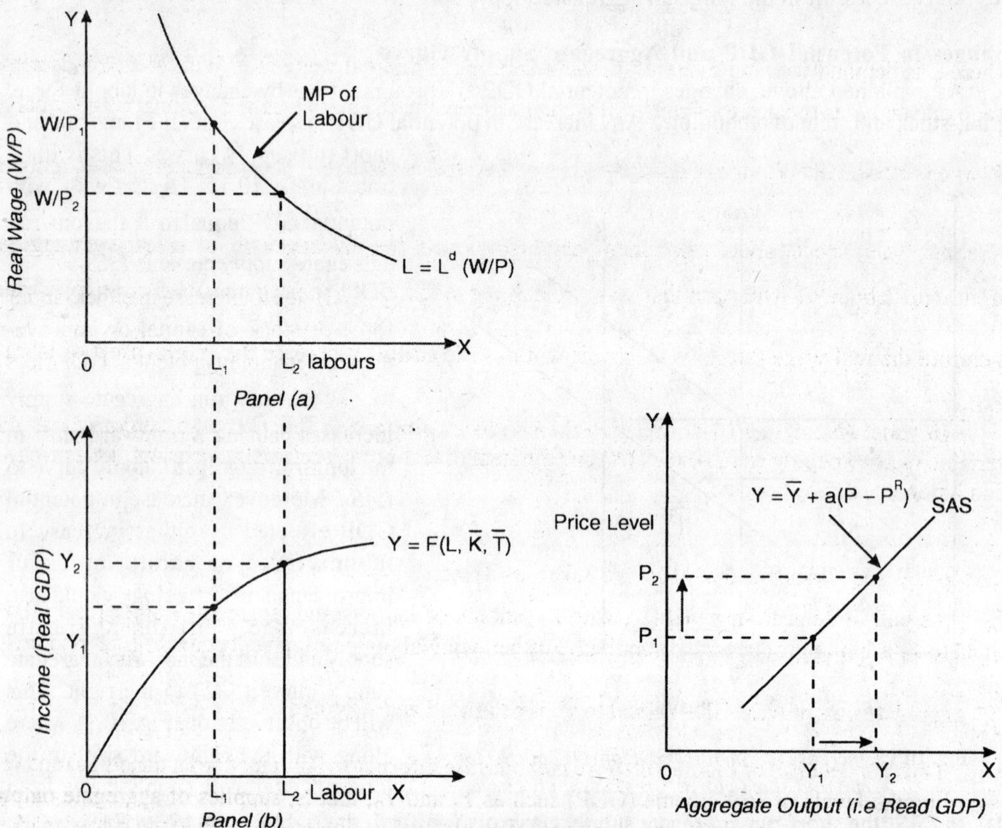

Figure 10.16. *Deriving Short-run Aggregate Supply Curve : Stickly Wage Model*

The above factors account for stickiness of nominal wages in the short run. Recall that short-run aggregate supply curve shows how the quantity of aggregate output (*i.e.* real GDP) changes in the short run when the actual price level deviates from the expected price level. As the actual price level rises in the short run, more quantity of the aggregate output (*i.e.* real GDP) is produced and supplied. That is, the short-run aggregate supply slopes upward to the right. Now, what accounts for the upward-sloping nature of the short-run aggregate supply curve. *Since the nominal wages are sticky in the short run, a rise in the actual price level in the short run lowers the real wage rate of workers. The lower real wage induces the firms to employ more labour. The increase in labour employment will lead to the increase in aggregate output (i.e. real GDP). Thus, when actual price level increases above the expected price level in the short run, the quantity of aggregate output or real GDP increases.* That is, short-run aggregate supply curve slopes upward to the right. It is worthwhile to note that the greater quantity of aggregate output could be produced and supplied in the short run only *at a higher actual price* because of employment of more labour in the short run, quantity of capital and the state of technology remaining the same, leads to the rise in marginal cost of production of the firms. Therefore, higher price of output is required to cover this higher marginal cost of production as expansion in aggregate output takes place in the short run.

How the short-run aggregate supply curve is derived in the sticky wage model is illustrated in figure 10.16. In panel (*a*) of this figure we show the determination of labour employment through demand for labour function. This labour demand function of labour is given by marginal product curve and can be stated as under.

$$L = L^d\left(\frac{W}{P}\right)$$

where L is demand for employment of labour and $\frac{W}{P}$ is the real wage rate. With W as the nominal wage rate and P as the price level. It will be seen from panel (*a*) that given the nominal wage equal to W, when price level is P_1, the real wage equals $\frac{W}{P_1}$. At this real wage $\frac{W}{P_1}$, the firms employ L_1 amount of labour. This is because at L_1 amount of labour employed, the real wage rate $\frac{W}{P_1}$ is equal to marginal product of labour. If, with nominal wage remaining stuck at W, actual price level rises to P_2 and therefore the real wage rate falls to $\frac{W}{P_2}$, it will pay the firms to increase the employment of labour to L_2.

In panel (*b*) of fig. 10.17 we give the short-run production function with labour (L) as the variable factor, keeping capital stock (K) and the state of technology remaining constant. This production function can be stated as

$$Y = F(L, \bar{K}, \bar{T})$$

Bars on K and T shows that they are taken as fixed.

As will be seen from panel (*b*), with L_1 amount of labour used, aggregate output (real GDP) equal to Y_1 is being produced and supplied. Further, with labour employment equal to L_2 at real wage $\frac{W}{P_2}$ aggregate output (real GDP) equal to Y_2 is produced and supplied.

Thus in panel (*C*) of Figure 10.16 we combine the information obtained from panels (*a*) and (*b*) regarding the levels of real income (GDP) such as Y_1 and Y_2, that is, supplies of aggregate output corresponding to price levels P_1 and P_2 respectively (determined by equilibrium in the labour market and the given production function, $Y = F(L, \bar{K}, \bar{T})$) and plot them to get a short-run aggregate supply curve *SAS*. It will be seen from panel (*C*) that short-run aggregate supply curve so obtained slopes upward to the right.

It will be seen from panel (*d*) that short-run aggregate supply curve (*SAS*) slopes upward to the right. It is worth nothing *that the short-run supply curve slopes upward because with money wage rate being fixed, as the actual price level rises, real wage rate declines which induces the firms to employ more labour resulting in more aggregate output (real GDP) produced and supplied.* In terms of aggregate supply equation, namely, $Y = \bar{Y} + \alpha(P - P^e)$ when actual price level (P) deviates from expected price level (P^e) which formed the basis of fixation of nominal wages (W), the real wage rate

$\left(\frac{W}{P}\right)$ will fall below the target wage rate and will therefore raise the amount of labour employed and aggregate output produced.

Short-run and Long-run Aggregate Supply Curve

Note that when actual price level (P) equals the expected price level (P^e), $P - P^e$ in the aggregate supply equation $Y = \overline{Y} + \alpha(P - P^e)$ will be zero and therefore aggregate output (or real GDP) will be equal to potential GDP ($\overline{Y}$). Therefore, when the actual price level and the expected price level are equal, the short-run aggregate supply (*SAS*) curve will intersect the long-run aggregate supply curve (*LAS*) at the level of current real price level as shown by point E in Figure 10.17. When the actual price level rises above the expected price level ($P > P^e$ or $P - P^e > 0$). the real wage rate will fall and consequently more labour will be employed resulting in more aggregate output. With this we will move towards right form E on short-run supply curve *SAS*. This implies that the level of unemployment will fall below the natural rate of unemployment.

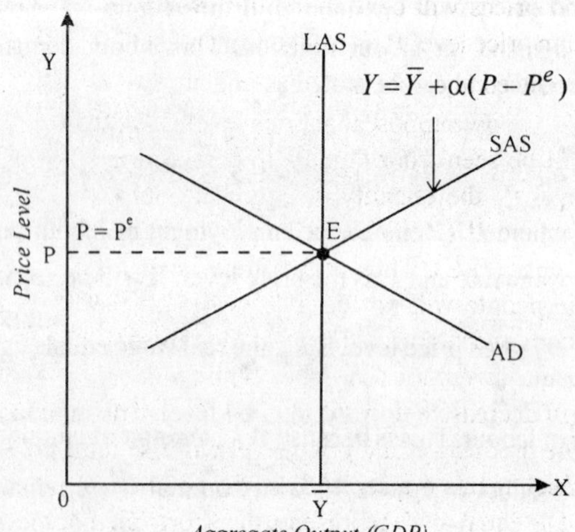

Figure 10.17. *Short-Run and Long-Run Aggregate Supply Curve*

On the other hand, when actual price level falls below the expected price level ($P < P^e$ or $P - P^e < 0$) real wage rate will rise above the target wage rate. This will induce the firms to reduce the quantity of labour employed resulting in smaller aggregate output produced. As a result, with the initial equilibrium at point E, the economy will be move to the left of point E. With this, real GDP will be below the potential GDP ($\overline{Y}$) and rate of unemployment well rise above the natural rate of unemployment.

MACROECONOMIC EQUILIBRIUM : AS-AD MODEL

Having explained the concepts of aggregate demand and aggregate supply with variable price level. Now we shall explain how macro equilibrium is reached between the aggregate supply and aggregate demand to determine the amount of real GDP and the price level. As there is difference between the long-run and the short run aggregate supply curves, the long-run equilibrium differs from the short-run macroeconomic equilibrium. while long-run equilibrium is the state toward which the economy is moving short-run equilibrium is the actual state of the economy in the short run as it fluctuates around potential GDP. The purpose of AS-AD model is to explain how the various events, fiscal and monetary policies bring about changes in real GDP and the price level. We explain below both the short-run and long-run macroeconomic equilibrium.

Short-run Macroeconomic Equilibrium

Short-run macroeconomic equilibrium occurs at the price level at which aggregate output demanded equals aggregate supply of output. That is, short-run equilibrium is reached at the price level at which aggregate demand curve *AD* intersects the short-run aggregate supply curve *SAS*. This is shown in fig. 10.18 where *AD* is the aggregate demand curve and *SAS* is the aggregate supply curve. It will be seen that the short-run macroeconomic equilibrium occurs at point E at which the price level is P_0 and the real GDP is Y_0. If price level is different from P_0, the economy will not be in equilibrium. Suppose, for example, price level is P_2, the quantity of the real GDP demanded P_2 is less than the quantity $P_2 B$ of real GDP supplied. This means the firms will not be able to sell all their output. As a result ,unintended inventories well pile up and firms will cut both production and prices. The process of cutting production and prices will continue until the equilibrium price level P_0 is reached and real GDP produced and sold is Y_0.

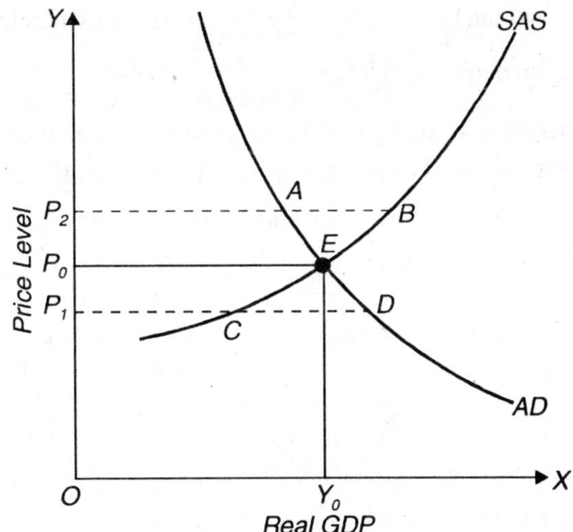

Fig. 10.18. *Short-run Macroeconomic Equilibrium : Joint Determination of GDP and Price Level*

Now suppose that price level is P_1. It will be seen from Fig. 10.18 that at price level P_1 the quantity of aggregate output demanded ($P_1 D$) exceeds the aggregate supply ($P_1 C$). Thus at the price level P_1, the people will not be able to get all the goods and resources they want to buy. As a result, inventories of goods with the firms will decrease below the desired level. This will induce firms to increase production and raise prices. The production and price level will rise until price level P_0 is reached and real GDP produced is Y_0 which meets the demands of the people fully at the price level P_0. Thus, the price level P_0 and real GDP equal to Y_0 represents the short-run macroeconomic equilibrium.

It is worthwhile to note that in the short-run the money wage rate is fixed. *It does not adjust to bring macro equilibrium at full-employment level of real GDP.* Thus, in the short run macro equilibrium can be attained with real GDP less than or greater than potential GDP (*i.e.* the level of GDP at which there is full employment of labour) depending on the level of aggregate demand. It is only in the long run when money wage rate adjusts that equilibrium is restored at potential GDP.

Further, it may be noted that fluctuations in the economy occur due to changes in the factors that cause changes in either aggregate demand or aggregate supply. For example, changes in money supply, the government expenditure, taxes, investment demand by business firms or consumption demand of households will bring about changes in aggregate demand and cause shift in the short-run macroeconomic equilibrium. On the other hand, changes in money wage rate and other resource prices such as oil price stock will cause a shift in aggregate supply curve and bring about a change in the short-run macroeconomic equilibrium

It is important to note that according to Keynes, this equilibrium at less than full-employment level when there prevails recession in the economy comes into existence in the short run due to deficiency of aggregate demand caused by a fall in private investment by the business class. He argued that unless the Government intervenes in the economy through adoption of expansionary fiscal policy (that is, increasing its expenditure and cutting taxes) and finance its budget deficit through deficit financing, a free market economy cannot be brought into equilibrium at full employment. (*i.e.* potential GDP) level. He emphasized that a free market economy was not self correcting through any adjustment in wages and prices to restore equilibrium at full employment level. According to him, without intervention by the Government, under-employment equilibrium with recession prevailing in the economy will persist in the long run. Keynes therefore did not discuss how through adjustment of wages and prices the long-run equilibrium of a free market economy is reached. On the other hand, classical economists, monetarists and New Classical economists believe in the establishment of long-run equilibrium at full employment level through automatic adjustments in wages and prices . We explain below their viewpoint.

Long-Run Macroeconomic Equilibrium

The long-run macroeconomic equilibrium occurs at the price level where the aggregate demand curve intersects the long run aggregate supply curve which is vertical at the potential GDP level. Thus, long-run equilibrium occurs *when real* GDP *equals potential* GDP. *But this long-run equilibrium of price level and real* GDP *is reached when money wage rate adjusts so that the short-run aggregate supply curve shifts to intersect the long-run aggregate supply curve (LAS) at the point at which*

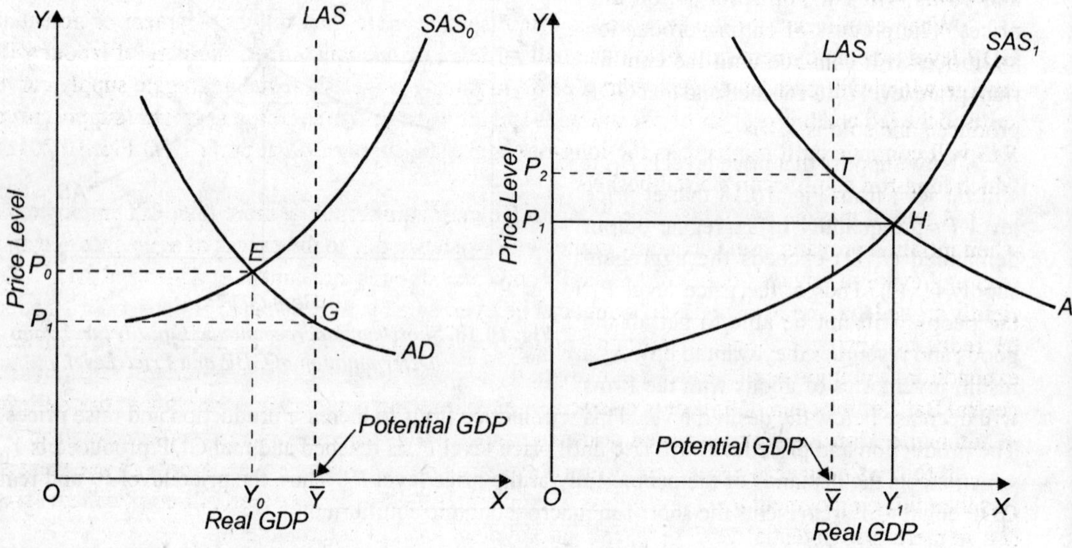

Fig. 10.19. *Short-run Equilibrium at less than full-employment (or Potential GDP).*

Fig. 10.20. *Short run Equilibrium at more than Full-Employment Level with Inflation.*

aggregate demand curve intersects the latter. The long-run macro equilibrium and how it is reached is illustrated in Figure 10.19 & 10.20. From Fig. 10.19 it will be seen that the short-run aggregate supply curve SAS_0 *intersects the given aggregate demand curve AD at point E and determines the price level equal to* P_0 *and real* GDP *equal to* Y_0 *in the short run. Thus in this short-run macroeconomic equilbrium, real GDP which is equal to* Y_0 *is less than the potential GDP (remember that the potential GDP corresponds to full employment of labour, with the given stock of capital and the given state of technology). The difference* $Y_0\bar{Y}$ *between the short-run equilibrium GDP and the potential GDP is called recessionary gap which exists because at the short-run equilibrium price level* P_0 *aggregate demand is not sufficient for the purchase of potential GDP. Besides, the production of less than potential GDP implies that in the short-run equilibrium, there will exist cyclical unemployment, that is, the rate of unemployment will exceed the natural rate of unemployment.*

If money wage rate is flexible as classical economists, monetarists and new classical economists think they are, then in the short run equilibrium at point *E* with more than natural rate of unemployment, money wage rate will fall. As a result, short-run aggregate supply curve (*SAS*) will shift to the right. This rightward shift in the short-run aggregate supply curve will continue until it intersects the long-run aggregate supply curve (*LAS*) at point *G* (see Figure 10.19) where the given aggregate demand cuts the latter. At the new equilibrium point *G* price level has fallen to P_1 and aggregate quantity of output demanded has increased to the potential GDP. Point *G* in the of Figure 10.19 represents the long-run equilibrium at full-employment level, that is, the level at which only natural rate of unemployment prevails.

Let us consider the opposite case when the short-run equilibrium is initially at more than potential GDP, that is, above full employment level. Suppose initially with aggregate demand curve *AD* and the short-run aggregate supply curve SAS_1, the short-run equilibrium is at point *H* at which the price level is P_1 and real GDP is Y_1 which is greater than potential GDP equal to $\bar{Y}$. (see Fig. 10.20).

Now, the question may be asked how real GDP has risen to the level which is more than the potential GDP. The answer is that even beyond potential GDP, real GDP rises as labour-employment increases by reduction in rate of unemployment more than the natural rate and the given capital stock is utilised more intensively. The amount $\bar{Y}Y_1$ by which real GDP which is equal to Y_1 exceeds potential GDP ($\bar{Y}$) represents the *inflationary gap* as this gap creates inflationary pressures in the economy

When equilibrium of the economy is established at more than full-employment or potential GDP level, unemployment falls below the natural level of unemployment, shortage of labour will emerge which will push up wages. With the rise in money wages short-run aggregate supply curve shifts to the left and this process of rise in wages and leftward shift in short run aggregate supply curve *SAS* will continue until it intersects the long-run aggregate supply *LAS* at point *T* (in Fig. 10.20) at which long-run equilibrium is estabilieshed.

Again, it may be noted that, according to Keynes, equilibrium at more than full employment when inflation prevails in the economy comes into existence due to the excess of aggregate demand over aggregate supply cannot be automatically corrected through adjustment in wages and prices. He rightly argued that inflation in the economy can be overcome by *demand management policy*, that is, by reducing aggregate demand through contractionary fiscal policy *(i.e.,* reducing Government expenditure and imposing taxes) and tightening of monetary policy (*i.e.* raising interest rates) by the central Bank of the country. It is only classical, monetarists and new classical economists that believe in automatic adjustment of wages and prices to achieve long-run equilibrium at full-employment.

It follows from above that equilibrium between aggregate and aggregate supply can be there at less than full-employment level (*i.e.* at less than potential GDP), at more than full-employment level (*i.e.* at more than potential GDP or at full employment level of potential GDP.

Friedman's Natural Rate Hypothesis : Explained Through AD-AS Model

Having explained the meaning of natural rate of unemployment, we are now in a position to explain natural rate hypothesis put forward by Friedman. According to this hypothesis, *Flucluations in aggregate demand affect output and employment in the short run, in the long run, the economy returns to the level of natural unemployment.* Recall that the natural rate of unemployment corresponds to level of full-employment or potential GDP. In essence this model implies that level of full employment of classical economists, or what is also called potential GDP is determined by different factors than the short-run levels of employment and output which are determined by fluctuations in aggregate demand. This is in fact one expression of classical dichotomy.

We explain natural rate hypothesis with short-run aggregate supply curve (*SAS*) derived in chapter 10. The short-run aggregate supply curve is represented by the following equation.

$$Y=\bar{Y}+\alpha(P-P^e)$$

where Y is actual output $\bar{Y}$ is potential level of output or GDP corresponding to natural rate of unemployment. P^e is the expected price level and P is the actual price level.

The above equation describes that the deviations of actual output level (Y) from the natural output level ($\bar{Y}$) depends on the deviation of actual price level from the expected price level. To explain natural rate hypothesis we introduce aggregate demand curve along with short-run aggregate supply curve (*SAS*) representing the equation, $Y=\bar{Y}+\alpha(P-P^e)$ and long-run aggregate supply curve (LAS) drawn at the natural level of output (or employment) which are shown in Figure 10.21. It is worth mentioning that short-run aggregate supply (*SAS*) is drawn with a given expected price level and changes in expected price level will cause a shift in this short-run aggregate supply curve.

Now in Figure 10.20A short-run aggregate supply curve SAS_0 and aggregate demand curve AD_0 intersect at point E on the given long-run aggregate supply LAS. Thus at point E the equilibrium is at the natural level of output, that is, at natural level of unemployment. Now suppose aggregate demand unexpectedly increases to AD_1 and as a result new equilibrium at point K is reached at which actual price rises to P_1 and aggregate output or national income increases to Y_1 which implies unemployment will fall below the natural unemployment level. Thus equilibrium at point K represents the boom period. However, the workers are surprised at the rise in actual price level to P_1 against their expected price level P_0, $(P_0 = P_0^e)$. This causes rise in expected price level to P_1 and as a result short-run supply curve will shift upward and continue shifting upward till the expected price becomes equal to the actual price. Such a short-run supply curve is given by SAS_1 which intersects aggregate demand curve AD_1 and long-run aggregate supply curve LAS at point H with expected price level P^e_2 equal to the actual price level P_2. As equilibrium point H also lies at the long-run supply curve LAS drawn at potential GDP, that is, at natural level of unemployment. Thus we find though in the short run the economy deviated from the natural level of output and unemployment $\overline{Y}$ due to unexpected increase in aggregate demand in the long run it returns to the natural level of unemployment. This, *according to Milton Friedman, movement along short-run aggregate supply curve due to changes in aggregate demand involves trade off between inflation and output (or between inflation and unemployment), in the long-run there is no such trade off as the economy remains at natural level of the unemployment.*

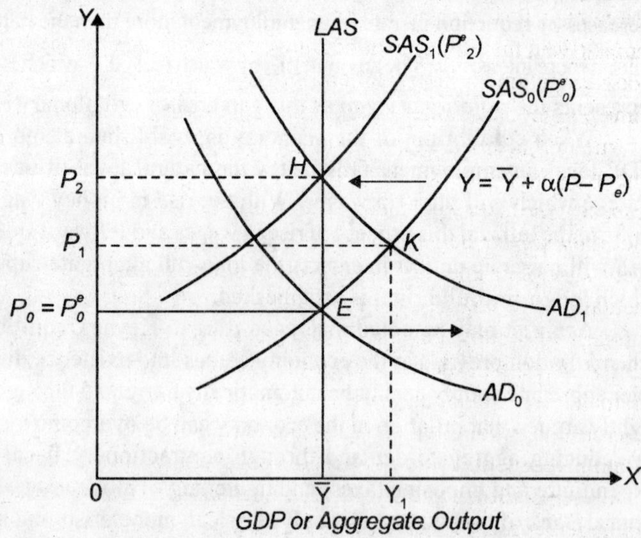

Fig. 10.20A. *Natural Rate Hypothesis Graphically Represented*

We now turn to explain the opposite case when aggregate demand decreases causing recession in the economy which is graphically shown in Fig. 10.20B. To begin with, the equilibrium of the economy is at point E where upward-sloping short-run aggregate supply curve $SAS_0(P_0^e)$ intersects both the given aggregate demand curve AD_0 and long-run aggregate supply curve LAS at point E. Price level is P_0 and we assume that this price level also

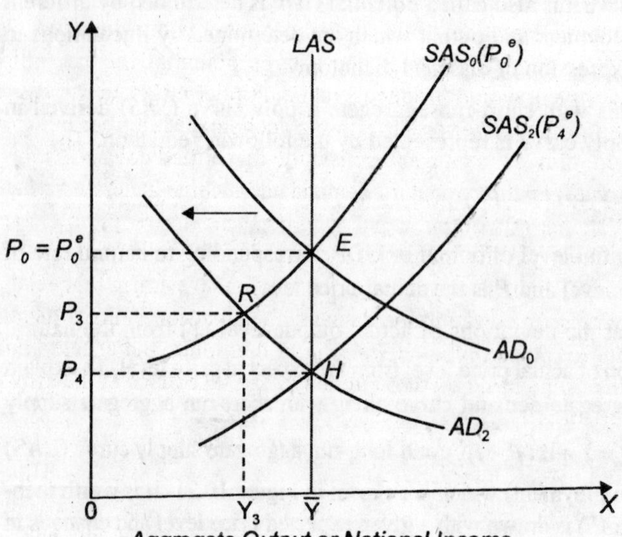

Fig. 10.20B. *Natural Rate Hypothesis : Case of Decrease in Aggregate Demand*

prevailed in the previous period. Therefore, the expected price level of workers is P_0, ($P_0^e = P_0$). Now suppose aggregate demand decreases and *AD* curve shifts to the left to AD_2 which intersects the short-run aggregate supply curve $SAS(P_0^e)$ at point *R*. In this new short-run equilibrium at point *R*, price level falls to P_3 and level of national income (*i.e.*, aggregate output) decreases to Y_3 and causes unemployment to increase more than the natural unemployment level. Thus, the fall in aggregate demand to AD_2 has resulted in recession in the economy. However, according to Friedman, since the fall in actual price level to P_3 is against their expected price level P_0, the expected price level will be revised to P_3. As a result, short-run aggregate supply curve will shift to the right and rightward shifting in the short-run aggregate supply curve will continue until SAS_2 is reached when expected price level becomes equal to actual price ($P_4 = P_4^e$). It will be seen from Fig.10.20B that short-run supply curve SAS_2 intersects aggregate demand curve AD_2 and long-run aggregate supply curve *LAS* at point *T*. Thus, the economy has come back to be in equilibrium at national income $\overline{Y}$ corresponding to natural level of unemployment.

To sum up though there are economic fluctuations in the short run due to changes in aggregate demand (which may be brought about by changes in money supply or investment demand) but in the long run equilibrium at natural level of unemployment is restored.

ECONOMIC FLUCTATIONS : AS-AD MODEL

The purpose of *AS-AD* model is to explain economic fluctuations or what are called business cycles. In this model the business cycles or economic fluctuations occur because aggregate demand and short-run aggregate supply fluctuate but the money wage rate does not adjust quickly enough to maintain real *GDP* at the level of potential *GDP*. The economy fluctuates around potential GDP, sometimes recessionary and sometimes boom conditions prevail in the economy. The changes in aggregate demand and short-run aggregate supply bring about fluctations in real GDP and price level. Figures 10.21 and 10.22 shows how changes in aggregate demand bring about fluctuations in GDP and price level.

Decrease in Aggregate Demand

Let us fist show how decrease in aggregate demand brings about changes in

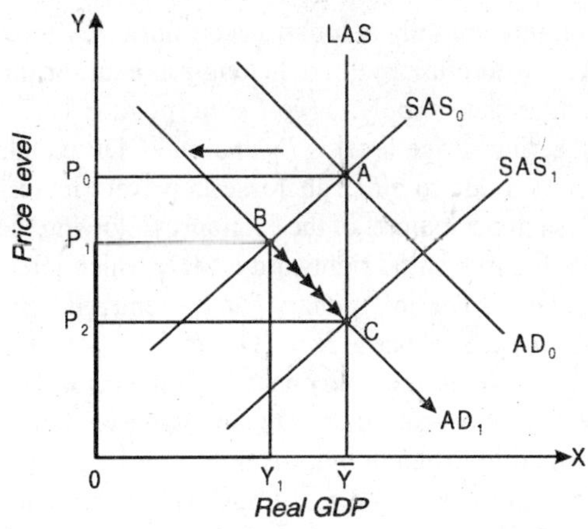

Fig. 10.21. *Impact of Decrease in Aggregate Demand on Real GDP and Price Level.*

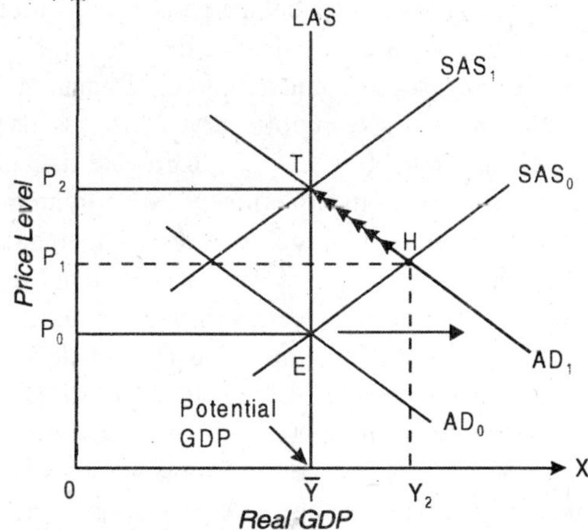

Fig. 10.22. *Impact of Increase in Aggregate Demand on Real GDP and Price Level.*

real GDP and price level. Aggregate demand consists of consumption demand (*C*), investment demand (*I*), government expenditure (*G*) and net exports (X_n). Decrease in any of these components of demand will shift the aggregate demand curve to the left. Keynes emphasised that private investment is very volatile. When profit expectations of business men in future become dim, they reduce investment which through the working of the multiplier adversely affects consumption demand too. In developing countries like India where agriculture is also still a relatively important sector failure of monsoon resulting in loss of output can cause reduction in consumption demand of the farmers and bring about a shift in aggregate demand to the right. Thirdly, when government reduces its investment expenditure, it will also cause a leftward shift in aggregate demand if it is not matched by the increase in private investment. Lastly, the world trade also affects the aggregate demand of an economy. Suppose the world trade declines in a year and, as a result, the demand for Indian exports decreases, it will also reduce aggregate demand in India.

If there is adverse change in any of the above components of aggregate demand, aggregate demand curve shifts to the left, say from AD_0 to AD_1 (see Figure 10.21). In Figure 10.21 initially the long-run equilibrium between aggregate demand curve AD_0 and short-run aggregate supply curve SAS_0 is at point A. Price level is OP_0 and real GDP is $\bar{Y}$. The leftward shift in aggregate demand curve from AD_0 to AD_1, the new short-run equilibrium is at B at which price level has fallen to P_1 and real GDP has declined to Y_1. The recessionary gap $\bar{Y}Y_1$ has emerged and therefore there are recessionary conditions in the economy. Not being able to sell their total output, the firms will reduce prices of their output. The money wage rate remaining sticky, the lower price level will increase the real wage rate. As a result, the firms' costs will increase relative to the prices of their outputs. Since real GDP has declined below potential GDP, unemployment in the economy will increase more than the natural rate of unemployment. The existence of a large amount of unemployment will put downward pressure on wages. Thus, eventually recessionary conditions will lead to fall in money wage rates if they are flexible. With the fall in wage rate, short-run aggregate supply curve will shift rightward and real GDP will tend to rise. However, since wage rate falls gradually, the real GDP will increase slowly to potential GDP equal to $\bar{Y}$. As a result price level will fall to P_2. Thus long-run equilibrium is established at point C of the long-run aggregate supply curve LAS. As mentioned in an earlier section above, the fall in price level equal to P_0P_2 or AC will be relatively equal to the fall in wage rate.

Increase in Aggregate Demand.

Let us now see what happens when, with the economy initially in long-run equilibrium, aggregate demand increases. This is depicted in figure 10.22 where inially there is long-run equilibrium between aggregate demand curve AD_0 and long-run aggregate supply curve LAS at point E where short-run aggregate supply curve (SAS_0) is also intersecting. Price level is P_0 and real GDP equals potential GDP. Now suppose aggregate demand increases due to either increase in private investment, or increase in Government expenditure or increase in net exports of the economy following the expansion in world trade. As a result, aggregate demand curve shifts rightward to AD_1 which intersects the short-run aggregate supply curve SAS_0 at point H. The inflationary gap has emerged and consequently price level has risen to P_1 and real GDP to Y_2. Since now real GDP exceeds potential GDP, rate of unemployment has fallen below the natural rate of unemployment. This means lobour shortage will emerge. But, it will be recalled that along a short-run aggregate supply curve money wage rate remains unchanged. Thus, with the short-run equilibrium at point H in Figure 10.22 with price level being higher and money wages remaining unchanged, the real wages (*i.e.* purchasing power of wages) of the workers will fall. The economy cannot therefore remains stable at point H because the workers will demand higher wages to maintain their real income. In view of the fact that labour-shortages have arisen because rate of unemployment has fallen below the natural rate of unemployment and being anxious to maintain their labour employment and output levels the firms will concede to the demand for higher wages.

As wage rates rise the short-run aggregate supply curve (SAS) will begin to shift to the left. Since the wage rates gradually adjust, the short-run aggregate supply curve will slowly move along the higher aggregate demand curve AD_1 toward SAS_1. The new equilibrium will be eventually reached at point T on the long-run aggregate supply curve LAS where the short-run aggregate supply curve SAS_1 intersects the aggregate demand curve AD_1. With equilibrium at point T, real GDP returns to the level of the potential GDP and price level has risen to P_2. Note that the rise in long-run price level from P_0 to P_2 (which is equal to ET) will be equal to the ultimate percentage rise in wage rate.

It is evident from above that fluctuations in aggregate demand can cause short-run fluctuations in output, employment and price level. This is how AS-AD model explain business cycles in the economy. But the second important cause of fluctuations in real GDP, employment and price level is the changes in aggregate supply. This is explained below.

Shift in Short-run Aggregate Supply Curve and Stagflation

Let us now turn to examine the effect of changes in aggregate supply, aggregate demand remaining constant. With the advent of *supply-side economics and new classical macroeconomics* embodying rational expectations in recent years economists are increasingly concerned with shifts in aggregate supply curve. Important factors that cause a shift in supply are changes in factor-prices and availability of resources, change in productivity and expectations about future inflation. Institutional factors such as Government regulations that affect resource use efficiency also cause shift in aggregate supply curve.

An important cause of shift in aggregate supply curve is the *rise in prices of resources such as large increase in oil price by OPEC* in 1973-74 and again in 1979-80. The rise in oil prices causes the aggregate supply curve to shift to the left as shown in Figure 10.23 where due to the higher per unit resource cost aggregate supply curve has shifted leftward from SAS_0 to SAS_1. The aggregate demand curve AD remaining constant, with the leftward shift in aggregate supply curve from AS_0 to AS_1, leads to the new macro-economic equilibrium being established at T, at which price level is higher and aggregate output smaller than before.

The emergence of rise in price level or inflation due to the leftward shift in aggregate supply curve is called *cost-push inflation.* There is important differences between deman pull inflation cost-push inflation. *Whereas in case of demand-pull inflation, price rises along with rise in GDP, in case of cost-push inflation price level rises but GDP declines.*

Thus, in Fig. 10.23 leftward shift in the SAS curve leads to rise in the price level from P_0 to P_1, while national output falls from Y_0 to Y_1. ***When both inflation and recession occur simultaneously, economists call this situation as stagflation.*** We thus see that increase in costs or resource prices are both inflationary and recessionary.

It may be noted that stagflation is also said to occur when instead of absolute fall in aggregate output there is *slowdown in economic growth rate* when inflation rate remains steadly high and also unemployment levels are quite high.It is evident from above that stagflation occurs as a result of supply shock, that is, rise in price of essential inputs such as crude oil which causes a shift in the short-run aggregate supply curve to the left. Given the aggregate demand curve, the new equilibrium is reached at a higher price level (*i.e.* inflation) and at the same time reduced aggregate output (*i.e.* GDP) which generates unemployment in the economy.

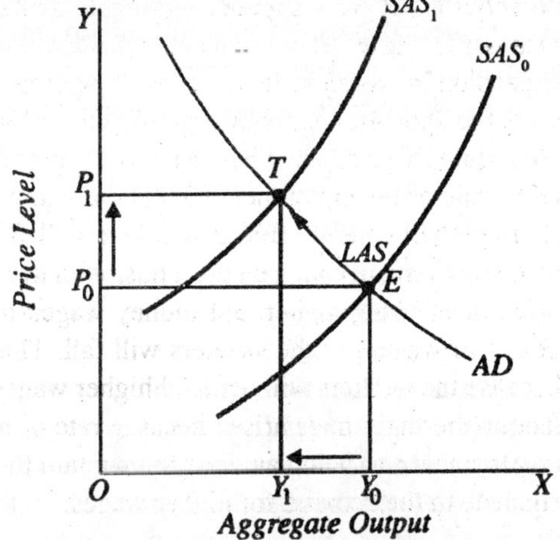

Fig. 10.23. ***Emergence of stagflation due to leftward shift in aggregate supply curve***

We have explained above stagflation as a result of sharp rise in price of crude oil effected by restriction of oil output by callusive agreement of OPEC. In India stagflation can arise when there is decline in agricultural output due to failure of monsoon. The decline in agricultural output causes *food inflation* which in turn leads to rise in wages of workers which cause a shift in the short-run aggregate supply curve to the left. Besides, drastic decline in agricultural output also leads to the rise in prices of raw materials provided by agricultural sector to industries. The rise in raw material prices for industries shifts aggregate supply curve to the left causing both inflation and reduction in output.

Solution. To solve the problem of stagflation is a difficult task. In the seventies when the problem of stagflation was first faced efforts were made to solve it through demand management policies. However, when to reduce inflation, steps were taken to reduce aggregate demand by cutting expenditure, the result was decline in aggregate output which further worsened the unemployment problem. On the other hand, when to reduce unemployment attempt was made to increase aggregate expenditure through expansionary fiscal and monetary policies the result was acceleration in inflation.

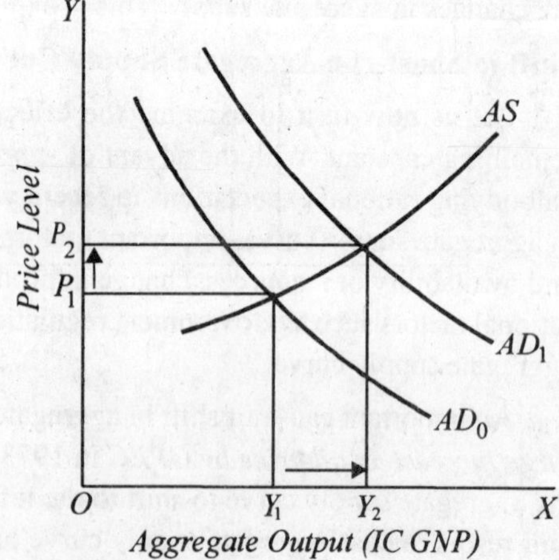

Fig. 10.24. *Keynesian View :* *Expansionary Fiscal and Monetary Policies in times of recession lead to more increase in GNP and less rise in Price Level.*

The proper solution of stagflation is to shift the short-run aggregate supply curve to the right by reducing cost through raising productivity levels. The productivity in both industry and agriculture can be raised through technological improvements and more capital accumulation. Besides rightward shift in short-run aggregate supply can be made by reducing indirect taxes such as excise duties, sales tax, customs duties not only on final products but also on essential inputs used in the production of commodities.

Role of Fiscal and Monetary Policies in Keynesian, Monetarist and Classical Models

With this aggregate demand-aggregate supply model, popularly known as *AD-AS* model, we can explain the effects of fiscal and monetary policies on aggregate output (*i.e., GNP*) and price level in the economy. For example, if Government steps up its expenditure without increasing taxes, this will cause aggregate demand curve *AD* to shift to the-right and thereby will lead to the increase in Gross-National Product (*i.e.*, National Income) and the price level as is illustrated in Figure 10.24. Likewise, expansion in money supply, increase in private investment, or reduction in taxes without reducing Government expenditure will also result in shift in the aggregate demand curve to the right causing price level and national output to increase

An important result follows from this *AD*–AS model with flexible prices when under the influence of expansionary policies aggregate demand curve shifts to the right. *To what extent it will affect the national output and the price level depends on the elasticity of aggregate supply curve.* Keynesian economists *i.e.* followers of Keynes are of the view that the aggregate supply curve is relatively elastic (*i.e.* flat), especially in times of recession, and therefore most of the response to expansion in aggregate demand will be the increase in output rather than rise in the price level as is shown in Figure 10.24. On the other hand, moneterists think that the supply curve is *steep as is shown* in Fig. 10.25 and in this case the expansionary fiscal and monetary policies causing outward shift in *AD* curve will bring about rise in price more than the increase in output. In the extreme case of *perfectly elastic aggregate supply curve* which Keynes assumed in his analysis of depression increase in aggregate demand will not affect the price level and its full effect will be to raise the level of GDP.

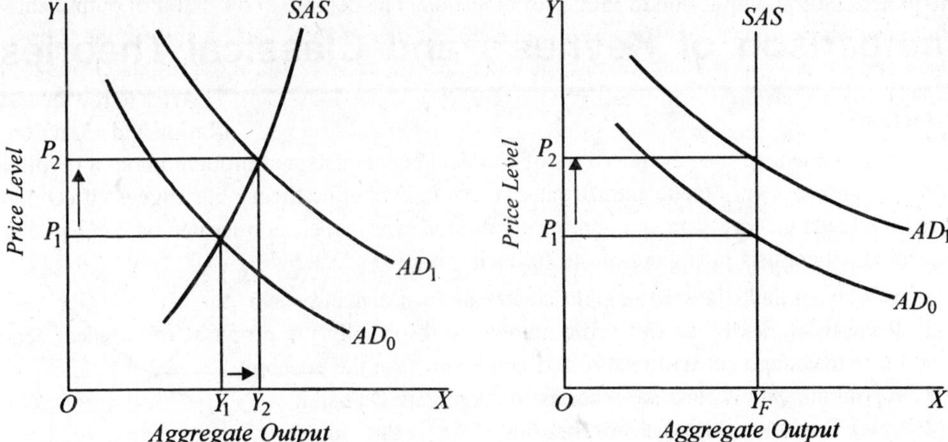

Fig. 10.25. *Moneterist Short-run View :* *When aggregate supply curve is steep, expansionary fiscal and monetary policies cause price level to increase more as compared to increase in aggregate output*

Fig. 10.26.*Classical View :* *With full-employment of resources aggregate supply curve is vertical straight line and an increase in aggregate demand will cause price level to rise without change in aggregate output*

Lastly, when the economy is operating at the level of capacity output (*i.e.* full complement level) as the classical economists assumed, increase in aggregate demand in this case will lead only to higher price level or inflation in the economy without affecting aggregate output (national income). The view of classical economists is illustrated in Figure 10.26 where aggregate supply curve *AS* is a vertical straight linc at thc full-employment level of output OY_F. It will be seen from this figure that when as a result of expansionary fiscal and monetary policies aggregate demand curve shifts outward to the right from AD_0 to AD_1, price level rises from P_1 to P_2 whereas aggregate output remains constant at OY_F level.

QUESTIONS FOR REVIEW

1. Briefly explain AS–AD model of determination of national product. With this model explain the impact of (1) increase in aggregate demand and (2) decrease in aggregate supply on price level and aggregate output.
2. Derive the aggregate demand curve (with varying price level). Why does it slope downward? Show the effect of an increase in nominal money stock on aggregate demand curve.
3. Compare the Keynesian and Classical aggregate supply curve. Briefly explain their policy implications.
4. With AS–AD model explain the multiplier effect of increase in Government expenditure on private investment when (1) price level remains constant and (2) when price level rises.
5. What is stagflation? Explain with AS–AD model what can cause stagflation.
6. Distinguish between short-run aggregate supply and long-run aggregate supply. What are the factors that cause shift in them?
7. Derive a short-run aggregate supply curve when nominal wages are stricky. Give reasons for the stickiness of nominal wages.
8. With AS–AD model explain economic fluctuations in the economy. Explain the impact of increase and decrease in aggregate demand on GDP and price level in the economy.
9. What is natural rate hypothesis ? Explain it with AS-AD model with flexible prices.

APPENDIX TO CHAPTER 10

Comparison of Keynes's and Classical Theories

Introduction

Keynes challenged the several views of classical economists and brought about a revolution in economics. He not only made significant changes in economic theory but suggested economic policies to overcome depression and control inflation. Keynesian economics can be compared with the classified economists in respect of the following issues

1. Validity of Say's law that supply creates its own demand.
2. Wage-price flexibility and full employment, especially the proposal of classical economists that wage cut will restore full employment in the economy.
3. Keynesian versus classical theories of Aggregate Demand.
4. The Classical and Keynesian Theories of Aggregate Supply.
5. Saving-Investment Relationship : Are Savings Automatically Invested?
6. Classical Dichotomy and Role of Money
7. Explanation of Depression
8. Explanation of Inflation
9. Determination of rate of Interest

As regards the first issue of Say's law the detailed comparison has been made between the views of classical economists and Keynes in Chapter 3. The second issue of wage-price flexibility and full employment has been discussed in chapters 3 and 11. The ninth issue of Keynesian and Classical theories of determination of interest rate is the subject matter of chapter 18. The Keynesian challenge to the classical views in regard to the other six issues listed above are explained below.

Keynesian Versus Classical Theories of Aggregate Demand

A key difference between Keynes and the classics relates to the theory of aggregate demand. The classical theory does not have an explicit theory of aggregate demand. The quantity theory of money of classical economics provides an implicit classical theory of aggregate demand. According to the quantity theory of money :

$$MV = PY$$

or $$P = \frac{MV}{Y}$$

where M is the quantity of money, V is the income velocity of circulation, Y is the level of national product and P is the price level.

Velocity of circulation (V) is assumed to be constant. Therefore, given the value of V, the amount of output purchased, that is, PY is determined by the given amount of money (M). From this it follows that the amount of real national output (Y) which can be purchased depends on (1) the given

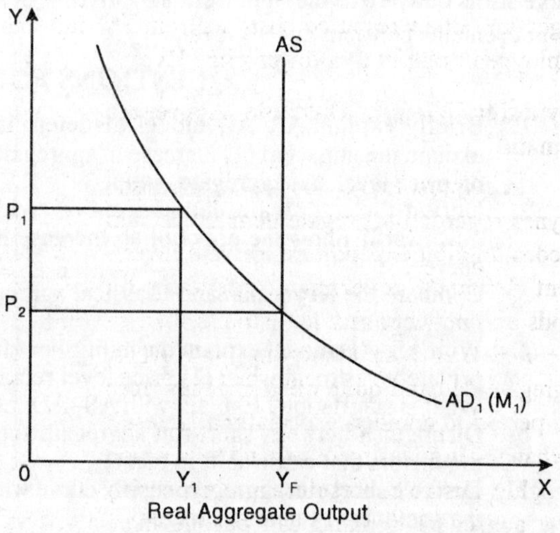

Fig. 10A.1. *The Classical View of Aggregate Demand*

quantity of money (M) in circulation and (2) the purchasing power of money as determined by the price level. Aggregate demand curve as visualised by the classical theory is drawn in Figure 10A.1 where aggregate demand curve AD_1 is drawn, given the quantity of money equal to M_1. With a higher price level, say P_1, the given quantity of money will be capable of purchasing the smaller amount of real output Y_1. With the fall in price level to P_2 (which means each rupee can now buy greater quantity of goods), more can be purchased, say Y_F, with the given quantity of money. Thus given a fixed supply of money, the price level and real national output are inversely related. Since money supply is given we move downward along the aggregate demand curve, the percentage fall in price level is matched by same the percentage increase in real national output. This implies that the classical aggregate demand curve is a rectangular hyperbola. It will be observed from Fig 10A.1 that only at price level P_2 full-employment output Y_F will be demanded.

It is worth noting that, given the money supply, classical aggregate demand curve is reasonably stable as, according to classical economists, the other variable determining the effective supply of money, namely, velocity of circulation (V) is likely to remain constant. It is increase in the money supply that will shift the aggregate demand curve to the right. This is of crucial importance as, according to classical economists, given the aggregate supply, increase in money supply will shift the aggregate demand curve to the right and cause demand-pull inflation. Therefore, the classical economists stressed that to achieve price stability or control inflation, the government or central bank must control the supply of money to prevent inflation. It may be interesting to note that modern monetarists hold the view similar to that of as classical economists regarding money supply as the crucial factor determining aggregate demand and the price level. Friedman, the pioneer of modern monetarists write, "inflation is always and everywhere a monetary phenomenon". Prof. McConnel rightly writes, "*present-day monetarists has its intellectual roots in classical economics. One reason is that both classical economists and modern monetarists focus upon the money supply as the basic determinant of aggregate demand and the price level*".[1]

It may be noted that if decrease in money supply will cause a leftward or downward shift in the aggregate demand curve resulting in fall in the price level. However, as explained earlier, the decrease in aggregate demand, according to classical economists, will not cause unemployment, though its immediate effect will be the excess supply of output of goods and services. This is because the classical economists asserted that as a result of this excess supply of output prices, wages and other resource costs will quickly fall and the new equilibrium will be reached at full employment output at a lower price level.

Keynesian View : Unstable Aggregate Demand

In contrast to the classical economists, Keynes regarded aggregate demand as sum of consumption expenditure, private investment demand, government spending on goods and services and net exports. ($AD = C + I + G + NX$). According to Keynes, aggregate demand quite often changes from one period to another, especially as a result of changes in investment expenditure which is highly unstable. Besides, in Keypnesian view aggregate demand can change even when money supply remains unchanged. And it is the fluctuations in aggregate demand that

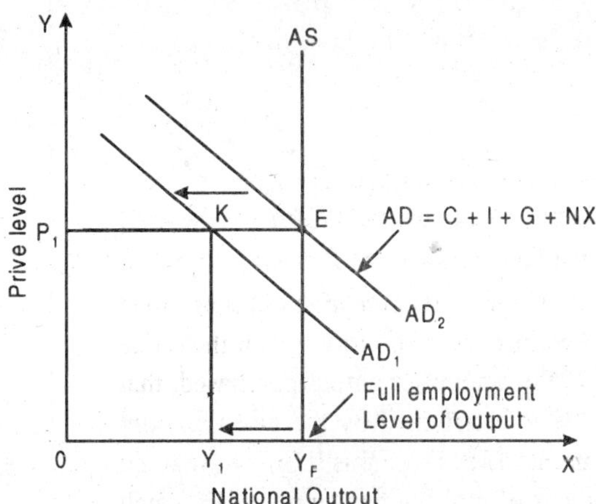

Fig. 10A.2. *Keynes's View of Aggregate Demand*

1.Campbell R. McConnel and Stanley Brue, *Economics*, 11th edition, McGraw-Hill 1990, p.210.

cause business cycles in a free market economy. It was decline in investment demand due to the collapse of marginal efficiency of capital that according to Keynes resulted in the great depression of 1930s. Consider Figure 10A-2 where if with the decline in investment demand aggregate demand curve shifts to the left from AD_2 to AD_1, the new equilibrium is achieved at point K where real national output has fallen below the full employment level to Y_1 with price level remaining unchanged. As a result, unemployment of labour will emerge. Keynes believed that unless the government intervenes through fiscal and monetary policy measures to raise aggregate demand the economy will permanently stay at less than full-employment equilibrium at Y_1. Keynes explained that money wages are rigid, that is, inflexible downward and will therefore not adjust to bring back the full-employment equilibrium.

In contrast to the Keynesian view, the classical economists thought aggregate demand was stable as long as there was no significant changes in the money supply. According to them, even if aggregate demand did decrease, prices, wages and other resource costs would automatically adjust to bring the economy back into full-employment equilibrium.

The Classical and Keynesian Theories of Aggregate Supply

A key difference between the classical and Keynesian theories relates to the nature of aggregate supply curve. The classical aggregate supply curve is a vertical straight line at the level of full employment or potential GDP as shown by AS in Figure 10A.3. According to the classical economists, the economy operates at the full-employment level because of Say's law, and flexibility of wages, prices and rate of interest. Whenever there is excess supply of labour, wage rate quickly adjusts to equate demand for and supply of labour so that at wage rate so determined all who are willing to work at the equilibrium wage rate are in fact employed. Since classical aggregate supply curve is vertical, *output and employment in this theory is completely supply-determined and the level of aggregate demand does not play any role in determining national output and employment.*

A significant feature of the classical aggregate supply curve is that national output does not change in response to changes in aggregate demand or the price level. It will be observed from Fig. 10A.3. that when price level falls from P_1 to P_2 in response to the decrease in aggregate demand from AD_1 to AD_2, real national product remains unchanged at Y_F. This appears to be contrary to the general perception that fall in price level causes the quantity supplied of goods to fall. This is because the lower prices make production of goods less profitable and would therefore cause producers to offer less output and generally employ fewer workers. However, according to classical economists, this does not happen because *along with fall in prices of goods, money wages, and profits and other input costs also fall in the same proportion so that real wages and profits remain unchanged* and therefore levels of national product and employment remain at the full-employment level.

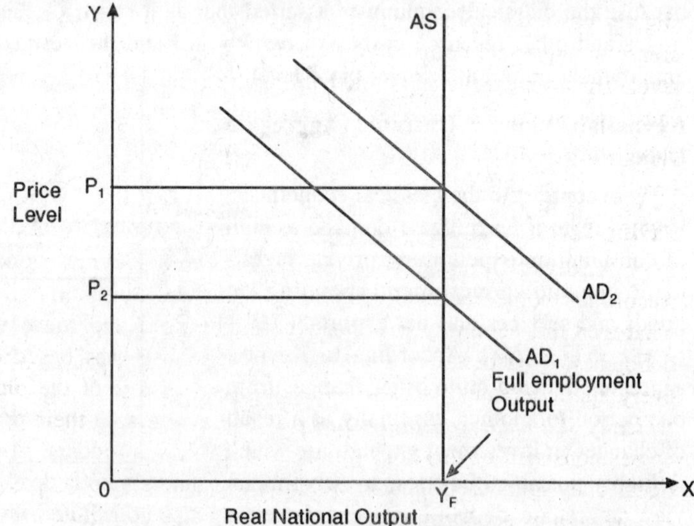

Fig. 10A.3. *Classical Aggregate Supply Curve and Price-Output Determination*

Keynesian View. In sharp contrast to the classical view, according to Keynes, short-run aggregate supply curve is a horizontal straight line (*i.e.* flat) at levels of output below full-employment and becomes vertical at the level of full-employment or potential GDP as shown in Figure 10A.4.

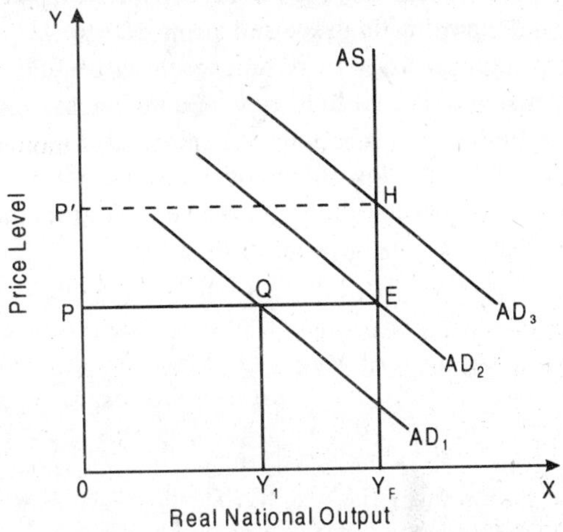

Fig. 10A.4. *Keynes's Aggregate Supply Curve: Effect of Increase in Aggregate Demand on Output and Price Level*

The Keynesian view of aggregate supply lays stress on the stickiness of money wages and failure on the part of workers to perceive the change in real wage correctly due to suffering from *money illusion*. As a result, labour market will not always be in equilibrium at full employment. Keynes emphasised that actual level of output and employment is not completely determined by supple-side factors that determine only full-employment or potential GDP. The followers of Keynes, who are called Keynesians, mainly agreed with the Keynes's view but point out that in the short run, especially when the economy approaches close to full employment level, aggregate supply curve is gently upward-sloping due to slight rise in wages and other input costs and becomes vertical at full-employment level. Therefore, some Keynesians divide aggregate supply curve into three ranges. (1) The *Keynesian range* when aggregate supply curve is quite flat, (2) the *intermediate range* when the aggregate supply curve is gently sloping upward, and (3) the classical range when the aggregate supply curve becomes a vertical straight line.

However, an important thing to note is that in *Keynesian view the level of aggregate demand is an important factor determining the level of output and employment, if the economy is working at less than full employment level*. Shift in the aggregate demand curve to the right as shown in Figure 10A.4) in the horizontal portion will increase the level of national income and employment without bringing about rise in the price level. Further, in the intermediate range, that is, in the slightly upward-sloping part of short run aggregate supply curve (not shown in Fig. 10A.4), increase in aggregate demand will cause large increase in national output with a small rise in price level. However, at the full-employment or potential GDP level, increase in aggregate demand will cause rise in price level with national output remaining unchanged. Thus when aggregate demand curve shifts from AD_2 to AD_3, price level rises from P to P' national output remains constant at Y_F level.

Saving-Investment Relation : Are Savings automatically Invested ?

A key difference between classics and Keynes related to savings and investment. According to the classical economists there was always a full-employment equilibrium because whatever the economy produced could be sold and there was no any problem of demand deficiency. This belief of the classical economists was based on Say's law according to which every supply creates its own demand. This was true of the old economy where producers were *typically self-employed individual producers* who sold their products in the market and their incomes consisted of the sales proceeds from these products. Financial markets had not yet developed. They spent their income either on consumers' goods or for buying tools, machines, buildings etc. In such as economy every act of saving also constituted the act of investment. As a matter of fact, saving in such an economy was investment, not a distinct separate process. Thus the classical economists argued that income generated by a fully-employed labour force must be either saved and invested or spent on consumption. More precisely, all saving (*i.e.* the part that is not spent on consumption) must be automatically invested. With the structural changes in the economy, the production was carried out in corporate firms who used hired factors such a labour for use in the production process and further financial markets developed from which they could borrow money and also could keep their savings with them.

According to classical economists, even then saving were automatically invested. They argued that there were certain forces at work in the economy that ensured that at full-employment level of income, all savings would be invested and therefore it was not possible for the emergence of deficiency of aggregate demand resulting in depression. The occasional bouts of unemployment associated with downswing of the business cycles was dismissed as 'temporary disturbance' which would be rectified through automatic adjustment. In the new free-market economy that emerged, the managers of business firms decided how much they should invest, and the rich and middle class, households (even working classes) decided how much they should save.

Though the close link of earlier days between saving and investment were broken, the classical economists still believed that the changes in interest rate provided a mechanism which ensured equality of saving and investment. For example, suppose that for some reason households decide to save a higher proportion of their income than the businessmen plan to invest, will this not mean that some savings by households will not be invested? In the event of failure of some saving to find an outlet in investment, will it not lead to insufficient demand causing a fall in national output and employment? No, said the classical economists. This is because, according to them, whenever saving exceeded investment, the supply of loanable funds will exceed the demand for loanable funds and as a result rate of interest will fall. The fall in rate of interest will induce businessmen to undertake more investment. Besides, the fall in interest rate will discourage saving because return on saving will now be lower. The rate of interest will continue to fall until saving and investment are brought back into equilibrium. Thus, according to classics, adjustment in rate of interest is a mechanism which will automatically ensure that whatever be the savings at the full employment level of national output, these savings will be invested. There may be temporary departure from this equality but changes in rate of interest will automatically bring them back into balance.

Keynes's View. Keynes' made a basic departure from the classical view of saving and investment and explained that the classical theory was quite invalid because it failed to take account of the changes in income that come about from any change in saving or investment. Besides, the classics failed to realise that what people intend to save and what they actually save are in certain circumstances quite different. Let us illustrate the Keynes's analysis with two examples. Consider

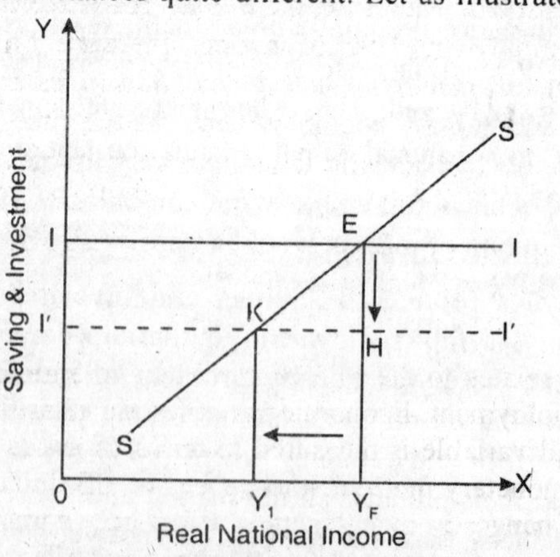

Figure 10A.5. *Saving-Investment Relation*

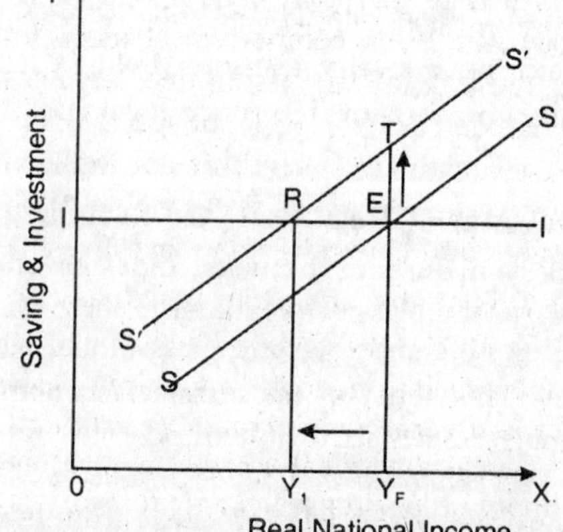

Figure 10A.6. *Saving Investment Relation*

Figure 10A.5. where macroeconomic equilibrium is shown through saving and investment functions. In Figure 10A.5. intended saving and investment are in equilibrium at full employment level of income Y_F where saving function curve *SS* intersects intended investment. Curve *II*.

Now suppose that due to fall in expected rate of profit (*i.e.* marginal efficiency of capital) investment falls and the new investment curve is II' (dotted). Thus investment falls short of saving at full-employment income Y_F by *EH*. The classical economists argued that the excess of saving over investment would cause interest rate to fall and at lower rate of interest more investment would take place to bring back the equality between the two. Keynes challenged this classical view by pointing out that this ignored the effect of decline in investment on level of national income. According to him, the fall in investment would lead to the decline in level of income. The decline in income will be much more than the decline in investment due to the multiplier effect. It will be seen from Fig. 10A.5. that new equilibrium between saving and investment is established at point *K*, that is, at the lower level of national income Y_1 which is less than full-employment level of income Y_F.

Now consider Figure 10A.6. Here also intended saving and investment functions are in equilibrium at Y_F level of real national income which is a full employment level. Now suppose that at Y_F level of income households decide to save *ET* more and therefore saving functions shifts above to $S'S'$. As a result, saving exceeds investment which remains equal to *OI or* EY_F. Classical economists believed that increase in saving will lower the rate of interest and at lower rate of interest more investment would be forthcoming so that saving and investment would once again become equal. But Keynes rightly pointed out that the classical economists ignored the fact that increase in saving implied decline in consumption demand. Decline in consumption expenditure would also lead to the multiple decrease in income through the working of multiplier. It will be seen from Figure 10A.6. that as a result of upward shift in the saving curve from *SS* to $S'S'$ (dotted) the saving and investment function are again in equilibrium at point *R* but at a less than full-employment level of national income Y_1. Thus the classical view that saving and investment are always equal at full-employment level of income is not valid.

It follows from above that investment does not become automatically equal to saving at full employment level of income or, in other words, saving at full employment level of national income is not automatically invested. So quite often investment is not sufficient to fill the saving gap at full employment level of income. As Keynes rightly pointed out, saving or consumption is mainly a function of income and as income increases, consumption increases but less than the increase in income (*i.e. MPC* is less one). Besides, saving function which is determined by various subjective and objective factors is stable in the short run. On the other hand, investment is volatile in the short run as it is determined by profit expectations of businessmen. Therefore, there is no guarantee that investment will be inevitably equal to saving at full-employment level of income. Investment and saving may well be in equilibrium at much less than full-employment level of national income reflecting the state of depression and large-scale involuntionary unemployment. At the time of great depression (1929 – 1933) though the rate of interest had actually fallen to a very low level, even then adequate investment was not forthcoming to achieve full-employment equilibrium. This shows how wrong was the classical view that changes in rate of interest would automatically bring about equilibrium between saving and investment at full employment level.

Classical Dichotomy and Role of Money

A key difference between classics and Keynes relates to the role of money in determining real variables such as national output, real wages, employment. Economic variables are classified into either *real variables* or *nominal variables.* A real variable is measured in terms of goods or services whereas a nominal variable is measured in monetary units such as rupees or US dollars. The important proposition of classical theory is that changes in money supply affect only nominal variables, such as price level, money wages, nominal rate of interest and do not have any effect on the real variables such as national output, real wages and employment. These real variables, according to the classical theory, depend on such factors as labour supply (which is governed by work-leisure preferences), factor endowments such as capital stock, technology etc. and further that money plays no role in determining output, employment and real wagers. This is known as *Classi-*

cal dichotomy according to which while money determines nominal variables such as price level, money wages nominal interest rate etc. it is neutral in the determination of real variables such as output, real wages and employment. On the other hand, in Keynes's theory money supply determines rate of interest which influences investment which, in turn, plays an important role in determining output and employment in the economy. Let us first graphically illustrate classical dichotomy. This has been done in Figure 10A.7. where in panel (*a*) determination of price level through classical vertical aggregate supply curve *AS* and downwards-sloping aggregate demand curve *AD* is shown. With money supply equal to M_0, aggregate demand curve is AD_0 which intersects aggregate

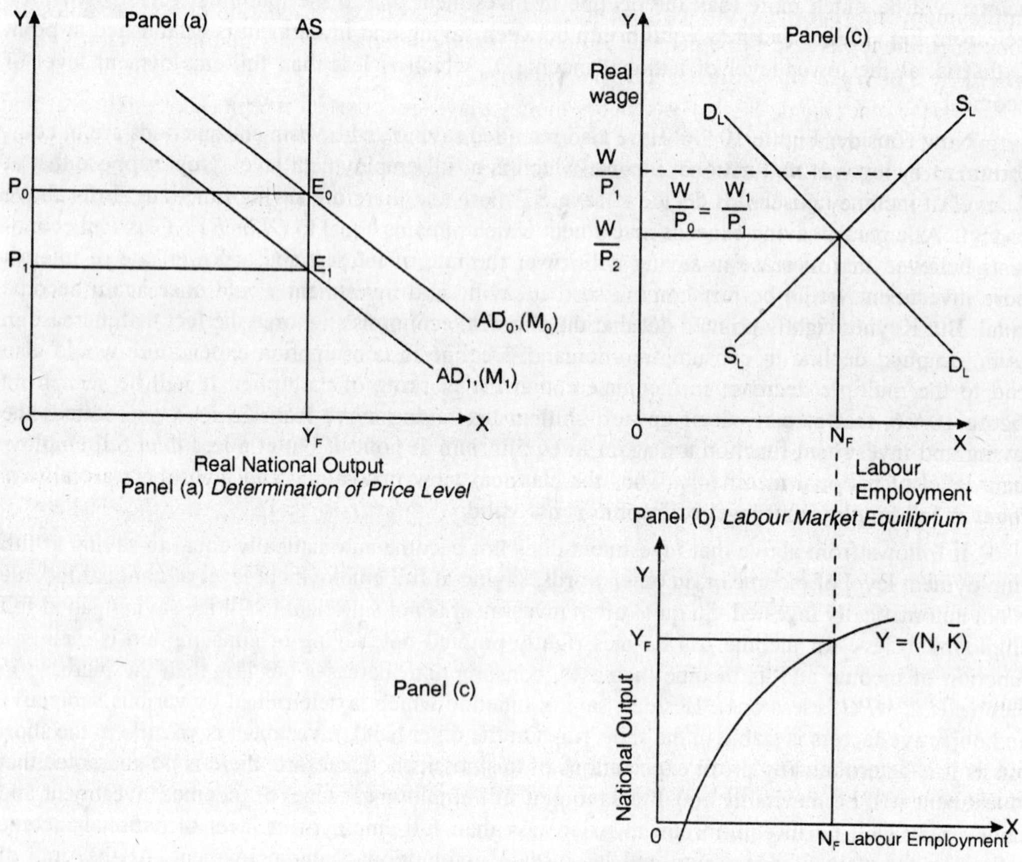

Fig. 10A.7. *Classical Dichotomy*

supply curve *AS* at point E_0 and determine price level P_0. Panel (*b*) of Fig 10.A.7. shows labour market equilibrium which determines real wage rate equal to $\frac{W}{P_0}$ and labour employment equal to ON_F. From panel (*C*) it will be observed that with ON_F amount of labour employed, full-employment level of output Y_F is determined.

Now suppose that money supply is reduced to M_1 resulting in the fall in aggregate demand curve to AD_1 which causes price level to fall to P_1 while *real national output remains unchanged at* Y_F. Now, with the money wage equal to *W*, the fall in price level will bring about rise in real wage rate to $\frac{W}{P_1}$. But, with this higher real wage rate labour market will be thrown into disequilibrium with emergence of excess supply of labour (see panel (*b*) of Fig. 10A.7.). According to classical theory, to restore labour-market equilibrium money wage rate quickly falls to W_1 so that real wage returns to the original level $\frac{W}{P_0}$ $\left(\text{Note that } \frac{W_1}{P_1} = \frac{W}{P_0}\right)$.

Besides, in labour market equilibrium, labour employment remains at full employment level ON_F. In panel (*c*), with ON_F amount of labour employed, national output remains at Y_F though the quantity of money has been reduced from M_0 to M_1.

It follows from above that with the decrease in money supply, though nominal variables such as price level, money wage rates have fallen, the real variables such as real national output, labour employment and real wage rate remain unchanged. Thus, so far determination of real variables are concerned money is said to be neutral. Supply of money determines only nominal variables.

Keynes's Theory : Money affects real variables

On the other hand, in Keynes's theory money plays an important role in determination of real output and employment. In fact, *Keynes brought about integration of money market and real goods market.* Keynes was able to do so because he showed that rate of interest was determined by demand for money (to which he gave the name liquidity preference) and supply of money. For example, increase in the supply of money will lower the rate of interest. Since investment depends on the rate of interest and marginal efficiency of capital, at the lower rate of interest more investment will be undertaken. The higher investment will lead to the greater level of real national income and employment through the operation of investment multiplier. In this way, Keynes showed that changes in money supply working through changes in rate of interest exercise important influence on the levels of real national income and employment. In fact Keynesian analysis brings out that monetary policy can play significant role in influencing the real variables and controlling business cycles. However, Keynes pointed out that *effect of increase in money supply depends on interest elasticity of demand for money (i.e. liquidity preference curve) and interest sensitivity of investment demand.* The greater the elasticity of demand for money, and the lower the elasticity of investment demand curve, the smaller will be the effect of changes in money supply on national income and employment. Though during the period of great depression (1929 – 33), Keynes pointed out that demand for money was highly elastic and therefore he argued that effect of monetary policy would not be enough to lift the economy out of depression and therefore he emphasised that expansionary fiscal policy should be adopted to raise aggregate demand and thereby real income and employment.

However, empirical evidence after Keynes has revealed that demand for money is not absolutely elastic and also investment demand is quite elastic. Therefore, the modern Keynesian economists emphasise the roles of both monetary and fiscal policy to achieve economic stability.

How Keynes integrates money market and real goods market is illustrated in Figure 10A.8. where where in panel (a) money market equilibrium is shown. Given money supply equal to M_1, money supply curve MS_1 intersects money demand curve M^d at rate of interest r_1. It will be seen from panel (*b*) that at rate of interest r_1, investment is I_1. Then in panel (*c*) with the consumption function curve C and investment equal to I_1, aggregate demand curve is $C + I_1$ which intersects the income line OZ at point E and determines level of real national income equal to Y_1.

Now suppose that there is increase in money supply from M_1 to M_2 which causes shifts in money supply curve from MS_1 to MS_2. As a result, rate of interest falls from r_1 to r_2, investment increases from I_1 to I_2. With this increase in investment (ΔI), aggregate demand curve shifts above to the position $C + I_2$. With this increase in aggregate demand, level of real national income increases from Y_1 to Y_2. Corresponding to this increase in real national income the level of labour employment will also rise.

It is evident from above that Keynes succeeded in integrating money market with goods market and with this he showed that money supply plays an important role in determining real variables such as real investment (*i.e.* addition to the stock of capital), real national output and employment.

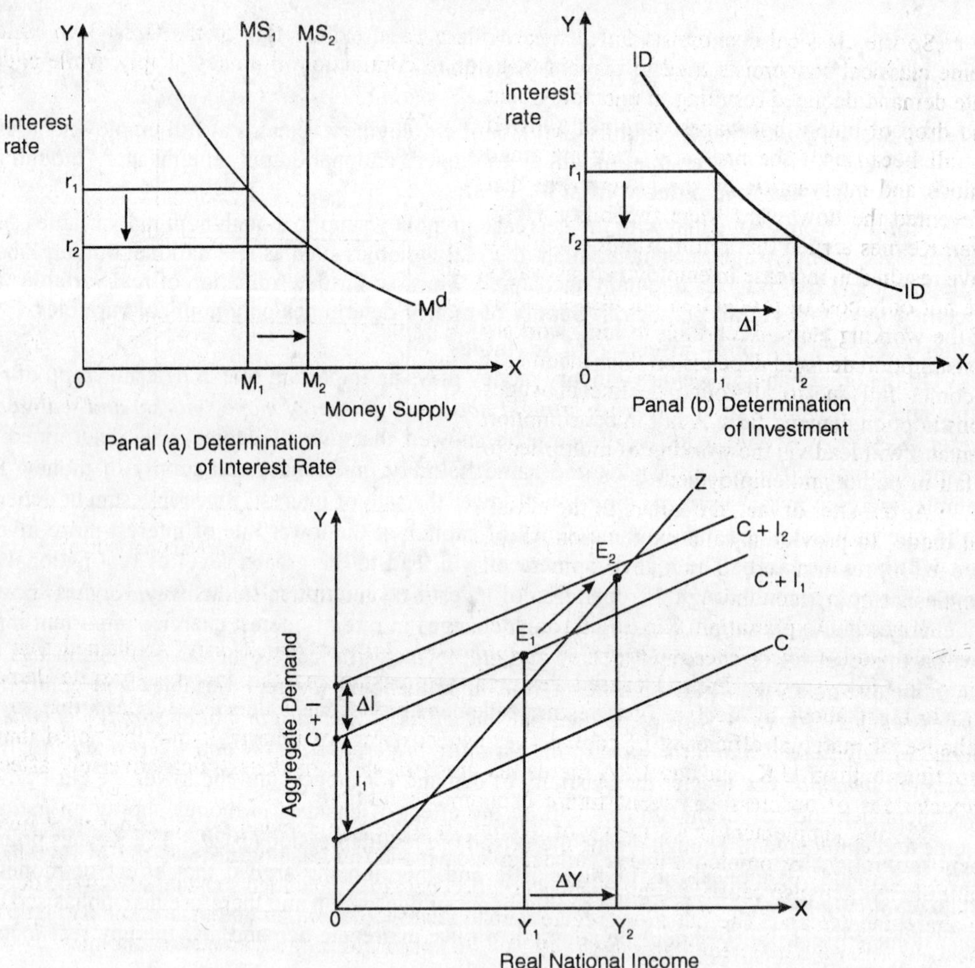

Fig. 10A. 8. *Keynesian Theory : Integration of Money Market with Commodity Market*

Explanation of Depression : Keynes Versus Classics

Perhaps the most important drawback of classical theory is its failure to explain the Great Depression (1929-33). During this depression, in the USA 20 per cent decline in output was recorded and price level too sharply fell. The rate of unemployment went up to 25 per cent of labour force. In the classical model, aggregate supply curve is vertical and the aggregate demand can fall and therefore aggregate demand curve will shift to the left only due to the contraction in money supply. In the fifties, Freidman supporting the classics pointed out that in fact there was a decline in money supply during the period 1928-32 which fell by 25 per cent to 33 per cent in the capitalist economies. This contraction in money supply, according to him, was responsible for Great Depression[1] . But, as will be seen from Figure 10A.9 the leftward shift in aggregate demand curve will lower the price level but would not cause a decline in real national output due to the vertical aggregate supply curve. Thus, whereas in the classical model, only price level falls and output remains constant, but actually during depression of 1029-33 both national output and price level fell, that is, prices were strongly procyclical[2] which is contrary to the classical model. In the classical model, aggregate supply of output (*i.e.* real national product or GDP) can decline if the real factors such as capital stock, technology, availability of labour force decline but that did not happen during the Great Depression.

2. See Friedman and Schwartz, "The *Great Depression*, 1965
3. Procyclical means prices fall when GDP falls and prices rise when GDP rises.

So the classical economists failed to provide a valid explanation of the Great Depression. Some classical economists tried to explain that due to contraction in money supply, while aggregate demand declined resulting in unemployment and drop of output but wages were not allowed to fall because of the pressure of strong trade unions and intervention by the government that prevented the downward wage flexibility. However, Keynes argued that fall in wages would not have resulted in increase in employment as wages are not only cost of production but also incomes of the working class. According to him, workers consumption demand depends on their income. If incomes fall due to all round decline in wages consumption demand falls. A fall in consumption demand will lead via the working of multiplier to a fall in output and employment.

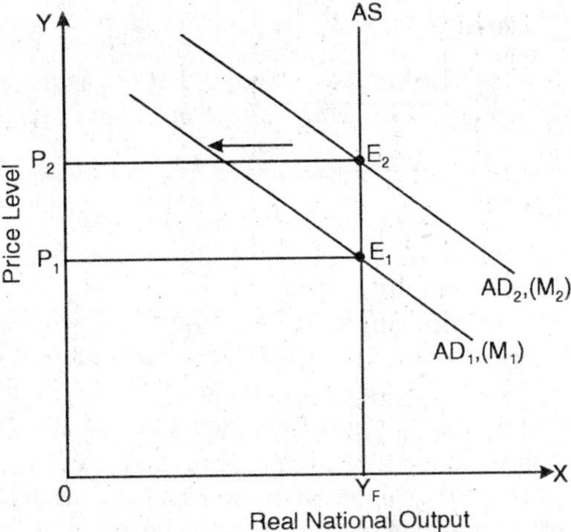

Figure 10A.9. *Classical View of Depression*

As a matter of fact, the failure of the classical model to provide a valid explanation of the Great Depression led to the development of Keynesian macroeconomics.

Keynes's Explanation. Keynes in his path-breaking work *"The General Theory of Employment, Interest and Money*" explained that the sharp fall in aggregate demand caused the great Depression and this fall in aggregate demand was brought about by decline in investment demand. Investment demand declined due to the collapse of marginal efficiency of capital (i.e. expected rate of return). It may be noted that at that time both in U.K. and the USA there was crash in stock markets which adversely affected expectations of businessmen about future economic conditions.

Keynes supplemented his theory of decline in aggregate demand by the concept of investment multiplier. He pointed out that fall in investment led to the reverse working of investment multiplier which also caused decline in consumption demand and added substantially to the decline in aggregate demand. The fall in aggregate demand caused decline in output, income and employment. In this way the Great Depression (1929 – 33) occurred in the capitalist economies.

Explanation of Inflation : Classics Vs Keynes

The Classical and Keynes's theories also differ in providing explanation of inflation. Inflation is a percentage rate of change of price level from one period to another. Therefore, the quantity theory of money with which the classical economists explained the determination of price level is also used to explain inflation. As explained above, the aggregate demand for good and services in the classical theory is determined by the quantity of money, velocity of circulation money (or, propensity to bold money in terms of Cambridge version of the quantity theory) remaining the same. Writing the Cambridge version of the quantity theory we have

$$M = kPY$$

or
$$P = \frac{M}{kY} \quad \text{... }(i)$$

where k is fraction of nominal national income (PY) which people want to hold in the form of money. In other words, k is propensity to hold money[4]. Assuming k and Y to remain constant, price level (P) is determined by the quantity of money (M).

Since inflation is percentage rate of change of price level from one period to another, it will be proper to express the above quantity theory *in growth terms*. With k remaining constant, the quantity theory (as given in equation (i) above) can be written in growth terms as follows:

$$\frac{\Delta P}{P} = \frac{\Delta M}{M} - \frac{\Delta Y}{Y} \quad \text{... }(ii)$$

4.Note that $k = \frac{1}{V}$, where V is velocity of circulation of money.

That is, rate of inflation $\left(\frac{\Delta P}{P}\right)$ depends on the growth of money supply $\left(\frac{\Delta M}{M}\right)$ *minus* the growth of aggregate supply of output or real national income $\left(\frac{\Delta Y}{Y}\right)$. As explained above, the classical economists explained that the aggregate supply of output equal to full-employment level of output is determined by labour-market equilibrium and remains constant. Therefore, in strict version of the quantity theory rate of inflation depends on the growth of money supply $\left(\frac{\Delta M}{M}\right)$.

Thus, the classical explanation is that inflation occurs due to rapid growth of money supply. The increase in the money supply causes aggregate demand to rise and, aggregate output remaining the same, results in inflation.

Keynes criticised the quantity theory of money and explained that increase in the quantity of money is just one of the possible causes of inflation. The empirical studies of relationship between money growth and inflation conducted in the US, UK and India shows that though there is relation between the two, growth in money supply does not fully explain inflation in these countries. This is because, as Keynes pointed out, propensity to hold money (k), that is velocity of circulation (V), and real national output do not remain constant. As Farmer writes, "*the connection between money growth and inflation is not particularly strong because real GDP growth and changes in propensity to hold money have been almost as important as the rate of money creation in determining the rate of inflation.*"[5] Of course, if propensity to hold money does not change to offset the increase in money supply or if growth in real GDP is very small, the large increases in money supply will result in high rate of inflation.

Thus, to quote Farmer again, "the connection between money growth and inflation is strong in countries with very high inflation because movements in the propensity to hold money and movements in real GDP are very small relative to huge movements in the stock of money."[6]

Keynes's View. Keynes viewed aggregate demand as a sum of consumption expenditure, investment expenditure, Government spending and net exports ($AD = C + I + G + NX$). Any component of aggregate demand can increase to trigger inflation. According to him, inflation occurs because aggregate demand exceeds aggregate supply of output at current price level. Thus Keynes's explanation of inflation is of demand-pull variety, with aggregate demand considered as stated above. Keynes argued that when during depression there was excess productive capacity and a lot of involuntary unemployment of labour and consequently aggregate supply curve was a horizontal straight line, increase in aggregate demand would not result in inflation. Of course, according to him, when the economy approaches full-employment, aggregate supply curve may be slightly upward sloping; there will be some inflation when aggregate demand increases. However, according to Keynes, true inflation occurs beyond the level of full-employment output, when aggregate supply curve cannot increase in response to the rise in aggregate demand.

As regards relationship between money growth and inflation, Keynes was of the view that increase in money supply affects aggregate demand through its effect on rate of interest. According to him, increase in money supply, money demand function remaining the same, lowers rate of interest. The lower interest rate will cause increase in investment expenditure which through the working of multiplier will raise aggregate demand. In the face of rising aggregate demand, what would be rate of inflation depends on the elasticity of aggregate supply curve. Keynes laid stress on the fact that *there was no any simple and direct relationship between money supply and inflation*. Much depends on the interest-elasticity of money demand function (*i.e.* liquidity preference curve), the sensitivity of investment demand to changes in rate of interest and elasticity of aggregate supply curve. For example, if money demand function is highly elastic, or sensitivity of investment to changes in interest rate is small and if aggregate supply curve is quite elastic, then according to Keynes, increase in money supply would not cause much inflation.

5. Roger E.A. Farmer, *Macroeconomics,* 2nd edition, Thomson, 2002, p. 130.
6. Ibid, p. 131-132.

CHAPTER 11

Unemployment, Full Employment and Wage-Price Flexibility

Introduction

In the last few chapters we have explained how the equilibrium level of income and employment is determined. When the economy is in equilibrium at less than full-employment level of output, unemployment comes into existence. There are several types of unemployment depending upon the different factors which cause it. Further, the nature and causes of unemployment in developing countries like India are different from those of developed countries. One of the frequent causes of labour unrest in moderns societies, both developed and developing, is unemployment among workers and the insecurity of employment. The specter of unemployment constantly haunts the working classes. Full employment has therefore become the goal of all countries. In what follows we will explain the various types of unemployment and their causes. We shall also explain the concept of full employment and what policies should be pursued to eliminate unemployment and achieve full employment.

Meaning of Unemployment. Technically speaking, *unemployment is defined as a state of affairs when in a country there are a large number of able-bodied persons of working age who are willing to work but cannot find work at the current wage levels.* People who are either unfit for work for physical or mental reasons, or don't want to work, *e.g., sadhus*, are excluded from the category of the unemployed.

Mere engagement in some productive occupation does not necessarily mean absence of unemployment. People, who are only partially employed or are engaged in inferior jobs, though they can do better jobs, are not adequately employed. It is called a state of *underemployment* which is equally bad for the prosperity of a country. Under capitalism, it seems some amount of unemployment is inevitable. The best that can be done is to keep the number of the unemployed as low as possible.

TYPES OF UNEMPLOYMENT

There are three main types of unemployment: (1) frictional unemployment, (2) structural unemployment; and (3) cyclical unemployment. In order to understand the concept of full employment the difference between these types of unemployment needs to be grasped.

Frictional Unemployment

There is always some minimum amount of unemployment that prevails in the economy among workers who have voluntarily quit their previous jobs and are searching for new better jobs or looking for employment for the first time. They are said to be *between jobs*. They are not able to get jobs immediately because of frictions such as lack of market information about availability of jobs and lack of perfect mobility on the part of workers. The distinguishing feature of frictionally unemployed persons is that the number of job vacancies equal to them are available in the economy. They remain unemployed for a relatively short period of time before they are able to get new jobs. This is because some time is required for job searchers to have information about the availability of jobs. When presently fractionally unemployed persons get jobs, the new frictionally unemployed persons come into existence and thus there is always some frictional unemployment prevailing in the economy due to imperfections or lack of market information about the availability of jobs. Since frictionally unemployed are those who have either quit their old jobs voluntarily and are looking for better jobs or those who have entered into the labour force *for the first time* and searching for jobs according to their acquired skills or those who had re-entered the labour force for some time, for example, after having children, the frictional unemployment is considered as voluntary unemployment.

Structural Unemployment

Structural unemployment is another type of unemployment which always exists to some extent in a growing economy. Structural unemployment refers to the mismatch between the unemployment persons and the demand for specific types of workers for employment occurs because whereas demand for one kind of labour is expanding, the demand for another kind of labour is declining either due to the changes in the structure (*i.e.*, composition) of demand for the industrial products or due to the changes in technology that take place in an economy. *The distinguishing feature of structural unemployment is that the unemployed workers lack skills required by the expanding industries.* Structural unemployment also occurs because of the mismatch between the location of job-vacancies of the expanding industries and the present location of the unemployed workers.

Let us give an example of structural unemployment. In a growing economy techniques of production are constantly changing with the result that people are likely to lose their jobs when these are replaced by newer and more efficient techniques. The unemployment created in this way is structural unemployment and is inevitable consequence of technological progress. These structurally unemployed persons will need to acquire new skills and training before they will be absorbed in the new technologically superior jobs. Take another example, when computerisation of banks, offices occurred in India recently some workers were rendered unemployed. But computerisation created new job opportunities. On being given training in computer operations some of them again got jobs. But for some time they remain unemployed. Further, due to changes in demand for some goods, the output of industries producing them declines rendering some people unemployed. On the other hand, those industries the demand for whose products are increasing, new jobs are created and unemployed workers are absorbed in them but before getting jobs in the expanding industries they remain unemployed.

Structural unemployment tends to last much longer than frictional unemployment because more time is required for people to get new training or acquire new skills or to move to new locations of expanding industries. Structural unemployment is more serious than frictional unemployment. This is because frictionally unemployed are likely to get jobs in a relatively short period of time as job vacancies exist for them. On the other hand, structurally unemployed have no immediate job prospects as they have to get training or acquire new skills required for the jobs available. The structurally unemployed persons can be expected to get only low paying unskilled types of jobs in the immediate future. Some accept such jobs while others prefer to remain unemployed and go on searching for better jobs which match their skills.

It may be noted that frictional and structural types of unemployment together constitute what is called **natural rate of unemployment** which may be of the order of 4 to 5 per cent of labour force in free-market economies. Thus, natural rate of unemployment arises due to labour market frictions and structural changes in a free market economy. Note that *when unemployment is equal to the natural rate of unemployment, full employment is said to exist.* In the late nineties, natural rate of unemployment was estimated to be 5.2 per cent of labour force in the United States. In 2003 actual unemployment rate rose to 6.2 percent in the United States. This higher than natural rate of unemployment was due to recessionary conditions prevailing in the American economy. Thus, *full employment is said to prevail despite the existence of natural rate of unemployment which is unavoidable in a changing economy.*

Cyclical Unemployment

This unemployment is due to deficiency of effective demand. It is also called cyclical '*Keynesian unemployment*'. Advanced capitalist countries have been suffering from time to time from this type of unemployment. This type of unemployment greatly increases during periods of recession or depression. Since recession or depression is one phase of the business cycles that generally occur in the industrialised developed economies this type of unemployment is called cyclical unemployment. This type of unemployment is due to the fact that the total effective demand of the community is not sufficient to absorb the entire production of goods that can be produced with the available stock of capital. In a private enterprise economy, production takes place in response to the profit motive. When businessmen cannot sell their entire output, their profit expectations are not fulfilled so that their reaction in the next period is to reduce their output. The factors of production earn their incomes because of their participation in the process of production and when entrepreneurs decide to reduce their production, some factors of production become unemployed. Since employment is the major source of income for a great majority of the people, a fall in employment signifies a fall in their incomes also.

The deficiency of aggregate demand as an explanation of involuntary unemployment in the industrially advanced countries is associated with the name of J.M. Keynes. Classical and Neo-classicial economists often denied the very existence of the problem. In the view of classical economists, symbolised in *Say's Law of Markets*, a freely competitive capitalist economy could never suffer from a deficiency of aggregate effective demand. The argument advanced by Say (a French economist) and accepted implicity by many others in support of this contention was that there could never be a problem of general over-production and that if there was any unemployment it was because of hindrances placed in the working of the freely competitive price system by artificial monopolistic action on the part of trade unions, employers or the government.

Now, it is true that supply does create a demand for goods and services because various factors of production earn their incomes in the process of production by helping to create additional supply of output. When factors of production are employed to produce a good they get their reward in the form of wages, rents, interest and profit. But from this it does not follow that the entire supply of national output will always be demanded by them. The incomes of the factors of production are necessarily equal to the value added in the productive process but it does not mean that the entire income will be automatically spent on goods and services created in a given time period. A part of income will be saved so that this part of income is not available to create demand for goods and services. Unless investors are willing to invest to an equivalent extent of intended savings, the total effective demand which consists of demand for consumers' goods and producers' good ($C + I$) will not be sufficient to absorb the entire available supply of output. And if it happens like this, producers will not be able to sell their entire output, their profits will fall and they will reduce their production and this will create unemployment.

In a given period, consumers are planning to spend a given part of their income and save the rest. Similarly, entrepreneurs are planning to invest in factories, machines, etc., to a given extent. The total effective demand is the sum of the consumption and the investment demand. Savers are saving for different reasons than the investors whose investment is determined by different factors and in a private enterprise economy there is no mechanism to ensure that what savers are planning to save is just equal to what investors are planning to invest. If there is any discrepancy between planned saving and investment, output, income and employment will change to correct this discrepancy. If planned investment is greater than planned saving, the current output will not be sufficient to meet the emerging demand and hence income, output and employment will increase and vice versa. Thus, we see that the basic weakness of Say's law arises because of lack of any agency to ensure that intended savings are just equal to intended investment and that since savings and investment are undertaken by different persons and for different reasons a discrepancy between the two is bound to arise and when it arises the necessary mechanism to correct it is through changes in the volume of employment and income.

Involuntary Unemployment and Labour Market Equilibrium

Let us explain through labour market equilibrium how Keynes explain the emergence of cyclical involuntary unemployment. As stated above, *involuntary unemployment refers to those workers who are seeking work or willing to work at the prevailing wage rate but are unable to get jobs.* According to Keynes, this involuntary unemployment happens to prevail in an economy on a large scale in times of depression due to fall in aggregate demand for goods and services. Classical economists thought that at times of recession wages and prices would fall to eliminate involuntary unemployment and ensure full employment. Keynes challenged this Classical viewpoint on two grounds. First, he pointed out that *money wages are rigid and fail to adjust even when there exists involuntary unemployment due* to lack of aggregate demand for output. Secondly, even if money wages are flexible downward or there is all-round cut in money wages, involuntary unemployment will not be removed. Consider Figure 1 where we have shown labour market equilibrium. *DD* is the demand curve of labour which is sloping downward to the light.

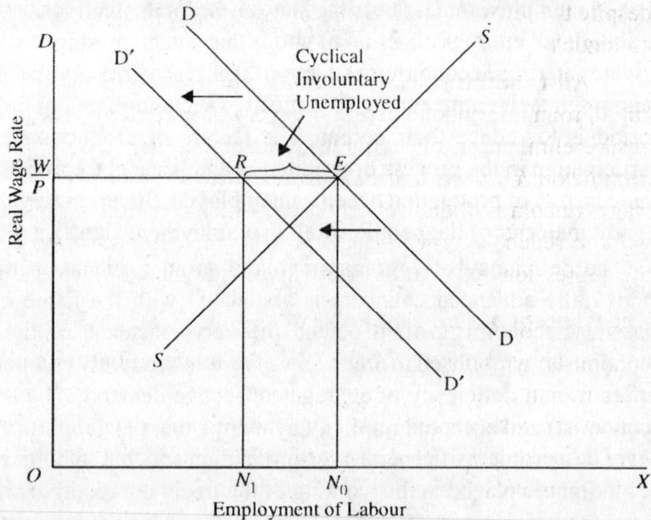

Fig. 11.1: *Labour Market Equilibrium and Involuntary Unemployment*

This shows that at lower wage rates more labour is demanded and employed and vice versa. *SS* is the supply curve of labour which is sloping upward to the right. This shows that at higher wages more labour is supplied and vice versa. These demand and supply curves of labour intersect at point *E* at which real wage rate $\frac{W}{P}$ and labour employment of ON_0 are determined. At the wage rate $\frac{W}{P}$, all those who are willing to work and supply their labour services are employed. Thus, at this labour market equilibrium, there is full employment of labour and involuntary unemployment does not prevail.

Now suppose aggregate demand for output of goods and services declines, as it happens in times of recession. *Demand for labour is a derived demand.* Decline in aggregate demand for output causes demand curve of labour to shift to the left to *D'D'*. Now, at the given real wage rate, $\frac{W}{P}$ the quantity ON_1 labour will be demanded, whereas supply of labour at this real wage rate remains ON_0. Thus, *RE* number of workers will be rendered unemployed who are willing to work at the prevailing wage rate but their services are not demanded by the economy.

According to classical economists, this involuntary unemployment cannot persist for long. The excess supply of labour and competition among unemployed workers will bring down the real wage rate and at lower real wage rate more labour will be demanded and employed. In this way, according to classical economists, due to downward adjustment in wages as well as prices of goods involuntary unemployment of labour will be eliminated and full employment will be restored.

Rigid Money Wages. However, Keynes contended that *money wages are rigid* and do not fall and as a result involuntary unemployment continue to prevail. There are a number of reasons for rigidity of money wages. First, workers strongly resist a reduction in money wages. Second, there is usually a wage contract between workers (or their trade unions) with the employers for a period of two to three years during which wage rates cannot be changed. Thirdly, there are minimum wages fixed by the government below which employers are not permitted to pay wages to the workers.

Lastly, employers themselves may not be interested in reducing wages, as lower wages are likely to reduce efficiency or productivity of labour. Thus, if in Figure 11.1, wages remained rigid at $\frac{W}{P}$ despite the leftward shift in the demand curve of labour to $D'D'$, involuntary unemployment would continue to exist.

All-round Cut in Wages and Employment. However, Keynes argued that even if wages are cut all round during the period of recession caused by lack of effective demand, even this will not ensure elimination of involuntary unemployment. This is because *wages are not only costs of production for firms and industries but are also incomes of workers.* In case of all-round cut in wages, incomes of the working class, which constitutes a majority in a society, will fall which will work to reduce aggregate demand for output. Reduction in aggregate demand will further deepen the depression and result in more involuntary unemployment rather than removing it.

The Concept of Full Employment

The above analysis of the types of unemployment requires us to make the concept of full employment clear. Full employment may be defined as the situation wherein all those who are willing and able to work at prevailing wage rates are in fact employed for the work in which they are trained. Two things must be noted in regard to this definition. First, full employment does not mean that every one is employed. Some people like children, old men and physically or mentally handicapped people are not able to work. There can be no question of their being employed. In fact these people are not included in the labour force of the country. Full employment will exist in spite of their not working. Secondly, some people called 'idle rich' though able to work are not willing to work because they get enough unearned incomes to live. These people are also not included in the labour force of the country.

From above it follows that *the unemployed people are those who are involuntarily idle. They are able and willing to work but the economy does not provide them jobs.*

Another important qualification to the above definition is worth noting. It is that, at any given time, there is bound to be some frictional and structural unemployment owing to labour-saving technological improvements or a change in consumer tastes for the product of some individual industries, some workers are in the process of voluntarily changing jobs. Some time may elapse before they get a new job after leaving the old one and, therefore, they remain temporally unemployed. Similarly, some amount of seasonal unemployment is also in evitable. Experience indicates that the total amount of frictional and structural unemployment may amount to 4 to 6 per cent of the labour force.

Thus, *full employment is said to exist in the economy even if there is prevailing some amount of frictional and structural unemployment in the economy.* If the number of unemployed is greater than frictional and structural unemployment, only then we shall say that full employment does not prevail.

Keynesian full employment is, by definition, the maximum level of employment that private enterprise countries can attain without experiencing strong inflationary pressure. But for purposes of practical policy it is necessary to reduce the concept to quantitative terms. It should be possible to say precisely when employment is less than full so that remedial action is called for. The concept, as defined above, raises two quantitative problems, namely, how to determine (1) the amount of employment sought by those who at the ruling wage-rates wish to be employed, and (2) the inevitable minimum amount of frictional and structural unemployment? The first, in turn, depends upon (a) the number of people able and willing to work for wages, and (b) the average number of hours of work which each of them wants to be employed. The number of wage-employment seekers depends upon the following: the size of the population of working age, the number who, having sufficient unearned incomes, choose to remain idle; the number who, being in command of the requisite means of production, are self-employed; and the prevailing wage-rates and other incentives provided. Normally, apart from the size of the population of working age, these factors are likely to be more or less stable over short-periods. For instance, the span of life regarded as falling within the working age, while subject to variation as a result of changes in the period of schooling or in the normal age for retirement consequent on changes in health standards and longevity, is likely to remain unchanged in the short period.

Again, since most workers have no large unearned incomes or accumulated savings, they are compelled to try to remain continuously in employment. They cannot, therefore, throw their labour power in the market or withhold it therefrom in some unpredictable manner. Accordingly, the number who choose to remain idle is unlikely to vary much in any short period. And so on. Moreover, even when some of these factors change somewhat, the net quantitative effect may not be important. *Higher wages, for instance, may induce some of the older workers to postpone their retirement while these may impel some of the married women workers, now that their husbands are better off, to relinquish their jobs. The net effect of a rise in a wages will not, therefore, be quantitatively important.*[1] *The same applies to other of factors.* The size of the population of working age too, though not invariant, is measurable as it changes according to definite trends. It follows that the number of wage-seeking population can be determined with a great measure of accuracy. And since the average number of hours of work which each wage-employment seeker wants to put in is likely to be more or less stable in any short period, the total amount of wage-employment sought is quite precisely measurable.

Similar observations may be made regarding the permissible allowance for structural and frictional unemployment. It varies from year to year, in accordance with the magnitude of the structural shifts in demand and production that together with immobility of labour and lack of adequate information about the availability and locations of new jobs cause structural and frictional unemployment. It may, therefore, be better defined as a range rather than as a precise figure. Since normally structural shifts in demand and production are unlikely to be violent or spasmodic and since in industrialised countries the incidence of frictional, unemployment is bound to be quite low, the allowance for frictional and structural unemployment needs to be very small. A US study has suggested that this allowance need not be beyond a range of 4 to 5.5 per cent of the available labour force.

The possibility of measuring the size of the available labour force and the inevitable minimum of frictional and structural unemployment makes full employment a determinate quantity. As suggested by a UN study, as a necessary step in the effective implementation of full-employment policies, each country should fix a full-employment target expressed in terms of the permissible range of frictional and structural unemployment. Unemployment in excess of the fixed target would indicate a lapse from full employment calling for a remedial action. The fixation of such a target would help to reduce the chances of government inaction and vacillation in the face of growing unemployment. It may also help to maintain confidence among businessmen whose pessimism ordinary plays a notable part in magnifying the downswing. There is, of course, the danger of the government acting on a false scent. For at times unemployment may exceed the level of frictional and structural unemployment due to causes other than insufficient demand. This danger may be minimized by allowing the government the discretion to disregard the signal if it has clear evidence that rise in unemployment is not due to the demand deficiency.

WAGE CUT AND EMPLOYMENT

The relationship between wages and employment has been a highly controversial issue between Keynes and classical economists. As seen earlier, classical economists believed that a cut in money wages would increase employment and help in removing unemployment. Keynes pointed out that workers would strongly resist any attempt to cut *money wages*, though they might be prepared to agree to cuts in *real wages* caused by rise in prices. Therefore, according to him, money wages remain rigid and any cut in money wages for the purpose of promoting employment was not a practical policy proposal. However, though wage cuts may not be practically possible, it is important to know whether it is a theoretically valid proposition that wage cuts or downward wage-flexibility will promote employment and help in removing unemployment.. In fact, Keynes made two-pronged attack on the classical view of cutting wages to remove unemployment. First, he challenged the classi-

1. Pigou, A.C., *Lapses from Full Employment,* 1945, p. 45.

cal view that wage cuts would promote employment at times of depression on grounds of practical feasibility. Second, he showed that even theoretically downward wage-price flexibility would not promote employment and attain full employment of labour. We discuss below both classical and Keynesian viewpoints about the relationship between wage-price flexibility and employment.

Wage Cut and Unemployment : Classical View

The analysis of wage reduction on employment is important because, according to classical economists, wage flexibility provides the economy with a self-adjusting mechanism that worked to restore full-employment equilibrium when there is recession and involuntary unemployment. Wage rigidity, according to them, was to blame for any prevailing unemployment. The classical view was simple; if there was an excess supply of labour (*i.e.* involuntary unemployment), wage rate must be too high and if unemployment was to be eliminated, wage rate must fall.

For analysing the effect of wage cuts on employment the classical economists applied partial or micro-economic analysis to the macro level. They argued that if wages fell, the prices of products made by labour would also fall. The price of products will fall because reduction in wages causes reduction in marginal costs of production. Since they used partial equilibrium analysis they assumed that the demand for the output of an industry would remain unaffected when cut in wages was made. They argued that with a fall in price of the product of the industry consequent to the cut in wages, the amount of product produced would increase and the new price - output equilibrium will be established at a lower price and larger quantity of the product. The expansion in output of the products will lead to the increase in employment of labour and other inputs. The extent of expansion in output (and therefore increase in employment) following the cut in wages and consequent fall in the price of the product depends on the elasticity of demand for output made by labour. On the basis of this partial equilibrium analysis of the impact of wage cut on price, output and employment in an industry the classical economists applied this result to the impact of *all-round* cut in wages on the increase in output and employment in the economy.

Keynes's Critique of the Classical View

Keynes challenged the classical viewpoint regarding the impact of all-round cut in money wage on output and employment of labour. According to him, while in case of the analysis of price and output determination of an individual industry, it is justified to assume that a cut in wages by the industry would not significantly affect the demand for the product of that industry because most of the demand for the product of that industry comes from the workers and persons employed in other industries. However, to assume that demand curve for output of *all industries* will remain unchanged when *cut in wages in all industries together* is made is not valid. In other words, to apply the result of partial equilibrium analysis of the determination of price, output and employment to the economy as a whole is quit misleading and invalid. This is because wages are not only costs from the viewpoint of individual industries, they also constitute incomes of the workers and these incomes determine the demand for the products of various industries. When all-round cut in wages is made in all industries, it will reduce the aggregate demand for the products because workers would have now less incomes and therefore would spend less on goods and services. With reduced demand for the products of industries smaller output will be produced. Therefore, smaller amount of labour will be demanded and employed. To quote Stonner and Hague, *"When there is general unemployment, a general cut in wages in all industries cannot be assumed to leave demand unchanged, for part of that demand results from spending out of wages. It is thus quite clear that a general cut in wages will merely cause a reduction and will not in itself remove unemployment".*[2] Thus, we see that classical economists neglected the adverse effect of all-around cut in wages on the level of aggregate demand. Instead, Keynes argued that unemployment had come into existence due to fall in aggregate demand.

2. Stonier and Hague, *A Textbook of Economic Theory*, Fourth Edition, 1977, p. 397.

The effect of all-around reduction in wages on aggregate output is illustrated through *AS-AD* in Fig. 11.2 where short-run aggregate curve supply curves SAS_0 and aggregate demand curve AD_0 intersect at point *E* and determine aggregate output Y_0 which is less than full employment level of output Y_F. Thus in macro equilibrium at point *E* there is recession in the economy and involuntary unemployment will prevail. According to classical viewpoint, cut in wages will cause a downward shift in aggregate supply curve, say to the new position SAS_1 with the result that new equilibrium is established at full-employment output Y_F. But, according to Keynes, all-round cut in wages will reduce incomes of the workers and therefore expenditure made by them which will cause a leftward shift in the aggregate demand curve *AD*, say to the new position AD_1. If the decrease in aggregate demand is proportional to the increase in aggregate supply, then equilibrium might be reached at the original output Y_0. Besides, if fall in the price level is in proportion to the cut in wages, the real wage rate will remain the same. Consequently, level of employment will remain below the full-employment level.

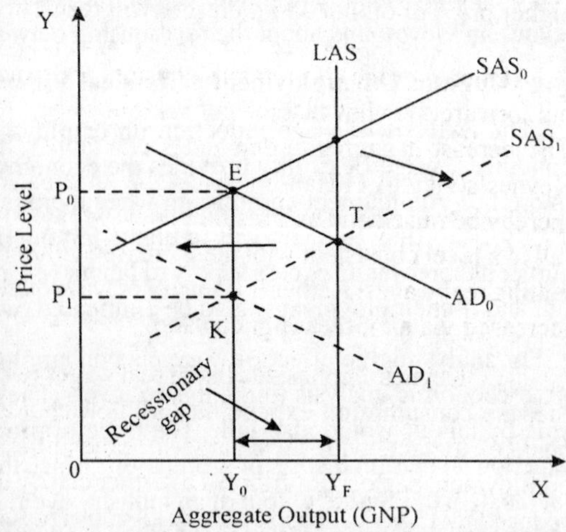

Fig. 11.2. *Impact of All-round cut in Wage on Aggregate Output and Employment*

It may be noted that the classical view was based on the two fundamental theoretical foundations, namely, (1) The Law of Diminishing Returns, and (2) The Theory of Marginal Productivity of Distribution. According to the law of diminishing returns, as more workers are employed, given a fixed amount of capital equipment and given the state of technology, the less would each additional worker produce and the marginal productivity theory say the average wages rate of the workers employed would be equal to the value of the product produced by the last worker employed. Taken both these principles together, the classical economists put forth the view that if more men are to employed, the average wage must be lower. Therefore, the classics said '*cut wages and employment will rise*'.

The interesting thing about Keynes's view is that he accepted both of the above classical premises. He agreed that as employment and output increase in the short run, marginal product per man will diminish. And he also agreed that it was true that the men employed will be paid the average wage equal to the value of the marginal product of the last man employed. How did then Keynes refute the conclusion of the classical economists that for increasing employment one must reduce real wages ? In fact, *Keynes turned the classical theory upside down.* He showed that we need not reduce real wages to get more employment, but we should raise employment to get a reduction in real wages.

This brings us to distinguish between money wages and real wages. Real wages represent the amount of goods a man can buy with his money wage, that is, real wages mean the purchasing power of the money wages. Real wages increase if a person buys more with his given money wages. If *W* stands for money wage and *P* stands for the price level, then $\frac{W}{P}$ measures the level of real wages. Keynes believed as did the classics that real wages and employment are inversely related. This follows from the principle of diminishing marginal productivity of labour. The classical economists argued that money wages (*W*) should be reduced to reduce real wages $\left(\frac{W}{P}\right)$. Keynes opposed the reduction of money wages as he thought it would reduce aggregate demand and therefore adversely affect employment. Instead, Keynes argued that, keeping *money wage* rate constant, one should increase the level of employment by raising aggregate demand. Given the downward-sloping marginal product curve of labour, the increase in employment of labour under increasing marginal cost conditions cause higher price of output and therefore will result in lower real wage rate $\left(\frac{W}{P}\right)$.

If money wage (W) remains constant and price level (P) rises, real wages will fall. Thus, Keynes put forward the view that the cut in money wage rate is not an effective way to increase employment. The increase in aggregate demand is a far more effective policy to raise employment. Thus, explaining Keynes's view A.H Hansen writes, "With substantially stable money wage rates employment could thereby be raised and as a result, real wage rate (under conditions of increasing marginal cost) would fall to a level consistent with the increased volume of employment. Thus employment is not raised by cutting real wages. Rather it is the other way round real wage rates fall because employment has been increased via an increase in demand."[3]

Keynes emphasized that if real wages remain unchanged then there can be no reason to expect that the consumption expenditure by households or investments expenditure by businessmen will change. In fact, with no change in expenditure or aggregate demand, no change in output and employment can occur further. To further clarify this point, consider that money wages of workers are reduced by 15 per cent and prices of all goods produced by them also fall by 15 per cent, then real wages $\left(\frac{W}{P}\right)$ will remain constant. As a result, output and employment will remain unaffected. Consider Figure 11.2 again where as a result of reduction in money wages, the short-run aggregate supply curve shifts from SAS_0 to SAS_1. But with the reduction of money incomes of workers, aggregate demand curve also shifts downward from AD_0 to AD_1. The shifts in aggregate supply curve and aggregate demand curve together cause a fall in the price level from P_0 to P_1. It is assumed that fall in price level is proportionately equal to the fall in money wages so that real wages remain constant. It will be seen from the Figure 11.2 that at the new equilibrium point K, the aggregate output (GNP) remains unchanged at Y_0, the previous recessionary level and hence the amount of unemployment remains the same.

Though the assumption in our above analysis that reduction in money wages will cause equal proportionate fall in the price level is not strictly true, but it clearly brings out a fundamental flaw in the classical theory that downward flexibility in money wages and prices will secure reduction in real wages and moves the economy back to full employment. The classical view ignores the effect of cut in money wages on aggregate demand for goods and services. In short, while on the basis of marginal productivity theory the classical theory indicated that a cut in real wages was needed to secure, increase of labour employment, in practice it was not possible to achieve it through cut in money wages as it would adversely affect aggregate demand.

However, it may be noted that a cut in money wages will not generally lead to proportionate reduction in prices. This is because wages account for only a part of the sale proceeds of goods produced the other elements in the sale proceeds such as incomes of profits, rent and interest would not fall, at least immediately. Therefore, a general reduction in money wages by 15 per cent might lead to 10 per cent fall in prices. Real wages would therefore fall only by 10 per cent. However, as explained below, Keynes stressed that the favourable effect on employment of the reduction in real wages would not be large enough to offset the adverse effect on employment of the fall in consumption demand of the workers whose money incomes have been reduced.

Wage Cut, Aggregate Demand and Employment

As illustrated in Figure 11.2 that wage-price flexibility when real wages remain unchanged does not guarantee the restoration of full-employment when the economy is in the grip of recession. Even when, as is likely the case, real wages fall to same extent as a result of cut in money wages, this would not lead to increase in employment because of the adverse effect of cut in money wages on aggregate

3. A.H. Hansen, *A Guide to Keynes,* McGraw-Hill, New York, 1953, p. 23.

demand. This is because consumption demand of workers who constitute majority in a society would fall as their incomes have been reduced. Consumption demand, it will be recalled, depends on income. Besides, a fall in consumption will lead via the working of the multiplier to a further fall in output and employment.

Keynes recognised that income of entrepreneurs, that is, profits, incomes of rentiers, that is, interest, dividends, rent may increase at least for some time following the reduction in money wages. But Keynes rightly thought that the higher consumption demand of the recipients of higher incomes in the form of profits, interest, rent, etc. would not be large enough to offset lower consumption demand of wage earners and that the net effect of the original cut in money wages would still be to depress output and employment.[4]

A General Equilibrium Analysis of the Effect of Wage Cut on Employment

It may however be noted that the impact of a wage cut on aggregate demand is more complicated than described above. As a matter of fact, as a result of all-round cut in wages the extent to which aggregate demand will decline depends on several factors such as its effect on propensity to consume, rate of interest, marginal efficiency of capital etc. But the classical analysis that there is a direct link between wage cuts and rising employment through reduction in cost of production is also not valid because it neglects the role of aggregate effective demand when all-round cut in money wages is made. Professors Stoner and Hague rightly write, "*A general equilibrium analysis of wage cuts is futile unless it pays attention to the problem of whether aggregate demand will rise or fall as wages are reduced.*"[5]

Whether employment will rise or fall when wages are cut depends on whether aggregate demand in terms of money will remain constant, will it fall less than in proposition to the cut in money wages or will it fall more than in proportion to cut in money wages. In Keynesain macroeconomic analysis, the impact of cut in money wages is explained through its effect on the three main determinants of aggregate demand, namely, (1) propensity to consume, (2) rate of interest and (3) marginal efficiency of capital.

We have seen above that classical economists' suggestion of cutting money wages can be rarely put into practice, although workers might accept cut in real wages through rise prices. We have in an earlier chapter the various reasons for money wage-rigidity or sticky wages which explains the persistence of involuntary unemployment despite the fact that labour market is in disequilibrium. However, Keynes opposed cut in money wages to promote employment during depression not only on practical grounds of rigidity of money wages but also on theoretical grounds. He argued that even if wages and prices were flexible downward, they were not likely to lead to the increase in employment in a free market economy.

However, Keynes argued that while in partial equilibrium analysis, it was theoretically right to take the demand for the product of an individual industry as given when cut in money wages is made by it, to extend this conclusion to the macro level or general equilibrium framework was not justified. Thus, according to Keynes, we need to analyse whether aggregate demand or aggregate monetary expenditure will rise or fall as wages are reduced all-round in the economy (that is, in all industries together). Keynes examined the effect of reduction in wages on employment by considering its effect on the following determinants of aggregate demand:

1. Propensity to consume
2. The rate of internest
3. The marginal efficiency of capital

After having examined the effect of cut in money wages on the above determinants of aggregate demand he reached the conclusion that when all things are considered, cut in money wages is likely to

4. See Michael Stewart, *Keynes and After,* Penguin Books, 1967, p. 134.
5. Stonier and Hague, *op. cit.* p.575

affect aggregate effective demand adversely and will therefore be unable to remove unemployment in the economy. In any case, according to him, *favourable effect of wage-price flexibility on aggregate demand and employment occurs through reduction in rate of interest which gives a boost to investment demand.* But reduction in rate of interest can be easily achieved through expansion in money supply in the economy and therefore for that purpose it is not a sound policy to adopt the policy of cutting money wages of workers. We examine below the effect of wage cuts on three determinants of aggregate demand.

Propensity to Consume. The effect of reduction in money wages is likely to reduce consumption demand by adversly affecting proensity to consume. All-round cut in money wages will reduce prices of products since wages are an important element of cost. The greater the ratio of wage costs to total production costs, the greater the fall in prices of products. The *reduction in money wages and fall in prices of products are likely to lead to the redistribution of real income from wage earners to those sections of the society whose money incomes have not been reduced.* Since propensity to consume of wage earners is higher than the non-wage earners who happen to be relatively richer sections of a society, this redistribution of income is likely to reduce propensity to consume causing a decline in aggregate consumption demand.

Another type of redistributive effect of falling prices is that redistribution of income from debtors to creditors occurs which also reduces consumption expenditure. The debit repayments are usually fixed in money terms so that fall in prices due to all-round reduction in wages which was not expected when debts were incurred causes an increase in the real value of mortgage and instalment payments by debtors to creditors which usually happen to be individual savers and banks. Even banks receive funds from individuals and companies who save and deposit their savings. This redistribution of income also reduces aggregate consumption demand, because creditors spend a relatively small part of the addition to their income due to fall in prices whereas debtors have to reduce their consumption greatly to meet their higher real interest payments caused by fall in prices.

It follows from above that cut in money wages will have an adverse effect on propensity to consume and will therefore reduce aggregate demand.

Marginal Efficiency of Capital. The effect of cut in money wages on marginal efficiency of capital is quite uncertain. This effect depends on what has been called *expectation effect*. If entrepreneurs expect that although money wages have been reduced in the present, they will rise again in the future, this will have a favourable effect on marginal efficiency of capital in the present. This is because higher money wages in the future will ensure better prospects of future demand for goods which will raise marginal efficiency of capital. Further, the fact that entrepreneurs expect money wages and therefore prices to rise in future, the people will prefer to buy goods in the present rather than in the future. This will improve prospects of making profits temporarily in the present and will therefore raise marginal efficiency of capital. However, this favourable effect of wage cut on marginal efficiency of capital is unlikely to be significant.

But the expectation effect of fall in wages and prices is likely to have more adverse affect on marginal efficiency of capital. If fall in wages and prices lead people to expect that they will fall even further in the future, it will reduce consumption demand. This will make entrepreneurs to become pessimistic about future economic prospects. As a result, marginal efficiency of capital will fall which will cause a reduction in investment demand.

It follows from above that the effect of a wage cut and fall in price on the marginal efficiency of capital is uncertain because much depends in expectations of entrepreneurs. However, cut in money wages is likely to reduce consumption demand which ultimately determines the future prospective yields from investment. It is believed by Keynesians that cut in wages and falling prices make future prospects of selling consumer goods less rosy and therefore adversely affect marginal efficiency of capital.

KEYNES'S EFFECT, PIGO EFFECT AND EMPLOYMENT

Rate of Interest : Keynes's Effect

The cut in money wages and consequent fall in prices is likely to reduce the rate of interest which will favourably affect investment demand. This is generally referred to as Keynes's effect as compared to Pigou effect which traces out the favourable effect of money wage cuts on consumption demand. According to Keynes, when cut in money wages is made and consequently prices fall, transactions demand for money will decline which will cause increase in the money supply for speculative motive. This increase in money supply for speculative motive will cause a reduction in the rate of interest. At a lower rate of interest, more investment will be forthcoming which will raise the level of aggregate demand and employment. It is important to notice here that in Keynesian analysis the hope of stimulus to investment following the cut in money wages and resultant fall in prices lies in the *lowering of rate of interest.* However, Keynes asserted that rate of interest can be easily lowered through expansion in money supply. Therefore, according to Keynes, theoretically "*We can produce the same effect on the rate of interest by increasing the quantity of money while keeping the level of wages unchanged*".[6] Further, according to him, expansionary monetary policy to reduce rate of interest is preferable to the policy of reducing money wages since the latter will not only be strongly resisted by workers but also an all-round wage cut will reduce consumption demand for goods and will therefore adversely affect employment. Keynes scarstically remarks that while the flexible wage policy and monetary policy produce the same effect on investment demand through lowering rate of interest but there is a "World of difference between them in practice only a foolish person would prefer a flexible wage policy to a flexible monetary policy"[7]

However, Keynes emphasised that expansionary monetary policy (and for that matter flexible wage policy so far its effect on rate of interest is concerned) will not necessarily ensure full employment. To *what extent increase in money supply will succeed in lowering rate of interest and boost investment demand depends first on interest-elasticity of the liquidity preference curve and secondly on interest-elasticity of investment demand curve.* If the liquidity preference curve is highly elastic, (or in the extreme case, the economy is in the region of *liquidity trap*), the increase in quantity of money would not bring about much fall in the rate of interest. Again, if the investment demand curve is relatively inelastic, then even the fall in rate of interest as a consequence of expansion in money supply would not be able to achieve much increase in investment.

Thus, Keynes was not hopeful of securing adequate increase in employment through either flexible wage policy or flexible monetary policy at times of depression.

Real Balance Effect or Pigou Effect

All-round cut in wages and consequent fall in prices produces a favourable effect on aggregate demand and employment in another way which was first pointed out by Pigou and is, therefore, known after his name as Pigou effect. According to Pigou effect, when wage cut causes a fall in prices, *real value of money balances increases* making people richer which induces them to increase their consumption expenditure and raises aggregate demand and employment. Though Keynes and his followers admitted that real balance effect operated but they expressed doubts about its *quantitative significance.* Of course, Pigou effect or real balance effect is theoretically possible but empirical evidence shows that it is not strong enough to raise aggregate demand sufficiently to ensure full employment.

It may be noted that 'Pigou effect' has been subsequently developed by Don Patinkin under the title of *real balance effect*. Don Patinkin[8] tried to revive the classical economics and tried to show that

6. J.M. Keynes, *The General Theory of Employment, Interest and Money*. P. 267.
7. Ibid, pp. 267-268
8. Don Patinkin, *Money, Interest and Prices,* Evanston, 1956

Keynes was wrong for advancing the view that the free market economy did not have a mechanism to restore full employment equilibrium after an initial disturbance. Like the Pigou effect, real balance effect means that when the economy goes into recession and depression, wages and prices fall and as result *real value or purchasing power of money balances increases*. This enables people to buy more than they could before. At lower prices they will actually purchase more than they did before. This increase in demand will lead to rise in output and employment. Thus the operation of real balance effect, according to Patinkin, will bring the economy back automatically to full employment.

Of course, there may be some increase in output and employment as a result of the working of the real balance effect. But the crucial question, is whether it is quantitatively strong enough to get the economy out of depression and restore full employment. As mentioned above, the real balance effect is not very significant to ensure the return to full employment. Thus Steward writes, "*The process of falling prices was limited in its extent, it was not possible for the expansionary effect of its purchasing power to be more than a minor effect to the contractionary effect of falling incomes, consumption and investment, particularly when account was taken of the multiplier.*"[9]

Insider-Outsider Model

A recent approach about wage-employment relation known as insider-outsider model is worth mentioning[10]. According to this approach, those who become unemployed as a result of fall in aggregate demand resulting in recession in the economy lose their influence on the wage-setting process and do not participate in wage negotiation with the employers. This is because the unemployed often lose their status as union members and therefore neither the employers nor the labour union care about them. As a result, while the unemployed workers would want firms to cut wages so as to create more jobs which would enable them to get back employment but the firms ignore them and negotiate with the workers who have jobs and are members of unions. It may be noted that it is quite expensive for the firms to often turnover the workers as costs have to be incurred for hiring new workers, training them and when not required retrenching them. Therefore, insiders have advantage over the outsiders who are seeking employment. Therefore, it is difficult for the firms to cut wages of the insiders (*i.e.*, their employed labour force), especially if their labour-union is strong. Even threats by the firms to the workers that they will be fired and rendered jobless if they do not accept wage cuts may not succeed.

Even if the workers yield to these threats and accept cut in wages to retain their employment it may not be in the interest of the firms themselves to lower wages as it is likely to adversely affect the morale, effort and productivity of workers. The firms will therefore think it better for them to deal with the insiders and pay them good wages even if there are unemployed workers outside who are eagerly seeking employment even at lower wages. Thus, "*The insider outsider model* predicts that wages will not respond substantially to unemployment and thus another reason why we do not quickly return to full employment once the economy experiences recession."[11]

Some economists believe that the insider-outsider model provides an important explanation of the persistent high unemployment in the European countries for the last about three decades starting in early 1980s. This is because labour unions in the European Countries are quite strong and force the firms to bargain with the insiders and ignore the outsiders, the unemployed. This keeps the wages at high levels despite the existence of large unemployment in the European countries. However, if the labour union were not strong, the firms might hike to hire the outsiders (*i.e.*, unemployed at lower wages and thereby reduce unemployment and the new firms might be set up to take advantage of cheap labour and provide employment. This would reduce European unemployment but the strong

9. Michael Stewart, *Keynes and After*, 2nd edition 1972 Penguin Books, pp. 139 – 40.
10. See Assar Lindech and Dennis Snower, *The Insider-Outsider Theory of Employment and Unemployment* (Cambridge, M.A: MIT Press 1988).
11. Dornbusch, Fisher and Startz, *Macroeconomics*, Tata McGraw-Hill, 8th edition, 2002. p.116

unions would resist lowering of wages. As a result there is persistent high unemployment in European countries.

Summing up. Let us now sum up the debate between Keynes and the classical economists on pursuing a flexible wage policy to ensure full employment. In the recent years the quantitative importance of Keynes's effect and real balance effect has been hotly debated. Many modern economists doubt the importance of real balance effect though its theoretical possibility is not denised. Again, as regards the choice between flexible wage policy and flexible monetary policy for increasing investment demand through lowering the rate of interest is concerned one is likely to achieve much less success by reducing the level of money wages than by increasing the supply of money. Besides, there are strong practical objections to following a flexible wage policy as an alternative to monetary policy. First, as has been mentioned above, workers and their trade unions will strongly oppose all-round cut in money wages for every section of workers. It is much easier to lower interest rate through expansionary monetary policy than by cuts in money wages. Secondly, it is inequitable and unreasonable to expect that workers alone should accept cut in their money wages while other sections of the society continue enjoying higher money incomes. Thus, to increase the supply of money to reduce unemployment during depression is preferable to cutting wages. Thirdly, reduction in money wages and consequent fall in prices would increase the real burden of debt whereas expansionary monetary policy would reduce it.

Thus, there is wide agreement among modern economists that, in practice, cut in money wages are unlikely to brought about to make them a practical policy of achieving full employment. Further what can be achieved by cuts in money wages can be easily achieved through increase in money supply to raise aggregate demand and employment.

ANTI-RECESSIONARY POLICY TO REMOVE CYCLICAL UNEMPLOYMENT

As explained in a previous chapter, when aggregated demand falls short of aggregate supply at full-employment level of resources, a deflationary or recessionary gap emerges in the economy. This gap or demand deficiency arises due to the fact that investment demand is not large enough to be equal to the amount of savings at full-employment level of income. Investment demand depends upon expected rate of profit. When businessmen have adverse expectations about future profits, the expected rate of return on capital falls causing decline in investment demand. The decline in investment demand leads to the multiple fall in overall aggregate demand resulting in unemployment of resources, especially unemployment of labour. This is recession (*if it is very severe, it is called depression*). To pull the economy out of recession or depression, the adoption of measures to raise aggregate demand is called for. We spell out below the various measures for raising aggregate demand so as to correct demand deficiency.

1. Deficit Budgeting : Expanding Aggregate Demand

An important fiscal measure to correct demand deficiency is to plan for deficit budgets. Deficit budgets can be attained in two ways. First, government should increase its expenditure on goods and services without being matched by imposition of fresh taxes or without raising the rates of old taxes. In 1930's when all capitalist economies of the world suffered from severe depression Keynes recommended the increase in government expenditure on *public works programmes* such as constructions of roads, railways, canals, school buildings, irrigation works, electrification of villages etc., to tackle the problem of demand deficiency. It should be noted that increase in public expenditure will have a multiplier effect on raising income and employment, that is, income and employment will not rise to the extent of increase in government expenditure but by much more than that depending upon the magnitude of multiplier. The magnitude of the multiplier which is generally denoted by the letter k in turn depends upon the marginal propensity to consume. Thus, $k = \frac{1}{1 - mpc}$. The greater the marginal propensity to consume, the higher the multiplier and therefore the greater the effect of public expenditure on income employment.

If government increases its expenditure by ₹ 5,000 crores and multiplier is 3, then national income and output will expand by ₹ 15,000 crores. Corresponding to this expansion in national output there will be three-fold increase in employment of labour, given the labour-output ratio.

It is important to note that for maximum effect on income and employment, deficit budget should be financed not by *borrowing* from the general public but by creating *new money* (*i.e.*, issuing of new notes) by Reserve Bank of India. Thus deficit budget should be financed by what is called *deficit-financing* which would lead to the expansion in money supply in the economy.

2. Reduction in Taxes : Increasing Disposable Income

Another fiscal measure to raise aggregate demand is cutting down taxes. With reduction in taxes, people's disposable income will rise and consequent to this, their spending on goods and services will rise. If corporate taxes are reduced, this will increase the profitability of investment due to which business class will be induced to invest more. Thus, with reduction in taxation the two components of aggregate demand, namely, consumption demand and investment demand will increase. This would help in taking the economy out of depression. In 1964 on the advice of the Keynesian economists government in US made significant cut in income tax. And this did a miracle in reviving the American economy and soon output and employment increased substantially. The recession was thus overcome with the help of fiscal policy. In June 2003, present President of the United States announced a tax cut of 3.5 billion dollars to revive the American economy which is presently experiencing recession.

3. Monetary Policy : Expanding Credit

Monetary policy can also be used to overcome depression by removing demand deficiency. The following three types of monetary measures may be taken under monetary policy to raise aggregate demand. Whereas the first measure works to raise the *cost of credit*, the other two increase the *availability of credit*. When there is a depression in the economy, the central bank tries to overcome it by lowering the bank rate. As a result of the fall in the bank rate, the market rates of interest also fall. With the fall in the market rates of interest, investment is stimulated which brings about the increase in aggregate demand and helps to remove depression.

Another method to stimulate expansion in credit supply is lowering of *Cash Reserve Ratio* (CRR). With lower cash reserve ratio banks will have more available funds which they will be willing to lend to business firms for investment purposes. This will raise aggregate demand in the economy leading to the expansion in income and employment. Likewise, statutory liquidity ratio (SLR) can also be lowered which will also increase the availability of credit by banks.

4. Export Promotion to Raise Aggregate Demand

Deficiency in aggregate demand can also be corrected through promotion of exports of goods. When domestic demand or market for goods is limited or has shrinked due to the operation of some adverse factors, the goods can be sold abroad. But growth of expors of a country can depend upon several factors. The first important factor is the prices of the goods to be exported. We can export those goods which can be produced comparatively at lower costs and therefore can be sold abroad at competitive prices. That is, expansion in exports of those products can be achieved in which the country has a comparative advantage. We can also lower the cost of production by modernisation and upgradation of technology in export industries. Industrial licensing policy may also be suitably modified so that export industries are able to enjoy the economies of scale.

To achieve growth in exports we should also pay attention in the *quality* of exports. If the quality of our goods to be exported is superior, they can favourably compete with the goods of other countries.

Besides, we should enter into bilateral agreements with other countries to ensure that our exports do not suffer from heavy tariff duties. The developed countries have taken several steps chief among which are heavy import duties to protect their industries. Efforts should be made through bilateral talks as well as through international forums to convice and pressure them to remove thee tariff barriers on the exports from the developing countries.

To expand exports substantially we have to diversify our exports. Not only the exports of products of agro-based industries such as tea, cotton textiles, hides and skins, jute manufactures, tobacco and iron-ore, which are our traditional exports, have to be promoted but also exports of new manufactured goods such as engineering goods, chemicals, leather and leather products and handicrafts. India now exports a wide range of light manufactured goods such as typewriters, plastic goods, sewing machines, electric fans, cycles, transistors, some types of machinery. Exports of all these need to be encouraged by providing suitable incentives.

QUESTIONS FOR REVIEW

1. What is meant by involuntary unemployment ? Explain Keynes's theory of involuntary unemployment.
2. Explain the following types of the unemployment. What factors are responsible for their existence ?
   1. Frictional Unemploymnt
   2. Structural Unemployment
   3. Cyclical Unemployment.
3. Explain the concept of full employment. Is it consistent with the existence of natural rate of unemployment ? Explain the measures that can be adopted to achieve it.
4. What is natural rate of unemployment ? How do the unemployment benefits affect it ?
5. What is full employment ? Discuss with the help of a diagram the different ways of attaining full employment ?
6. Distinguish between fiscal policy and monetary policy. How is monetary policy helpful in generation of employment opportunities in the economy ?
7. What is meant by disguised unemployment ? How can the problem of disguised unemployment in developing countries be solved ?
8. Discuss the nature of unemployment in developing countries like India. Explain the limitations of Keynesian policy prescription, namely, defect financing to increase aggregate demand, to solve the problem of unemployment.
9. Discuss the causes of unemployment and underemployment in developing countries like India. What policy measures would you suggest to solve the unemployment problem in these countries?
10. Explain Insider-Outsider Model. How does it explain the persistent high unemployment rate in Western European Countries ?

PART II

IS-LM MODEL, INFLATION-UNEMPLOYMENT TRADE-OFF AND RECENT DEVELOPMENTS IN MACRO-ECONOMICS

- The IS-LM Curve Model : The Integration of Commodity and Money Markets
- Stagflation and Supply-Side Economics
- Inflation-Unemployment Trade-off : Phillips Curve
- The New Classical Economics : Rational Expectations Model
- The New Keynesian Economics

CHAPTER 12
The IS-LM Curve Model

THE GOODS MARKET AND MONEY MARKET : LINKS BETWEEN THEM

The Keynes in his analysis of national income explains that national income is determined at the level where aggregate demand (i.e., aggregate expenditure) for consumption and investment goods (C + I) equals aggregate output. In other words, in Keynes' simple model the level of national income is shown to be determined by the *goods market equilibrium.* In this simple analysis of equlibirum in the goods market Keynes considers investment to be determined by the rate of interest along with the marginal efficiency of capital and is shown to be independent of the level of national income. The rate of interest, according to Keynes, is determined by money market equilibrium by the demand for and supply of money. In this Keynes' model, changes in rate of interest either due to change in money supply or change in demand for money will affect the determination of national income and output in the goods market through causing changes in the level of investment. In this way changes in money market equilibrium influence the determination of national income and output in the goods market. However, there is apparently one flaw in the Keynesian analysis which has been pointed out by some economists and has been a subject of a good deal of controversy. It has been asserted that in the Keynesian model whereas the changes in rate of interest in the money market affect investment and therefore the level of income and output in the goods market, *there is seemingly no inverse influence of changes in goods market i.e., (investment and income)* on the money market equilibrium.

It has been shown by J.R. Hicks and others that with greater insights into the Keynesian theory one finds that the changes in income caused by changes in investment or propensity to consume in the goods market also influence the determination of interest in the money market. According to him, the level of income which depends on the investment and consumption demand determines the transactions demand for money which affects the rate of interest. Hicks, Hansen, Lerner and Johnson have put forward a complete and integrated model based on the Keynesian framework wherein the variables such as investment, national income, rate of interest, demand for and supply of money are interrelated and mutually interdependent and can be represented by the two curves called the *IS* and *LM* curves. This extended Keynesian model is therefore known as *IS-LM* curve model. In this model they have shown how the level of national income and rate of interest are jointly determined by the simultaneous equilibrium in the two interdependent goods and money markets. Now, this *IS-LM* curve model has become a standard tool of macroeconomics and the effects of monetary and fiscal policies are discussed using this *IS* and *LM* curves model.

GOODS MARKET EQUILIBRIUM : THE DERIVATION OF THE *IS* CURVE

The *IS-LM* curve model emphasises the interaction between the goods and money markets. The goods market is in equilibrium when aggregate demand is equal to income. The aggregate demand is determined by consumption demand and investment demand. In the Keynesian model of goods market equilibrium we also now introduce the rate of interest as an important determinant of investment. With this introduction of interest as a determinant of investment, the latter now becomes an endogenous variable in the model. When the rate of interest falls the level of investment increases and vice versa. Thus, changes in the rate of interest affect aggregate demand or aggregate expenditure by causing changes in the investment demand. When the rate of interest falls, it lowers the cost of investment projects and thereby raises the profitability of investment. The businessmen will therefore undertake greater investment at a lower rate of interest. The increase in investment demand will bring about increase in aggregate demand which in turn will raise the equilibrium level of income. *In the derivation of the IS Curve we seek to find out the equilibrium level of national income as determined by the equilibrium in goods market by a level of investment determined by a given rate of interest. Thus IS curve relates different equilibrium levels of national income with various rates of interest.* As explained above, with a fall in the rate of interest, the planned investment will increase which will cause an upward shift in aggregate demand function ($C + I$) resulting in goods market equilibrium at a higher level of national income.

The lower the rate of interest, the higher will be the equilibrium level of national income. Thus, the *IS* curve is the locus of those combinations of rate of interest and the level of national income at

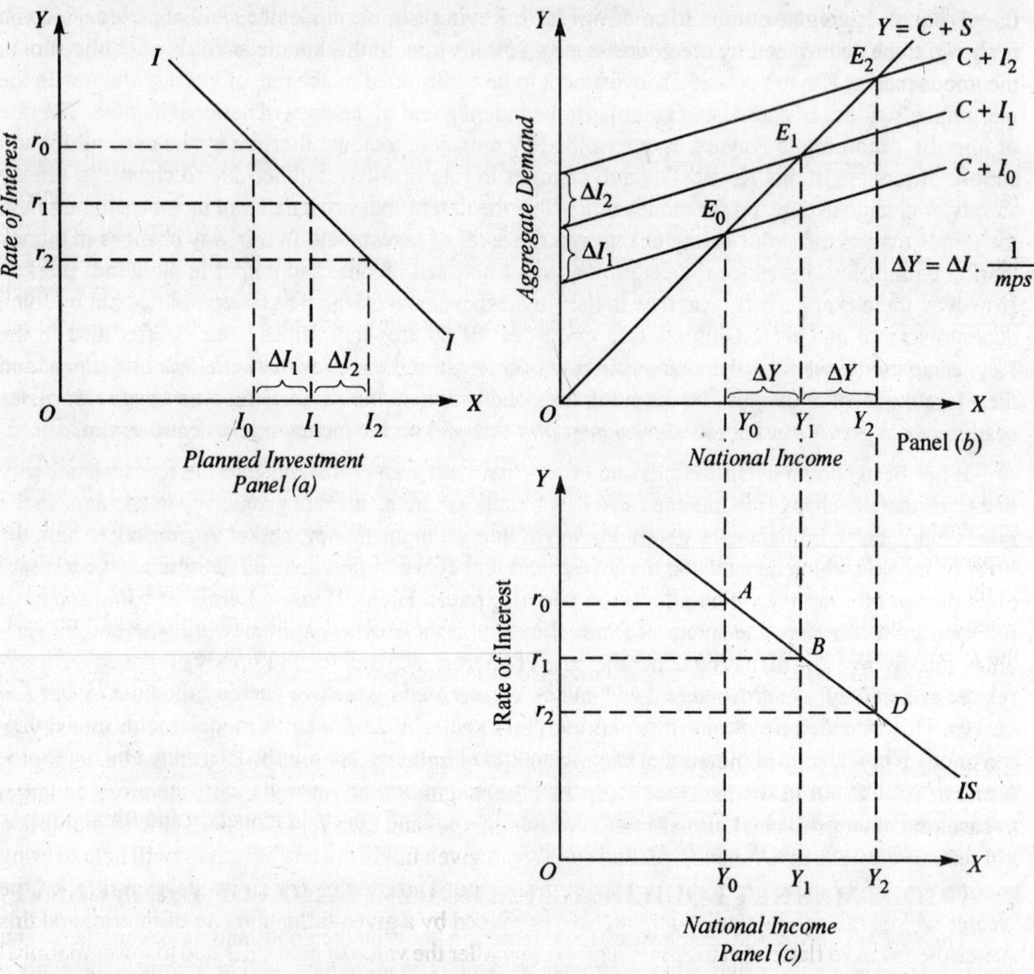

Fig. 12.1. *Derivation of IS Curve : Linking Rate of Interest with National Income through Investment and Aggregate Demand*

which goods market is in equilibrium. How the *IS* curve is derived is illustrated in Fig. 12.1. In panel (a) of Fig. 12.1 the relationship between rate of interest and planned investment is depicted by the investment demand curve *II*. It will be seen from panel (*a*) that at rate of interest Or_0 the planned investment is equal to OI_0. With OI_0 as the amount of planned investment, the aggregate demand curve is $C + I_0$ which, as will be seen in panel (*b*) of Fig. 12.1 equals aggregate output at OY_0 level of national income. Therefore, in the panel (*c*) at the bottom of the Fig. 12.1, against rate of interest Or_0, level of income equal to OY_0 has been plotted. Now, if the rate of interest falls to Or_1, the planned investment by businessmen increases from OI_0 to OI_1 [see panel (*a*)]. With this increase in planned investment, the aggregate demand curve shifts upward to the new position $C + I1$ in panel (*b*), and the goods market is in equilibrium at OY_1 level of national income. Thus, in panel (c) at the bottom of Fig. 12.1 the level of national income OY_1 is plotted against the rate of interest, Or_1. With further lowering of the rate of interest to Or_2, the planned investment increases to OI_2 (see panel *a*). With this further rise in planned investment the aggregate demand curve in panel (*b*) shifts upward to the new position $C + I_2$ corresponding to which goods market is in equilibrium at OY_2 level of income. Therefore, in panel (*c*) the equilibrium income OY_2 is shown against the interest rate Or_2. By joining points A, B, D representing various interest-income combinations at which goods market is in equilibrium we obtain the *IS* Curve. It will be observed from Fig. 12.1 that the *IS* Curve is downward sloping (*i.e.*, has a negative slope) which implies that when rate of interest declines, the equilibrium level of national income increases.

Why does *IS* Curve Slope Downward?

What accounts for the downward-sloping nature of the *IS* curve. As seen above, the decline in the rate of interest brings about an increase in the planned investment expenditure. The increase in investment spending causes the aggregate demand curve (*i.e*, $C + I$ curve) to shift upward and therefore leads to the increase in the equilibrium level of national income. Thus, a lower rate of interest is associated with a higher level of national income and vice-versa. This makes the *IS* curve, which relates the level of income with the rate of interest, to slope downward.

Steepness of the IS curve depends on (1) the elasticity of the investment demand curve, and (2) the size of the multiplier. The elasticity of investment demand signifies the degree of responsiveness of investment spending to the changes in the rate of interest. Suppose the investment demand is highly elastic or responsive to the changes in the rate of interest, then a given fall in the rate of interest will cause a large increase in investment demand which in turn will produce a large upward shift in the aggregate demand curve. A large upward shift in the aggregate demand curve will bring about a large expansion in the level of national income. Thus when investment demand is more elastic to the changes in the rate of interest, the investment demand curve will be relatively flat (or less steep). Similarly, when investment demand is not much sensitive or is less elastic to the changes in the rate of interest, the *IS* curve will be relatively more steep.

The steepness of the IS curve also depends on the magnitude of the multiplier. As has been explained in a previous chapter the value of multiplier depends on the marginal propensity to consume (*mpc*). It may be noted that the higher the marginal propensity to consume, the aggregate demand ($C + I$) curve will be more steep and the magnitude of multiplier will therefore be large. In case of a higher marginal propensity to consume (*mpc*) and therefore a higher value of multiplier, a given increment in investment demand caused by a given fall in the rate of interest will help to bring about a greater increase in equilibrium level of income. Thus, the higher the value of multiplier, the greater will be the rise in equilibrium income produced by a given fall in the rate of interest and this makes the *IS* curve flatter. On the other hand, the smaller the value of multiplier due to lower marginal propensity to consume, the smaller will be the increase in equilibrium level of income following a given increment in investment caused by a given fall in the rate of interest. Thus, in case of smaller size of multiplier the *IS* curve will be more steep.

Shift in *IS* Curve

It is important to understand what determines the position of the *IS* curve and what causes shifts in it. It is the level of autonomous expenditure which determines the position of the *IS* curve and changes in the autonomous expenditure cause a shift in it. *By autonomous expenditure we mean the expenditure, be it investment expenditure, the Government spending or consumption expenditure which does not depend on the level of income.* The government expenditure is an important type of autonomous expenditure. Note that the Government expenditure which is determined by several factors as well as by the policies of the Government, does not depend on the level of income and the rate of interest. Similarly, some consumption expenditure has to be made by individuals if they have to survive even by borrowing from others or by spending their savings made in the past year. Such consumption expenditure is a sort of autonomous expenditure and changes in it do not depend on the changes in income.

Further, autonomous changes in investment can also occur. In the goods market equilibrium of the simple Keynesian model the investment expenditure is treated as autonomous or independent of the level of income and therefore does not vary as the level of income increases. However, in the complete Keynesian model, the investment spending is thought to be determined by the rate of interest along with marginal efficiency of investment. Following this complete Keynesian model, in the derivation of the *IS* curve we consider the level of investment and changes in it as determined by the rate of interest along with marginal efficiency of capital. However, there can be changes in investment spending autonomous or independent of the changes in rate of interest and the level of income. For instance, growing population requires more investment in house construction, school buildings, roads, etc., which does not depend on changes in level of income or rate of interest. Further, autonomous changes in investment spending can also take place when new innovations come about, that is, when there is progress in technology and new machines, equipment, tools etc., have to be built embodying the new technology. Besides, Government expenditure is also of autonomous type as it does not depend on income and rate of interest in the economy. As is well-known government increases its expenditure for the purpose of promoting social welfare and accelerating economic growth. Increase in Government expenditure or autonomous increase investment and consumption will cause a rightward shift in the *IS* curve.

MONEY MARKET EQUILIBRIUM : DERIVATION OF *LM* CURVE

Derivation of the *LM* Curve

The *LM* curve can be derived from the Keynesian theory from its analysis of money market equilibrium. According to Keynes, demand for money to hold depends upon transactions motive and speculative motive. It is the money held for transactions motive which is a function of income. The greater the level of income, the greater the amount of money held for transactions motive and therefore higher the level of money demand curve.

The demand for money depends on the level of income because they have to finance their expenditure, that is, their transactions of buying goods and services. The demand for money also depends on the rate of interest which is the cost of holding money. This is because by holding money rather than lending it and buying other financial assets, one has to forgo interest.

Thus demand for money (M^d) can be expressed as:

$$Md = L(Y, r)$$

where M^d stands for demand for money, Y for real income and r for rate of interest. Thus, we can draw a family of money demand curves at various levels of income. Now, the intersection of these various money demand curves corresponding to different income levels with the supply curve of money fixed by the monetary authority would gives us the *LM* curve. The *LM* curve relates the level of income with the rate of interest which is determined by money-market equilibrium corresponding to different levels of demand for money. The *LM* curve tells what the various rates of interest will be (given the quantity of money and the family of demand curves for money) at different levels of income. But the money demand curve or what Keynes calls the liquidity preference curve alone cannot tell us what exactly the rate of interest will be. In Fig. 12.2 (*a*) and (*b*) we have derived the *LM* curve from a family of demand curves for money. As income increases, money demand curve shifts outward and therefore the rate of interest which equates supply of money with demand for money

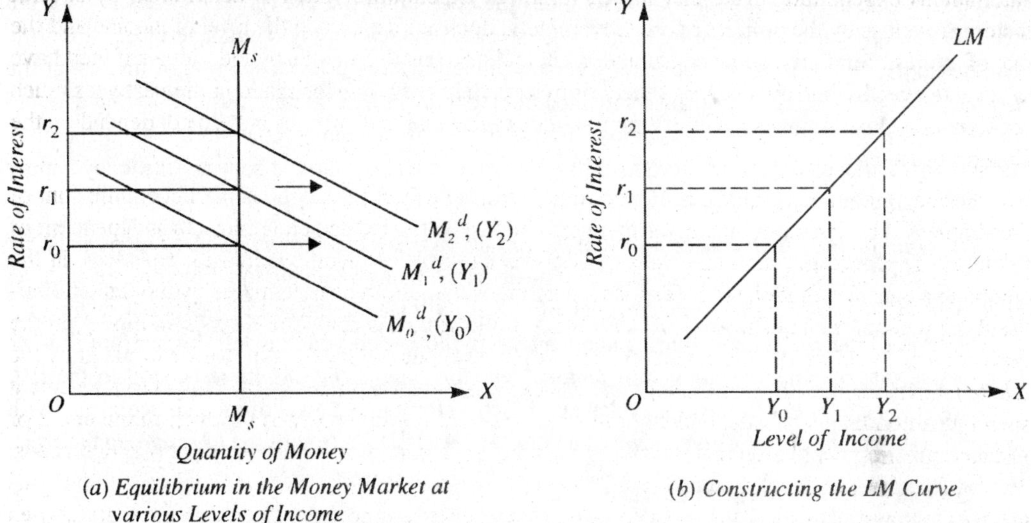

(a) Equilibrium in the Money Market at various Levels of Income

(b) Constructing the LM Curve

Fig. 12.2. *Derivation of LM Curve*

rises. In Fig. 12.2 (*b*) we measure income on the *X*-axis and plot the income level corresponding to the various interest rates determined at those income levels through money market equilibrium by the equality of demand for and the supply of money in Fig. 12.2 (*a*).

Slope of *LM* Curve

It will be noticed from Fig. 12.2 (*b*) that the *LM* curve slopes upward to the right. This is because with higher levels of income, demand curve for money (M^d) is higher and consequently the money market equilibrium, that is, the equality of the given money supply with money demand curve occurs at a higher rate of interest. This implies that rate of interest varies directly with income. It is important to know the factors on which the slope of the *LM* curve depends. There are two factors on which the slope of the *LM* curve depends. First, *the responsiveness of demand for money (i.e., liquidity preference) to the changes in income.* As the income increases, say from Y_0 to Y_1, the demand curve for money shifts from $M_0{}^d$ to $M_1{}^d$, that is, with an increase in income, demand for money would increase for being held for transaction motive, M^d or $L_1 = f(Y)$. This extra demand for money would disturb the money market equilibrium and for the equilibrium to be restored the rate of interest will rise to the level where the given money supply curve intersects the new demand curve corresponding to the higher income level. It is worth noting that in the new equilibrium position, with the given stock of money supply, money held under the transactions motive will increase whereas the money held for speculative motive will decline. The greater the extent to which demand for money for transactions motive increases with the increase in income, the higher the rise in the rate of interest and consequently the steeper the *LM* curve. $r = f(M_1{}^d, M_2{}^d)$ where r is the rate of interest, $M_1{}^d$ is the stock of money available for transaction motive and $M_2{}^d$ is the money demand or liquidity preference for speculative motive.

The second factor which determines the slope of the *LM* curve is the *elasticity or responsiveness of demand for money to the changes in rate of interest*. The lower the elasticity of demand for money for speculative motive with respect to the changes in the rate of interest, the steeper will be the *LM* curve. On the other hand, if the elasticity of money demand-function to the changes in the rate of interest is high, the *LM* curve will be flatter or less steep.

Shifts in the *LM* Curve

Another important thing to know about the *IS-LM* curve model is that what brings about shifts in the *LM* curve or, in other words, what determines the position of the *LM* curve. As seen above from Feb. 2012, a *LM* curve is drawn by keeping the stock of money supply fixed. Therefore, when the money supply increases, given the money demand function, it will lower the rate of interest at the given level of income. This is because with income fixed, the rate of interest must fall so that demand for money for speculative and transactions motive increases to become equal to the greater money supply. This will cause the *LM* curve to shift outward to the right. On the contrary if money supply decreases *LM* curve will shift to the left.

The other factor which causes a shift in the LM curve is the change in liquidity preference (i.e., money demand function) for a given level of income. If the money demand function for a given level of income shifts upward, this, given the stock of money, will lead to the rise in the rate of interest for a given level of income. This will bring about a shift in the *LM* curve to the left. It therefore follows from above that *increase in the money demand function causes the LM* curve to shfit to the left. Similarly, on the contrary, if the money demand function for a given level of income declines, it will lower the rate of interest for a given level of income and will therefore shift the *LM* curve to the right.

The *LM* Curve : The Essential Features

From our analysis of the *LM* curve, we arrive at its following essential features:"

1. The *LM* curve is a schedule that describes the combinations of rate of interest and level of income *at which money market is in equilibrium.*
2. The *LM* curve slopes upward to the right.
3. The *LM* curve is flatter if the interest elasticity of demand for money is high. On the contrary, the *LM* curve is steep if the interest elasticity demand for money is low.
4. The *LM* curve shifts to the right when the stock of money supply is increased and it shifts to the left if the stock of money supply is reduced.
5. The *LM* curve shifts to the left if there is an increase in the money demand function which raises the quantity of money demanded at the given interest rate and income level. On the other hand, the *LM* curve shifts to the right if there is a decrease in the money demand function which lowers the amount of money demanded at given levels of interest rate and income.

SIMULTANEOUS EQUILIBRIUM OF THE GOODS MARKET AND MONEY MARKET

The *IS* and the *LM* curves relate the two variables: (*a*) income and (*b*) the rate of interest. Income and the rate of interest are therefore determined together at the point of intersection of these two curves, *i.e.*, *E* in Fig. 12.3. The equilibrium rate of interest thus determined is Or_2 and the level of income determined is OY_2. At this point income and the rate of interest stand in relation to each other such that (1) the goods market is in equilibrium, that is, the aggregate demand equals the level of aggregate output, and (2) the demand for money is in equilibrium with the supply of money (*i.e.*, the desired amount of money is equal to the actual supply of money). It should be noted that LM curve has been drawn by keeping the supply of money fixed.

Thus, the *IS-LM* curve model is based on: (1) the investment-demand function, (2) the consumption function, (3) the money demand function, and (4) the quantity of money. *We see, therefore, that according to the IS-LM curve model both the real factors, namely, saving and investment, productivity of capital and propensity to consume and save, and the monetary factors, that is, the demand for money (liquidity preference) and supply of money play a part in the joint determination of the rate of interest and the level of income. Any change in these factors will cause a shift in IS or LM curve and will therefore change the equilibrium levels of the rate of interest and income.*

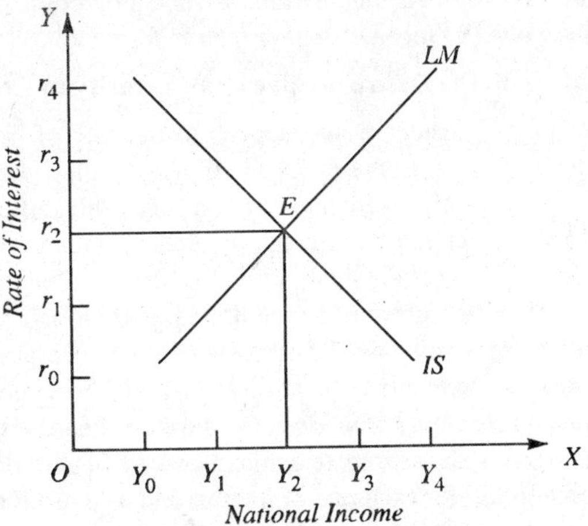

Fig. 12.3. *The IS and LM Curves Combined: The Joint Determination of the Interest Rate and the Income Level*

The *IS-LM* curve model explained above has succeeded in integrating the theory of money with the theory of income determination. And by doing so, as we shall see below, it has succeeded in synthesising the monerary and fiscal policies. Further, with the *IS-LM* curve analysis, we are better able to explain the effect of changes in certain important economic variables such as desire to save, the supply of money, investment, demand for money on the rate of interest and level of income.

Effect of Changes in Supply of Money on the Rate of Interest and Income Level

Let us first consider what will happen if the supply of money is increased by the action of the Central Bank. Given the liquidity preference schedule, with the increase in the supply of money, more money will be available for speculative motive at a given level of income which will cause the interest rate to fall. As a result, the *LM* curve will shift to the right. With this rightward shift in the *LM* curve, in the new equilibrium position, rate of interest will be lower and the level of income greater than before. This is shown in Fig. 12.4 where with a given supply of money, *LM* and *IS* curves intersect at point *E*. With the increase in the supply of money, *LM* curve shifts to the right to the position *LM'*, and with *IS* schedule remaining unchanged, new equilibrium is at point *G* corresponding to which rate of

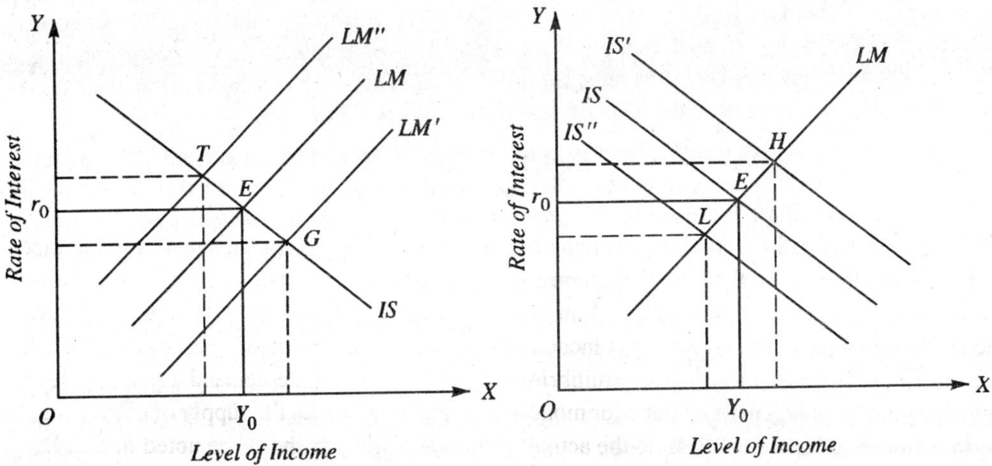

Fig. 12.4. *Impact of Change in Supply of Money*

Fig. 12.5. *Impact of Change in Propensity to Save*

interest is lower and level of income greater than at *E*. Now, suppose that instead of increasing the supply of money, Central Bank of the country takes steps to reduce the supply of money. With the reduction in the supply of money, less money will be available for speculative motive at each level of income and, as a result, the *LM* curve will shift to the left of *E*, and the *IS* curve remaining unchaned, in the new equilibrium position (as shown by point *T* in Fig. 12.4) the rate of interest will be higher and the level of income smaller than before.

Changes in the Desire to Save or Propensity to Consume

Let us consider what happens to the rate of interest when desire to save or in other words, propensity to consume changes. When people's desire to save falls, that is, when propensity to consume rises, the aggregate demand curve will shift upward and, therefore, level of national income will rise at each rate of interest. As a result, the *IS* curve will shift outward to the right. In Fig. 12.5 suppose with a certain given fall in the desire to save (or increase in the propensity to consume), the *IS* curve shifts rightward to the dotted position *IS'*. With *LM* curve remaining unchanged, the new equilibrium position will be established at *H* corresponding to which rate of interest as well as level of income will be greater than at *E*. Thus, *a fall in the desire to save has led to the increase in both rate of interest and level of income*. On the other hand, if the desire to save rises, that is, if the propensity to consume falls, aggregate demand curve will shift downward which will cause the level of national income to fall for each rate of interest and as a result the *IS* curve will shift to the left. With this, and *LM* curve remaining unchanged, the new equilibrium position will be reached to the left of *E*, say at point *L* (as shown in Fig. 12.5) corresponding to which both rate of interest and level of national income will be smaller than at *E*.

Changes in Autonomous Investment and Government Expenditure

Changes in autonomous investment and Government expenditure will also shift the IS curve. If either there is increase in autonomous private investment or Government steps up its expenditure, aggregate demand for goods will increase and this will bring about increase in national income through the multiplier process. This will shift *IS* schedule to the right, and given the *LM* curve, the rate of interest as well as the level of income will rise. On the contrary, if somehow private investment expenditure falls or the Government reduces its expenditure, the *IS* curve will shift to the left and, given the *LM* curve, both the rate of interest and the level of income will fall.

Changes in Demand for Money or Liquidity Preference

Changes in liquidity preference will bring about changes in the *LM* curve. If the liquidity preference or demand for money of the people rises, the *LM* curve will shift to the left. This is because, greater demand for money, given the supply of money, will raise the rate of interest corresponding to each level of national income. With the leftward shift in the *LM* curve, given the *IS* curve, the equilibrium rate of interest will rise and the level of national income will fall.

On the contrary, if the demand for money or liquidity preference of the people falls, the *LM* curve will shift to the right. This is because, given the supply of money, the rightward shift in the money demand curve means that corresponding to each level of income there will be lower rate of interest. With rightward shift in the *LM* curve, given the *IS* curve, the equilibrium level of rate of interest will fall and the equilibrium level of national income will increase.

We thus see that changes in propensity to consume (or desire to save), autonomous investment or Government expenditure, the supply of money and the demand for money will cause shifts in either *IS* or *LM* curve and will thereby bring about changes in the rate of interest as well as in national income. The integration of goods market and money market in the *IS-LM* curve model clearly shows that Government can influence the economic activity or the level of national income through monetary *and fiscal measures*. Through adopting an appropriate monetary policy (*i.e.*, changing the supply of money) the Government can shift the *LM* curve and through pursuing an appropriate fiscal policy (expenditure and taxation policy) the Government can shift the *IS* curve. Thus both monetary and fiscal policies can play a useful role in regulating the level of economic activity in the country.

The Critique of the *IS-LM* Model

The *IS-LM* model makes a significant advance in explaining the simultaneous determination of the rate of interest and the level of national income. It represents a more general, inclusive and realistic approach to the determination of interest rate and level of income. Further, the *IS-LM* model succeeds in integrating and synthesising fiscal with monetary policies, and theory of income determination with the theory of money. But the *IS-LM* model is not without limitations. Firstly, it is based on the assumption that the rate of interest is quite flexible, that is, free to vary and not rigidly fixed by the Central Bank of a country. If the rate of interest is quite inflexible, then the appropriate adjustment explained above will not take place. Secondly, the model is also based upon the *assumption that investment is interest-elastic*, that is, investment varies with the rate of interest. If investment is interest-inelastic, then the *IS-LM* model breaks down since the required adjustments do not occur. Thirdly, Don Patinkin[1] and Milton Friedman have cirticised the *IS-LM* model as being too artificial and over-simplified. In their view, division of the economy into two sectors – monetary and real – is artificial and unrealistic. According to them, monetary and real sectors are quite interwoven and act and react on each other. Further, Patinkin has pointed out that the *IS-LM* model has ignored the possibility of changes in the price level of commodities. According to him, the various economic variables such as supply of money, propensity to consume or save, investment and the demand for money not only influence the rate of interest and the level of national income but also the prices of commodities and services. Patinkin has suggested a more integrated and general equilibrium approach which involves the simultaneous determination of not only the rate of interest and the level of income but also of the prices of commodities and services.

DERIVING AGGREGATE DEMAND CURVE WITH IS-LM MODEL

In a later chapter we will use IS-LM model to explain how national income and rate of interest are determined, treating price level as fixed. We can now use IS-LM model to derive aggregate demand curve with variable price level. It is this aggregate demand curve with variable price level that through intersection of aggregate supply curve determines the level of national income and the general price level. In the *AS-AD* model, aggregate demand curve describes the relationship between the price level and aggregate output demanded. Note that the in macroeconomic equilibrium the aggregate effective demand for output equals national income or *GDP*. Viewed in this way aggregate demand curve shows the relationship between the price level and the level of national income. As seen before, this aggregate demand curve with variable price level slopes downward to the right. How this is derived from IS-LM model is depicted in figure 12.6.

For any given money supply when price level falls the supply of *real money balances* increases. The increase in real money balances causes a shift in the *LM* curve as shown in the upper panel of Figure 12.6. With price level equal to P_1, LM_1 is the *LM* curve and its intersection with the given *IS* curve determines Y_1 level of national income or output. With the fall in price level to $P_2 (P_2 < P_1)$, *LM* curve shifts to the right to LM_2 position and its intersection with the given *IS* curve, determines Y_2 level of national income or output. Thus with this rightward shift in the *LM* curve from LM_1 to LM_2 as a result of fall in price level, equilibrium national income (output) which was Y_1 with LM_1 curve with price level equal to P_1 has risen to Y_2 with LM_2 curve at a lower price level P_2. Accordingly, in the panel at the bottom of Figure 12.6 we have plotted income or output level Y_1 against price level P_1 and higher output level Y_2 against the lower level P_2. With this we get the downward-sloping aggregate demand curve *AD*. Note that along with this aggregate demand curve *AD* both goods market and money market are in equilibrium.

1. Don Patinkin, *Money, Interest and Prices*, Harper and Row, 1965.

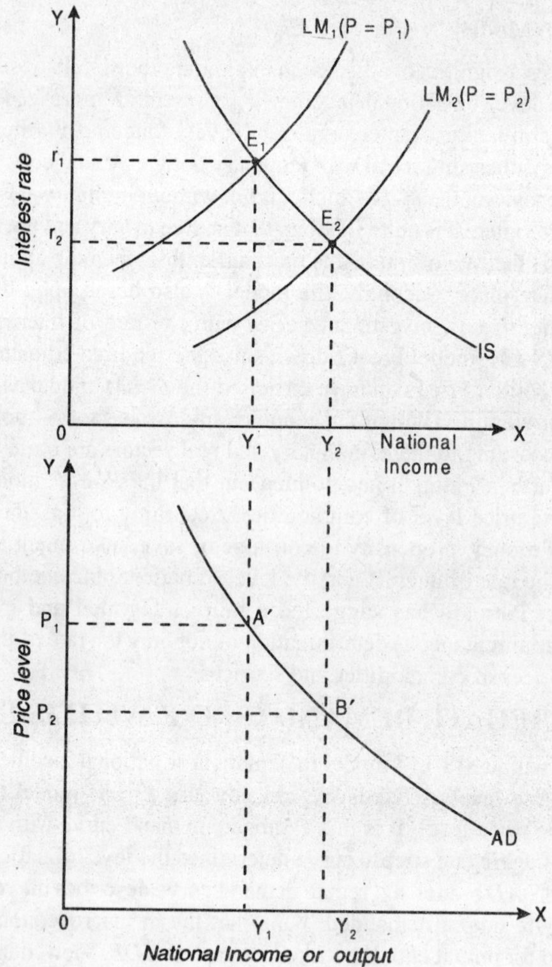

Figure. 12.6. *Deriving Aggregate Demand Curve with IS-LM Model*

Factors Causing a Shift in Aggregate Demand Curve

Now, what will bring about a shift in the aggregate demand curve. This can also be known from the results of *IS-LM* model. The factors which cause a shift in either *IS* or *LM* curve (with a given price level) will bring about a shift in the aggregate demand curve. As we know changes in money supply or government expenditure or taxes bring about a change in the short-run macroeconomic equilibrium as explained by *IS-LM* model, they will also shift the aggregate demand curve. This is shown in figure 12.7.

For example, expansionary fiscal policy which involves increase in government expenditure or reduction in taxes will cause a shift in the *IS* curve to the right in the *IS-LM* model for a given price level as in seen from the upper pannel of Fig. 12.7. This will cause increase in the national income (output) at a given price level and therefore lead to the shift in the aggregate demand curve to the right as shown in the lower panel of Figure 12.7. It may however be noted that increase in national income or output (*i.e.* ΔY) will not be equal to increase in government expenditure (ΔG) times the multiplier $\left(i.e., \Delta G \frac{1}{1-MPC} \right)$ but, as seem from upper part of Fig. 12.7, less than this. This is because with the

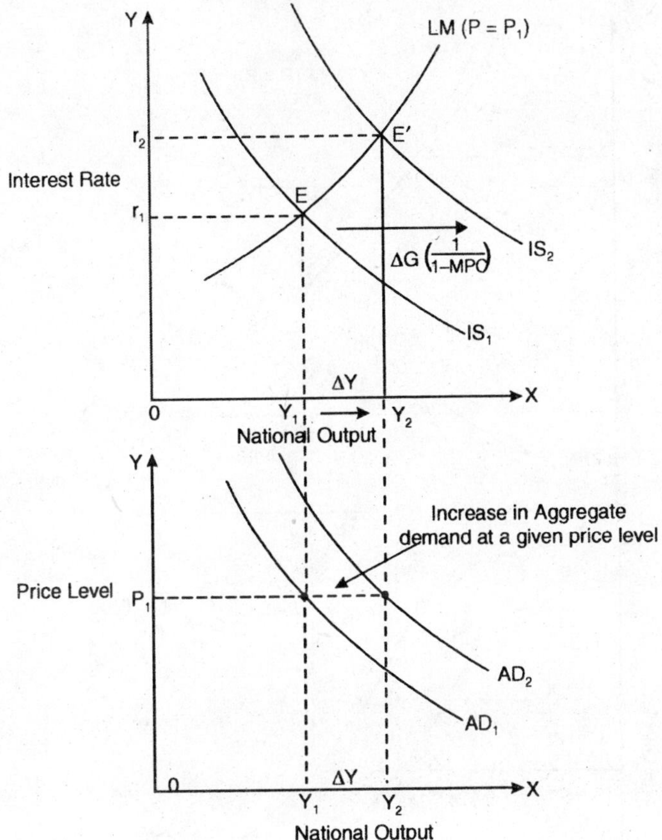

Fig. 12.7. *Shift in Aggregate demand Curve due to Increase in Government Expenditure*

shift in the *IS* curve to IS_2, new equilibrium with the given *LM* curve is reached at lower level of national output or income.

Similarly, if there is a *decrease* in government expenditure or increase in taxes, this will cause a *shift in the IS curve to the left* at a given price level in the *IS-LM* model and will lead to the decrease in national income or output for a given price level. As a result, aggregate demand curve will shift to the left in this case.

Changes in Money Supply and Shift in Aggregate Demand Curve

Changes in money supply in the *IS-LM* model affects national income or output by causing shifts in the *LM* curve for a given price level. For example, when Central Bank of a country adopts an expansionary monetary policy and accordingly there is increase in money supply, *LM* curve shifts to the right from LM_1 to LM_2 for a given price level (see upper panel (*a*) in Fig. 12.8 (given on the *next* page). With the given *IS* curve, shift in *LM* curve from LM_1 to LM_2 leads to the increase in national output from Y_1 to Y_2. It will be observed from the lower panel (*b*) of Fig. 12.8 that with the shift in the *LM* curve from LM_1 to LM_2 for a given price level, aggregate demand curve shifts from AD_1 to AD_2 so that at a given price P_1, national output produced and demanded increases from Y_1 to Y_2. Similarly, if there is a decrease in money supply with the adoption of contractionary monetary policy, *LM* curve will shift to the left for a given price level causing a shift in the aggregate demand curve to the left.

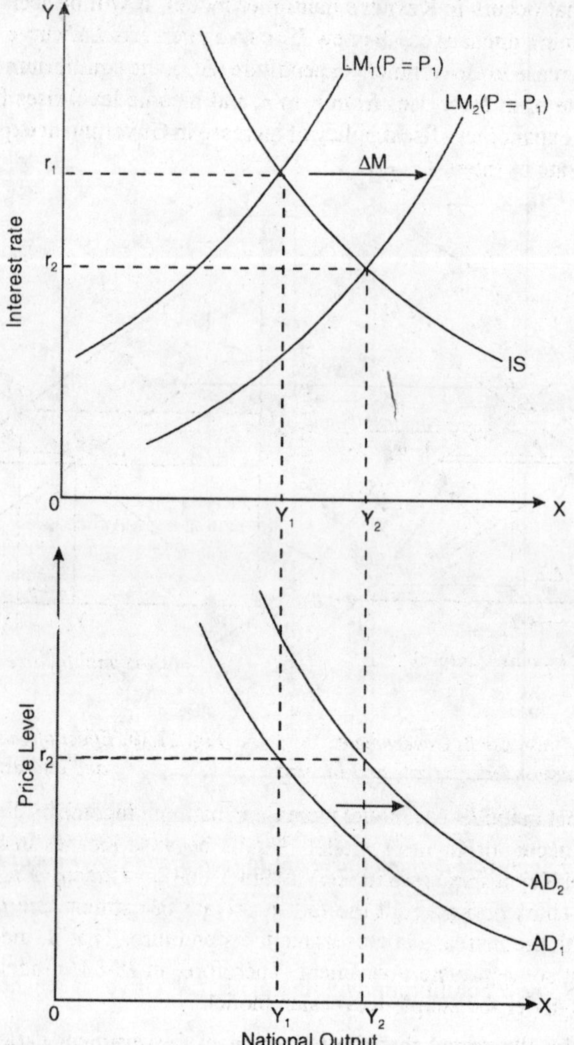

Figure 12.8. *Shift in Aggregate Demand Curve due to Expansion in Money Supply*

IS-LM CURVE MODEL : EXPLAINING ROLES OF FISCAL AND MONETARY POLICIES

With the help of *IS-LM* curve model we can explain how the *intervention by the Government* with proper fiscal and monetary policies can influence the level of economic activity, that is, inocme and employment level. We explain below the impact of changes in fiscal and monetary policy on the economy in the *IS-LM* model.

Effect of Fiscal Policy

Increase in Government Expenditure. Let us first explain how *IS-LM* model shows the effect of increase in Government expenditure on level of income. This is illustrated in Fig. 12.9. As explained above, increase in Government expenditure which is of autonomous nature raises aggregate demand for goods and services and thereby causes an outward shift in *IS* curve, as is shown in Fig. 12.9 where increase in Government expenditure leads to the shift in IS curve from IS_1 to IS_2. Note that the horizontal distance between the two *IS* curves is equal to $\Delta G \times \frac{1}{1-MPC}$ which shows the increase in income that occurs in Keynes's multiplier model. It will be seen from Fig. 12.9 that with the *LM* curve remaining unchanged, the new IS_2 curve intersects *LM* curve at point *B*. Thus, in *IS-LM* model with the increase in Government expenditure (ΔG), the equilibrium moves from point *E* to *B* and with this the rate of interest rises from r_1 to r_2 and income level rises from Y_1 to Y_2. Thus, *IS-LM* model shows that expanoinary fiscal policy of increase in Government expenditure raises both the level of income and rate of interest.

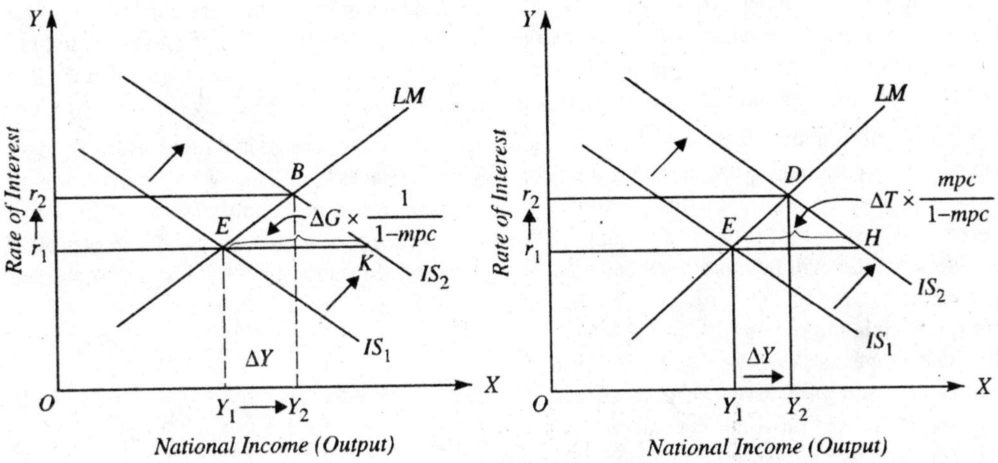

Fig. 12.9. *Impact of Increase in Government Expenditure on Interest rate and Income*

Fig. 12.10. *Effect of Cut in Taxes on Income and Interest Rate*

It is worth noting that in the *IS-LM* model increase in national income by Y_1Y_2 in Fig. 12.9 is less than *EK* which would occur in Keynes's model. This is because Keynes in his simple multiplier model (popularly called Keynesian cross model) assumes that investment is fixed and autonomous, whereas *IS-LM* model takes into account the fall in private investment due to the rise in interest rate that takes place with the increase in Government expenditure. That is, increase in Government expenditure crowds out some private investment. Therefore, in *IS-LM* model increase in national inocme is less than that under the simple Keynesian model.

Likewise, it can be illustrated that the reduction in Government expenditure will cause a rightward shift in the *IS* curve, and given the *LM* curve unchanged, will lead to the fall in both rate of interest and level of income. It should be noted that Government often cuts expenditure to control inflation in the economy.

Reduction in Taxes. An alternative measure of *expansionary fiscal policy* which may be adopted is the reduction in taxes which through increase in disposable income of the people raises consumption demand of the people. As a result, cut in taxes causes a shift in the *IS* curve to the right as is shown in Fig. 12.10, from IS_1 to IS_2. It may however noted that in the Keynesian multiplier model, the horizontal shift in the IS curve is determined by the value of *tax multiplier* which is equal to $\Delta T \times \frac{MPC}{1-MPC}$ and causes level of income to increase by *EH*. However, in the *IS-LM* model, with the shift of the *IS* curve from IS_1 to IS_2 following the reduction in taxes, the economy moves from equilibrium point *E* to *D* and as is evident from Fig. 12.10, rate of interest rises from r_1 to r_2 and level of income increases from Y_1 to Y_2. Due to the rise in rate of interest increase in national income as a reduction in tax is less than *EH* $\left(=\Delta T \frac{MPC}{1-MPC}\right)$ that would occur in the simple Keynesian model.

On the other hand, if the Government intervences in the economy to *reduce inflationary pressures, it will raise the rates of personal taxes to reduce disposable income of the people. Rise in personal taxes will lead to the decrease in aggregate demand.* Decrease in aggregate demand will help in controlling inflation. This case can also be shown by *IS-LM* curve model.

Impact of Monetary Policy

Through making appropriate changes in monetary policy the Government can influence the level of economic activity. Monetary policy may also be expansionary or contractionary depending on the prevailing economic situation. *IS-LM* model can be used to show the effect of expansionary and tight monetary policies. As has been explained above, a change in money supply causes a shift in the *LM* curve; expansion in money supply shifts it to the right and decrease in money supply shifts it to the left.

Suppose the economy is in grip of recession, the Government (through its Central Bank) adopts the expansionary monetary policy to lift the economy out of recession. Thus, it takes measures to increase the money supply in the economy. The increase in money supply, state of liquidity preference or demand for money remaining unchanged, will lead to the fall in rate of interest. At a lower interest there will be more investment by businessmen. More investment will cause aggregate demand and income to rise. This implies that with expansion in money supply *LM* curve will shift to the right as is shown in Fig. 12.11. As a result, the economy will move from equilibrium point *E* to *D* and with this the rate of interest will fall from r_1 to r_2 and national income will increase from Y_1 to Y_2. Thus, *IS-LM* model shows the expansion in money supply lowers interest rate and raises income. We have also indicated what is called *monetary transmission mechanism*, that is, *IS-LM* curve model shows how the expansion in money supply leads to the increase in aggregate demand for goods and services. We have thus seen that increase in money supply lowers the rate of interest which then stimulates more investment demand. Investment demand through multiplier process leads to a greater increase in aggregate demand and national inocme.

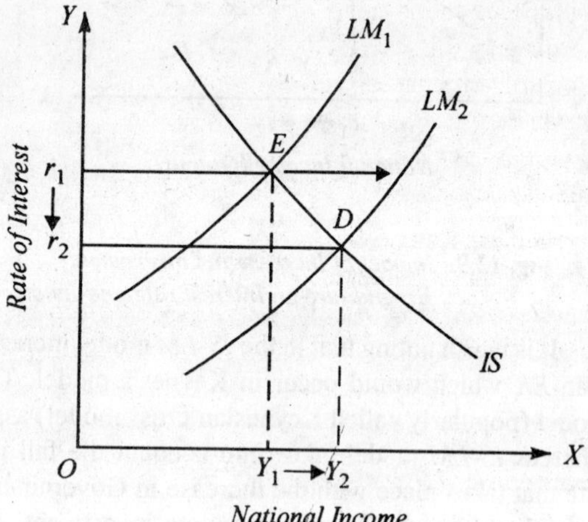

Fig. 12.11. *Effect of Expansion in Money Supply on Interest Rate and Income*

If the economy suffers from inflation, the Government will like to check it. Then its Central Bank should adopt tight or contractionary monetary policy. That is, it should reduce the money supply. *IS-LM* model can be used to show, as we have seen above in case of expansionary monetary policy. *The reduction in money supply will cause a leftward shift in LM curve and will lead to the rise in interest rate and fall in the level of income.*

ELASTICITY OF *LM* CURVE AND RELATIVE EFFECTIVENESS OF MONETARY AND FISCAL POLICIES

Between Keynesian and monetarists, there has been a great controversy about relative effectiveness of fiscal and monetary policy. Monetarists think that *only money matters* and fiscal policy is quite ineffective as greater Government expenditure will crowd out private investment. On the other hand, Keynesians, especially early Keynesians, believe that money does not matter and it is active fiscal policy that is effective in controlling economic fluctuations. The source of controversy is the assumption that Keynesians and monetarists make about the elasticity of *LM* curve.

Keynesian Range. Early Keynesians believe that at relatively higher rate of interest, liquidity preference curve is *interestic-elastic* but at a certain low rate of interest, liquidity preference curve becomes perfectly elastic ($e = \infty$). This perfectly elastic part of the liquidity preference curve known as liquidity trap. An increase in money supply over this range does not affect interest rate and therefore investment does not increase. This makes the *LM* curve flat at a certain minimum rate of interest as shown in Figure 12.12. The range i_0 to *K* of the *LM* curve is horizontal due to the liquidity trap in the liquidity preference curve and therefore represents what is called the Keynesian range.

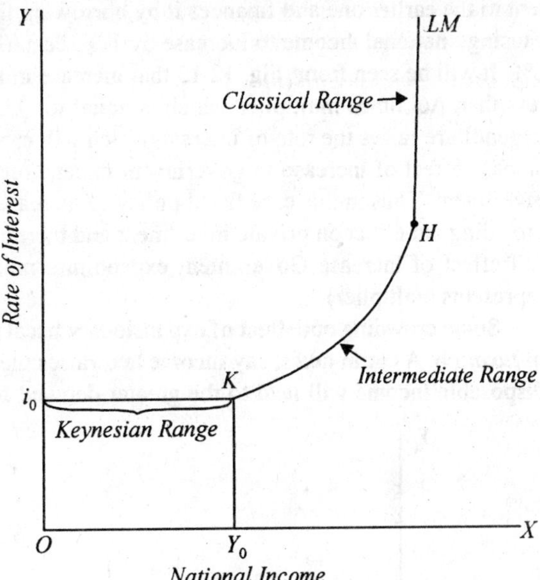

Fig. 12. 12. *LM Curve with Different Ranges*

Classical Range. On the other extreme, early monetarists followed the classical viewpoint that money is primarily demanded for transaction purposes and is interest inelastic (e = 0). According to this classical assumption, *LM* Curve is of vertical shape as shown by the *LM* curve in Figure 12.12 from point *H* upward. This vertical portion of *LM* curve is therefore called classical range.

Intermediate Range. In between the Keynesian and classical range is the intermediate range over which *LM* curve is interest-elastic ($0 < e < \infty$). In Figure 12.12 the portion of *LM* curve between points *K* and *H* over which *LM* curve slopes upward and is interest elastic represents the intermediate range.

The relat1ive effectiveness of fiscal and monetary policies varies in different ranges of *LM* curve. We discuss them below.

Effectiveness of Fiscal Policy

Efficiency of fiscal policy in affecting national income is different in different ranges of *LM* curve. As explained above, the different ranges of *LM* curve are based on different assumptions regarding interest-elasticity of demand for money. In Figure 12.13 (Given on the *next page*) we reproduce *LM* curve with Keynesian, intermediate and classical ranges. Let us consider the effect of expansionary fiscal policy in the Keynesian range. Suppose to begin with economy is in equilibrium at point *E* where IS_0 curve intersects *LM* curve in the Keynesian range and the Government increases its expenditure and finances it through borrowing from the Reserve Bank of India. Increase in Government expenditure will cause a shift in *IS* curve, say from IS_0 to IS_1 in Figure 12.13. It will be seen from this figure that shift in the *IS* curve from IS_0 to IS_1 as a result of increase in Government expenditure causes increase in national income from Y_0 to Y_1. It may be noted that this increase in income will be equal to ΔG times multiplier ($\Delta Y = \Delta G \times$ multiplier). If the increase in Government expenditure is financed by *selling Government bonds* to the public, even then the effect will be the same in this range because in this range there is excess liquidity with the public and the purchase of Government bonds and by them will not affect their demand for money for transaction purposes and the rate of interest. Since interest rate remains the same, private investment will not be affected. Therefore, with shift of *IS* curve from IS_0 to IS_1 will bring about increase in national income equal to ΔG times the multiplier.

Thus, in the Keynesian range expansionary fiscal policy is very effective in causing expansion in national output and employment

Intermediate range. Now suppose initially the economy is in equilibrium at point D in the intermediate range of LM curve in Fig. 12.13. If the Government increases its expenditure equivalent to the earlier one and finances it by borrowing from the public), IS curve shifts from IS_2 to IS_3 causing national income to increase by Y_2Y_3 *i.e.* ($\Delta Y = Y_2Y_3$) and rate of interest rises from 5% to 6%. It will be seen from Fig. 12.13 that increase in income (ΔY) in this intermediate range will be less than ΔG times multiplier which is equal to DJ. This is because as increase in Government expenditure raises the rate of interest, which will crowd out some private investment. Thus expansionary effect of increase in government expenditure has been partly offset by decline in private investment. Thus in this case fiscal policy of increase in Government expenditure has caused some crowding out effect on private investment and therefore national income increases but less than the full effect of increase Government expenditure multiplied by the multiplier ($\Delta Y < \Delta Gk$ where k represents multiplier).

Some crowding out effect of expansionary fiscal policy will occur even if it is of the form of *cut in taxation*. A cut in taxes, say income tax, raises the disposable income of the people. The higher disposable income will lead to the greater demand for money for transaction purposes. To obtain

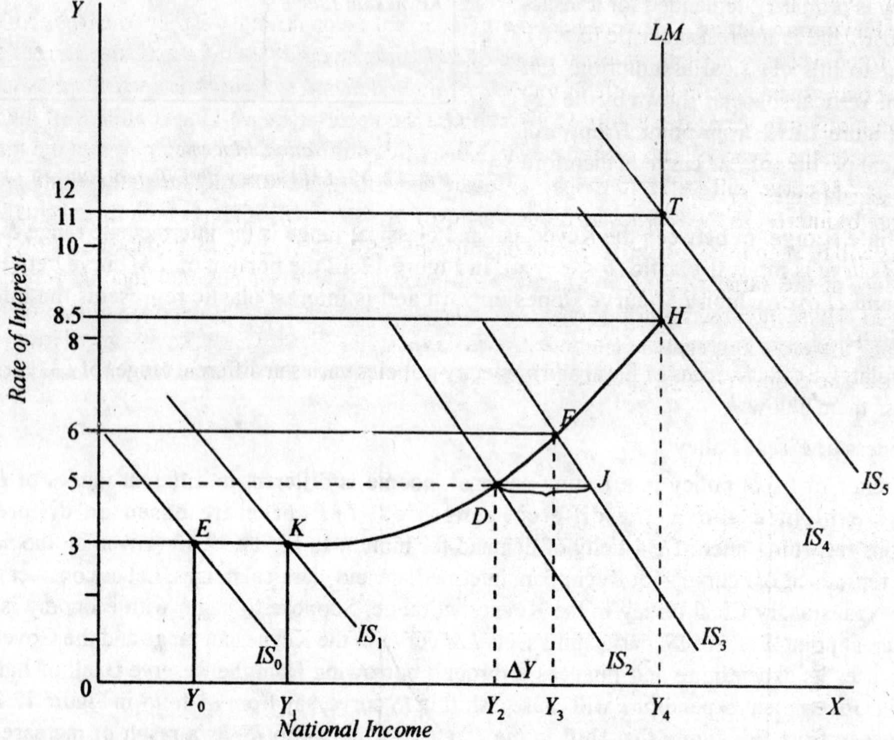

Fig. 12.13. *IS-LM Curve Model : Efficacy of Fiscal Policy*

more money to fulfil transaction motive, the public will sell bonds which will cause fall in bond prices or increase in interest rate. This increase in interest rate will crowd out some private investment and will threfore offset some of the expansionary effect of reduction in taxes.

Classical Range. Now, consider the effect of expansionary fiscal policy in the classical range of LM curve which is a vertical line in this range. A glance at Figure 12.13 will reveal that increase in Government expenditure in this classical vertical range of LM curve equivalent to the earlier one causes a shift in the IS curve from IS_4 to IS_5 will lead to the rise in interest from 8.5 per cent to 11 per cent with no effect on national income which remains constant at Y_4 level. The reason for unchanged level of national income despite the increase in Government expenditure is that there is *full crowding-*

out effect on private investment. Rise in rate of interest as a result of increase in Government expenditure causes decline in private investment which fully cancels out the expansionary effect of increase in Government expenditure. It is due to their belief in this classical range of *LM* curve that monetarists argue that fiscal policy is quite ineffective in expanding national output and employment.

It thus follows from above, fiscal policy is most effect in the Keynesian range, relatively less effective in the intermediate range and completely ineffective in the classical range. This is because there is no crowding out effect in the Keynesian range, some crowding out effect in the intermediate range and full crowding out effect in the classical range of *LM* curve.

Effectiveness of Monetary Policy

Whether monetary policy is effective or not has been a highly controversial issue between Keynesian and monetarists. The shape of *LM* curve with its three ranges has a significant influence on the effectiveness of monetary policy. As explained earlier, a *LM* curve is derived with a given stock of money supply. Now when with adoption of expansionary monetary policy the money supply is increased, *LM* curve shifts to the right. The impact of increase in money supply on rate of interest and level of income is different in different ranges of *LM* curve. We explain below the effectiveness of monetary policy in these three ranges of *LM* curve.

The Keynesian Range. Let us consider the effect of expansion in money supply when the economy happens to be working in the Keynesian range of *LM* curve. Recall that the Keynesian range of the *LM* curve occurs at a certain low rate of interest at which demand for money is perfectly elastic and there is liquidity trap. Consider Figure 12.14 suppose the economy is working at point *K* of the LM_1 curve at which the given IS_1 curve intersects it. Now, of Central Bank of a country raises the money supply, the *LM* curve will shift to the right, IS_1 curve remaining unchanged. Due to the liquidity trap at low rate of interest in the Keynesian range the new LM_2 curve will coincide with the original LM_1 curve. As will be seen from Figure 12.14 the equilibrium between *IS* curve IS_1 and the new LM_2 curve also occurs at the same point *K*, with rate of interest and level of national income remaining unchanged. Thus, *increase in money supply is quite ineffective* in raising the level of real national income and therefore aggregate employment. This has been the view of early Keynesians. How do we explain it ? The economy being operating in the Keynesian range of *LM* curves, *the whole increase in*

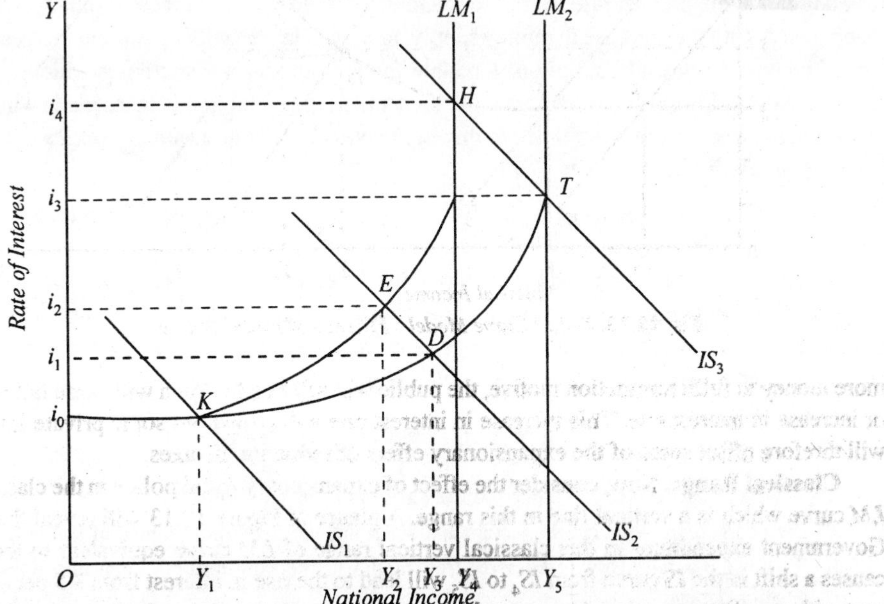

Fig. 12.14. *IS-LM Curve Model : Inpact of increase in Money Supply Over Three Ranges of LM Curve*

money supply is kept as idle cash balances due to the perfectly elastic demand for money and no money goes to fulfil transaction purposes, national income is therefore not affected. Further, since the rate of interest also remains the same due to the economy working in the liquidity-trap portion of the *LM* curves, investment also does not increase and therefore does not influence national income. It is worth noting this ineffectiness of expansionary policy in the Keynesian range confirms the view of early Keynesians that "*money does not matter*".

Intermediate Range. Let us now assume that to begin with economy is operating in the intermediate range, say at point *E* on the LM_1 curve in Figure 12.14 where the IS_2 curve intersects it. Now, suppose there is increase in money supply by the Central Bank of the country and as a result *LM* curve shifts from LM_1 to LM_2. As will be seen from Figure 12.14 the new LM_2 curve intersects the given IS_2 curve at point *D* resulting in fall in rate of interest from i_2 to i_1 and increase in national income from Y_2 to Y_3. How can we explain it ? Increase in money supply causes cash balances with public to rise and, with a given income, this induces the public to buy corporate bonds or supply more money for lending purposes. As a result, bond price rises and rate of interest falls. The decline in the rate of interest causes investment to increase. With the increase in investment, national income increases. Further, with increase in national incomes demand for money for transaction purposes increases and a part of increase in cash balances is used for transaction purposes.

It therefore follows that in the intermediate range expansionary monetary policy is effective to some extent in raising national income and employment. It may be noted that new Keynesians think that monetary policy can have useful and effective role in raising national income and therefore they believe in the intermediate range of *LM* curve. With slight difference *modern* monetarists also believe in the working of economy in the intermediate range of *LM* curve.

The Classical Range. Let us assume that initially the economy is in equilibrium at point *H* where LM_1 and IS_3 curves intersect in the classical range. Recall that in the classical range over which *LM* curve is of vertical shape demand for money is interest-inelastic. Now suppose that Central Bank increases the money supply through open market operations. As a result, *LM* curve shifts from LM_1 to LM_2. It will be seen from Figure 12.14 that the new LM_2 curve intersects the given IS_3 curve at point *T* causing fall in the interest rate from i_4 to i_3 and increase in national income from Y_4 to Y_5. How has it happened ? With the increase in money supply, money balances with the public increases at a given level of income As a result, supply of lendable funds in the market increases which causes rate of interest to fall. At lower rate of interest more investment in capital goods takes place which results in increase in national income. We thus see that *in the classical range monetary policy is fully effective in raising national income.*

Conclusion. From the foregoing analysis, it follows that monetary policy is completely ineffective in the Keynesian range as the whole increase in money supply is kept as inactive or idle monetary balances. In the intermediate range, monetary policy is relatively effective due the decline in rate of interest and consequently there is some increase in investment and national income but monetary policy is fully effective in the classical range as it results in large decline in interest rate and consequently substantial increase in investment and national income.

QUESTIONS FOR REVIEW

1. What is *IS* curve ? How is it derived from goods market equilibrium ?
2. Define *IS* curve. What are the factors that determine the slope or steepness of *IS* Curve ?
3. What is *LM* curve ? How is it derived from money market equilibrium ? On factors does its slope and position depend ?

4. How do the product and money markets interact to determine the short-run equilibrium level of national income and the rate of interest ?
5. Using IS-LM model analyse the impact of an increase in money supply on the equilibrium level of income and rate of interest.
6. Using *IS-LM* model, show that fiscal policy is more effective at low rate of intrest and low level of income, while monetary policy is more effective when the levels of income and rate of interest are high.
7. Explain how far expansionary monetary policy is effective in increasing the level of national income in each of the three ranges of *LM* curve. In which range is fiscal policy most effective.
8. Using *IS-LM* curve model analyse the impact of an increase in the money supply on the equilibrium level of national income and the rate of interest.
9. What do the *IS* and *LM* curves signify ? Under what conditions would the *IS-LM* model be unstable.
10. What is crowding out effect of Government's fiscal policy ? Is it very significant ? What role does interest elasticity of investment play in determining the slope of *IS* curve ?
11. Explain and show graphically how product market is in equilibrium along *IS* curve.
12. Explain *IS* and *LM* curves. What is the role of these two curves in simultaneous determination of equilibrium rate of interest and level of income ?
13. (*a*) Derive *IS* curve for an economy. What are the factors which determine slope of the *IS* curve ?

    (*b*) Show how *IS* curve will change as a result of increase in Government expenditure.
14. Why does *IS* curve slope downward ? How is *IS* curve related to investment multiplier in the Keynesian income theory ? What are the factors which cause a shift in *IS* curve ?
15. Discuss the features of *IS* and *LM* curves. Is the equilibrium between *IS* and *LM* curves always stable?
16. How is *LM* curve derived from money market equilibrium ? Why does *LM* curve slope upward ? How will *LM* curve shfit with increase in money supply in the economy ?
17. Explain with the aid of *IS-LM* curves role of monetary policy for stabilisation of the economy.
18. Explain with the help of *IS-LM* curve model role of fiscal policy in overcoming recession in the economy.

APPENDIX TO CHAPTER 12
IS-LM MODEL : ALGEBRAIC ANALYSIS

In the foregeing chapter we have explained the IS-LM curve model with graphs. In this section we make algebraic analysis IS-LM curves model. We first derive the equations for IS and LM curves and then combine them to show how level of national income and rate of interest are jointly determined through the simultaneous equilibrium of goods and money markets. This algebraic analysis of IS-LM model provides additional insights into how fiscal and monetary policy instruments affect national income and rate of interest.

The Derivation of Equation for IS Curve : Algebraic Method.

The IS curve is derived from goods market equilibrium. The IS curve shows the combinations of levels of income and interest at which goods market is in equilibrium, that is, at which aggregate demand equals income. Aggregate demand, as explained earlier, consists of consumption demand investment demand, government expenditure on goods and services and net exports. Consumption demand is function of disposable income. Disposable income is level of income minus taxes ($Y_d = Y - T$) where Y_d stands for disposable income and T for taxes. However, in a two sector model where we do not incorporate taxation by the government, $Y_d = Y$.

Investment depends on rate of interest. With a given level of income, a higher rate of interest reduces investment demand and a lower rate of interest leads to more investment, that is, investment is negatively related to rate of interest. Thus

$$I = \overline{I} - di$$

Therefore, we have the following equation for aggregate demand (AD)

$$AD = C + I + G + NX \qquad \ldots(1)$$

where $C = a + bY$ (Consumption function)

$I = \overline{I} - di$ (Investment function)

Where $\overline{I}$ is autonomous investment, that is, independent of income and rate of interest

G is government expenditure on goods and services and NX is net exports, that is, exports – imports.

Product market is in equilibrium when

$$Y = AD = C(Y) + I(i) + G + NX \qquad \ldots(2)$$

or

$$Y = (a + bY) + (\overline{I} - di) + G + NX$$

$$Y - bY = a + \overline{I} - di + G + NX$$

$$Y(1-b) = a + \overline{I} - di + G + NX$$

$$Y = \frac{1}{1-b}(a + \overline{I} + G + NX) - \frac{di}{1-b} \qquad \ldots(3)$$

The above equation (3) describes *IS* curve Terms in the brackets are all automous expenditure and are independent of both income and rate of interest. If we denote all these autonomous items by $\overline{A}$, then equation (3) for *IS* can be written as

$$Y = \frac{1}{1-b}(\bar{A}) - \frac{1}{1-b}(di)$$

or
$$Y = \frac{1}{1-b}(\bar{A} - di) \quad \ldots (4)$$

$\frac{1}{1-b}$ is the income multiplier and b is marginal propensity to consume. Given the value of automous expenditure, we can obtain value of Y at different rates of interest to draw an *IS* curve. It is worth noting that the value of automous $(\bar{A})$ determines the intercept of the *IS* curve, d in the term di in equation (3) shows the sensitivity of investment to the changes in rate of interest and determines the slope of *IS* curve. Since fall in interest rate increases investment spending, it will raise aggregate demand and thus the equilibrium level of income. Besides, the slope of the *IS* curve depends on the size of income multiplier.

NUMERICAL PROBLEMS ON *IS* CURVE :TWO SECTOR MODEL

Problem 1. The following equations describe an economy :

$C = 10 + 0.5Y$ (Consumption function)

$I = 190 - 20\,i$ (Investment function)

Derive the equations for *IS* curve and represent it graphically

Solution :

IS curve describes the equation for product market equilibrium at various combinations of level of income and rate of interest.

$$Y = AD = C + I$$

Thus, Y
$$= 10 + 0.5Y + 190 - 20\,i$$

$$Y - 0.5Y = 200 - 20\,i$$

$$Y(1 - 0.5) = 200 - 20\,i$$

$$\frac{1}{2}Y = 200 - 20i$$

$$Y = 400 - 40\,i$$

Thus, *IS* curve is : $Y = 400 - 40\,i$

Alternative Method

Alternative way to get *IS* curve is to directly use *IS* curve equation and fill in it the values of various parameters and variables.

The equation for *IS* curve is given by :

$$Y = \frac{1}{1-b}(\bar{A} - di)$$

where $\bar{A} = a + \bar{I}$ (*i.e.* the sum of autonomous consumption (a) and investment expenditure $(\bar{I})$, b is marginal propensity to consume, d is sensitivity of investment to changes in rate of interest. Y and i are level of income and rate of interest respectively.

Substituting the values of various parameters we have the following *IS* equation :

$$Y = \frac{1}{1-0.5}[(10+190)-20i]$$

$$= \frac{1}{0.5}(200-20i)$$

$$= 400 - 40\,i$$

or equation for *IS* curve : $Y = 400 - 40\,i$

Graphic Representation : We can represent the *IS* equation graphically by taking some values of interest and calculate the level of income using the *IS* equation.

Suppose rate of interest is 5 per cent. Substituting this value of interest in *IS* equation we have

$$Y = 400 - 40\,i$$

$$= 400 - 40 \times 5$$

$$= 400 - 200 = 200$$

Thus, at 5 per cent rate of interest level of income is 200,

Now, suppose rate of interest is 2, then the level of income,

$$Y = 400 - 40 \times 2$$

$$= 400 - 80 = 320$$

At 2 per cent rate of interest, level of income is 320.

We have now two combinations of interest and income. We can plot these and obtain *IS* curve. This is done in Figure 12A.1

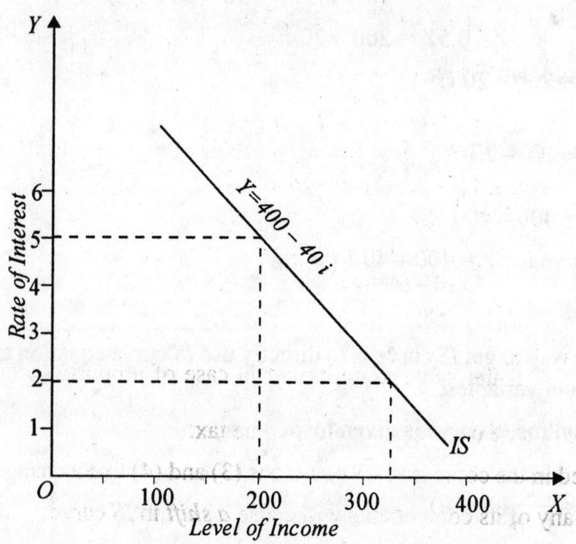

Fig. 12A.1. *Graphic Representation of IS Curve*

IS Curve : Three Sector Model with Taxation and Transfer Payments

In the last section we have derived the *IS* curve taking government expenditure G on goods and services without considering taxation and transfer payments by it. In fact the concept of consumption function conceives consumption as a function of disposable income and is therefore written as

$$C = a + bY_D \quad \ldots (1)$$

Now, disposable income Y_D is obtained from deducting tax and adding transfer payments by the government. Thus

$$Y_D = Y - T + R$$

where T is tax revenue and R is the transfer payments by the government. Whereas a tax reduces disposable income, transfer payment raises it.

Further, whereas transfer payments are assumed as lump sum amount, tax can be lump sum tax or levied as proportion of income. If we assume proportionate income tax, then,

$$T = tY$$

where t is the proportion of income which is taken away by way of tax. . . . (2)

Let us derive *IS* equation incorporating proportionate income tax and lump sum transfer payments.

$$Y = AD = C + I + G + NX$$

$$Y = a + bY_D + I + G + NX$$

$$= a + b(Y - tY + R) + \bar{I} - di + G + NX$$

$$= a + bY - btY + bR + \bar{I} - di + G + NX$$

$$= a + b(1-t)Y + bR + \bar{I} - di + G + NX$$

$$Y = \bar{A} + b(1-t)Y - di \quad \ldots (3)$$

where $\bar{A} = a + bR + \bar{I} + G + NX$

Rearranging equation (3) we have

$$Y - b(1-t)Y = \bar{A} - di$$

or $Y[1 - b(1-t] = \bar{A} - di$

$$Y = \frac{1}{1-b(1-t)}(\bar{A} - di) \quad \ldots (4)$$

where $\frac{1}{1-b(1-t)}$ is the value of multiplier in case of proportionate income tax. Equation (4) represents *IS* curve in case of proportionate income tax.

It may be noted in the context of *IS* equations (3) and (4) that a change in autonomous spending ($\bar{A}$) as a result of any of its components will cause *a shift* in *IS* curve.

NUMERICAL PROBLEMS ON THE *IS* CURVE : THREE SECTOR MODEL (With Taxation)

Problem 1. The following equations describe an economy

$$C = 100 + 0.75\, Y_d$$
$$I = 50 - 25i$$
$$T = G = 50$$

where C is aggregate consumption, Y_d is disposable income, I is aggregate investment, T is taxes, G is government purchases and i is the interest rate. Derive the *IS* curve for the economy.

Solution. $Y = C + I + G$

Now, $C = 100 + 0.75\, Y_d = 100 + 0.75\,(Y - T)$

$$C = 100 + 0.75\,(Y - 50)$$
$$I = 50 - 25\,i$$
$$G = 50$$
$$T = 50$$
$$Y = 100 + 0.75\,(Y - 50) + 50 - 25i + 50$$
$$Y = 200 + 0.75\,Y - 0.75 \times 50 - 25i$$
$$Y - 0.75Y = 200 - 37.5 - 25i$$
$$Y\,(1 - 0.75) = 162.5 - 25i$$
$$\frac{1}{4}Y = 162.5 - 25i$$
$$Y = 650 - 100\,i$$

IS equation is : $Y = 650 - 100\,i$

DERIVATION OF EQUATION FOR *LM* CURVE : ALGEBRAIC ANALYSIS

Having derived algebraically equation for *IS* curve we now turn to the derivation of equation for *LM* curve. It will be recalled that *LM* curve is a curve that shows combinations of interest rates and levels of income at which money market is in equilibrium, that is, at which demand for money equals supply of money. We explain the derivation of *LM* curve in two steps. First, we show how money demand depends on interest rate and level of income. It is worth noting that in their demand for money people care more about the purchasing power of money, that is, people's demand is for *real money balances* rather than nominal money balances. Real money balances are given by $\frac{M}{P}$ where M stands for nominal money demand and P for price level.

The demand for real money balances depends on the level of real income and interest rate. Thus $M_d = L(Y,\ i)$. As explained earlier, demand for real money balances increases with the rise in level of income and decreases with rise in rate of interest. Let us assume that money demand function is linear. Then

$$L(Y, i) = kY - hi \qquad k,\ h > 0 \qquad \ldots (5)$$

Parameter k represents how much demand for real money balances increases when level of income rises. Parameter h represents how much demand for real money balances decreases when rate of interest rises. The equilibrium in the money market is established where demand for real money balances equals supply of real money balances and is given by

$$\frac{M}{P} = kY - hi \qquad \ldots (6)$$

Money supply (M) is set by the central bank of a country and we assume it to remain constant for a period. Besides, we assume the price level (P) to remain constant.

Solving the equation (6) for interest rate we have

$$i = \frac{1}{h}(kY - \frac{M}{P}) \qquad \ldots (7)$$

The above equation (7) describes the equation for *LM* curve. To be precise it gives us the equilibrium interest rate for any given value of level of income (Y) and real money balances. In drawing *LM* curve, real money balances are assumed to be constant. Thus *LM* curve describes money market equilibrium for different values of income and rate of interest, given a fixed value of real money balances $\left(\frac{M}{P}\right)$. Thus, given the real money balances $\left(\frac{M}{P}\right)$, we can obtain a rate of interest for different values of income.

Let us state some conclusions about *LM* curve as given by equation (7). First, since in equation (7) for *LM* curve, the coefficient (k) of income (Y) is positive, *LM* curve will slope upward. That is, higher income requires higher interest rate for money market to be in equilibrium, given the supply of real money balances. Second, since the coefficient of real money balances is negative, the expansion in real money balances will cause a shift in the *LM* curve to be right, and decrease in the real money balances will shift *LM* curve to the left.

From the coefficient of income k/h, we can know whether *LM* curve is steep or flat. If demand for money is not much sensitive to level of income, then k will be small. Therefore, in case of small k (*i.e.* low sensitivity of interest with respect to changes in income), small change in interest rate is required to offset a small increase in money demand caused by a given *increase in income.*

NUMERICAL PROBLEMS

Problem 1. *Given the following data about the monetary sector of the economy* :

$$M_d = 0.4Y - 80\,i$$

$$Ms = 1200 \text{ crores.}$$

where M_d is demand for money, Y is level of income, i is rate of interest and M_s is the supply of money

1. *Derive the equation for LM function*
2. *Give the economic interpretation of the LM curve. Draw LM curve from the above data*

Solution :

For money market to be in equilibrium

$$M_d = M_s$$

$$0.4\,Y - 80\,i = 1200$$

$$80\,i = 0.4\,Y - 1200$$

$$i = \frac{0.4Y}{80} - \frac{1200}{80}$$

$$i = \frac{1}{200}Y - 15$$

Thus we get the following *LM* function :

$$i=\frac{1}{200}Y-15 \qquad \ldots (i)$$

Alternatively, *LM* equation or function can also be stated as :

$$Y = 200\,i + 3000 \qquad \ldots (ii)$$

LM curve means what would be rate of interest when money market is in equilibrium, given the level of income. Thus, if level of national income is ₹ 4000 crores, then using *LM* equation (*i*) we have

$$i=\frac{1}{200}\times 4000-15$$

$$= 20 - 15 = 5\%$$

Thus, at income of ₹ 4000 crores, rate of interest will be 5 per cent when money market is in equilibrium.

Now, if level of income is ₹ 4400 crores, equilibrium rate of interest will be

$$i=\frac{1}{200}Y-15$$

$$=\frac{1}{200}\times 4400-15$$

$$= 22 - 15 = 7\%$$

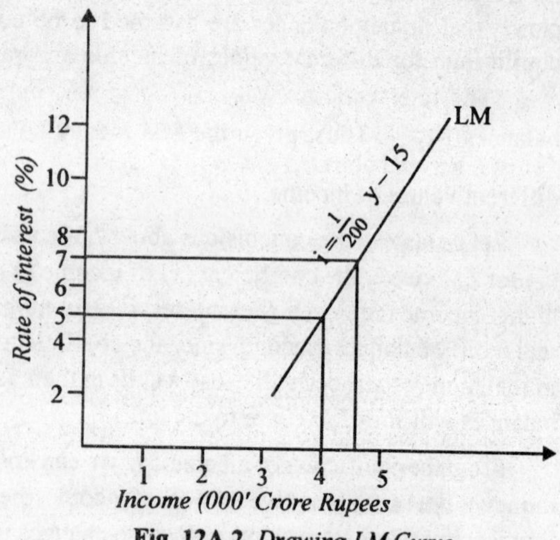

Fig. 12A.2. *Drawing LM Curve*

With two combinations of interest rate and income level when money market is in equilibrium we can draw *LM* curve as shown in 12A.2.

Problem 2. *The following data is given for the monetary sector of the economy.*

Transaction demand for money, $M_t = 0.5Y$. *Speculative demand for money,* $M_{sp} = 105 - 1500\,i$

Money supply $M_s = 150$

Derive *LM equation from the above data*

Solution. Total demand function for money can be obtained by adding up the transactions demand for money (M_t) and speculative demand for money (M_{sp}). Thus

$$M_d = M_t + M_{sp}$$

$$M_d = 0.5Y + 105 - 1500\,i$$

In money market equilibrium

$$M_d = M_s$$

$$0.5Y + 105 - 1500i = 150$$

$$1500\,i = 0.5Y + 105 - 150$$

$$i=\frac{0.5Y}{1500}-\frac{45}{1500}$$

$$=\frac{1}{3000}Y-\frac{3}{100}$$

Thus, *LM* equation is :

$$i=\frac{1}{3000}Y-\frac{3}{100}$$

Alternatively, *LM* equation can be written as

$$Y=3000i+\frac{3}{100}\times 3000$$

$$Y=3000\,i+90$$

IS-LM MODEL : ALGEBRAIC ANALYSIS
(Joint Equilibrium of Income and Interest Rate)

The intersection of *IS* and *LM* curves determines joint equilibrium of income and interest rate. Mathematically, we can obtain the equilibrium values by using the equations of *IS* and *LM* curves derived above. Thus,

Equation for *IS* curve : $Y=\frac{1}{1-b}(\bar{A}-di)$ ... (*i*)

Equation for *LM* curve : $i=\frac{1}{h}(kY-\frac{M}{p})$ ... (*ii*)

Joint determination of equilibrium values of income and interest rate requires that both the *IS* and *LM* equations hold good. In this way both the goods market and money market equilibrium will be achieved at the same interest and income levels in the two markets. To find such equilibrium values we substitute the interest rate from the *LM* equation (*ii*) into the *IS* equation (*i*). Doing so we have

$$Y=\frac{1}{1-b}\left[\bar{A}-\frac{d}{h}(kY-\frac{M}{P})\right]$$

$$Y=\frac{1}{1-b}\left[\bar{A}-\frac{d}{h}(kY)+\frac{d}{h}\left(\frac{M}{P}\right)\right] \quad ...(iii)$$

The equation shows that the equilibrium level of income depends on exogenously given autonomous variables $(\bar{A})$ such as automous consumption, autonomous investment, government expenditure on goods and services, and the real money supply $\left(\frac{M}{P}\right)$ and further on the size of multiplier $\left(\frac{1}{1-b}\right)$. It will be noticed from equation (*iii*) that higher the autonomous expenditure, the higher the level of equilibrium income. Further, the greater the real money supply, the higher the level of national income.

NUMERICAL PROBLEMS ON IS-LM MODEL

Problem – 1. *For an economy the following functions are given :*

$C = 100 + 0.8\,y$

$S = -100 + 0.2\,y$

$I = 120 - 5\,i$

$M^s = 120$

$M^d = 0.2y - 5i$

Find out (1) IS equation, (2) LM equation, (3) equilibrium level of income and interest rate

Solution :

IS curve : $Y = \left[\frac{1}{1-b}(a+\bar{I}) - di\right]$

where $b = MPC$, a and $\bar{I}$ are autonomous consumption and autonomous investment respectively, d is sensitivity of investment demand to changes in rate of interest (i).

Substituting the values of various parameters we have

$$Y = \frac{1}{1-0.8}[(100+120) - 5i]$$

$$= \frac{1}{0.2} = (220 - 5i)$$

$$Y = 5(220 - 5i)$$

$$Y = 1100 - 25i$$

Thus *IS* curve is :

$$Y = 1100 - 25i \quad \ldots (i)$$

Derivation of *LM* Equation :

For money market equilibrium

$$M^d = M^s$$

$$0.2Y - 5i = 120$$

$$5i = 0.2Y - 120$$

$$i = \frac{0.2}{5}Y - 24$$

LM curve is :

$$i = \frac{0.2}{5}Y - 24 \quad \ldots (ii)$$

Substituting the value of i in the *IS* equation (i) we have

$$Y = 1000 - 25\left(\frac{0.2}{5}Y - 24\right)$$

$$= 1100 - (1Y - 600)$$

$$Y = 1100 - Y + 600$$

$$2Y = 1700$$

$$Y = \frac{1700}{2} = 850$$

Thus the equilibrium level of income is 850. To obtain the equilibrium rate of interest we substitute the value of Y in LM equation (*iii*) obtained above we have

$$i = \frac{0.2}{5}(850) - 24$$

$$= \frac{1}{25}(850) - 24$$

$$= 34 - 24 = 10$$

Thus equilibrium rate of interest is 10 per cent.

Problem 2. *Consider the following economy :*

$$C = 100 + 0.8 Y_d$$

$$I = 50 - 25i$$

$$G = T = 50$$

$$\frac{M^s}{P} = 200$$

$$M^d = Y - 25\,i$$

1. *Calculate the IS and LM curves.*
2. *Calculate the equilibrium levels of output and interest.*

Solution :

$$Y = C + I + G$$

Substituting the values of C, I and G we have

$$Y = 100 + 0.8\, Y_d + 50 - 25\,i + 50$$

$$Y = 100 + 0.8\,(Y - T) + 50 - 25i + 50$$

or $$Y = 100 + 0.8\,(Y - 50) + 50 - 25\,i + 50$$

$$Y = 200 + 0.8Y - 40 - 25\,i$$

$$= 160 + 0.8Y - 25i$$

$$(Y - 0.8Y) = 160 - 25\,i$$

$$Y(1 - 0.8) = 160 - 25\,i$$

$$0.2Y = 160 - 25\,i$$

$$Y = 800 - 125i$$

IS curve is : $Y = 800 - 125\,i$ ... (*i*)

Money Market Equilibrium : Money market is in equilibrium when $M^d = \frac{M^s}{P}$

Thus, in equilibrium

$$M^d = \frac{M^S}{P}$$

$$Y - 25i = 200$$

$$Y = 200 + 25\,i$$

Thus, *LM* curve is : $Y = 200 + 25\,i$ ... *(iii)*

Since in equilibrium *IS* and *LM* curves intersect (or *IS* = *LM*) we have

$$200 + 25i = 800 - 125i$$

$$150\,i = 800 - 200 = 600$$

$$i = \frac{600}{150} = 4$$

Thus equilibrium rate of interest is 4%

Substituting the value of *i* in *IS* equation (*i*) we have :

$$Y = 800 - 125 \times 4$$

$$= 800 - 400 = 400$$

Thus, the equilibrium rate of interest is 4 per cent and equilibrium level of income is 200

Problem 3. *Consider an economy with the following features*

Consumption, $C = 100 + 0.9\,Y_d$

Income tax, $t = \frac{1}{3}Y$

Investment, $I = 600 - 30\,i$

Government expenditure, $G = 300$

Transaction demand money for $M_d = 0.4Y$

Speculative demand for money, $M_2 = -50\,i$

Nominal money supply $\bar{M} = 1040$

Price level = 2

(where Y_d *stands for disposable income, and i for rate of interest)*

Derive the IS and LM equations and fund out the equilibrium levels of income and rate of interest.

Solution :

(i) Obtaining *IS* equation :

$$Y = C + I + G$$

$$= 100 + 0.9\,Y_d + 600 - 30i + 100$$

$$= 100 + 0.9\left(Y - \frac{1}{3}Y\right) + 600 - 30i + 300$$

$$= 1000 + 0.9y - 0.3y - 30\,i$$

$$Y - 0.9y + 0.3Y = 1000 - 30\,i$$

$$Y(1 - 0.9 + 0.3) = 1000 - 30\,i$$

$$0.4Y = 1000 - 30\,i$$

$$Y = 1000 \times \frac{10}{4} - \left(30 \times \frac{10}{4}\right)i$$

$$= 2500 - 75i$$

Thus *IS* equation is : $Y = 2500 - 75\,i$ . . . (*i*)

(*i*) Obtaining *LM* equation :

For money market equilibrium :

$$M^d = M^S$$
$$M^d = M_1 + M_2$$
$$= 0.4y - 50i$$

Real money supply $M^S = \frac{\bar{M}}{P} = \frac{1040}{2} = 520$

Therefore, $0.4Y - 50i = 520$

$$0.4Y = 520 + 50i$$

$$Y = 520 \times \frac{10}{4} + (50 \times \frac{10}{4})i$$

$$= 1300 + 125i$$

LM function is : $1300 + 125i$

In equilibrium *IS* = *LM*

$$2500 - 75\,i = 1300 + 125\,i \quad \ldots (ii)$$

$$125i + 75i = 2500 - 1300$$

$$200i = 1200$$

Therefore, interest, $i = \frac{1200}{200} = 6\%$

Substituting the value of $i = 6$ in *IS* equation we have

$$Y = 2500 - 75 \times 6$$
$$= 2500 - 450$$
$$= 2050$$

Thus, equilibrium income is 2050 and equilibrium interest is 6 %.

Problem 4. (Four Sector Model) : *The major macro aggregates for an economy are given as follows* :

Consumption, $C = 60 + 0.8Y_d$ (Y_d *is disposable income*)

Investment $I = 100 - 5i$

% Interest rate $i = 6$

Government expenditure, $G = 76$

Lump-sum Tax, $T = 15$

Transfer payments, $TR = 60$

Exports $X = 70$

Imports $M = 12 + 0.2Y$

1. *Derive the IS curve using the above data*
2. *Calculate equilibrium level of income*
3. *Calculate foreign trade multiplier*

Solution :

$$Y = C + I + G + X - M \qquad \ldots (i)$$

$$\text{and } Y_d = Y - T + TR$$

Substituting the values of variables in equation (*i*) we have

$$Y = 60 + 0.8\,(Y - 15 + 60) + 100 - 5i + 76 + 70 - (12 + 0.2Y)$$

$$= 60 + 0.8Y + 0.8X\,45 + 100 + 76 + 70 - 12 - 0.2Y - 5i$$

$$Y - 0.8Y + 0.2Y = (60 + 36 + 100 + 76 + 58) - 5i$$

$$Y(1 - 0.8 + 0.2)\,Y = 330 - 5\,i$$

$$0.4Y = 330 - 5i$$

or

$$\frac{2}{5}Y = 330 - 5i$$

$$Y = 330 \times \frac{5}{2} - \frac{5}{2} \times 5i$$

$$Y = 825 - 12.5\,i$$

(*i*) Equation for *IS* curve is : $Y = 825 - 12.5\,i$

(*ii*) Equilibrium level of income when rate of interest is 6 per cent

$$Y = 825 - 12.5 \times 6$$

$$= 825 - 75 = 750$$

(*iii*) Foreign trade multiplier $= \dfrac{1}{1 - b + m}$

where $b = MPC = 0.8$

m = marginal profensity to import = 0.2

Thus, foreign trade multiplier $= \dfrac{1}{1 - 0.8 + 0.2} = \dfrac{1}{0.4} = \dfrac{5}{2} = 2.5$

Problem 5. *The follow data are given for an an economy*

Consumption : $C = 40 + 0.75y$

Investment : $I = 140 - 10i$

Government expenditure : $G = 100$

Lump sum tax $T = 80$

Money demand, $M^d = 0.2\,Y - 5i$

Money supply, $M^S = 85$

(*i. is % interest rate; other figures in Rs. crores*)

(*a*) *Find out the equilibrium income, Y and interest rate i*

(*b*) *Suppose the government increases its expenditure on education and health services by Rs. 65 crores what would be its effect on equilibrium income and rate of interest.*

Solution. In order to obtain equilibrium income, we have to find out first the equations for *IS* and *LM* curves.

$$Y = C + I + G$$

where $C = 40 + 0.75\ Y_d$ and $I = 140 - 10\ i$ and $G = 100$

Therefore, $Y = 40 + 0.75\ Y_d + 140 - 10\ i + 100$

$$= 40 + 0.75\ (Y - 80) + 140 - 10\ i + 100$$

$$= 40 + 0.75Y - 60 + 140 - 10\ i + 100$$

$$Y - 0.75\ Y = 220 - 10\ i$$

$$0.25\ Y = 220 - 10\ i$$

$$\frac{1}{4}Y = 220 - 10i$$

$$Y = 880 - 40\ i$$

Thus *IS* equation : $Y = 880 - 40i$ . . . (*i*)

To obtain *LM* function, we equate demand for money with supply of money.

$$M^d = M^S$$

$$0.2Y - 5i = 85$$

$$5i = 0.2Y - 85$$

$$i = \frac{0.2}{5}Y - 17$$

Thus, *LM* function is

$$i = 0.04\ Y - 17 \qquad \text{. . . (ii)}$$

Substituting the value of *i* in the *IS* function equation (*i*) we have

$$Y = 880 - 40\ (0.04\ Y - 17)$$

$$= 880 - 1.6Y + 680$$

$$Y + 1.6Y = 880 + 680$$

$$2.6Y = 1560$$

$$Y = 1560 \times \frac{10}{26} = 600$$

Thus, equilibrium level of national income is 600 crores

Substituting the value of 600 for *Y* in *IS* equation (i) we have

$$600 = 880 - 40\ i$$

$$40\ i = 880 - 600 = 280$$

$$i = \frac{280}{40} = 7$$

The equilibrium rate of interest is 7 per cent.

---

* The students can check this with the general equation for *IS* curve, that is, $Y = \frac{1}{1-b+m}(\bar{A} - di)$ where A is the sum of automous factors, that is, $\bar{A} = a + bTR - bT + \bar{I} + \bar{G} + \bar{X} - \bar{M}$ and $\frac{1}{1-b+m}$ is foreign trade multiplier

(*b*) With the increase in Government expenditure by Rs. 65 crores

New Income, $Y' = C + I + G + \Delta G$

$$Y' = 40 + 0.75\,(Y'-80) + 140 - 10\,i + 100 + 65$$

$$= 40 + 0.75Y' - 60 + 140 - 10\,i + 100 + 65$$

$$Y' - 0.75\,Y' = 285 - 10\,i$$

$$Y'(1 - 0.75) = 285 - 10\,i$$

$$\frac{1}{4}Y' = 285 - 10i$$

$$Y' = 1140 - 40i$$

New equation for *IS* curve is = $Y' = 1140 - 40i$

Substituting the value of *i* from *LM* function equation (*ii*) we have

$$Y' = 1140 - 40(0.04\,Y' - 17)$$

$$Y' = 1140 - 1.6Y' + 680$$

$$Y' + 1.6Y' = 1820$$

$$Y'\,(1 + 1.6) = 1820$$

$$2.6Y' = 1820$$

$$Y' = 1820 \times \frac{10}{26} = 700$$

Now, substituting the value of Y in the *LM* equation (*ii*) we have

New interest $i = 0.04\,(700) - 17$

$$= 28.00 - 17 = 11$$

$$= 11$$

Thus, the new equilibrium income is 700 crores and interest rate is 11 per cent

Problem 6. *An economy shows the following features :*

Consumption, $C = 50 + 0.9\,(Y - T)$

Tax Revenue, $T = 100$

Investment, $I = 150 - 5i$

Government expenditure, $G = 100$

Money demand, $L = 0.2\,Y - 10\,i$

Real money supply, $\frac{M}{P} = 100$

Exports, $X = 20$

Imports, $M = 10 + 0.1\,Y$

where Y = income, i = rate of interest figures in Rs. crores.

(a) *Obtain the IS and lM equations of the economy*

(b) *Find out equilibrium income and rate of interest atom*

(c) *Find the balance of trade*

Solution :

Let us first obtain the *IS* equation

$$Y = C + I + G + (X–M)$$
$$= 50 + 0.9\,(Y - 100) + 150 - 5i + 100 + 20 - (10 + 0.1Y)$$
$$= 50 + 0.9Y - 90 + 150 - 5i + 100 + 20 - 10 - 0.\,1Y$$
$$Y - 0.9\,Y + 0.1Y = 50 - 90 + 150 - 5i + 100 + 20 - 10$$
$$Y(1–0.9 + 0.1) = 220 - 5\,i$$
$$0.2Y = 220 - 5\,i$$
$$Y = 220 \times 5 - 25i$$
$$Y = 1100 - 25i \qquad \ldots (i)$$

In money market equilibrium :

$$M^d = M^s$$
$$0.2Y - 10i = 100$$
$$0.2Y = 100 + 10\,i$$

LM Equation is : $Y = 500 + 50\,i$

In equilibrium $IS = LM$

$$1100 - 25i = 500 + 50i$$
$$75i = 600$$
$$i = \frac{600}{75} = 8\%$$

Substituting the value of $i = 8$ in *IS* equation (*i*) we have

$$Y = 1100 - 25i = 1100 - 25 \times 8 = 1100 - 200 = 900$$

Balance of Trade (BOT) $= X - M$

$$X = 20$$

Imports, $M = 10 \times 0.1Y$

As found above $Y = 900$

Imports, $M = 10 + 0.1 \times 900$

$$= 10 + 90 = 100$$
$$\text{BOT} = 20 - 100 = -80$$

Trade Deficit = 80

Alternative Method :Using Straight away the *IS* equation

$$Y = \frac{1}{1-b+m}(\bar{A} - di)$$

where $\bar{A} = a - bT + \bar{I} + G + \bar{X} - \bar{M} - di$

$$Y = \frac{1}{1-0.9+0.1}[(50-90+150+100+20-10)-5i]$$
$$= \frac{1}{0.2}(220-5i)$$
$$= 5(220-5i)$$
$$Y = 1100 - 25i$$

CHAPTER 13

Inflation–Unemployment Trade-off : Phillips Curve and Rational Expectations Theory

Introduction

In the simple Keynesian model of an economy, the aggregate supply curve (with variable price level) is of inverse L-shape, that is, it is a horizontal straight line up to the full-employment level of output and beyond that it becomes horizontal. This means that during recession or depression when the economy is having a good deal of excess capacity and large-scale unemployment of labour and idle capital stock, the aggregate supply curve is perfectly elastic. When full employment level of output is reached, aggregate supply curve becomes perfectly inelastic. With this shape of aggregate supply curve assumed in the simple Keynesian model, increase in aggregate demand before the level of full employment, causes increase in the level of real national output and employment with price level remaining unchanged. That is, no cost has to be incurred in the form of rise in the price level (i.e., inflation rate) for raising the level of output and reducing unemployment. In the Keynesian model, once the full-employment level of output is reached and aggregate supply curve becomes vertical, further increase in aggregate demand caused by the expansionary fiscal and monetary policies will only raise the price level in the economy. That is, in this simple Keynesian model, inflation occurs in the economy only after full-employment level of output has been attained. Thus, *in the simple Keynesian model with inverse L-shaped aggregate supply curve there is no trade off or clash between inflation and unemployment.*

INFLATION-UNEMPLOYMENT TRADE -OFF: PHILLIPS CURVE

However, the actual empirical evidence did not fit well in the above simple Keynesian macro model. A noted British economists, A.W. Phillips[1] published an article in 1958 based on his good deal of rasearch using historical data from the U.K. for about 100 years in which he arrived at the conclusion that *there in fact existed an inverse relationship between rate of unemployment and rate of inflation.* This inverse relation implies a trade-off, that is, for reducing unemployment, price in the form of a higher rate of inflation has to be paid, and for reducing the rate of inflation, price in terms of a higher rate of unemployment has to be borne. On graphically fitting a curve to the historical data Phillips obtained a downward sloping curve exhibiting the inverse relation between rate of inflation and the rate of unemployment and this curve is now named after his name as *Phillips Curve.* This Phillips curve is shown in Fig. 13.1 where along the horizontal axis the rate of unemployment and along the vertical axis the rate of inflation is measured. It will be seen that when rate of inflation is 10 per cent, the unemployment rate is 3 per cent, and when rate of inflation is reduced to 5 per cent per annum, say by pursuing contractionary fiscal policy and thereby reducing aggregate demand, the rate of unemployment increases to 8 per cent of labour force. The actual Phillips curve drawn from the data of sixties (1961-69) for the United States also shows the inverse relation between unemployment rate and rate of inflation (see Fig. 13.2). Such empirical data

1. A.W. Phillips, "Relation between Unemployment and Rate of Change in Money Wages in the United Kingdom, 1861-1957." *Economica* 25 (Nov. 1958), pp. 283-299.

pertaining to the fifties and sixties for other developed countries seemed to confirm the Phillips curve

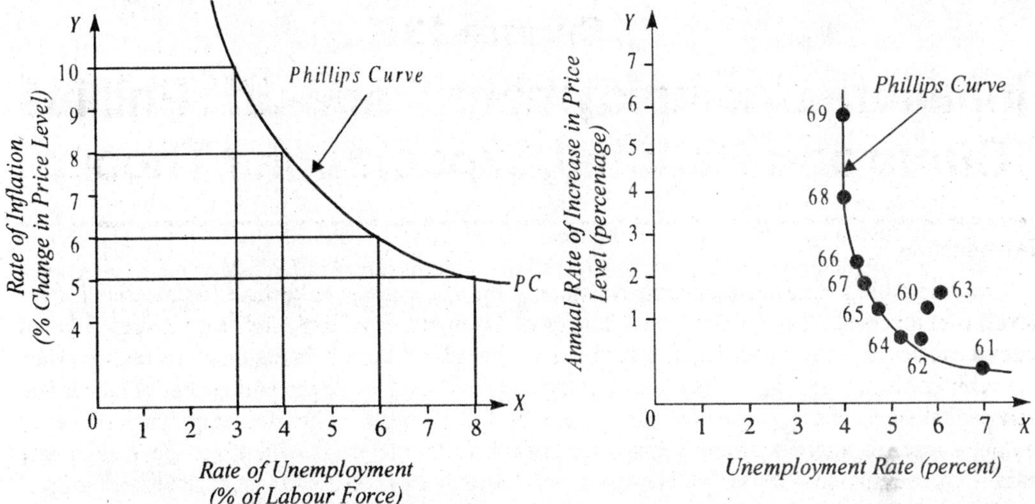

Fig. 13.1. *Phillips Curve showing Negative Relationship between Rates of Inflation and Unemployment*

Fig. 13.2. *Phillips Curve of the Sixties of the United Statesin the Sixties*

concept. On the basis of this, many economists came to believe that there existed a *stable Phillips curve* which depicted a predicatable inverse relation between inflation and unemployment. Further, on the basis of a *stable Phillips curve* for a country, they emphasised the trade off that confronts the economic policy makers. This trade off presents a dilemma for the policy makers; should they choose a higher rate of inflation with lower unemployment or a higher rate of unemployment with a low inflation rate. In what follows we first explain the rationale underlying the Phillips curve, that is, how the inverse relationship between inflation and unemployment can be theoretically explained. We will further explain why this concept of stable Phillips curve depicting inverse relation between inflation and unemployment broke down during seventies and early eighties. During seventies a strange phenomenon was witnessed in the USA and Britain when there existed *a high rate of inflation side by side with high unemployment rate*. This was contrary to both Phillips curve concept and the simple Keynesian model. This simultaneous existence of both high rate of inflation and high unemployment rate (or low level of real national product) during the seventies and early eighties has been described as *stagflation* which has been explained in the previous chapter.

Keynesian Explanation of Phillips Curve

Let us first provide an explanation for the Phillips curve. Both Keynesians and Moneterists agreed to the existence of the Phillips curve. The explanation of Phillips curve by the Keynesian economists is quite simple and is graphically illustrated in Fig. 13.3. It may be noted that Keynesian economists assume the upward-sloping short-run aggregate supply curve. In fact, Keynes himself recognised that the curve *SAS* is upward sloping in intermediate range, that is, as the economy approaches near full employment level, the aggregate supply curve slopes upward. According to Keynesian economists, short-run aggregate supply curve is upward sloping for two reasons. First, as output is increased by the firms in the economy, diminishing returns to variable factors, especially to labour, accure resulting in fall in marginal physical product (MPP_L) of labour. With money wage rate (W) as given and fixed, the fall in the marginal physical product of labour causes the rise in the marginal cost (MC) of production $\left(\text{Note that } MC = \dfrac{W}{MPP_L}\right)$. With the fall in the *MPP* of labour, wage rate remaining constant, the term $\frac{W}{MPP_L}$ measuring marginal cost (*MC*) will rise.

The second reason for the marginal cost to go up is the rise in the wage rate as employment and output are increased. When under pressure of aggregate demand for output, demand for labour increases, its wage rate tends to rise, supply curve of labour being upward sloping. Even Keynes himself believed that as the economy approached near full employment, labour shortage might appear in some sectors of the economy causing increase in the wage rate. Thus, marginal cost of firms increases as more labour is employed due to diminishing marginal physical product of labour and also because wage rate also rises. In fact Phillips himself while discussing the relationship between inflation and unemployment, considered the relationship between rate of increase in wage rate (as a proxy for the rate of inflation) on the one hand and unemployment rate on the other.

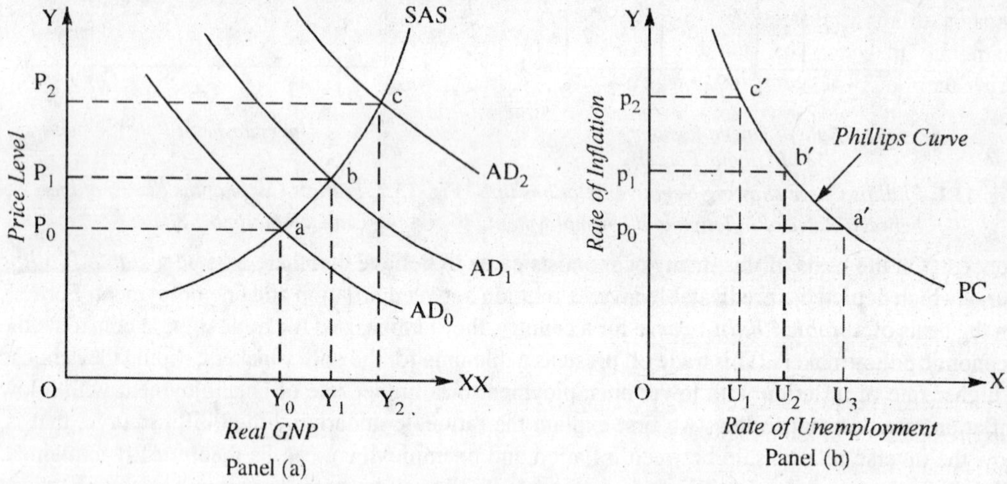

Fig. 13.3. *Keynesian Explanation of Phillips Curve*

Now, it will be seen from panel (*a*) of Fig. 13.3 that with the initial aggregate demand curve AD_0 and the given aggregate supply curve *AS*, the price level P_0 and output level Y_0 are determined. Now, suppose the aggregate demand curve increases from AD_0 to AD_1, it will be seen that price level rises to P_1 and aggregate national output increases from Y_0 to Y_1. Note that increase in aggregate national product means increase in employment of labour and therefore reduction in unemployment rate. Thus the rise in the price level from P_0 to P_1 (*i.e.*, occurrence of inflation) results in lowering of unemployment rate showing inverse relation between the two. Further, if aggregate demand increases to AD_2, the price level further rises to P_2 and national output increases to Y_2 which will further lower the rate of unemployment. The greater the rate at which aggregate demand increases, the higher will be the rate of inflation which will cause greater increase in aggregate output and employment resulting in much lower rate of unemployment. Thus, ***a higher rate of increase in aggregate demand and consequently a higher rate of rise in price level is associated with the lower rate of unemployment and vice-versa.*** This is what is represented by Phillips curve. Consider panel (*b*) of Fig. 13.3 where point *a′* on the downward sloping Phillips curve *PC* corresponds to point *a* of panel (*a*) of Fig. 13.3. In panel (*b*) of the Fig. 13.3 we have shown the rate of unemployment equal to U_3 corresponding to the price level P_0 of panel (*a*). When the aggregate demand shifts to AD_1, there is a certain rate of inflation and price level rises to P_1 and aggregate output expands to Y_1. As seen above, this increase in aggregate output leads to the increase in employment of labour bringing about decline in unemployment rate. Suppose the rate of rise in the price level (*i.e.*, the rate of inflation) when it increases from P_0 to P_1 in panel (*a*) following the increase in aggregate demand is greater than the rate of rise in the price level of the previous period, we obtain a lower rate of unemployment U_2 than before corresponding to a higher inflation rate p_1 in the Phillips curve *PC* in panel (*b*). With a still higher rate of inflation, say p_2, when price level rises from P_1 to P_2 in panel (*a*) following the increase in aggregate demand to AD_2, we have a further lower rate of unemployment equal to U_1 in panel (*b*) corresponding to point *c′* on the Phillips curve *PC*. This gives us a downward-sloping Phillips curve *PC*.

It is clear from above the through increase in aggregate demand and upward-sloping aggregate supply curve, Keynesians were able to explain the downward-sloping Phillips curve showing the negative relation between rates inflation and unemployment.

Collapse of Phillips Curve in the USA (1971-91)

During the sixties Phillips curve became an important concept of macro-economic analysis. The stable relationship described by it suggested that policy makers could have a lower rate of unemployment if they could bear with a higher rate of inflation. On the contrary, they could achieve a low rate of inflation only if they were prepared to reconcile with a higher rate of unemployment. But a stable Phillips curve could not hold good during the seventies and eighties, especially in the United States. Therefore, experience in the two decades (1971-91), has prompted some economists to say that the stable Phillips curve has disappeared. Figure 13.4 shows that data regarding the behaviour of inflation and unemployment during the seventies and eighties in the United States which do not conform to a stable Phillips curve. *In these two decades we have periods when rates of both inflation and unemployment increased (that is, a high rate of inflation was associated with a high unemployment rate, which shows the absence of trade off.* We have shown the data of inflation rate and unemployment in case of the United States in Fig. 13.4. From the data it appears that instead of remaining stable, the Phillip curve shifted to the right in the seventies and early eighties and to the left during the late eighties. (see Fig. 13.4).

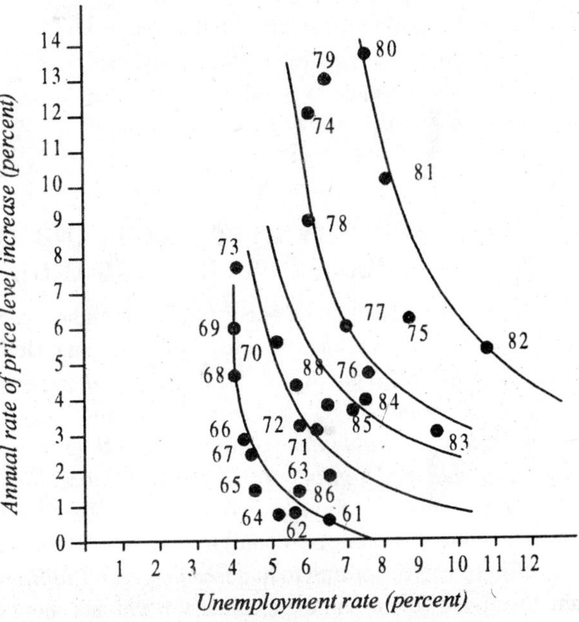

Fig. 13.4. *Shift in Phillips Curve : United States*

Causes of Shift in Phillips Curve

Now, what could be the cause of shift in the Phillips curve. There are two explanations for this. First, according to Keynesians, the occurrence of higher inflation rate along with the increase in unemployment rate witnessed during the seventies and early eighties was due to the *adverse supply shocks* in the form of four fold increase in the prices of oil and petroleum poducts delivered to the American economy first in 1973-74 and then again in 1979-80. Consider Fig. 13.5 where AD_0 and AS_0 are in equilibrium at point *E* and determine price level OP_0 and aggregate national output OY_0. The hike in price of oil by *OPEC*, the Cartel of Oil Producing Middle East Countries brought about a rise in the cost of production of several commodities for the production of which oil was used as an energy input. Further, the oil price hike also raised the transportation costs of all commodities.

The increase in cost of production and transportation of commodities caused a shift in the aggregate supply curve upward to the left. This is generally described as adverse supply shock which raised the unit cost at each level of output. It will be seen from Fig. 13.5 that due to this adverse supply shock aggregate supply curve has shifted to the left to the new position AS_1 which intersects the given aggregate demand curve AD_0 at point H. At the new equilibrium point H, price level has risen to P_1 and output has fallen to OY_1 which will cause unemployment rate to rise. Thus, we have a higher price level with a higher unemployment rate. This explains the rise in the price level with the rise in the unemployment rate, the phenomenon which was witnessed during the seventies and early eighties in the developed capatalist countries such as the U.S.A. Note that *this has been interpreted by some economists as a shift in the Phillips curve and some as demise or collapse of the Phillips curve.*

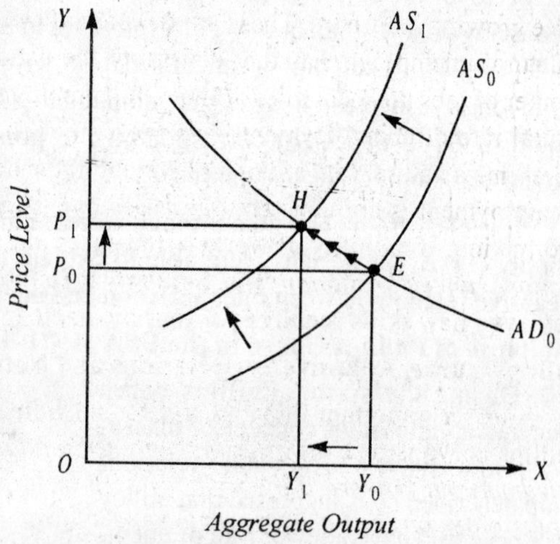

Fig. 13.5. *Adverse Supply Shock Giving Rise to Stagflation and Break-down of Phillips Curve*

NATURAL RATE HYPOTHESIS AND ADAPTIVE EXPECTATIONS: FRIEDMAN'S VIEW REGARDING PHILLIPS CURVE

A second explanation of occurrence of a higher rate of inflation simultaneously with a higher rate of unemployment was provided by Friedman.[2] He challenged the concept of a *stable* downward-sloping Phillips curve. According to him, *though there is a trade off between rate of inflation and unemployment in the short run, that is, there exists a short-run downward sloping Phillips curve, but it is not stable and it often shifts both leftward or rightward. He argued that there is no long-run stable trade off between rates of inflation and unemployment.* According to Friedman's natural rate hypothesis though there is trade-off between inflation and unemployment in the short run, in the long run economy comes back to be in stable equilibrium at the natural rate of unemployment. Therefore, according to him, *the long-run Phillips curve is a vertical straight line.* He argues that misguided Keynesian expansionary fiscal and monetary policies based on the wrong assumption that a *stable* Phillips curve exists result in increasing the rate of inflation. In a previous chapter we explained the natural rate hypoteheses with the help of short-run aggregate supply curve and long-run aggregate supply. Here we will explain Friedman's natural rate hypothesis with his version of Phillips curve concept.

Natural Rate of Unemployment

It is necessary to explain first the concept of natural rate of unemployment on which the concept of long-run Phillips curve is based. *The natural rate of unemployment is the rate at which in the labour market the current number of unemployed is equal to the number of jobs available. These unemployed workers are not employed for the firctional and structural reasons, though the equivalent number of jobs are available for them.* For instance, due to lack of information or lack of mobility the fresh entrants to the labour force may spend a good deal of time in searching for the jobs before they are able to find work. This is called *frictional unemployment.* Besides, some industries may be registering a decline in their production rendering some workers unemployed, while

2. Milton Friedman, Inflation and Unemployment, *Journal of Political Economy*, 1977.

others may be growing and therefore creating new jobs for workers. But the unemployed workers may have to be provided new training and skills before they are employed in the newly created jobs in the growing industries. These are *strucutrally unemployed* workers. Thus, it is these frictional and structural unemployments that constitute the natural rate of unemployment. Since the equivalent number of jobs are available for them, full employment is said to prevail even in the presence of this natural rate of unemployment. It is presently believed that 4 to 5 per cent rate of unemployment represents a natural rate of unemployment in the developed countries. However, this natural rate of unemployment is not constant but varies over time due to changes in mobility and availability of information. If mobility of workers increases and quick information about new jobs are available *frictional unemploymation* falls. Similarly if facilities for training unemployed workers and equiping them with new skills required for jobs available increase structural unemployment will decline.

Phillips Curve, Adaptive Expectations and Natural Rate Hypothesis

Another important thing to understand from Friedman's explanation of shift in the short-run Phillips curve is that *expectations about the future rate of inflation play an important role in it. Friedman put forward a theory of adaptative expectations according to which people form their expectations on the basis of previous period rate of inflation, and change or adapt their expectations only when the actual inflation turns out to be different from their expected rate.* According to this Friedman's theory of adaptive expectations, there may be a trade off between rates of inflation and unemployment in the short run, but there is no such trade off in the long run.

The view of Friedman and his follower monetarists illustrated in Figure 13.6. To begin with SPC_1 is the short run Phillips curve and the economy is at point A_0, on it corresponding to the natural rate of unemployment equal to 5 per cent of labour force. The location of this point A_0 on the short-run Phillips curve depends on the level of aggregate demand. Further, we assume that the economy has been experiencing a rate of inflation equal to 5%. The other assumption we make is that nominal wages have been set on the expectations that 5 per cent rate of inflation will continue in the future.

Now, suppose for some reasons the government adopts expansionary fiscal and monetary policies to raise aggregate demand. The consequent increase in aggregate demand will cause the rate of inflation to rise, say to seven per cent. Given the level of money wage rate which was fixed on the basis that the 5 per cent rate of inflation would continue to occur, the higher price level than expected would raise the profits of the firms which will induce the firms to increase their output and employ more labour. As a result of the increase in aggregate demand resulting in a higher rate of inflation and more output and employment, the economy will move to point A_1 on the short-run Phillips curve SPC_1 in Figure 13.6, where unemployment has decreased to 3.5 per cent while inflation rate has risen to 7%. It may be noted from Figure 13.6 that in moving from point A_0 to A_1, on SPC_1 the economy accepts a higher rate of inflation as the cost of achieving a

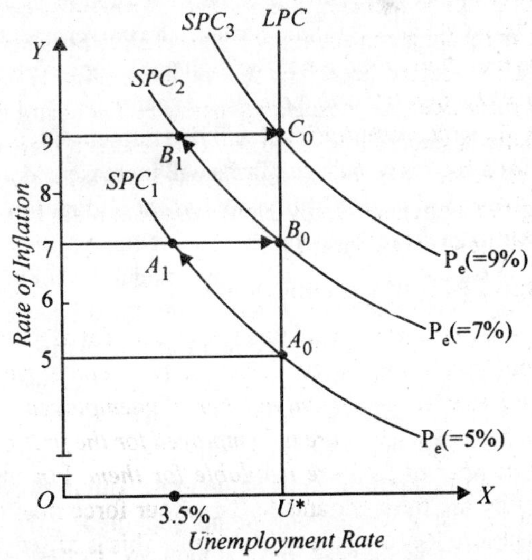

Fig. 13.6. *Shift in Short-run Phillips Curve and Long-run Phillips Curve.*

lower rate of unemployment. Thus, this is in conformity with the concept of Phillips curve explained earlier. However, the advocates of natural unemployment rate hypothesis interprets it in a slightly different way. They think that lower rate of unemployment achieved is only a temporary phenomenon. They think *when the actual rate of inflation exceeds the one that is expected, unemployment rate will fall below the natural rate only in the short run. In the long run, the natural rate of unemployment will be restored.*

Long-Run Phillips Curve and Adaptive Expectations. This brings us to the concept of long-run Phillips curve, which Friedman and other natural rate theorists have put forward. According to them, the economy will not remain in a stable equilibrium position at A_1. This is because the workers will realise that due to the higher rate of inflation than the expected one, their real wages and incomes have fallen. The workers will therefore demand higher nominal wages to restore their real income. But as nominal wages rise to compensate for the higher rate of inflation than expected, profits of business firms will fall to their earlier levels. This reduction in their profit implies that the original motivation that prompted them to expand output and increase employment resulting in lower unemployment rate will no longer be there. Consequently, they will reduce employment till the unemployment rate rises to the natural level of 5%. That is, with the increase is nominal wages in Figure 13.6 the economy will move from A_1 to B_0, at a higher inflation rate of 7%. It may be noted that the higher level of aggregate demand which generated inflation rate of 7% and caused the economy to shift from A_0 to A_1 still persists.

Further, at point B_0, and with the actual rate of inflation equal to 7 per cent, the workers will now expect this 7 per cent inflation rate to conitnue in future. As a result, the short-run Phillips curve *SPC* shifts upward from SPC_1 to SPC_2. It therefore follows, according to Friedman and other natural rate theoriests, the movement along a short-run Phillips curve *SPC* is only a temporary or short-run pheonomenon. In the long when nominal wages are fully adjusted to the changes in the inflation rate and consequently unemployment rate comes back to its natural level, a new short-run Phillips curve is formed at the higher expected rate of inflation.

However, the above process of reduction in unemployment rate and then its returning to the natural level may continue further. The Government may misjudge the situation and think that 7 per cent rate of inflation is not too high and adopt expansionary fiscal and monetary policies to increase aggregate demand and thereby to expand the level of employment. With the new increase in aggregate demand, the price level will rise further with nominal wages lagging behind in the short run. As a result, profits of business firms will increase and they will expand output and employment causing the reduction in rate of unemployment and rise in the inflation rate. With this, the economy will move from B_0 to B_1 along their short-run Phillips curve SPC_2. After sometime, the workers will recognise the fall in their real wages and press for higher normal wages to compensate for the higher rate of inflation than expected. When this higher nominal wages are granted, the business profits decline which will cause the level of employment to fall and unemployment rate to return to the natural rate of 5%. That is, in Figure 13.6 the economy moves from point B_1 to C_0. The new short run Phillips curve will now shift to SPC_3 passing through point C_0. The process may be repeated again with the result that while in the short run, the unemployment rate falls below the natural rate and in the long run it returns to its natural rate. But throughout this process the inflation rate continuously goes on rising. On joining points such as A_0, B_0, C_0 corresponding to the given natural rate of unemployment we get a vertical long run Phillips curve *LPC* in Figure 13.6. Thus, *in the adaptive expectations theory of the natural rate hypothesis while the short run Phillips curve is downward sloping indicating that trade-off between inflation and unemployment rate in the short run, the long run Phillips curve is a vertical straight line showing that no trade off exists between inflation and unemployment in the long run.*

It is important to remember that adaptive expectations theory has also been applied to explain the *reverse process of disinflation,* that is, fall in the rate of inflation as well as inflation itself. Suppose in Figure 13.6 the economy is originally at point C_0 with 9% rate of inflation. Now, if a decline in aggregate demand occurs, say as a result of contraction of money supply by the Central Bank of a country. This will reduce inflation rate below the 9 per cent expected rate. As a result, profits of business firms will decline because the prices will be falling more rapidly than wages. The decline in profits will cause the firms to reduce employment and consequently unemployment rate will rise. Eventually, firms and workers will adjust their expectations and the unemployment rate will return to the natural rate. The process will be repeated and the economy in the long run will slide down along the vertical long-run Phillips curve showing falling rate of inflation at the given natural rate of unemployment.

It follows from above that *according to adaptive expectations theory any rate of inflation can occur in the long run with the natural rate of unemployment.*

LONG-RUN PHILLIPS CURVE : RATIONAL EXPECTATIONS

In the end we explain the viewpoint about inflation and unemployment put forward by Rational Expectations Theory which is the corner stone of recently developed macroeconomic theory, popularly called *new classical macroeconomics.* As explained above, Friedman's adaptive expectations theory assumes that nominal wages lag behind changes in the price level. This lag in the adjustment of nominal wages to the price level brings about rise in business profits which induces the firms to expand output and employment in the short run and leads to the reduction in unemployment rate below the natural rate. But according to the rational expectations theory, which is another version of natural unemployment rate theory, there is no lag in the adjustment of nominal wages consequent to the rise in price level. The advocates of this theory further argue that nominal wages are *quickly* adjusted to any expected changes in the price level so that there does not exist the type of Phillips curve that shows trade off between rates of inflation and unemployment. According to them, as a result of increase in aggregate demand, there is no reduction in unemployment rate. The rate of inflation resulting from increase in aggregate demand is *fully and correctly anticipated* by workers and business firms and get completely and quickly incorporated into the wage agreements resulting in higher prices of products. Thus, as shown in Fig. 13.7, it is the price level that rises, the level of

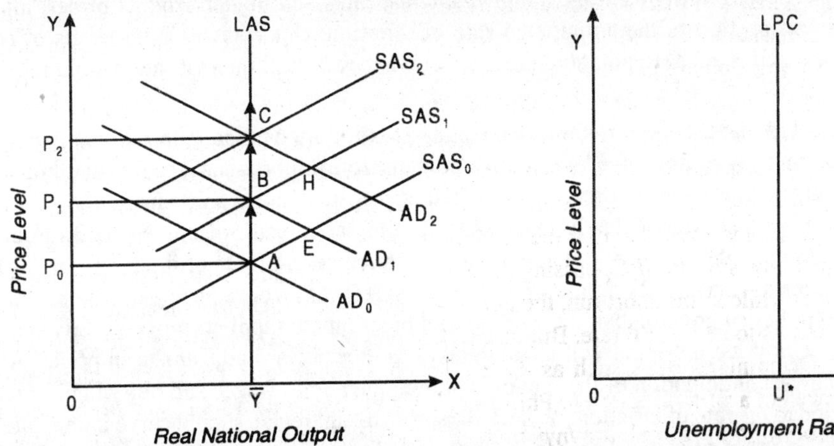

Fig. 13.7. *Inflation and National Output : Rational Expectations Theory*

Fig. 13.8. *According to Ratunal Expectations Theory, Long run Phillips Curve is a Vertical Straight Line.*

real output and employment remaining unchanged at the natural level. Hence, aggregate supply curve according to the rational expectations theory is a vertical straight line at the potential GNP level, that is, at the natural rate of unemployment, given the resources and technology. Long-run Phillips curve, according to rational expectations theory, corresponds to this long-run aggregate supply curve and is a vertical straight line at the natural unemployment rate as shown in fig. 13.8.

Rational expectations theory rests on two basic elements. First, according to it, workers and producers being quite rational have a correct understanding of the economy and therefore correctly anticipate the effects of the Government's economic policies *using all the available relevant information.* On the basis of these anticipations of the effects of economic events and Government's policies they take correct decisions to promote their own interests.

The second premise of rational expectations theory is that, like the classical economists, *it assumes that all product and factor markets are highly competitive.* As a result, wages and product prices are highly flexible and therefore can quickly change upward and downward. Indeed, the rational expectations theory considers that new information is quickly assimilated (*i.e.*, taken into account) in the demand and supply curves of markets so that new equilibrium prices immediately adjust to the new economic events and policies, be it a new technological change or a supply shock such as a drought or act of OPEC oil cartel or change in Government's monetary and fiscal policies.

Figure 13.7 illustrates the standpoint of rational expectations theory about the relation between inflation and unemployment. In this $O\bar{Y}$ is the level of real potential output corresponding to the full-employment of labour (with a given natural rate of unemployment). *LAS* is aggregate supply curve at $O\bar{Y}$ level of real potential long-run output. To begin with, AD_0 is the aggregate demand curve which intersects the aggregate supply curve *LAS* at point *A* and determines price level equal to P_0. and SAS_0 is the short-run aggregate supply curve. Suppose Government adopts an expansionary monetary policy to increase output and employment. As a consequence, aggregate demand curve shifts upward to the new position AD_1. According to rational expectations theory, people (*i.e.*, workers, businessmen, consumers, lenders) will correctly anticipate that this expansionary policy will cause inflation in the economy and they would take prompt measures to protect themselves against this inflation. Accordingly, workers would press for higher wages and get it granted, businessmen would raise the prices of their products, lenders would hike their rates of interest. All these increases would take place immediately. It is thus clear that the increase in aggregate demand (*i.e.*, aggregate expenditure) brought about by expansionary monetary policy will cause the equlbrium to shift to point *B* and price level will rise to P_1. Thus, the increase in aggregate demand or expenditure will be fully reflected in higher wages, higher interest rates and higher product prices, all of which will rise in proportion to the anticipated rate of inflation. Consequently, the levels of real national product (which is equal to potential GNP), real wage rate, real interest rate, would remain unchanged.

It should be noted that the like Friedman's adaptative expectations theory, in rational expectations theory the economy does not move temporarily from macro equilibrium at *A* to *E* in the short run along the short-run aggregate supply curve SAS_0. When aggregate demand shifts from AD_0 to AD_1, short-run supply curve shifts immediately from SAS_0 to SAS_1 as a result of immediate and quick adjustment in wages and other input prices due to correct anticipation of rate of inflation. Similarly, when aggregate demand curve shifts rightward from AD_1 to AD_2 as a consequence of expensionary monetary or fiscal policy of government, the workers and other inputs suppliers will correctly anticipate the further rise in price level and will make qucikly further upward adjustment in prices. And again due to the correct anticipation of the rate of inflation, the rise in wages and other input prices will be in proportion to the rate of inflation. As a result, short-run aggregate supply curve immediately shifts from SAS_1 to SAS_2 and price level rises to P_2 corrresponding to the new equilibrium point *C*.

It is clear from above that people's anticipations or expectations of inflation and acting upon them in their decision making when expansionary monetary policy is adopted frustrate or nullify the intended effect (that is, increase in real output and employment) of Government's monetary policy. In other words, *according to the rational expectations theory, the intended effect of expansionary monetary policy on investment, real output and employment does not materialise.* As seen above, in Fig. 13.7 it is due to the anticipation of inflation by the people and quick upward adjustments made in wages, interest etc., by them that the price level instantly rises from P_0 to P_1 and from P_1 to P_2, the level of output OY remaining constant. That is why, according to the rational expectations theory, aggregate supply curve is a vertical straight line. *The vertical aggregate supply curve means that there is no trade off between inflation and unemployment, that is, downward-sloping Phillips curve does not exist.* Thus, according to rational expectations theory, the increase in aggregate demand or expenditure as a consequence of easy monetary policy of the Government will fail to reduce unemployment and instead will only cause inflation in the economy.

It is important to note that according to rational expectations theory long-run aggregate supply curve is a vertical straight line at potential GNP level such as *LAS* in figure 13.7. This is due to the correct anticipation of rate of inflation by the workers and other suppliers of inputs. If inflation rate was more than the expected or anticipated rate, the unemployment rate would have fallen below the natural level and GNP would have been greater than the potential level.

Since according to rational expectations theory aggregate supply curve *LAS* is vertical in the long run, the long run Phillips curve is also vertical at the natural unemployment rate. *The long-run Phillips curve shows relationship between inflation and unemployment when the actual inflation rate equals the anticipated (i.e. expected) inflation rate.* The vertical long-run Phillips curve shows that whatever the anticipated inflation rate the long-run equilibrium is at the natural unemployment rate. As depicted by AS-AD model in Fig. 13.8, the long-run Phillips curve corresponds to the vertical long-run aggregate supply curve at the potential GNP level.

Relationship between Short-run Phillips Curve and Long-run Phillips Curve

It is important to know the relationship between short-run Phillips curve and long-run Phillips curve. The *position of a short-run Phillips curve (SPC) which passes through a point on the long-run Phillips curve (LPC) depends on the anticipated inflation rate.* Short-run Phillips curve is like the short-run aggregate supply curve (*SAS*) which is drawn with a given expected price level. Short-run Philips curve is also drawn with an anticipated (*i.e.* expected) inflation rate and it will shift as the expected inflation rate changes. This is depicted in Figure 13.9. If the expected inflation rate is 9 per cent a year, then, as will be seen from Figure 13.9, the short-run Phillips curve SPC_0 passes through the corresponding point *A* on the long-run Phillips curve *LPC* with natural unemploy ment rate of 5 per cent. As explained above, the movement along a short-run Phillips curve occurs as a result of changes in aggregate demand. When there is unanticipated increase in aggregate demand, inflation rate rises more than the expected rate and GNP increases causing a fall in unemployment rate, we move upward to the left from point *A* on the short-run Phillips curve SPC_0. On the other hand, when there is unanticipated decrease in aggregate demand, inflation rate fall and unemployment rate increases above the natural rate and as a result we move downward to the right from point *A* along the short-run Phillips curve SPC_0.

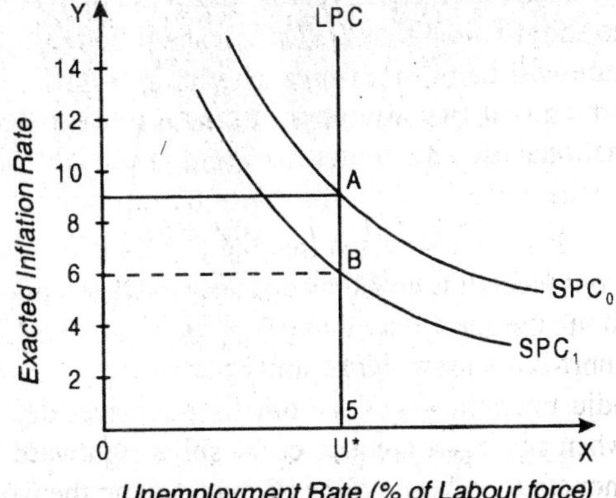

Fig. 13.9. *Long-run Phillips Curve and Shift in Short-run Phillips Curve*

However, *when the expected inflation rate changes, the short-run Phillips curve shifts.* For example, when the expected inflation rate is 9 per cent a year, the short-run Phillips curve is SPC_0 in Fig. 13.9. If the expected inflation rate falls to 6 per cent a year, the short-run Phillips curve shifts below to SPC_1. The new short-run Phillips curve passes through long-run Phillips curve at the new expected inflation rate of 6 per cent. The distance by which the short-run Phillips curve shifts to a lower position is equal to the change in the expected rate of inflation.

Now, the question arises as to why the short-run Phillips curve shifts downward when the expected inflation rate falls. To begin with, the expected inflation rate of 9 per cent a year prevails. To check this inflation rate the central bank of a country will take steps to lower the growth in money supply. As resutl, actual inflation rate falls to 6 per cent a year. However, at first the fall in actual inflation rate is unanticipated and therefore the wages and other input prices continue to rise at their original rate consistent with 9 per cent expected inflation rate and there is rightward movement along the short-run Phillips curve SPC_0 resulting in fall in GNP and increase in unemployment rate. However, when the inflation rate remains steady at 6 per cent a year, this rate eventually comes to be anticipated. As this happens, increase in wage rate and other input prices slows down and with the expected increase in aggregate demand, GNP increases and unemployment rate falls to the natural level. As a result, the short-run a Phillips curve shifts downward to the new position SPC_1 that corresponds to the new lower expected inflation rate of 6 per cent a year (see Fig. 13.9).

SACRIFICE RATIO AND POLICY OF DISINFLATION

Reducing rate of inflation or disinflation policy has been the objective of policy makers. But disinflation or reduction in inflation rate involves the cost to the society in terms of loss of output. The loss of output results from increase in unemployment, that is, reduction in labour employment. This implies, as seen above, trade off between inflation and unemployment suggested by short-run Phillips curve as shown in Fig. 13.10. It will be seen from this figure that reduction in rate of inflation from 10% to 8% causes 2% increase in unemployment rate. Note that increase in unemployment will bring about loss of output. This amount of loss of output from a given reduction in inflation rate is measured by the sacrifice ratio. Precisely stated, the *sacrifice ratio "is the ratio of cumulative loss of GDP (as a result of disinflation policy) to the reduction of inflation that is actually achieved"*.[3]

Though short-run Phillips curve implies that reduction in inflation causes increase in unemployment, but since increase in unemployment involves reduction in output, sacrifice ratio is generally measured in terms of loss of output following the policy of disinflation. To reduce inflation, policy makers must know the loss of output caused by it. This loss or sacrifice of output can be compared with the benefits from reduction in inflation rate. This will help them in taking proper decisions.

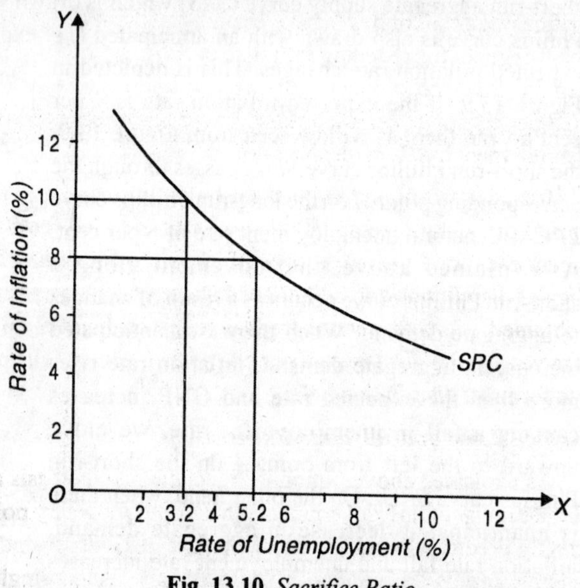

Fig. 13.10. *Sacrifice Ratio*

Studies of empirical data of the United States before the eighties conducted to estimate the quantitative relation between inflation and output found sacrifice ratio was typically equal to 5% of one year's GNP, that is, 5% of one year's GNP

3. R. Dornbusch, Stanley Fischer, and R Startz, *Macroeconomics* (New York: Tata McGraw-Hill, 2002), Ninth Edition, p. 472.

had to be foregone to reduce inflation by 1 percentage age point. However, the estimates of sacrifice ratio made in other studies vary a good deal. For example, a study for the eighties of the effects of disinflation policy pursued by Reagan-Volcker in the United States found that it resulted in very large unemployment but succeeded in reducing inflation. In an important study of this period Lawrence Ball has found that sacrifice ratio was 1.83 for the eighties which was much lower than the earlier estimates of 5. The success of reduction in inflation by Reagan and Volcker shows that *credibility of policy makers play an important role in reducing inflation.* If people believe that Government or Central Bank of the country is highly committed to disinflation policy and making sincere and tough measures to bring down inflation, their inflationary expectations will be reduced and this itself will reduce inflation. To win credibility the government has to make a drastic cut in its expenditure and also to reduce substantially the growth in money supply in the economy. It is these measures that helped to ensure credibility of Reagan and Volker (then Chairman of Federal Bank of the US) and played an important role in reducing inflation during the eighties.

Sacrifice Ratio in Terms of Unemployment

Sacrifice ratio can be expressed in terms of unemployment. In terms of unemployment, sacrifice ratio means how much unemployment rate has to increase to reduce inflation by one percentage point. Thus if we take 5 as sacrifice ratio in terms of GNP, then given the relation between unemployment and GNP we can find out the sacrifice ratio in terms of unemployment. For this we take the help of **Okun's law** *which states that 1 per cent point increase in unemployment causes 2 per cent fall in GNP*. This means that given 5 as sacrifice ratio in terms of GNP, then 2.5 percentage point increase in unemployment will cause fall by 5 per cent of yearly GNP.

Using Sacrifice Ratio

Using the sacrifice ratio we can find out by how much and how long unemployment must rise to reduce inflation by certain percentage points. For example, given 5 as a sacrifice ratio in terms of GNP, then to reduce inflation by 4 per cent points, say from 8% to 4%, how much percent of yearly GNP will have to be foregone and how much increase in unemployment will occur. Since the sacrifice rate of 5 implies that for reducing inflation by 1 percent point 5 per cent of yearly GNP has to be foregone, for reducing inflation by 4 percentage points 20 percent of yearly GNP will have to given up. Since according to Okum's law 1 percentage point of cyclical unemployment is associated with 2 per cent of a year's GNP, then to reduce 20 per cent of a year's GNP means increase in cyclical unemployment by 10 percentage points.

It is also worth nothing that the policy of disinflation (*i.e.* reducing inflation can take various forms. For example, rapid inflation or what is called **'cold turkey'** solution can lower output by 10 per cent each for 2 years (*i.e.* total of 20 per cent decline of year's GNP). Alternatively, a moderate policy of disinflation can be followed under which 5 per cent tall in GNP per year for 4 years has to be obtained. Further, a more gradual policy of disinflation may be decided under which 2 per cent fall in yearly GNP for 10 years period can be planned. The policy maker has to make a choice among these forms of disinflation policy.

Sacrifice Ratio and Rational Expectations

As explained above, rational expectations hypothesis assumes that people use all the available information including government's fiscal and monetary policies to predict the future. Further, they correctly predict what would be the impact of Government's fiscal and monetary policies and other economic events on inflation in the economy. Accordingly, workers and firms who have rational expectations can *quickly incorporate* the changes in their expected inflation for fixing wages and prices. Therefore, according to advocates of rational expectations, downward sloping short-run Phillips curve showing trade-off between inflation and unemployment does not represent the right options that are available for policy makers. They argue, given the rational expectations, Phillips curve is in fact vertical which implies that there is no trade-off between inflation and unemployment or between inflation and GNP.

They argue that if there is credibility of policy makers among the people about their commitment to reduce inflation, the people will quickly respond by lowering their expectations of inflation when they adopt anti-inflationary policies. In this way inflation will be reduced without much rise in unemployment or fall in GNP. Therefore, the advocates of rational expectations argue that the estimates of sacrifice ratio are not useful for evaluating the impact of alternative economic policies. They think that if Government or Central Bank of the country is committed to reduce inflation and if there is credibility of government among the people, then inflation can be reduced in a painless *manner*, that is, without foregoing any output or employment. Thus advocates of rational expectations believe in *painless disinflation* provided government credibility about fighting inflation is quite high among the people. Thus Mankiw points out that there are two requirements for having painless disinflation. First, the policy to reduce inflation must be announced before workers and firms who have to fix wages and prices form their expectations. Second, the workers and firms must in fact believe in the commitment of Government or Central Bank to reduce inflation when it makes announcement of such a policy. If people do not have faith in government or Central Bank pursuing its announced anti-inflationary policy, they will not lower their inflationary expectations. If both requirements are fulfilled short-run Phillips curve representing trade off between inflation and unemployment will shift downward as shown in Figure 13.11. This will cause reduction in inflation without increase in unemployment. To conclude in the words of Mankiw, "*Although the rational expectations approach remains controversial almost all economists agree that expectations of inflation influence the short-run trade off between inflation and unemployment. The credibility of a policy to reduce inflation is therefore one determinant of how costly the policy will be. Unfortunately, it is often difficult to predict whether the public will view the announcement of a new policy as credible.*[4]

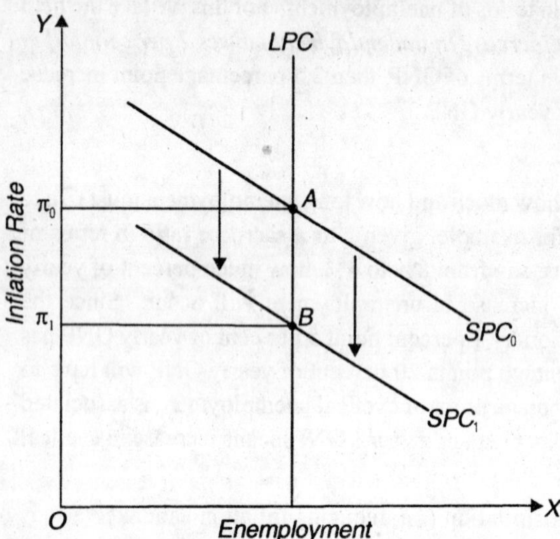

Fig. 13.11. *Downward Shift in Short-Run Phillips Curve As a Result of Painless Disinflation*

QUESTIONS FOR REVIEW

1. What is the Phillips Curve ? What kind of trade-off between unemployment rate and inflation rate does it imply ?
2. What is Phillips Curve ? What are its policy implications ?
3. Explain the factors causing downward-sloping Phillips Curve. What is the policy significance of its downward sloping ?

4. B.N. Gregory Mankiw, op. cit. p. 360

4. What is meant by trade-off between the rate of inflation and unemployment ? Explain the Keynesian explanation of this trade-off.
5. What is meant by adaptive expectations ? Explain how with their help Friedman proves that short-run Phillips curve is downward-slopping while the long-run Phillips curve is vertical.
6. What is *natural rate hypothesis. How does Friedman explain it will his concepts* of Phillips curve and adaptative expectation.
7. While there is trade off between inflation and unemployment in the short-run, there is no such trade off between them in the long run. Explain how Friedman explains with his concepts of short-run and long-run Phillips curves.
8. What effect do expectations regarding rate of inflation have on the short-run Phillips curve ? Can this help to explain stagflation ?
9. What is meant by rational expectations ? How does rational expectations theory show that aggregate supply curve is a vertical straight line and that there is no trade-off between rate of inflation and rate of unemployment.
10. Distanguigh between short-run and long-run Phillips curve. Explain why long-run Phillips curve is vertical, while the short-run Phillips curve is negatively sloping.
11. What is meant by sacrifice ratio ? Express it in terms of both output and unemployment.
12. Explain sacrifice ratio in the context of policy of disinflation. How is sacrifice related to short-run Phillips Curve ?

Appendix To Chapter 13

Derivation of Phillips Curve from Aggregate Supply Curve

As explained in the foregoing chapter, the short-run Phillips curve and short-run aggregate supply curve convey the same information, namely, inflation and unemployment are inversely related; the higher the inflation rate, the lower the rate of unemployment and vice versa. Therefore, short-run Phillips curve can be mathematically derived from short-run aggregate supply curve. According to the Phillips curve concept, inflation depends on three factors:

1. Anticipated or expected rate of inflation ;
2. The extent to which unemployment rate deviates from the natural rate, the is, the extent of cyclical unemployment ; and
3. Supply shocks to the economy.

The above three factors are expressed through the following equation of the Phillips curve;

$$\pi = \pi^e - \beta(U - \bar{U}) + v \qquad \ldots(1)$$

where π is inflation rate, π^e is anticipated or expected inflation rate, U is total unemployment and $\bar{U}$ is natural unemployment. Therefore, $U - \bar{U}$ represents cyclical unemployment. v is supply shock to the economy; β is the parameter which measures the degree of responsiveness of inflation rate to the rate of cyclical unemployment. The minus sign before β shows that inflation rate and cyclical unemployment are inversely related; the high rate of cyclical unemployment reduces inflation and vice versa.

The above short-run Phillips curve can be easily derived from the equation of short-run aggregate supply. As mentioned in a previous chapter, the short-run aggregate supply curve is written as

$$P = P^e + \frac{1}{\alpha}(Y - \bar{Y}) \qquad \ldots(2)$$

where P is the price level and P^e is the expected price level, $Y - \bar{Y}$ is the deviation of level of income *i.e.* GNP (or Y) from full-employment output.

We add the term v which represents supply shock to the economy to the right side of equation (2). Note that v is an exogenous fact such as change in world oil prices. This exogenous factor will change the price level and cause a shift in the short-run aggregate supply curve. Thus adding v to the right side of the above equation (2) we have

$$P = P^e + \frac{1}{\alpha}(Y - \bar{Y}) + v$$

Subtracting the previous year's price level (P_{-1}) from both sides of the above equation we have

$$P - P_{-1} = P^e - P_{-1} + \frac{1}{\alpha}(Y - \bar{Y}) + v$$

The term $P–P_{-1}$ on the left hand side of the above equation represents the change in price level from the previous year's price level, that is, $P–P_{-1}$ represents inflation rate and can therefore be written as π. The term $P^e - P_{-1}$ on the right side of the above equation (2) measures the deviation of expected price level from the last year's price level, that is, expected inflation rate which can also be written as π^e. Thus, to rewrite the above equation (2)

$$\pi = \pi^e = \frac{1}{\alpha}(Y - \bar{Y}) + v \qquad \ldots (3)$$

Now in order to derive the short-run Phillips curve we have to replace GNP (i.e. output) *i.e.,* Y and potential GNP (i.e. $\bar{Y}$) by unemployment (U) and natural unemployment rate ($\bar{U}$) respectively. This requires the help of Okun's law. According to Okun's law, the deviation of GNP from potential GNP is *inversely* related to the deviation of unemployment from the natural rate of unemployment. This relation can be written as

$$\frac{1}{\alpha}(Y - \bar{Y}) = -\beta(U - \bar{U})$$

Substituting the above Okun's law relationship in equation (3) we have

$$\pi = \pi^e = -\beta(U - \bar{U}) + v \qquad \ldots (4)$$

The *equation (4) represents the short-run Phillips curve as stated in the beginning.*

It follows from above that short-run Phillips curve equation provides the same information as the short-run aggregate supply equation. Whereas the short-run aggregate supply curve is more relevant and helpful to use when we are analyzing the relationship between GNP and the price level, the short-run Phillips curve is more relevant and useful when we analyze the relation between inflation and unemployment. In fact, the short-run Phillips curve and aggregate supply curve are the two sides of the same coin.

Classical Dichotomy and Short-run Phillips Curve

A useful result can be obtained from the short-run aggregate supply curve and Phillips curve. The relation described by both the equations shows that the classical dichotomy does not apply in the short run. As will be remembered, according to classical dichotomy, changes in money supply affects only the price level and therefore nominal variables such as money wages, nominal GNP and do not affect the real variables such as real GNP, employment and real wages. Such conclusion does not follow from the short-run aggregate supply curve or equation and short-run Phillips curve. Whereas the short-run aggregate supply equation $\left[P = P^e + \frac{1}{\alpha}(Y - \bar{Y})\right]$ shows that a short-run deviation of *real GNP* (*i.e.* Y) from the potential GNP (*i.e.* $\bar{Y}$) depends on the unanticipated or unexpected changes in price level or inflation rate which is influenced by the changes in money supply. And short-un Phillips curve or equation ($\pi = \pi^e - \beta U - \bar{U}$) shows that the deviation of unemployment rate from the natural rate depends on the unexpected changes in the inflation rate which is determined by changes in money supply.

Thus, short-run Phillips curve and short-run aggregate supply curve show that changes in money supply can bring about changes in real variables such as real GNP and level of employment and unemployment. To conclude, "Both equations (i.e. short-run aggregate supply equation and Phillips curve equation) show a link between real and nominal variables that causes the classical dichotomy to break down in the shortrun". In a previous chapter we have also shown through AS-AD Model how business cycles in real output and employment are caused by short-run changes in aggregate demand. And the changes in aggregate demand can occur as a result of changes in money supply.

1. Gregory Mankiw, *Macroeconomics* (New York: Worth Publishers), Fifth Edition 2003, p. 360.

CHAPTER 14
Stagflation and Supply-Side Economics

Introduction

Keynes put forward his theory of income and employment during the Great Depression of 1930s, when a large percentage of labour force was rendered unemployed (almost 25%) in today's developed capitalist economies such as U.K., U.S.A. In the fifties and sixties, Keynesian theory got great prominence when rate of inflation in these economies was a modest, about 2 to 3 per cent per annum, and the substantial unemployment rate prevailing at that time became a major concern of economic policy. The Keynesian policy to reduce this unemployment rate was to raise aggregate demand or expenditure. On the other hand, during the periods of high inflation and low unemployment, Keynesian economists recommended reduction in aggregate expenditure to fight inflation. Thus Keynesian economics emphasised management of aggregate demand through the adoption of proper fiscal and monetary policies. These policies could prove successful when there was either high inflation or high unemployment, that is, when high inflation and high unemployment did not exist simultaneously.

As mentioned in the last chapter, during the sixties Phillips curve concept describing inverse relation between inflation and unemployment became popular among economists. According to the Phillips curve, a high rate of inflation is accompanied by a low rate of unemployment or a low rate of inflation is accompanied by higher unemployment which shows that the goal of reduced inflation conflicts with the objective of reduced unemployment. This posed a great dilemma for policy makers. However, Keynesian economists advocated that Government should seek some socially acceptable short-run compromise. That is, it should try to achieve some combination of inflation and unemployment lying on the economy's Phillips curve. Monetarists led by Friedman recommend slow growth of money stock to fight inflation, while they thought unemployment would be automatically eliminated through the fee working of labour market.

The above was the general belief among economists until 1970s when stagflation appeared as a big problem for many economies of the world, especially those of USA and Britain. *Stagflation implies a high inflation rate prevailing simultaneously with a high unemployment rate.* Keynesian policy prescription of managing aggregate demand could not solve both high inflation and high unemployment existing simultaneously. If steps are taken to reduce aggregate demand to fight inflation, this would worsen the unemployment problem and, on the other hand, if measures aimed at increasing aggregate demand to reduce unemployment were taken, they would add fuel to the inflationary fire. Thus, the emergence of stagflation cast Keynesian theory into doubt. Some sounded the breakdown of Keynesian economics to tackle the problem of stagflation. Even monetarists could not provide any solution to reduce high inflation and high unemployment existing simultaneously. The search began for new ways of analysing and solving the twin problems of high inflation and high unemployment. This gave birth to a new economic thought which is now popularly called *supply-side economics* in contrast to the *demand-side* Keynesian economics. In what follows we will first explain in detail the meaning and causes of stagflation and then examine how supply-side macroeconomics offers a solution for this complicated problem. It may be noted that supply-side economics emphasises management of supply to fight against stagflation (*i.e.*, inflation and stagnation) rather than management of demand as recommended by Keynesian economics.

STAGFLATION

As mentioned above, stagflation refers to a situation when a high rate of inflation occurs simultaneously with a high rate of unemployment The existence of a high rate of unemployment means the reduced level of GNP. The term stagflation was coined in the seventies when several developed countries of the world, received a supply stock in terms of rapid hike in oil prices. In 1973, the Cartel of Oil Producing Countries OPEC raised the price of oil. There was a four times increase in the oil prices. In the United States during 1973-75 the higher costs of fuel-oil and other petroleum products brought about a sharp increase in the prices of manufactured goods. The rate of inflation went upto over 12 per cent during 1974 in USA. A severe recession, the worst since 1930s, also hit the American economy during the period 1973-75. The real GNP declined between the late 1973 and early 1975. As a consequence, the rate of unemployment shot upto nearly 9 per cent. Thus, both inflation and unemployment were unusually very high during this period (1973-75). This simultaneous occurrence of high inflation and high unemployment was also seen in case of other free market developed countries such as Britain, France and Germany. The recovery from recession began in 1975 and over the next few years GNP rose and unemployment declined. Inflation rate also declined from over 12 per cent to the range of 5 to 7 per cent.

But, again in 1979 when a revolution in Iran created a crises in world oil market, OPEC doubled the price of oil. This brought back stagflation again in 1979 in the developed countries. Real GNP fell at a rapid rate during 1979-81. Inflation rate again went upto over 10 per cent in these countries during this period.

India also could not escape from the oil price shocks in 1973 and 1979. But, in case of India, oil price triggered cost-push inflation but did not give rise to stagflation as the term is usually interpreted in 1973 and 1979. The public investment in India picked up from 1974 which generated economic growth.

Causes of Stagflation

Different explanations of stagflation have been given by eminent economists. It is worth noting that causes of stagflation in India during 1991-94 are different from those given by the economists for stagflation of 1973-75 and 1979-81 in the developed capitalist economies such as those of USA, Great Britain. We will first explain stagflation in USA, Great Britain and other developed capitalist countries during 1973-1975 and again in 1979-81 and then dwell on stagflation in India.

Adverse Supply Shocks. The main reason why typical stagflation arose in the developed capitalist economies during seventies and early eighties was the adverse supply shocks that occurred during these two periods. As mentioned above, there was four fold increase in oil prices by OPEC following Arab-Israel war in 1973 and then again doubling of oil prices by it in 1979 following the Iranian Revolution which pushed up the energy costs of the economies and resulted in higher product prices. In terms of aggregate supply curve, this cost-push factor delivered by oil price shock is interpreted as a decrease or leftward shift in the aggregate supply curve. How this adverse supply shock caused stagflation in the developed capitalist world is illustrated in Fig. 14.1 where initially aggregate demand curve AD_0 and aggregate supply curve

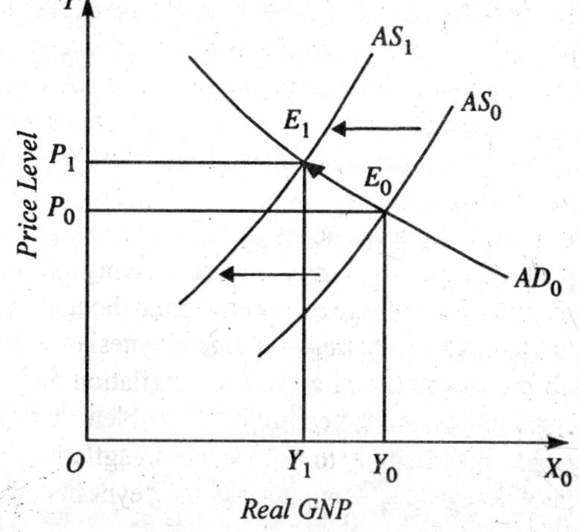

Fig. 14.1. *Stagflation Arising From an Adverse Supply Shock*

AS_0 intersects at E_0 and determines the price level equal to P_0. Since adverse supply shock delivered by hike in oil prices raises the cost per unit of production, aggregate supply curve shifts upward to the left to the new position AS_1. With the aggregate demand curve AD_0 remaining unchanged, the new aggregate supply curve AS_1 intersects it at E_1. It will be seen that in the new equilibrium position price level rises to P_1 and *GNP* falls to Y_1. Thus, adverse supply shock causes cost-puch inflation along with a reduction in the level of *GNP*. A reduction in *GNP* implies an increase in unemployment rate and occurrence of recession. Thus, an adverse supply shock causes both high inflation and high unemployment rate. It may be noted that in order to get out of recession and to reduce unemployment, if Government seeks to raise aggregate demand to the higher level AD_1 by adopting expansionary fiscal and monetary policies, the new equilibrium is reached at point E_2 (see Fig. 14.2) and as a result price level rises to P_2, while the real GNP comes back to the original higher level Y_0 where full employment of labour prevails.

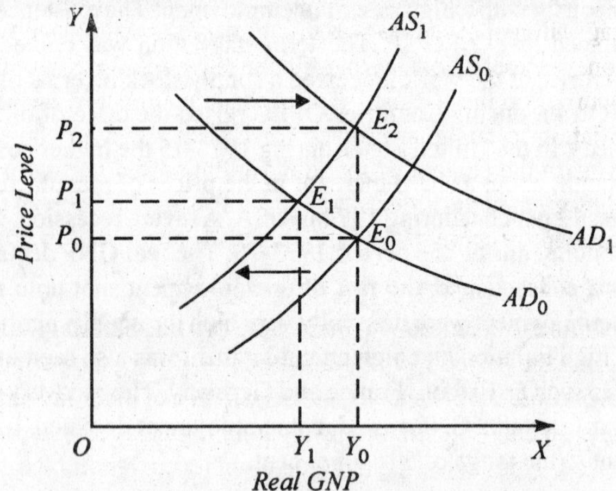

Fig. 14.2. *Further Surge in Inflation Rate if Aggregate Demand is Raised to Get Out of Stagflation.*

Thus in this context of stagflation in the economy attempts by the Government to raise aggregate demand to get out of recession and reduce unemployment result in further rise in the inflation rate. This shows that mere management of demand is quite inappropriate to solve the problem of stagflation. Though rise in oil prices has been a chief supply shock received by all the economies of the world which imported oil from Middle East Countries causing stagflation of 1970s and early 1980s, there are also other types of adverse supply shocks which occur. In different countries different types of supply shocks may occur bringing about rise in unit cost of production and causing a leftward shift in the aggregate supply curve. This has caused stagflation episodes from time to time. In case of USA, besides oil price shocks, the other supply shocks explained below also contributed to the stagflation of 1973-75.

An important supply shock operating in the USA was *the shortage in supplies of agricultural products* during this period. This happened because a good amount of American agricultural products had to be exported to Asia and the Soviet Union where severe shortfall in production occurred in 1972 and 1973. Larger exports reduced the domestic supplies of agricultural products used as raw material in the production of industries producing food and fibre products. This raised the unit cost of production of these commodities and their higher costs were passed on to the consumers as higher prices. This resulted in shifting of the aggregate supply curve to the left. It is important to note that the higher prices of agricultural commodities such as sugar cane, cotton, foodgrains which may occur due to either shortfall in production or due to the increase in their procurement prices has often been working also in the Indian economy which has resulted in higher costs to the industries processing these agricultural products.

Another adverse supply shock that occurred in the USA during the period of 1971-73 causing stagflation episode of 1973-75 was *depreciation of dollar*. Depreciation of dollar means that price of dollar in terms of foreign currencies was reduced. This raised the prices of American imports. To the extent the imports were used as inputs in American industries, unit production costs went up causing a shift in the aggregate supply curve to the left. In the period of 1973-75, *removal of wage and price controls* which had been imposed earlier also produced a supply stock to the American economy. As these wages and price controls were lifted, workers got their wages increased and business firms pushed up the prices of their products. This also contributed to stagflation of 1973-75 in the USA.

Inflationary Expectations. Besides supply shocks explained above, another important cause of stagflation of seventies was inflationary expectations which were prevailing at that time. These inflationary expectations at that time in the USA were caused by greatly increased military expenditure incurred on the Vietnam War in the late 1960s. In the early seventies workers with expectations of inflation to continue pressed for higher wages to compensate for accelerating inflation. Business firms in the context of mounting inflation did not resist labour demand for higher nominal wages. They granted the higher wages which raised unit cost of production and resulted in shifting of aggregate supply curve to the left. This also contributed to bringing stagflation.

End of Stagflation in the USA : 1982-88

As explained above, there were two bouts of stagflation in the several countries of the world, first during the period 1973-75 and, second, during the period 1979-81. However, during 1982-88 due to *favourable* supply shocks and occurrence of other favourable factors, stagflation of the earlier period came to end. The important favourable supply shocks was the decline in oil prices by OPEC in this period. This caused the aggregate supply curve to shift to the right bringing about fall in both inflation and unemployment.

Another important factor contributing to the demise of stagflation in 1982-88 in USA was the deep recession that overtook the American economy in 1981-82 which was mainly caused by tight monetary policy pursued by Federal Bank. Such was the severity of recession that unemployment in USA rose to 9.7 per cent in 1982. Due to this high unemployment rate workers accepted smaller increases in their nominal wages or in some cases accepted even reduction in their wages. Further, due to still foreign competition and their eagerness to maintain relative shares in domestic and foreign markets, business firms were restrained to raise prices of their products. This also worked to bring stagflation to end.

It is important to note that while during the periods of stagflation in 1970s and early 1980s, both inflation and unemployment simultaneously increased, during the expansion period of 1982-88 when stagflation nearly subsided both inflation and unemployment rates fell simultaneously.

SUPPLY-SIDE ECONOMICS

Keynesian economics was born during the great depression of the 1930s, when a large percentage of labour force (about 25%) was rendered unemployed and also a good deal of productive capacity (*i.e.*, capital stock) lay idle resulting in a huge decline in Gross National Product (GNP) of the economies. The prices were actually falling during this depression period. When after the Second World War, problem of inflation rather than unemployment became the major concern of the economists. Keynesian economists explained it in terms of excess aggregate demand and therefore called it demand-pull inflation. As seen in the previous chapters that Keynes and his followers laid emphasis on the *management of aggregate demand* to bring about short-run stability in the economy. They recommended expansionary fiscal and monetary policies to raise aggregate demand to pull the economy out of depression or recession and thereby to reduce unemployment. On the other hand, to fight inflation, they advocated contractionary fiscal and monetary policies to reduce aggregate demand.

However, the problem of stagflation encountered in the USA and Great Britain during the seventies and early eighties when both high inflation and high unemployment prevailed simultaneously did not admit of easy solution through the Keynesian demand management policies. In fact, attempts to remedy the stagflation through Keynesian demand management worsened the situation.

Against this backdrop an alternative school of thought about macroeconomics was put forward.

This alternative thought laid stress on supply-side of macroeconomic equilibrium, that is, *it focused on shifting the aggregate supply curve to the right* rather than causing a shift in aggregate demand curve. Thus, supply-side economics prefers to solve the problem of stagflation, that is, simultaneous existence of high inflation and high unemployment through *management of aggregate supply* rather than management of aggregate demand. Further, supply-side economics stresses the determinants of long-run growth instead of causes of short-run cyclical changes in the economy. Supply-side economists lay emphasis on the factors that determine the incentives to work, save and invest which ultimately determine the aggregate supply of output of the economy.

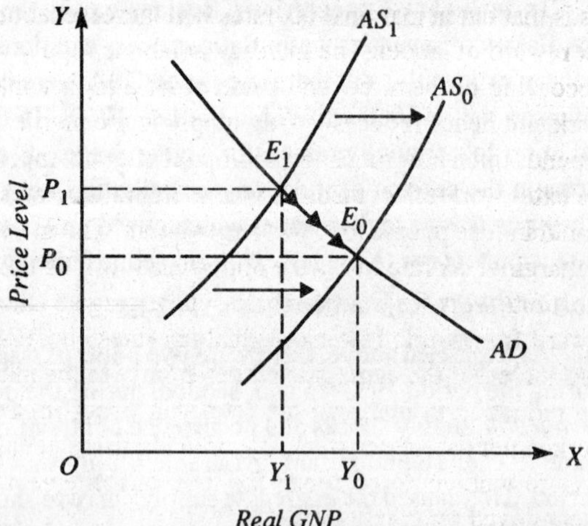

Fig. 14.3. *Supply-Siders seek to shift aggregate supply curve to the right by stimulating incentives to work, save and invest.*

Difference in the approaches of Keynesian demand-side theory and alternative supply-side theory can be understood with reference to Fig. 14.3 which illustrates the emergence of stagflation as a consequence of a shift in the aggregate supply curve due to the cost-push factors and decline in productivity. Suppose aggregate supply curve shifts upward to the left from AS_0 to AS_1 due to some cost-push factors (*e.g.*, rise in oil price). As a result, it will be seen from Figure 14.3 that price level would rise to P_1 and output (*i.e.*, real GNP) would fall to Y_1 (which will cause increase in unemployment). This high inflation and high unemployment configuration represents the state of stagflation. Now, the supply-side economists argue that to get out of stagflation, aggregate supply curve should be shifted to the right. As is evident from the Fig. 14.3 with the rightward shift of the aggregate supply curve from AS_1 to AS_0, the economy moves from the equilibrium point E_1 to point E_0 showing that *while price level falls, aggregate national output increases (which will reduce unemployment)*. Thus, in this way, through management of aggregate supply, the economy can be lifted out of stagflation.

It is worth mentioning that if to tackle this problem of stagflation Keynesian policy of increasing aggregate demand, that is, shifting the aggregate demand curve from AD_0 to AD_1 (see Fig. 14.2) through expansionary fiscal and monetary measures is adopted to reduce unemployment, it will cause price level to rise further to P_2 and will thus worsen the inflationary situation. On the other hand, if to tackle inflation, aggregate demand is reduced to AD_0, though i will cause the price level to fall, it will result in reduction in real aggregate output (GNP) causing unemployment to increase further and thus deepen the recession. Therefore, supply-side economists contend that Keynesian demand-management policy fails to provide a solution for the problem of stagflation. The supply-side economists, the prominent among whom is Arthur Laffer, are of the view that economic policy, especially of taxation, can be used to stimulate incentive to work, save and invest and task risks which cause increases in aggregate supply and yield higher growth in productivity. This leads to higher growth of real GNP and lower both rates of inflation and unemployment. We explain below the basic elements of supply-side economics and then critically evaluate it.

Basic Propositions of Supply-Side Economics

As mentioned above, supply-side economists emphasise the importance of effects of tax incentives on labour supply, saving and investment for promoting growth of output. They further lay stress on the favourable effects of tax cuts on Government revenue and thereby to achieve reduction in budget deficit. The following are the basic propositions of supply side economics:

1. **Taxation and Labour-Supply.** The first important basic proposition of supply-side economics is that cut in marginal tax rates will increase labour supply or work effort as it will raise the after-tax reward of labour. The increase in labour supply will cause growth in aggregate supply of output. According to them, beyond some point a higher marginal tax rate reduces people's willingness to work and hence reduces labour supply in the market. They argue that how long individual will work depends upon how much the additional after tax income (i.e., after-tax wage rate) will be earned from the extra work-effort made. Lower marginal tax rates by increasing after tax earnings of extra labour would induce people to work longer hours. The increase in after-tax earnings as a result of reduction in marginal tax rate raises the opportunity cost of leisure and provide incentives to the individuals to substitute work for leisure. As a result, aggregate labour supply increases. Further, by ensuring higher reward from work, lower marginal tax rates encourage more people to enter the labour force. This also increases the aggregate labour supply in the market. Thus, increase in labour supply following the reduction in marginal tax rates can occur in several ways by increasing the number of hours worked per day or per week, by inducing more people to enter the labour force, by providing incentives to workers to postpone the time of retirement, and by discouraging workers from remaining unemployed for a long period.

Reduction in marginal tax rates on business income raises the after-tax return on labour employed. This will encourage businesses to demand and employ more labour. Thus reduction in marginal tax rates on incomes will increase both the supply of labour and demand for it.

2. **Incentives to Save and Invest.** The second basic proposition of supply-side economics is that reduction in marginal tax rates will increase the incentives to save and invest more. According to it, a high marginal tax rate on incomes reduces the after-tax return on saving and investment and therefore discourages saving and investment. Suppose an individual saves Rs. 1000 at 10 per cent rate of interest, he will earn Rs. 100 as interest income per annum. If marginal tax rate is 60 per cent, his after-tax interest income will be Rs. 40. This means that after-tax interest on his savings has fallen to 4 per cent $\left(\frac{40}{1000} \times 100 = 4\right)$.

Thus, whereas an individual might be willing to save at 10 per cent rate of return on his saving, he might prefer to consume more rather than save when the return he gets is only 4 per cent. To promote savings, it may be noted, is essential for raising investment and capital accumulation which in the long run determines growth of output. The supply-side economists emphasise lower marginal tax rates on income to encourage savings. They also argue for lower tax rates especially on income from investment such as business profits to induce businessmen and firms to invest more. It will be recalled that investment in an economy depends to a great extent on expected rate of profits (or what is called marginal efficiency of investment). A higher tax on business profits and corporate income discourages investment by reducing the after-tax net profit on investment. Thus, lower marginal tax rates on business profits will encourage saving and investment and step up capital accumulation. With more capital per worker, labour productivity will rise which will tend to reduce unit labour cost and lower the rate of inflation. Moreover, the higher rate of capital accumulation, will ensure greater growth of productive capacity. The lower unit labour cost and the higher rate of capital accumulation made possible by greater saving and investment will cause aggregate supply curve to shift to the right. This will lower the price level, increase the growth of output and reduce unemployment.

3. **Cost-Push Effect of the Tax Wedge.** Another important proposition of supply-side economics is that the substantial growth of public sector in the modern economies has necessitated a large increase in the tax revenue to finance its activities. The tax revenue has increased both absolutely and as a percentage of national income. The Keynesian economists view the tax revenue as withdrawal of money income from the people which operates to reduce aggregate demand. Thus, in the Keynesian

view the mobilisation of resources for the public sector through taxation have an anti-inflationary effect. On the contrary, supply-side economists think that sooner or later most of the taxes, especially excise duties and sales taxes, are incorporated in the business costs and shifted to the consumers in the form of higher prices of products. Thus, in their view, imposition of higher taxes, like higher wages, have a cost-push effect. Referring to the period of seventies and early eighties in the USA, which was plagued by the great stagflation, they point out that huge increases made in sales and excise taxes by the state and local Governments and substantial hike in payroll taxes by Fed Government in the USA during this period had greatly pushed up the business costs resulting in higher product prices. In fact, supply siders contend that many taxes constitute a wedge between the costs incurred on resources and the price of a product. With the substantial growth of the public sector, the funds required to finance it have greatly increased resulting in a greater tax wedge. This has worked to shift the aggregate supply curve to the left.

4. **Underground Economy.** Another important contention of supply-siders is that higher marginal tax rates encourage people to work in the underground economy (which in India is popularly called black or parallel economy) where their income cannot be traced by the income tax department. In India, this underground economy is very large. Not only individual businessmen evade income taxes, corporate firms also have devised several illegal ways to evade taxes on their profits. It is not only taxes on personal income and company profits but also excise duties and sales taxes which are not paid fully by individuals and companies. In line with the supply-side view, the former Finance Minister Dr. Manmohan Singh has often argued in favour of reduction in taxes. According to him, *lower tax rates would increase tax compliance* which increases the amount of income which people will report to the taxation authorities. Thus, the supply-side economists think that reduction in taxes will in fact raise the tax revenue by discouraging people from evading taxes and from operating in the underground economy.

5. **Tax Revenue and Laffer Curve.** By far the most important proposition of supply-side economics is that the lower marginal taxes will increase tax revenue. In seventies and eighties American economy was not only facing the problem of stagflation but also of large budget deficits of the Government. The supply-siders contend that through raising tax revenue, the reduction in tax rates will not only reduce inflation and unemployment by bringing about increase in aggregate supply but will also reduce budget deficits of the Government. An eminent supply-side economist, Arthur Laffer has argued that lower tax rates are quite consistent with the increase in tax revenue. He has shown the relationship between tax rates and the total tax revenue collected with the help of a curve named after him as Laffer Curve. *Laffer curve* shows that after a certain point increase in tax rates can reduce tax revenue as incentives to work, save and investment are adversely affected. The higher tax rates after a certain point prove to be counter-productive as they reduce supply of labour and capital accumulation through providing disincentives to work, save and invest. Therefore, these higher tax rates reduce national output and income. Remember that total tax revenue (TR) collected is equal to the tax rate, which we denote by t multiplied by the total income which we denote by Y. Thus, total tax revenue $TR = tY$. According to Laffer, when tax rate t is raised beyond a certain point the national out-

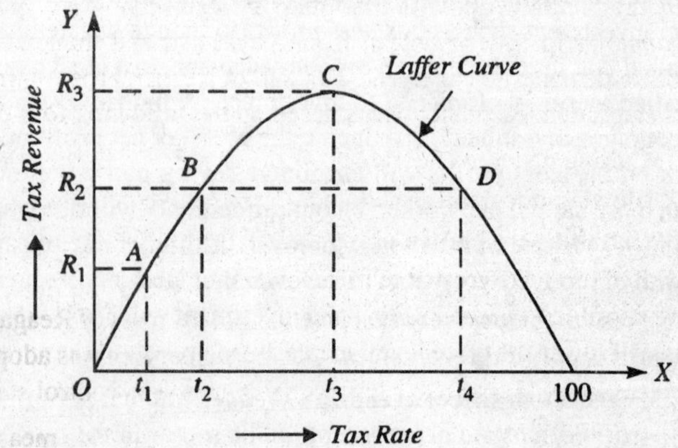

Fig. 14.4. *Laffer Curve : Relationship between Tax Rate and Tax Revenue Collected*

put and income Y which constitutes the base of taxation declines so much that total tax revenue t_Y falls. Laffer curve has been drawn in Fig. 14.4. The Laffer curve starts from the origin which means when the tax rate is zero, total tax revenue will also obviously be zero. Upto point C, Laffer curve is rising which shows that as tax rate rises to t_3, tax revenue collected increases. But if the tax rate is raised beyond t_3, Laffer curve slopes downward showing that tax revenue decreases as tax rate is increased above t_3 for the reasons explained above. At tax rate t_3, the tax revenue collected R_3 is the maximum. For instance, if tax rate is raised from t_3 to t_4, the tax revenue falls from R_3 to R_2. As explained above, when tax rate is raised beyond some point, tax revenue decreases. This is because *higher tax rates serve as disincentives to work, save and invest, innovate and take business risks and therefore the tax base,* (*that is, the level of national output, income and employment*) *decreases.* This can be easily understood if the tax rate is raised to 100 per cent. At 100 per cent tax rate no body would have any incentive to work, save and invest or engage in any productive activity and therefore the tax revenue will be reduced to zero. Production of goods and earning of income (i.e., tax base) would come to a halt at this consfiscatory (100 per cent) tax rate.

Most of the economists agree with Laffer that beyond a certain tax rate, the tax revenue will fall. However, *the moot point is at which point on Laffer curve the position of the economy is presently located.* For example, if the economy is presently at point D with tax rate t_4, that is, on the downward portion of the Laffer curve, the reduction in tax rate from t_4 to t_3 will raise the tax revenue from R_2 to R_3. If there is drastic cut in the tax rate from t_4 to t_2, the tax revenue remains unaffected.

It may be noted that with the reduction in tax rate, the tax revenue increases because of two additional reasons. First, as explained earlier, *the reduction in tax increases tax compliance and tends to reduce tax evasion and tendency to indulge in underground or black market activities.* Lower tax rates also reduce the inclination of people to avoid taxes through the use of various tax shelters (such as buying National Saving Certificates) investment in which is exempted from taxes. Second, the supply-side economists also argue that by promoting the growth of production and employment, lower tax rates will reduce Government transfer payments, such as unemployment allowances.

REAGANOMICS AND SUPPLY-SIDE ECONOMICS

Supply-side economics became popular when President Reagan of the USA actually put it into practice after winning the election in 1981. Reagan came into power at a time when the American economy was facing the problem of stagflation with higher rates of both inflation and unemployment. Though Reagan economic programme cannot be fully equated with supply-side economics, it contained the fundamentals of the latter. Reagan economic programme is generally described as *Reaganomics* to differentiate it from Keynesian and moneterist economics which were based on aggregate demand-management. The aim of Reagan programme was to pull the American economy out of stagflaion. Reaganomics is based on the following four pillars:

1. Cutting down the tax rates;
2. Slowing down the growth of Government expenditure;
3. Curtailing the burden of regulations; and
4. Reducing the growth of money supply.

We discuss below these fundamental policy steps of Reaganomics. The first three measures are features of supply-side economics. The fourth measure was adopted by Reagan to control inflation as a supplementary measure to supply-side approach to control stagflation.

Reduction of Taxes. The most important supply-side measure adopted by Reagan was to make a drastic cut in taxes. A 25 per cent reduction in personal income-tax rates over the three years was made. With this the highest rate of personal income was reduced to 33 per cent. Most of the Americans were brought in the bracket of 15 per cent tax rate. As seen above, such low tax rates are aimed at promoting incentives to work, save and invest and thereby increase aggregate supply of output. Further, in line with the view of supply-side economics, Reagan programme allowed a *higher depreciation allowance* to business firms to cover the cost of machinery and equipment installed. This virtually lowered the tax-burden on the companies which increased their incentives to invest in capital accumulation. Besides, another measure of tax reduction was *lowering of capital gains tax rates* to boost investment incentives. In 1986 tax reform, Reagan *reduced the corporation income tax*. This, according to supply-siders, promoted investment incentives by raising the profitability of investment and also making available more investible funds from within the internal resources of the companies.

As we will examine below, the reduction in taxes by Reagan became a highly controversial issue because of prevailing high inflation in USA at that time. Keynesian economists argued that these cuts in taxes will increase the disposable incomes with the individuals and companies and would bring about increase in aggregate demand resulting in higher inflation rate. Besides, they pointed out that tax cuts would lower the Government revenue and increase budget deficits.

Reducing the Burden of Government Regulation. Supply-siders argued that a high degree of Government regulation was also responsible for poor performance of the American economy in the past some decades. According to them, Government regulation of some industries such as transport and communication created monopolies and thus protected them from competition by rivals.

In the absence of competition, these monopolistic firms created through Government regulations tended to become inefficient which raised the cost of production in the regulated industries. Second, but more importantly, the supply-siders argue, there has been a substantial increase in the number of Government regulations and controls regarding protection of environment from pollution, safety of products (such as of insecticides, pesticides etc.) safety and health of workers, equal access to job opportunities. Supply-siders argue that these Government regulations and controls have raised the costs of production and of doing business. This have resulted in higher prices of goods and sluggish growth in output and has thus tended to give rise the problem of stagflation.

A Critical Apparaisal of Supply-Side Economics

As seen above, a central idea of supply-side economics is that the reduction in rates of certain type of taxes will increase aggregate supply of output by increasing both the supply of labour and capital. Taxes can certainly be cut in some ways that raise the rewards for working and saving and thereby provide incentives to work more and save more. If people actually respond positively to these incentives, then tax cuts would lead to the increase in supplies of labour and capital and cause a rightward shift in the aggregate supply curve. However, critics point out that there is no guarantee that tax cuts would induce people to actually work more and save more. According to them, those people whose aim is to earn a fixed targeted income to buy goods and services they want, at higher rewards for working resulting from tax cuts, they will be able to earn targeted incomes with fewer hours of work. Thus, the higher monetary reward per unit of work hour will enable them to enjoy more leisure and earn the same amount of income as before. As regards the people who behave positively to increased reward for working, it is pointed out that the increase in work-effort (*i.e.*, labour supply) obtained in this way may not be very large.

Similarly, cut in taxes raises the reward for saving, but we cannot certainly say whether this will cause people to save more. Those people who want to have a given amount of savings, they would find that their saving goals can be achieved by saving less when return on saving has been raised by reducing taxes. Thus, lower taxes can encourage some people to do greater saving and investment but at the same time they can also discourage others to save more. It has been pointed out by critics *that following tax cuts in USA by Reagan in 1981 the saving rate in the United States fell.* Commenting on the emperical evidence in this regard Baumol and Blinder write, "Most of the statistical evidence suggests that we should expect tax reduction to lead to only small increase in either labour supply or household savings"[1]

The Threat of Inflation: Demand-Side Effects of Tax Cuts: The second important criticism made against supply-side economics is that it underestimates the effect of tax cuts on increasing

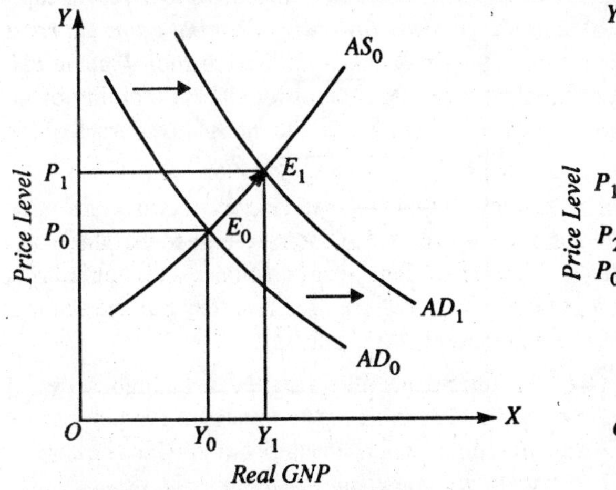

Fig. 14.5. *Effect of Tax Cut on Aggregate Demand and Inflation : Keynesian View*

Fig. 14.6. *Effect of Tax Cut on Aggregate Supply and Demand, and Inflation Rate : Supply-Side View*

aggregate demand and thus adding to the inflationary pressures in the economy. As we know that reduction in personal income tax increases the disposable income of the people and will therefore cause an increase in the demand for consumer goods. Similarly, the cuts in business taxes will raise the profitability of investment and thereby induce the firms to invest in expanding productive capacity. This will lead to the increase in demand for investment goods. Thus, reduction in taxes will cause aggregate demand for goods to increase which tend to raise the inflation rate. This is illustrated in Fig. 14.5 where initially aggregate demand curve AD_0 and aggregate supply curve AS_0 intersect at E_0 and determine price level P_0. If aggregate supply curve AS_0 remains constant, the increase in aggregate demand from AD_0 to AD_1 due to tax cuts establishes equilibrium at point E_1 and thereby determines new price level P_1 which is much higher than the initial price level P_0 (that is, rate of inflation is high).

On the other hand, supply-side economists argued that the increase in aggregate supply of goods stimulated by reduction in taxes will be large enough to counteract any inflationary pressures due to higher aggregate demand arising from tax cuts. Fig. 14.6 illustrates the supply-side view of the effect of tax cuts made to solve stagflation. Originally, aggregate demand and aggregate supply are in equilibrium at point E_0 where price level is P_0 and real GNP is equal to Y_0. This equilibrium situation is one of stagflation when there is high rate of inflation and lower GNP (and therefore high level of unemployment). According to supply-siders, the tax cuts through stimulating work effort, saving and investment substantially shift the aggregate supply curve to the right. Of course, it also shifts the aggregate demand curve upward. But the supply-side effect dominates resulting in *only small increase in the price level from P_0 to P_2 (that is, rate of inflation is quite low) and large expansion in real GNP from Y_0 to Y_1 which will cause unemployment to fall.* But, as we have pointed out above, this is a very optimistic view of the effect of tax cuts.

Empirical evidence reveals that tax cuts have only a small effect on increasing aggregate supply, whereas they have substantial effect on raising aggregate demand and inflation. Figure 14.7

1. Baumol, William J. and Blinder, Allan S., *Economics : Principles and Policies*, Harcourt Publishers, Fifth Edition, 1991

illustrates how a large effect on aggregate demand of tax cuts is stronger than their favourable impact on increasing the aggregate supply. With reduction in taxes, there is a large shift in aggregate demand curve from AD_0 to AD_2 but only a small increase in aggregate supply from AS_0 to AS_2. As a result, price level jumps to P_1, showing a higher rate of inflation (see Fig. 14.7).

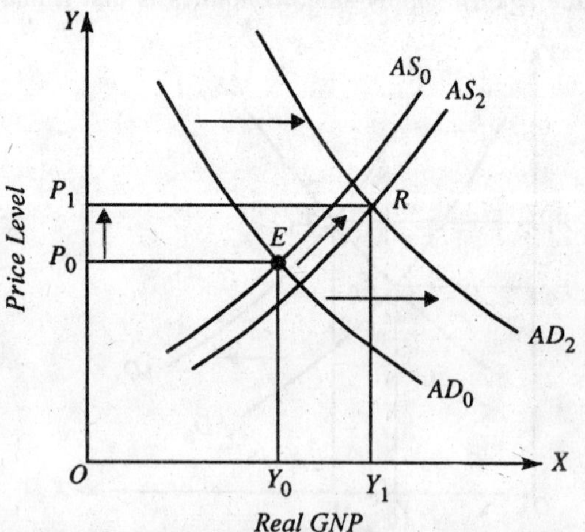

Fig. 14.7. *Whem the effect of tax cut an aggregate supply is much smaller than its effect on raising aggregate demand curve, tax cut causes a higher rate of inflation.*

It is worth mentioning here that perhaps recognising the demand-side effect of tax cuts and contrary to supply-side view President Reagan in his fiscal package, also made reduction in Government spending to cancel out the demand-side effect of generating }inflationary pressures in the economy. As we know whereas tax cuts increases aggregate demand, reduction in Government expenditure reduces it and thus cancels out the effect of the former. By combining the tax cuts with reduction in Government expenditure of the right magnitude aggregate demand curve could be held constant which would make it possible to retain the favourable impact of tax cuts on aggregate supply. However, the problem with this fiscal strategy is that large cuts in Government expenditure are also to be made simultaneously, if aggregate demand is to be kept constant. However, in case of President Reagan's fiscal programme, many economists in the early 1980s felt that reduction in Government expenditure in Reagan's fiscal package was smaller than the tax cuts.

It follows from above that tax cuts of supply-side economics which was originally propounded to cure both inflation and stagnation, could be expected to make not more than a small dent in the inflation rate because of the demand-side effects they create. However, in case of USA, implementation of Reagan's economic programme did not actually lead to higher rate of inflation, despite the increase in budget deficits. But this was not because of successful effect of supply-side tax cuts but due to tight monetary policy adopted by Federal Reserve System of America to check inflation at that time.[2] It is this tight money policy that helped to contain aggregate demand by restraining the growth of money supply. Thus, credit for checking inflation must go to Federal Reserve's tight money policy rather than to tax cuts of supply-side economists.

Increase in Budget Deficits

Another important shortcoming of supply-side cuts in taxes is that they are likely to increase budget deficits. When a country is facing the problem of budget deficits, cut in taxes will cause reduction in Government revenue and will therefore raise budget deficits. It may be noted that in 1981 when on the advice of supply-side economists Reagan made large tax cuts, his critics argued that these would further increase the budget deficits, as he had made only small cuts in Government spending. Extreme supply-siders however denied that large tax cuts would raise budget deficits. As has been explained above, they argued that higher marginal tax rates were encouraging tax evasion and avoidance and also causing more and more activities to be done in the underground economy, and thus escaping from the tax net. Reduction in taxes, they argued, would increase tax compliance which

2. It should be noted that in the USA Federal Reserve System works independently of Government or President of the USA. Interestingly, the former Governor of Reserve Bank of India, Dr. C.R. Rangarajan also demanded independence of RBI from Government

will increase the Government revenue. Besides, they, especiailly an eminent supply-side economist Arthur Laffer, pointed out that lower taxes need not lead to reduction in tax revenues because they were bound to raise the tax base. An important graphic concept called as Laffer curve was developed to prove that reduction in taxes would increase tax revenue and help in reducing budget deficits. Tax base refers to the real GNP or national income. Tax cuts, according to them, stimulate work effort, saving and investment which cause a large increase in aggregate supply of goods (that is, real GNP). It is this greater tax base which will ensure increase in tax revenue.

However, in case of tax cut made by President Reagan during 1981-83 in the United States, the supply-side view proved wrong. In reality federal tax revenue fell sharply after the reduction in taxes during 1981-83 by President Reagan resulting in larger budget deficits.

Effect on the Distribution of Income

Another problem with supply-side economics is that it leads to the increase in inequilities of income distribution. Though increasing incomes of the richer sections of the society is not its explicit primary objective, the cut in taxes recommended by supply-side economics increases the incomes and wealth of the already affluent sections of the society. This is because it is the rich who earn most of capital gains, interest and dividend and tax cuts on them therefore greatly benefit them. Besides, it is the rich people who own the business corporations and tax cuts on corporate profits will also benefit them. Thus, the supply-side economics tilt income distribution towards the rich.

Conclusion

To sum up, it follows from above that supply-side theorists have too optimistic view of the favourable effect of tax cuts on inflation. Tax cuts have both supply-side and demand-side effects. Effects of tax cuts on raising aggregate supply through stimulating saving and business investment in plant and machinery *will accrue more slowly than their effect on increase in aggregate demand. Therefore, supply-side policies should not be considered as substitutes for short-run stabilisation policy which focuses on management of aggregate demand but rather they should be used to promote rapid growth of output in the long run.* Furthermore, the effect of tax cuts on raising aggregate demand is likely to be much greater than their effect on raising aggregate supply, at least in the short run. In view of the smaller supply-side effect as compared to the demand-side effect, tax cuts are unlikely to make any contribution to lowering the inflation rate. Further, the supply-side measures are likely to increase income inequalities as they benefit the rich more than the poor. Lastly, tax cuts of supply-side economics, if not accompanied by appropriate cuts in government spending would lead to larger and not smaller budget deficits.

CHAPTER 15

The New Classical Economics : Rational Expectations Model

Introduction

An important post-Keynesian development in macroeconomics is the rational expectations model propounded by an American economist, Robert Lucas in the the seventies[1]. Since rational expectations model re-establishes many classical concepts and policy prescriptions, it is also called '*New Classical Economics.*' The rational expectations model was developed against the background of both high inflation and high unemployment that prevailed in the US economy in the 1970s. As the coexistence of both high rate of inflation and high rate of unemployment seemed to contradict the Keynesian theory, there was a lot of dissatisfaction with it calling for new explanation of the then prevailing situation of high inflation and high unemployment.

It many be noted that both the Friedman's *moniterism* and the new classical rational expectations models are similar as both are rooted in some aspects of classical economics and also reach the same conclusion of non-interventionist policy by the Government in regulating or fine tuning the economy so as to achieve macroeconomic stabilisation. In fact, Lucas and his followers, new classical economists, are even more skeptical than monetarists about the usefulness of activist monetary and fiscal policies to stabilise the economy. However, as we will explain later there are important differences in Friedman's monetarism and Lucas rational expectations model. The new classical model of rational expectations is a more basic critique of Keynesian theory than the monetarist model. New classical economists describe the Keynesian theoretical system as '*fundamentally flawed*'.

In what follows we first explain the critique of Keynesian macroeconomic theory made by new classical economists, especially Robert Lucas. Having done so we will explain in detail rational expectations model and its policy implications. Like the classical economists, the new classical economists question the usefulness of activist monetary and fiscal policies of the government for achieving macroeconomic stability as they show that demand management policies do not affect the real variables such as output and employment. Thus the new classical economists believe that monetary and fiscal policies cannot achieve macroeconomic stability through management of aggregate demand. This is generally referred to as '*policy ineffectiveness postulate*' of new classical economics.

It is worth mentioning that the economic policy stance of the new classical economics differes also from that of the monetarists. Whereas the monetarists think that *discretionary economic policies* (especially, the discretionary fiscal policy) do not affect output and employment in the long run and are therefore neither necessary nor desirable. They believe that *systematic* (i.e. non-discretionary) monetary policy does have real effect on output and employment *in the short run*. On the other hand, Lucas and his followers, other new classical economists, question the desirability of activist fiscal and monetary polices for achieving macroeconomic stability *both in the short run and long run.*

1. Some important contributions to Rational Expectations Model are (1) Robert Lucas, "Rules, Discretion and the Role of Economic Advisor" in Stanley Fischer, ed., *Rational Expectations and Economic Policy* (Chicago; University of Chicago Press, 1980) and (2) Robert Lucas and Thomas Sargent, *After Keynesian Macroeconomics'* in *After the Philips Curve. Persistence of High Inflation and High Unemployment* (Boston : Federal Reserve Bank of Boston, 1978).

Therefore, the challenge of new classical economists to the Keynesian theory is more fundamental and far-reaching than that of monetarists.

Rational Expectation : Meaning

New classical economics is *based on rational expectations hypothesis put forward by Robert* Lucas of the University of Chicago[2]. According to rational expectations hypothesis, economic agents such as workers and firms do not know the future with certainty and therefore base their decisions on their expectations of the future. The economic agents make rational expectations of future if they *use all available information* to make best *possible forecasts*. Prior to Lucas, analysis of relation between inflation and unemployment relied on simplistic Phillips curve model which visualised higher inflation led to lower unemployment. But these simple Phillips curve models assumed that the firms and workers did not use all available information to make forecasts and therefore would make same mistakes again and again. For example, in these previous theories higher inflation was assumed to raise workers willing to supply more labour as they thought their higher money wages brought about by high inflation meant higher real wages as they did not realise the prices of all commodities had risen because of this. Thus, they were continually being fooled into believing that their real wages rose when actually their money wages had risen due to inflation. The focus of Lucas rational expectations approach is that people's forecasts may not always be correct but in forming expectations *they do not make systematic errors*. According to Robert Barro, an advocate of rational expectation approach. "In Lucas theory *people can be confused temporarely by monetary surprises....... In particular, an unanticipated expansion of money and the general price level may temporarily fool workers* into thinking that their wages had risen in real terms. Similarly, producers might believe that the prices of the goods they were selling had risen relative to the prices of other goods. Through these channels, a monetary stimulus might cause a temporary boom, but one that must end soon after the errors in expectations were recognised"[3]. A further important aspect of rational expectations model is that it believes in *equilibrium in which markets clear immediately*. That is, they have no faith in either money-wage stickiness or price-stickiness. Having rational expectations, if firms fix prices and wages on that basis, then on an average, prices and wages will be set at the levels at which products and labour markets will be in equilibrium.

KEYNESIAN THEORY AND THE NEW CLASSICAL (LUCAS) CRITIQUE

Keynesian Theory. The Keynesian economists such as Tobin and Franco Modigliani point out that for ensuring macroeconomic stability in a market economy the Government should pursue active demand-management policy. On the other hand, Lucas and other new classical economists believe that real variables such as output and employment cannot be stabilised by management of aggregate demand through the activist monetary and fiscal policies. This is because they show that the values of such real variables cannot be affected in both the short run and long run by any systematic aggregate-demand management policies.

To understand the new classical critique of the Keynesian macroeconomic model, it will be useful to review in brief the Keynesian analysis of relationship between aggregate demand on the hand, and output and employment on the other. This is illustrated in Figure 15.1 where in left-hand panel (*a*) we show the equilibrium in the product market and in the right-hand panel (*b*) we show the labour-market equilibrium. *LAS* is long-run aggregate supply curve drawn at potential output level Y_0 at which only natural rate of unemployment exists, P_0^e is the expected price level which, according to the Keynesian model, is based on the price level prevailing in the previous period.

2. Robert E. Lucas "Expectations and the Neutrality of Money" *Journal of Political Economy*, April 1972
3. Robert J. Barro, *Nothing is Sacred, Economic Ideas for the New Millenium*, MIT, 2002 pp. 27-28.

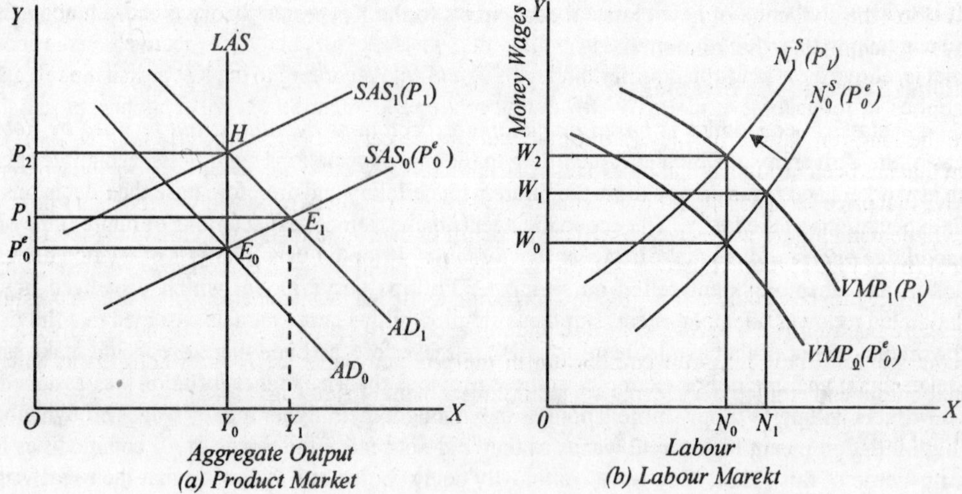

Fig. 15.1. *The Keynesian Model : Short-run and Long-run Effect of Increase in Aggregate Demand.*

The people expect that this past period price level will continue to prevail in the current period. The short-run aggregate supply curve based on this expected price level (P_o^e) is SAS_0 which passes through the long-run aggregate supply curve at the level of this expected price level P_0^e. With the given aggregate demand curve AD_0, the macroeconomic equilibrium is at point E_0 corresponding to potential aggregate output Y_0 (i.e. at natural rate of unemployment). It is important to note that expected price level (P_o^e) remains constant during the short run and therefore the corresponding short-run aggregate supply curve SAS_0 remains fixed in the short run. In the left-hand panel (*b*) of Figure 15.1, the VMP_0 is the curve of the value of marginal product of labour which represents the demand curve for labour (Note that $VMP_0 = MPP_N \times P_o^e$ where MPP_N is marginal physical product of labour). Given the expected price level P_o^e, the labour supply curve is N_o^s which is sloping upward. The given labour-supply function is written as

$$N_0^s = f\left(\frac{W}{P_0^e}\right)$$

where N^S is the supply of labour W is the *money wage rate* and P_0^e is the expected price level and $\frac{W}{P_0^e}$ is therefore the expected real wage rate. Labour market is in equilibrium at wage rate W_0 so that real wage determined is $\frac{W_0}{P_0^e}$

Now suppose that aggregate demand increases, say as a result of increase in money supply, causing a shift in the aggregate demand curve to AD_1 (see Panel (a) of Fig. 15.1). Since short-run aggregate supply curve of output remains fixed the short-run equilibrium is at E_1 at which new higher price level of output P_1 is determined. With rise in price of product from P_0^e to P_1 in the short run and consequently lowering of the real wage rate, $\frac{W_0}{P_1} < \frac{W_0}{P_0^c}$, demand curve for labour shifts to VMP_1. With short-run supply curve of labour remaining the same at N_0^s, the labour employment increases to N_1 and money wage rate rises W_1. *It must be remembered that in the Keynesian model the workers' short-run supply of labour is governed by the past price level P_0^e which they expect will continue to prevail in the shrot run whatever the current changes in the price level.*

It is evident from Figure 15.1 that as a result of increase in aggregate demand brought about by increase in money supply, both output and employment increase to Y_1 and N_1 respectively in the short run, that is, above their long-run equilibrium levels Y_0 and N_0. According to the Keynesian model (and this applies to monetarist model as well), output and employment levels will continue to remain above the long-run equilibrium levels until the workers perceive correctly the rise in price level of output that has been brought about by expansinary monetary policy. When in the long run the workers perceive that price level of output has risen from P_0^e to P_1 as a result of expansionary monetary policy, they will demand higher wages which will cause a shift in their labour supply curve to the left to N^S_1 in panel (*b*) of Fig. 15.1 and together with the new higher labour demand curve VMP_1 will determine a higher wage rate W_2. Thus, in the long run, according to the Keynesian theory, this will cause a shift in the aggregate supply curve *SAS* to the left and this process of leftward shift in labour-supply curve will continue until new long-run equilibrium in the product market at *H* is established at which original output and employment levels are restored [see panel (*a*) of Fig. 15.1].

Lucas Critique

The new classical economists, Lucas and others do not agree with the Keynesian and monetarist analysis that the workers form their expectations of current price level and inflation rate on the basis of past behaviour of price level. They question the Keynesian and monetarist view that there is slow adjustment of price expectations and for analysis of the effects of a policy these expectations can be assumed to remain constant in the short run. The advocates of rational expectations argue that such formulation of expectations formation is quite simplistic and naive. The firms and workers cannot continue to form expectations on the basis of the past behaviour of prices resulting from changes in policy when they are proved to be systematically wrong. Therefore, according to them, as explained above, people quickly form and revise their expectations *using all available information and intelligently predict* the changes in prices and form their expectations on that basis.

Thus, if expectations are rational, private economic agents use all informations to predict the price level following the adoption of expansionary monetary policy. If the expectations are rational, then the policy change by the government will be anticipated by the people. Firstly, either the government has announced the policy change or the people may anticipate the change because the policy maker, the Central Bank or government, is known to *respond in a certain systematic way*. For example if the Central Bank of a country is known to respond systematically to follow expansionary monetary policy when the situation of unemployment of labour emerges, then people anticipate that the Central Bank will expand the money supply to tackle the unemployment problem and further that this will result in rise in price level. According to John Muth, the pioneer of the concept of rational expectations, *"rational expectations are essentially the same as the predictions of the relevant economic theory"*[4].

For understanding of New Classical (Lucas) model of rational expectations, it is necessary to explain Lucas aggregate supply function and aggregate demand function.

The Lucas Aggregate Supply Function

The key element in New Classical Theory is the particular specification of aggregate supply function that was formulated by Robert Lucas. According to this, the real aggregate output is a function of the difference between the actual price level (*P*) and the expected price level (P^e). Lucas supply function is written as

$$Y = Y^* + \alpha (P - P^e) \qquad \ldots (i)$$

where *Y* is actual aggregate output in a period, Y^* is the potential output corresponding to the level of natural unemployment. From the above Lucas supply function it is evident that if actual price level (*P*)

4. John Muth, Rational Expectations and the Theory of Price Movements, *Econometrica* Nol. 29, (July 1961) p. 316.

exceeds expected price level (P^e), actual aggregate output in the short run (Y) would be greater than the potential output Y^*. The extent to which Y will exceed Y^* depends on the value of α. On the other hand, if actual price level (P) happens to be less than expected price level (P^e) the actual aggregate output (Y) will be less than the potential aggregate output (Y^*). In the Lucas approach, actual price level of output is variable in the shrot run, it responds to the changes in aggregate demand. Further, in his approach wages are not just given on the basis of the last period's equilibrium as the Keynesians believe but they are fixed in the beginning of the current period at the market clearing level, given the expected price level as determined by the anticipated demand conditions for the current period. In other words, money wages are set on the basis of *forward-looking expectations* of what the aggregate demand will be in the current period.

The difference between the actual price level and the expect price level ($P-P^e$) is described as *price surprise*. In the beginning of each period, a firm expects a certain price level for that period. If actual price level happens to be different, there is price surprise. For example, if actual price level exceeds the average expected price level, the firm will learn about it only slowly since only after a certain time lag it realises that *all prices* have risen. However, the firm knows quickly that the price *of its* own product has risen. Thus, the firm perceives, though incorrectly, that the price of its product has risen relatively to others. Thus the firms are 'fooled' in believing that their relative prices have risen. In response to the rise in its relative price, the firm will increase its output.

Likewise, when there is positive price surprise workers too are fooled in believing that their price, that is, their real wage has risen relative to other prices. In other words, with positive price surprise they erroneously believe that their real wage rate has risen, though real wage rate has not actually risen and in response they supply more work hours. Thus when the actual price level is higher than the expected level, the economy will produce more output and employ more labour than when the price level is at their expected level. Thus, rationale for Lucas supply function is that "*Unexpected increase in the price level can fool workers and firms into thinking that their relative prices have changed causing them to alter the amount of labour or goods they choose to supply*"[5].

However, it may be emphasised that with rational expectations, as assumed by the *Lucas, the firms and workers will not make any systematic errors in expecting the price level* so that the actual price level will not differ from the expected price level. Thus with the changes in money supply and hence in aggregate demand, only the price level and money wages will change, leaving output and employment unchanged. Therefore, like the classicals, Lucas and others advocates of rational expectations believe that money is neutral.

Aggregate Demand Function

The second element in the rational expectations theory is the nature of aggregate demand. It is fluctuations in aggregate demand that bring about changes in price level and output. In Lucas new classical approach aggregate demand is generally considered in terms of quantity theory as given below :

$$AD : MV = PY \qquad \ldots (ii)$$

where M is the money supply, V is income velocity of money, P is the price level and Y is real income or aggregate output. Aggregate demand in this approach is given mainly by money supplied multipled by the velocity (*i.e. MV*).

In terms of growth of the variables the above quantity theory equation can be written as

$$\frac{\Delta M}{M} = \frac{\Delta P}{P} + \frac{\Delta Y}{Y}$$

5. Karal E. Case and Ray C. Fair, *Principles of Economics*, Pearson Education, 6th edition 2002, p.66

Note that velocity V is assumed to be constant, it disappears in the equation written in terms of growth of these variables.

Rewriting the above equation we have

$$\frac{\Delta P}{P}=\frac{\Delta M}{M}-\frac{\Delta Y}{Y}$$

$\frac{\Delta Y}{Y}$ which measures growth rate of output is generally written as g. Doing so we have

$$\frac{\Delta P}{P}=\frac{\Delta M}{M}-g \qquad \text{. . . }(ii)$$

The expected inflation rate by the private economic agents (i.e. firms and workers) will depend on the expected growth rate of money supply $\left(\frac{\Delta M}{M}\right)$ and the expected growth rate of output (g).

$$\left(\frac{\Delta P}{P}\right)^e=\left(\frac{\Delta M}{M}\right)^e-(g)^e \qquad \text{. . . }(iv)$$

Having explained the essential elements of both supply function and demand function of Lucas rational expectations approach we now turn to explain and illustrate the complete Lucas rational expectations model in terms of AS–AD curves rather than in algebric equations which complicate the issues involved. *To further simplify the model we take expected price level (P^e) as determined by expected money supply (M^e) and expected output level (Y^e) rather than expected growth rates of these variables.*

THE NEW CLASSICAL (LUCAS) RATIONAL EXPECTATIONS MODEL

In view of rational expressions by the people, the new classical economists modify the effects of a policy change, say of expansionary monetary policy, explained by the Keynesian and monetarists models as illustrated in Figure 15.1. The crucial departure that the new classical economists make from Keynesian and monetarists rests on the variables that determine position of labour supply curve and the aggregate supply curve of output. It is therefore important to mention on what factors these curves depend. As in the Keynesian theory, in rational expectations model also labour supply curve depends on the expected real wage rate. Thus,

$$N^S=f\left(\frac{W}{P^e}\right)$$

Thus, the position of labour supply curve N^S and therefore shrot-run aggregate supply curve of output depends on the expected price level, P^e. The increase in the expected price level will lower the real wage rate leading to the demand for higher money wages which will cause a shift in the labour supply curve and the aggregate supply curve of output to the left.

In the rational expectations model, expected price level depends on the expected levels of the variables within the model that actually determine the price level which becomes the expected price level by the workers and suppliers of output. These price-determining variables on the demand side are the expected level of money supply (M^e), government expenditure (g^e), tax collected (t^e) and the amount of autonomous investment (I^e). On the supply side, oil prices, custom duties, excise duties,

3. Milton Friedman, "A Theoretical Framework for Monetary Analysis" in Robert Gordon, ed., *Milton Friedman's Monetary Framework*, University of Chicago Press, 1974, p. 27

prices of raw materials and capital goods are important factors determining price level of output. In this new classical model the position of labour supply curve and aggregate supply curve of output depends on the expected values of these policy variables such as M^e, g^e, I^e which determine the price level.

Let us describe how the rational expectations model explains the effect of a *fully-anticipated expansion in money supply*, say from M_0 to M_1. Consider panel (a) of Figure 15.2 where to begin with AD_0 is the aggregate demand curve which is determined by the given money supply M_0, government expenditure g_0, tax collection t_0 and autonomous investment I_0. SAS_0 is the aggregate supply curve which depends on price level P_0 which is determined by money supply (M_0). With the increase in money supply from M_0 to M_1, other determining variables remaining the same, aggregate demand curve shifts to AD_1. As a result, price level rises to P^e_1, short-run aggregate supply curves remaining the same at the level SAS_0. Now, in panel (*b*) of Fig. 15.2, with the rise in price level to P_1^e, labour demand curve in panel (*b*) shifts to N_1^d which intersects the labour supply curve N^S_0 at point *B* and determine wage rate W_1 and as a result labour employment increases to N_1. In the Keynesian model

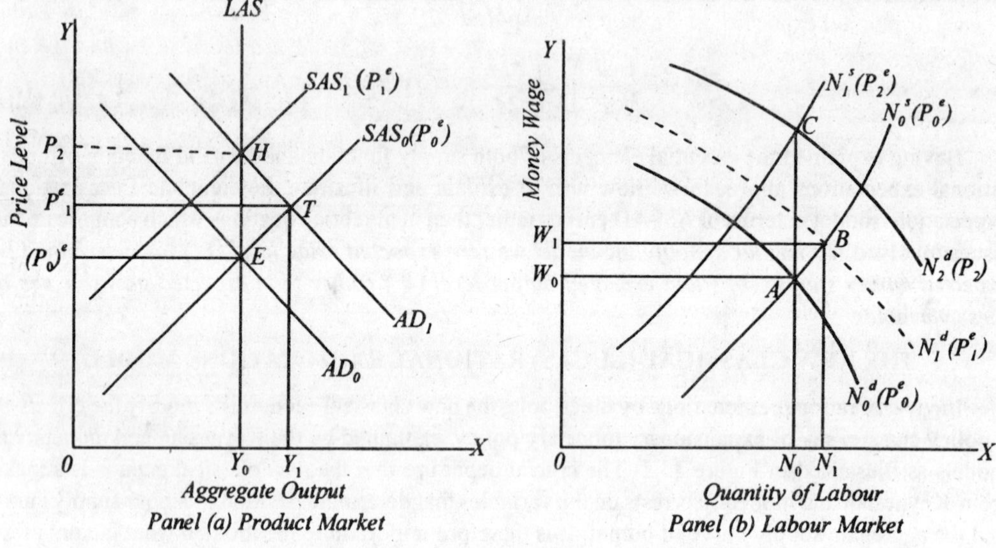

Fig.15.2. *Rational Expectations Model : The Effect of Expansionary Monetary Policy*

where the expected price level is unrelated to the *current* level of policy variables and therefore aggregate supply curve and labour supply curve *remains fixed in the short run*, the analysis ends here so far as the short-run period is concerned.

However, in the rational expectations model, the positions of aggregate supply curve of output and labour supply curve do not remain fixed in the short run. This is because in *the rational expectations model the adoption of expansionary policies are fully anticipated in response to the situation of recession or rise in unemployment that may emerge*. As a result, it is anticipated by the public that money supply would be increased resulting in rise in their expected price level to P_1^e. This is because with rational expectations, the workers who supply their labour services fully know that increase in money supply will cause the rise in price level to P_1^e. The rise in the expected *price level* will cause workers to demand more money wages and will therefore result in leftward shift in the labour supply curve to $N_1^s(P^e_1)$ in panel (*b*) of Fig. 15.2 and leftward shift in the aggregate supply curve of output to the new position $SAS_1(P^e_1)$ in panel (*a*) of Figure 15.2. It will be seen from panel (a) that the new short-run aggregate supply curve SAS_1 intersects the new aggregate demand curve AD_1 at point *H* and determines a higher price P_2.

With the rise in price level to (P_2), the labour demand curve will further shift to the left to the new position N_2^d (P_2) *and as a result wage rate will further rise. Such changes in wage rate and aggregate supply curves will continue until the new equilibrium in the labour market and product market is established where the output and labour employment are restored to their original levels, namely.* N_0 *and* Y_0 *respectively*. Wage rate rises to the same extent as the rise in price level. Thus, in rational expectations model it is only price level and money wage rate rise permanently while output and employment remain the same. It is important to note that with rational expectations the original levels of output and employment are restored in the short run itself and there is no time lag in the adjustment process because workers correctly perceive the change in price level as the money supply is increased by the policy maker.

Policy Implications of New Classical Approach : Ineffectiveness of Economic Policies

Since despite the adoption of expansionary monetary policy, in rational expectational model the real variables output and employment remain unaffected, this model leads to the conclusion of *ineffectiveness (or irrelevance) of economic policy*. Emphasising this conclusion of the new classical theory of rational expectations Richard Froyen write. "*If expectations are formed rationally, anticipated aggregate demand policy actions will not affect real output or employment, even in the shrot run. Notice that, because the public will learn any systematic "rules" of policy action such as hypothetical response of the money stock to unemployment .... any such set of systamatic policy actions will come to be anticipated and will not affect the behaviour of output or employment. The values of real variables such as output and employment will be unsensitive to systematic changes in aggregate demand management policeis*"[6]. The new classical economists regard the discretionary demand management policies, both monetary and fiscal, to achieve economic stability as ineffective or irrelevant in view of rational expectations by labour-suppliers and other economic agents. This is because the new classical economists believe that with rational expectations workers do not make *systematic mistakes* in their price predictions. In the rational expectations not only policy action by the Government (or the Central Bank in case of monetary policy) but also the price effects of that policy are correctly predicted. As a result, they immediately respond to their anticipated or expected price and this renders the economic policy ineffective in having any influence on the levels of output and employment.

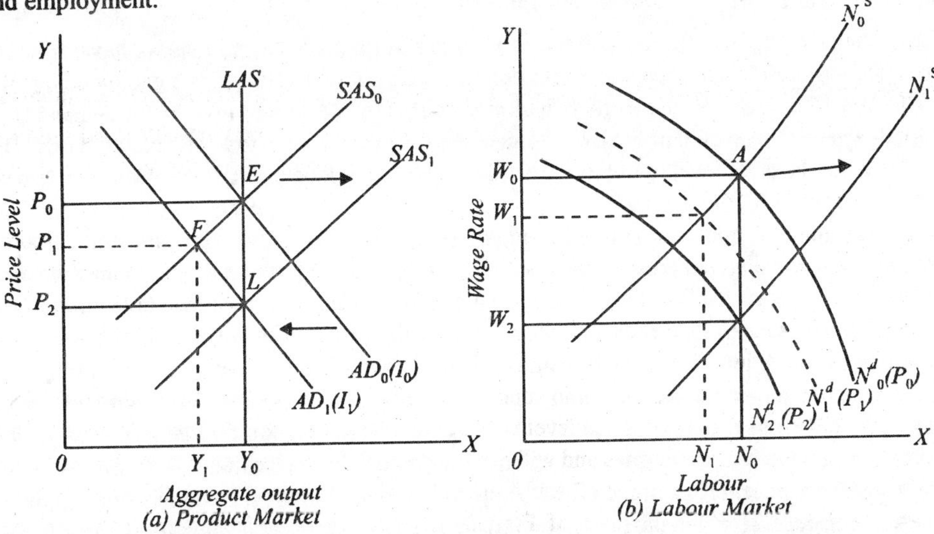

Fig. 15.3. *Rational Expectations Model: Irrelvance of Expansionary Fiscal Policy to Offset Decline in Private Investment Demand*

6. Richard, T. Froyen, *Macroeconomics, Theories and Policies*, (Singapore : Addison Wisley Longman), 6th edition, 1999, p. 237.

To show further the ineffectiveness of policy aimed at stabilising output and employment we consider Keynesian policy prescription of adopting expansionary fiscal or monetary policy to offset the decline in private autonomous investment demand so as to stabilise output and employment.

The new classical view of the effects of decline in private investment demand is illustrated in Figure 15.3. To start with, in the panel (*a*) of Fig. 15.3 showing the product market the aggregate demand curve with private investment demand equal to I_0 is AD_0. and aggregate supply curve is SAS_0. The intersection of aggregate demand curve AD_0 and the short-run aggregate supply curve SAS_0 determine equilibrium price level P_0 and output Y_0. Corresponding to this situation in the product market the demand curve of labour is N_0^d, given the price level P_0 determined in the product market, In panel (*b*) representing the labour market, N_0^s is the supply curve of labour. The supply curve of labour N_0^s and demand curve of labour N_0^d determine wage rate equal to W_0.

Now suppose the private autonomous investment declines, say from I_0 to I_1 and causes leftward shift in the aggregate demand curve from AD_0 to AD_1 (In the brackets I_0 and I_1, are given to show the aggregate demand curves corresponding to them). With the new aggregate demand curve AD_1 and the given aggregate short run supply curve SAS_0 the price level falls to P_1 and output falls to Y_1. With this fall in price, demand *curve of labour in panel* (*b*), *shifts* downward to the new position N_1^d (Remember the labour demand curve represents the curve of value of marginal product of labour (VMP_N) where VMP_N is given by $MPP_N \times$ price of output.) Therefore, with fall in price level, labour demand curve shifts downward to N_1^d as $P_1 < P_0$. With this new labour demand curve N_1^d and the initial given supply curve of labour N_0^s, the wage rate falls to W_1 and employment falls to N_1. Thus, in the short run equilibrium with the fall in money wage rate and price level of output, employment and output have declined to N_1 and Y_1 respectively. *These effects in the new classical theory are the final ones if the decline in private investment was unanticipated by the economic agents including the suppliers of labour*. These short run effects of unanticipated decline in private autonomous investment demand in the new classical theory are the same as we obtain from the Keynesian and monetarist models. However it is important to note that the new classical model assumes that economic agents have rational expectations but they do not have perfect information. There may be some unanticipated or surprise changes that may bring about changes in aggregate demand. The unanticipated changes in aggregate demand which may be the result of changeş in fiscal and monetary policies or changes in some other factors[7].

But, in the new classical theory with the assumption of rational assumptions we have different shrot-run effects if these changes in economic policies are *anticipated* by private economic agents. Consider Figure 15.3 again. If the workers had *anticipated* the decline in investment demand they with rational expectations would have also predicted the fall in price level to P_1 as a result of this. The workers expecting the price level to fall to P_1, would supply more labour as their real wages rise with the fall in price level to P_1, money wages remaining at W_0, As a result, supply curve of labour in panel (*b*) shifts to the right to N_1^s indicating more labour will be supplied. With this rightward shift in labour supply curve, short-run aggregated supply curve of output will also shift to the right to new position SAS_1 in panel (*a*) of Figure 15.3. This new aggregated supply curve SAS_1 together with the new aggregate demand curve AD_1 determine price level P_2 and the original output Y_0. It will be seen from panel (b) that with price level equal to P_2 labour demand curve shifts further to the left to the new position N_2^d which together with labour supply curve N_1^S determine wage rate W_2 and employment N_0 which represent full employment of labour. Thus, in the new short-run equilibrium in case of anticipated change and with the assumption of rational assumptions, prices and wages have fallen sufficiently to restore equilibrium at the initial levels of potential output and employment, Y_0 and N_0 respectively. Therefore, like the classical economists, *the new classical economists conclude that there is no need for adopting expansionary fiscal or monetary policy to offset the decline in private*

7. Though we are hare considering unanticipated changes in aggregate demand, changes or shocks may be on the supply side also.

investment demand for stabilisation of output and employment. According to the new classical economists with their assumption of rational expectations, the economy is *self-stabilising* with respect to changes in demand shocks such as decline in private investment. This shows irrelevance of activist economic polices to stabilise the economy.

Unanticipated Change

It is worth noting that in the view of new classical economists, even in case of unanticipated changes, say a demand shock in the form of decline in private autonomous investment, the adoption of economic policy to stabilise the economy, even though desireable, is not feasible. If the decline in private autonomous investment is unanticipated, this could not be predicted by economic agents such as suppliers of labour services on the basis of any available information. The new classical economists argue that like other economic agents, the government or the Central Bank of the country too would have been unable to anticpate the decline in private autonomous investment. Being unable to forecast the policy makers, that is, the Government or Central Bank could not adopt the policy to offset it and stabilise the economy. Once the decline in private investment has occurred it will lower output and employment, the policy makers could take fiscal and monetary measures to raise aggregate demand if the low private investment *was expected to continue in future periods. But if low investment was expected to continue in future*, there is no need for intervention by Government and the Central Bank to adopt corrective measures because even private economic agents such as workers and employers could also anticipate this and, as shown above, suitable adjustments would be made in wage and prices to restore the equilibrium at the initial level of output and employment. Thus, according to Richard Froyen, "*as long as the shock is unanticipated, policy makers lack the knowledge needed to act to offset the shock. Once the shock is anticipated by other economic agents including labour supplies there is no need to offset the shock*".[8]

Summing up. From the foregoing analysis we reach the conclusion that according to the new classical economists there is no need for the Government and Central Bank of the country to adopt fiscal and monetary policies for management of aggregate demand to stabilise aggregate output and employment. This is known as *ineffectiveness or irrelevance* of policies aimed at stabilising output and employment. Thus, like the classical economics, the new classical economists, believe in *non-intervention by the Government or Central Bank.* Besides, like the classical economists, with the assumption of rational expectations by economic agents, they believe that in case of anticipated changes in aggregate demand or supply, wages of labour and price level of output change in a way that restore equilibrium at full-employment level of output. Because of these two similarities, the rational expectations model is generally referred to as new classical economics and their advocates as new classical economists.

Rational Expectations, Monetary and Fiscal Policies

New Classical belief in non-interventionist policy is the same as of monetarists led by Friedman, though for different reasons. Like monetarists, new classical economists favour a monetary policy of having a '*money growth rule*' rather than adopting a discretionary monetary policy. Such a policy rule will ensure that there will be no uncertainty due to unanticipated changes in money supply which is likely to drive the economy away from full-employment level of output by causing economic agents to make errors in anticipating future prices. Besides, a stable rate of money growth rate would ensure stability in inflation rate and if money growth is fixed at a low level, it will cause low rate of inflation.

In the case of fiscal policy too, the new classical economists favour stability in it and the avoidance of large budget deficits which are financed by creation of new money and lead to inflation. Commenting on rational expectations view about the activist and discretionary fiscal policy, Froyen writes, "Instability in fiscal policy causes uncertainty making it difficult for agents forming rational

8. Richard T. Froyen, op. cit. p. 240
9. Richard, T. Froyen, op. cit. p. 241

expectations to correctly anticipate the course of the economy. Moreover ... a credible non-inflationary monetary policy cannot coexist with a fiscal policy that generates large deficits. Huge deficits put great pressure on the monetary authority to increase money growth in order to help finance the deficit."[9] Sargent, a strong advocate of rational expectations theory, writes, "rational expectations view denies that there is any inherent momentum to the present process of inflation. This view maintains that the firms and workers have come to expect high rates of inflation in the future and that they strike inflationary bargains in light of these expectations. However, it is held that people expect high rates of inflation in the future precisely because the government's current and prospective monetary and fiscal policies warrant those expectations..... Thus, inflation only seems to have a momentum of its own; it is actually the long-term government's policy of persistently running large deficits and creating money at high rates which imparts momentum to the inflation rate.[10]

An important policy implications of Lucas' rational expectations is that the short-run Phillips curve showing trade-off between inflation and unemployment does not present a true picture of the options available to the policy makers. Lucas and other advocates of rational expectations think that if Government and monetary authorities have a credible commitment to reduce inflation, with rational expectations the private economic agents will understand the commitment and as a result immediately lower their expectations of inflation. Thus, according to rational expectations approach, reduction in inflation can be achieved merely by reducing inflationary expectations of the people without suffering from the reduction in output and a rise in unemployment. That is, according to rational expectations, the estimates of *sacrifice ratio* based on downward sloping short-run Phillips curve are not useful as a guide for evaluating the impact of alternative economic policies. Under a credible policy, the cost of reducing inflation is much less than that found by an estimate of sacrifice ratio.

Rational Expectations and Business Cycles

According to the new classical theory with its assumption of rational expectations, the economy experiences business cycles or economic fluctuations due to *unanticipated changes in aggregate demand.* We have seen above, that with rational expectations private economic agents such as firms and workers are *able to anticipate the changes in aggregate demand and its effect on prices and wages and therefore immediately adjust* so that only price level and money wages change, level of output remaining at full-employment level. In the new classical theroy, as seen above, if there is *unanticipated increase* in aggregate demand, price level will rise in the short run resulting in increase aggregate output and employment.

On the other hand, if *decrease* in aggregate demand occurs and it *is not anticipated* by the firms and workers, the price level will fall causing increase in *real wages*. As a result, labour employment and aggregate output will fall. Thus, in the new classical theory it is only *unanticipated fluctuations in aggregate demand* that are not taken into account in wage agrements

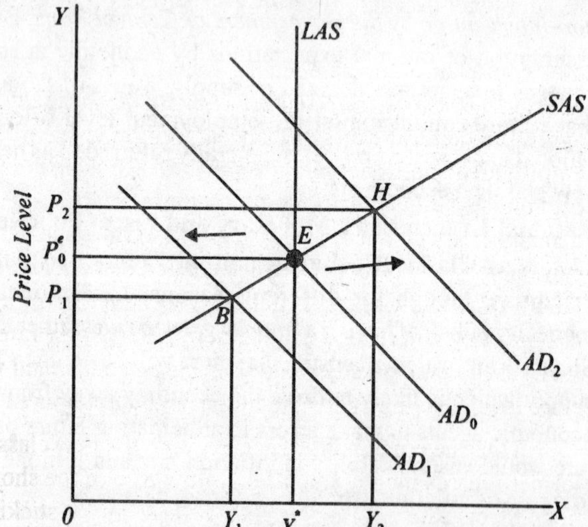

Fig.15.4. *In New Classical Theory, Unanticipated Changes in Aggregate Demand are the Cause of Fluctuations in Output and Employment.*

10.Thomas J. Sargent "The Ends of Four Big Inflations", in Robert E. Hall, ed. *Inflation, Causes and Effects* (Chicago : University of Chicago Press, 1982).

cause changes in aggregate output and employment in the economy. The new classical view of business cycles is illustrated in Figure 15.4 where *LAS* is the long run aggregate supply curve at the potential GDP level of Y^* which corresponds to the level of natural unemployment. To begin with, aggregate demand curve is AD_0 and with expected price level is P_0^e, *SAS* is the shrot-run aggregate supply curve. Point *E* represents long-run equilibrium. Suppose there is *unanticipated decrease* in aggregate demand which causes a shift in aggregate demand curve to the left to AD_1. As a result, price level falls to P_1 and output declines to Y_1. This unanticipated fall in price level, money wage rate remaining constant, will cause real wage rate to rise and as a result employment will fall and unemployment will rise above the natural level, that is, cyclical unemployment will emerge.

Now suppose that there is increase in unanticipated aggregate demand so that aggregate demand curve shifts from AD_0 to AD_2. As a result, price level rises to P_2 and aggregate output increases to Y_2. With this unanticipated or *unexpected rise in price level*, money wage remaining unchanged, *real wage will fall* inducing the firms to employ more labour. This increase in employment will lead to fall in unemployment below the natural level.

It therefore follows from above that *only changes in aggregate demand that are unanticipated and* are therefore not taken into account in money wage contracts cause fluctuations in output and employment. On the contrary, anctipated changes in aggregate demand bring about appropriate changes in price level and money wages, leaving aggregate output and employment unchanged and therefore do not cause business cycles.

Comparison with the New Keynesian Economics

It will be interesting to compare the new classical approach to business cycles outlined above with the *New Keynesian theory*. New Keynesian economists, like the new classical economists, believe that money wages are influenced by rational expectations of the price level. But New Keynesians lay stress on the long-term nature of wage contracts. According to them, the money wages in the present period are influenced by rational expectations of the recent past which were based on the then available information which might now be incorrect. After having made a long-term wage contracts on the old information, the private economic agents (i.e. firms and workers) might anticipate a change in aggregate demand according to which the new price level will be anticipated necessaitating fixation of a new money wage. But since the firms and workers are locked in their long-term contract, they could not change the money wages. *Thus, according to the new Keynesians, money wages are sticky*. In view of this stickiness of money wages, even anticipated (i.e. expected) changes in aggregate demand causing changes in price level will bring about changes in aggregate output and employment and become a source of a business cycle. On the other hand, the new classical economists believe that long-term contracts are re-negotiated when there are changes in aggregate demand. They do not consider that long-term wage agreements hinder change in money wages if the contracting parties recognise the changed demand conditions. Thus, according to the new classicals, if both firms and workers anticipate the change in the aggregate demand and expect the price level to change, they will renegotiate the new money wage rate that reflects the changed demand conditions. As a result, anticipated changes in aggregate demand will bring about changes in money wages and price level, leaving aggregate output and employment level unchanged.

Thus the crucial difference between the new classicals and the new Keynesians is that while the former regards money wage-flexibility even in the short run due to their version of rational expectations theory, the new Keynesians believe in the stickiness of money wages in the short run due to long-term nature of wage contracts, they also believe that people make rational expectations.

---

11. Robert Barro, "Unanticipated Money, Output and the Price Level in the United States", *Journal of Political Economy*, August 1978.

A Critical Evaluation of Rational Expectations Theory

An important prediction of rational expectations model is that anticipated changes in monetary policy will have no effect on output and employment. Earlier studies by one of its advocate Robert Barro[11] found evidence consistent with the rational expectations hypothesis that only unanticipated changes is money supply affect output. However, further empirical studies found no such evidence in its favour. Thus, Dornbush, Fisher and Startz using the US data of quarterly M_2 growth from 1960 to 1996 and its effect on output growth have found that "*there is a strong positive relation between anticipated money growth and output growth*"[12] which contradicts rational expectations model that anticipated changes in money stock are neutral. Likewise, Christina Romer and David Romer[13] in their research in case of the USA's six episodes of changes in monetary policy adopted to lower inflation found in each such case that contractionary monetary policy had a recessionary effect which is inconsistent with rational espectations hypothesis of neutrality of monetary policy. Thus whatever intellectual appeal rational expectations model may have, there is not much empirical support for it.

The other criticism of this model is that its assumption of rational expectations is quite unrealistic. The argument against this assumption is that it requires firms and workers to know too much. It is unrealistic to believe that decision makers such as firms and workers know as much they are required to know to form rational expectations. In our view even econometricians and economists are often unable to make correct forcasts of the consequences of changes in monetary and fiscal policies.[14] To expect that ordinary managers and workers of firms would correctly anticipate the effects of economic policies in their decision making on prices and inflation is to demand too much from them. Further, making comments on rational expectations model Case and Fair write, "People must know the true model (or at least approximation of true model) to form rational expectations, and this is a lot to expect. Even if firms and households are capable of learning the true model (or good approximation of it) may not be worth the cost"[15].

Although the assumption of rational expectations is quite consistent with satisfaction–maximising and profit-maximising principles of microeconomic theory, it is quite extreme and more demanding because to make rational expectations it requires a lot of information on the part of firms and workers. This model requires that these private economic agents to know much more about the working of overall economy in response to changes in monetary and fiscal policies than they are likely to know about it.

Thus Roger Farmer writes, "Rational expectations ascribe a degree of knowledge to households and firms that many economists find *implausible*. In order to form a rational expectation of the future inflation rate, households and firms must be able to predict the future rate of money growth. Predicting future money growth is difficult because the policies of the Federal Reserve Board are constantly changing as policy makers respond to changing circumstances".[16]

Further, the critics point out that contrary to the new classical view about the ineffectiveness monetary and other policies, economic policies do matter and influence the working of the market economy and help in stabilising it. According to the new classical theory, only unanticipated policy changes lead to changes in national output and further that systematic policy change will be

---

12. Dornbusch, Fischer and Startz, *Macroeconomics*, Tata McGraw Hill, 8th edition, 2001, p 507.
13. Christina D. Romer and David H. Romer, "Does Monetary Policy Matter ? A New Test in the Spirit of Friedman" *NBER Macroeconomic Annual*, 1989.
14. In various budgets of the Central Government in India containing large fiscal deficites during NDA Government from 1998 to 2004 even as able an economist as Dr. Manmohan Singh described them highly inflationary but actually inflation rate turned out to be quite low despite large fiscal deficits and higher growth of money supply.
15. Karl E. Case and Ray C. Fair, *Principles of Economics*, Pearson Education, 2002, p. 660.
16. Roger E. A. Farmer, *Macroeconomics,* South-Western, 2nd edition, 2002, p. 420.

predictable and will have no real effect. This view is not acceptable to most economists. This is for two reasons. First, it is thought that there is so much inertia in price and wage setting behaviour that it is not easy to re-negotiate contracts when a policy change is announced. Besides, "policy makers have some leverage over real economic activity, even when making policy changes that are predictable."[17]

The second reason for the lack of quick adjustment to changes in economic policies is that "the massive complexity of the economy makes it impossible for individuals agents to know how shock will affect all the relevant prices and quantities that matter to them over any specified period of time. The idea of everyone knowing the exact nature of some policy disturbance and solving the equations of the economy to determine the outcome and of their acting to anticipate these outcomes is far-fetched"[18].

QUESTIONS FOR REVIEW

1. Explain the main features of the New Classical Economics. How does the New Classical Model differ from the Classical Model ?
2. What are rational expectations ? How is monetary policy neutral in the rational expectations hypothesis ?
3. Compare the New Classical Economics based on rational expectations with the (*a*) traditional Keynesian Model and (*b*) the New Keynesian Model.
4. The rational expectations approach suggests that anticipatory monetary policy is neutral even in the short run. Explain.
5. Show how rational expectations model of the New Classical Economists proves the ineffectiveness of economic policy to ensure economic stability.
6. Explain the concept of rational expectations. How does it differ from the *adaptive expectations* ?
7. Explain how the New Classical view differs from the Keynesian view of the way in which labour markets functions.
8. Compare the New Classical and Monetarist views concerning the usefulness and effectiveness of demand management policies to stabilise output.

---

17. Richard G Lipsey and K. Alex Chrystal, *Economics* Oxford University Press, 10th edition, 2004, p. 586.
18. Lipsey and Chrystal, op. cit. p.586

CHAPTER 16

The New Keynesian Economics

Introduction

It has been observed that short-run fluctuations in aggregate demand cause deviations of output and employment from the potential GDP. The classical and new classical economists maintain that due to wage-price flexibility changes in aggregate demand produce appropriate changes in wages and prices, so that aggregate output and employment remain unaffected. On the other hand, Keynes and his earlier followers assumed that wages and prices are rigid or sticky, therefore fluctuations in aggregate demand do not affect wages and prices in the short run and instead cause change in levels of output and employment. According to Keynes and earlier Keynesians, due to stickiness of price level, short-run aggregate supply curve is a horizontal straight line as shown by the curve *SRAS* in Fig. 16.1.

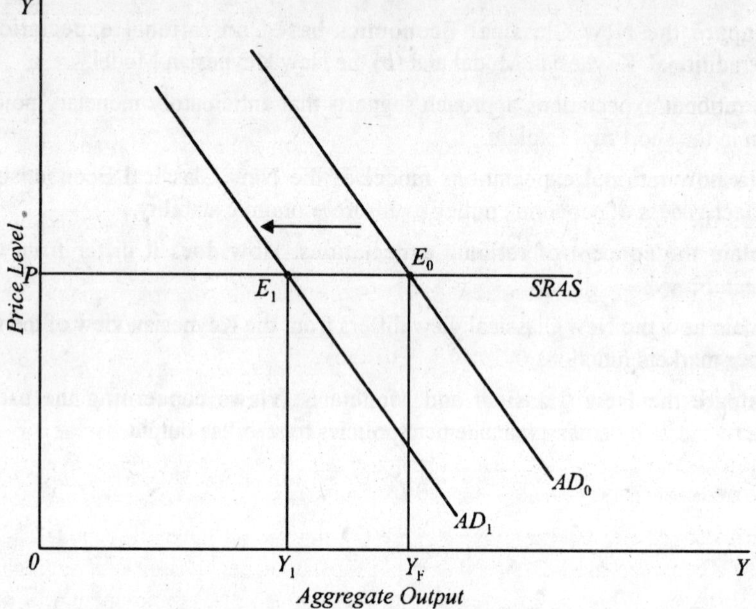

Fig. 16.1. *With price stickiness a fall in aggregate demand causes output and therefore employment to fall.*

With aggregate demand curve AD_0 and horizontal short-run aggregate supply curve *SRAS*, full-employment level of output (i.e, potential GDP) Y_F is determined. Now, if aggregate demand decreases, say due to decline in investment demand or decrease in money supply, aggregate demand curve shifts to the left to AD_1. As a result, new equilibrium output falls and causes recession in the economy.

The New Classical Economics based on rational expectations express doubts on the validity of the assumption of price rigidity or stickiness of the traditional Keynesian model and point out that it is not based on firm **foundations of microeconomics** which was based on rational and profit-maximising principle.

As stated above, a key element in the traditional Keynesian model is that money wages and prices are sticky or slow to adjust to changes in economic conditions. But, why are prices sticky ? The New Keynesians have attempted to *explain* this short-run price stickiness with the help of microeconomic theory and has thus put it on a firmer theoretical foundations. **A number of models based on microeconomics principles to explain price stickiness and which make some improvement over the traditional Keynesian model but still remaining within the framework of the earlier Keynesian model are called New Keynesian Economics or New Keynesian Models.**

The New Keynesian economics is based on the imperfect competition unlike the traditional Keynesian model which assumed perfect competition under which a firm faces a horizontal demand curve. The horizontal demand curve facing a perfectly competitive firm shows that it can sell as much as it likes at the prevailing price as determined by demand for and supply of a commodity. On the other hand, the downward-slopping demand curve of an imperfectly competitive firm implies that cut in price by it will cause some increase in sales but rival firms are likely to cut their prices too so that it may not be profitable to change or adjust prices. Besides, the New Keynesian Models are based on optimal behavior of firms working rationally.

Some Common Elements of New Keynesian Models

Though there are more than one New Keynesian Model differing from each other in some respects, we will explain the New Keynesian Model as propounded by N. Gregory Mankiw[1]. Before explaining Mankiw model of price stickiness, it is important to note what are the common elements of all New Keynesian models. They are stated below.

1. A new Keynesian model generally assumes some form of imperfect competition. Therefore, this differs from the perfect competition assumption of the earlier Keyneisan model.
2. Whereas the focus of the old Keynesian model was on money-wage rigidity, the New Keynesian Models also focus on *price stickiness*
3. In addition to the rigidity of *money wages and prices*, the new Keynesian models assume the stickiness of real variables such as *real wages, relative price levels* in the face of changes in aggregate demand.
4. **Output is demand determined.** Like the traditional Keynesian model, in the New Keynesian economics, it is assumed that the firms set prices and produce whatever is demanded. Therefore, when demand increases, firms *produce and sell more output* even if they do not change their prices
5. Wage rigidity causes unemployment. Like the traditional Keynesian model, according to the New Keynesian models, firms' demand for labour depends on *real* aggregate demand and *real* wages. When aggregate demand for output falls, employment will decline and hence unemployment will rise. If wage rate is rigid, then unemployment will increase more.

Mankiw's New Keynesian Model

In the traditional Keynesian model it was assumed that perfect competition prevailed in the product market. In Mankiw's Model, as in other New Keynesian models, it is maintained that a firm *must not* be working under perfect competition. This is because under perfect competition in the product market, prices are determined by demand for and supply of a product, an individual firm has no control over the price of the product. A perfectly competitive firm can sell all it can produce at the prevailing price. Now, suppose price as determined by demand for and supply of the product under perfect competition falls from ₹ 100 to ₹ 80 per unit. Now, if the firm dos not reduce its price and goes on charging price of ₹100, its sales would fall to zero. Therefore, a perfectly competitive firm will

---

1. See N. Gregory Mankiw, "Small Menu Costs and Large Business Cycles" A Macroeconomic Model of Monopoly, *uarterly Journal of Economics*, May, 1985.

lower the price if it has to produce the product. Thus under perfect competition there is no scope for stickiness of prices.

On the other hand, Mankiw and other New Keynesian economists explain that under imperfect competition (monopolistic competition or oligopoly) in the product market, the firms are *likely to keep their prices constant* (*i.e. sticky*) when there is decrease in aggregate demand. Under imperfect competition demand curve for a firm's product is downward-sloping. If in the face of a fall in aggregate demand, say due to the contraction of money supply in the economy, an imperfectly competitive firm *does not adjust or lower its price, it will lose some consumers but not all of them*. For example, when aggregate demand decreases and as a result demand for Maruti Cars decreases. The Maruti car company can continue to sell cars at the previous high prices and may not lower its prices, that is, price may remain sticky in the face of decrease in demand. Elaborating on this point Richard Froyen writes "Monopolistic competitors and oligopolies have some control over the price of their products. In fact, the incentive to lower prices may be fairly weak for those types of firms. If they hold to their initial price when demand falls, they will lose sales, but the sales they retain will still be at the relatively high initial price. Also, if all firms hold to the initial price, no individual firm will lose sales".[2]

However, it may be noted that when the demand for a product decreases, a firm gains or benefits from lowering price even under conditions of imperfect competition. Due to downward-sloping demand curve facing an imperfectly competitive firm the reduction of price by it will cause the quantity demanded of its product will increase and as a result, there may be some gain in profits. So the question arises why then the firm does not lower price when there is decline in aggregate demand?

Menu Costs. According to Mankiw and other new Keynesian economists, one reason why the firms do not change or adjust prices when demand for their products changes is that they have to incur costs for making adjustment in prices. To change prices, a firm has to print a new catalogue and send it to its customers, distribute new price list among its sales staff. Such costs of making price adjustments are called *Menu Costs*. This term originates from the practice of restaurants. When restaurants change prices, they print new menus and incur cost on it.

Mankiw and other new Keynesian economists argue that the firm will change prices only when gains or benefits of changing price *outweights costs*. However, some economists are sceptical of this new Keynesian viewpoint. They have pointed out that menu costs are quite small and therefore they cannot explain stickiness of price in the face of decrease in aggregate demand. They question as to how small menu costs explain recession which result from price-stickiness and prove very costly for the society. But Mankiw has argued that "small does not mean inconsequential; even though menu costs are small, they can have a large effects on the economy as a whole".[3]

In defence of his viewpoint Mankiw points to the *aggregate demand externality*. He emphasises that there are beneficial externalities to price adjustment by one firm that must be recognised. According to this beneficial externality effect, a price reduction by a firm will benefit other firms. If a firm which is initially charging a high price, reduces its price it will result in slightly lower average price level that will lead to the expansion in aggregate income by causing a rightward shift in LM curve. This expansion in aggregate income will benefit other firms through its effect on the demands for their products. Therefore, this has been called *aggregate demand externality*. But, according to Mankiw, since this beneficial effect is *external* to the firms, they ignore it in their decision making about charging of price for their products. To quote Mankiw, "The firm makes decision by comparing the benefit of a price cut – higher sales and profits – to the cost of price adjustment. Yet because of the aggregate demand externality, the benefits to society of the price cut would exceed the benefits to the

---

2. Richard T. Froyen, *Macroeconomics,* Pearson Education, 6th Edition 1999, p.262.
3. N. Gregory Mankiw, *Macroeconomics*, Worth Publishers 6th Edition, 2003, p.510.

firm. *The firm ignores this externality* when making its decision, so it may decide not to pay the menu cost and cut its price even though the price cut is socially desirable. Hence sticky prices may be optimal for those setting prices, even though they are undesirable for the economy as a whole"[4]

Other Reasons for Sticky Prices

Two other important reasons have been given for sticky prices by the new Keynesian economists. They are :

An important costs of not adjusting prices is the *potential loss of consumer goodwill.* Though the consumer goodwill is lost when a firm raises its prices, but the cut in prices by a firm at times of recession implies that it will raise them when the economy recovers from recession. This change in relative price quite often harms the goodwill of a firm among its customers. The consumers understand the firm raising its prices when they know the costs of the firm have risen. But changing prices in response to changes in demand of the consumers is not well received by the consumers. Therefore, firms prefer to keep prices sticky.

A second possible perceived cost of cutting price at times of recession is that *it may lead to higher price cuts by the rival firms or it may even lead to price war* which harms every firm. This response is more relevant in case of oligopolistic markets where rival firms keep their eyes on the pricing decisions of their rival firms.

If the above costs of price adjustments are high enough, there will be price stickiness. If prices do not adjust in response to changes in aggregate demand, the fluctuations in demand cause business cycles, that is, recessions and booms in the economy.

Mankiw's New Keynesian Model in Mathematical Form

Let us present the New Keynesian Model in mathematical form. We assume that an economy consists of many firms, each having some monopoly power (Note that firms working under monopolistic competition and oligopoly enjoy some monopoly power over its product). Let Y_i represents demand facing each firm, P_i is the *relative* price of the product of a firm to the overall price level (P) and Y is the aggregate demand for the product. The demand function for each firm's product can be written as

$$Y_i = \left(\frac{P_i}{P}\right)^{-e} Y \quad e>1 \qquad \ldots (1)$$

The above equation (1) shows that demand for a firm's product depends on its relative prices $\left(\frac{P_i}{P}\right)$, price elasticity of demand (e) and aggregate demand (Y).

To simplify the model Mankiw assumes that real aggregate demand (Y) is determined by the real money supply, that is, $Y = \frac{M}{P}$. Substituting $\frac{M}{P}$ for Y in equation (1) we have

$$Y_1 = \left(\frac{P_i}{P}\right)^{-e} \cdot \frac{M}{P} \qquad \ldots (2)$$

The equation (2) tells us that demand facing a firm depends on its relative price to the overall price $\left(\frac{P_1}{P}\right)$ and real money supply $\left(\frac{M}{P}\right)$ which determines aggregate demand. Besides, the relative

4. Mankiw op. cit. p. 510. See also N. Gregory, Mankiw, "Small Costs and Large Business Cycles : A Macroeconomic Model fo Mnopoly" *Quarterly Journal of Economics*, May 1985.

price of a firm determines its relative position in the given aggregate demand for the product.

An imperfectly competitive firm will set its price by adding a mark-up over marginal cost. Thus

$$P_i = \frac{e}{e-1} \frac{W}{MP_L} \qquad \ldots (3)$$

Where $\frac{e}{e-1}$ is mark-up and $\frac{W}{MP_L}$ is marginal cost. A firm's profits which we denote by π can be obtained by multiplying the difference between price and marginal cost multiplied by the amount of output demanded and sold. Thus

$$\text{Profit } (\pi) = \left(P_i - \frac{W}{MP_L} \right) Y_i \qquad \ldots (4)$$

Now suppose the nominal money supply decreases which results in decrease in aggregate demand, with price P_i remaining unchanged. In terms of equation (2) with the fall in M, demand for output of each firm, Y_1 will decline whcih will result in recession, price of each firm remaining unchanged.

To maintain output in the face of a fall in demand requires reduction in prices by the firms. Reduction in price by a firm facing downward-sloping demand curve will lead to more sales and profits. However, according Mankiw, *price adjustment by a firm would yield only second order gain and even small menu costs exceed it.* Therefore, firms will not adjust (i.e. cut) prices. As a result, average price level will not get adjusted to the new reduced demand conditions for output, the recession will occur in the economy. With reduced output (Y_i) of the firm, the profits as measured by equation (4) will fall.

It may be noted that Mankiw explains that as compared to menu costs of price adjustment, potential gain from price cutting will be very small, that is, of second order under the following two conditions.

1. If the difference between the existing price and profit-maximising (i.e. optimal) price is small, the potential gain of making price adjustment is very small.

2. If price elasticity of demand for firm's product is low, the increase in profit is less sensitive to adjusting price to the exactly new profit-maximising level.

It may be stressed again that firms do not adjust prices in the face of changes in demand because in their price-making decisions they do not take into account the external demand benefits of adjusting their prices. As a result, overall price level (P) and the relative prices of the firms remain unchanged. The fall in aggregate demand therefore results in reduction in output i.e. recession.

Price Adjustment and Coordination Failures

Some New Keynesian economists including Gregory Mankiw think that not adjusting prices in the face of a fall in aggregate demand results in recession. In recession, levels of output and employment are low, a number of factories do not work or work below their capacity. This is a socially undesirable happening. If a society fails to attain its potential GDP and full employment that is socially desirable, then it follows that the members of a society have failed to coordinate among them in some way. The coordination problem is relevant to the explanation of stickiness of prices of the firms which set them by anticipating the actions of the others. While setting their prices firms anticipate what prices other firms will be setting. But they take these decisions under uncertainty about what prices the other firms will charge.

To see how price stickiness and therefore recession occurs due to failures of coordination when aggregate demand decreases we consider that the economy consists of two firms A and B and therefore we have a market situation of oligopoly. With the decrease in aggregate demand (say as a result of fall in money supply) each firm has to decide whether it should cut its price to achieve profit - maximising state or keep its price at the existing high level. It is important to note that each firm's profits depends on not only its own price decision but also the pricing decision of the other. In the following table we give payoff matrix of the two firms of various possible combinations of pricing decisions of the two firms.

Pay off Matrix

Firm B (*in crores*)

		Cut price	**Keeping price high**
Firm A	**Cut Price**	Firm A'S Profits : 50 Firm B'S Profits : 50	Firm A'S profits : 10 Firm B'S profits : 25
	Keeping price high	Firm A'S Profits : 25 Firm B'S profits : 10	Firm A'S Profits : 20 Firm B'S Profits : 20

It will be seen from the table that if both firms decide not to cut price and accordingly keep their prices at the existing high level each of them will make profits of ₹ 20 crores (see right-hand side bottom box). In this case of price stickiness the result is fall in output and employment and hence recession. On the other hand, if both of them cut their prices, each of them will get profits of ₹ 50 crores. This is not only most profitable for the two firms individually but also represents a social optimum. This is because lowering of prices by both of them will result in reduction in overall price level and this will stimulate aggregate demand. The recession would therefore not occur in this case.

Further, if firm A cuts its price, while the firm B keeps its price at the existing high level, firm A's profits are ₹ 10 crores while firm B's profits are 25 crores. (See right-hand side upper box of the table). This is because not cutting price by firm B results in recession and as a result firm A's profits are smaller due to both lower output and lower price. Similarly, if firm B cuts its price but firm A keeps its price at the existing high level, firm A's profits are 25 cores and firm B's profits are ₹ 10 crores (see bottom box of left-side of payoff matrix of the above Table). Although both firms would like to avoid recession, neither can achieve this by its action alone. Each firm's decision affects the profit opportunities available to the other firm. When a firm cuts its price, it benefits other due to beneficial aggregate demand externality (in the terms of improved profits) created by it. But since each firm ignores this beneficial externality and are therefore likely to land themselves in recession due to the absence of coordination between them.

Of course, if each firm expects that the other will cut its price, both will cuts prices and the result will be desirable outcome not only for them individually but for the society as a whole because the cut in prices by them will cause the reduction in overall price which will enable them to avoid recession in terms of loss of output and employment. On the other hand, if each firm expects that the other will keep its price at the present high level both will keep prices unchanged at the present relatively high level. Therefore, outcome in this case is recession which is not only bad for both the firms individually but also for the society as a whole. Though both outcomes are possible but the new keynesian economists generally believe the later inferior outcome, that is, not cutting or adjusting prices leading to recession is more probable because of *coordination failure*. Thus, Gregory writes, "If the two firms could coordinate, they would both cut their price and reach the preferred outcome. In the real world........ coordination is often difficult because the number of firms setting prices is large. *The moral of the story is that prices can be sticky simply because people expect them to be sticky, even though stickiness is in no one's interest*'.[5]

QUESTION FOR REVIEW

1. What is New Keynesian Economics ? How does it differ from the New Classical Economics.
2. Explain the four important features of the New Keynesian Models. Why do most New Keynesian Model rely on imperfect competition.
3. Prices can be sticky even though the menu costs of adjusting price are quite small. Explain.
4. New Keynesian models attempt to reintegrate aggregate demand, especially sticky prices with solid microeconomic foundation.
5. What are the key features of Mankiw's menu-cost model ? How does it explain recession?
6. Compare the Lucas model of aggregate supply with Mankiw's menue cost model of aggregate supply.
7. Explain how the new keynesian economics explains business cycles.

5. Gregory Mankiw, *Macroeconomics*, 6th edition, p.512.

PART III
MONETARY DEMAND AND SUPPLY

- Money : Nature, Functions and Role
- Credit and Commercial Banking
- Role of Central Banking
- Monetary Policy in a Developing Economy
- Supply of Money and Its Determinants
- The Demand for Money and Keynes's Liquidity Preference Theory of Interest
- Post Keynesian Theories of Demand for Money :

  Tobin's Porfolio Approach, Baumol's Inventory and Friedman's Theories

CHAPTER 17

Money : Nature, Functions and Role

Difficulties of Barter System and Invention of Money

Money was not used in the early history of man. Exchanges were few since each family was self-sufficient. Whatever exchanges there were, they took the form of barter, that is, exchange of goods for the other goods. Various difficulties were faced by the people in the barter economy. There was no acceptable means of payment for the direct purchase of goods and services in the barter economy. In other words, in a purely barter system, there was no generally acceptable medium of exchange in the form of a particular good or asset which could be used to buy goods and services and do other types of transactions. The following are the main difficulties which were found in the barter system.

1. **Double Coincidence of Wants.** Owning to lack of generally acceptable medium of exchange, a difficult problem of double coincidence of wants was faced by the persons who wanted to sell and buy goods. For exchange of goods persons desiring to exchange goods must specifically want those goods what others offers in exchange. Thus, an individual who wants to have a good he must locate another person who offers to give up the good wanted by him and who is willing to accept in exchange the good offered by him. Thus, under barter system only when wants for buying and selling goods of different persons coincided the exchange of goods was possible. A good deal of time was spent by a person in searching for a man with whom wants coincided. Halm rightly says, "It is next to impossible that all wishes of bartering individuals should coincide as to the kind, quality and quantity and value of things which are mutually desired, especially in a modern economy in which on a single day millions of persons may exchange millions of goods and services."[1]

2. **Lack of a Standard Unit of Account.** A barter economy lacked not only a common medium of exchange but also a standard unit of account in which prices could be measured and quoted. In the absence of a common unit of account, the number of exchange ratios (that is, prices of goods expressed in terms of each other) between goods would be very large. For example, two cows for one horse, one cow for two quintals of wheat, one pen for three pencils and so on. Thus, lack of a standard unit of account with which to measure values of different goods and services made exchange or trade difficult.

3. **Impossibility of Subdivision of Goods.** Another problem faced under the barter system for exchange of goods was impossibility of subdivision of goods without loss of their value. For instance, if a person has a cow and wants to have 5 kg of wheat, obviously, it is too costly to give one cow for 5 kg of wheat he requires. Then, to do this transaction cow has to be divided. But cow cannot be divided or cut into pieces because cow will lose much of its value if it is divided. Thus, impossibility of division of goods for the purpose of exchange posed a great difficulty and obstructed the growth of trade.

4. **Lack of Information.** Another problem found in the barter system was that in it traders required a good deal of information for exchange of goods. For example, if Amit wants to have a saw in exchange of a wooden table which he has made. Not only should Amit be able to assess the value of saw but the maker of a saw should also be able to determine the value of the wooden table which Amit wishes to exchange. All this required a lot of information about goods for which people must spend a

1. G.N. Halm, *Monetary Theory*, 1946, p. 1.

good deal of time and resources to obtain such information. If there exists a medium of exchange, it will solve half the problem. However, Amit will still have to determine the value of the table in terms of the medium of exchange. Thus, if there exists a medium of exchange, with well-known characteristics, it will reduce the information costs of trading. Without the medium of exchange information cost will indeed be very large.

5. **Production of Large and Very Costly Goods not Feasible.** Another problem of barter economy relates to the production of large costly goods. Suppose an individual who has technical skill and equipment to manufacture a car will not have much incentive to manufacture it in the barter economy. This is because he can exchange a car with a person who has enough goods having a value equal to a car so that their exchange with a car can take place. The car maker must obtain food, clothing and several other commodities of day-to-day consumption in exchange for a car. It will be very difficult, almost impossible to find a prospective buyer who has enough of these goods and services to give in return for a car.

It is evident from above that barter system could work in a primitive economy where life was simple and man was self-sufficient. As man made some economic progress, division of labour or specialisation and large-scale production came to exist, barter system could not fulfil the increasing needs for exchange of goods. Due to the difficulties of exchange barter economy would have no large-scale production, no advantage of the use of capital-intensive specialised machinery and no easy and cheap means in which wealth could be stored. *The range of goods produced must be much smaller than those produced in the modern developed economies. To meet the needs for a common unit of account and also as a generally accepted medium of exchange and thereby to overcome the difficulties faced under the barter system, money was invented.*

Evolution of Money

Commodity Money. Today when in India we think of money, it is generally in terms of rupee notes, in the USA it is in terms of dollar notes and in Great Britain it is in terms of Pound Sterling, and all of these are mostly made of paper. However, in the beginning it was commodities which was selected as a medium of exchange and thus came to be used as money. Bows, sea shells, beads, arrows, furs and skin etc. were adopted as money at different times in the early stages of development, especially in the hunting stage of human development. With further development and in the pastoral stage, animals such as sheep and cattle (goats and cows) were started being used as money, that is, as a medium of exchange of goods. The use of cattle and other animals as money suffered from certain disadvantages. Since all cows and goats were not identical, they could not serve as a standard unit of measurement. Secondly, the supply of animals such as cows, sheep and goats were subject to large and abrupt fluctuations. Thirdly, ordinary commodities and animals cannot serve as a satisfactory store of value.

Metalic Money. In view of the above limitations of ordinary commodities and animals for being used as money and with further progress of human civilisation, ordinary commodities and animals were replaced by precious metals such as gold and silver for being used as money. Crowther thus sum up the superiority of precious metals like gold and silver for monetary use "They are easily handled and stored, they do not deteriorate, they have the just the right degree of scarcity and they can be relied upon neither to increase nor to diminish in quantity except gradually."[2] But with invention of coinage, it was coins made of gold and silver which began to be widely used as money rather than simple and plain bits of gold and silver whose value were difficult to be ascertained. It is important to note that precious metals were used as money not because they were valuable but because they were scarce. *For a thing to serve as money scarcity is more important than value.* These days, *it is the scarcity of paper money which is responsible for its efficiency as money*; its lack of value is no

2. G. Crowther, An Outline of Money.

hindrance for it to serve as money.

Paper Money. As it came to be firmly realised for a sound money, scarcity is more important than value, precious metals were replaced by *paper money*. In the beginning paper money, that is, paper notes were simple claims to and substitutes for metallic money. But in the course of time paper money came to be regarded as money itself. Paper money took the form of bank notes which were not mere substitutes but were considered as an addition to the supply of money. At first, notes could be issued by all commercial banks but with the passage of time when paper money became inconvertible into metallic money issuing of notes became the monopoly of the Central Bank of a country. Central Bank of India is named as Reserve Bank of India.

Bank Deposits as Money. Finally, there was further development in the form of money. In the developed countries the main type of money is not paper notes issued by the central bank but the *bank deposits* (especially, *demand deposits*) which people hold with the commercial banks and against which cheques can be drawn. In India too *bank money* (*i.e.* bank deposits) or which is also called credit money has become a significant part of the total money supply. It is worth mentioning that chequeable bank deposits held by the public in the banks serve as money because through drawing cheques on them we can use them for making payments for purchase of goods and services and assets.

An essential pre-requisite of money which needs to be emphasised is that it should be generally acceptable in a society as a medium of exchange. You accept paper notes in payment for goods or services you sell because you are confident that others will accept them from whom you wish to buy goods or services. If people lose confidence in any money, they will not accept it in payment for goods and services. Thus, when people lose confidence in any money as, for instance, when its value is fast depreciating, the money ceases to be generally acceptable. Indeed, in that case it ceases to be money. In the early twenties this happened to 'Mark' in Germany and it may happen to 'Rouble' of Soviet Russia at present as its value in the recent past is fast depreciating.

Definition of Money

To give a precise definition of money is a difficult task. Various authors have given different definitions of money. Professor D.H. Robertson defines money as *"any thing which is widely accepted in payment for goods or in discharge of other kinds of business obligations". According to Crowther, "Money can be defined as anything that is generally acceptable as a means of exchange and that at the same time acts as a measure and a store of value"*.

Two important things about money emerge from the above two definitions of money. First, Money has been defined in terms of the functions it performs. That is why some economists have said that money is what money does. That is, money is any thing which performs the functions of money. Secondly, *an essential requirement of any kind of money is that it must be generally acceptable to every member of the society*. Money has a value for 'A' only when he thinks that 'B' will accept it in exchange for the goods. And money is useful for 'B' only when he is confident that 'C' will accept it in settlement of debts. But the general acceptability is not the physical quality possessed by a good. General acceptability is a social phenomenon and is conferred upon a good when the society by law or convention adopts it as a medium of exchange.

Functions of Money

There are four main functions of money which are summed up in the following couplet:

"Money is a matter of functions four,
A medium, a measure, a standard, a store

We explain below these four functions of money in some detail.

1. **Medium of Exchange.** The most important function of money is that it serves as a medium of exchange. In the barter economy a great difficulty was experienced in the exchange of goods as the exchange in the barter system required double coincidence of wants. Money has removed this diffi-

culty. Now a person A can sell his goods to B for money and then he can use that money to buy the goods he wants from others who have these goods. As long as money is generally acceptable, there will be no difficulty in the process of exchange. By serving as a very convenient medium of exchange money has made possible the complex division of labour or specialisation in the modern economic organisation.

2. **Measure of Value.** Another important function of money is that it serves as a common measure of value or a unit of account. Under barter economy there was no common measure of value in which the values of different goods could be measured and compared with each other. Money has also solved this difficulty. Money serves as a yardstick for measuring the value of goods and services. As the value of all goods and services is measured in a standard unit of money, their relative values can be easily compared.

3. **Standard of Deferred Payment.** Another function of money it that it serves as a standard for deferred payments. Deferred payments mean those payments which are to be made in the future. If a loan is taken today, it would be paid back after a period of time. The amount of loan is measured in terms of money and it is paid back in money. A large number of credit transactions involving huge future payments are made daily. Money performs this function of standard for deferred payments because its value remains more or less stable.

If the prices are falling, *i.e.*, the value of money is rising, the creditors will gain in real terms and the debtors will lose. Conversely, if the prices are rising (or value of money is falling) creditors will be the losers. Thus if the money is to serve as a fair and correct standard for deferred payments, its value must remain stable. In case the value of money is changing very much, the creditors or debtors will be put to much loss and sufferings. Thus when there is severe inflation or deflation, money ceases to serve as a standard for deferred payments.

4. **Store of Value.** Lastly, money acts as store of value. Money being the most liquid of all assets is a convenient form in which to store wealth, that is, *money can be held as an asset*. Thus store of value function is also called *asset function of money*. It is, therefore, essential that the good chosen as money should be such as can be easily stored without deterioration or wastage. That is why gold was popular in the past as money material. Gold could be kept safely without deterioration. But in the modern times even paper money can be kept as deposits in banks to serve as asset. Of course, there are other assets like houses, factories, bonds, shares etc., in which wealth can be stored. But money performs the store of value function with a difference. Money being the most liquid of all assets has the advantage that an individual or a firm can buy with it anything at any time. But this is not the case with other assets. Other assets like houses and shares have to be sold first and converted into money and only then they can be used to buy other things.

Money would perform the store of value function properly if it remains stable in value. For example, if there is a high rate of inflation in the economy, real value or purchasing power of money goes on falling. This adversely affects the store of value function of money. Since a high rate of inflation erodes the real value of money, it discourages people to save. Besides, a high rate of inflation induces people to invest whatever savings they do in unproductive assets such as gold and jewellery, real estate etc. rather than storing their savings in cash money or deposits in bank with a fixed rate of interest.

From above it is clear that money has removed the difficulties of barter system. It has facilitated trade and has made possible the complex division of labour and specialisation of the modern economic system. Without the use of money, modern economy will not run smoothly and the production will get a serious setback. For these reasons, monetary economy is preferred to barter economy.

FORMS OF MONEY

Money of Account. Money of account is the monetary unit in terms of which the accounts of country are kept and transactions settled, *i.e.*, in which general purchasing power, debts and prices are expressed. The rupee is, for instance, our money of account, sterling is the money of account of Great Britain and mark that of Germany. Money of account need not however be actually circulating in the country. During 1922-24 the mark in Germany depreciated to such an extent that it ceased to be money of account. The paisa in India has not in circulation and yet it is money of account. In the circulation and yet it is money of account. In the words of Keynes, "Money of account is the description of little title money is the thing which answers to the description."

Limited and Unlimited Legal Tender : Coins may be limited legal tender or unlimited legal tender. *A legal tender currency is one in terms of which debts can be legally paid.* It is an offence to refuse to accept payment in legal tender money. *A currency is unlimited legal tender when debts upto any amount can be paid through it.* It is limited legal tender when payments only up to a given limit can be made by means of it.For instance, rupee coins and rupee notes are unlimited legal tender in India. And so is the half-rupee coin. But coins of lower denominations are only limited legal tender. They are legal tender only up to ten rupees.

When a coin is worn out and become light beyond a certain limit, then it ceases to be a legal tender. When one rupee and half-rupee coins are more than 20% below the standard weight they are not longer legal tender. A Government may take away the legal tender quality of a currency. For instance, the old rupee coins of one hundred and eighty grains 11/12 fine are no longer legal tender in India. In 1978 the Government declared currency notes of rupees one thousand denomination and above as no longer legal tender. it is usually done to bring such currency out of the hoards. However, recently notes of Rs. 1000 have again been issued by ReserveBank of India and have unlimited legal tender status.

Standard Money. Standard money is that in which the value of goods as well as all other forms of money are measured. Thus, in India all prices of goods are measured in terms of rupees. Moreover, the other forms of money such as two-rupee notes, ten rupee notes, hundred rupee notes and one half rupee coin are expressed in terms of rupees. Thus rupee is the standard money of India. Standard money is always made the unlimited legal tender money. In old days the standard money was a *full-bodied money, i.e.*, its face value was equal to the real or intrinsic worth of the metal it contained. But now-a-days in almost all countries of the world, even the standard money is only a *token money i.e.*, the material contained in it is very much less than the face value written on it. Thus, the rupee in India is available in the form of paper notes which have no intrinsic worth. Even the rupee coin has a metallic value much less than its face value. Rupee coin has been called a '*note printed on nickel*' (Rupee coin these days is made of nickel).

Token Money. As explained above, the token money is that the metallic value of which is much less than the real or intrinsic worth of the metal it contains. Rupee and all other coins in India are all token money.

Bank Money. Demand deposits of banks are usually called bank money. Bank deposits are created when somebody deposits money with them. Banks also create deposits when they advance loans to the businessmen and traders. Today these demand deposits are the important constituent of the money supply in the country.

It is important to note that bank deposits are generally divided in two categories : *demand deposits and time deposits*. Demand deposits are those deposits which are payable on demand through cheques and without any serving prior notice to the banks. On the other hand, time deposits are those deposits which have a fixed term of maturity and are not withdrawable on demand and also cheques cannot be drawn on them. Clearly, it is only the demand deposits which serve as a medium of exchange, for they can be transferred from one person to another through drawing a cheque on them as and when deired by them. However, since even time or fixed deposits can be withdrawn by foregoing some interest and can be used for making payments, they are included in the concept of broad money, generally called *M*3. It may be noted that latest addition to the forms of money are *credit cards* issued by the banks which are these days extensively used for making purchases.

MODERN MONETARY SYSTEM OR MANAGED CURRENCY STANDARD

Paper money has come to occupy a very important place in the modern monetary system of almost all the countries of the world. The term paper money only applies to Government notes and the notes issued by the Central Bank of the country. In early times when notes were introduced they were backed by an exactly equal amount in gold or silver kept in reserve by the issuing authority. Such notes could be exchanged for gold or silver coins when demanded and did nothing more than representing metallic coins. Such paper money or notes are therefore called *representative paper money*. Paper money now-a-days is not wholly backed by gold or silver. Representative paper money is now not found anywhere in the world.

Convertible Paper Money. For a long time, paper money remained a convertible paper money. Under this, money is convertible into standard coins made of gold or silver. Under it the paper currency issued by the Central Bank was fully backed by the reserves of gold and silver of equal value kept by it. Therefore, this paper currency system was called "*Full Reserve System*". But with the passage of time it was thought that a cent per cent reserve against paper currency issued was not needed and instead only proportion of 30 to 50 per cent was enough to convert the notes presented for conversion into gold. Therefore, *proportional reserve system* was adopted. According to this, the issuing authority was called upon to keep a 30 to 50% of the total amount of notes issued as gold reserves. A percentage of 30 to 50 was considered enough to honour the notes when they were presented for exchange into gold. It was based upon the fact that people found notes very convenient and they seldom thought of presenting them to the issuing authority. Therefore, full backing of gold was not required. In India, this proportional reserve system was adopted in 1927 and continued till 1957.

Inconvertible Money. Thus, now-a-days paper money is of *inconvertible type*. Under the incovertible paper money system, money is not convertible into gold or other precious metals. Thus, when paper money is inconvertible, the issuing authority is not responsible to convert the paper notes into gold or gold coins. The currency notes that are issued by Reserve Bank of India are **'fiat' paper money**, that is, they are issued by the fiat *i.e.* order) of the Government. As they are legal tender, they are generally acceptable in exchange for goods and services and for payment of debt. It may be noted that 'promises to pay' written on the currency notes are not 'promises to pay' something else. For these notes, only other paper notes can be given whose value would be equal to the face value of the note you present for payment

Minimum Reserve System. But as time passed even proportional reserve system was thought to be inadequate for the monetary needs of a growing economy. Therefore, it was abonded in India in 1957 and was replaced by the minimum reserve system. According to this, Reserve Bank was required to keep only a minimum amount of gold and other approved securities (such as dollar and Pound Sterling) of the value of Rs. 200 crores. Out of these reserves it was required that gold must not be less than the value of Rs. 115 crores. On the basis of these minimum reserves, Reserve Bank of India could issue *any number of notes or currency* subject to the economic conditions of the country.

Managed Paper Currency Standard : Its Advantages

Paper currency standard or managed currency system which prevails in the modern economy has several advantages and disadvantages. Its main advantage is that under it the quantity of money can be easily increased according to economic needs of the country. When any country is under gold standard, it cannot increase the quantity of money unless the quantity of gold with it increases, despite the fact that the country needs expansion in money supply badly for purpose of promoting economic growth. Therefore, paper or fiat currency standard, which delinks the creation of money from gold, facilitates expansion in the quantity of money for promoting economic growth. The process of economic growth brings about an increase in output of goods and services in agriculture, industry, transport and communication. As a result, there is need for financing these activities so that transactions involving a larger amount of goods and services take place easily. But this requires the availability of the sufficient amount of money. If the required amount of money is not forthcoming, as is the case under gold and silver standards, then the process of economic growth will be retarded.

In times of depression there is need to increase the aggregate demand in the economy so that the state of full employment is reached. The best way to increase aggregate demand is the creation of new money by the Government and spending it on various public works. Following the increase in aggregate demand, production will expand and employment for workers will increase causing their incomes to rise. But, as we have seen above, only under paper currency standard, the quantity of money can be increased easily, whereas under gold standard, without the increase in the quantity of gold, money supply cannot be increased. In this way we see that paper currency standard is helpful to overcome depression and to achieve the objective of full employment.

On the other hand, when inflation occurs in the economy the Government can make a surplus budget and in this way it can withdraw the extra money from the public. This will lower the aggregate demand which will help in controlling inflation. With the appropriate monetary and fiscal policies price stability can be achieved. But these appropriate monetary and fiscal policies are possible only under paper currency standard. J.M. Keynes also supported the managed currency standard on the ground that, as compared to gold standard or any other monetary standard, this is very elastic and under it the quantity of money can be varied according to the needs of the economy.

Unlike the gold and silver standard, paper currency is not a fair weather friend. This standard is very helpful to the Government in situations of crisis such as war, drought, etc. when it needs extra quantity of money. By creating new paper money the Government can conduct the war successfully. With the newly created money the Government can buy real resources and goods when sufficient quantity of money cannot be procured through taxes. Under gold and silver standards, money cannot be increased unless the quantity of gold or silver increases. This is true that under paper currency standard Governments are tempted to issue excessive notes which results in inflation. But if proper controls are applied and production of goods expands, the issue of more money within reasonable limits to match the extra output does not result in inflation.

Besides, paper currency standard is very economical. As compared to the prices of metals, the price of paper is very low. Even those countries can adopt this standard who have no or few resources of gold and silver. Besides this, with the adoption of paper currency standard the gold and silver are saved which can be used for industrial and productive purposes. Lastly, under the paper currency standard, rate of foreign exchange automatically changes according to the conditions of demand and supply and therefore disequilibrium in the balance of trade is automatically removed. According to a foreign exchange specialist, Agnas, "*the beauty of paper system is that as soon as any disequilibrium between demand and supply occurs, sharp fluctuation in the price of foreign exchange immediately takes place which by its immediate action on both exports and imports rapidly restores equilibrium.*"

Disadvantages of Paper or Managed Currency Standard

But paper currency standard has several disadvantages too. First, it creates foreign exchange instability. Due to excessive changes in the foreign exchange rate, the prices of exports and imports of a country go on changing rapidly which affects foreign exchange earnings of the country. As a result of this, the country has to continually face foreign exchange instability and this instability is very dangerous for those countries who predominantly depend on foreign trade. These days when most of the countries of the world have floated their currencies (*i.e.*, foreign exchange rate is left to be determined by demand and supply), foreign exchange instability has assumed serious proportions. Therefore, many suggestions have been put forward to reform the international monetary system so that the problem of foreign exchange instability is avoided. Secondly, it is also asserted that even internal economic stability cannot be achieved with paper currency standard. The over-issue of paper currency can lead to inflation in the economy. This has been actually so in India where too much new paper money has been created to finance ever increasing Government expenditure. This has caused serious inflationary pressures in the Indian economy. Thus, the paper currency standard can give rise to both internal and foreign exchange instability. However, for this paper currency system should not be blamed. Desired benefits from paper currency system can be obtained if the Government properly manages it. If the adoption of paper currency system causes instability in the economy, the Government is responsible for it and not the paper currency system. The paper currency system is very elastic and its main advantage is that the quantity of money can be increased or decreased according to the requirements of the economy. But if improper use of its elastic nature is made by the Government by creating excessive quantity of money, the Government should be blamed and not the standard.

IMPORTANCE OR SIGNIFICANCE OF MONEY

Classical economists thought that money is a just veil and does not affect the real volume of goods and services in the economy, that is, the level of national product. According to them, money only affects the price level in the economy with no effect on the levels of real income and employment. They contended that what we really want was goods and services which satisfy the wants of the people and promote their welfare. Therefore, according to them, we must go behind the veil of money to see changes in the total output of goods and services or in real income. It is true that what we really want is not money but the goods and services which money can buy. It is the goods and services which satisfy the wants of the people and not money as such. But it must not be concluded from this that money is of no real importance. Modern economic life based on the complex division of labour or specialization which has added so greatly to the productivity of the economy will not be possible without money. The following are some of the advantages of money which show that money plays a vital and significant role in the modern economy.

1. **Moeny has Facilitated Exchange and Promoted Trade.** In the first place by serving as a medium of exchange and a common measure of value, money has removed the difficulties of the barter system and promoted trade in the economy. The difficulties of the barter system, namely, lack of double coincidence of wants, lack of division and lack of common measure of value are well known. By removing these difficulties, money has greatly facilitated the process of exchange. In the absence of money, trade and exchanges must have been few and far between and entailed a great waste of time and energy.

2. **Money Promote Division of Labour and Productivity.** Money is of great importance as it promotes division of labour and productivity in the modern economies. Since under the barter system, exchange was difficult, a man had to be self-sufficient, that is, produced most of the goods for himself. In the absence of money there were great difficulties in exchanging goods and services. This worked as an obstacle to the division of labour and specialisation among various individuals and nations. Long ago Adam Smith clearly brought out in his now well-known book "*Wealth of Nations*" how the division of labour and specialisation enhance productivity and efficiency of labour force. It is this division of labour and specialisation that has made the use of more efficient machines and advanced technology possible for production of goods. Indeed, it is because of the output-augmenting effect of division of labour that *Adam Smith regarded increase in the division of labour as progress in technology*. By opening up the opportunities of effecting division of labour, and through facilitating exchange and trade of goods and services money contributes to the expansion of production. Therefore, money enables the increase in the amount of production and variety of goods and services produced. "*If a modern economy were somehow deprived of the monetary mechanism and were driven back to a system of barter, the level of output would be much lower and the variety of goods and services much smaller than is enjoyed with a money system.*"[3] In fact money serves as a 'factor of production' which enables us to increase and diversify output

3. A.A. Walters, *Money and Banking*, Pengiun Readings, pp. 8-9.

3. **Money Promotes Saving.** A great significance of money is that it contributes a great deal to the increase in saving of the economy. Money has made saving easier than in the barter system. Increase in saving leads to the increase in investment which determine economic growth of a country. Further, money has made easier the acts of borrowing and lending and has given birth to various financial institutions which promote saving. Investment which is made possible by saving raises the rate of capital formation in the economy. The higher level of output in the modern economy is mainly due to the extensive use of capital in the production process.

4. **Moeny helps in Maximising Satisfaction or Profits by Consumers and Producers.** Fifthly, money is of immense advantage both to the consumers and producers. To the consumers money represents a general purchasing power. He can buy anything with money he has and at any time convenient to him. Since the values of goods are expressed in terms of common measure *i.e.* money, the consumer can easily compare the relative money prices of the goods and expected utilities from them. A consumer can easily spend his given money income on various goods in such a way that marginal utilities goods are proportional to their prices. With this he will be maximising his satisfaction from his given income. Thus the existence of money helps the consumer to maximise his satisfaction by acting on the principle of equi-marginal utility.

Money helps the producer too. The producer can easily compare the money cost and money income of the different levels of output. He can thus easily decide about the level of output which maximises his profits by equating marginal cost with marginal revenue ($MC = MR$). He can also easily decide about the units of a factor to be employed by comparing its marginal revenue product with the money payment he has to make to it. To maximise profits he can easily equate marginal revenue product (*MRP*) of a factor with the marginal factor cost (*MFC*) on that factor. Moreover, the workers engaged by a producer want goods and services to satisfy their wants. They want food, clothing, shelter and so many other things. The producer cannot supply them all these things easily. But what be can do is to pay them in money with which they buy the commodities they like at their own convience and when they need them.

5. **Money can Help in Reviving the Economy from Recession or Depression.** According to modern economists, money may play an important role in bringing about real changes. They point out that at times of recession or depression when there exists a lot of idle productive capacity and unemployment of labour, expansion of money supply, say through Government's deficit budget financed by the creation of new money will cause aggregate expenditure or demand to shift upward. This increase in aggregate expenditure or demand will cause output and employment in the economy to rise and thus will help the economy to recover from recession or depression.

Beneficial effect on output and employment of expansion in money supply can be obtained even if Central bank of a country takes steps to expand money supply in the economy say through reduction in Cash Reserve Ratio (*CRR*) and through buying securities in the open market. These steps by the central bank aim at expansion in credit availability for the businessmen. The greater credit availability will lead to more private investment which through multiplier process will cause income, output and employment to rise. It, therefore follows that ***money is not neutral in its effect on real income and employment.*** **In fact, as seen just above,** ***it plays an important role in the determination of the level of real economic activity.***

It is evident from above ***money helps us to avoid double conincidence of wants***. It enables the complex system of a large of number of prices of goods and services in terms of each other that prevail under barter system which makes it difficult to compare various prices and take optimal decisions. For example, if I sell my services as an economist, I need to know only money price of that service and money prices of the goods and services that I will buy; I do not require a complete list of various offers of goods as price of my service. In view of this significant role of money in the modern complex production system and transactions of goods and services that enhances productive capacity of the economy that **it is not proper to call money as a mere '*veil*** and intrinsically unemployment as a *mere* medium of exchange. Of course, money is a veil in the sense that what matters most is that the amount of goods and services that one can purchase with money. Thus, while considering the amount of money one should keep in mind money's purchasing power of goods and services. Therefore, in order to stress the importance of purchasing power of money, economists have evolved the concept of ***real money balances.*** *By real money balances we mean the value of money balances in terms of goods and services that we can buy.* Real money balances are measured by dividing the money balances divided by the price level as measured by price index. Thus, real money balances are equal to $\frac{M}{P}$ where M is the magnitude of money balances and P is the price level.

ROLE OF MONEY IN ECONOMIC DEVELOPMENT OF THE DEVELOPING COUNTRIES

Economic development is generally believed to be dependent on the growth of real factors such as capital accumulation, technological progress, and increase in quality and skills of labour force. This view does not adequately stress the role of money in the process of economic development. It is said that money is a mere veil and instrinsically unimportant. What matters is the real goods and productive factors which money buys. However, this extreme view about the unimportance of money as such is no longer believed. Not only is money an important factor without which modern complex economic organisation is impossible, but it is also an important factor for promoting economic development. We discuss below the importance of money in the process of economic development.

In the economy today money performs several functions. Money serves as a standard of value in which other values are measured. Money is a store of value, that is, the means in which wealth can be held. It acts as a standard for deferred payments. However, the most important function of money which distinguishes it from other goods is that it serves as a medium of exchange. That is, money is a means of payment for goods and services. It is this use of money that distinguishes a monetary economy from a barter economy. A monetary economy is one in which goods are sold for money and money is used to buy goods.

Money Promotes Productivity and Economic Growth. Barter system was full of difficulties of exchanging goods and services between individuals. In the absence of easy exchange of goods and services the barter system worked as an obstacle to the division of labour and specialisation among individuals which is an important factor for increasing productivity and economic growth. Further, the process of economic growth leads to the expansion of production of goods and services and consequential rise in incomes of the people. As a result, volume of transactions in the developing economy increases. This raises the demand for money to finance the increased transactions brought about by the expanded level of economic activity. Thus, the process of economic growth would be held in check if adequate supply of money is not forthcoming to meet the requirements of increase in the level of economic activity.

Money Promotes Investment. From the viewpoint of development another important role of money lies in making the magnitude of investment independent of the current level of savings. In a barter system, the goods not consumed constitute the savings as well as investment. That is, investment is not different from current savings. The greater the current savings, the greater the investment. However, in a modern economy, this is not so. Whereas it is households which save in the form of money, it is the firms which invest money in capital goods. Therefore, investment can differ from saving because investment activity is separated from the act of saving. More importantly, investment in a monetary economy can exceed the current level of savings. This excess of investment over savings is possible because new money can be created by the Government in the form of currency or by banks in the form of bank deposits. And this is what is important for the purpose of economic development.

In the developed countries in times of depression when idle productive capacity exists, the increase in investment made possible by creation of new money by the Government or banks would lead to the increase in aggregate demand for goods and services. In such times the supply of goods and services is elastic due to the existence of excess capacity. Therefore, increase in aggregate demand generated by the investment financed by created money brings about expansion in output of goods and services and thereby causes an increase in the level of employment.

In developing countries, the created money can play a useful role in promoting economic development. Rapid economic development can be achieved by stepping up the rate of investment or capital formation. But additional resources are required to increase the rate of investment. But in a country where a majority of the people are living at the bare subsistence level, voluntary savings, taxation. Government borrowing cannot by themselves provide sufficient investible resources for development. The government therefore attempts to increase the volume of investible resources beyond what is possible on the basis of current level of savings through creating new money. The newly created money can be spent on investment projects both in the industrial and agricultural fields which would lead to the increase in output, income and employment.

Money and Investment in Quick-Yielding Projects. It is widely believed that any increase in the supply of money in developing countries would lead to the rise in prices or to the emergence of inflationary pressures. However, this is not always true. A reasonable amount of newly created money helps the development of the economy by raising the level of investment. In the developing economies a lot of natural and human resources lie unutilised and underutilised which can be employed for productive purposes. If the newly created money is used for investment in those projects such as small irrigation works, land reclamation schemes, flood control and anti-soil erosion measures, cottage industries which yield quick returns, then the danger of inflation will not be there. These quick-yielding projects will increase the production of essential consumer goods in the short run and will therefore prevent the rise in prices. Further, if development strategy is such that a higher priority is assigned to agriculture and other wage goods industries and further that organisational and institutional reforms are undertaken to provide all farmers with irrigation facilities, fertilizers and high-yielding varieties, agricultural output can be raised in the short period. In this framework, new money can be created to increase the level of investment without much adverse effect on prices.

Money and Inflationary Financing of Economic Development. In his famous model of development with unlimited supply of labour, Arthur Lewis[4] has shown how the creation of new credit money can accelerate investment or capital formation in a developing economy. According to Lewis, in an economy marked by scarcity of capital and abundance of labour and idle natural resources, creation of credit or bank money would lead to the increase in capital accumulation in the same way as does a more respectable source, that is, savings out of profits.

However, according to him, capital formation resulting from a net increase in the money supply would be accompanied by rise in prices. But this would be a short-lived phenomenon. When the modern sector expands through more capital formation and surplus labour employed in it is paid out of the created money, the immediate effect would be rise in prices. What happens is that while the purchasing power in the hands of workers immediately increases, the output of consumer goods remains constant for a time. However, when the newly formed capital created by credit money is put to use, the output of consumer goods also increases. Thus, after a time lag output of consumer goods catches up with the increased purchasing power and the prices would start taking the downturn.

Further, the inflationary process would also be made to die away through another mechanism that operates simultaneously. With the creation of money and consequent accumulation of capital and expansion of the modern sector, not only do the output and employment increase but also the profits.

4. See Arthur Lewis, Economic Development with Unlimited Supplies of Labour, The *Manchester School*, May 1954.

As the profits increase relatively to national income, so will do the savings. Therefore, as the profits increase, the amount of investment being financed out of created money would go on diminishing. Ultimately, with the increase in voluntary savings, the seeds of inflation would be completely killed when the voluntary savings catch up with the inflated level of investment. Once equilibrium is restored, new investment made thereafter could be financed without the creation of new money. With the savings growing into equilibrium with investment, the rise in prices would eventually peter out.

Money and Forced Savings. It is important to note that even if prices permanently rise following the increase in investment or capital accumulation financed by the created money, even then new money fulfils the purpose of augmenting savings in the economy. The rise in prices of goods brought about by the monetary expansion for investment purposes, compels some people in the society to curtail their level of consumption. The completed investment projects represents the savings of the society. Thus, the resources for investment which could not be obtained from voluntary savings, have actually been procured through forced savings caused by the inflation or rise in prices. It is argued by some economists that economic development requires savings, voluntary or forced. If adequate amount of resources through voluntary savings and taxation are not forthcoming, recourse can be made to forced savings enforced by the creation of new money and resultant rise in prices.

Whether economic development should be financed through such inflationary method is however a very controversial issue. Critics have pointed out several adverse effects of inflation on saving propensity of the people and the pattern of investment, but we shall not go into this controversy here. Suffice it to say here that *newly created money can be used for development purposes to a good extent without causing a rise in prices if it is used for specific quick-yielding projects and in the framework of a development strategy which assigns a high priority to agriculture and other wage goods industries.*

Monetisation and Economic Growth. Further, as is well known, most underdeveloped countries have a large non-monetised (*i.e.* barter) sector where production is for the purpose of subsistence only. To break the subsistence nature of economic activity and thus generate new forces for economic growth, its monetisation is required. The introduction of money helps in bringing it in contact with the modern sector. This contact of the subsistence sector with the modern sector will lead to the expansion of its output. In order to obtain the products of the modern industrial sector, the people engaged in the subsistence sector will make efforts to raise their output. Thus, a surplus of output over their self-consumption will be generated in this way which will ultimately break subsistence nature. It is supported by the past history of the developing countries. During the colonial period, the monetisation of the peasant sector led the expansion in exports in exchange for the imported industrial products. This stepped up their agricultural development to a good extent.[5]

Similar to the growth of production for exports the introduction of money in the subsistence agricultural sector and its contact with the modern sector, would lead to the increase in marketable surplus of foodgrains and other agricultural products which is an important factor in economic development. If some rise in agricultural prices occurs as a result of increase in investment financed by the created money, as is likely the case, it would serve as an incentive to produce more foodgrains and supply it the market. The stimulated demand for industrial products would accelerate this process.

Further, the monetisation of the subsistence sector will also help in raising the volume of savings. Monetisation will bring this sector in contact with the financial institutions such as commercial and cooperative banks and insurance companies. The opportunities of earning more income through

5. See H. Myint, *The Economics of the Developing Countries*, Hutchinson University Library, London, 3rd edition, 1967, Ch. 3.

interest on saving will raise the propensity to save of the people in the present-day subsistence sector. If proper monetary policies are pursued, then instead of consuming or hoarding all their incomes, these people can deposit a part of them in the financial intermediaries.

QUESTIONS FOR REVIEW

1. What is money ? Show how it has removed the difficulties of barter system.
2. Define money. Describe its functions in a modern economy.
3. What is the necessary condition which makes something money ? How is the store of value function of money derived from its function as a medium of exchange ?
4. Money is what money does. Discuss
5. Define money. Explain tis important functions.
6. Explain the following forms of money.
   (a) Demand Deposits
   (b) Paper money
   (c) Legal Tender money
   (d) Convertible and inconvertible money.
   (d) Fiat money.
7. What is money ? Would you include time deposits in money supply ?
   [**Hints.** At present there are various measures of money supply such as M_1, M_2, M_3. Time deposits are not included in M_1 measure of money supply but they are an important part of M_3 measure of money supply. It may also be noted that these days measure M_3 of money supply is extensively used. For details see Chapter 17.]
8. Distinguish between money and near money. Why is time deposits considered as near money whereas demand deposits are regarded as money.
9. Discuss the various functions of money. What would happen to an economy if money supply suddenly disappeared ?
10. Explain the paper monetary system as it prevails today in the modern economies. Is for issuing new money Government or Reserve Bank of India has to keep proportionate amount of gold as reserve ? Explain the advantages and disadvantages of paper monetary system.
11. Explain the significance of money in the economy for promoting (*a*) division of labour, (*b*) saving, (*c*) income and employment.
12. Explain the importance of money for economic development of a developing country.
13. Money which is a source of so many blessings to mankind becomes, unless we control it ,a source of peril and confusion". Disucss.
14. Under what circumstances money does not perform well as a *store of value function*. What are its consequences.
15. Is it proper to call money as a mere '*veil*' ? Discuss. In this connection explain why economists distinguish between '*money balances and real money balances* ?
16. What is meant by 'double confidence of wants'? How does money enable us to avoid this problem.
17. "If a modern economy were some how deprived of monetary mechanism and were driven back to a system of barter, the level of output would be much lower and the variety of goods and services much smaller than is enjoyed with a money system" (A.A. Walters), Discuss.

CHAPTER 18

Credit and Commercial Banking

Credit : Meaning and Functions

With the introduction and use of money credit also came into existence. Credit is created when one party (a person, a firm or an institution) lends money to another party, the borrower. Thus, credit is generally understood to mean the finance provided to others at a certain rate of interest. The act of lending and borrowing creates both credit and debit. Whereas debt means the obligation to pay the finance borrowed, the credit means the claim to receive this money payments from the other party. Every credit involves debt, that is, obligation to pay money and therefore creates claim.

The act of borrowing and lending and thereby the creation of credit is a special type of exchange transaction which involves future payment of the principal sum borrowed as well as the rate of interest on it. The lending and borrowing of money and the institution of money lending came into vogue ever since money was invented by man. In the modern times there are a variety of institutions which specialise in borrowing and lending of money. The bank credit is only one form of credit. Money lenders, indigenous bankers, credit cooperative societies, commercial and cooperative banks, industrial financial institutions, L.I.C., export finance houses etc. are all credit institutions and do the business of borrowing and bending money. Different credit institutions lend money for different purposes and are collectively called the financial system. Thus commercial banks are only one segment, though an important one, of the financial or credit system of an economy.

Credit institutions can be differentiated according to the type and purpose of credit they offer. There are credit institutions which lend money only for agriculture. There are others which provide credit only to industries and still others to finance exports only. Credit institutions also differ in respect of the duration of period for which they lend money to their clients. Some provide short-term credit, some medium-term credit and others only long-term credit. We shall study only one type of credit-institution, namely, the commercial banks.

Functions of Credit

The main function of credit is to relieve the constraint imposed by balanced budgets on economic agents, that is, to meet the financial requirements of investors who have to spend more on trade and investment than their own savings. Accordingly, it is through the means of credit that the surplus funds with some individuals and institutions are made available to the deficit spenders, that is, those who are required to spend more than their resources, for instance, traders, companies, investors. It is the performance of this function, that is, the transferring surplus funds of some to meet the spending by the businessmen and investors, that the banking and other segments of the financial system are able to promote savings and investment, to ensure better allocation of financial resources and thereby to encourage economic growth in the economy.

But, for the credit system to perform these functions, it needs to be efficiently managed and controlled. If credit is not efficiently managed, it can cause inflation or deflation, recession and unemployment in the economy. Besides, the mismanagement of credit can lead to misallocation of investible resources and thereby hinder economic growth. It can also cause concentration of economic power in a few hands and exploitation of weaker sections and thus work against the achievement of social justice.

Purpose or End-Uses of Credit

Credit is required for different purposes and by all sectors of the economy. Therefore, there is need for the proper allocation of credit between different uses and sectors if the society is to achieve its objectives. When credit is demanded and used for productive purposes, it may be used to finance the needs of working capital or for fixed investment (*i.e.* capital equipment, machinery etc.). The broad categories of economic activity for which credit for productive purposes is demanded are (*a*) agriculture, (*b*) industry, (*c*) construction, and (*d*) trade, both domestic and foreign. Further, in each of these categories, the allocation of credit between different users is of crucial importance from the viewpoint of economic growth and social justice. Thus, in agriculture allocation of credit between large landowners and small farmers has been a matter of serious debate. Likewise, the allocation of credit between the large-scale industries and small-scale industries has been a major concern in India's credit policy. Credit policy in India in recent years has emphasised certain priority sectors such as agriculture, small-scale industries, export and weaker sections of society such as small and marginal farmers, young entrepreneurs for whom greater amount of credit is to be made available.

Origin and Evolution of Commercial Banking

A Commercial Bank is a business organisation which deals in money; it borrows and lends money. In this borrowing and lending of money, it makes profit. The distinction between money lender and a commercial bank may be noted. Whereas money lender only lends money to others and that too from his own sources; a commercial bank does both the lending and borrowing businesses. A commercial bank raises its resources through borrowing from the public in the form of deposits and lends them to the businessmen. Its lending rate of interest is greater than that it pays to its depositors. It is because of this difference in lending and borrowing rates of interest that it is able to make profits.

Now, a curious student will ask the question how the institution of banking originated and evolved. The banking owes its origin to the activities of goldsmiths in England. In the Seventeenth Century, goldsmiths in England possessed strongest safe vaults where valuable goods such as gold, silver, diamonds could be kept safely. Therefore, the rich people in England at that time used to keep their valuable things such as gold and silver with the goldsmiths and obtained receipts from them for their deposits of gold and silver. At a later stage it was found that these deposits with goldsmiths could serve as money, that is, a medium of exchange. The person who had a deposits of gold and silver with a goldsmith could pay off his debt simply by endorsing the deposit receipt in favour of the person to whom he has to pay back the loan. In this way gold and silver got automatically transferred to another person even though they remained in the safe custody of the goldsmiths. It was soon discovered that there was no need for endorsing the whole deposit receipt in favour of the other person. With a deposits of gold and silver a person could issue a letter to his goldsmith instructing him to transfer a certain amount of gold or silver to another person. Obviously from this practice emerged the present-day system of payment through cheques.

Another important development took place when goldsmiths realised that a good amount of gold deposited with them remained idle for long as only the ownership of them changed through transfer. From this they concluded that they could issue more deposit receipts than the actual deposits of gold and silver with them to meet the financial needs of some persons and started charging some interest on them. In this practice one can see the beginning of the creation of deposits or credit by the modern banks which will be described in detail later in this chapter.

BALANCE SHEET OF A BANK: LIABILITIES AND ASSETS STRUCTURE

Balance sheet of a bank is of great importance for understanding the sources of funds it possesses and the uses to which these funds are put. As is well known, a balance sheet of an institution indicates its liabilities and assets. The liabilities of a bank shows the sources of its funds and assets show its uses by it. The balance sheet of Bank of Baroda as on 31st March 1997 is given below :

(Rs. in crores)

Liabilities		*Assets*	
Capital	254.3	Cash and Balances with RBI	3,048.2
Reserves and Surplus	1,733.4	Balances with other banks and money at call and short notice	4,683.4
Deposits	32,156.7	Investment in Govt. and other securities	10,927.2
Borrowings	339.9	Advances	16,531.6
Other Liabilities and Provisions	3,155.4	Fixed Assets	570.1
		Other Assets	1,872.2
Total	37,639.7	Total	37,639.7

Liabilities

It will be observed from the balance sheet of a bank given above that deposits constitute a very large proportion of the total funds available with a bank. It should be borne in mind that these deposits are bank's liabilities as they are depositors' claim against the bank. Deposits are mainly of two types: (1) demand deposits, (2) time deposits. Demand deposits are payable on demand and therefore can be withdrawn by the public through cheques. On the other hand, the time deposits are repayable by the bank only after a certain fixed period of time. In addition to these, in India there is another type of deposits called Savings Bank Deposits. Though money in such deposits can be withdrawn through cheques, there are limits to the amount withdrawable in a week or month.

Banks also borrow from the Central Bank of the country and these borrowings also constitute its liabilities and source of funds. In the balance sheet, these borrowings from the Reserve Bank of India (*i.e.*, Central Bank of India) are included in other items of the liabilities. When supply of money is very tight, the borrowings from Central Bank is of immense help to the banks.

Assets Structure : Liquidity Vs. Profitability

The asset side of the balance sheet of a bank shows for what purposes it has used the funds obtained from the depositors. As pointed out above, a viable bank has to operate so as to make reasonable profits. On the other hand, in order to meet the demands for withdrawals by the public and thus to retain faith and creditibity, it has to keep some ready cash with it, that is, it has to ensure some liquidity. Profitability and liquidity are the two major considerations that weigh with the commercial banks in deciding about the composition of its assets. If all of its deposits are kept by the bank in the form of cash, it will have perfect liquidity in this case but will make no profits at all. But if the bank advances all its deposits as long-term loans to the industries it will lose liquidity and will be unable to honour the demands of withdrawals by the depositors. Therefore, a bank has to keep such an asset structure (that is, a combination of different types of assets) that strikes a balance between liquidity and profitability.

A glance at the balance sheet of a commercial bank given above shows that *cash in hand* and with other banks, which is a liquid asset, constitutes about 8 per cent of the total assets of a bank. There is another quite a good liquid asset, namely, *money at call and short notice*, which is about 12 per cent of the total assets. Another important liquid asset is the *investment in government and other securities*. Investment in government securities and other securities by the bank are also liquid as they can be sold in a short time and cash realised therefrom. It may be noted that in India the banks are by law required to invest a given percentage of their deposits in government securities. But legal requirements apart, the investment in government securities by the banks ensures their liquidity position such as these can be readily converted into cash. It will be seen from the balance sheet of the bank that investment in Government and other securities by the bank constitutes about 29 per cent of its assets.

Loans and advances by the banks to industries and traders are the most profitable item of asset. It is against these profitable assets that liquid assets, mentioned above, have to be balanced. It will be noticed that loans and advances account for about 44 per cent in the asset structure of the banks.

It is worthwhile to note that asset structure of different banks will vary depending upon the composition of their deposits. A bank that has relatively more demand deposits, will have to keep a greater proportion of its assets in liquid form. On the other hand, if a bank possesses more time deposits, it will need to hold a relatively smaller proportion of its assets in liquid form.

FUNCTIONS OF COMMERCIAL BANKS

The main functions of the commercial banks can be summed up in one sentence : *the banks borrow to lend*. To receive deposits and to advance loans are thus the two main functions of all commercial banks. They borrow in the form of deposits and lend in various types of advances. Besides, there are other miscellaneous functions of commercial banks which have developed according to the needs of the society.

(*a*) Accepting Deposits

The banks borrow in the form of deposits. This function is important because banks mainly depend on the funds deposited with them by the public. The deposits received by the banks may be of the following types.

(*i*) **Demand Deposits or Current Account Deposits.** If a depositor deposits money in the bank in the current account (*i.e.*, demand deposits), he can withdraw it in part or in full at any time he likes without notice. These accounts are generally kept by businessmen whose requirements of making business payments are quite uncertain. Usually no interest is paid on them, because the bank cannot utilise these short-term deposits for lending purposes and must keep almost cent per cent reserve against them. But in return for these current account deposits, the banks offer some facilities or concessions to the account holders. The most important is the cheque facility made available to them, that is, the account holders make payment to the parties through cheques on these accounts. Further, on behalf of the holders of current account deposits, banks collect cheques, drafts, dividend warrants, postal orders, etc.

(*ii*) **Fixed Deposits or Time Deposits**. These deposits are made for a fixed period of time, which varies from fifteen days to a few years. These deposits cannot, therefore, be withdrawn before the expiry of that period. However, a loan can be taken from the bank against the security of these deposits within that period. A higher rate of interest is paid on the fixed deposits. As the fixed deposits carry a good rate of interest, they are a good source of investment by the people who are in a position to save. In India, the increase in the rates of interest on fixed deposits of various durations has attracted a good deal of savings in the banks. Since June, 1998, the interest on these deposits for 6 months and above but less than 1 year is 8 per cent, on deposits for one year and above is not regulated by RBI but varies from 9 per cent to 12 per cent depending on the period.

(*iii*) **Savings Bank Deposits.** In this case the depositor can generally withdraw money usually once a week. Sometimes there are also restrictions as to the total amount that can be withdrawn at one time and the total amount that can be placed in one deposit. These deposits are generally made by the people of small means, usually, people with fixed salaries, for holding their short-term savings. Like the current account deposits, the saving bank deposits are payable on demand and also they can be drawn upon through cheques. But in order to discourage people to use the savings bank deposits very frequently, there are some restrictions on the number of times withdrawals (through cheque or otherwise) that can be made from these accounts. The saving deposits carry lower rate of interest than the fixed deposits. Since March 1, 1996, the interest on savings bank deposits in India is 4.5 per cent per annum.

(b) Advancing Loans

Another function of the bank is to give loans to others. If the bank does not lend the deposited money to others, how can it pay the interest on the deposits to depositors? Banks give loans to businessmen and firms usually for short periods only. This is so because the bank must keep itself ready to meet the demands of the people who have deposited money for short period only. In advancing loans, the bank has to shoulder a heavy responsibility. The bank makes profit by advancing loans. But the bank deals in other people's money and it has to keep some ready cash to meet the depositors' demands. Hence a great care has to be exercised in the matter of lending and keeping resources. The bank must strike a fine balance between liquidity and profitability. If it keeps its assets in too liquid a form, it loses profit and if it tries to make too much profit, it may not be able to meet the depositor's demand. It must aim at both liquidity and profitability. Banks advance loans in the following ways.

1. By allowing an overdraft. Those people who keep current account with the banks are sometimes given the right to overdraw their accounts. In other words, people make arrangements with the banks that if a cheque has been drawn by them which is not covered by the deposit, then the bank should grant the overdraft and honour the cheque. Thus under overdraft arrangements, people can get more than they have deposited but they have to pay interest on the extra amount which has to be paid back within a short period. Overdraft facilities are generally granted to businessmen who can pay off the money after the sale of the goods.

2. Cash-Credit Loan. Under the cash-credit system, borrower is sanctioned a credit limit up to which he can borrow from the bank. But before granting a credit limit the bank satisfies itself about the credit-worthiness of the borrower. However, the actual utilisation of the credit limit by the borrower depends on his withdrawing power. Withdrawing power of a borrower is determined by his current assets which consists of stocks of goods, that is, stocks of raw materials, semi-finished goods and payments receivable from others. The borrower has to submit periodically a list of his assets showing his borrowing power. The interest payable by the borrower is calculated on the amount of the credit limit actually drawn.

3. Demand Loans. Demand loans granted by a bank are those loans which can *be recalled on demand by the bank any time*. The entire sum of demand loan granted to a borrower is paid in lump sum by crediting it to his account. Therefore, the interest is payable on the entire sum of demand loan granted. Usually demand loans are granted to stock-brokers whose need for credit fluctuates from day to day.

4. Short-Term Loan. Short-term loans are given as personal loans against security. Car loans, computer loans, housing loans are some examples of short-term loans. Short-term loans are also given to finance needs for working capital of business men. In case of short-term loans also the whole amount of loan granted is paid in lump-sum by crediting it to the loan account of the borrower. The interest is payable on the entire sum of loan granted.

(c) Discounting Bills of Exchange or Hundies

A very important function of a modern bank is to discount bills or hundies of businessmen. It is like this, a businessman buys goods and is granted credit, say, for a month. The seller of the goods draws a bill of exchange which the purchaser is asked to sign. The bill orders the purchaser to pay a certain sum after the expiry of one month. If the seller goes on selling goods on this basis, he will soon find that all his stock is gone and he has got only these hundies in his cash box. Unless these hundies are changed into cash, his business will come to a standstill. He, therefore, does not keep these hundies with him till they mature for payment. But he takes them to the bank and gets the present worth of the hundies, leaving the bank to realise them when the date of payment comes. This is called discounting a bill. It is obvious that the bank has advanced money to the businessman for the period of the currency of the bill.

Bill discounting is considered a very suitable investment for a bank. The bills are certain to be paid on maturity. They can be rediscounted with the central bank, if necessary. They set up a regular flow of incomings and outgoings of cash. Being negotiable instruments, the bills do not create any difficulty at the time of payment and do not involve the bank in any litigation. It represents a short-term investment, which suits the bank very well because most of its deposits are also of short term. For all these reasons this form of advance represents the most suitable investment from the bank's point of view. That is why it is sometimes remarked that a good banker knows the difference between a bill and a mortgage.

(*d*) Transfer of Money

Banks transfer money from one place to another for their customers. Banks remit the funds of the people by means of a bank draft or a cheque. This is a cheap as well as safe method of transferring money from one place to another.

(*e*) Miscellaneous Functions

A bank now-a-days serves its customers in various other ways. It has lockers or 'safe deposit vaults'. They are meant to keep the valuables of customers in safe custody. Further, a bank collects interest on behalf of its customers as well as pays dividends on behalf of joint-stock companies. It purchases and sells stocks and shares of companies for its clients. It pays insurance premium on behalf of their customers from their deposits. It executes the wills of deceased customers and acts for them as a trustee.

From the above discussion it follows that these days the functions of banks are many and varied. Banks are not merely the *traders of money* but they are also the *manufacturers of money*. In other words, they not only deal in money, *i.e.*, borrow and lend money but also manufacture or make money. They create money through credit creation. Bank deposits these days are as much money as any other form of money.

ROLE OF COMMERCIAL BANKS IN ECONOMIC DEVELOPMENT

As is well known, the rate of economic development depends to a large measure on the rate of capital formation. The rate of capital formation in turn depends on the rate of savings and investment and the proper allocation of investible funds among different sectors and users. The banking system helps economic growth in all these ways, that is, by (*a*) promoting savings, (*b*) mobilizing savings, and (*c*) allocating savings among alternative uses and users. Let us explain how commercial banking, which is an important part of the financial system of the country, performs these functions.

(*a*) Promotion of Savings

People save for various reasons. Thus people save to provide for future needs such as periods of unemployment, old age, sickness, to provide for education and marriage of their children, to own property such as real estate, houses etc. in future, and to purchase durable consumer goods. But they require assets in the form of which they should keep their savings in safe custody and earn a rate of return as well. Commercial banks promote savings by providing a wide range of deposits with varying combinations of liquidity and rate of interest to suit the needs and preferences of different savers. It has been found that with the growth of commercial banking in unbanked and under-banked regions, the household savings go up. As a store of value, bank deposits enjoy certain advantages over tangible assets (physical capital, inventories of commodities) and other financial assets. The bank deposits are convenient to hold as store of value and are more safe and more liquid, *i.e.*, they can be converted into cash easily. They are also greatly divisible and less risky. With all these advantages, they earn varying rates of interest depending upon the type of deposits into which the savers put their savings. These advantages of bank deposits induce households to save more and encourage the habit of thrift.

It is worth noting that the commercial banks would perform well this function of promoting savings in the framework of price stability. If the prices of goods are rising, that is, inflation grips the economy, then the savers would prefer to use their savings to buy gold and silver, other commodities, and real estate whose prices are also rising. This is because the real rate of interest on bank deposits goes down to the extent of rise in prices. This underlines the importance of keeping prices stable, if savings by households are to be promoted.

(b) Mobilisation of Savings

Not only do the banks encourage savings but they also mobilise savings done by serveral households and make them available for the purposes of production and investment to the entrepreneurs in various sectors of the economy. This function of mobilizing savings is of crucial importance because in the modern monetary economy, the act of saving has been separated from the act of real investment. Savings are done by millions of households and firms, whose individual savings may be very small, savings of some may be of short-term and of others of long-term nature. Banks and other financial intermediaries collect or mobilise these savings before these can be made available to the producers or investors. Without the banks (and other financial intermediaries), these savings would have remained scattered and also idle, that is, would not have been utilised for productive and investment purposes. As pointed out above, banks mobilise savings of households and firms through offering variety of deposits to suit the needs and preference of different households possessing surplus funds.

It follows from above that the *commercial banks, like other financial institutions, provide a link between those who have savings (i.e. surplus funds) and those who are in need of such funds to use them for production and investment purposes.* If commercial banks and other financial intermediaries were not there, those with surplus funds would have to search for appropriate borrowers and strike individual bargains with them and bear risks of lending them. The existence of commercial banks makes the tasks of lenders easy and with the control over commercial banks by the Government or central bank of the country, the risks of depositors have almost been eliminated. This enables the banks to mobilise more resources for production and investment purposes.

It is evident from above that banks act as a financial intermediary between lender and borrower. The financial assets can be classified into two categories (1) primary securities, (2) secondary securities. Equity shares, debentures, and company deposits of corporate firms represent primary securities. When households buy these securities they directly invest or lend money to the investor and bear risk of such investment. On the other hand, bank deposits represent secondary securities and when households go in for them, they provide their savings to banks who allocate them among competing borrowers—traders, producers and investors. In this way it is the banks who bear risks of lending, whereas the depositors' money and interest are safe and certain. Those savers who are risk averters find the secondary securities (bank deposits) more acceptable than the primary securities.

(c) Allocation of Funds

Allocation of funds or economic surplus among different sectors, users and producers so as to make maximum social return and thus to ensure optimum utilisation of savings is an other important function performed by the banks. Whereas the corporate firms can raise resources through sale of equity shares and debentures, the noncorporate firms and borrowers depend greatly on banks for financing the needs of both working capital and fixed capital. Through the lending rates of interest determined by market mechanism or fixed by the central bank of the country credit advanced by the banks get rationed among various potential borrowers and sectors. Further, before lending banks take into account the credit-worthiness or capacity to pay back the loans. Thus the banks are in a better position to judge the returns or productivity from the uses for which the funds are lent out. This helps in maximisation of returns from scarce financial resources.

However, it may be mentioned, that commercial banks do not always work and allocate resources in the way that maximises production or social welfare. For instance, before nationalisation in 1969 the commercial banks in India in their allocation of funds neglected socially highly desirable sectors such as agriculture, small-scale industries and the weaker sections of the society such as small and marginal farmers, the young entrepreneurs seeking self-employment. On the contrary, they preferred to invest funds collected from the public in the business concerns of the big business houses which controlled these banks. Therefore, it was thought necessary to nationalise them so that they should allocate resources in socially desirable directions.

(*d*) Promotions of Trade, Production and Investment

By encouraging inducement to save and also mobilising savings from the public, banks help to increase the aggregate rate of investment in the economy. It may also be noted that banks not only mobilise the saved funds from the public, but also themselves create deposits or credit which serve as money. The new deposits are created by the banks when they lend money to the investors or other users. These deposits are by the banks in excess of the cash reserves they obtain through deposits by the public. These days, the bank deposits, especially demand deposits, are as much good money as the currency issued by the Government or Reserve Bank of India. This creation of credit, if it is used for productive purposes, greatly larges production and investment and thus promotes economic growth.

CREDIT CREATION BY BANKS

Creation of credit is one of the most outstanding functions of a modern bank. A bank has sometimes been called a factory for the manufacture of credit. How credit is created? It is an open secret that the banks do not keep cent per cent reserves against deposits in order to meet the demands of depositors. The bank is not a cloak room where you can keep your currency notes or coins and claim those very notes or coins back when you desire. It is generally understood that money received by the bank is meant to be advanced to others. A depositor has to be content simply with the bank's promise or undertaking to pay him whenever he makes a demand. Thus the banks are able to do with a very small reserve, because all the depositors do not come to withdraw money simultaneously; some withdraw, while others deposit at the same time. The bank is thus enabled to erect a vast superstructure of credit on the basis of a small cash reserve. The bank is able to lend money and charge interest without parting with cash, as the bank loan creates simply a deposit or it creates a credit for the borrower. This is what is meant by creation of credit.

Similarly, the bank buys securities and pays the seller with its own cheque which again is no cash; it is just a promise to pay cash. The cheque is deposited in some bank and a deposit is created or credit is created for the seller of the securities. This is credit creation. The term 'credit creation' implies a situation, to use Benham's words, when "a bank may receive interest simply by permitting a customer to overdraw their accounts or by purchasing securities and paying for them with its own cheques, thus increasing the total bank deposits."

Let us see the actual process. Let us assume that there is only one bank in the country. Suppose a customer deposits Rs. 1,000 in the bank. The bank has to pay him interest. Therefore, the bank must seek a safe and profitable investment for this amount. It must lend it to somebody. But this amount is not actually paid out to the borower; it is retained by the bank to meet its obligations, *i.e.,* to pay to those of its depositors who need cash and draw cheques for the purpose. The bank's experience tells him that for this purpose only a certain percentage of cash reserves to total liabilities need be kept. In countries like England, they keep nearly 10 per cent. The ratio of cash reserves to liabilities is much higher in countries like India, where banking habit has yet to develop.

Suppose the bank, in which a depositor has deposited Rs. 1,000, keeps 20 per cent cash reserve to meet the demand of depositors. This means that, as soon as the bank has received Rs. 1,000 it will make up its mind to advance loans up to the amount of Rs. 5,000 (only one-fifth reserve is kept). When, therefore, a businessman comes to the bank with a request for a loan of Rs. 5,000, he may be sure of being granted accommodation to this extent, provided of course, his credit is good. The bank lends Rs. 5,000, although it has only Rs. 1,000 in cash. It is here that credit comes in. This transaction is rendered possible because the borrower is not given the loan in cash; only an account is opened in his name and the amount is credited to his account. He is simply given the cheque book, *i.e.*, the right to draw cheques as and when he needs money. Even when he withdraws cash, it will be deposited in the bank by the recipients, because businessmen do not raise funds to keep them locked up in a cash box but to run their business and to make payments to their creditors. When this particular businessman draws cheques on this bank to pay his creditors, these cheques are passed on by them to their own banks, where the amount is deposited in their account. Cash is seldom withdrawn. The banks adjust their mutual obligations through a system of bank clearing. Thus the bank has succeeded in creating a credit of Rs. 5,000 against a cash reserve of Rs. 1,000.

The bank also creates credit when it purchases securities. The bank can purchase securities without paying any cash. It issues its own cheque to pay the purchase price. The cheque is deposited in this bank or some other bank and the small cash reserve which the bank keeps is sufficient to meet an obligation arising from this transaction too. It is thus that, on a small cash foundation, a vast superstructure of credit is built up.

Let us now understand the process of credit creation when there are *several* banks in the country, as they are in the real world. In the case of several commercial banks in the country, one individual bank cannot create all the credit as described above. But what no single bank can do individually, the banking system as a whole can do, *i.e.,* create credit. We shall explain the process of credit creation or the expansion of money supply in the country by the banking system collectively with the help of *balance sheets* of the banks. We shall illustrate how deposit of Rs. 1,00,000 of currency in a commercial bank enables the banking system as a whole to expand deposits by another Rs. 4,00,000, that is, deposits of Rs. 1,00,000 in currency leads to a total deposits of Rs. 5,00,000 in the banking system.

Banks, as other business firms, show their financial condition on a balance sheet. A simple balance sheet has two columns, its left column represents all the *assets* of a bank and its right column represents all the *liabilities* of a bank. Assets are all the things or claims a bank owns, liabilities, on the other hand, are claims against those assets; some of the claims are of creditors and some of them are of owners of the banks themselves. Because assets show everything that a bank owns and because liabilities represent claims against those assets, the two sides of the balance sheet, that is, assets and liabilities must equal each other.

Let us suppose that an individual or a firm deposits Rs. 1,00,000 in cash with a bank A. Ignoring everything else in the balance sheet, let us know how the balance sheet of bank A will look like with this fresh deposit of Rs. 1,00,000 in currency with it. The cash of Rs. 1,00,000 which the bank A will receive will become its assets, and at the same time individual's deposits of Rs. 1,00,000 will be its liabilities, the assets and liabilities of bank A will therefore be equal to each other.

BANK A
Balance Sheet

Assets		*Liabilities*	
Cash	Rs. 1,00,000	Deposits	Rs. 1,00,000

Let us assume that cash reserve ratio is 20%. Now the bank does not require all the Rs. 1,00,000 in cash against the deposits of Rs. 1,00,000. The bank A requires only 20% of it, that is, Rs. 20,000 cash against its deposits of Rs. 1,00,000. The bank can lend or invest in securities the remaining amount of Rs. 80,000. Actually if the bank does not lend or invest it will suffer a loss, since it will pay the interest to the depositor with no profit from the cash it possesses.

Therefore, the bank A will lend Rs. 80,000 to the business firms or individuals whom it finds creditworthy. Now, when a bank lends to a person or firm it does not give him cash immediately. The bank makes deposits in the name of the person whom he lends the money and gives him the right to draw cheques against it when required. It is a new deposit, one that did not exist before. The person or firm getting loans from the bank will, however, after some time completely withdraw the money through cheques from his deposits. When the loan of Rs. 80,000 has been sanctioned to a person, but before that person starts withdrawing his money, the balance sheet of bank A will look like as follows:

BANK A
Balance Sheet

(When the bank sanctions loan of Rs. 80,000 but before loan is cashed)

Assets		*Liabilities*	
Cash	Rs. 1,00,000	Deposits	Rs. 1,00,000
Loan	Rs. 80,000	New Deposits (Created)	Rs. 80,000
	Rs. 1,80,000		Rs. 1,80,000

In this balance sheet, loan of Rs. 80,000 becomes asset of the bank, while the new deposits created constitute the liability of the bank, since the person getting the loan has the right to draw upon these deposits.

Now, when the person wholly withdraws his deposits through cheques and the recipients of these cheques deposit them in some other bank, say bank B, then the bank A will have to surrender to bank B cash money equal to Rs. 80,000. After the whole newly created deposits of Rs. 80,000 have been thus withdrawn, the balance sheet of bank A will now look like as follows:

BANK A
Balance Sheet

Assets		*Liabilities*	
Cash	Rs. 20,000	Original Deposits	Rs. 1,00,000
Loan	Rs. 80,000	New Deposits	0
Total	Rs. 1,00,000	Total	Rs. 1,00,000

As said above, cheques worth Rs. 80,000 against Bank A are deposited in Bank B, for the Bank B these will constitute new cash money and will therefore become the assets of bank B. But Rs. 80,000 will also be the liability of the bank B in the form of deposits in the name of those persons who have deposited the cheques with it. Ignoring other assets and liabilities of bank B and taking into account only this above transaction, the balance sheet of bank B will be as follows:

BANK B
Balance Sheet

Assets		*Liabilities*	
Cash	Rs. 80,000	Deposits	Rs. 80,000

Now against the deposits of Rs. 80,000 bank B rcquires to keep its 20%, that is, Rs. 16,000 and it can lend or invest the remaining amount of Rs. 64,000. When bank B lends Rs. 64,000 to a firm, it will create deposits for that firm. Before the firm draws upon that deposits, the balance sheet of bank B will took like:

BANK B
Balance Sheet

Assets		*Liabilities*	
Cash	Rs. 80,000	Deposits	Rs. 80,000
Loan	Rs. 64,000	New Deposits Created	Rs. 64,000
Total	Rs. 1,44,000	Total	Rs. 1,44,000

Now, when the firm which has got loan from bank B completely withdraws Rs. 64,000 through cheques, the balance sheet of bank B will be as follows. As a result of the firm spending the loan money of Rs. 64,000, the bank B will transfer cash of Rs. 64,000 to another bank, say C, in which the cheques drawn by the firm are deposited. As a result of this, the cash with bank B will fall to Rs. 16,000 (Rs. 80,000 – Rs. 64,000 = Rs. 16,000).

BANK B
Balance Sheet

Assets		*Liabilities*	
Cash	Rs, 16,000	Deposits	Rs. 80,000
Loan	Rs. 64,000	New Deposits	0
Total	Rs. 80,000	Total	Rs. 80,000

Now when the bank C will get Rs. 64,000, it will also require to keep 20% of it (*i.e.*, Rs. 12,800) and the remaining amount of Rs. 51,200 will be lent out or invested by it.

From the foregoing analysis it is clear that the currency deposits of Rs. 1,00,000 led to the creation of deposits of Rs. 80,000 by Bank A, Rs. 64,000 by Bank B, Rs. 51,200 by Bank C. But the process of expansion of deposits will not stop here, it will go on as the money lent out by one bank is spent through cheques and these cheques are deposited in other banks, till the total deposits of Rs. 5,00,000 in all the banks (including original deposits of Rs. 1,00,000) are created. But it should be remembered that at each stage the new deposits created by a bank goes on declining. This is because at each stage a bank is required to keep 20% of the money it receives as cash reserves and therefore lends and creates deposits equal only to the remaining amount. Thus bank A created deposits of Rs. 80,000, bank B created deposits of Rs. 64,000, bank C created deposits of Rs. 51,200 and so on.

We are now in a position to state how much deposits have been created by the banking system out of the currency deposits of Rs. 1,00,000.

Total Deposits = Rs. 1,00,000 + 80,000 + 64,000 + 51,200 + ... = Rs. 5,00,000

Out of the total deposits of Rs. 5,00,000, the deposits of Rs. 1,00,000 in cash was made in the banking system, the remaining deposits have been created by the banking system itself, as if out of thin air.

$$\left.\begin{array}{r}\text{Deposits created by the}\\ \text{banking system}\end{array}\right\} \begin{array}{l}= \text{Rs. } 5{,}00{,}000 - 1{,}00{,}000\\ = \text{Rs. } 4{,}00{,}000\end{array}$$

It should be further noted that the *total expansion of deposits by the banking system depends upon the cash reserve ratio* (CRR). The smaller the cash reserve ratio the large the expansion of deposits or credit. Thus, in the above case, we noted that, given the cash reserve ratio of 20%, the total deposits expansion from the cash deposits of Rs. 1,00,000, was equal to Rs. 5,00,000. Thus the total deposits expanded to was five times the original cash deposits. Therefore the deposits of cash in the banking system leads to multiple expansion in the total deposits. This is known as *deposits* or *credit multiplier.* In our above case, the deposits or credit multiplier is 5. It should be remembered that the *magnitude of deposits multiplier depends on the cash reserve ratio.*

Deposit multiplier $d_m = \frac{\Delta D}{\Delta R} = \frac{1}{r}$

where r stands for cash reserve ratio.

Thus deposit multiplier is the reciprocal of cash reserve ratio (CRR) which we have denoted by r in the measure of deposit multiplier.

Thus, when the cash reserve ratio is 20%, that is, 0.20 or 1/5, the deposit multiplier.

$$= \frac{1}{\frac{1}{5}} = 5$$

Now, if the cash reserve ratio is raised by Reserve Bank to 25 per cent, that is, 0.25, the deposit multiplier,

$$d_m = \frac{1}{0.25} = \frac{1}{1/4} = 4$$

Thus, *the greater the cash reserve ratio, the lower will be the value of deposit multiplier.* In other words, increase in the cash reserve ratio *(CRR* or *r)* will lead to the contraction of credit created by the banks, and vice versa

Similarly, if the cash reserve ratio is 10%, *i.e.,* 1/10, then the deposits multiplier = 1/1/10 = 10.

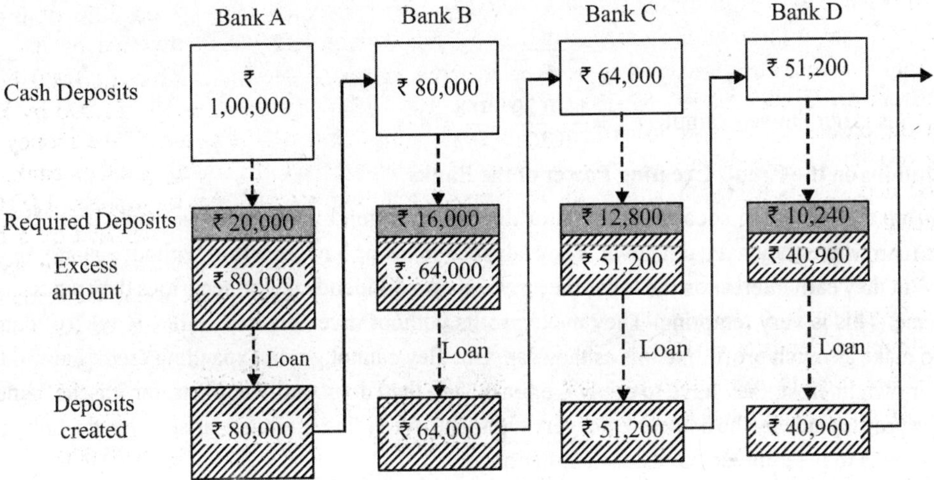

Fig. 18.1. *Credit Creation by Banks*

In this case initial deposits of some cash amount in the banking system will lead to ten times expansion in the total deposits. Figure 18.1 makes clear the process of deposits expansion by the banking system.

Deposit Multiplier and Credit Multiplier

Some economists distinguish between deposit multiplier and credit multiplier. In our above example, original or primary deposits of ₹ 100,000 made by the public in the banking system, given the cash reserve ratio (r) equal to 20 per cent (*i.e.* 0.20), resulted in the increase in total deposits in the banking system equal to ₹ 500,000. If we denote total increase in deposits by ΔD and original increase in cash deposits as ΔR, then the deposit multiplier can be written as

$$d_m = \frac{\Delta D}{\Delta R} \quad ...(i)$$

or, in our first example, $$d_m = \frac{\Delta D}{\Delta R} = \frac{1}{r} = \frac{1}{0.20} = 5 \qquad ...(i)$$

Now, in our above example the primary cash deposits of ₹ 100,000 led to the creation of deposits (*i.e.* increase in credit) equal to ₹ 4,00,000 by the banking system itself when making loans or creating credit for businessmen. The credit multiplier measures the extent by which the banking system creates credit as a result of new increase in primary deposits which they use as reserves. If we denote credit created by the banks as ΔC and the increase in primary deposits as cash with the banks as ΔR, then credit multiplier can be written as

$$C_m = \frac{\Delta C}{\Delta R} \qquad ...(ii)$$

Where C_m represents credit multiplier

Since $$\Delta C = \Delta D - \Delta R$$

$$C_m = \frac{\Delta D - \Delta R}{\Delta R} = \frac{\Delta D}{\Delta R} - \frac{\Delta R}{\Delta R} = \frac{\Delta D}{\Delta R} - 1$$

$$\frac{\Delta D}{\Delta R} = d_m$$

Therefore, $$C_m = d_m - 1$$

$$= \frac{1}{r} - 1$$

$$= \frac{1-r}{r} \qquad ...(iii)$$

Thus is our above example $C_m = \frac{1-0.20}{0.20} = \frac{0.8}{0.2} = 4$

Limitations on the Credit Creating Power of the Banks

From the foregoing account of credit or deposits creation by the banks, it would seem that the banks reap where they have not sown. They advance loans or buy securities without actually paying cash. But they earn interest on the loans they give or earn dividends on the securities they purchase all the same. This is very tempting. They make profits without investing cash. They would, of course, like to make as much profit like this as they can. But they cannot go on expanding credit indefinitely. In their own interest, they have to apply the brake, and they do actually apply it, for it is well-known that the profits made by the banks are not very high. The overriding limitation arises from the obligation of the banks to meet the demands of their depositors.

Benham has mentioned three limitations on the powers of the banks to create credit:

(*i*) The amount of cash in the country;

(*ii*) The amount of cash which the public wishes to hold; and

(*iii*) The minimum percentage of cash to deposits, called cash revenue ratio which the banks have to maintain.

(*iv*) The amount of money which the public wants to hold as deposits in the banks.

As for (*i*), it may be said that credit can be created on the basis of cash. *The larger the cash (i.e., legal tender money) the larger the amount of credit that can be created.* But the amount of cash that a bank may have is subject to the control of the central bank. The central bank has the monopoly of issue of cash. It may increase it or decrease it, and credit will expand or contract accordingly. The power of the central bank to control currency helps it to control the extent of credit that the banks have the power to create.

The second limitation arises from *the habit of the people regarding the use of cash i.e. currency.* If people are in the habit of using cash and not cheques, as in India, then as soon as credit is granted by the bank to a borrower, he will draw the cheque and get cash. When the bank's cash reserves is thus reduced, its power to create credit is correspondingly reduced. On the other hand. If people use cash only for very small and odd transactions, then the cash reserve of the banks is not much drawn upon and their power of creating credit remains unimpaired. This is the case in advanced countries like the U.S.A., England and other European countries. There the banks hardly keep 10 per cent cash reserve.

The third limitation is the most important. It arises from the *cash reserve ratio cash, which the banks must maintain* to ensure the safety of the bank and to retain the degree of liquidity that is considered desirable. It is clear that when a bank creates a credit or grants a loan, it undertakes a liability. There is an increase in its liabilities and there is correspondingly a fall in cash reserve ratio. The bank will not let the cash reserve ratio fall below a certain minimum. When that minimum is reached, the power of the bank to create credit comes to an end. To grant any further credit will be risky unless the bank's experience is reassuring enough to permit the adoption of a lower percentage. Then that would be the limit.

The other important limitation on the credit creating power of banks is *the amount of money which the public choose to hold as deposits in banks.* The more money which the public deposits with the banks, the more reserves banks would have and therefore more credit they will be able to create and vice versa. It may noted that public can use their saved money in more than one way. The public can buy shares or debenture of the companies, it can invest in mutual funds of both public and privates sectors. But the credit creation by the banks depends on the money the public deposits in them. It is important to note than rate of interest paid by the banks on deposits determines to a good extent the amount of money deposits with them by the public. Other things being equal, the higher the rate of interest, the greater the amount of money the public will deposit money with the banks.

To these may be added the fourth limitation. *The bank cannot create credit without acquiring some asset.* An asset is a form of wealth. Thus the bank only turns immobile wealth into mobile wealth. Hence, as Crowther observes, "the bank does not create money out of thin air, it transmutes other forms of wealth into money." However, banking system today has become quite advanced. These days banks give credit on the basis of personal goodwill rather than on the basis of any form of wealth.

QUESTIONS FOR REVIEW

1. Explain credit creation. Describe the factors which determine the volume of credit which can be created.
2. Explain the process of credit creation through the 'Balance Sheet Approach'. What factors limit credit creation ?
3. What are functions of a Commercial Bank
4. Explain the role of commercial bank in the economic development of India.
5. Explain the process of creation of credit by commercial banks. What are the limitation on the credit creating power of banks ?
6. Explain how commercial banks create credit. Are there any limit to credit creation by them? If cash deposits ratio changes from 0.1 to 0.2, will there be any change in the credit creating power of banks ?
7. Explain the functions of Commercial Banks. How is Commercial bank different from the Central Bank ?
   (*a*) Explain why commercial banks should be concerned about liquidity.
   (*b*) Is there a conflict between the profit motive of a bank and the need for liquidity ?
   (*c*) Which assets are a bank's principal sources of profitability

CHAPTER 19
Central Banking

In the monetary system of all countries, the central bank occupies an important place. The central bank is an apex institution of the monetary system which seeks to regulate the functioning of the commercial banks of a country. The central bank of India is called the Reverse Bank of India which was set up in 1935. As explained in the previous chapter, the commercial banks keep only a fraction of their deposits in cash and the rest they lend out to the traders and investors. Therefore, the commercial banking is often known as *fractional reserve system.* In view of the fact that commercial banks keep only a fraction of their deposits in cash, they will run into difficulties if at a time there is rush of depositors to withdraw their money. This indicates the need for an institution which should come to the rescue of the commercial banks and provide them the money required to meet the excessive demand of the depositors. The central bank fulfills this need. However, in the modern times, the central bank not only provides monetary aid to the commercial banks in time of crisis but performs many other functions. Indeed, the control over cost and availability of credit in the economy and regulation of the growth of money supply are special responsibilities of the central bank .

The Principles of Central Banking

The central bank of a country enjoys a special status in the banking structure of the country. The principles on which a central bank is run differ from the ordinary banking principles. An ordinary bank is run for profits. A central bank, on the other hand, is primarily meant to promote the financial and economic stability of the country. "The guiding principle of a central bank", says DeKock, "is that it should act only in the public interest and for and welfare of the country and without regard to profit as primary consideration". Earning of profit for a central bank is thus a secondary consideration.

The central bank is thus not a profit hunting institution. It does not act as rival of other banks. In fact, it is a monetary authority of the country and has to function in a manner so as to promote economic stability and development. The functions of the central bank especially the Reserve Bank of India have increased enormously in recent years. Not only does the Reserve Bank of India regulate credit and money supply in the country but it promotes economic development and price stability. Guiding principles of the Reserve Bank are to operate its most instruments in a way that serves the objectives of economic policy laid down by the Government and Planning Commission.

FUNCTIONS OF CENTRAL BANK

The following are the main functions of a central bank :

1. It acts as a note issuing agency.
2. It acts as the banker to the state.
3. It acts as the banker's bank.
4. It controls credit.
5. It acts as the lender of the last resort.
6. It manages exchange rate.

Note Issuing Agency

The central bank of the country has the monopoly of issuing notes or paper currency to the public. Therefore, the central bank of the country exercises control over the supply of currency in the country. In India with the exception of one rupee notes which are issued by the Ministry of Finance of the Government of India, the entire note issue is done by the Reserve Bank of India. In the past the central bank of various countries used to keep as reserves some gold and foreign exchange securities against the notes issued. The percentage of the reserves to be kept against the total amount of notes issued was fixed by law and is subject to change by the Government. Theoretically, there is no need of the backing of gold reserves against the notes issued. It may be pointed out that paper notes these days cannot be converted into gold or some other precious metals; they are inconvertible. This is called *proportional reserve system.* Before 1956 in India also, there was proportional reserve system of issuing currency or notes. According to this, the Reserve Bank was required to keep as reserves 40 per cent of the total notes issued in the form of gold and foreign exchange securities. Since 1956 this system has been given up and instead *minimum reserve system* has been adopted according to which the Reserve Bank is required to keep only a *minimum amount of reserves* in the form of gold and foreign exchange securities and given this minimum reserve it can issue notes as much as it thinks desirable in view of the needs and conditions of the economy. There is even no need for backing of gold for the currency issued by the Government or the central bank. From the economic point of view what matters is the production of real goods and services and not the amount of gold supporting a currency. The real value of a currency depends on how much it can buy goods and services and not how much gold or silver is kept as reserve against it.

Thus, ultimately the credibility of the currency of a country depends not upon whether it is convertible into gold or silver but upon to what extent it is possible to maintain the stability of its value by suitable monetary control.

Banker to the Government

Another important function of the central bank is to act as the banker to the Government. All the balances of the Government are kept with the central bank. On these balances the central bank pays no interest. The central bank receives and makes all payments on behalf of the Government. Further, the central bank has to manage the public debt and also to arrange for the issue of new loans on behalf of the Government. The central bank also provides short-term loans to the Government. This is usually done through the central bank discounting the Government treasury bills either directly or when presented by other banks. Thus the central bank performs a number of services to the Government. In fact, the central bank is the fiscal agent of the Government and advises the latter in matters relating to currency and exchange as well as finance.

Bakers' Bank

Broadly speaking, the central bank acts as a bankers' bank in three capacities: (*i*) as the custodian of the cash reserves of the commercial banks; (*ii*) as the lender of the last resort; and (*iii*) as bank of central clearance, settlement and transfers. All other banks in the country are found by law to keep a fixed portion of their total deposits as reserves with the central bank. These reserves help the central bank to control the issue of credit by commercial banks. They in return can depend upon the central bank for support at the time of emergency. This help may be in the form of a loan on the strength of approved securities or through rediscounting of bills of exchange. Thus the central bank is the lender of the last resort for other banks in difficult times because on such occasions there is no hope of getting help from any competing institution.

In India, scheduled banks have to keep deposits with the Reserve Bank not less than 5% of their current demand deposits and 2% of their fixed deposits as reserves. In return they enjoy the privilege of rediscounting their bills with the Reserve Bank as well as securing loans against approved securities when in need.

Clearing function is also performed by the central bank for the banks. Since banks keep cash reserves with the central bank, settlement between them may be easily effected by means of debts and credits in the books of the central bank. If clearing go heavily against some bank, its cash reserves with the central bank will fall below the prescribed limit and therefore the bank concerned will have to make up the deficiency.

Control of Credit

The chief objective of the central bank is to maintain price and economic stability. Price instability—both inflation and deflation—has harmful effects. Moreover, fluctuations in overall economic activity, that is, trade cycles entail a lot of human sufferings. Main reason for the fluctuations in prices as well as in overall economic activity is the changes in aggregate demand. Aggregate demand, especially the investment demand, depends upon the supply of money. And credit these days is the important constituent of the money supply. Thus the supply of credit greatly affects the prices, national income and employment through changes in investment demand.

Now it is the responsibility of the central bank of a country to guide the money market, *i.e.*, the commercial banks regarding supply of credit so as to maintain stability in prices as well as in overall economic activity. To overcome inflation it has to restrict the supply of credit and to prevent or get rid of depression and deflation it has to expand the credit. There are various methods by which the central bank can control the supply of credit in the economy. These methods are: (*a*) varying the bank rate; (b) engaging in open market operations; and (*c*) changing the reserve ratio, and (*d*) exercising selective credit controls. We shall explain these methods of credit in detail in later sections of this chapter.

It is through controlling the supply of credit and cost of credit (*i.e.*, rate of interest on it) that the central bank of a country tries to bring about stability in prices as well as in overall level of economic activity. The central bank is the monetary authority of the country and monetary policy is one of the important measures which are taken to avoid and cure both depression and inflation. To remedy inflation central bank tries to restrict the supply of credit by raising the bank rate and using other weapons of credit control. To overcome depression it tries to expand credit by lowering the bank rate and cash reserve ratio and also by buying securities from the open market.

In India Reserve Bank which is the central bank of the country has been making important contribution to the achievement of the objective of price stability. To achieve price stability Reserve Bank has been setting forgets of expansion in money supply which are consistent with the growth of output. Control of inflation by checking excessive expansion in credit supply has been the major concern of monetary policy imposed by Reserve Bank of India.

Lender of the Last Resort

As mentioned above, the commercial banks operate on the basis of fractional reserve system. Therefore, even a well-managed commercial bank can run into difficulty if there is a great rush of demand for cash by the depositors, because with a fraction of its deposits in cash, it will not be able to meet a sudden and large demand for cash. The central bank must therefore come to their rescue at such times. Thus, central bank is the last source of supply of credit. It is the duty of the central bank to meet demand for cash by a bank at the time of emergency when panic prevails among the public and people's confidence has been shaken and when other banks have refused to supply credit. The central bank boldly steps forward to supply cash and allay panic. The central bank must meet situation of high liquidity preference.

To Promote Economic Development

A very important function of central bank these days in developing countries like India is to promote economic development. It can help in both agricultural and industrial development in the country. The central bank can promote agricultural and industrial growth by providing finance or credit to agriculture and industry. Central bank adopts such a monetary policy as is conducive to economic growth. In order to accelerate the rate of investment or capital formation, the central bank takes steps to make more credit available for investment at lower lending rates of interest. In the developing countries, the role of central bank as promoter of economic development is very important.

Thus, in India apart from regulatory function, Reserve Bank of India has been playing a promotional role. RBI has been making important contribution for building up appropriate financial institutions such as Industrial Finance Corporation of India, State Finance Corporations to promote saving and investment. By ensuring adequate supply of agricultural credit, term finance to industries, credit for exports, RBI has performed a useful promotional role in encouraging economic growth.

Managing Exchange Rate of the National Currency

An important function of a central bank is to maintain the exchange rate of the national currency. For example, the Reserve Bank of India has the responsibility of maintaining the exchange value of the rupee. When a country has adopted flexible exchange rate system under which value of a currency is determined by demand for and supply of a currency, the value of a currency, that is, its exchange rate with other currencies is subject to large fluctuations which are harmful for the economy. Under these circumstances, it is the duty the central bank to prevent undue depreciation or appreciation of the national currency. Since 1991 when the rupee has been floated, the value of Indian rupee, that is, its exchange rate with US dollar and other foreign currencies has been left to be determined by market forces, RBI has been taking several steps from time to time to stabilise the exchange rate of rupee, especially in terms of US dollar.

There are several ways by which RBI can manage or maintain the exchange rate of the rupee. First, if due to speculative activities of foreign exchange operators, the rupee starts depreciating fastly, RBI can intervene in the market. It can use its reserves of dollars and supply dollars in the market from its own reserves. With the increase in supply of dollars, the rupee will be prevented from depreciation. It may however be noted that the success of this step depends on the amounts of dollar reserves with Reserve Bank of India. This is illustrated in Fig. 15.1 where we have depicted demand and supply curves of US dollars which intersect at point E and determine exchange value of rupee equal to Rs. 43 per U.S. dollar. Now suppose that demand for dollars by Indian traders, companies and market operators increases so that demand curve for dollar shifts to the right to $D'D'$ position. It will be seen that the intersection of this new demand curve for the US dollars $D'D'$ intersects the supply curve SS of dollars at point H and determine the exchange rate of rupee for the US dollars equal to Rs. 44 per dollar. Thus with increase in demand for dollars

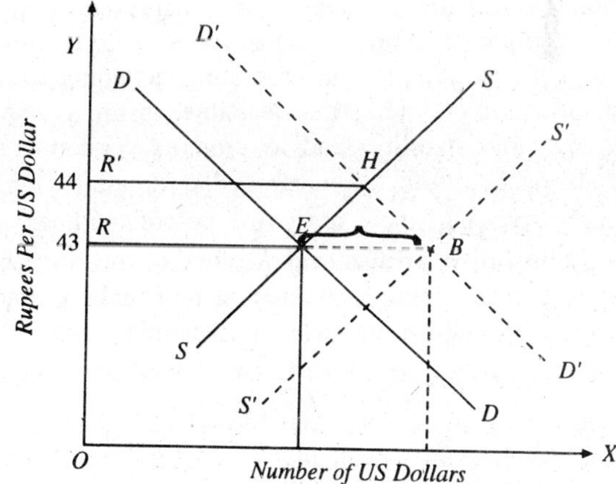

Fig. 15.1. *Intervention by Central Bank to Maintain Exchange Rate*

rupee has depreciated (and the US dollar appreciated). Now, if RBI intervenes and from its foreign exchange reserves, it supplies extra dollars equal to *EB*, the supply curve of dollars will shift to the right to the position *S′S′* which intersects the higher demand curve *D′D′* of dollars at point *B* so that again Rs. 43 becomes the equilibrium exchange rate of rupees for the US dollar. In this way by its intervention and supplying extra dollars from its foreign exchange reserves, RBI can succeed in maintaining the exchange rate of rupee at Rs. 43 per dollar. In actual practice in January 1996 and again in Aug.-Sept. 1998, when rupee was depreciating RBI intervened and succeeded in preventing the fast depreciating rupee against US dollar.

Another method by which RBI can manage the exchange rate of rupee is adopting measures which will reduce the demand for dollars. Some importers, foreign investors, foreign exchange operators try to avail of cheap credit facilities of banks and borrow rupee funds from the banks and try to convert them into dollars. This raises the demand for dollars and leads to the depreciation of the Indian rupee. Such a situation occurred in July-September 1998. RBI intervened and raised the Cash Reserve Ratio (CRR) and increased its repurchase rates. This succeeded in mopping up the excess liquidity with the banks and reduced their lending capacity. This led to the reduction in the demand for dollars and helped in preventing the rupee from depreciating.

On the contrary, if rupee is appreciating against the US dollar and it is thought desirable to check undue appreciation of the Indian rupee, RBI can interveue to check its further appreciation. For this purpose, it can buy dollars from the market. This will raise the demand for dollars in the foreign exchange market and appreciation of Indian rupee will be checked

METHODS OF CREDIT CONTROL

The central bank of a country has the responsibility of controlling the volume and direction of credit in the country. Bank credit has become these days an important constituent of the money supply in the country. The volume and direction of bank credit has, therefore, an important bearing on the level of economic activity. Excessive credit will tend to generate inflationary pressures in the economy, while deficiency of credit supply may tend to cause depression or deflation. Lack of the availability of cheap credit may also hinder economic development of a country. At times of depression, there is a need to expand credit and at times of booms there is need to contract credit. For promoting economic development, expansion of cheap credit (credit at low rates of interest) is desirable. In order to prevent booms and depressions (*i.e.*, to maintain economic stability) and to promote economic growth, central bank seeks to control credit in accordance with the needs of the situation.

Broadly speaking, there are two types of methods of controlling credit.

(1) **Quantitative or General Methods.** These methods seek to change the total quantity of credit in general. These are three in number: (*i*) changing the bank rate; (*ii*) open market operations; (*iii*) changing the cash reserve ratio.

(2) **Qualitative or Selective Control Methods.** These methods aim at changing the volume of a specific type of credit. In other words, the selective control method affect the use of credit for particular purposes.

We discuss below these methods in detail.

Bank Rate Policy

Bank rate is the minimum rate at which the central bank of a country provides loans to the commercial bank of the country. Bank rate is also called discount rate because in the earlier days central bank used to provide finance to the commercial banks by rediscounting bills of exchange. Through changes in the bank rate, the central bank can influence the creation of credit by the commercial banks. Bank credit these days is an important component of the supply of money in the economy. Changes in money supply affect aggregate demand and thereby output and prices. For instance, when the central bank raises the bank rate, the cost of borrowings by the commercial banks from the central bank would rise. This would discourage the commercial banks to borrow from the central bank. Further, when the bank rate is raised, the commercial banks also raise their lending rates. When the lending rates of interest charged by the commercial banks are higher, businessmen and industrialists would feel discouraged to borrow from commercial banks. This would tend to contract bank credit and hence would result in the reduction of money supply in the economy. The reduction in the supply of money would reduce aggregate demand or money expenditure. This would reduce prices and check inflation in the economy. Thus when the economy is gripped by inflation or rising prices, the bank rate is generally raised to contract credit creation by the banks.

On the other hand, when there is recession or depression in the economy, the bank rate is lowered to overcome it. A fall in the bank rate will cause the reduction in lending interest rates of the commercial banks. With credit or loans from banks becoming cheaper, businessmen would borrow more from the commercial banks for investment and other purposes. This would lead to the increase in aggregate demand for goods and services and help in overcoming recession and bringing about recovery of the economy.

If a country permits the free flow of funds in and out of the country, then the changes in the bank rate will also have an effect on the external flows. For instance, as said above, when the bank rate is raised all interest rates in the market would also generally rise. With the rise in the deposit rates of interest of the banks, funds from outside would be attracted to the banks of the country. Further, with the rise in deposit rates, outflow of funds from the banks to the other countries would be prevented. Therefore, these effects on the inflow and outflow of funds of the rise in bank rate will have a favourable effect on the balance of payments of the country.

It is important to note that the *changes in bank rate affect the credit creation by banks through altering the cost of credit.* Changes in the cost of credit affect borrowings by the commercial banks from the central bank and also affect the demand for credit by businessmen from the commercial banks.

Limitations of Bank Rate Policy

Bank rate policy does not have always the desired effect on investment, output and prices. There are certain conditions which must be met for the successful working of the bank rate policy. These conditions are:

(1) All other rates should follow the bank rate in its movement so that bank credit should expand or contract as desired. This will not happen if the commercial banks have considerable reserves of their own at their disposal and, therefore, their dependence on borrowed funds from the central bank may be very less. Further, for the changes in the bank rate to cause changes in all other interest rates in the market, a well-organised money market is needed. If well-organised money market does not exist as is the case in India where indigenous bankers contribute a good part of the money market, changes in the bank rate would not be followed by the appropriate changes in all rates.

(2) The second important condition for the successful working of the bank rate policy is the responsiveness of businessmen to the changes in the lending rates of interest. If businessmen and investors reduce their borrowings when the bank rate and hence the lending rates of commercial bank are raised, and increase their borrowings for investment when the bank rate and lending rates of the banks are reduced, the changes in the bank rate will have the effect, predicted in the bank rate theory. However, empirical studies conducted recently have shown that rate of interest does not exercise a strong influence on borrowings for investment and other purposes. When there is inflationary situation in the economy, the rate of interest will have to be raised very high in order to have desirable effects. Similarly, the response of investment to the fall in the rate of interest is never vigorous. Demand by businessmen for loans for investment purposes from the banks depends on the economic situation prevailing in the economy. When the economy

is gripped by severe depression and consequently prospects for making profits are bleak, businessmen would be reluctant to borrow for investment even though the lending rates of interest have been lowered considerably to induce them to borrow. It has been aptly remarked that 'you can bring the horse to water but you cannot make it drink'.

The present belief is that bank rate policy will play only a subsidiary role in the monetary control. The bank rate at the best could check a boom and inflation but could not bring about a recovery if the country was suffering from recession or depression. Thus it has much greater potential effectiveness if it is desired to arrest credit expansion than when it is sought to stimulate credit. But used in conjunction with other methods it can still play an useful role. The bank rate has the value as a signal. If the traditions are that a signal must be obeyed, the bank rate policy can fulfil its purpose since it will be in keeping with respectable conduct.

Open Market Operations

Open market operations are another important instrument of credit control, especially in the developed countries. The term open market operations means the purchase and sale of securities by the central bank of the country. The theory of open market operations is like this: The sale of securities by the central bank leads to the contraction of credit and the purchase thereof to credit expansion. When the central bank sells securities in the open market, it receives payment in the form of a cheque on one of commercial banks. If the purchaser is a bank, the cheque is drawn against the purchasing bank. In both cases the result is the same. The cash balance of the bank in question, which it keeps with the central bank, is to that extent reduced. With the reduction of its cash, the commercial bank has to reduce its lending. Thus, credit contracts. When the central bank purchases securities, it pays through cheques drawn on itself. This increases the cash balance of the commercial banks and enables them to expand credit. "Take care of the legal tender money and credit will take care of itself" is the maxim.

The open market operations method is sometimes adopted to make the bank rate policy effective. If the member-banks do not raise lending rates following the rise in the bank rate due to surplus funds available with them, the central bank can withdraw such surplus funds by the sale of securities and thus compel the member-banks to raise their rates. Scarcity of funds in the market compels the banks directly or inidirectly to borrow from the central bank through rediscounting of bills. If the bank rate is high, the market rate of interest cannot remain low.

Limitations of the Open Market Operations. It is obvious that this method will succeed only if certain conditions are satisfied. The limitations are discussed below:

(1) According to the theory of open market operations, when the central bank purchases securities, the cash reserves of the member-banks will be increased and, conversely, the cash reserves will be decreased when the central bank sells securities. This, however, may not happen. The sale of securities may be offset by return of notes from circulation and hoards. The purchase of securities, on the other hand, may be accompanied by a withdrawal of notes for increased currency requirements or for hoarding. In both the cases, therefore, the cash reserves of the member-banks may remain unaffected.

(2) But even if the cash reserves of the member-banks are increased or decreased, the banks may not expand or contract credit accordingly. The percentage of cash to credit is not rigidly fixed and can vary within quite wide limits. The banks will expand and contract credit according to the prevailing economic and political circumstances and not merely with reference to their cash reserves.

(3) The third condition is that when the commercial bank's cash balances increase, the demand for loans and advances should increase too and vice versa. This may not happen. Owing to economic or political uncertainty, even cheap money rate may not attract borrowers. Conversely when trade is good and prospects of profits bright, entrepreneurs would borrow even at high rates of interest.

(4) Finally, the circulation of bank credit should have a constant velocity. But the velocity of bank deposits is rarely constant. It increases in periods of rising business activity and decreases in periods of depression. Thus, a policy of contracting credit may be neutralised by increased velocity of circulation, and vice versa.

Open market operations as an instrument of credit control have proved to be quiet successful in regulating the availability of credit in developed countries. This is for two reasons. First, when the central bank purchases or buys securities, the reserves of the commercial banks automatically expand or contract. The changes in the reserves of the banks directly affect their capacity to lend. Unlike in the case of instrument of bank rate, the success of the market operations does not depend on the attitude or responsiveness of the commercial banks; their capacity to provide credit is affected automatically. Secondly, the open market operations can be managed in a way that the cash reserves of the banks increase or decrease to the desired extent.

Since for the success of market operations it is necessary that there should be broad and active market in short and long-term government securities, and such markets exist only in the U.S.A. and Great Britain and other developed countries, this method of credit control has been most effectively used in these countries.

Open market operations which did not play a significant role as an instrument of credit control in India has now become important and are being used extensively by RBI.This is because market for Government securities in India has now become quite wide and there is excess liquidity in the banking system. General public do not buy more than a fraction of government securities. Besides in view of the excess liquidity in the banking system, banks are willingly investing in Government securities more than the statutary limits.

Changing the Cash Reserve Ratio (CRR)

Another method to vary the quantity of credit is to change the cash reserve ratio. By law, banks have to keep a certain amount of cash money with themselves as reserves against the deposits. If the legal minimum cash reserve ratio, for example, is 20%, the bank will have to keep Rs. 4,000 as reserves against the deposits of Rs. 20,000. Now the central bank of a country has the authority to vary the cash reserve ratio. If now the central bank increases the cash reserve ratio from 20% to 25%, then the reserves of Rs. 4,000 could support only deposits of Rs. 16,000 and therefore the banks having reserves of Rs. 4,000 will have to reduce their deposits form Rs. 20,000 to Rs. 16,000. That means the contraction of credit.

On the other hand, if the central bank reduces the cash reserve ratio from 20% to 10% then the reserves of Rs. 4,000 could support the deposit of Rs. 40,000. Therefore the banks having reserves of Rs. 4,000 can increase their deposits, *i.e.*, expand credit to Rs. 40,000. To sum up, increase in the legal cash reserve ratio leads to the contraction of credit and decrease in the legal reserve ratio leads to the expansion of credit. An increase in the legal cash reserve ratio will succeed in contracting credit only when banks have to excess reserves. If banks are holding excess reserves, the increase in the legal reserve ratio will not bring about the contraction of credit. On the other hand, the reduction in the cash reserve ratio will have the desired effect of expanding credit only if the borrowers respond favourably. As a result of decrease in the cash reserve ratio, the availability to lend of the banks increases and the banks tend to make more credit available to borrowers, or to make it available at lower rates. Now, if the borrowers for one reason or another do not respond favourably, *i.e.*, are not prepared to borrow, credit will not be expanded.

SELECTIVE CREDIT CONTROLS

The methods of credit control described above are known as quantitative or general methods as they are meant to control the availability of credit in general. Thus, bank rate policy, open market operations and variations in cash reserves ratio expand or contract the availability of credit for all purposes. On the other hand, selective credit controls are meant to regulate the flow of credit for particular or specific purposes. Whereas, the general credit controls seek to regulate the total available quantity of credit (through changes in the high powered money) and the cost of credit, the selective credit control seek to change the distribution or allocation of credit between its various uses. The selective credit controls have both the positive and negative aspects. In its positive aspect, measures are taken to stimulate the greater flow of credit to some particular sectors considered as important. Thus in India, agriculture, small and marginal farmers, small artisans, small-scale industries are the priority sectors to which greater flow of bank credit has been sought to be encouraged by the Reserve Bank of India. In its negative aspect, several measures are taken to restrict the credit flowing into some specific activities or sectors which are regarded as undesirable or harmful from the social point of view. The selective credit controls generally used are:

(1) Changes in the minimum margin for lending by banks against the stocks of specific goods kept or against other types of securities.
(2) The fixation of maximum limit or ceiling on advances to individual borrowers against stocks of particular sensitive commodities.
(3) The fixation of minimum discriminatory rates of interest chargeable on credit for particular purposes.
(4) Prohibition of the discounting of bills of exchange involving sale of sensitive commodities.

The selective credit controls originated in U.S.A. to regulate the flow of bank credit to the stock market (*i.e.*, the market for shares). They were also used to restrict the volume of credit available for purchasing durable consumer goods during the period of the Second War. However, in India, the selective credit controls are being used by the Reserve Bank to prevent speculative hoarding of commodities so as to check the rise in prices of these commodities. The selective credit controls in India are being used in the case of foodgrains, oilseeds, vegetable oils, cotton, sugar, gur and khandsari.

Though, all the above techniques of selective credit control are used, in India it is the first technique, namely, the changes in the minimum margin against stocks of commodities or other securities that has been mostly used. It may be noted that the central bank of a country has the power to vary the minimum margin requirements against the security of stocks of commodities. While lending advances to businessmen, the commercial banks leave a margin of the value of stock kept as security to be financed by the businessmen from their own sources and lend funds to them equal to the remaining amount of the value of the stock. This minimum requirement of the value of the stock left to be financed by the borrowers themselves is known as margin. Suppose the margin fixed for a stock of particular commodity is 60 per cent. In this case the businessmen can borrow up to the value of 40 per cent of the stock of that commodity while the 60 per cent of the value of stock will be financed by the businessmen themselves. Now, if the bank raises the margin to 70 per cent, then businessmen can borrow from the bank to the extent of 30 per cent of the value of the stock of that commodity. This will lead to the contraction of credit for holding the stock of the commodity by the businessmen. If the businessmen are not able to finance the holding of 10 per cent extra stock of the commodity, they will be forced to sell that in the market and thus raising market supply of the commodity. This will lower the prices of the commodity, other things remaining the same.

In developed countries, the selective credit controls are generally used to prevent excessive speculation in share market. In the share market, the buyers purchase a good amount of shares by making a small payment and the remaining value of shares are paid by brokers through borrowing from the banks against the shares thus purchased. When the central bank raises the margin, the buyers of shares have to pay a larger sum of money for the shares purchased and as a result bank credit contracts and the speculative activity in the stock market is discouraged.

Conditions Necessary for Success of Selective Credit Controls

Some conditions are necessary for the successful operations of selective credit controls of commodities. However, the clever businessmen can obtain credit from the banks by offering other securities and use the funds so obtained to finance the speculative holdings of the stocks of sensitive commodities. Therefore, if the selective credit controls are to succeed in preventing the rise in prices of sensitive commodities, they have to be accompanied by general credit controls aimed at reducing the capacity of banks to lend money. It also follows from above that end-use or purpose of all credit ought to be taken into account by the banks and credit advanced accordingly if selective credit controls are to be effective.

In India the selective credit controls have been in operation since 1956 to check the rise in prices of sensitive commodities. However, the success of selective credit controls in achieving its objective of restraining the rise in commodity prices depends upon certain conditions explained below:

1. The Use of Quantitative Credit Controls. Selective Credit Controls are effective only when they are accompanied by the general quantitative credit controls such as variation in bank rate and cash reserve ratio. This is because the selective credit controls operate through regulating credit against particular securities or stocks.

2. The Availability of Non-Bank Finance. The success of the selective credit control also depends upon the exent to which the funds from non-bank sources (*i.e.*, from their own funds and also from the unregulated credit market) is available to the businessmen. When the bank credit for a particular purpose is reduced, the businessmen can use their own funds or borrow from non-regulated markets to indulge in speculative holding of inventories. In India today the businessmen have large quantities of black money with them which they generally use for speculative holding of inventories of sensitive commodities and in this way succeed in defeating the purpose of selective credit controls.

Moral Suasion

Central bank sometimes makes use of moral suasion to affect the credit policies of the commercial banks. Moral suasion means the employment by the central bank of policy statements, public announcements, or outright appeals and advices that excessive expansion or contraction of bank credit may lead to evil consequences. Banks often regard the central bank as their leader and guide, and generally act in accordance with wishes and advice of the central bank .

QUESTIONS FOR REVIEW

1. What are the main functions of a Central Bank ? How does a Central Bank control the *direction of credit.*
2. How are the main functions of a Central Bank diffrent from the functions of a commercial bank.
3. Explain the quantitative methods of credit control. Do you think these methods are adequate for effective control of credit supply ?
4. How fare are the quantiative methods of credit control effective in developing countries like India.
5. Discuss the functions of a Central Bank between bank rate and open market operations which is more effective as an instrument of credit control.
6. Explain the various methods of selective credit control. Explain their significance in an economy like India.
7. Explain the qualitative methods of Credit Control adopted by a Central Bank. Which of the methods – quantitative or qualitative – is better for India.?
8. Explain how Reserve Bank India tries to maintain exchange rate of rupee. Illustrate digrammatically.

CHAPTER 19A

Monetary Policy of Reserve Bank in India

Introduction

Monetary policy is concerned with the measures taken to regulate the supply of money, the cost and availability of credit in the economy. Further, it also deals with the distribution of credit between uses and users and also with both the lending and borrowing rates of interest of the banks. In developed countries the monetary policy has been usefully used for overcoming depression and inflation as an anti-cyclical policy. However, in developing countries it has to play a significant role in promoting economic growth. As Prof. R. Prebisch writes, "The time has come to formulate a monetary policy which meets the requirements of economic development, which fits into its framework perfectly." Further, along with encouraging economic growth, the monetary policy has also to ensure price stability, because the excessive inflation not only has adverse distribution effect but hinders economic development also.

It is important to understand the distinction between *objectives* or *goals*, *targets* and *instruments* of monetary policy. Whereas goals of monetary policy refer to its objectives which, as mentioned above, may be price stability, full employment or economic growth, *targets refer to the variables such as supply of money or bank credit, interest rates which are sought to be changed through the instruments of monetary policy so as to attain these objectives*. The various instruments of monetary policy are changes in the supply of currency, variations in bank rates and other interest rates, open market operations, selective credit controls, and variations in reserve requirements. We have explained these instruments in detail in a previous chapter. We shall first explain below the objectives or goals of monetary policy in a developing economy with special reference to those adopted by Reserve Bank of India. After having explained the objectives we shall explain role of monetary policy in promoting economic growth in a developing country like India. In the end we will explain monetary policy of reserve Bank of India in different periods of planned development, especially soft-interest and liberal credit policy adopted by Reserve Bank of India since 1996.

OBJECTIVES OF MONETARY POLICY

Before explaining in detail the monetary measures undertaken by RBI to regulate credit and growth of money supply, it is important to explain the objectives of monetary policy pursued by RBI in formulation of its policy. Since monetary policy is one instrument of economic policy, its objectives cannot be different from those of overall economic policy. The three important objectives of monetary policy are:

1. ensuring *price stability,* that is, containing inflation.
2. to encourage *economic growth.*
3. to ensure *stability of exchange rate of the rupee,* that is, exchange rate of rupee with the US dollar, pound sterling and other foreign currencies.

Let us explain below these objectives in some detail.

Price Stability or Control of Inflation

It may be noted that each instrument of economic policy is better suited to achieve a particular objective. Monetary policy is better suited to the achievement of price stability, that is, containing inflation. To quote C. Rangarajan, a former Governor of Reserve Bank of India, "Faced with multiple objectives that are equally relevant and desirable, there is always the problem of assigning to each instrument the most appropriate target or objective. Of the various objectives, *price stability is perhaps the one that can be pursued most effectively by monetary policy.* In a developing country like ours, acceleration of investment activity in the context of supply shocks in the agricultural sector tends to be accompanied by pressures on prices and, therefore, monetary policy has much to contribute in the short-run management."[1]

Thus, achieving price stability has remained the dominant objective of monetary policy of Reserve Bank of India. It may however be noted that price stability does not mean absolutely no change in price at all. In a developing economy like ours where structural changes take place during the process of economic growth some changes in relative prices do occur that generally put upward pressure on prices. Therefore, some changes in price level or, in other words, a certain rate of inflation is inevitable in a developing economy. Thus, *price stability means reasonable rate of inflation.* A high degree of inflation has adverse effects on the economy. First, *inflation raises the cost of living of the people and hurts the poor* most. Therefore, inflation has been described as enemy No. 1 of the poor. Inflation sends many people below the poverty line. Secondly, *inflation makes exports costlier and, therefore, discourages them*. On the other hand, due to higher prices at home people are induced to import goods to a large extent. Thus, inflation has an adverse effect on the balance of payments. Thirdly, when due to a higher rate of inflation *value of money is rapidly falling, people do not have much incentives to save*. This lowers the rate of saving on which investment and economic growth depend. Fourthly, a high rate of inflation *encourages people to invest in the unproductive assets* such as gold, jewellery, real estate etc.

An expert committee on monetary reforms headed by Late Prof. S. Chakravarty suggested 4 per cent rate of inflation as a reasonable rate of inflation and recommended that monetary policy by RBI should be so formulated that ensures that rate of inflation does not exceed 4 per cent per annum. Emphasising the importance of price stability from the viewpoint of India's balance of payments, Prof. Rangarajan writes, "*The increasing openness of the economy, the need to service external debt and the necessity to improve the share of our exports in a highly competitive external environment require that the domestic price level not be allowed to rise unduly, particularly since our major trading partners have had notable success in recent years in achieving price stability.*[2]

Economic Growth

Promoting economic growth is another important objective of the monetary policy. In the past Reserve Bank has often been criticised that it pursued the objective of controlling inflation and achieving price stability and neglected the objective of promoting economic growth. Monetary policy can promote economic growth through ensuring adequate availability of credit and lower cost of credit. There are two types of credit requirements of businesses. First, they have to finance their requirements of working capital and for importing needed raw materials and machines from abroad. Secondly, they need credit for financing investment in projects for building fixed capital. Easy availability of credit at low interest rate stimulates investment and thereby quickens economic growth.

However, during the periods of high inflation, Reserve Bank followed a tight monetary policy under which Cash Reserve Ratio (CRR) and Statutory Liquidity Ratio (SLR) were raised to restrict

1. C. Rangarajan, "*Issues in Monetary Management*" printed in *Indian Economy* : Essays on Money and Finance, 1998, p. 6.
2. *Op. cit.*, p. 7.

the availability of credit for private sector. Besides, by raising bank rate and repo rate at which banks borrow from Reserve Bank of India lending rates of interest of banks were kept at high levels which discouraged private investment. This tight monetary policy worked against promoting growth. However, in the opinion of Prof. Rangarajan, *there is no conflict between the objectives of price stability and growth.* Price stability, according to him, is a means to ensure economic growth. To quote him, "*It is price stability which provides the appropriate environment under which growth can occur and social justice can be ensured.*" However, in our opinion, this may be true in the long run but in the short run there exists *trade off between growth and inflation.* To ensure higher economic growth the adequate expansion of money supply and greater availability of credit at a lower rate of interest is needed. But large expansion in money supply and bank credit leads to the increase in aggregate demand which tends to cause a higher rate of inflation. This raises the issue of what is *acceptable trade off between growth and inflation, that is, what rate of inflation is acceptable to promote growth through appropriate monetary policy.*

Expert Committee on monetary policy headed by Late Prof. Chakravarty suggested a target of 4 per cent as "the acceptable rise in prices". According to it, the growth of money supply and availability of credit should be so regulated that rate of inflation does not exceed 4 per cent per annum. However, C. Rangarajan, former Governor of Reserve Bank, fixed a higher target, namely, 5 to 6 per cent rate of inflation in the context of objective of achieving 6 to 7 per cent rate of economic growth. To quote him, "keeping the price and growth objectives in view the money supply growth should be so regulated that inflation rate comes down, eventually to 5 to 6 per cent. That indeed must be the goal of monetary policy."[3]

It may be noted that in the context of the openness of the economy and floating exchange rate system, as is the case of the Indian economy today, the objective of achieving higher rate of economic growth through monetary measures may also conflict with objective of exchange rate stability, that is, value of rupee in terms of the US dollar and other foreign currencies. Whereas prevention of the depreciation of rupee requires tightening of monetary policy, that is raising of interest rate, reducing liquidity of the banking system so that banks restrict their credit supply, the promotion of growth objective requires lower lending rates of interest and greater availability of credit for encouraging private investment. It is this dilemma of conflicting objectives of supporting higher economic growth or achieving price stability through control of inflation by RBI which is being presently faced in India (2012-13).

Exchange Rate Stability

Until 1991, India followed fixed exchange rate system and only occasionally devalued the rupee with the permission of IMF. The policies of floating exchange rate and increasing openness and globalisation of the Indian economy, adopted since 1991, have made the exchange rate of rupee quite volatile. The changes in capital inflows and capital outflows and changes in demand for and supply of foreign exchange, particularly US dollar, arising from the imports and exports cause great fluctuations in the foreign exchange rate of rupee. In order to prevent large depreciation and appreciation of foreign exchange rate Reserve Bank has to take suitable monetary measures to ensure foreign exchange rate stability. Owing to the fixed exchange rate system prior to 1991 the concern about foreign exchange rate had not played a significant role in the formulation of monetary policy.

Today, the exchange rate of rupee is determined by demand for and supply of foreign exchange (say, US dollar). When there is mismatch between demand for and supply of foreign exchange, external value of rupee changes. For instance, from August 2011 to December 2011 depreciation

3. C. Rangarajan, "*The Changing Context of Monetary Policy*". Address at 31st Convocation of the Indian Statistical Institute, March 31, 1997.

of rupee as against US dollar had been caused by the increase in demand for dollars from (1) the corporate sector for financing their imports, (2) Foreign Institutional Investors (FII) who wanted to take out their dollars from India (*i.e.,* capital outflow) to the US risen and (3) increase in demand for US dollar by the Indian banks on the instructions of the public sector undertakings for financing necessary imports from abroad. Since export earnings and capital inflows which determine the supply of dollars had not risen adequately, mismatch between dollars and supply of dollars had arisen causing the depreciation of rupee as against the US dollar.

Thus when there is large current account deficit (CAD) that exceeds comfortable level (which in Indian situation is estimated at 2.5 per cent of GDP as it can be financed by normal capital inflows), it tends to depreciate the Indian rupee. In 2011-12 there was current account deficit (CAD) of 4.2 per cent and for 2012-13 it is expected that current account deficit (CAD) will be around 5 per cent of GDP. This is too high current account deficit which is putting downward pressure on the exchange rate of rupee. The depreciation of rupee raises the costs of imports which adds to the inflationary pressures in the Indian economy. Therefore, reducing current account deficit (CAD) to the comfortable level is not only essential for exchange rate stability but also for controlling inflation and achieving price stability. According to D. Subbarao, the present Governor of RBI, the widening of current account deficit in India during the last two years (2011-12 and 2012-13) has emerged as a major constraint on easing of monetary policy as causing lower lending interest rates and large availability of funds with banks will lead to more imports which will add to the current account deficit.

To arrest the fall in value of rupee Reserve Bank raises the bank rate and repo rate and thus sending signals to the banks to raise their lending rates. It also raises cash reserve ratio (CRR) to reduce the liquidity in the banking system and thus reducing lendable resources of the banks. Thus, through rise in the cost of credit and reduction in the availability of credit, borrowing from the banks are discouraged which is expected to reduce the demand for dollars. The higher interest rates in India would also discourage foreign institutional investors and Indian corporates to invest abroad. This will also work to reduce the demand for dollars which will prevent the fall in the value of the rupee.

Alternatively, to prevent the depreciation of the rupee, Reserve Bank can release more dollars from its foreign exchange reserves. The release of more dollars by Reserve Bank will increase the supply of US dollars in the foreign exchange market and will therefore tend to correct the mismatch between demand for and supply of the US dollars. This will help in stabilising the exchange rate of the rupee.

It is clear from above that in the context of flexible exchange rate system, Reserve Bank has to intervene frequently to achieve stability of exchange rate at a reasonable level.

ROLE OF MONETARY POLICY FOR PROMOTING ECONOMIC GROWTH

Economic growth implies the expansion in productive capacity or capital stock in the economy so that increases in real national output or income are attained. As is well known, economic growth can be speeded up by accelerating the rate of savings and investment in the economy. This requires the following steps:

(*a*) Increase in the aggregate rate of savings in the economy,

(*b*) Mobilisation of these savings so that they are made available for the purpose of investment and production,

(*c*) Increase in the rate of investment,

(*d*) allocation of investment funds for productive purposes and priority sectors of the economy.

Proper monetary policy can help in producing favourable effects on the above requirements of economic growth. We explain below the appropriate monetary policy to promote growth in developing countries.

(*a*) Monetary Policy and Savings

Several monetary measures can be adopted to raise the aggregate rate of saving. First, a high interest rate policy can promote savings. In the fifties and sixties of the 20th Century it was widely believed that interest rate reflected the price of capital and since capital was scarce in developing countries, the real interest rates should be kept at higher levels to promote saving so that capital accumulation is speeded up. However, this argument in favour of higher real interest rates in developing countries was based upon the belief or assumption that *savings were positively elastic or sensitive to the interest rate.*

It is worthwhile to mention an opposite view point regarding interest rate policy which has gained large support in recent years. According to this view (emphasised by Keynes in his monetary theory), rate of interest represents the cost of investment, and lower the rate of interest, the greater will be inducement to invest. However, Keynes was of the view that investment was not much sensitive or elastic to lower rate of interest Dr. K.N.Raj argued that *since investment is an important factor determining economic growth in developing countries, it should be promoted by lowering the interest rates*. However, this is not fully correct. This is because whereas inducement to invest may be promoted by lowering the interest rates the adequate amount of savings or resources needed to finance larger investment may not be forthcoming at lower interest rates. Further, a low interest rate policy in developing countries like India is likely to promote more investment in inventories and luxury consumer goods such as cars, airconditioners, luxury houses rather than that in fixed capital goods.

In our view therefore in a developing economy *a reasonably positive real interest rate policy* should be pursued to provide incentives for more savings so that large sources are made available for investment in fixed capital stock. If monetary policy in a developing country is to promote economic growth it must aim at raising the rate of saving. It may be recalled that *real rate of interest is nominal rate of interest minus rate of inflation.* In our view real rate of interest should not be allowed to fall below 5 per cent per annum, if it is to provide reasonable rate of return on savings. Therefore, with the rise in rate of inflation nominal rate of interest should also be raised to keep incentives for saving intact. It may be noted that in recent years (2011-12 and 2012-13) in India low deposit rates offered to the public by banks have prompted the people to invest their savings in unproductive assets such as gold, jewellery, real estate. *This led to the fall in financial saving* required for productive investment. This has led the Finance Minister, Mr. Chidambaram, in his budget for 2013-14 to announce issuing of **inflation-indexed bonds** on which nominal interest rate will automatically rise with the increase in inflation rate.

Besides, the monetary policy can play a strategic role in increasing national savings by promoting the expansion of banking facilities and other financial intermediaries in the developing countries, especially in their rural areas. With more bank branches in under-banked and under-developed regions, the people who consume away their surplus incomes, will be induced to save them in the form of bank deposits which are quite safe as a store of value. The commercial banking encourages thrift or propensity to save by offering a return on savings in the form of interest rate on bank deposits. It also induces more savings by providing outlets for mutual funds which can be equity linked and other saving schemes for fruitful investment of the savings by the people who would have otherwise put them to unproductive or wasteful uses such as buying land, real estate, gold and jewellery. But to tap and raise savings sufficiently and to prevent its unproductive use banks and other financial institutions need to be numerous and dispersed throughout the economy in both the urban and rural areas. Speaking from the development experience of various countries. Prof. Lewis, a development economist, has emphasised that the volume of savings depends partly upon how widespread banking and other financial institutions are. To quote him, "*if the saving institutions are placed under the individual's nose, people save more than if the nearest saving institutions is some distance away.*"[4]

4. Arthur Lewis, *Theory of Economic Growth*, George Allen and Unwin, 1960.

Thus growth in saving in the form of bank deposits will be greater, if a reasonable real rate of interest policy is pursued. Similarly, with the expansion of other financial institutions, the people will feel induced to save more for buying financial assets. It is generally agreed that the rapid expansion of banking facilities after the nationalisation of major commercial banks in 1969 promoted by the Reserve Bank of India has contributed considerably to the growth of aggregate savings. While the aggregate saving rate has gone up from 16.5 per cent in 1969-70 to 22.7 per cent in 1982-83, bank deposits which accounted for 8.7 per cent of total domestic savings in 1969-70, accounted for 22.5 per cent of these savings in 1982-83. The number of commercial banks offices increased from 8,262 in July 1969 to 44,521 in 1984 and to 62,350 in 1995. Although it is difficult to establish a precise quantitative relationship between expansion of bank branches and savings in the form of bank deposits, its significant contribution to the promotion of savings cannot be denied. Therefore, the future branch expansion policy must fully take into account the untapped saving potential of under-banked and under-developed regions.

It may be noted that in order to facilitate mobilisation of an increasing proportion of savings by the banking system it is essential to maintain a reasonable price stability. Dr. Manmohan Singh, when he was Governor of Reserve Bank of India, pointed out, "*It is only under conditions of reasonable price stability that people will have less attraction for savings in the form of physical assets such as gold, real estate and excessive accumulation of inventories.*" Further, if banks are to mobilise adequate amount of savings in the form of bank deposits, interest rates on bank deposits must remain positive in real terms. That is, the rate of interest be maintained at a higher level than the rate of inflation. If through excessive rise in prices, real rate of interest becomes negative, people will be discouraged to save.

(*b*) Monetary Policy and Investment.

Monetary policy has an important role to play in boosting up the level of investment by making available savings or resources mobilised by banks for purposes of investment and production. The banks fulfil this task by offering bank credit for investment to business and industry.

Cost of Credit. It may be noted that Keynesian theory of monetary policy emphasises that the effect of a change in the supply of money on the level of production and investment operates through the changes in the rate of interest. The increase in the supply of money by the monetary authority will cause the market rate of interest to fall. At lower rate of interest, the entrepreneurs will be induced to invest more. Accordingly, Keynesian monetary theory has been described as "*cost of credit*" theory. However, Keynes himself and several economists after him believed that this effect of changes in money supply on investment which operates through rate of interest is not very vigorous. It has been asserted that investment in fixed capital is interest inelastic. That is why Keynes did not have much faith in the effectiveness of monetary policy and instead emphasised the role of fiscal policy in influencing the level of economic activity. However, it is now generally believed by the economists that since interest is an important cost of investment, *investment demand is fairly interest elastic.* Therefore, to promote investment, the easy monetary policy should be adopted. It may be noted that in the post-was reform period from 1996 to 2003 easy or low interest rate policy adopted to promote private investment so as to revive the industrial sector whose growth slowed down from 1996-97 to 2002-03. Following the soft-interest rate policy of Reserve Bank of India prime lending rates of interest of commercial banks which varied between 15 and 16 per cent prior to 1996, were reduced over a period of time to 9 to 10 per cent in 2003. Again when in September 2008 global financial crisis occurred as a result of bust of housing bubble in the US, there was worldwide (including India) economic slowdown, Reserve Bank of India in October 2008 reduced its repo interest rate from 9 per cent in July 2008 to 7 per cent in October 2008 and further to 4.75 per cent on March 4, 2009, to promote private investment so as to prevent sharp economic slowdown in India.

However, the soft interest rate policy does not always, especially during recession, achieve much success in stimulating private investment. This is because when there are sluggish demand conditions, the existing fixed capital is underutilised, it is not profitable to make more investment for expanding fixed capital stock, private enterprises are therefore not willing to make further investment despite lower interest rates. It is for such economic conditions that it has been said that *'you can bring the horse to water but you cannot make it drink'*. However, in normal circumstances cheap interest rate policy promotes private investment and therefore helps to achieve higher economic growth.

Availability of Credit. It is noteworthy that in the recent times monetary theory emphasises the **credit-availability effect on investment** of the changes in the supply of money. According to this, an increase in the supply of money causing expansion in the reserve money with the banks directly enlarges the availability of bank credit for investment purposes and thereby raises the level of investment in the economy. On the contrary, contraction in money supply, will directly reduce the availability of credit and hence tend to decrease investment in the economy.

Further, in this context it is noteworthy that in developing countries, Government or public investment plays a crucial role in the development of their economies. Therefore, monetary policy requires to promote not only private investment but also public investment by making available adequate amount of credit for it.

Monetary Policy and Public Investment. Let us first explain the promotion of the public investment through monetary policy. Monetary policy has to ensure that the banking system contributes to the financing of the planned public investment. For this a good part of bank deposits mobilised by the banks should be invested in Government and other approved securities so that the government should be able to finance its planned investment, especially in infrastructure. At present in India, there is lack of infrastructure such as power, roads, highways, ports, irrigation facilities which is obstructing economic growth. Besides, when industry faces demand recession, public investment is an ideal tool to develop infrastructure and to increase the demand for industrial products through the operation of multiplier. This will stimulate private investment. Therefore, in our view, policy of raising public investment will *crowd in* private investment rather than *crowding it out*. In India a new technique of monetary policy has been designed to secure larger resources from the banking system for financing public investment. This technique has been described as *Statutory Liquidity Ratio* (SLR). According to this, *in addition to cash reserve requirements* banks in India are required to keep a minimum proportion of its total demand and time deposits in the form of specified liquid assets. And the most important specified liquid asset for this purposes is the investment in Government and other securities. To raise the lendable resources of the banks, cash reserve ratio of the banks must be kept at low level.

Monetary Policy and Private Investment. If the private sector plays an important role in the development process, as it does in India after economic reforms undertaken since 1991, monetary policy has also to ensure that the need for bank credit for investment and production in the private sector are fully met. The banks must provide adequate bank credit to meet at least essential working capital requirements of industry and agriculture. Both large-scale and medium industries require funds for investment in fixed capital, working capital and for maintaining inventories. Subject to appropriate norms fixed for inventory holdings, the credit needs of the private sector should be met if existing capacities in the private sector are to be fully used and also more productive capacity is to be built up. In India banks have been asked by the Reserve Bank of India to give specific percentage of loans at concessional rates of interest to some priority sectors such as agriculture and small and medium enterprises.

(*c*) Allocation of Investment Funds

Mobilisation of savings alone would not do. Proper canalisation of these into suitable directions of investment is or perhaps more important than mobilisation itself. The monetary policy should restrict the growth of wasteful lines of investment which are inimical to economic growth. It should be able to direct investment in productive channels. In this regard, the monetary policy has to play a selective or qualitative role in so far as it is possible through its operations to *discriminate between productive and unproductive outlays. It should give a fillip to the former and stint* the growth of the latter. Further, it has to be designed as to influence the specific sectors and industries which are most significant to affect the growth of the economy. In fact, the particularised application of credit can greatly activise the process of economic growth. Therefore, it is necessary to operate the *selective credit rationing with a view to influence the pattern of investment*. However, in the gamut of monetary policy, there are selective credit control measures of both general and specific nature. In the general category are included measures such as voluntary credit restriction and moral suasion. In the category of specific measures there exist measures to control credit institutions.

For the purpose of regulating the individual credit institutions, the method of varying the reserve requirements is quite effective. On the other hand, in order to divert the financial resources into desired channels, the method of **credit rationing** should be used by the Central Bank. This may be done by fixation of a ceiling on the aggregate portfolio of the commercial banks, thereby making it incumbent that loans and advances do not exceed the fixed ceiling. Alternatively, it may be done by directly allocating funds that can be granted and used. Besides, policies such as the selective rediscount policy, prior deposit requirement policy and the fixation of deposit requirement policy can also be adopted to achieve similar goals. However, it may be pointed out that the potency of credit planning depends upon the extent of the area over which it operates. The developing economies must strive for an extension of credit planning over wider areas.

Credit control measures such as noted above promote growth by directing the stream of domestic savings into the desired lines of investment. Measures such as lengthening the periods of repayment, lowering of margin requirements, providing rediscounting facilities at rates below the bank rate, provision of special loans by commercial banks to be used for specific purposes or the setting up of special Investment institutions such as Industrial Development Bank can provide the required inducement to channelise savings in the desired directions. In the indirect sense, these measures may prove conducive to growth in two ways. Firstly, the qualitative credit control measures prevent the savings from being wasted in unproductive channels. Through their application it becomes possible to deny or discourage certain lines of investment that are inimical to the growth of the economy. However, the extent to which such measures can help providing resources for investment in the desired directions depends on the extent to which the flow of credit towards the undesirable channels can prevented.

Secondly, such measures may go a long way in galvanising the process of growth by restraining inflation and its adverse effects. When inflationary tendencies set in, generally the bank advances to businessmen tend to rise. In this way certain undesirable and unproductive enterprises may grow and flourish. For instance, activities such as speculative demand for building up inventories, accumulation of precious metals for purchase of foreign exchange and real estate get a fillip. Growth of these and such other unproductive activities can be held in check by raising the margin requirements for the blackballed collaterals. Further, the monetary authority can fix a ceiling by holding the loans and advances of the value of the collateral. Thus, it *serves the dual purpose of curbing inflation and protecting certain essential productive forms of investment from being restricted.*

In the context of the planned development of the underdeveloped countries, the use of methods of selective credit controls and credit rationing are not only necessary but also essential. They greatly widen the horizons of development along predetermined and desired directions. They are not only helpful in preventing inflation but also *act as a positive means of directing the process of economic development on the desired lines*. Furthermore, the policy of selective credit controls is especially suited to the needs of underdeveloped countries where the orthodox monetary techniques have limited applicability. As it is, the structure of these economies is not very conducive to the general methods of credit control.

The huge investment expenditure made by the government in the public sector in its endeavour to accelerate the process of growth is not amenable to control by the monetary authority. The monetary authority is, in fact, subversive to the wishes of the government in the matter of providing resources for development. Further, in order to help government borrowings, the bank rate policy of the Reserve Bank tends to become more or less inflexible. Besides, for the sake of supporting government loans, the institutions such as SEBI (Stock Exchange Board of India) is also required to stabilise the securities market.

MONETARY POLICY OF RESERVE BANK OF INDIA

Monetary Policy is an important instrument of economic policy to achieve multiple objectives. Like all central banks in the developing countries, Reserve Bank of India has been playing both a *regulatory and promotional* (*i.e.,* developmental) roles in achieving social objectives. Monetary policy of Reserve Bank has been changing from time to time depending on the prevailing economic situation and circumstances. It is important to note that changes in monetary policy, unlike in case of fiscal policy, can be made at any time during a year. It needs to be emphasised that *monetary policy acts through influencing the availability and cost of credit and growth of money supply in the economy.* The effectiveness of monetary policy depends on the institutional framework available for transmitting impulses released by the monetary policy of the central bank.

In its developmental or promotional role, RBI adopted measures to deepen and widen the financial system to promote saving and investment in the Indian economy. RBI was instrumental in the setting up *apex* institutions for ensuring provision of agricultural credit, providing *term finance* to industries and adequate credit for export.

Monetary Policy during the Pre-Reforms Period (1972–1991): Tight Monetary Policy

It is worth noting that prior to 1991 monetary policy in India has been framed in response to *fiscal policy* of the Government. Fiscal Policy in India during the seventies and eighties had been such that large fiscal deficits were incurred. A good part of fiscal deficit was monetised, that is, financed by borrowing from Reserve Bank which created money against treasury bills issued by the Government. This resulted in a very large increase in Reserve Bank credit to the Government which caused rapid growth in money supply. This highlights the close link between the fiscal policy and monetary policy and further that there is a need for coordination between two policies. Monetary policy adopted in the seventies and eighties was concerned mainly with the task of *neutralising inflationary impact* of the growing budget deficits by continually mopping up large increases in *reserve money* (which in economic theory is also called *high-powered money*). The instruments used were changes brought about mainly in Cash Reserve Ratio (CRR) and Statutory Liquidity Ratio (SLR) which were quite often raised during seventies to offset the effect of budget deficits and consequently increase in reserve money.

Given the fully administered nature of interest rates during most part of this period, the excess liquidity in the banking system was mopped up by raising the cash reserve ratio to the legally maximum limit, namely, 25 per cent. Besides, since rates of interest on Government securities were much below the open market rates, excess liquidity from the banking system could not be withdrawn through open market operations. Further, in view of the below market rates of interest, banks and other financial institutions could not be induced to invest in Government securities to meet the borrowing requirements of the Government. Statutory Liquidity Ratio (SLR) had therefore to be progressively raised to meet the borrowing needs of the Government and eventually it was increased to the maximum limit of 38.5 per cent. To quote C. Rangarajan, a former Governor of Reserve Bank of India. "*Until the overall reform process was initiated in 1991, the basic goal of monetary policy was to neutralise the impact of the fiscal deficits*. . . . Monetary management took the form of compensatory increases in the cash reserve ratio (CRR) for banks, controls on growth of commercial credit (mainly to the enterprises sector) and adjustments of administered interest rates. The fixation of CRR and SLR at their maximum levels *crowded out* credit for the commercial sector. Thus, even when money supply was growing at a rapid rate, private sector could not get the needed credit for financing industry and trade."[5]

The banks were compelled to fund most of the large fiscal deficit at below the market rates of interest as they had to meet the high and rising SLR imposed on them by Reserve Bank of India. This is because rates of interest on Government securities were kept at lower levels than the prevailing market rates of interest.

Thus, Y.V. Reddy, the present Governor of Reserve Bank commenting on the monetary policy of Pre-reform period prior to 1991 writes, "given the command and controlled nature of the Indian economy, the RBI had to resort to direct instruments like interest rate regulation, selective credit control and Cash Reserve Rate (CRR) as major monetary instruments. *These instruments were used to neutralise the monetary impact of the Government's budgetary operations.*"

On the recommendation of S. Chakravarty Committee report, in the late eighties and early nineties the rates of interest on Government securities were raised close to the market levels. This had two implications. First, with market rates of interest on Government securities, Reserve Bank could now undertake open market operations. Secondly, with higher interest rates on Government securities banks and other financial institutions could now be induced voluntarily to invest more in Government securities. Accordingly, statutory liquidity ratio (SLR) was reduced below its maximum statutory level.

RECENT MONETARY POLICY STANCE OF RESERVE BANK OF INDIA

The major thrust of the Reserve Bank of India throughout has been to promote growth of the economy without inflation. The changes in domestic economy affect economic growth, price stability, and financial stability in the Indian economy. These changes pose serious challenges in the conduct of monetary policy. Depending on the particular situation facing the Indian economy at a particular time, RBI has been changing its monetary policy stance from time to time. RBI formulates its monetary policy on its estimates of economic growth and its target rate of inflation. Targets for growth of money supply and credit expansion by commercial banks are fixed keeping in view the twin objectives of facilitating growth keeping inflation under control.

RBI Dilemma : Inflation Vs Growth

RBI often finds itself in a dilemma as it often faces the problem of trade-off between inflation and growth. To control inflation tightening of monetary policy (that is, high interest rate and high cash reserve ratio (CRR) are required. But this tightening of monetary policy discourages investment and hurts economic growth. Therefore, when inflation is very high the RBI is prepared to sacrifice some growth to curb inflation. On the other hand, when to promote growth RBI follows expansionary or easy monetary policy, namely, lowering of interest rate and cash reserve ratio (CRR) it leads to increase in aggregate demand and causes inflationary pressures. Therefore, RBI has to adopt a monetary policy that balances its concerns for controlling inflation on the one hand and promoting growth on the other though in actual practice doing such balancing act is a difficult task. We discuss below monetary policy adopted by the RBI since 2006-07. During the last many years RBI has been changing its monetary policy stance depending on the prevailing economic situation and keeping in view its concern for controlling inflation and facilitating growth. Targets for growth of monetary policy and credit expansion are set so as to achieve growth with price stability.

Monetary Policy of RBi Since 2008-09

Beginning from March 2008 there was spurt in inflation rate which became serious as

5. C. Rangarajan, *op. cit.*

year-on-year inflation rate reached 9 per cent in June 2008, and then reached the two digit level of 10 to 11 per cent in July 2008 and reached the alarming figure of around 13 per cent in mid-August 2008 and then it came down to 11.8 per cent and 11.4 per cent in Oct. 2008 and further to 10.8 per cent and 8.4 per cent in Nov. 2008. In order to tackle this inflation RBI raised the cash reserve ratio (CRR) to a high level of 9 per cent and repo rate also to 9 per cent as shown in Table 19A.1. It is these tight monetary measures that reduced liquidity in the banking system and growth of credit and money supply was brought down. The year-on-year inflation rate fell from peak of 12.6 per cent in Sept. 2008 to 11.4 per cent in Oct. 2008. Due to fall in international commodity prices and decline in price of crude oil from $ 147 per barral to $ 50 per barrel in Nov. 2008 inflation rate further came down to 8.4 per cent in end-Nov. 2008.

Reversal of Monetary Policy from Oct. 2008

In the mean time world financial crisis assumed alarming proportion. Foreign Institutional Investors (FII) started selling shares in capital market in India and repatriating dollars. This not only caused depreciation of Indian rupee and stock market crash but also created liquidity crunch in the banking system which restricted credit flow for investment purposes. To solve this liquidity problem and restore investors' confidence RBI reversed its monetary policy. In the first week of Oct. 2008, it reduced cash reserve ratio from 9 per cent to 7.5 per cent and repo rate from 9 per cent to 7.5 per cent. Such a large reduction in cash reverse ratio increased the liquidity in the banking system and it was expected to increase availability of credit for investment. Lowering of repo rate was expected to lower lending rates of interest and thus to ensure cheap credit for investment. Reduction in cash reserve ratio from 9 per cent to 7.5 per infused liquidity in the banking system to the turne of Rs. 1,25,000 crores. With these measures it was hoped that slowdown in rate of economic growth would be prevented. It was further expected that due to fall in international commodity prices and sharp decline in price of crude oil along with the improved supply of agricultural commodities would help in containing inflation. With inflation well under control, to give further boost to investment by increasing availability of credit, RBI further infused liquidity in the banking system by lowering cash reserve ratio (CRR) from 7.5 to 5.5 per cent in Oct. 31, 2008. Besides on Dec. 6, 2008 it further cut key interest rates signalling a further movement towards soft interest rate regime. To ensure that banks should reduce their landing rates it lowered its repo rate i.e. short-term lending rate for borrowing by banks from 7.5 per cent to 6.5 per cent on Dec. 6, 2008. Besides it cut *reverse repo rate* (i.e., the overnight rate at which banks park their surplus funds with RBI) from 6 per cent to 5 per cent. This was meant to encourage banks to give credit to private enterprises rather than keep liquid funds with RBI.

Table 19A.1: Monetary Policy Changes from the Second Half of 2008-09 to the First Half of 2009-10

Date	Repo Rate	Reverse Repo Rate	Cash Reserve Ratio (CRR)
August 30, 2008	9.0	6.0	9.0
October 3, 2008	7.5	6.0	7.5
October 31, 2008	—	—	5.5
December 6, 2008	6.5	5	—
January 2, 2009	5.5	4	5.0
March 4, 2009	5.0	3.5	5.0
April 21, 2009	4.75	3.25	5.0

Source GOI, *Economic Survey,* 2008-09 and 2009-10.

However, the above monetary measures taken during October-December 2008 did not have desired effects. The creation of credit for businesses and consumers remained subdued. In the beginning of 2009, there was a distinct evidence of further slowdown of the Indian economy as a consequence of global financial crisis and global meltdown. RBI cut its forecast for GDP growth rate of the Indian economy for 2008-09 to 7 per cent from 7.5 to 8 per cent. Though many banks had lowered their lending rates of interest, the others had yet to do so.

The US Federal Reserve had reduced its Federal Fund rate to almost zero to revive the American economy. The Central Banks of countries such as the UK, Germany, Euro area and Japan too lowered their benchmark interest rates to overcome recession.

In the environment of sluggish exports and drop in manufacturing output in the third quarter (Oct.–Dec. 2008) of 2008-09, Reserve Bank of India on January 2, 2009, further reduced its three key policy rates, namely, cash reserve ratio (CRR), repo rate and reverse repo rate in an attempt to allow banks to cut lending interest rates further. RBI reduced its cash reserve ratio from 5.5 per cent to 5 per cent. With this it injected additional liquidity of ₹ 20,000 crores in the Indian financial system bringing the total infusion of liquidity in the banking system to over ₹ 300,000 crore since Sept. 2008 to revive the growth of credit for businesses for investment and for consumers buying houses and automobiles. On January 2, 2009 repo rate was reduced from 6.5 per cent to 5.5 per cent and on March 4, 2009 this was further cut to 5 per cent. This was expected to reduce further lending rates by banks and thus making credit cheaper for business and for those taking housing and auto loans. Reverse repo rate was also reduced from 5 per cent to 4 per cent on January 2, 2009 and further to 3.5 per cent on March 4, 2009 which was expected to discourage banks for parking their surplus funds with RBI and instead lend them to business for productive purposes.

Evaluation of Easy Monetary Policy of 2008-09

With the adoption of above measures by the RBI, banks lowered their lending rates but not to the extent by which the RBI reduced their short-term interest rate, that is, repo rate and the extent to which the cash reserve ratio was lowered to increase the liquidity of the banks. As a result of monetary policy measures adopted, bank credit during 2008-09 increased by 17.3 per cent as against 22.3 per cent in 2007-08. It was the public sector banks which issued more credit, private sector banks and foreign banks lagged far behind. Even this modest achievement RBI was not only able to contain inflation as measured by WPI but also along with the expansionary fiscal policy helped to achieve 6.7 per cent growth of GDP in 2008-09. However, as a result of RBI's measures banks were saddled with huge liquid resources as **credit off-take** remained subdued reflecting moderation in demand for credit. To keep their profitability the banks invested in government securities, mutual funds and were also keeping their surplus funds in reverse repo window of Liquidity Adjustment Facility (LAF) of RBI. The usual response of the banks in such a high liquidity condition is to cut lending rates of interest so that private firms borrow more for investment and other purposes. One limitation that banks faced in reducing their lending rates was because they had raised deposits at higher interest rates to meet the demand for credit in the high growth period of first half of financial year 2008-09 and before. These high interest rates on deposits came in the way of cutting lending rates to stimulate investment demand. However, *banks reduced their deposit rates and also reduced their lending rates sufficiently* and with the increase in their liquidity position more credit was made available for private sector. However, off-take of credit was relatively very poor and as a result banks were flush with the liquidity.

In India easy monetary policy adopted from Oct. 2008 had not been much successful to boost credit growth and to prevent slowdown in economic growth. This is for two reasons. As mentioned above, due to global meltdown, stock market crash and sluggish demand conditions businessmen were quite pessimistic about future profitable investment opportunities. Therefore, they were reluctant to make further investment despite lowering of interest rate. This is more so when due to recessionary conditions there is a great deal of uncertanity about adequate demand conditions for goods and as a consequence even their existing capital stock remains under-utilised. In this context it has been said that *'you can bring horse to water but you cannot make it drink'*.

Besides, in times of recession even banks are hesitant to give loans to businesses because of risk that due to default by them they may not get back their money and these loans may get converted into bad debt or non-performing assets. It was therefore observed that despite infusion of liquidity of over ₹ 3,88,000 crores in the Indian banking system from Oct. 2008 to Jan. 2009, the bank credit did not increase adequately and instead due to risk aversion banks were parking their surplus funds with RBI under reverse repo rate system. Besides, banks preferred to invest in Government bonds which are risk free rather than lending to the private sector. In fact, about 388,000 crore liquidity created by RBI had been bagged by Central Government by issuing bonds which were largely purchased by banks. Thus despite the infusion of large liquidity in the banking system and lowering of its key interest rates slowdown in the Indian economy continued from Oct. 2008 to Feb. 2009. In fact there was a drop in manufacturing output during this period.

Monetary Policy Stance During 2009-10

The monetary policy in 2008-09 had to address the emerging economic situation, wherein the position in the second half of the year was substantially different from the first half. The policy had to contend with the spill-over effects of the global financial crisis on the country's growth path. The liquidity situation had improved significantly towards the end of 2008-09 in the wake of measures taken by the RBI. For the year 2009-10, RBI had envisaged a macroeconomic scenario with the real GDP growth at 6.0 per cent and WPI inflation to be around 4.0 per cent by end-March 2010. Taking into account the need to respond to sluggish economic growth witnessed lately, the RBI envisaged growth in money supply (M3) for 2009-10 at 17.0 per cent in April 2009 which was later (July 28) raised to 18 per cent as an indicative projection. Consistent with this, the growth in aggregate deposits of scheduled commercial banks has been projected to grow at 18.0 per cent and non-food credit by 20.0 per cent in 2009-10 as against 17 per cent in 2008-09. The Annual Policy Statement for 2009-10 was announced on April 21, 2009. In it marginal reductions in the key rates were announced. The salient points of Annual Monetary Policy Announcement of April 21, 2009 and Quarterly Review of July 28, 2009 while, the bank rate was retained unchanged at 6.0 per cent. Besides the repo rate under the liquidity adjustment facility (LAF) was reduced by 25 basis points from 5.0 per cent to 4.75 per cent with immediate effect from April 21. In the Annual Policy Statement for 2009-10 the cash reserve ratio (CRR) of scheduled banks was retained unchanged at 5.0 per cent of net demand and time liabilities (NDTL).

In first quarterly review (July 28, 2009), the wholesale price inflation was expected to rise to 5 per cent by the end of March 2010, which would make it imperative for the RBI to start tightening monetary policy. The RBI felt overall macroeconomic scenario continued to be uncertain, although stimulus measures were expected to boost demand in 2009-10 and ensure economic growth and boost private sector investment. "*The task for the Reserve Bank is to maintain the accommodative monetary stance till demand conditions further improve and the credit flow takes hold, but to be ready with a roadmap to reverse the expansionary stance quickly and effectively thereafter,*" said RBI Governor, D. Subbarao. Thus, in its Quarterly Review (28 July 2009) RBI visualised *monetary tightening* (*i.e.* revising repo rate, reverse repo rate of interest and cash reserve ratio (CRR) upward) when inflation was expected to rise after Sept. 2009. Exact timing of monetary tightening was said to depend on the situation of inflation.

Tightening of Monetary Policy Stance in the Second Half of 2009-10. In the later half of 2009-10 there was a significant improvement in the economic situation. While recovery of the Indian economy gained momentum with overall growth in GDP estimated to rise to 7.5 per cent and manufacturing growth rising to over 11 per cent. However, despite this higher growth rate, problem of inflation worsened during the second half of 2009-10. While inflation as measured by WP1 on year-on-year basis went up to 8 per cent in Jan. 2010, food inflation rose to about 18 per cent and it was feared that food inflation would soon spill over to general inflation. It was widely felt that to tackle the problem of inflation in the third Quarter Review of monetary policy of 2009-10, RBI would tighten its monetary policy. However, some believed that tightening of monetary policy, especially raising of interest rates (*i.e.*, repo rate and reverse repo rate) by RBI would adversely affect economic growth and retard the recovery process. Thus, to tackle inflation it was not easy to exit the expansionary monetary policy without hurting economic growth.

Even in its second quarterly review of its monetary policy in Oct. 2009 RBI signalled that the situation required to shift its stance from "*management of crisis*" to "*management of recovery*" and hinted at tightening its monetary policy if inflation became worse. Even then (in Oct. 2009) in its policy review RBI shut all windows for refinance by it and also raised statutory liquidity ratio (SLR) from 24 per cent to 25 per cent so that liquidity with the banks be reduced. One per cent hike in statutory liquidity ratio for the banks meant that banks' holding of more Government bonds and less money in the banks' kitty for providing-loans to the private commercial sector. But this measure proved quite ineffective because banks had already invested about 28 per cent of their deposits in Government bonds. This means raising of statutory liquidity ratio (SLR) from 24 to 25 per cent could not have any effect on liquidity. Similarly, withdrawal of refinance facilities for non-banking financial companies, housing finance firms, mutual funds and exporters and for swapping banks foreign exchange liabilities hardly made any difference because these were rarely used.

Hike in Cash Reserve Ratio (CRR) in January 2010. To check inflationary expectations in its third quarterly review of its credit policy in January 29, 2010, RBI raised cash reserve ratio (CRR) from 5 per cent to 5.75 per cent. In doing so RBI sucked out ₹ 36000 crore from the banking system. However, in its Jan. 29 review of the policy, contrary to the expectations, it kept its key interest rates, namely, repo rate, reverse repo rate and bank rate unchanged. RBI refrained from raising its short-term interest rates as it thought such a policy action would deal a below to the economic recovery by adversely affecting private investment demand and consumption expenditure whose increase was necessary to keep the growth momentum. It pointed out that till Oct. 2009, growth was primarily driven by Government's fiscal stimulus but since then private consumption and private demand had started picking up and therefore dependence on Government's fiscal stimulus for keeping growth momentum had declined. It further emphasised that Government must begin the process of fiscal consolidation (*i.e.* reduce fiscal deficit by withdrawing cuts in taxes and reduce its expenditure.

In its view RBI thought withdrawal of liquidity from the banking system through hike in CRR would be enough to curtial inflationary expectations without having any adverse effect on economic growth. "In its interview, defending the hike in CRR while keeping interest rate unchanged D. Subbarao says, "*The recovery is not broad based and we need to encourage more investments in supply before the output gap gets closed. So, it's important that we support the recovery process in order to control inflationary pressures from the demand side.* Also, on growth-inflation trade-off, it's important to recognize that even as there is some trade-off in the short term, if you look slightly beyond the short term, inflation will anyway continue. So we had to take into account inflation concerns and growth considerations. *We expect that the CRR hike will anchor inflationary expectations without hurting growth impulses.*"

As a matter of fact RBI could not completely reverse its policy of monetary accomodation as long as Government did not reduce its borrowing from the market. In 2009-10 to meet its large fiscal deficit of 6.8% of GDP. Government had to borrow heavily from the market (mainly banks). Such Government borrowing required enough liquid funds with the banks so as to lend them to the Government. Therefore, the RBI urged upon the Government to return to the path of fiscal consolidation so as to make it easier for the RBI to take strong anti-inflationary measures such as hike in repo rate of interest. On Jan. 29, 2010 statement as a policy measure 75 bps hike in CRR was considered as a more potent instrument than a combination of a 50 bps hike in CRR and 25 bps rise in repo rate that legal cash reserves kept in RBI by the banks do not earn any interest rate. Therefore, a very high increase in CRR would compel the banks to keep their liquid funds at zero rate of interest instead of earning 3.5 per cent interest by keeping funds under reverse repo window. This implies that without raising repo rate, through steep hike in CRR, RBI was able to raise the cost of money lending for the banks who were expected to raise their lending rates sooner or later. When in the end of first week of March general inflation shop up to 9.89 per cent year-on-year basis RBI raised its repo rate and reverse rupee rate by 25 bps. *Therefore, in middle of March 2010 RBI raised repo rate from 4.75 per cent to 5 per cent and reverse repo rate from 3.25 per cent to 3.50 per cent. In our view it was "too little and too late a measure" to control inflation.*

RBI found that credit during 2009-10 was not high, it was actually around 15 per cent till January 2010 against the earlier projection of 18 per cent by the RBI. It was therefore felt that large hike in repo interest rate would slowdown the growth of credit for productive and investment purposes and adversely affect the recovery process. In view of the poor credit off-take till Jan. 2010, it even lowered its target of credit expansion from 18 per cent to 16 per cent. It even found that money supply growth of 16.5 per cent till Jan. 2010 was modest. Thus RBI found that growth of bank credit and money supply expansion was very modest and could not be held responsible for inflation which as measured by WPI on year-on-year basis reached 7.31 per cent by end of Dec. 2009 and was estimated to rise to 8.5 per cent by middle of Jan. 2010. However, even in first week of March inflation, based on WPI, shot up to 9.89 per cent. Food inflation was very high at around 18 per cent in Feb. 2010. But RBI emphasized that food inflation was due to supply-side factors and not due to excessive increase in aggregate demand. Further, according to it food inflation was spilling over to general inflation.

Thus RBI maintained that hike in repo interest rate would lead to immediate increase in lending rates by the banks and would further slowdown credit growth and adversely affect the recovery process and economic growth. Thus keeping the repo interest rate and bank rate unchanged even in its. Third Quarterly Review of its policy for 2009-10 RBI in Jan. 28, 2010 showed that it continued *to maintain a positive pro-growth stance*. Even in its credit policy review in Oct. 2009, RBI noted that growth was primarily driven by fiscal stimulus (*i.e.* increase in public expenditure and cuts in taxes) by the Government but after Oct. 2009, private consumption and private demand had picked up to ensure growth. Therefore, RBI Governor urged upon the Government to begin the process of fiscal consolidation so that excessive borrowing by it from the market be reduced.

Lastly, RBI noted inflation in India, especially food inflation during 2009-10, *was so far primarily due to supply-side factors as failure of adequate monsoons caused drought conditions in many parts of the country in 2009-10* and rate of agricultural growth was negative (– 0.2 per cent). It pointed out that monetary policy of higher interest rates and reduction in liquidity helped to check demand-pull inflation and was not appropriate to tackle inflation driven by supply-side factors. In fact the main *emphasis of latest credit policy of RBI was that it was moving from a mode of crisis management to that of handling the recovery process.*

Comments

The inflationary situation again emerged in 2010. Inflation which was initially food driven was late getting generalised. Though RBI substantially raised cash reserve ratio (CRR) by 75 bps and it sucked out mere 36000 crore from the system whereas the size of reverse repo operations indicated that liquidity in the banks was of the order of around ₹ 80,000 crore at that time. Therefore, after the rise in CRR by RBI, there still remained a large amount of liquidity in the banking system. In view of the ample liquidity with the banks, it was unlikely that they would raise their lending rates to curtail demand for credit. By keeping its key interest rates at relatively low levels and not taking enough measures to reduce surplus liquidity in the system it *served* to promote private investment to strengthen the recovery process and to achieve higher growth. For anti-inflationary measures it urged the Government to reduce fiscal deficit and cut its fiscal stimulus. In fact, the Governor of the RBI in its credit policy announcement emphasised that to exit expansionary monetary policy to tackle inflation without hurting growth was a very difficult task in the then prevailing complex situation.

Monetary Policy Stance During 2010-11 : Further Tightening of Monetary Policy.

The accommodative expansionary monetary policy which was purused starting mid-Sept. 2008 instilled confidence in investors and producers and reduced the adverse impact of global financial crisis on the Indian Economy. As a result, the Indian economy started recovering ahead of most other economies. However, when in the second half of 2009-10, food inflation rose with the risk of it raising inflationary expectations, the RBI started *exit* from the expansionary monetary policy beginning from Oct. 2009. However, its anti-inflationary policy in the second half of 2009-10 merely consisted in giving warning that it would tighten its monetary policy if serious inflation problem emerged for its policy was not to hurt economic growth by raising its short-term rates, namely, repo rate and reverse repo rate and increasing cash reserve ratio (CRR). It is only in the end of the FY 2009-10 in the months of February and March 2010 that it raised CRR by 25 bps from 5.50 to 5.75 (see Table 19A.3) to suck out some liquidity from money market and also raised by 25 bps repo rate from 4.75 to 5 per cent and reverse repo rate from 3.50 to 3.75 per cent to control inflation. Thus in 2009-10 only half -hearted monetary measures were taken by the RBI to control inflation. This was explained by pointing out that inflation then was driven by supply-side factors and monetary policy was inappropriate for fighting inflation driven by supply-side shocks.

The monetary policy stance in the Annual Policy Statement for the year 2010-11 announced on April 20, 2010 was guided by the following considerations.

1. The need to move in a calibrated manner in the direction of normalising the monetary policy instruments to control inflation without hurting growth.
2. The need to ensure that demand-side inflation did not become entrenched.

Table 19A.2. Movements in Key Policy Rates in 2010 and 2011

Effective Since	Repo Rate	Reverse Repo Rate	Cash Reserve Ratio (CRR)
April 21, 2009	4.75 (– 0.25)	3.25 (– 0.25)	5.0
Feb. 13, 2010	4.75	3.25	5.50 (+ 0.50)
Feb. 27, 2010	4.75	3.25	5.75 (+ 0.25)
March 19, 2010	5.00 (+ 0.25)	3.50 (+ 0.25)	5.75
April 20, 2010	5.25 (+ 0.25)	3.75 (+ 0.25)	5.75
April 24, 2010	5.25	3.75	6.00 (+ 0.25)
July 2, 2010	5.50 (+ 0.25)	4.00 (+ 0.25)	6.0
July 27, 2010	5.75 (+ 0.25)	4.50 + 0.50	6.0
Sep. 16, 2010	6.00 (+0.25)	5.00 (0.50)	6.0
Nov. 2, 2010	6.25 (+ 0.25)	5.25 (+ 0.25)	6.0
Jan. 25, 2011	6.50 (+ 0.25)	5.50 (+ 0.25)	6.0
March 17, 2011	6.75 (+ 0.25)	5.75 (+ 0.25)	6.0
May 17, 2011	7.25 (+ 0.50)	6.25 (+ 0.50)	6.0
June 16, 2011	7.50 (+ 0.25)	6.50 (+ 0.25)	6.0
July 26, 2011	8.00 (+ 0.50)	7.0 (+ 0.50)	6.0

3. The need to balance the monetary policy objective of controlling inflation by absorbing liquidity while ensuring that credit was available to both the Government and the private sector.

Significant developments took place subsequent to the announcement of the monetary policy in April 2010. Though recovery of economic growth was consolidating, problem of inflation worsened. The upward revision in administered fuel prices on June 25, 2010 also influenced inflation in the subsequent months. In the First Quarterly Review on July 2, 2010, the RBI raised repo rate and reverse repo rate under LAF by 25 bps each. As will be seen from Table 19A.2, on July 2, 2010 repo rate was raised from 5.25 to 5.50 per and reverse repo rate was raised from 3.75 per cent of per cent to 4 per cent while cash reserve rātio was kept unchanged at 6 per cent. Again on July 27, 2010 due to further rise in WPI inflation rate, repo rate was further raised to 5.75 per cent and reverse repo rate was increased from 4 per cent to 4.50 per cent. Besides, on July 27, 2010, in its First Quarter Review

(July 2010) the RBI revised upward its projections for real GDP growth for the year 2010-11 to 8.5 per cent and raised its projection for WPI inflation for March 2011 to 6.0 per cent. The monetary policy action during 2010-11 was intended to moderate inflation by reining in demand pressures and inflationary expectations and to maintain financial conditions conducive to sustained growth.

With worsening of inflation, the RBI, in its *Mid-Quarterly Review* on Sept. 16, 2010, further increased the repo rate under LAF by 25 basis points from 5.75 per cent to 6 per cent and the reverse repo rate by 50 bps from 4.5 per cent to 5.0 per cent, keeping cash reserve ratio unchanged.

Monetary Policy Stance in 2011-12: Continuation of Tight Monetary Policy

In its Annual Monetary Policy for 2011-12 the Reserve Bank announced on May 3, 2011 aggressive monetary measures to control inflation. The inflation which was previously confined to food inflation became quite generalised in the preceding three months. The RBI move was guided by the fact that headline WP inflation which stood at 9 per cent in March 2011 was expected to remain at an elevated level and might even get worse during the year due to some risk factors that were working to raise it. The Reserve Bank which in its earlier policy measures during 2010-11 was avoiding to hurt growth, for the first time it pointed out that it was necessary to check inflation even by sacrificing some growth in the short run so as to achieve *sustained growth in the medium term.* According to the Annual Monetary Policy statement, *inflation is inimical to sustained growth as it harms growth by creating uncertainty*". It further states that current elevated rates of inflation pose significant risks to future growth. Bring them down therefore even at the cost of some growth in the short run should take precedence.

To control inflation the Reserve Bank raised the rate at which it lends to the banks by 50 bps from 6.75% to 7.25 per cent and reverse Repo rate, the rate at which banks park their surplus funds with it from 5.75% to 6.25 per cent on May 3, with effect from May 17, 2011. For the first time in 19 years it raised saving bank rate from 3.5 per cent to 4 per cent, cash reserve ratio (CRR) and statuary liquidity ratio were left unchanged. It lowered its estimate of rate of growth of the Indian economy from 8.6 per cent for the year 2011-12 to 8 per cent. Besides, it estimated that inflation would be moderated to 6% with an upward bias by the end of March 2012 while it would remain high till September 2011. In view of hike in repo rate the target for credit growth during the year 2011-12 was fixed at 19 per cent.

Since in May 2011 banks were working under tight liquidity conditions, the monetary transmission mechanism of the hike in repo rate was thought to be effective and the banks were expected to pass on the increase in cost of funds resulting from hike in repo rate to constomers. As a result, cost of auto-loans and house loans which are highly interest-sensitive was expected to go up. As a result, credit for purchase of automobiles and houses would decline.

The *RBI expressed doubts whether the government would be able to meet its fiscal deficit target of 4.5%* of gross domestic product for the year 2011-12 with many assumptions getting thrown into the winds. "Critical assumption that petroleum and fertiliser subsidies would be capped is bound to be seriously tested at prevailing high crude oil prices," said Subbarao. Even though adjustment of administered retail prices of petroleum products may add to inflation in the short run, the Reserve Bank believes this needs to be done as soon as possible. Otherwise, the consequent increase in fiscal deficit will counter the moderating trend in aggregate demand." To ensure more credit flow to industry, the RBI barred banks from investing more than 10% of their net worth in liquid schemes of mutual funds.

Justification for Aggressive Credit Policy in 2011. Justifying the very aggressive credit policy in 2011, Dr. D. Subbarao pointed out that as compared to the last year the conditions in 2011 were changed. The last year the domestic economy was facing uncertainty and inflation was more due to high food inflation and supply-side factors. This year the economy is on firm footing and inflation has spread from food to non-food manufactured products and has been generalised and demand-side pressures have been working to bring it about. He further emphasised that the aim of our strategy this year, now in 2011, is to check inflation by restraining demand and force the conditions for sustained growth by bringing environment of price stability. *The baby step approach was good for last year's growth-inflation dynamics. The dynamics have changed now and we have hiked more than we have done so far.*

Explaining the causes of persistent inflation despite increasing repo interest rate several times in the last year and projections of inflation of the RBI going wrong he said that there were *a series of unexpected supply shocks such as vegetable crisis and adjustment in coal prices and escalating demand pressures which made our projections go off track.* Producers were able to pass on higher input prices to consumers due to demand pressures. The aim of the RBI is to attain sustained growth in the environment of low inflation.

RBI indicated some risks that may lead to more inflationary pressures than anticipated. First, if monsoon is not normal, then food supply may not keep pace with the growth of demand. Second, food inflation may lead to increase in wages which would cause cost-push inflation. Third, subsidy bill of the Government may increase due to higher oil prices causing larger fiscal deficit which would add to demand pressure.

The RBI again laid stress that Government must check its fiscal deficit which is important for the success of monetary policy in controlling inflation. The Government should stick to its fiscal deficit targets against the backdrop of rising global crude oil prices and other commodity prices. The RBI wanted the Government to raise domestic retail prices of petroleum products to cut expenditure on subsidies in order to fight inflation, Dr. D. Subbarao, the Governor of RBI says "*Even though adjustments of administered retail prices of petroleum products may add to inflation in the short run, the Reserve Bank believes that this needs to be done as soon as possible. Otherwise, the consequent increase in the fiscal deficit will counter the moderating trend in aggregate demand.*"

Mid-Quarterly Review (15 June 2011). Since the announcement of Annual Monetary Policy on May 3, 2011, macroeconomic environment underwent a change and a high inflation rate (9.06% year on year basis) prevailed in May 2011, despite raising interest rate by it earlier. Further **core inflation** (*i.e.*, inflation other than food and fuel) hardened at 8.71 per cent at May 2011 compared to 7.93% in April 2011. Thus the main worry for the Central Bank was non-food manufactured products. Accordingly, to check inflation it increased the repo rate under liquidity adjustment facility by another 25 bps *from 7.25 per cent to 7.5 per cent* on May 2011. Similarly, in tandem with repo rate reverse repo rate was raised to 6.5 per cent and marginal standing facility (MSF) rate to 8.5%.

The RBI said that inflation persisted at an uncomfortable level and headline inflation rate then understated the inflationary pressures because the then domestic fuel prices had yet to reflect the global crude oil prices. While at that time the government had raised patrol prices sharply but delayed the decision to increase diesel, kerosene and cooking gas prices. It was felt that increased diesel prices would cause high inflationary pressures as it would raise transportation costs that would lead to rise in product prices through cascading effect.

The industry associations called for a halt or pause in interest rate increases as, according to them, demand for industrial products was slowing. One industrialist pointed out, "*For infrastructure companies looking for a debt instrument, this hike will come as a death sentence.*" Though industrial production slowed in the preceding two quarters the RBI was of the view that slowdown was not particularly sharp or severe.

Continuing with a Firm Anti-Inflationary Stance : First Quarterly Review of Monetary Policy 2011-12 on July 26, 2011

In its first quarterly review of its credit policy on July 26, 2011, Reserve Bank of India raised its repo and reverse repo rates by 50 basis points each. Accordingly, it raised repo rate from 7.5 per cent to 8 per cent and reverse repo rate from 6.5 per cent to 7 per cent with immediate effect. In its credit policy review cash reserve ratio (CRR) and statuary liquidity ratio (SLR) were remained unchanged. This was in sharp contrast to small 25 bps hike each time in these interest rates in previous reviews of its monetary policy ten times since March 2010. Through these large hike in the interest rates, Reserve Bank sought to give strong signals to the market and industry that this time it is determined to check inflation and anchor inflationary expectations. As a matter of fact, in its previous reviews hike in interest rate by 25 bps each time for ten reviews since March 2010, failed to check inflation. The inflation rate based on WPI in June 2011 was found to be 9.44% which was likely to be revised to 10% when the rise in oil prices made in June 2010 was fully reflected in WPI. This inflation rate was more than that estimated by RBI. In its new macroeconomic assessment it made a forecast that inflation rate will fall to 7% by March 2012 against its earlier forecast of 6%. In fact the earlier small hike in policy rates popularly called baby steps did not produce the desired effect of reining in inflation as they were quite on expected lines and were factored in by the business class while adjusting the prices of their products.

Against this large rise in interest rate by RBI it was argued by the critics of RBI that it would hurt economic growth as this would discourage investment by raising the cost of funding the investment projects. By raising the cost of borrowing it was expected to affect adversely the growth of interest-sensitive sectors such as automobiles, houses, (*i.e.,* real estate) etc.

RBI in this 11th time hike in interest rates rightly thought that *infaltion was going to remain at an elevated level in the short run and therefore substantial hike in interest rate was called for to moderate inflation.* Some sacrifice in growth in the short term was necessary to control inflation if 8 per cent sustained growth in GDP was to be achieved in the medium term.

RBI pointed out that even with these relatively high rise in interest rates, inflation rate in India could still rise further if world commodity prices, especially of oil, do not soften fast enough, if debt crisis in Europe and the US squeeze the dollar flows that finances our imports and further if food prices spurt on a week monsoon during 2010-11 and, lastly, if fiscal deficit of the Government is not reduced to ease demand pressure. The *Reserve Bank made a strong case that in the absence of complementary policy measures such as reduction in fiscal deficit by cutting government expenditure, especially on subsidies which have outlived their utility, and make a shift in its expenditure toward investment in infrastructure and agriculture so as to overcome supply-side bottlenecks to ease supply-side pressures it was difficult to control inflation.*

A Critical Evaluation of Tight Monetary Policy to Fight Inflation

The Reserve Bank raised its overnight repo interest rate at which it lends to the banks 11 times since March 2010 till July 2011 through a series of baby steps, i.e. raising it each time by 0.25% except on two occasions when it increased it by 0.50 per cent. By doing so it raised the cost of borrowing through which it sought to limit the growth of bank credit. It kept the cash reserve ratio (CRR) unchanged at 6 per cent and therefore the *availability of credit* had not been affected.

The hikes in repo rate lowered the demand for credit for interest-sensitive sectors such as automobiles, houses (real estate) and other durable consumer goods. As a result, growth in consumption demand slowed down. But investment demand by the corporate sector had not been affected and credit had been made available to them. Therefore, the growth of bank credit has only marginally declined. However, a relatively large reduction in bank credit is essential to bring inflation under control. Inflation which from the later half of 2009-10 began with food inflation became generalised in 2010-11 and 2011-12 and spread to non-food manufactured products. The series of 11 hikes in interest rates (repo and reverse repo rates) till July 26, 2011 failed to check WPI inflation rate. Headline inflation (i.e., WPI inflation) rate rose to 9.44 per cent year-on-year basis in June 2011 and to 10 per cent in Sept. 2011 making life tough for the people. Inflation rate will further rise if global commodity prices, particularly oil do not soften fast enough; if debt crisis in Europe and America reduce the capital flows that finance our imports; if food prices spurt in the later half of 2011 due to below normal monsoon in 2011 (as is now expected); and if fiscal deficit increases. All these events will tend to raise inflationary pressures in the economy. The RBI's projected target of inflation of 5.5 percent in WPI inflation (which had been raised to 7 per cent) by March 2011 went wrong and actually stood at 9 per cent. Now, despite its several hikes in repo rate WPI inflation in Sept. 2011 went up to 10 per cent. Despite hike in repo rate to 8 per cent in Oct. 2011 and then to 8.5 per cent in Nov. 2011, inflation rate remained at an elevated level. It was estimated at 9.72 per cent year-on year basis in Oct. 2011 and at 9.11 per cent in November 2011. Due to the sharp decline in food inflation headline WPI inflation came down to 7.47% in 2011.

It is worth noting that even after latest hike in repo rate to 8 per cent on July 26, 2011, it was still below 9 per cent that prevailed prior to global financial crisis which started affecting India in September 2008. The private corporate sector and their supporters raise hue and cry when hike in repo interest rate is made on the ground that it would discourage investment and growth. However, they ignore the fact that despite 11 times hike in interest till July 2011 since March 2010, fixed deposit rates of banks for 1 year to 2 years duration were around 6 to 8 per cent in different banks and therefore with around 10 per cent rate of WPI inflation in Oct. 2011, *real rate* of interest for savers, was still in *negative* territory. That is, monetary policy still favoured the borrowers and investors at the cost of savers, especially the persons with fixed incomes and those who live on their past savings while inflation continue unabated. This is not only unjust but will discourage savings which finance investment. Already, due to negative real interest rates on bank deposits people had started investing their savings in gold, jewellery, real estate which are unproductive investment. As a result, there has been diversion of bank deposits to these unproductive types of investment and currency holding by the people.

Further, as stressed by the Reserve Bank of India in its monetary policy review of July 26, 2011 that tight monetary policy alone will not succeed in controlling inflation, the government must also contribute to it by fiscal consolidation by preventing wasteful Government expenditure and targeting subsidies to the really needy people so as to check the excess demand in the system. The Government can also help in controlling inflation if it steps up its *investment in infrastructure and agriculture so as to remove supply-side bottlenecks that feed inflation.*

In our view RBI's monetary policy had not been very effective in controlling inflation because government was incurring high fiscal deficit which led to the increase in inflationary pressures in the Indian economy. Besides, global situation regarding high oil prices also contributed to the inflationary pressures in the Indian economy. These high prices could not be passed on to the consumers which added to the subsidy bill of the government which contributed to the high **fiscal deficit** of the government. Besides, inflation was partly driven by supply-side factors and therefore tight monetary policy could not be able to check it, while it discouraged growth. Further, RBI in its conduct of tight monetary policy there could not successfully resolve the problem of inflation-growth trade-off. It sent confused signals regarding controlling inflation but at the same time supporting growth.

It needs to be emphasized that in a growing economy though in the short run there is trade-off between inflation and growth, in the long run there is no trade-off between them. This is because *investment has a dual effect, demand effect and capacity effect.* In the short run investment leads to the increase in aggregate demand and causes increases in inflation. This should be tackled through supply management by the government. But its effect on increase in productive capacity materialises in the long run and therefore leads to the increase in aggregate supply of goods in the economy and therefore counters the inflationary tendency in the economy. Monetary policy should be so conducted that while high interest rates should be pursued to discourage demand, especially of gold, automobiles, real estate, luxury consumer durable goods, whose demand is interest-elastic, at the same time they should promote investment in productive sectors of the economy which augments aggregate supply in the long run by making adequate funds available for them.

In 2011-2012 throughout inflation persisted at an elevated level. It was only in its First Quarterly Review in July 2011 that RBI talked of *sacrificing some growth in the short run to achieve price stability for the sake of sustained growth in the long run.* However, at that time inflation was getting out of hand because not only the demand pressure on non-food manufactured products increased but also because of higher food inflation resulted in increases in wages which gave rise to cost-push inflation as well. *By then inflation was being driven by both the demand-side and supply-side factors and became quite generalised by spreading to non-food manufactured products.* Such inflation cannot be bought under control merely by tightening monetary policy but proper fiscial policy aimed at fiscal consolidation through reduction in Government wasteful expenditure was also needed to tackle it. Besides, demand management through appropriate monetary and fiscal policies, efforts should be made to augment supply of those goods which are in great demand by raising their production and lowering cost of production through increasing productivity. To ensure that shortage of some goods should not emerge, efforts and investment should be so directed that supply must match demand, if price stability is to be achieved.

Monetary Policy Changes in 2012-13

During the financial year, 2012-13 growth has slowed markedly, even as inflation remained above the Reserve Bank's comfort level. Monetary Policy responded to this evolving growth-inflation dynamics through calibrated easing. After lowering the cash reserve ratio (CRR) by 125 basis points (bps) during Q4 of 2011-12, the Reserve Bank made a reduction in its repo rate by 50 bps in April 2012. Even as elevated inflation and the twin deficits severely restricted the room for further easing of the policy rate since April 2012, subsequent measures were directed towards ensuring adequate liquidity to facilitate a turnaround in credit deployment to productive sectors for supporting growth. As part of liquidity management measures, the CRR was reduced in two stages : first on Jan. 28, 2012 from 6 per cent to 5.50 per cent and then on March 3, 2012 to 4.75 per cent to ease monetary and liquidity conditions. Also, the statutory liquidity ratio (SLR) of scheduled commercial banks (SCBs) was reduced from 24 per cent since May 2012 to 23 per cent in August 2012 to improve the credit conditions facing the private sector (Table 19A.3).

Table 19A.3. Movements in Key Policy Variables During 2011-12

(Percent)

Effective since	Repo Rate		Reverse Repo Rate		Cash Reserve Ratio*		Statutory Liquidity Ratio*	
1	2		3		4		5	
May 3, 2011	7.25	(+0.50)	6.25	(+0.50)	6.00		24	
June 16, 2011	7.50	(+0.25)	6.50	(+0.25)	6.00		24	
July 26, 2011	8.00	(+0.50)	7.00	(+0.50)	6.00		24	
September 16, 2011	8.25	(+0.25)	7.25	(+0.25)	6.00		24	
October 25, 2011	8.50	(+0.25)	7.50	(+0.25)	6.00		24	
January 28, 2012	8.50		7.50		5.50	(–0.50)	24	
February 13, 2012	8.50		7.50		5.50		24	
March 10, 2012	8.50		7.50		4.75	(–0.75)	24	
April 17, 2012	8.00	(–0.50)	7.00	(–0.50)	4.75		24	
June 18, 2012	8.00		7.00		4.75		24	
August 11, 2012	8.00		7.00		4.75		23	(–1.00)
September 22, 2012	8.00		7.00		4.50	(–0.25)	23	
November 3, 2012	8.00		7.00		4.25	(–0.25)	23	

Figures in parentheses indicate changes in policy rates/ratios.

* : Per cent of Net Demand and Time Liabilities.

Furthermore, apart from supplying liquidity through daily liquidity adjustment facility (LAF), the Reserve Bank made active use of the auctions under outright open market operations (OMOs) and injected primary liquidity of about ₹ 1.1 trillion coupled with liquidity injection of around ₹ 229 billion through anonymous trading platform (NDS-OM) in 2012-13 upto January-end 2013. The judicious use of the two sets of instruments, *i.e.,* keeping the policy rate unchanged since April 2012 and proactive liquidity easing measures conferred dual benefits that were evident as inflation gradually declined from its peak and credit off-take showed signs of improvements during most of November and December 2012. Inflation, however, continued remain above the Reserve Bank's level.

Global economic and financial conditions continued to deteriorate during this period and with a sharper reduction in domestic growth, the growth-inflation trade-off needed a revisit. In the assessment of the Reserve Bank of India, keeping in view the inflation in the country, further reduction in policy rates at this juncture (during September 2012 to 28 January 2013) could accentuate inflationary pressures rather than supporting growth. Further, since the risk to inflation was also arising from the high fiscal deficit, uncertainty in international prices of crude oil and structural imbalances in demand-supply of food (particularly protein foods), a cautious monetary policy stand was preferred by the RBI. However, the actions taken by the Government since September, particularly with regard to the *increase in the administered prices of diesel, fixing cap on the use of* LPG, *announcement of fiscal road map with clear medium term fiscal deficit targets and initiatives to improve investor perception* had created a favourable environment and had signalled a shift towards investment and capacity addition. Some of the inflationary pressures from excess demand was expected to be alleviated by these government measures the RBI would have room for more accommodative monetary policy.

The slowdown of economic activity was also getting reflected through a moderation in money supply and bank credit growth. While liquidity conditions continued to remain manageable, a widening of the gap between deposit and credit growth combined with a seasonal pick-up in credit demand are likely to keep up the pressure on liquidity. Policy actions in terms of reduction in CRR and SLR in the recent months had been supportive and tended to pre-empt a prospective tightening of liquidity conditions and reinforce the growth stimulus.

RBI Adopts Growth - Supporting Monetary Policy in the Third Quarter of 2012-13

Reserve Bank of India in its third quarterly review on July 29, 2012, cut its key policy rates, repo rate and cash reserve ratio (CRR) by 25 basis points each to revive the growth momentum. After holding the repo rate constant for nine months, RBI on Jan. 29, 2013, cut it from 8 per cent to 7.75 per cent. Along with it RBI also cut cash reserve ratio (CRR) from 4.25 to 4 per cent. This cut in CRR was estimated to release ₹ 18,000 crore for the bank to lend. The simultaneous cut in repo rate and cash reserve ratio was to ensure effective transmission of monetary policy to low lending rates by bank so as to promote investment and growth.

RBI justified its relaxation of monetary policy on the basis of three considerations. The first was, according to it, inflation had moderated, both headline wholesale inflation and core inflation (*i.e.,* non-food manufacturing inflation). Further, RBI thought that momentum of inflation was coming down. The second factor related to the deceleration of growth. The growth in the first quarter of 2012-13 was 5.4 per cent and in the second quarter was 5.3 per cent. The deceleration of economic growth, according to it, was not just due to fall in investment but also of net exports and consumption demand. The third consideration that weighed with RBI was liquidity, which was quite tight over the last few months.

It's Been a Long Wait

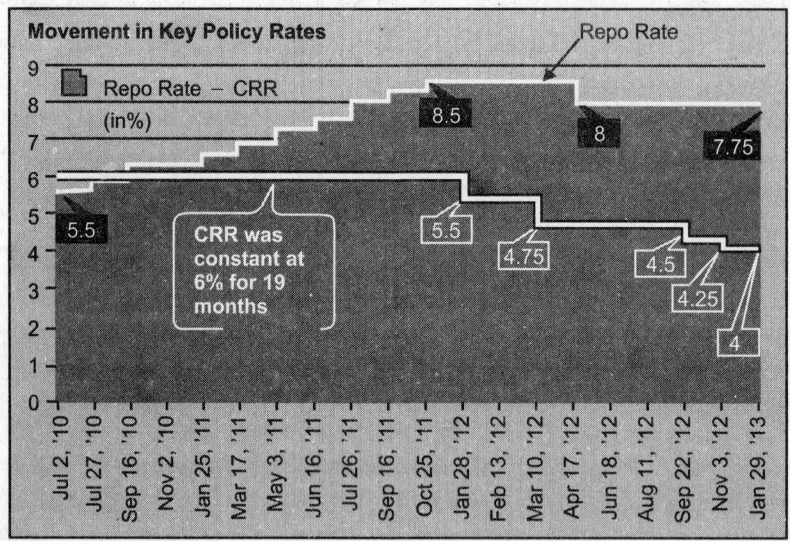

The daily drawings at the liquidity adjustment facility in the month of January 2013 averaged ₹ 90,000 crore despite RBI pumping in ₹ 82,000 crore through CRR cut and open market operations. This suggested that there was a structural liquidity deficit and that prompted the CRR decision in addition to the rate action.

Risk Factors to Growth

There are five risk factors to economic grwoth that IBI indicated. The first risk factor related to twin deficits : risk arising from *high current account deficit* (CAD) and *large fiscal deficit;* the second risk was from global outlook, implications of which were for financing our current account deficit (CAD); the third risk factor related to the *inflation outlook:* even as demand pressures has ebbed, sustained reduction in inflation would have to come from vigorous supply response; the fourth risk factor was *about investment*, which was very important because the key to stimulating growth was a vigorous and sustained revival in investment; finally RBI also mentioned the *bank asset quality.* Banks and indeed the RBI were quite understandably concerned about the high level of bad loans but it was also concerned that the high bad loans should not cut into the flow of credit to productive sectors of the economy. RBI pointed out that decline in inflation provided some room for relaxation of monetary policy to give greater emphasis to growth risk.

Risk of Inflation. However, RBI pointed out that despite the recent decline in inflation there were upside risks to inflation in future. The first risk was about food inflation. Both in WPI and CPI, the share of food inflation had been high and that could put upward pressure on inflationary expectations and there would be pressure and obligation on monetary policy to respond to entrenched inflationary expectations. The second risk came from the monthly diesel price increases. This was a good thing for long-term inflation management but in the short term it would put inflationary pressures and thereby have implications for inflationary expectations.

The third risk to inflation related to *global crude prices.* They had plateaued in the last couple of months. Crude oil prices, going forward, will depend on economic, financial and geo-political factors. As far as the RBI was concerned, crude oil price also depended on the exchange rate movement.

The fourth risk factor to inflation is *suppressed inflation.* The RBI expected that coal prices would be adjusted later this year, perhaps in April. There will be a consequent adjustment in electricity prices. Hence, some of the suppressed inflation would come out and that would exert inflationary pressure.

Finally, there was the *pressure from wages*. Rural wages continued to go up. What was of concern was that this increase was not accompanied with commensurate improvement in productivity.

Risk of Current Account Deficit

By far the biggest risk, according to RBI, for inflation and for macroeconomic management was the CAD in the context of slowing growth and high fiscal deficit. For the first half of FY 2013, CAD was 4.7 per cent of GDP. Third quarter trade numbers were quite disturbing for which CAD was estimated at 6.7 per cent of GDP. It was a problem because it had implications for financing the CAD and for our exchange rate stability.

Caution for Future Monetary Policy

RBI in its third quarterly review of the year 2012-13 cautioned that if inflation and current account deficit did not improve as expected by it, then the scope for further easing of monetary policy would be limited.

Evaluation of Easing of Monetary Policy in Third Quarterly Review (2012-13)

At long last RBI yielded to pressure put by Government and the corporate sector and on January 29, 2013, cut its repo interest rate and cash reserve ratio by 25 basis points each. It apparently justified its decision by pointing out the recent fall in headline WPI inflation and core inflation (*i.e.* non-food manufacturing inflation) in the third quarter of 2012-13 and much loss of rate of economic growth during this period. Its decision just ignored CPI inflation which was estimated at around 11 per cent (*i.e.* a double digit figure) in January 2013. In our view inflationary expectations depend more on CPI inflation since food prices which have risen sharply in the last two years play an important role in influencing inflationary expectations and lead to high wages which sets wage-price spiral into motion.

Further, it is not clear whether the recent decline in WPI headline inflation and core inflation will be sustained. Besides, the RBI itself points out that risk of suppressed inflation persists since as Government raises fuel prices, electricity and food prices to reduce its subsidy but the suppressed inflation will come into open. This raises the question whether RBI will follow through and continue to cut its policy rates in the year 2013.

As regards growth, it is unlikely to pick up in the short run. Demand may have bottomed out as RBI points out but the supply side has lagged for many years now. The supply-side bottlenecks such as of coal production, iron ore production, power generation and issues relating to land acquisition will limit the supply-side responses to achieve higher rate of economic growth. Besides, the need to curtail the fiscal deficit will mean that big push to the infrastructure spending by the government is unlikely in the near future. Already to reduce fiscal deficit for the year 2012-13 to 5.2% of GDP, the finance minister had cut capital and plan expenditure. The easing of monetary policy cannot solve the supply-side bottlenecks to growth.

Further, as high inflation reduced the *real* rate of interest on bank deposits led the people to move their saving funds to physical assets such as gold, real estate as hedge against inflation. This increased gold imports in a very large quantity and led to the sharp increase in our current account deficit (CAD) which reduced the value of Indian rupee adding to inflation. Besides, contrary to the RBI intentions, the cut in repo rate and cash reserve ratio has eased the liquidity of banks which has prompted the banks to reduce deposit rates to keep their margins. This will further induce the people to shift their savings to physical assets and thus reducing the financial savings with its adverse effect on investment which RBI wanted to raise.

QUESTIONS FOR REVIEW

1. Discuss the objectives of monetary policy in a developing economy.
2. What is meant by price stability ? "Of the various objectives price stability is perhaps the one that can be pursued most effectively by monetary policy" (C. Rangarajan). Discuss.
3. "The objective of achieving price stability through monetary policy clashes with its objective of economic growth". Do you agree ? Discuss.
4. "Both the large depreciation and appreciation of rupee is bad" Explain the measures that have been taken by RBI from time to time to ensure exchange rate stability.
5. Explain the role of monetary policy to promote economic growth in the economy.
6. Explain the role of monetary policy in promoting saving and investment in developing countries.
7. Explain the role of monetary policy in ensuring price stability in a developing economy. What tools of monetary have been used by Reserve Bank to control inflation in the Indian economy and with what success ?
8. Explain monetary policy of Reserve Bank of India before 1996. Was it targeted only at controlling inflation in the Indian economy ?
9. From Oct. 2008 to Jan. 2009 Reserve Bank of India followed easy monetary policy to promote private investment and revive the Indian economy from recession. Explain what monetary steps it had taken in this direction and how far they succeeded in raising investment.
10. What are repo rate and reverse repo rate ? How are they used to regulate liquidity in the Indian economy ?
11. Monetary policy faces the ticklish problem of trade-off between inflation and growth. Has RBI successfully tackled this problem since 1996 ? Explain.
12. To get rid of recession, monetary policy is ineffective and fiscal policy can be successfully used to revive the economy. In the light of this Keynes's view, comment on the success of policies adopted in the US and India to tackle recession/slowdown during 2007-09.
13. Explain the tight monetary policy adopted by the Reserve Bank of India from the second half of 2009-10. Discuss why it failed to control inflation.
14. Despite raising repo rate 13 times from Jan. 2010 to Nov. 2011, by the Reserve Bank of India, inflation remained at the elevated level of above 9 per cent year-on-year basis. Discuss why this dear monetary policy failed to check inflaton.
15. Explain '*growth as inflation*' dilemma faced by the Reserve Bank of India in the conduct of its tight monetary policy.

CHAPTER 20
Supply of Money and its Determinants

Money supply plays a crucial role in the determination of price level and interest rate. In the present chapter we shall explain what determines the money supply in an economy. In economic analysis it is generally presumed that money supply is determined by the policy of Central Bank of a country and the Government. However, this is not fully correct as in the determination of money supply, besides Central Bank and Government, the public and commercial banks also play an important role. There are various measures of money supply depending upon which types of deposits of banks and other financial institutions are included in it. We will explain various measures of money supply later in this chapter.

Importance of Money Supply

Growth of money supply is an important factor not only for acceleration of the process of economic development but also for the achievement of price stability in the economy. What constitutes the money supply and what factors causes variation and growth in money supply will be explained in the present chapter. There must be controlled expansion of money supply if the objective of development with stability is to be achieved. A healthy growth of an economy requires that there should be neither inflation nor deflation. Inflation is the greatest headache of a developing economy. A mild inflation arising out of the creation of money by deficit financing may stimulate investment by raising profit expectations and extracting forced savings. But a runaway inflation is highly detrimental to economic growth. The developing economies have to face the problem of inadequacy of resources in initial stages of development and it can make up this deficiency by deficit financing. But it has to be kept strictly within safe limits. Thus, increase in money supply affects vitally the rate of economic growth. In fact, it is now regarded as a legitimate instrument of economic growth. Kept within proper limits it can accelerate economic growth but exceeding of the limits will retard it. Thus, management of money supply is essential in the interest of steady economic growth.

THE CONCEPT OF MONEY SUPPLY AND ITS MEASUREMENT

By money supply we mean the total stock of monetary media of exchange available to a society for use in connection with the economic activity of the country. According to the standard concept of money supply, it is composed of the following two elements :

1. Currency with the public,
2. Demand deposits with the public.

Before explaining these two components of money supply two things must be noted with regard to the money supply in the economy. First, the money supply refers to the total sum of money available to the public in the economy *at a point of time*. That is, money supply is a *stock concept* in sharp contrast to the national income which is a flow representing the value of goods and services produced *per unit of time*, usually taken as a year. Secondly, money supply always refers to the amount of money *held by the public*. In the term public are included households, firms and institutions other than banks and the government. The rationale behind considering money supply as held by the public is to separate the producers of money from those who use money to fulfil their various types of demand for money. Since the Government and the banks produce or create money for the use by the public, the money (cash reserves) held by them are not used for transaction and speculative purposes and are excluded from the standard measures of money supply. This *separation of producers of money from the users of money is important from the viewpoint of both monetary theory and policy.*[1]

Let us explain the two components of money supply at some length.

Currency with the Public

In order to arrive at the total currency with the public in India we add the following items:

1. Currency notes in circulation issued by the Reserve Bank of India.
2. The number of rupee notes and coins in circulation.
3. Small coins in circulation.

It is worth noting that *cash reserves* with the banks has to be deducted from the value of the above three items of currency in order to arrive at the total currency with the public. This is because cash reserves with the banks must remain with them and cannot therefore be used for making payments for goods or by any commercial banks' transactions. It may further be noted that these days paper currency issued by Reserve Bank of India (RBI) are not fully backed by the reserves of gold and silver, nor it is considered necessary to do so. Full backing of paper currency by reserves of gold prevailed in the past when gold standard or silver standard type of monetary system existed. According to the modern economic thinking the magnitude of currency issued should be determined by the monetary needs of the economy and not by the available reserves of gold and silver. As mentioned in the last chapter, as in other developed countries, since 1957 Reserve Bank of India follows Minimum Reserve System of issuing currency. Under this system, minimum reserves of Rs. 200 crores of gold and other approved securities (such as dollars, pound sterling, etc.) have to be kept and against this any amount of currency can be issued depending on the monetary requirements of the economy.

As stated earlier, RBI is not bound to convert notes into equal value of gold or silver. In the present times currency is inconvertible. The word written on the note, say 100 rupee notes and signed by the governor of RBI that 'I promise to pay the bearer a sum of 100 rupees' is only a legacy of the past and does not imply its convertibility into gold or silver. Another important thing to note is that paper currency or coins are *fiat money*, which means that currency notes and metallic coins serve as money on the bases of the *fiat* (*i.e.* order) of the Government. In other words, on the authority of the Government no one can refuse to accept them in payment for the transaction made. That is why they are called *legal tender*.

Demand Deposits with the Public

The other important component of money supply are demand deposits of the public with the banks. These demand deposits held by the public are also called *bank money* or *deposit money*. Deposits with the banks are broadly divided into two types: demand deposits and time deposits. Demand deposits in the banks are those deposits which can be withdrawn by drawing cheques on them. Through cheques these deposits can be transferred to others for making payments from whom goods and services have been purchased. Thus, cheques make these demand deposits as a medium of exchange and therefore make them to serve as money. It may be noted that demand deposits are *fiduciary money proper*. Fiduciary money is one which functions as money on the basis of *trust of* the persons who make payment rather than on the basis of the authority of Government. Thus, despite the fact that demand deposits and cheques through which they are operated are not legal tender, they functions as money on the basis of the trust commanded by those who draw cheques on them. They are money as they are generally acceptable as medium of payment.

---

1. S. B. Gupta, *Monetary Economics : Institutions, Theory and Policy*, S. Chand & Co., New Delhi, 3rd Edition, 1997, p. 272.

Bank deposits are created when people deposits currency with them. But far more important is that banks themselves create deposits when they give advances to businessmen and others. On the basis of small cash reserves of currency, they are able to create a much larger amount of demand deposits through a system called *fractional reserve system* which will be explained later in detail.

In the developed countries such as USA and Great Britain deposit money accounted for over 80 per cent of the total money supply, currency being a relatively small part of it. This is because banking system has greatly developed there and also people have developed banking habits. On the other hand, in the developing countries banking has not developed sufficiently and also people have not acquired banking habits and they prefer to make transactions in currency. However in India after 50 years of independence and economic development the proportion of bank deposits in the money supply has risen to about 50 per cent.

FOUR MEASURES OF MONEY SUPPLY

Several definitions of money supply have been given and therefore various measures of money supply based on them have been estimated. First, different components of money supply have been distinguished on the basis of the different functions that money perform. For example, demand deposits, credit card and currency are used by the people primarily as a medium of exchange for buying goods and services and making other transactions. Obviously, they are money because they are used as a medium of exchange and are generally referred to as M_1. Another measure of money supply is M_3 which includes both M_1 and time deposits held by the public in the banks. Time deposits are money that people hold as store of value.

The main reason why money supply is classified into various measures on the basis of its functions is that effective predictions can be made about the likely affects on the economy of changes in the different components of money supply. For example, if M_1 is increasing fastly it can be reasonably expected that pepole are planning to make a large number of transactions. On the other hand, if time-deposits component of money-supply measure M_3 which serves as a store of value is increasing rapidly, it can be validly concluded that people are planning to save more and accordingly consume less. Therefore, it is believed that for monetary analysis and policy formulation, a single measure of money supply is not only inadequate but may be misleading too. Hence various measures of money supply are prepared to meet the needs of monetary analysis and policy formulation.

Recently in India as well as in some developed countries, four concepts of money supply have been distinguished. The definition of money supply given above represents a narrow measure of money supply and is generally described as M_1. From April 1977, the Reserve Bank of India has adopted four concepts of money supply in its analysis of the quantum of and variations in money supply. These four concepts of measures of money supply are explained below.

1. Money Supply M1 or Narrow Money. This is the narrow measure of money supply and is composed of the following items:

$$M_1 = C + DD + OD$$

where C = Currency with the public

DD = Demand deposits with the public in the Commercial and Cooperative Banks.

OD = Other deposits held by the public with Reserve Bank of India.

The money supply is the most liquid measure of money supply as the money included in it can be easily used as a medium of exchange, that is, as a means of making payments for transactions.

Currency with the public (C) in the above measure of money supply consists of the followings:

(*i*) Notes in circulation.

(*ii*) Circulation of rupee coins as well as small coins

(*iii*) Cash reserves on hand with all banks.

Note that in measuring demand deposits with the public in the banks (*i.e.*, *DD*), inter-bank deposits, that is, deposits held by a bank in other banks are excluded from this measure.

In the other deposits with Reserve Bank of India (*i.e.*, *OD*) deposits held by the Central and State Governments and a few others such as RBI Employees Pension and Provident Funds are excluded. However, these other deposits of Reserve Bank of India include the following items.

(*i*) Deposits of Insititutions such UTI, IDBI, IFCI, NABARD etc.

(*ii*) Demand deposits of foreign Central Banks and Foreign Governments.

(*iii*) Demand deposits of IMF and World Bank.

It may be noted that other deposits of Reserve Bank of India constitute a very small proportion (less than one per cent).

Money Supply *M*2

M_2 is a broader concept of money supply in India than M_1. In addition to the three items of M_1, the concept of money supply M_2 includes savings deposits with the post office savings banks. Thus,

$M2 = M1$ + Savings deposits with the post office savings banks.

The reason why money supply M_2 has been distinguished from M_1 is that saving deposits with post office savings banks are not as liquid as demand deposits with Commercial and Co-operative Banks as they are not chequable accounts. However, saving deposits with post offices are more liquid than time deposits with the banks.

Money Supply *M*3 or Broad Money

*M*3 is a broad concept of money supply. In addition to the items of money supply included in measure M_1, in money supply M_3 time deposits with the banks are also included. Thus

$M3 = M1$ + Time Deposits with the banks.

It is generally thought that time deposits serve as store of value and represent savings of the people and are not liquid as they cannot be withdrawn through drawing cheque on them. However, since loans from the banks can be easily obtained against these time deposits, they can be used if found necessary for transaction purposes in this way. Further, they can be withdrawn at any time by forgoing some interest earned on them.

It may be noted that recently *M*3 has become a popular measure of money supply. The working group on monetary reforms under the chairmanship of Late Prof. Sukhamoy Chakravarty recommended its use for monetary planning of the economy and setting target of the growth of money supply in terms of *M*3. Therefore, recently RBI in its analysis of growth of money supply and its effects on the economy has shifted to the use of M_3 measure of money supply. In the terminology of money supply employed by the Reserve Bank of India till April 1977, this *M*3 was called *Aggregate Monetary Resources* (AMR).

Money Supply M4

The measure *M*4 of money supply includes not only all the items of M_3 described above but also the total deposits with the post office savings organisation. However, this excludes contributions made by the public to the national saving certificates. Thus, $M4 = M3$ + *Total Deposits* with *Post Office Savings Organisation*.

Let us summarise the four concepts of money supply as used by Reserve Bank of India in the following tabular form:

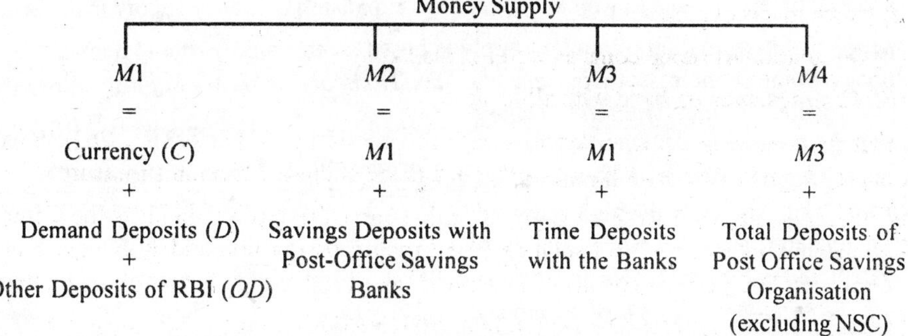

DETERMINANTS OF MONEY SUPPLY : MONEY MULTIPLIER THEORY

In order to explain the determinants of money supply in an economy we shall use M_1 concept of money supply which is the most fundamental concept of money supply. We shall denote it simply by M rather than M_1. As seen above this concept of money supply is composed of currency held by the public (C_p) and demand deposits with the banks (D). Thus

$$M = C_p + D \qquad ...(1)$$

where
M = Total money supply with the public
C_p = Currency with the public
D = Demand deposits held by the public

The two important determinants of money supply as described in (1) are (*a*) the amounts of high-powered money which is also called *Reserve Money* by the Reserve Bank of India and (*b*) the size of money multiplier. We explain below the role of these two factors in the determination of money supply in the economy.

1. **High-Powered Money (*H*).** The high-powered money which we denote by H consists of the currency (notes and coins) issued by the Government and the Reserve Bank of India. A part of the currency issued is held by the public, which we designate as C_p and a part is held by the banks as reserves which we designate as R. A part of these currency reserves of the banks is held by them in their own cash vaults and a part is deposited in the Reserve Bank of India in the Reserve Accounts which banks hold with RBI. Accordingly, the high-powered money can be obtained as sum of currency held by the public and the part held by the banks as reserves. Thus

$$H = C_p + R \qquad ...(2)$$

where
H = the amount of high-powered money
C_p = Currency held by the public
R = Cash Reserves of currency with the banks.

It is worth noting that Reserve Bank of India and Government are *producers of the high-powered money* and the commercial banks do not have any role in producing this high-powered money (H). However, commercial banks are *producers of demand deposits* which are also used as money like currency. But for producing demand deposits or credit, banks have to keep with themselves cash *reserves of currency* which have been denoted by R in equation (2) above. Since these cash reserves with the banks serve as a basis for the multiple creation of demand deposits which constitute an important part of total money supply in the economy, it provides high poweredness to the currency issued by Reserve Bank and Government. A glance at equations (1) and (2) above will reveal that the difference in the two equations, one describing the total money supply and the other high-powered money is that whereas in the former, demand deposits (D) are added to the currency held by the public, in the later it is cash reserves (R) of the banks that are added to the currency held by the public. In fact, it is against these cash reserves (R) that banks are able to create a multiple expansion of credit or demand deposits due to which there is large expansion in money supply in the economy.

The theory of determination of money supply is based on the supply of and demand for high-powered money. Some economists therefore call it '*The H Theory of Money Supply*[2]. However, it is more popularly called '*Money-multiplier Theory of Money Supply*' because it explains the determination of money supply as a certain multiple of the high-powered money. How the high-powered money (H) is related to the total money supply is graphically depicted in Fig. 20.1. T*he base of this figure shows the supply of high-powered money (H), while the top of the figure shows the total stock of money* supply. It will be seen that the total stock of money supply (that is, the top) is determined by a multiple of the high-powered money (H). It will be further seen that whereas currency held by the public (C_p) uses the same amount of high-powered money, that is, there is one-to-one relationship between currency held by the public and the money supply. In sharp contrast to this, bank deposits (D) are a multiple of the cash reserves (R) of the banks which are part of the supply of high-powered money. That is, one rupee of high-powered money kept as bank reserves gives rise to much more amount of demand deposits. Thus, the relationship between money supply and the high-powered money is determined by the money multiplier. The money multiplier which we denote by m is the ratio of total money supply (M) to the stock of high-powered money, that is, $m = \frac{M}{H}$. The size of money multiplier depends on the preference of the public to hold currency relative to deposits, (that is, ratio of currency to deposits which we denote by K) and banks' desired cash reserves ratio to deposits which we call r. We explain below the precise multiplier relationship between high-powered money and the total stock of money supply.

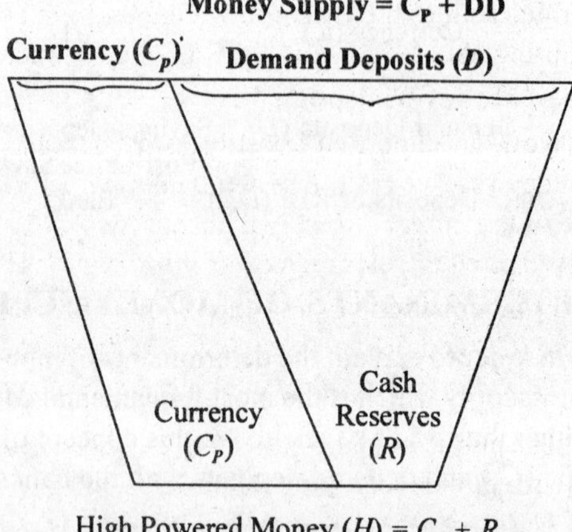

Fig. 20.1. *The High Powered Money and the Stock of Total Money-Supply*

It follows from above that if there is increase in currency held by the public which is a part of the high powered money with demand deposits remaining unchanged, there will be a direct increase in the money supply in the economy because this constitutes a part of the money supply. If instead currency reserves held by the banks increase, this will not change the money supply immediately but will set in motion a process of multiple creation of demand deposits of the public in the banks. Although banks use these currency reserves held by the public which constitutes a part of the high-powered money to give more loans to the businessmen and thus create demand deposits, they do not affect either the amount of currency or the composition of high-powered money. The *amount of high-powered money is fixed by RBI by its past actions. Thus, changes in high-powered money are the result of decisions of Reserve Bank of India or the Government which own and controls it.*

2. **Money Multiplier.** As stated above, money multiplier is the degree to which money supply is expanded as a result of the increase in high-powered money. Thus

$$m = \frac{M}{H}$$

Rearranging we have,

$$M = H.m \qquad ...(3)$$

2. See S.B. Gupta, *Monetary Economics: Institutions Theory and Policy*, 3rd Edition, 1992, S. Chand & Co., New Delhi.

Thus money supply is determined by the size of money multiplier (m) and the amount of high-powered money (H). If we know the value of money multiplier we can predict how much money will change when there is a change in the amount of high-powered money. As mentioned above, change in the high-powered money is decided and controlled by Reserve Bank of India, the money multiplier determines the extent to which decision by RBI regarding the change in high-powered money will bring about change in the total money supply in the economy.

Size of Money Multiplier

Now, an important question is what determines the size of money multiplier. It is the cash or currency reserve ratio r of the banks (which determines deposit multiplier) and currency-deposit ratio of the public (which we denote by k) which together determines size of money multiplier. We derive below the expression for the size of multiplier.

From equation (1) above, we know that total money supply (M) consists of currency with the public (C_p) and demand deposits with the banks. Thus

$$M = C_p + D \qquad \ldots (1)$$

The public hold the amount of currency in a certain ratio of demand deposits with the banks. Let this currency-deposit ratio be devoted by k,

$$C_p = kD$$

Substituting kD for C_p in equation (1) we have

$$M = kD + D = (k + 1)D \qquad \ldots (2)$$

Now take equation which defines high powered money (H) as

$$H = C_p + R \qquad \ldots (3)$$

where R represents cash or currency reserves which banks keep as a certain ratio of their deposits and is called cash-reserve ratio and is denoted by r. Thus

$$R = rD$$

Now substituting rD for R and kD for C_p in equation (3) we have

$$H = kD + rD$$

$$H = (k + r)\, D \qquad \ldots (4)$$

Now money multiplier is ratio of total money supply to the high powered money, therefore we divide equation (1) by equation (4), to get the value of multiplier, which we denote by m. Thus

$$m = \frac{M}{H} = \frac{(k+1)D}{(k+r)D} = \frac{k+1}{k+r}$$

or, Money multiplier $(m) = \dfrac{M}{H} = \dfrac{1+k}{r+k}$

or

$$M = H\frac{1+k}{r+k} \qquad \ldots (4)$$

where r = Reserve ratio of the *banks*

k = Currency-deposit ratio of the *public.*

From above it follows that money supply is determined by the high powered money (which is also called reserve money) times the *money multiplier which is equal to* $\dfrac{1+k}{r+k}$. Thus the following factors determine money supply in the economy:

1. H, that is, the amount of high powered money.

2. r, that is, *cash reserve ratio* of banks (*i.e.*, ratio of currency reserves to deposits in the banks). This cash reserve ratio of banks determines the magnitude of money multiplier. The smaller the cash reserve ratio of the banks, the larger is the money multiplier.
3. k, that is, *currency-deposit ratio of the public*. The smaller the currency-deposit ratio of the public, the larger is the size of money multiplier.

From the equation (4) expressing the determinants of money supply, it follows that *money supply will increase* :

1. When the supply of high-powered money (*i.e.*, reserve money) H increases;
2. When the currency-deposit ratio (k) of the public decreases[3]; and
3. When the currency reserves-deposit ratio (*i.e.*, cash reserve ratio) of the banks (r) falls.

The Reserve Ratio and the Deposit Multiplier

In a later chapter we will see that because of *fractional reserve system*, with a small increase in cash reserves with the banks, they are able to create a multiple increase in total demand deposits which are an important part of money supply. The ratio of change in total deposits to a change in reserves is called the *deposit multiplier* which depends on cash reserve ratio. The value of deposit multiplier is the reciprocal of cash reserve ratio, $\left(d_m = \frac{1}{r}\right)$ where d_m stands for deposit multiplier. If cash reserve ratio is 10 per cent of deposits, then $d_m = \frac{1}{0.10} = 10$. Thus deposit multiplier of 10 shows that for every ₹ 100 increase in cash reserves with the banks, there will be expansion in demand deposits of the banks by ₹ 1000 assuming that no leakage of cash to the public occurs during the process of deposit expansion by the banks. In India, this currency-reserve ratio of banks is called Cash Reserve Ratio (CRR) and is regulated by RBI.

Currency-Deposit Ratio and Multiplier

However, in the real world, with the increase in reserves of the banks, demand deposits and money supply do not increase to the full extent of deposit multiplier. This is for two reasons. First, the public does not hold all its money balances in the form of demand deposits with the banks. When as a result of increase in cash reserves, banks start increasing demand deposits, the people may also like to have some more currency with them as money balances. This means during the process of creation of demand deposits by banks, some currency is leaked out from the banks to the people. This drainage of currency to the people in the real world reduces the magnitude of expansion of demand deposit and therefore the size of money multiplier. Suppose the cash reserve ratio is 10 per cent and cash or currency of ₹ 100 is deposited in a bank A. The bank A will lend out ₹ 90 and therefore create demand deposits of ₹ 90 and so the process will continue as the borrowers use these deposits for payment through cheques to others who deposit them in another bank B. However, if borrower of bank A withdraws ₹ 10 in cash from the bank and issue cheques of the remaining borrowed amount of ₹ 80, then bank B will have only ₹ 80 as new deposits instead of ₹ 90 which it would have if cash of ₹ 10 was not withdrawn by the borrower. With these new deposits of ₹ 80, bank B will create demand deposits of ₹ 72, that is, it will lend out ₹ 72 and keep

3. It will be noticed that in the equation $M = H\frac{1+k}{r+k}$, k appears both in the numerator and denominator. *While in the numerator k is added to unity, in the denominator it is added to fraction.* Mathematically, it means that a fall in k will affect the denominator relatively more than the numerator. Therefore, with fall in k, the value of multiplier term $\frac{1+k}{r+k}$, will increase. Thus, with decrease in k, the money supply will increase and *vice versa*.

₹ 8 as reserves with it $\left(80\times\frac{10}{100}=8\right)$. The drainage of currency may occur during all the subsequent stages of deposit expansion in the banking system. The greater the leakage of currency, the lower will be the money multiplier. We thus see the currency-deposit ratio, which we denote by k is an important determinant of the actual value of money multiplier.

It is important to note that deposit multiplier works both ways, positively when cash reserves with banks increase, and negatively when the cash reserves with the banks decline. That is, when there is a decrease in currency reserves with the banks, there will be multiple contraction in demand deposits with the banks.

Excess Reserves

In the explanation of the expansion of demand deposits or deposit multiplier we assumed that banks do not keep currency reserves in excess of the *required* cash reserve ratio. The ratio r in the deposit multiplier is the *required cash reserve ratio* fixed by Reserve Bank of India. However, banks like to keep with themselves some excess reserves, the amount of which depend on the extent of liquidity (*i.e.* availability of cash with them) and profitability of making investment and rate of interest on loans advanced to business firms. Therefore, the *desired reserve ratio* is greater than the statutory minimum required reserve ratio. Obviously, the holding of excess reserves by the banks also reduce the value of deposit multiplier.

Conclusion

Theory of determination of money supply explains how a given supply of high-powered money (which is also called *monetary base or reserve money*), leads to multiple expansion in money supply through the working of money multiplier. We have seen above how a small increase in reserves of currency with the banks leads to a multiple expansion in demand deposits by the banks through the process of deposit multiplier and thus causes growth of money supply in the economy. Deposit multiplier measures how much increase in demand deposits (or money supply) occur as a result of a given increase in cash or currency, reserves with the banks depending on the required cash reserve ratio (r) if there are no cash drainage from the banking system. But in the real world drainage of currency does take place which reduce the extent of expansion of money supply following the increase in cash reserves with the banks. Therefore, *the deposit multiplier exaggerates the actual increase in money supply from a given increase in cash reserves with the banks*. In contrast, money multiplier takes into account these leakages of currency from the banking system and therefore measures actual increase in money supply when the cash reserves with the banks increase. *The money multiplier can be defined as increase in money supply for every rupee increase in cash reserves (or high powered money), drainage of currency having been taken into account. Therefore, money multiplier is less than the deposit multiplier.*

It is worth noting that rapid growth in money supply in India has been due to the increase in high-powered money H, or what is also called Reserve Money by Reserve Bank of India, the money multiplier remaining almost constant.

The money supply in a country can be changed by Reserve Bank of India by undertaking open market operations, changing minimum required currency reserve-deposit ratio, and by varying the bank rate. The main source of growth in money supply in India is creation of credit by RBI for Government for financing its budget deficit and thus creating high-powered money. Further, though the required currency reserve-deposit ratio of banks can be easily varied by RBI, the actual currency reserve-deposit ratio cannot be so easily varied as reserves maintained by banks not only depend on minimum required cash reserve ratio but also on their willingness to hold excess reserves.

Lastly[4], an important noteworthy point is that though money multiplier does not show much variation in the long run, it can change significantly in the short run causing large variations in

4. Note that Reserve Bank of India calls the high-powered money as *Reserve Money* (RM).

money supply. This unpredictable variation in money multiplier in the short run affecting money supply in the economy prevents the Central Bank of a country from controlling exactly and precisely the money supply in the economy.

FACTORS DETERMINING MONEY SUPPLY : RBI'S APROACH

In its analysis of factors determining money supply in India and sources of variation in it, Reserve Bank of India does not follow any explicit theory of money supply such as money multiplier theory explained above. It provides only purely *accounting or ex-post analysis* of variations in money supply and the factors or sources causing these variations. Although Reserve Bank provides figures of the high powered money in its analysis, it virtually clubs high powered money with the ordinary money to calculate the total money supply in the country and therefore does not give due importance to the high powered money as an important factor causing variation in money supply in the economy. Further, *Reserve Bank also does not lay emphasis on the two behavioural ratios, namely, desired currency-deposit ratio (k) of the public and desired cash reserve ratio* (*r*) of the banks as determinants of money supply, though it provides *ex-post* or realised figures of these ratios. We explain below Reserve Bank's analysis of sources of variation in money supply.

Reserve Bank of India classifies factors determining money supply into the following categories:

(a) Government borrowing from the banking system;
(b) Borrowing of the private or commercial sector from the banking system;
(c) Changes in net foreign assets held by the Reserve Bank of India caused by changes in balance of payments position; and
(d) Government's currency liabilities to the public.

Bank Credit to the Government. When the Government expenditure exceeds government revenue and there is deficit in government's budget, then *it may* resort to borrowing from Reserve Bank of India which creates new currency notes for the purpose. This creation of new currency for financing the deficit of the Central Government Budget is known as *monetiztion of deficit*. It was previously called *deficit financing*. Monetization of deficit is an important source of change in money supply in the economy. It may noted here that since 1995 when Fiscal Responsibility and Budget Management (FRBM) Act was passed Central Government fiscal deficit is financed by borrowing through selling Government bonds to the banks. This has caused a stoppage of RBI's credit to the Government through monetisation of fiscal deficit. However, for the year 2008-09 and 2009-10 the Government is thinking of *directly borrowing from RBI* by selling its bonds to it and thus monetising a part of its fiscal deficit which has greatly risen due to large increase in Government expenditure incurred to prevent slowdown in economic growth. Thus in recent years budget deficit of the Central Government has been largely financed by borrowing from the Commercial banks and other financial institutions who buy government securities or bonds.

The commercial banks also lend money to the Government for purchase of foodgrains by the Food Corporation of India. The creation of credit by the banks when they lend to the Government leads to the increase in money supply in the economy. When the Government uses this bank credit for meeting its expenditure, money supply with the public increases.

Bank Credit to the Commercial or Private Sector. The private sector also borrows from the banking system when its own resources are less than its total expenditure. This also adds to the money supply with the public because when the banks lend they create credit or deposits. Bank deposits, as we have seen above, is a part of money supply in the economy. This also affects the money supply in the same manner as the Government borrowing from the banking system. There is, however, an important difference. However, the Central Bank can influence the credit supply by the banks to the private sector by changing liquidity with the banks through making changes in cash reserve ratio.

Changes in Net Foreign Exchange Assets. Changes in the foreign exchange assets held by the Reserve Bank can also bring about a change in the money supply. The change in the net foreign assets may be caused by balance of payment situation. Suppose there is deficit in balance of payments and therefore available foreign exchange is less than the country needs to pay for its imports, both visible and invisible. In order to meet this deficit in balance of payments the country will have to dispose of some of its foreign exchange assets. If there is a net deficit in balance of payments, rupees would flow into the Reserve Bank which pays out foreign exchange reserves in return for the rupee currency. This would have the effect of reducing the *Reserve Money* (*i.e.* the high powered money) in India and the contraction of money supply with the public. Opposite result would follow when there is a net surplus in balance of payments of a country.

It follows from above that a deficit in the balance of payments decreases the supply of rupee currency (that is, high powered or reserve money) in the economy and thereby causes contraction in money supply with the public. On the contrary, a surplus in the balance of payments will increase the foreign exchange assets and thereby will lead to the expansion in reserve money and money supply in the economy.

It may also be noted that apart from surplus in balance of payments foreign exchange reserves or assets may also come through *capital inflows* by either foreign aid or deposits in Indian banks by NRI or foreign direct investment made by foreign companies in India or by portfolio investment by foreign institutional inverstors (FII). For example, in years 2005 to 2008 there had been a large-scale inflow of foreign exchange through investment made by foreign companies in India. As a result, our foreign exchange reserves substantially went up which resulted in the issue and expansion of rupee currency in circulation. But RBI neutralised its monetary impact to a large extent by moping up liquidity of the banks through open market operations by selling them Government bonds.

The plenty of foreign exchange receives posed a problem of its optimal use during 2005-2008. One proposal was to use foreign exchange reserves to finance the infrastructure projects which are crucial for accelerating economic growth. But argument against this was that the use of foreign exchange reserves will lead to expansion in money supply which would cause higher rate of inflation. The other proposal was these foreign exchange reserves should be used to import goods in short supply which help in lowering inflation rate. But since September 2008, the opposite problem of *capital outflows* arose due to foreign institutional investors selling shares in Indian stock market and repatriating dollars abroad following the global financial crisis. These capital outflow increased the demand for dollars and caused depreciation of Indian rupee. In order to prevent the rapid depreciation of rupee, RBI sold dollars from its reserves and in return got rupees resulting in decline in the number of rupees in circulation, that is, decrease in money supply.

(*d*) Government's Currency Liabilities to the Public. Changes in money supply in the economy are also brought about by Government's currency liabilities to the public. Coins and one-rupee notes represent Government's currency liabilities to the public. On Jan. 28, 2005, there were Rs. 7374 crores of coins and one rupee notes as compared to Rs. 7296 crores on March 31, 2004. If Government's currency liabilities increase, the money supply also increases.

BUDGET DEFICITS AND MONEY SUPPLY

A budget deficit is also an important source of expansion of money supply in the economy. There are two possible links between budget deficit and growth in money supply. First, when following an expansionary fiscal policy the government raises its expenditure without financed by extra taxation and thereby causing a budget deficit, it will tend to raise interest rate. This happens when budget deficit is financed through borrowing from the market. As a result, demand for money or loanable funds increases which, given the supply of money, causes interest rate to rise. Rise in interest rate tends to reduce or crowd out private investment. If the Central Bank is following the policy of a fixed interest rate target, when the government resorts to borrowing to finance the budget deficit, then to prevent the rise in interest rate the Central Bank will take steps to increase the money supply in the economy.

The second link between budget deficit and expansion in money supply is direct. This occurs when the Central Bank itself purchases government securities when the government resorts to borrowing.[5] The Central Bank is said to *monetise* budget deficit when it purchases government securities as it prints new notes for the purpose and gives it to the government for meeting public expenditure. In some countries such as the US, Federal Reserve (which is the Central Bank of the USA) enjoys a good deal of independence from the Treasury (*i.e.,* the Government) and voluntarily decides when and how much to purchase government securities to finance its budget deficit.

Central Bank's Dilemma

The Central Bank of a country faces a dilemma in deciding whether or not to monetise budget deficit. If the central Bank does not monetise budget deficit to meet its increased expenditure, the government will borrow from the market and in the absence of any accomodating monetary policy this will tend to raise interest rate and thereby *reduce or crowd out private investment.* Referring to the policy of Federal Reserve of the United States, Dornbusch, Fischer and Startz write, " There is accordingly a temptation for the Federal Reserve to prevent crowding out by buying government securities thereby increasing the money supply and hence allows an expansion in income without a rise in interest rates"[7]

But the policy of monetisation of budget deficit by the Central Bank involves a risk. If the economy is working near full employment level, that is, at near full production capacity, monetisation of budget deficit will cause inflation in the economy. However, if the economy is in the grip of a severe depression, the risk of causing inflation through monetisation of budget deficit and consequent growth in money supply is not much there.

It follows from above that in any particular case the Central Bank, if it enjoys freedom from the Government, has to judge whether it should adopt accomodatory monetary policy to achieve its goal of interest-targeting or allow fiscal expansion through monetisation of budget deficit accompanied by the tight monetary policy to check inflation. It is the latter course of action that was adopted by Reserve Bank of India before 1995 when government's fiscal deficit was high and a good part of it was monetised by it.

MONEY SUPPLY AND THE OPEN ECONOMY

The transactions of an open economy also affects the growth of money supply in it. In the open economy there is free flow of goods and services through trade with foreign countries. Besides, in the open economy there are flows of capital between countries. The impact of transactions of an open economy on the money supply can be letter understood from national income identity of an open economy. National income of the open economy is written as

$$Y = C + I + G + NX \quad ...(1)$$

or

$$NX = Y - (C + I + G) \quad ...(2)$$

where NX stands for net exports or trade balance. In the trade balance if we also include exports and imports of services (*i.e.,* invisibles), then NX can be taken as current account balance.

The current account balance (NX) can be either positive or negative. If in equation (2) above aggregate expenditure ($C + I + G$) exceeds national output (Y), current account balance or NX will be negative, that is, imports will be greater than exports. In other words, there will be deficit in current account of the balance of payments. On the other hand, if aggregate expenditure is less than national

5. It is important to note that when government borrows from the market, it does so through sale of its securities (i.e. bonds)
7. Dornbusch, Fischer, and Startz, *op.cit.* 9th edition, 2004, p.275

income [$(C+I+G)<NX$], there will be surplus in current account balance of payments. This implies our exports will be greater than imports.

Now, if in a year there is deficit in current account, that is, *NX* is negative, it means our demand for foreign exchange, say the US dollars, for imports of goods and services will exceed the supply of foreign exchange. This situation is depicted in Fig. 20.2 where the curve *DD* represents demand curve for foreign exchange (US $) and *SS* is the supply curve of foreign exchange (US $) at exchange rate (₹ per US dollar) is *OR* and *LK* represents deficit in current account.

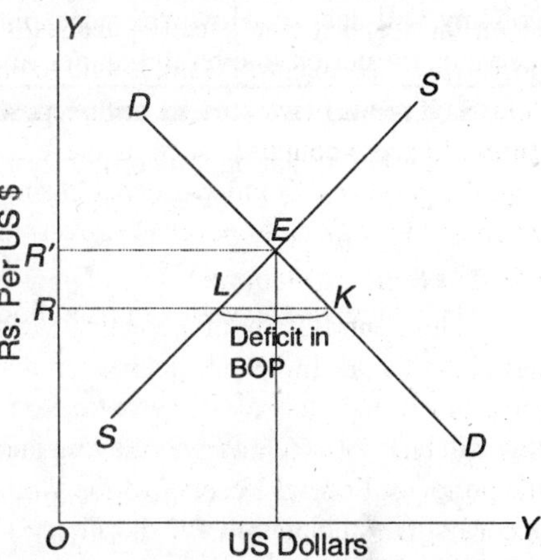

Fig. 20.2. *Deficit in Balance of Payments and Foreign Exchange Market*

If the economy is under flexible exchange rate regime and the Central Bank of the country does not intervene at all, the exchange rate will change to *OR′* and as a result deficit in current account balance will be eliminated and equilibrium restored at the new exchange rate. If there is such a situation, there is no impact on the money supply. However, if the Central Bank wants to maintain the exchange rate at *OR*, then current account deficit equal to *LK* has to be met. If there are no capital inflows, then to maintain the exchange rate at *OR*, the Central Bank of the country has to supply foreign exchange equal to *LK* out of the reserves held by it. But when the Central Bank (RBI in case of India) pays out foreign exchange from its reserves, *it will receive money (i.e., rupees in India)* from *importers of goods and services in return for foreign exchange paid to them to meet the deficit*. Thus some money (say Indian rupees) will flow into the Central Bank and thus withdrawn from circulation. As a result of Central Bank intervention to meet the current account deficit and to maintain the exchange rate money supply in the economy decreases. It is important to note that the Central Bank of the country cannot go on supplying foreign exchange reserves, year after year, for a long time because foreign exchange assets with the Central Bank are available in limited amount.

The above analysis of expansion in money supply as a result of use of foreign exchange reserves to meet the current account deficit is based on the two assumptions. First, it is assumed that there are no capital flows to meet the deficit in current account balance. Second, it is assumed the exchange rate is not allowed to change as result of inbalance between demand and supply of foreign exchange due to current account deficit.

Capital inflows. However, if there are sufficient net capital inflows accruing from the capital account of balance of payments, then deficit in current account (*i.e.*, negative *NX*) can be met by these capital inflows. In this case there will be no impact of deficit in current aczcount balance of payments on money supply in the economy.

Now take the opposite case of surplus in current account balance (*i.e.*, when *NX* is positive). This implies that the supply of foreign exchange exceeds demand for it. In the absence of capital out- flows this excess supply of foreign exchange will have to by purchased by the Central Bank if exchange rate is to be maintained. The Central Bank (RBI) will print new notes to pay for the purchase of foreign exchange. This will lead to the increase in money supply in the economy. However, if exchange rate is allowed to change, as the case under flexible exchange rate system, the exchange rate will adjust to bring supply and demand for foreign exchange in equilibrium.

Overall Balance of Payments and Capital Inflows

When in an open economy with flexible exchange rate regime there is *deficit in overall balance of payments* (*i.e.*, on both current and capital accounts), it means that capital inflows are insufficient to bridge the gap in the balance of payments, then, in case of India, this has to met with use of foreign exchange reserves by the Reserve Bank of India. When Reserve Bank of India pays foreign exchange (*e.g.* US $) to finance the deficit in overall balance of payments, it get rupees in return. Thus rupee currency flows into the RBI. As a result, money supply (rupee currency) in the economy will decline. However, an explained above, under flexible, rate system, if RBI does not intervene, the deficit in overall balance of payments will cause rupee to depreciate.

Saving and Investment and Open-Economy Capital Flows

According to national income identity of an open economy

$$Y = C + I + G + NX \quad ...(i)$$

or

$$Y - C - I - G = NX \quad ...(ii)$$

Deducting Tax revenue (T) from both sides of the above equation and after adjustment we have

$$(Y - T - C) - I + (T - G) = NX$$

Now, $Y - T - C$ = Private Saving and $T - G$ = Government Saving or Budget Surplus

The total saving (S) of the economy is

$$S = Y - T - C + T - G$$

or

$$S = Y - C - G$$

Now substituting $S = Y - C - G$ in equation (*ii*) above we have

$$S - I = NX \quad ...(iii)$$

Where S and I are domestic saving and investment.

When NX is negative, this implies that $I > S$, that is, excess of investment over domestic saving is financed by *capital inflows.* On the other hand, if NX is positive (*i.e.,* there is surplus in current account), it implies that $S > I$. In this case a part of national saving will be invested abroad.

Now suppose there is *surplus in overall balance of payment* as capital inflows exceed the deficit in current account. The large capital inflows can occur due to heavy foreign direct investment (FDI) and portfolio investment by foreign institutional investors (FII) as it happened in some years in India, especially in 2006-07, 2007-08 and recently in 2010-11. In the absence of intervention by RBI under the flexible exchange rate system, these large capital inflows will cause appreciation of Indian Rupee. In fact, though RBI has been intervening in foreign exchange market from time to time, its intervention has been only limited. As a result, between Oct. 2006 and Oct 2007, rupee appreciated by 15 per cent. By making our exports relatively expensive the appreciation of rupee has adversly affected our exports and therefore growth in GNP and employment. Besides, appreciation of rupee has made imports relatively cheaper and has led to large imports of goods and materials and thereby harming our domestic manufacturing industries.

To prevent the high appreciation of the Indian Rupee RBI has been purchasing US dollars from the foreign exchange market from time to time. When RBI purchases dollars from the foreign exchange market, it pays rupees to the sellers of foreign exchange. To do so more rupee currency is printed by RBI to pay for US dollars purchased by it. In this way more rupee currency (*i.e.,* high–powered money) comes into existence in the economy. Thus intervention by RBI to prevent appreciation of rupee results in increase in money supply in the economy.

The effect of large capital inflows and its effect on appreciation of currency and money supply in the Indian economy is illustrated in Fig. 20.3 where exchange rate of rupee for US dollars (₹ per US $) is measured on the Y-axis and number of US dollars are measured on the X-axis.

Initially the equilibrium between demand for and supply of dollars in the Indian foreign exchange market and equilibrium exchange rate is ₹ 48 per US $. As a result of large capital inflows supply curve of US dollars shifts to the right to $S'S'$. As a result, at the existing exchange rate of ₹ 48 per US dollar, *EH* is the increase in capital inflows. Now if under a variable exchange rate regime as it exists today the exchange rate is allowed to adjust freely, rupee will rise to ₹ 45 per US dollar. If Reserve Bank wants to manage it and tries to maintain it at ₹ 48 per US dollar it will have to buy US dollars equal to *EH* from the market. By buying US dollars equal to *EH* it will cause the demand curve for US dollars to shift to the right to the new position *D′D′* and the new equilibrium is at point *H* which corresponds to ₹ 48 per US dollar.

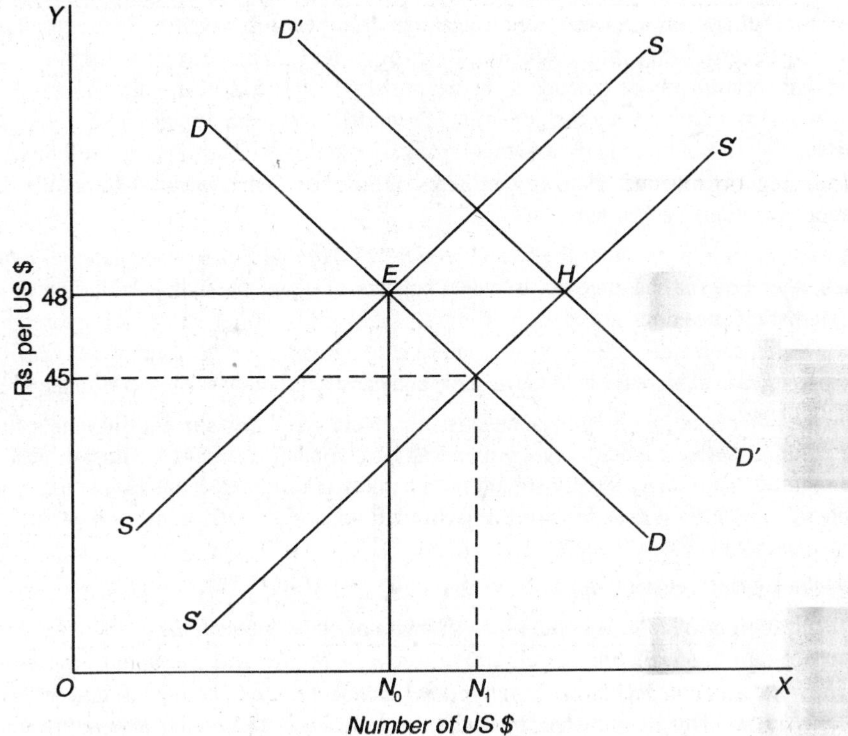

Fig. 20.3. *Capital Inflows and Appreciation of Rupee*

But for buying US dollars equal to *EH*, RBI will have to print new rupee currency to pay for US dollars. Thus more high powered money (*i.e.*, rupee currency) would come into circulation in the Indian economy. But why RBI did not intervene sufficiently to prevent the appreciation of rupee. This is because such intervention leads to the increase in money supply that is likely to cause inflation in the Indian economy. Therefore, RBI intervened only to a small degree and let the rupee to appreciate to some extent.

On the other hand, in 2011 the RBI faced the opposite problem when after August 2011, there was net *large capital outflow* from India due to uncertainty caused by European debt crisis and economic slowdown in the US. The FIIs which started selling Indian equity and bonds and converting rupees into US dollars. This led to the increase in demand for dollars resulting in appreciation of US dollar and *depreciation of Indian rupee*. The value of rupee which was around ₹ 45 to a US dollar in the first week of September 2011 depreciated to around ₹ 53 in the second-week of November 2011 and further to ₹ 54 in mid-December 2011. This depreciation of rupee will make our imports constlier which will tend to raise inflation if not matched by fall in international commodity prices. To prevent sharp depreciation of rupee the RBI intervened in the foreign exchange market by selling dollars in the market. As a result in the first week of January 2012 it moved in the range of ₹ 51 to ₹ 52 to a US dollar. Again its intervention was only limited. In fact, the RBI has no fixed target for maintaining exchange rate of rupee at any level and instead its policy is to *allow exchange rate of rupee to fluctuate within a band. In fact, RBI faces a dilemma which we discuss below.*

RBI Dilemma : External Balance and Internal Balance

RBI faces a dilemma because if it does not intervene in the face of large capital inflows rupee will appreciate much which will adversely affect our exports and therefore growth of GNP and employment in our economy. On the other hand, if it intervenes and purchases enough US dollars from the market to prevent any appreciation of rupee, it will cause large increase in money supply that would cause higher rate of inflation. A major objective of RBI is to control inflation. Therefore, RBI has to strike a balance between the two alternatives. It has been intervening in the foreign exchange market to prevent large appreciation of rupee. But it cannot buy inflows of foreign exchange indiscriminately as it leads to higher inflation. RBI has also resorted to *sterilization* of increase in money supply by selling government securities to the banks and thereby getting back the money issued by it. But there is limit to this sterilization operations as it has not unlimited amount of government securities to sell them to the banks. Hence the dilemma faced by it. We explain the sterilization operations by RBI later.

It follows from above that the two objectives of external balance and internal balance clash with each other External balance occurs when balance of payments is in equilibrium or close to it. When external balance does not exist the Central Bank will be either go on losing foreign exchange reserves which it cannot do so for long or it will be gaining foreign exchange reserves which also poses a problem as it leads to increase in money supply and causes inflationary pressures in the economy.

On the other hand, internal balance exists when the economy is in equilibrium at full employment or full productive capacity level without any inflationary pressures. Thus, to ensure internal balance requires that money supply should not be allowed to increase much. Since the two require different types of policy measure by the Central Bank, they clash with each other. Hence, the dilemma faced by the Central Bank.

Sterilization by the Central Bank

Sterilization provides a way out of the problem of clash between the goals of external balance and internal balance. *Sterilization refers to the action by the Central Bank of a country to offset or cancel the impact of its foreign exchange market intervention on the money supply through open market operations.* The sterilization measures can be used both to offset the reduction in money supply when in case of current account deficit the Central Bank of the country sells foreign exchange in the market and also when the Central Banks offsets the effect of increase in money supply when it buys foreign exchange from the market in case of surplus in balance of payments or when large capital inflows are coming into the economy.

Let us first explain sterlisation operation by the Central Bank in case of deficit in current account of the balance of payments. As seen above, the deficit in current account balance requires that the Central Bank to sell foreign exchange from its reserves to prevent the depreciation of domestic currency (that is, to maintain the exchange rate constant). The sale of foreign exchange in foreign exchange market by the Central Bank causes money supply in the economy to decrease that has deflationary effect on the economy. To avoid this adverse effect, the Central Bank buys government securities (*i.e.,* bonds) through open market operations. When it does so the Central Bank prints domestic currency to pay for the bonds it purchases. In this way money supply in the economy increases which offsets the decrease in money supply brought about by the Central Bank when it sells foreign exchange to prevent the depreciation of the domestic currency. Thus, provided it has enough foreign exchange assets, with sterilization operations by the Central Bank *persistent* deficit in balance of payments is possible because it *insulates* the money supply changes in the domestic economy from the Central Bank intervention in the foreign exchange market.

Sterilization Operations in Case of Surplus in Balance of Payments or Large Capital Inflows

Now, we take up the opposite case when there is surplus in balance of payments or when large capital inflows are taking place. This situation requires that Central Bank intervenes in the foreign exchange market and buys foreign exchange inflows from the market to maintain the foreign exchange rate or to prevent the appreciation of domestic currency. As mentioned above, in the two years (2006 - 08) due to large net capital inflows in the Indian economy there has been a quite large appreciation of the Indian rupee against US dollar that has produced undesirable effects. Therefore Reserve Bank has intervened in the foreign exchange market by buying US dollars to prevent too much appreciation of the Indian rupee. The purchase of foreign exchange (US dollars) from the foreign exchange market by the Reserve Bank has led to the increase in money supply in the Indian economy that has caused inflationary pressures. To sterilize the effect of this increase in money supply RBI has undertaken open market operations by *selling* government securities to the banks which have paid rupees to it. In this way through the sale of government securities some rupee currency has been withdrawn from the economy. In this way inflationary pressures created by the original increase in money supply through intervention in foreign exchange market have been offset.

QUESTIONS FOR REVIEW

1. Explain the concept of money supply. What are the factors responsible for the rapid increase in money supply.
2. Explain how supply of money depends upon the high powered money, the currency deposit ratio and cash reserve ratio.
3. Explain the impact of budget deficit on the supply of money in the economy. Explain the Central Bank's dilemma in this connection ?
4. Explain the impact of (1) deficit in balance of payments, and (2) large capital inflows on the money supply in the open economy. Explain sterilization operations by the central Bank of the country in each case.
5. Explain the Reserve Bank's dilemma in the face of large capital inflows in the Indian economy ?

CHAPTER 21
Demand for Money and Keynes's Liquidity Preference Theory of Interest

Introduction

Why people have demand for money to hold is an important issue in macroeconomics. The level of demand for money not only determines the rate of interest but also prices and national income of the economy. *Classical economists considered money as simply a means of payment or medium of exchange.* In the classical model, people therefore demand money in order to make payments for their purchase of goods and services. In other words, they want to keep money for transactions purposes. *On the other hand, J.M. Keynes laid stress on the store of value function of money.* According to him, money is an asset and people want to hold it so as to take advantage of changes in the price of this asset, that is, the rate of interest. Therefore, Keynes emphasised another motive for holding money which he called speculative motive. As will be explained in detail below, under speculative motive people demand to hold money balances to take advantages from the future changes in the rate of interest, or what means the same thing, from the future changes in bond prices.

An essential point to be noted about people's demand for money is that what people want is not *nominal* money holdings but *real money balances* (This is also referred to as simply *real balances*). This means that people are interested in the purchasing power of their money holdings, that is, the value of money balances in terms of goods and services which they could buy. Thus, people would not be interested in merely nominal money holdings irrespective of the price level, that is, the number of rupee notes and bank deposits. If with the doubling of price level, nominal money holdings are also doubled, their *real money balances* would remain the same. If people are merely concerned with nominal money holdings irrespective of the price level, they are said to suffer from *money illusion.*

The demand for money has been a subject of lively debate in economics. Interest in the study of demand for money has been due to the important role that monetary demand plays in the determination of the price level, interest and income. Till recently there were three approaches to demand for money, namely, transactions approach of Fisher, Cash-balance approach of Cambridge economists, Marshall and Pigou and Keynes theory of demand for money. However, in recent years Baumol, Tobin and Friedman have put forward new theories of demand for money. We critically examine below all these theories of demand for money.

FISHER'S TRANSACTIONS APPROACH TO DEMAND FOR MONEY

In his theory of demand for money Fisher[1] and other classical economists laid stress on the medium of exchange function of money, that is, money as a means of buying goods and services. All transactions involving purchase of goods, services, raw materials, assets require payment of money as value of the transaction made. If accounting identity, namely value paid must equal value received is to occur, value of goods, services and assets sold must be equal to the value of money paid for them. Thus, in any given period, the value of all goods, services or assets sold must equal to the number of

1. Irving Fisher, *Purchasing Power of Money,* Macmillan, 1911.

transactions T made multiplied by the average price of these transactions. Thus, the total value of transactions made is equal to PT.

On the other hand, because value paid is identically equal to the value of money flow used for buying goods, services and assets, the value of money flow is equal to the nominal quantity of money supply M multiplied by the average number of times the quantity of money in circulation is used or exchanged for transactions purposes. The average number of times a unit of money is used for transactions of goods, services or assets is called *transactions velocity of circulation* and denote it by V.

Symbolically, Fisher's equation of exchange is written as under :

$$MV = PT \qquad ...(1)$$

where

M = the quantity of money in circulation

V = transactions velocity of circulation

P = Average price

T = the total number of transactions.

The above equation (1) is an identity, that is true by definition. However by taking some assumptions about the variables V and T, Fisher transformed the above identity into a theory of demand for money.

According to Fisher, the nominal quantity of money M is fixed by the Central Bank of a Country (note that Reserve Bank of India is the Central Bank of India) and is therefore treated as an exogeneous variable which is assumed to be a given quantity in a particular period of time. Further, the number of transactions in a period is a function of national income; the greater the national income, the larger the number of transactions required to be made. Further, since Fisher assumed that full employment of resources prevailed in the economy, the level of national income is determined by the amount of the fully employed resources. Thus, with the assumption of full employment of resources, the volume of transactions T is fixed in the short run.

But most important assumption which makes Fisher's equation of exchange as a theory of demand for money is that velocity of circulation (V) remains constant and is independent of M, P and T. This is because he thought that *velocity of circulation of money (V) is determined by institutional and technological factors involved in the transactions process*. Since these institutional and technological factors do not vary much in the short run, the transactions velocity of circulation of money (V) was assumed to be constant.

As we know that for money market to be in equilibrium, nominal quantity of money supply must be equal to the nominal quantity of money demand. In other words, for money market to be in equilibrium

$$M_s = M_d = M$$

where M is fixed by the Central Bank of a country.

With the above assumptions, Fisher's equation of exchange can be rewritten as

$$M_d = \frac{PT}{V}$$

or

$$M_d = \frac{1}{V}.PT \qquad ...(2)$$

Thus, according to Fisher's transactions approach, demand for money depends on the following three factors:

(1) the number of transactions (T)

(2) the average price of transactions (P)

(3) the transaction velocity of circulation of money

It has been pointed out that Fisher's transactions approach represents some kind of a mechanical relation between demand for money (M_d) and the total value of transactions (PT). Thus Prof. Suraj Bhan Gupta says that in Fisher's approach the relation between demand for money M_d and the value of transactions (PT), "betrays some kind of a mechanical relation between it (*i.e.* PT) and M_d as PT represents the total amount of *work to be done* by money as a medium of exchange. This makes demand for money (M_d) a technical requirement and not a behavioural function"[2].

In Fisher's transactions approach to demand for money some serious problems are faced when it is used for empirical research. First, in Fisher's transactions approach, not only transactions involving current production of goods and services are included but also those which arise in sales and purchase of capital assets such as securities, shares, land etc. are also included. Due to frequent changes in the values of these capital assets, it is not appropriate to assume that T will remain constant even if Y is taken to be constant due to full-employment assumption.

The second problem which is faced in Fisher's approach is that it is difficult to define and determine a general price level that covers not only goods and services currently produced but also capital assets just mentioned above.

The Cambridge Cash-Balance Theory of Demand for Money

Cambridge Cash-Balance theory of demand for money was put forward by Cambridge economists, Marshall and Pigou[3]. This Cash-Balance theory of demand for money differs from Fisher's transaction approach in that it *places emphasis on the function of money as a store of value or wealth* instead of Fisher's emphasis on the use of money as a medium of exchange. It is worth noting that the exchange function of money eliminates the need to barter and solves the problem of double coincidence of wants faced in the barter system. On the other hand, the function of money as a store of value lays stress on holding money as a general purchasing power by individuals over a period of time between the sale of a good or service and subsequent purchase of a good or service at a later date. Marshall and Pigou focussed their analysis on the factors that determine individual demand for holding cash balances. Although, they recognised that current interest rate, wealth owned by the individuals, expectations of future prices and future rate of interest determine the demand for money, they however believed that changes in these factors remain constant or they are proportional to changes in individuals' income. Thus, they put forward a view that individual's demand for Cash-balances (*i.e.* nominal money balances) is proportional to the nominal income (*i.e.* money income). Thus, according to their approach, aggregate demand for money can be expressed as

$$M_d = kPY$$

where Y = real national income

P = average price level of currently produced goods and services

PY = nominal income

k = proportion of nominal income (PY) that people want to hold as cash balances

Cambridge Cash-balance approach to demand for money is illustrated in Fig. 21.1 where on the X-axis we measure nominal national income (PY) and on the Y-axis the demand for money (M_d). It will be seen from Fig. 21.1 that *demand for money (M_d) in this Cambridge Cash-balance approach is a linear function of nominal income*. The slope of the function is equal to k, that is, $k = \frac{M_d}{P_y}$. Thus

2. S.B. Gupta, *Monetary Economics, Theory Policy and Institutions*, 4th edition, 1997, p. 183.
3. A.C. Pigou, Value of Money, *Quarterly Journal of Economics*, Vol. 32, 1917, pp. 38-65.

important feature of Cash-balance approach is that *it makes the demand for money as function of money income alone.* A merit of this formulation is that it makes the relation between demand for money and income as behavioural in sharp contrast to Fisher's approach in which demand for money was related to total transactions in a mechanical manner.

Although, as mentioned above, Cambridge economists recognised the role of other factors such as rate of interest, wealth as the factors which play a part in the determination of demand for money but these factors were not systematically and formally incorporated into their analysis of demand for money. In their approach, these other factors determine the proportionality factor k, that is, the proportion of money income that people want to hold in the form of money, *i.e.* cash balances. It was J.M. Keynes who later emphasised the role of these other factors such as rate of interest, expectations regarding future interest rate and prices and formally incorporated them explicitly in his analysis of demand for money. Thus, Glahe rightly writes, "*Cambridge approach is conceptually richer than the transactions approach, the former is incomplete because it does not formally incorporate the influence of economic variables just mentioned on the demand for cash balances... John Maynard Keynes first attempted to eliminate this shortcoming.*"[4]

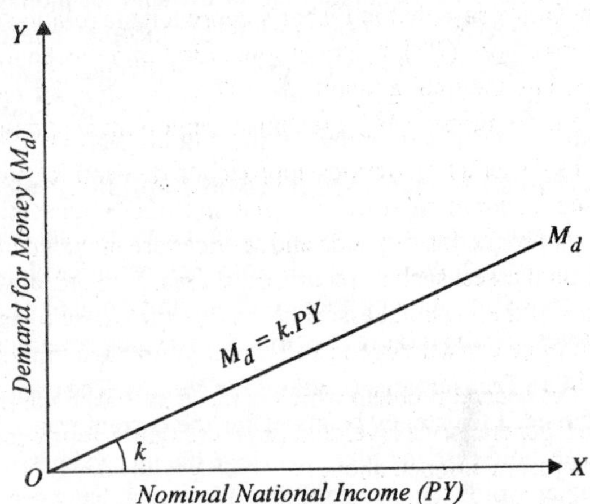

Fig. 21.1 : *Demand for Money : Cambridge Cash Balance Approach*

Another *important feature of Cambridge demand for money function is that the demand for money is proportional function of nominal income* ($M_d = kPY$). Thus, it is proportional function of both price level (P) and real income (Y). This implies two things. First, income elasticity of demand for money is unity and, secondly, price elasticity of demand for money is also equal to unity so that any change in the price level causes equal proportionate change in the demand for money.

Criticism. It has been pointed out by critics that other influences such as rate of interest, wealth, expectations regarding future prices and rate of interest have not been formally introduced into the Cambridge theory of the demand for cash-balances. These other influences remain in the background of the theory. "It was left to Keynes, another Cambridge economist, to highlight the influence of the rate of interest on the demand for money and change the course of monetary theory."[5]

Another criticism levelled against this theory is that income elasticity of demand for money may well be different from unity. Cambridge economists did not provide any theoretical reason for its being equal to unity. Nor is there any empirical evidence supporting unitary income elasticity of demand for money. Besides, price elasticity of demand is also not necessarily equal to unity. In fact, changes in the price level may cause non-proportional changes in the demand for money. However, these criticisms are against the mathematical formulation of cash-balance approach, namely, $M_d = kPY$. They do not deny the important relation between demand for money and the level of income. Empirical studies conducted so far point to a strong evidence that there is a significant and firm relation between demand for money and level of income.

4. Fred R. Glahe, *Macroeconomics: Theory and Policy*, 2nd Edition, 1977, Harcourt, p. 164.
5. S.B. Gupta, *op. cit.*, p. 184.

KEYNES'S THEORY OF DEMAND FOR MONEY

In his well-known book[6], Keynes propounded a theory of demand for money which occupies an important place in his monetary theory.

It is also worth noting that for demand for money to hold Keynes used the term what he called *liquidity preference*. How much of his income or resources will a person hold in the form of ready money (cash or non-interest-paying bank deposits) and how much will he part with or lend depends upon what Keynes calls his "*liquidity preference*." Liquidity preference means the *demand for money to hold* or the desire of the public to hold cash.

Demand for Money or Motives for Liquidity Preference : Keynes's Theory

Liquidity preference of a particular individual depends upon several considerations. The question is: Why should the people hold their resources liquid or in the form of ready money when he can get interest by lending money or buying bonds? The desire for liquidity arises because of three motives : (*i*) the transactions motive, (*ii*) the precautionary motive, and (*iii*) the speculative motive.

The Transactions Demand for Money. The transactions motive relates to the demand for money or the need for money balances for the current transactions of individuals and business firms. Individuals hold cash in order "to bridge the interval between the receipt of income and its expenditure". In other words, people hold money or cash balances for transactions purposes, because receipt of money and payments do not coincide. Most of the people receive their incomes weekly or monthly while the expenditure goes on day by day. A certain amount of ready money, therefore, is kept in hand to make current payments. This amount will depend upon the size of the individual's income, the interval at which the income is received and the methods of payments prevailing in the society.

The businessmen and the entrepreneurs also have to keep a proportion of their resources in money form in order to meet daily needs of various kinds. They need money all the time in order to pay for raw materials and transport, to pay wages and salaries and to meet all other current expenses incurred by any business firm. It is clear that the amount of money held under this business motive will depend to a very large extent on the turnover (*i.e.*, the volume of trade of the firm in question). The larger the turnover, the larger, in general, will be the amount of money needed to cover current expenses. It is worth noting that money demand for transactions motive arises primarily because of the use of money as a medium of exchange (*i.e.* means of payment).

Since the transactions demand for money arises because individuals have to incur expenditure on goods and services during the receipt of income and its use of payment for goods and services, money held for this motive depends upon the level of income of an individual. A poor man will hold less money for transactions motive as he spends less because of his small income. On the other hand, a rich man will tend to hold more money for transactions motive as his expenditure will be relatively greater.

The demand for money is a demand for *real* cash balances because people hold money for the purpose of buying goods and services. The higher the price level, the more money balances a person has to hold in order to purchase a given quantity of goods. If the price level doubles, then the individual has to keep twice the amount of money balances in order to be able to buy the same quantity of goods. Thus the demand for money balances is demand for *real* rather than *nominal* balances.

According to Keynes, the transactions demand for money depends only on the real income and is not influenced by the rate of interest. However, in recent years, it has been observed empirically and also according to the theories of Tobin and Baumol transactions demand for money also depends on the rate of interest. This can be explained in terms of *opportunity cost* of money holdings. Holding one's asset in the form of money balances has an opportunity cost. The cost of holding money

6. J.M. Keynes, *General Theory of Employment, Interest and Money*, Macmillan, 1936.

balances is the interest that is foregone by holding money balances rather than other assets. The higher the interest rate, the greater the opportunity cost of holding money rather than non-money assets. Individuals and business firms economise on their holding of money balances by carefully managing their money balances through transfer of money into bonds or short-term income yielding non-money assets. Thus, at higher interest rates, individuals and business firms will keep less money holdings at each level of income.

Precautionary Demand for Money. Precautionary motive for holding money refers to the desire of the people to hold cash balances for unforeseen contingencies. People hold a certain amount of money to provide for the danger of unemployment, sickness, accidents, and the other uncertain perils. The amount of money demanded for this motive will depend on the psychology of the individual and the conditions in which he lives.

Speculative Demand for Money. The speculative motive of the people relates to the desire to hold one's resources in liquid form in order to take advantage of market movements regarding the future changes in the rate of interest (or bond prices). The notion of holding money for speculative motive was a new and revolutionary Keynesian idea. Money held under the speculative motive serves as a store of value as money held under the precautionary motive does. But it is a store of money meant for a different purpose. The cash held under this motive is used to make speculative gains by dealing in bonds[7] whose prices fluctuate. If bond prices are expected to rise which, in other words, means that the rate of interest is expected to fall, businessmen will buy bonds to sell when their prices actually rise. If, however, bond prices are expected to fall, *i.e.*, the rate of interest is expected to rise, businessmen will sell bonds to aboid capital losses. Nothing is certain in the dynamic world, where guesses about the future course of events are made on precarious basis, businessmen keep cash to speculate on the probable future changes in bond prices (or the rate of interest) with a view to making profits.

Given the expectations about the changes in the rate of interest in future, less money will be held under the speculative motive at a *higher current* rate of interest and more money will be held under this motive at a *lower current* rate of interest. The reason for this inverse correlation between money held for speculative motive and the prevailing rate of interest is that at a lower rate of interest less is lost by not lending money or investing it, that is, by holding on to money, while at a higher current rate of interest holders of cash balance would lose more by not lending or investing.

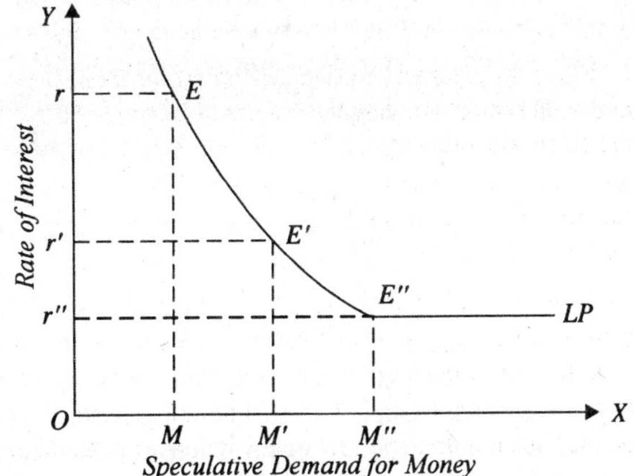

Fig. 21.2. *Liquidity Preference Curve and Liquidity Trap*

Thus the demand for money under speculative motive is a function of the current rate of interest, increasing as the interest rate falls and decreasing as the interest rate rises. Thus, demand for money under this motive is a decreasing function of the rate of interest. This is shown in Fig. 21.2. Along *X*-axis we represent the speculative demand for money and along the *Y*-axis the current rate of interest The liquidity preference curve *LP* is a downward sloping towards the right signifying that the higher the rate of interest, the lower the demand for money for speculative motive, and vice versa. Thus at the high current rate of interest Or, a very small amount *OM* is held for speculative motive. This is because at a high current rate of interest more money would have been lent out or used for buying bonds and therefore less money would be kept as inactive balances. If the rate of interest falls to *Or'*, then a greater amount of money *OM'* is held under speculative motive. With the further fall in the rate of interest to Or', money held under speculative motive increases to OM.

Liquidity Trap. It will be seen from Fig. 21.2 that the liquidity preference curve LP becomes quite flat *i.e.*, perfectly elastic at a very low rate of interest; it is horizontal line beyond point E'' towards the right. This perfectly elastic portion of liquidity preference curve indicates the position of *absolute liquidity* preference of the people. That is, at a very low rate of interest people will hold with them as inactive balances any amount of money they come to have. This portion of liquidity preference curve with absolute liquidity preference is called *liquidity trap* by the economists because expansion in money supply gets trapped in the sphere of liquidity trap and therefore cannot affect rate of interest and therefore the level of investment. According to Keynes, it is because of the existence of liquidity trap that monetary policy becomes ineffective to tide over economic depression.

But the demand for money to satisfy the speculative motive does not depend so much upon what the current rate of interest is, as on expectations about changes in the rate of interest. If there is a change in the expectations regarding the future rate of interest, the whole curve of demand for money or liquidity preference for speculative motive will change accordingly. Thus, if the public on balance expect the rate of interest to be higher (*i.e.*, bond prices to be lower) in the future than had been previously supposed, the speculative demand for money will increase and the whole liquidity preference curve for speculative motive will shift upward.

Aggregate Demand for Money : Keynes's View

If the total demand of money is represented by M_d we may refer to that part of M held for transactions and precautionary motive as M_1 and to that part held for the speculative motive as M_2. Thus $M_d = M_1 + M_2$. According to Keynes, the money held under the transactions and precautionary motives, *i.e.*, M_1, is completely interest-inelastic unless the interest rate is very high. The amount of money held as M_1, that is, for transactions and precautionary motives, is mainly a function of the size of income and business transactions together with the contingencies growing out of the conduct of personal and business affairs. We can write this in a functional form as follows:

$$M_1 = L_1(Y) \qquad \text{...(i)}$$

where Y stands for income, L_1 for demand function, and M_1 for money demanded or held under the transactions and precautionary motives. The above function implies that money held under the transactions and precautionary motives is a function of income.

On the other hand, according to Keynes, money demanded for speculative motive, *i.e.*, M_2, as explained above, is primarily a function of the rate of interest. This can be written as:

$$M_2 = L_2(r) \qquad \text{...(ii)}$$

where r stands for the rate of interest, L_2 for demand function for speculative motive.

Since total demand of money $M_d = M_1 + M_2$, we get from (*i*) and (*ii*) above

$$M_d = L_1(Y) + L_2(r)$$

Thus, according to Keynes' theory of total demand for money is an *additive demand function* with two separate components. The one component, $L_1(Y)$ represents the transactions demand for money arising out of transactions and precautionary motives is an increasing function of the level of money income. The second component of the demand for money, that is, $L_2(r)$ represents the speculative demand for money, which depends upon rate of interest, is a decreasing function of the rate of interest. Keynes' additive form of demand for money function has now been rejected by the modern economists. It has been pointed out that money represents a single asset, and not the several ones.

---

7. All securities and other such papers as yield a fixed and known rate of interest over a period of time are known as bonds.

There may be more than one motive to hold it and the same unit of money can serve several motives. Therefore, the demand for money cannot be divided into separate compartments independent of each.

Further, as has been argued by Tobin and Baumol, the transactions demand for money also depends upon the rate of interest. Others have explained that speculative demand for money is an increasing function of the total assets or wealth. If income is taken as a proxy for total wealth then even speculative demand for money will depend upon the size of income, apart from the rate of interest. In view of all these arguments, the Keynesian total demand for money function is written in the following modified form

$$M_d = L(Y, r)$$

where it is conceived that demand for money function (M_d) is increasing function of the level of income, it is a decreasing function of the rate of interest. The presentation of the demand for money function in the above revised and modified form, $M_d = L(Y, r)$ has been a highly significant development in monetary theory.

Critique of Keynes's Theory. By introducing speculative demand for money, Keynes made a significant departure from the classical theory of money demand which emphasized only the transactions demand for money. However, as seen above, Keynes' theory of speculative demand for money has been challenged. The main drawback of Keynes' speculative demand for money is that *it visualises that people hold their assets in either all money or all bonds*. This seems quite unrealistic as individuals hold their financial wealth in some combination of both money and bonds. This gave rise to portfolio approach to demand for money put forward by Tobin, Baumol and Freidman. The portfolio of wealth consists of money, interest-bearing bonds, shares, physical assets etc. Further, while according to Keynes' theory, demand for money for transaction purposes is insensitive to interest rate, the modern theories of money demand put forward by BaUmol and Tobin show that money held for transaction purposes is interest elastic. We will discuss in the next chapter the Post-Keynesian theories of demand for money put forward by Tobin, Baumol and Friedman.

Further, *Keynes additive form* of demand for money function, namely, $M_d = L_1(Y) + L_2(r)$ has now been rejected by the modern economists. It has been pointed out that *money represents a single asset*, and not the several ones. There may be more than one motive to hold money but the same units of money can serve several motives. Therefore, the demand for money cannot be divided into two or more different departments independent of each other.

In view of all these arguments, the Keynesian total demand for money functions is written in the following modified form

$$M_d = L(Y, r)$$

where it is conceived that demand for money function (M_d) is increasing function of the level of income, it is a decreasing function of the rate of interest. The presentation of the demand for money function in the above revised and modified form, $M_d = L(Y, r)$, has been a highly significant development in monetary theory.

KEYNES'S LIQUIDITY PREFERENCE THEORY OF RATE OF INTEREST

In his epoch-making book "*The General Theory of Employment, Interest and Money*", J.M. Keynes gave a new view of interest. According to him, the rate of interest is a purely monetary phenomenon and is determined by demand for money and supply of money. According to him "*interest is a reward for parting with liquidity for a specified period.*" Since people prefer liquidity or want to hold money to meet their various motives, they need to be paid some reward for surrendering liquidity or money. And this reward is the rate of interest that must be paid to them in order to induce them to part with liquidity or money. Further, according to Keynes, rate of interest is determined by liquidity preference or demand for money to hold and the supply of money known as *Liqudity Preference Theory.*

The Demand for Money in a Two Asset Economy. In order to explain the demand for money and interest-rate determination. Kenyes assumed a simplified economy where there are two assets which people can keep in their portfolio balance. These two assets are : (1) money in the form of currency and demand deposits in the banks which earn no interest, (2) long term bonds. It is important to note that rate of interest and bond prices are inversely related. When bond prices go up, rate of interest rises and vice versa. The demand for money by the people depends upon how they decide to balance their portfolios between money and bonds. This decision about the portfolio balance can be influenced by two factors.

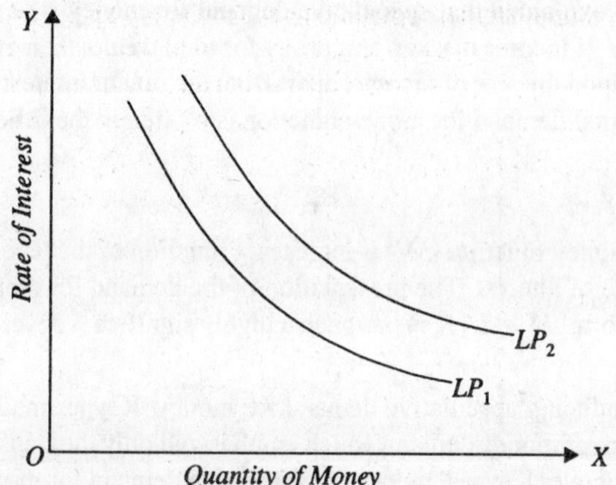

Fig. 21.3. *Demand for Money (Liquidity Preference) Rate of Interest and Level of income*

First, the higher the level of nominal income in a two asset economy people would want to hold more money in their portfolio balance. This is because of transactions motive according to which at the higher level of nominal income, the purchases by the people of goods and services in their daily life will be relatively larger which require more money to be kept for transactions purposes.

Second, the higher the nominal rate of interest, the lower the demand for money for speculative motive. This is firstly because a higher nominal rate of interest implies a higher opportunity cost for holding money. At higher rate of interest holders of money can earn more incomes by holding bonds instead of money. Secondly, if the current rate of interest is higher than what is expected in the future, the people would like to hold more bonds and less money in their portfolio. On the other hand, if the current rate of interest is low (in other words, if the bond prices are currently high), the people will be reluctant to hold larger quantity of bonds (and instead they could hold more money in their portfolio) for the fear that bond prices would fall in the future causing capital losses to them.

Money Demand Curve. It follows from above that quantity of money demanded increases with the fall in the rate of interest or with the increase in level of nominal income. At a given level of nominal income, we can draw a money demand curve showing the quantity of money demanded at various rates of interest. As demand for money is inversely related to the rate of interest, the money demand curve at a given level of income say, will be downward-sloping as is shown by the curve LP_1 in Figure 21.3. When the level of money income increases, suppose from Y_1 to Y_2, the curve of demand for money shifts upward to the new position LP_2.

Determination of Rate of Interest : Equilibrium in the Money Market

The rate of interest, according to J.M. Keynes, is determined by demand for money (Liquidity Preference) and supply of money. The factors which determine demand for money has been explained above. The supply of money, at a given time, is fixed by the monetary authority of the country. In Figure 21.4 *LP* is the demand curve for money at a given level of nominal income. *MS* is the money supply curve which is a vertical straight line showing that 200 crores of rupees is the money supply fixed by the monetary authority. It will be seen that quantity demanded of money equals the given money supply at 10 per cent rate of interest. So the money market is in equilibrium at 10 per cent rate of interest. There will be disequilibrium if rate of interest is eighter higher or lower than 10 per cent.

Suppose the rate of interest is 12 per cent. It will be seen from Figure 21.4 that at 12 per cent rate of interest, supply of money exceeds the demand for money. The excess supply of money reflects the fact that people do not want to hold as much money in their portfolio as the monetary authority has

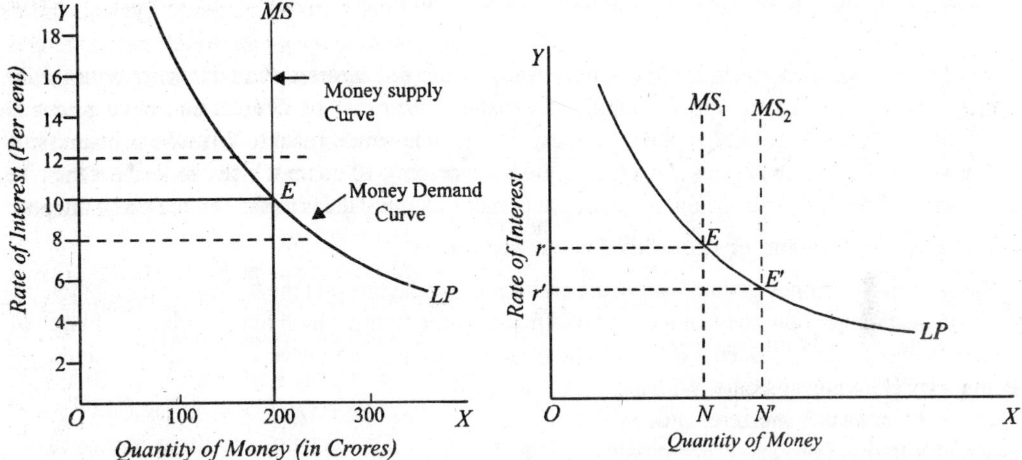

Fig. 21.4. *Money Market Equilibrium*

Fig. 21.5. *Effect of Increase in Money Supply on the Rate of Interest.*

made it available to them. The people holding assets in the present two-asset economy would react to this excess money supply with them by buying bonds and thus buying bonds and thus replace some of money in their replace some of money in their portfolios with bonds. Since the *total money supply* at a given moment remains fixed, it cannot be reduced by buying bonds by individuals. What the bonds-buying spree would lead to the rise in prices of bonds. The rise in bond prices mean the fall in the rate of interest. As will be seen from the Figure with the fall in the interest rate from 12 per cent to 10 per cent, quantity demand of money has increased to be once again equal to the given supply of money and the excess supply of money is entirely eliminated and money market is in equilibrium.

On the other hand, if the rate of interest is lower than the equilibrium rate of 10 per cent, say it is 8 per cent, then as will be seen from Figure there will emerge *excess demand for money.* As a reaction to this excess demand for money, people would like to sell bonds in order to obtain a greater quantity of money for holding at lower rate of interest. The stock of money remaining fixed, the attempt by the people to hold more money balances at a rate of interest lower than the equilibrium level through sale of bonds will only cause the bond prices to fall. The fall in bond prices implies the rise in the rate of interest. Thus, the process started as a reaction to the excess demand for money at an interest rate below the equilibrium will end up with the rise in the interest rate of the equilibrium level.

Effect of an Increase in Money Supply

Let us now examine the effect of increase in money supply on the rate of interest. In Fig. 21.5, *MD* is the demand for money for satisfying various motives. To begin with, *ON* is the quantity of money available. Rate of interest will be determined where the demand for money is in balance or equal to the fixed supply of money *ON*. It is clear from Fig. 21.5 that demand for money is equal to

ON quantity of money at *Or* rate of interest. Hence *Or* is the equilibrium rate of interest. Assuming no change in expectations and nominal income, an increase in the quantity of money (through buying securities by the Central Bank of the country from the open market), will lower the rate of interest. In Fig. 21.5, when the quantity of money increases from *ON* to *ON*, the rate of interest falls from *Or* to *Or′* because the new quantity of money *ON′* is in balance with the demand for money at *Or′* rate of interest. In this case we move down on the curve. Thus, given the money demand curve or curve of liquidity preference, an increase in the quantity of money brings down the rate of interest.

Let us see how increase in money supply leads to the fall in the rate of interest. With initial equilibrium at *Or*, when the money supply is expanded from *ON* to *ON′*, there emerges excess supply of money at the initial *Or* rate of interest. The people would react to this excess quantity of money supplied by buying bonds. As a result, the bond prices will go up which implies that the rate of interest will decline. This is how the increase in money supply leads to the fall in rate of interest.

Shifts in Money Demand or Liquidity Preference Curve

The position of money demand curve depends upon two factors: (1) the level of nominal income, (2) the expectations about the changes in bond prices in the future which implies changes in rate of interest in future. As has been explained above, a money demand curve is drawn by assuming a certain level of nominal income. With the increase in nominal income, money demand for transactions and precautionary motives increase causing an upward shift in the money demand curve.

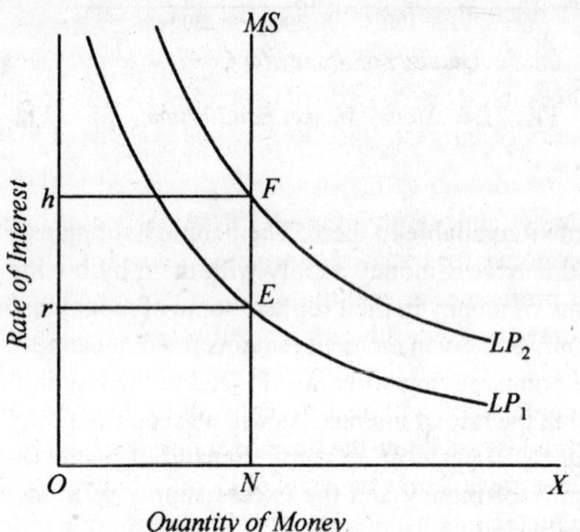

Fig. 21.6. *Effect of Increase in Liquidity Preference on the Rate of Interest.*

Shift in money demand curve (or what Keynes called liquidity preference curve) can also be caused by changes in the expectations of the people regarding changes in bond prices or movements in the rate of interest in the future. If some changes in events leads the people on balance to expect a higher rate of interest in the future than they had previously supposed, the money demand or liquidity preference for speculative motive will increase which will bring about an upward shift in the money demand curve or liquidity preference curve and this will raise the rate of interest.

In Fig 21.6 assuming that the quantity of money remains unchanged at *ON*, the rise in the money demand or liquidity preference curve from LP_1 to LP_2, the rate of interest rises from *Or* to *Oh* because *at Oh*, the new speculative demand for money is in equilibrium with the supply of money *ON*. It is worth noting that when the liquidity preference curve rises from LP_1 to LP_2, the amount of moneyheld does not increase; it remains *ON* as before. Only the rate of interest rises from *Or* to *Oh* to equilibrate the new liquidity preference or money demand with the available quantity of money *ON*.

Thus we see that Keynes explained interest in terms of purely monetary forces and not in terms of real forces like productivity of capital and thrift which formed the foundation-stones of both classical and loanable fund theories. According to him, demand for money for speculative motive together with the supply of money determines the rate of interest. He agreed that the marginal revenue product of capital tends to become equal to the rate of interest but the rate of interest is not determined by marginal revenue productivity of capital. Moreover, according to him, interest is not a reward for saving or thriftiness or waiting but for parting with liquidity. Keynes asserted that it is not the rate of interest which equalises saving an investment. But this equality is brought about through changes in the level of income.

Critical Appraisal of Keynes's Liquidity Preference Theory of Interest

1. *Keynes ignored the role of real factors in the determination of interest.* Firstly, it has been pointed out that rate of interest is not purely a monetary phenomenon. Real forces like productivity of capital and thriftiness or saving also pay an important role in the determination of the rate of interest. Keynes makes the rate of interest independent of the demand for investment funds. In fact, it is not so independent. The cash-balances of the businessmen are largely influenced by their demand for capital investment. This demand for Capital investment depends upon the marginal revenue productivity of capital. Therefore, the rate of interest is not determined independently of the marginal revenue productivity of capital (marginal efficiency of capital) and investment demand. When investment demand increases due to greater profit prospects or, in other words, when marginal revenue productivity of capital rises, there will be greater demand for investment funds and the rate of interest will go up. But Keynesian theory does not account for this. Similarly, Keynes ignored the effect of the availability of savings on the rate of interest. For instance, if the propensity to consume of the people increases, savings would decline. As a result, supply of funds in the market will decline which will raise the rate of interest.

2. *Keynesian theory is also indeterminate.* Now, exactly the same criticism applies to Keynesian theory itself on the basis of which Keynes rejected the classical and loanable funds theories. Keynes's theory of interest, like the classical and loanable funds theories, is indeterminate.

According to Keynes, rate of interest is determined by liquidity preference (*i.e.* demand for money) and supply of money. However, as we have seen, liquidity preference, especially demand for money for transactions motive depends on level of income. Now, when income increases, liquidity preference curve (that is, money demand curve will shift to the right and, given the supply of money, new equilibrium rate of interest will be obtained. Thus at different levels of income there will be different liquidity preference curve or money demand curve. As a result, at different levels of income, there will be different equilibrium rates of interest. Thus, we cannot know the rate of interest unless we know the liquidity preference curve, and also we cannot know the liquidity preference curve unless know the level of income. However, we cannot know the level of income unless we first know the rate of interest. This is because rate of interest influences investment which in turn determines the level of income. Thus, Keynes's theory is indeterminate, that is, we are not able to arrive at a single determinate rate of interest; rate of interest various as income varies.

Thus, Keynes's analysis at the most help as to obtain *LM* curve which shows what will be the rate of interest at different levels of income and not any unique or particular rate of interest. Thus, the Keynesian theory, like the classical theory, is indeterminate. "In the Keynesian case the supply and demand for money curves cannot give the rate of interest unless we already know the income level, in the classical case the demand and supply schedules for saving offer no solution until the income is known. Precisely the same is true of loanable funds theory. Keynes' criticism of the classical and lonable funds theories applies equally to his now theory[8].

3. *No liquidity without savings.* According to Keynes, interest is a reward for parting with liquidity and in no way a compensation and inducement for saving or waiting. But without saving how can the funds be available to be kept as liquid and how can there be the question of surrendering liquid-

8. A. H. Hansen, *Guide to Keynes*. p. 141

ity if one has not already saved money. Jacob Viner rightly maintains, "*Without saving there can be no liquidity to surrender.*" Therefore, the rate of interest is vitally connected with saving which is neglected by Keynes is the determination of interest.

If follows from above that keynesian theory of interest is also not without flaws. But importance Keynes gave to liquidity preference as a determinant of interest is correct. A valid and an adequate explanation of interest must incorporate this important factor of demand for money to hold.

HICKS–HANSEN SYNTHESIS: IS-LM CURVE MODEL

We have noted above that both the Classical theory and Keynes' liquidity preference theory ot interest are indeterminate and quite inadequate. Renowned economists, Hicks and Hansen, have brought about a synthesis between the Classical and Keynes' theories of interest and have thereby succeeded in propounding an adequate and determinate theory of interest through the intersection of what are called *IS* and *LM* curves. They are of the opinion that the classical and loanable funds theories amount to the same thing. According to them, the difference between these two theories, *i.e.*, classical and loanable funds, lies only in the meaning of savings. The Pigovian supply schedule of savings amounts to the same thing as the Robertsonian or Swedish supply of loanable funds. Through derivation the *IS* curve from the classical theory and *LM* curve from Keynes' liquidity preference theory they have brought about a synthesis between the classical and Keynes' theories of interest to provide an adequate and determinate theory of the rate of interest. From the classical theory they get a family of saving curves at various income levels.

From these various saving curves at various income levels together with the given investment demand curve, the *IS* curve is derived. This *IS* curve tells us what will be the various rates of interest at different levels of income, given the investment demand curve and a family of saving curves at different levels of income. On the other hand, from Keynes' formulation, the *LM* curve is obtained from a family of liquidity preference curves corresponding to various income levels together with the given stock of money supply. This-is because as the level of income increases, people would like to hold more money under the transactions motive. That is, the higher the level of income, the higher would be the liquidity preference curve. With the given supply of money, the different levels of liquidity preference curves corresponding to various levels of income would determine different rates of interest. This yields *LM* curve which depicts the various combinations of interest and income level at which *money market* is *in equilibrium*. Now, Hicks and Hansen show that with the intersection of *IS* and *LM* curves, both the interest and income are simultaneously determined. Thus the classical and Keynes' theories taken together help us in obtaining an adequate and determinate theory of interest. In what follows we explain how the *IS* curve is derived from the classical theory, and the *LM* curve from Keynes' theory. Further, we will explain what factors determine the shape and the levels of *IS* and *LM* curves.

Derivation of the IS Curve

In Fig. 21.7 *IS* curve is derived. As the income rises, the savings curve shifts to the right and the rate of interest which equalises savings and investment falls. In Fig. 21.7 (b) we measure income (Y) on the X-axis and plot the corresponding rates of interest determined by the equality of savings and investment on the Y-axis. Thus, when income is Y_2 the relevant savings curve is S_2Y_2 in Fig. 21.7(a) and the corresponding rate of interest that equalizes savings and investment is r_4. Similarly, for other levels of income rates of interest that equalise savings and investment can be obtained and plotted. Since, as income increases, rate of interest falls, the *IS* curve slopes downward.

Thus, *IS* curve relates the rates of interest with the levels of income at which intended savings and investment are equal. In otherwords, the *IS* curve depicts the various combinations of levels of interest and income at which, intended savings equal investment, *goods-market is in equilibrium.* Since with the increase in income the savings curve shifts to the right. its intersection with the investment demand curve will lower the rate of interest, the level of income and rate of interest are inversely related. That is, the *IS* curve slopes downward as shown in Figure 21.7 (*b*). Further, the steepness of the *IS* curve depends upon the elasticity or sensitiveness of investment demand to the

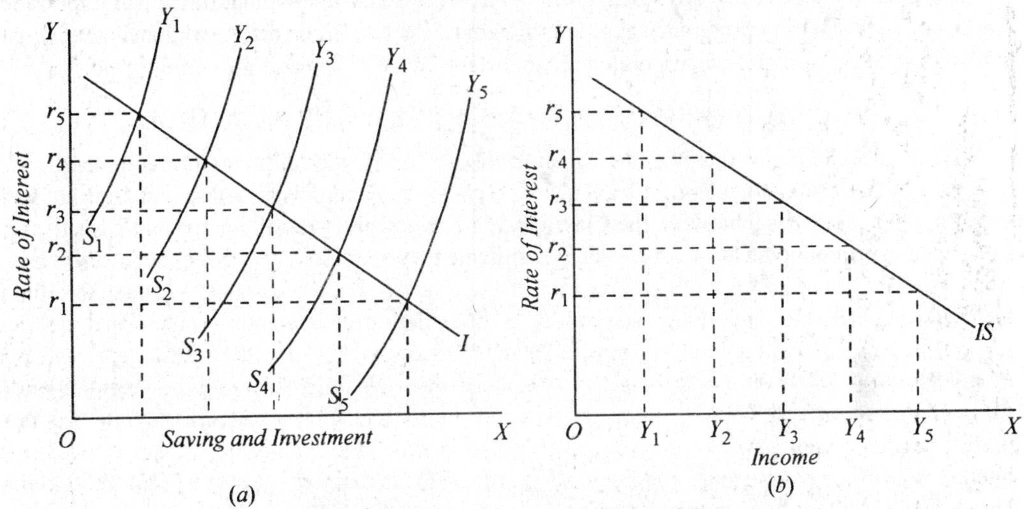

Fig. 21.7. *Derivation of IS Curve from Classical Theory*

changes in rate of interest. If the investment demand is highly elastic, that is, very sensitive to the changes in the rate of interest, a given change in interest will produce a large change in investment and thereby cause a large change in the level of income. Thus when investment demand is greatly elastic or highly sensitive to the rate of interest, the *IS* curve will be flat (*i.e.* less steep). On the other hand, when investment demand is not very sensitive to the changes in rate of interest, the *IS* curve will be relatively steep.

Now, what determines the position of *IS* curve and what would cause changes in its level. *It is the level of autonomous expenditure such as Government expenditure, transfer payments, autonomous investment which determines the position of the IS curve.* If the Government expenditure or any other type of autonomous expenditure increases, it will increase the equilibrium level of income at the given rate of interest. This will cause the *IS* curve to shift to the right. How much does the *IS* curve shift following an increase in expenditure depends on the size of multiplier. A reduction in Government expenditure or transfer payments will shift the *IS* curve to the left.

Derivation of the *LM* Curve from Keynes's Liquidity Preference Theory

The *LM* curve can be derived from the Keynesian liquidity preference theory of interest. Liquidity preference or demand for money to hold depends upon transactions motive and speculative motive. It is the money held for transactions motive which is a function of income. The greater the level of income, the greater the amount of money held for transactions motive and therefore the higher the level of liquidity preference curve. Thus, we can draw a family of liquidity preference curves at various levels of income. Now, the intersection of these various liquidity preference curves corresponding to different income levels with the supply curve of money fixed by the monetary authority would give us the *LM* curve which relates the rate of interest with the level of income as determined by *money-market equilibrium* corresponding to different levels of liquidity preference curve (Fig.21.8). The *LM* curve tells us what the various rates of interest will be (given the quantity of money and the family of liquidity preference curves) at different levels of income. But the liquidity preference curves alone cannot tell us what exactly the rate of interest will be. In

Fig. 21.8 (*a*) and (*b*) we have derived the *LM* curve from a family of liquidity preference curves. As income increases, liquidiy preference curve shifts outward and therefore the rate of interest which equates supply of money with demand for money rises. In Fig. 21.8 (*b*) we measure income on the

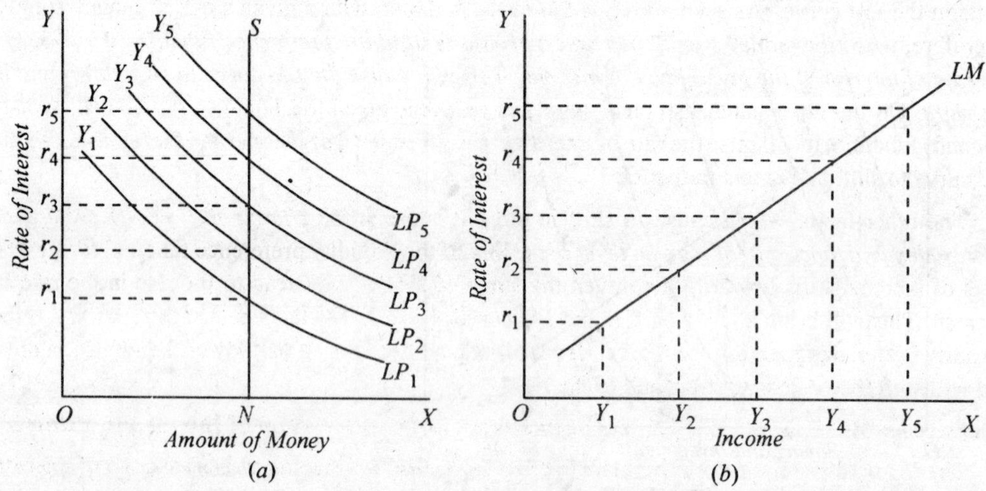

Fig. 21.8. *Derivation of LM Curve from a Family of Keynes's Liquidity Preference Curves*

X-axis and plot the income levels corresponding to the various interest rates determined at those income levels through money-market equilibrium by the equality of demand for and supply of money in Fig. 21.8 (*a*).

The Slope and Position of the *LM* Curve

It will be noticed from Figure 21.8 (*b*) that the *LM* curve slopes upward to the right. This is because with higher levels of income, demand for money (that is, the liquidity preference curve) is higher and consequently the money-market equilibrium, that is, the equality of the given money supply with liquidity preference curve occurs at a higher rate of interest. This implies that rate of interest varies directly with income. It is important to know which factors determine the slope of the *LM* curve. There are two factors on which the slope of the *LM* curve depends. First, *the responsiveness of demand for money (i.e., liquidity preference) to the changes in income.* As the income increases, say from Y_1 to Y_2, the liquidity preference curve shifts from LP_1 to LP_2, that is, with an increase in income, demand for money would increase for being held for transactions motive, $L_1 = f(Y)$. This extra demand for money would disturb the money-market equilibrium and for the equilibrium to be restored the rate of interest will rise to the level where the given money supply curve intersects the new liquidity preference curve corresponding to the higher income level. It is worth noting that in the new equilibrium position, with the given stock of money supply, money held under the transactions motive will increase whereas the money held for speculative motive will decline. The greater the extent to which demand for money for transactions motive increases with the increase in income, the greater the decline in the supply of money available for speculative motive and, given the liquidity preference schedule for speculative motive, the higher the rise in the rate of interest and consequently the steeper the *LM* curve. According to Keynes' liquidity preference theory, $r = f(M_2, L_2)$ where M_2 is the *stock of money available for speculative motive and* L_2 *is the money demand or liquidity preference function for speculative motive.*

The second factor which determines the slope of the *LM* curve is *the elasticity or responsiveness of demand for money (i.e., liquidity preference for speculative motive)* to the changes in rate of interest. The lower the elasticity of liquidity preference with respect to the changes in interest rate, the steeper will be the *LM* curve. On the other hand, if the elasticity of liquidity preference (money-demand function) to the changes in the rate of interest, is high, the *LM* curve will be relatively flat or less steep.

Another important thing to know about the *IS-LM* curve model is to know what brings about shifts in the *LM* curve. As seen above, a *LM* curve is drawn with a given stock of money supply. Therefore, *when the money supply increases, given the liquidity preference function, it will lower the rate of interest at the given level of income. This will cause the LM curve to shift down and to the right.* On the other hand, if money supply is reduced, given the liquidity preference (money demand) function, it will raise the rate of interest at the given level of income and therefore cause the *LM* curve to shift above and to the left.

The other factor which causes a shift in the *LM* curve is the *change in liquidity preference (money demand function) for a given level of income.* If the liquidity preference function for a given level of income shifts upward, this, given the stock of money, will lead to the rise in the rate of interest. This will bring about a shift in the *LM* curve above and to the left. On the contrary, if the liquidity preference function for a given level of income declines, it will lower the rate of interest and will shift the *LM* curve down and to the right.

Intersection of the *IS* and *LM* Curves : Simultaneous Determination of Intrest and Income

The *IS* curve and the *LM* curve relate the two variables : (*a*) income and (*b*) the rate of interest. Income and the rate of interest determined together at the equilibrium rate of interest are therefore-determined together at the point of intersection of these two curves, *i.e.*, *E* in Fig.21.9. The equilibrium rate of interest thus determined is Or_3 and the level of income determined is OY_2. At this point, income and the rate interest stand in relation to each other such that (1) investment and saving are in equilibrium and (2) the demand for money is in equilibrium with the supply of money (*i.e.*, the desired amount of money is equal to the actual supply of money). It should be noted that *LM* curve has been drawn by taking the supply of money as fixed.

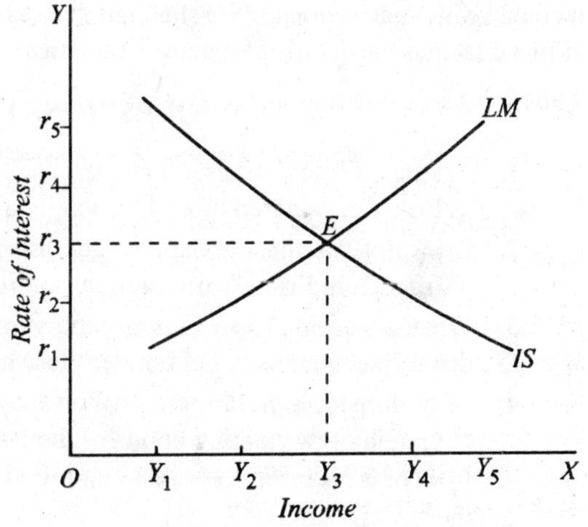

Fig. 21.9. *Simultaneous Determination of Interest and Income*

Thus, a determinate theory of interest is based on : (1) the investment-demand function, (2) the saving function (or, conversely, the consumption function), (3) the liquidity preference function, and (4) the quantity of money. We see, therefore, that according to Hicks and Hansen, both monetary and real factors, namely, productivity, thrift, and the monetary factors, that is, the demand for money (liquidity preference) and supply of money play a part in the determination of the rate of interest. Any change in these factors will cause shift in *IS* or *LM* curve and will therefore change the equilibrium level of the rate of interest and income.

Hicks-Hansen theory explained above has suceceded in integrating the theory of money with the theory of income determination. And by doing so, as we shall see below, it has succeeded in synthesising the monetary and fiscal policies. Further, with Hicks-Hansen analysis, we are better able to explain the effect of changes in certain important economic variables such as desire to save, the supply of money, investment, liquidity preference on the rate of interest.

A Crtique of Hicks-Hansen Synthesis or *IS-LM* Curve Model

Hicks-Hansen synthesis of Classical and Keynesian theories of interest makes a significant advance in explaining the determination of the rate of interest. It represents a more general, inclusive and realistic approach to the interest rate determination. Further, Hicks-Hansen integration succeeds in synthesising fiscal with monetary policies, and theory of income determination with the theory of money. But Hicks-Hansen synthesis of interest theories is not without limitations. Firstly, it is based upon the assumption that the rate of interest is quite flexible, that is, free to vary and not rigidly fixed by a Central Bank. If the rate of interest is quite inflexible, then the appropriate adjustments explained above will not take place. Secondly, the synthesis is also based upon the assumption that investment is interest-elastic, that is, investment varies with the rate of interest. If investment is interest-inelastic, as suggested by a good deal of empirical evidence, then also the Hicks-Hansen synthesis breaks down since the required adjustments do not occur. Thirdly, Don Patinkin[9] and Milton Freidman have criticised Hicks-Hansen synthesis as being too artificial and over-simplified. In their view, division of the economy into two sectors monetary and real is artificial and unrealistic. According to them, monetary and real sectors are quite interwoven and act and react on each other. Further, Patinkin has pointed out that Hicks-Hansen synthesis has ignored the possibility of changes in the price level of commodities. According to him, the various economic variables such as supply of money, propensity to consume or save, investment, and liquidity preference not only influence the rate of interest and the level of income but also the prices of commodities and services. He has suggested a more integrated and general equilibrium approach which involves the simultaneous determination of not only the rate of interest and the level of income but also of prices of commodities and services. We shall not discuss here the views of Professor Patinkin because that will land us into the details of macro-economics.

QUESTIONS FOR REVIEW

1. Exkplain Fisher's transactions approach to demand for money. Classical economists such as Fisher considered money as simply a medium of exchange. Examine critically.
2. Critically examine the Cambridge Cash-Balance Theory of Demand for money. How does it differ from Fisher's transactions approach to demand for money ?
3. What, according to Keynes, are the motives for holding money. What are the factors that determine the money held under these motives ?
4. Why do people hold money when they can earn interest by lending it to others or by buying interest yielding bonds of the companies ?
5. In what ways is the Keynesian theory of demand for money a departure from the classical theory ? Discuss. *[D.U. B.Com. (Hons) 1998]*
6. Explain the speculative motive for holding money ? Why is it interest elastic.
7. What is meant by liquidity preference ? Explain various motives of liquidity preference. What role does it play in determining rate interest ?
8. Explain why demand for money is considered to be declining function of rate of interest. *[D.U. B.Com. (Hons), 1995]*
9. Why does an increase in interest rate cause a decline in bond prices ? What is its effect on demand for money ?
10. Explain the Keynesian theory of interest. How is the Keynesian theory of interest different from the classical theory ? *[D.U. B.Com (Hons) 1999]*
11. Explain Keynes' liquidity preference theory of interest. Why is it considered to be indeterminate. Show that at best we can get *LM* curve from it. *[D.U. B.Com (Hons), 1998]*

---

9. Don Patinkin, *Money, Interest and Prices*, Harper and Row, 1965.

12. What is meant by liquidity trap ? How does its existence make the expansionary monetary policy ineffective at times of depression ?
13. Keynes' criticism that classical theory of interest is indeterminate "applies equally to his own theory" (A.H. Hansen). Discuss.
14. "It was left to Keynes to highlight the influence of rate of interest on the demand for money and change the course of monetary theory" Discuss.
15. How did J.R. Hicks and A.H. Hansen bring about synthesis between Classical and Keynes's theories of interest through *IS-LM* curves ? Explain.
16. Explain through *IS-LM* curves model how the following will affect rate of interest.
    (*a*) Expansion in money supply
    (*b*) Increase in propensity to consume
    (*c*) Increase in Government expenditure
    (*d*) Decline in investment demand
    (*e*) Fall in the liquidity preference of the people
17. Hicks-Hansen synthesis of Classical and Keynes' theories of interest succeeds in integrating the theory of income determination with the theory of money.
18. What is LM Curve ? How is LM Curve derived from Keynesian analysis of interest rate determination ?

CHAPTER 22
Post-Keynesian Theories of Demand for Money

By introducing speculative demand for money, Keynes made a significant departure from the classical theory of money demand which emphasized only the transactions demand for money. However, as seen above, Keynes' theory of speculative demand for money has been challenged. The main drawback of Keynes' speculative demand for money is that *it visualises that people hold their assets in either all money or all bonds*. This seems quite unrealistic as individuals hold their financial wealth in some combination of both money and bonds. This gave rise to portfolio approach to demand for money put forward by Tobin, Baumol and Freidman. The portfolio of wealth consists of money, interest-bearing bonds, shares, physical assets etc. Further, while according to Keynes' theory, demand for money for transaction purposes is insensitive to interest rate, the modern theories of money demand put forward by Baumol and Tobin show that money held for transaction purposes is interest elastic. We discuss below the Post-Keynesian theories of demand for money put forward by Tobin, Baumol and Friedman.

TOBIN'S PORTFOLIO APPROACH TO DEMAND FOR MONEY

An American economist James Tobin[1], in his important contribution explained that rational behaviour on the part of the individuals is that they should keep a portfolio of assets which consists of both bonds and money. In his analysis he makes a valid assumption that people prefer more wealth to less. According to him, an investor is faced with a problem of what proportion of his portfolio of financial assets he should keep in the form of money (which earns no interest) and interest-bearing bonds. The portfolio of individuals may also consist of more risky assets such as shares. *According to Tobin, faced with various safe and risky assets, individuals diversify their portfolio by holding a balanced combination of safe and risky assets.* According to Tobin, individual's behaviour shows *risk aversion.* That is, they prefer less risk to more risk at a given rate of return. In the Keynes' analysis an individual holds his wealth in either all money or all bonds depending upon his estimate of the future rate of interest. But, according to Tobin, individuals are uncertain about future rate of interest. If a wealth holder chooses to hold a greater proportion of risky assets such as bonds in his portfolio, he will be earning a high average return but will bear a higher degree of risk. Tobin argues that a risk averter will not opt for such a portfolio with all risky bonds or a greater proportion of them.

On the other hand, a person who, in his portfolio of wealth, holds only safe and riskless assets such as money (in the form of currency and demand deposits in banks) he will be taking almost zero risk but will also be having no return and as a result there will be no growth of his wealth. Therefore, people generally prefer a mixed diversified portfolio of money, bonds and shares, with each person opting for a little different balance between riskiness and return.

It is important to note that a person will be unwilling to hold all risky assets such as bonds unless he obtains a higher average return on them. In view of the desire of individuals to have both safety and reasonable return, they strike a balance between them and hold a mixed and balanced portfolio

1. James Tobin, Liquidity Preference as Behaviour Towards Risk, Review of Economic Studies Vol. 25 (1958)

consisting of money (which is a safe and riskless asset) and risky assets such as bonds and shares though this balance or mix varies between various individuals depending on their attitude towards risk and hence their trade-off between risk and return.

Tobin's Liquidity Preference Function

Tobin derived his liquidity preference function depicting relationship between rate of interest and demand for money (that is, preference for holding wealth in money form which is a safe and "riskless" asset[2]. He argues that with the increase in the rate of interest (*i.e.* rate of return on bonds), wealth holders will be generally attracted to hold a greater fraction of their wealth in bonds and thus reduce their holding of money. That is, at a higher rate of interest, their demand for holding money (*i.e.*, liquidity) will be less and therefore they will hold more bonds in their portfolio. On the other hand, at a lower rate of interest they will hold more money and less bonds in their portfolio. This means, like the Keynes's speculative demand for money, in Tobin's portfolio approach demand function for money as an asset (*i.e.* his liquidity preference function curve) slopes downwards as is shown in Fig. 22.1, where on the horizontal axis asset demand for money is shown. This downward-sloping liquidity preference function curve shows that the asset demand for money in the portfolio increases as the rate of interest on bonds falls. In this way Tobin derives the aggregate liquidity preference curve by determining the effects of changes in interest rate on the asset demand for money in the portfolio of individuals. Tobin's liquidity preference theory has been found to be true by the empirical studies conducted to measure interest elasticity of the demand for money. As shown by Tobin through his portfolio approach, these empirical studies reveal that aggregate liquidity preference curve is negatively sloped. This means that most of the people in the economy have liquidity preference function similar to the one shown by curve M_d in Fig. 22.1.

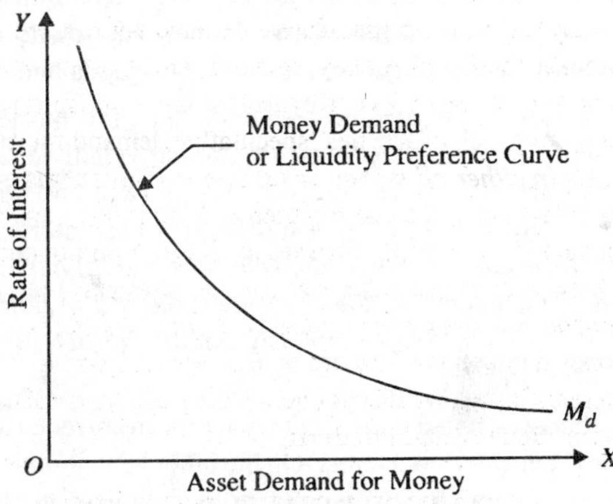

Fig. 22.1. *Tobin's Liquidity Preference Curve*

Evaluation

Tobin's approach has done away with the limitation of Keynes' theory of liquidity preference for speculative motive, namely, individuals hold their wealth in *either all money or all bonds*. Thus, Tobin's approach, according to which individuals simultaneously hold both money and bonds but in different proportion at different rates of interest yields a *continuous* liquidity preference curve. Further, Tobin's analysis of simultaneous holding of money and bonds is not based on the erroneous Keynes's assumption that interest rate will move only in one direction but on a simple fact that individuals do not know with certainty which way the interest rate will change. It is worth mentioning that Tobin's portfolio approach, according to which liquidity preference (*i.e.* demand for money) is determined by the individuals attitude towards risk, can be extended to the problem of asset choice when there are several alternative assets, not just two, of money and bonds.

2. Note that riskless is written in quotes because strictly speaking even money defined as currency and demand deposits is also not completely riskless in view of the frequent changes in prices of commodities. If inflation occurs, it reduces the value of money and thus inflicts a capital loss on its holders.

BAUMOL'S INVENTORY APPROACH TO TRANSACTIONS DEMAND FOR MONEY

Instead of Keynes's speculative demand for money, Baumol concentrated on transactions demand for money and put forward a new approach to explain it. Baumol explains the transaction demand for money from the viewpoint of the inventory control or inventory management similar to the inventory management of goods and materials by business firms. As businessmen keep inventories of goods and materials to facilitate transactions or exchange in the context of changes in demand for them, Baumol asserts that individuals also hold *inventory of money* because this facilitates transactions (*i.e.* purchases) of goods and services.[3]

In view of the cost incurred on holding inventories of goods there is need for keeping *optimal inventory* of goods to reduce cost. Similarly, individuals have to keep *optimum inventory of money* for transaction purposes. Individuals also incur cost when they hold inventories of money for transactions purposes. They incur cost on these inventories as *they have to forgone interest which they could have earned if they had kept their wealth in saving deposits or fixed deposits or invested in bonds*. This interest income forgone is the cost of holding money for transactions purposes. In this way *Baumol and Tobin emphasised that transaction demand for money is not independent of the rate of interest.*

It may be noted that by money we mean currency and demand deposits which are quite safe and riskless but carry no interest. On the other hand, bonds yield interest or return but are risky and may involve capital loss if wealth holders invest in them. However, saving deposits in banks, according to Baumol, are quite free from risk and also yield some interest. Therefore, Baumol asks the question why an individual holds money (*i.e.* currency and demand deposits) instead of keeping his wealth in saving deposits which are quite safe and earn some interest as well. According to him, it is for convenience and capability of it being easily used for transactions of goods that people hold money with them in preference to the saving deposits. Unlike Keynes both *Baumol and Tobin argue that transactions demand for money depends on the rate of interest.* People hold money for transaction purposes "*to bridge the gap between the receipt of income and its spending.*"[4] As interest rate on saving deposits goes up people will tend to shift a part of their money holdings to the interest-bearing saving deposits.

Individuals compare the costs and benefits of funds in the form of money with the interest-bearing saving deposits. According to Baumol, the cost which people incur when they hold funds in money is the *opportunity cost of these funds*, that is, interest income forgone by not putting them in saving deposits.

Baumol's Analysis of Transactions Demand

Baumol analyses the transactions demand for money of an individual who receives income at a specified interval, say every month, and spends it gradually at a steady rate. This is illustrated in Fig. 22.2. It is assumed that individual is paid ₹ 12000 salary cheque on the first day of each month. Suppose he gets it cashed (*i.e.* converted into money) on the very first day and gradually spends it daily throughout the month. (₹ 400 per day) so that at the end of the month he is left with no money. It can be easily seen that his average money holding in the month will be ₹ = $\frac{12000}{2}$ ₹ 6,000 (before 15th of a month he will be having more than ₹ 6,000 and after 15th day he will have less than ₹ 6,000). Average holding of money equal to ₹ 6,000 has been shown by the dotted line.

3. See James Tobin, "The Interest Elasticity of Transactions Demand for Cash," *Review of Economics and Statistics*, Vol. 38 (1956).
4. W.J. Baumol, The Transactions Demand for Cash: an Inventory Theoretic Approach, *Quarterly Journal of Economics*, Vol. 66 (Nov. 1952).

Now, the question arises whether it is the optimal strategy of managing money or what is called optimal cash management. The simple answer is no. This is because the individual is losing interest which he could have earned if he had deposited some funds in interest-bearing saving deposits instead of withdrawing all his salary in cash on the first day. He can manage his money balances so as to earn some interest income as well. Suppose, instead of withdrawing his entire salary on the first day of a month, he withdraws only half of it *i.e.* (₹ 6,000 in cash and deposits the remaining amount of ₹ 6,000 in saving account which gives him interest of 5 per cent, his expenditure per day remaining constant at ₹ 400. This is illustrated in Fig. 22.3. It will be seen that his money holdings of ₹ 6,000 will be reduced to zero at the end of the 15th day of each month. Now, he can withdraw ₹ 6,000 on the morning of 16th of each month and then spends it gradually, at a steady rate of 400 per day for the

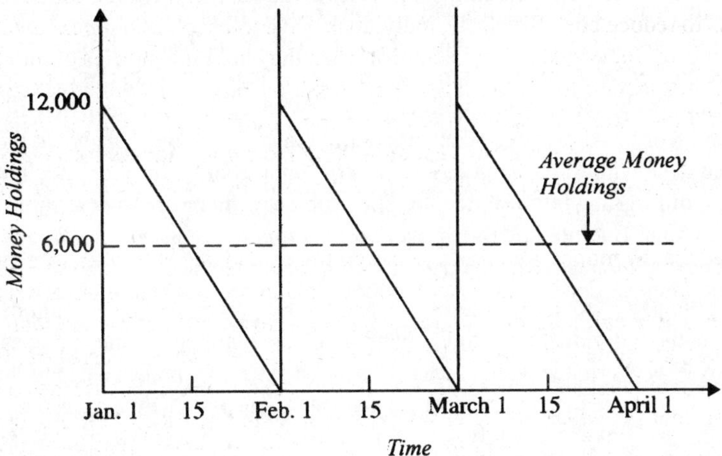

Fig. 22.2. *Stream of Cash Payments and Transactions Demand for Money*

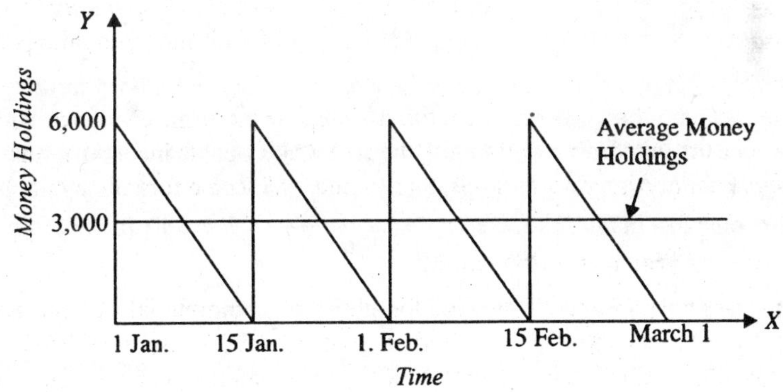

Fig. 22.3. *Transactions Demand for Money and Stream of Cash Payments*

next 15 days of a month. This is a better method of managing funds as he will be earning interest on ₹ 6,000 for 15 days in each month. Average money holdings in this money management scheme is

₹ $\frac{6000}{2} = 3000$.

Likewise, the individual may decide to withdraw ₹ 4,000 (*i.e.*, 1/3rd of his salary) on the first day of each month and deposits ₹ 8,000 in the saving deposits. His ₹ 4,000 will be reduced to zero, as he spends his money on transactions, (that is, buying of goods and services) at the end of the 10th day and on the morning of 11th of each month he again withdraws ₹ 4,000 to spend on goods and services till the end of the 20th day and on 21st day of the month he again withdraws ₹ 4,000 to spend steadily till the end of the month. In this scheme on an average he will be holding ₹ $\frac{4000}{2} = 2000$ and will be investing remaining funds in saving deposits and earn interest on them. Thus, in this scheme he will be earning more interest income.

Now, which scheme will he decide to adopt? It may be noted that investing in saving deposits and then withdrawing cash from it to meet the transactions demand involves cost also. Cost on brokerage fee is incurred when one invests in interest-bearing bonds and sells them. Even in case of saving deposits, the asset which we are taking for illustration, one has to spend on transportation costs for making extra trips to the bank for withdrawing money from the Savings Account. Besides, one has to spend time in the waiting line in the bank to withdraw cash each time from the saving deposits. Thus, the greater the number of times an individual makes trips to the bank for withdrawing money, the greater the broker's fee he will incur. If he withdraws more cash, he will be avoiding some costs on account of brokerage fee. Thus, individual faces a *trade-off problem*; the greater the amount of pay cheque he withdraws in cash, less the cost on account of broker's fee but the greater the opportunity cost of forgoing interest income. The problem is therefore to determine an optimum amount of money to hold. Baumol has shown that *optimal amount of money holding is determined by minimising the cost of interest income forgone and broker's fee.* Let us elaborate it further.

Let the size of the pay cheque (*i.e.* salary) be denoted by *Y*, the average amount of the cash he withdraws each time the individual goes to the bank by *C*, the number of times he goes to the bank to withdraw cash by *T*, broker's fee which he has to bear each time he makes a trip to the bank by *b*. In the first scheme of money management when he gets his whole pay-cheque cashed on the first day of every month he incurs broker's fee only once since he makes only a single trip to the bank. Thus *T* in our first case is equal to one $T = \frac{Y}{C} = \frac{12000}{12000} = 1$ because in this case C = Y. In the second case, $T = \frac{12000}{6000} = 2$ and in the third case $T = \frac{12000}{4000} = 3$.

Interest income lost by holding money is the average amount of money holding multiplied by the interest rate. As seen above, average money held is one half of cash withdrawn each time $\left(i.e., \frac{C}{2}\right)$. Thus, interest income lost in the first case is $\frac{rC}{2} = \frac{5}{100} \times \frac{1200}{2}$ = ₹ 300, in the second case interest lost $= r.\frac{C}{2} = \frac{5}{100} \times \frac{6000}{2} = 150$ and in the third case it is $\frac{5}{100} \times \frac{4000}{2} = 100$.

Thus the total cost incurred on broker's fee and interest income forgone is given by

$$\text{Total Cost} = bT + \frac{r.C}{2}$$

where b stands for broker's fee.

$$\text{As seen above, } T = \frac{Y}{C}$$

$$\text{Therefore,} \quad \text{Total Cost} = \frac{Y}{C}b + \frac{r.C}{2}$$

Baumol has shown that average amount of cash withdrawal which minimises cost is given by

$$C = \sqrt{\frac{2bY}{r}}$$

This means that average *amount of cash withdrawal which minimise cost is the square root of the two times broker's fee multiplied by the size of individual's income (Y) and divided by the interest rate*. This is generally referred to as *Square Root Rule*. For this rule, it follows that a higher broker's fee will raise the money holdings as it will discourage the individuals to make more trips to the bank. On the other hand, a higher interest rate will induce them to reduce their money holdings for transaction purposes as they will be induced to keep more funds in saving deposits to earn higher interest income. That is, at a higher rate of interest transactions demand for money holdings will decline.

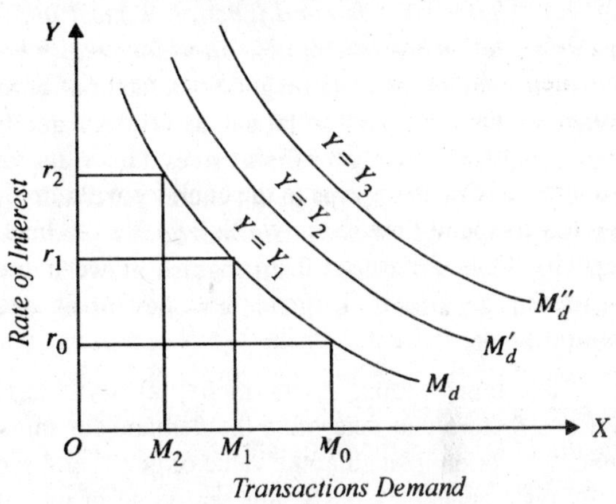

Fig. 22.4. *Transactions Demand for Money : Baumol-Tobin Approach*

As we have studied earlier, Keynes thought that transactions demand for money was independent of rate of interest. According to him, transactions demand for money depends on the level of income. However, Baumol and Tobin have shown that transactions demand for money is sensitive to rate of interest. As explained above, *interest represents the opportunity cost of holding money instead of bonds, saving and fixed deposits*. The higher the rate of interest, the greater the opportunity cost of holding money (*i.e.* the greater the interest income forgone for holding money for transactions). Therefore, *at a higher rate of interest people will try to economise the use of money and will demand less money for transactions*. At a lower interest rate on bonds, saving and fixed deposits, the opportunity cost of holding money will be less which will prompt people to hold more money for transactions. Therefore, according to Baumol and Tobin, transactions demand curve for money slopes downward as shown in Fig. 22.4. At higher interest rates, bonds, savings and fixed deposits are more attractive relative to money holding for transactions. Therefore, at higher interest rates people tend to hold less money for transaction purposes. On the other hand, when the rates of interest are low, opportunity cost of holding money will be less and, as a consequence, people will hold more money for transactions. Therefore, the curve of transaction demand for money slopes downward.

It will be observed from the square root rule given above that transactions demand for money varies directly with the income (Y) of the individuals. Therefore, the higher the level of income, the greater the transactions demand for money at a given rate of interest. In Fig. 22.4. the three transactions demand curves for money M_d, M_d' and M_d'', for three different income levels, Y_1, Y_2, Y_3 are shown. It will be known from the square root rule that optimum money holding for transactions will increase less than proportionately to the increase in income. Thus, transactions demand for money, according to Baumol and Tobin, is function of both rate of interest and the level of income.

$$M_{td} = f(r, Y)$$

where M_{td} stands for transactions demand for money, r for rate of interest and Y for the level of income.

FRIEDMAN'S THEORY OF DEMAND FOR MONEY

A noted monetarist economist Friedman put forward demand for money function which plays an important role in his restatement of the quantity theory of money and prices. In this section we shall be concerned with Friedman's money demand function and will explain in a later chapter money which shows how the changes in money supply affect the price level in the economy. *Friedman believes that money demand function is most important stable function of macroeconomics. He treats money as one type of asset in which wealth holders can keep a part of their wealth.* Business firms view money as a capital good or a factor of production which they combine with the services of other productive assets or labour to produce goods and services. Thus, according to Friedman, individuals hold money for the services it provides to them. It may be noted that the service rendered by money is that it serves as a general purchasing power so that it can be conveniently used for buying goods and services. *His approach to demand for money does not consider any motives for holding money*, nor does it distinguish between speculative and transactions demand for money. Friedman considers the demand for money merely as an application of a general theory of demand for capital assets.

Like other capital assets, money also yields return and provides services. He analyses the various factors that determine the demand for money and from this analysis derives demand for money function. Note that the value of goods and services which money can buy represents the real yield on money. Obviously, this real yield of money in terms of goods and services which it can purchase will depend on the price level of goods and services. Besides money, *bonds* are another type of asset in which people can hold their wealth. Bonds are securities which yield a stream of interest income, fixed in nominal terms. Yield on bond is the *coupen rate of interest* and also anticipated capital gain or loss due to expected changes in the market rate of interest.

Equities or Shares are another form of asset in which wealth can be held. The yield from equity is determined by the dividend rate, expected capital gain or loss and expected changes in the price level. The fourth form in which people can hold their wealth is the *stock of producer and durable consumer commodities*. These commodities also yield a stream of income but in kind rather than in money. Thus, the basic yield from commodities is implicit one. However, Friedman also considers an explicit yield from commodities in the form of expected rate of change in their price per unit of time.

Friedman's nominal demand function (M_d) for money can be written as

$$M_d = f\left(W, h, r_m, r_b, r_e, P, \frac{\Delta P}{P}, U\right)$$

As demand for *real money balances is nominal demand for money divided by the price level*, demand for real money balances can be written as

$$\frac{M_d}{P} = f\left(W, h, r_m, r_b, r_e, \frac{\Delta P}{P}, U\right)$$

where M_d stands for *nominal* demand for money and $\frac{M_d}{P}$ for demand for real money balances, W stands for wealth of the individuals, *h* for the proportion of human wealth to the total wealth held by the individuals, r_m for rate of return or interest on money, r_b for rate of interest on bonds, r_e for rate of return on equities, *P* for the price level, $\frac{\Delta P}{P}$ for the change in price level (*i.e.* rate of inflation), and *U* for the institutional factors.

1. **Wealth** (*W*): The major factor determining the demand for money is the wealth of the indi-

vidual (W). In wealth Friedman includes not only *non-human wealth* such as bonds, shares, money which yield various rates of return but also *human wealth* or *human capital.* By human wealth Friedman means the value of an individual's present and future earnings. Whereas non-human wealth can be easily converted into money, that is, can be made liquid. Such substitution of human wealth is not easily possible. Thus human wealth represents illiquid component of wealth and, therefore, the proportion of human wealth to the non-human wealth has been included in the demand for money function as an independent variable.

Individual's demand for money directly depends on his total wealth. Indeed, the total wealth of an individual represents an upper limit of holding money by an individual and is similar to the budget constraint of the consumer in the theory of demand. The greater the wealth of an individual, the more money he will demand for transactions and other purposes. As a country, becomes richer, its demand for money for transaction and other purposes will increase. Since as compared to non-human wealth, human wealth is much less liquid, Friedman has argued that as the proportion of human wealth in the total wealth increases, there will be a greater demand for money to make up for the illiquidity of human wealth.

2. Rates of Interest or Return (r_m, r_b, r_e). Friedman considers three rates of interest, namely, rm, r_b and r_e which determine the demand for money. r_m is the own rate of interest on money. Note that money kept in the form of currency and demand deposits does not earn any interest. But money held as saving deposits and fixed deposits earns certain rates of interest and it is this rate of interest which is designated by r_m in the money demand function. Given the other rates of interest or return, the higher the own rate of interest, the greater the demand for money.

In deciding how large a part of his wealth to hold in the form of money the individual will compare the rate of interest on money with rates of interest (or return) on bonds and other assets. As mentioned earlier, *the opportunity cost of holding money is the interest or return given up by not holding these other forms of assets.* As rates of return on bond (r_b) and equities (r_e) rise, the opportunity cost of holding money will increase which will reduce the demand for money holdings. Thus, the *demand for money is negatively related to the rate of interest (or return) on bonds, equities and other such non-money assets.*

3. Price Level (P). Price level also determines the demand for money balances. A higher price level means people will require a larger *nominal money balances* in order to do the same amount of transactions, that is, to purchase the same amount of goods and services. *If income (Y) is used as proxy for wealth (W) which, as stated above, is the most important determinant of demand for money, then nominal income is given by $Y.P$* which becomes a crucial determinant of demand for money. Here Y stands for real income (*i.e.* in terms of goods and services) and P for price level. As the price level goes up, the demand for money will rise and, on the other hand, if price level falls, the demand for money will decline. As a matter of fact, people adjust the nominal money balances (M) to achieve their desired level of real money balances $\left(\frac{M}{P}\right)$.

4. The Expected Rate of Inflation $\left(\frac{\Delta P}{P}\right)$. If people expect a higher rate of inflation, they will reduce their demand for money holdings. This is because inflation reduces the value of their money balances in terms of its power to purchase goods and services. If the rate of inflation exceeds the nominal rate of interest, there will be negative rate of return on money. Therefore, when people expect a higher rate of inflation they will tend to convert their money holdings into goods or other assets which are not affected by inflation.

On the other hand, if people expect a fall in the price level, their demand for money holdings will increase.

5. **Institutional Factors (*U*).** Institutional factors such as mode of wage payments and bill payments also affect the demand for money. Several other factors which influence the overall economic environment affect the demand for money. For example, if recession or war is anticipated, the demand for money balances will increase. Besides, instability in capital markets, which erodes the confidence of the people in making profits from investment in bonds and equity shares will also raise the demand for money. Even political instability in the country influences the demand for money. To account for these institutional factors Friedman includes the variable U in his demand for money function.

Simplifying Friedman's Demand for Money Function

A major problem faced in using Friedman's demand for money function has been that due to the non-existence of reliable data about the value of wealth (*W*), it is difficult to estimate the demand for money. To overcome this difficulty Friedman suggested that since the *present value of* walth or $W = \frac{Y_P}{r}$ (where Y_p is the permanent income and *r* is the rate of interest on money.), permanent income Yp can be used as a proxy variable for wealth. Incorporating this in Friedman's demand for money function we have

$$M_d = \left(Y_p, h, r_m, r_b, r_e \frac{\Delta P}{P}, U \right)$$

If, we assume that no price change is anticipated and institutional factors such as *h* and *U* remain fixed in the short run and also all the three rates of interest return are clubbed into one, Friedman's demand for money function is simplified to

$$M_d = f(Y_p r)$$

QUESTIONS FOR REVIEW

1. Explain Tobin's Portfolio Approach to demand for money. Why, according to Tobin, asset demand for money increases as the rate of interest on bonds falls ?
2. How does Tobin's approach to liquidity preference differ from Keynes's liquidity prefernce function ?
3. How does Baumol-Tobin model explain that the transaction demand for money is a function of interest rate and level of income.
4. Explain why the transactions demand for money depends not only on the level of income but also on the rate of interest.
5. Explain Friedman's theory of demand for money. How does it differ from Keynes' theory of demand for money ?
6. Why, according to Freidman, are the main factors that determine demand for money. How do the stock of wealth and rate of interest influence the demand for money ?
7. State and explain Friedman's Quantity Theory of Demand for Money. Friedman thinks that his theory is closely related to Cambridge version of quantity theory of money while Don Patinkin holds that Friedman provides us a most elegant and sophisticated statement of Keynesian theory demand for money. Discuss.

PART IV

Money, Prices and Inflation

- Money and Prices : Quantity Theory of Money
- Money and Prices : Keynesian Monetary Theory
- Friedman's Modern Quantity Theory of Money and Monetarism
- Monetarism Vs. Keynesianism
- Inflation: Nature, Causes and Effect

CHAPTER 23

Money and Prices : Quantity Theory of Money

Value of Money and the Price Level

Value in economics means value-in-exchange. The value of a commodity means what it can be exchanged for or what it can buy. It means the purchasing power of a commodity. Similarly, the value of money means its purchasing power in terms of goods and services in general. The purchasing power of money obviously depends on the prevalent price level. If the prices are high, money will buy less and its value will be low. Conversely, if the price level is low, the value of money is high. The value of money is thus inversely proportional to the price level, or the value of money is the reciprocal of price level.

QUANTITY THEORY OF MONEY: FISHER'S TRANSACTIONS APPROACH

We are now in a position to explain how the general level of prices is determined, that is, why at sometimes the general level of prices rises and sometimes it declines. Sometime back it was believed by the economists that the quantity of money in the economy is the prime cause of fluctuations in the price level. The theory that increase in the quantity of money leads to the rise in the general price was effectively put forward by Irving Fisher.[1] They believed that the greater the quantity of money, the higher the level of prices and vice versa. Therefore, the theory which linked prices with the quantity of money came to be known as quantity theory of money. In the following analysis we shall first critically examine the quantity theory of money and then explain the modern view about the relationship between money and prices and also the determination of general level of prices.

The quantity theory of money seeks to explain the value of money in terms of changes in its quantity. Stated in its simplest form, the quantity theory of money says that the level of prices varies directly with quantity of money. "Double the quantity of money, and other things being equal, prices will be twice as high as before, and the value of money one-half. Halve the quantity of money and, other things being equal, prices will be one-half of what they were before and the value of money double." The theory can also be stated in these words: *The price level rises proportionately with a given increase in the quantity of money. Conversely, the price level falls proportionately with a given decrease in the quantity of money, other things remaining the same.*

There are several forces that determine the value of money and the general price level. The general price level in a community is influenced by the following factors:

(*a*) the volume of trade or transactions;

(*b*) the quantity of money;

(*c*) velocity of circulation of money.

The first factor, the volume of trade or transactions, depends upon the supply or amount of goods and services to be exchanged. The greater the amount or supply of goods in an economy, the

1. Irving Fisher, *Purchasing Power of Money*, Macmillan, 1911.

larger the number of transactions and trade, and *vice versa*. But the classical and neoclassical economists who believed in the quantity theory of money assumed that *full employment* of all resources (including labour) prevailed in the economy. Resources being fully employed, the total output or supply of goods (and therefore the total trade or transactions) cannot increase. Therefore, those who believed in the quantity theory of money assumed that the total volume of trade or transactions remained the same.

The second factor in the determination of general level of prices is the quantity of money. It should be noted that the quantity of money in the economy consists of not only the notes and currency issued by the Government but also the amount of credit or deposits created by the banks.

The third factor influencing the price level is the velocity of circulation. A unit of money is used for exchange and transactions purposes not once but several times in a year. During several exchanges of goods and services, a unit of money passes from one hand to another. Thus, if a single rupee is used five times in a year for exchange of goods and services, the velocity of circulation is 5. Hence, the velocity of money is the *number of times* a unit of money changes hands during exchanges in a year. The work done by one rupee which is circulated five times in a year is equal to that done by the five rupees which change hands only once each.

Let us illustrate the quantity theory of money. Suppose in a country there is only one good, wheat, which is to be exchanged. The total output of wheat is 2,000 quintals in a year. Further suppose that the government has issued money equal to ₹ 25,000 and no credit is issued by the banks. We further assume that one rupee is used four times in a year for exchange of wheat. That is, velocity of circulation of money is four. Under these circumstances, 2,000 quintals of wheat are to be exchanged for ₹ 1,00,000, (25,000 × 4 = 1,00,000). The price of wheat will be $\frac{1,00,000}{2,000}$ = ₹ 50 per quintal. Suppose the quantity of money is doubled to ₹ 50,000, while the output of wheat remains at 2,000 quintals. As a result of this increase in the quantity of money, the price of wheat will rise to $\frac{2,00,000}{2,000}$ = ₹ 100 per quintal. Thus with doubling of the quantity of money, the price has doubled. If the quantity of money is further increased to ₹ 75,000, the amount of wheat remaining constant, the price level will rise to $\frac{3,00,000}{2,000}$ = ₹ 150 per quintal. It is thus clear that if the volume of transactions, *i.e.*, output to be exchanged remains constant, the price level rises with the increase in the quantity of money.

Fisher's Equation of Exchange

An American economist, Irving Fisher, expressed the relationship between the quantity of money and the price level in the form of an equation, which is called 'the equation of exchange'. This is:

$$PT = MV \quad \ldots(1)$$

or

$$P = \frac{MV}{T} \quad \ldots(2)$$

where P stands for the average price level:

T stands for total amount of transactions (or total trade or amount of goods and services, raw materials, old goods etc.)

M stands for the quantity of money; and

V stands for the transactions velocity of circulation of money.

The equation (1) or (2) is an accounting identity and true by definition. This is, because *MV* which represents money spent on transactions must be equal to *PT* which represents money received from transactions.

However, the equation of exchange as given in equations (1) and (2) has been converted into a theory of determination of general level of prices by the classical economists by making some assumptions. First, it has been assumed that *the physical volume of transactions is constant* because it is determined by a given amount of real resources, the given level of technology and the efficiency with which the given available resources are used. These real factors determine a level of aggregate output which necessitates various types of transactions. Another crucial assumption is that *transactions velocity of circulation (V) is also constant.* The quantity theorists accordingly believed that velocity of circulation (*V*) depends on the methods and practices of factor payments such as frequency of wage payments to the workers, and habits of the people regarding spending their money incomes after they receive them. Further, velocity of circulation of money also depends on the development of banking and credit system, that is, the ways and speed with which cheques are cleared, loans are granted and repaid. According to them, these practices do not change in the short run. This assumption is very crucial for the quantity theory of money because when the quantity of money is increased this may cause a decline in velocity of circulation of money, then *MV* may not change if the decline in *V* offsets the increase in *M*. As a result, increase in *M* will not affect *PY*.

The quantity theorists believed that the volume of transactions (*T*) and the changes in it were largely independent of the quantity of money. Further, according to them, changes in velocity of circulation (*V*) and price level (*P*) do not cause any change in volume of transactions except temporarily. Thus classical economists who put forward the quantity theory of money believed that the number of transactions (which ultimately depends on aggregate real output) does not depend on other variables (*M*, *V* and *P*) in the equation of exchange. Thus we see that the assumption of constant *V* and *T* converts the equation of exchange ($MV = PT$), which is an accounting identity, into a theory of the determination of general price level.

The quantity of money is fixed by the Government and the Central Bank of a country. Further, it is assumed that quantity of money in the economy depends upon the monetary system and policy of the central bank and the Government and is assumed to be autonomous of the real forces which determine the volume of transactions or national output.

Now, with the assumptions that *M* and *V* remain constant, the price level *P* depends upon the quantity of money *M*; the greater the quantity of *M*, the higher the level of prices. Let us give a numerical example. Suppose the quantity of money is ₹ 5,00,000 in an economy, the velocity of circulation of money (*V*) is 5; and the total output to be transacted (*T*) is 2,50,000 units, the average price level (*P*) will be:

$$P = \frac{MV}{T}$$

$$= \frac{5,00,000 \times 5}{2,50,000} = \frac{2,500,000}{2,50,000}$$

$$= ₹\ 10 \text{ per unit.}$$

If now, other things remaining the same, the quantity of money is doubled, *i.e.*, increased to ₹ 10,00,000 then:

$$P = \frac{10,00,000 \times 5}{2,50,000} = ₹\ 20 \text{ per unit}$$

We thus see that according to the quantity theory of money, price level varies in direct proportion to the quantity of money. A doubling of the quantity of money (M) will lead to the doubling of the price level. Further, since changes in the quantity of money are assumed to be independent or autonomous of the price level, the changes in the quantity of money become the cause of the changes in the price level.

Quantity Theory of Money: Income Version

Fisher's transactions approach to quantity theory of money described in equation (1) and (2) above considers such variables as total volume of transaction (T) and average price level of these transactions are conceptually vague and difficult to measure. Therefore, in later years quantity theory was formulated in income form which considers real income or national output (*i.e.*, transactions of final goods only) rather than all transactions. As the data regarding national income or output is readily available, the income version of the quantity theory is being increasingly used. Moreover, the average price level of output is a more meaningful and useful concept. Indeed, in actual practice, the general price level in a country is measured taking into account only the prices of final goods and services which constitute national product. It may be noted that even in this income version of the quantity theory of money, the function of money is considered to be a means of exchange as in the transactions approach of Fisher. In this approach, the concept of *income velocity of money* has been used instead of transactions velocity of circulation. *By income velocity we mean the average number of times per period a unit of money is used in making payments involving final goods and services*, that is, national product or national income. In fact, income velocity of money is measured by $\frac{Y}{M}$ where Y stands for real national income and M for the quantity of money.

In view of the above, the income version of quantity theory of money is written as under:

$$MV = PY \qquad \ldots (3)$$

$$P = \frac{MV}{Y} \qquad \ldots (4)$$

where

M = Quantity of money

V = Income velocity of money

P = Average price level of final goods and services

Y = Real national income (or aggregate output)

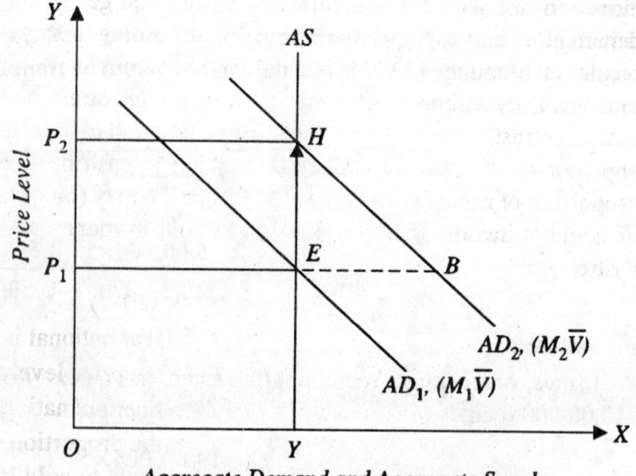

Fig. 23.1. *Quantity Theory of Money*

Like that in the transactions approach, in this new income version of the quantity theory also the different variables are assumed to be independent of each other. Further, income velocity of money (V) and real income or aggregate output (Y) are assumed to be given and constant during a short period. More specifically, they do not vary in response to the changes in M. In fact, real income or output (Y) *is assumed to be determined by the real sector forces such as capital stock, the amount and skills of labour, technology etc.* But as these factors are taken to be given and constant in the short run, and further full employment of the given resources is assumed to be prevailing due to the operation of Say's law and wage-price flexibility supply of output is taken to be inelastic and constant for purposes of determination of price level.

It follows from equations (3) and (4) above that with income velocity (V) and national output (Y) remaining constant, price level (P) is determined by the quantity of money (M).

Classical quantity theory of money is illustrated in Fig. 23.1 through aggregate demand and aggregate supply model. It is worth noting that the quantity of money (M) multiplied by the income velocity of circulation (V), that is, MV gives us aggregate expenditure in the quantity theory of money. Now with a given quantity of money, say M_1 and constant velocity of money $\overline{V}$, we have a given amount of monetary expenditure ($M_1 \overline{V}$). Given this aggregate expenditure, at a lower price level more quantities of goods can be purchased and at a higher price level, less quantities of goods can be purchased. Therefore, in accordance with classical quantity theory of money aggregate demand representing $M_1 \overline{V}$ slopes downward as shown by the aggregate demand curve AD_1 in Fig. 23.1. If now the quantity of money is increased, say to M_2, aggregate demand curve representing new aggregate monetary expenditure $M_2 \overline{V}$ will shift upward.

As regards, aggregate supply curve, due to the assumption of wge-price flexibility, it is perfectly inelastic at full-employment level of output as is shown by the vertical aggregate supply curve AS in Fig. 23.1. Now, with a given quantity of money equal to M_1, aggregate demand curve AD_1 cuts the aggregate supply curve AS at point E and determines price level OP_1. Now, if the quantity of money is increased to M_2, the aggregate demand curve shifts upward to AD_2. It will be seen from Fig. 23.1 that with the increase in aggregate demand to AD_2 consequent to the expansion in money supply to M_2, excess demand equal to EB emerges at the current price level OP_1. This excess demand for goods and services will lead to the rise in price level to OP_2 at which again aggregate quantity demanded equals the aggregate supply which remains unchanged at OY due to the existence of full employment in the economy.

QUANTITY THEORY OF MONEY: THE CAMBRIDGE CASH BALANCE APPROACH

The equation of exchange has been stated by Cambridge economists, Marshall and Pigou, in a form different from Irving Fisher. Cambridge economists explained the determination of value of money in line with the determination of value in general. Value of a commodity is determined by demand for and supply of it and likewise, according to them, the value of money (*i.e.*, its purchasing power) is determined by the demand for and supply of money. As studied in cash-balance approach to demand for money Cambridge economists laid stress on the store of value function of money in sharp contrast to the medium of exchange function of money emphasised by in Fisher's transactions approach to demand for money. According to cash balance approach, the public likes to hold a proportion of nominal income in the form of money (*i.e.*, cash balances). Let us call this proportion of nominal income that people want to hold in money as k. Then cash balance approach can be written as:

$$M^d = kPY \quad \text{...(1)}$$

where
Y = *real* national income (*i.e.*, aggregate output)
P = the price level
PY = *nominal* national income
k = the proportion of nominal income that people want to hold in money
M^d = the amount of money which public want to hold

Now, for the achievement of money-market equilibrium, demand for money must equal worth the supply of money which we denote by M. It is important to note that the supply of money M is exogenously given and is determined by the monetary policies of the central bank of a country. Thus, for equilibrium in the money market.

$$M = M^d$$

As $$M^d = kPY$$

Therefore, $$M = kPY \qquad ...(2)$$

It is worth mentioning that k in the equations (1) and (2) is related to velocity of circulation of money V in Fisher's transactions approach. Thus, when a greater proportion of nominal income is held in the form of money (*i.e.*, when k is higher), V falls. On the other hand, when less proportion of nominal income is held in money, V rises. In the words of Crowther, "The higher the proportion of their real incomes that people decide to keep in money, the lower will be the velocity of circulation, and vice versa."[2]

It follows from above that $k = \frac{1}{V}$. Now, rearranging equation (2) we have cash balance approach in which P appears as dependent variable. Thus, on rearranging equation (2) we have

$$P = \frac{1}{k} \cdot \frac{M}{Y} \qquad ...(3)$$

Like Fisher's equation, cash balance equation is also an accounting identity because k is defined as:

$$\frac{\text{Quantity of Money Supply}}{\text{National Income}}, \text{ this is, } \frac{M}{PY}$$

Now, Cambridge economists also assumed that k remains constant. Further, due to their belief that wage-price flexibility ensures full employment of resources, the level of real national income was also fixed corresponding to the level of aggregate output produced by full employment of resources.

Thus, from equation (3) it follows that with k and Y remaining constant price level (P) is determined by the quantity of money (M); changes in the quantity of money will cause proportionate changes in the price level.

Some economists have pointed out similarity between Cambridge cash-balance approach and Fisher's transactions approach. According to them, k is reciprocal of V $\left(k = \frac{1}{V} \text{ or } V = \frac{1}{k}\right)$. Thus in equation (2) if we replace k by , we have

$$M = \frac{1}{V} PY$$

or $$MV = PY$$

Which is income version of Fisher's quantity theory of money. However, in spite of the formal similarity between the cash balance and transactions approaches, there are important conceptual differences between the two which makes cash balance approach superior to the transactions approach. First, as mentioned above, Fisher's transactions approach lays stress on the medium of exchange function of money, that is, according to it, people want money to use it as a means of

2. Crowther, *Outline of Money*, p. 150.

payment for buying goods and services. On the other hand, cash balance approach emphasizes the store-of-value function of money. They hold money so that some value is stored for spending on goods and services after some lapse of time.

Further, in explaining the factors which determine velocity of circulation, transactions approach points to the mechanical aspects of payment methods and practices such as frequency of wages and other factor payments, the speed with which funds can be sent from one place to another, the extent to which bank deposits and cheques are used in dealing with others and so on. On the other hand, k in the cash balance approach is *behavioural in nature*. Thus, according to Prof. S.B. Gupta, "*Cash-balance approach is behavioural in nature: it is built around the demand for money, however simple. Unlike Fisher's V, k is a behavioural ratio. As such it can easily lead to stress being placed on the relative usefulness of money as an asset.*"[3]

Thirdly, cash balance approach explains determination of value of money in a framework of general demand-supply analysis of value. Thus, according to this approach value of money (that is, its purchasing power is determined by the demand for and supply of money).

To sum up cash balance approach has made some improvements over Fisher's transactions approach in explaining the relation between money and prices. However, it is essentially the same as the Fisher's transactions approach. Like Fisher's approach it considers substitution between money and commodities. That is, if they decide to hold less money, they spend more on commodities rather than on other assets such as bonds, shares, real property, durable consumer goods. Further, like Fisher's transactions approach it visualises changes in the quantity of money causes proportional changes in the price level. Like Fisher's approach, cash balance approach also assumes that full-employment of resources will prevail due to the wage-price flexibility. Hence, it also believes the aggregate supply curve as perfectly inelastic at full-employment level of output.

An important limitation of cash balance approach is that it also assumes that the proportion of income that people want to hold in money, that is, k, remains constant. Note that . In practice it has been found that proportionality factor k or velocity of circulation has not remained constant but has been fluctuating, especially in the short run.

Besides, cash-balance approach falls short of considering *demand for money as an asset*. If demand for money as an asset were considered, it would have a determining influence on the rate of interest on which amount of investment in the economy depends. Investment plays an important role in the determination of level of real income in the economy. It was left to J.M. Keynes who later emphasised the role of demand for money as an asset which was one of the alternative assets in which individuals can keep their income or wealth. Finally, it may be mentioned that other criticisms of Fisher's transactions approach to quantity theory of money discussed above equally apply to the Cambridge cash balance approach.

Keynes's Critique of the Quantity Theory of Money

The quantity theory of money has been widely criticised. The following criticisms have been levelled against the quantity theory of money lay by Keynes and his followers.[4]

1. **Useless truism.** With the qualification that velocity of money (V) and the total output (T) remain the same, the equation of exchange ($MV = PT$) is a *useless truism*. The real trouble is that these things seldom remain the same. They change not only in the long run but also in a short period. Fisher's equation of exchange simply tells us that expenditure made on goods (MV) is equal to the value of output of goods and services sold (PT).

---

3. S.B. Gupta, *op. cit.*, p. 206.
4. For detailed analysis of Keynes' theory of money and prices, See Chapter 21.

2. Velocity of money is not stable. *Keynesian economists has challenged the assumption that velocity of money remains stable.* According to them, velocity of money changes inversely with the change in money supply. They argue that increase in money supply, demand for money remaining constant, leads to the fall in the rate of interest. At a lower rate of interest, people will be induced to hold more money as idle cash balances (under speculative motive). This means velocity of circulation of money will be reduced. Thus, *if a decline in interest rate reduces velocity, then increase in the money supply will be offset by reduction in velocity,* with the result that price level, need not rise when money supply is increased.

3. Increase in quantity of money may not always lead to the increase in aggregate spending or demand. Further, according to Keynes' the quantity theory of money is based upon two more *wrong assumptions*. Basically, for the quantity theory to be true, the following two assumptions must hold:

(*i*) An increase is money supply must lead to an increase in spending, that is, aggregate demand *i.e.*, no part of additional money created should be kept in idle hoards.

(*ii*) The resulting increase in spending or aggregate demand must face a totally inelastic output.

Both the assumptions according to Keynes, lack generality and, therefore, if either of them does not hold, the quantity theory cannot be accepted as a valid explanation of the changes in price level.

Let us take the first assumption. Under this assumption, the entire increase in the quantity of money must express itself in the form of increased spending. If spending does not increase, there is no question of a change in prices or output. But, is it valid to make such an assumption? Obviously, *there is no such direct link* between the increase in the quantity of money and the increase in the volume of total spending or aggregate demand. No one is going to increase his expenditure simply because the government is printing more notes or the banks are more liberal in their lending policies. Thus, if the demand for money is highly interest-elastic, the increase in money supply will not lead to any appreciable fall in the rate of interest. With no significant fall in rate of interest, the investment expenditure and expenditure on durable consumer goods will not increase much. As a result, increase in money supply may not lead to increase in expenditure or aggregate demand and therefore price level may remain unaffected.

This is not to say, however, that changes in the quantity of money have no influence whatsoever on the volume of aggregate spending. As we shall show below, changes in the quantity of money are often capable of inducing changes in the volume of aggregate spending. What Keynes and his followers deny is the assertion that there exists a direct, simple, and more or less a proportional relation between variation in money supply and variation in the level of total spending.

4. Assumption of constant volume of transactions or constant level of aggregate output is not valid. Keynes asserted that the assumption of constant aggregate output valid only under conditions of full employment. It is only then that we can assume a totally inelastic supply of output, for all the available resources are being already fully utilised. In conditions of less than full employment, the supply curve of output will be elastic. Now, if we assume that aggregate spending or demand increases with an increase in the quantity of money, it does not follow that prices must necessarily rise. If the supply curve of output is fairly elastic, it is more likely that effect of an increase in spending will be more to raise production rather than prices. Of course, at full-employment level every further increase in spending or aggregate demand must lead to the rise in the price level as output is inelastic in supply at full-employment level. Since full-employment cannot be assumed to be a normal affair, we cannot accept the quantity theory of money as a valid explanation of changes in the price level in the short run.

QUESTIONS FOR REVIEW

1. **Explain the Quantity Theory of Money. Will a doubling of money supply always lead to a doubling of general price level ?**
2. **Does increase in money supply always lead to a proportional increase in prices ? Give reasons in support of your answer.**
3. **Critically examine the Quantity Theory of Money. Does an increase in money supply always lead to a proportionate increase in prices ?**
4. **Explain Keynes's criticism of the quantity Theory of money.**
5. **Discuss Fisher's and Keynes' approach to the relationship between the quantity of money and price level.**
6. **Explain Fisher's equation of exchange. It is asserted by some that Fisher's equation of exchange is a '*useless truism*' Do you agree ? Discuss.**
7. **Explain Cambridge Cash Balance Approach of the Quantity Theory of Money. How does it differ from Fisher's transactions approach ?**
8. **Cash Balance Approach of the Quantity Theory of Money is behavioural in nature and is built around the demand for money. Discuss.**

CHAPTER 24
Keynes's Monetary Theory : Money, Income and Prices

Introduction : Integrating Money Market with Goods Market

The main thrust of Keynes's criticism of classical quantity theory of money was directed at its conclusion that (*i*) velocity of circulation is constant, and (*ii*) full employment of resources is the natural state of a free market economy. Keynes believed that velocity of circulation was volatile and there often existed underemployment of resources due to recessionary conditions in the economy. As seen in the previous chapters, classical economists believed that people demanded money only for transactions purpose and money balances held for transactions purposes were proportional to nominal income. Keynes challenged this viewpoint and held that people could hold income-earning assets such as bonds instead of holding money balances. To the transactions motive for holding money, Keynes added precautionary motive and speculative motive (that is demand for money as an asset) for holding money. Income or interest earned on assets such as bonds is the opportunity cost of holding money. The higher the rate of interest on these assets, the less money will be held by the public. It is worth noting that people adjust their money holdings until what they demand equals what they actually have. If people have more money than what they demand, they will spend either on consumer goods and services or invest more. On the other hand, if their demand for money to hold is greater than what they presently have, they will try to acquire more money either by reducing expenditure on goods and services or selling some of their assets such as bonds and shares. Keynes laid stress on financial investment in bonds as a major way to reduce one's money holdings.

The task of a monetary theory is to explain the influence of changes in money supply on the level of economic activity (*i.e.*, levels of real income, output and employment) and the price level. *Keynes's monetary theory explains the effect of variation in money supply on the level of economic activity through its effect on the rate of interest which determines investment in the economy.* In what follows we first explain the impact of expansion in money supply on the levels of real income and employment. In the second stage of our analysis of Keynes's monetary theory we show how changes in money supply affect the price level in the economy.

KEYNES'S MONETARY THEORY : THE EFFECT OF MONEY SUPPLY ON THE LEVEL OF ECONOMIC ACTIVITY

The effect of money supply on rate of interest and the effect of rate of interest on aggregate demand provides a mechanism through which changes in money supply affect the level of economic activity. We know from the study of money market that monetary policy have a profound effect on the rate of interest. Thus, if rate of interest is reduced as a result of an increase in money supply, the rate of investment will rise and the increase in investment will lead to increase in income *via* the multiplier. If this happens, there will be an increase in aggregate expenditure (*i.e.*, aggregate demand) and as a result real national income (aggregate output) increases.

---

* This Chapter is meant for Higher Level Courses in Macroeconomics.

Transmission Mechanism. How, according to Keynes, the change in money supply leads to the increase real income output and employment is shown in the following scheme:

$$M^S \xrightarrow{(1)} r\downarrow \xrightarrow{(2)} I\uparrow \xrightarrow{(3)} AD\ (\text{or } C+I+G+X_n)\uparrow \xrightarrow{(4)} Y\ (i.e.,\ GNP)$$

The first link in the transmission mechanism is the effect of expansion in money supply on the rate of interest which depends on how far demand for money holdings is sensitive *(i.e.,* elastic) to the changes in rate of interest. The expansion in money supply (M^S) causes the rate of interest to fall. The second step in the transmission mechanism is the influence of change in rate of interest on the rate of investment, which is determined by the elasticity of investment with respect to rate of interest. The fall in rate of interest leads to the increase in investment in the economy. The next step in the process is the effect of increase in investment on aggregate demand and therefore on national income (aggregate output) and employment in the economy. The effect of investment on income, output and employment is determined by the size of multiplier.

We explain below at length the above factors and show how the increase in money supply affects the level of economic activity. It may be noted that expansion in money supply which leads to the increase in aggregate demand will affect both the real national income (*i.e., GNP*) and the price level jointly. However for better understanding of the subject by the students we shall explain the Keynesian monetary theory with regard to the relation between money supply and price level separately as well.

Money Supply and Rate of Interest. Rate of interest, according to Keynes, is a purely monetary phenomenon. Demand for money to hold depends on the level of income and rate of interest. At a higher current rate of interest, less money is demanded by the people to hold and vice versa. Therefore, money demand curve (M^d) or what Keynes calls liquidity reference curve slopes downward as shown by M^d curve in Fig. 24.1. Rate of interest determined by demand for money and supply of

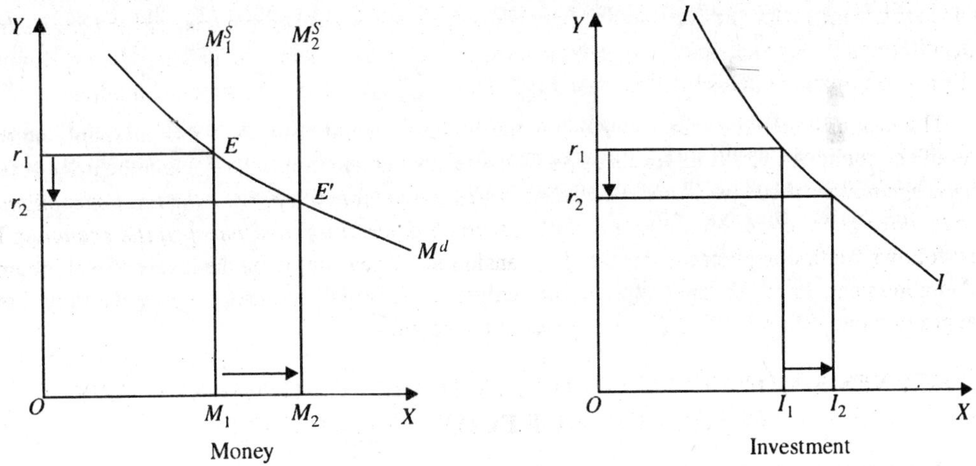

Fig. 24.1. *Money Supply and Rate of Interest* **Fig. 24.2.** *Rate of Interest and Investment*

money. This is shown in Fig. 24.1 where the quantity of money fixed by the Government is OM_1 so that money supply curve is $M_1{}^S$. The intersection of demand for money curve M^d and the supply of money curve $M_1{}^S$ determines r_1 rate of interest. Thus at rate of interest r_1, demand for money to hold is equal to the available supply of money M_1. Now, observing that there is unemployment of labour and other resources and recessionary conditions prevail in the economy, the central bank takes steps to raise money supply. The central bank can raise money supply by purchasing Government securities from the market (that is undertaking open market operations) or lowering cash-reserve ratio (*CRR*) of the banks. Suppose ultimately these steps lead to the expansion in money supply to M_2. It will be seen from Fig. 24.1 that with the increase in money supply from M_1 to M_2, rate of interest falls to r_2 at which demand for money holdings equals the increased supply of money M_2.

It may however be noted that the extent to which rate of interest falls as a result of expansion in money supply depends on the elasticity of demand for money holdings with respect to the rate of interest. The higher the elasticity of demand for money with respect to the rate of interest, the smaller the fall in rate of interest as a result of increase in money supply by the central bank of a country.

Rate of Investment. The next link in the chain of causation is the effect of change in rate of interest on investment in the economy. In the Keynesian system, investment in the economy depends on the rate of interest on the one hand and marginal efficiency of investment *(MEI)* on the other. Marginal efficiency of investment *(i.e.,* expected rate of profit), it may be emphasised, depends on the expectations of entrepreneurs.

The determination of investment is shown in Fig. 24.2 where *II* is investment demand curve whose position depends on the profit expectations of the entrepreneurs which determine marginal efficiency of investment. At the rate of interest r_1, investment equal to I_1 will be made. Now, if the expansion in money supply results in fall in rate of interest to r_2, investment increases to I_2. It is worth noting that the *increase in investment as a result of change in the rate of interest depends on the responsiveness (that is, elasticity) of investment demand to the changes in rate of interest.* The higher the elasticity of investment expenditure to the changes in the rate of interest, the greater will be the increase in investment for a given fall in the rate of interest.

Investment and Aggregate Demand. Next step in the transmission mechanism of the effect of money supply on the national income and price level is concerned with the impact of increase in investment on aggregate demand. Aggregate demand which we may write as *AD* is determined in the Keynesian theory by the sum of private consumption expenditure, private investment expenditure *(I)*, Government's expenditure on goods and services *(G)* and net exports (X_n) that is, excess of exports over imports. Thus

$$AD = C + I + G + X_n$$

When the rate of interest is reduced as a result of expansion in money supply and causes investment to increase, it will shift the aggregate demand curve upward. This is depicted in Fig. 24.3 where initially with investment equal to I_1 along with other variables, aggregate demand curve is AD_1 or $C + I_1 + G + X_n$. When due to the expansion in money supply and resultant fall in rate of interest investment increases from I_1 to I_2, aggregate demand curve shifts upward to the new position $C + I_2 + G + X_n$. The upward shift in aggregate demand curve is equal to the increase in investment from I_1 to I_2.

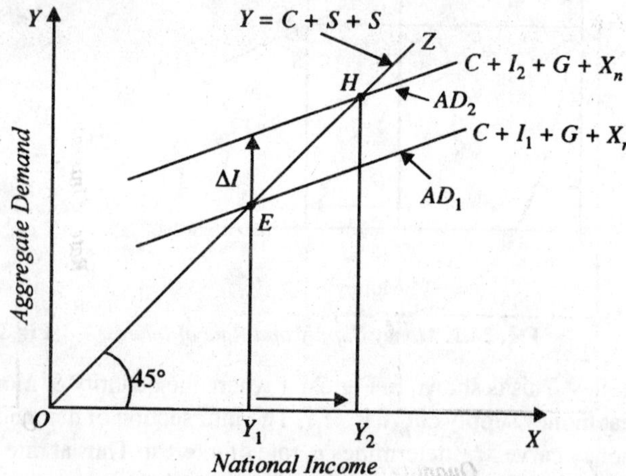

Fig. 24.3. *The Effect of Increase in Investment on Aggregate Demand and National Income*

Multiplier and National Income. Finally, the effect of increase in investment and aggregate demand on real national income (GNP) depends on the size of multiplier. The size of multiplier depends on the marginal propensity to consume *(MPC)* of a community. The higher the marginal propensity to consume, the greater the size of the multipier $\left(\text{Multiplier}=\frac{1}{1-MPC}\right)$. Thus increase in national income (GNP) following increase in investment by ΔI will be equal to $\Delta I\frac{1}{1-MPC}$. This is illustrated in Fig. 24.3 where we have assumed marginal propensity to consume being equal to 0.5 and the size of multiplier equal to 2. Thus when investment increases from I_2 to I_2 (*i.e.*, ΔI), national increases from Y_1 to Y_2 (*i.e.*, ΔY) which is twice the increase in investment.

It follows from above that the *effect of expansion in money supply on national income and employment depends on the elasticity of demand curve for money holding, on the elasticity of investment to changes in rate of interest, and on the size of multiplier.*

Ineffectiveness of Monetary Policy: Keynes's View

It may however be noted that Keynes and early Keynesians were not very optimistic about the success of expansionary monetary policy in lifting the economy out of depression. They point out various weak links in the chain of causation in the process of increase in money supply leading to the rise in aggregate demand. The first weak link occurs at the stage of increase in money supply causing lowering of the rate of interest. Keynes was considering an economy which was in the grip of depression and rate of interest prevailing then was already at a low level and therefore they did not expect any further fall. Whatever expansion in money supply is made at that time, all of it would be held by them rather than investing it in bonds. In other words, according to Keynes and his earlier followers. The demand for money (*i.e.*, liquidity preference curve) was perfectly elastic at a very low rate of interest as shown in Fig. 24.4 where at rate of interest r_3 demand for money becomes perfectly elastic. It is said that at a very low rate of interest economy gets caught up in the **liquidity trap** in times of depression.

Thus. if the rate of interest is already very low, as is usually the cause in times of depression. the expansion in the quantity of money will not be able to reduce it still further. As shown in Fig. 24.4 when the rate of interest is already at a low level so that people demand any amount of money (*i.e.*, the economy is caught in the liquidity trap) at it, the rate of interest will not fall further

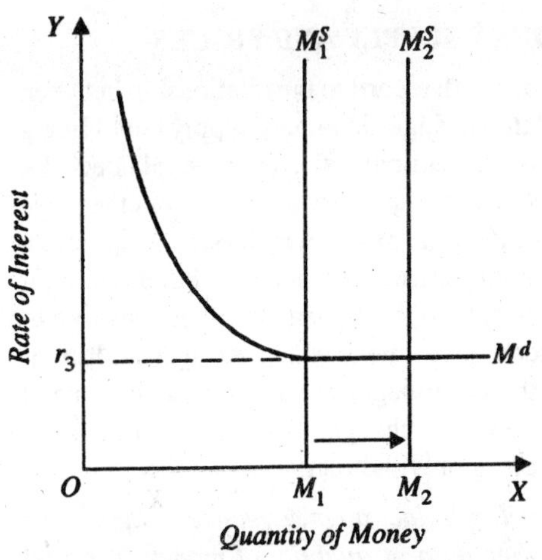

Fig .24.4. *In liquidity-trap situation increase in money supply does not cause fall in interest rate.*

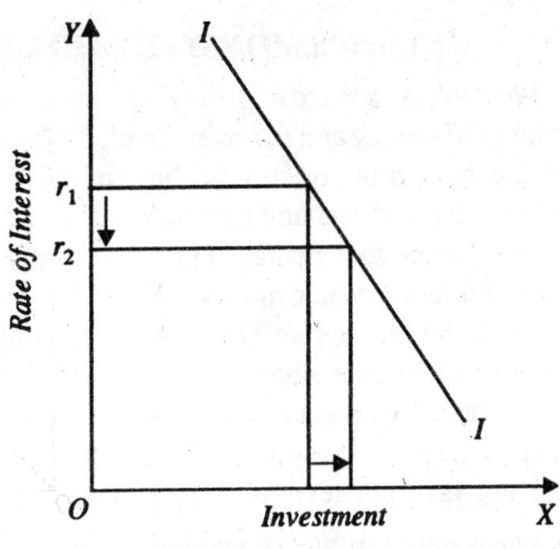

Fig. 24.5. *Investment is interest inelastic*

even when the supply of money is increased. The curve M^d is the money demand curve with a horizontal segment (*i.e.*, liquidy trap) on the right side. Suppose the quantity of money is initially

M_1. With the given money demand curve M^d and the money supply M_1 the rate of interest Or_3 is determined which is very low. Now. if the money supply is increased to M_2. the rate of interest does not fall; all the additional money is held by the people with themselves and not lent out or used for buying bonds or debentures. Thus, when we are operating along the perfectly elastic part of the liquidity preference or money demand curve the rate of interest cannot be reduced by the increase in money supply. With no fall in the rate of interest, investment demand curve remaining the same, the rate of investment will not increase and if investment does not increase, aggregate demand and expenditure will not increase.

Another weak link in the transmission mechanism occurs in the effect of change in the rate of interest on the investment. Keynes and early Keynesians believed that investment demand curve is not much sensitive to the rate of interest, that is, interest-elasticity of investment demand is very low. If this is so them even if there is a large fall in the rate of interest brought about by increase in money supply by the central bank, investment will not increase much. This is illustrated in Fig. 24.5 where we have drawn an inelastic investment demand curve II. It will be seen from Fig. 24.5 that when rate of interest falls from r_1 to r_2, there is only small increase in investment because investment demand curve is not sensitive to the rate of interest. Therefore, when investment does not increase much even when there is a large fall in rate of interest as a result of expansion in money supply, aggregate demand or expenditure will not increase much.

Thus, there are circumstances, especially when recessionary conditions prevail in the economy with large scale unemployment and excess capacity in the economy, expansionary monetary policy may fail to increase the level of aggregate demand or expenditure. With no increase in aggregate demand, real national income, that is, GNP will not increase. Besides, in this Keynesian system, when due to ether highly interest-elastic nature of the money demand curve *(i.e.,* due to liquidity trap) or due to the interest-inelastic nature of the investment demand curve, increase in money supply fails to raise aggregate demand, it will not cause rise in the level of national income.

It is thus clear from above that the *Keynesian theory traces the effect of the increase in money supply on the level of economic activity (i.e., income, output and employment) via its effect on the rate of interest.* Thus, in the Keynesian monetary theory the relationship between money-supply and national income is not direct but it is thought to be much more indirect and uncertain than is assumed in the Friedman's' modern quantity theory of money.

KEYNES'S MONETARY THEORY : MONEY SUPPLY AND PRICES

We know turn to explain the Keynes's monetary theory with regard to the relationship between the supply of money and the price level. Keynes believed that changes in money supply could being about changes in the price level but contrary to the classical economists' view he explained that there was no any direct and proportionate relationship between the quantity of money and the price level. He showed that changes in money supply indirectly affect the price level through its effect on the rate of interest. When money supply is increased, given the demand for money holdings curve, it leads to the fall in the rate of interest depending upon how far money demand curve is sensitive to the rate of interest. A change in the rate of interest affects investment which through multiplier process affects aggregate expenditure or demand. It is then the magnitude of aggregate demand relative to aggregate supply of output that causes price level to change. Thus, relation between money and the price level far from direct and proportionate is only indirect.

The Keynesian theory emphasises that the price level is in fact a consequence of aggregate demand or expenditure relative to aggregate supply rather than of quantity of money. The real cause of fluctuations in price level is to be found in fluctuations in the level of aggregate expenditure. Therefore, changes in the quantity of money can bring about changes in the level of prices only if they change aggregate demand in relation to the supply of output. Unless aggregate expenditure increases, there can be no increase in demand for goods. And if demand for goods does not increase, the question of rise in price level does not arise. However, even if aggregate demand or expenditure does increase, prices may still not rise if the supply curve of output is fairly elastic. Therefore, the effects of a change in quantity of money on the price level depend on the following factors:

(i) effect of changes in money supply on the level of aggregate demand or spending;

(ii) relation between aggregate spending and the volume of production.

As regards the volume of aggregate expenditure or aggregate demand, in the Keynesian theory it depends on the following:

(a) rate of interest which is determined by the demand for money and the supply of money;

(b) the investment demand curve which determines the increase in investment demand following a fall in the rate of interest; and

(c) the propensity to consume which determines the magnitude of the multiplier effect of increase in investment.

(d) supply of money.

Transmission Mechanism. The mechanism through which increase in money supply can lead to the rise in aggregate demand and price level can be represented by the following scheme:

$$M^S \uparrow \longrightarrow r \downarrow \longrightarrow I \uparrow \longrightarrow AD \uparrow \longrightarrow Y \uparrow \text{ and } P \uparrow$$

where M^S = supply of money

r = rate of interest

I = amount of investment

AD = aggregate demand

Y = level of national income, that is, aggregate output

P = price level

The above scheme represents the chief proposition of Keynesian monetary theory. According to this, expansion in money supply *(MS)* causes the rate of interest to fall. Then, given the investment demand function, at a lower rate of interest, there is more demand for investment. This higher rate of investment boosts up the level of aggregate demand or expenditure through multiplier process. However, as we will see below, *whether or not this increase in aggregate demand or expenditure will cause the rise in the price level depends upon the nature of aggregate supply curve.*

It is evident from above that in the Keynesian theory the general price level is determined by the same forces which determine the level of national income and employment, that is, the level of aggregate demand and aggregate supply. It needs to be emphasised that price level and national income *(i.e.,* aggregate output) are determined jointly by aggregate demand and aggregate supply. However, in the analysis of determination of real national income in the framework of 45° line diagram, we have used the concept of aggregate demand with a given fixed price level. But to explain the Keynesian theory of money and prices, we need to use the concept of *aggregate demand with varying price level.* Aggregate demand (with varying price level) is the sum of total expenditure, which consumers, businessmen, Government and foreigners are willing to make on aggregate output of goods and services at different price levels during a given period. That is, aggregate demand (with flexible prices) shows how much output, the consumers, businesses, Government and foreigners are willing to buy at various price levels. Thus aggregate demand curve in Keynesian theory is $C + I + G + X_n$ at various price levels.[1] At higher price levels, aggregate output demanded or purchased is less at a higher price level and it increases at a lower price level. In other words,

1. Note that in sharp contrast to Keynes' theory, in the quantity theory of money aggregate demand at various price levels is determined by *MV.*

aggregate demand ($C + I + G + X_n$) curve with variable price level slopes downward as shown in Fig. 24.6. Three factors account for the downward sloping nature of the aggregate demand curve. These three factors are *real balance effect, interest effect and foreign trade effect* of the change in the price level which have been explained in an earlier chapter concerning *AD-AS* model (with flexible prices).

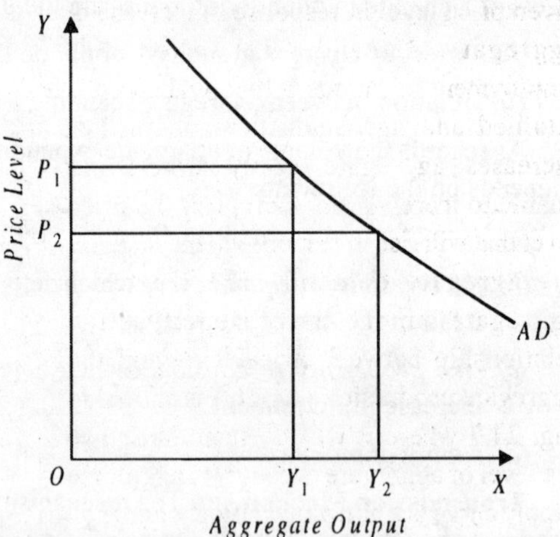

Fig. 24.6. *Aggregate Demand Curve and Varying Price Level*

As explained in an earlier chapter concerning *AD-AS* model (with flexible prices), the sum of aggregate demand for consumption, investment and net exports increases with a fall in the price level and declines with a rise in the price level. This means that aggregate demand curve showing relationship between aggregate output demanded and the general price level slopes downward to the right as is shown in Fig. 24.6

Aggregate demand curve is derived from changes in aggregate expenditure caused by changes in the price level. If there is a change in the *non-price factors such as money supply, investment demand, Government expenditure, taxation,* the aggregate demand curve will shift. Thus, when money supply is increased by the central bank of a country, it will lower the rate of interest. As seen above, at a lower rate of interest more investment is undertaken depending on the elasticity of investment demand curve. Further, with more investment expenditure the entire aggregate demand curve (with variable price level) depicting $C + I + G + X_n$ will shift to the right implying thereby that at each price level, the aggregate quantity demanded will increase.

Money Supply, Aggregate Demand and Price Level

But what happens to the equilibrium price level and real national product as a result of change in money supply, we must consider aggregate supply as well. Thus, even if aggregate demand or expenditure increases it does not follow that prices must necessarily rise. Whether or not the increase in aggregate demand will cause a rise in price level depends upon the nature of aggregate supply curve. If the supply curve of output is fairly elastic, it is more likely that the effect of increase in aggregate demand or spending will be more to raise production or real income than prices. In the model of determination of general price level, the concept of aggregate supply curve with variable price level is used. Precisely speaking, in this sense, *aggregate supply curve shows the various amounts of aggregate supply which the producers in the economy are willing to produce and sell in the market at various price levels.* The classical economists assumed that there normally prevailed full employment of resources in the economy. According to them, if at any time there is deviation from this full employment level, the wages, interest and prices quickly and automatically adjust or change to restore equilibrium at the full employment level. Thus, in the classical theory, the aggregate supply curve of output is perfectly inelastic (*i.e.,* a vertical straight line) at the output level corresponding to the full employment level of resources.

As mentioned above, Keynes considered the situation of economic depression when the economy was operating at less than full employment level of resources. He further believed that in such a situation money wage rates were sticky, *i.e.,* remain stable. He further assumed that average and margined products of labour remain constant when more of it is employed following the increase in aggregate demand. With these assumptions, more aggregate output is produced and supplied at the given price level in response to increase in aggregate demand. But when full employment of labour and capital stock is attained and aggregate demand further increases, aggregate supply curve being unable to increase any more, it is the price level that will rise in response to the increase in aggregate demand. The Keynes's aggregate supply curve depicting the relationship between price level and the aggregate production (supply) is shown in Fig. 24.7 where it will be seen that up to the level of aggregate output OY_F aggregate supply curve is a horizontal straight line (*i.e.*, perfectly elastic) showing thereby that more is produced and supplied at the same price level *OP*. OY_F is the full employment level of aggregate production (*i.e.*, potential GNP) and therefore beyond that aggregate supply curve becomes vertical (*i.e.*, perfectly inelastic). It may however be noted that Keynes recognised that as the aggregate supply approaches close to the full employment level cost of output per unit tends to rise due to the rise in wage rate and also due to diminishing returns to extra units of factors employed. But, according to Keynes, the rise in price level before full employment or less than capacity output will not be much.

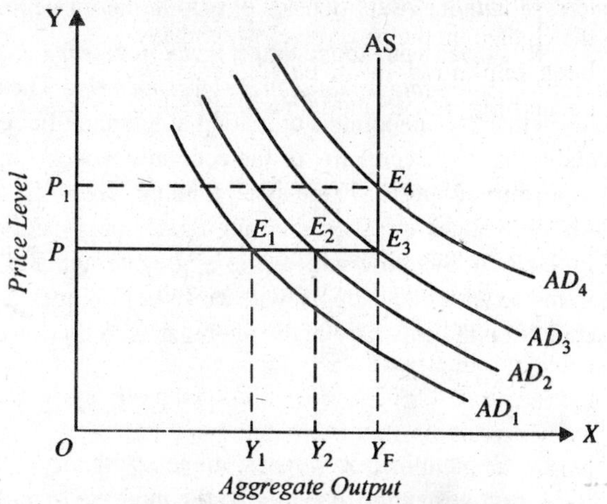

Fig. 24.7. *Effect of Increase in Money Supply on Price Level: Keynes's Model*

Suppose the economy is in state of depression so that a lot of resources including labour are lying idle. Initially, the aggregate demand curve is AD_1 which cuts the aggregate supply curve *AS* at point E_1 and as a result price level *OP* is determined (see Fig. 24.7). Now suppose that expansion in money supply succeeds in raising aggregate demand curve to AD_2. It will be seen from Fig. 24.7 that the new aggregate demand curve stills cuts the aggregate supply curve in its horizontal range at point *E2*. Thus increase in aggregate demand to AD_2 caused by expansionary monetary policy has led to the increase in aggregate output (*i.e.*, real national income) from Y_1 to Y_2 without any rise in general price level. If money supply is further increased and as a result aggregate demand curve shifts upward to AD_3, and cuts aggregate supply curve *AS* at point E_3 even then only aggregate output rises to its full employment level Y_F, price level remaining unchanged. Thus, with aggregate demand curve AD_3 economy is operating at full employment level of output Y_F. Now, if there is further expansion in money supply causing aggregate demand curve to rise above AD_3, say to AD_4 in Fig. 24.7, resources bring already fully utilised supply of output will not respond to the increased demand and will cause the price level to rise to P_1 This happens when firms try to hire more workers and other resources for expanding

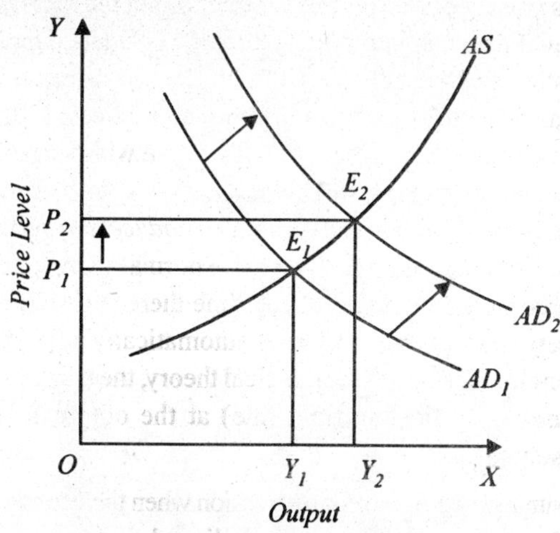

Fig. 24.8. *Impact of Increase in Aggregate Demand on Prive Level and Output*

output to meet the increased demand. In view of full employment of resources have been already achieved, they will only bid up wages and their cost of production. Hence the price level will rise. Thus when full employment is prevailing increase in aggregate demand for goods brought about by increase in money supply leads only to higher price level and not to higher output..

It is clear from above that *it is not necessary that even if expansion in money supply succeeds in raising aggregate demand, price level must rise.* The effect of increase in aggregate demand depends on whether the economy is operating at less than fun employment level when there are recessionary conditions in the economy or the economy is working at full employment level at which aggregate supply curve is perfectly inelastic. It may however be noted that the modern Keynesians believe that in normal times the short-run aggregate supply curve slopes upward and is elastic as shown in Fig. 24.8. In this case increase in aggregate demand say from AD_1 to AD_2 in Fig. 24.8 caused by expansion in money supply will cause both output and price level to rise, the extent of their rise depends on the elasticity of the aggregate supply curve.

QUESTIONS FOR REVIEW

1. Explain briefly Keynes' monetary theory. Show how, according to Keynes, expansion in money supply can lead to the increase in national income and employment.
2. What, according to Keynes, are the factors which determine the effect of changes in money supply on the level of income and employment in the economy ? Explain with the help of Keynes' monetary theory.
3. Explain how Keynes showed that monetary policy is ineffective in tackling recession/ depression and thereby revive the economy. What policy did he suggest for this purpose ?
4. Explain the relationship between money supply and price level as established by Keynes. Explain how he proved that there is no direct and proportionate increase in the general price level as a result of increase in money supply in an economy.
5. According to J.M. Keynes price level is in fact the consequence of aggregate expenditure rather than of quantity of money. Discuss.
6. What is real balance effect ? How does it affect aggregate demand ? Is it strong enough to cancel out the adverse effect on employment of all-round cut in wages in the economy ?
7. What is liquidity trap ? Why does in the presence of liquidity trap increase in money supply does not affect the level of economic activity.

CHAPTER 25

Monetarism : Friedman's Modern Quantity Theory of Money

Monetarism : An Introduction

The quantity theory of money as put forward by classical economists emphasised that increase in the quantity of money would bring about an equal proportionate rise in the price level. The quantity theory of money had come into disrepute, together with the rest of classical economists as a result of the Great Depression of the 1930s. J.M. Keynes criticised quantity theory of money and brought out that expansion in money supply did not always cause the price level to rise. Keynes and his *early* followers, often called *early* Keynesians[1], believed that money was not important in influencing the level of economic activity and that depression was not caused by contraction in money supply by the central banks of the countries. Keynes and his early followers argued that demand for money at a low rate of interest was almost infinetely elastic (that is, liquidity trap existed in the demand for money) so that increase in money supply would not succeed in lowering the rate of interest. As a result, investment would not increase following the expansion in money supply. They further argued that investment demand was very much less interest-elastic which made it doubly sure that expansionary monetary policy was quite ineffective in giving boost to investment and thereby the level of economic activity. Briefly speaking Early Keynesians thought that money was unimportant or *"Money does not matter"*.

However, in the fifties and sixties, the new thinking emerged under the influence of Milton Friedman, an eminent American economist and a Nobel Laureate in economics, who laid stress on the importance of money not only in determining the general price level but more importantly in influencing the level of economic activity. Friedman asserted that events of 1930s had been wrongly assessed and did not in fact offer evidence against the quantity theory of money. He however realised that there was a need to restate or *reformulate the quantity theory of money* which should re-establish the importance of money determining the level of economic activity and the price level. However, in his restatement of the quantity theory of money he took account of Keynes's contribution to monetary theory, especially his emphasis on the demand for money as an asset. We may describe Friedman's monetarism into the following three propositions:

1. The level of economic activity in current rupee terms, that is, the level of *nominal income* is determined *primarily* by the stock of money.
2. In the long run, the effect of expansion in money supply is primarily on the price level and other *nominal* variables. In the long run, the level of economic activity in real terms, that is level of real output and employment are determined by the real factors such as stock of capital goods, the state of technology, the size and quality of labour force. Therefore, long-run aggregate supply curve of output (LAS) is a vertical straight line.
3. In the short run price level as well as the level of real national income (*i.e.*, real output) and employment are determined by the supply of money and demand for money. In the short run changes in the quantity of money are the dominant factor causing cyclical fluctuations in output and employment.

1. Note that later Keynesians, often called modern or *New Keynesians*, hold slightly different views from the early Keynesians.

We shall explain below the above three propositions of Friedman's monetary theory. The above conclusions derived by Friedman depends on the restatement of the quantity theory of money. It is important to note that Friedman's modern quantity theory of money is in fact based on his theory of demand. Therefore, in our analysis below we start from Friedman's theory of demand for money. We then explain how his theory of money demand explains the determination of the level of economic activity and the price level, both in the short run and long run.

Demand for Money and Friedman's Restatement of Quantity Theory of Money

Friedman's modern quantity theory of money is very close to the Cambridge's cash balance approach. Friedman and other modern monetarists have emphasised that k in Cambridge approach should be interpreted as proportion of nominal income that people *desire* or *demand to hold* in the form of money balances. Interpreting k in this *desired or ex-ante* sense helps to convert the Cambridge equation of exchange into a *theory of nominal income*. Thus, rewriting Cambridge equation as demand for money (M^d) we have:

$$M^d = kPY \qquad ...(1)$$

where k is assumed to be constant. PY is the nominal income obtained by multiplying the real income (Y) with the price level (P). Like Cambridge economists, Friedman regards the quantity of money being fixed exogenously by the central bank of the country. If M represents the quantity of money set exogenously by the central bank we have the equation which describes the Cambridge theory of determination of nominal income.

$$M = M^d = \bar{k}PY \qquad ...(2)$$

or

$$M.\frac{1}{\bar{k}} = PY \qquad ...(3)$$

According to Cambridge equation (3) nominal income is determined by the supply of money (M) multiplied by the reciprocal of constant k. Now, Friedman *introduced changes in the above Cambridge theory of money demand* incorporating important aspects of Keynes's theory of demand for money. Keynes emphasised the *role of money as an asset* apart from its role in meeting transactions demand.

In studying the factors that determine demand for money as an asset relative to other assets, he simplified his analysis by lumping together all non-monetary assets under a single category '*bonds*'. He then examined what determined people's allocation of their wealth between money and bonds. According to him, the level of income and rate of interest determined the allocation of wealth between money and bonds. According to Keynes, rate of interest was the most important determinant of k in the Cambridge cash balance approach. It may be recalled that k in Cambridge theory indicates how much proportion of income people hold as money. However, Keynes regarded k as the proportion of income that people want to hold in money as an asset. *Friedman accepted Keynes's emphasis on the role of money as an asset* and presented his own theory of demand for money. In his analysis of determinants of money demand, Friedman included not only level of income and rate of interest on bonds but also rates at return on other assets such as equity shares, durable goods including real property. Thus, Friedman's theory demand for money can be written as follows:

$$M^d = F(P, Y, r_B, r_E, r_D)$$

where
P = price level
Y = level of real income
r_B = rate of interest on bonds
r_E = rate of return on equity shares
r_D = rate of return on durable goods

It will be seen from Friedman's money demand function that the product of the first two variables, namely, P and Y give us the level of nominal income. It therefore follows that, in Friedman's function, demand for money depends on nominal income. The higher the level of nominal income, the greater the demand for money. It is worth mentioning that for a given level of nominal income, in Friedman's money demand function as in that of Keynes, demand for money depends on the rates of return on non-monetary alternative assets. But, unlike Keynes, *Friedman regards money demand function is stable.* Stability of money demand function implies that it will not shift erratically and that variables in the function will determine the quantity of money that will be demanded. Friedman's theory of demand for money can be used to restate the Cambridge money demand equation so as to bring out the important role of money demand function in the determination of the level of economic activity. Thus Friedman money demand function can be restated as follows:

$$M^d = k\,(r_B, r_E, r_D)\,PY \qquad ...(4)$$

It is worth noting that whereas in Cambridge cash balance equation, k, that is, the proportion of income that is held in money, is mainly dependent on the transactions demand for money in Friedman's theory, it has been taken to be a function of rates of return on alternative non-monetary assets such as bonds, equity shares, durable goods. Any rise in the rates of return on these alternative assets, it will cause k to fall showing the increased desirability of alternative non-monetary assets. "In these terms Friedman can be seen to have restated the quantity theory, providing a systematic explanation of k, an explanation that takes account of the Keynesian analysis of money's role as an asset."[2]

Money Market Equilibrium: Friedman's Analysis. In terms of Friedman money demand function, the condition for equilibrium in the money market can be stated as under:

$$M = M^d = k\,(r_B, r_E, r_D)PY$$

where M stands for the supply of money which is determined by the central bank policies. k is the proportion of nominal income (PY) that is held in the form of money and is determined by the rates of return (r_B, r_E, r_D) on alternative non-monetary assets such as bond, equity shares, durable goods respectively. Friedman assumes that money demand function is stable. *Given the stable money demand function, any increase in money supply by the central bank will cause either increase in nominal income (PY) or decline in rates of return so that k rises or alternatively some increase in nominal income (PY) and some rise in k.* Friedman believes that much of the effect of exogenous increase in money supply will be to bring about increase in nominal income (PY) rather than k. Thus Friedman concludes that quantity of money is an important determinant of the level of economic activity, that is, output, employment and prices. Here the short-run and long-run effects of exogenous increase in money supply must be distinguished. In the short run, the increase in money supply will lead to a change partly in real income (*i.e.*, real aggregate output or Y) and partly in the price level (P). That is, in the short run the effect of increase in money supply will be distributed between change in real income (Y) and change in price level (P) depending upon the elasticity of the aggregate supply curve. Friedman recognised that at times of depression, aggregate supply curve was fairly elastic so that the effect of the increase in money will be more in the form of expansion in real output and less in the form of rise in the price level. But, in the long run, the aggregate supply curve is perfectly inelastic at full-employment level and, therefore, the exogenous increase in money supply will be reflected in the rise in price level.

DETERMINATION OF NOMINAL INCOME : FRIEDMAN'S APPROACH

Let us show how in Friedman's modern quantity theory nominal income is determined. To show this Friedman makes some strong assumptions about the behaviour of k. Friedman converts his money demand function into a theory of nominal income by assuming that variables in his

2. Richard Froyen, *Macroeconomics: Theories and Policies*, 3rd edition, Macmillan, New York, p. 278.

money demand function other that nominal income (PY), that is, r_B, r_E, r_D have little effect on k. With this assumption, money held as a proportion of income will be nearly constant. It may be noted by taking this assumption Friedman's theory comes very close to Cambridge theory of determination of nominal income. With this assumption Friedman's theory of nominal income can be derived as follows:

$$M^d = k\,(r_B, r_E, r_D)\,PY$$

With variables r_B, r_E, r_D having little or no effect on k, k can be assumed to be constant. Therefore,

$$M^d = kPY$$

Rearranging we have

$$PY = \frac{1}{k} M^d$$

since $\frac{1}{k} = V$, we can write

$$PY = VM^d$$

In equilibrium demand for money (M^d) equals money supply (M) which is *exogenously* given, we have

$$PY = VM$$

or

$$PY = \frac{1}{k} M$$

The last condition shows that *nominal income is determined by the supply of money, k being remaining constant.* The determination of nominal income in the short run is graphically shown in Fig. 25.1 where we measure nominal income (PY) on the Y-axis, and the supply and demand for money on the Y-axis. Suppose the Central Bank sets money supply equal to OM. With OM as the supply of money, supply curve of money is a vertical straight line M^S. It will be seen that at the level of nominal income P_0Y_0, money market is in equilibrium as at it demand for money (M^d) equals the supply of money (M). Let us explain how this equilibrium level of nominal income is determined. Suppose the level of nominal income is P_1Y_1. It will be seen from Fig. 25.1 that at nominal income P_1Y_1, money

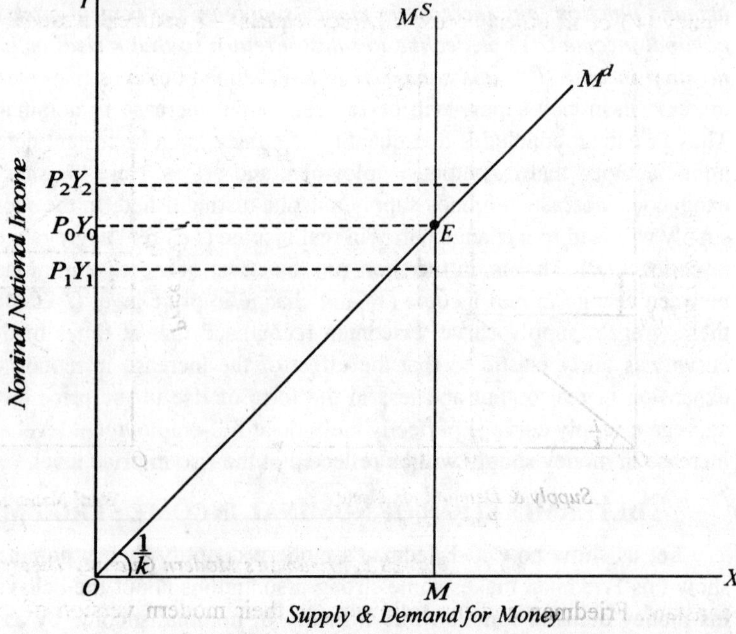

Fig. 25.1. *Determination of Nominal Income : Monetarist Theory*

supply OM exceeds money demand (M^d). Given the stable money demand function and constant **k**, Friedman argues that this excess money supply will be spent by the people on goods and services so as to bring demand for money in equilibrium with the supply of money. As a result, nominal income will increase to the level P_0Y_0 at which money demand becomes equal to money supply (OM). If the period we are considering is the short run when there prevails depression and unemployment in the economy, the increase in nominal income will be more in terms of real income (*i.e.*, real GDP) and less in terms of price level (P).

On the other hand, if at a level of nominal income money supply (M^S) is less than the demand for money ($M^S < M^d$) as it is at nominal income P_2Y_2 in Fig. 25.1. The people will react to such a situation by spending less on goods and services so that their demand for money decreases to become equal to the given supply of money OM. The decline in expenditure by the people on goods and services will cause nominal income to decrease to the level P_0Y_0. Again this decline in nominal income from P_2Y_2 to P_0Y_0 may occur partly in real income (Y) and partly in terms of fall in price (P) depending on the elasticity of short-run aggregate supply curve of output. It follows from above that nominal income is in equilibrium at the level where demand for money equals available quantity of money supply.

Increase in Money Supply and the Price Level

Let us explain in more detail how in Friedman's monetarist approach increase in money supply will affect the price level and national income. We will also spell out the transmission mechanism through which increase in money supply operates to bring about rise in the price level and income. Consider again the equation for money equilibrium,

$$kPY = M^S$$

$$PY = \frac{1}{k} M^S \qquad ...(5)$$

Now, if k and Y are constant, then it follows from (5) above that price is directly proportional to money supply. This is the viewpoint of the old quantity theory of money which thought velocity of money (V) or in other words, k [which equals $\frac{1}{v}$] and real national income or output remained

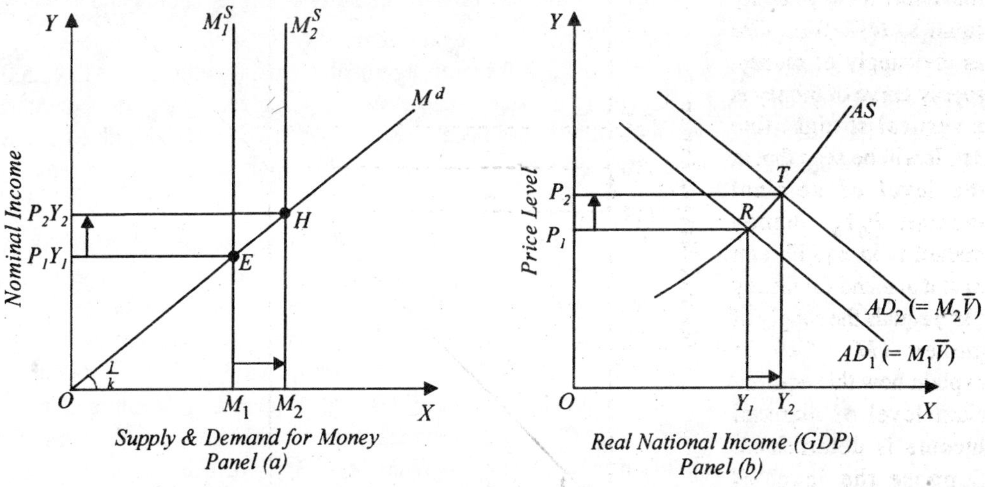

Fig. 25.2. *Friedman's Modern Quantity Theory*

constant. Friedman and his followers, in their modern version of quantity theory of money or demand for money assume k to be stable, the effect of expansion in money supply will be distributed between the increase in real income (*i.e.*, Y) and increase in price level (P) in the short run. They further explain that if in the short run the economy is working below the full employment level of output the increase in money supply will cause increase in real income (*i.e.*, output) much more than the rise in price level. Thus, according to them, *if in the short run the economy is in recession, then the effect of increase in money supply, with k or V remaining constant, is likely to lead to the increase in output or real income (i.e., Y) more than rise in the price level (P).* However, Friedman and his followers, as shall be explained in detail later,think that since in the long run the aggregate supply curve is a vertical straight line at the full employment level of output and Y and k remain constant the increase in money supply will raise the price level or cause inflation in the economy, real GDP remaining constant.

To consider fully Friedman's new quantity theory, look at panel (a) in Fig. 25.2. Let us suppose the supply of money is raised from M_1 to M_2. As will be seen from the figure, the expansion in money supply causes the nominal income to rise. In panel (a) of Fig.25.2 with M_1 as the supply of money and M^d as the curve of demand for money, money market is initially in equilibrium at point E with P_1Y_1 as the equilibrium level of nominal income. When the supply of money is increased from M_1 to M_2 and as a result money supply curve shifts to the left to M_2^S, then at nominal income P_1Y_1, money supply becomes excessive relative to the demand for money to hold at it. As a result, people will be induced to spend the excess money supply and thereby increase the aggregate demand for goods and services. This increase in aggregate demand for or expenditure on goods and services leads to the increase in nominal income. With this increase in nominal income demand for money increases and the new money market equilibrium is reached at point H at the new nominal income level P_2Y_2. How much increase in nominal income will occur in terms of increase in real income (*i.e.* physical output) and how much in terms of rise in price level can be explained in the framework of aggregate demand (*AD*) and aggregate supply (*AS*) curves with flexible prices. This is shown in panel (*b*) of Fig. 25.2 where on the *X*-axis we measure aggregate demand and aggregate supply and on the *Y*-axis price level is measured. The concept of aggregate demand curve in this framework needs to be spelled out. In the monetarist view aggregate demand curve is determined by the quantity of money supply (*M*) and the velocity of circulation (*V*). That is, aggregate demand or aggregate expenditure in this approach is obtained from multiplying a given quantity of money supply by the velocity of circulation (*V*) which is assumed to remain constant. Note that velocity of circulation (*V*) is equal to $\frac{1}{k}$. Thus, if ₹4000 crores is the quantity of money supply and velocity of circulation is 5, the aggregate expenditure or aggregate demand (*MV*) will be equal to ₹ 20,000 crores. Now, if money supply is raised to ₹ 5,000 crores, aggregate demand will increase to ₹ 25,000 crores, velocity of circulation remaining constant at 5. Now, with a given aggregate expenditure (*MV*), aggregate demand curve slopes downward because at a lower price level, with given quantity of money more quantity of goods and services can be purchased, velocity of circulation remaining constant.

Now, a glance at panel (*b*) of Fig. 25.2 reveals that with money supply equal to M_1, the aggregate demand curve is AD_1 with the constant velocity V. Aggregate demand curve AD_1 and aggregate supply curve *AS* determines the price level P_1 and *real* national income equal to Y_1. Now, when in panel (*a*), money supply is increased from M_1 to M_2, and as a result nominal income rises to P_2Y_2, in panel (*b*) aggregate demand curve based on $M_2\bar{V}$ shifts upward to AD_2 and its intersection with the given aggregate supply curve *AS*, determines higher level of real national income equal to OY_2 and new higher price level P_2. It is thus evident that increase in nominal income from P_1Y_1 to P_2Y_2 as a result of expansion in money supply from M_1 to M_2 is distributed or absorbed as increase in real national income (*i.e.*, physical output) by the amount Y_1Y_2 and as rise in price level from P_1 to P_2. According to Friedman and other monetarists, this occurs in the short run, especially when the economy is operating in recessionary conditions and therefore less than full-employment level of national income. Thus, to what extent real income as a result of expansion in money supply increases depends on the elasticity of short-run aggregate supply curve *AS*. Thus, Friedman writes, "I regard the description of our position as 'money is all that matters for changes in nominal income and for short-run changes in real income as an exaggregation but one that gives the right flavour to our conclusion."[3]

As seen above, according to the monetarist view, the impact of increase in the money supply on prices and real income is direct. The expansion in money supply is seen as putting more money in the hands of both consumers and investors. Since monetarists believe that demand for money to hold (M_d) is a stable function of nominal income, expansion in money supply leads to the excess money supply or, in other words, excess cash balances with the people relative to their demand for money holdings. The excess money balances are soon spent leading to the increase in aggregate demand for goods and services. Unlike the transmission mechanism of Keynesian analysis wherein increase in money supply first reduces the rate of interest and thereby raises investment and aggregate demand and then affects prices, in the analysis of Friedman and other modern monetarists, the expansion in *money supply has a direct impact on prices and income through increase in aggregate demand.* Liquidity trap and inelastic nature of investment demand are not involved in this adjustment process which in Keynesian analysis could prevent or curtail the effect of monetary expansion on prices and national income.

However, many modern monetarists (including Friedman) aggree to the Keynesian idea that expansionary macroeconomic policy may lead to the increase in national output and employment and this enabies the economy to come out of recession quickly. It may be recalled that Keynes laid stress on the use of expansionary fiscal policy (expansion in Government expenditure and lower taxation) as the proper instrument to tide over recession. Keynes believed that in view of the liquidity trap and interest-unresponsive nature of investment demand in times of recession, expansionary monetary policy will not help much to get the economy out of recession. However, monetarists emphasize that since expansion in money supply directly causes increase in aggregate demand through people spending the excess money supply, expansionary monetary policy can help in curing recession and achieving full employment.

Short-run and Long-run Impact of Expansion in Money Supply on Price Level and Real National Income

Monetarists believe that perfectly elastic aggregate supply curve envisaged by Keynes actually represents the recessionary state of the economy in the short run. According to the monetarists, though short run aggregate supply curve of output at times of recession is elastic, the long-run aggregate supply curve of output is perfectly inelastic, that is, it is a vertical straight line. As mentioned above, the position of long-run vertical supply curve is determined by the amounts of real resources such as labour force, capital stock, availability of infrastructure, state of

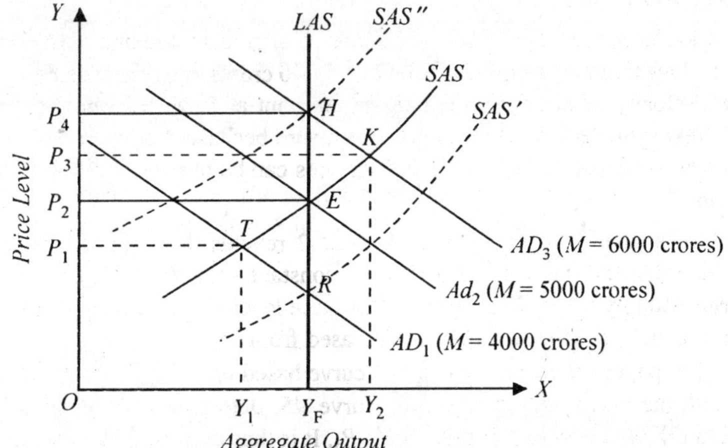

Fig. 25.3. *Long run Impact of Expansion in Money Supply on the Price Level*

3. Milton Friedman, "A Theoretical Framework for Monetary Analysis" in Robert Gordon, ed., *Milton Friedman's Monetary Framework*, University of Chicago Press, 1974, p. 27

technology. Besides, according to Friedman, in the long run wages and prices are perfectly flexible. Therefore, in the long run with a given vertical aggregate supply curve any increase in aggregate demand brought about by increase in money supply will cause price level to rise, (that is well cause inflation), real national income (GDP) remaining the same. However, according to them, in the short run wages are temporarily fixed and short-run aggregate supply curve (SAS) is sloping upward. Therefore, in their analysis of impact of increase in money supply, Friedman and his followers make distinction between short run and long run. The monetarist view is portrayed in Fig. 25.3. Assume that aggregate demand curve is initially at AD_1 corresponding to the available money supply equal to ₹ 4000 crores, and a given velocity of circulation (V), cuts the short-run aggregate supply curve *SAS* at point *T* and thus determines the price level equal to P_1 and the income level Y_1 which is less than full employment level of output Y_F. In such an equuilibrium situation idle or unutilized productive capacity would prevail causing unemployment of labour. Thus, in equilibrium at point *T*, the economy will find itself in the grip of recession. However, according to Friedman and his followers, this only represents a short-run situation. They argue that if in such a situation the money supply and aggregate demand curve were held constant, then in view of the prevailing unutilized capacity and unemployment, prices and wages would **eventually** fall so that equilibrium at point *R* will be reached in the long run. The point *R* represents full-employment equilibrium though at a lower price level and lower wages.

However, Friedman and other modern monetarists accept that if instead of waiting for the downward adjustment in prices and wages, money supply is increased, say from ₹ 4000 crores to ₹ 5000 crores, raising the aggregate demand curve from AD_1 to AD_2, the new equilibrium is attained at point *E* where the effect of increase in money supply has been divided into rise in price level from P_1 to P_2 and increase in real national income (GDP) from Y_1 to Y_F. The extent to which price level will rise and output will increase depends on the elasticity of short-run aggregate supply curve. Further, if money supply is increased further to ₹ 6000 crores so that aggregate demand curve rises to AD_3 the price level will rise to P_3 and output will increase to Y_2 in the short-run. However, with some time lag wages would rise causing a shift in the short-run aggregate supply to short upwards to *SAS″* which cuts the long-run aggregate supply curve *LAS* at point *H*. Thus, it will be seen from Fig. 25.3 that in the long run only price level will rise to P_4, aggregate (*i.e.*, real income) output remaining unchanged, at Y_F.

Monetarists are Opposed to the Active Discretionary Monetary Policy

It is however worthnoting that most of the modern monetarists are opposed to the use of active monetary policy to tide over recession since they believe that prices and wages are quite flexible and downward adjustment in them will take place fairly rapidly to restore equilibrium at full-employment level of output. Second, monetarists are opposed to pursuing active monetary policy because they feel very much concerned about inflation as a result of *discretionary and active monetary policy.* They think than in its bid to overcome recession monetary authority is likely to *overshoot* and expand money supply much greater than that required to achieve equilibrium at full employment level of national income and thus causing inflation in the economy. As will be seen from Fig. 25.3, when aggregate demand increases to AD_3 level, as a result of the expansion of money supply to ₹ 6000 crores when only ₹ 5000 crores were needed to achieve equilibrium at full employment level, price level rises to P_4 and thus inflation emerges in the economy as a result of discretionary active monetary policy.

KEY PROPOSITIONS OF MONETARISM

We state below the key propositions of monetarism and in a later section we shall compare them with Keynesian proposition of macroeconomics.

1. **Money Demand Function.** Miltion Friedman, the pioneer of modern monetarism, rests his monetary theory on the demand function for money which is written as under

$$M^d = k\,(r_B, r_E, r_D)\,PY$$

That is, demand for money is a function of nominal income (*PY*) and *k* which is proportion of nominal income held in the form of money and this proportion is determined by the rate of returns on alternative non-monetary assets such as bonds, equity consumer durables. Together with stock of money supply this money demand function determines price level, output and rates of return on assets.

2. **The quantity of money supply, given the money demand function, determines the level of nominal income** (*PY*). If the quantity of money increases rapidly, so will nominal income. The velocity of money circulation or *k* in the money demand function is fairly stable and predictable. However, it takes time for changes in money supply to affect nominal income. This time lag between growth of money supply and its effect on nominal income, according to Friedman, is about 6 to nine months.

3. **Increase in money supply affects output in the short run only.** This short run, according to Friedman, may mean five to ten years. Over the long run, according to monetarists, the old quantity theory of money holds. That is, in the long run increase in money supply affects only prices. Thus, according to a fundamental proposition of monetarism, in the long run *inflation is always and everywhere a monetary phenomenon.* This means that in the long run inflation cannot occur without a *more rapid increase in the quantity of money than in output.* In fact, monetarists claim that sustained increase in the growth rate of money will, in the long run when all adjustments have taken place, lead to an equal increase in the rate of inflation.

4. **Money alone matters.** In sharp contrast to the views of early Keynesians, as seen above, Friedman and other modern monetarists argue that money has significant effect on price level or inflation in the economy in the long run and have real effects on output and employment in the short run. Thus, contrary to the views of early Keynesians who thought that "*money does not matter*" in view of the above effects of the growth of money supply, monetarists think '*Money alone matters*'.

5. **The output or real national income in the long run is determined by the real factors** such as stock of capital, propensity to save, supplies of other resources such as labour, natural resources, state of technology. An increase in the money supply has no long run effects on the level of output. Thus, according monetarists, there is no long-run trade off between inflation and output or for that matter, between inflation and unemployment. According to monetarists, in the long run Philips Curve is vertical. However, monetarists adviets that there is trade off in the short run and accordingly, short run Phillips Curve slopes downward to the right. (This proposition of monetarists will be explained at length in a later chapter concerning this issue).

6. **Milton Friedman and other modern monetarists oppose the use of active counter cyclical monetary policy to control economic fluctuations in the economy.** Instead they recommend a *rule of constant money growth rate* to ensure economic stability in the economy. Monetary policy should be conducted in a manner that should ensure money supply to grow at a constant rate. However, monetarists have suggested different constant money growth rate which varies from 2 to 5.

This monetary policy of constant money growth rate implies that monetary policy should not respond to disturbances in the economy unless these are major disturbances such as the Great Depression that occurred in industrialised countries during 1929–33. To quote Friedman, "*By setting itself a steady course and keeping to it, the monetary authority could make a major contribution to promoting economic stability. By making that course one of steady but moderate growth in the quantity of money, it would make a major contribution to avoidance of either inflation or deflation of prices.*"[3]

It therefore follows from above that Friedman and other monetarists oppose activist policy of "*Fine tuning*". By *fine tuning* we mean policy variables are continuously adjusted in response to small disturbances in the economy so as to ensure economic stability at full-employment level of output. Dornbusch and Fischer explain the monetarists position on fine tuning in the following words.

"The major" argument of monetarist against fine tuning is that in actual practice policy makers do not in fact behave as suggested—making only small adjustments in response to small disturbances. If allowed to do anything they may do too much. Instead of merely trying to offset disturbances, policy makers shift towards fine tuning to keep the economy always exactly at full employment, with the risk of overdoing a good thing. The 'full employment bias in policies risks creating inflation".[4]

7. **Money Supply and Interest Rate Targets.** Another controversial issue between monetarists and Keynesians is what should be the target variable of monetary policy, that is, whether monetary authority should have fix targets of money supply growth or target of interest rate as an appropriate monetary variable for formulating monetary policy. In the fifties and sixties in the USA, emphasis of monetary policy was entirely on controlling interest rates — a policy suggested by Keynesians Monetarists are opposed to it and support the money stock target for a monetary policy. They argue that increase in the money supply leads ultimately to inflation and therefore only by keeping in money supply growth moderate, inflation in the economy can be avoided. They point out that while the Central Bank of a country keeps its eye on interest rate target, the money supply growth rate and inflation rate often tend to rise.

As a result of the above monetarist critique of interest rate as a target variable of monetary policy, in recent years, not only in the USA but in other countries as well emphasis has been shifted to proper *money supply growth rate* as target variable of monetary policy. In India however, since 1996, both money supply growth and interest rate targets are being used as policy variables of monetary policy.

8. **Inherent Stability of the Private Sector.** Monetarists believe that private sector is inherently stable but the fluctuations in the economy are caused by wrong policies and mistakes of the Government or the Central bank of the country. They try to show that even occurrence of Great depression of 1929–33, especially its severity was due to failure of Federal Reserve System (which is the name of Central Bank of the United States) to prevent bank failures and reduction of the money supply from 1929 to 1933. Likewise, major inflation occurs due to the more rapid expansion in money supply than growth in output. In addition to this, they argue that left to itself and without interference by the Government and trade unions the price wage flexibility will ensure equilibrium at natural rate of unemployment (*i.e.* full employment level) in the long run. They are therefore opposed to the active role of government in the economy and adoption of counter-cyclical discretionary monetary and fiscal policies.

A Critique of Monetarism.

The observation of data belonging to the United States of the sixties and seventies and upto late eighties indicates that inflation rate and growth rate of money supply *broadly moved together*. Until the late seventies upward trend in both the rate of inflation and rate of money growth was observed and during the seventies downward trend in both had been seen. From this it may appear that Friedman's monitary theory has proved to be correct. But, as has been rightly pointed out by

3. Milton Friedman, "The Role of Monetary Policy", *American Economic Review*, March 1968.
4. Dornbusch, Fischer & Startz, *Macroeconomics*, Tata McGraw Hll, 8th edition 2002, p. 176

Dornbusch and Fischer, the relationship between growth of money and rate of inflation has been *very rough with large gaps between their growth lines* that persist for several years and this means change in output growth and/or velocity changes have affected inflation.[5]

Thus, it shows that monetarism has not been fully correct in explaining rate of inflation in terms of growth of money supply alone. Examining the relationship between rate of inflation and rate of money growth *after adjusting for growth in output* they observe that during the sixties and seventies and to a lesser extent during the eighties hold somewhat but *during the nineties the relationship between growth in M_2 and rate of inflation seems to have broken down*" in the united states. Further, they find that "relationship between money growth and inflation is much looser if we *measure growth of money supply in terms of* $M1$. "To obtain a stable relationship between money growth and inflation we need a stable real money demand function or equivalently stable velocity."[6] It is this velocity of money circulation which has been found to be largely fluctuating as

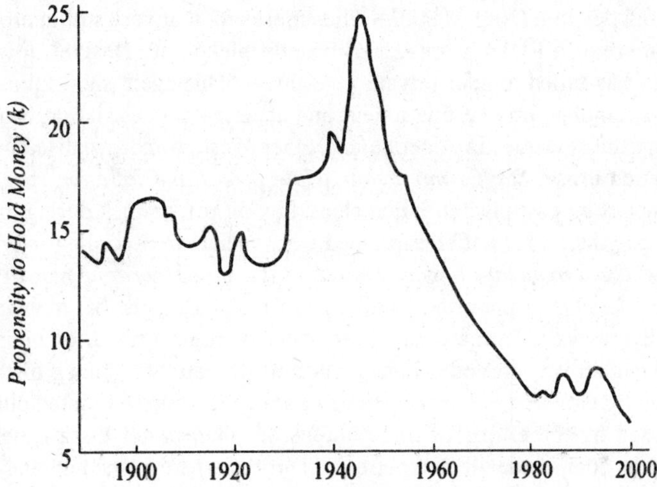

Fig. 25.4. *The Propensity to Hold Money (k) in the United States*

will be observed from Figure 25.4 where on the *Y*-axis we have measured *k* which stands for the proportion of income which people are willing to hold in cash balances to (Recall that $k=\frac{1}{v}$). It will be seen from the graph of *k* in Figure 25.4 that velocity of money has been greatly fluctuating that has disturbed the close relationship between money growth and rate of inflation. It will be seen from the graph that proportion of national income that people want to hold as money balances (*k*) has fallen to a very low level which provides explanation why relationship between money growth and inflation is not close.

It will be seen from Fig. 25.4 that the propensity to hold money has fluctuated considerably since 1890. In the early part of the century it was relatively stable. During the 1930s and 1940s it increased dramatically, reaching a peak of nearly 25 weeks of income in 1946. Since the end of World War II it has been falling. This vindicates the viewpoint of Keynesians that *k* or *v* is not stable and may move in opposite direction to the growth in money supply and this has disturbed the close relation between the two.

Recent Experience. Since the end of nineties till today (July 2003), the united States economy has been experiencing recession and in order to revive the American economy and stimulate invest-

5. Dornbusch, Fischer and Startz, *Macroeconomics*, Tata McGraw Hill, 2002, p. 422
6. Op. cit. p. 423.

ment money supply was increased by Reserve System (Central Bank of the United States) and also in the last two years, it reduced bank rate more than seven times and recently in July, it had been reduced to as low as 0.75 per cent per annum, but without much success. Thus, monetary policy had been tried again in the United States to overcome recession but has failed as was predicted by Keynesians. This again shows the failure of monetarism. That is why in the United States fiscal policy measures such reduction in taxes to the tune of 3.5 billion US dollars in 2001-02 and increase in Government expenditure have been adopted to get rid of recession.

The conclusion of ineffectiveness of monetary policy also appears to hold in India too. Since 1996 Reserve Bank of India has been following expansionary and liberal monetary and credit policy by reducing significantly the cost of credit and also making more bank credit available but it has achieved little success in stimulating private investment. Bank rate which was 9 per cent in 1995 has been reduced over successive periods to 6 per cent in April 2003 (the lowest in the last four decades). As a result, prime lending rates of bank which were around 16.5 per cent have now been reduced to 10 to 10.5 per cent (August 2003). Thus more credit at very soft interest rates have been made available but credit off take has not significantly picked up. Besides, low interest rate and liberal credit policy has failed to spur private investment. This again shows the ineffectiveness of monetary policy to stimulate private investment and accelerate industrial growth.

Besides, during the seventies in America and other Western industrialised countries a ticklish problem of stagflation arose. *Stagflation means while prices and inflation rose, output declined.* This was brought about by cost-push inflation caused by oil price shock during the seventies. Cost-push inflation and stagflation cannot be explained by monetarism according to which "*Inflation is always and everywhere a monetary phenomenon and is caused by rapid growth in the quantity of money than output*" Lastly, an important challenge to monetarism is that monetarism *direction of causation* is not always valid. According to monetarists, rapid growth of money supply causes inflation and not the other way around. Monetarists consider rate of money growth as an exogenous variable determined by Government or the Central Bank. Critics have pointed out that when wages of workers are raised by the efforts of trade unions or when prices of raw materials, especially energy inputs (such as coal, crude oil, and petroleum products) are pushed up, they are passed on to the buyers as price hikes resulting in cost-push inflation. Critics rightly point out that the increase in the money supply that is often observed to accompany inflation can also be explained as *accommodating response* of Central bank that increases money growth in order to avoid recession or prevent decline in GDP. In this case money growth is the *effect* of inflation, not its *cause*.

QUESTIONS FOR REVIEW

1. Explain the *restatement of Quantity Theory of Money* as made by Friedman. How does it differ from Fisher's version of the Quantity Theory of Money ?
2. Discuss briefly the relation between the supply of money and price level in terms of Friedman's Quantity Theory of Money. What are the main shortcomings of this theory ?
3. According to Friedman's modern quantity theory of money, changes in the quantity of money would affect output as well as prices in the short run. Discuss.
4. Referring to his restatement of the theory Friedman says, "the quantity theory of money is not the tautology of the equation, it is rather an analysis of the factors determining the quantity of money that the community wishes to hold". Discuss ?
5. "The substantial changes in prices or nominal income are *almost invariably the result* of changes in the nominal supply of money" (Friedman). Discuss.
6. 'Inflation is always and everywhere a purely monetary phenomenon" (Friedman). Discuss ?
7. According to monetarists, increase in money supply causes price level to rise, real income remaining the same. Do you agree ? Discuss why monetarists are opposed to the adoption of active discretionary monetary policy to fight recessionary conditions.
8. How, according to Friedman, nominal national income is determined ? How does the impact of increase in money supply is distributed between changes in price level and real national income in the short run.

CHAPTER 25A

Monetarism and Keynesianism Compared

The old monetarists like Irving Fisher put forward quantity theory of money which explained that changes in money supply had a direct and proportionate relationship with the price level. However, modern monetarists led by Prof. Milton Friedman of Chicago University have put forward an alternative macroeconomics to the Keynesian macroeconomic theory. Accordingly, they not only explain the changes in the general price level but also changes in output and employment. Monetarists hold that the money supply is the prime determinant of nominal GNP in the short run and changes in price level in the long run. In what follows we compare the two theories in detail and in the end will bring out how in recent years the difference between the two approaches has quite narrowed down.

It is important to note that the main difference between the monetarists and Keynesians lies in their approaches to the determination of aggregate demand. While Keynesians hold that many different factors such as consumption investment Government expenditure, taxes, exports and money determine aggregate demand, monetarists argue it is the changes in money supply that are primary factor in determining aggregate demand which affect both output and prices. Besides, there is important ideological differences between the monetarists and Keynesians. Monetarists believe that a private market economy is inherently stable and if left free will automatically adjust itself to full-employment level of output. Therefore, they argue that there is no need for Government intervention in the economy. In fact, they point.out that it is the discretionary monetary and fiscal policies pursued by the monetary authorities and Government that are responsible for much instability in the private economies. On the other hand, Keynesians believe that private economy is inherently unstable and for its stabilisation and growth, the Government should play an active role by adopting proper discretionary fiscal and monetary policies.

1. Two Different Approaches to Aggregate Demand

Keynesians focus on aggregate demand as a determinant of income and employment and view it as a sum of consumption, investment, Government expenditure and net exports (that is, exports–imports). In symbolic terms Keynesian aggregate demand is written as

$$AD = C + I + G + (X - M)$$

Keynesians equate it with value of goods and services produced to determine equilibrium level of national income or national product. Thus,

$$C + I + G + X - M = Y$$

where Y is national income or Gross National Product (GNP).

On the other hand, monetarists focus on only money supply as a primary determinant of aggregate demand. The fundamental equation of monetarists is the equation of exchange which is as under :

$$MV = PQ$$

Where M is the quantity of money

V is income velocity of money

P is general price level

Q is level of physical output of goods and services

MV in the above equation represents aggregate expenditure or aggregate demand in the monetarist approach. Thus, in monetarist approach aggregate demand is simply the sum of money multiplied by its velocity. *PQ* in the above equation of exchange represents nominal income or nominal GNP. Thus, in monetarist model,

$$MV = \text{Nominal GNP}$$

Since monetarist believe that velocity (*V*) is stable and predictable, there is direct relationship between money supply and nominal income or GNP. With *V* as stable, when money supply increases, consumers and businesses find themselves with excess money balances which they spend on goods and services. As a result of this increase in aggregate demand caused by the expansion in money supply, *PQ* or nominal GNP rises.

It is clear from above that though aggregate demand may be equal in the two approaches, the fundamental difference lies in the conception of aggregate demand. Keynesians view it as $C + I + G + (X - M)$, monetarists view it as simply *MV*. The question which has been debated which approach provides a better explanation of determination of income, employment and prices and which therefore can be made a basis for formulation of economic policy.

2. Growth of Money Supply is the Prime Determinant of Growth in Nominal GNP

A fundamental principal of monetarism is that "*Only money matters*". As seen above, like the Keynesian approach, monetarism is basically a theory of aggregate demand. They view aggregate demand as being equal to *MV*. With their belief that *V* is stable, aggregated demand is influenced primarily by changes in money supply. From the equation of exchange, $MV = PQ$, if *V* is stable the only force that can affect nominal income *PQ* is supply of money (*M*). According to monetarists, changes in money play a more and direct role in determining nominal income or GNP. They emphasise that while fiscal measures such as changes in amount and pattern of Government expenditure and taxation is important for determining how much is allocated to defence, private consumption or investment but the important macroeconomic variables such national output, employment and prices are determined mainly by money supply.

On the other hand, as seen above, Keynesians view aggregate demand as $C + I + G + X - M$ which determines the level of national income, output and employment. In the Keynesian model, the effect of increase in money supply on national income and employment is very indirect and operates through its effect on investment component of aggregate demand. According to it, expansion in money supply causes a fall in rate of interest. At a lower interest rate, more private investment is undertaken. When the economy is in the grip of depression and there is a lot of idle productive capacity, more investment through multiplier process leads to the increase in aggregate demand and therefore in national income and employment. It may however be noted that early Keynesians regarded this effect of changes in money supply through its effect on interest and investment very weak because they thought money demand curve (*i.e.* liquidity preference curve) at low rates of interest is *quite flat* and investment demand curve *quite steep.* Therefore, the early Keynesians thought that monetary policy did not play an important role in reviving the depressed economy. However, modern Keynesians have veered round to the view that changes in money supply can play a significant role in raising national output and employment. But unlike monetarists they trace the effect of changes in money supply on the real macroeconomic variables through its effect on interest and investment.[1]

3. Differences Regarding Shape of Aggregate Supply Curve

Another important difference between monetarist and Keynesian theories revolves around the shape of economy's aggregate supply curve. It is important to note that in monetarist approach it is the elasticity or steepness of the aggregate supply curve that determines how changes in nominal

1. This is explained in detail in a later section of this chapter.

GNP (*i.e., PQ*) will be divided between the change in output (*i.e.,* real income) and change in the price level. Monetarists believe that short-run aggregate supply curve is relatively steep so that when aggregate demand increases consequent to the expansion in money supply, it results in rise in price level (*P*) much more than the expansion in output (*Q*).

In other words, in case of steep aggregate supply curve, increase in nominal income leads more to rise in price than to increase in output. This is illustrated in panel (*a*) of Fig. 25A.1. It will be seen from panel (*a*) where a relatively steep short-run aggregate supply is drawn that when due to the expansion in money supply (ΔM) aggregate demand increases from AD_1 to AD_2, price level rises sharply from P_1 and P_2 whereas *real* GNP (that is, aggregate output) increases relatively much less from Q_1 and Q_2. Thus, it is clear how division of *nominal GNP* into change in price level and change in output depends on the steepness of aggregate supply curve.

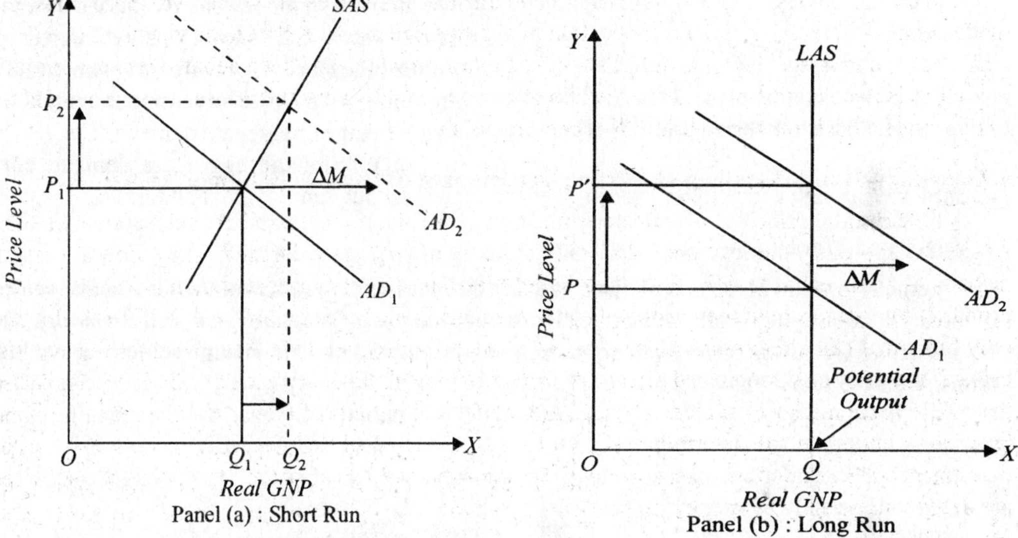

Fig. 25A.1. *Monetarism : Effect of Expansion in Money Supply in the Short Run and Long Run*

It is important to note that, according to monetarists, long-run aggregate supply is vertical because they believe that *due to wage-price flexibility,* long-run equilibrium is established at the level of potential output (that is, full-employment level of output). In panel (*b*) of Fig. 25A.1 vertical straight *LAS* represents long-run aggregate supply curve. Now, in this case of long-run vertical aggregate supply curve when aggregate demand shifts upward from AD_1 to AD_2 due to the expansion in money supply (ΔM), price level rises sharply from *P* to *P′* whereas real GNP remains constant. Thus, according to monetarists, in the long run expansion in money supply only causes price level to rise, level of output remaining unaffected.

On the other hand, Keynesians believe that the short-run aggregate supply curve is quite flat (in the extreme cause it is a horizontal straight line), the effect of increase in aggregate demand is more on raising real GNP with little rise in the price level. This is shown in Fig. 25A.2 where it will be observed that the part *SR* is a short-run aggregate supply curve which is quite flat. According to Keynesians, this flat short-run aggregate supply curve represents the situation of an economy which is having depression or recession and therefore has a lot of idle capacity and a large unemployment of labour in the economy. In such a situation when aggregate demand increases, say through increase in investment, from AD_1 to AD_2, it leads to a large expansion in real GNP with only a small rise in price level from P_1 to P_2. Similarly, when aggregate demand increases from AD_2 to AD_3, real GNP increases by a large amount with only a relatively small rise in price from P_2 to P_3.

However, Keynesians' point out that when the economy is operating at the level of full-employment or potential output, aggregate supply curve takes a vertical shape. Thus, with vertical

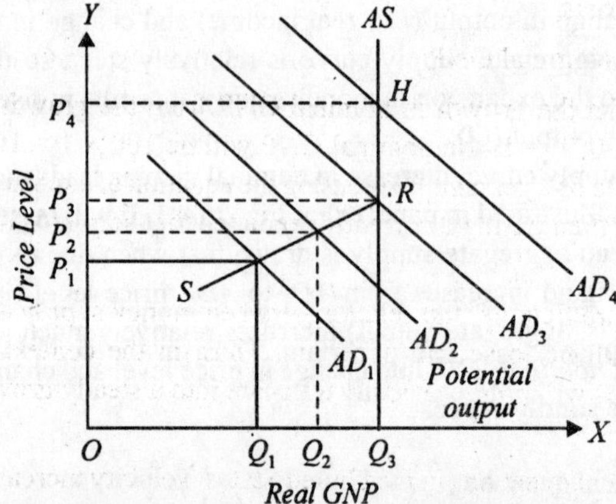

Fig. 25A.2. *Keynesianism : Impact of Increase in Aggregate Demand on Real GNP.*

aggregate supply curve at full-employment level of output, any increase in aggregate demand in this case from AD_3 to AD_4 will cause a sharp rise in price level from P_3 to P_4 with no effect at all on real GNP which remains constant at Q_3.*

It is important to note that, in Keynesian theory, the effect of changes in money supply on aggregate demand and consequently on output and prices is quite indirect and operates through its effect on interest. According to it, the increase in money supply pushes down the rate of interest. The lower market interest rate encourages more private investment. The increase in private investment which is a component of aggregate demand $(C + I + G + X - M)$ shifts the aggregate demand curve upward and through a multiplier process leads to higher output, employment and prices.

4. Velocity of Money : Stable or Unstable

A crucial issue involved in the debate between the monetarists and Keynesians is whether velocity of money is stable or unstable. *Velocity is the average number of times per year that the money stock is used in making payments for final goods and services.* Let us explain income velocity in symbolic terms. We have found above that

$$MV = PQ = \text{Nominal GNP}$$

$$V = \frac{PQ}{M}$$

Since $PQ = \text{nomimal GNP}$

$$V = \frac{\text{Nominal GNP}}{M}$$

Thus, income velocity of money (V) is the average number of money stock (M) used to buy nominal GNP which is the value of final goods and services produced in a year. It follows from the above definition of velocity that, according to monetarists, given the money stock M, if we can *predict* the income velocity of money V, we can predict the level of nominal GNP (that is, nominal income). Further, if velocity was *constant,* changing the money supply would result in proportionate changes in nominal income.

Note that modern monetarists do not assert that velocity is constant but that it is stable and predictable. Velocity depends on the methods of payment, duration of pay periods, use of more rapid means of making payments such as cheques and credit cards. Changes in these factors alter the velocity of money. Monetarists argue that the *factors which alter velocity change gradually and predictably.* Hence, changes in velocity from year to year can be easily anticipated. Moreover, monetarists contend that velocity does not change in response to changes in supply of money.

The assumption of stable and predictable V is crucial to the monetarist theory. If V is stable, it follows from the equation of exchange that there is a direct predictable relationship between money

* Some Keynesians believe that short-run aggregate supply curve during periods of depression is a horizontal straight line. In this case when aggregate demand is raised, it leads only to expansion in real GNP with no effect on price level at all.

supply and nominal GNP. According to monetarists.

$$MV = \text{Nominal GNP}$$

If V is stable and predictable we can predict the growth in nominal GNP from the growth in money supply. For instance, if in a year $M = 100$, $V = 1$, the nominal GNP will be $100 \times 1 = 100$. Suppose velocity annually increases at a stable rate of 2 per cent. Now, using the equation of exchange, if there is 5 per cent in increase inmoney supply, then it can be correctly predicted that nominal GNP will grow by 7 Per cent.

On the other hand, if V is unstable and unpredictable, the relation between money supply and nominal GNP (that is, between M and PQ) will be losse and uncertain. Thus, in the context of variable V, a steady growth in money supply (M) will not necessarily translate into a steady growth in nominal GNP.

Now, if velocity is stable or not is an empirical question. In the United States, velocity increased predictably (steadily at the rate of 3.4% per annum) in the 1960s and 1970s and during this period many economists became monetarist in their approach not only in the USA but in many other countries as well. But then during the 1980s and 1990s in the USA and other countries there was a sharp fall in velocity and it behaved quite erratically and unpredictably many economists abandoned monetarism. However still the debate between monetarists and Keynesians go on as there is a difference of opinion about the proper interpretation of the data from which change in velocity is estimated.

Keynesian View : V is Unstable. Quite opposite to the monetarists' view Keynesians believe that *velocity of money is variable and unpredictable.* Moreover, according to Keynesians, velocity of money is affected by changes in money supply and rate of interest. According to Keynesians, money is demanded not only for transaction purposes but also for *holding it as an asset,* which was called speculative demand for money by Keynes. Money demanded for transactions purposes is termed as *active* money because it changes hands and circulates through income-expenditure stream during a period. In other words, money meant for transaction purposes has a certain *positive velocity,* say, five in a year. But money demanded and held as an asset *remains idle* and does not flow through the transactions involving final goods and services and, therefore, its velocity is zero. It follows therefore that *overall velocity of money depends on how public divides the total money supply between transaction and asset balances.* The greater the extent to which money is demanded for transaction motive, the larger will be the overall veloxity of money. Conversely. the greater the proportion of money held as an asset, the lower will the velocity of money.

Keynesians also challenge the transmission mechanism of changes in moiney affecting changes in GNP. They argue that if a large proportion of expansion in money supply goes into asset demand for money, velocity of money will fall. In the extreme case when all additional money is held as an asset balances, then the increase in money supply will be accompanied by the offsetting decline in velocity so that in that case the size of nominal GNP will remain unaffected.

Keynesians viewpoint can be better understood with their notion of demand for money. According to Keynesians, total demand for money is a function of rate of interest and level of national income. In symbolic terms,

$$M_d = L\,(i, Y)$$

where i denotes interest, Y denotes income and L stands for function

Now rewriting the velocity of money by replacing money supply (M_s) with M_d we have[2]

$$V = \frac{\text{Nominal GNP}}{M_s} = \frac{\text{Nominal GNP}}{M^d}$$

Let us write Y for nominal GNP and $L\,(i, Y)$ for M_d we have

$$V = \frac{Y}{L(i, Y)}$$

Now, *if increase in money supply lowers the interest rate,* it will lead to the public holding *more money* as an asset. This is because lower interest rate means cost of holding money is less. This will induce the public to hold large amount of money as asset balances which have a zero velocity. As a result, *expansion* in money supply will cause *decline* in velocity of money and vice-versa. Thus, *in the Keynesian view velocity of money varies (1) inversely with the supply of money (2) and directly with the rate of interest.*

In view of the variable velocity of money, Keynesians hold that stable relationship between money supply (M) and nominal GNP as visualised by monetarists' transmission mechanism *does not hold good as* V varies as money supply and interest change.

5. Price-Wage Flexibility

Another important difference between Keynesians and monetarists revolves around wage-price flexibility. According to monetarists, money is the prime determinant of nominal GNP and prices and wages are fairly flexible so that wages and prices are so adjusted in the long run that the long-run equilibrium is established at potential GNP or full-employment level of output. According to them, though changes in money supply affect *both output and prices in the short run,* in the long run equilibrium is achieved through appropriate changes in wages and prices at full-employment level of output. Thus, according to monetarists, long-run aggregate supply curve is vertical at full-employment level of output. In the long run, according to monetarists, as a result of changes in money supply *only price level changes,* equilibrium level of GNP remains constant at full-employment or potential level.

On the other hand, Keynesian economists think that *wages and prices are sticky,* especially in the downward direction. Therefore, according to them, wages and prices do not adjust fully to restore the equilibrium at full-employment level of output. The difference in the two approaches is illustrated in Fig. 25A.3 where SAS_0 and LAS are short-run and long-run aggregate supply curves respectively. To begin with, economy is in equilibrium at point R where LAS and SRS_0 intersect the aggregate demand curve AD_0 at point R. As a result, equilibrium exists at the level of potential or full-employment output Q_F. Suppose due to contraction in money supply aggregate demand curve shifts downward to the new position AD_1. From Fig. 25A.3, it will be seen that new short-run equilibrium is established at GNP level Q_1 or point T where SAS_0 intersects the new aggregate demand curve AD_1. Thus, in the short run, GNP has declined to Q_1 and price level to P_1. This fall in GNP in the short run will cause the emergence of involuntary unemployment. Keynesian economists stop at this point because they contend that wages cannot fall and therefore price level cannot decline further.

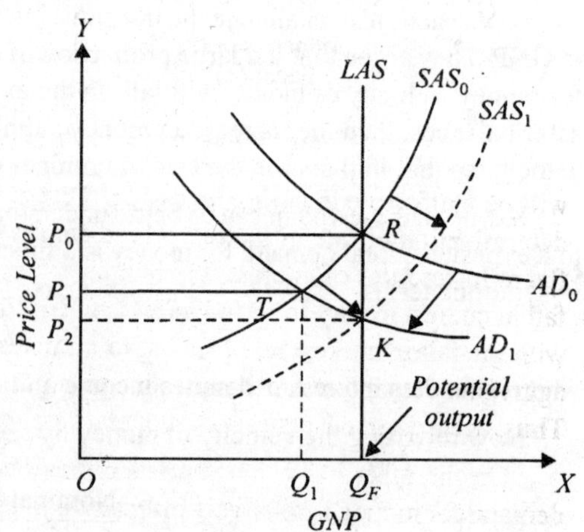

Fig. 25A.3. *Wage-Price Flexibility : Monetarists Vs. Keynesians.*

However, monetarist believe that pressure of unemployment will force the workers to bid down wages. When wages fall, cost of production will decrease causing short-run aggregate supply curve to shift below till it reaches the position SAS_1 where it intersects the aggregate demand curve AD_1 and LAS at point K. At point K, new long run equilibrium is established at potential level Q_F of GNP and price level has further fallen to P_2 level. Thus, according to monetarists, in the long run wages and prices change so that equilibrium is achieved at full-employment level. To conclude, according to monetarists in the long run only wages and prices change, while GNP remains unchanged at potential level.

6. Role of Monetary Policy

The difference in the theoretical viewpoints about the effect of money supply on output and prices leads to their divergent views about the effectiveness of monetary policy. On the basis of their monetary theory, monetarists believe that monetary policy can play a much more important role in stabilisation of the economy than do the Keynesians. While Keynesians agree that *money also matters* but they contend that expansionary monetary policy alone will be quite ineffective in lifting the economy out of depression. Keynesians argue that during recession demand for money curve (that is, liquidity preference curve) is quite flat so that expansion in money supply does not reduce very much market rate of interest. Besides, they believe that private investment is relatively insensitive to interest rates (that is, investment demand curve is steep) as it depends primarily on business expectations about possibilities of profit makeing. This suggests that a slight fall in interest rate consequent to the expansion in money supply will not lead to much increase in investment. As a result, aggreagate demand will rise only by a small amount. Hence, expansionary monetary policy

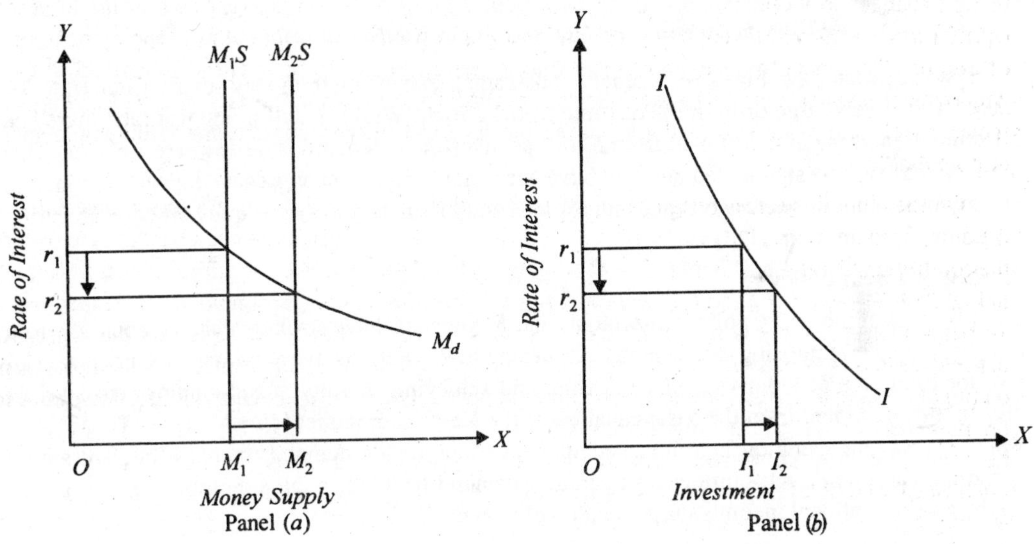

Fig. 25A.4. *Ineffectiveness of Monetary Policy : Keynesian View.*

will be ineffective in curing recession. This is illustrated in Fig. 25A.4 where Pnael (*a*) depicts the determination of rate of interest where demand for money is shown by the curve M_d which is quite flat at lower rates of interest. When money supply is increased from M_1 to M_2, there is only a small fall in interest from r_1 to r_2. In Panel (*b*) of Fig. 25A.4, since investment demand is relatively inelastic, with the fall in interest rate from r_1, to r_2, investment increases by only a small amount. As a result, aggregate demand will not rise much to produce any significant effect on output and employment. Thus, according to Keynesians, monetary policy as an instryment of stabilisation is quite ineffective.

On the other hand, monetarists believe tha demand for money curve is quaite steep (that is, demand for money is relatively insensitive to interest rates) so that small expansion in money supply causes a large reduction in interest rate. Besides, according to monetarists, investment is very sensitive to interest rates (that is, investment demand curve is relatively flat so that a fall in interest rate causes a large increase in investment demand with a significant effect on otuput and employment. Thus, monetarists argue that monetary policy is very effective and can become an important tool for stabilisation. This monetarists' view is graphically shown in Fig. 25A.5.

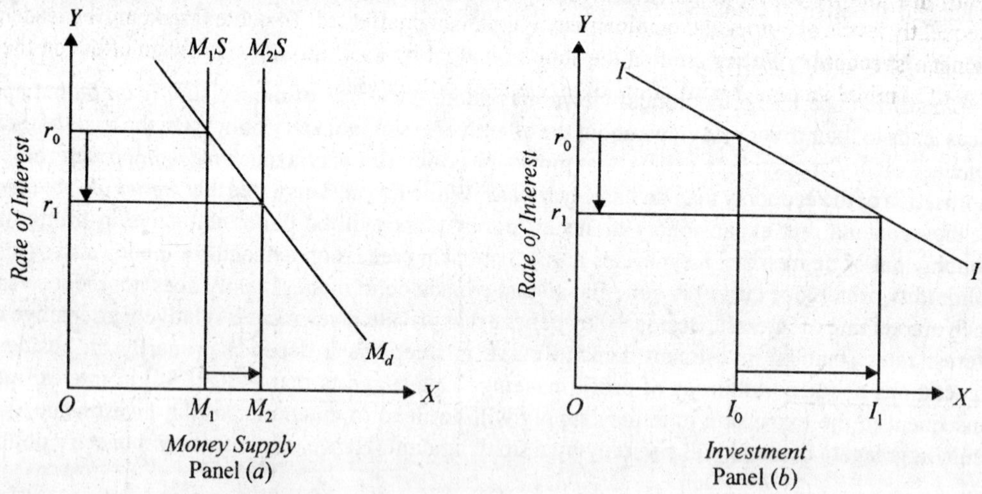

Fig. 25A.5. *Expansionary Monetary Policy is Effective : Monetarist's View.*

It will be seen from Fig. 25A.5 panel (*a*) that small expansion in money supply from M_1 to M_2 causes a relatively large drop in interest rate from r_0 to r_1. With this fall in interest rate, there is a substantial increase in investment from I_0 to I_1 as investment demand is quite interest-elastic. This large increase in investment demand will have appreciable effect on aggregate demand, output and employment. Thus, monetarists argue that expansionary monetary policy is quite effective in curing recession or depression.

7. Role of Fiscal Policy

Like that of monetary policy monetarists and Keynesians have strongly debated about the role of fiscal policy in stabilising the economy. According to Keynesians, fiscal policy is a more powerful tool for lifting the economy out of depression and achieving stability at full-employment level of output. this is evident from the basic equation of the Keynesian model $[C + I + G + (X - M) = Y]$ where investment spending is a direct component of aggregate demand. Increase in government spending therefore directly influences aggregate demand which through a multiplier effect pushes up the level of national income, output and employment.

As regards fiscal policy measure of taxation, it has also a significant effect on consumption and investment demand. for instance, lower taxes increase profits from investment by businesses. Thus, lower taxes boost both consumption and investment demand components of aggregate demand curve.

According to Keynesians, for containing inflation also, role of fiscal policy plays an important role. At times of inflationary pressures in the economy reduction in Government expenditure and increase in taxes will reduce aggregate demand and thus help in stabilising prices.

On the other hand, monetarists argue that fiscal policy has an insignificant effect on aggregate demand and therefore does not serve as an important tool of stabilisation. They believe that fiscal policy is quite weak and ineffective because of the *crowding out effect* of Government expenditure. Monetarists point out that when Government makes a deficit budget and finances it through borrowing from the market, it will be completing with private businesses for funds. As a result, demand for money will increase which, given the money supply, will push up the interest rate. higher interest rate will cause a large reduction in private investment due to investment demand being highly sensitive to the interest rates. Thus, increase in Government expenditure through its large borrowing from the market *crowds out* substantial amount of private investment which other wise would have been possible. Monetarists therefore contend that due to crowding out effect increase in government expenditure simply replaces private investment with little effect on aggregate demand and consequently levels of output and employment will remain unaffected. To quote Friedman, the leader of monetarist school "...in my opinion the state of budget by itself has not significant effect on the course of nominal income, on inflation, or an cyclical fluctuations."[1]

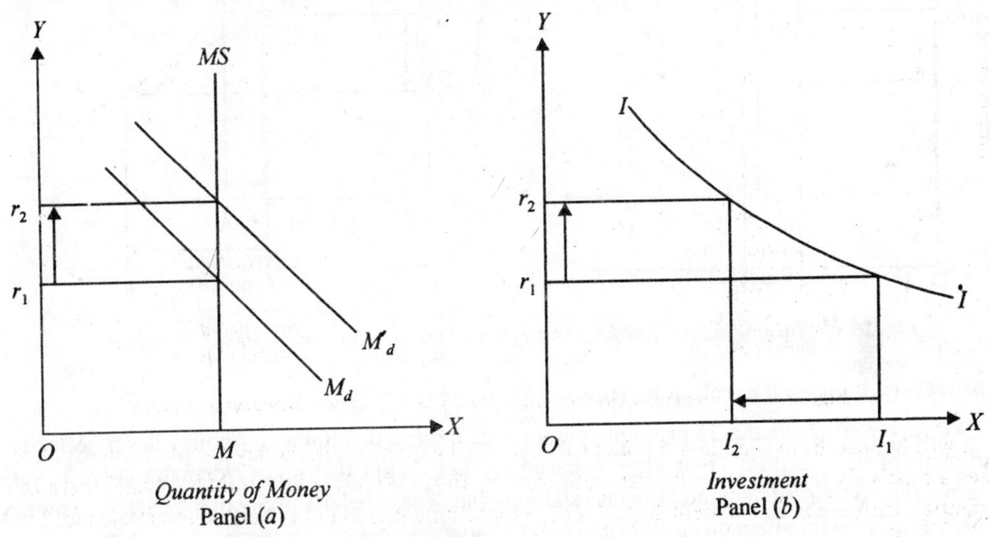

Fig. 25A.6. *Crowding Out Effect of Rise in Government Expenditure*

Crowding out effect of Government expenditure is illustrated in Fig. 25A.6. The increase in Government expenditure pushes up the demand curve for money from M_d to M'_d and, given the omeny supply *OM*, raises the interest rate form r_1 to r_2. From Panel (*b*) of Fig. 25A.6 it will be seen that rise in interest rate from r_1 to r_2 causes a reduction in private investment from I_1 to I_2. Thus, a good amount of private investment has been crowded out as a result of expansion in government expenditure financed by borrowing from the market.

Of course, if budget deficit or increase in Government expenditure is financed by issuing new money, it will have no effect on demand for money and interest rate. As a result there will be no crowding out effect. But monetarists argue that this would not be due to the fiscal policy of increase in Government expenditure but due to the *creation of additional money*.

It may however be noted that most of the Keynesians admit that some crowding out effect of fiscal policy may be there but they strongly contend that the *net effect* of expansionary fiscal policy on real national income and employment will be substantial. Keynesians argue that demand for money curve is relatively flat because demand for money is highly sensitive to changes in interest rate [see Panel (*a*) of Fig. 25A.7] so that increase in money demand brought about by increase in Government expenditure, given the money supply, does not lead much to the rise in rate of interest. Besides, according to them, investment demand is relatively steep because investment is insesitive to changes in interest rate [see Panel (*b*) of Fig. 25A.7]. Under these circumstance, increase in Government expenditure will cause only a little rise in interest rate which due to the steep investment demand curve will result in a very small decrease in private investment. Thus, Keynesians believe that crowding-out effect of expansionary fiscal policy is quite insignificant.

1. Milton Friedman and Walter Heller, *Monetary vs. Fiscal Policy* (New York : W.W. Norton and Company, (1969) p. 51

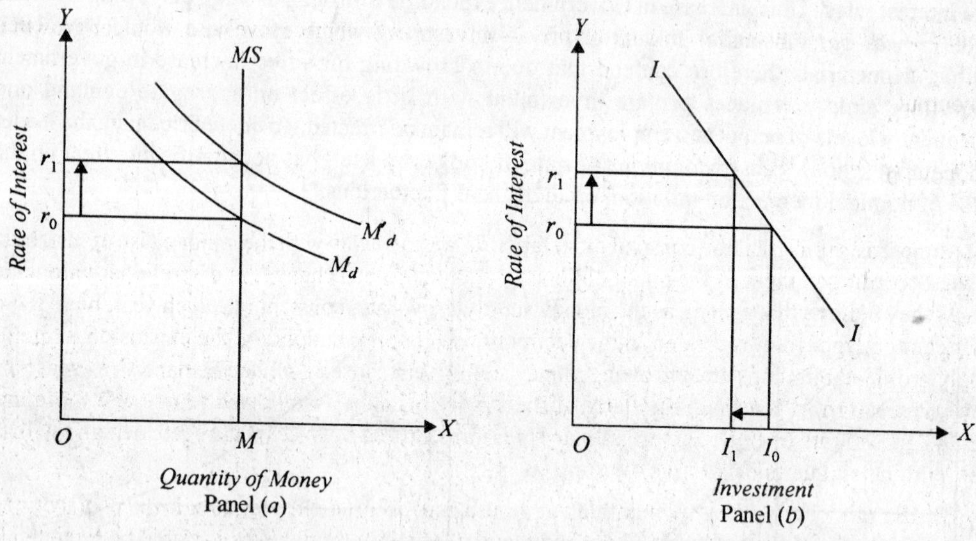

Fig. 25A.7. *Insignificant Crowding-Out Effect of Increase in Government Expenditure*

8. Monetary Policy : Discretion or Rules

We have seen above that in principle monetarists believe that monetary policy is very effective instrument of stabilisation. Their view is based on their belief that money demand curve is very steep and the investment demand curve is relatively flat. These beleifs imply that a change in money supply has a powerful effect on equilibrium level of *nominal* income. However, most monetarists do not recommend *active* use of monetary policy to stabilise the economy. This is because they believe that private economy is inherently stable and central bank of a country through its erratic and improper discretionary monetary policy tends to destabilise rather than stabilise the economy. Friedman, on the basis of historical evidence from the United States contended that discretionary changes in money supply made by the monetary atuhorities had in fact been a destabilising influence on the American economy.

Moreover, monetarists argue that *changes in money supply affect output only after long, irregular and variable lags* which make it very difficult to formulate a proper monetary policy *at right time* to achieve stability. Therefore, monetarists advocate the adoption of *Constant monetary rule* in preference to the discretionary monetary policy, According to the constant monetary rule which they recommend *money supply should be increased each year at the same annual rate as the potential growth of real* GNP. For instance, if the annual potential growth of real GNP is 3 per cent, money supply should be expanded also by 3 per cent; if potential growth in real GNP is 5 per cent money supply should also be increased every year by 5 per cent.

The rationale behind constant monetary rule can be explained with the equation of exchange ($MV = PQ$) behind constant monetary rule can be explained with the equation of exchange ($MF = PQ$). If the money supply (M) grows at the same rate as our ability to produce (Q) and if velocity (V) is constant, then the price level will remain stable. This can be shown mathematically. In growth terms equation of exchange can be written as

$$\frac{\Delta M}{M} + \frac{\Delta V}{V} = \frac{\Delta P}{P} + \frac{\Delta Q}{Q}$$

where $\frac{\Delta M}{M}$ stand for growth of money supply, $\frac{\Delta P}{P}$ for growth in price level and $\frac{\Delta Q}{Q}$ for growth in real output.

Now, if $\frac{\Delta M}{M} = \frac{\Delta Q}{Q}$ and $\frac{\Delta V}{V} = 0$ it follows from above equation that $\frac{\Delta P}{P} = 0$.

Monetarists think that the constant monetary rule will do away with the major cause of instability which, according to them, is the pursuit of erratic and capricious changes in discretionary monetary policy. they believe that as long as the money supply grows at a constant rate each year, be it 3, 4 or 5 per cent emergence of recession in the economy will be only temporary. the expansion in money supply provided by a constatnly growing money supply will cause aggregate demand to increase and prevent recession to last long. Similarly, if the supply of money is allowed to rise at a more than average growth rate of GNP, any inflationary pressures caused by excess aggregate demand will get itself eliminated due to lack of money supply.

On the other hand, Keynesians think it would not be prudent to follow a fixed or constant monetary rule. they argue that in view of the fact that velocity of money is variable both cyclically and secularly, a constant annual rate of growth of money supply would in fact cause substantial fluctuations in aggregate demand and would therefore promote instability.

QUESTIONS FOR REVIEW

1. What is monetarism ? Campare monetarism with Keynesian theory of income, prices and employment.
2. How does Keynes's approach to aggregate demand differ from that of Milton Friedman ? Explain
3. According to Friedman, growth of money supply is prime determinant of nominal national income. How does Keynesian view differ from it ?
4. According to monetarists, in the long run wages and prices change so that equilibrium is determined at full employment. How do Keynesians differ from this ?
5. How does monetarists view regarding the impact of monetary and fiscal policies on the level of economic activity differ from that of Keynes ?

Chapter 26
Inflation: Nature and Causes

Meaning

Having discussed the relationship between quantity of money and price level in the previous chapter, we are now in a position to explain the nature and causes of inflation. By inflation we mean *a general rise in prices.* To be more correct, inflation is a persistent rise in the general price level rather than a once-for-all rise in it. On the other hand, *deflation represents persistently failing prices.* These days all the economies of the world, underdeveloped as well as developed, suffer from inflation. Inflation or persistently rising prices is a major problem in world today. Rate of inflation during the seventies and eighties was very high as compared to the rates of inflation experienced earlier during peace periods. Since the late nineties, rate of inflation in several countries (including India) has declined. However, in some countries, it still remain very high.

Causes of Inflation

Let us understand how the inflation originates or what causes it. Depending upon the specific causes, four types of inflation have been distinguished: (1) *Demand-pull inflation* (2) Excessive growth in money supply (3) *Cost-push inflation,* (4) *Structural inflation.* An important cause of inflation is the excessive growth of money supply in the economy. We will explain this cause in *Monetarist Theory of Inflation.* We will explain and discuss below these four types of inflation. At the end of this discussion, we will explain how inflation in the developing countries like India can be explained.

DEMAND-PULL INFLATION

This represents a situation where the basic factor at work is the increase in aggregate demand for output either from the government or the entrepreneurs or the households. The result is that the pressure of demand is such that it cannot be met by the currently available supply of output. If, for example, in a situation of full employment, the government expenditure or private investment goes up, this is bound to generate an inflationary pressures in the economy. Keynes explained that inflation arises when there occurs an *inflationary gap* in the economy which comes to exist when aggregate demand exceeds aggregate supply at full employment level of output. Basically, inflation is caused by a situation whereby the pressure of aggregate demand for goods and services exceeds the available supply of output (both being counted at the prices ruling at the beginning of a period). In such a situation, the rise in price level is the natural consequence. Now, this imbalance between aggregate demand and supply may be the result of more than one force at work. As we know aggregate demand is the sum of consumers' spending on consumer goods and services, government spending on consumer goods and services and net investment being contemplated by the entrepreneurs. The ordinary functioning of an economy should result in distributing and spending income in such a manner that aggregate demand for output is equivalent to the cost of producing total output including profits and taxes. At times, however, the government, the entrepreneurs or the households may attempt to secure a larger part of output than would thus accrue to them. If other sectors are not prepared to acquiesce in this increase in the share of output used by any one sector, all of the sectors together will be trying to get more of the national output than production has provided. This is the basic cause for inflation to start. *When aggregate demand for all purposes—consumption, investment and government, expenditure—exceeds the supply of goods at current prices, there is a rise in prices.*

To illustrate the above point, let us assume that the government adopts expansionary fiscal policy under which it increases its expenditure on education, health, defence and finances this extra expenditure by borrowing from Reserve Bank of India which prints new notes for this purpose. This will lead to increase in aggregate demand ($C + I + G$). If aggregate supply of output does not increase or increases by a relatively less amount in the short run, this will cause demand-pull inflation in the economy, that is, general rise in price level from one period to another.

If the government is insistent on securing additional resources, it will get them in one way or another—by issuing currency or by borrowing from the central bank or from commercial banks. If other sectors, particularly the active sectors—entrepreneurs and wage earners—are unwilling to contract their investment or consumption by the amount of these additional resources used by the government, an inflationary process will be initiated. Similarly, an inflationary process will be initiated if entrepreneurs wish to use more of national output than the ordinary functioning of the economy provides (through savings out of profits and savings lent to them or invested by the public) while other sectors do not wilingly reduce their demands for resources to the extent that entrepreneurs want to use them more.

It is important to note that Keynes in his booklet *How to Pay for the War* published during the Second World War explained inflation in terms of excess demand for goods relative to the aggregate supply of their output. His notion of the *inflationary gap* which he put forward in his booklet represented excess of aggregate demand over full-employment output. This inflationary gap, according to him, leads to the rise in prices. Thus Keynes explained inflation in terms of demand-pull forces. Therefore, the theory of demand-pull inflation is associated with the name of Keynes. Since beyond full-employment level of aggregate supply, output cannot increase in response to increase in emand this results in rise in prices under the pressure of excess demand.

Demand-pull inflation can be illustrated with aggregate demand and supply curves. Consider Fig. 26.1 in which aggregate demand and aggregate supply are measured along the X-axis and general price level along the Y-axis. Curve AS represents the aggregate supply which rises upward in the beginning but when full-employment level of aggregate supply OY_F is reached, aggregate supply curve AS takes a vertical shape. This is because after the level of full employment, supply of output cannot be increased. When aggregate demand curve is AD_1, the equilibrium is at less than full-employment level where price level OP_1 is determined. Now, if the aggregate demand increases to AD_2, price level rises to OP_2 due to the emergence of excess of demand at price level OP_1. It will be noticed that here the rise in price level has also brought about increase in aggregate output supplied from OY_1 to OY_2. If the aggregate demand further increases to AD_3, the price level rises to OP_3 under the pressure of more demand. But since the aggregate supply curve is yet sloping upward, increase in aggregate demand from AD_2 to AD_3 has caused the increase in output from OY_2 to OY_F. If aggregate demand further increases, say to AD_4, only price level rises to OP_4 with output remaining constant at YF. OY_F is the full-employment level of output and aggregate supply curve is perfectly inelastic at Y_F.

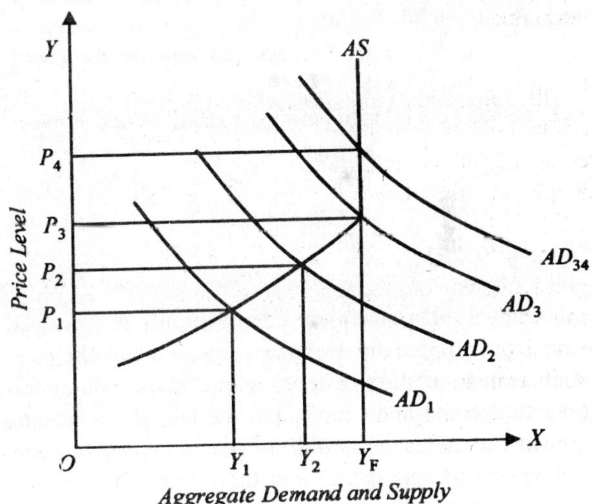

Fig. 26.1. *Demand-Pull Inflation*

Demand-Pull Inflation and Wage Price Spiral

If the total claims on output exceed the available supply of output, prices will rise. The rise in prices provides the necessary mechanism whereby the real resources being currently used by inactive sectors are reduced so that they should be used by the more active sectors. If, for example, the initiative for the inflationary pressure comes from the government demand for more resources, the only way that the government can have more resources is by the consumers and private entrepreneurs having less of them (assuming that all the resources are fully employed already). If they are not willing to reduce their claims on resources voluntarily, the prices will rise and the result will be that the value of spending by these sectors will be reduced and to that extent resources will be made available for use by the government.

But that will not be the end of the story. A rise in prices reduces the real consumption of the wage earners. They will, therefore, press for higher money wages to compensate them for the higher cost of living. Now, an increase in wages, if granted, will raise the prime cost of production and, therefore, entrepreneurs will be tempted to raise the prices. This adds fuel to the inflationary fire. A further rise in prices raises the cost of living still further and the workers ask for still higher wages. In this way, wages and prices chase each other and the process of inflationary rise in prices gathers momentum. If unchecked, this may lead to *hyper-inflation* which signifies a state of affairs where wages and prices chase each other at a very quick speed.

Monetarist Theory of Inflation

We have explained above the Keynesian theory of demand-pull inflation. It is important to note that both the original quantity theorists and the modern monetarists, prominent among whom is Milton Friedman, also explain inflation in terms of excess demand for goods and services. But there is an important difference between the monetarist view of demand-pull inflation and the Keynesian view of it. Keynes explained inflation as arising out of real sector forces. In his model of inflation excess demand comes into being as a result of *autonomous* increase in expenditure on investment or consumption, that is, the increase in aggregate expenditure or demand occurs independent of any increase in the supply of money. On the other hand, monetarists explain the emergence of excess demand and the resultant rise in prices on account of the increase in money supply in the economy. To quote Friedman, *"Inflation is always and everywhere a monetary phenomenon........* and can be produced only by a more rapid increase in the quantity of money than in output.[1]

Friedman holds that when money supply is increased in the economy, then there emerges an excess supply of real money balances with the public over the demand for money. This disturbs the equilibrium. In order to restore the equilibrium, the public will reduce the money balances by increasing expenditure on goods and services. Thus, according to Friedman and other modern quantity theorists, the excess supply of real monetary balances results in the increase in aggregate demand for goods and services. If there is no proportionate increase in output, then extra money supply leads to excess demand for goods and services. This causes inflation or rise in prices. The whole argument can be presented in the following scheme:

$$M^S > kPY \rightarrow AD\uparrow \rightarrow P\uparrow \qquad \ldots(1)$$

M **stands for quantity** of money and P for the price level. Therefore, $\frac{M}{P}$ represents real cash balances.

Y stands for national income and k for the ratio of income which people want to keep in cash balances. Hence kY represents demand for cash balances (*i.e.*, demand for money)

1. Milton Friedman, The Role of Monetary Policy, *American Economic Review,* 1968, March 1-17.

AD represents aggregate demand for or aggregate expenditure on goods and services which is composed of consumption demand (*C*) and investment demand (*I*).

In the above scheme it will be seen that when the supply of money (M^S) is increased, it creates excess supply of real cash balances. This is expressed by $M^S > kPY$. This excess supply of real money balances leads to (→) the rise (↑) in aggregate demand (*AD*). Then increase (↑) in aggregate demand (*AD*) leads to (→) the rise (↑) in prices (*P*).

Friedman's monetarist theory of inflation can be better explained with quantity equation $\left(P=\frac{MV}{Y}=\frac{M}{Y}\cdot\frac{1}{k}\right)$ written in percentage from which is written as below taking *V* or *k* as constant

$$\frac{\Delta P}{P}=\frac{\Delta M^S}{M^S}-\frac{\Delta Y}{Y} \qquad \ldots (2)$$

$\frac{\Delta P}{P}$ is the rate of inflation, $\frac{\Delta M^S}{M^S}$ is the rate of growth of money supply and $\frac{\Delta Y}{Y}$ is the rate of growth of output. Thus, according to equation (2), rate of inflation $\left(\frac{\Delta P}{P}\right)$ is determined by growth of money supply $\left(\frac{\Delta M^S}{M}\right)$ and rate of growth of output $\left(\frac{\Delta Y}{Y}\right)$, with velocity of circulation (*V*) or *k* remaining constant. Friedman and other monetarists claim that *inflation* is predominantly a monetary phenomenon which implies that changes in velocity and output are small.

It thus follows that when money supply increases, it causes disturbance in the equilibrium, that is, $M^S > kPY$. According to Friedman and other monetarists, the reaction of the people would be to spend the excess money supply on goods and services so as to bring money supply in equilibrium with the demand for money. This leads to the increase in aggregate demand or expenditure on goods and services which, *k* remaining constant, will lead to the increase in *nominal* national income (*PY*). They further argue that the real national income or aggregate output (*i.e.*, *Y* in the demand for money function stated above) remains stable at full employment level in the long run due to the flexibility of wages. Therefore, according to Friedman and his followers (modern monetarists), in the long run, the increase in nominal national income (*PY*) brought about by the expansion in money supply and resultant increase in aggregate demand will cause a proportional increase in the price level. However, in the short run, like Keynesians, they believe that the economy may be working at less than full employment, that is, in the short run there may prevail excess capacity and unemployment of labour so that expansion in money supply and consequent increase in nominal income partly induces expansion in real income (*Y*) and partly results in rise in the price level as shown in Fig. 26.2. To what extent price level increases depends upon the elasticity of supply

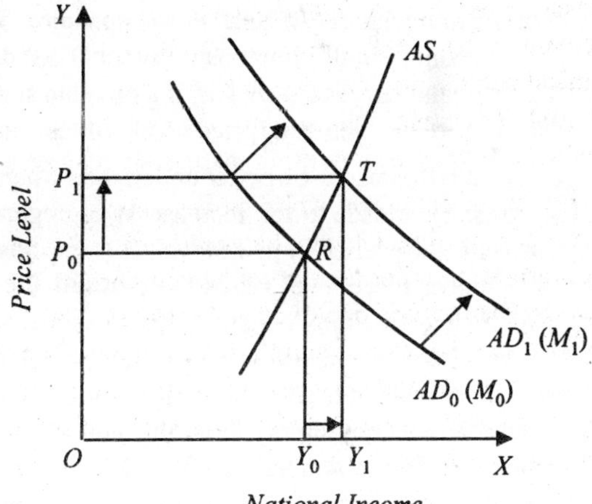

Fig. 26.2. *The Effect of expansion in money supply in the short run is split up into price rise and increase in Real National Income: Friedman's Monetarist Approach.*

or aggregate output. It will be seen from Fig. 26.2 that effect of increase in money supply from M_0 to M_1 and resultant increase in aggregate demand curve for goods and services from AD_0 to AD_1 is split up into the rise in price level (from P_0 to P_1) and the increase in real income or aggregate output (from Y_0 to Y_1).

It should be noted that Friedman and other modern quantity theorists believe that in the short run full-employment of labour and other resources, may not prevail due to recessionary conditions and, therefore, they admit the possibilities of increase in output. But they emphasise that when the growth in money supply is greater than the growth in output, the result is excess demand for goods and services which causes rise in prices or demand-pull inflation.

It follows from above that both Friedman and Keynesians explain inflation in terms of excess demand for goods and services. Whereas Keynesians explain the emergence of excess demand due to the increase in *autonomous expenditure,* independent of any increase in money supply. Friedman explains that inflation is caused by *proportionately greater increase in money supply than the increase in aggregate output.* In both views inflation is of demand-pull variety.

Money and Sustained Inflation

Many economists believe in the monetarist view of inflation. Increase in money shifts the aggregate demand curve to the right and if the economy is operating at full capacity (i.e. along the vertical part of the aggregate supply curve), the upward shift in aggregate demand curve will cause price level to rise. A big drawback of this approach is that it assumes that supply of output does not increase sufficiently to counter this effect of expansion in money supply on aggregate demand. In this context there is a need to distinguish between a *one-time increase* in the price level and *sustained inflation* which occurs when the general price level continues to rise over a long period of time. It is generally believed by most of the economists that whatever be the initial cause of inflation (demand-pull, cost-push or inflationary expectations), for the price level to continue rising, period after period, it must be *accommodated* by expansion in money supply. *Sustained inflation is therefore considered as a purely monetary phenomenon.* It is not possible for the price level to continue rising if the money supply remains constant. The increase in money supply continues shifting the aggregate demand curve to the right; if aggregate supply does not increase sufficiently to match the increase in aggregate demand, price level will continue rising.

Sustained inflation can be better understood when Government increases its expenditure without raising taxes. This leads to the increase in aggregate demand which, *aggregate supply remaining constant*, will cause a rise in price level. It is important to know what happens when the price level rises. The higher price level raises the demand for money to rise for transaction purposes. With supply of money remaining constant, the greater demand for money causes interest rate to rise. The rise in interest rate *crowds out* private investment. If the Central Bank of a country wants to prevent the fall in the private investment, it will expand the money supply to keep the interest constant. But this expansion in money supply through its effect on aggregate demand will cause the price level to rise further if increase in more supply of output is not possible. This further rise in price level will again cause greater demand for money leading to higher interest rate. And the Central Bank, if it is committed to keep the interest rate constant so that private investment does not decline, it will further expand the money supply which will cause further inflation. This process could lead to *hyper inflation* which represents *a rapid* and *continuous rise in price level*, period after period. The historical experience shows this hyperinflation in some countries when the Central Bank or Government of these countries kept pumping in more and more money either to finance its persistent budget deficit of the government year after year or to prevent the interest rate to rise. However, as mentioned above, hyperinflation disrupts the payment system and people's loss of credibility of the currency. This leads to a deep crisis in the economy. If hyper inflation is to be avoided, then the process of rapid expansion in money supply must be halted.

Inflationary Expectations

Inflationary expectations are an important cause of inflation. The expectations of future prices play a significant role in decision-making by firms regarding price and output. If a firm expects that its rival firms will raise their prices, it may also raise its own price in anticipation. Suppose inflation has been occurring at a rate of 8 per cent per annum in the past, a firm will expect this inflation rate to continue in future too and therefore it will raise its price by 8 per cent. If every firm expects that other firm will raise their prices by 8 per cent, every one will raise its prices by 8 per cent. As a result, inflation rate of about 8 per cent will occur. This is how inflationary expectations cause inflation. Elaborating on this, Case and Fair write, "*Expectations can lead to an inertia that makes it difficult to stop an inflationary spiral. If prices have been rising and if people's expectations are adaptive, that is, if they form their expectations on the basis of past pricing behaviour – that firms may continue raising prices even if demand is slowing.*"[1a] Therefore, to check inflation, steps should be taken to break the inflationary expectations.

COST-PUSH INFLATION

We can visualise situations where even though there is no increase in aggregate demand, prices may still rise. This may happen if there is increase in costs independent of any increase in aggregate demand. Three such autonomous increases in costs which generate cost-push inflation have been suggested. They are:

1. Wage-push inflation
2. Profit-push inflation
3. Increase in prices raw materials, especially energy inputs such as rise in crude oil prices.

It may be noted that rise in prices of raw materials, especially of energy inputs (petrolium products) which have a cost push effect are also called *supply shocks*. We discuss these below:

Wage-Push Inflation. It has been suggested that the growth of powerful trade union is responsible for the spread of inflation, especially in the industrialized countries. When trade unions push for higher wages which are not justifiable either on grounds of a prior rise in productivity or of cost of living they produce a cost-push effect. The employers in a situation of high demand and employment are more agreeable to concede to these wage claims because they hope to pass on these rises in costs to the consumers in the form of hike in prices. If this happens we have cost-push inflation. It may be noted that as a result of cost-push effect of higher wages, aggregate supply curve of output shifts to the left and, given the aggregate demand curve, this results in higher price of output.

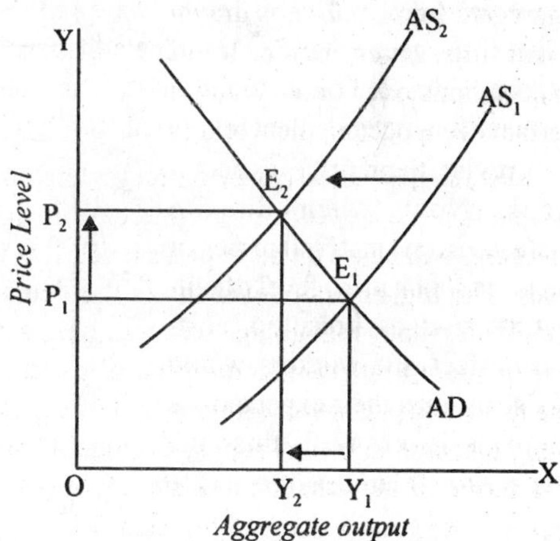

Fig. 26.3. *Cost-Push Inflation*

Profit-Push Inflation. Besides the increase in wages of labour without any increase in its productivity, there is another factor responsible for cost-push inflation. This is the *increase in the profit margin by* the firms working under monopolistic or oligopolistic conditions and as a result charging higher prices from the consumers. In the former case when the cause of cost-push inflation is the rise in wages it is called *wage-push inflation* and in the latter case when the cause of cost-push

1a. Karl E. Case, and Race C. Fair, *Principles of Economics*, Pearson Education, 6th Edition, 2002, inflation is the rise in profit margins, it is called *profit-push inflation*. The increase in profit margins also produces a cost-push effect and results in shift in the aggregate supply curve to the left.

Rise in Raw material Prices or Oil Price Shock. In addition to the rise in wage rate of labour and increase in profit margins, in the seventies the other supply-shocks causing increase in marginal cost of production became more prominent in bringing about cost-push inflation. During the seventies, rise in prices of raw materials, especially energy inputs (hike in crude oil price made by OPEC resulting in rise in prices of petroleum products). The sharp rise in world oil prices during 1973-75 and again in 1979-80 produced significant supply shocks resulting in cost-push inflation.

The cost-push inflation can also be illustrated with the aggregate demand and supply curves. Consider Fig. 26.3, where aggregate supply and demand are measured along the X-axis and price level along the Y-axis. AD is the aggregate demand curve and AS_1 and AS_2 curves are aggregate supply curves. Now, when wages increase, and as a result cost of production rises, the aggregate supply curve would shift upward to the left. As will be seen in Fig. 26.3 when there is an upward shift in the aggregate supply curve from AS_1 to AS_2 due to the rise in wages, price level rises from OP_1 to OP_2. Thus, in this case when aggregate demand curve remains the same, price level rises due to rise wages which has caused leftward shift in the supply curve. *An important feature of cost-push inflation is that this causes not only rise in price level but brings about a fall in aggregate output.* Thus in Fig. 26.3 when price level rises from OP_1 to OP_2, aggregate output falls from OY_1 to OY_2. This situation of high inflation and lower output is generally diescribed **as stagflation.**

Indirect Effect of Increase in oil prices or other raw material prices. In addition to the direct effect of oil price shocks and increase in other raw material prices, there are indirect effects of such supply shocks which cause further rise in rate of inflation. It may be noted that an aggregate supply curve is drawn assuming given price level expectations over time. When a certain event occurs, the workers will revise their price expectations. Now, when due to increase in raw material prices or oil price shock price level of output has risen as a result of cost-push effect, the workers would revise upward their expectations of price level. With this, the *expected real wage* rate $\left(\frac{W}{P}\right)$ will decline and therefore less labour will be supplied at a given money wage rate. Besides, this fall in expected real wage rate will decline and as a result the workers will demand higher wages. Thus, with the increase in expected price level, aggregate supply curve will further shift to the left as a result of this *indirect effect* through the upward revision of expected price level. This indirect effect is illustrated in 26.4. Initially, aggregate demand curve AD and aggregate supply curve AS_1 (with P_1 as the expected price level) determine price level P_1 and output Y_1. Now, due to oil price shock, aggregate supply curve shifts to the left to $AS_2(P_1)$ and price level rises to P_2. Since price

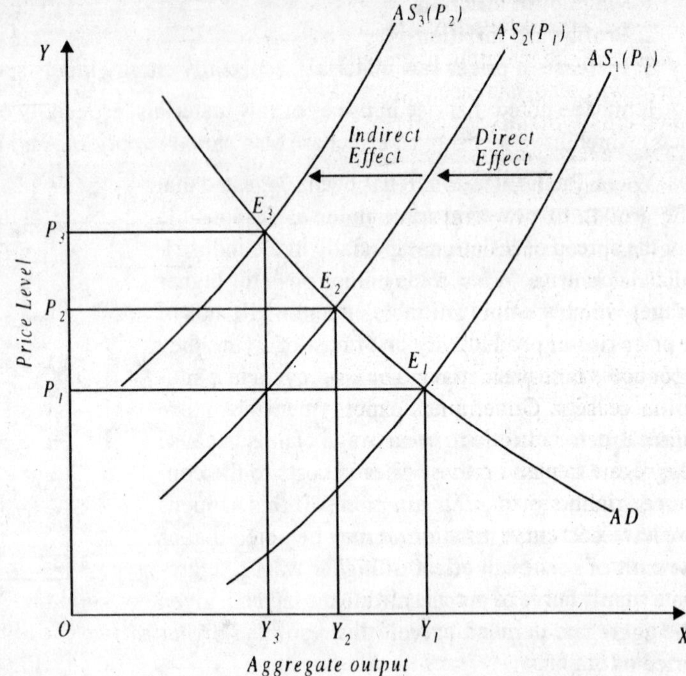

Fig. 26.4. *Cost-Push Inflation: Accounting for both Direct and Indirect Effects of Oil Price Shock*

level has risen, workers will adjust their expected price level upward, say to P_2 and demand higher wages. The hike in wages will cause a further shift in the aggregate supply curve to $AS_3(P_2)$ and further rise in price level to P_3.

Interaction between Demand-Pull and Cost-Push Inflation.

Many economists think inflation in the economy is generally caused by the interaction of the demand pull and cost-push factors. The inflation may be started in the first instance either by cost-push factors or by demand pull factors both work and interact to cause sustained inflation over time. Thus, according to Machlup, "there cannot be a thing as cost push inflation because without an increase in purchasing power and demand, cost increases will lead to unemployment and depression, not to inflation"[1] Likewise, Cairncross writes, "*there is no need to pretend that demand and cost inflation do not interact or that excess demand does not aggrevate wage inflation, of course it does*."[2]

We will explain this interaction, first with inflationary process starts with cost push factor and then secondly when inflation begin with shift in aggregate demand. In both cases rate of inflation over time is the result of interaction of demand-pull and cost-push factors.

1. Let us consider the Figure 26.5 where to begin with aggregate demand curve *AD* and aggregate supply curve *AS* intersect at point E_0 and determine price level P_0 and output level Y_0. Further suppose that Y_0 is the full capacity (*i.e.*, full-employment) level of output and therefore long-run aggregate supply curve *LAS* is vertical at Y_0 level of output. Suppose there is increase in oil prices which causes shifts in aggregate supply curve to the left from *AS* to AS_1. As a result, price level rises to P_1 but output falls from Y_0 to Y_1. With decline in output unemployment will also increase. This is a cost-push inflation which has caused a recessionary conditions in the economy. The Government and Central Bank are likely to adopt expansionary monetary and fiscal policies in order to avoid recession. Consequent to the adoption of expansionary policies, (for example, increase in money supply or increase in Government expenditure or reduction in taxes), aggregate demand curve will shift to the right, say to AD_1, which intersects AS_1 curve and *LAS* curve at point E_2. Though as a result of this accommodatary policy while output level has increased to the original full capacity level Y_0, price level has further risen to P_2 level. This later rise in price level from P_1 to P_2 is the result of demand-pull Inflation. It is thus clear that both cost-push and demand-pull inflation interact to cause inflation in the economy.

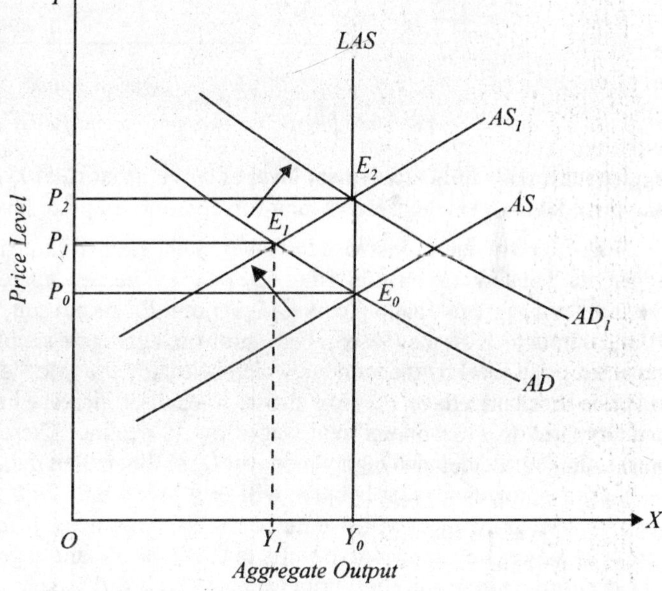

Fig. 26.5. *Interaction of Cost-Push and Demand-Pull Inflation*

2. Let us now explain inflationary process which starts with demand-pull inflation in the first instance. Consider Figure 26.6. where to begin with aggregate demand curve AD_0 and aggregate

1. Fritz Machlup, "Another View of Cost-Push and Demand-Pull Inflation" in *Review of Economics and Statistics* Vol. 42. 1960.
2. Alec Cairncross *Inflation Growth and International Trade* George Allen and Unwin, 1975.

supply curve AS_0 intersect at E_0 and determine level of price P_0 and aggregate output Y_0. Assume long-run aggregate supply curve *LAS* also passes through point E_0 so that equilibrium level of output

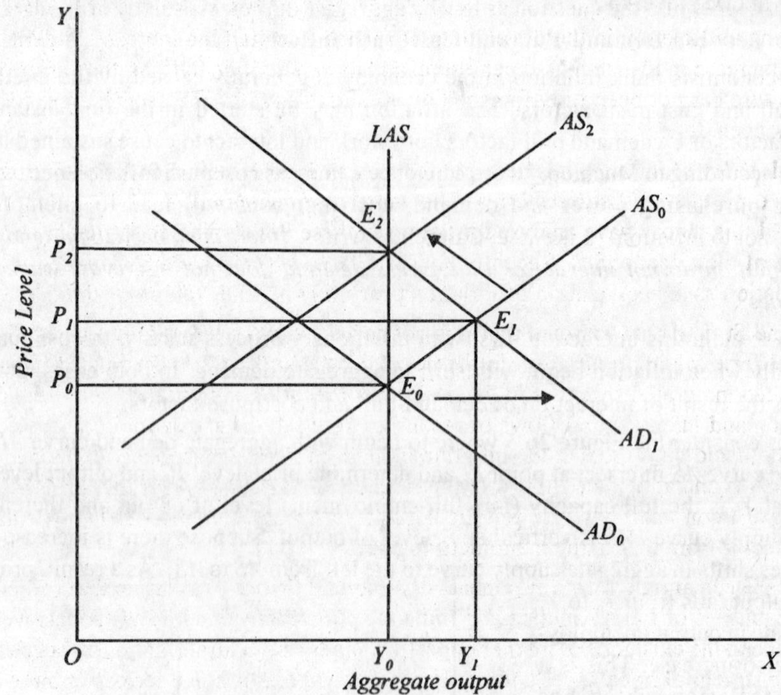

Fig. 26.6. *Interaction betwen Demand-Pull and Cost-Push Inflation*

Y_0 also represents full-employment level of output (that is, at Y_0 only natural unemployment exists) and price level P_0 also represents long-run equilibrium price level.

Now suppose due to increase in Government expenditure financed by creation of new money aggregate demand curve shifts from AD_0 to AD_1.The new aggregate demand curve AD_1 intersects the short-run aggregate supply curve AS_0 at point E_1. As a result, in the short run price level rises to P_1 and output to Y_1. It may be recalled, short-run aggregate supply curve is drawn assuming a given expected price level by the workers which is usually the price level prevailing in the last few years which is here taken to be P_0. Now that as a result of increase in aggregate demand price level has actually risen to P_1, workers' real wages would decline. Therefore, in order to restore their real wages, they would demand higher money wages. When their demand for higher wages are conceded to, short-run aggregate supply curve will shift to the left. With this leftward shift in the aggregate supply curve, price level will rise further. In this way *wage-price spiral* will go on operating until short-run aggregate supply curve shifts to the level AS_2 and together with aggregate demand curve AD_1 determine a long-run equilibrium at point E_2. It will be seen that both demand-pull inflation and cost-push inflation have operated together to raise price level from P_0 to P_2.

To conclude, demand-pull inflation and cost-push inflation are intertwined and operate together to determine rate of inflation over time. *It is difficult to say in actual practice what part of inflation is due to demand-pull factors and what due to cost-push factors*, though, as seen above, theoretically speaking, we can distinguish between demand-pull and cost-push inflation.

STRUCTURALIST INFLATION

But there is another important theory of inflation known as *structuralist inflation* which explains inflation in the developing-countries in a slightly different way. The structuralists argue that increase in investment expenditure and the expansion of money supply to finance it are the only proximate and not the ultimate factors responsible for inflation in the developing countries. According to them, one should go deeper into the question as to why aggregate output, especially of foodgrains, has not been increasing sufficiently in the developing countries to match the increase in demand brought about by the increase in investment expenditure, and money supply. Further, they argue why investment expenditure has not been fully financed by voluntary savings and as a result excessive deficit financing has been done.[3]

Structural theory of inflation has been put forward as an explanation of inflation in the developing countries especially of Latin America. The well-known economists, Myrdal and Streeten who have proposed this theory have analysed inflation in these developing countries in terms of structural features of their economies. Recently Kirkpatrick and Nixon have generalised this structural theory of inflation as an explanation of inflation prevailing in all developing countries.[4]

Myrdal and Streeten have argued that it is not correct to apply the highly aggregative demand-supply model for explaining inflation in the developing countries.[5] According to them, there is a lack of balanced integrated structure in them where substitution possibilities between consumption and production and inter-sectoral flows of resources between different sectors of the economy are not quite smooth and quick so that the inflation in them cannot be reasonably explained in terms of aggregate demand and aggregate supply. In this connection it is noteworthy that Prof. V.N. Pandit of Delhi School of Economics has also felt the need for distinguishing price behaviour in the Indian agricultural sector from that in the manufacturing sector.[6]

Thus, it has been argued by the exponents of structural theory of inflation that economies of the developing countries of Latin America and India are structurally underdeveloped as well as highly fragmented due to the existence of market imperfections and structural rigidies of various types. The result of these structural imbalances and rigidies is that whereas in some sectors of these developing countries, we find shortages of supply relative to demand, in others under-utilisation of resources and excess capacity exist due to lack of demand. According to structuralists, these structural features of the developing countries make the aggregate demand-supply model of inflation inapplicable to them. They therefore argue for analysing disaggregative and sectoral demand-supply imbalances to explain inflation in the developing countries. They mention various sectoral constraints or bottlenecks which generate the sectoral imbalances and lead to rise in prices. Therefore, to explain the origin and propagation of inflation in the developing countries, the forces which generate these bottlenecks or imbalances of various types in the process of economic development need to be analysed. A study of these bottlenecks is therefore essential for explaining inflation in the developing countries. These bottlenecks are of three types : (1) Agricultural bottlenecks which make supply of agricultural products inelastic, (2) resources constraint or Government budget constraint, and (3) foreign exchange bottleneck. Let us explain briefly how these structural bottlenecks cause inflation in the developing countries.

Agricultural Bottlenecks. The first and foremost bottlenecks faced by the developing countries relate to agriculture and they prevent supply of food grains to increase adequately. Of special mention of the structural factors are disparities in land ownership, defective land tanure system which act as disincentives for raising agricultural production in response to increasing demand for them arising from increase in people's incomes, growth in population and urbanisation. Besides, use of backward agricultural technology also hampers agricultural growth. Thus, in order to control inflation, these

3. G.Myrdal, *Asian Drama, An Enquiry into the Poverty of Nations*, 1968, Penguin Books.
4. C. Kirkpatrick and F., Nixon, Inflation and Stabilisation policy in LDC's in N. Gemmel (ed.), *Surveys in Development Economics*, 1987 Basil, Blackwell.
5. P. Streeten, *The Frontiers of Development Studies*, 1972, London, MacMillan.
6. See V.N. Pandit, "An Analysis of Inflation in India, 1950-75, *Indian Economic Review*, Vol. 22, 1978

bottlenecks have to be removed so that agricultural output grows rapidly to meet the increasing demand for it in the process of economic development.

Resources Gap or Government's Budget Constraint. Another important bottleneck mentioned by structuralists relate to the lack of resources for financing economic development. In the developing countries planned efforts are being made by the Government to industrialise their economies. This requires large resources to finance public sector investment in various industries. For example, in India, huge amount of resources were used for investment in basic heavy industries started in the public sector. But socio-economic and political structure of these coun tries is such that it is not possible for the Government to raise enough resources through taxation, borrowing from the public, surplus generation in the public sector enterprises for investment in the projects of economic development. Revenue raising from taxation has been relatively very small due to low tax base, large scale tax evasion, inefficient and corrupt tax administration. Consequently, the government has been forced to resort to excessive deficit financing (that is, creation of new currency) which has caused excessive growth in money supply relative to increase in output year after year and has therefore resulted in inflation in the developing countries. Though rapid growth of money supply is the proximate cause of inflation, it is not the proper and adequate explanation of inflation in these economies. For proper explanation of inflation one should go deeper and enquire into the operation of structural forces which has caused excessive growth in money supply in these developing economies. Besides, resources gap in the private sector due to inadequate voluntary savings and under-development of the capital market have led to their larger borrowings from the banking system which has created excessive bank credit for it. This has greatly countributed to the growth of money supply in the developing countries and has caused rise in prices. Thus, Kirkpatrick and Nixon write, "*the increase in the supply of money was a permissive factor which allowed the inflationary spiral to manifest itself and become cumulative—it was a system of the structural rigidities which give rise to the inflationary pressures rather than the cause of inflation itself.*"[7]

Foreign Exchange Bottleneck. The other important bottleneck which the developing countries have to encounter is the shortage of foreign exchange for financing needed imports for development. In the developing countries ambitious programme of industrialisation is being undertaken. Industrialisation requires heavy imports of capital goods, essential raw materials and in some cases, as in India, even foodgrains have been imported. Besides, imports of oil on a large scale are being made. On account of all these imports, import expenditure of the developing countries has been rapidly increasing. On the other hand, due to lack of export surplus, restrictions imposed by the developing countries, relatively low competitiveness of exports, the growth of exports of the developed countries has been sluggish. As a result of sluggish exports and mounting imports, the developing countries have been facing balance of payment difficulties and shortage of foreign exchange which at times has assumed crisis proportions. This has affected the price level in two ways. First, due to foreign exchange shortage domestic availability of goods in short-supply could not be increased which led to the rise in their prices. Secondly, in Latin American countries as well as in India and Pakistan, to solve the problem of foreign exchange shortage through encouraging exports and reducing imports devaluation in the national currencies had to be made. But this devaluation caused rise in prices of imported goods and materials which further raised the prices of other goods as well due to cascading effect. This brought about cost-push inflation in their economies.

Physical Infrastructural Bottlenecks. Further, the structuralists point out various *bottlenecks* such as lack of infrastructural facilities *i.e.*, lack of power, transport and fuel which stands in the way of adequate growth in output. At present in India, there is acute shortage of these infrastructural inputs which are hampering growth of output. Sluggish growth of output on the one hand, and excessive growth of money supply on the other have caused what is now called *stagflation*, that is inflation which exists along with stagnation or slow economic growth.

7. Kirkpatrick and Nixon, Op. Cit.

According to the structuralist school of thought, the *above bottlenecks and constraints are rooted in the social, political and economic structure of these countries*. Therefore, in its view a broad-based strategy of development which aims to bring about social, institutional and structural changes in these economies is needed to bring about economic growth without inflation. Further, many structuralists argue for giving higher priority to agriculture in the strategy of development if price stability is to be ensured. Thus, we see that structuralist view is greatly relevant for explaining inflation in the developing countries and for the adoption of measures to control it. Let us further elaborate the causes of inflation in the developing countries.

INFLATION IN DEVELOPING COUNTRIES: DEMAND-PULL OR COST-PUSH INFLATION

Now, the question arises as to which theory of inflation can explain inflation in developing countries. Of course, the rise in prices has come about as a result of excess of aggregate demand over aggregate supply. In other words, inflation in the developing countries is mainly of demand-pull variety. However, how this excess demand for goods and services has been caused is issue at dispute. In our view both the Keynesian and Friedman's views are relevant to explain the emergence of excess demand for goods. To promote rapid economic growth a hunge investment expenditure has been made in India in successive development plans. If this increase in investment expenditure had been financed by raising resources through taxation, Government borrowings from the public, profits of public undertakings, then the increase in investment expenditure would have been matched by increase in savings with the result that excess demand for goods had not arisen. As a matter of fact, a good deal of increase in investment expenditure has been financed by deficit financing *i.e.*, through creating of new money by the central bank. Besides, the increase in private investment expenditure has also been financed to a good extent by expansion of credit or demand deposits by the commercial banks. This increase in investment expenditure for promoting economic growth has been made possible by the expansion in money supply, which as emphasized by Friedman and other monetarists, causes prices to rise through creating excess demand for goods and services. Thus, it is hard to distinguish whether it is increase in investment expenditure as such or expansion in money supply to finance it which has caused demand-pull inflation in the face of slow growth of output of goods, especially foodgrains and other essential consumer goods. Indeed, both have played a part in causing inflationary situation in India.

What has caused the inflationary pressures in India's developing economy? To think that only demand-pull factors or excess demand generated by huge budget deficits and huge growth in money supply are responsible for the problem of inflation facing the Indian economy would not be fully correct. As a matter of fact, both types of factors, namely, demand-pull and cost push factors have operated to cause inflation in India, which crossed the two-digit figure in some years. As a result of rapid growth in Government expenditure without corresponding increase in mobilisation of resources, the Government has resorted to heavy deficit financing (*i.e.*, the creation of new money). This has further created the conditions of excess demand in the economy which have led to the rise in general price level. Besides, the increase in petroleum prices, many times during the last few years, the hike in administered prices of steel, cement, coal, fertilizers, increase in indirect taxes on several commodities, increase in railway fares and freights have all led to the *cost-push inflation* or what is also called *supply-side inflation*.

Now, when due to the demand pull inflation, the general price-level rises, the demand for rise in wages and dearness allowance are made by the working classes and they have to be conceded to in view of the rising cost of living. The rise in wages and dearness allowance of the workers raises the cost of production. The increases in cost of production due higher wages and dearness allowance also cause the aggregate supply curve shift to the left and brings about cost-push or supply side inflation. Thus there has been persistent rise in prices under the combined impact of demand-pull factors caused by the large budget deficits and cost-push factors due to the hike in administrated prices of petroleum, steel, cement, coal etc., and increase in indirect taxes on commodities such as sugar, cloth, cooking gas, soaps, cold-drink, etc.

Let us illustrate graphically how the operation of the various demand-pull and cost-push factors resulting in persistent rise in general price level. Consider Fig. 26.7, where AD_0 represents aggregate demand curve and AS_0 the aggregate supply curve and the two intersect at point E_0 and the price level P_0 is determined. With huge budget deficits and large expansion in money supply generating conditions of excess demand cause upward shift in the aggregate demand curve to AD_1. The general price level rises to P_1 corresponding to the new equilibrium point E_1. Now, the increase in cost of production brought about by either independently of the rise in price caused by increase in aggregate demand or by rise in wages and dearness allowances induced by the demand-pull inflation in the first instance, aggregate supply curve shifts to the left to AS_1. With this the price level further rises to P_2 under the influence of cost push factors. The price equilibrium moves from E_0 to E_1 and then to E_2. This process of joint operation of demand-pull and cost-push factors has been going on year after year and is responsible for the persistent rise in prices in the Indian economy. Therefore, to check and moderate this inflationary process not only the budget deficits have to be drastically cut but also steps should be taken to prevent the increase in cost of production by avoiding the frequent hike in administered prices and indirect taxes.

It is evident from above that huge investment expenditure by the Government and the private sector under five year development plans are being made to increase the *rate of capital formation and thus to obtain rapid economic growth. This huge investment expenditure leads to a sharp increase in aggregate demand for consumers' goods, especially the agricultural products. When in India's emerging economy there is shortfall in output of consumer goods and their supply cannot be increased sufficiently to match the increase in demand for them this leads to inflationary rise in prices*. In recent years, Government in India is heavily spending on education and health, and on anti-poverty schemes such as NREGA (National Rural Employment Gurantee Act) which have led to a large increase in incomes of the rural people and generated demand for goods and services.

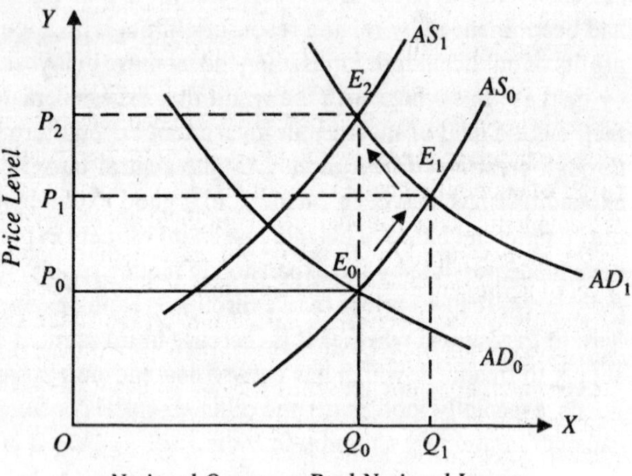

Fig. 26.7. *Rise in General Price Level as a Result of Joint Impact of Demand-Pull and Cost-Push Factors*

It is worth noticing that it is the food prices which first start rising rapidly in a developing economy. Rise in food prices is then followed by the rise in the prices of other consumers' goods. This is so because a greater part of the increase in demand generated by the investment expenditure is spent on the foodgrains such as wheat and rice and further the supply of foodgrains cannot be sufficiently increased in the short run due to the failure of monsoons, lack of irrigation facilities, HYV seeds, fertilizers and inefficient techniques of cultivation. Besides, in India's five year plans adequate investment in agriculture has not been made and as a result, growth rate in agriculture has been law. On the other hand, *income elasticity of demand for food is very high because the vast majority of the people are undernourished. Thus, as a result of huge investment expenditure by the government and private sector there is a sharp rise in demand for foodgrains, leading to increases in food prices.*

In developing countries like India, which are predominantly agricultural, the prices of agricultural commodities, especially of foodgrains, hold the key position in the price structure of the country. Any rise in agricultural prices leads to a distortion in the whole price structure. A steep rise in food prices increases the cost of living of the people. Consumers are hit hard as their incomes do not increase so easily to offset the increase in prices. Workers whose cost of living rises press for higher wages. When wage increases are conceded to, the cost of production of manufactured articles rises and this, in turn, increases their prices, and so on. Moreover, some agricultural products are raw materials for industries and increase in their prices will directly increase the cost of production of industrial goods. Hoarding of and speculation in both agricultural and industrial products add fuel to the inflationary fire. Thus *once the prices of agricultural goods rise they are likely to cause inflationary spiral in the economy.*

A factor which deserves special mention in this connection is the *mode of financing development plans*. The developing countries, especially India, are not in a position to finance their plans fully through voluntary savings of the people and taxes by the government. They have often made resort to fiscal deficit (*i.e.*, borrowing by the Government from the Central Bank and Commercial banks) as a method of financing their development plans. In the past in India up till 1996, the Government in India borrowed heavily from the Central Bank (i.e. RBI) which often led to the large increase in high powered money. Increase in the high-powered money as a result of borrowing from RBI, which was then called *deficit financing was highly inflationary.*

Deficit financing which is now called *money financing* or *monetisation of fiscal deficit* to some extent is good and can be absorbed by the economy without experiencing inflation. This is so because as the economy grows, its monetary sector expands and also there is an increase in production as a result of economic growth for which extra money is needed. But owing to acute shortage of finance the developing countries had often indulged in deficit financing to an excessive degree. Sharp increase in the money supply with the public as a result of excessive deficit financing added greatly to the level of aggregate demand for consumers' goods. On the other hand, the supply of consumers' goods, especially of food products, could not be increased rapidly and sufficiently. The pressure of demand, therefore, led to the inflationary rise in prices. In recent years in India (after 1996) the Government does not generally borrow directly from RBI but to finance its fiscal deficit, it borrows from commercial banks through sale of its bonds to them. A high degree of fiscal deficit increases greatly government expenditure and leads to excess demand conditions which exert inflationary pressures in the economy.

It may, however, be pointed out that investment expenditure made by the government under the development plans not only generates the additional demand for goods, it also increases the productive capacity. *Investment has a dual effect. On the one hand, it generates demand or income, on the other it increases the productive capacity.* As a result of increase in productive capacity, more output of goods can be obtained which will counteract inflationary tendencies. But, in the earlier stages of development, investment expenditure is largely made on huge dams, steel plants and other heavy and basic industries which have long-gestation periods. In other words, the long-term projects can help in increasing the supply of consumers' goods only in the long run. In the short-run, prices generally shoot up under the pressure of excessive demand for goods. And once inflationary spiral starts operation, it is difficult to control it. However, if increase in Government expenditure takes place on financing its consumption expenditure which does not lead to any durable productive assets, it has a large inflationary potential

It is often said that inflation in India is due to the emergence of imbalance between demand and supply. As we have said above, increase in aggregate demand is due to the increase in Government expenditure, which has been financed largely by either by money financing or borrowing from the market. Besides, commercial banks have also created a good amount of bank money or credit to finance private investment. As a result, the aggregate expenditure increased very much and has brought about a huge expansion in aggregate demand. On the other hand, the production of foodgrains and other consumer goods industries did not increase adequately and this brought about a rapid rise in prices.

It may however be noted that *strategy of economic development*, adopted in our Five Year Plans, prior to 1991 gave high priority to basic heavy industries and relatively neglected agriculture and consumer goods industries. This is the structural reason why output of foodgrains and other essential consumers goods did not increase adequately to meet the rising demand for them resulting in inflation. After 1991 economic reforms undertaken also gave higher priority to industrialisation and did not accord due importance to agriculture. As a result, there has been slower growth of agriculture even after 1991.

Global Factors. In recent, years inflation in India has been affected by global developments with prime movers being the spurt in the prices of crude oil, minerals and metal related products. This shows the growing integration of the Indian economy with the other economies of the world. However, in some years inflationary pressures were contained below 7 per cent by importing goods such as wheat, rice, fertilizers, edible oils when their domestic supplies fell short of domestic demand. Liberalisation of foreign trade has helped in this process of importing goods in short supply.

Is Monetarist Theory a Valid Explanation of Inflation

In India from the above explanation it should not be concluded that classical quantity theory of money or Friedman modern monetarist theory of inflation applies to India quite well. *In our view it is not true that inflation in India is purely monetary phenomenon*, though rapid growth is money supply in the past has contributed to the inflation in India. However, recent experience shows that

Table : 26.1. Growth in Money Supply and Rate of Inflation in India (1991–2011)]

Year	Annual Growth in Money Supply M_3	Rate of inflation based on WPI (1999– 2002 = 100) (52-week average % Change)	Rate of Inflation based on CPI (IW)	Growth rate in GDP at constant Prices
1991–92	19.3	13.7	13.5	1.1
1992–93	14.8	10.1	9.6	5.1
1993–94	18.4	8.4	7.5	5.9
1994–95	22.4	12.5	10.1	7.2
1995–96	13.6	8.0	10.2	7.5
1996–97	16.2	4.6	9.4	8.2
1997–98	18.0	4.4	6.8	4.9
1998–99	19.4	5.9	13.1	6.4
1999–2000	14.6	3.3	3.4	6.2
2000–2001	16.8	7.1	3.8	4.4
2001–2002	14.2	3.6	4.3	5.8
2002–2003	14.7	3.4	4.0	4.0
2003-2004	16.8	5.5	3.9	8.5
2004-2005	12.3	5.1	4.2	7.5
2005-2006	17.0	4.3	4.9	9.5
2006-2007	21.7	6.5	6.7	9.6
2007-2008	21.4	4.8	5.5	9.3
2008-2009	19.3	8.0	9.2	6.8
2009-2010	16.8	3.6	12.37	8.0
2010-2011	16.5	9.6	11.5	8.5
1991–92-1995-96	17.5	10.5	10.2	5.4
1996–97-2005-06	16.0	4.6	5.7	6.5
2005-06-2009-10	19.2	5.5	–	8.6

despite relatively higher growth in money supply during the last 8 years rate of inflation remained at low level. It will be seen from Table 1 that whereas rate of growth money supply has been quite high (it has varied from 14 per cent a year to 19 per cent a year, but rate of inflation has been relatively low. This shows that growth in money supply alone is not the cause of inflation. Even after adjusting for rate of GDP growth rate during the period 1995-2008 there still remains a large gap between money supply growth and rate of inflation. In addition to growth in GDP which works to reduce inflation rate, several cost-push factors such as rise in oil prices, rise in procurement prices of food grains, other administrated prices and fiscal policy of the Government, agricultural performance in a period also play an important role in determining rate of inflation in an economy.

In addition to growth in GDP which works to reduce inflation rate, several cost-push factors such as rise in oil prices, procurement prices of food grains, other administrated prices and fiscal policy of the Government, agricultural performance in a period also play an important role in determining rate of inflatiion in an economy. An important conclusion from the above evidence regarding growth of money supply and inflation is that there is *no direct* relation between growth in money supply and inflation rate. First in addition to increase in money supply, growth of output that is, GDP, especially growth in agricultural output, plays an important role in determining rate of inflation. Let us explain this with Fisher's equation of exchange.

$$PY = MV$$

or

$$P = \frac{MV}{Y}$$

where Y is, real gross national product M is the money supply and V is the velocity of circulation. Since, old monetarists assume that V and Y remain constant, change in price is directly related to the quantity of money (M). However, in a growing economy such as ours *GDP* (i.e. Y)is *increasing* every year and from the equation it follows that it works to reduce the price level. Besides, as seen above, many cost-push and structural factors also play an important role in determining the changes in price level. It therefore follows that quantity that theory of money does not fully apply to India though growth in money supply is one important factor that determines aggregate demand and influences inflation.

INFLATION AND INTEREST RATE : THE FISHER EFFECT

Interest rate is an important macroeconomic variable as it dermines saving and investment in the economy that play an important rate in the determination of national income and employment. Through its effect on saving and investment, interest links the present with the future. It is therefore important to understand the relation between interest rate and inflation. To understand the relation between interest rate and inflation, it is necessary to know the distinction between *nominal interest rate and real interest rate.* Nominal interest rate is the stated interest rate which a bank provides to its depositors on the saving account and the fixed deposits of different maturity periods. Nominal interest is also the agreed nominal rate at which the lenders lend money to the borrowers. If your bank gives you 8 per cent interest rate on the fixed deposit of one year, then 8 per cent is the nominal interest rate.

On the other hand, real interest rate means how fast the purchasing power of your deposits in the *bank increases over a year*. The rate of increase in purchasing power of your money deposits over time depends not only on the nominal interest rate but also on the inflation rate that takes place over time. For example, if nominal interest rate on a fixed deposit for a year is 8 per cent and inflation rate in the year is 5 per cent, then 5 per cent of purchasing power of nominal interest rate has been wiped out by infaltion. Therefore, in this case 8 per cent minus 5 per cent, that is, 3 per cent is the *increase in purchasing power of your deposits* and therefore represents the real rate of interest.

Thus real interest rate can be obtained from nominal interest rate by adjusting for inflation rate that takes place in a year. Thus relationship among the real rate of interest, nominal rate of interest and inflation rate can be stated as under.

Real interest rate=nominal interest rate – inflation rate.

If we denote real interest rate by r, nominal interest rate by i and inflation rate by π, then

$$r = i - \pi \quad \ldots (i)$$

Fisher Equation and Effect

An important principle of Classical theory is that money is neutral, that is, it does not affect the real variables. Changes in money supply determine only the changes in price level or rate of inflation in the economy. This principle has an important application in the determination of relation between nominal interest rate, real interest rate and inflation rate.

Rearranging the equation (i) we have

Nominal interest rate = real interest rate + rate of inflation

In symbolic terms,

$$i = r + \pi \quad \ldots (ii)$$

The above equation (2) shows that change in nominal interest rate (i) can occur due to the reasons : (1) changes in real interest rate, and (2) changes in rate of inflation. The relationship between nominal interest rate, real interest rate and inflation rate described in equation (2), namely, *nominal interest rate is the sum of real interest rate and inflation rate is called Fisher Equation* after the economist. Irving Fisher (1867 – 1947) who first of all stated this relation.

The viewing nominal interest rate as the sum of real interest rate and inflation rate is quite useful as entirely different forces determine the real interest rate and the inflation state which together determine the nominal interest rate. As has been studied earlier, according to classical theory, real interest rate is determined by saving and investment (or, according to neo-classical theory, demand for and supply of loanable funds), rate of inflation is determined by rate of growth of money supply. According to Classical theory, rate of inflation is determined by rate of growth of money supply. Growth of many supply does not influence real interest rate. As a matter of fact, real interest rate is a real variable, and, as stated above, according to the important classical principle of monetary neutrality, changes in money supply do not affect the real variables.

Fisher Effect. An important macroeconomic issue is how nominal interest rate adjusts to change in inflation rate which in turn is determined by growth of money supply. When Central Bank of a country increases money supply in the economy, it will cause rate of inflation to rise. Since nominal interest rate is the sum of real interest rate and rate of inflation, rise in inflation rate will raise the nominal interest rate, real interest rate remaining unchanged. In fact there is one-for-one adjustment of nominal interest rate to changes in inflation rate. *Adjustment of nominal interest rate to changes in inflation rate is called Fisher effect*. Let us take an example. Suppose on your fixed deposit for a year your bank pays you 8 per cent. Further suppose inflation rate in the economy is 5 per cent per annum. Writing them in Fisher equation we have

$$i = r + \pi$$

$$8 = 3 + 5$$

Now, if as a result of higher growth of money supply rate of inflation rises to 6 per cent per annum, then given the real interest rate as 3 per cent, nominal interest rate will rise to 9 per cent. This is because

$$9 = 3 + 6$$

If follows from above nominal interest rate adjusts to change in rate of inflation. The higher the rate of inflation, the higher will be the nominal interest rate.

The historical experience shows that nominal interest rate and rate of inflation are closely associated in recent years. Chile and Brazel have experienced high rates of inflation. In recent years

Chile experienced an annual inflation rate of around 30 per cent with nominal interest rate of 40 per cent. Brazil experienced a still higher inflation rate and in it inflation rate and nominal interest rate were about 40 per cent *per month.*

THE COST OF INFLATION

Inflation has been a highly debated issue in economics. One of the goals of modern Government is to control inflation and ensures price stability in the economy. The finance minister of a country has to ensure that his budget proposals do not contribute to rise in inflation rate in the economy. Similarly, the Central Bank of a country such as Reserve Bank of India has to manage the growth of money supply in the economy in a way that it does not cause inflation. Generally, the Central Bank of a country announces a target rate of inflation beyond which it will not allow the inflation rate to rise and in order to keep inflation rate within that limit, it takes appropriate monetary measures.

Now, in what follows we explain why inflation is of serious concern for both policy makers and the general public.

Is there an Inflation Fallacy ?

The widespread view among people is that inflation is had because it reduces the purchasing power of their hard-earned money income. When prices rise, each rupee of income earned buys a smaller amount of goods and services. In this way, according to popular perception, inflation erodes real income of the people and therefore lowers their living standards.

However, some economists on the basis of Classical theory calls it as inflation fallacy.[8] According to them, when inflation occurs, the buyers of goods and services pay more for what they buy, but at the same time sellers of goods and services receive more for what they sell. Thus, according to this view, on account of inflation, people lose with one hand, but gains with the other. As a result, there is no net loss due to inflation. According to this the view, people earn their income by selling their *services*, physical or mental. When inflation takes place prices of services also rise to the same extent along with the rise in prices of goods. Thus inflation does not reduce the real income of the people. To quote Mankiw, "*Because most people earn their incomes by selling their services such as their labour, rise in incomes goes hand in hand with the rise in prices. Thus, inflation does not in itself reduce people's purchasing power.*"[9]

According to this view, people believe in this common falacy about the adverse effect of inflation on purchasing power because they do not recognise that expansion in money is neutral in its effect on real variables such as real income. The real income or purchasing power of the people is determined by their productivity which in turn depends on the availability of physical capital, human capital (i.e. skills and education of the people), natural resources and production technology used for production. On the other hand, *nominal incomes* of the people are determined by inflation rate which depends on the growth of money supply. According to this view, inflation that is caused by growth of money supply determines only nominal incomes and not real incomes or purchasing power.

A Critical Evaluation. Though this so-called fallacy about inflation is often emphasised by some American economists and believe that there are no or little social costs of inflation, it is not true under all circumstances and in all countries. If prices of *all services* increase to the same extent when prices of all goods increase, then there is no problem about inflation. In the United States, where prices of services may increase in response to anticipated inflation, nominal incomes from services keep pace with the rising prices of goods, there is no adverse effect of inflation on real incomes of the people. But what is true of the United States of America is not true of all countries

8. See N.G Mankiw, *Principles of Economics*, Second Edition, p. 6.41
9. Mankiw, op. cit. p. 641

such as India. In the case of India, prices of services do not adjust or adjust only partially and therefore rising prices of goods erode the purchasing power of their nominal incomes and therefore adversely affect the living standards of the people. In India, as in many other developing countries, the organised sector is only a small part of the economy. A large part of the economy is unorganised where people do not automatically raise the prices of their services. Even in the organised sector rise in money wages lag much behind the rise in price level. Landless agricultural workers, casual labour in both the rural and urban areas who work on petty wages which do not change over years even there is rapid inflation in the economy. Therefore, these poor people suffer a lot due to inflation. It is therefore rightly said that *inflation is enemy No. 1 of the poor people*. Even small farmers who have little marketable surplus to sell in the market, petty self-employed groups such as artisans, weavers etc. who are unable to change the prices of their services and goods find themselves robbed of the purchasing power and therefore poorer due to inflation. In all these cases inflation has a social cost and to say that there is fallacy about the adverse impact of inflation on their real incomes is not correct. In view of this harmful effect of inflation in India, as in other developing countries, fiscal and monetary policies of government are so designed as to check inflation and ensure price stability.

The Social Cost of Inflation

Having discussed the so called inflation falacy we proceed to explain in detail the social cost of monopoly. Apart from reducing the purchasing power of people's incomes, inflation inflicits some other costs on the society. To explain such costs of inflation it is necessary to distinguish between anticipated inflation and unanticipated (i.e. unexpected) inflation. As noted above, in case of anticipated inflation, the expected rise in price level is taken into account while making economic transactions, for example, in negotiating wage rate of labour etc.

Costs of Anticipated Inflation

Suppose in an economy there has annual inflation rate of 5 per cent for a long time in the past and every body expects that this 5 per cent rate of inflation will continue in the future too. In such a case all contracts made by the people such as loan agreements with borrowers, wage contracts with labour, property lease contracts will provide for 5 per cent annual rise in rates of interest, wages, rent to compensate for inflation of that order. That is, in any contract in which passage of time is involved 5 per cent rate of inflation will be taken into account and rates will be agreed to rise per period equal to the anticipated rate of inflation. If rates of interest, wages, rent etc are agreed to rise at the anticipated rate of inflation, then there will be no cost of inflation except the following two types of costs – shoe-leather costs and mence costs which are not very high. We explain below both these types of costs.

1. **Shoe-leather costs.** This type of cost occurs because on account of inflation cost of holding money in the form of currency i.e. (notes and coins) rises with the increase in inflation rate. Such cost arises because no interest is paid on holding currency, while money kept in deposits with the bank or used for keeping bonds earns interest. When inflation rate rises, the nominal interest rate on bank deposits rises, the interest lost by holding currency by the people therefore increases. In order to reduce the cost of holding currency people will tend to reduce their holdings of currency for transaction purposes. Accordingly, at a time people will hold less currency with them and keep as long as possible greater amount of money in bank deposits that yield interest. Therefore, rather than withdrawing a large amount of currency from banks at a time, they will withdraw less money which is sufficient for meeting daily expenses for a few days, say for a week. But for doing so the people will make more trips to withdraw cash. More trips to a bank in a month involves greater cost to the people. These costs have to be incurred on spending on petrol if car is used for making trips, more wear and tear of car, the time spent for making a trip. These costs of making more trips to the bank for withdrawing currency is metaphorically called *shoe-leather costs* of inflation, as walking to banks more often, one's shoes wear out more rapidly and one has to spend money on new shoes more often.

2. **Men Costs.** The second type of anticipated inflation is menu costs, a term derived from a restaurant's cost of printing a new menu. Menu costs arise because high inflation requires them to change their listed prices more often. Changing prices is somewhat more expensive because the firms have to print new catalogues listing new prices and distribute them among their customers. They have even to incur expenditure on advertisements to inform the public about their new prices.

3. **Macroeconomic inefficiency in resource allocation.** A third cost of inflation arises because firms having menu costs change their prices quite infrequently. Given the reluctance to change prices frequently, the higher the rate of inflation, the greater the variability in relative prices of a firm. Suppose a firm issues a new catalogue listing prices of its products once in a year, say in the month of January of every year. If during the year inflation occurs, there will be change in the relative prices of a firm to the general price level. If inflation rate of one per cent per month lakes place in a year the firm's relative prices to the general price level will *fall* by 12 per cent by the end of the year. As a result, his sales will tend to be lower in the early part of the year (when its prices are relatively high) and higher in the later part of the year (when its prices are relatively low). Thus when due to inflation relative prices of a firm vary during a year as compared to the overall price level, it causes destortion in production and therefore leads microeconomic inefficiencies in resource allocation.[10]

4. **Inconvenience of Living.** Lastly, another social cost of inflation is the *inconvenience of living* in a world with a changing price level. Money is the yardstick with which we measure the value of transactions. When inflation is taking place the value of money changes and as a result it becomes difficult to correctly estimate the value of transactions in real terms every time a transaction is made during a year. The rising price level makes it difficult to make optimal decisions about saving and investment and thus do the rational financial planning covering a long period of time. To quote Mankiw, "A dollar saved today and invested at a fixed nominal interest rate will yield a fixed dollar amount in the future. Yet the real value of that dollar amount – which will determine the retiree's living standard – depends on the future price level. *Deciding how much to save would be much simpler* if people could count on the price level in 30 years being similar to its level today."[11]

Conclusion. Taking account of all costs of anticipated inflation one finds that the cost of anticipated inflation are quite small or trivial and if these alone are considered, it is then surprising why inflation it a matter of serious concern for the policy makers and politicians. In our opinion the above view of costs of inflation does not consider the true cost of inflation which, as mentioned above, refers to the reduction in purchasing power or real incomes of the people which lowers their standard of living. Besides, there is ample cross country evidence that *high rates of inflation lead to low rate of sustanced economic growth* [12].

It may be further noted that in the above analysis of cost of inflation it is assumed that there is only small to moderate inflation rate, say a single digit rate of inflation occurs so that it does not disrupt the payment system. With such a low to moderate inflation, costs of inflation are small. The hyperinflation has more harmful effect as it disrupts the payment system which leads to the collapse of the economy.

Cost of Unanticipated Inflation

Unanticipated inflation has a more substantial and harmful effect as compared to the cost of anticipated infllation rate. The significant effect of unanticipated inflation is that it *arbitrarily re-distributes wealth* among individuals. Consider the value of assets fixed in nominal terms. Between 1995 and 2006, price level in India rose by about 100 per cent. This implies that those who

10. See N. Gregory Mankiw, *Macroeconomics*, 6th edition, Worth Publishers, New York, 2003.
11. Mankiw, op. cit., p. 98
12. Stanley Fisher, Macroeconomic Factors in Economic Growth, *Journal of Monetary Economics*, Dec. 1993.

held *claims on assets fixed in nominal terms in 1996*, their real value in terms of purchasing power would have declined significantly. Thus, a person who bought government bound of 10 years maturely with a face value of Rs. 1000 bearing 8 per cent nominal interest rate in 1996 will find that Rs.1000 he gets bank in 2006 has far less value than when he purchased the bond in 1996.

Similarly, unanticipated inflation harms the individuals, who retire on pensions fixed in rupee terms. After some years of inflation, the real value or purchasing power of the fixed nominal pension will greatly decline and will therefore reduce his standard of living in his old age. Thus inflation hurts individuals with fixed pensions. Workers and the private firms often agree on fixed nominal pension payable to the workers after retirement. Workers are greatly harmed when inflation is higher than anticipated. Likewise, higher than anticipates inflation rate hurts the creditors who give loans to the others and get back the principal amount after the stipulated period. Thus *inflation redistributes wealth in favour of debtors*.

EFFECTS OF INFLATION*

Inflation is a very unpopular happening in an economy. Opinion surveys conduced in India, the U.S.A. and other countries reveal that inflation is the most important concern of the people as it badly affects their standard of living. The political fortunes of many political leaders (Prime Ministers and Presidents) and Governments in India and abroad have been determined by how far they have succeeded in tackling the problem of inflation. So much sc that some American presidental candidates called '*inflation as enemy number one*'. Same is the case in India where inflation is the most hotly debated issue during the general elections for the Parliament and Assemblies. A high rate of inflation makes the life of the poor very miserable. It is, therefore, described as anti-poor. It redistributes income and wealth in favour of some and greatly harms others. By making the rich richer and the poor poorer, it militates against social justice. Besides, inflation lowers national output and employment and impedes long-run economic growth, especially in developing countries like India. We shall discuss below all these effects of inflation.

Anticipated and Unanticipated Inflation

The difference between anticipated inflation and unanticipated inflation is of crucial importance as the effects of inflation, especially its redistributive effect, depend on whether it is anticipated or not. If rate of inflation is anticipated, then people take steps to make suitable adjustments in their contracts to avoid the adverse effects which inflation could bring to them. For example, if a worker correctly anticipates the rate of inflation in a particular year to be equal to 10 per cent and if his present wage rate is Rs. 5000 per month, he can enter into contract with the employer that to compensate for the 10 per cent rise in prices his money wage per month next year be raised by 10 per cent so that next year he gets Rs. 5500 per month. In this way he has been able to prevent the erosion of his real income with the automatic revision of his money wage depending on the anticipated rate of inflation.

Take another example. You lend Rs. 10,000 to a person at a rate of 10 per cent per annum. After a year you will receive Rs. 11,000. But if it is anticipated that during the year there will be 8 per cent rate of inflation, then 8 per cent of your income will be offset by the rise in prices that would occur so that you will get only 2 *per cent real rate of interest*. Therefore, in order to receive 10 per cent real rate of interest, in view of 8 per cent anticipated inflation rate you must demand 18 per cent nominal rate of interest.

On the other hand, effects of unanticipated inflation are unavoidable because in this case you do not know what would be the rise in the price level. That is, unanticipated inflation catches you by surprise. In what follows we shall examine the *effects of unanticipated inflation*. The effects of inflation can be divided into three categories:

---

*Some effects of taxation we have discussed above under the heading 'Costs of Inflation". Therefore, many points will be repeated in the discussion of effects of taxation.

1. Effect on real income;
2. Effect on distribution of income and wealth;
3. Effect on output; and
4. Effect on long-run economic growth.

Inflation Erodes Real Incomes of the People

To examine the effect of inflation it is important to note the difference between money income and real income. It is the change in the general price level that creates the crucial difference between the two. Money income or what is also called nominal income means the income such as wages, interest, rent *received in terms of rupees*. On the other hand, *real income* implies the amount of goods and services which you can buy. In other words, real income means the purchasing power of your income. If your money or nominal income increases at a lower rate than the rate of rise in the general price level (*i.e.*, the rate of inflation), you will be able to buy less goods and services, that is, your real income will decline. Real income will rise only if nominal income rises faster than the rate of inflation. For illustration, take the case of workers who enter into contract with their employer at an agreed wage rate of Rs. 5000 per month for the period, say 5 years. Now, suppose the rate of inflation is 10 per cent per annum. This means after a year, with money wage rate of Rs. 5,000 workers will be able to buy less goods and services. That is, their real income will decrease and therefore their standard of living will fall.

Take another example. Suppose you deposit your saving of Rs. 100 in a saving account which carries 5 per cent rate of interest. After a year you will receive Rs.105. However, if during that year rate of inflation has been 12 per cent, you will be a loser in real terms. In fact your real interest-income will be negative as, with 12 per cent rate of inflation, Rs. 105 after a year will buy less goods and services than what you can purchase with Rs. 100 today.

The above two examples clearly show that inflation reduces the purchasing power of money and thereby adversely affects real income of the people.

Effect on Distribution of Income and Wealth

An important effect of inflation in that it redistributes income and wealth in favour of some at the cost of others. Inflation adversely affects those who receive relatively fixed incomes and benefits businessmen, producers, traders and others who enjoy flexible incomes. Inflation brings windfall profits for the producers and traders. Thus, all do not lose as a result of inflation, rather some gain from it. We examine below how inflation redistributes income and wealth and thereby harms some people and benefits others.

Creditors and Debtors. Unanticipated inflation harms creditors and benefits debtors and in this way redistributes income in favour of the latter. As explained above, value of money declines due to inflation. For creditors (including financial institutions such as banks and insurance companies) who enter into agreement with the borrowers to provide loans at fixed nominal rate of interest, the real value of money in terms of goods and services which they will receive at the end of the period would be much less if during the period prices rise sharply. Thus, the debtors or borrowers gain because they would return the loan-money when its real value has declined greatly due to the unexpected rapid rate of inflation.

Fixed Income Groups. Those who get fixed incomes stand to lose from inflation. Workers and salaried people who earn fixed wages and salaries are hit hard by unanticipated inflation. These people often enter into contract with the employers regarding wages or salaries fixed in nominal terms. When inflation occurs, the purchasing power of their nominal incomes falls greatly causing a decline in their levels of living. Thus, when inflation persists for some years there are demands for revision of wages and salaries. It may be mentioned that now-a-days workers and other salaried people get dearness allowances to compensate them for the rise in cost of living due to inflation. However, these dearness allowances do not fully neutralise the rise in price level and therefore they also demand revision of wages and pay scales.

Pensioners. They also come in the category of the people who get income in fixed nominal terms. For the people who retired in 1984 with the monthly pension of Rs. 2000, the real value of their pension in Oct. 1998 would been reduced to one third as compared to 1984 as there has been more than 300 per cent rise in the price level during this period. It may also be noted that in order to reduce the hardship of the pensioners, some dearness allowance is also provided on pension. But effects of inflation on the real value of their pension are only partly offset in this way.

Businessmen : Producers and Traders. Businessmen, that is, entrepreneurs and traders, stand to gain by inflation. During periods of inflation, the prices of goods produced by entrepreneurs rise relatively faster than the cost of production because wages lag behind the rise in prices of goods. Consequently, *inflation increases the profits of businessmen.* The value of the inventories or stocks of goods and materials kept by the entrepreneurs and traders increases due to rise in prices of goods which brings about an increase in their profits.

Wealth Holders of Cash, Bonds and Debentures. Inflation also adversely affects wealth holders who hold their wealth in the form of cash money, demand deposits, saving and fixed deposits and interest-bearing bonds and debentures. These wealth holders are severely hurt by inflation as inflation reduces the real value of their wealth. Saving and demand deposits, bonds and debentures represent assets whose value is fixed in terms of money. The rise in prices reduces the purchasing power of these fixed-value money assets such as saving and time deposits, bonds and debentures which bear a fixed nominal rate of interest.

Inflation, therefore reduces the real rate of interest earned by them. Consequently, it has been observed that during periods of rapid inflation people try to convert their holdings of money and near money into goods and physical property so as to avoid the loss due to inflation. It may also be noted that if inflation is anticipated and all expect equal rates of inflation the nominal rates of interest are adjusted upward so as to obtain targeted real rate of interest. Thus, if creditors want real rate of interest equal to 10 per cent and anticipate rate of inflation is equal to 8 per cent, they will try to have nominal rate of interest fixed at 18 per cent. This is known as **Fisher effect** *which states that market or nominal rate of interest is equal to the real rate of interest (based on productivity of capital and rate of time preference) plus the anticipated rate of inflation.* Thus nominal rate of inflation includes what is called *inflation premium* to prevent the erosion of purchasing power due to inflation.

Effect on Output

There is a good deal of uncertainty and also disagreement as to whether inflation will adversely or favourably affect national output. The effect of inflation on output also depends on whether it has been caused by demand-pull or cost-push factors. Further, the effect of inflation on output depends on whether it is moderate or very rapid or whether it is anticipated or unanticipated. Let us examine the likely effects of inflation in each of these cases.

Demand-pull Inflation and Output. Till recently a large number of economists favoured a mild or modest inflation and they argued that rising prices are caused by increase in aggregate demand which are accompanied by expansion in output. Indeed, according to them, rising prices create a tonic effect on the level of investment and employment of labour and other resources by raising the marginal efficiency of capital (*i.e.*, expected rate of profits). We know the level of output and employment depend on aggregate demand, given the aggregate supply curve. In a previous chapter we have explained that short-run aggregate supply curve has three ranges: in range 1 aggregate supply curve is horizontal, in range 2 when the economy is near full employment level or potential level of output, aggregate supply curve mildly slopes upward and in range 3 aggregate supply curve becomes vertical. To start with, aggregate demand is low. For instance, if in Fig. 26.8 it is AD_0, the economy will produce level of output Y_0 and will be far below the full-employment level of output Y_3. Now, if aggregate demand increases to AD_1, the price level will remain stable and output will rise to Y_1. But if aggregate demand further increases to AD_2, it will intersect the AS curve in range 2, where it is sloping upward mildly. In this range 2, price level will increase but output and employment will also increase. Even if aggregate demand further increases upto AD_3, aggregate output increases to Y_3 and is accompanied by rise in the price level to P_2. Thus, in range 2 of aggregate supply curve until the full-employment output Y_3 is reached, increase in aggregate demand causes moderate inflation and also raises aggregate output and employment. It is only when aggregate demand increases beyond full-employment output that it leads to a higher rate of inflation without affecting output. Thus, so far as economy finds itself in range 2, moderate inflation has to be tolerated if higher levels of output and employment are to be achieved. Therefore, some economists have argued that there exists trade-off between output and inflation or between employment and inflation. Some inflation has to be accepted if you want higher output (and therefore less unemployment). However, this viewpoint has been criticised in recent years and it has been asserted that any trad-off between rate of inflation and output (or unemployment) is only a short-run phenomenon and there is no such trade-off in the long run.

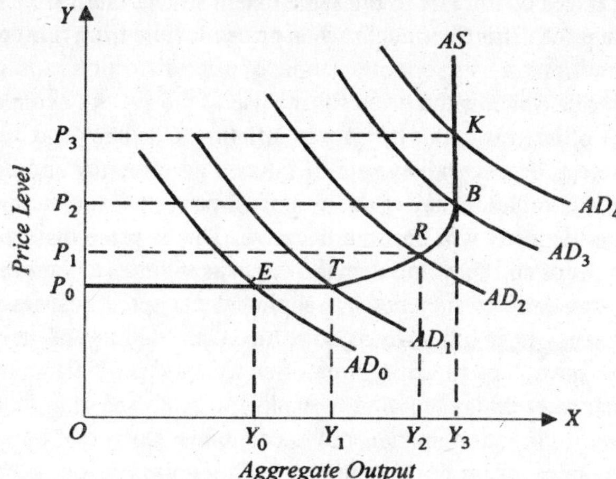

Fig. 26.8. *Effect of Inflation on Output*

Cost-Push Inflation and Output. But, as seen above, the economic events in recent years have thrown up another type of inflation which is generally described as cost-push inflation which is caused by leftward shift in the aggregate supply curve due to rise in prices of crucial inputs such as petroleum oil, wages of labour etc. In the cost-push inflation, rise in price level is associated with a fall in aggregate output as will be seen from Fig. 26.9. In the early years of 1970s and again in 1979–80 when oil price shock given by *OPEC* created cost-push inflation, prices rose but at the same time output fell and unemployment went up. Such a situation has been described as *stagflation* which implies occurrence of inflation with static or lower output and higher unemployment.

From the above it is clear that there is no necessary relationship between inflation and output. Inflation may come about with either a higher or a lower level of output and employment. To quote Samuelson, "*Today, macroeconomists believe that there is no necessary relationship between prices and output. An increase in aggregate demand will increase both prices and output, but a supply shock shifting up aggregate supply curve will raise prices and lower output.*"[13]

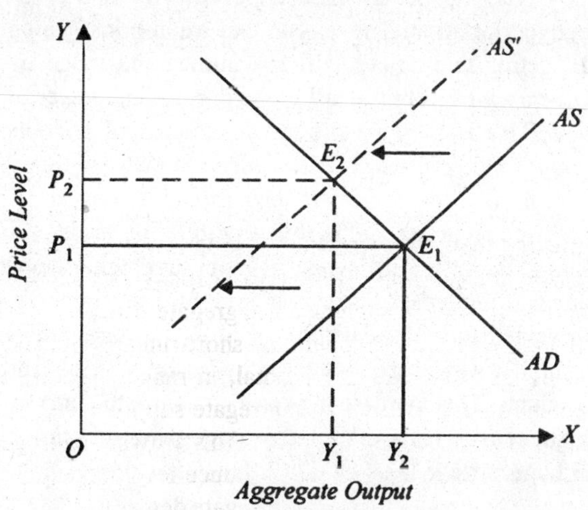

Fig. 26.9. *Effect of Cost-Push Inflation an Output*

Loss of Economic Efficiency

It is generally believed that inflation causes misallocation of resources and

13. Samuelson, P.A. & Nordhuas, W.D., *Economics*, Fourteenth edition, McGraw-Hill, 1992

therefore results in loss of economic efficiency. Inflation causes distortions in prices which misallocate resources and result in inefficiency. This distortion in prices occurs because, as a result of inflation, all prices do not rise to the same extent so that there are changes in relative prices. It may be noted that price distortions occur when prices deviate from right prices as determined by costs and demand conditions. An important example of price distortion caused by inflation is the *change in real rate of interest* which is the price for the use of money. As explained above, real rate of interest is money rate of interest minus the rate of inflation. Currency and demand deposits generally do not earn any interest, that is, money rate of interest on currency and demand deposits is zero. However, when there is inflation, say at the rate of 12 per cent per annum, the real rate of interest on currency and bank deposits will become negative. This is price distortion which causes people to unload their stocks of currency and demand deposits in times of rapid inflation and buy other assets. This leads to economic inefficiency as people have to spend real resources for trying to economise the use of currency or, in other words, to reduce their holdings of currency and demand deposits. For example, they have to go to banks more often to withdraw their money holdings. They use up their shoes and such other things in going to banks too often and also spend a good deal of their valuable time. In times of inflation, in their bid to economise the use of currency, the business firms also spend some resources for proper management of their cash funds.

Another important price distortion caused by inflation is in respect of taxes. In a progressive income tax structure Gpeople will have to pay higher rates of taxes as their money income increases as a Gresult of inflation. As money incomes of the people increase due to inflation, the Gaverage rate of tax automatically rises as they are pushed into higher income tax slabs. This is generally called inflation *tax*. As a result of this inflation their rewards for work or other factor services go below what is justified by the real productivity of their work or other factor services. This causes misallocation of labour and other factors which create economic inefficiency and unnecessary loss of output. It is due to this adverse effect of taxes on resources allocation that in some countries taxes are also indexed, that is, adjusted in tune with the rise in general price level so that inflation induced distortion be avoided.

Hyperinflation and Economic Crisis

When inflation is extremely rapid, it is called hyperinflation. The effect of hyperinfilation on national output and employment turns out to be devastating. This hyperinflation is generally caused when Government issues too much currency which greatly adds to the money supply in the economy. However, some economists are of the view that even mild or creeping inflation may ultimately lead to hyperinflation. They argue that when prices go on creeping upward for some time, people start expecting that prices will rise futher and value of money will depreciate. In order to protect Gthemselves from the fall in the purchasing power of money in the future, they try to spend money now. That is, they try to beat the anticipated price increases. This raises the aggregate demand for goods in the present. Businessmen too increase their purchases of capital goods and build up larger than normal inventories if they anticipate rise in prices. Thus, inflationary expectations raise the pressure on prices and in this way inflation feeds on itself. Further, the rise in prices and the cost of living, under the influence of rising aggregate demand, prompts the workers and their unions to demand higher wages to compensate them for the rise in the prices. During the periods of boom these demands of the workers for hike in wages are generally conceded. But rise in labour costs due to higher wages are recovered by business firms from the consumers by raising the prices of their products. This increase in prices gives rise to demand for further increases in wages resulting in still higher costs. Thus, cumulative wage-price inflationary spiral starts operating which may culminate in hyperinflation.

Hyperinflation not only has disruptive redistributive effect, it also brings about economic crisis and may even cause collapse of the economic system. Hyperinflation encourages speculative activity on the part of people and businessmen who shy away from productive activities, as they find it highly profitable to hoard both finished goods and materials expectations of further rise in prices. But such hoardings of goods and materials restrict the supply and availability of goods and tend to intensify the inflationary pressures in the economy. Instead of making productive investment, people and businesses tend to invest in unproductive assets such as gold and jewellery, real estate, houses etc., as a means of protecting themselves from inflation.

In the extreme when, as a result of issuing too much money supply or working of wage-price spiral, inflation becomes extremely rapid or what economists called hyperinflation, normal working of the economy collapses. In this sitation, "prices are so rapidly rising and consequently purchasing power of money so much dwindling that businessmen do not know what to charge for their products and consumers do not know what to pay. Resource suppliers will want to be paid with actual output rather than with rapidly depreciating money. Creditors will avoid debtors to escape the rapayment of debts with cheap money. Money becomes virtually worthless and ceases to do its job as a measure of value and a medium of exchange. The economy may be literally thrown into a state of barter. Production and exchange grind towards a halt and the net result is economic, social and political chaos." [14]

Such grim and gloomy situation created by hyperinflation did occur in the Germany during 1920s and in Hungary and Japan in the forties. At that time, money depreciated so much that for some time barter system came to prevail and after some time, the new currency had to be issued. It is therefore desirable that appropriate anti-inflationary measures be taken so that inflation should not go out of control and get transformed into hyperinflation.

Effects of Inflation on Long-run Economic Growth

Some Economists have argued that inflation of a creeping or mild variety has a tonic effect on the long-run economic growth. In their support they give the example of today's industralised countries in the Eighteenth and Nineteenth Centuries when the rate of growth of output had been more rapid during long periods of inflation witnessed in these countries. The driving force in the process of economic growth, according to them, has been *high profit margins* created by inflation. They argue that wages lag behind the rise in general price level and thus creating higher profit margins for businessmen and industrialists. This tends to increase the profit share in national income. The businessmen and industrialists who receive profits as income belong to the upper income brackets whose propensity to save is higher as compared to the workers. As a result, savings go up which ensures higher rate of investment. With greater rate of investment more accumulation of capital is made possible. More rapid capital accumulation generates a higher rate of long-run economic growth.

Looking at the problem from an alternative angle, with wages lagging behind rise in prices, inflation causes a large shift of resources away from the production of consumer goods for the wage earners to the production of capital goods. The higher rate of expansion in capital stock raises the growth of productive capacity of the economy and productivity of labour. This generates rapid economic growth.

Bad Effect of Inflation on Economic Growth

However, it is now widely recognised that, far from encouraging savings and generating higher rate of economic growth, inflation slows down the rate of capital accumulation. There are several reasons responsible for this. First, as seen above, when due to rapid inflation value of money is declining, people will not like to keep money with themselves and will, therefore, be eager to spend it before its value goes down heavily. This raises their consumption demand and therefore lowers their saving. Besides, people find that the rapid inflation will erode the real value of their savings.

14. McConnell and Brue, *Economics*, 11th edition, McGraw-Hill, 1990, p. 175

This discourages them to save. Thus, *inflation or rapid rise in prices serves as a disincentive to save*. Further, as a consequence of the rise in prices, a relatively greater part of the income of the people is spent on consumption to maintain their level of living and therefore little is left to be saved. Thus, not only does inflation reduce the willingness to save, it also slashes their ability to save.

Secondly, *inflation or rising prices lead to unproductive form of investment* in gold, jewellery, real estate, construction of houses etc. These unproductive forms of wealth do not add to the productive capacity of the economy and are quite useless from the viewpoint of economic growth. Thus, inflation may lead to more investment but much of this is of unproductive type. In this way economic surplus is frittered away in unproductive investment.

Thirdly, a highly undesirable consequence of inflation, especially in developing countries, is that *it accentuates the problem of poverty in these countries*. It is often said inflation is enemy number one of the poor people. Due to rising prices poor people are not able to meet their basic needs and maintain minimum subsistence level of consumption. Thus inflation sends many people to live below the poverty line with the result that the number of people living below the poverty line increases. Besides, due to inflation, consumption of a large number of poor people is reduced much below what may be regarded as *productive consumption*, that is, essential consumption required to maintain health and productive efficiency. In India, rapid inflation in recent years is as much responsible for the mounting number of people below the poverty line as the lack of employment opportunities.

Fourthly, *inflation adversely affects balance of payments* and thereby hampers economic growth, especially in the developing countries. When prices of domestic goods rise due to inflation, they cannot compete abroad and as a consequence exports of a country are discouraged. On the other hand, when domestic prices rise relatively to prices of foreign goods, imports of foreign goods increase. Thus, falling exports and rising imports create disequilibrium in the balance of payments which may, in the long run, result, in a foreign exchange crisis. The shortage of foreign exchange prevents the country to import even essential materials and capital goods needed for industrial growth of the economy. The Indian experience during 1988–92 when foreign exchange reserves declined to abysmally low level and created an economic crisis in the country, shows the validity of this argument.

There is no agreement among economists whether or not moderate or mild inflation encourages saving and therefore ensures higher rate of capital accumulation and economic growth. However, there is complete unanimity that a rapid inflation discourages saving and hinders economic growth. However, barring the special case of hyperinflation, whether or not saving is encouraged by inflation depends on whether there exists *wage lag*.[15] While there is sufficient evidence in the industrialised countries such as the U.S.A. Great Britain, France etc., about the existence of wage lag in the period *before the World War II*, in the period after this there is no solid evidence of it. In the present wages quickly catch up with the rising prices. Indeed, there is evidence in some developed countries that the share of profits in national income has declined and that of wages has gone up during the post World War II period. Therefore, "To the extent that rate of long-run economic growth depends on the rate of capital accumulation, *a major basis for the conclusion that inflation promotes rapid economic growth is undermined given that wages no longer lag during inflation as they apparently did in time of past*."[16]

However, it may be noted that in the developing countries like India where labour is mostly unorganised and trade unions of labour are not strong and further there is a lack of information which causes wages lagging behind prices during periods of inflation. This itself will cause greater

15. See D. Felix, "Profit Inflation and Industrial Growth, "*Quarterly Journal of Economics, August* 1956, pp. 441-63 and E.J. Hamilton, Prices as a Factor in Business Growth, *Journal of Economic History*, December 1952, pp. 325-49.
16. E. Shapiro, *Macroeconomic Analysis*, Harcourt, Fourth Edition, 1978, p. 443 (*Italics added*)

proportion of national income going to profits and other business incomes which should ensure higher saving rate. However, in India, businessmen are prone to make unproductive investment in speculative activities, gold, jewellery, real estate and palatial houses whose prices rise rapidly during periods of inflation. Such kind of investment is not only counter-productive and anti-growth but is repugnant to social justice as it further accentuates inequalities in the distribution of income and wealth.

Is Deflation (i.e. Falling Prices) Desirable?

Now, when the rising prices as a goal of monetary policy are ruled out, the question is whether falling prices will be the desirable objective to be pursued by the *monetary authority*. Falling prices can be favoured on various grounds. *First*, falling prices means increase in the real wages and income of the workers and other fixed *encomists*. It is argued that only through falling prices that workers and other people with fixed money incomes can benefit automatically from economic growth without the necessity of fighting for higher wages. *Secondly*, falling prices check speculative activities in the economy. This is because when prices are falling it is not profitable to hoard commodities. This will discourse speculation. *Thirdly*, falling prices imply the rising value of money. This will increase the willingness or propensity to save of the people. Besides, rise in real incomes as a result of falling prices will raise the ability to save of the people. The increase in savings, it is argued, will enable more investment which in turn will accelerate economic growth. *Fourthly*, falling prices will favourably affect the balance of pyments of the country. With lower prices, exports will rise and imports will decline, thereby generating a favourable effect on balance of trade.

But falling prices also involve severe dangers. With falling prices, profit expectations of the entrepreneurial class will become bleak which will adversely affect investment in the economy. The decline in investment, if large, will cause recession or depression in the economy which will spread unemployment in the economy and cause the national output and income to fall. Therefore, some economists believe that falling prices or deflation is more serious than inflation. Thus, even falling prices are not considered as desirable objective of the monetary policy.

Prices Stability : The Desirable Objective

When both rising prices and falling prices are ruled out as desirable policies of a monetary authority, the third alternative is the policy of price stabilisation. The policy of price stabilisation has gained wide support in recent years as it has been realised that inflation has caused much unrest in the country and has also impeded economic development. It has been argued by some that if money is only to serve as instrument of exchange and be nothing else except an intermediary, it must be "*neutral*" and should not affect some adversely and others beneficially. If money is to be "*neutral*" prices must be kept stable. Besides, stable prices will promote saving and investment and therefore be conducive to growth.The stable prices will also not cause any labour unrest and social tensions which prevail when prices are rising. Stable prices will also not disturb the planning process by ensuring adequate financial resources to achieve physical target of the plans.

Thus, much can be said for the policy of price stabilisation. But what is exactly meant by price stabilisation? Does it mean prices of all commodities must remain stable? The answer is in the negative. Under conditions of consumer sovereignty and a free market economy with a significant role for private sector and free market mechanism the productive activity is continually adjusted and readjusted in response to changing consumer's preferences. Broadly speaking, those activities in which consumer demand is increasing, other things remaining the same, would experience price and profit increases and thus become relatively more attractive to investors than other activities. In a free market economy large or small demand for commodities relatively to their supply is indicated through the beacons of price rises and decreases. In a free market economy, price stability will prevail if price-rising tendency of some commodities is offset by the falling tendency of others leaving the general price level constant. In a planned economy like that of India, the price stability will be attained if such monetary and fiscal policies are adopted which ensure general price index to remain constant. This implies that if in a planned mixed economy, prices of some commodities rise due to their shortage, efforts should be made by monetary authority to either increase the output of the commodities in short supply or to bring down the prices of some other commodities, if price index is to remain constant.

MEASURES TO CONTROL INFLATION

Measures to Correct Excess Demand

As has been explained above, inflation occurs due to the emergence of excess demand for goods and services relative to their supply of output at the prevailing prices. Inflation of this type is called *demand-pull inflation.* Various fiscal and monetary measures can be adopted to check this inflation. We discuss below the efficacy of the various policy measures to check inflation which is caused by excess aggregate demand.

1. Fiscal Policy: Reducing Budget Deficit

The budget deals with how a Government raises its revenue and spends it. If the total revenue raised by the Government through taxation, fees, surpluses from public undertakings is less than the expenditure it incurs on buying goods and services to meet its requirements of defence, civil administration and various welfare and developmental activities, there emerges a deficit in its budget. It may be noted here that the budget of the government has two parts: (1) *Revenue Budget*, (2) *Capital Budget.* In the revenue budget on the receipts side revenue raised through taxes, interests, fees, surpluses from public undertakings are given and on the expenditure side consumption expenditure by the government on goods and services required to meet the needs of defence, civil administration, education and health services, subsidies on food, fertilizers and exports, and interest payments on the loans taken by it in the previous years are important items. In the capital budget, the main items of receipts are market borrowings by the government from the Banks and other financial institutions, foreign aid, small savings (*i.e.*, Provident Fund, National Savings Schemes etc.). The important items of expenditure in the capital budget are defence, loans to public enterprises for developmental purposes, and loans to states and union territories.

The fiscal deficit can be financed by two ways : First, by borrowing from the Reserve Bank of India which is the nationalised central bank of the country and has the power to create new money, that is, to issue new notes. Thus, to finance its budget deficit, the Government can borrow from Reserve Bank of India against its own securities. This is only a technical way of creating new money because the Government has to pay neither the rate of interest nor the original amount when it borrows from Reserve Bank of India against its own securities. It is thus clear that budget deficit implies that Government incurs more expenditure on goods and services than its normal receipts from revenue and capital budgets. This excess expenditure by the Government financed by newly created money leads to the rise in incomes of the people. This causes the aggregate demand of the community to rise to a greater extent than the amount of deficit financing undertaken through the operation of what Keynes called *income multiplier*.

In the opinion of many economists, the expansion in money supply caused by monetisation of fiscal deficit leads to the excess aggregate demand in the economy, especially when aggregate supply of output is inelastic. To some extent the creation of new money may not generate demand-pull inflation because if the aggregate output increases, especially of essential consumer goods such as foodgrains, cloth, the extra demand arising out of newly created money would be matched by extra supply of output. However, if the increase in money supply is not accompanied by sufficient increase in output, this contributes a good deal to the general rise in prices and has been an important factor responsible for inflation in the Indian economy. Second, the fiscal deficit can be financed by borrowing from the market by the Government. In Inida at present to finance its fiscal deficit the Government usually borrows from the market by issuing its bonds. It is the banks, big business firms, insurance companies etc. which generally buy these Government bonds. The Government pays annually interest on these bonds.

To reduce fiscal deficit and keep borrowing within a safe limit, the Government can mobilise more resources through raising (*a*) taxes, both direct and and indirect, (*b*) raising small savings such as receipts from Provident Funds. National Saving Schemes (NSC and NSS) by offering suitable incentives. On the other hand, it can reduce fiscal deficit by curtailing its wasteful and inessential expenditure. In India, it is often argued that there is a large scope for pruning down non-planned expenditure on defence, police and General Administration and on subsidies being provided on food, fertilizers and petroleum products. Though it is easy to suggest cutting down of Government expenditure, it is difficult to implement it in practice. However, in our view, there is a large-scale inefficiency in resource use and also a lot of corruption involved in the spending by the Government, expenditure can be curtailed to a good extent. Thus, both by greater resource mobilisation on the one hand and pruning down of wasteful and inessential Government expenditure on the other, the fiscal deficit and consequently borrowing by the Government can be reduced.

2. Monetary Policy: Monetary Tighening

Monetary policty refers to the adoption of suitable policy regarding *interest rate* and the *availability of credit*. Monetary policy is another important measure for reducing aggregate demand to control inflation. As an instrument of demand management, monetary policy can work in two ways. First, it can affect the *cost of credit* and second, it can influence the *credit availability* for private business firms. Let us first consider the cost of credit. The higher the rate of interest, the greater the cost of borrowing form the banks by the business firms. As anti-inflationary measure, the rate of interest has to be kept high to discourage businessmen to borrow more and also to provide incentives for saving more. In the fifties and early sixties, the cheap credit policy (*i.e.*, lower interest rates) was recommended on the ground that lower rate of interest will promote more private investment which is an important factor determining economic growth. Keeping in view this consideration, cheap money policy was adopted in India upto 1964 and accordingly bank rate was kept low. However, private investment demand has been empirically found to be *interest-inelastic*. This implies that changes in the rate of interest do not affect much the inducement to invest. Therefore, rationale behind cheap money policy was not based upon valid grounds.

Since the mid-sixties the dear money policy (that is, higher interest '*rate policy*') has been pursued in India to curb the inflationary pressures in the Indian economy. As mentioned above, the higher rate of interest on saving and fixed deposits will induce more savings by the households and help in cutting down aggregate consumption expenditure. Besides, higher rates of interest will discourage more investment in inventories and consumer durables and will help in reducing aggregate demand. Not only the bank rate has to be raised but also the deposit and lending rates of commercial banks if full effect of the monetary measures are to be achieved.

It is noteworthy that a recent monetary theory emphasizes that it is the changes in the credit availability rather than cost of credit (*i.e.*, rate of interest) that is a more effective instrument of regulating aggregate demand. There are several methods by which credit availability can be reduced. Firstly, it is through *open market operations* that the central bank of a country can reduce the availability of credit in the economy. Under open market operations, the Reserve Bank sells Government securities. Those, especially banks, who buy these securities will make payment for them in terms of cash reserves. With their reduced cash reserves, their capacity to lend money to thc business firms will be curtailed. This will tend to reduce the supply of credit or loanable funds which in turn would tend to reduce investment demand by the business firms.

However, in India open market operations do not play a significant role as an instrument of credit control to fight against inflationary situation. This is because market for Government securities is narrow as well as captive. General public do not buy more than a fraction of Government securities. It is the institutions such as commercial banks, LIC, GIC and Provident Funds which are required by law to invest a certain proportion of their funds in buying Government securities. Thus, in the context of captive market for Government securities open market operations cannot be usefully used for checking inflation.

In India, it is the *Cash Reserve Ratio* (*CRR*) which can be raised to curb inflation. By law banks have to keep a certain proportion of cash money as reserves against their deposits. This is called cash reserve ratio. To contract credit availability Reserve Bank can raise this ratio. In recent years to squeeze credit for checking inflation, cash reserve ratio in India has been raised from time to time.

Another instrument for affecting credit availability is the Statutory Liquidity Ratio (SLR). According to statutory liquidity ratio, in addition to *CRR*, banks have to keep a certain minimum proportion of their deposits in the form of specified liquid assets. And the most important specified liquid asset for this purpose is the Government securities. To mop up extra liquid assets with banks which may lead to undue expansion in credit availability for the business class, the Reserve Bank has often raised statutory liquidity ratio.

Limitations of Tight Monetary Policy

However, tight monetary policy for controlling inflation is not without its limitations. First, monetary transmission mechanism may be weak and raising of short-term interest rates by the RBI may not actually lead to the restriction of bank credit. First, the banks may have surplus liquidity (i.e., cash reserves) with them and therefore they may not follow tight monetary policy and raise their lending rates. As a result, supply of credit by banks will not be restricted. Secondly, if the economic environment is such that boom conditions prevail in the economy and aggregate demand for products is quite high, demand for credit may not be much affected by higher lending rates. As emphasized by J.M. Keynes investment is determined more by marginal efficiency of capital (that is, expected rate of return) rather than rate of interest. Thirdly, at present in India corporate firms are more easily able to borrow from foreign capital markets (i.e., external commercial borrowing, ECB), especially when rates of interest in the US, European zone and Japan are extremely low. Therefore, unless this debt-capital inflow (i.e. ECB) is checked, RBI's monetary policy may not be effective to check the supply of credit to control inflation in the economy.

Thirdly, when the stock market prices are rising and aggregate demand is quite high, the corporate sector is able to raise funds itself more easily from the capital market. This will also offset the impact of tight monetary policy of the RBI to control inflation. Fourthly, if adequate internal funds are available with the corporate firms as a result of *retained profit earnings* by the companies they can use them to finance their expansion plans and thereby add to the aggregate expenditure or demand. This will also nullify the tight monetary policy of the RBI to curb inflation.

Lastly, if inflation in the economy has originated from the supply-side factors, for example if production of foodgrains and other essential food articles such as milk, vegitables, fruits etc. in a year declines or does not increase adequately to meet the growing demand for them due to certain supply-side bottlenecks, this will cause the *demand-supply imbalances* leading to the rise in inflation. Such supply-side inflation cannot be checked by raising interest rates under the tight monetary policy. This happened in 2009-10 when due to the shortage of monsoon rainfall drop in agricultural production was expected, inflationary pressures emerged in the Indian economy raising food-inflation to around 20 per cent in December 2009. This food inflation continued to prevail at double digit level till February 2011. Tight monetary policy which is aimed at management of aggregate demand rather than augmentation of supply is ineffective in tackling this supply-side inflation as in case of food inflation in 2010-11. Similarly, supply-side inflation arises when prices of (petroleum products) arise which is passed on to the domestic consumers and cannot be tackled with use of tight monetary policy.

Now to control food inflation what is required to take long-term measures to augment supply of foodgrains and other food articles by raising agricultural productivity by undertaking appropriate technological changes and land-reform measures. In the short run to control food inflation what is needed is to release food stocks through public distribution system (PDS) which should be properly monitored to check black-market. Besides, to control rise in food prices in the short run release of food stocks for sale in the open market should be made. However, this pre-supposes enough food stocks with the Government. Further, to check food-inflation foodgrains, pulses, oilseeds and other feed articles in short-supply can be imported.

It may however be noted that when inflationary expectations arise as a result of emergence of shortage of supply of some essential commodities there is tendency on the part of traders to hoard stocks of goods in short supply for speculative purposes. To discourage such speculative hoarding of goods in short supply monetary policy of high interest rates can be helpful. Besides, as will be explained below, selective credit controls of monetary policy can also be used to check excessive hoarding of foodgrains, oil-seeds and other essential commodities.

Selective Credit Controls

By far the most important anti-inflationary measure in India is the use of selective credit control. The methods of credit control described above are known as quantitative or general methods as they are meant to control the availability of credit in general. Thus, bank rate policy, open market operations and variation in cash reserves ratio expand or contract the availability of credit for all purposes. On the other hand, selective credit controls are meant to regulate the flow of credit for particular or specific purposes. Whereas the general credit controls seek to regulate the total available quantity of credit (through changes in the high powered money) and the cost of credit, the selective credit control seeks to change the distribution or allocation of credit between its various uses. These selective credit controls are also known as *Qualitative Credit Controls*. The selective credit controls have both the positive and negative aspect. In its positive aspect, measures are taken to stimulate the greater flow of credit to some particular sectors considered as important. Thus in India, agriculture, small and marginal farmers, small artisans, small-scale industries are the priority sectors to which greater flow of bank credit has been sought to be encouraged by the Reserve Bank of India. In its negative aspect, several measures are taken to restrict the credit flowing into some specific activities or sectors which are regarded as undesirable or harmful from the social point of view. The selective credit controls generally used are:

(1) Changes in the minimum margin for lending by banks against the stocks of specific goods kept or against other types of securities.

(2) The fixation of maximum limit or ceiling on advances to individual borrowers against stock of particular sensitive commodities.

(3) The fixation of minimum discriminatory rates of interest chargeable on credit for particular purposes.

In India, the selective credit controls are being used by the Reserve Bank to prevent speculative hoarding of commodities so as to check the rise in prices of these commdities. The selective credit controls in India are being used in case of foodgrains, oilseeds, vegetable oils, cotton, sugar, gur and Khandsari.

Though, all the above techniques of selective credit controls are used, in India it is the first technique, namely, the changes in the minimum margin against stocks of commodities or other securities that has been mostly used. It may be noted that the Reserve Bank of India has the power to vary the minimum margin requirements against the security of stocks of commodities. While lending advances to businessmen, the commercial banks leave a margin of the value of stock kept as security to be financed by the businessmen from their own sources and lend money equal to the remaining amount of the value of the stock. This minimum requirement of the value of the stock left to be financed by the borrowers themselves is known as margin. Suppose the margin fixed for a stock of particular commodity is 60 per cent. In this case, the businessmen can borrow up to the value of 40 per cent of the stock of that commodity and the remaining 60 per cent of the value of stock will be financed by he businessman himself. Now, if the Reserve Bank raises the margin to 70 per cent, then he can borrow from the bank to the extent of 30 per cent of the value of the stock of that commodity. This will lead to the contraction of credit for holding the stock of the commodity by the businessman. If the businessmen are not able finance the holding of 10 per cent extra stock of the commodity, they will be forced to sell that in the market and thus raising market supply of the commodity. This will lower the prices, other things remaining the same.

Some conditions are necessary for the successful operations of selective credit controls of commodities. First, they should be accompanied by general credit control measures. This is because the clever businessmen can obtain credit from the banks by offering other securities and use the funds so obtained to finance the speculative holdings of the stocks of sensitive commodities. Therefore, if the selective credit controls are to succeed in preventing the rise in prices of sensitive commodities, they have to be accompanied by general credit controls aimed at reducing the capacity of banks to lend money. It also follows from above that end-use or purpose of all credit ought to be taken into account by the banks and credit advanced accordingly if selective credit controls are to be effective. In India the selective credit controls have been in operation since 1956 to check the rise in prices of sensitive commodities.

The success of the selective credit controls also depends upon the extent to which the funds from *non-bank sources* (*i.e.*, from their own funds and also from the unregulated money market) is available to the businessmen. When the bank credit for a particular purpose is reduced, the businessmen can use their own funds or borrow from non-regulated money markets for speculative holding of inventories. In India today the businessmen have large quantities of black money with them which they generally use for speculative holding of inventories of sensitive commodities and in this way succeed in defeating the purpose of selective controls.

3. Supply Management through Imports

To correct excess demand relative to aggregate supply, the latter can also be raised by importing goods in short supply. In India, to check the rise in prices of foodgrains, edible oils, sugar etc., the Government has often taken steps to increase imports of goods in short supply to enlarge their available supplies. When inflation is of the type of *supply-side inflation*, imports are increased to augment the domestic supplies of goods. To increase imports of goods in short supply the Government can reduce customs duties on them so that their imports become cheaper and therefore their imports help in containing inflation. For example, in 2008-09 the Indian Government removed customs duties on imports of wheat and rice and reduced them on oilseeds, steel etc. to increase their supplies in India. Besides, to increase the domestic supplies the government can ban the exports of some commodities for some time. Thus, in 2010 the Indian Government banned the exports of onions and pulses.

At times of inflationary expectations, there is a tendency on the part of businessmen to hoard goods for speculative purposes. The attempt by the Government to import goods in short supply would compel the hoarders to release their hoarded stocks. This will have a favourable impact on prices of these goods. However, when international prices of commodities are high, their imports cannot be very helpful for tackling domestic inflation. This was the case in 2009-10 and 2010-11 in India when commodities such as sugar, wheat, oil seeds could not be imported sufficiently to augment domestic supplies because of their high world prices.

4. Incomes Policy: Freezing Wages

Another anti-inflationary measure which has often been suggested is the avoidance of wage increases which are unrelated to improvements in productivity. This requires exercising control over wage-income. As seen in the previous chapter, it is through wage-price spiral that inflation gets momentum. When cost of living rises due to the initial rise in prices, workers demand higher wages to compensate for the rise in cost of living. When their wage demands are conceded to, it gives rise to cost-push inflation. And this generates inflationary expectations which add fuel to the fire. To check this vicious circle of wages-chasing prices, an important measure will be to exercise control over wages. However, if wages are raised equal to the increase in the productivity of labour, then it will have no inflationary effect. Therefore, the proposal has been to *freeze wages* in the short run and wages should be linked with the changes in the level of productivity over a long period of time. According to this, wage increases should be allowed to the extent of rise in labour productivity only. This will check the net growth in aggregate demand relative to aggregate supply of output.

However, freezing wages and linking it with productivity only irrespective of what happens to the cost of living has been strongly opposed by trade unions. It has been validly pointed out why freeze wages only to ensure social justice the other kinds of income such as rent, interest and profits should also be freezed similarly. Indeed, effective way to control inflation will be to adopt a broad-based incomes policy which should cover not only wages but also profits, interest and rental incomes.

It is thus clear that with the adoption of various monetary, fiscal and other policy measures, the aggregate demand can be reduced on the one hand and the aggregate supply of output can be increased on the other. This would help in bridging the gap between aggregate demand and aggregate supply which would enable us to contain the inflationary pressures in the economy.

QUESTIONS FOR REVIEW

1. What is meant by '*inflationary gap*' How does it cause a continuous and presistent increase in general price level ?
2. Define demand-pull inflation. How, is it caused by the Government's insistence of keeping the market rate of interest low so as to stimulate investment.
3. What are the main factors that cause cost-push inflation ? Suggest measures to control cost-push inflation ?
4. Distinguish between demand-pull inflation and cost-push inflation. How are they often intertwined ?
5. Inflation may originate because of cost-push but it cannot be sustained for long unless it is supported by demand-pull inflation.
6. Inflation in the less developed countries can be explained in terms of the structural features of these economies
7. Inflation is inevitable in an economy attempting to grow rapidly in the presence of structural bottlenecks, Discuss.
8. An inflationary process may begin on the supply side but it will not continue for long unless there is increase in demand. Discuss.
9. Distinguish between demand-pull and cost-push inflation. How can demand-pull inflation be controlled?
10. Inflation is a purely monetary phenomenon. Explain your viewpoint making use of Fisher's equation of exchange.
11. Define inflation. Explain its effects on (*a*) creditors and deletors (b) persons of fixed income group.
12. Explain the effects of inflation on output and distribution of income.
13. How does inflation distort the pattern of production and distribution in an economy?

14. Define inflation. What measures would you suggest to control it?
15. What are the main causes of inflation in India? Which policies of government has helped to check rise in prices ?
16. What is meant by inflation falacy ? It it valid in case of India.
17. State the Fisher's equation describing the relation between real rate of interest, inflation rate and nominal interest rate. What is the effect of inflation rate on real rate of interest and nominal rate of interest.
18. What is Fischer effect ? Show how nominal interest rate depends on inflation rate.
19. What are social costs of inflation ? Are they significant ?
20. Explain the role of monetary policy for controlling inflation. Point out the limitations of tight monetary policy for curbing inflation.
21. Explain how fiscal policy can be used to check inflation. Comment on its efficacy.
22. What is supply-side inflation ? How can it be tackled ?

APPENDIX TO CHAPTER 26

MEASUREMENT OF INFLATION AND PRICE INDICES : WPI AND CPI

We have explained above that inflation has been one of the important problems facing the economies of the world. Precisely stated, *inflation is the rate of change of general price level during a period of time*. And the general price level in a period is the result of inflation in the past. Through rate of inflation economists measure the *cost of living* in an economy. Let us explain how rate of inflation is measured. Suppose P_{t-1} represents the price level on 31st March 2012 and P_t represents the price level on 31st Mach 2013. Then the rate of inflation in year 2012-13 wIll be equal to

$$\pi = \frac{P_t - P_{t-1}}{P_{t-1}}$$

where p represents rate of inflation. Suppose Consumer Price Index (CPI) on March 31 , 2012 which was 250, it rose to 275 on March 31, 2013, rate of inflation in 2012-13 will be

$$\pi = \frac{275-250}{250} \times 100 = \frac{25}{250} \times 100 = 10\%$$

Thus rate of inflation during 2012-13 will be 10 per cent. This is called *point-to-point inflation* rate. There are 52 weeks in a year, average of price indexes of 52 weeks of a year (say 2011-12) can be calculated to compare the average of price indexes of 52 weeks of year 2012-13 and find the inflation rate on the basis of average weekly price levels of a year. In both these ways rate of inflation in different years is measured and compared. We now explain in detail how inflation is measured with the help of various price indices.

Measuring Inflation with Price Indices

Having explained the meaning of inflation we will now explain how inflation rate is measured. As inflation means rate of change in average or general price level over a period time we need to explain how the prices of various individual goods are aggregated to obtain the measure of general price level. This is done through construction of price index numbers. There are a number of price indices that are prepared to assess the changes in price level (i.e. inflation). The following types of price indices are generally used :

1. The Consumer Price Index Number (CPI)
2. The Wholesale Price Index (WPI)
3. GDP Deflator

In India inflation is generally measured by changes in wholesale price index (WPI), while in the developed countries such as US it is consumer price index (CPI) that is used for this purpose. We explain below all these three price indices.

Consumer Price Index (CPI)

The Consumer Price Index (CPI) is used to measure *cost of living* of the people and is based on *retail prices* of the selected goods constituting the consumption basket of a particular group of consumers. For instance, in India CPI is prepared for (1) industrial workers (CPI-IW) and for its preparation retail prices of those goods are selected which generally form the consumption basket of industrial workers. Second, consumer price index for agricultural labour (CPI-AL) is prepared and this includes the retail prices of consumer goods that constitutes the consumption basket of agricultural labour. Third, CPI for urban non-manual employees (CPI-UNME) is constructed to measure retail prices of those consumer goods and services purchased by urban non-manual employees.

Method of Constructing Consumer Price Index (CPI)

We now proceed to explain the method used for constructing consumer price index (CPI). The first step is to *choose the basket of consumer goods and services* that is generally purchased by a specific group of consumers, for example, industrial workers.

The second step in the construction of CPI is to select the base year. In India at present the year 2001 is selected as the base year for the construction CPI for industrial workers. It is the retail prices in the base year with which retail prices of the current year are compared that enable us to obtain the relative price.

The third step is collecting the retail prices for the current year of various goods included in the consumption basket of the specific group of consumers. The price data from different centres or locations in the country is gathered for this purpose. The fourth step involves choosing weights to be given to the prices of different items in the consumption basket of the specific group of consumers. If simple average prices of various items of consumption are used, it would mean treating all items equally for the specific group. However, this is not realistic as consumers spend different amounts on various items. Therefore, different weights are assigned to different items in consumers' basket of goods. The weight assigned to an item is the proportion of expenditure on an item to the consumers' total expenditure on the consumption basket. It is calculated as follows :

Expenditure on an item in the base year = $P_i^0 Q_i^0$

Superscript '0' in the above expression stands for the base year P_i stands for price of an item and Q_i for the quantity of the item. The total expenditure of all items in the consumption basket in the base year is give by :

$$\text{Total expenditure} = \sum_{i=1}^{n} P_i^0 Q_i^0$$

Thus weight assigned to an item is given by

$$W_i = \frac{P_i^0 Q_i^0}{\sum_{i=1}^{n} P_i^0 Q_i^0} \qquad \ldots (1)$$

Suppose expenditure on a commodity of a household, say rice, in a week is ₹ 500 (i.e., $P_i^0 Q_i^0$ = ₹ 500 and total expenditure on all items in its consumption basket is ₹ 1500 (i.e. $\sum_{i=1}^{n} P_i^0 Q_i^0$ = ₹ 1500), then weight to be assign to the item 'rice' will be 500 ÷ 1500 = 0.33).

As said above, a consumer price index expresses the current price relative to its price in the base period. Thus the consumer price index for a period *t* is given by

$$CPI_t = \frac{P^t}{P^0} \times 100 \qquad \ldots (2)$$

Thus, if price of rice in the base year is ₹ 5 per kg and the price in the current period *t* is ₹ 9 per kg. then

$$CPI_t = \frac{9}{5} \times 100 = 180$$

This means the price of rice in the current period has risen by 80 per cent.

But the expression $\frac{P_t}{P_0}$ is price index of and individual item. A general consumer price index is *weighted average* of various items in the consumption basket. Therefore, general consumer price index is written as

$$\text{CPI} = \sum W_i \left(\frac{P_i^t}{P_i^0}\right) \times 100 \quad \ldots (3)$$

Substituting the value of W_i in (3)

We have

$$CPI_i = \sum \left(\frac{P_i^0 Q_i^0}{\Sigma P_i^0 Q_i^0}\right)\left(\frac{P_i^t}{P_i^0}\right) \times 100$$

Simplifying

$$CPI = \frac{\sum Q_i^0 . P_i^t}{\sum Q_i^0 . P_i^0} \times 100 \quad \ldots (4)$$

The expression (4) of consumer price index is known as *Laspeyre's index* as in it takes base year's quantity while finding weighted average of the relative prices of different items.

As example will make clear the process of calculating CPI . This is done in the following table.

Table 26A.1. Calculating CPI

Item	Quantity Q_i^0	Price in 2001 P_i^0	Expenditure in 2001, $P_i^0 Q_i^0$	Price in the Current Period (2012)	Expenditure in the current period $P_i^t . Q_i^t$
Rice	25 kg	₹ 5/kg	₹ 125	₹ 10/kg	250
Pulses	5 kg	₹ 10/kg	₹ 50	₹ 25/kg	125
Clothing	5 m	₹ 20/m	₹ 100	₹ 50/m	250
Housing	1 room set	₹ 500 per one room set	₹ 500	₹ 800	800
			$\sum P_i^0 Q_i^0 = 775$		$\sum P_i^t . Q_i^0 = 1425$

This implies that price in 2012 is 84 per cent higher compared to the base year 2001.

$$\text{CPI} = = \frac{\sum P_i^t Q_i^0}{\sum P_i^0 Q_i^0} \times 100 = \frac{1425}{775} \times 100 = 184$$

Wholesale Price Index (WPI)

While consumer price index is based on retail prices of a few consumer goods making up the consumption basket of a specific group of consumers, wholesale price (WPI) is constructed to measure the *average wholesale prices of all commodities* produced and/or transacted in the economy. Two things must be noted in this regard. First, wholesale price index (WPI) measures wholesale prices of commodities, and not their retail prices. Second, it is based on all commodities produced and/or transacted in the economy. Thus it includes not only consumer goods but also raw materials used in industrial production such as coal, cotton, steel and capital goods such as machines, tractors, pump sets and other equipment. However, WPI does not cover the prices of services such as health, education, transport communication.

The commodities included in the construction of WPI are classified into the following three categories.

1. Primary articles such as food, non-food and minerals
2. Manufactured goods
3. Fuel, power, light and lubricants

In India at present wholesale price index is prepared with 2004-05 as the base year as the base year. Movements in WPI over a period of time is used to measure inflation rate. Since WPI is based on changes in prices of all commodities, from change in inflation rate it can be ascertained which particular group of commodities, for example, whether changes in prices of food products or manufactured goods or of fuel and power are responsible for rise in general price level.

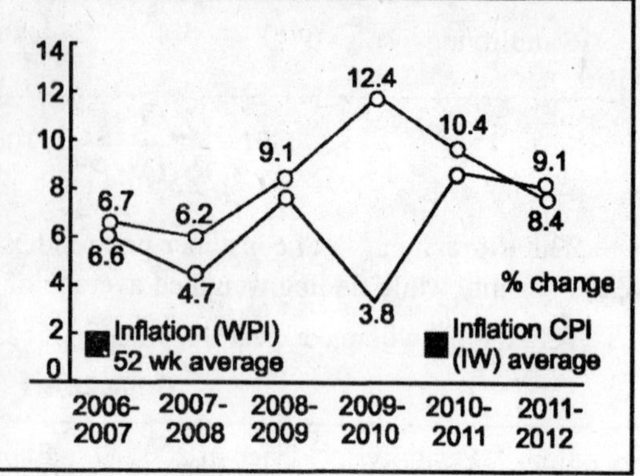

Fig. 26A.1. India's Inflation rate based on CPI (IW) and WPI

The method of constructing WPI is the same used in case of CPI. *The WPI is the weighted average of wholesale prices of all commodities*. The weights to various commodities are assigned on the basis of relative values of different commodities to the total value of commodities produced and/or transacted in the economy. For preparing WPI, price data is collected from all important wholesale markets or centres in the country like that of construction of CPI, Laspeyre's formula is used to construct WPI, namely, base-year's values of commodities produced or transacted are used as weights in its preparation. Thus $\text{WPI} = \dfrac{\sum P_i^t Q_i^0}{\sum P_i^0 Q_i^0} \times 100$

The above formula indicates the percentage change in the price level of commodities in period *t* compared to the base year. If wholesale price index for the year 2011 is 198 with base year 2004-05, then it implies that in 2011 general wholesale price level is 98 per cent higher than in 2004-05. We have depicted in Fig. 26A.1 infaltion rate in India since 2006-07 both in terms of CPI and WPI.

GDP Deflator

As a measure of changes in price level or inflation rate GDP deflator is important because besides all goods it also includes *all services* that go to make up the Gross Domestic Product (GDP). It shows the relation between nominal GDP and real GDP as the two differ because of the changes in prices of commodities and services over a period of time. It may be noted that nominal GDP is the value of GDP at *current prices*, while real GDP is the value of GDP at constant prices (i.e. prices of a certain year taken as the base year).

$$\text{Thus, GDP Deflator} = \frac{\text{Naminal GDP}}{\text{Real GDP}} \times 100$$

Since GDP of a country consists of market value of all *final* goods and services produced in a year,GDP deflator does not include value of *intermediate goods* to avoid double counting. Besides, since the quantities of goods and services in both the nominal GDP and real GDP refer to the current year, weights computed for the construction of WPI will not be fixed but will vary from year to year.

It needs to be emphasized that since GDP deflator measures the changes in prices of goods and services produced domestically, it does not capture the changes in prices of goods imported from abroad, such as patrol and petroleum products.

The calculation of GDP deflator in India is illustrated in the following table where we have calculated it from India's GDP at current prices and GDP at constant prices with 2004-05 as the base year. The last column in this table shows GDP deflator.

Table. 26A.2. GDP Deflator

Year	GDP at current prices (in lakh crore)	GDP at constant prices (2004-05 = 100) (in lakh crore)	GDP Deflator = $\frac{\text{GDP at current prices}}{\text{GDP at 2004-05 prices}} \times 100$
2004-05	29.5	29.5	$\frac{29.5}{29.5} \times 100 = 100$
2005-06	33.6	32.3	$\frac{33.6}{32.3} \times 100 = 104.0$
2006-07	39.2	35.4	$\frac{39.2}{35.4} \times 100 = 110.7$
2007-08	45.6	36.8	$\frac{45.6}{36.8} \times 100 = 123.9$
2008-09	52.5	41.4	$\frac{52.5}{41.4} \times 100 = 126.8$
2009-10	61.0	44.6	$\frac{61.0}{44.6} \times 100 = 136.7$

In India the wholesale price Index (WPI) of all commodities with base year 1993-94 price level at the end of fiscal year is used to measure rate of inflation and is widely reported in the media. Since the wholesale price index does not truly indicate the cost of living, separate consumer price index (CPI) for agricultural labourers and consumer price index (CPI) for industrial workers (with base 1982 = 100) at the end of fiscal year) are constructed to measure rate of inflation. In constructing the consumer price index (CPI) the price of a *basket* of goods which a typical consumer industrial worker or agricultural labourer as the case may be are taken into account. We will explain the nature and causes of inflation in a separate chapter.

PART V

BUSINESS CYCLES AND MACROECONOMIC POLICY

- Analysis of Business Cycles :
- Hicks, Kaldor and Goodwin's Models of Business Cycles
- Monetarist Theory of Business Cycles
- Lucas' New Classical (Rational Expectations) Theory of Business Cycles
- Real Business Cycle Theory
- Economic Stabilisation : Role of Fiscal Policy
- Economic Stabilisation : Monetary Policy

CHAPTER 27
Analysis of Business Cycles

Introduction

Many free enterprise capitalist countries such as USA and Great Britain have registered rapid economic growth during the last two centuries. But economic growth in these countries has not followed steady and smooth upward trend. There has been a long-run upward trend in Gross National Product (GNP), but periodically there have been large short-run fluctuations in economic activity, that is, changes in output, income, employment and prices around this long-term trend. The period of high income, output and employment has been called the period of *expansion, upswing* or *prosperity,* and the period of low income, output and employment has been described as *contraction, recession, downswing* or *depression.* The economic history of the free market capitalist countries has shown that the period of economic prosperity or expansion alternates with the period of contraction or recession. *These alternating periods of expansion and contraction in economic activity has been* called business cycles. They are also known as *trade cycles.* J.M. Keynes writes, "A trade cycle is composed of periods of good trade characterised by rising prices and low unemployment percentages with periods of bad trade characterised by falling prices and high unemployment percentages."[1]

A noteworthy feature about these fluctuations in economic activity is that they are recurrent and have been occurring periodically in a more or less regular fashion. Therefore, these fluctuations have been called business cycles. It may be noted that calling these fluctuations as 'cycles' mean they are periodic and occur regularly, though perfect regularity has not been observed. The duration of a business cycle has not been of the same length; it has varied from a minimum of two years to a maximum of ten to twelve years, though in the past it was often assumed that fluctuations of output and other economic indicators around the trend showed repetitive and regular pattern of alternating periods of expansion and contraction. However, actually there has been no clear evidence of very regular cycles of the same definite duration. Some business cycles have been very short lasting for only two to three years, while others have lasted for several years. Further, in some cycles there have been large swings away from trend and in others these swings have been of moderate nature.

A significant point worth noting about business cycles is that they have been very costly in the economic sense of the word. During a period of recession or depression many workers lose their jobs and as a result large-scale unemployment, which causes loss of output that could have been produced with full-employment of resources, come to prevail in the economy. Besides, during depression many businessmen go bankrupt and suffer huge losses. Depression causes a lot of human sufferings and lowers the levels of living of the people. Fluctuations in economic activity creates a lot of uncertainty in the economy which causes anxiety to the individuals about their future income and employment opportunities and involve a great risk for long-run investment in projects. Who does not remember the great havoc caused by the great depression of the early thirties of the present century? Even boom when it is accompanied by inflation has its social costs. Inflation erodes the real incomes of the people and makes life miserable for the poor people. Inflation distorts allocation of resources by drawing away scarce resources from productive uses to unproductive ones. Inflation redistributes income in favour of the richer

1. J.M. Keynes, *The General Theory of Employment, Interest and Money*, 1936.

sections and also when inflation rate is high, it impedes economic growth. About the harmful effects of the business cycles Crowther writes, "On the one hand, there is the misery and shame of unemployment with all the individual poverty and social disturbances that it may create. On the other hand, there is the loss of wealth represented by so much wasted and idle labour and capital."[2]

Phases of Business Cycles

Business cycles have shown distinct phases the study of which is useful to understand their underlying causes. These phases have been called by different names by different economists. Generally, the following phases of business cycles have been distinguished :

1. Expansion (Boom, Upswing or Prosperity)
2. Peak (upper turning point)
3. Contraction (Downswing, Recession or Depression)
4. Trough (lower turning point)

The four phases of business cycles have been shown in Fig. 27.1 where we start from trough or depression when the level of economic activity *i.e.*, level of production and employment is at the lowest level. With the revival of economic activity the economy moves into the expansion phase, but due to the causes explained below, the expansion cannot continue indefinitely, and after reaching peak, contraction or downswing starts. When the contraction gathers momentum, we have a depression. The downswing continues till the lowest turning point which

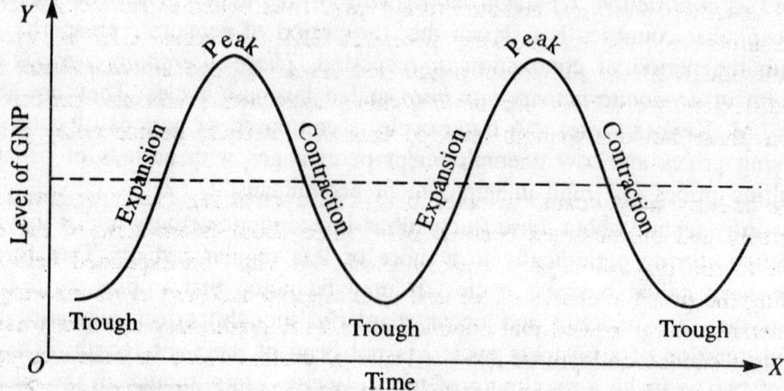

Fig. 27.1. *Four Phases of Business Cycles without Growth Trend*

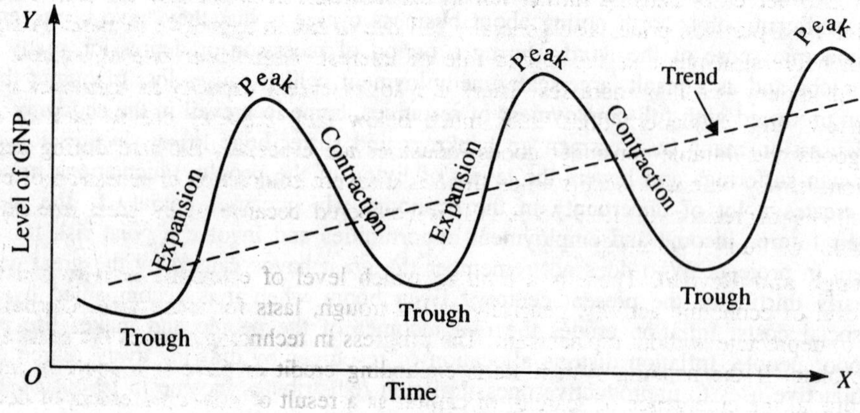

Fig. 27.2. *Cycles with Trend (i.e., Growth)*

2. G. Crowther, *An Outline of Money*, (London 1962), p. 192.

is also called trough is reached. In this way cycle is complete. However, after remaining at the trough for some time the economy revives and again the new cycle starts. Haberler in his important work[3] on business cycles has named the four phases of business cycles as (1) Upswing, (2) Upper turning point, (3) Downswing, and (4) Lower turning point.

There are two types of patterns of cyclic changes. One pattern is shown in Fig. 27.1 where fluctuations occur around a stable equilibrium position as shown by the horizontal line. It is a case of dynamic stability which depicts change but without growth or trend. The second pattern of cyclical fluctuations is shown in Fig. 27.2 where cyclical changes in economic activity take place around a growth path (*i.e.,* rising trend). J.R. Hicks in his model of business cycles explains such a pattern of fluctuations with long-run rising trend in economic activity by imposing factors such as autonomous investment due to population growth and technological progress causing economic growth on the otherwise stationary state. We briefly explain below various phases of business cycles.

Expansion and Prosperity. In its expansion phase, both output and employment increase till we have full-employment of resources and production is at the highest possible level with the given productive resources. There is no involuntary unemployment and whatever unemployment prevails is only of frictional and structural types. Thus, when expansion gathers momentum and we have prosperity, the gap between potential GNP and actual GNP is zero, that is, the level of production is at the maximum production level. A good amount of net investment is occurring and demand for durable consumer goods is also high. Prices also generally rise during the expansion phase but due to high level of economic activity people enjoy a high standard of living.

Then something may occur, whether banks start reducing credit or profit expectations change adversely and businessmen become pessimistic about future state of the economy that bring an end to the expansion or prosperity phase. As shall be explained below, economists differ regarding the possible causes of the end of prosperity and start of downswing in economic activity. Monetarists have argued that contraction in bank credit may cause downswing. Keynes have argued that sudden collapse of expected rate of profit (which he calls marginal efficiency of capital, MEC) caused by adverse changes in expectations of entrepreneurs lowers investment in the economy. This fall in investment, according to him, causes downswing in economic activity.

Contraction and Depression. As stated above, expansion or prosperity is followed by contraction or depression. During contraction, not only there is a fall in GNP but also level of employment is reduced. As a result, involuntary unemployment appears on a large scale. Investment also decreases causing further fall in consumption of goods and services. At times of contraction or depression prices also generally fall due to fall in aggregate demand. A significant feature of depression phase is the fall in rate of interest. With lower rate of interest people's demand for money holdings increases. There is a lot of excess capacity as industries producing capital goods and consumer goods work much below their capacity due to lack of demand. Capital goods and durable consumer goods industries are especially hit hard during depression. Depression, it may be noted, occurs when there is a severe contraction or recession of economic activities. The depression of 1929-33 is still remembered because of its great intensity which caused a lot of human suffering.

Trough and Revival. There is a limit to which level of economic activity can fall. The lowest level of economic activity, generally called trough, lasts for some time. Capital stock is allowed to depreciate without replacement. The progress in technology makes the existing capital stock obsolete. If the banking system starts expanding credit or there is a spurt in investment activity due to the emergence of scarcity of capital as a result of non-replacement of depreciated

3. See G. Haberler, *Prosperity and Depression, A Theoretical Analysis of Cyclical Movements,* Harward University Press, 1960.

capital and also because of new technology coming into existence requiring new types of machines and other capital goods. The stimulation of investment brings about the revival or recovery of the economy. The recovery is the turning point from depression into expansion. As investment rises, this causes induced increase in consumption. As a result industries start producing more and excess capacity is now put into full use due to the revival of aggregate demand. Employment of labour increases and rate of unemployment falls. With this the cycle is complete.

Features of Business Cycles

Though different business cycles differ in duration and intensity they have some common features which we explain below:

1. Business cycles occur *periodically.* Though they do not show same regularity, they have some distinct phases such as expansion, peak, contraction or depression and trough. Further the duration of cycles varies a good deal from minimum of two years to a maximum of ten to twelve years.
2. Secondly, business cycles are *Synchronic.* That is, they do not cause changes in any single industry or sector but are of all embracing character. For example, depression or contraction occur simultaneously in all industries or sectors of the economy. Recession passes from one industry to another and chain reaction continues till the whole economy is in the grip of recession. Similar process is at work in the expansion phase, prosperity spreads through various linkages of input-output relations or demand relations between various industries. and sectors.
3. Thirdly, it has been observed that fluctuations occur not only in level of production but also simultaneously in other variables such as employment, investment, consumption, rate of interest and price level.
4. Another important feature of business cycles is that investment and consumption of durable consumer goods such as cars, houses, refrigerators are affected most by the cyclical fluctuations. As stressed by J.M. Keynes, investment is greatly volatile and unstable as it depends on profit expectations of private entrepreneurs. These expectations of entrepreneurs change quite often making investment quite unstable. Since *consumption of durable consumer goods* can be deferred, it also fluctuates greatly during the course of business cycles.
5. An important feature of business cycles is that consumption of *non-durable goods and services* does not vary much during different phases of business cycles. Past data of business cycles reveal that households maintain a great stability in consumption of non-durable goods.
6. The immediate impact of depression and expansion is on the *inventories of goods.* When depression sets in, the inventories start accumulating beyond the desired level. This leads to cut in production of goods. On the contrary, when recovery starts, the inventories go below the desired level. This encourages businessmen to place more orders for goods whose production picks up and stimulates investment in capital goods.
7. Another important feature of business cycles is *profits fluctuate more than any other type of income.* The occurrence of business cycles causes a lot of uncertainty for businessmen and makes it difficult to forecast the economic conditions. During the depression period profits may even become negative and many businesses go bankrupt. In a free market economy profits are justified on the ground that they are necessary payments if the entrepreneurs are to be induced to bear uncertainty.
8. Lastly, business cycles are *international in character.* That is, once started in one country they spread to other countries through trade relations between them. For example, if there is a recession in the USA, which is a large importer of goods from other countries, will cause a fall in demand for imports from other countries whose

exports would be adversely affected causing recession in them too. Depression of 1930s in USA and Great Britain engulfed the entire capital world.

THEORIES OF BUSINESS CYCLES

We have explained above the various phases and common features of business cycles. Now, an important question is what causes business cycles. Several theories of business cycles have been propounded from time to time. Each of these theories spells out the factors which cause business cycles. Before explaining the modern theories of business cycles we first explain below the *earlier* theories of business cycles as they too contain important elements whose study is essential for proper understanding of the causes of business cycles.

Sun-Spot Theory

This is perhaps the oldest theory of business cycles. Sun-spot theory was developed in 1875 by Stanley Jevons. Sun-spots are storms on the surface of the sun caused by violent nuclear explosions there. Jevons argued that sun-spots affected weather on the earth. Since economies in the olden world were heavily dependent on agriculture, changes in climatic conditions due to sun-spots produced fluctuations in agricultural output. Changes in agricultural output through its demand and input-output relations affect industry. Thus, swings in agricultural output spread throughout the economy.

Other earlier economists also focused on changes in climatic or weather conditions in addition to those caused by sun-spots. According to them, weather cycles cause fluctuations in agricultural output which in turn cause instability in the whole economy. Even today weather is considered important in a country like India where agriculture is still important. In the years when due to lack of monsoon there are drought in the Indian agriculture, it affects the income of farmers and therefore reduce demand for the products of industires. This causes industrial recession. Even in USA in the year 1988 a severe drought in the farm belt drove up the food prices around the world. It may be further noted that higher food prices reduce income available to be spent on industrial goods.

Critical Appraisal. Though the theories of business cycles which emphasise climatic conditions for business cycles contain an element of truth about fluctuations in economic activity, especially in the developing counties like India where agriculture still remains important, they do not offer an adequate explanation of business cycles. Therefore, much reliance is not placed on these theories by modern economists. Nobody can say with certainty about the natue of these sun-spots and the degree to which they affect rain. There is no doubt that climate affects agricultural production. But the climate theory does not adequately explain periodicity of the trade cycle. If there was truth in the climatic theories, the trade cycles may be pronounced in agricultural countries and almost disappear when the country becomes completely industrialised. But this is not the case. Highly industrialised countries are much more subject to business cycles than agricultural countries which are affected more by famines rather than business cycles. Hence variations in climate do not offer complete explanation of business cycles.

Hawtrey's Monetary Theory of Business Cycles

An old monetary theory of business cycles was put forward by Hawtrey.[4] His monetary theory of business cycles relates to the economy which is under gold standard. It will be remembered that economy is said be under gold standard when either money in circulation consists of gold coins or when paper notes are fully backed by gold reserves in the banking system. According to Hawtrey, increases in the quantity of money raises the availability of bank credit for investment. Thus, by increasing the supply of credit expansion in money supply causes rate of interest to fall. The lower rate of interest induces businessmen to borrow more for investment in capital goods and also for investment in keeping more inventories of goods. Thus, Hawtrey argues that lower rate of interest will lead to the expansion of goods and services as

4. R.G. Hawtrey, *Good and Bad Trade,* Constable and Co., London, 1913.

a result of more investment in capital goods and inventories. Higher output, income and employment caused by more investment induces more spending on consumer goods. Thus, as a result of more investment made possible by increased supply of bank credit economy moves into the expansion phase. The process of expansion continues for some time. Increases in aggregate demand brought about by more investment also causes prices to rise. Rising prices lead to the increase in output in two ways. First, when prices begin to rise businessmen think they would rise further which induces them to invest more and produce more because prospects of making profits increase with the rise in prices. Secondly, the rising prices reduces the real value of idle money balances with the people which induces them to spend more on goods and services. In this way rising prices sustain expansion for some time.

However, according to Hawtrey, the expansion process must end. He argued that rise in incomes during the expansion phase induces more expenditure on domestically produced goods as well as more on imports of foreign goods. He further assumes that domestic output and income expand faster than foreign output. As a result, imports of a country increase more than its exports causing *trade deficit* with other countries. If exchange rate remains fixed, trade deficit means there will be *outflow of gold* to settle its balance of payments deficit. Since the country is on gold standard, outflow fo gold will cause reduction in money supply in the economy. The decrease in money supply will reduce the availability of bank credit. Reduction in the supply of bank credit will cause the rate of interest to rise. Rising interest rate will reduce investment in physical capital goods. Reduction in investment will cause the process of contraction to set in. As a result of reduced order for inventories, producers will cut production which will lower income and consumption of goods and services. In this state of reduced demand for goods and services, prices of goods will fall. Once the prices begin to fall businessmen begin to expect that they will fall further. In response to it traders will cut order of goods still causing further fall in output. The fall in prices also causes real value of money balances to rise which induce people to hold larger money holdings with them. In this way contraction process gathers momentum as demand for goods start declining faster and with this economy plunges into depression.

But after a lapse of some time depression will also come to an end and the economy will start to recover. This happens because in the contraction process imports fall drastically due to decrease in income and consumption of households, whereas exports do not fall much. As a result, *trade surplus* emerges which causes *inflow of gold*. The inflow of gold would lead to the expansion of money supply and consequently availability of bank credit for investment will increase. With this, the economy will recover from depression and move into the expansion phase. Thus, the cycle is complete. The process, according to Hawtrey, will go on being repeated regularly.

Critical Appraisal. Hawtrey maintains that the economy under gold standard and fixed exchange rate system makes his model of business cycles self-generating as there is built-in tendency for the money supply to change with the emergence of trade deficit and trade surplus which cause movements of gold between countries and affect money supply in them. Changes in money supply influence economic activity in a cyclical fashion. However, Hawtrey's monetary theory does not apply to the present-day economies which have abandoned gold standard in 1930s. However, Hawtrey's theory still retains its importance because it shows how changes in money supply affects economic activity through changes in price level and rate of interest. In modern monetary theories of trade cycles this relation between money supply and rate of interest plays an important role in determining the level of economic activity.

Under-Consumption Theory

Under-consumption theory of business cycles is a very old one which dates back to the 1930s. Malthus and Sismodi criticised Say's Law which states '*supply creates its own demand*' and argued that consumption of goods and services could be too small to generate sufficient demand for goods and services produced. They attribute over-production of goods due to lack of consumption demand for them. This over-production causes piling up of inventories of goods which results in recession.

Under-consumption theory as propounded by Sismodi and Hobson was not a theory of recurring business cycles. They made an attempt to explain how a free enterprise economy could enter a long-run economic slowdown. A crucial aspect of Sismodi and Hobson's under-consumption theory is the distinction they made between the rich and the poor. According to them, the rich sections in the society receive a large part of their income from returns on financial assets and real property owned by them. Further, they assume that the rich have a large propensity to save, that is, they save a relatively large proportion of their income and therefore, consume a relatively smaller proportion of their income. On the other hand, less well-off people in a society obtain most of their income from work, that is, wages from labour and have a lower propensity to save. Therefore, these less well-off people spend a relatively less proportion of their income consumer goods and services. In their theory, they further assume that during the expansion process, the incomes of the rich people increase relatively more than the wage-income. Thus, during the expansion phase, income distribution changes in favour of the rich with the result that average propensity to save falls, that is, in the expansion process saving increases and therefore consumption demand declines.[5]

According to Sismodi and Hobson, increase in saving during the expansion phase leads to more investment expenditure on capital goods and after some time lag, the greater stock of capital goods enables the economy to produce more consumer goods and services. But since society's propensity to consume continues to fall, consumption demand is not enough to absorb the increased production of consumer goods. In this way, lack of demand for consumer goods or what is called under-consumption emerges in the economy which halts the expansion of the economy. Further, since supply or production of goods increases relatively more as compared to the consumption demand for them, the prices fall. Prices continue falling and go even below the average cost of production bring losses to the business firms. Thus, when under-consumption appears, production of goods becomes unprofitable. Firms cut their production resulting in recession or contraction in economic activity.

Karl Marx and Under-Consumption. It is worth mentioning that Karl Marx, the philosopher of scientific socialism had also predicted the collapse of the capitalist system due to the emergence of under-consumption. He predicted that capitalism would move periodically through expansion and contraction with each peak higher than its previous peak and each crash (*i.e.*, depression) deeper than the last. Ultimately, according to Marx, in a state of acute depression when the cup of misery of working class is full, they will overthrow the capitalist class which exploits them and in this way the new era of socialism or communism would come into existence.

Like other under-consumption theorists, Marx argues that driving force behind business cycles is ever increasing income inequalities and concentration of wealth and economic power in the hands of the few capitalists who own the means of production. As a result, the poor workers lack income to purchase goods produced by the capitalist class resulting in under-consumption or over-production. With the capitalist producers lacking market for their goods, capitalist economy plunges into depression. Then the search for ways of opening of new markets is started. Even wars between capitalist countries take place to capture other countries to find new markets for their products. With the discovery of new methods of production of finding new markets, the economy recovers from depression and the new upswing starts.

Critical Appraisal. The view that income inequalities increase with growth or expansion of the economy and further that this causes recession or stagnation is widely accepted. Therefore, even many modern economies suggest that if growth is to be sustained (that is, if recession or stagnation is to be avoided), then consumption demand must be increasing sufficiently to absorb the increasing production of goods. For this deliberate efforts should be made to reduce in-

5. J.A. Hobson, *The Economics of Unemployment*, London: Allen & Union Ltd., 1922.

equalities in income distribution. Further, under-consumption theory rightly states that income redistribution schemes will reduce the amplitude of business cycles.

Besides, the suggested behaviour of average propensity to save and consume of the property owners and wage earners in this theory have been found to be consistent with the observed phenomena. Even in the theory of economic development the difference in average propensity to save (APS) of the property owners and workers has been widely used.

It is clear from above that under-consumption theory contains some important elements, especially the emergence of the lack of consumption demand as the cause of recession but it is regarded as too simple. There are many features other than growing income inequalities which are responsible for causing recession or trade cycles. Although under-consumption theory concentrate on a significant variable, it leaves too much unexplained.

Over-Investment Theory

It has been observed that over time investment varies more than that of total output of final goods and services and consumption. This has led economists to investigate the causes of variation in investment and how it is responsible for business cycles. Two versions of over-investment theory have been put forward. One theory offered by Hayek emphasises monetary forces in causing fluctuations in investment. The second version of over-investment theory has been developed by Knut Wickshell which emphasises spurts of investment brought about by innovation. We explain below both these versions of over-investment theory. It is worth noting that in both the versions of this theory distinction between natural rate of interest and money rate of interest plays an important role. Natural rate of interest is defined as the rate at which saving equals investment and this equilibrium interest rate reflects marginal revenue product of capital or rate of return on capital. On the other hand, money rate of interest is the rate at which banks give loans to the businessmen.

Hayek's Monetary Version of Over-investment Theory. Hayek[6] suggests that it is monetary forces which cause fluctuations in investment which are prime cause of business cycles. In this respect Hayek's theory is similar to Hawtrey's monetary theory except that it does not involve inflow and outflow of gold causing changes in money supply in the economy.

To begin with, let us assume that the economy is in recession and businessmen's demand for bank credit is therefore very low. Thus, lower demand for bank credit in times of recession pushes down the money rate of interest below the natural rate. This means that businessmen will be able to borrow funds, that is, bank credit at a rate of interest which is below the expected rate of return in investment projects. This induces them to invest more by undertaking new investment projects. In this way, investment expenditure on new capital goods increases. This causes investment to exceed saving by the amount of newly created bank credit. With the spurt in investment expenditure, the expansion of the economy begins. Increase in investment causes income and employment to rise which induces more consumption expenditure. As a result, production of consumer goods increases. According to Hawtrey, the competition between capital goods and consumer goods industries for scarce resources causes their prices to rise which in turn push up the prices of goods and services.

But this process of expansion cannot go on indefinitely because the excess reserves with the banks come to an end which force the banks not to give further loans for investment, while demand for bank credit goes on increasing. Thus, the inelastic supply of credit from the banks and mounting demand for it cause the money rate of interest to go above the natural rate of interest. This makes further investment unprofitable. But at this point of time there has been over-investment in the sense that savings fall short of what is required to finance the desired investment. When no more bank credit is available for investment, there is decline in investment

6. F.A. Hayek, *Monetary Theory and Trade Cycle,* New York Harcourt Brace, 1933 and also *'Profits, Interest and Investment,* London, Routledge, 1935.

which causes both income and consumption to fall and in this way expansion comes to an end and the economy experiences downswing in economic activity.

However, after a lapse of some time the fall in demand for bank credit lowers the money rate of interest which goes below the natural rate of interest. This again gives boost to investment activity and as a result recession ends. In this way alternating periods of expansion and contraction occur periodically.

Wicksell's Over-investment Theory. Over-investment theory developed by Wicksell[7] is of non-monetary type. Instead of focusing on monetary factors it attributes cyclical fluctuations to spurts of investment caused by new innovations introduced by entrepreneurs themselves. The introduction of new innovations or opening of new markets make some investment projects profitable by either reducing cost or raising demand for the products. The expansion in investment is made possible because of the availability of bank credit at a lower money rate of interest. The expansion in economic activity ceases when investment exceeds saving. Again it may be noted that there is over-investment because the level of saving is insufficient to finance the desired level of investment. The end of investment expenditure causes the economy to go into recession. However, another set of innovations occurs or more new markets are found which stimulates investment. Thus, when investment picks up as a result of new innovations, the economy revives and moves into the expansion phase once again.

Appraisal. Though the over-investment theory does not offer an adequate explanation of business cycles, it contains an important element that fluctuations in investment are the prime cause of business cycles. However, it does not offer a valid explanation as to why changes in investment take place quite often. Many exponents of this theory point to the behaviour of banking system that causes diverges between money rate of interest and natural rate of interest. However, as Keynes later on emphasised, investment fluctuates quite often because of changes in profit expectations of entrepreneurs which depends on several economic and political factors operating in the economy. Thus, the theory fails to offer adequate explanation of business cycles.

KEYNES'S THEORY OF BUSINESS CYCLES

J.M. Keynes in his seminal work '*General Theory of Employment, Interest and Money*' made an important contribution to the analysis of the causes of business cycles. According to Keynes's theory, in the short run, the level of income, output or employment is determined by the level of aggregate effective demand. In a free private enterprise, the entrepreneurs will produce that much of goods as can be sold profitably. Now, if the aggregate demand is large, that is, if the expenditure on goods and services is large, the entrepreneurs will be able to sell profitably a large quantity of goods and therefore they will produce more. In order to produce more they will employ a larger amount of resources, both men and materials. In short, a higher level of aggregate demand will result in greater output, income and employment. On the other hand, if the level of aggregate demand is low, smaller amount of goods and services can be sold profitably. This means, that the total quantity of national output produced will be small. And a small output can be produced with a small amount of resources. As a result, there will be unemployment of resources, both labour and capital. Hence, the *changes in the level of aggregate effective demand will bring about fluctuations in the level of income, output and employment.* Thus, according to Keynes, the fluctuations in economic activity are due to the fluctuations in aggregate effective demand. Fall in aggregate effective demand will create the conditions of recession or depression. If the aggregate demand is increasing, economic expansion will take place.

Now the question arises : What causes fluctuations in aggregate demand? The aggregate demand is composed of demand for consumption goods and demand for investment goods. Thus

---

7. Knut Wicksell, *Interest and Prices,* London: Macmillan, 1936.

aggregate demand depends on the total expenditure of the consumers on consumption goods and entrepreneurs on investment goods. Propensity to consume being more or less stable in the short run, fluctuations in aggregate demand depend primarily upon the fluctuations in investment demand. Keynes shows that the fundamental cause of fluctuations in aggregate demand and hence in fluctuations in economic activity is the fluctuations in investment demand. *Investment demand is very unstable and volatile and brings about business cycles in the economy.*

Let us start from the phase of economic expansion to explain Keynes's theory of business cycles. We first explain how in Keynesian theory expansion comes to end and recession or depression sets in. During an economic expansion two factors eventually work to cause investment to fall. First, during the expansion phase increase in demand for capital goods due to large-scale investment activity leads to the rise in prices of capital goods due to rising marginal cost of their production. Higher prices of capital goods raise the cost of investment projects and thereby reduce marginal efficiency of capital (that is, expected rate of return). Secondly, as income rises during expansion phase, the demand for money increases which raises interest rate. Higher interest rate makes some potential, projects unprofitable. Thus, fall in marginal efficiency of capital on the one hand and rise in interest rate on the other cause decline in investment demand. Declining trend of investment, according to Keynes, raises doubts about the *prospective yield on capital goods* which is more important factor determining marginal efficiency of capital than cost of investment projects and rate of interest. When among businessmen pessimism sets in about future profitability of investment projects stock prices tumble. The crash in stock prices worsens the situation and causes investment to fall even more. Besides, fall in prices of shares reduces wealth of households. Wealth, according to Keynes, is an important factor determing consumption. Thus, the decline in stock prices reduces autonomous consumption demand of households. With the fall in both investment and consumption demand aggregate demand declines which result in accumulation of unintended inventories with the firms. This induces the firms to cut production of goods.

It follows from above that besides the rise in cost of capital goods and rise in rate of interest towards the end of the expansion phase, it is the fall in expected prospective yield that reduces the marginal efficiency of capital and causes investment demand to fall. This induces a wave of pessimistic expectations among businessmen and speculators. These pessimistic expectations cause stock prices to tumble which work like adding fuel to the fire. They cause a further fall in the marginal efficiency of capital. *The turning point from expansion to contraction is thus caused by a sudden collapse in marginal efficiency of capital.* In terms of graph, a sudden fall in the marginal efficiency of capital causes on leftward shift in the investment demand curve, for example from I_0I_0 to I_1I_1 in Figure 27.3 resulting in decline in investment from I_0* to I_1* at the given rate of interest. Note that decrease in investment does not automatically decrease in rate of interest to offset the fall in the marginal efficiency of capital.

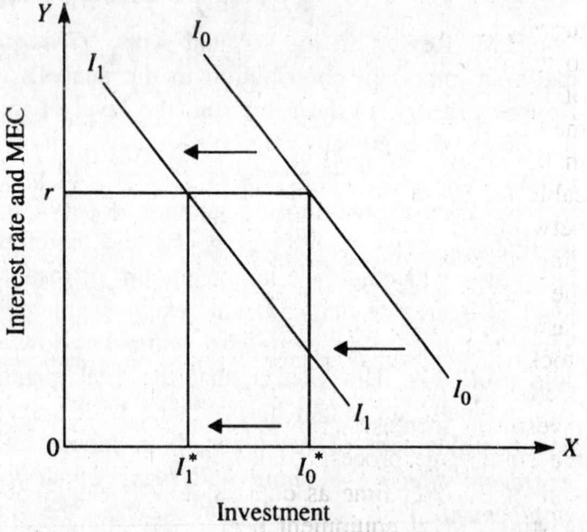

Fig. 27.3. *A Decline in Investment Expenditure due to Fall in Marginal Efficiency of Capital*

However, additional factor that makes Keynes's business cycle theory potent is the working of multiplier which was an important discovery of J.M. Keynes. According to Keynes, a decrease in investment expenditure causes a decline in income which in turn reduces consumption expenditure. The reduction in consumption expenditure further reduces income and this process of reduction in income continues further. The total fall in income (ΔY) due to an initial decline in investment (ΔI) will be equal to $\Delta I \times \frac{1}{1 - MPC}$ where $\frac{1}{1 - MPC}$ is the value of multiplier. If marginal propensity to consume is 0.75, the multiplier will be equal to 4. Thus, a decline in investment by 100 crores will lead to the decline in income by 400 crores. Note that multiplier here works in reverse. Thus, the multiplier process magnifies the effect of decline in investment expenditure on aggregate demand and income and further deepens the depression. As income and output are falling rapidly under the multiplier effect, the employment also goes tumbling down. Thus, the Keynes theoryof income multiplier plays a significant role in causing magnified changes in income, output and employment following a reduction in investment.

It is important to note that, in Keynes's views, wages and prices are not flexible enough to offset the decline in investment expenditure and thereby restore full employment. This is in sharp contrast to the classical theory where changes in wages and prices ensure continuous full employment. In Keynes model wages and prices are "sticky" downward which implies that though wages and prices do not remain constant but when demand falls wages and prices will fall but not sufficient to restore full employment in the economy.

Since wage and price flexibility does not ensure the recovery of the economy out of the state of depression, Keynes thinks that marginal efficiency of capital must rise to stimulate investment. During depression investment falls to a very low level, capital stock begins to wear out and requires replacement. Further, some existing capital equipment becomes technologically obsolete and has to be abandoned. This generates demand for replacement investment. A long period of time is necessary for existing capital to depreciate because most capital goods are durable as well as irreversible. By durability of capital goods we mean that they last for a long time and by irreversibility we mean that they cannot be used for purposes other than those for which they are meant.

Thus, just as the collapse of marginal efficiency of capital is the main cause of the upper turning point, similarly the lower turning point, *i.e.*, change from recession to recovery is due to the revival of the marginal efficiency of capital, that is, expected rate of profit. Restoration of business confidence is the most important, yet the most difficult factor to achieve. Even if the rate of interest is reduced, the investment will not increase. This is because of the fact that in the absence of confidence the profitability of investment may remain so low that no practicable reduction in the rate of interest will stimulate investment. The interval which will elapse between the upper turning point and the start of recovery is conditioned by two factors: (*i*) the time necessary for wearing out of durable capital assets, and (*ii*) the time required to absorb the excess stocks of goods left over from the boom. Just as the expected rate of profit was pushed down by the growing abundance of capital during the period of boom, similarly as the stocks of capital goods are depleted and there grows a scarcity of capital goods, then the expected rate of profit rises thereby inducing the businessmen to invest more. When the level of investment increases, income increases by a magnified amount due to the multiplier effect. So the cumulative process starts upward.

Thus, over time as depreciation of capital stock occurs without replacement and also some existing capital equipment becomes technologically obsolete, the size of capital stock declines. New investment must be undertaken even to produce reduced depression level of output. Thus with the emergence of scarcity of capital, marginal efficiency of capital rises which boosts investment. Once investment increases, it induces further rise in income and consumption demand through the multiplier process. Now, the multiplier works to magnify the effect of increase in investment on raising aggregate demand. The mood of bussinessmen changes from pessimism to optimism which drives up stock prices. All these factors work to lift the economy out of depression and puts it on the road to prosperity.

However, it is noteworthy that the recovery process from depression takes a very long time. Keynes argued that Government should not wait for long for the natural recovery to occur. This is because persistence of depression creates a lot of human sufferings. He, therefore, advocated for the active intervention by the Government to raise aggregate through fiscal policy, that is, stepping up its expenditure or reducing taxes. Thus, he argued for the adoption of policy of deficit budget to boost aggregate demand so that economy is lifted out of depression.

It may be noted that Keynes' business cycle theory is self-generating. In it the economy passes through a long phase of expansion. But eventually some forces automatically work for example, the growing abundance of capital stock, which reduces marginal efficiency of capital. Pessimisin overtakes businessmen. This causes reduction in investment which is responsible for bringing about downswing in the economy. The idea that it is the fluctuations in investment that bring about the fluctuations in the level of economic activity is an important contribution made by Keynes. Of course, even before Keynes, it was believed that the fluctuations in the investment demand have something to do with the business cycles, but a systematic exposition was lacking. Keynes propounded a definite relationship between a change in investment and the resulting change in income and employment. This relationship is embodied in his famous theory of multiplier.

The Critical Appraisal of Keynes's Theory

J.M. Keynes has made three important contributions to the business cycle theory. First, it is fluctuations in investment that cause changes in aggregate demand which bring about changes in economic activity (*i.e.*, income, output, and employment). Secondly, fluctuations in investment demand are caused by changes in expectations of businessmen regarding making of profits (that is, marginal efficiency of capital). Thirdly, Keynes put forward an important theory of multiplier which tells us how changes in investment bring about magnified changes in the level of income and employeemnt.

But the Keynesian theory of multiplier alone does not offer a full and satisfactory explanation of the trade cycles. A basic feature of the trade cycle is its cumulative character both on the upswing as well as on the downswing *i.e.*, once economic activity starts rising or falling, it gathers momentum and for a time feeds on itself. Thus, what we have to explain is the cumulative character of economic fluctuations. The theory of multiplier alone does not prove adequate for this task. For example, suppose that investment rises by 100 rupees and that the magnitude of multiplier is 4. From the theory of multiplier we know that national income will rise by 400 and if multiplier is the only force at work, that will be the end of the matter, with the economy reaching a new stable equilibrium at a higher level of national income. But in real life this is not likely to be so, for a rise in income produced by a given rise in investment will have further repercussions in the economy. This reaction is described in the *principle of the accelerator*. According to the principle of acceleration, a change in national income will tend to induce changes in the rate of investment. *While multiplier refers to the change in income as a result of change in investment, the acceleration principle describes the relationship between a change in investment as a result of change in income.*

In the above example, when income has risen by 400 rupees, people's spending power has risen by an equivalent amount. This will induce them to spend more on goods and services. When the demand for goods rises, initially this will be met by overworking the existing plant and machinery. All this leads to an increase in profits with the result that businessmen will be induced to expand their productive capacity and will instal new plants, *i.e.*, they will invest more than before. Thus, *a rise in income leads to a further induced increase in investment.* The accelerator describes this relation between an increase in income and the resulting increase in investment. Thus, Samuelson combined the accelerator principle with the multiplier and showed that the interaction between the two can bring about cyclical fluctuations in economic activity.

SAMUELSON'S MODEL OF BUSINESS CYCLES : INTERACTION BETWEEN MULTIPLIER AND ACCELERATOR

We have briefly explained above the Keynes made an important contribution to the understanding of the cyclical fluctuations by pointing out that it is the ups and downs in investment demand, depending as it is on the profit expectations of the entrepreneurs, that causes changes in aggregate demand which affect the levels of income, output and employment. Further, by putting forward the theory of multiplier, Keynes has shown how the efect of increase and decrease in investment on output and employment get magnified when multiplier is working during either the upswing or downswing of a business cycle. However, Keynes did not explain the cyclical and cumulative nature of the fluctuations in economic activity. This is because Keynes did not give any importance to the accelerator in his explanation of business cycles. Samuelson in his seminal paper[8] convincingly showed that it is the interaction between the multiplier and accelerator that gives rise to cyclical fluctuations in economic activity. The multiplier alone cannot adequately explain the cyclical and cumulative nature of the economic fluctuations. An autonomous increase in the level of investment raises income by a magnified amount depending upon the value of the multiplier. This increase in income further induces the increases in investment through the acceleration effect. The increase in income brings about increase in aggregate demand for goods and services. To produce more goods we require more capital goods for which extra investment is undertaken. Thus the relationship between investment and income is one of mutual interaction; investment affects income which in turn affects investment demand and in this process income and employment fluctuate in a cyclical manner.

We have shown below in Fig. 27.4 how income and output will increase by even larger amount when accelerator is combined with the Keynesian multiplier.

where ΔI_a = Increase in Autonomous Investment

ΔY = Increase in Income.

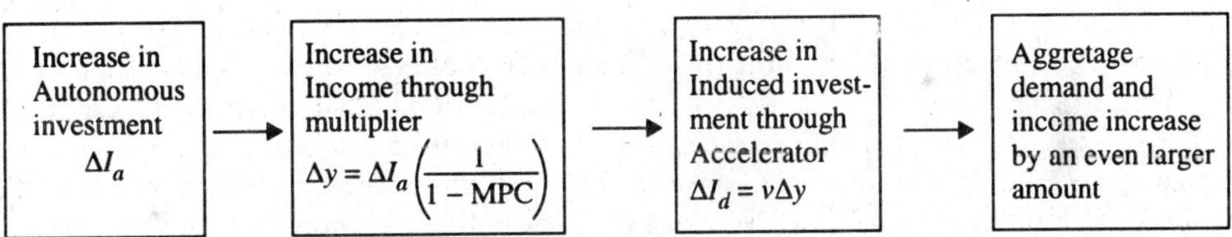

Fig. 27.4. *Combining Accelerator with Keynesian Multiplier*

$\frac{1}{1 - MPC}$ = Size of Multiplier where MPC = Marginal Propensity to Consume.

ΔI_d = Increase in Induced Investment

v = Size of accelerator.

Fluctuations in investment are the main cause of instability in a free private-enterprise economy. This instability further increases due to the interaction of the multiplier and accelerator. The changes in any component of aggregate demand produce a multiplier effect whose magnitude depends upon the marginal propensity to consume. When consumption, income and output increase under the influence of multiplier effect, they induce further changes in investment and the extent of this induced investment in capital goods industries depends on the capital-output ratio, that is, the interaction between the multiplier and accelerator without any external shocks can give rise to the business cycles whose pattern differs depending upon the magnitudes of

8. Samuelson, P.A. "Interaction Between the Multiplier Analysis and the Principle of Acceleration" in *Review of Economic Statistics,* May 1939, p. 751.

the marginal propensity to consume and capital-output ratio. The model of interaction between multiplier and accelerator can be mathematically represented as under:

$$Y_t = C_t + I_t \quad ...(i)$$

$$C_t = C_a + c\,(Y_{t-1}) \quad ...(ii)$$

$$I_t = I_a + v\,(Y_{t-1} - Y_{t-2}) \quad ...(iii)$$

Where Y_t, C_t, I_t stand for income, consumption and investment respectively for a period t, C_a stands for autonomous consumption, I_a for autonomous investment, c for marginal propensity to consume and v for the capital-output ratio or accelerator.

From the above equations it is evident that consumption in a period t is a function of income of the previous period Y_{t-1}. That is, one period lag has been assumed for income to determine the consumption of a period. As regards induced investment in period t, it is taken to be the function of the change in income in the previous period. This means that there is two periods gap for changes in income to determine induced investment. In the equation (*iii*) above, induced investment equals $v(Y_{t-1} - Y_{t-2})$ or $v(\Delta Y_{t-1})$. Substituting equations (*ii*) and (*iii*) in equation (*i*) we have the following income equation which states how changes in income are dependent on the values of marginal propensity to consume (c) and capital-output ratio v (*i.e.*, accelerator).

$$Y_t = C_a + c(Y_{t-1}) + I_a + v\,(Y_{t-1} - Y_{t-2}) \quad ...(iv)$$

In static equilibrium, the level of income determined will be:

$$Y = C_a + cY + I$$

This is due to the fact that in static equilibrium, given the data of the determining factors, the equilibrium level of income remains uncharged, that is, in this case, $Y_t = Y_{t-1} = Y_{t-2} = Y_{t-n}$ so that period lags have no influence at all and accelerator is reduced to zero. Thus, in a dynamic state when autonomous investment changes, the equation (*iv*) describes the path which a disequilibrium system follows to reach either a final equilibrium state or moves away from it. But whether the economy moves towards a new equilibrium or deviates away from it depends on the values of marginal propensity to consume (c) and capital-output ratio v (*i.e.*, accelerator).

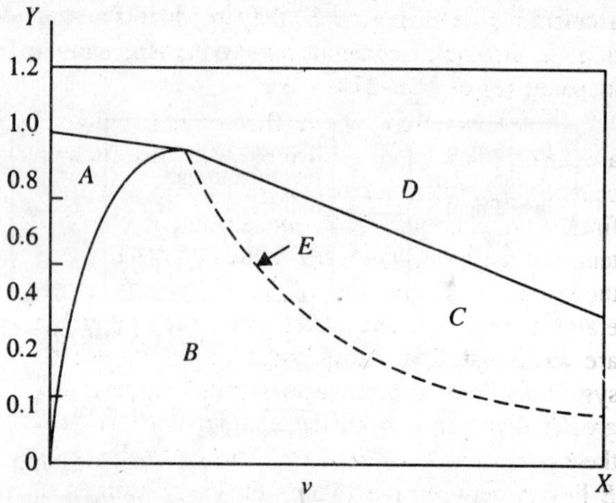

Fig. 27.5. *Combinations of c & v*

By taking different combinations of the values of marginal propensity to consume (c) and capital-output ratio (v), Samuelson has described different paths which the economy will follow. The various combinations of the values of marginal propensity to consume and capital-output ratio (which respectively determine the magnitudes of multiplier and accelerator) are shown in Fig. 27.5. The four paths or patterns of movements which the economic activity (as measured by gross national product or income) can have depending upon various combinations of the values of marginal propensity to consume (c) and capital-output ratio (v) are depicted in Fig. 27.6. When the combinations of the value of marginal propensity to consume (c) and capital-output ratio (v) lie within the region marked A, with a change in autonomous investment, the gross national product or income moves upward or downward at a decreasing rate and finally reaches a new equilibrium as is shown in panel (*a*) of Fig. 27.6. If the values of c and v are such that they lie within the region B, the change in autonomous investment or autonomous consumption will generate fluctuations in income which follow the pattern of a series of *damped cycles* whose amplitudes go on declining until the cycles disappear as is shown in panel (*b*) of Fig. 27.6.

The region *C* in Fig. 27.6 represents the combinations of *c* and *v* which are relatively high as compared to the region *B* and determine such values of multiplier and accelerator that bring about explosive cycles, that is, the fluctuations of income with successively greater and greater amplitude. The situation is depicted in panel (*c*) of Fig. 27.6 which shows that the system tends to explode and diverges greatly from the equilibrium level. The region *D* provides the combinations of *c* and *v* which cause income to move upward or downward at an increasing rate which has somehow to be restrained if the cyclical movements are to occur. This is depicted in panel (*d*) of Fig. 13.6. Like the values of multiplier and accelerator of region *C*, their values in region *D* cause the system to *explode* and diverge from the equilibrium state by an increasing amount.

In a special case when values of *C* and *V* (and therefore the magnitudes of multiplier and accelerator) lie in region *E*, they produce fluctuations in income of *constant amplitude* as is shown in panel (*e*) of Fig. 27.6.

It follows from above that region *A* and *B* are alike, they after a disturbance caused by a change in autonomous investment or consumption finally bring about stable equilibrium in the system. On the other hand, the values of *c* and *v* and therefore the magnitudes of multiplier and accelerator of region *C* and *D* resemble each other but are such that they cause great instability in the system as both of these values cause successively greater divergence from the equilibrium level and the system tends to explode. The case of region *E* lies in between the two as the combinations of values of *c* and *v* in it are such that cause cyclical movements of income which neither move toward nor away from the equilibrium.

It is worth noting that all the above five cases do not give rise to cyclical fluctuations or business cycles. *It is only combinations of c and v lying in regions B, C and E that produce business cycles.* The values of accelerator and multiplier in the region *A* are such that with a disturbance caused by a change in autonomous investment or autonomous consumption, the economic activity (as measured by the level of in-

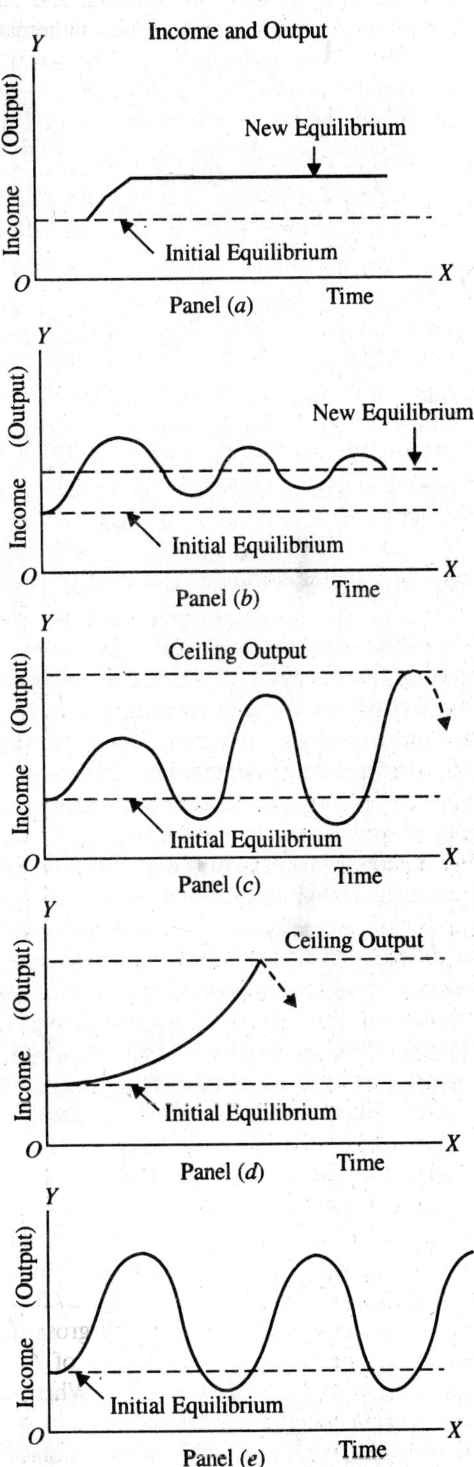

Fig. 27.6. *Interaction between Multiplier and Accelerator: Different Patterns of Income (output) movements for various values of c and v*

come or Gross National Product) moves smoothly from an initial equilibrium to a new equilibrium with no cyclical fluctuations or oscillations. On the other hand, the values of c and v (and therefore of multiplier and accelerator) of the region B produce cyclical fluctuations which are of the type of *damped oscillations* that tend to disappear over time, that is, the amplitude of the cycles shrinks to zero over a period of time. However, this contradicts the historical experience which reveals that there is no tendency for the cyclical movements to disappear or die out over time. However, it is worth noting that the case B explains the impact of a single disturbance on income and employment. For example, the effect of a one time increase in autonomous investment goes on diminishing over time if no other disturbance takes place. However, in reality, further disturbances such as technological advances, innovations, natural disasters and man-made disasters such as security scam in India in 1991-92 do take place quite frequently and at random intervals and in a way they provide shocks to the system.[9] Thus, *the values of c and v of region B can generate cyclical fluctuations over time without dying out if the above-mentioned disturbances are occurring frequently at random.* This results in business cycles whose duration and amplitude are quite irregular and not uniform. As a matter of fact, the business cycles in the real world also reveal such irregular pattern. To sum up, "*what otherwise shows up as a tendency for the cycle to disappear in case B may be converted into unending sequence* of cycles by the addition of randomly disturbed erratic shock system."[10]

In case of the values of multiplier and accelerator falling within the region C, though they generate continued oscillations, the cycles produced by them tend to become 'explosive' (*i.e.* their amplitude tends to increase greatly). But they are not consistent with the real world situation where oscillations do not become explosive. However, the values of multiplier and accelerator falling within region C can be made consistant with the actual world situation by incorporating in the analysis the so called buffers. Buffers are the factors which impose upper limit or ceiling on the expansion of income and output on the one hand or impose a lower limit or floor on the contraction of output and income on the other. With the inclusion of these buffers the otherwise explosive upward and downward fluctuations arising out of values of multiplier (or *MPC*) and accelerator (or capital-output ratio) of the region C can become limited cyclical fluctuations, characteristic of the real world situation.

What has been said about case C above also applies to region D where the values of multiplier and acclerator are such that give rise to *directly explosive upward or downward movement* which can be restrained by the factors determining the ceiling and floor. However, the adequate explanation of the business cycles in this case would require the reasons why the system starts moving in the reverse direction, say, after striking the ceiling. Hicks in his famous theory of the business cycles provides the reasons which cause movement of the system in the reverse direction after it hits the ceiling or the floor as the case may be. Hicks theory of business cycles will be explained below at length.

Lastly, the case E represents a situation where the business cycles neither try to disappear, nor try to explode, they go on continually with a *constant amplitude*. This however contradicts the real world situation and is quite impossible. This is because in the real world situation, business cycles differ a good deal in amplitude and duration.

Summing Up. We have explained the interaction of multiplier and accelerator in case of various values of marginal propensity to consume (c) and capital-output ratio (v). On the basis of the interaction of the multiplier and accelerator the two categories of business cycle theories have been put forward. One category of these business cycle theories assumes the values of multiplier and accelerator which generate explosive cycles. For example, Hicks' theory of busi-

9. The concept of erratic shocks has been put forward by a Nobel Prize winner in economics R. Frisch "Propagation Problems and Impulse Problems in Dynamic Economics" in *Economic Essays in Honour of Gustav Cassel.* Allen and Unwin, 1993, pp. 171-205.
10. Shapiro Edward, *Macroeconomic Analysis,* Fourth Edition, 1978, p. 378.

ness cycles falls in this category. On the other hand, Hansen has propounded a business cycle theory based on the interaction of multiplier with a *weak* accelerator which produces only damped oscillations. Further, as indicated above, the interaction theories have been modified either by incorporating in the analysis erratic shocks or random disturbances or by including so called buffers which check the upward movement of income and output by imposing ceiling of expansion and checking a downward movement by imposing a floor on the contraction of output. One of the famous theories of business cycles based on the interaction of multiplier and accelerator which also incorporate buffers in his analysis of fluctuations is that put forward by the noted English economist J.R. Hicks. We discuss below his theory of business cycles in detail.

Table 27.1. A Multiplier-Acceleration Interaction Model

Period 1	*Autonomous Investment* 2	*Induced Consumption (c = 2/3)* 3	*Induced Investment (v = 2)* 4	*Change in Income from the base period t* 5
	Rs. in Crores	Rs. in Crores	Rs. in Crores	Rs. in Crores
t	0	0	0	0
t + 1	10	0	0	10
t + 2	10	6.7	13.4	30.1
t + 3	10	20.0	26.6	56.6
t + 4	10	37.8	35.6	83.4
t + 5	10	55.6	35.6	101.2
t + 6	10	67.6	23.8	101.2
t + 7	10	67.6	0.2	67.8
t + 8	10	51.8	–10.0	51.8
t + 9	10	34.6	–10.0	33.8
t + 10	10	23.0	–10.0	23.0
t + 11	10	15.4	–10.0	15.4
t + 12	10	10.2	–10.0	10.2
t + 13	10	6.8	– 6.8	10.0
t + 14	10	6.6	+ 0.2	16.8

A Numerical Example of the Interaction of the Multiplier and Accelerator

How the interaction between the multiplier and accelerator gives rise to the cyclical movements in economic activity (as measured by income or output) will become clear from Table 27.1. In formulating this table we have assumed that marginal propensity to consume (c) being equal to 2/3 or 0.66 and capital-output ratio (v) or accelerator being equal to 2. Further, one period time lag has been assumed which implies that an increase in income in a period induces the increase in consumption in the next period. It is assumed that initially in period $t + 1$, autonomous investment is of Rs. 10 crores. In period $t + 3$, with autonomous investment being maintained constant at Rs. 10 crores, the deviation of total income in the period $t + 3$ as compared to the base period will be equal to 10 + 20 + 26.6 = Rs. 56.6 crores. Similarly, the changes in induced consumption and induced investment and hence in income brought about by the initial increase in autonomous investment of Rs. 10 crores which is maintained throughout, can be found out. It will be seen from column 5 of the Table 13.1 that there are large fluctuations in income. Under the influence of the interaction between the multiplier and acceelrator, the income increases up to the period $t + 6$. In other words, period up to $t + 6$ represents the expansion phase or upswing of the business cycle. Therefore, the period $t + 6$ is the upper turning point of the business cycle beyond which the contraction phase or downswing of the business cycle begins. It will be further observed that beyond the period $t + 13$, income again starts rising, that is, *recovery from the depression begins.* Thus, $t + 13$ represents the lower turning point of the business cycle. In this way we see that the interaction between the multiplier and accelerator can give rise to the cyclical movements of the economic activity and its various phases. It is worth mentioning that we have taken particular values of marginal propensity to consume (which determine the size of the multiplier) and capital-output ratio (which determines the size of the accelerator). The other values of multiplier and accelerator that have been explained above would give rise to the different patterns of fluctuations.

HICKS' THEORY OF BUSINESS CYCLES

Hicks[11] put forward a complete theory of business cycles based on the interaction between the multiplier and accelerator by choosing certain values of marginal propensity to consume (c) and capital-output ratio (v) which he thinks are representative of the real world situation. According to Hicks, the values of marginal propensity to consume and capital-output ratio fall in either region C or D of Fig. 27.5. As seen above, in case values of these parameters lie in the region C, they produce *cyclical movements* (*i.e.*, oscillations) whose amplitude increases over time and if they fall in region D they produce an *explosive upward movement* of income or output without oscillations. To explain business cycles of the real world which do not tend to explode, Hicks has incorporated in his analysis the role of buffers. On the one hand, *he introduces output ceiling* when all the given resources are fully employed and prevent income and output to go beyond it, and, on the other hand, he visualises a *floor or the lower* limit below which income and output cannot go because some autonomous investment is always taking place.

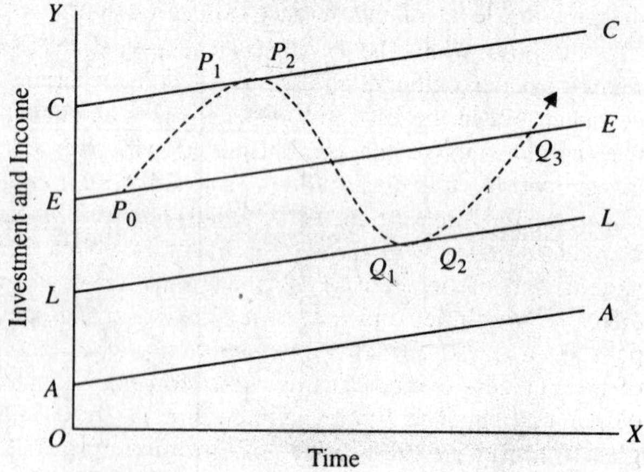

Fig. 27.7. *The Hicks' Model of Business Cycles*

Another important features of Hicks' theory is that business cycles in the economy occur in the background of economic growth (*i.e.*, the rising trend of real income of output over time). In other words, cyclical fluctuations in real output of goods and services take place *above and below this rising line of trend* or growth of income and output. Thus in his theory he explains business cycles along with an equilibrium rate of growth. In Hicks's theory of long-run equilibrium growth that is determined by rate of increase of autonomous investment over time and, therefore, long-run equilibrium growth of income is determined by the autonomous investment and the magnitudes of multiplier and accelerator. Hicks assumes that autonomous investment, depending as it is on technological progress, innovations and population growth, grows at a constant rate. With further assumptions of stable multiplier and accelerator, equilibrium income will grow at the same rate as autonomous investment. It follows therefore that the failure of actual output to increase along the equilibrium growth path, some times to move above it and some times to move below it determines the business cycles.

Hick's Theory of business cycles has been explained with the help of the Fig. 27.7. In this figure, AA line represents autonomous investment. Autonomous investment is that investment which is not induced by changes in income and is made by entrepreneur as a result of technological progress or innovations or population growth. Hicks assumes that autonomous investment grows annually at a constant rate given by the slope of the line AA. Given the marginal propensity to consume, the simple multiplier is determined. Then the magnitude of multiplier and autonomous investment together determine the equilibrium path of income shown by the

11. Hicks, J.R., A *Contribution to the Theory of Trade Cycles,* Oxford University Press, p. 50.

line *LL*. Hicks calls this the floor line as this sets the lower limits below which income (output) cannot fall because of a given rate of growth of autonomous investment and the given size of the multiplier. But induced investment has not yet been taken into account. If national income grows from one year to the next, as it would move along the line *LL*, there is some amount of induced investment via accelerator. The line *EE* shows the equilibrium growth path of national income determined by autonomous investment and the combined effect of the multiplier and accelerator. *FF* is the full employment ceiling. It is a line that shows the maximum national output at any period of time when all the available resources of the economy are fully employed. Given the constant growth of autonomous investment, the magnitude of multiplier and the induced investment determined by the accelerator, the economy will be moving along the *equilibrium growth* path line *EE*. Thus starting from point *E*, the economy will be in equilibrium moving along the path *EE* determined by the combined effect of multiplier and accelerator and the growing level of the autonomous investment.

Suppose when the economy reaches point P_0 along the path *EE*, there is an *external shock*—say an outburst of investment due to certain innovation or jump in governmental investment. When the economy experiences such an outburst of autonomous investment it pushes the economy above the equilibrium growth path *EE* after point P_0. The rise in autonomous investment due to external shock *causes national income to increase at a greater rate than that shown* by the slope of *EE*. This greater increase in national income will cause further increase in induced investment through acceleration effect. This increase in induced investment causes national income to increase by a magnified amount through multiplier. So under the combined effect of multiplier and accelerator, national income or output will rapidly expand along the path from P_0 to P_1. Movement from P_0 to P_1 represents the upswing or expansion phase of the business cycle. But this expansion must stop at P_1 because this is the full employment output ceiling. The limited human and material resources of the economy do not permit a greater expansion of national income than shown by the ceiling line *CC*. Therefore, when point P_1 is reached the rapid growth of national income must come to an end. Prof. Hicks assumes that the full employment ceiling grows at the same rate as autonomous investment. Therefore, *CC* slopes gently unlike the very steep slope of the line from P_0 to P_1. When point P_1 is reached the economy must grow at the same rate as the usual growth in autonomous investment.

For a short time the economy may crawl along the full employment ceiling *CC*. But because national income has ceased to increase at the rapid rate, the induced investment via accelerator falls off to the level consistent with the modest rate of growth determined by the constant rate of growth of autonomous investment. But the economy cannot crawl along its full employment ceiling for a long time. The sharp decline in growth of income and consumption when the economy strikes the ceiling causes a sharp decline in induced investment. Thus with the sharp decline in induced investment when national income and hence consumption ceases to increase rapidly, the contraction in the level of the income and business actually must begin. Once the downswing starts, the accelerator works in the reverse direction. That is, since the change in income is now negative the inducement to invest must begin to decrease. Thus there is slackening off at point P_2 and national income starts moving toward equilibrium growth path *EE*. This movement from P_2 downward therefore represents the downswing or contraction phase of the business cycle. In this downswing investment falls off rapidly and therefore multiplier works in the reverse direction. The fall in national income and output resulting from the sharp fall in induced investment will not stop on touching the level *EE* but will go further down. The economy must consequently move all the way down from point P_2 to point Q_1. But at point Q_1 the floor has been reached.

Whereas the upswing was limited by the output ceiling set by the full employment of available resources, in the downswing the national income cannot fall below the level of output represented by the floor. This is because the floor level is determined by simple multiplier and autonomous investment growing at constant rate, while during the downswing after a point accelerator ceases to operate. It may be noted that during downswing the limit to negative investment (disinvestment) and therefore the limit to the contraction of output is set by the depreciation of capital stock. There is no way for the businessmen to make disinvestment at a desired rate higher than the depreciation. When during downswing such conditions arise, accelerator becomes inoperative. After hitting the floor the economy may for some time crawl along the floor through the path Q_1 to Q_2. In doing so, there is some growth in the level of national income. This rate of growth as before induces investment and both the multiplier and accelerator come into operation and the economy will move towards Q_3 and the full employment ceiling CC. This is how the upswing of cyclical movement again starts.

Critical Appraisal

But Hicks' theory of trade cycles is not without critics. A major weakness of Hicks' theory, according to Kaldor, is that it is based on the principle of acceleration in its rigid form.[12] If the rigid form of acceleration principle is not valid, then the interaction of the multiplier and accelerator which is the crucial concept of the Hicksian theory of trade cycles is not valid. Thus Duesenberry writes, "the basic concept of multiplier-accelerator interaction is important one but we cannot really accept to explain observed cycles by a mechanical application of that concept."[13] and, according to him, Hicks in his business cycle theory actually tries to do so.

It may be noted that Kaldor puts forward a theory of business cycles which does not make use of the rigid or strict form of the acceleration principle. In his trade cycle theory Kaldor provides for investment being *directly related* to the level of income and *inversely related* to the stock of capital. Thus Kaldor's approach which is also supported by Goodwin abandons the rigid and inflexible relation of investment to changes in income (output) as implied by the rigid acceleration principle [*i.e.*, $I_t = I_a + v\ (Y_{t-1} - Y_{t-2})$] and instead has used the following form of the investment function

$$I_t = I_a + gY_{t-1} - jK_t$$

where I_t stands for investment in period t, I_a for autonomous investment, Y_{t-1} for income in the previous period, K_t for the stock of capital, and g and j are constants.

A look at the above investment function used by Kaldor will reveal that investment is directly related to the income and inversely related to the stock of capital. Thus in Kaldor-Goodwin investment function, the increase in income, the capital stock remaining constant, will cause an increase in investment which will enlarge the stock of capital. On the other hand, according to this new investment function, if capital stock increases, output or income remaining constant, investment will fall due to its being negatively related to capital stock. Thus, Kaldor-Goodwin approach to investment while gives up the rigid acceleration principle but still retains the basic idea of investment related to income because in this approach investment will cause the capital stock to expand towards the stock of capital as desired for the production of output of the preceding year.

However, despite the shortcomings of Hicks' theory of business cycles, this is a valuable contribution to the theory of business cycles. Even its critics such as Kaldor though indicating some of its weaknesses acknowledge its merit. Thus Kaldor writes that Hicks's theory of trade cycles provides us many brilliant and original pieces of analysis". Duesenberry considers it as an "ingenious piece of work".

QUESTIONS FOR REVIEW

1. Explain briefly characteristics of a trade cycle.

12. See Kaldor N., "Hicks on the Trade Cycles" in *Economic Journal*, Dec. 1951, pp. 833-478.
13. Duesenberry, J.S. "Hicks on the Trend and Cycles" in *Quarterly Journal of Economics*, August 1950, pp. 464-76.

2. Explain briefly the different phases of business cycle.
3. Explain Hawtrey's Monetary theory of business cycle. Show that his model of business cycles is self-generating.
4. What is meant by under-consumption? What factors, according to Karl Marx, are responsible for it ? How does under-consumption cause trade cycles in the economy ?
5. Critically examine Hayek's overinvestment theory of business cycles. Compare it with Wicksell's overinvestment theory of business cycles.
6. Explain Keynes's Contribution to business cycle theory. Is his theory a sufficient explanation of business cycles.
7. What is accelerator? What role does it play in explaining business cycles in the economy?
8. Explain how the interaction of multiplier and accelerator explain cyclical fluctuations in the economy.
9. Critically examine Hicks' model of trade cycles. What determines floor and ceiling in his model ?

CHAPTER 27A

Kaldor and Goodwin's Models of Business Cycles

Introduction

We have explained in the previous chapter that J.R. Hicks[1] explained business cycles through interaction of multiplier and accelerator subject to the ceiling or upper limit fixed by full-employment and the floor. In his analysis of business cycles he combined cycles with growth. Another significant Keynesian non-linear model of business cycles is that of Kaldor[2]. Two other important models of trade cycles have been put forward by R.M. Goodwin and Milton Friedman. Like Hicks, Goodwin explains cycles around a growth trend and is a non-linear dynamic model of business cycles. Friedman uses his monetarist theory to analyze business cycles and is therefore known as Friedman's monetarist theory of trade cycles. We first explain Kaldor's model of trade cycles.

KALDOR'S MODEL OF BUSINESS CYCLES

Kaldor in his model uses saving and investment functions which are of peculiar shape. The intersection of Kaldor's investment and saving functions determines the level of economic activity (that is, the level of aggregate employment and output). The intersection of investment and saving functions, as shall be seen below, yields three equilibria, two stable and one unstable. We first explain investment and saving functions used by Kaldor in his model of trade cycles.

Kaldor's Investment Function. According to Kaldor's investment function, investment is a function of income Y (i.e. level of economic activity) and the stock of capital (K). His investment function can be stated as follows:

$$I = f(Y, K)$$

$$\text{where } \frac{\partial I}{\partial y} > 0$$

$\frac{\partial I}{\partial y}$ represents marginal propensity to invest.

Note that Kaldor's investment function is not the accelerator relationship.

According to the conventional principle of accelerator, investment or demand for capital goods depends upon the *rate of change* of income (*i.e.* rate of change of the level of economic activity) while, in Kaldor's investment function, investment or demand for capital goods depends upon the *level of income* or economic activity. It should be noted that in Kaldor's analysis the level of economic activity means the level of aggregate employment or aggregate output or income. Further, in the Hicksian analysis accelerator or investment demand does not consider the effect of capital accumulation on the productive capacity and therefore on the new investment decisions by the entrepreneurs. In Kaldor's model of trade cycle, capital accumulation by raising the productive capacity affects the investment decisions of the entrepreneurs. The effect of the capital accumulation

1. J.R. Hicks, *A Contribution to the Theory of Trade Cycles*, Oxford: Oxford University Press, 1950
2. N. Kaldor, A Model of Trade Cycles, *Economic Journal*, Vol. 50, 1940, pp. 78-92.

on the investment decision of the entrepreneurs makes the investment function non-linear. As we shall see abow, it is especially through non-linear investment function and non-linear saving function

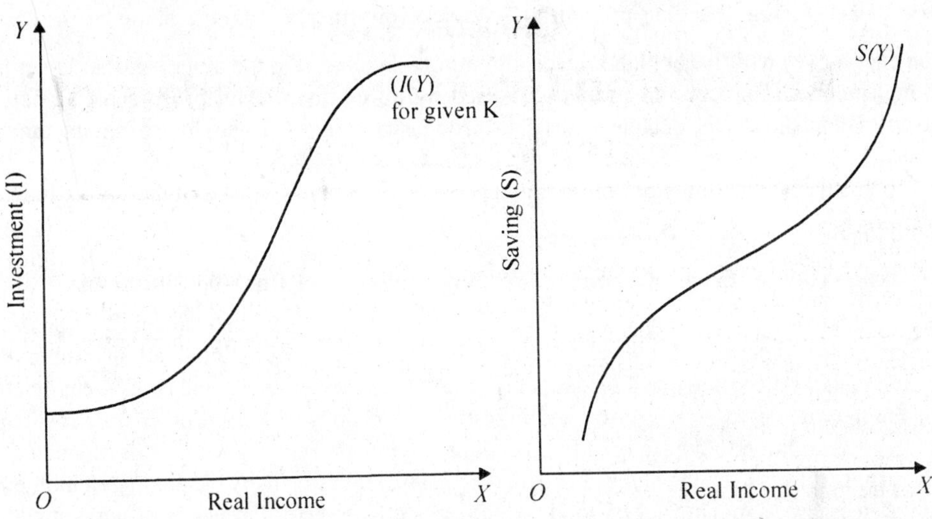

Fig. 27A.1. *Kaldor's Non-Linear Investment Function* **Fig. 27A.2.** *Kaldor's Non-Linear Saving Function*

that Kaldor explains trade cycles. Kaldor's non-linear investment function is shown in Figure 27A.1. According to this investment function, there is normal level of marginal investment propensity $\left(\frac{\partial I}{\partial Y}\right)$ in the middle range of real income or the level of economic activity. That is, marginal propensity to invest is assumed to be small at both the high and low levels of economic activity. The declining slope (i.e. marginal investment propensity) of investment function at lower level of real income (*i.e.* economic activity) is due to decrease in profit opportunities for investment. At higher level of economic activity, due to decrease in economies of scale and rise in financial costs of production, marginal investment propensity $\frac{\partial I}{\partial Y}$ becomes small.

Further, Kaldor assumes that there is inverse relation between investment and capital stock. When level of investment is high, there is large accumulation of capital stock which reduces the range of available investment opportunities. This implies that as a result of large capital accumulation level of investment falls for each level of income (*i.e.* economic activity). Thus, with accumulation of more capital stock due to higher levels of investment in the upper portion, investment function curve will shift downward.

Kaldor's Saving Function: Kaldor uses the following Keynesian saving function:

$$S = f(Y), \frac{dS}{dY} > 0$$

where $\frac{\partial S}{\partial Y}$ represents marginal propensity to save.

As in case of investment function Kaldor uses non-linear saving function which is also of a peculiar shape and is shown in Fig. 27A.2. In this saving function, used by Kaldor, at middle range of national income, there is a normal value of marginal propensity to save $\left(\frac{dS}{dY}\right)$. When due to higher levels of investment, level of national income is high, profits to the capitalists will also be larger because the marginal propensity to save of the rich capitalists is greater than that of the workers. Thus, marginal saving propensity $\left(\frac{dS}{dY}\right)$ or, in other words, the slope of the saving-function curve, $S(Y)$ will rise at higher levels of national income. On the other hand, at lower level of national income (*i.e.* economic activity) caused by lower investment, profit share in national income will fall leading to the decline in marginal propensity to save (*i.e.* the slope of saving function. It is due to this particular behaviour of marginal propensity to save $\left(\frac{dS}{dY}\right)$ that the saving function) curve, $S(Y)$ takes the peculiar shape as shown in Fig. 27A.2.

Determination of Level of Economic Activity: Stable and Unstable Equilibria

Kaldor explains the occurrence of trade cycles through saving and investment functions which by their interaction determine the level of activity, that is, the level of national output, employment and income. It is worth noting that Kaldor uses *planned* (*i.e. ex-ante*) saving and investment functions and not the *actual* (*i.e. ex-post*) saving and investment functions. Planned or *ex-ante* investment means intended addition to the stock of fixed capital and inventories of goods. This planned or *ex-ante* investment differs from the realised or actual or *ex-post* investment by the amount of unintended increase or decrease in inventories of goods which arise due to the difference between planned and realised sales of goods. Similarly, *planned* or *ex-ante* saving means the savings they intend to make for a period if they had accurately forecast their incomes. Therefore unexpected changes in the level of income will make the *realised* or *ex-post* savings different from the *planned* or *ex-ante* savings.

Kaldor uses the Keynesian equality of planned (*ex-ante*) investment and saving to explain the determination of equilibrium level of national income (economic activity). Given the peculiar non-linear investment and saving function curves three equilibria at points *A*, *B* and *C* of national income are possible for any given level of capital stock, as shown in Figure 27A.3.

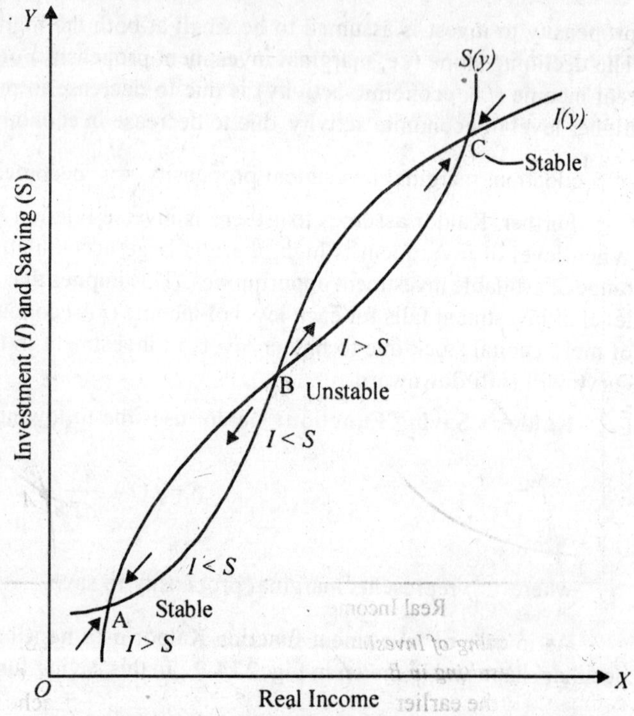

Fig. 27A.3. *Kaldor's Business Cycle Theory : Stable and Unstable Equilibria*

Equilibrium at *B* is quite unstable both upward and downward. Above the equilibrium point *B*, planned investment exceeds planned saving and therefore when as a result of some disturbance or shock, planned investment exceeds saving, the national income (*i.e.* the level of activity) will go on moving upward until point *C* is reached. On the other hand, with equilibrium position at point *B*, if as a result of some disturbance in the economy, the planned investment falls short of planned saving, the national income will go on moving downward until point *A* is reached. Thus, the equilibrium in the middle point *B* is quite unstable and, as explained above, if some economic disturbance or shock causes the economy to shift from point B, then the economic forces will operate in a way that takes the economy away from the equilibrium position B rather than bringing it back to the position B.

The equilibrium point C where both investment and saving are high is stable one and at it the economy is enjoying a high level of income and employment. This is because above the equilibrium point C planned investment is less than saving ($I < S$) which will tend to reduce national income until point C is reached once again. And below the equilibrium point C, planned investment exceeds planned saving ($I > S$) which will cause level of income to rise until equilibrium is once again reached at point C. Thus point C represents the position of stable equilibrium. Similarly, point A represents a position of stable equilibrium.

Explanation of Business Cycles

Given the non-linear saving and investment functions (for a given capital stock), Kaldor explains how business cycles occur. According to him, the equilibria of economic activity at points A and C (Figure 27A.3) are stable only in the short run because as activity continues at either of these points, with time forces generally accumulate which render them unstable. This is because saving function ($S = f(Y)$) and investment function ($I = f(Y)$ assume a given stock of capital and hence a constant real income corresponding to a given level of activity. It is through changes in the stock of capital resulting in the *shifts* in the investment and saving functions that Kaldor explains the self-generating trade cycles found in free market economies. Suppose to start with in Fig. 27A.3 the economy is in equilibrium at point C where it is enjoying higher levels of income and employment as levels of both investment and saving are high. The high level of investment at point C will cause capital stock (K) to be increasing and so the output of consumer goods. There are two consequences of this. First, with the rapid increase in capital stock as a result of high level of investment, the opportunities for further investment become temporarily restricted which will tend to make investment fall. As a result of this, investment function curve will shift downward.

On the other hand, with level of investment being high at point C (Fig. 27A.3), both the consumption and saving increase for any given level of activity which will cause a shift in the saving function [$S(Y)$] curve upward. As a consequence of these shifts in investment function, $I(Y)$ and saving function, $S(Y)$, point C is gradually shifted leftward and point B rightward so as to come closer to one another (See Fig. 27A.4) and with this level of activity or real income will be reduced

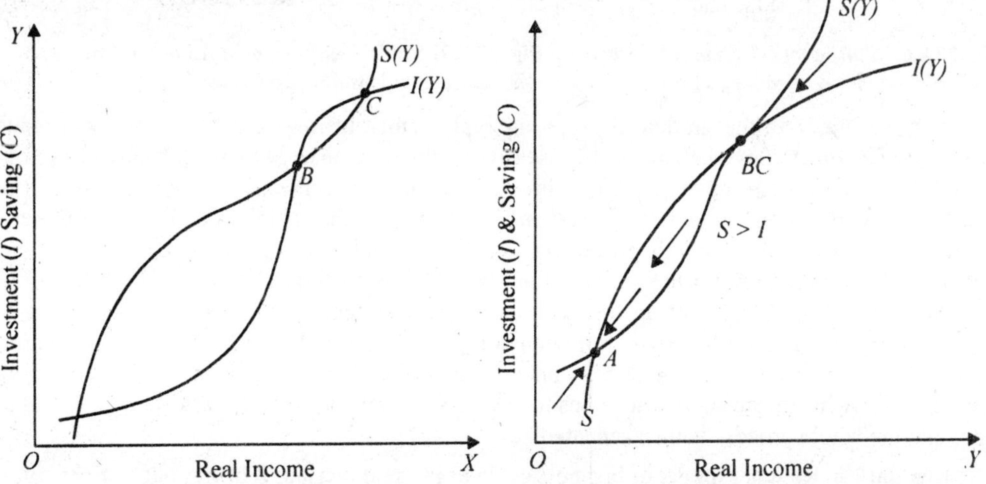

Fig. 27A.4. *Shifting of Investment Saving Curves resulting in B & C coming closer.*

Fig. 27A.5. *Shifting of Investment and Saving Curves resulting in B and C joining together.*

as compared to the earlier situation. The critical point is reached when as a result of gradual shifting of the two curves, the two points coincide and combined point BC is reached (See Fig. 27A.5).

However, the combined equilibrium point *BC* in Figure 27A.5 is unstable in the downward direction and stable in the upward direction. Therefore, after some disturbance, due to saving being greater than investment ($S > I$) the level of activity (that is, real income) will fall rapidly until a new *stable equilibrium* point *A* is reached. But stable equilibrium *A* represents a low activity equilibrium where levels of income and employment are very small. In other words, at equilibrium point *A*, there is recession or depression in the economy.

However, the economy will not remain at the low-activity equilibrium at point *A* for ever. This is because forces will again accumulate which will cause *shift in ex-ante investment and saving* curves. When low-level activity continues at point *A* for some time, investment becomes insufficient to cover even depreciation of fixed capital, negative net induced investment will occur. With this the investment opportunities again become available which would cause upward shift in the investment curve. Kaldor points out this upward tendency in the level of activity may be reinforced by the new innovations which require further investments. This will give further boost to the level of activity.

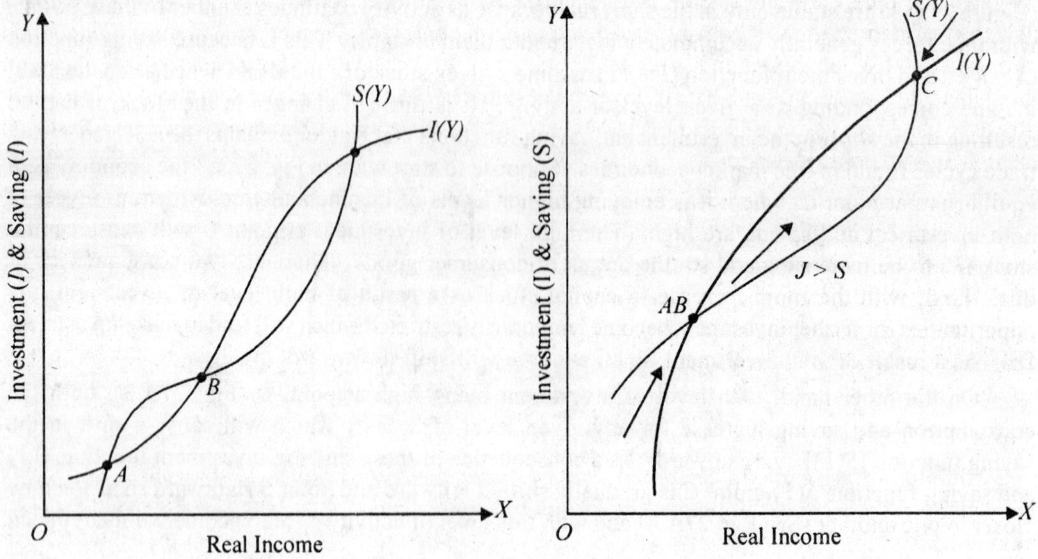

Fig. 27A.6. *Shifting of I & S curves resulting in A & B coming closer.*

Fig. 27A.7. *Stable Equilibrium at AB in the Downward Direction and Unstable upwards.*

Furthermore, with the gradual decrease in capital stock at low activity point A will reduce income per person employed. This will cause saving function curve $S(Y)$, to shift downward over time. Thus after a while upward shift of investment function curve and downward shift in the saving curve will cause *A* to shift rightward and *B* leftward so that points A and B come closer to each other (see Fig. 27A.6 and this process will continue until a tangency point *AB* is reached (See Fig. 27A.7). This new equilibrium point *AB* in Fig. 27A.7 is stable in the downward direction but is unstable in the upward direction because planned investment (*I*) exceeds planned saving (*S*) above the tangency point *AB*. Thus, following a shock, capital will go on accumulating and real income will go on rising until point *C* is once again reached (See Fig. 27A.7). At point *C* the economy experiences a strong boom. Thus the circle is complete. After some time the cycle starts again and the whole process is then repeated.

Evaluation. Kaldor's model of business cycle has a great merit as it brings out self-generating nature of business cycles. The business cycle will occur even if one of the two curves is linear. For example, cyclical nature of economic activity does not change significantly if saving function curve is linear. It may be noted that due to the great appeal of Kaldor's model of business cycle it has been reformulated by Chang and Smyth and Schinasi.

GOODWIN'S MODEL OF BUSINESS CYCLES

Introduction

Goodwin's model of business cycles like that of Hicks is an extension of the multiplier-accelerator model of business cycles. Like Hicks he thinks there is need to combine growth and cycles. However, he thinks that Hicks' introduction of growth in his model of trade cycles by means of exponentially growing autonomous investment is not fully sufficient. According to him, growth in labour force and improvements in techniques are crucial factors in determining economic to growth. These two factors, in his view, cause persistent growth in productive capacity but not necessarily equal to growth in demand. According to Goodwin, adequate growth in demand is achieved through occasional bursts of innovational investment.

Thus, to quote him, "The existence of a cycle means that aggregate demand is not always adequate to realize the full productive capacities of capitalism and at first we might be tempted to wonder that they are ever realized. In general, new techniques require heavy investment outlays which swell demand so that both increased output per labourer and the increased number of labourers are absorbed. When the economy has achieved its new higher levels of output and capital, it cannot hold them because the great bursts of investment (both innovational and accelerational) is necessary to create the effective demand, and when it ceases, demand and output drop, thus creating unemployed capital and unemployed labour"[3].

Goodwin assumes that structural coefficients of the economy such as propensity to consume or save and capital-output ratio are such as to give 'explosive oscillations'.[4] According to him, investment once begun carries the free market economy to full employment and this upper limit rises rapidly with accumulation of capital which allows the realisation of the technological progress. Thus, the expansion of the economy is constrained by the full-employment ceiling. However, after remaining at the peak, certain forces push it downward again. Thus, in the absence of lags, Goodwin's model visualizes a two-phase cycle, full employment and deep depression.

Formal Framework of Goodwin's Model

Goodwin takes capital stock rather than income as the central explanatory variable. He rejects the simple proportionality of capital and output (i.e. constant capital-output ratio) and explains investment on the basis of comparison of desired capital stock with the actual capital stock. He uses '*flexible accelerator*' as the explanatory principle for investment. According to this principle, net investment will be undertaken as long as desired capital stock is greater than existing capital and disinvestment will occur if desired capital stock is less than the existing capital stock. Thus the crucial equation of his model of cyclical growth is that of factors which determine desired capital (K^*) stock and is stated as under:

$$K^* = VY + \beta(t) \qquad \ldots (1)$$

where V is the acceleration coefficient (*i.e.* capital-output ratio), Y is the output, and (βt) is a parameter representing a change in technique or technology. According to equation (1), innovation or technological advance implies that more capital is desired with a *given output* and the accelerator (v) implies that more capital is desired with *increased output*. Thus equation (1) describes the principle of '*flexible accelerator*'.

---

3. R.M. Goodwin, "A Model of Cyclical Growth" in E. Lumberg (Ed.), *The Business Cycle in the Post-War World* (London: Macmillan, 1955)
4. How the interaction of multiplier whose value is determined by propensity to consume and acceleration coefficient whose value depends on capital-output ratio gives rise to explosive oscillations. See the previous chapter 27)

Goodwin argues that even if $\beta(t)$ in equation (1) is ignored, it does describe the *conventional accelerator principle which assumes a perfect adjustment of capital to output at all times.* On the contrary, in Goodwin's model it is assumed that "with a given stock of capital we can produce more (by overtime, etc.) than it was designed to produce, and obviously also less. Furthermore, in designed capacity there is usually some stand-by or peak-load capacity which can be used. The point is that this high-level operation involves higher variable costs, strain on staff and equipment, delays, etc. all of which create a pressure to expand capital and capacity. Therefore, the short-run is characterized by "failure to exemplify the acceleration principle"[5]

The pressure to expand capital stock through investment is proportional to the difference between desired capital stock (K^*) and the actual capital stock (K) subject to two non-linear constraints. The upper limit is set by maximum output of new capital goods obtainable with given capital stock and labour and therefore corresponds to the full-employment ceiling visualized by J.R. Hicks. The lower limit is set by the rate at which capital can be scrapped at zero gross investment. (Note : Zero gross investment implies that depreciation allowances are not spent on replacement of capital.)

It follows from above that, according to Goodwin,

$$I = \lambda (K^* - K) \qquad \dots (2)$$

where λ is proportion of the gap between the desired capital stock (K^*) and the actual capital stock (K) which determines investment. Since investment leads to the expansion in productive capacity, the equation (2) represents the supply side of the model. Demand in Goodwin's model is given by the Keynesian multiplier and can be stated as under:

$$Y = f(I) \qquad \dots (3)$$

The relation between income or output (Y) and investment (I) depends on the size of multiplier which is governed by marginal propensity to consume or save. Goodwin notes that propensity to save is rather small which ensures higher value of multiplier in the downswing of a business cycle because expenditure is difficult to be reduced when incomes decline.

We now proceed to derive the complete version of Goodwin's model. To do so, we substitute the value of K^* of equation (1) in equation (2) and get

$$I = \lambda[v\,Y + \beta(t) - K]$$

Since $Y = f(I)$

$$I = \lambda[vf(I) + (\beta(t)) - K]$$

$$I = \lambda vf(I) + \lambda\beta(t) - \lambda K$$

$$\lambda K = \lambda vf(I) + \lambda\beta(t) - I$$

Dividing both sides by λ we have

$$K = v.f(I) + \beta\, t - \frac{I}{\lambda} \qquad \dots (4)$$

From the above equation (4) it follows that *capital stock (K) depends on investment and technological change (i.e. innovations).*

Explaining Business Cycles

The above macro-model is used by Goodwin to explain business cycles. The net investment in the model depends on the difference between the *actual* capital stock and the *desired* capital stock. Suppose for some reasons desired capital stock is greater than the actual capital stock ($K^* > K$), then this gap between the two determines investment or capital accumulation. But this gap

5. Goodwin, op. cit

cannot be filled immediately because the given capital stock cannot produce more than a certain amount of capital goods which is determined by the actual capital stock in capital goods producing industries and capital-output ratio. Net investment in a period will be equal to fixed gross investment minus depreciation.

On the other hand, if desired capital stock is equal to the actual capital stock, then net investment will be zero. If desired capital stock is less than the actual capital stock, then net investment will be negative and will be equal to $-D$ where D stands for depreciation. We summarise these conclusions as follows:

If $K^* > K$, then $I^n = I - D$

If $K^* = K$, then $I^n = 0$

If $K^* < K$, then $I^n = -D$

Now suppose technological advance (*i.e.* innovations) or $\beta(t)$ is absent and the economy is presently in the upswing, and the desired capital stock exceeds capital stock, then net investment (I^n) will occur in each period over time until actual capital stock (K) becomes equal to the desired capital stock (K^*). During the period net investment or capital accumulation is taking place, it will bring about expansion in output, income and employment through interaction of multiplier and accelerator and the economy will move up till the upper limit.

When the desired capital stock is reached investment will slacken. This will cause the economy to move downward through the interaction of multiplier and accelerator which will now cause rapid fall in output and employment. This downward movement continues until gross investment (I^g) falls to zero, that is, even depreciation allowances are not spent. The depreciation continues to occur until the capital stock falls below the low level required in the depression. In this way we see that, according to Goodwin, sharp booms are periodically accompanied by prolonged depression.

There is a lower limit or floor to the downswing set by the minimum investment required to replace capital that is scrapped in each period. It is worth noting that the floor of economic activity in Goodwin's model also rises with each successive cycle because of greater expenditure and associated fixed outlay during the previous boom period. Hence there is limit to which the desired capital stock falls. Thus the economy surges forward and plunges down but does not go back to the old level.

Growth and Cycles

The above analysis ignores the two sources of economic growth which, according to Goodwin, play crucial role in determining the cyclical growth. As mentioned above, *two sources of economic growth are: (1) the increase in size of labour force and (2) increase in productivity of labour due to innovations or technological progress.* As a result of the operation of these two forces, there is rise in full-employment ceiling level. Goodwin assumes that all growth in the full-employment ceiling occurs during the boom. When there is enough growth of capital stock resulting in boom, full-employment output may rise rapidly because the capital is accumulated to equip the increased labour force with newest techniques. But his output rises above the previous peak and carries the economy into the range of the large secular multiplier. Along with accelerator this causes large increases in desired capital stock with the rising output levels. Thus, to quote Goodwin, "The achieved rate of rise in full-employment output, say 4 per cent or 5 per cent per year, fixes the rate of growth of desired capital and this in combination with the slowly accelerating capital stock, determines the length of boom".[6]

6. R.M. Goodwin, A Model of Cyclical Growth in E. Lunberg (Ed.), *The Business Cycles in the Post-War Period*, Macmillan, London.

Finally, when it is recognized that innovation (*i.e.* technological advance) and consequently rising labour productivity will generally require additional investment, we get a result closer to reality, namely, prolonged boom period and short depression period in Goodwin's model of business cycle. As M.J.C. Surrey comments, "*A steady rise in $\beta(t)$ will further prolong the boom and shorten the depression, while variation in $\beta(t)$ may account for differences betwees cycles both over time and between countries*".[7]

Evaluation

Goodwin, like J.R. Hicks, assumes an economy whose behaviour is characterized by tendency towards 'explosive oscillations'. Therefore, these oscillations must be constrained by '*ceilings*' and '*floors*' if business cycles of reasonably regular amplitude are to be explained. This has been rightly done so by Goodwin in his model of business cycle. But if economy's inherent tendency is towards 'damped cycles', then persistent cycles cannot be accounted for by Goodwin's theory. Ragnar Frisch, the Nobel prize winner in economics, has given a correct answer in terms of *persistent random shocks* to the system".[8] Random shocks means erratic changes in any or all of the variables, whether exogenous or endogenous. Thus *accelerator-multiplier interaction models as of Goodwin and Hicks along with random shocks to the economy, as pointed out by Surrey, provide a reasonable explanation of trade cycles with fairly regular amplitude.* M.J.C. Surrey is right when the writes, "Informally random shocks keep the systems in motion and prevent its settling down to a stable equilibrium, but the frequency of the cycles which the system follows is governed by multiplier-accelerator interaction. There is some tentative empirical evidence that this is indeed a plausible view to take of the generation of business cycles"[9]

7. M.J.C. Surrey, *Macroeconomic Themes* (Ed.), London: Oxford University Press, 1976.
8. R. Frisch, "Propagation Problems and Impulse Problems in Dynamic Economies" in R. Gordon and L. Klein (Eds), *Beadings in Business Cycles*, AER, 1966.
9. M.J.C. Surrey, op. cit. p. 255

CHAPTER 27B

Monetarist and New Classical (Rational Expectations) Theories of Business Cycles

We have explained in the previous chapters several theories of business cycles including Keynes's theory, Samuelson's theory of interaction between accelerator and multiplier, Hicks's theory, Kaldor's theory and Goodwins theory. The later theories are in the tradition of original Keynesian economics and make some improvement and modification in Keynes's explanation of trade cycles. However, in the post Keynesian era, Friedman led a revolution in macroeconomics and propounded a new theory called *"Monetarist Theory of Business Cycles"* and from the beginning of nineteen eighties Robert Lucas, a nobel laureate in economics, brought about another revolution in macroeconomics which dominated in the eighties and nineties. Lucas propounded a new theory of business cycles called '*New Classical Theory*' or '*Rational Expectations Theory*' of business cycles. To counter these some Keynesian economists put forward a new theory based on the original Keynesian economics but made some improvements and modifications in it and their theory is therefore called '*New Keynesian Theory of Business Cycles*'. In the present chapter we discuss these new theories of business cycles.

FRIEDMAN'S MONETARIST THEORY OF BUSINESS CYCLES

A different explanation of occurrence of business cycles has been propounded by Friedman and Schwartz [1] of Chicago University. They argue that *instability in growth of money supply is the source of most cyclical fluctuations in economic activity*. Therefore, their theory is called *monetarist theory of business cycles*. Friedman and his followers consider the free market economy as being inherently stable. According to them, it is the exogenous money shocks (*i.e.* money supply changes) that affect aggregate demand which in turn causes cyclical changes in output and employment in the economy.

Friedman and Schwartz start from the historical data for the United States which show a high correlation between cyclical movements in economic activity and cyclical changes in money stock. They admit that *cyclical correlation does not prove direction of causality,* namely, changes in exogenous money supply leading to the cyclical movements in economic activity. Quoting the historical evidence from the US economy Friedman and Schwartz conclude that there is a causal linkage running from changes in money supply to the changes in levels of economic activity rather than other way around. Thus "Friedman and Schwartz adduce evidence from particular historical periods which suggests, first, that changes in activity have always been accompanied by changes in money stock while there have not been (major) disturbances in the money stock which have not been accompanied by changes in activity and, secondly, changes in money can be attributed to specific historical events rather than systematically to changes in activity"[2]

This raises two questions First, how is Friedman's monetarist theory opposed to the conventional cyclical theories, especially, the Keynesian one. Second, what is the *transmission mechanism* that links changes in money stock with occurrence of fluctuations in economic activity. Friedman, as

---

1. M. Friedman and Anna Schwartz, Money and Business Cycles, *Review of Economics and Statistics* (Supplement), 1963.
2. M.T.C. Surrey, *Macroeconomic Themes,* Edited Readings in Macroeconomics, Oxford University Press, 1976, p. 255.

opposed to Keynes, lays stress on the *exogenous changes* in *money stock* that causes fluctuations in aggregate demand and hence in economic activity while Keynes emphasized *autonomous changes in investment* that bring about changes in aggregate demand and hence in economic activity. Besides, Friedman and other monetarists put forward the *concept of money multiplier* which relates the statistical relationship between changes in money stock with changes in real income (*i.e.* $\frac{\Delta Y}{\Delta M}$ is money multiplier where ΔY stands for change in national income and ΔM stands for change in money stock in a given period) as against *investment multiplier* of Keynes, which states the relationship between change in autonomous investment (ΔI) and resulting change in income (ΔY), that is, $\frac{\Delta Y}{\Delta I}$ measures the size of multiplier. According to Friedman and other monetarists, money multiplier shows greater stability than the Keynesian investment multiplier which varies depending on the various leakages such as the extent of imports and the degree of taxation of income. They assert that apparently greater stability of money multiplier shows *prima facie* evidence in favour of the *monetarists* explanation of cyclical fluctuations"[3]

Finally there is issue of *transmission mechanism* through which changes in money supply affect the level of national output and employment. Friedman explains it through *portfolio adjustment* consequent to changes in money stock where portfolios are considered to be comprising a *spectrum of assets ranging from money (liquid funds) through financial assets (bonds and equities to physical assets, durable producer and consumer goods.* When there is increase in money stock by the Central Bank of the country, individuals and firms would have temporarily more money balances (*i.e.*, cash or liquid funds) in their portfolio of assets than desired by them, they readjust their portfolio by spending some of the extra money balances on consumer goods and services; some part of extra money balances goes to purchasing new bonds and equity shares, some part to durable consumer goods such as houses. The new expenditure on bonds and shares raise their prices and lead to the fall in the rate of interest. The fall in interest and increase in wealth of the people will induce more investment and consumption demand. More investment will cause rise in demand for capital goods. Thus increase in money stock causes increase in aggregate demand for goods and services either directly through portfolio adjustment or indirectly through increase in wealth and fall in rate of interest caused in this adjustment process. The transmission process is quite complex as it involves not only readjustment of portfolio of the individuals but also of firms, banks and other financial institutions.

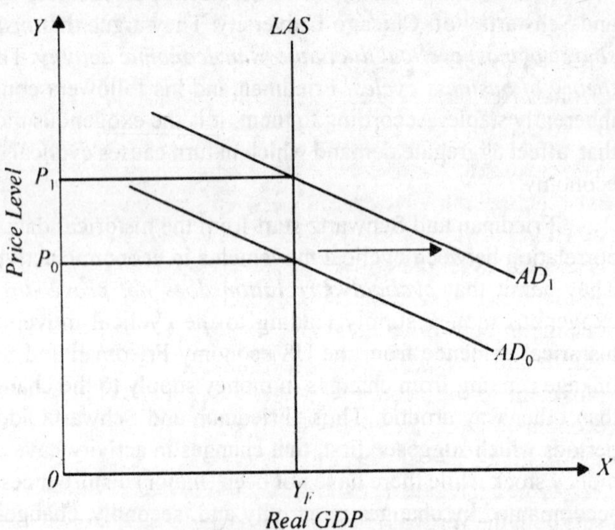

Fig. 27B.1. *Monetarist Theory* : Changes *in money supply do not affect real GDP in the long run ; they affect only the price level.*

As regards response of changes in supply of goods, monetarists led by Friedman distinguish between short run and long run. The long-run aggregate supply of goods, according to them, is determined by the real factors such as the availability of labour force, capital stock, infrastructure facilities

3. M.J.C. Surrey, *op. cit.* p. 254.

energy resources and state of technology and is a vertical straight line at the level of potential GDP as shown by LAS as a vertical straight line in Fig. 27B.1. It is important to note that in the equation of exchange, $M = kPY$ generally used by the monetarists to explain the changes in price level, they assume that real national income (*i.e.* Y) remains constant at potential GDP or full-employment level. Besides, they assume that k which is a proportion of income level held in the form of money to remain constant (note that k is inverse of income velocity of money, *i.e.*, that is, $k = \frac{1}{V}$). With k or V remaining stable (as is assumed by Friedman and other monetarists) and the real national income remaining constant at the potential GDP level (or full-employment level of output), increase in money supply brings about rise in price level only, real national income remaining constant.

Thus by making some assumptions about the behaviour of certain variables, namely, k and Y they turn equation of exchange into the theory of economic behaviour. Consider Fig. 27B.1 where long-run aggregate supply curve (LAS) is a vertical straight line at potential GDP level Y_F. The increase in money supply that causes aggregate demand curve to shift from AD_0 to AD_1 brings about rise in price level from P_0 to P_1, level of GDP remaining fixed at Y_F. But the monetarists explain business cycles on the one hand by the changes in money supply and, on the other hand, by the short-run supply curve which is assumed to be sloping upward. This upward-sloping short-run supply curve implies that both price level and aggregate output (real national income) change as aggregate demand curve shifts upward due to the increase in money supply. The short-run aggregate supply curve (SAS) slopes upward as money wages (W) are temporarily sticky in the short run and with the rise in price level (P), *real wage rate* $\left(\frac{W}{P}\right)$ *falls*. At lower real wage rate more labour is employed which produces more output or real income.

On the other hand, decrease in money supply or slowdown in its growth causes decline in aggregate demand causing both price level and aggregate output to fall.

Monetarist Theory and Business Cycles

Let us explain how monetarist theory explains business cycles with upward sloping short-run aggregate supply curve and changes in money supply or changes in growth of money supply. We first take the case how recession is caused in this theory. According to monetarists, when there is slow-down in growth in money stock by the action of the Central Bank of the country, aggregate demand decreases. With the upward sloping short-run aggregate supply curve, given the wage rate, the decrease in aggregate demand brings about decline in both price level and national output and employment causing unemployment in the economy. That is, the economy experiences recession. This is shown in Fig. 27B.2 where to begin with AD_0 is the aggregate demand curve which cuts both the vertical long run aggregate supply curve LAS and the upward-sloping short-run aggregate supply curve SAS at point E. At point E the system is in long-run equilibrium. Now if there is a slow-down in growth of money supply causing a leftward shift in aggregate demand curve from AD_0 to AD_1. As a result, the economy moves to the new equilibrium point B at which aggregate demand AD_1 cuts the short-run aggregate

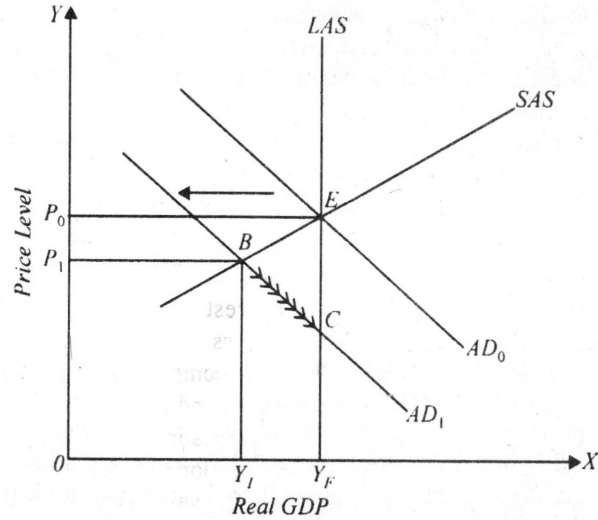

Fig. 27 B. 2 *Explaining Recession: Monetarist Theory.*

supply curve *SAS*. It will be seen from Fig. 27B.2 that at point *B* aggregate output is smaller than the potential GDP level, unemployment in the economy will emerge. However, as mentioned above, monetarists believe that *wage rate is only temporarily sticky*. When aggregate demand decreases due to slowdown in growth of money supply and causes increase in unemployment, money wage rate will *eventually* begin to fall. As shown in Fig. 27B.2, with the fall in money wage rate short-run aggregate supply curve (*SAS*) shifts downward resulting in fall in price level. Short-run aggregate supply curve (*SAS*) goes on shifting downward until the equilibrium is reached at point *C* at the level of potential GDP level Y_F where full employment prevails. Thus, according to monetarist theory, through adjustment in money wage rate and price, the economy again reaches full-employment equilibrium and unemployment is eliminated. In this way monetarists explain how with the fall in growth of money supply, the economy goes into recession and then through adjustment in wage rate and price level new full-employment equilibrium is automatically achieved at *lower* wage rate and price level.

Explaining Expansion

Expansion phase of business cycle is explained by monetarists through a positive monetary shock, that is, *exogenous increase in money supply or higher rate of growth in money supply*. This is illustrated in Fig. 27 B.3 where initially the full-employment equilibrium is at point *E* where aggregate demand curve AD_0 intersects *LAS* and SAS_0 at point *E*. Now, a speed up in growth in money stock causes an upward shift in aggregate demand curve to AD_2 resulting in increase in aggregate output (GDP) along the short-run aggregate supply curve SAS_0 which is drawn with a given wage rate.

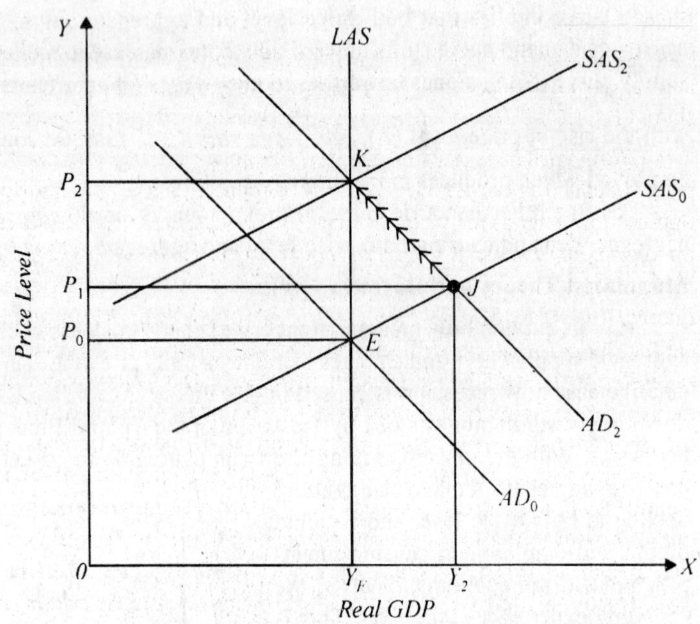

Fig. 27B. 3. *Monetarist Explanation of Expansion*

It will be seen from Fig. 27B.3 that with the sticky wages, the higher aggregate demand curve AD_2 cuts SAS_0 curve at point *J* at which the new equilibrium is established at GDP equal to Y_2 which is greater than potential GDP equal to Y_F. Equilibrium at a level higher than potential GDP implies that *unemployment has fallen below the natural level of unemployment*. (It should be recalled that in full-employment situation at Y_F, the frictional and structural unemployments exist which together are called natural level of unemployment). However, the equilibrium at point *J* is only temporary. Eventually, due to the emergence of shortage of labour at GDP level Y_2 wage rate will start rising and cause shift in *SAS* to the left until it reaches SAS_2 which intersects AD_2 curve at point *K* where new full-employment equilibrium is reached at price level P_2 and the potential GDP level Y_F. Thus, in the long run, according to monetarists the economy automatically returns to the full-employment equilibrium (*i.e.* potential GDP level) without any intervention by Government and Central Bank of the country. Prof. Parkin of the University of Ontario, US rightly says, "The monetarist business cycle is like a rocking horse. *It needs an outside force to get it going*, but once going it rocks back and forth (but just once). It does not matter in which direction the force initially hits. If it is a money growth slowdown, the economy cycles with a recession followed by expansion. If it is money growth speed up, the economy cycles with an expansion followed by recession."[1] It follows from above that monetarists believe that *changes in money supply* has a destabilising influence on the economy. They think that money shocks to the economy are the prime movers of cyclical fluctuations around the full-employment level of output in the economy.

Importance of lags

If the monetarist theory would have stopped at explaining that changes in money supply are the major source of cyclical fluctuations in the economy, it would not have been much impressive as many Keynesian also believe that changes in money supply are important source of macroeconomic instability. There must be more in monetarist theory as it emerged as an important alternative to Keynesian explanation of cyclical fluctuations in the economy. However, *monetarists view of cyclical fluctuations has been founded as much on emperical evidence as on theoretical reasoning in terms of money shocks to the economy causing cyclical fluctuations.* Friedman and his followers quoted a lot of evidence of historical episodes in favour of their viewpoint but also showed that there is a time lag between changes in money supply and their actual effect on aggregate demand and the real economy and further that this time lag is quite uncertain. That is, changes in money supply do not immediately affect aggregate demand or spending on goods and services. The initial effect of changes in money supply is on interest rate and wealth. The initial expansion in money supply is spent on financial assets, *i.e.* bonds and shares etc. driving their prices up and thereby lowers interest rate. Eventually lower interest rate and increase in their wealth leads to increase in investment demand for capital goods and demand for consumer goods and services (note that rise in prices of bonds and shares causes wealth of individuals to increase).

How this changes in aggregate demand for goods, both capital and consumer goods, affect the price level and aggregate output (GDP) depends on, as explained above, on the response of supply of output to it. It needs to be emphasized that the lag between the increase in money supply and its effect on aggregate demand is *uncertain and variable.* It may be a few months, a year or more for a given increase in money supply to produce its effect on aggregate demand and hence on price level and output. It is errors of judgement on the part of Government or monetary authority about when recession starts in the economy. It may happen that the Central Bank injects more money supply to fight recession when trough of recession might be several months in the past. If so, the injection of more money supply at such time may magnify the expansion already in progress and possibly may cause the economy to *overheat* so that aggregate demand increases beyond the potential GDP level. According to the monetarists, such excessive aggregate demand pressure generally prompts the Central Bank to contract money supply (or reduce the growth of money supply) which will cause AD curve to shift to the left and ease demand pressure. However, according to them, the Central Bank may decide to contract the money supply when aggregate demand is already slowing down on its own. If such is the case, the contraction of money supply at this time could push the economy into recession. Thus, according to monetarists, intervention by the Central Bank through changes in money supply only aggravate the natural tendency of cyclical fluctuations to be of small amplitude. These small natural fluctuations, according to them, are caused by imperfect information, weather shocks and changes in international factors.

Critical Evaluation

Most economists, even Keynesians, believe that large money supply changes have a destabilising effect on the economy. But the monetarists view that money supply changes *alone* are responsible for cyclical fluctuations does not appear to be correct. As Keynes asserted even without any significant money supply changes, changes in investment demand due to changes in marginal efficiency of capital (*i.e.,* expected return on capital) are important factors that determine changes in aggregate demand and cause cyclical fluctuations in economic activity. Besides, it has been observed that when

1. Michael Parkin, *Economics*, 4th Edition, Addison Wesley, 1998, p. 748

to pull the economy out of recession, the Central Bank takes steps to increase the money supply it may have no effect on aggregate spending due to lack of investors' confidence and bleak prospects for profit making. For example, in 2007-08 when worst ever recession took place since the Great Depression of 1930s, the Federal Reserve had pumped into the economy a large amount of money, reduced its lending rate to almost zero, but it did not lead to greater investment and consumption spending. In fact, those who got the extra money decided to hold on to it rather than spending it due to uncertain future economic environment. Because of the limitation of monetary expansion to revive the American economy, along with the expansionary monetary policy the adoption of fiscal stimulus policy measures helped the recovery of the US economy.

Further, monetarists think that economy is inherently stable and left to itself it would *automatically* correct itself through adjustment in wages and prices to restore equilibrium at full-employment (*i.e.* potential GDP) level. Therefore, they are of the view that Central Bank or Government of the Country should pursue non-interventionist policy. However, the experience of past (most recently recession of 2007-09) has abundantly showed that the automatic correction has failed to occur. Therefore, an important lesson from the past experience is that the roles of Government and Central Banks to fight recession and curb inflation are of paramount importance.

LUCAS' NEW CLASSICAL (RATIONAL EXPECTATIONS) THEORY OF BUSINESS CYCLES

Introduction

Rational expectations theory, also known as *New Classical Theory* was put forward by Nobel Laureate Robert E. Lucas of the University of Chicago. From the early eighties to 1997 Lucas New Classical Theory dominated macroeconomics. Lucas has been said to bring about a revolution in macroeconomics. He has plenty of differences with Keynes and leaned towards monetarist theory. However, he made an improvement over monetarist explanation of business cycles by introducing rational expectations in his analysis.

The cornerstone of Lucas new classical theory is the concept of rational expectations. *By rational expectations Lucas means that people use all available relevant information to make economic forecasts about price level.* This information includes not only explicit changes in money supply, Government's fiscal policy, international developments (which determine exports and prices of fuel, raw materials, and other commodities) but also economic theory about how the economy works.

According to rational expectations theory money wages are determined by rational expectations of the price level. Robert Lucas is of the view that **it is only *unanticipated* changes in aggregate demand that are the cause of cyclical fluctuations in the economy**. A greater than anticipated increase in aggregate demand causes expansion in the level of output and employment and less than anticipated increase in aggregate demand brings about recession and therefore decline in output and employment. Any factor that affects aggregate demand, for example, *larger than expected changes* in money stock, Government's fiscal deficit or changes in taxes or interest rate and unanticipated changes in international developments (that affect exports, prices of fuel and other commodities). According to Lucas, if changes in aggregate demand are anticipated, then money wages and prices would adjust so that equilibrium remains undisturbed. Thus, in his view, on the basis of all available information people estimate the future increase in money supply in forming their expectations and, if wages and prices are flexible, they are set on the basis of these expectations. Therefore, anticipated increase in aggregate demand based on these expectations in money supply changes would have no effect on the level of output and employment. This is because wages and prices would be raised in anticipation of increase in money supply and the short-run aggregate supply curve would shift to the left by the same amount as the rightward shift in aggregate demand. This is illustrated in Fig. 27B.4 where to begin with aggregate demand curve AD_0 intersects the long-run aggregate supply curve *LAS* and short-run aggregate supply curve *SAS* at point *E* and determine equilibrium price level P_0 and potential GDP level Y_F. Now, if on the basis of certain anticipated increase in money supply, aggregate demand curve shifts upward to AD_1, the anticipated price will be P_1. Now, the wages will be fixed immediately at a higher level in accordance with the new expected price level P_1. Now the wage rate will be immediately fixed at the higher level, *SAS* curve would also shift upward to SAS_1, by the same extent as the increase in aggregate demand curve to AD_1. With this, as will be seen from Fig. 27B.4, price level and wage rate have risen, the aggregate output remains at the potential GDP level. Therefore, according to Lucas, New Classical Theory based on rational expectations concept, *only unanticipated change in money supply* would affect output and employment as in the absence of adjustment in wage rate, in the short run, the response to the increase in aggregate demand the economy will move along the given short-run aggregate supply curve SAS_0. What is true of unanticipated changes in money supply and its impact on aggregate demand and output also applies to the effect of unanticipated changes in other factors.

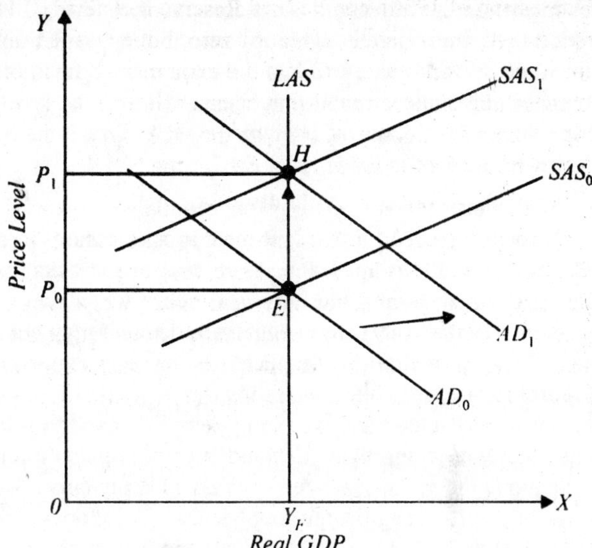

Fig. 27B.4 *Rational Expectation Theory : The Impact of Anticipated Increase in Aggregate Demand*

In what follows we explain how new classical theory explains cyclical fluctuations in economic activity (*i.e.* levels of output and employment.

Rational Expectations : Explaining Recession

We first explain how new classical theory based on rational expectations explains the emergence of recession in the economy. Consider Fig. 27B.5 where EAD is expected aggregate demand curve which intersects the long-run aggregate supply curve *LAS* and short-run aggregate supply curve *SAS* and equilibrium is at potential GDP level Y_F with price level equal to P_0. Suppose there is unanticipated decrease in the aggregate demand due to unexpected decrease in money supply growth by the Central Bank of a country or due to unexpected imposition of a higher tax or unanticipated decline in demand for country's exports. Since this decline in aggregate demand is unanticipated, wage rate will not rise in the short run. As a result of unanticipated downward shift in aggre-

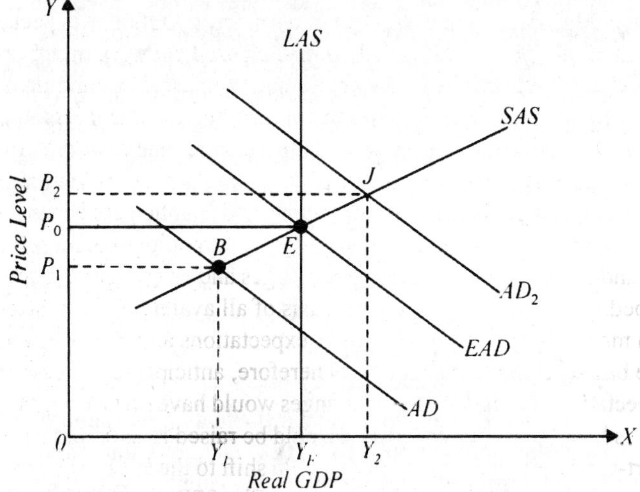

Fig. 27B.5. *Rational Expectations Theory of Business Cycles*

gate demand curved to AD_1, the economy will move along the given short-run aggregate supply curve SAS_0. With this the price level falls to P_1 and aggregate output (GDP) decreases to Y_1 causing unemployment in the economy. This indicates the situation of recession in the economy. Now, if the decline in aggregate demand is anticipated, price level will be expected to fall and therefore firms and workers will immediately agree to lower money wage rate. By doing so they will prevent the rise in real wage rate and therefore avoid the increase in unemployment. Thus it is only unanticipated decrease in aggregate demand that causes fall in price level and decline in real GDP below the full-employment level causing unemployment to rise. This recession persists until aggregate demand increases to the anticipated level *EAD*.

Rational Expectations Explaining Expansion

Now, we proceed to explain the opposite case of expansion in economic activity with Lucas' rational expectations approach. As in case of recession, according to rational expectations theory, expansion in economic activity will occur when there is *unanticipated increase in aggregate demand.* Such an increase in aggregate demand may occur due to larger than expected increase in money supply or due to unexpected increase in exports or lowering of taxes causing increase in disposable income. This is also shown in Fig. 27 B.5. *EAD* is the expected demand curve. Suppose there is unanticipated increase in aggregate demand to AD_2 due any of the factors mentioned above. Since increase in aggregate demand is unanticipated money wages will not rise, the economy will move along the given short-run aggregate supply curve *SAS*. The new aggregate demand curve AD_2 intersects short-run aggregate supply curve *SAS* at point *J* resulting in rise in price level to P_2 and real GDP level to Y_2. Since GDP has risen more than potential GDP level Y_F, unemployment will fall below the natural level of unemployment. This points to the emergence of expansion in economic activity. The new equilibrium will remain at point *J* until aggregate demand decreases to the level of expected aggregate demand curve *EAD*.

It follows from above that unanticipated fluctuations in aggregate demand such as changes from AD_1 to AD_2 around *EAD* cause changes in price level and GDP around the potential GDP level Y_F at which unemployment is at natural level (that is, at which full-employment prevails).

Critical Evaluation

Lucas' rational expectations theory has come under attack by New Keynesian economists assume that as soon as anticipated aggregate demand increases money wage rate will quickly rise. The new Keynesians point out that money wage rate does not rise quickly because labour-employer are locked in long-term contracts about money wage rate. It is only when new employer-labour contracts are renegotiated after the expiry of old ones that money wage rates can be raised. Thus, *according to new Keynesians, short-run aggregate supply curve SAS shifts only after sometime. In the meantime even anticipated increase in aggregate demand will lead to the rise in both the price level and GDP in the short run, SAS remaining unchanged.* On the contrary, according to supporters of new classical theory based on rational expectations, the employer-labour contracts are renegotiated immediately when conditions change. Therefore, they think employer-labour contracts do not impose any impediments to money wage rate flexibility. However, in our, view this can happen only if both parties agree to recognise the changed conditions.

Further, according to rational expectations theory, *anticipated policy change* brings about change in price level only with no change in real GDP and level of employment. This is because, as explained above, when policy changes are anticipated wage rate changes quickly causing *SAS* curve to shift immediately offseting the effect of policy change on real GDP and employment. As seen above, this is not correct as there is always some time lag before change in money wage rate takes place.

Like monetarist theory, new classical theory also explain cyclical fluctuation on the basis of exogenous (*i.e.* outside) forces such as changes in money supply, fiscal (*e.g.* taxation), international; developments (e.g. changes in export demand for goods and services of a country) which affect aggregate demand. *In this theory there is no any endogenous mechanism to generate cyclical movements in economic activity.*

CHAPTER 27C

Real Business Cycle Theory

Introduction

In the previous chapters we have discussed theories which explain business cycles through changes in aggregate demand, though the factors responsible for changes in aggregate demand differ in these various demand-side theories, namely, Keynesian, Kaldor and Hicks, Friedman's monetarist and Lucas' new classical theory of rational expectations. However, in the 1980s a number of economists[1] after a good deal of research put forward the view that the *major source of cyclical fluctuations in output is shift in aggregate supply (AS) rather than shift in aggregate demand (AD)*. Since the theory they developed emphasizes real factors that cause shift in aggregate supply (AS), it is called real business cycles theory. The basic idea behind the cause business cycles theory is that the same supply-side factors that explain growth over a long period are also responsible for short-run cyclical fluctuations in real GDP and employment.

Real Business Cycle Theory

In explaining real business cycle theory we use the following simple growth equation :

$$Y_t = A_t f(K_t, L_t)$$

where Y_t stands for output, K_t and L_t for capital and labour inputs respectively in time period t. In the above equation A_t represents the state of technology. It is the term A_t the changes in which represent *technology shocks* that causes shift in the production function. The technology shocks changes factor productivity (of labour, capital or both) that leads to the change in output for given levels of labour and capital inputs. The technology shock, also called supply shock, may be positive or negative. A positive technology shock increases factor productivity and thereby raises real GDP and a negative technology shock causes a decline in factor productivity and thereby reduces real GDP.

The definition of technology shock is quite comprehensive and includes more than technological innovations such as the microchip or the optic communication system which brought about revolution in information technology. Technology shock includes change in any factor that changes factor productivity. Thus oil price shock of 1973-74 and of 1979 and rise in crude oil price in later years represents negative technology shock as it raised cost of production which is similar to the rise in cost caused by decline in productivity of labour or capital.

It follows from above that it is technological changes that cause changes in factor productivity and thereby changes in real GDP and employment. Sometimes technological change is rapid and causes faster growth in factor productivity, at other times technological change is slow and consequently productivity grows slowly. We explain below how a positive technology shock affects output and employment. We further assume that technology shock is temporary and lasts for one period only (we shall explain later the case of technology shock that lasts much longer). The technology shock is assumed to be exogenous and is represented in our production function equation above by a change in the term A_t. Thus with the given amounts of K_t and L_t, output Y_t increases due to positive

1. The real business cycle theory has been put forward by Edward Prescott, Finn Kydland, John Long and Charles Plosser

technology shock. The effect of this positive technology shock is shown in Fig. 27C.1. To begin with, the technology term in the production function A_t is assumed to be equal to A_{0t} and therefore

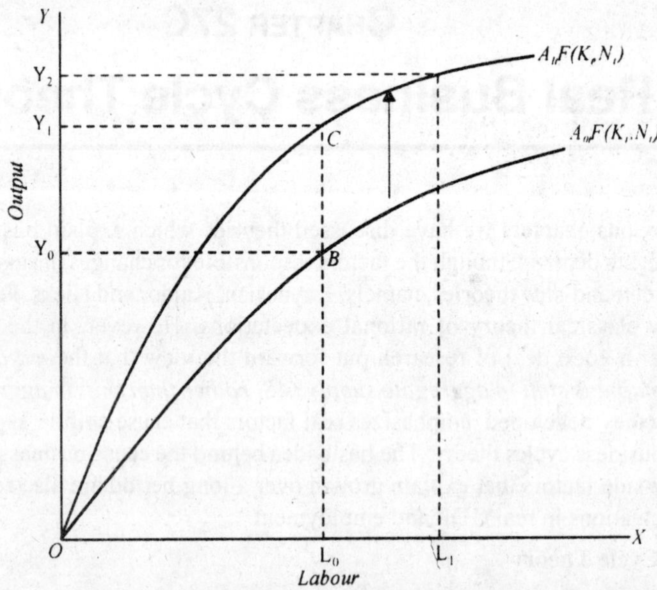

Fig. 27C.1. *Real Business Cycle Theory : The Effect of Positive Technology Shock on Output and Employment*

the production function curve is given by $A_{0t}F(K_t, L_t)$. Suppose that a given number of workers comprising a society chooses to put in OL_1 amount of labour behaving rationally to maximise their satisfaction. Given the production function, $A_{0t}\,F(K_t, L_t)$ with OL_0 as labour input, Y_0 level of output is produced. Now, as a result of positive technology shock production function shifts upward to $A_{1t}\,F(K_t, L_t)$. It will be seen from Fig. 27C.1 that as a result of positive technology shock with the use of OL_0 labour input, the level of output rises to Y_1. Moreover, with the upward shift in the production function due to technology shock the production function $(A_{1t}F(K_t, L_t)$ becomes steeper than the initial production function $(A_{0t}F(K_t, L_t)$. It may be recalled that the slope at the production at a given input level measures marginal product of an input. This shows marginal product of labour (MP_L) will be greater at point *C* on the new production function $(A_{1t}\,F(K_t, L_t))$ as compared to point *B* on the initial production function $(A_{0t}\,F(K_t, L_t))$. It is the rise in labour productivity due to positive technology shock that even with given labour input L_0, output rises to Y_1. However, as marginal product of labour at the given labour input L_0 rises, in a competitive economy this will lead to the rise in real wage rate. The workers' response to this increase in productivity (*i.e.*, return to labour) and therefore rise in real wage rate will be to increase their labour input from L_0 to L_1. More labour employment will cause rise in total output. Thus, in Fig. 27C.1 in equilibrium employment of labour rises to L_1 causing output to increase to Y_2.

Now, the workers must decide how the increase in output has to be distributed between consumption and saving. They are not likely to consume all the increase in output especially when the technology shock is only temporary. Usually, workers will consume a part of additional output and a part will be saved $(\Delta Y = \Delta C + \Delta S)$. As a result, saving in a period will increase as a result of higher output brought about by positive technology shock. Now, the higher saving in a period will lead to the increase in investment that will cause addition to the stock of capital in the next period.

As a result of greater capital stock, output in the future periods will be higher than it, would have been in the absence of technology shock. This will hold even if the *direct effect* of the positive technology shock lasted for one period since the effect of addition to the stock of capital would have long-lasting effect. Thus, the effect of increase in saving and investment on addition to the capital stock will lead to the increase in output and employment for many periods in future.

We have explained above the effect of positive technology shock on expansion in output and employment for a long period. Similarly, if there is a negative technology shock, it will also cause decline in output and employment not only in one period but its effect will persist longer for some more periods. The real business cycle theorists are of the view that the effect of technology shocks lasts for long and with it they explain persistent cyclical fluctuations in output and employment. Thus, Richard T. Froyan writes, "Real business Cycle theorists argue that dynamic responses of optimising agents to changes in economic conditions...... have long lasting effects. These responses can explain periods of persistently high or low economic activity".[2]

In our dynamic analysis of real business cycles we have confined ourselves to explaining the effects of technology shocks on cyclical fluctuations in economic activity. The other supply shocks whose effects on fluctuations in economic activity are analysed by real business cycle theorists are changes in world fuel prices (for example, oil price shock of 1973-74 and 1979), Changes in international environment affecting exports of a country, changes in taxes by the Government.

Real GDP and Price Level

Let us now explain how in real business cycle theory technology shocks affect real GDP and price level. As explained above, a positive technology shock leads to higher labour productivity and increase in employment. The expansion in employment brings about increase in potential real GDP which causes increase in aggregate supply. This causes a shift in long-run aggregate supply curve to the right as depicted in Figure 27C.2 where as a result of a positive technology shock, long-run aggregate supply curve shifts to the right from LAS_0 to LAS_1. Since positive technology shock raises labour productivity, it leads to the expansion in output which is divided between increases in consumption and saving. As a result of higher saving, investment in the economy will rise causing a rightward shift in the aggregate demand curve from AD_0 to AD_1 in Fig. 27C.2. It is worth noting that in real business cycle theory there is no short-run aggregate supply curve since it is assumed that money wage rate is quite flexible and adjusts freely so that real wage rate keeps labour market in equilibrium. Thus, in real business cycle theory long-run aggregate supply curve is vertical at potential GDP level where there is full employment of labour. It will be seen from Fig. 27C.2 that initially equilibrium is at point E at which potential real GDP is Y_0 and price level is P_0. As a result of positive technology shock long-run supply curve shifts to LAS_1 and aggregate demand curve to AD_1. With these shifts, the new equilibrium is established at

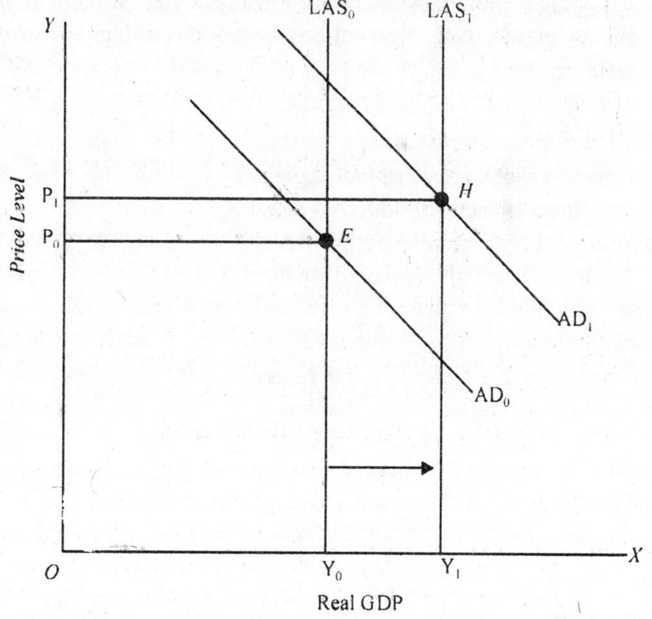

Fig. 27C.2. *Change in real GDP and Price Level in Real Business Cycle Theory*

2. Richard T. Froyen, *Macroeconomics : Theories and Policies,* Sixth Edition, p.256.

point *H* and potential GDP (*i.e.*, full employment level of output) increases to Y_1 and price level rises to P_1. This means economic expansion has taken place.

On the other hand, negative technology shock causes labour productivity to fall due to a downward shift in the production function ($Y_t = A_t F(K_t, L_t)$) which leads to the decrease in employment. The decrease in labour employment would cause a decline in real GDP. As a result *LAS* will shift to the left. Besides, the decrease in employment would also lead to the decline in aggregate demand causing shift in aggregate demand curve to the left. As a result of leftward shift in *LAS* and *AD* curves potential GDP and price level would fall. This means that economy would go in recession.

Has Money any Role in Real Business Cycle Theory ?

In real business cycle theory it is *real factors* and not the monetary ones that cause cyclical fluctuations in economic activity. Like the classical theory, changes in money supply affect only the price level with no real effects on the use of resources and no change in potential GDP or employment level. In the real business cycle theory this outcome occurs because aggregate supply curve is vertical at potential GDP or full employment level. Therefore, when aggregate demand curve *AD* shifts to the right due to the increase in money supply, only the price level rises, potential GDP remaining the same as shown in Fig. 27C.3. Thus in real business cycle theory, like that in Classical theory money has no role in influencing real GDP and employment level.

Critique of Real Business Cycle Theory

Real business cycle theory has come in for severe attack for its incredible assumptions. Critics point out to that in the real world *money wage rate is sticky* and to assume that it is quite flexible, both downward and upward, and its free adjustment keeps labour market equilibrium at full employment level is just not right. Besides, intertemporal adjustment assumed in the theory is too weak to explain large fluctuations in labour productivity and employment with small real wage changes.

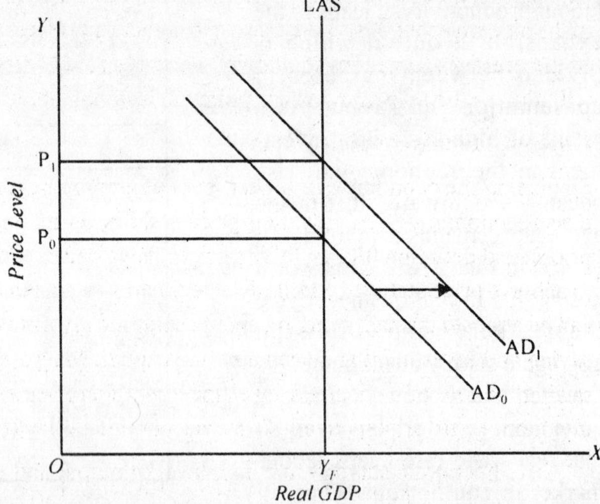

Fig. 27C.3. *Change in Money supply affects only price level, Real GDP remains unchanged*

However, a crucial criticism of real business cycle theory is that technology shocks alone cannot explain fluctuations in factor productivity and hence in levels of employment and real GDP. It has been rightly pointed out that these changes in productivity and employment are likely the result of changes in aggregate demand rather than shocks to technology. Changes in aggregate demand occur due to changes in investment as explained by Keynes or due to changes in money supply as pointed out by monetarists. In fact, the correlation between changes in GDP and changes in factor productivity observed from empirical evidence are due to changes in GDP causing changes in factor productivity rather than the other way around and further that it is changes in aggregate demand that cause fluctuations in both GDP and productivity. As one critic[3] says, "*fluctuations in productivity do not cause the cycle but are caused by it.*"

3. Michael Parkin, *Economics*, 4th edition, Addison-Wesley, 1998. p.754.

CHAPTER 28
Economic Stabilisation : Fiscal Policy

Introduction: Macroeconomic Policy and Stabilisation

The economy does not always work smoothly. There often occur fluctuations in the level of economic activity. At times the economy finds itself in the grip of recession when levels of national income, output and employment are far below their full potential levels. During recession, there is a lot of idle or unutilised productive capacity, that is, available machines and factories are not working to their full capacity. As a result, unemployment of labour increases along with the existence of excess capital stock. On the other hand, at times the economy is *'overheated'* which means inflation *(i.e.* rising prices) occurs in the economy. Thus, in a free market economy there is a lot of economic instability. The classical economists believed that an automatic mechanism works to restore stability in the economy; recession would cure itself and inflation will be automatically controlled. However, the empirical evidence during the 1930s when severe depression took place in the Western capitalist economies and also the evidence of post Second World II period amply shows that no such automatic mechanism works to bring about stability in the economy. That is why Keynes argued for intervention by the Government to cure depression and inflation by adopting appropriate tools of macroeconomic policy. *The two important tools of macroeconomic policy are fiscal policy and monetary policy.* According to Keynes, monetary policy was ineffective to lift the economy out of depression. He emphasized the role of fiscal policy as an effective tool of stabilising the economy. However, in view of the modern economists both fiscal and monetary policies play a useful role in stabilising the economy. In the present chapter we shall dwell upon the role of fiscal policy for stabilising the economy and will discuss the role of monetary policy in bringing about stabilisation in the next chapter.

Goals of Macroeconomic Policy

Stabilising the economy at a higher level of employment and national output is not the only goal of macroeconomic policy. Ensuring price stability is its another goal. Both inflation, (that is, rising prices) and deflation (that is, falling prices) have bad economic consequences. It is therefore desirable to achieve price stability. Similarly, every nation wants to raise the level of living of its people which can be attained through bringing about economic growth which in turn depends on raising the rates of saving and investment and accumulating capital. Macro-economic policies can play a useful role in raising the rate of saving and investment and therefore ensure rapid economic growth. Thus, three important goals or objectives of macroeconomic policy (both fiscal and monetary) are follows :

1. Economic stability at a high level of output and employment.
2. Price stability.
3. Economic growth.

In the present chapter we shall confine ourselves to the discussion of the role of fiscal policy in achieving economic stability at full employment level and in controlling inflation and deflation and thus attaining price stability. The role of monetary policy for encouraging economic growth will be discussed at length in a later chapter.

DISCRETIONARY FISCAL POLICY FOR STABILISATION

Fiscal policy is an important instrument to stabilise the economy, that is, to overcome recession and control inflation in the economy. Fiscal policy is of two kinds : *Discretionary fiscal policy and Non-discretionary fiscal policy of automatic stabilisers.* By discretionary policy we mean deliberate change in the Government expenditure and taxes to influence the level of national output and prices. Fiscal policy generally aims at managing aggregate demand for goods and services. On the other hand, non-discretionary fiscal policy of automatic stabilisers is a built-in tax or expenditure mechanism that automatically increases aggregate demand when recession occurs and reduces aggregate demand when there is inflation in the economy without any special deliberate actions on the part of the Government. In this section we shall confine ourselves to the discussion of discretionary fiscal policy.

At the time of recession the Government increases its expenditure or cuts down taxes or adopts a combination of both. On the other hand, to control inflation the Government cuts down its expenditure or raises taxes. In other words, *to cure recession expansionary fiscal policy and to control inflation contractionary fiscal policy is adopted.* It is worth mentioning that fiscal policy aims at changing aggregate demand by suitable changes in Government spending and taxes. Thus, *fiscal policy is mainly a policy of demand management.* It should be further noted that when the Government adopts expansionary fiscal policy to cure recession, it raises its expenditure without raising taxes or cuts down taxes without changing expenditure or increases expenditure and cuts down taxes as well. With the adoption of any of these types of expansionary fiscal policy Government's budget will have a deficit. Thus expansionary fiscal policy to cure recession and unemployment is a deficit budget policy. If, on the other hand, to control inflation, Government reduces its expenditure or increases taxes or adopts a combination of the two, it will be planning for a budget surplus. *Thus policy of budget surplus, or at least reducing budget deficit is adopted to remedy inflation.* In what follows we will discuss fiscal policy first to cure recession and then to control inflation.

Fiscal Policy to Cure Recession

As we know, the recession in an economy occurs when aggregate demand decreases due to a fall in private investment. Private investment may fall when businessmen become highly pessimistic about making profits in future, resulting in decline in marginal efficiency of investment. As a result of fall in private investment expenditure, aggregate demand curve shifts down creating a *deflationary or recessionary gap*. It is the task of fiscal policy to close this gap by increasing Government expenditure, or reducing taxes. Thus there are two fiscal methods to get the economy out of recession.

(*a*) Increase in Government Expenditure

(*b*) Reduction of Taxes.

We discuss below both these methods.

(*a*) **Increase in Government Expenditure to Cure Recession.** For a discretionary fiscal policy to cure depression, the increase in Government expenditure is an important tool. Government may increase expenditure by starting public works, such as building roads, dams, ports, telecommunication links, irrigation works, electrification of new areas etc. For undertaking all these public works, Government buys various types of goods and materials and employs workers. The effect of this increase in expenditure is both direct and indirect. The direct effect is the increase in incomes of those who sell materials and supply labour for these projects. The output of these public works also goes up together with the increase in incomes. Not only that, Keynes showed that increase in Government expenditure also has an *indirect effect* in the form of the working of a multiplier. Those who get more incomes spend them further on consumer goods depending on their marginal propensity to consume. As during the period of recession there exists *excess capacity* in the consumer goods industries, the increase in demand for them brings about expansion in their output which further generates employment and incomes for the unemployed workers and so the new incomes are spent and respent further and the process of multiplier goes on working till it exhausts itself.

How large should be the increase in expenditure so that equilibrium is established at full employment or potential level of output. This depends on the magnitude of GNP gap caused by deflationary gap on the one hand and the size of multiplier on the other. It may be recalled that the size of the multiplier depends on the marginal propensity to consume. The impact of increase in Government expenditure in a recessionary condition is illustrated in Fig. 28.1. Suppose to begin with the economy is operating at full-employment or potential level of output Y_F with aggregate demand curve $C + I_2 + G_2$ intersecting 45° line at point E_2. Now, due to some adverse happening (say due to the crash in the stock market), investor's expectations of making profits from investment projects become dim causing a decline in investment. With the decline in investment, say equal to E_2B, aggregate demand curve will shift down to the new position $C + I_1 + G_1$ which will bring the economy to the new equilibrium position at point E_1 and thereby determine Y_1 level of output or income. The fall in output will create involuntary unemployment of labour and also excess capacity (*i.e.* idle capital stock) will come to exist in the economy. Thus emergence of deflationary gap equal to E_2B and the reverse working of the multiplier has brought about conditions of recession in the economy. It will be observed from Fig. 28.1 that, to overcome recession if the Government increases its expenditure by E_1H, the aggregate demand curve will shift upward to original position $C + I_2 + G_2$ and as a result the equilibrium level of income will increase to the full-employment or potential level of output Y_F and in this way the economy would be lifted out of depression. Note that the increase (ΔY) in national income or output by Y_1Y_F is not only equal to the increase in Government expenditure by ΔG or E_1H but a multiple of it depending on the marginal propensity to consume. Thus, increase in national income is equal to $\Delta G \times \dfrac{1}{1 - MPC}$ where $\dfrac{1}{1 - MPC}$ is the value of multiplier.

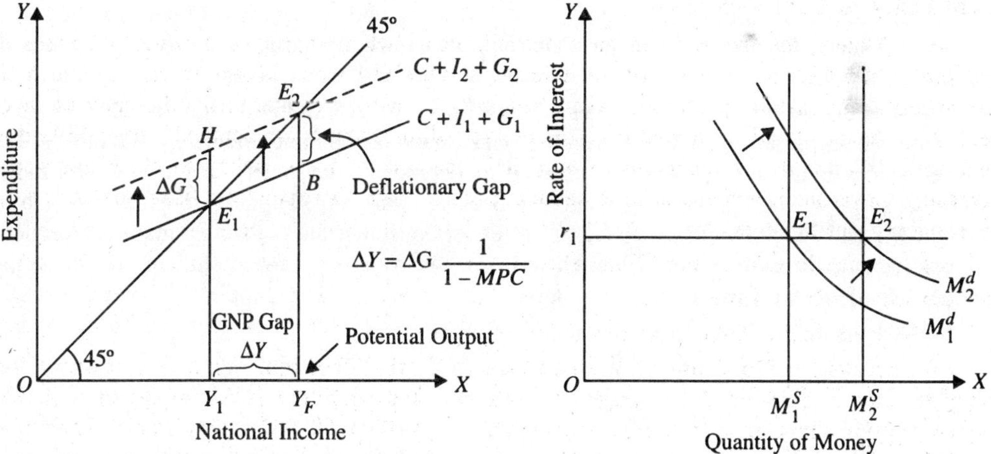

Fig. 28.1. *Increase in Government Expenditure to Cure Recession*

Fig. 28.2. *Expansion in Money Supply to Keep the Rate of Interest Unchanged*

It may also be further noted that increase in Government expenditure without raising taxes (and therefore the policy of deficit budgeting) will fully succeed in curing recession if rate of interest remains unchanged. With the increase in Government expenditure and resultant increase in output and employment demand for money for transactions purposes is likely to increase as is shown in Fig. 28.2 where demand for money curve shifts to right from M_1^d to M_2^d as a result of increase in transactions demand for money. Money supply remaining constant, with increase in demand for money rate of interest is likely to rise which will adversely affect the private investment. The decline in private investment will tend to offset the expansionary effect of rise in Government expenditure. Therefore, if fiscal policy of increase in Government expenditure (or of deficit budgeting) is to succeed in overcoming recession, the Central Bank of the country should also pursue expansionary monetary policy and take steps to increase the money supply so that increase in Government expenditure does not lead to the rise in rate of interest. It will be noticed from Fig. 28.2 that if money supply is increased from M_1^S to M_2^S, the rate of interest does not rise despite the increase in demand for money. With rate of interest remaining unchanged, private investment will not be adversely affected and increase in Government expenditure will have full effect on raising national income and employment.

Financing Increase In Government Expenditures and Budget Deficit

An important question is how to finance the increase in Government expenditure which is undertaken to cure recession. This increase in Government expenditure must not be financed by raising taxes because rise in taxes would reduce disposable incomes and consumers' demand for goods. As a matter of fact, rise in taxes would offset the expansionary effect of rise in Government spending. Therefore, proper discretionary fiscal policy at times of recession is to have the budget deficit if expansionary effect is to be realisted.

Borrowing. A way to finance budget deficit is to borrow from the public by selling interest-bearing bonds to them. However, there is a problem in adopting borrowing as a method of financing budget deficit. When the Government borrows from the public in the money market, it will be competing with businessmen who also borrow for private investment. The Government borrowing will raise the demand for loanable funds which in a free market economy, if rate of interest is not administered by the Central Bank, will drive up the rate of interest. We know the rise in rate of interest will reduce or crowd out some private investment expenditure and interest-sensitive consumer spending for durable goods.

Creation of New Money. The more effective way of financing budget deficit is the creation of new money. By creating new money to finance the deficit, the crowding out of private investment can be avoided and full expansionary effect of rise in Government expenditure can be realised. Thus, creation of new money for financing budget deficit or what is called *monetisation of budget deficit* has a greater expansionary effect than that of borrowing by the Government.

(*b*) **Reduction in Taxes to Overcome Recession.** Alternative fiscal policy measure to overcome recession and to achieve expansion in output and employment is reduction of taxes. The reduction in taxes increases the disposable income of the society and causes the increase in consumption spending by the people. If tax reduction of Rs. 200 crores is made by the Finance Minister, it will lead to Rs. 150 crores in consumption, assuming marginal propensity to consume is 0.75 or 3/4. Thus reduction in taxes will cause an upward shift in the consumption function. If along with the reduction in taxes, the Government expenditure is kept unchanged, aggregate demand curve $C + I + G$ will shift upward due to rise in consumption function curve. This will have an expansionary effect and the economy will be lifted out of recession, and national income and employment will increase and as a result unemployment will be reduced. Note that reduction in taxes, with Government expenditure remaining constant, will also result in budget deficit which will have to be financed either by borrowing or creation of new money.

It is worth noting that *reduction in taxes has only an indirect effect on expansion and output* through causing a rise in consumption function. But, like the increase in government expenditure, the increase in consumption achieved through reduction in taxes will have a multiplier effect on increasing income, output and employment. As we have shown in a previous chapter the value of *tax multiplier*, as it is called, is given by

$$\Delta T \times \frac{MPC}{1 - MPC} \text{ or } \Delta C \times \frac{MPC}{1 - MPC}$$

The effect of reduction in taxes in curing recession and in causing expansion in income and output can be graphically shown by figure such as Fig. 28.1. In case of reduction in taxes, instead of increase in Government expenditure *G*, it is increase in consumption *C* which will cause upward shift in the aggregate demand curve ($C + I + G$) and will result in, through the working of multiplier, a higher level of equilibrium national income.

There are some instances in the history of the capitalist world, especially U.S.A. when taxes were reduced to stimulate the economy. In 1964, the President Kennedy reduced personal and business taxes by about $12 billion to give a boost to the American economy when there was high unemployment and lower capacity utilisation in the American economy. This tax cut was quite successful in reducing unemployment substantially and expanding national income through full utilisation of excess capacity. Again, over the period 1981-84, President Reagan made a very large tax reduction to get out of recession and to achieve expansion in national income to reduce unemployment. There is some debate whether President Reagan's tax cut alone had positive effect on national income as some economists attribute the recovery in that period to the monetary expansion that took place. However, tax reduction by President Reagan did play a significant role for bringing about the recovery.

Fiscal Policy Option: Increase in Government Expenditure or Reduction in Taxes

Is it better to use Government expenditure or changes in taxes to stabilise the economy at full employment and potential-level of output. The answer depends to a great extent upon one's view regarding the role of public sector. Those who think that public sector should play a significant role in the economy to meet various failures of a free market system will recommed the increase in Government expenditure during recession on public works to achieve expansion in output and employment. On the other hand, those economists who think that public sector is inefficient and involves waste of scarce resources would advocate for reduction in taxes to stimulate the economy.

The choice between tax reduction and increase in Government expenditure depends on the basis of another factor, namely, the magnitude of the effect of expenditure multiplier and tax multiplier. The value of tax multiplier is less than the Government expenditure multiplier. Ignoring the signs of the multipliers, it should be noted that whereas expenditure multiplier is equal to $\frac{1}{1-MPC}$, the tax multiplier equals $\frac{MPC}{1-MPC}$ or $MPC \times \frac{1}{1-MPC}$ which is less than $\frac{1}{1-MPC}$. Suppose marginal propensity to consume is 0.75 or 3/4 so that value of expenditure multiplier is 4. Increase in Government expenditure by Rs. 100 crores will raise national output by Rs. 400 crores. On the other hand, reduction in taxes by Rs. 100 crores will increase income and output by $100 \times \frac{MPC}{1-MPC} = 100 \times \frac{3/4}{1-3/4}$ = Rs. 300 crores. Thus, the effect of reduction in taxes by an equal amount as the increase in Government expenditure has a smaller impact on national income than that of increase in Government expenditure. This difference in the effects of the two methods of expanding output has implications for the size of the Government deficit. If we want to achieve expansion in income by the same amount, we need to cut taxes by more than we would need to increase Government expenditure because the size of the tax multiplier is less than that of expenditure multiplier. In other words, in case we adopt the policy of tax reduction, to achieve expansion by a given amount the budget deficit planned will to have to be much greater.

However, the size of expenditure multiplier relative to the size of the tax multiplier is not the sole deciding factor for the choice of a policy option. For example, reduction in taxes are greatly welcomed by the people as it directly increases their disposable incomes. Further, it is individual or households who themselves decide how to spend their extra disposable income made possible by a tax cut, while in case of increase in expenditure the Government decides how to spend it.

Fiscal Policy to Control Inflation

When due to large increases in consumption demand by the households or investment expenditure by the entrepreneurs, or bigger budget deficit caused by too large an increase in

Government expenditure, aggregate demand increases beyond what the economy can potentially produce by fully employing its given resources, it gives rise to the situation of *excess demand* which results in inflationary pressures in the economy. This inflationary situation can also arise if too large an increase in money supply in the economy occurs. In these circumstances *inflationary gap* occurs which tend to bring about rise in prices. If successful steps to check the emergence of exceeds demand or close the inflationary gap are not taken, the economy will experience a period of inflation or rising prices. For the last some decades, problem of demand-pull inflation has been faced by both the developed and developing countries of the world[1]. An alternative way of looking at inflation is to view it from the angle of business cycles. After recovery from recession, when during upswing an economy finds itself in conditions of boom and become overheated prices start rising rapidly. Under such circumstances *anticyclical fiscal policy* calls for reduction in aggregate demand. Thus, *fiscal policy measures to control inflation are* (1) *reducing Government expenditure and* (2) *increasing taxes*. If in the beginning the *Government is having balanced budget*, then increasing taxes while keeping Government expenditure constant will yield budget surplus. The creation of budget surplus will cause downward shift in the aggregate demand curve and will therefore help in easing pressure on prices. If there is a balanced budget to begin with and the Government reduces its expenditure, say on defence, subsidies, transfer payments, while keeping taxes constant, this will also create budget surplus and result in removing excess demand in the economy.

It is important to mention that in the developing countries like India, the main factor responsible for inflationary pressures is *heavy budget deficit* of the Government for the last several years resulting in excess demand conditions. Rate of inflation can be reduced not necessarily by planning for budget surplus which is in fact impracticable but by *trying to take steps to reduce budget deficits*. It has been estimated that the aim should be to reduce fiscal deficit[2] to 3 per cent of GNP to achieve price stability in the Indian economy.

How the reduction in Government expenditure will help in checking inflation is shown in Fig. 28.3. It will be seen from this figure that an aggregate demand curve $C + I + G_1$ intersects 45° line at point E and determines equilibrium national income at full-employment level of income Y_F. However, if due to excessive Government expenditure and a large budget deficit, the aggregate demand curve curve shifts upward to $C + I + G_2$, this will determine Y_2 level of income which is greater than full employment or potential output level Y_F. Since output cannot increase beyond Y_F, income will rise only in money terms through rise in prices, real income or output remaining unchanged. To put in other words, while the economy does not have labour, capital and other resources sufficient to produce Y_2 level of income or output, the households, businessmen and Government are demanding Y_2 level of output. This excess demand pushes up the price level so that level of only *nominal income* increases, real income or output remaining constant. It is thus clear that with the increase in aggregate demand beyond the full-employment level of output to $C + I + G_2$ causes excess demand equal to EA to emerge in the economy. It is this excess demand EA relative to full-employment output Y_F which causes the price level to rise and thus creates inflationary situation in the economy. This excess demand EA at full-employment level has therefore been called inflationary gap. *The task of fiscal policy is to close this inflationary gap by reducing Government expenditure or raising taxes.* With equibrium at point H and nominal income equal to Y_2, if Government expenditure equal to HB (which is equal to inflationary gap AE) is reduced, aggregate demand curve will shift downward to $C + I + G_1$ which will restore the equilibrium at the full-employment level Y_F. The reduction in Government expenditure equal to HB through the operation of multiplier will result in a multiple decline in the level of national income or output. It will be seen from Fig. 28.3 that the decrease in Government expenditure by HB has led to a much bigger decline in output by Y_2Y_F. Ideally Government expenditure should cut down its expenditure on non-development or unproductive heads such as defence, unnecessary subsidies. It may however be noted that in India to control inflation the Government has been reducing *capital expenditure* which is mainly of development nature and has therefore been validly criticised.

1. It is worth noting that in the mid nineties in the developed countries inflation has become very moderate which is currently at the rate of about 4 per cent per annum.
2. There is some difference in the meaning of *budget deficit* and *fiscal deficit*. However, we shall not go into this issue and will be treating them to be of the same meaning.

Raising Taxes to Control Inflation. *As an alternative to reduction in Government expenditure, the taxes can be increased to reduce aggregate demand.* For this purpose especially personal direct taxes such as income tax, wealth tax, corporate tax can be raised. The hike in taxes reduces the disposable incomes of the people and thereby force them to reduce their consumption demand. Note that in Fig. 28.3 as a result of hike in personal taxes it is the decrease in consumption-demand (C) component which will cause the aggregate demand curve $C + I + G_2$ to shift downward. Since, as shown above, the magnitude of tax multiplier is smaller than the expenditure multiplier, the tax revenue will be raised by a greater amount to achieve contraction in national income by Y_2Y_F.

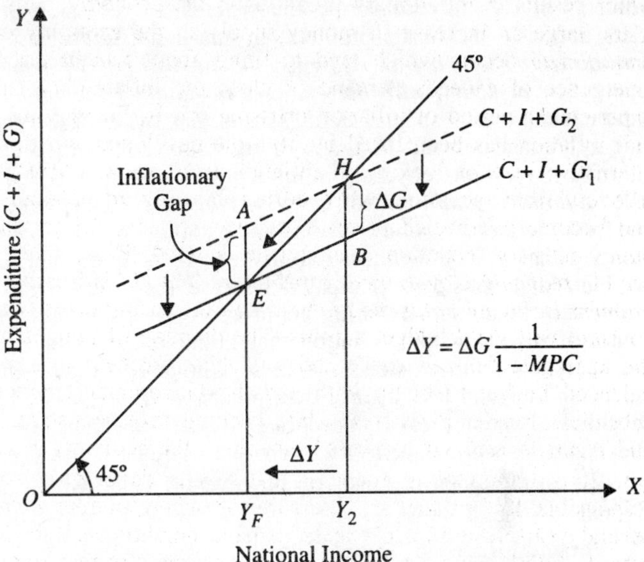

Fig. 28.3. *Reducing Expenditure to Check Inflation*

Disposing of Budget Surplus. We have seen above to control demand-pull inflation, the Government either reduces its expenditure or raises taxes to lower aggregate demand for goods and services. Reduction in expenditure or hike in taxes results in decrease in budget deficits (if occurring before such steps) or in the emergence of budget surplus if the Government was having balanced budget prior to the adoption of anti-inflationary fiscal policy measures. Let us assume that anti-inflationary fiscal policy results in budget surplus. Anti-inflationary impact of budget surplus depends to a good extent on how the Government disposes of this budget surplus. There are two ways in which budget surrplus can be disposed of : (1) reducing or retiring public debt and (2) impounding public debt.

We examine below the anti-inflationary effects of these two ways of disposing of the budget surplus

1. **Retiring Public Debt**. The budget surplus created by anti-inflationary policy can be used by the Government to pay back the outstanding debt. However, using budget surplus for retiring public debt will weaken its anti-inflationary effect. In paying off the debt held by the public, the Government will be returning the money to the public which it has collected through taxes. Further, this will also add to the money supply with the public. The general public will spend a part of the money so received which will raise consumption demand. Besides, retiring of public debt will result in the expansion of money supply in the money market which will tend to lower the rate of interest. The lower rate of interest will stimulate consumption and investment demand while anti-inflationary policy requires that they should be reduced.

2. **Impounding of Public Debt.** To realise a large anti-inflationary effect of budget surplus it is desirable to impound the surplus fund. The impounding surplus funds means that they should be kept idle. Thus by impounding the budget surplus, the Government shall be withdrawing some income or purchasing power from the income-expenditure stream and thus will not create any inflationary pressures to offset the deflationary impact of the budget surplus. To conclude, the impounding of budget surplus is a better method of disposing of budget surplus than of paying off public debt.

NON-DISCRETIONARY FISCAL POLICY: AUTOMATIC STABILIZERS

There is an alternative to the use of discretionary fiscal policy which generally involves problems of lags in recognising the problem of recession or inflation and lag of taking appropriate action to tackle the problem. In this non-discretionary fiscal policy, *the tax structure and expenditure pattern are so designed that taxes and Government spending vary automatically in appropriate direction with the changes in national income*. That is, these taxes and expenditure pattern *without any special deliberate action* by the Government and Parliament automatically raise aggregate demand in times of recession and reduce aggregate demand in times of boom and inflation and thereby help in ensuring economic stability. These fiscal measures are therefore called *automatic stabilizers* or *built-in stabilizers*. Since these automatic stabilizers do not require any fresh deliberate policy action or legislation by the government, they represent non-discretionary fiscal policy. Built-in-stability of tax revenue and Government expenditure of transfer payments and subsidies is created because they vary with national income. These taxes and expenditure automatically bring about appropriate changes in aggregate demand and reduce the impact of recession and inflation that might occur in an economy at some times. This means that because of the existence of these automatic or built-in stabilizers recession and inflation will be shorter and less intense than otherwise be the case. Important automatic fiscal stabilisers are personal income taxes, corporate income taxes, transfer payments such as unemployment compensation, welfare benefits, corporate dividends.

We discuss below these taxes, revenue from which varies directly with the change in national income.

Personal Income Taxes. The tax rate structure is so designed that revenue from these taxes directly varies with income. Moreover, personal income taxes have progressive rates; the higher rates are charged from the upper income brackets. As a result, when national income increases during expansion and inflation, increasing percentage of the people's income are paid to the Government. Thus, through causing a decline in their disposable income these taxes automatically reduce people's consumption and therefore aggregate demand. This decline in aggregate demand because of imposition of progressive personal income taxes tends to check inflation from becoming more severe. On the other hand, when national income declines at times of recession, the tax revenue declines as well which prevents aggregate demand from falling by the same proportion as the decline in income.

Corporate Income Taxes. Companies, or corporations as they are called now, also pay a percentage of their profits as tax to the Government. Like personal income taxes, corporate income tax rate is also generally higher at higher levels of corporate profits. As recession and inflation affect corporate taxes greatly, they have a powerful stabilising effect on aggregate demand; the revenue from them rises greatly during inflation and boom which tends to reduce aggregate demand, and revenue from them falls greatly during recession which tends to offset the decline in aggregate demand.

Transfer Payments : Unemployment Compensation and Welfare Benefits. When there is recession and as a result unemployment increases, the Government has to spend more on compensation for unemployment and other welfare programmes such as food stamps, rent-subsidies, subsidies to farmers. This hike in Government expenditure tends to make recession short-lived and less intense. On the other hand, when at times of boom and inflation national income increases and therefore unemployment falls, the Government curtails its programme of social benefits which result in lowering Government expenditure. The smaller spending by the Government helps to control inflation.

Corporate Dividend Policy. With economic fluctuations, corporate profits also rise and fall. However, corporations do not so quickly increase or reduce dividends in tune with fluctuations in profits and follow a *fairly stable dividend policy*. This permits the individuals to spend more during recession and spend less than would have the case if dividends were lowered in time of recession and raised in conditions of boom and inflation. Thus, fairly stable dividends tend to cushion a recession and curb inflation by stabilising consumption expenditure.

Conclusion

It follows from above that automatic stabilisers reduce the intensity of business fluctuations, that is, both recession and inflation. However, the automatic or built-in stabilizers cannot alone correct the recession and inflation significantly. According to an estimate made for the U.S.A., automatic stabilizers have been able to reduce fluctuations in national income only by one-third. Therefore, the role of discretionary fiscal policy, namely, deliberate and explicit changes in tax rates and amount of Government expenditure are required to cure recession and curb inflation.

CROWDING OUT AND EFFECTIVENESS OF FISCAL POLICY

The critics of Keynesian theory has pointed out that expansionary effect of fiscal policy is not as much large as Keynesian economists suggest. In the Keynesian theory it is asserted that when Government increases its expenditure without raising taxes or when it reduces taxes without changing expenditure, it will have a large expansionary effect on national income. In other words, deficit budget would lead to the large increase in aggregate demand and thereby help to expand national output and income. However, it has been pointed that the above analysis of effect of expansionary fiscal policy of budget deficit ignores the effect of increase in Government expenditure or budget deficit on private investment. It has been argued that increase in Government expenditure or creation of budget deficit adversely affects private investment which offsets to a good extent the expansionary effect of budget deficit. This adverse effect comes about as increase in Government expenditure or reduction in taxes causes rate of interest to go up. There are two ways in which rise in rate of interest is explained. First, within the framework of Keynesian theory increase in Government expenditure leads to the rise in national output which raises the transactions demand for money. Given the supply of money in the economy, the increase in transactions demand for money will cause the rate of interest to go up. Secondly, in order to finance its budget deficit the Government will borrow funds from the market. This will raise the demand for loanable funds which will bring about rise in the rate of interest.

Whatever the mechanism the budget deficit or increase in Government expenditure to achieve expansion in national income and output will cause the rate of interest to go up. The rise in the rate of interest will discourage private investment. As we know from the theory of investment, at a higher rate of interest, private investment declines. Thus, *increase in Government expenditure or fiscal policy of budget deficit crowds out private investment.* This fall in private investment as a result of

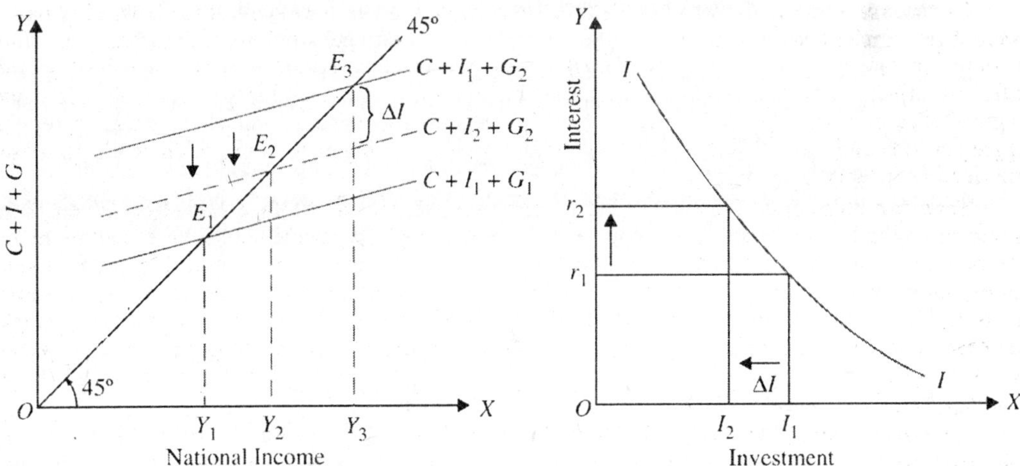

Fig. 28.4. *Effect of Crowding Out on National Output or Income*

Fig. 28.5. *Crowding Out of Private Investment*

the rise in rate of interest will offset or cancel out a part of the expansionary effect of increase in Government expenditure. The magnitude of this crowding out effect depends on the elasticity of the investment demand. If investment demand is more elastic, the decrease in private investment consequent to the rise in rate of interest will be quite substantial and will greatly offset the expansionary effect of the increase in Government expenditure. On the contrary, if investment demand is relatively inelastic, the rise in rate of interest will lead to only a small decline in private investment and therefore crowding out effect will be relatively small.

It, therefore, follows that the magnitude of crowding out weakens the effectiveness of fiscal policy. The crowding out effect of expansionary fiscal policy and its effect on national output and employment is graphically shown in Fig. 28.4. and 28.5. To begin with the economy is in equilibrium at Y_1 level of income where aggregate demand curve $C + I_1 + G_1$ intersects the 45° line and determines Y_1 level of income. Let us assume that this is much below the potential or full-employment level of output. Suppose in order to raise the level of national income and output, the Government raises its expenditure from G_1 to G_2 so that the aggregate demand curve shifts upward to the new position $C + I_1 + G_2$ which intersects the 45° line at point E_3. With increase in Government expenditure national income will rise by $\Delta G \times$ multiplier, that is, by $\Delta G \times \left(\frac{1}{1-MPC}\right)$. In the absence of crowding out effect, national income will rise to Y_3. This change in national income, ΔY or by Y_1Y_3 is equal to the increase in Government expenditure (G) times the value of multiplier $\frac{1}{1-MPC}$. However, as explained above, the increase in Government expenditure or the creation of budget deficit causes the rate of interest to rise, say from r_1 to r_2 (See Figure 28.5). It will be seen from Fig. 28.5 that with the rise in interest from r_1 to r_2, private investment decreases from I_1 to I_2. Now, with the decline in private investment expenditure, aggregate expenditure curve in Fig. 28.4 shifts below to the new lower position $C + I_2 + G_2$ (dotted) and as a result new equilibrium is reached at Y_2 level of income. Thus, net result of increase in Government expenditure (ΔG) and crowding out of private investment equal to I_1I_2 or ΔI is the expansion in national income equal to only Y_1Y_2 which is relatively very small as compared to the rise in income by Y_1Y_3 in the absence of crowding out effect. Thus, the crowding out effect has weakened the expansionary effect of fiscal policy.

However, in view of this author crowding out effect has been blown out of all proportions by the critics of Keynes. As a matter of fact, when Government raises its expenditure, it leads to a large increase in aggregate demand for several goods and services through working of the multiplier. This rising aggregate demand improves investment climate by raising expectations of making profits by the private sector. As a result, the investment demand curve II shown in Fig. 28.5 will shift outward to the right showing that at each rate of interest more private investment will be forthcoming. Thus, while negative crowding out effect takes place as a result of moving upward along the given investment demand curve, there is positive effect of increase in aggregate demand on private investment which occurs as a result of rightward shift in the investment demand curve. Thus, we see that crowding out effect is a highly controversial issue of macroeconomics.

QUESTIONS FOR REVIEW

1. What is meant by fiscal policy? Why did Keynes argue for the adoption of proper fiscal policy as an instrument of demand management to get out of depression.
2. Explain the various objectives of fiscal policy in the advanced developed economies.
3. Explain the role of fiscal policy in overcoming recession and in achieving economic stability at full-employment level.
4. What is meant by discretionary fiscal policy? How does it differ from the fiscal policy of automatic stabilizers? Explain the effectiveness of discretionary fiscal policy in curing recession and attaining equilibrium at full employment level.
5. Expansionary fiscal policy and expansionary monetary policy are complementary with each other.

6. What is effective demand ? How will it change if the Government covers its entire expenditure by (*a*) raising tax or (*b*) printing more currency.
7. Explain fiscal policy measures to control inflation. How far do you think they can be effective?
8. In an inflationary situation, the task of fiscal policy is to close the inflationary gap by reducing government expenditure or raising taxes. Discuss.
9. What is balanced budget multiplier ? Explain that even balanced budget multiplier has an expansionary effect.
10. Derive mathematically to show that the balanced budget multiplier is equal to one.
11. What is meant by crowding out effect ? Show how the expansionary effect of fiscal policy is reduced by the crowding out effect.
12. Increase in government expenditure, especially financed by borrowing from the open market, crowds out private investment. Discuss.
13. How does mechanism of crowding out of private investment work? Does it always occur ?"
14. How is private investment affected if increase in Government spending is financed by sale of Government bonds ? Do you think borrowing from the Central Bank to finance budget deficit is preferable if desired expansionary effect is to be realised ?

CHAPTER 29

Economic Stabilisation : Monetary Policy

Introduction

Monetary policy is another important instrument with which objectives of macroeconomic policy can be achieved. It is worth noting that it is the Central Bank of a country which formulates and implements the monetary policy in a country. In some countries such as India the Central Bank (the Reserve Bank is the Central Bank of India) works on behalf of the Government and acts according to its directions and broad guidelines. However, in some countries such as the USA the Central Bank (*i.e.*, Federal Reserve Bank System) enjoys an independent status and pursues its independent policy. Like the fiscal policy the broad objectives of monetary policy are to establish equilibrium at full-employment level of output, to ensure price stability and to promote economic growth of the economy. Monetary policy is concerned with changing the supply of money stock and rate of interest for the purpose of stabilizing the economy at full-employment or potential output level by influencing the level of aggregate demand. More specifically, at times of recession monetary policy involves the adoption of some monetary tools which tend the increase the money supply and lower interest rates so as to stimulate aggregate demand in the economy. On the other hand, at times of inflation, monetary policy seeks to contract the aggregate spending by tightening the money supply or raising the rate of interest.

It may however be noted that in a developing country such as India, in addition to achieving equilibrium at full employment or potential output level, monetary policy has also to promote and encourage economic growth both in the industrial and agricultural sectors of the economy. Thus, in the context of developing countries the following three are the important goals or objectives of monetary policy:

(1) to ensure economic stability at full-employment or potential level of output;

(2) to achieve price stability by controlling inflation and deflation; and

(3) to promote and encourage economic growth in the economy.

In line with the above goals of monetary policy it has often been asserted by Governors of Reserve Bank of India that *growth with price stability is the goal of monetary policy of the Reserve Bank of India*. The role of monetary policy in achieving economic stability at a higher level of output and employment will be discussed below and its role in promoting economic growth in developing country with special reference to India will be explained and critically examined at length in a later chapter.

Tools of Monetary Policy

There are four major tools or instruments of monetary policy which can be used to achieve economic and price stability by influencing aggregate demand or spending in the economy. They are:

1. Open market operations;
2. Changing the bank rate;
3. Changing the cash reserve ratio; and
4. Undertaking selective credit controls.

How these three tools of monetary policy work to influence aggregate spending and economic activity has been explained in a previous chapter. We shall explain how these various tools can be used for formulating a proper monetary policy to influence levels of aggregate output, employment and prices in the economy. In times of recession or depression, *expansionary monetary policy* or what is also called *easy money policy* is adopted which raises aggregate demand and thus stimulates the economy. On the other hand, in times of inflation and excessive expansion, *contractionary monetary policy* or what is also called *tight money policy* is adopted to control inflation and achieve price stability through reducing aggregate demand in the economy. We discuss below both these policies.

EXPANSIONARY MONETARY POLICY TO CURE RECESSION OR DEPRESSION

When the economy is faced with recession or involuntary cyclical unemployment, which comes about due to fall in aggregate demand, the central bank intervenes to cure such a situation. Central bank takes steps to expand the money supply in the economy and/or lower the rate of interest with a view to increase the aggregate demand which will help in stimulating the economy. The following three monetary policy measures are adopted as a part of an expansionary monetary policy to cure recession and to establish the equilibrium of national income at full employment level of output

1. The central bank undertakes open market operations and *buys securities in the open market.* Buying of securities by the central bank, from the public, chiefly from commercial banks will lead to the increase in reserves of the banks or amount of currency with the general public. With greater reserves, commercial banks can issue more credit to the investors and businessmen for undertaking more investment. More private investment will cause aggregate demand curve to shift upward. Thus buying of securities will have an expansionary effect.

2. The Central Bank *may lower the bank rate or what is also called discount rate*, which is the rate of interest charged by the central bank of a country on its loans to commercial banks. At a lower bank rate, the commercial banks will be induced to borrow more from the central bank and will be able to issue more credit at the lower rate of interest to businessmen and investors. This will not only make credit cheaper but also increase the availability of credit or money supply in the economy. The expansion in credit or money supply will increase the investment demand which will tend to raise aggregate output and income.

3. Thirdly, the *central bank may reduce the Cash Reserve Ratio (CRR) to be kept by the commercial banks*. In countries like India, this is a more effective and direct way of expanding credit and increasing money supply in the economy by the central bank. With lower reserve requirements, a large amount of funds is released for providing loans to businessmen and investors. As a result, credit expands and investment increases in the economy which has an expansionary effect on output and employment. In April 1996, when *Reserve Bank* lowered the CRR from 14 per cent to 13 per cent, it was estimated that this would release funds equal to Rs. 5,000 crores for the banks and thereby would significantly increase their lending capacity.

Similar to the Cash Reserve Ratio (CRR), in India there is another monetary instrument, namely, *Statutory Liquidity Ratio* (SLR) used by the Reserve Bank to change the lending capacity and therefore credit availability in the economy. As explained in a previous chapter, according to Statutory Liquidity Ratio, in addition to the Cash Reserve Ratio (CRR) banks have to keep a certain minimum proportion of their deposits in the form of some specified liquid assets such as Government securities. To increase the lendable resources of the banks, Reserve Bank can lower this Statutory Liquidity Ratio (SLR). Thus, when Reserve Bank of India lowers statutory liquidity Ratio (SLR), the, credit availability for the private sector will increase.

It may be noted that the use of all the above tools of monetary policy leads to an increase in reserves or liquid resources with the banks. Since reserves are the basis on which banks expand their credit by lending, the increase in reserves raises the money supply in the economy. Thus, *appropriate monetary policy at times of recession or depression can increase the avail-*

ability of credit and also lower the cost of credit. This leads to more private investment spending which has an expansionary effect on the economy.

How Expansionary Monetary Policy Works : Keynesian View

Now, it is important to understand how expansionary monetary policy works to cause increase in output and employment and thus help the economy to recover from recession. In the Keynes' theory, rate of interest is determined by the demand for and supply of money. According to Keynesian theory, expansion in money supply causes the rate of interest to fall. And this fall in the rate of interest will encourage businessmen to borrow more for investment spending. As is well known, *rate of interest is the opportunity cost of funds invested for purchasing capital goods.* As rate of interest falls, it becomes profitable to invest more in producing or buying capital goods. Thus, fall in the rate of interest raises the investment expenditure which is an important component of aggregate demand. The increase in aggregate demand causes expansion in aggregate output, national income and employment. How, according to Keynesian view, expansion in money supply can help to cure recession is illustrated in Fig. 29.1. In panel (*a*) of Fig. 29.1 it will be seen that when as a result of some measures taken by the central bank, the money supply increases from M_1 to M_2, the rate of interest falls from r_1 to r_2. It will be seen from panel (*b*) that with this fall in rate of interest, investment increases from I_1 to I_2. Now, in panel (*c*), it is shown how the increase in investment expenditure from I_1 to I_2 shifts the aggregate demand curve $(C + I_1 + G)$ upward so that the new aggregate demand curve $C + I_2 + G$ intersects the 45° line at point E_2 and thus establishes equilibrium at full-employment output level Y_F. It may be noted that with the given increase in investment how much aggregate output or national income will increase depends on the size of income multiplier which is determined by marginal propensity to consume. The greater the size of multiplier, the greater the impact of increment in investment on expansion of output and income.

From above, it is clear that monetary policy can play an important role in stimulating the economy and ensuring stability at full employment level. But it is worth mentioning that there are several weak links in the full chain of increase in money supply achieving a significant expansion in economic activity. In fact, *Keynes himself was of the view that in times of depression, monetary policy will be ineffective in reviving the economy and therefore he laid stress on the adoption of fiscal policy to overcome depression.*

The first weak link in the above argument of expansionary monetary policy relates to the elasticity of money-demand (*i.e.*, liquidity preference) curve M^d in panel (*a*) of Fig. 29.1. As shall be explained at length below, if demand for money curve M^d is nearly flat (*i.e.*, highly elastic), the increase in money supply by the central bank will not greatly affect the rate of interest and consequently further steps of significant expansion in investment and aggregate demand will not be realised. Besides, even if money demand curve is elastic and, therefore, expansion of money supply lowers the rate of interest significantly, the investment may not rise much. This is because if the investment demand curve is steep or inelastic, that is, investment is not sensitive to the changes in rate of interest, the fall in the rate of interest will fail to cause any significant increase in investment. As a result, aggregate demand curve will not change much and expansionary effect on output and employment will not be realised.

Further, the effect of increase in investment on output and employment depends on the size of multiplier. If there are several leakages in the multiplier process, even increase in investment may not bring about much change in output and employment. Thus, because of several weak links in the process or chain of expansion in money supply bringing about expansion, Keynes remarked that *there are many a slip between the cup and the lip*. Therefore, for all these reasons (especially because of the liquidity trap in the demand for money curve at lower rates of interest), Keynes was of the view that monetary policy is not an effective instrument in bringing about revival of the economy from the depressed state.

It may however be noted that modern Keynesians do not share the pessimistic view of the effectiveness of monetary policy. They think that liquidity preference curve is not flat and further that investment demand is fairly sensitive to the changes in the rate of interest. Therefore,

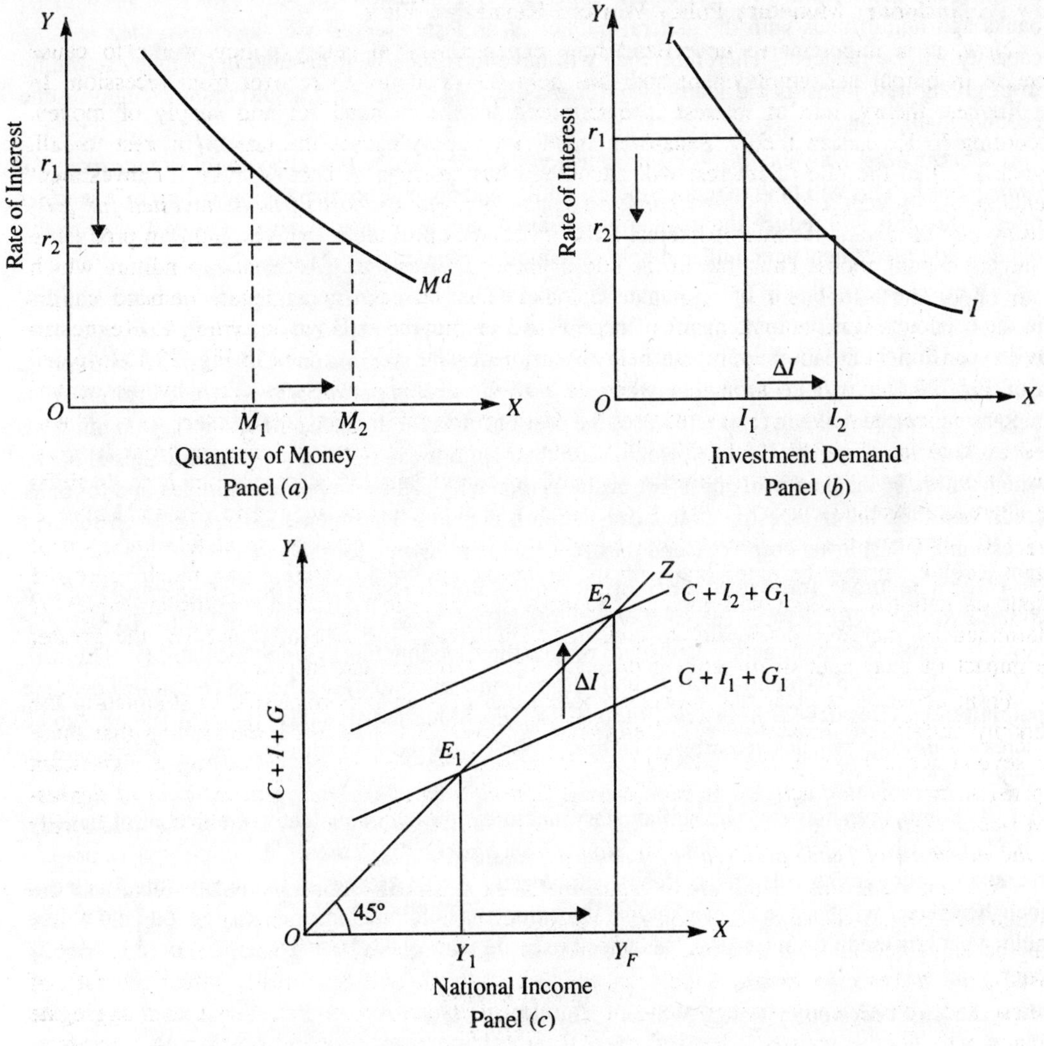

Fig. 29.1. *How Expansionary Monetary Policy Works: Keynesian View*

modern Keynesians equally advocate for the adoption of discretionary monetary policy as for the discretionary fiscal policy to get rid of recession.

TIGHT MONETARY POLICY TO CONTROL INFLATION

When aggregate demand rises sharply due to large consumption and investment expenditure or, more importantly, due to the large increase in Government expenditure relative to its revenue resulting in huge budget deficits, a demand-pull inflation occurs in the economy. Besides, when there is too much creation of money for one reason or the other, it generates inflationary pressures in the economy. To check the demand-pull inflation which has been a major problem in India and several other countries in recent years the adoption of *contractionary monetary policy* which is popularly called *tight monetary policy* is called for. Note that tight or restrictive money policy is one which reduces the availability of credit and also raises its cost. The following monetary measures which constitute tight money policy are generally adopted to control inflation:

1. *The Central Bank sells the Government securities to the banks, other depository institutions and the general public through open market operations.* This action will reduce the reserves with the banks and liquid funds with the general public. With less reserves with the banks, their lending capacity will be reduced. Therefore, they will have to reduce their demand deposits by refraning from giving new loans as old loans as old loans are paid back. As a result, money supply in the economy will shrink.

2. *The bank rate may also be raised which will discourage the banks to take loans from the central bank.* This will tend to reduce their liquidity and also induce them to raise their own lending rates. Thus this will reduce the availability of credit and also raise its cost. This will lead to the reduction in investment spending and help in reducing inflationary pressures.

It may be noted that in India changes in bank rate has not been generally used to bring stability in the economy. It is the instruments of **repo rate and reverse repo rate changes** that have often been used to fight inflation and recesseonary situation. *Repo rate is the interest rate at which Reserve Bank of India lends funds to the commercial banks for a short period of time.* To control inflation repo rate is raised. Hike in repo rate raises the cost of funds for the banks which, if they do not have excess reserves or enough liquidity, would raise their lending rates. The rise in lending rates of banks which will raise the borrowing costs for business men will lead to the reduction in demand for bank credit and thus lower investment and consumpiton demand. The opposite happens when to fight recession the RBI lowers repo rate and thus reducing lending rate for the banks.

3. The most important anti-inflationary measures is *raising of statutory Cash Reserve Ratio (CRR).* Rise in cash reserve ratio (CRR) reduces cash reserves of banks. To meet the new higher resrve requirements, banks will reduce their lending that is credit availability. This will ave a direct effect on the contraction of money supply in the economy and help in controlling demand pull inflation. Besides Cash Reserve Ratio (CRR), the Statutory Liquidity Ratio (SLR) can also be increased through which excess reserves of the banks are mopped up resulting in contraction in credit.

4. Fourthly, an important anti-inflationary measure is the use of qualitative credit control, namely, *raising of minimum margins for obtaining loans from banks against the stocks of sensitive commodities* such as foodgrains, oilseeds, cotton, sugar, vegetable oil. As a result of this measure, businessmen themselves will have to finance to a greater extent the holding of inventories of goods and will be able to get less credit from banks. This selective credit control has been extensively used in India to control inflationary pressures.

How the Tight Monetary Policy Works : Keynesian View

It is important to understand how tight monetary policy works to check inflation. As explained above, tight monetary policy seeks to reduce the money supply through contraction of credit in the economy and also raising the cost of credit, that is lending rates of interest. The reduction in money supply itself raises the rate of interest. The higher interest rate reduces investment spending which results in lowering of aggregate demand curve ($C + I + G$). The decrease in aggregate demand tends to restrain demand pull inflation. How tight money policy helps in checking inflation is graphically shown in Fig. 29.2. Let us assume that full-employment level of national income is Y_F as depicted in panel (*c*) of Fig. 29.2. Now, if due to a large budget deficit and excessive creation of money supply, aggregate demand curve shifts to $C + I_2 + G_2$; inflationary gap of E_1H comes to exist at full-employment level. That is, the sum of consumption expenditure, private investment spending and Government expenditure exceeds the full-employment level of output by E_1H. This creates a demand-pull inflation causing rise in prices. Though with aggregate demand curve $C + I_2 + G_2$ equilibrium reaches at point E_2 and as a result national income increases but only in money terms ; real income or output level remaining constant at OY_F.

Now, it will be seen from panel (*a*) that if tight money policy succeeds in reducing money supply from M_2 to M_1 the rate of interest will rise from r_1 to r_2. Panel (*b*) of Fig. 29.2 shows that at a higher interest rate r_2, private investment falls from I_2 to I_1. This reduction in investment expenditure shifts aggregate demand curve $C + I_2 + G_2$ downward to $C + I_1 + G_1$ and in this way inflationary gap is closed and equilibrium at full-employment output level Y_F is once again established. In our figure it

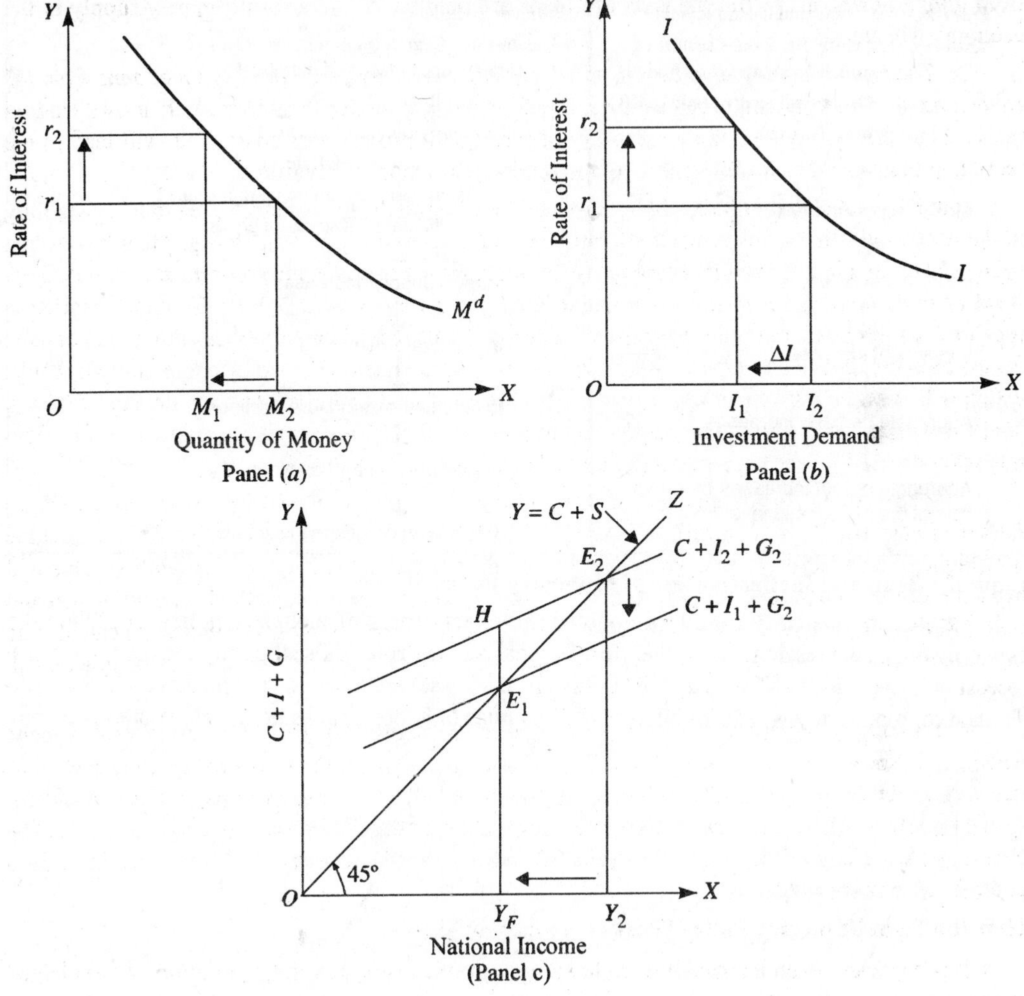

Fig. 29.2. *How Anti-inflationary Monetary Policy Works : Keynesian View*

has been assumed that there is contraction of money supply from M_2 to M_1 and as a result rise in rate of interest form r_1 to r_2 is sufficient to reduce investment expenditure equal to $I_2 - I_1$ which is equal to inflationary gap and in this way macroeconomic equilibrium without any inflationary pressure is established at output leave Y_F.

It should be further remembered that in our analysis of the successful working of the tight monetary policy it is assumed that demand for money curve (*i.e.*, liquidity preference curve) is fairly steep so as to push up the rate of interest from r_1 to r_2 and further that investment demand curve *II* in panel (*b*) of Fig. 29.2 is fairly elastic so that rise in rate of interest from r_1 to r_2 is sufficient to reduce investment by $I_2 - I_1$ or ΔI. If these conditions regarding the slopes of the money demand curve and investment demand curve represent the real world situation, then tight monetary policy will succeed in controlling inflation and ensuring price stability.

To sum up, Keynesian view of how expansionary and contractionary (tight) monetary policies work to achieve the twin goals of price stability and equilibrium at full-employment level of output is shown in the accompanying box.

Monetary Policy : Keynesian View

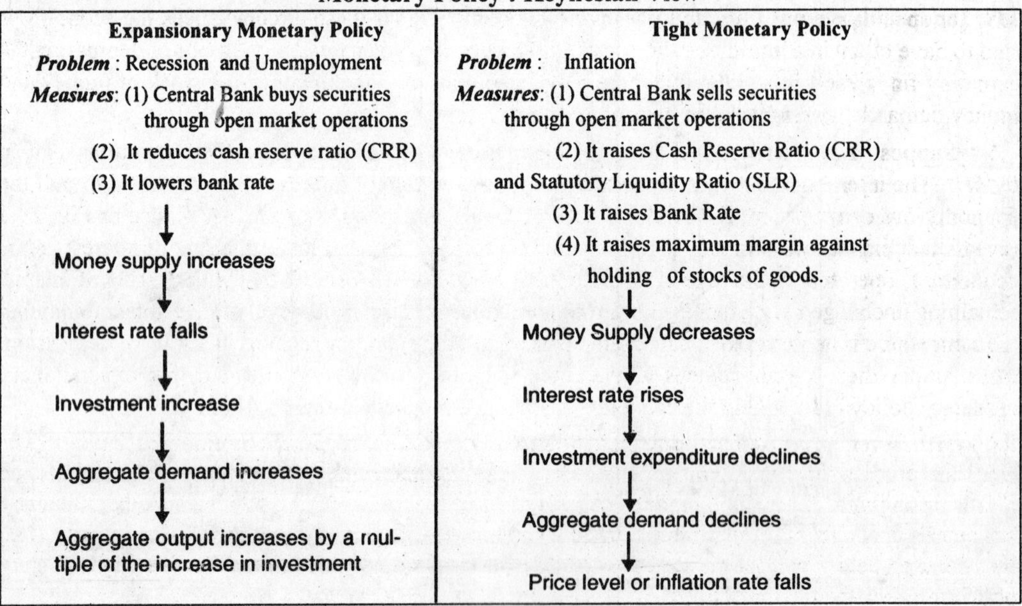

Expansionary Monetary Policy	Tight Monetary Policy
Problem : Recession and Unemployment	***Problem*** : Inflation
Measures: (1) Central Bank buys securities through open market operations (2) It reduces cash reserve ratio (CRR) (3) It lowers bank rate	***Measures***: (1) Central Bank sells securities through open market operations (2) It raises Cash Reserve Ratio (CRR) and Statutory Liquidity Ratio (SLR) (3) It raises Bank Rate (4) It raises maximum margin against holding of stocks of goods.
↓ Money supply increases ↓ Interest rate falls ↓ Investment increase ↓ Aggregate demand increases ↓ Aggregate output increases by a multiple of the increase in investment	↓ Money Supply decreases ↓ Interest rate rises ↓ Investment expenditure declines ↓ Aggregate demand declines ↓ Price level or inflation rate falls

Liquidity Trap and Ineffectiveness of Monetary Policy

Keynes and his early followers doubted the effectiveness of monetary policy in pulling the economy out of depression. They therefore emphasized the role of fiscal policy for fighting severe recession. According to Keynes and his followers, during severe recession people have a high elastic demand for money at low rates of interest. At low rates of interest banks hold on to whatever money

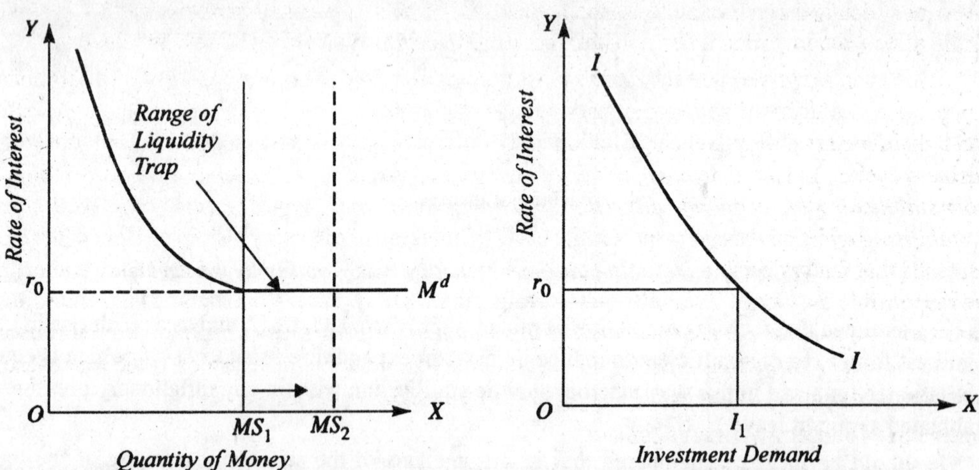

Fig. 29.3. *Liquidity Trap and Increase in Money Supply* **Fig. 29.4.** *Investment Demand*

reserves they happen to get and the people in general also hold on to whatever money they spare. According to Keynes, demand for money or what he calls liquidity preference is determined mainly by transactions and speculative motives. Whereas transactio@ns demand for money is determined by the level of national income, the speculative demand for money depends on the expectations regarding future rates of interest. During depression, current rate of interest may fall so low that most of the people expect the interest rate to rise in future and therefore they hold on to their money for the present. This makes the demand for money absolutely elastic at a low rate of interest as is shown in Fig. 29.3. It will be seen from Fig. 29.3 that at a low rate of interest r_0 demand curve for money M^d is absolutely elastic showing people demand or hold on to all the increases in money supply beyond MS_1 for speculative purposes and not invest in bonds. Under these circumstances the economy is said to have fallen in a liquidity trap. A liquidity trap occurs when under conditions of depression the economy finds itself in a situation where people hold all the increments in the stock of money and money demand curve M^d takes a horizontal shape.

Suppose during a recession, stock of money is equal to MS_1 and money demand curve is given by M^d. The interaction between these two determines r_0 rate of interest. Suppose now, to pull the economy out of recession, the stock of money supply is expanded to MS_2. A glance at Fig. 29.3 reveals that expansion in money supply from MS_1 to MS_2 does not lower the rate of interest as the economy is operating in the rage of liquidity tap. Now, Fig. 29.4 shows that with the rate of interest remaining unchanged at r_0, the level of investment does not rise. With level of investment remaining the same, there is no increase in aggregate demand and the economy remains in a state of depression. Thus, under these circumstances Keynes and his early followers contended that expansionary monetary policy did not help the economy in staging a recovery from recession.

It may, However, he noted that the concept of liquidity trap is not supported by empirical studies. The empirical studies show that demand for money (liquidity preference) never becomes flat and instead it falls throughout. Therefore, modern Keynesians and toehr economists now believe that monetary policy can play a useful role in stabilising the economy at full employment level. However, as shall be discussed below, it is the *monetarists* led by Friedman who do not favour discretionary monetary policy to check cyclical instability.

MONETARY POLICY : MONETARIST VIEW

Though most of the modern economists regard both fiscal and monetary policies as important tools for stabilising the economy there is a group of economists known as *monetarists* led by Friedman who thick that changes in money supply are the key determinants in the level of economic activity and the price level. They contend that demand curve for money is quite steep and the investment demand curve is quite elastic so that when there is a change in money supply, it significantly affects the investment demand and therefore the equilibrium level of nominal income.

However, surprisingly, enough, the most monetarists do not advocate the use of discretionary monetary policy, namely, an expansionary or easy money policy, to lift the economy out of recession and tight monetary policy to check inflationary boom and thereby correct the 'downs' and 'ups' of the business cycles. In fact, *Friedman, the chief exponent of monetarism, contends that, historically, far from stabilising the economy, discretionary changes in money supply or rates of interest have a destabilising effect on the economy.* On the basis of his study of monetary history of United States, he contends that faulty decision regrading changes in money supply, made by the monetary authorities, are responsible for a lot of instability that prevailed during the period of his study. Thus, according to monetarists, *it is not the presence of certain inherent destabilising factors in a free-market economy but the monetary mismanagement* by the discretionary monetary policies which is the root cause of economic instability that has been existing in the free market economies.

Source of Monetary Mismanagement

According to monetarists, there are two important sources of monetary mismanagement. (1) *variable time lags* concerning the effect of money supply on the nominal income and (2) *treating interest rate as the target of monetary policy* for influencing investment demand for stabilising the economy. We examine below both these sources of monetary mismanagement.

1. Variable Time Lags. First there is a problem of variable long time lags that occur for changes in money supply to bring about desirable effect on nominal income. From his empirical studies Friedman concludes that it takes six months to two years for the changes in money supply to produce a significant effect on nominal income. Monetarists argue that since it is extremely difficult to know the time lag involved in a specific monetary policy measure adopted to tackle the problem, it is impossible to determine *when* a particular policy measure should be taken and *which policy measure*, expansionary or tight, is suitable under the given situation. In fact, according to the monetarists, in view of the uncertainty about the exact duration of time lags involved, the use of discretionary monetary policy to stabilise the economy may backfire and further intesify the cyclical instability. For example, if expansionary monetary policy is adopted because the various economic indicators show the situation of mild recession then, due to the time lags involved, say six to eight months, for the policy to yield results, the economic situation might change and becomes reverse during that period and becomes one of mild inflationary situation. Expansionary monetary policy which produce the effect after 6 to 8 months may, therefore, acutally intensify the inflationary situation.

2. Interest rate as a Wrong Target Variable. The second source of money mismanagement is the wrong target variable chosen by the monetary authorities. Monetarists have asserted that monetary authorities have tried to control the interest rates to stabilise the economy. It has been argued that Central Bank cannot simultaneously stabilise both the interest rate and money supply. By controlling the interest rate it has actually destabilised the economy. For example, if the economy is recovering from recession and is presently approaching full employment with aggregate demand, output, employment and prices all registering a rise, the transactions demand for money will increase. This increase in transactions demand for money will cause the rate of interest to rise. But if the monetary authorities have chosen to stabilise the interest rate, they would adopt tight monetary policy to prevent the interest rate from going up. Demand when the economy is recovering from recession, and will again cause the recessionary omy unstable. Similarly, when the economy is going into recession, it will result in lowering aggregate output and prices. This fall in aggregate output and prices will cause a decline in the transactions demand for money. And the decrease in transactions demand will lead to the fall in interest rate. To prevent this fall in interest rate, if money supply is increased, it will generate stability in the economy rather than removing it.

Monetary Rule : Monetary Policy Prescription

From the above analysis it follows that monetarists are not in favour of stabilising the interest rate they advocate for the *adoption of a rule rather than pursuing discretionary monetary policy* to stabilize the economy. They prescribe a *rule for the growth of the money supply* to achieve economic grow with stability. According to the monetary rule suggested by Friedman, *money supply should be allowed to grow at the rate equal to the rate of growth of output*. If the economy is expected to growth annually at the rate of 3, 4 or 5 per cent, money supply should also grow at this rate. The growth of output of an economy will absorb the extra money supply created as per this rule, without generating inflationary or recessionary conditions, and will thus ensure stability in the economy. To quote Ritter and Silber, "such a rule would eliminate the major cause of instability in the economy—the capricious and unpredictable impact of counter cyclical monetary policy. As long as the money supply grows at a constant rate each year, be it 3, 4 or 5 per cent, any decline into recession will be temporary. The liquidity provided by a constantly growing money supply will cause the aggregate demand to expand. Similarly, if the supply of money does not rise at a ore than average rate, any inflationary increase in spending will burn itself out for lack of fuel."[1]

Monetary rule has been criticised by the Keynesian economists. They have argued that monetary rule will have a destabilising effect. Given that the velocity of money (V) is unstable or variable, increase in money supply (M), according to this rule, may not ensure growth of aggregate demand (which, according to monetarist theory, is equal to MV) equal to the rate of growth of output in a year

which is difficult to predict. Thus, money supply increase may sometimes exceed the growth of output and sometimes fall short of it and as result may cuase sometimes demand-pull inflation and sometimes necessary conditions. Thus, according to Keynesian economists, policy of monetary rule does not guarantee economic stability and it may itself create economic instability.

QUESTIONS FOR REVIEW

1. What is meant by monetary policy ? Briefly explain the instruments of monetary policy.
2. Expaling the objectives of monetary policy.
3. Explain monetary policy measures that should be adopted for curing recession (or depression) and reviving the economy. How does expansionary monetary policy work ? How does Keynesian view in this regard differe the onetarist view ?
4. What are the factors that determine the effectiveness of monetary policy in reviving the economy from recession. Why Keynes thought that monetary policy was ineffective in reviving the economy from depression ?
5. What is liquidity trap ? How does it make the expansionary monetary policy ineffective in reviving the economy from recession ?
6. Explain the main instruments of monetary policy that can be adopted to control inflation in the economy.
7. Explain the mechanism through which tight monetary policy works to check inflation. Illustrate diagrammatically.
8. Descritionary monetary policy can play an important role in stabilising the economy at full employment. Discuss.
9. Explain the views of Friedman and his follower modern monetarists regarding monetary policy as a tool of economic stabilisation. In this connection also comment on the monetarist view that interest rate is a wrong target variable of proper monetary policy.
10. What is meant by 'time lags' ? How do they affect the efficiency of monetary policy to stabilise the economy?
11. What are the instruments of monetary policy ? Explain the role of changes in bank rate and open market operations in controlling trade cycles.
12. "Monetary policy for its success depends on fiscal policy." Explain and critically examine this statement.

PART VI

GOVERNMENT AND THE MACROECONOMY : GOVERNMENT'S BUDGET CONSTRAINT AND FISCAL POLICY

- Government in the Macroeconomy : Public Expenditure
- Financing of Government Expenditure : Taxation
- Role of Fiscal Policy and Taxation in Mobilisation for Economic Growth
- Government Borrowing and Debt-Financing of Budget Deficit
- Government Budget Constraint : Money Financing of Budget Deficit
- Fiscal Deficit and Economic Growth

Chapter 30

Government in the Macroeconomy

CHAPTER 30

Government in the Macroeconomy : Public Expenditure

What is Public Finance?

In public finance we study the finances of the Government. Thus, public finance deals with the question how the Government raises its resources to meet its ever-rising expenditure. As Dalton puts it, *public finance is "concerned with the income and expenditure of public authorities and with the adjustment of one to the other."*[1] Accordingly, effects of taxation, Government expenditure, public borrowing and deficit financing on the economy constitutes the subject matter of public finance. Thus, Prof. Otto Eckstein writes "*Public Finance is the study of the effects of budgets on the economy, particularly the effect on the achievement of the major economic objects—growth, stability, equity and efficiency*"[2] Further, it also deals with fiscal policies which ought to be adopted to achieve certain objectives such as price stability, economic growth, more equal distribution of income. Economic thinking about the role that public finance is expected to play has changed from time to time according to the changes in economic situation. Before the Great Depression that gripped the Western industrialised countries during the thirties, the role of public finance was considered to be raising sufficient resources for carrying out the Government functions of civil administration and defence from foreign countries. During this period, the classical economists considered it prudent to keep expenditure to the minimum so that taxing of the people is avoided as far as possible. Further, it was thought that Government budget must be balanced. Public borrowing was recommended mainly for production purposes. During a war, of course, public borrowing was considered legitimate but it was thought that the Government should repay or reduce the debt as soon as possible.

The Concept of Functional Finance

But under the impact of the Great Depression of thirties and the Keynesian explanation of it, the thinking about and role of public finance underwent a sea change. The classical view of public finance could not meet the requirements of the then prevailing situation. In order to increase aggregate effective demand and thereby raise the level of income and employment in the country, public finance was called upon to play an active role. During the second world war and after, the Western economies suffered from serious inflationary pressures which was attributed to the excessive aggregate demand. So, in such inflationary conditions, the public finance was expected to check prices .through reducing aggregate demand. Thus the budget which was previously meant to raise resources for limited activities of the Government assumed a *functional role* to serve as an instrument of *economic regulation.*

It came to be realised that government's taxing and spending policies could go a long way in mitigating economic fluctuations. Balanced budgets are no longer considered sacrosanct and the governments can spend beyond their resources without offending canons of sound finance to restore the health of the economy. Public borrowing and consequent increase in public debt at the time of depression raises aggregate demand and thereby helps in raising the level of income and employment. Therefore, deficit budget and increase in public debt at such times is

1. Dalton, *Public Finance,*
2. O. Eckstein, *Public Finance,* Prentice Hall of India Private Ltd., 3rd Edition, p. 53.

a thing to be welcomed. It was further demonstrated by Keynes that deficit spending by the Government could activise a depressed economy by creating income and employment much more than the original amount of deficit financing through the process of multiplier. Thus, after Keynesian revolution public finance assumed a functional role of *maintaining economic stability at full employment level.* Therefore, the present view of public finance is not one of mere resource-raising for the Government but one of serving as an instrument for maintaining stability through management of demand. Therefore, this present view of public finance has been described by A.P. Lerner as one of "*Functional Finance*".

In developing countries, public finance has to perform another important role. Whereas in the developed industrialised countries, the bask problem in the short run is to ensure stability at full employment level and in the long run to ensure steady rate of economic growth, that is, growth without fluctuations, the developing countries confront a more difficult problem of how to generate and sustain a higher rate of economic growth so as to tackle the problems of proverty and unemployment. Therefore, public finance has to play a special role of promoting economic growth in the developing countries besides maintaining price stability. Further, for developing countries mere economic growth is not enough; the composition of growing output and distribution of additional incomes ought to be such as will ensure removal of poverty and unemployment in the developing countries. Therefore, public finance has not only to augment resources foı development and to achieve optimum allocation of resources, but also to promote fair distribution of income and expansion in employment opportunities. This is the functional view of public finance in the context of the developing countries.

PUBLIC EXPENDITURE

Of the two main branches of public finance, namely, public revenue and public expenditure, we shall first study the public expenditure. The classical economists did not analyse in depth the effects of public expenditure, for public expenditure throughout the nineteenth century was very small owing to the very restricted Government activities. The Governments followed *laissez faire* economic policies and their functions were only confined to defend the country from foreign aggression and to maintain law and order within their territories. But now, the expenditure of Government all the world over have greatly increased. Therefore, the modern economists have started analysing the effects of public expenditure on production, distribution and the levels of income and employment in the economy.

Importance of Public Expenditure

Thanks to the macroeconomic theory advanced by J.M. Keynes, the role of public expenditure in the determination of level of income and its distribution is now well recognised. Keynesian macroeconomics provides a theoretical basis for recent developments in public expenditure programmes in the developed countries. The public expenditure can be used as a lever to raise aggregate demand and thereby to get the economy out of recession. On the other hand, through variation in public expenditure, aggregate demand can be managed to check inflation in the economy. Public expenditure can also be used to improve income distribution, to direct the allocation of resources in the desired lines and to influence the composition of national product. In the developing countries also, the role of public expenditure is highly significant.

In the developing countries, the variation in public expenditure is not only to ensure economic stability but also to generate and accelerate economic growth and to promote employment opportunities. The public expenditure policy in developing countries also plays a useful role in alleviating mass poverty existing in them and to reduce inequalities in income distribution. In what follows, we shall study the types of public expenditure, the causes of growth of public expenditure and its effects on production, distribution and economic growth in both the developed and the developing countries.

Classification of Public Expenditure

Revenue Expenditure and Capital Expenditure. Public expenditure has been classified into various categories. Firstly, Government expenditure has been classified into *revenue expenditure* and *capital expenditure*. Revenue expenditure is a current or consumption expenditure incurred on civil administration (*i.e.*, police, jails and judiciary), defence forces, public health and education. This revenue expenditure is of recurrent type which is incurred year after year. On the other hand, capital expenditure is incurred on building durable assets. It is a non-recurring type of expenditure. Expenditure incurred on building multipurpose river projects, highways, steel plants etc., and buying machinery and equipment is regarded as capital expenditure.

Transfer Payments and Expenditure on Goods and Services. Another useful classification of public expenditure divides it into transfer payments and non-transfer payments. *Transfer payments refer to those kinds of expenditure against which there is no corresponding transfer of real resources (i.e., goods and services) to the Government.* Expenditure incurred on old-age pensions, unemployment allowance, sickness benefits, interest on public debt during a year etc., are examples of transfer payments because the Government does not get any service or goods against them in the particular year. On the other hand, *expenditure incurred on buying or using goods and services is a non-transfer payment as against such an expenditure, the Government receives goods or services.* It is therefore called expenditure on goods and services. It may be noted that expenditure on defence, education, health etc., are non-transfer expenditure as in return for these, Government obtains the services of army personnel, teachers, doctors etc., as well as some goods or equipments used in these activities. Investments expenditure is undoubtedly a non-transfer expenditure as through it Government obtains capital goods. It is worthwhile to mention that whereas in case of transfer payments, it is the beneficiaries that decides about the use of resources, in the case of non-transferable type of expenditure, the Government itself decides about the use of real resources, especially whether they are to be used for consumption or investment purposes.

Developmental and Non-Development Expenditure. Another useful classification of public expenditure rests on whether a particular expenditure by the Government promotes development. All those expenditures of Government which promote economic growth are called developmental expenditure. Expenditure on irrigation projects, flood control measures, transport and communication, capital formation in agricultural and industrial sectors are described as developmental. On the other hand, expenditure on defence, civil administration (*i.e.*, police, jails and judiciary), interest on public debt etc., are put into the category of non-development expenditure. It may be noted that, till recently, expenditure on education and health were regarded as non-developmental type. It has now been realised that the expenditure on education and public health promotes the growth of what is called *human capital* which promotes economic growth as much as physical capital, if not more. Therefore, these days, expenditure on education, research and health are generally regarded as developmental expenditure.

It is worth noting that division of Government expenditure into developmental or non-developmental is the modern counterpart of the distinction drawn by classical economists between *productive* and *unproductive public expenditure*, which has been a subject of great controversy. For instance, it has been pointed out that even Government expenditure on defence and civil administration helps to maintain conditions in which productive activity can be carried out. It is, therefore, claimed by some that indirectly, expenditure on defence, and civil administration is also productive. Thus, we see that what Government expenditure is developmental or productive and what non-developmental or unproductive is not based on any objective or fool-proof criteria and is therefore somewhat arbitrary.

GROWTH OF PUBLIC EXPENDITURE

Public expenditure has phenomenally increased all the world over. A pertinent question is what are the causes of this phenomenal growth in public expenditure. It will be useful to discuss this with reference to India. This is because the factors responsible for a large increase in public expenditure over time in India are generally applicable to other countries too. It will be interesting to mention here two laws about the growth of public expenditure.

Wagner's Law of Increasing State Activity. First, there is *Wagner's Law of Increasing State Activity.* According to Wagner, a German economist, there are inherent tendencies for the activities of the Government to increase both extensively and intensively. In other words, according to this law as an economy develops over time, the activities or functions of the Government increase. With the development of the economy, new functions and activities are undertaken by the Government and old functions are performed more thoroughly. The expansion in the Government functions and activities leads to the increase in public expenditure. Though Wanger based his law on the historical evidence drawn from economic growth of Germany, this applies equally to other countries, both developed and developing ones.

Wiseman-Peacock Hypothesis. The second hypothesis about the growth of public expenditure has been put forward by Wiseman and Peacock in their study of public expenditure of U.K. According to this *Wiseman-Peacock hypothesis,* Government expenditure does not increase at a steady rate continuously but in jerks and step-like manner. However, in the view of the present author, both these factors, one making for a continuous increase in Government activity and consequently public expenditure as emphasised by Wagner and others like war and depression causing the public expenditure to rise by jerks as emphasised by Wiseman and Peacock have been responsible for the enormous increase in public expenditure. In what follows, we shall explain the factors responsible for growth in public expenditure with special reference to the Indian economy.

1. **Defence.** An important factor responsible for public expenditure is the mounting defence expenditure incurred by countries all the world over. It is not only during actual wars that defence expenditure has been rising but even during peace time, the countries have to remain in the state of military preparedness demanding large defence expenditure. There is arms race going on between countries. A poor country like India has to safeguard its hard earned freedom and this involves a lot of expenditure on building up efficient and adequate armed forces. India is wedged in between two enemies, namely, expansionist China and aggressive Pakistan, which have been strengthening their armed forces. India had to fight three wars since independence. India has thus to remain in a state of military preparedness. Internally also in view of clash of linguistic, territorial and political interests, lot of expenditure has to be incurred on maintaining internal security.

2. **Population Growth and Urbanisation.** Another factor responsible for the increase in public expenditure is the growth in population and urbanisation of the economies. Population has been increasing in almost all countries of the world, though at varying rates. In India the population has been increasing at an alarming rate since independence. The population of India which was 36 crores in 1951 has now gone upto about 100 crores. The scale of government activities such as providing education, public health, roads and transport facilities has to increase in harmony with the growth of population. Further, when population increases, more has to be spent on administrative services (police, jails, judiciary etc.) to maintain law and order in the country.

With the progress of the economy and the growth of population, the extent of urbanisation increases. In India, the proportion of urban population to the total population has risen from 11.3 per cent in 1921 to 25.5 per cent in 1991 and to 27.8 per cent in 2001. As a result of the increasing urbanisation, the existing towns expand and the new ones come up. Urbanisation calls for greater per capita expenditure on social and administrative services. Therefore, the increase in urbanisation in India has tended to increase the government expenditure.

3. **Activities of a Welfare State.** The Government activities and functions have been increasing due to the change in the nature of State. The modern States are no longer Police States concerned mainly with the maintenance of law and order. They have now become Welfare States. *A Welfare State is one which provides for social insurance of its citizens against old age, sickness, unemployment etc.* The modern Governments have therefore to incur a lot of expenditure on social security measures such as old age pensions, unemployment allowances, sickness benefits.

4. **Maintaining Economic Stability.** As pointed out by Wagner, state functions increase with the advancement and progress of the economy. In the nineteenth and early twentieth century, the Government followed *laissez-fair* policy. Now, need for active intervention of the Government has been increasingly felt. Thanks to J.M. Keynes whose macroeconomic theory clearly brought out that the working of free-market mechanism does not ensure economic stability at full employment level. According to his theory, lapses from full employment or depressions are caused by deficiency of aggregate demand due to the slackened private investment activity. In order to compensate for this shortfall in private investment, the Government has to step up its expenditure on public works. The increase in Government expenditure raises aggregate demand manifold through the working of what Keynes has called income multiplier. This helps to push the economy out of depression and to raise levels of income and employment. Now, this compensatory fiscal policy is being followed by all the world over, since achievement of full employment and maintenance of economic stability has become an important objective of the Government.

It is in line with the objective of employment that in India, the Government has taken over several *private sick mills* and incurs a lot of expenditure on them so that workers employed in them are not rendered unemployed. Further, the Indian Government, both Central and States, incur a lot of expenditure on relief public works in rural areas when drought and other natural calamities occurs. Besides, a lot of public expenditure is being incurred on special employment schemes to promote employment in the economy.

5. **Economic Growth and Development.** The most important factor in developing countries such as ours that has led to a phenomenal increase in public expenditure is the expansion in developmental activities of the Government. In countries like India which have socialistic tendencies the public sector plays an important role in promoting economic growth and development. Not only public utility services such as water supply, electricity, post and petroleum and transport services have been undertaken by the public sector, but also the Government has invested a huge sum of resources in industrial and agricultural development of the economy. Several steel plants, multipurpose irrigation projects, fertilizer factories, coal mining, exploration and production of oil and petroleum, different kinds of machine-making industries and chemical plants have been started and are being operated in the public sector. On these a huge amount of expenditure is being incurred by the Government in India. Owing to these developmental activities of the Government in India, the proportion of developmental expenditure to the total Government expenditure has greately increased and is greater than that of non-developmental expenditure. In 2003-04, Central Governments plan expenditure, which is mainly development expenditure, was 122.3 thousand crores which rose to 137.4 thousand crores in 2004-05.

6. **Mounting Debt Service Charges.** The Governments in all developing countries (including India) has been borrowing heavily in recent years to finance their increasing activities. Not only the debt money has to be paid back when it matures, interest payments have also to be made annually to the creditors. These debt service charges have resulted in enormous increase in public expenditure. It should be noted that the Government in India has not only been borrowing from within the country but also from abroad through foreign aid or commerical loans from private capital markets to finance her development plans. It has been estimated that for

the year 1998-99, Rs. 75,000 crores were spent on the interest payments which went up to Rs. 125,900 crores in 2004-05 by the Central Government.

7. **Mounting Expenditure on Subsidies.** Governments, both in the developed and developing countries, incur a lot of expenditure on subsidies to the various sections of population. In India, the Government has been providing subsidies on food, fertilizers, exports and education, and expenditure on them has been increasing at a rapid rate which is the main cause of large fiscal deficit in India. For example while, in 2002-2003, the Central, Government expenditure on subsidies was of the order of Rs. 44.6 thousand crores and for the year 2004-2005 it was estimated to go up to Rs. 46.5 thousand crores. The expenditure of Central Government's expenditure on subsidies on food, fertilizers, exports now account for about 7 per cent of budget expenditure. While the aim of giving food subsidy is to help the people below the poverty line, the aim of fertilizer subsidy is to promote the growth of agriculture and help small farmers.

8. **Anti-Poverty Schemes.** Another important cause of increasing public expenditure in India is huge expenditure which he Government is incurring on employment generating anti-poverty schemes. It has now been realised that economic growth alone will not eradicate poverty, at least in the short run. Therefore, various employment schemes have been started by the Government for the people living below the poverty line. Prominent among these anti-poverty schemes in India are Jawahar Rozgar Yojna, Prime Minister's Employment Scheme and Integrated Rural Development Scheme (IRDP). Expenditure on these schemes has greatly risen in recent years.

Conclusion

We have seen above that several factors have been working to cause increase in public expenditure in all the economies of the world. Though most of the factors are common operating all the world over, there are some additional factors in developing countries like India which have adopted socialist path to economic development wherein public sector plays a dominant role in the process of socio-economic development. This calls for more rapid growth of public expenditure.

EFFECTS OF PUBLIC EXPENDITURE ON PRODUCTION AND DISTRIBUTION

Having studied the causes of large increase in public expenditure, it will be useful to explain the effects of public expenditure on the production and distribution in the economy. Public expenditure, if properly allocated and efficiently used, can have a wholesome effect on the economy. Public expenditure can augment productive capacity of the economy and improve productivity of its working class. It can also reduce inequalities in income distribution, if properly designed. In the following we shall spell out in detail the impact of public expenditure on production and income distribution in the economy.

Effect of Public Expenditure on Production

It is generally pointed out that all kinds of expenditure by Government is not productive. For instance, Government expenditure on defence and civil administration (police, jail and judiciary) is said to be unproductive for it does not apparently add to the volume of production of the economy. It is true that public expenditure on defence and civil administration are unproductive *directly*, but even they can *under certain circumstances* in an indirect way promote production and employment. This will be made clear a bit later. Further, the effects of public expenditure on production may be different in the case of a developed economy from that of a developing economy, for the circumstances in them differ a good deal. Let us first take the case of a developed economy.

Effect of Public Expenditure on National Output at Times of Depression

Developed economies often find themsleves in the grip of a depression or recession caused by lack of aggregate effective demand. At certain times in the developed countries effective demand falls due to the decline in private investment. At times of depression in an industrialised developed economy, there is idle productive capacity on the one hand and unemployed manpower on the other. Under these circumstances, the increase in Government expenditure on public works or any other type of investment or even expenditure on defence and civil administration will lead to the manifold increase in income and employment through the process of multiplier, as has been explained by J.M. Keynes. The increase in aggregate demand will cause fuller utilization of the existing productive capacity and unemployed manpower resulting in expansion in volume of production, employment and national income. This will become clear from Fig. 30.1 where along the X-axis we measure national product or income and on the Y-axis aggregate demand which comprises consumption demand (C) and investment demand (I). It will be seen from Fig. 30.1 that prior to the Government expenditure the aggregate demand curve cuts the 45° line representing aggregate supply curve at point E. Thus OY_1 is the equilibrium level of national product or income determined by aggregate demand and supply.

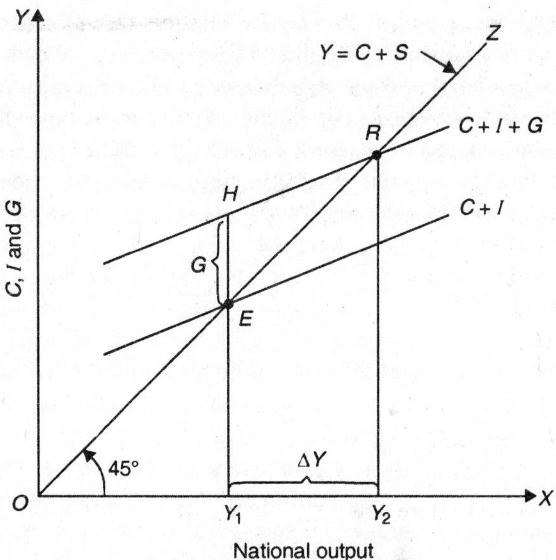

Fig. 30.1. *Effect of Government Expenditure on National Output and Income*

Now, as has been explained in the chapters relating to macroeconomic theory that this equilibrium level may not be established at full-employment level. Suppose full employment of labour and other resources corresponds to OY_2 level of national product. This implies that in equilibrium at OY_1, level of income aggregate demand is not sufficient to ensure full employment. If under these circumstances the Government undertakes extra expenditure, say equal to EH or G, then the aggregate demand curve will shift upward to $C + I + G$ position (dotted). As will be seen from the figure the increase in Government expenditure will cause the equilibrium level to shift to OY_2 level of national product resulting in higher level of employment. It will be further noticed that the increase in national output (*i.e.*, income) equal to Y_1Y_2 (*i.e.*, ΔY) will be greater than the Government expenditure (G) depending upon the magnitude of multiplier. It may be noted that the magnitude of multiplier depends upon the marginal pro-pensity to consume of the people.

From the foregoing analysis we conclude that the increase in Government expenditure preferably financed by borrowings from the banks or printing new notes at times of depression will raise aggregate demand and thereby lead to the multiple increase in national output and employment. But once the level of full employment is attained the increase in Government expenditure cannot raise production through raising aggregate demand. Instead, prices will rise.

However, even in the developing countries such as India there are ways in which government expenditure, if judiciously planned, can promote production. First, if the Government expenditure is incurred on *investment projects for capital formation,* for instance on building of canals, railways, and other infrastructural facilities, it will expand productive capacity and generate long-term economic growth. Secondly, if public expenditure is directed to *scientific research and development (R & D),* it will ensure progress in technology and raise productivity or power to produce of workers. Thirdly, it has now been found that Government expenditure on education and public health helps in building "*human capital*" which also greatly enhances productivity or power to produce of the people. Against these, it may be pointed out that certain types of Government expenditure may adversely affect production. Government expenditure on social insurance like health insurance, unemployment insurance, and old age pensions is said to be of such a type. By insuring against their future and uncertain contingencies like sickness, unemployment and old age, they blunt the edge of the desire to work and save more. The social security expenditure by the Government makes the people indifferent towards the future and makes them neglect savings. This is bound to affect adversely productive efforts in present. Because of the future security, people will work less and save less. However, in our view, if such social security expenditure is kept within proper limits and if it is used to help the really needy and helpless, the adverse effects of social security expenditure on production efforts and savings may be negligible. Further, Government expenditure on social security makes the working people contented and create healthy social environment and industrial peace which is conducive to production.

Apart from augmenting total production, the Government expenditure also affect *allocation of resources* as between different industries and can divert resources to socially desirable channels. Through subsidies and grants and also through its purchase policy, the Government may succeed in diverting resources to hitherto neglected industries. Thus, besides raising the level of production, the Government expenditure can influence *the pattern of production or composition of output.* Likewise, by diverting resources through subsidies and bounties to the backward regions it can promote growth of output in backward regions. We thus see that public expenditure, if wisely conducted, can promote production by raising the levels of productivity or powers to produce and save. It can also cause reallocation of resources between industries and regions and exert wholesome influence on the pattern of production work by the Government undertaken through public enterprises.

Effects of Public Expenditure on Distribution

In the modern times the Government modifies the free working of market mechanism in respect of income distribution not only through devising proper tax structure but also through various forms of public expenditure. Through public expenditure the Government redistributes income in favour of the poor. Too large inequalities in income distribution as produced by the free working of market system is not only socially unjust, but also not conducive to the maximisation of social welfare. Not all types of public expenditure reduce inequalities in income distribution. The following forms of public expenditure redistribute income in favour of the poor and thus reduce inequalities.

1. **Social Security Measures.** Expenditure on unemployment insurance, sickness benefits, old age pensions are some of the social security measures which help the people at times of contingencies. In India only in recent years some State Governments such as those of Haryana, Punjab, Delhi have introduced old age pension scheme. In capitalist countries such as U.S.A., Great Britain the social security system to help the people emerged with the idea of a Welfare State and in these countries Governments spend a large sum of money on the social security system.

2. **Expenditure on Subsidies.** Expenditure on various types of subsidies have also a redistributive effect. In India subsidies on food, sugar, kerosene oil, handloom cloth, fertilizers are provided to the people and Government spend a good part of its budget on these subsidies. Food, sugar, kerosene oil are sold through ration shops *(i.e.,* public distribution system) at prices below the market prices and the difference is borne by the Government as a subsidy. It may be noted that at present benefits of these subsidies are enjoyed not only by the poor but all those who are relatively well off. *If the public expenditure on subsidies is to have a real redistributive effect, these subsidies should be targeted to the poor.*

3. **Expenditure on Social Infrastrucure.** Public expenditure by the Government on social infrastructure such as education, health care of the people, housing for the poor also

tend to reduce income inequalities. With free or subsidised education, free or highly subsidised health care facilities the poor people's real income go up. The modern government spend a lot of money on schools, colleges, etc., to promote education. In most states in India education upto the middle class is free and for higher levels wards of the poor people are either given free education or charged only low fees.

Similarly, the Governments spend a lot on public hospitals and dispensaries to provide health care to the poor people. Likewise, in many countries poor people are given financial aid by the Government to build houses : In India under Indra Awas Yojna, poor people are being given aid to build their low cost houses.

4. Expenditure on Anti-Poverty Programmes. An important step for increasing incomes of the poor people is starting of several employment' generating anti-poverty schemes. Prominent among these anti-poverty schemes in India are Jawahar Rozgar Yojna, Employment Assistance Scheme (EAS), Integrated Rural Development Programme (IRDP). In 1995-96 about 2955 crores were spent on Jawahar Rozgar Yojna, 1816 crores were spent on Employment Assistance Scheme and 655 crores were spent on Integrated Rural Development Programme. By generating employment these schemes raise incomes of the poor.

5. Encouragement to Labour-intensive Industries. The Indian Government gives various types of subsidies to the cottage and small-scale Industries which adopt labour-intensive technique. Being labour-intensive, the growth of these industries generate a large number of employment opportunities which improve income distribution.

6. Negative Income Tax to Achieve More Equal Distribution of Income. Last but not the least, to achieve more equal distribution of income and make a big dent into the poverty problem, a proposal which has been recently put forward by some economists in the USA and Great Britain is introduction of negative Income Tax. Though the name shows it is a tax, but in fact it is a form of expenditure, called *transfer expenditure.* In this negative income tax scheme, payments are made by the Government to the poor to raise their incomes. Under this system, the Government has first to define *poverty income standard* for families of different sizes. Then it makes payment in the form of direct money transfer to bring the incomes of all families upto that standard or at least to close a large part of the gap between their income and poverty income standard.

But the use of public expenditure to reduce inequalities in income distribution has certain bad effects also. The first and foremost evil effect is that it *adversely affects incentives to work and save of the people.* Thus, when people know that in times of difficulties such as unemployment, old age, sickness, the Government will come to their help they will be less willing to work hard. The poor would not work more when they know whatever their income, the gap between the minimum income and their will be filled by the Government. Likewise, many people save to live comfortably in old age, in periods of sickness. But when all these difficult periods are taken care of by the Government their willingness to work more and save more will be badly hurt. Thus, *expenditure to reduce income inequalities will tend to affect adversely incentives to work, save and invest more. All these discourage production and growth.*

It is important to note that *redistributive effects of public expenditure must be considered in the light of how it is financed.* For example, if redistributive public expenditure is financed through taxation and if the tax system of the country is regressive, it will work against the desirable distributive effects of public expenditure. For example, if public expenditure is financed through deficit financing, as has been the case in India for several years, it causes inflation in the economy. This inflation hurts the poor most and will therefore cancel out the desired dis-tributive effects of public expenditure. Thus, if reduction in income inequalities has to be achieved not only the pattern of public expenditure, but also method of financing it and the system of taxation has to be suitably designed and adjusted.

QUESTIONS FOR REVIEW

1.. Explain Wagner's Law and Wiseman–Peacock Hypothesis of growth in public expenditure. How do they explain rising expenditure in the developing countries ?
2.. What are the canons of public expenditure. Describe the factors responsible for rising public expenditure in Inida.
3.. Explain the main causes of rapid growth of public expenditure in India. Is this growth justifiable?
4. Explain the effects of public expenditure on production and distribution in an economy.
5. How does public expenditure reduce inequality in income distribution.?
6. What are the principles of public expendtirue? What are the effects of public expenditure on production and distribution of income?

CHAPTER 31

Financing of Government Expenditure : Taxation

Government Budget Constraint

Having studied the increasing importance of public expenditure in both the developed and developing countries and its effects on production and distribution, we now turn to study of financing Government expenditure. The Government can finance its expenditure including interest payments on accumulated public debt by using taxation, borrowing from the market (i.e. sale of new bonds) and use of printed money. *The Government budget constraint refers to the limit on government expenditure imposed by the extent it can mobilise resources through taxation, borrowing from the market and the use of printed money.* Government's budget constraint equation can be written as

$$G = T + \Delta B + \Delta M \qquad \ldots (i)$$

Where G stands for Government expenditure, T for tax revenue, ΔB for new borrowing (i.e. issue of new bonds) and ΔM for new money created.

Rearranging government budget constraint (i) we have

$$G - T = \Delta B + \Delta M \qquad \ldots (ii)$$

When G exceeds T, we have a budget deficit. *Budget constraint equation (ii) says that budget deficit must be financed either by new borrowing by the Government (ΔB) or by using printed money (ΔM).* In this chapter we will explain taxation as a mean of financing Government expenditure and use of borrowing (*i.e.* debt financing) and printed money (*i.e.* money financing) will be explained in the next few chapters.

What is Tax?

A tax is a *compulsory payment* levied on the persons or companies to meet the expenditure incurred on conferring *common benefits* upon the people of a country. Two aspects of taxes follow from this definition : (1) A tax is a compulsory payment and no one can refuse to-pay it. (2) Proceeds from taxes are used for *common benefits* or *general purposes* of the State. In other words, there is no direct *quid pro quo* involved in the payment of a tax. This implies that an individual cannot expect or demand that the Government should render him a specific service in return for the tax paid by him. However, this does not imply that Government does nothing for the people from whom it receives taxes. In fact. Government spends the tax money for the general or common benefits of all the people rather than conferring any special benefit on a particular tax payer. To quote Taussig. "The essence of a tax, as distinguished from the other charges by Government is the absence of any direct *quid pro quo* between the tax payer and the public authority."[1]

Tax should be carefully distinguished from a *fee.* Fee is also compulsory payment made by a person who receives in return a particular benefit or service from the Government. For paying fee on a television or radio, a person gets the benefits of programmes relayed by the Government on television or radio. Likewise, students who pay the education fee in schools and colleges, obtain the benefits of teaching arranged by the Government. The amount of fee is always less than the cost of service rendered by the Government in return and therefore covers only a part of the cost of service rendered. Thus, even in case of fee, there is a general public interest or common benefit of the service rendered by the Government. In this case, the Government undertakes a service for the common benefits of the citizens and obtains a fee from those who avail of that service to cover a part of the cost of service

1. Taussig, *Principles of Economics.*

CLASSIFICATION OF TAXES

The taxes have been variously classified. Taxes can be direct or indirect, they can be progressive, proportional or regressive, and indirect taxes can be *specific* or *ad-valorem.* We spell out below the meanings of these different types of taxes.

Direct and Indirect Taxes. The distinction between direct and indirect taxes is based on whether or not the burden of a tax can be shifted wholly or partly to others. If a tax is such that its burden cannot be shifted to others and the person who pays it to the Government has also to bear it, it is called a direct tax. Income tax, annual wealth tax, capital gains tax are examples of direct taxes. In case of a direct tax there is a direct contact between the tax payer and tax levying public authority.

On the other hand, indirect taxes are those whose burden can be shifted to others so that those who pay these taxes to the Government do not bear the whole burden but pass it on wholly or partly to others. For instance, excise duty on the production of sugar is an indirect tax because the manufactures of sugar include the excise duty in the price and pass it on to buyers. Ultimately, it is the consumers on whom the incidence of excise duty on sugar falls as they will pay higher price for sugar than before the imposition of the tax. Thus, though excise duties are on the production of commodities but they can be shifted to the consumers. Likewise, sales tax on commodities can also be passed on to buyers or consumers in the form of higher prices charged for the commodities. Therefore, excise duties and sales taxes on commodities are examples of indirect taxes. They are also known as *commodity taxes.* In the case of indirect taxes, there is an indirect relation, between the Government and those who ultimately bear the burden of the taxes.

Specific and Ad-Valorem Taxes. Indirect taxes can be either *specific* or *ad-valorem.* A specific tax on a commodity is a tax *per unit* of the commodity, whatever its price. Thus the amount of total specific tax will vary in accordance with the changes in total output or sales of the commodity and not with the total value of output or sales. On the other hand, an ad-valorem type of an indirect tax is levied according to the value of the commodity. For instance, sales tax in India is an ad-valorem tax as the rate of sales tax in case of several commodities is 10 per cent of the value of sales of the commodities. Ad-valorem taxes are progressive in their burden on consumers whereas specific taxes are regressive.

Progressive, Proportional and Regressive Taxes. According to another classification, taxes can be progressive, proportional or regressive. In case of proportional tax, the *same rate* of the tax is charged, whatever be the magnitude of the base on which it is levied. For instance, if rate of income tax is 25 per cent whatever the size of income of a person, it will then be a proportional income tax. Likewise, if rate of wealth tax is 5 per cent, it will be porportional wealth tax. Thus, in case of proportional tax it is the *rate* which is fixed and not the *absolute* amount of the tax. Thus with the rate of 25 per cent proportional income tax, a person with income of Rs. 25,000 will pay Rs. 6,250 as the tax, and a person with income of 50,000 will pay Rs. 12,500 as the tax. Thus, even under proportional income tax, a richer person has to pay greater amount of tax though rate of the tax is the same.

On the other hand, in case of a progressive tax, rate of the tax increases as the amount of the tax base (income, wealth or any other object) increases. The principle underlying a pro-gressive tax is that greater the tax base, the higher the tax rate. In India income tax, an important direct tax levied by the Central Government, is progressive. Its rate at present (1998-99) varies from 10 per cent in the slab of Rs. 40,000 to 60,000 to 30 per cent in the slab of income above Rs. 1,50,000. Under progressive income tax, the richer person pays not only absolutely more tax but also a higher rate of the tax. Thus, the burden of progressive tax falls more heavily on the richer persons as compared to proportional income tax.

A regressive tax is the opposite of a progressive tax. In case of a regressive income tax, the rate is lowered as the income rises. Thus, under regressive tax system, the burden of the tax is relatively more on the poor than on the rich. A regressive tax is therefore inequitable and no civilised Government in the world today will levy such a tax.

PRINCIPLES OR CANONS OF A GOOD TAX SYSTEM

A good tax system must fulfil certain principles if it is to raise adequate revenue and fulfil certain social objectives. Adam Smith had explained four canons of taxation which he thought a good tax must fulfil. These four canons are: of (1) *Equality,* (2) *Certainty,* (3) *Convenience,* and (4) *Economy.* These are still regarded as characteristics of a good tax system. However, there has been significant developments in economic theory and policy since Adam Smith wrote his book *"The Wealth of Nations"*. Activities and functions of Government have enormously increased. Now, the Governments are expected to maintain economic stability at full employment level, they are to reduce inequalities in the income distribution, and they are also to perform the functions of a Welfare State. Above all, they are to promote economic growth and devel-opment, especially in the developing countries, not only through encouraging private enterprise but to undertake the task of production in some strategic industries. Thus, in order to devise a good tax system, these objectives and functions of Government's economic policy must be kept in view.

It may be noted that Adam Smith was basically concerned with how the wealth of nations or, in other words, production capacity of the economy can be increased and he thought that private enterprise working on the basis of free market mechanism would ensure efficient use of resources and, if left unfettered would bring about rapid economic growth. His ideas about public finance were influenced by his economic philosophy of virtues of free private enterprise. In proposing the above mentioned canons of taxation, he was guided only by the sole objective that Government should be able to raise sufficient revenue to discharge its limited functions of providing for defence, maintaining law and order, and, public utility services. However, as men-tioned above, both the objectives and functions of modern Governments have increased neces-sitating large resources. Therefore, the modern economists have added other principles or characteristics which taxation system of a country must satisfy if the objectives of modern Governments are to be achieved. In what follows we shall spell out in detail the principles and characteristics of a good tax system starting with the explanation of Smith ian canons of taxation.

1. Principle or Canon of Equality

The first canon or principle of a good tax system emphasised by Adam Smith is of equality. According to the canon of equality, every person should pay to the Government according to his ability to pay, that is in proportion of the income or revenue he *et jove onder* the protection of the State. Thus under the tax system based on equality principle the richer persons in the society will pay more than the poor. On the basis of this canon of equality or ability to pay Adam Smith argued that taxes should be proportional to income, that is, everybody should pay the same rate or percentage of his income as tax. However, modem economists interpret equality or ability to pay differently from Adam Smith. Based on the assumption of diminishing marginal utility of money income, they argue that ability to pay principle calls for progressive income tax, that is, the rate of tax increases as income rises. Now, in most of the countries, progressive system of income and other direct taxes have been adopted to ensure equality in the tax system.

We shall discuss at length later in this chapter the principle of ability to pay. It may, however, be mentioned here that there are two aspects of ability to pay principle. First is the concept of *horizontal equity.* According to the concept of horizontal equity, those who are equal, that is, similarly situated persons ought to be treated equally. This implies that those who have same income should pay the same amount of tax and there should be no discrimination between them. Second is the concept of *vertical equity.* The concept of vertical equity is concerned with how people with different abilities to pay should be treated for the purposes of division of tax burden. In other words, what various tax rates should be levied on people with different levels of income, A good tax system must be such as will ensure the horizontal as well as vertical equity.

2. Canon of Certainty

Another important principle of a good tax system on which Adam Smith laid a good deal of stress is the canon of certainty. To quote Adam Smith, 'The tax which each individual is bound to pay ought to be certain and not arbitrary. The time of payment, the manner of payment, the quantity to be paid ought all. to be clear and plain to the contributor and to every other person."[2] A successful function of an economy requires that the people, especially business class, must be certain about the sum of tax that they have to pay on their income from work or investment. The tax system should be such that sum of tax should not be arbitararily fixed by the income tax authorities. While taking a decision about the amount of work effort that a person should put in or how much investment should he undertake under risky circumstances, he must know with certainty the definite amount of the tax payable by him on his income. If the sum of tax payable by him is subject to much discretion and arbitrariness of the tax as-sessment authority, this will weaken his incentive to work and invest more. Moreover, lack_ of certainty in the tax system, as pointed out by Smith, encourages corruption'in the tax admini-stration. Therefore in a good tax system, "individuals should be secure against unpredictable taxes levied on their wages or other incomes. The law should be clear and specific; tax collectors should have little discretion about how much to assess tax payers, for this is a very great power and subject to abuse."[3] In the opinion of the present author the Indian tax system violates this canon of certainty as under the Indian income tax law a lot of discretionary powers have been given to the income tax officers, which have been absued with impunity. As a result, there is a lot of harassment of the tax payers and corruption is rampant in the income tax department.

3. Canon of Convenience

According to the third canon of Adam Smith, the sum, time and/manner of payment of a tax should not only be certain but the time and manner of its payment should also be convenient to the contributor. If a land revenue is collected at the time of harvest, it will be convenient since at this time farmers reap their crop and obtain income. In recent years efforts have made to make the Indian income tax convenient to the tax payers by providing for its payments in instalments as advance payments at various times during the year. Further, income tax in India is levied on the basis of *income received* rather than *income accrued* during a year. This also makes the income tax system convenient, However, there is a lot of harassment of the tax payers as they are asked to come to the income tax office several times during a year for clarifications of their income tax returns.

4. Canon of Economy

The Government has to spend money on collecting taxes levied by it- Since collection costs of taxes add nothing to the national product, they should be minimized as far as possible. If the collection costs of a tax is more than the total revenue yielded by it, it is not worthwhile to levy it. More complicated a tax system, more elaborate administrative machinary will be employed to collect it and consequently collection costs will be relatively larger. Therefore, even for achieving economy in the tax collection, the taxes should be as simple as possible and tax laws should not be subject to different interpretations.

Other Principles or Characteristics of a Good Tax System

We have explained above the Smithian canons of a good tax system. Adam Smith viewed the problem of devising a good tax system chiefly from the viewpoint of devising a good tax payers. Taxation system should also be such that it meets the requirements of increasing state activity and

2. Adam Smith, *The Wealth of Nations*, Vol. *II*, p. 327.
3 Otto Eckestein, *Public Finance*. Prentice Hall of India Private Ltd., 3rd Edition, p. 53.

achieves the objectives the society has placed before it. We explain below the characteristics and principles of a good tax system, especially in the context of the developing countries.

1. Productivity or Fiscal Adequacy: An important principle of a good tax system for a developing country is that it should yield adequate amount of resources for the Government so that it should be able to perform its increasing welfare and developmental activities. If the tax system fails to yield enough resources, the Government will resort to deficit financing. An excessive dose of deficit financing is bound to raise prices which are harmful for the society. To make the tax system sufficiently productive it should be broad-based and both direct and indirect taxes find place in it. Moreover, taxes should be progressive so that the revenue from them rises with the increase in income of tr)e people.

2. Elasticity of Taxation : Another principle of taxation suitable for the developing coun* tries is the principle of elasticity of taxation. According to the concept of elasticity of the taxation system, as national income increases as a result of economic growth, the Government revenue from taxes should also increase. In developing countries, the share of tax revenue as a proportion of national income is low as compared to the developed countries. This share of tax revenue will rise as national income increases, if the tax system is sufficiently elastic. Pro-gressive taxation of income and wealth provides this elasticity to the tax system. Impositions of higher indirect taxes on luxury goods having a high income elasticity of demand also makes the tax system elastic.

3. Diversity : A good tax system should follow the principle of diversity. This implies that there should not be a single or a few taxes from which Government seeks to raise large revenue. This is because if a Government tries to get large revenue from a single tax or few taxes, it will have to raise the rates of taxation too high which will not only adversely affect the incentives to work, save and invest but also encourage evasion of taxes. Therefore, the tax system should be a multiple tax system with a large variety of taxes so that all those who can contribute to the public revenue should be made to do so. This calls for a mix of various direct and indirect taxes. With the diverse tax system, the principles of fiscal adequacy and equity will also be better satisfied. Commending a diversity in the tax system Arthur Young writes, "If I were to define a good system of taxation, it should be that of bearing lightly on an infinite nurpber of points, heavily on none". Similarly, another expert of public finance writes, "Excessive reliance on any one base may produce adverse economic effects because the rates may become too high. Therefore, a tax system may do less economic damage if it raises moderate amounts from several bases rather than large amounts from one or two."[4]

4. Taxation as in Instrument of Economic Growth : In a developing economy such as ours, taxation should serve as an instrument of economic growth. Economic growth is primarily a function of rate of capital formation. If in the development strategy public sector has been assigned an eminent place, then capital formation in the public sector must occur at a relatively higher rate. This calls for mobilization of resources by the Government so as to finance capital formation in public sector. Therefore, a good tax system for a developing country will be such as will enable the Government to mobilise adequate resources for capital formation or economic growth. This it can do in the following two ways.

(*a*) **Mobilisation of Economic Surplus.** An important principle for a developing country is that it should mobilise economic surplus found in the economy. Economic surplus is the "surplus of national income over *essential consumption*". It is the task of taxation system that it should restrain non-essential or unproductive consumption through appropriate system of pro-gressive direct and indirect taxes and thereby mobilize economic surplus. "In an underdeveloped economy, there are particular economic sectors and classes of people where the economic surplus is generally found and which therefore should receive the special attention of tax authoritics in such countries.[4]

(*b*) **Increase in the Intermental Saving Ratio.** A good tax system not only tries to mobilise the

4. T. Mathcw, *Tax Policy: Some Aspects of Theory and Indian Experience*, p. 31.

existing economic surplus but also seeks to raise it with a view to mop up relatively greatei amount of increase in national income for the purpose of capital formation. Thus taxation in *s* developing economy has not only to restrain current unproductive consumption but also to check the large increases in consumption when with the increase in national income, economic surplus goes up. This will ensure rise in the incremental or marginal saving ratio which is a prime determinant of continuous economic growth. In other words, through the means of taxation consumption should not be allowed to increase in proportion to increase in incomes. Expansion in economic surplus accruing to the individuals should be mobilised and invested in the public sector for further growth. Progressive income tax and indirect taxes on goods with higher income elasticity will ensure this,

5. Taxation as sn Instrument for Improving Income Distribution: A good tax system for a developing economy should also serve as an instrument for reducing economic inequalities. The purpose of a good tax system for a developing economy is not merely to raise revenue for the Government but also to ensure that burden of taxes falls more on the rich. This requires that the rates of progressive direct taxes on income, wealth, expenditure, capital gains etc., must be sufficiently high. This objective of reducing income inequalities will be better served if a good part of the ,tax revenue is used for proverty alleviation programmes.

6. Taxation for Ensuring Economic Stability: A tax system must also ensure economic stability. Economic fluctuations have been a big problem in the developed countries and for reducing these fluctuations taxation can play a useful role. For this purpose, tax system must have built-in-flexibility. To have built-in-flexibility, the taxation system must be progressive in relation in the changes in national income. This will ensure that when national income rises, an increasing part of the rise in income should automatically accrue to the Government. On the other hand, when national income falls, as in a recession or depression, the revenue obtained progressive from taxes will fall more rapidly than the decline in national income. Built-in-flexi-bility attained through progressive taxation ensures that when incomes are increasing* during the period of boom or inflation, the relatively greater amount of tax revenue accruing to Government will moderate the increase in purchasing power with the people and aggregate demand and thus help in keeping prices under check. Likewise, under progressive taxation at times of depression or recession, tax revenue will fall faster than the income so that purchasing power of thc pcople does not fall as fast as their pre-tax income. This will serve to check decline in economic activity.

However, in developing countries, the problem is more of restraining inflation so as to achieve price stability. By discouraging or restraining consumption, especially of non-essential or unproductive type, taxation can pay a useful role in controlling inflation in the developing countries.

Conclusion

From the foregoing analysis, we conclude that in the world today taxation is called upon to achieve several socio-economic objectives. It is not just a means of raising revenue for the limited functions of the State. *Neutrality principle* of taxation, that is, leave them as you find them, no longer finds favour with the modern economists. Tax system today has to play a more positive role. It is intended to bring about rapid economic growth, reduce inequalities of incomes, promote stability and to achieve other socio-economic objectives.

PRINCIPLE OF EQUITY IN TAXATION

An important question widely discussed in public finance is what kind of tax system is fair, just or equitable. As seen above, equity in taxation was the first cajion of taxation on which Adam Smith laid a good deal of stress. A fair tax system is not merely an issue in pure economic analysis but also in social philosophy. There are two prominent theories put forward to devise a fair or equitable tax system. They are (1) Benefits Received Theory and (2) Ability to pay Theory. We discuss below these two theories of equity in taxation.

Benefits Received Theory

According to this theory of taxation, citizens should be asked to pay taxes in proportion to the benefits they receive from the services rendered by the Government. This theory is based upon the assumption that there is an exchange relationship or *quid pro quo* between the tax payer and Government. The Government confers some benefits on the tax payers by performing various services or providing them what are called social goods. In exchange for these benefits individuals pay taxes to the Government. Further, according to this theory, equity or fairness in taxation demands that an individual should be asked to pay a tax in proportion to the benefits he receives from the services rendered by the Government.

However, there are some difficulties in application of this theory. The most Crucial problem faced by benefits received approach is that it is *difficult to measure the benefits* received by an individual from the services rendered by the Government. For instance, how much benefit an individual tax payer derives from providing for national defence and education, and maintaining law and order by the Government cannot be measured with any objective criterion. Secondly, most of the Government expenditure is incurred on common indivisible benefits so that the division of benefits of Government expenditure is not possible.

Further, benefits received theory miltilates against the very notion of a tax. A tax is defined as a payment for general purposes of the State and not in return for a specific service. The benefit theory can have meaning if the benefits of the Government services to the community as a whole is considered. But this will only indicate how much total tax revenue the community should pay to the Government. This will not help us in dividing the tax liability among various individuals comprising the community. It may be noted that most important common benefits are peaceful enjoyment of life, liberty and property. So far as life and liberty are concerned, Government's protection is the same for all. This will indicate levying of a toll tax. But toll tax has long been discarded as it was found to be highly regressive and also a small yielder of revenue.

The benefit principle is applicable only in cases where the beneficiaries can be clearly identified. Thus benefit principle is applied to the collection of road tax from vehicle owners. This is also applied when local bodies collect special levies for the services such as construction of sewers and roads they render to the people of their locality. The benefit principle is also applied to social security programmes for workers. Social security contributions, or what are called payroll taxes, which are collected from workers are kept in reserves out of which benefit payments are made to them. To conclude, therefore, "at best the benefit principle can provide a partial solution to the problem of fairness in taxation."[5]

Ability to Pay Theory

The ability to pay is another criterion of equity or fairness in taxation. This theory requires that individuals should be asked to pay taxes according to their ability to pay. The rich have greater ability to pay, therefore they should pay more tax to the Government than the poor. Essentially, the ability to pay approach to fairness in taxation requires that *burden of tax* falling on the various persons should be the same. In the discussion of various characteristics of a good tax system, we mentioned about the two concepts of equity, namely horizontal equity and vertical equity based on the principle of ability to pay. According to the concept of horizontal equity, equals should be treated equally, that is, persons with the same ability to pay should be made to bear the same amount of tax burden. According to the vertical equity, unequals should be treated unequally, that is, how the tax burden among poeple with different abilities to pay be divided. In both these cencepts of equity, what excatly do we mean by ability to pay and what are the objective measures of ability to pay are crucial. Some have explained the ability to pay treating it as a subjective concept. Others have treated the ability to pay in terms of

5. Otto Eckstein, *op. cit.*, p. 54.

some objective bases such as income, wealth, consumption expenditure etc. We shall explain below both these approaches to the measurement of ability to pay.

Ability to Pay : Subjective Approach

In the subjective approach to tax paying ability, the concept of *sacrifice* undergone by a person in paying a tax occupies a crucial place. In paying a tax, a person feels a pinch or suffers from some disutility. This pinch or disutility felt by a tax payer is the sacrifice made by him. In this subjective approach to ability to pay, tax burden is measured in terms of sacrifice of utility made by the tax payers. The following three principles of sacrifice have been put forward by various authors:

1. The Principle of Equal Absolute Sacrifice;
2. The Principle of Equal Proportional Sacrifice; and
3. The Principle of Equal Marginal Sacrifice (or Minimum Aggregate Sacrifice).

The principle of equal absolute sacrifice implies that the tax burden in terms of utility sacrificed should be the same for all tax payers. If U stands for total utility, Y stands for income and T for the amount of tax paid, then the principle of equal absolute sacrifice requires that $U(Y) - U(Y - T)$ should be the same for all individuals. The term $U(Y)$ implies that total utility of a given income Y and $U(Y - T)$ implies the total utility of the post-tax income $(Y - T)$. If the equal absolute sacrifice principle is applied, none will be exempted from taxation and every body will pay same amount of the tax. Now, the pertient question is what type of tax, propor-tional or progressive, follows from this principle. If marginal utility of money income falls, as is generally believed, and if this fall in marginal utility of money income equals the rate of increase in income, then this principle will suggests proportional income tax. However, if the fall in marginal utility of income is greater than the rate of increase in income, then equal absolute sacrifice principle will suggest progressive income tax.

Equal Proportional Sacrifice. This principle requires that every person should be made to pay so much tax that the sacrifice of utility as a proportion of his income is the same for all tax payers. In terms of the notation used above, this implies that $\frac{U(Y) - U(Y - T)}{U(Y)}$ of all tax payers should be equal. If a person enjoying higher income is to bear same proportion of sacrifice, then given the falling marginal utility of income, he will have to pay income tax at a higher rate. This means progressive income tax.

Equal Marginal Sacrifice. According to this principle, tax burden should be so apportioned among various individuals that marginal sacrifice of utility of each person paying the tax should be the same. This approach seeks to minimize the aggregate sacrifice of the society as a whole. When all persons pay so much tax that their marginal sacrifice of utility is the same, the loss of total utility by the society will be minimum. Thus, the principle of equal marginal sacrifice looks at the problem of dividing the tax burden from the point of view of welfare of the whole society. The social philosophy underlying this principle is that the total sacrifice imposed by taxation on the community ought to be minimum. Assuming that marginal utility of income falls, the principle of equality of marginal sacrifice implies very high marginal rates of taxation. Indeed, in the extreme this principle can be used to recommend 100 per cent rate of tax on the people in highest income bracket in the society. Thus this principle recommends a highly progressive tax structure. This principle of taxation has been recommended among others by Edgeworth, Pigou and Musgrave who consider this as the ultimate principle of taxation. It is worthwhile to quote Edgeworth, a chief exponent of this principle. "The minimum sacrifice is the sovereign principle of taxation. If one is utilitarian and believes not only in the measurability of utility but also in the view that the law of diminishing utility is applicable to money also, then this principle would involve a high level of minimum exemption and a very steep pro-gression as income increases .... The less the aggregate sacrifice, the better the distribution of tax ourden in the community. The State exists to maximize human welfare. This it will be able to do by minimizing the sacrifices involved."

Comments. The whole subjective approach to ability to pay based on the sacrifice of utility has been termed as invalid because utility being a subjective entity cannot be measured in cardinal sense. Further, it is alleged there is no definite evidence that marginal utility of money income falls as income increases. Interpersonal comparison of utility which the sacrifice approach requires is held to be unscientific. However, in the view of the present author, these objections against ability to pay or sacrifice principle are not valid. We may not be able to measure utility of money income in exact absolute terms but a sufficiently good measure of utility of income can be obtained and this is enough for the application of this principle of ability to pay in terms of sacrifice. Observations in the world clearly indicate that people in the lower income brackets spend most of their incomes on buying necessaries, while people in the higher income groups spend a relatively greater proportion of their incomes on luxuries and non-essential goods. In view of this it is quite valid to assume diminishing marginal utility of money for purpose of taxation.

Ability to Pay : Objective Approach

The objective approach to the ability to pay principle considers what should be objective base of taxation which measures ability to pay correctly. There is even no agreement on this question also. However, income is generally considered to be the best measure of ability to pay. This is because a person's income determines a person's command over resources during a period to consume or to add to his wealth. However, it may be noted that ability to pay does not increase in direct proportion to money income. Ability to pay increases more than propor-tionately to the amount of income. Justification of progressive income tax is based on this. Further, in order to ensure equity in taxing income distinction ought to be made between earned income and unearned income, and considerations should also be given for a number of depend-ents on the person paying the tax.

Wealth of a person is another objective measure of ability to pay that has been suggested as a tax base. The ownership of the property or wealth of an individual determines how much resources he has accumulated. Saving from every year's income adds to his wealth. The wealth or property is therefore said to be a better index of taxable capacity.

It may however be noted that wealth alone is not considered to be adequate measure of taxable capacity and instead a combination of income and wealth taxes is regarded as a better measure from the viewpoint of ability to pay. Thus, according to Prof. Kaldor, *"Only a combi-nation of income and property taxes can give approximation to taxation in accordance with ability to pay"*.[6] Arguing the case for levying annual wealth tax in India, he writes "income taken by itself is an inadequate yardstick of taxable capacity as between income from work and income from property, and also as between different property owners". He further writes, "the ownership of property in the form of disposable assets endows the property-owner with a taxable capacity as such quite apart from the money income which that property yields."

It follows form above that a combination of income tax and wealth tax will be a better measure of ability to pay.

Prof. Kaldor has also advocated another base for taxation. He has been a strong advocate of *levying of expenditure tax* in both the developed and developing countries.[7] It should be noted that his expenditure tax is in fact a tax on consumption, that is, income minus saving. He claims that, IY *is consumption that is a fair or equitable base of taxation.* According to him, it is consumption that measures the resources that a person actually withdraws from the economy for his personal use. The part of his income not consumed, that is, savings lead to the increase in the capital stock and thus add to society's productive capacity. If a person consumes more than his income, he should the made to pay a higher tax because he reduces the capital stock of the country.[8] *The imposition of expenditure*

6. See Nicholas Kaldor, *An Expenditure Tax,* Alien and TJnwin, 1955.
7. *Ibid.*

tax, according to Kaldor, is particularly relevant for developing countries where high consumption expenditure of richer classes reduces the rate of capital accumulation. Imposition of expenditure tax will discourage consumption by taxing it heavily and promote savings *by* exempting it. In 1958 on the recommendation of Kaldor expenditure tax was levied in India. But after some years it was withdrawn on the ground that it was difficult to administer it and also that the revenue from it was very small.

Conclusion. In conclusion it may be said that it is *better to levy taxes on various bases instead of a single base.* As explained in the section of characteristics of a good tax system, *diversity of tax bases is preferable not only from the viewpoint of a measure of ability to pay but also because it will have less adverse economic effects.* Eckstein rightly points out, "Ex-cessive reliance on any one base may produce adverse economic effects because the rates may become too high. Therefore, a tax system may do less economic damage if it raises moderate amounts from several bases rather than larger amounts from one or two."[9] Perhaps it is because of these reasons that in actual practice, a good variety of taxes are levied. In India, income tax, corporation tax, wealth tax and union excise duties are the most important taxes levied by the central Government, while sales tax, land revenue, and certain excise duties are the important taxes at the state level.

DIRECT TAXES VS. INDIRECT TAXES

We have explained above the characteristics of a good tax system. A controversial issue in public finance is concerned with whether in tax structure of an economy direct or indirect taxes should be preferred. Indeed, both direct taxes and indirect taxes have their merits and demerits and therefore a good tax system should contain a proper mix of these two types of taxes. Direct taxes, it may be .recalled, are those which are levied directly on the indi-viduals and firms and their burden is borne by those on whom they are levied. Persona! income tax, corporate income tax, wealth tax, expenditure tax, gift tax are some examples of direct taxes. On the other hand, indirect taxes are levied on production and sale of commodities and services. A small or a large part of the burden of an indirect tax is passed on to the consumers. Excise duties on the production of commodities, sales tax, service tax, tax on railway or bus fare are some examples of the indirect tax. The Indian tax system contains a combination of both direct and indirect taxes. We discuss below the merits and demerits of both direct and indirect taxes. It should be noted that tax has to be judged especially from the following viewpoints:

1. Equity;

2. Efficiency in allocation of resources;

3. Economic growth. that is, whether it promotes or discourages supply of work effort (labour), saving and investment on which economic growth depends;

4. Buoyancy, that is, to what extent revenue from tax increases with the increase in income; and

5. Economic stability, Merits of Direct Taxes

1. An important merit of direct taxes is that they can be selected and their rate structure be *so designed which is closely related to the ability jo pay principle.* The direct taxes can be made progressive and the degree of progression among different income brackets can be deter-mined so as to satisfy the principle of ability to pay. The larger burden of these progressive taxes fall on the rich people who have capacity to bear them and the poor people with less ability to pay have to bear less burden.

---

8. Nicholas Kaldor, *Indian Tax Reforms.*
9. Otto, Eckstein, *op. cit.,* p. 56.

2. Direct taxes are *important instrument of deducing inequalities of income and wealth.* A progressive income tax, imoposition of progressive wealth tax and estate duties have been used in different countries to reduce inequalities in income distribution. Large inequalities are harmful for maximization of social welfare. They are even bad from the viewpoint of achieving economic stability.

3. Another important merit of direct taxes is that unlike indirect taxes *they do not cause distortion in the allocation of resources.* As a result, they leave the consumers better off as compared to indirect taxes. Direct taxes such as general income and wealth taxes do not affect relative prices of goods and services and therefore leave the relative profitability of different industries unchanged. As a result, resource allocation among them remain unaffected. Therefore, from the viewpoint of efficiency in resource allocation direct taxes are preferred to indirect taxes.

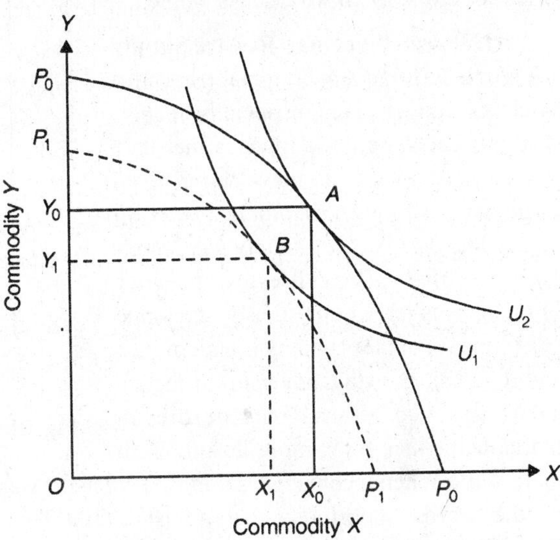

Fig. 31.1. *Direct Taxes do not Cause Inefficiency in Resource Allocation*

That the direct taxes have no effect on allocation of resources except to withdraw resources from private use is illustrated in Fig. 31.1. Suppose there are two commodities X and Y. A production possibility curve P_0P_0 of a community is drawn. U_1, U_2 are the indifference curves of the community showing successively higher levels of welfare. In equilibrium and without a direct tax, the economy is producing X_0 of commodity X and Y_0 of commodity Y. Allocation of resources is efficient as by producing X_0 of good X and Y_0 of good Y, the community is reaching the highest possible indifference curve U_2. With this social welfare is maximum because marginal rate of transformation in production is equal to marginal rate of substitution of the community between the two commodities

Now suppose a certain amount of revenue is collected by leying a direct tax, say personal income tax. Since through this tax private purchasing power has been cut, some resources will be freed for Government use. The new production possibility curve for private economy shifts downward to P_1P_1. Now, the private economy will &e in equilibrium at point 5, where P_1P_1 is tangent to the community indifference curve U_1 and X_1 of good X and Y_1 of good Y are being produced. At point B, marginal rate of substitution between X and Y of the community (MRS_{xy}) equals marginal rate of transformation (MRT_{xy}) in production between the two goods. Thus, resource allocation between the two goods remain efficient. Of course, resources for the use of private sector have been reduced.

4. Fourthly, *revenue elasticity of direct taxes, especially if they are of progressive type is quite high.* As the national income increases, the revenue from these taxes also rises a great deal. It is due to this fact that progressive direct taxes serve as *automatic stabilizers.* When during upswing the economy gains momentum and boom conditions emerge, a relatively larger fraction of increasing income are siphoned of through the progressive direct taxes. This acts as a brake on the economy getting into serious inflationary situation. Similarly, when during downswing the income and employment of the community is falling due to the progressive nature of the direct taxes, a relatively smaller part of income is taken away by way of these taxes. Therefore, the consumption demand does not fall to the same extent as the decrease in income. This prevents further slowdown of the economy which turns around and thereby recovery of the economy starts.

Demerits of Direct Taxes

We have seen above from the viewpoints of achieving equity, efficiency, economic stability that direct taxes are desirable. However, there are some demerits of direct taxes which we discuss below:

1. Direct Taxes may Reduce Supply of Work Effort. An important harmful effect of* direct taxes, especially if their marginal rates are quite high, is that they *reduce people's will-ingness to put forth larger productive y effort, that is, as a result of, say income tax, They supply less labour for produc-tive work.* With lesser productive effort or smaller labour supply economic per-formance of the economy is undermined and economic growth is adversely af-fected. There are two alternatives before an individual: either enjoy more leisure or do more work. When income tax is imposed, after-tax wage rate, that is, re-turn from work diminishes or, in other words, opportunity cost of leisure falls. This induces the individual to substitute leisure for work effort. As a result, sup-ply of work effort is reduced. To quote Eckstein, "If a worker has to pay taxes, say one half of his income from extra work, perhaps a lawyer working week-ends, a doctor taking on additional pa-tients or a sales-person making evening calls—his incentives will certainly be reduced." He further writes about direct taxes, "if their high rates are diminishing effort substantially through-out the economy, we are giving up a lot of economic performance for the sake of equity."[10]

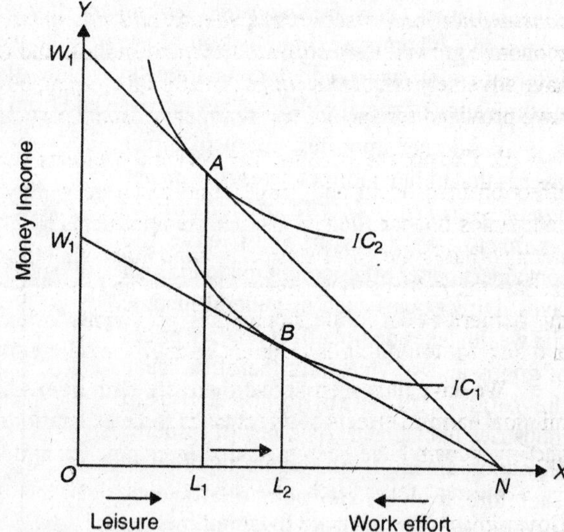

Fig. 31.2. *Effect of Income Tax on Supply of Work Effort*

Let us illustrate the harmful effect of a direct tax, say income tax, on supply of work effort (*i.e.*, labour). In Fig. 31.2 we have drawn the indifference curves of an individual between income and leisure. Suppose before taxation, the wage rate is depicted by the slope of the wage line NW_1. The individual is in equilibrium at point *A* on indifference curve IC_2 where he is enjoying OL_1 leisure and working NL_1 hours.

Suppose a proportional income tax at the rate of 50% is levied. As a result, after-tax wage rate is reduced and after-tax wage line shifts below to NW_2. The individual moves to equilibrium point *B* on indifference curve IC_1. In this equilibrium situation *B* the individual has increased his leisure to OL_2 and reduced hi- work effort to NL_2. Thus, as a result of levying of income tax and consequently lowering of the wage rate the individual has substituted leisure for work, resulting in the decrease of labour supply (*i.e.*, work effort). This is a normal behaviour. Of course, there are some exceptions to this normal behaviour.

2. Direct Taxes Reduce Incentives to Save and Invest. A significant adverse effect of direct taxes is that *they reduce incentives to save and invest.* People save and invest their savings by sacrificing present consumption. Investment of savings yields a return. Here the *choice is between present consumption and saving for investment.* A direct tax, say income tax, reduces the rate of return on investment since a part of the return is taken away through tax. Thus, with the imposition of income tax, rate of return on investment is reduced which induces the individuals to substitute present consumption for saving and investment. As a consquence, *levying of income tax induces more*

10. Otto, Eckstein, *Public Finance,* Prentice Hall.

consumption and discourages saving and investment. The lower saving and investment retards economic growth. Empirical studies made in India and USA have shown that high rates of direct taxes have adversely affected savings. It is for this reason, budgets in India and the industrialised countries have provided for special tax treatment of some particular forms of saving and investment.

3. Corporate Income Tax Adversly Affects Investment. It is corporate income tax and its effect on investment and growth that has been widely discussed. Corporations, that is, joint stock companies finance their investment requirements by using their internal savings. It is these internal savings that is the chief source of capital accumulation by the companies. Imposition of corporate income tax reduces their investible funds and thereby ratards investment and growth. To overcome this demerit of corporate income tax, provisions for exempting depreciation funds from income tax and also for providing investment credit have been generally made in the budgets.

We have thus seen above there are both merits and demerits of direct taxes. In order to have minimal harmful effects of direct taxes some exemptions, special tax treatment of depreciation, saving and investment have been provided in income tax and wealth tax laws.

Indirect taxes such as excise duties and sales tax are important source of revenue for the Government. The revenue from indirect taxes has shown a great deal of buoyancy. In India revenue from indirect taxes has been continuously increasing.

Merits of Indirect Taxes

1. Convenient to Pay and Less Cumbersome. A significant merit of indirect taxes is *that they are convenient to pay and less cumbersome as compared to direct taxes.* In case of indirect taxes such as an excise duty or a costum duty people have to pay these taxes *bit by bit* when they produce, sell and buy these commodities. This piecemeal payment of an indirect tax makes it easier for the tax payers who do not feel its pinch in contrast to direct taxes. Indirect taxes are also not difficult to collect as they are collected from the firms and traders who pass them on to the buyers in the form "of higher prices of goods.

2. Large Revenue Potential. Another important merit of indirect taxes.is that *they have a large revenue potential* for the Government. Through indirect taxes even the poor and low-income people can be brought in the tax net. Whoever, rich or poor, buys commodities ultimately bears the burden of indirect taxes. But direct taxes such as income tax cannot be levied on the poor as cost of collection from them will be much higher and also there is need for some exemption limit. For example in India with a population of over 900 million only about 8 million people pay income tax. On the other hand, a much large number of people pay indirect taxes such as excise duties, sales tax, tax on railway and bus fare. Thus through indirect taxes, *a large amount of resources can be raised* for meeting increasing requirements of the Government.

A large revenue potential of indirect taxes has a special importance for the developing countries like India where resources are needed by the Government not only to run the general administration and provide for defence but also for *investment and economic growth.* For accelerating capital formation and economic growth, the developing countries cannot rely on reve-nue from direct taxes alone. Revenue from indirect taxes can be increased substantially by bringing more commodities under their purview and increasing their rates. It has been found that revenue from indirect taxes show a great deal of *buoyancy,* that is, revenue from them increases very much with the growth of national income.

3. Important Instrument for Influencing Pattern of Production and Investment An-other merit of indirect taxes is that it serves as an important tool for influencing pattern of production and investment in an economy. The working of market mechanism, left to itself, does not always ensure desirable or optimum pattern of productions and investment allocation. For example, left to itself market mechanism may lead to greater investment in producing,harm-ful goods such as alcohol, cigarettes, luxury goods such as airconditioners, washing machines, luxury cars. By imposing heavy excise and sales taxes, the production and investment in these industries can be discouraged. Similarly, indirect tax structure can be so designed as to encourage employment generation and the use of appropriate technology. For example, in India heavy excise duties have been levied on mill-made cloth while handloom cloth has been exempted from them. This has been done to promote the production of handloom cloth, a labour-intensive product, to promote employment generation. The point which is being emphasised is that *indirect faxes can be selective commoditywise and ratewise* so as to affect the prices of different com-modities to promote higher priority industries and discourage low priority ones.

Demerits of Indirect Taxes

Indirect taxes have been criticized for some of their shortcomings which we explain below

1. Indirect Taxes are Regressive. An important criticism of indirect taxes is that they are *regressive,* that is, people with lower incomes bear a higher burden as compared to the rich people. Rich or poor has to pay the same rate of excise duty or sales tax levied on commodities irrespective of their ability to pay. Thus, the fact that same rate of an excise duty on sugar, mill-made cloth etc., has to be paid both by the poor and rich, violates the principle of equity as poor people have lower ability to pay than the rich. However, the regressive nature of indirect taxes has been sought to be removed by levying higher taxes on luxuries which only rich people buy.

2. Indirect Taxes are Inflationary. Another important ground on which indirect taxes have been opposed is that they are *inflationary,* that is, they cause a rise in prices of commodities. In India before 1991 in order to raise more revenue rates of indirect taxes were often raised by Finance Ministers. Even essential commodities such as sugar, cloth, petroleum products were subjected to heavy excise duties and sales taxes. These taxes were wholly or partly added to the prices of goods which caused *cost-push inflation.*

In this connection it is to important to mention the *cascading effect* of indirect taxes which add to their inflationary potential. Cascading effect refers to the effect of indirect taxes on the prices of inputs of the industrial commodities. Higher prices of inputs as a result if levying indirect taxes on them lead to the rise in prices of industrial products in whose production they are used as inputs. In this way through cascading effect much higher rise in price of industrial goods occur when *their several inputs* are subjected to indirect taxes.

3. Excess Burden of Indirect Taxes or Inefficiency in Resource Allocation. The most important harmful effect of indirect taxes is that they make the allocation of resources inefficient and cause *excess burden* on the consumers. As explained above, resource allocation is efficient when resources are so allocated to the production of goods as maximises social welfare. This is achieved when the pattern of production of goods is such that marginal rate of transformation (MRT_{xy}) between goods in production equals marginal rate of substitution between them of' consumers (MRS_{xy}). Indirect taxes distort the pattern of production or resource allocation from this ideal one and thereby cause inefficiency and loss of consumer welfare. The prices of com-modities on which indirect taxes are levied rise causing reduction in their quantities demanded and as a result less resources are devoted to^D their production. Resources so released are used for the production of those goods which are not covered by indirect taxes. Thus indirect taxes cause distortion in the prices of goods and thereby reallocate resources away from the efficient or optimum state. Thus, consumer welfare decreases more as a result of indirect taxes than in case of direct taxes.

Graphic Illustration of Inefficient Resource Allocation of Indirect Taxes

Consider Fig. 31.3 where *AB* is the production possibility curve between two commodities *X* and *Y* before taxation. IC_1, IC_2, IC_3 are social indifference curves. Equilibrium is reached at point *H* where production possibility curve is tangent to social indifference curve IC_3 and the quantities of the two goods produced are indicated by the point *H*. At point *H*, the community is at the highest possible indifference curve and therefore social welfare is maximum. It should be noted that at the tangency point *H*, MRT_{xy} in production equals MRS_{xy} of consumers.

Now, suppose excise duty is levied on commodity *X*, while commodity *Y* remains untaxed. As a result, price of *X* rises, while price of *Y* remains unchanged. With this, the price line shifts to PL_2. Further, as a result of withdrawal of resources by the Government through indirect tax on *X*, the production possibility curve for private use shifts to the left to *CD*. Now, the equilibrium of the private economy will be at point *K* of the production possibility curve *CD* where the new price line PL_2 is tangent to the indifference curve IC_1. Thus, consumers suffer a loss of welfare as they have been shifted from a higher indifference IC_3 to the lower indifference curve IC_1 as a result of imposition of indirect tax on commodity *X*. Resource allocation at *K* is inefficient because slope of the price line *PL^* showing MRS_{xy} is greater than MRT_{xy} as measured by the slope of the tangent *tt'*. If a direct tax (say income tax) of *equal yield* is levied by the Government, the society will reach at point *R* on indifference curve IC_2. The social indifference curve IC_2 is higher than IC_1 which was reached by levying indirect tax on X. Thus indirect tax causes inefficient allocation of resources and reduces social welfare more than a direct tax. That is, an indirect tax causes an excess burden on consumers by distorting prices.

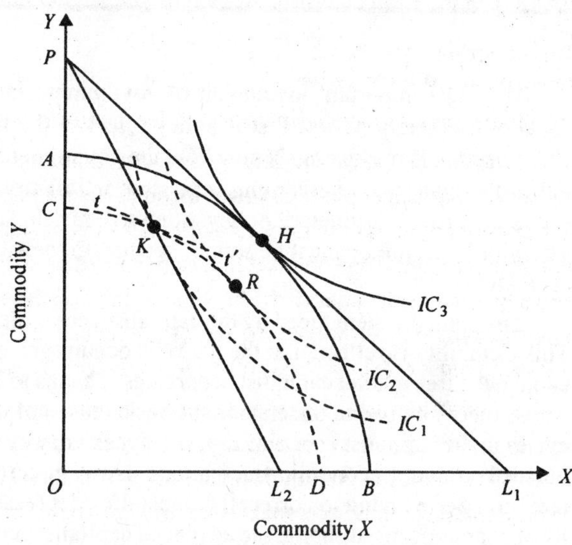

Fig. 31.3. *An Indirect Tax Causes Inefficiency in Resource Allocation.*

QUESTIONS FOR REVIEW

1. Describe the characteristics of a good tax system. How do you rate the Indian tax system in this context ?
2. Discuss the merits and demerits of direct and indirect taxes. Do you think indirect taxes are regressive ?
3. Distinguish between direct tax and indirect tax. Explain the role of indirect tax in the Indian economy.
4. Distinguish between progressive and proportional taxation. What are the effects of a progressive tax system ?
5. Explain the various canons of taxation. Discuss the principle of equity in taxation in a country like India.
6. Discuss the various objectives of taxation policy in India.
7. Explain the objectives and role of fiscal policy in a developing economy.
8. Discuss the role of fiscal policy in an economy. Do you think its role is expanding in the real world ?
9. Explain the main features of the Indian tax structure and examine the role of indirect taxes in a developing economy like India.

CHAPTER 32

Role of Fiscal Policy and Taxation in Resource Mobilisation for Economic Growth

Introduction

The most important instrument of government intervention in the economy today is that of fiscal or budgetary policy. Fiscal policy refers to the taxation, expenditure and borrowing by the Government. The economists now hold the government intervention through fiscal policy is essential in the matter of overcoming recession or inflation as well as of promoting and accelerating economic growth. Monetary policy alone will not do. There is no doubt that the Government budgetary or fiscal policy must be sound, keeping in view the needs and requirements of a developing economy.

The main problem faced by the capitalist economies is economic instability prevailing in them. This instability is reflected in the periodic occurrence of trade cycles which are a general phenomenon in the free market capitalist economies. Thanks to J.M. Keynes, an eminent English economist, whose theory helped to understand the basic reason of the fluctuations in economic activity or trade cycles in the capitalist economies. It is Keynes's theory which has a profound effect on fiscal policy pursued to avoid economic fluctuations. Now, governments have learned to take suitable fiscal measures before hand to correct the impending depression or severe inflation. Therefore, the severity of economic instability in the advanced capitalist economies has declined due to the adoption, by Governments, of fiscal measures suggested by J.M. Keynes.

During a recession or depression fiscal policy should help in increasing demand. For this purpose, the government can increase its expenditure and spend more on public works. This will provide employment to more people. The government can also increase its expenditure on subsidies to producers of consumer goods so as to increase consumption spending. Similarly, the government can lower its tax rates so as to stimulate consumption and investment. Thus, a budget deficit during a depression helps greately in removing unemployment. On the other hand, during periods of inflation, there is too much of demand and hence the government should reduce its own expenditure and curb private spending by increasing taxes. Thus in periods of inflation, we should have surplus budgets. Therefore, there is no inherent superiority in a balanced or a surplus budget. It all depends on the prevailing economic situation. This view of public finance is called as *functional finance* because, according to this view, public revenue and expenditure of the Government are not to be considered as being governed solely by the requirements of government finances but by the requirements of attaining and maintaining full employment, and price stability.

Objectives of Fiscal Policy in Developing Countries

In developing countries, taxation, the Government expenditure, taxation and borrowing have to play a very important role in accelerating economic development. In fact, fiscal policy is a powerful instrument in the hands of the Government by means of which it can achieve the objectives of development. There are several peculiar characteristics of a developing country which necessitate the adoption of a special fiscal policy which ensures a rapid economic growth. There are vast and diverse resources, human and material, which are lying underutilised. Such countries have weak infrastructure, *i.e*, they lack adequate means of transport and communications, roads, ports, highways, irrigation and power. They also lack technical know-how. Their population is increasing at an explosive rate which necessitates rapid economic development to meet the requirements of the rapidly-growing population. Above all, these countries suffer from deficiency of capital. They are caught up in a vicious circle of poverty. In order to overcome these handicaps, a suitable fiscal and taxation policy is called for.

The principal objectives of fiscal policy in a developing economy are:

1. to mobilise resources for economic growth, especially for the public sector;
2. to promote economic growth in the private sector by providing incentives to save and invest;
3. to restrain inflationary forces in the economy in order to ensure price stability; and
4. to ensure equitable distribution of income and wealth so that fruits of economic growth are fairly distributed.

ROLE OF FISCAL POLICY FOR MOBILISATION OF RESOURCES FOR ECONOMIC GROWTH

In developing economies, the Government has to play a very active role in promoting economic development and fiscal policy is the instrument that the state must use. Hence the great importance of public finance in underdeveloped countries desirous of rapid economic development. In a democratic society, there is an inherent dislike for direct (physical) controls and regulation by the state. The entrepreneurs would not like to be orderd about to produce this or that, how much to produce or where to produce. Fiscal incentives in the form of tax concessions, rebates or subsidies are, therefore, preferable. Similarly, the consumers would not like to be told directly to curtail their consumption or to consume this and not to consume that. Taxation of articles whose consumption is to be discouraged is therefore preferable. Hence, a democratic state must rely on indirect methods of control and regulation and this is done through fiscal and monetary policies. Thus, in democratic countries, fiscal policy is a powerful and least undesirable weapon on which the states can rely for promoting economic development.

Capital formation is of strategic importance in the matter of rapid economic development and the developing economies suffer from capital deficiency. It is, therefore, necessary to achieve a higher ratio of savings to national income. In early days of capitalism, payment of low wages and the existence of inequalities of income helped capital formation in the present-day developed countries. But no democratic country can adopt this method in modern times; the effort rather is to raise wages and reduce inequalities of income and wealth. Under a regime of socialist dictatorship, capital formation is brought about by ruthlessly curtailing consumption and keeping down the standards of living. But in modern democracies with every adult person having a right to cast vote very low levels of living for a long time is not feasible. *Hence the state must rely on instruments of fical policy to mobilise resources for economic development.* Taxation can be used to to raise collective savings for public investment and also at the same time to promote private investment. A well-conceived scheme of taxation is an important way of raising ratio of savings to national income which is one of the crucial determinants of the rate of economic growth. As Nurkse says, "*public finance assumes a new significance in the face of the problem of capital formation in underdeveloped countries.*"[1]

On the expenditure side, there is positive need for public investment, especially in those branches of economic activity where the private investments are not easily attracted, for example, the development of power resources, means of transport and communications, basic heavy industries, education and research. Such investments are very often the very foundations of rapid economic advance. Thus, fiscal policy is of crucial importance in accelerating the pace of development in developing countries.

1. Ragnar Nurkse, *Problems of Capital Formation in Under-developed Countries.*

We explain below in detail how fiscal policy measures can be used to achieve the objectives of economic growth, more equal distribution of income and price stability in the developing countries.

As mentioned above, capital formation is an imoportant determinant of economic growth. For accelerating the rate of capital formation, savings and investment rate in the economy has to be stepped up. For this purpose savings have to be mobilised and channelled into productive investment. Due to the severe limitations of alternative ways of mobilising resources for economic growth such as government borrowing and money financing the role of taxation in performing this task assumes greater importance. Fiscal policy, if properly designed, is an efficient and equitable way of mobilising resources for augmenting public investment. Through it not only collective public savings can be raised for financing public investment but also at the same time private savings and investment can be encouraged. "In fact, according to the Indian Taxation Commission, *taxation may be the most effective means of increasing the total volume of saving and investment in an economy where the propensity to consume is normally high.*" Further, the fiscal policy can be so devised that not only the objective of rapid capital accumulation or growth, but also other objectives of economic policy such as equitable distribution of income and wealth, price stability and promotion of employment opportunities can be achieved.

In what follows we shall explain how the various instruments of fiscal policy such as taxation and Government borrowing can be used to mobilise resources for economic development.

Taxation and Resource Mobilisation for Growth

Taxation is an important instrument for fiscal policy which can be used for mobilising resources for capital formation in the public sector. To raise ratio of savings to national income and thereby raise resources for development, it is necessary that marginal saving rate be kept higher than the average saving rate. By imposition of direct progressive taxes on income and profits and higher rates of indirect taxes such as excise duties and sales tax on luxury goods for which income elasticity of demand is higher, the marginal saving rate can be made higher than the average saving rate. This will cause a continuous increase in the saving rate of the economy. An important merit of taxation is that it is not only a good instrument of resource moblisation for development but it also cuts down consumption of goods and thereby helps in checking inflation. Whereas direct taxes on income, profits and wealth reduce the disposable incomes of the people and thereby tend to reduce aggregate demand in the economy, indirect taxes directly discourages the consumption of the goods on which they are levied by raising their prices.

Direct Taxes and Mobilisation of Resources. Now the question arises what should be the taxation structure of a developing economy which will mobilise the potential economic surplus to the maximum, that is, what kinds of taxes be levied, how much progressive should be their rates and what should be the exemptions and concessions in various taxes. This is, however, a highly controversial issue. It has been suggested that an appropriate tax which would mobilise resources or mop up economic surplus is the progressive income tax. In India and the other developing countries income has been regarded as a good base for direct taxation. And the imposition of highly progressive income tax not only mops up relatively greater amount of resources but also tend to reduce inequalities of income. However, a progressive income tax with a high marginal rates of taxes adversely affects private saving and investment and also raises the propensity to evade the tax. In view of this, two proposels have been put forward to make the income tax both as an effective instrument of resource mobilisation for the public sector and of providing incentives to save and invest. First, Prof. Kaldor of Cambridge University, who in 1956 was invited by Government of India to suggest reforms in the Indian tax system for mobilising resources for development, suggested that whereas the marginal rate of income tax be reduced to, say, 45 to 50 per cent, expenditure tax be levied to discourage the people belonging to upper income brackets from dissipating

2. See, S. Gulati, *Capital Taxation in India*, Orient Longman, 1957.

their income in conspicuous consumption. According to him, this will also reduce the tendency to evade income tax on the one hand and promote private savings on the other. The second proposal to reform the income tax put forward by others is that whereas marginal rates of income tax be kept high but some exemptions for approved forms of saving and investment be allowed to the individuals. This will channel individual savings along desired lines and at the same time mobilise resources for development.

Apart from the income tax on individuals and companies, the imposition of other direct taxes such as wealth tax, gift tax, and estate duty are also needed to mobilise sufficient resources for capital formation. Unlike income tax, these capital taxes do not have any adverse effects on incentives to save and invest.[2] They are also important instruments of reducing inequalities of income and wealth. Because of these advantages, Professor Kaldor in his report of taxation reforms in India recommended the imposition of these capital taxes and this recommendation was accepted and the annual wealth tax and gift tax were levied in 1957 with estate duty having been already introduced in 1954.

Agricultural Taxation and Resource Mobilisation. A major part of national income in India and other developing countries originates in the agricultural sector which has substantial economic surplus which can be tapped for capital formation. This economic surplus mainly goes to rich farmers, landlords, merchants and other intermediaries and, in the absence of suitable taxation on agriculture, this is used for conspicuous consumption and for investing in unproductive activities such as buying gold, jewellery, real estate. Thus, according to Professor Kaldor, "*the taxation of agriculture by one means or another has a critical role to play in the acceleration of economic development*."[3] Further, owing to economic growth in general and agricultural development in particular income of the agricultural class and therefore economic surplus enormously increases and therefore need to be mopped up for further development. Besides, the agricultural sector has to be taxed not only because it has a potential surplus but also to achieve maximium utilisation of land through devising a system of land taxation which would penalise poor use of good land. In this regard, a progressive land tax "the effective rates of taxation of which vary with the total value of landholdings of the family unit" may be suitable one. Besides this, progressive agricultural income tax with appropriate exemption may be levied to tap resources from affluent sections of the agricultural sector.

It may be noted that as compared to the non-agricultural sector, agricultural sector in India and other developing countries is quite under-taxed. Land revenue which was at one time the greatest source of revenue for government has now become an insignificant yielder of revenue. In the context of India, Agricultural Taxation Committee under the Chairmanship of Dr. K.N. Raj recommended Agricultural Holdings Tax (AHT) which was to be imposed at a progressive rate on the rateable value of an agricultural holdings of ₹ 5000 and above. It was expected to yield annually ₹ 200 crores. However, Agricultural Holdings Tax was found to be difficult to assess and administer. In our view, a *graded surcharge on the existing land revenue* will be far easier to assess and administer and make land revenue a more elastic source of revenue. However, it may be noted that in India agricultural taxation is a state subject and there is lack of political will on the part of the State Governments to raise the level of land taxation in a country. But if sufficient resources are to be mobilised for development, the level of agricultural taxation has to be raised.

Merits of Direct Taxes for Resource Mobilisation, As seen above, as an instrument of resource mobilisation for development direct taxes enjoy several advantages. (1) They raise resources in a non-inflationary way. Indeed, they tend to check inflation by curtailing consumption demand. (2) They help to reduce inequalities of income and wealth, and (3) They discourage

3. N. Kaldor, The Role of Taxation in Economic Development, in E.A.G. Robinson (ed.), *Problems in Economic Development*, 1965, p. 177.

conspicuous and non-necessary consumption and thereby enlarge economic surplus. But the direct taxation of agricultural and non-agricultural sectors has its own limits. In India there is a great potential for raising resources through direct taxes. At present 2.7 crores people out of more than 100 crores population pay income tax. As economic growth takes place incomes of the people increase and as a result their taxable capacity also increases. There is a considerable evasion of income tax and corporation tax in India. If this evasion is checked more resources can be raised. Yield from other direct taxes such as wealth tax, gift tax is quite meagre due to very small coverage, low rates and considerable evasion of them. Therefore, more revenue from these taxes can also be obtained by making suitable reforms in them.

Role of Indirect Taxes in Resource Mobilisation

As a result of limitations of direct taxes, developing countries have resorted to extensive use of indirect taxes. *In India, almost all commodities have been brought within the net of indirect taxes such as excise duties and sales tax. Besides, there are custom duties* (*i.e., taxes on imports and exports*). Indirect taxation is an important source of development funds in a developing country. In the last five decades of planned development, revenue from several indirect taxes has been rising as a percentage of total revenue as well as of national income. It has been found that indirect taxes are better suited to the conditions obtaining in developing countries for reducing current consumption and mobilising resources for development. This is because in such countries quite a large proportion of national income tends to be diverted to current consumption instead of being productively invested. The average propensity to consume in such countries is much higher than is the case in advanced countries. Indirect taxes which reduce consumption must thus play a more important part. They will raise the rate of savings which are so essential for economic growth.

"High rates of taxes on commodities with a high income elasticity of demand are quite effective in siphoning a substantial proportion of increase in output into the resources of the public sector needed for development financing and a stiff rate of commodity taxes on luxury articles tends to introduce an element of progressiveness in an otherwise predominantly regressive tax structure in developing countries."[4] But in order to make sure that the resources raised through commodity taxes are adequate, it will be necessary to extend their coverage to include some articles of mass consumption. In the poor countries, it is not possible to exempt entirely goods of general and necessary consumption, because they are the only goods that provide a base broad enough to assure an adequate amount of resources. The rates of two important indirect taxes, namely, excise duties and customs duties which yielded increasingly greater revenue for government before 1991 had to be reduced under economic reforms initiated since 1991. To promote free trade customs duties had to the reduced as a part of agreement under WTO. Excise duty had to the reduced so that domestic industries could compete with imports from abroad after the adoption of liberal foreign trade policy. However, to compensate for the loss in revenue due to reduction in customs duties and excise duty, new *service* tax (which is an indirect tax) has been imposed. Service tax which now covers more than 100 services has become a good source of tax revenue. Besides in the States, sales tax has been replaced by value added tax (VAT) which is also yielding more revenue.

Limitations. But there are some limitations of raising resources through indirect taxes. First, they lead to *cost-push inflation*. The burden of indirect taxes are passed on to the consumers in the form of higher prices charged from them. In India excise duties on sugar, cloth, kerosene oil, petrol etc., has raised the prices and have contributed a good deal to cost-push inflation witnessed in last several years. Secondly, levying of custom duties on imports of capital goods, raw materials used for industrial production have accelerated cost-push inflation in the Indian economy. Thirdly, imposition of custom duties on imports of goods also protect inefficiency in domestic industries. This also contributes to high-cost production and promotes inefficiency. Lastly, indirect taxes are

4. R.N. Tripathy, *Public Finance in Developing Countries*, 1966, p. 200.

regressive in nature; both the rich and poor have to pay the same rate on the taxed commodities. The regressive character of indirect taxes have been attempted to be reduced by imposing higher rates of excise and custom duties on luxury items and smaller rates of duties on goods of mass consumption. However, the need for mobilising greater resources have forced the finance ministers to levy higher indirect taxes even on articles of mass consumption.

Role of Taxation in Promoting Private Saving and Investment

It is worth mentioning that in a mixed economy such as ours, there is need to raise not only the public savings and investment but also to promote private saving and investment so that the overall rate of saving and investment in the economy is stepped up. This implies that taxation measures should not impair incentives to save and invest of the people. Therefore, a developing economy encounters a crucial dilemma in augmenting larger resources for public investment on the one hand and to promote private savings and investment on the other. Thus, according to Prof. Heller, "Tax Policy faces a basic dilemma in its role as a an instrument of capital formation for economic development. On the one hand, high levels of taxes are necessary to finance that part of the development which falls in the government share and to mobilise for investment the private resources that might otherwise be dissipated. On the other hand, the lower the taxes the greater will be the inducement to private investment... The dilemma is worsened by the fact that those taxes which are most effective in capturing a large share of the gains for further capital formation are the ones most likely to affect the returns from private investment. *Only way of the dilemma may be to combine high rates of taxation in general, with preferential treatment for categories of desired development activity.*"

However, as Kaldor pointed out in its recommendations for tax reforms in India, very high rates of income tax cause evasion of the tax and also discourage incentive to save and invest. Besides, according to Laffer Curve concept, on which supply-side economics is based, if rate of income tax is raised beyond a point (above the range of 30 to 35%), revenue from tax decreases. This has been confirmed by the Indian experience as under the economic reforms initiated since 1991, marginal rates personal income tax has been reduced to 30 per cent and this has led to substantial increase in tax revenue from both personal income tax and corporate income tax. Therefore, the policy of moderate direct taxes with preferential treatment for some desired forms of saving and investment is ideal one for resource mobilisation for economic growth.

Thus, while the policy of moderate rates of taxation on income and profit may be adopted but even with this private saving and investment can be promoted through preferential treatment of them. Besides the adoption of moderate rate of income tax, private savings can be promoted in several other ways. First, interest on several types of private savings such as bank deposits, investment in units of Unit Trust of India and National Savings Certificates, and other approved forms of saving be totally or substantially exempted from taxation. This will encourage private savings through raising the rate of return on savings as the savers would earn interest income free of income tax. Secondly, voluntary savings in certain selective lines such as voluntary contributions to provident fund, life insurance premium, certain specific units (of UTI) and National Savings Certificates be substantially exempted from income tax. This will also stimulate private savings by raising the rate of return on these savings. For, people will not only earn rate of interest or dividend but will save a good amount of income tax on these approved forms of savings. Thirdly, some economists have suggested that if progressivity in tax rates is avoided (that is, if rates of income taxes do not increase much with the increase in income) private saving and investment will be boosted up. However, this is based upon a questionable assumption that richer people in countries like India have high propensity to save. In view of the present author, the lower marginal rates of taxes will place more disposable income in the hands of higher income brackets which will tend to raise their conspicuous consumption, especially when goods catering to their frivolous wants are available in abundance these days through both domestic production and imports. As mentioned above, this is reinforced by the international demonstration effect which exercises a strong influence on the consumption behaviour of the richer sections of the Indian society.

Besides private savings, private investment can be directly encouraged through taxation. Firstly, in order to stimulate private investment, the *retained profits* which are reinvested by the business firms instead of distributing them among the shareholders can be exempted from taxation or taxed at preferential rates. Secondly, to boost private investment *liberal depreciation and investment allowances* may also be allowed to the business firms which will be used for purposes of investment in new plant, equipment and machinery. Further, "subsidies on investment can also be provided by the Government which generally prove to be a very effective way of promoting private investment".

Another important fiscal method of stimulating private investment in developing countries is *granting of tax holidays or relief from tax on the profits of new enterprises* for some specified period of time. Further, indirect taxes can also be manipulated in a variety of ways to promote private investment in certain selected fields of industrial activity. Thus exmption or lowering of sales tax or excise duties on some domestically produced important raw materials or lowering of import duties on raw materials and capital goods from abroad can provide a boost to private investment. Likewise, reduction of export duties may also bring about a healthy effect on investment outlook.

It needs to be stressed that various incentives to promote private savings and investment will prove effectively only if they are kept as simple, certain and stable as possible. A complicated schemes of incentives with frequent and arbitrary changes are likely to defeat the very purpose of these incentive schemes. Prof. Prest rightly points out, "*If the main purpose of investment incentives is to raise the long-term level of investment rather than offset cyclical downturns and this clearly is the case in underdeveloped countries ... the emphasis should be on the stability of these tax arrangements rather than their variability.*"[5]

It is important to note that private investment depends upon several factors such as size of the market, cost of inputs, availability of infrastructural facilities such as power, coal, oil, transport, availability of technical know-how. Tax incentives will prove effective only if conditions regarding these other factors are not unfavourable. Further, unless there is an efficient and competent system of tax administration it is very likely that incentives become tax loopholes. The businessmen in the developing countries tend to take advantages of these tax exemptions on bogus basis without fulfilling and carrying out the underlying intent of such concessions. An honest and efficient administrative machinery, therefore, remains the basic precondition for the purposeful use of incentives.[6]

FISCAL POLICY, EQUITY AND PRICE STABILITY

Fiscal Policy and Equitable Income Distribution

Let us now explain how fiscal policy can be used to achieve equitable distribution of income. Attainment of a wider measure of equality in incomes, wealth and opportunities must form an integral part of economic development and social advance. Existence of gross inequalities is a social evil and no measure of economic development will increase economic welfare unless an equitable distribution of the rising national product is assured. Instrument of taxation, therefore, must be used as a means of bringing about a redistribution of income in favour of the poorer sections of the society. A caution is, however, necessary. It is essential to strike a balance between the two objectives of lessening economic inequalities and that of sustaining and strengthening incentives to invest and increase production. Fiscal policy must maintain unimpaired the flow of savings and

---

5. See Prest, A.R. Fiscal Measures and Capital Accumulation in Agarwala and Singh (ed.), *Accelerating Investment in Developing Countries*, Oxford University Press.
6. A.R. Prest. *op. cit., p.* 445.

investment which makes for continued progress of productive enterprises. Larger production and greater equality are both objectives of high importance in relation to general economic and social policy. Higher incomes can be taxed without adverse repercussions on private productive effort and enterprise. Optimum rate of growth and maximum social welfare are not irreconcible. It will be possible to reconcile these two objectives by the formulation of a well-balanced fiscal programme.

But lessening inequalities through taxing higher incomes is only one form of fiscal operations. A better and complementary fiscal policy consists of *increasing public expenditure for promoting welfare of the less privileged classes.* Increasing public expenditure on anti-poverty programmes such as construction of rural public works, employment guarantee schemes will ensure equity in income distribution. Stepping up of public expenditure on primary education and public health will greatly improve the economic conditions of the poor people. In fact, international experience shows that active public expenditure policies aimed at raising the consumption of the poor are far more effective in promoting equity as compared to tax policies aimed at containing the incomes of the rich.

Fiscal Policy for Achieving Price Stability

India as well as other developing countries have been experiencing the problem of rising prices or inflation. Inflation in them has been of both demand-pull and cost-push types. The main cause of demand-pull inflation has been the *fiscal deficit* in Government's budgets which has arisen because they have not been able to finance the mounting public expenditure through revenue from taxes and public sector surpluses In India in the year 1990-91, fiscal deficit rose to 8.3 per cent of GDP (Gross Domestic Product) and even after 14 years of efforts, the Indian Government has been able to achieve a only a modest reduction in fiscal deficit. In 2004-05, fiscal deficit is estimated to be of the order of 6.1 per cent of GDP, whereas to achieve price stabilisation IMF recommended its reduction to 3 per cent of GDP. A huge fiscal deficit in Government is financed in two ways: (1) by Government borrowing from the market, (2) by monetising the deficit which is commonly called deficit financing in India. A high degree of fiscal deficit leads to excess market borrowing by the Government which causes expansion in bank credit to the Government and therefore increase in money supply in the economy causing prices to rise. Besides, excessive Government borrowing from the market leads to the rise in interest rate which discourages private investment. Further, a part of fiscal deficit that is monetisedthrough borrowing from Reserve Bank of India which issues new currency (which is a reserve or high powered money) for the Government. This causes greater expansion in money supply through the process of money multiplier and generates inflationary situation in the economy. Thus, to check the rate of inflation, fiscal deficit has to be reduced through both raising revenue of the Government and reducing Non-developmental Government expenditure. In what follows we first explain the concepts of fiscal deficit revenue deficit, primary deficit. We will then explain various measures in the Indian context that can be adopoted to reduce fiscal deficit and thereby to reduce inflationary pressures in the economy.

CHAPTER 33

Government Borrowing or Debt-Financing of Budget Deficit

Government borrowing is another fiscal method by which savings of the community may be mobilised for economic development. In developing economies, the Governments resort to borrowing in order to finance schemes of economic development. Government or what is also called public borrowing becomes necessary because taxation alone cannot provide sufficient funds for economic development. Besides, too heavy taxation has an adverse effect on private saving and investment. It may noted that when there is fiscal deficit (i.e. budget deficit). It can be financed in two ways. First, by borrowing by the Government from the market and this borrowing leads to the increase in public debt. Borrowing as a means to finance the fiscal deficit is therefore called **debt-financing of budget deficit.** Second, budget or fiscal deficit can be financed by *printing new money* and therefore it is called **money financing of fiscal deficit**. The debt-financing of budget deficit will be discussed in the present chapter and money financing of fiscal or budget deficit will be discussed in the next chapter.

How much resources should be mobilised through creation of money, that is, through money financing depends on whether or not newly printed money is used for productive purposes which generates higher growth in GDP. In our view in a developing economy such as ours, a fine balance needs to be striked between how much resources have to be raised through taxation, borrowing (i.e., debt financing) and newly created money (i.e. money financing).

DEBT FINANCING OF BUDGET DEFICIT

A popular method of financing budget deficit is borrowing by the government which issues bonds and sells it to the public. Generally, sale of interest-bearing bonds to the public is indirect through financial intermediarises such as banks. Banks buy the bonds floated by the government with the currency deposits of the public. Therefore, debt-financing of budget deficit is also known as *bond-financing of budget deficit*. With the borrowed money in this way the government is able to expand its expenditure but at the same time it adds to public debt which has both short-run and long run consequences. It may also be noted that budget deficit also comes about when taxes are reduced, keeping government expenditure constant. This type of budget deficit can also be financed through incurring debt by selling bonds to the banks or public. The government has not only to pay annually interest on borrowed funds but has to pay back also the principal sum borrowed for which it may levy higher taxes in future.

The Keynesians have emphasised the expansionary effect of debt financing of government **expenditure or budget deficit. In the Keynesian model with a fixed price level, the increase in government** expenditure through use of borrowed money causes an upward shift in aggregate expenditure ($C + I + G$) curve. If the economy is working at less than full-employment level of national income so that output gap exists in the economy, the increase in debt-financed government expenditure will bring about expansion in output or income. With the increase in income at the given tax rate, tax revenue collected will rise which will over time reduce the budget deficit or even ultimately eliminate it so that budget becomes balanced. This can also be illustrated through *IS-LM*

1. R. Dornbusch, S. Fischer, & R. Startz, *Macroeconomics*, Tata McGraw Hill, 8th edition, P.476.

model in Figure 33.1 where *IS* and *LM* curves are drawn, given the money supply in the economy. Y^* is the full employment level of output. Initially, the equilibrium is at income level Y_0. Now, with debt-financed increase in government expenditure *IS* curve shift to the right from IS_0 to IS_1 with *LM* curve

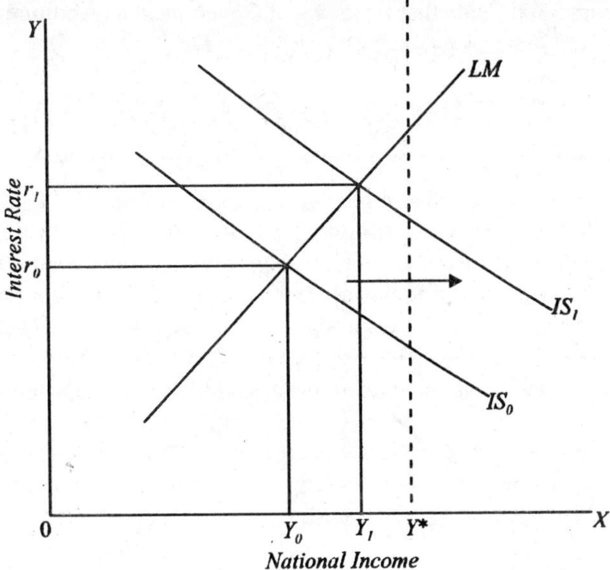

Fig. 33.1. *Expansionary Effect of Debt-financed Increase in Government Expenditure*

remaining the same. As a result, as will be seen from Fig. 33.1, national income increases to Y_1. This will bring about increase in tax revenue collected by the government and over time budget deficit will be reduced or even eliminated. It will be seen from Figure 33.1 that though interest rate also rises but it does not fully offset the expansionary effect of debt-financed increase in government expenditure.

However, critics have pointed out that debt-financed government expenditure is largely offset by the *crowding-out effect* of debt financing on private investment. The crowding-out effect on private investment takes place in a variety of ways. First, it has been pointed out that government's borrowing funds to finance budget deficit will lead to the increase in demand for lendable funds which will cause the rate of interest to rise. The rise in interest rate will cause private investment to decline. Thus debt-financed increase in government expenditure crowds out private investment. According to this view, due to crowding-out effect on private investment net expansionary effect of increase in government expenditure is negligible. On the other hand, the society will have to bear the burden of increase in public debt as a result of debt-financed expansion in government expenditure. If budget deficit arises due to reduction in taxes, keeping government expenditure constant, this will also lead to rise in interest rate and will therefore cause crowding-out effect on private investment. This happens because reduction in taxes stimulates consumption expenditure of the people which reduces savings. The decline in savings causes interest rate to rise resulting in fall in private investment.

Wealth Effect of Debt-Financing

In our above analysis we have not taken into account the wealth effect of debt financing. When the government issues bonds to finance its budget deficit, it creates private wealth. This is because bonds are considered as wealth by the people. Patinkin and Friedman in their models include wealth in there money demand function. That is, according to them, demand from money depends on the real value of wealth, apart from other factors. If this wealth effect of bond-financing of budget deficit is recognised, then it exercises an important influence on the dynamic behaviour of the economy. When through debt-financing of budget deficit, more bonds are issued and sold by the government, the wealth of the people increases which will raise the demand for money. The increase in demand for money, money supply remaining the same, causes a leftward shift in the *LM* curve, for instance, from LM_0 to LM_1 in Figure 33.2. (Note that financing of Government expenditure through creation

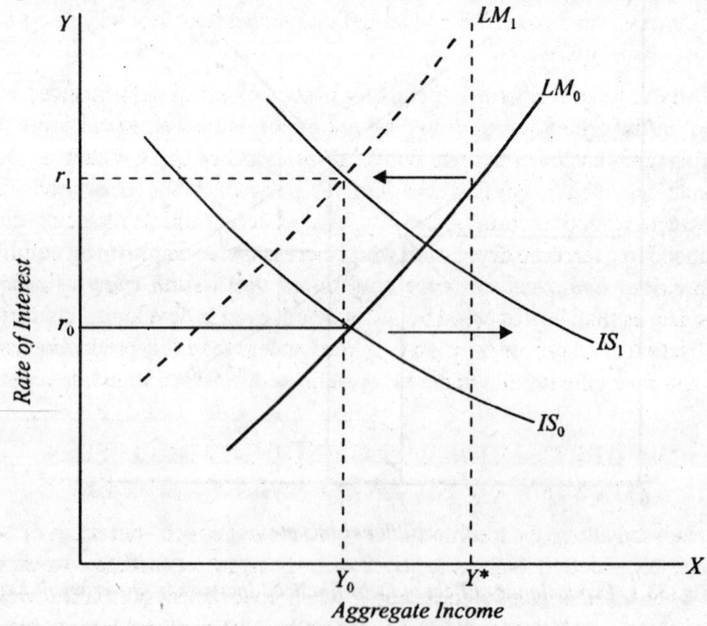

Fig. 33.2. *Debt-financing of Budget Deficit with Wealth effect of Bonds Sold by the Government*

of printed money, *LM* curve shifs downward (*i.e.* to the right). Thus, while with the increase in government expenditure *IS* curve shifts to the right to the new position IS_1 which tends to raise aggregate income, the wealth effect of bonds issued to finance the deficit causes leftward shift in the *LM* curve which tends to raise rate of interest and thereby crowds out private investment. According to Friedman, the wealth effect is quite substantial so that it completely offsets the expansionary effect of increase in government expenditure. In Figure 33.2, initially the equilibrium is at Y_0 level of income. With bond-financed increase in government expenditure *IS* curve shifts from IS_0 to IS_1 and due to wealth effect *LM* curve shifts leftward to LM_1. It will be seen that interest rate rises from r_0 to r_1 with no net effect on the level of income which remains unchanged at Y_0. Due to rise in interest, private investment declines so much that completely offsets the expansionary effect of debt-financed budget deficit. As a result, budget deficit persists and debt goes on accumulating and becomes unsustainable.

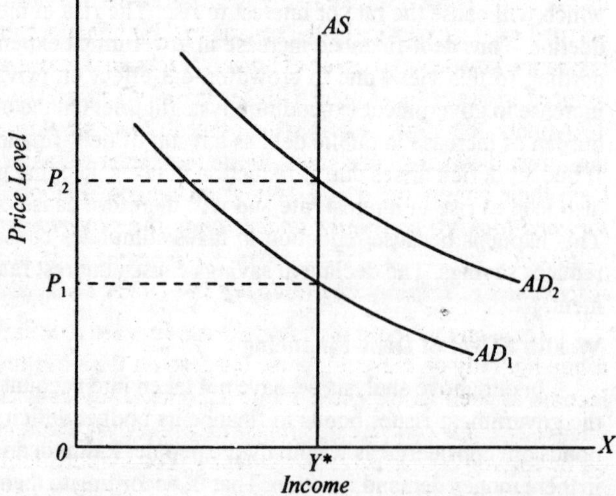

Fig. 33.3. *Rise in price level offsets the expansionary effect of debt financing of budget deficit.*

In the above analysis of crowding-out effect of debt-financing it is assumed that price level remains fixed. However, when the aggregate supply function is vertical as is the case when the economy is working at full capacity output (i.e., full-employment level), increase in aggregate demand (*AD*) brought about by debt-financed increase in government expenditure will result in rise in price level, equilibrium income remains unchanged as shown through *AS-AD* model in Figure 33.3. Since income remains unchanged, tax-revenue will not increase and therefore budget deficit persists and debt will go on accumulating and over time become unsustainable.

Conclusion: We have seen above that expansionary effect of debt-financed budget deficit has been challenged on the ground of its crowding-out effect. However, in our view the crowding-out effect of debt-financing has been belown out of all proportions. As a matter of fact, crowding-out effect of debt financing of budget deficit is negligible, especially when the economy is working at less than full-employment level of income. Generally, budget deficit and its financing through floating of bonds is recommend to overcome depression when there is under-employment equilibrium and therefore output gap exists. *Empirical evidence also shows that wealth effect of sale of bonds is not significant*. Besides, as shall be discussed below in detail, even in developing countries where there is gross under-utilisation of resources or when they work at less their full-production capacity, policy of budget deficits and financing it through debt is a useful instrument to stimulate economic growth and raise income.

DEBT-FINANCING OF BUDGET DEFICIT : THE VIEW OF RICARDIANCE EQUIVALENCE

We have analysed above the traditional Keynesian view of debt-financing of budget deficit. As noted earlier, the budget deficit may come about when government increases its expenditure without imposition of higher taxes or it may come about when government cuts taxes without reducing its expenditure. Recently, an alternative view of effects of debt-financed budget deficit has been put forth and this view is known as *Ricardian Equivalence* as this view was first of all put forward by David Ricardo but has been revived and further refined by some modern economists. According to this view, the consumers are forward looking and decide about their consumption expenditure not only on the basis of their disposable current income but also on their expected future income. This view of forward looking consumer underlies the post-Keynesian theories of consumption, namely, life saving model of Modigliani and permanent income consumption theory of Milton Friedman. A forward-looking consumer views the budget deficit financed by incurring debt by the government that at some point in future, the government will have to raise taxes to pay off the debt and interest accrued on it. Accordingly, the consumers think that present tax cut that causes budget deficit which is financed by debt (i.e. issue of bonds) *raises his income only temporarily* since it will be eventually reduced in future by imposing higher taxes to pay off the debt. Therefore, as a result of tax cut and debt-financed budget deficit in the present, *their permanent or life time income does not rise*. Thus the forward-looking consumers do not feel better off as a result of present cut in taxes and therefore keep their consumption and saving unchanged. Elaborating on this view, Mankiw writes, *"The forward-looking consumer understands the government borrowing today means higher taxes in future. The tax cut financed by government debt does not reduce the tax burden, it merely reschedules it. It therefore should not encourage the consumer to spend more"*[2].

Thus, on this view, if consumers are forward looking or foresighted they will base their expenditure not only on current income but also on their life-time income which consists of their present income as well as expected future income. *They consider government debt incurred to finance budget deficit is equivalent to future taxes because the debt incurred in the current year will be paid off by levying higher taxes in the future.* For forward-looking consumers therefore future taxes are equivalent to current taxes. Therefore, this concept is called Ricardian equivalence because it was

2. N. Gregory Mankiw, *Macroeconomics*, Fifth Edition, Worth Publishers, New York, 2003, p. 4, 6

David Ricardo who first put forward this idea of government debt being equivalent to future taxes. The concept of Ricardian equivalence implies that debt-financed cut in tax will not affect the present consumption of the people. To quote Mankiw again, "the implication of Ricardinan equivalence is that a debt-financed tax cut leaves consumption unaffected. *Households save the extra disposable income* to pay the future tax liability that the tax cut implies. This increase in private saving exactly offsets the decrease in public saving. National saving–the sum of private and public saving–remains the same. The tax cut therefore has none of the effects that traditional analysis predicts"[3]

Thus, according to the Ricardian equivalence, debt-financed tax cut does not cause increase in consumption expenditure and therefore aggregate demand. Therefore, the debt-financed tax cut will not succeed in stimulating the economy.

Robert Barro and Ricardian Equivalence

Robert Barro,[4] an eminent American economist, presents an alternative view of Ricardian equivalence. He also points out that debt-financed tax cut does not lead to increase in consumption expenditure and therefore cannot stimulate the economy. He assumes that people have perfect foresight about the future. Further, they do not discount the future because they care about the welfare of future generations as much as they care for their own. That is, according to him, future generations are the children and grandchildren of the current generation. Therefore, it is not correct to consider them independent or different economic agents. He argues that the assumption that the present generation cares about future generation as much as its own is proved by the fact that most people give gifts to their children, often in the form of bequests at the time of their deaths. The evidence of bequests shows that people are not willing to consume more at their children's expense. He considers an individual belonging to a family which lives for ever. Therefore, a debt-financed tax cut may raise an individual's income in the present or in his life time but it does not raise his family's income for ever. Instead of consuming his extra income accrued to him due to cut in tax, he saves it and leaves it to his children who will bear the future tax liability. We thus see that consumption expenditure does not increase and the economy therefore does not receive any stimulus on this count.

Conclusion. It follows from above that the consequence of government debt depends on the nature of consumption behaviour of people. However, the evidence in support of Ricardian equivalence hypothesis is quite weak. The effect of tax cut in stimulating the economy has been tested in some economies, such as that of the United States. President John Kenedy made a tax cut in 1964, and again President Reagan made a tax cut to stimulate the American economy. As a result of it government debt increased but the American economy was revived and got out of recession which gripped it earlier. These real-life experiments confirms the validity of the Keyneisan traditional analysis and disproves Ricardian equivalence hypothesis. Recently in the year 2000, President George Bush again tried to revive the American economy through tax cut and financed the budget deficit by sale of bonds. This again was quite successful and by the end of year 2003, American economy got out of recession.

GOVERNMENT BORROWING AND DEBT-FINANCING OF BUDGET DEFICIT : THE CASE OF INDIA

In India there has been a problem of persistent budget deficits which has been largely financed by borrowing from the banks and public and thus adding to the public debt. In 1991 as a measure of economic reforms IMF directed that fiscal deficit of the central government should be reduced to achieve economic stability. The economists associated with IMF and World Bank hold the view that large fiscal deficit raises inflation rate of the economy on the one hand and since it is financed largely by borrowing from the market, this raises rate of interest and therefore crowds out private investment

3. Mankiw, op. cit. p. 416.
4. Robet J. Barro, "Are Government Bonds Net Wealth," *Journal of Political Economy*, 81 (1974).

and adversely affects economic growth. Besides, it has been pointed out that the persistent budget deficit year after year adds to public debt and as a result ratio of public debt to national income (Debt/GDP ratio) will greatly increase which will land the country in debt trap[5].

In view of the above it is appropriate to discuss the above issues relating to debt-financing of budget deficit in the light of the recent Indian experience. It is worth mentioning that from the years 1997 to 2002-03 and again in 2008 and 2009 the Indian economy experienced slowdown in economic growth due to lack of aggregate demand resulting mainly from the fall in public investment and poor performance in agriculture. In this situation *output gap* in the Indian economy emerged as the existing production capacity was not fully utilised. Besides, there has been lack of infrastructure facilities which stands in the way of raising private investment.

With their focus on reducing fiscal deficit the government reduced its capital expenditure (i.e. investment expenditure) because it failed to curb its consumption expenditure and subsidies. Thus, Mihir Rakshit, a leading Indian macroeconomist, rightly states. "With their focus on fiscal deficit, policy makers seem to think that what matters primarily is curbing government expenditure .... irrespective of changes in their composition. The period 1995-2000 was marked by 9.6 per cent and 12.6 per cent growth in government consumption and subsidies respectively, but public accumulation grew at snail's pace of 1.9 per cent and its two crucial constituents, namely, investment in agriculture and infrastructure actually declined by 5.6 per cent and 0.2 per cent respectively"[6]

The consequences of debt-financed budget deficit in the case of India depends on whether or not output gap exists due to lack of demand and infrastructural facilities. If the output gap exists, then increase in government expenditure on consumption and subsidies will raise aggregate demand and help in utilising more fully the existing production capacity and over time will cause private investment to rise. But this will not raise public saving and public investment and therefore will not result in much higher growth of the economy. This may also raise ratio of public debt to GDP since due to slow growth in GDP, tax collection will not appreciably rise. Mihir Rakshit aptly points out that, "The Indian economy since 1997[7] has also been characterised by output gap, high fiscal deficit and growing debt/GDP ratio. The mainstream view in India is that despite the output gap fiscal deficits crowd out private investment and are unsustainable"[8].

The mainstream view of debt-financed fiscal deficit is not correct and has been rightly challenged by some prominent India economists such as Mihir Rakshit, V.N. Pandit and Prabhat Patnaik, among others. *Under the circumstances when there exists output-gap and under-utilisation of production capacity, the increase in government expenditure, especially of investment nature will crowd in private investment and speed up rate of economic growth.* To quote Mihir Rakshit, "contrary to wide spread perception among commentators *budget deficits associated with closing the output gap in fact crowds in private investment*.......... crowding in will be much more pronounced in countries like India where government's infrastructural investment favourably affects private investment even while projects are being executed : the fact that highways are being built in some area or that it will soon have abundant supply of power, communication facilities is likely to induce private investors to start setting up new units and expending existing ones even in the shrot run"[9].

5 For this view, see Shankar Acharya, former Chief Economic Advisor who puts forward this view in a forcefull manner in 'How Fiscal Deficit Hurts Economic Growth. We have explained in detail this mainstream view in the next chapter.

6. Mihir Rakshit, "Some Macroeconomics of India's Reforms Experience" in *India's Emerging Economy* (e.d.) Kaushik Basu, Oxford University Press, 2004, p,104.

7. Mihir Rakshit describes the situation that prevailed during 1997-2002-03.

8. Budget Deficit: Sustainability, Solvancy and Optimality, printed in Amaresh Bagchi, "*Readings in Public Finance*" Oxford University Press, 2005, pp. 342-343.

9. Mihir Rabshit, op. cit. p.345

When there is outgap in a developing economy such as India, even increase in Government's consumption expenditure will crowd in private investment through the former's demand effect. But, as has been pointed out by Dr. Mihir Rakshit, crowding-in effect of government's investment expenditure will be greater because it expands the infrastructural facilities (i.e. supply-side factors) badly needed for increase in private investment.

In our view, the expansionary effect of government's investment expenditure and also its crowding-in effect on private investment in a developing country like India is not confined to the situation when output gap and under-utilisation of capital stock exists due to demand deficiency but also when such an economy functions at its normal capacity. Besides, even in normal times, debt-financed government investment expenditure which brings about rapid economic growth, budget deficits and debt/GDP ratio over time can be reduced. **An important rule of public finance, which is sometimes described as a golden rule is that if borrowed money by the government is used for investment or developmental purposes, it leads to growth in GDP or national income.** Given the tax rate, this increase in income will ensure collection of more tax revenue possible. As a result, budget deficit or what is called fiscal deficit will be reduced and debt/GDP ratio will decline. This has actually happened in India.

As a matter of fact, long ago (in 1994) E.D. Domar had stated the **condition for sustainability of persistent budget deficits** and consequently of mounting public debit. According to Domar, debt-financed deficits *are sustainable if growth rate exceeds the rate of interest*. This is because economic growth means increase in income or GDP from which annual interest payments can be made and if growth in income exceeds the rate of interest, the part of increase in income may be used for retiring public debt. In this way with the growth of the economy budget deficit and debt/GDP ratio can be reduced Elaborating Domar's condition. Mihir Rakshit writes, "According to Domar, if the government finances part of its expenditure (amounting to a given fraction of full-employment output) through borrowing, in a growing economy public debt and the government interest outgo as proportion of GDP will be stable in the long run provided the growth rate exceeds the interest rate. The implication is that when this condition is satisfied, maintenance of full employment through debt financing of budget deficit does not erode fiscal viability or produce a debt trap"[10]

In case of India's macrodynamics the viability and sustainability can be explained through the following equation

$$Y = C(Y_d) + I_v(Y_1 - Y_{t-1}) + I_g + G \qquad \ldots (i)$$

where Y stands for national income (*i.e.* GDP_{FC}), Y_d for disposable income, C for consumption which depends on disposable income (Y_d), I_v for private investment which depends on change in national income (Y), I_g for government's investment expenditure, and G for government's consumption expenditure

Since $Y_d = Y - T$ where T stands for tax revenue. If t is the rate of income tax, then $T = tY$. Thus

$$Y_d = Y - tY = (1 - t)\,Y \qquad \ldots (ii)$$

Since budget deficit (BD) in our simple model is the difference between Government total expenditure on consumption (G) and investment (I_g) and the tax revenue collected, we have

$$BD = (Ig + G) - tY \qquad \ldots (iii)$$

Now substituting $(1 - t)Y$ for Y_d in equation (i) above we have

$$Y = C[(1 - t)Y)] + I_v(Y_t - Y_{t-1}) + Ig + G \qquad \ldots (iv)$$

The viability and sustainability of debt-financed budget deficits in a growing economy must be based on the magnitude of Government investment expenditure (I_g) in the total expenditure ($I_g + G$).

10. Mihir Rakshit, op. cit. (2005), p. 340.

Suppose the economy is working at the full capacity output, and government increases its investment expenditure, say, in infrastructure and finances the budget deficit through incurring debt. This increase in government investment expenditure will raise income through both demand effect and capacity effect and will therefore stimulate private investment which depends on change in income (i.e. $Y_1 - Y_{t-1}$). This increase in both government and private investment will over time cause rapid growth in income which in turn will result in more tax revenue. Thus, in this way budget deficit will be reduced with favourable effect on public debt/GDP ratio, if rate of growth in income (GDP) exceeds rate of interest.

It is thus clear that sustainability of budget deficit and public debt depends on *shifting the composition of government expenditure towards investment*. To quote Mihir Rakshit, "Budgetary viability requires an improvement in revenue balances in the medium term and the long run public investment in agriculture aided by crowding-in effect, raises agricultural productivity and acts as a stimulant to a rural economy, brings down poverty and *enables the government to reduce over time expenditure on food or fertilizer subsidies and poverty alleviation measures*. An increase in government investment in rural and urban infrastructural facilities will through increased revenue receipts and decreased subsidies will strengthen budgetary position not only in the medium term and the long run but in the short run as well"[11]. It is interesting to note that when with effect from year 2003 the Government investment expenditure in India has been raised, tax revenue collection has significantly risen and also fiscal deficit, revenue deficit and debt/GDP ratio have declined. Besides, private investment went up (i.e. croweded in) rather than crowding out by increase in debt-financed increase in government expenditure.

Thus, in the nineties when the focus in our strategy was to reduce fiscal deficit, no matter reducing capital expenditure of the government for this purpose, the Indian economy experienced slowdown in growth and our fiscal situation worsened. On the other hand, when from March 2003 we shifted the focus toward increase in government investment expenditure on power, ports, highways, rural roads in a big way, private investment also crowed in, generated higher economic growth which resulted in lower fiscal deficits and lower debt/GDP ratio.

Now-a-days, the Central Government borrows mostly from the market through sale of its bonds of different maturities carrying different rates of interest by RBI.

Borrowing is the quickest mode of raising funds. Financing through taxation is not so expeditious because passing of tax laws, assessment of taxes based on those laws and their collection involves considerable delay. On the other hand, bonds can be issued any time during a year. It is bankes, insurance companies, mutual funds that usually invest their funds in government bonds. **Public borrowing generates additional productive capacity.** The funds raised by public borrowing can be utilised for building up economic infrastructure for the economy through schemes for the development of irrigation, transport, power and communication. They can help also in building up of the agricultural and industrial base of the economy. All such investments facilitate further economic growth. There is no doubt, therefore, that the public borrowing plays a very useful and important role in accelerating economic development of underdeveloped economies. Public debt promotes saving and investment, the two most crucial determinants of economic growth.

But there are three problems concerning government borrowing. First, government borrowing leads to increase is public debt whose burden falls on future generations who have to pay higher taxes to the government for paying back the borrowed funds. Besides, every year the Government has to pay interest on the borrowed funds and these annual interest payments which are very large due to accumulated large public debt generally cause large deficit in revenue account of the Government budget. As a result, a large chunck of new borrowings every year are used to make

11. Mihir Rakshit, op. cit. 2005 p.105

interest payments. Thirdly, borrowing by the government from the market leads to increase in demand for loanable funds and *causes rise in interet* rate. At a higher interest rate private investment falls. Thus it is often asserted that *Government borrowing crowds out private investment.* However, when there is ample liquidity in the banking system, the banks can make adequate funds available for meeting the demand for funds for the corporate sector.

However, Government borrowing has often been used to finance Governments's current or consumption expenditure as there has been *large revenue deficit* year after year and Government borrowing has been used to meet this revenue deficit with the result that financing of capital expenditure through Government borrowing has been very small. *Golden rule of Government borrowing* is that it should be used for financing investment or productive projects so that it yields returns which can be used to pay interest on the borrowed funds as well as pay back the principal amount. In this way Government borrowing would not involve any burden on future generations and instead higher economic growth will occur which will benefit the future generations.

Another problem of Government borrowing to finance large fiscal deficit is that it causes large increase in government expenditure which leads to *excess demand conditions* in the immediate future which cause inflation in the economy. Therefore, financial prudence requires that fiscal deficit should be of reasonable degree and the funds borrowed by the Government should be used for investment and productive purposes so that inflationary pressures can be contained.

Obstacles. But there exist a number of obstacles which hinder the success of borrowing policy in developing countries. The resources of the organised financial market may be too inadequate to fulfil the needs both of the private and public sectors. Further, in the financial market the competition for funds between the government and the private sector will raise rate of interest and this will have a highly disincentive effect on the expansion of investment in the private sector. More borrowing by the Government leads to the rise in market rates of interest. The higher interest rates tends to reduce private investment. Therefore, it is often asserted that the *higher borrowing target by the Government 'crowds out' private investment*. In India the rates of interest on loans (on bonds or securities) of Government have been raised quite substantially. Since banks and others prefer to invest in Government securities because they are safe (*i.e.*, riskless). This has reduced funds for private investment. However, in our view, this can be avoided if RBI through its monetary measures ensure adequate availability of funds available with the banks so that rate of interest does not rise when investors borrow from the market.

For the success of government's borrowing policy, it is necessary that financial institutions be developed and extended into the rural areas of the economy in order to inculcate the habit of thrift in the population and to mobilise for productive purposes the amount of savings originating in this sector. Besides, for the mobilisation of savings it will be necessary to check and regulate the diversion of savings into unproductive investment such as real estate, gold and jewellery and inventory accumulation.

Suitable techniques of borrowing must also be devised. For example, bonds issued by the Government should be adjusted to the preferences of the general public; bonds of large denomination and long maturity may be offered to the institutional investors, whereas those of small denomination and short maturity may be reserved for the non-institutional public. If properly devised and conducted small savings campaign can mobilise a sizable amount of resources. Further, the mobilisation of the hoardings of gold and jewellery through government programmes constitutes a highly desirable source of resource mobilisation. Of course, suitable techniques of public borrowing for the mobilisation of these resources have to be evolved.

CHAPTER 33A

Government Budget Constraint : Money Financing of Budget Deficit

Government Budget Constraint : Introduction

The government normally finances its expenditure through receipts from taxes, both direct and indirect. When government expenditure increases and it finds it difficult to raise more resources from taxation, it resorts to borrowing from the public or printing money to finance its budget deficit. Increase in rates of income and other taxes not only adversely affects incentives to work more, save and invest more but also promotes tax evasion. Further, as Laffer curve concept shows increase in rate of a tax beyond a point causes revenue from taxes to decline. Thus there are limits to increasing revenue from taxes to finance the increased expenditure of the government. As result, when government finds it difficult to raise adequate resources to finance its increased expenditure fully through normal taxes, it faces a resource constraint resulting in *budget deficit* which in recent years is also called *fiscal deficit*. Thus government budget constraint *refers to the limit placed on the Government expenditure by the extent it can raise resources through taxation, borrowing from the market (i.e., through sale of its bonds) and using printed money*. The Government has to make a choice between the magnitude of borrowing from the market and the magnitude of using printed money to finance its budget deficit.

The general from of government budget equation is

$$G = T + \Delta B + \Delta M \qquad ...(1)$$

Where G stands for government expenditure (including subsidies and interest payments on past debt), T is tax revenue, ΔB is the new borrowing from the market (through sale of bonds or securities) and ΔM is the new printed money issued to finance Government expenditure. According to the budget constraint equation (1), government expenditure in a year can be financed by tax revenue (T), new borrowing (ΔB) by the government from the market (both within and outside the country) through sale of its bonds, and by creating new high powered money (ΔM) which is also called *money financing*. The Government budget constraint can be rewritten as

$$G - T = \Delta B + \Delta M \qquad ...(2)$$

$G - T$ represents *budget deficit* (also called *fiscal deficit*) that must be financed by new borrowing (ΔB) by the government through sale of bonds and creation of new high powered money (ΔM) which is called money financing. Thus

Fiscal or budget deficit = New market Borrowing (i. e., sale of Bonds) by Government + Printed Money

The budget deficit (fiscal deficit) can be financed either by *printing money* (also called *seiniorage*) by the government or by *selling bonds* to the public (which includes banks, insurance companies, mutual funds and other financial institutions). It is through sale of bonds that the government borrows from the market which adds to the government debt. The government has to pay interest annually on its debt and have also to pay back the principal sum borrowed at the maturity of bonds or securities. Besides, borrowing by the Government leads to the rise in interest rate which crowds out private investment. On the other hand it Government finances its budget deficit by using printed money, it can lead to inflation. Thus due to budget constraint, the Government has to make a difficult choice between borrowing from the market and using printed money to finance its budget deficit. Financing through the use of printed money is also called *money financing*.

In times of recessionary conditions which arise due to the deficiency of aggregate demand J.M. Keynes argued for the adoption of deliberate policy of framing a budget deficit to get rid of recession and restore full-employment equilibrium. In recent years there has been a considerable debate among economists about the appropriate methods of financing the budget deficits and their consequences. It is important to discuss the consequencies of budget deficit and the mode of its financing as there has been persistent large budget deficits year after year not only in developed countries such as the United States but also in the developing countries such as India resulting in mounting burden of public debt on the one hand and inflation on the other.

Budget Deficit and Growth of Money Supply

It is important to mention that budget deficit has often been accompanied by inflation. Since the popular perception is that it is growth in money supply that causes inflation in the economy, we therefore need to explain the link between budget deficit and money growth for explaining inflationary potential of budget deficit.

There are two possible links between budget deficit and growth of money supply. First, the budgetary deficit that is financed by borrowing by the government from the market reduces the supply of lendable resources for the private sector in the shrot run which causes market interest rate to rise. Higher market interest leads to decline in private investment. In this way *budget deficit financed by borrowing crowds out private investment.* If the Central bank is following the policy of targeting interest rate, then to prevent the interest rate from rising it will increase the money supply. To do so the Central Bank will buy a part of the securities or bonds issued by the government. This is generally called *accommodating the deficit.*

Note that in some countries such as the USA the Central Bank i.e. Federal Reserve System enjoys independence from the government. Therefore, it can decide independently whether to buy a part of the bonds or securities floated by the government. The Central bank prints money notes against these government securities or bonds held by it as an asset. In this way budget deficit leads to the growth of money and possibly causes inflation. The second way by which the budget deficit leads to growth in money stock is the deliberate policy of the government of financing the budget deficit through the use of printing high powered money by virtue by its sovereign right of creating money. In this method the government itself may print new money or in some countries by the Central Bank as in India where the Central Bank is a nationalised bank without having any independence from the government. In India the Central government when it wants to finance the budget deficit through printed money just issues its securities or bonds and the Reserve Bank prints new money notes and credit them in government account which the government can use them for spending to finance the deficit.[1]

Thus when Central Bank on its own buys government bonds or securities to accommodate the budget deficit so that its crowding-out effect on private investment does not take place, there is growth of money stock in the economy. Alternatively, when the government follows a deliberate policy of printing high powered money to finance its deficit it leads to growth in money supply in the economy. As we shall discuss below when money stock grows at a greater rate than the increase in output, it may lead to inflation. Thus risk of inflation acts as a constraint on printing money to finance budget deficit.

In what follows we will discuss first in detail financing of budget deficit through printed money or what is also called '*money financing of budget deficit*' and then financing of budget deficit through sale of bonds or securities issued by it or what is called '*bond or debt financing of budget deficit*'.

MONEY FINANCING OF BUDGET DEFICIT

As stated above, the government can finance its deficit and meet its increased expenditure by printing high powered money. The revenue raised through printing of money is also called *seignior-*

1. Note that State governments in India do not have the power to print new money.

age. When government finances its budget deficit through printing money, money supply in the economy increases. There are two views regarding the effect of increase in money supply on inflation. According to the Keynesean view, when money supply is increased in times of depression when both productive capacity and labour are lying idle due to deficiency of aggregate demand, price level is not likely to rise much and the effect of increase in money supply is to raise output or income. The increase in real income, given the rate of taxation will bring about increase in revenue from taxation, which will *tend to reduce budget deficit in the short run*. However, if the economy is operating at or near full employment, printing money to finance the deficit will cause inflation. Printing money to raise revenue for financing the budget deficit which causes inflation is like an *inflation tax*. This is because the government is able to get resources through printed money which causes inflation and reduces the real value of the holdings of money by the public.

Let us first explain the Keynesian model with a fixed price level when the economy is in recession due to demand deficiency and a lot of unemployment of resources prevails. The tax function can be written as

$$T = t(Y)$$

where t is the rate of tax and Y is real income and T is the total tax revenue. If G is government expenditure, then budget deficit (BD) is given by

$$BD = G - t(Y) \qquad \ldots (i)$$

If $G - t(Y) = 0$, budget deficit will be zero and therefore the budget will be balanced one. If $G - t(Y) > 0$ there will be budget deficit.

If the Government finances its deficit through money creation, then the short-run macro equilibrium can be written as

$$Y = Y(G, M) \qquad \ldots (ii)$$

The short run equilibrium in simple $IS-LM$ model is shown rated in Fig. 33A.1 where IS and LM curves intersect at point E and determine equilibrium income Y_0 and equilibrium interest rate r_0.

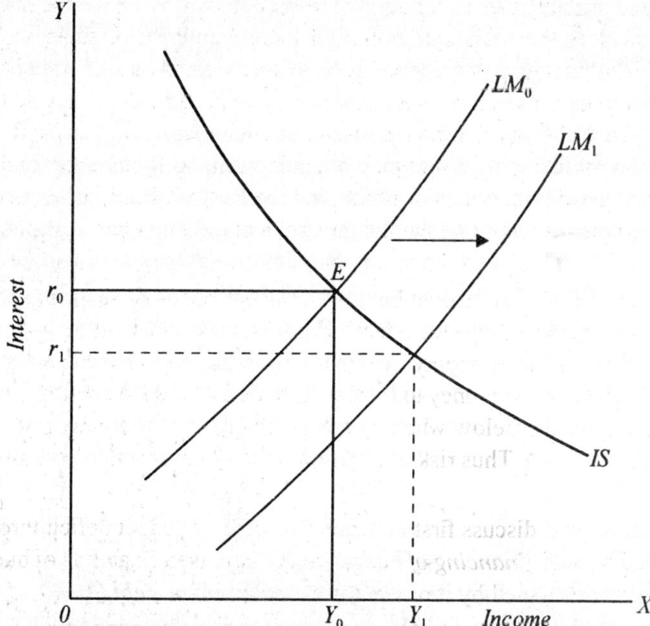

Fig. 33A.1. *IS-LM Model ; The Effect of Budget Deficit Financed by Printing Money*

Suppose in this equilibrium the government has a budget deficit so that $G - t(Y) > 0$. Further, government finances this budget deficit through creating high powered money. As a result, money supply in the economy increases and LM curve shifts to the right to the new position LM_1. With this, as will be seen from the figure, level of equilibrium income increases to Y_1 and rate of interest falls to r_1. Since we are assuming an economy with a depression, increase in demand brought about by expansion in money supply will not cause any rise in price level.

The adjustment process in this simple IS-LM model with a fixed price level when new money is created to finance budget deficit is shown as under

$$\frac{dM}{dt} = [P(G - t(Y)] \quad \ldots (iii)$$

Subsituting *Y* by *Y*(*M*, *G*) in equation (iii) above we have

$$\frac{dM}{dt} = P[G - t(YM, G)] \quad \ldots (iv)$$

The above equations (*iii*) and (*iv*) imply that growth of high powered money (*M*) over time to finance budget deficit is equal to budget deficit (*G*-*t*(*Y*) multiplied by the price level. If there is balanced budget that is, *G*–*t*(*Y*) = 0 over the years, from equation (*iii*) it follows that $\frac{dM}{dt} = 0$.

In the above model of an economy representing the period of recession price level remains unchanged as more money is created to finance budget deficit. In an important contribution. Fischer and Easterly explain the condition for non-inflationary printing of money. They write, "*the amount of revenue that the government can expect to obtain from the printing of money is determined by the demand for base or high-powered money in the economy, the real rate of growth of the economy and the elasticity of demand for real balances with respect to inflation and income*"[2]. Further, assuming income elasticity of demand equal to unity and currency to GNP ratio equal to 13, they conclude that "for every one percentage point that GNP increases, the government can obtain 0.13 percentage points of GNP is revenue through the printing of money that just meets the increased demand for real balances. With an annual economic growth rate of 6.5 per cent of GNP the government should be able to obtain nearly 0.9 per cent of GNP for financing the budget deficit through the non-inflationary printing of money, increasing the high powered money stock at an annual rate of 6.5 per cent".[3] If rate of growth of money exceeds this and, given a stable demand function for currency, inflation will result.

Printed Money and the Inflation Tax

It follows from above that if the economy is operating at full-employment level of GNP or growth rate of money due to persistent budget deficits over time is in excess of rate of growth of GNP, inflation will come about. It has been pointed out by some economists that inflationary financing through the creation of high powered money is an alternative to explicit taxation. Though in most of the industrialised economies (including the United States) the creation of high-powered money or inflationary financing of budget deficits is only a minor source of revenue, in other countries (including India), the creation of high-powered money has been a significant source of raising revenue to finance government expenditure. Before March 1997, in India the creation of money to finance the budget deficit was called 'deficit financing which has been a significant source of revenue for the Central Government in the sixties, seventies and eighties of the last century. Though, as explained above, it is not entirely correct that financing government expenditure through creation of high-powered money necessarily leads to inflation, traditionally every creation of high-powered money or deficit financing has been called inflationary.

Why is the creation of high powered money that causes inflation is called *inflation tax* and is an alternative to explicit taxation as a source of financing government expenditure. When government uses printed money to finance its deficit year after year, it uses it to pay for the goods and services it

---

2. Stanley Fischer and William Easterly, Economics of the Government Budget Constraint, *World Bank Research Observer*, Vol. 5 No. 2, July 1990, pp 127-42.
3. Fischer and Easterly, op. cit.

buys. Thus in this process the government get the resources to buy goods and services and as a result, money balances with the people increase a part of which they will save and the rest they will also spend on goods and services.

However, due to inflation *real value of money balances* held by the people decreases. That is, with their given money balances, people can buy fewer goods and services due to inflation. Thus when the government finances its budget deficit through creation of new high powered money and in the process causes inflation, the purchasing power of old money balances held by the public falls. Hence *inflation caused by creation of new money is like a tax on holding money. Though, apparently people do not pay inflation tax, but since their old money balances can buy fewer goods and services due to inflation they in fact bear the burden of inflation in terms of decline in their purchasing power.* To conclude in the words of Dornbusch and Fischer, *"Inflation acts just like a tax because people are forced to spend less than their income and pay the diference to the government in exchange for extra money*. The government thus can spend more resources, and the public less just as if the government had raised taxes to finance extra spending. When the government finances its deficit by issuing new printed money which the public adds to its holdings of nominal balances to maintain the real value of money balances constant we say the government is financing itself through the *inflation tax*.[4]

We can even estimate the revenue raised through inflation tax as under :

Inflation tax revenue = Inflation tax × real monetary base

Note that monetary base is the amount of the high powered money. It may be mentioned that in the eighties of the last century the inflation rate due to excess creation of high powered money in the Latin American Countries was very high and therefore the revenue raised through inflation tax was very high[5]. In fact some Latin American countries experienced *hyper inflation*. Thus, during 1983-1988 average annual inflation rate in Argentina was 359 per cent, in Boliva 1,797 per cent, Brazil 341 per cent, Mexico 87 percent and Peru 382 per cent.

Inflation Tax Revenue. In the Latin American countries, the governments raised large revenues due to high inflation rates caused by creation of large amount of printed money due to budget deficits year after year. From the above equation it is evident that inflation tax revenue of the government depends on the inflation rate and real money base. When the inflation rate is zero, inflation tax

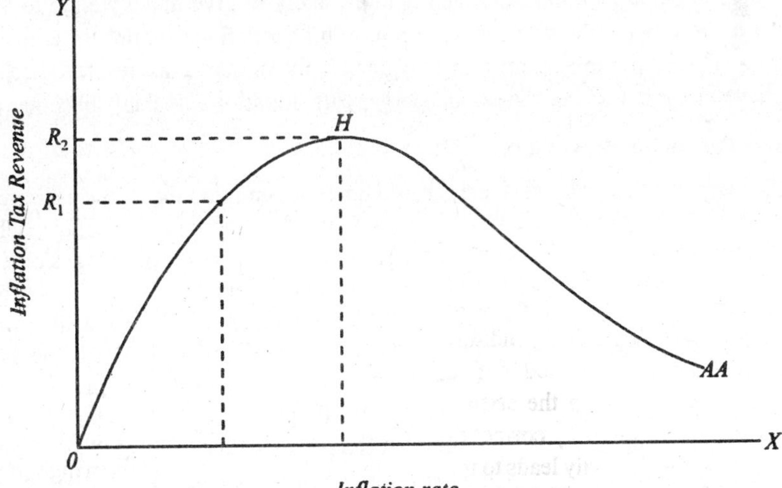

Fig. 33A.2. *Inflation Tax Revenue*

4. Rudiger Dornbusch, Stanley Fischer and Richard Startz, *Macroeconomics*, TATA McGRAW HILL, 8th edition, p. 436.
5. Ibid, p. 437.

revenue obtained by the government will also be zero. As the *inflation rate rises, the revenue obtained by the government through inflation tax increases*. But as the inflation rate rises, the people tend to reduce their holdings of the real money balances as the purchasing power of money holdings declines. As a result, as the inflation rate rises the public holds less currency and banks hold less excess reserves with them. With this the real money balances with the public and banks decline so much that inflation tax revenue collected by the government declines after a point.

The change in the tax revenue received by the government as the inflation rate rises is shown by *AA* curve in Figure 33A.2. Initially, in the economy there is no budget deficit and therefore no printing of money, inflation rate is zero, inflation tax revenue received by the government is also zero and the economy's situation lies at the point of origin. Now suppose the government reduces taxes, keeping its expenditure constant, budget deficit emerges which is financed by printing high powered money and suppose the resulting inflation rate is π at which the government collects tax revenue equal to OR_1. But as the inflation rate further rises as a result of increase in printed money, the tax revenue collected increases until inflation rate π^* is reached. At inflation rate π^* brought about by a certain amount of increase in printed money, the tax revenue collected by the government is OR_2. Beyond this growth in printed money and rise in inflation rate greater than π^*, tax revenue collected declines because real money balances with the public and banks decline, as explained above. Thus OR_2 is the maximum of tax revenue raised by the government through inflation tax and the corresponding inflation rate is π^*.

In the developed industralised countries where the real money base is relatively small, the government collects a small amount of inflation tax revenue. For example, in the United States where money base is only about 6 per cent of GDP the government raises revenue through inflation tax equal to only 0.3 per cent of GDP. corresponding to 5 per cent rate of inflation[6]. However, some developing countries such as Argentina, Brazil, Mexico, Peru have collected 3.5 per cent to 5.2 per cent of their GDP as inflation tax revenue[7]. But for this they had to pay a heavy price in terms of a very high rate of inflation. Dornbusch, Fischer and Startz righly comments, "In countries in which the banking system is less developed and in which people hold large amounts of currency, the government obtains more revenue from inflation and is more likely to give much weight to the revenue aspects of inflation in setting policy. Under conditions of high inflation in which the conventional tax system breaks down, the inflation tax revenue may be the government's last resort to keep paying its bills. But whenever the inflation tax is used on a large scale, inflation invariably becomes extreme".[8]

Evaluation of Inflation Tax Revenue

The above view of inflation tax revenue is based on the assumption that every increase in printed money causes inflation. In our view this is not correct. When the economy is working much below its full production capacity due to deficiency of aggregate demand as it happens at times of recession or depression, then more printed money can be created by the government to finance its projects. The increase in demand resulting from this will help in fuller utilisation of idle production capacity and will also generate employment for unemployed labour. This will not lead to inflation as output of goods and services will increase in this case to meet the increased demand. This case was analysed by J.M. Keynes who advocated for the adoption of budget deficit to overcome depression and financing it through printed money without causing inflation . It is only when there exists full employment in the economy that financing government expenditure through printed money causes inflation.

---

6. Dornbusch, Fischer, and Startz, op. cit. p. 438
7. Ibid, p. 438
8. *op. cit.* p. 439

Similarly, in developing countries like India where growth in GDP is taking place annually and also the economy is getting more monetised, the demand for money is increasing. Besides, a lot of resources are unutilised or underutilised in the Indian economy. Therefore, a reasonable amount of printed money can be created, which before 1997 was called deficit financing, to finance the investment expenditure of the government without causing inflation. Therefore, it is not true that the use of printed money for financing government expenditure necessarily leads to inflation. It all depends on whether or not newly printed money is used for productive purposes which generates higher growth in GDP. In our view in a developing economy such as ours, a fine balance needs to be striked how much resources have to be raised through taxation, borrowing (i.e., debt financing) and newly created money (*i.e.* money financing).

QUESTIONS FOR REVIEW

1. What is meant by fiscal deficit (budget deficit) ? How can it be financed ?
2. How is budget deficit (fiscal deficit) related to growth of money supply in the economy
3. Using IS-LM model explain the effects of financing the budget deficit through printed money.
4. What is meant by money financing of fiscal deficit ? Does it always lead to inflation in the economy ?
5. What is meant by inflation tax ? How does it enable the government to increase its revenue? Critically evaluate.

APPENDIX TO CHAPTER 33A

India's Fiscal Deficit and Economic Growth

Introduction

Government expenditure on goods and services and resources mobilised by it through taxes, etc., are important factors that determine aggregate demand in the economy. When there is a deficit in the budget of the government, it spends more than it collects resources through taxes and non-tax revenue. In recent years there have been huge fiscal deficits in India which have created large excess demand in the economy. This has resulted in inflation or sharp rise in the general level in prices. The deficit may occur either in the revenue budget or capital budget or in both taken together. When there is an overall budget deficit of the Government, it has to be financed by either borrowing from the market or from the Reserve Bank of India which is the nationalised central bank of the country. RBI has the power to create new money, that is, to issue new notes. Thus, to finance its fiscal deficit, the government may borrow from Reserve Bank of India against its own securities. This is only a technical way of creating new money because the government has to pay neither the rate of interest nor the original amount when it borrows from the Reserve Bank of India against its own securities. It is thus clear that fiscal deficit implies that government incurs more expenditure on goods and services than its normal receipts from taxes and non-tax revenue. This excess expenditure by the government is financed by either borrowing from the market or by newly created money which leads to the rise in incomes of the people. This causes the aggregate demand of the community rises to a greater extent than the actual amount of government expenditure through the operation of what is called *government expenditure multiplier.*

In the opinion of many economists, the expansion in government expenditure financed by either borrowing from the market or by monetisation of fiscal deficit leads to the excess aggregate demand in the economy, especially when aggregate supply of output is inelastic. The excess aggregate demand causes rise in the price level or brings about inflation in the economy.

Revenue Deficit

As mentioned above, the budget has two parts : ***Revenue Budget*** **and** ***Capital Budget.*** Receipts in the revenue account come from such sources as various types of direct and indirect taxes and also from non-tax sources such as interest received on loans given, dividend and profits of public enterprises. The items of expenditure in the revenue account are of the type that represents *collective consumption* of the society and therefore, creates no earning assets. The various types of expenditure on the revenue account are incurred on : (1) Interest payments on public debit, (2) Civil administration, (3) Defence, (4) Subsidies on food, fertilisers, exports and (5) Social services such as education, health, etc.

Revenue deficit refers to the excess of revenue expenditure over revenue receipts. Prudent management of public finance requires that receipts on revenue account should not exceed expenditure on revenue account. In other words, there should be surplus on revenue account so that this surplus should be used for investment in development projects or building assets which yield returns. In fact, surplus on revenue account of the budget represents *public or government savings* which can be used for financing developmental activities. However, in India, for the past several years, there has been deficit on the revenue account. That is, there has been *government dissaving* for the last some years in India. Therefore, borrowed funds from the capital account have been used to meet a part of consumption expenditure of the government. This has bad consequences for the economy. Revenue deficit as percentage of gross domestic product (GDP) has been quite high in recent years. Revenue deficit of the central government of India since 2000-01 is given in Table 33A.1.

Table 33A.1: Trends in Budget Deficit of Central Government as % of GDP

	Fiscal deficit	*Revenue deficit*	*Primary deficit*	*Revenue deficit as % of fiscal deficit*
2000-01	5.7	4.1	0.9	71.7
2001-02	6.2	4.4	1.5	71.1
2002-03	5.9	4.4	1.1	74.4
2003-04	4.5	3.6	0.0	79.7
2004-05	4.0	2.5	–0.1	62.6
2005-06	4.0	2.5	0.4	63.0
2006-07	3.3	1.9	–0.2	56.3
2007-08	2.5	1.1	–0.9	47.4
2008-09	6.0	4.5	2.6	–
2009-10	6.5	5.2	3.1	–
2010-11	4.8	3.2	1.7	–
2011-12	5.7	4.3	1.9	–
2012-13 (RE)	5.2	3.9	–	–
2013-14 (BE)	4.8	3.3	–	–

As per cent of GDP, revenue deficit rose from 2.4 per cent in 1996-97 to 4.4 per cent in 2002-03 but fell to 1.1 per cent in 2007-08. Fiscal Responsibility Budget Management (FRBM) Act passed in 2003 required to eliminate it by 2008-09. However, due to global financial crisis in 2008, it could not be achieved. As a part of fiscal stimulus package the government increased its expenditure and cut customs and excise duties in 2008 and 2009 to prevent large slowdown of economic growth following the global financial crisis. As a result, revenue deficit rose to 4.5 per cent of GDP in 2008-09 and 5.2% of GDP in 2009-10. Waving of loans of farmers in 2008-09 and rise in salaries of central government employees following the implementation of Sixth Central Payment Commission in 2008 and 2009 also caused the revenue deficit, to go up in 2008-09 and 2009-10.

Gross Fiscal Deficit as % of GDP

07-08	08-09	09-10	10-11	11-12*	12-13*
2.5	6.0	6.5	4.8	5.7	5.2

* BE

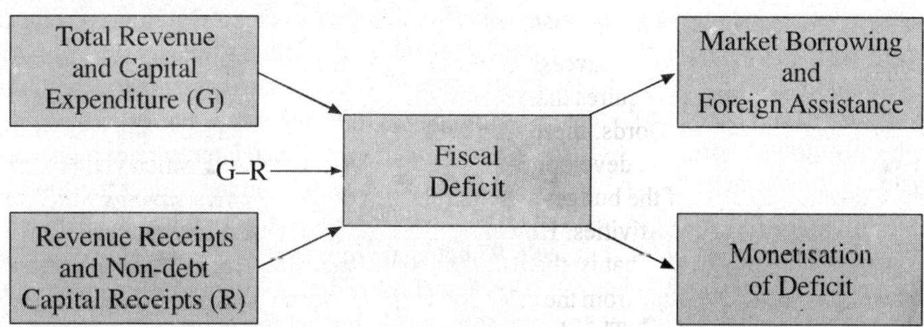

Fig. 33A.1. *Financing of Fiscal Deficit*

Since revenue deficit represents *negative savings* of the government it leads to lower investment by the government and slowsdown in economic growth of the country in the long run. Central government has been trying to achieve fiscal consolidation by raising more tax revenue by roll-back of tax concessions and withdrawing tax exemptions. As a result, revenue deficit in 2010-11 fell to 3.4% of GDP in 2010-11. Government borrowing to meet revenue deficit does not lead to increase in durable assets and therefore does not cause expansion in productive capacity to ensure sustained economic growth in future.

Fiscal Deficit

Fiscal deficit in the budget is an important measure of deficit. IMF and the World Bank generally prescribe targets for budget deficit in terms of fiscal deficit. *Fiscal deficit is the excess of total expenditure (both on revenue and capital accounts) over revenue receipts and non-debt type of capital receipts such as recoveries of loans.*

Thus,

Fiscal Deficit = (*Total Expenditure both on Revenue Account and Capital Account*) – (*Revenue Receipts + Non-debt Capital Receipts*)

Fiscal deficit is a more comprehensive measure of budgetary imbalances. Thus, we see that when the government's total expenditure, both revenue and capital expenditure, exceeds its receipts from taxes and other normal non-revenue and non-debt capital resources, *a fiscal deficit* is created. Now, this fiscal deficit can be financed in two ways as shown in Fig. 33A.1. First, through borrowing by the government from the market, both inside and outside the country. On this borrowing, the government has to pay rate of interest annually. Apart from that it has to pay back the internal and external debt taken. Secondly, the government can finance the fiscal deficit by borrowing from the Reserve Bank of India which issues new notes against government securities. Thus, government borrowing from the Reserve Bank against government securities results in expansion of high powered money in the economy and leads to *monetisation* of fiscal deficit which, if undertaken to an excessive degree, leads to inflation in the economy. On the other hand, Government borrowing from the market to finance fiscal deficit adds to the public debt and increases burden on future generations on whom heavy taxes have to be imposed for repaying the loans.

In the Table 33A.1, fiscal deficit of the Central Government of India has been calculated for the last fourteen years. Fiscal deficit which was 4.7% of GDP in 1997-98 rose to 6.2% of GDP in 2001-2002 but it fell to 2.5% of GDP in 2007-08. It will be seen from this that in the Indian economy, fiscal deficit was quite large prior to 2003-04 which led to inflation or rise in prices in the economy on the one hand and increase in public debt on the other. Therefore, it was decided to reduce it to 3 per cent of GDP by the year 2008-09 and Fiscal Responsibility Budget Management (FRBM) Act was passed to discipline Government's fiscal policy and reduce fiscal deficit.

Accordingly, the government did not borrow directly from RBI through privately placing bonds with it since 2003 (That is, did not monetise the fiscal deficit since 2002). However, for the years 2008-09 and 2009-10, the Government planned to monetise the deficit to some extent as fiscal deficit greatly went up due to fiscal stimulus packages adopted to overcome recessionary conditions in the Indian economy created by global financial crisis of 2008-09 and it was not considered prudent to finance its fully through borrowing from the market which would keep interest rates higher and crowd out private investment apart from raising the burden of public debt. In the budget for 2007-08, fiscal deficit was brought down to 2.5 per cent of GDP. In 1990-91, fiscal deficit was 8.3 per cent of GDP but came down to 4 per cent of GDP in 1996-97 but again rose to 5.7 per cent of GDP in 2000-2001 and to 6.2 per cent in 2001-2002. For 2008-09, actual fiscal deficit rose to 6 per cent of GDP and in 2009-10 to 6.5 per cent of GDP due to fiscal stimulus. In budget for 2010-11, the Finance Minister succeeded in to reducing it to 4.8 per of GDP (RE) (see Table 33A.1). However, in 2011-12 due to adoption of several welfare schemes fiscal deficit again shot up to 5.7 per cent of GDP which caused much increase in aggregate demand which has been responsible for rise in inflation rate. For 2012-13 against the budget target of 4.6% of GDP it was feared that fiscal deficit would go up to even 6 per cent of GDP because of less than estimated collection of taxes due to slowdown of the economy and decline in estimated funds from 2G Spectrum and disinvestment of public sector. However, the Finance succeeded in reducing government expenditure by cutting *planned expenditure* of over 91,000 crore though it was quite undesirable to do so. The States in India also have fiscal deficit of around 3 per cent of GDP.

Implications of Large Fiscal Deficit. There are four implications of fiscal deficit. First, a good part of it is financed through borrowing from within and outside the country. This *leads to the increase in public debt and its burden.* Secondly, a part of fiscal deficit is financed through money financing, that is, monetisation of fiscal deficit which leads to the creation of new money and *rise in prices or inflation.* The fiscal deficit is financed by borrowings, that is, drawing on the private sector's savings. If what the government wants to borrow is in excess of what the private sectors is willing to spare after meeting its own investment plans, the fiscal deficit will create excess demand, that is, aggregate demand in the economy would be in excess of the supply of goods and services, resulting in a combination of price rise and a wider current account deficit (CAD). By reining in the fiscal deficit, the pressure eases on both inflation and the current account deficit (CAD). To keep inflation under control and achieve price stability, IMF and World Bank have recommended that fiscal deficit in India should be reduced to 3 per cent of GDP in a phased manner. Thirdly, a large revenue deficit *adversely affects economic growth.* Due to large revenue deficit, a very large part of borrowed funds by the Government is used to finance current consumption expenditure of the Government. As a result, smaller amount of funds is left for productive investment in infrastructure and social capital (*i.e.*, education and health) by the Government. This lowers the rate of economic growth. Lastly, more borrowing by the Government leaves less resources for private sector investment.

To reduce fiscal deficit in his budget speech for 2013-14, the finance minister presented a roadmap for reducing fiscal deficit to 3% of GDP as shown in Fig. 33A. 3

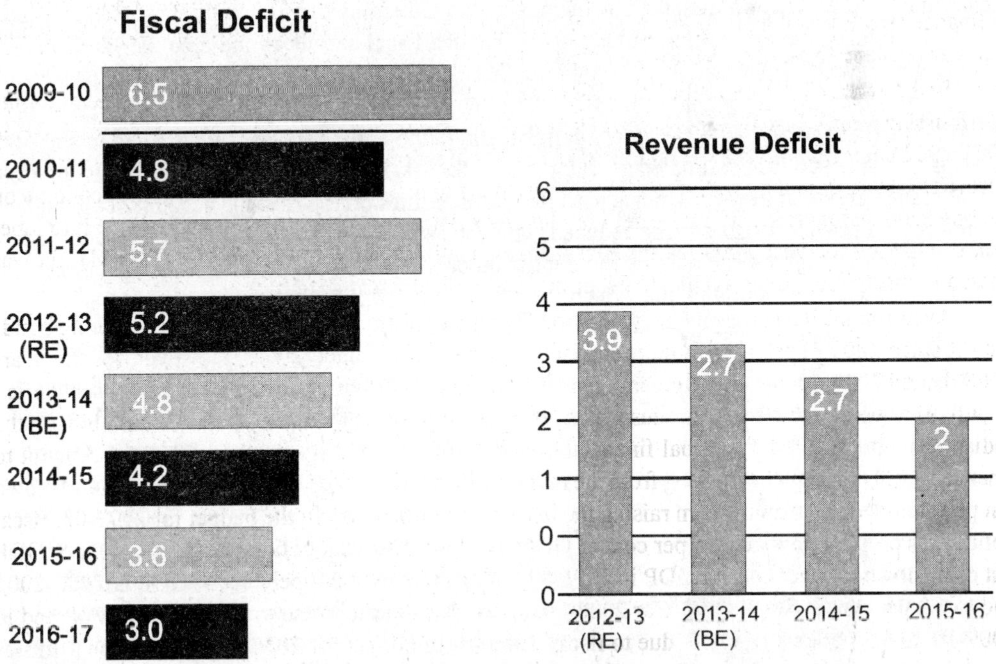

Fiscal Deficit
2009-10 6.5
2010-11 4.8
2011-12 5.7
2012-13 (RE) 5.2
2013-14 (BE) 4.8
2014-15 4.2
2015-16 3.6
2016-17 3.0

Revenue Deficit
6
5
4
3
2
1
0
0
3.9 2.7 2.7 2
2012-13 (RE) 2013-14 (BE) 2014-15 2015-16

Fig. 33A.3. *Roadmap of Reduction in Fiscal and Revenue in Deficits as per cent of GDP*

To reduce fiscal deficit to 3 per cent requires a drastic cut in non-productive revenue expenditure which is a difficult task. *In India, attempts have been made to reduce fiscal deficit by curtailing capital expenditure which is incurred on projects of capital formation and other developmental activities.* This is not a desirable way of reducing fiscal deficit because this adversely affects economic growth. For sound management of Government finances there is need to cut revenue expenditure and raise revenue receipts by mobilising resources through taxation. Attempts to reduce fiscal deficit by curtailing capital expenditure, as has been the practice in India so far, adversely affects economic growth and should therefore be avoided.

However, as shall be discussed below fiscal deficit, to a reasonable degree, is not bad. In times of recessionary situation or slowdown in economic growth such as the one that prevails in 2008-09 and 2009-10, is needed to fight recession and prevent slowdown in the economy. All over the world (including the US), the governments resort to a large dozes of fiscal deficit to stimulate the economy and prevent further deepening of recession and more losses of more jobs. It was for such a situation when private investment declines that J. M. Keynes recommended that Government should undertake deficit spending on a large scale to overcome recession and increase employment. In our view, though undertaking large fiscal deficit in recessionary or showdown in economic growth situation is desirable but in a developing country such as ours borrowed money should be used for *productive purposes* and not frittered away in spending on useless and wasteful projects.

Primary Deficit

Primary deficit is another important concept of budgetary deficit. Primary deficit is a measure of budget deficit which is obtained by deducting interest payments from fiscal deficit. Thus,

Primary Deficit = Fiscal Deficit – Interest Payments

Interest payments on public debt are transfer payments made by the government. The difference between the fiscal deficit and primary deficit shows the importance of interest payments on public debt incurred in the past. Huge interest payments are very largely responsible for causing a large fiscal deficits. In India, in recent years, interest payments on public debt has increased very much. The higher interest payments on the past borrowings by the Government has greatly increased the fiscal deficit. Therefore, primary deficit is much lower than the fiscal deficit. In India, in the year 1993-94 primary deficit was 2.1 per cent of GDP, whereas fiscal deficit was 6.3 per cent of GDP. The primary deficit came down to 0.0 per cent of GDP in 1995-96, went up to 0.7 per cent of GDP in 1999-2000 and to 1.5 per cent in 2001-2002. Primary deficit again fall to around 0.0 per cent of GDP in 2003-04, 2004-05 and 2005-06. It is estimated at –0.9 per cent for 2007-08 and 2.5 per cent of GDP 2008-09. As mentioned above, interest payments is an item of liabilities on the revenue account of the budget. Therefore, if fiscal deficit has to be reduced, interest payments on the revenue account should be reduced which can be done if past public debt is quickly retired by mobilising more resources and curtailing non-developmental public expenditure.

Monetisation of Fiscal Deficit

It may be noted that fiscal deficit can be financed by borrowing from the Reserve Bank of India by the central government against its own securities or treasury bills. The fiscal deficit is financed by borrowing from the Reserve Bank which issues new money or currency against government securities, which leads to the expansion in money supply. In the old terminology, it was known as *deficit financing in India.* Financing the fiscal deficit by issuing new money through borrowing by the government from the Reserve Bank against securities in the new terminology is called *monetisation of fiscal deficit*. It may be noted that in the earlier years separate data regarding the budgetary deficit and therefore, the magnitude of deficit financing undertaken in a year were provided by the government. However, in recent years the data regarding budgetary deficit is not separately provided by the government and it has become a part of fiscal deficit which is shown to be financed by *government borrowing and other new liabilities.* Now the data regarding these deficits, namely, (1) revenue deficit, (2) fiscal deficit and (3) primary deficit are provided in the budget documents.

MEASURES FOR FISCAL CONSOLIDATION

By fiscal consolidation we mean raising more resources and cutting government expenditure so as to reduce fiscal deficit to a reasonable level. Reducing fiscal deficit is a formiddle challenge for control of inflation and achieving 8 % annual growth in the near future.

Large fiscal deficit has two bad consequences. First, it leads to excessive Government borrowing from the market which causes rise in market interest rate. Higher market interest rate tends to reduce private investment. Further, it reduces the resources available for private sector investment. Second, the extent to which a large fiscal deficit is financed by borrowing from the Reserve Bank of India which issues new currency (which is called reserve money or high-powered money) for the government. This causes greater expansion in money supply through the process of money multiplier and generates inflationary situation in the economy. Thus, *to check the rate of inflation, fiscal deficit has to be reduced through both raising revenue of the government and reducing government expenditure.* In the Indian context, the following measures can be adopted to reduce fiscal deficit and thereby to reduce inflationary pressures in the economy. We first spell out the measures which may be adopted to reduce government expenditure and then describe measures for raising Government revenue.

Measures to Reduce Public Expenditure. In the context of the Indian economy, the following measures can be adopted to reduce public expenditure for reducing fiscal deficit and thereby check inflation.

1. A drastic reduction in expenditure on major subsidies such as food, fertilisers, and petroleum products is required to curtail public expenditure. A huge sum of money is spent on major subsidies on food, fertilisers, petroleum products by the central government. Without a drastic cut in subsidies over time it is difficult to reduce public expenditure to an appreciable degree. In June 2012, the government rightly decontrolled petrol so that its price is aligned with global price level. Besides, to reduce its expenditure on subsidies diesel prices were increased in September 2012 by ₹ 5 per litre and now it has been decided to increase diesel price by around 50 paise every month. As regards to check leakages direct cash transfer to the beneficiaries has been adopted. To reduce subsidy on LPG, the supply of subsidised LPG cylinder to each consumer was capped at 6 per annum which together with hike in diesel prices was expected to lower government expenditure by ₹ 2300 crore. However, in budget for 2013-14 expenditure on subsidies as per cent GDP is planned to be reduced marginally to 2 per cent of GDP compared to 2.2% of GDP for the years 2009-10 and 2010-11.
2. The huge sum of money is spent by the government on LTC (Leave Travelling Concessions), bonus, leave encashment etc. A reduction in expenditure on these is necessary if the government is determined to cut public expenditure.
3. Another useful measure to cut public expenditure is to reduce interest payments on past debt. In India, interest payments account for about 40 per cent of expenditure on revenue account of the central government. In our view, *funds raised through disinvestment in the public sector should be used to retire a part of old public debt rather than financing current expenditure.* Retirement of public debt quickly will reduce burden of interest payments in future.
4. Budgetary support to public sector enterprises other than infrastructure projects should be substantially reduced. Further, public sector enterprises should be asked to raise funds from the market and banks.
5. Austerity measures should be adopted to curtail non-plan expenditure in all government departments.

Increasing Revenue from Taxation

To reduce fiscal deficit and thereby check rise in inflation rate, apart from reducing government expenditure, government revenue has to be raised. However in recent years tax-GDP ration has declined. In 2007-08, tax GDP ratio was 12 per cent which came down to 10.4 per cent for the year 2012-13. Continuing on the path of fiscal consolidation with a view to narrowing the gap in Government spending and resources, the tax-GDP ratio has been targeted at 10.9 per cent in the 2013-14 (BE) with a nominal growth rate of 19.1 per cent. However, this is not enough for fiscal consolidation to reduce fiscal deficit to 3% of GDP. The Finance Minister has not made genuine efforts to raise more resources through taxation. He has in his budget for 2013-14, has only levied a surcharge of 10% on income of those earning ₹ 1 crore or more. This is two low to yield enough tax revenue. With current income tax rate of 30% in this income it will mean a super rich person will pay only ₹ 3 lakh more tax on his or her income of ₹ one crore per annum which is to small.

1. As regards mobilising resources to increase public revenue, it may be noted that the policy of moderate taxes with simplified taxation structure should be followed. This will help to increase public revenue rather than reduce it. High marginal rates of taxes should be avoided as they serve as disincentives to work more, save more and invest more. Further, high marginal rates of direct taxes cause evasion of taxes. However, *in our view, the present marginal rate of tax in India is 30 per cent for above 10 lakh income per annum*. This is too small. Besides, with this effective rate has been estimated to be around 20 per cent. Therefore there is need for introducing a higher income tax slab with 35% rate of income tax.
2. In India, the *tax base is narrow for both direct and indirect taxes*; only about 2.7 per cent of population pays income tax. To increase revenue from taxation, tax base should be broadened by taxing agricultural incomes and incomes derived from unorganised industrial and services sectors. *The various exemptions and deductions provided in the income and wealth taxes should be withdrawn to broaden the tax base and collect more revenue.* It may be noted that the Indian experience of the last 50 years reveals that these exemptions and deductions do not promote the intended objectives.
3. As is well known, there is a huge amount of black money in the Indian economy which has come into existence as a result of tax evasion. A good part of black money is parked in Swiss banks. In the last VDIS (Voluntary Disclosure Income Scheme) in 1997-98, more than, 10,000 crores of rupees were collected. However, there has been huge increase in the amount of black money since then. Not only the current black money has to be mopped up but also tax evasion that occurs every year has to be prevented by strict enforcement of the tax laws.
4. The past experience has shown that various tax concessions which have been given in income taxes and indirect taxes for promoting employment, industrial development of backward regions and for other such social objectives do not actually serve the intended purposes and are largely used for evading taxes. These *concessions should therefore be withdrawn to collect more revenue from taxes and the social objectives should be served by adopting more effective policy instruments.* Long-term capital gains on equity shares are exempted from income tax. In the context of boom conditions in the stock market, their exemption should be withdrawn to increase public revenue. They represent *unearned incomes* and canon of equity in taxation demands that this exemption should be withdrawn.
5. Lastly, there should be restructuring of public sector enterprises so that they should make some surpluses at least for their own growth so that their dependence on government's budgetary resources should be dispensed with. For this purpose, their pricing policy should be such that it recovers at least user cost.

To sum up, with the adoption of above measures of reducing public expenditure and enhancing public revenue, it will be possible to reduce fiscal deficit to a safe limit and thus achieve fiscal consolidation. The reduction in fiscal deficit will prevent the emergence of excess demand in the economy and thereby help in controlling inflation and achieving price stability.

FISCAL DEFICIT AND ECONOMIC GROWTH

How does fiscal deficit affect economic growth is a hotly debated issue. A number of Keynesian economists argue that fiscal deficit promotes growth. In India where in the last some years as between 1997-2003, a good deal of industrial capacity had been lying idle due to lack of aggregate demand, and there had been enough stocks of foodgrains, it was asserted that fiscal deficit would stimulate demand and thereby ensure rapid economic growth. In the economic situation especially from 1997 to 2003 the Indian economy was *demand-constrained economy* and therefore the increase in aggregate demand through larger fiscal deficit would not generate inflationary pressures in such a situation. In such a situation if the increase in public expenditure made possible by large borrowing is used for productive investment, especially for investment in infrastructure which will remove bottle-necks for expansion in supply of goods and therefore will boost production and help increase employment opportunities in the economy. In fact, increase in public investment in infrastructure such as irrigation, roads, highways, is doubly beneficial from the viewpoint of accelerating economic growth. It will helps in increasing aggregate demand on the one hand and help to reduce supply constraints on economic growth on the other.

So the focus should not be so much on reducing fiscal deficit but on reducing revenue deficit. Recall that revenue deficit is the excess of government revenue expenditure (*i.e.* current consumption expenditure) over revenue receipts. From the beginning of the nineties since economic reforms have been initiated, there has been large revenue deficits so that a large part of borrowings by the government has been used to bridge the revenue deficit. As a result, capital expenditure on investment in infrastructure and rural development as a percent of GDP declined which has adversely affected economic growth.

Alternative View

However, from the above it should not be understood that any amount of fiscal deficit or government borrowing is good for economic growth and employment generation. Higher fiscal deficit, that is, borrowing by the government involves payment of interest and raises the burden of public debt. The large increase in public debt involving large interest payments year after year will

Table 33A.2 : General Government Fiscal Trends, 1985-86 to 2002-03 (Centre and States Combined) (% of GDP)

	1985-86 to 1989-90	*1992-93 to 1996-97 (Eighth plan)*	*1996-97 to 2001-02 (Ninth plan)*	*2002-03*
Revenue deficit	2.6	3.6	6.1	6.9
Gross fiscal deficit	9.0	7.2	9.3	10.4
Interest payments	3.8	5.1	5.8	6.5
Capital expenditure	6.4	3.6	3.2	3.5
Current expenditure on social services	5.4	5.0	5.6	5.7
Expenditure on Physical Infrastructure (Irrigation + power + transport/GDP	4.7	3.5	3.5	3.8

Source : World Bank Study, *India: Sustaining Reforms, Reducing Poverty*, p.14

not only make the process unsustainable but adversely affect economic growth through reducing investible resources for spending on infrastructure and social sectors. Reviewing the Indian growth scenario World bank Study concludes "Interest payments consumed less than 20% of total revenues in the pre-crisis period, compared with over 30% during the Ninth Plan period (1997-2002). Revenue deficits doubled from less than 3% in the second half of the 1980s to 6% during the Ninth Plan period and beyond *representing a deterioration in the fiscal stance with spending on social and physical infrastructure crowded out by rising interest and other current payments*"[1].

It will be seen from Table 33A.2 that as compared to the later half of the Eighties, revenue and gross fiscal deficits (of the Centre and States Combined) sharply went up. As a result, interest payments as per cent of GDP greatly increased. The higher revenue deficits and large interest payments during the nineties caused a drastic decline in capital expenditure and public investment in physical infrastructure (irrigation + power + transport) as compared to the later half of the eighties (1985-86 to 1989-90). It will be seen from Table 33A.2 that current expenditure on social services (such as education, health, housing, anti-poverty schemes) remained almost stagnant. This shows fiscal and revenue deficits worked to lower economic growth.

Adverse impact of fiscal deficit on economic growth has also been shown through its effect on saving and investment in the Indian economy. For example, Shankar Acharya, a former chief economic adviser to the Government of India, has contended that a *large* fiscal and revenue deficits

Table 33A.3: Fiscal Deficit, Savings, Investment and Economic Growth

As per cent of GDP

1990-91	1990-91	1995-96	1999-2000	2000-01	2001-02	10th Plan 2002-07 (Annual average)
Fiscal Deficit (Centre & States)	9.4	6.5	9.4	9.6	9.9	8.4
Revenue Deficit (Centre & States)	4.2	3.2	6.2	6.6	7.0	4.26
Gross Domestic Savings	23.1	25.1	24.2	23.7	23.5	31.4
(a) Public Savings	1.1	2.0	-1.0	-2.3	-2.7	1.7
(b) Private Savings	22.0	23.0	25.2	26.1	26.2	29.7
Gross domestic investment	22.5*	26.8	25.3	24.4	23.1	31.4
Rate of economic growth (Annual % change in GDP_{FC})	5.6	7.3	6.1	4.4	5.8	7.8

Source : GOI, *Economic Survey*, 2005-06, 2007-08 and 2008-09.

* This pertains to the year 1991-92

after 1996 as compared to 1995-96 slowed down economic growth in India[2]. He argues that as a result of fiscal consolidation achieved between 1990-91 and 1995-96, combined fiscal deficit of Centre and States as percentage of GDP declined from 9.4 percent in 1990-91 to 6.5 percent in 1995-96 and revenue deficit fell from 4.2 percent in 1990-91 to 3.2 per cent in 1995-96 (See Table 33A.3). This freed resources for private investment and in fact brought about investment boom of 1993-96. Gross domestic investment rose from 22.5 percent of GDP in 1991-92 (to which it had fallen during the crisis) to a peak of 26.8 percent GDP in 1995-96 (See Table 33A.3). Gross domestic saving also rose to a record level of 25.1 per cent of GDP in 1995-56. This increase in gross domestic saving and investment, according to Dr. Shankar Acharya, "helped propelled India's growth to 7 per cent plus for three successive years in the mid nineties" (1995-96, 1996-97 and 1997-98).

1. The World Bank, *India : Sustaining Reforms, Reducing Poverty*, Oxford University Press, 2003, 17-18.
2. See his article 'How Fiscal Deficits Hurt Economic Growth, *The Economic Times*, Nov-1, 2001 and 'Why Large Fiscal Deficits are bad for *us* ? *The Economic Times*, January 2003.

As will be seen from Table 33A.3 after the mid nineties, fiscal deficit and revenue deficit increased which caused the decline in gross domestic saving and investment and thereby contributed to slowdown in economic growth. To quote Dr. Shankar Acharya, "*It would be hard to find more telling evidence of the adverse impact of deficits on savings and investment*"[3]. Of course, other factors were also dampening investment, including the slowdown in reforms, the higher uncertainties associated with coalition government and a worsening international economic environment. But increased borrowing by government (rising fiscal deficits) and the associated high real interest rates clearly played a role in slowing private investment. The drop in aggregate savings and investment took its toll of economic growth, which slowed from 7 percent plus of the mid nineties to around 5 percent in recent years"[4].

According to him, high fiscal deficits during the eighties also created balance of payments deficits as it was mainly financed by *external commercial borrowing* and therefore did not adversely affect economic growth. But in the later half of nineties rising fiscal deficits were financed by *domestic borrowings* which were largely used to meet current consumption expenditure and resulted in *public dissavings* (see Table 33A.3). It may be noted that the implementation during (1997-2000) of Fifth Pay Commission report enhancing the salaries of Government staff both at the Centre and States sharply increased the revenue expenditure of the governments and increased public dissavings. This adversely affected domestic rate of saving and investment and lowered rate of economic growth.

The high and rising fiscal deficits during the period from 1997 to 2002 which resulted in larger government borrowings from the market *preempted the needed resources for investment by the private sector*. This had an adverse effect on private investment and was mainly responsible for slowdown in economic growth.

Dr. Shankar Acharya's argument also applies to the growth experience in the 10th plan period (2002-07). As will be seen from Table 33A.3, in the five years of 10th plan on an average annual combined fiscal deficit of Centre and States was reduced to 8.4 per cent as compared to 9.4 to 9.9 per cent in the previous three years which resulted in higher domestic saving (28.2%) and higher domestic investment (27.2%) of GDP. As a consequence public saving turned positive (1% of GDP) and rate of economic growth rose to 7.8 per cent per annum during this period.

Thus in our view both supply-side and demand-side factors play a role in determining economic growth. The growth experience of a country cannot be explained by one type of factors alone.

Role of Fiscal Deficit and Economic Growth : Our View

However, we do not fully agree with Dr. Shankar Acharya's view which is similar to that of World Bank. They consider only supply-side factors determining economic growth. The fall in growth rate during the period from 1997 to 2002 was largely due to demand recession in the economy caused by (1) reduction in the capital expenditure by Government as a matter of new economic policy initiated since 1991, (2) sluggish performance in agriculture during the period, and (3) world-wide recession during the period. Thus demand recession caused a slowdown in the Ninth Plan period (1999-2002) As a result, gross saving and investment rate and GDP growth slowed down. As will be seen from Table 33.5 of the previous chapter, capital expenditure of government increased substantially in 2003-04 and 2005-06 and with multiplier effects led to the increase in aggeregate demand. This increase in demand also caused increase in private investment and the two together ensured a higher rate of economic growth. In the two years (2005-07) even when Government's capital expenditure as per cent of GDP fell, under pressure of rise in aggregate demand it was made up by increase in private investment in the two years 2005-06 and 2006-07 which kept the momentum of higher economic growth.

Thus in our view both supply-side and demand-side factors play a role in determining economic growth. The growth experience of a country cannot be explained by supply-side factors alone. In fact, in 2008 and 2009 as a result of global financial crisis there was economic slowdown in India which caused huge job losses. To prevent the situation from worsening further the Government

3. *Op. cit.*
4. Shankar Acharya, 'High Fiscal Deficit Hurts Growth, *The Economic Times*, Nov-1, 2003.

came out with three fiscal stimulus packages to keep the growth momentum. In these stimulus packages Government raised its expenditure, especially on infrastructure on the one hand and cut taxes on the other to stimulate aggregate demand. To increase its expenditure Government borrowed from the market about ₹ 300,000 crore in 2008-09 ₹ 400,000 crore in 2009-10. As a result, its fiscal deficit went up from 2.7 per cent of GDP in 2007-08 to 6.0 per cent in 2008-09 and 6.4% of GDP in 2009-10. *But this did not produce bad results for the private sector investment, nor did it result in higher rate of interest.* Of course RBI reduced cash reserve ratio to increase liquidity in the banking system and lowered its repo rate to enable banks to lower the lending rates of interest. As a matter of fact, increased borrowing and expenditure by the Government in 2008-09 and 2009-10 led to the increase in demand for the products of private sector. Therefore, from May 2009 onward there were signs of revival of the Indian manufacturing sector. Manufacturing sector output grew at 9.6% in Sept. 2009 year-on-year basis and this growth further picked up to 17.6% year-on-year basis in Dec. 2009. Manufacturing sector registered growth of 13.5 per cent in March 2010, 16.5% in April, 2010 and 11.1% in May 2010 year-on-year basis. This shows despite 6.0 per cent fiscal deficit in 2008-09 and 6.4 % in 2009-10 and consequently heavy borrowing by the government in these two years manufacturing output recorded high growth.

Besides, it is because of the fiscal stimulus packages and increase in government expenditure made possible by heavy borrowing and fiscal deficit that India could achieve 6.8 per cent rate of economic growth in 2008-09 and 8.6% in 2009-10, 9.3 % in 2010-11 which is quite high, especially when there were recessionary conditions in the US and Europe. So in our view fiscal deficit of more than 3% in a year is not always bad. All depends on the economic situation in the country and the purposes for which borrowed funds are spent. If there is recession or slowdown in the economy, the fiscal deficit of 6 to 7 per cent of GDP is necessary to lift the economy out of recession or to prevent sharp slowdown in the growth of the economy. If borrowed funds are spent by the Government for investment or building durable assets, it will lead to the expansion in productive capacity and therefore ensure sustained economic growth.

It is evident from above that larger fiscal deficit at the time of recession or economic slowdown far from reducing private saving and investment is helpful for fighting recession or keeping growth momentum of the economy. In fact, the present economic thinking is that even 3 per cent of fiscal deficit should be treated as *cyclically adjusted number*; that is, the fiscal deficit goes up at times of recession or economic slowdown and comes down in normal or boom period.

We have explained above the two alternative views regarding the impact of fiscal deficit on our economic growth. One view is of the Keynesian economists who think that in developing economies such as India when they suffer from demand constraint, fiscal deficit provides stimulus to economic growth by bringing about increase in aggregate demand. In the situation prevailing in India from 1997 to 2002, and then in 2008-2009 the Indian economy in fact suffered from lack of aggregate demand for manufactured products. This demand deficiency problem arose due to *bad agricultural performance in some years* (there was a negative agricultural growth in 1995-96, 1997-98 1999-2000 and 2000-01 and 2002-03 and also due to sharp *decline in public sector investment* which started in early nineties following the initiation of economic reforms since 1991.

Thus, during 1997-2002 there was a decline in public investment not only because a good deal of borrowing by the government was used to meet revenue deficit but also because of change in economic policy which aimed at reducing the role of public sector. Besides, public sector investment could not be raised also because of the fiscal policy stance of reducing fiscal deficit as recommended by IMF, World Bank and economists associated with these institutions. *In fact the focus of fiscal consolidation was reducing fiscal deficit rather than revenue deficit.* In fact, rates of income tax, corporation tax, excise and customs duties were reduced which resulted in fall in tax-GDP ratio till 2001-02 and caused revenue deficit to rise and therefore much of the borrowing by the government was used to bridge the revenue deficit. Thus, the fall in public investment was embedded in the new economic policy of reforms. *Fall in public sector investment resulted in decrease in aggregate demand on the one hand and shortage of infrastructure on the other which caused slowdown in economic growth during the period 1997-2002*. Again in 2008-09 and 2009-10 it was increase in Government expenditure made possible by heavy borrowing and large fiscal deficit that helped India to achieve GDP growth of 6.7% in 2008-09 and 8.6% in 2009-10.

After, 2003-04, the focus of the fiscal strategy of the Government has been to reduce fiscal deficit and revenue deficit by raising more resources through taxes. As a result, the Government succeeded in increasing tax-GDP ratio from 8.1 per cent in 2001-02 to 12.5 per cent in 2007-08, reducing revenue deficit to 1.1% of GDP and fiscal deficit to 2.5 percent in 2007-08. This enabled the Government to raise public sector investment and also private sector investment with the result that investment rate went up to 38 per cent of GDP in 2007-08. This caused on an average economic growth rate of over 9 per cent in three successive years, 2005-06, 2006-07 and 2007-08. Thus, *in order to ensure economic growth of 9 percent per annum on a sustained basis, focus should be shifted to reducing revenue deficit*. To reduce revenue deficit, steps should be taken to raise tax-GDP ratio and curtail unproductive consumption expenditure of the government so as to eliminate revenue deficit. The borrowings in the capital account should be used for financing public investment in physical infrastructure and social sectors. This will ensure sustained economic growth at the rate of 8 per cent per annum - the objective fixed under the Twelfth Year Plan (2012-17).

Here it may be recalled the **Golden Rule of Public Finance**, namely, *borrowing by the government should be used only for investment purposes and not to meet excess current consumption expenditure except during times of recession*. In times of recession even government consumption expenditure will promote GDP growth. Thus, the focus on merely reducing fiscal deficit at all times and treat it as fetish is not right. In fact, in a demand-constrained economy, a moderate doze of fiscal stimulus is needed. Fiscal responsibility should not be conceived in ritualistic terms of reducing fiscal deficit alone regardless of its effect on the public investment and the economy. In fact, the increase in public investment in infrastructure will also stimulate private investment. The question of containing Government consumption expenditure, except during periods of recession or economic slowdown, is important but reduction in fiscal deficit should not be elevated to a dogma. A moderate amount of fiscal deficit and associated borrowing is good as long as it is used for increasing public investment in physical infrastructure, education and health of the people. Even foreign investment depends on our success in improving infrastructure.

GOVERNMENT EXPENDITURE MULTIPLIER AND REVENUE BUOYANCY

To control inflation, achievement of fiscal consolidation without compromising growth is essential. But to achieve this requires not only efforts by the government to reduce revenue deficit but also to *proeprly direct its public expenditure*. In this context the two important economic concepts need to be explained, namely, *government expenditure multiplier* which is also called *fiscal multiplier*. According to this, an increase in Government expenditure generates the amount of income larger than the original increase in Government expenditure. The ratio of increase in income to the original increase in public expenditure measures the size of government expenditure multiplier. However, different forms of government expenditure have different multiplier effects. For instance, in India public investment expenditure, especially on infrastructure projects, induces increase in private investment thereby increases income directly and also indirectly through multiplier effect. Hence "*the fiscal multiplier of capital expenditure by the government turns out to be much stronger than the fiscal multiplier for current or revenue expenditure*".[5]

The other relevant economic concept of public finance is of *revenue buoyancy* which represents the percentage increase in revenue that would arise from a given percentage increase in income. In India the tax buoyancy has been on an average is around 1.3 which implies that one per cent increase in GDP leads to an additional 1.3 per cent increase in government revenue".[6]

From above it follows that the government multiplier and revenue buoyancy taken together implies that total revenue is not independent of government spending. The increase in government expenditure not only leads to the higher increase in income but also *higher revenue* for the

5 Sudipto Mundle, "Financing the Deficit" in the *Times of India*, Aug. 26, 2010.

government and that should be factored into the revenue projections while framing a government budget. According to the estimates of *National Institute of Public Finance and Policy*, on average increase in government expenditure by ₹ 100 leads to automatically generation of additional government revenue of about ₹ 60 as a result of the working of government expenditure multiplier and revenue buoyancy. This implies that to avoid increase in fiscal deficit, the remaining ₹ 40 be raised through imposition of new tax proposals or change in tax rates. It may be emphasised again that additional revenue flow will be less in case of increase in *revenue expenditure* by the government and more in case of capital expenditure because, as mentioned above, the latter has a higher expenditure multiplier. Thus, as compared to revenue expenditure a given amount of capital expenditure is much more effective for generating additional income as well as for additional revenue for the government. Thus, we agree with Prof. Sudipto Mundle that "*it is possible to achieve fiscal consolidation (i.e. to reduce fiscal deficit) without compromising growth*"[7]. For this purpose, the required fiscal strategy is to progressively reduce fiscal deficit to 6 to 7 per cent of GDP for the centre and states combined (each to 3% of GDP) on the one hand and at the same time to shift public expenditure in favour of capital expenditure.

To achieve fiscal consolidation, the 13th Finance Commission suggested that the public debt to GDP ratio be brought down below 68 per cent by 2014-15. This proposal had been accepted by the government. However, to lower the public debt to GDP ratio below 68 per cent requires reducing fiscal deficit of the centre and States combined to 6 per cent and to bring down the revenue deficit to zero by 2014-15. If this is achieved it will have favourable effect on growth of GDP which will enable us to return to the growth path of 8 per cent during the 12th Five year plan period (2012-17) which is the target set by the Planning Commission.

It may however be noted that reducing combined fiscal deficit to 6 to 7 per cent of GDP and to eliminate revenue deficit altogether require drastic decisions by the government. A part of revenue expenditure is on account of transfer to States for the items of capital expenditure which will enable us to reduce fiscal deficit cannot be reduced. Besides that, it is not easy to reduce revenue expenditure because a good part of it is committed such as interest payments on public debt and the wages and salaries of government employees including a large number of health workers, postal workers, security forces (i.e. police personnel), armed forces etc.

However, there is scope for reduction of subsidies on food, fertilizers and petroleum products. Subsidies on food can be reduced by better targetting them to the people below the poverty line (BPL) and plugging the leakages in the Public Distribution System (PDS). A better alternative will be to introduce *Cash transfer scheme* which will greatly help in stopping the leakages in the public distribution system. As regards subsidies on petroleum products, they can be eliminated if controls over them are lifted and their prices be determined by market forces or alternatively their prices be raised slowly over a period of time rather than sharply at one go.

But from above it should not be concluded that fiscal deficit and therefore borrowing by the Government can be made with impunity. This is because, as mentioned above, funding fiscal deficit involves interest payments and rising debt burden. It needs to be emphasized that fiscal deficit and government borrowing in normal times should be used for productive investment rather than current revenue (*i.e.* consumption) expenditure. The target or limit for fiscal deficit of government cannot be set before hand regardless of the situation in the economy. We think it is improper for Financial Responsibility and Budgetary Management (FRBM) Act to fix the date for achieving 3 percent fiscal deficit by the central government. When a large industrial capacity lies unutilised and the economy is experiencing economic recession or slowdown we can afford to have more than 3 percent central fiscal deficit to accelerate economic growth. It is worth mentioning that in the USA, there was a record level of fiscal deficits during 2002-03, 2003-04 and recently during 2007-08 and 2008-09 caused by cutting back on taxes and raising government expenditure. These fiscal deficits in the USA in fact succeeded in bringing about American recovery and increase in industrial production and employment.

---

6. *Ibid.*
7. Sudipto Mundle, op. cit.

PART VII
OPEN ECONOMY MACROECONOMICS

- Balance of Payments
- Monetary Approach to Balance of Payments
- Foreign Exchange Rate
- National Income and Foreign Trade Multiplier : Saving-Investment Approach
- Free Trade Versus Protection
- Mundell-Fleming Model of an Open Economy
- Globalisation, Commercial Policy and WTO

CHAPTER 34
Balance of Payments

Balance of Payments: Meaning

In the modern world, there is hardly any country which is self-sufficient in the sense that it produces all the goods and services it needs. Every country imports from other countries the goods that cannot be produced at all in the country or can be produced only at an unduly high cost as compared to the foreign supplies. Similarly, a country exports to other countries the commodities which those countries prefer to buy from abroad rather than produce at home.

"*The balance of payments is a systematic record of economic transactions of the residents of a country with the rest of the world during a given period of time.*" The record is so prepared as to provide meaning and measure to the various components of a country's external economic transactions. Thus, the aim is to present an account of all receipts and payments on account of goods exported, services rendered and capital received by residents of a country, and goods imported, services received and capital transferred by residents of the country. The main purpose of keeping these records is to know the international economic position of the country and to help the Government in reaching decisions on monetary and fiscal policies on the one hand, and trade and payments questions on the other.

Balance of Trade and Balance of Payments

Balance of trade and balance of payments are two related terms but they should be carefully distinguished from each other because they do not have exactly the same meaning. *Balance of trade refers to the difference in value of imports and exports of commodities only, i.e., visible items only.* Movement of goods between countries is known as visible trade because the movement is open and can be verified by the custom officials.

During a given period of time, the exports and imports may be exactly equal, in which case, the balance of payments of trade is said to be balanced. But this is not necessary, for those who export and import are not necessarily the same persons. If the value of exports exceeds the value of imports, the country is said to experience an *export surplus* or a favourable balance of trade. If the value of its imports exceeds the value of its exports, the country is said to have a *deficit or an adverse balance of trade.*

The terms "*favourable*" and "*unfavourable*" are derived from the mercantilist writers of the 18th century. In those days, settlements of the foreign transactions were made in gold. If India had exported ₹ 100 crores worth of goods but had imported ₹ 80 crores worth of goods, India would receive ₹ 20 crores worth of gold from the foreign countries. As gold was regarded as wealth and as the receipts of gold made a country wealthy, the mercantilist writers regarded exports surplus as being favourable to the country.

On the other hand, if India had exported ₹ 100 crores worth of goods, but imported ₹ 150 crores worth of goods, it had to pay ₹ 50 crores in gold to the foreigners. India would be losing gold and would be poorer to that extent. Therefore, an import surplus was regarded by the mercantilist writers as adverse balance. But in these days, the international transactions are not settled in terms of gold. Even then, the terms "*favourable*" and "*unfavourable*" balance of trades have continued to be used till today.

Exports and imports of a country are rarely equal. Balance of trade, in other words, will not balance. During any period a country may experience a favourable or an adverse balance of trade.

Distinction between Current Account and Capital Account

The distinction between the current account and capital account may be noted. The current account deals with payment for *currently produced goods and services*; it includes also interest earned or paid on claims and also gifts and donations. *The capital account, on the other hand, deals with payments of debts and claims*. The current account of the balance of payments affects the level of national income directly. For instance, when India sells its currently produced goods and services to foreign countries, the producers of those goods get income. In other words, current account receipts have the effect of increasing the flow of income in the country. On the other hand, when India imports goods and services from foreign countries and pays for them, money which would have been used to demand goods and services within the country flows out to foreign countries. The current account payments to foreigners involve reduction of the flow of income within the country and constitute a leakage. Thus, the current account or trade account of the balance of payments has a direct effect on the level of income in a country. The capital account, however, does not have such a direct effect an the level of income; it influences the volume of assets which a country holds.

It may be further noted that when there is a deficit in the current account, it has to be financed either by *using foreign exchange reserves* with Reserve Bank of Bank, if any, or by *capital inflows* (in the form of foreign assertance, funds flowing through FDI and portfolio investment by FIIs, commercial borrowing from abroad, non-resident deposits).

Determinants of Balance of Payments

There are several variables which determine the balance of payments position of a country, viz., national income at home and abroad, exchange rate of national currency, the prices of goods and factors, international oil and commodity prices, the supply of money, the rate of interest, etc. all of which determine exports, imports, and demand and supply of foreign currency. At the back of these variables lie the supply factors, production function, the state of technology, tastes, distribution of income, economic conditions, the state of expectations, etc. If there is a change in any of these variables and there are no appropriate changes in other variables, disequilibrium will be the result.

The main cause of disequilibrium in the balance of payments arises from imbalance between exports and imports of goods and services, that is, deficit or surplus in balance of trade. When for one reason or another exports of goods and services, of a country are smaller than their imports, disequilibrium in the balance of payments is the likely result. Exports may be small due to the lack of exportable surplus which in turn results from low production or the exports may be small because of the high costs and prices of exportable goods and severe competition in the world markets. Important causes of small exports are the inflation or rising prices in the country or over-valued exchange rate. When the prices of goods are high in the country, its exports are discouraged and imports encouraged. If it is not matched by other items in the balance of payments, disequilibrium emerges.

Balance of Payments on Current Account

Balance of payments is more comprehensive in scope than balance of trade. It includes not only imports and exports of goods which are visible items but also such invisible items as shipping, banking, insurance, tourism, interest on investments, gifts, etc.

A country, say India, has to make payments to the other countries not only for its imports of merchandise but also for banking, insurance and shipping services rendered by other countries; it has to pay further the royalties for foreign firms, expenditure of Indians in foreign countries, interest on foreign investments in India, or on loans obtained by India from other countries and such international organizations as the I.M.F., I.B.R.D., etc. These are debit items for India, since these transactions involve payments abroad. In the same way, foreign countries import goods from India, make use of Indian films and so on, for all of which they make payments to India. These are the credit items for India as the latter receives payments. Balance of payments thus gives a comprehensive picture of all such transactions including imports and exports of goods and services.

The Table 34.1 (given below) we give the position of India's balance of payments on current account for the years 2005-06 to 2011-12. In this table of balance of payments are given the visible as well as invisible items of trade. The *visible items* are export-import trade and the *invisible items of balance of payments on current account are travel, transportation and insurance, interest on loans given and other investment income and private transfers such as remittances from Indians living abroad.* Both visible and invisible items together make up the *current account.* Interest on loans, tourist expenditure, banking and insurance charges, etc., are similar to visible trade since receipts from selling such services to the foreigners are very similar in their effects to receipts from sales of goods; they provide income to the people who produce the goods or services.

Table 34.1. India's Balance of Payments on Current Account ***(in Billion US $)***

S.No. Items	2005-06	2006-07	2007-08	2008-09	2009-10	2010-11	2011-12
1. Exports	105.1	128.9	166.2	189.0	182.2	256.2	309.8
2. Imports	157.1	190.7	257.6	307.6	300.6	383.5	499.5
3. **Trade Balance**	–52.0	–61.8	–91.5	–118.6	–118.4	–127.3	–189.9
	(–6.2)	(–6.5)	(–7.4)	(–9.8)	(–8.6)	(–7.8)	(–10.1)
4. **Invisibles (Net)**	42.0	52.2	75.7	89.9	79.9	79.3	111.6
(*i*). Non-factor Services	23.2	29.5	38.9	49.6	35.7	44.1	64.1
(*ii*). Investment Income	–5.9	–7.2	–5.1	–4.0	–8.0	–17.9	–16.0
(*iii*). Private Transfers	24.5	29.8	41.7	44.6	52.3	53.1	63.5
5. **Goods and Services Balance**	–28.7	–32.3	–52.6	–69.0	–83.0	–83.2	–125.7
6. **Current Account Balance (Net)**	**–10.0**	**– 9.6**	**–15.7**	**–28.7**	**–38.4**	**–48.1**	**–78.2**
	(–1.2)	**(–1.0)**	**(–1.3)**	**(–2.4)**	**(–2.8)**	**(–2.7)**	**(–4.2)**

Source : RBI

Note : *Figures in brackets show per cent of GDP at market prices.*

It will be noted from Table 34.1 above that the most important item in the balance of payments on current account is balance of trade which refers to imports and exports of goods. In the Table 34.1 balance of trade does not balance and shows a deficit in all the seven years. In the years 2011-12 and 2012-13 trade deficit has substantially increased. Trade deficit was over 10 per cent of GDP in both these years. In fact, it is huge trade deficit in these two years that has caused huge current account deficit of over 4% of GDP in these two years Economic slowdown in advanced countries and its spill over effects in Emerging Market Economies coupled with high crude oil and gold prices were responsible for sharp increase in trade deficit. Due to *surplus in invisibles account,* there was a surplus on current account during 2001-2002, 2002-03 and 2003-04. In India's balance of payments on current account from 2004-05 onwards there has been a deficit. Contrary to popular perception, deficit on current account is not always bad provided it is within reasonable limits and can be easily met by non-debt capital receipts. In fact, *deficit on current account represents the extent of absorption of capital inflows in India during a year.*

It may be noted that when there is deficit on the current account, it is financed either by using *foreign exchange reserves* held by Reserve Bank of India or by *capital flows* that come into the country in the form of foreign direct investment (FDI) and portfolio investment by FIIs, external commercial borrowing (ECB) from abraod and by NRI deposits in foreign exchange account in our banks. However, due to global financial crisis in 2008-09, there was first slowdown and then decrease in exports. As a result, there was a large deficit of 2.4 of per cent of GDP on current account which could not be met by capital inflows as they were quite meagre ($ 8.6 billion) as a result of global financial crisis. Therefore, to finance the deficit on current account in 2008-09 we had to withdraw

US $ 20 billion from our foreign exchange reserves. Again in the last two years 2011-12 and 2012-13 the current account deficit (CAD) has been quite high.

It may be noted that high current deficit tends to weaken the rupee by raising the demand for US dollars. In 2011-12, current account deficit tended to weaken the rupee by raising the demand for US dollars. In 2011-12, the current account deficit was 4.2 per cent of GDP. Since capital inflows in this year were not adequate to finance the current account deficit, RBI had to withdraw 12.8 million US dollars from its foreign exchange reserves to meet the demand for US dollars (see Table 34.2) . In the year 2012-13 the current account deficit has been estimated to the even higher at 4.8 per cent of GDP, capital inflows through portfolio investment by FIIs have picked up in the latter half of 2012-13 but capital inflows through FDI have fallen. Therefore, to meet the current account deficit some US dollar will have to be withdrawn from foreign exchange reserves held by RBI. Thus current account deficit poses serious challenge to macroeconomic management of the economy. The dependence on volatile capital inflows through FIIs to meet the current account deficit is the unsustainable as these capital flows go back when global situation worsens and thereby causes sharp depreciation in exchange rate of rupee and crash in stock market prices.

Since in the recent years, 2011-12 and 2012-13 current account deficit has widened, this has increased the balance of payments vulnerability to sudden reversal of capital flows, especially when sizable flows are comprised of debt and volatile portfolio investment by FIIs. The priority has therefore been to reduce current account deficit (CAD) through improving trade balance. Efforts have been made to promote exports by diversifying the export commodity basket and export destinations. One way to limit imports is to bring prices up to the international level so that users bear the full cost. Accordingly, petrol has been decontrolled and diesel prices have been revised upward in Jan. 2013 to curtail subsidy on it. To discourage the imports of gold which has played a significant role in causing trade deficit, customs duty on its import has been raised from 4% to 6%.

Further, to improve the current account deficit emphasis has been on facilitating remittances and encouraging software exports that have been responsible for surplus on the invisible account. In recent years this surplus has lowered the impact of widening trade deficit on current account deficit (CAD) significantly. The two components together met nearly two thirds of the trade deficit that was more than 10 per cent of GDP in 2011-12. Remittances particularly are known to exhibit resistance when the country is hit by external shock as was evident during the global crisis of 2008

Balance of Payments on Capital Account

In the balance of payments on capital account given in Table 34.2 important items are borrowings from foreign countries and lending funds to other countries. This takes two forms: (*i*) *External assistance* which means borrowing from foreign countries under concessional rate of interest; (*ii*) *Commercial borrowing* under which the Indian Government and the Private sector borrow funds from world money market at higher market rate of interest. Besides *non-resident* deposits are another important item in capital account. These are the deposits made by non-resident Indians (NRI) who keep their surplus funds with Indian Banks. Another important item in balance of payments on capital account is *foreign investment* by foreign companies in India. There are two types of foreign investment. First is *portfolio investment* under which foreign institutional investors (FII) *purchase shares (equity) and bonds* of Indian companies and Government. The second is *foreign direct investment* (FDI) under which foreign companies set up plants and factories on their own or in collaboration with the Indian companies. Still another item in capital account is other capital flows in which the important source of funds is remittances from abroad sent by the Indian citizens working in foreign countries. The Table 34.2 gives the position of India's capital account for the years 2004 -05 to 2009-10.

Table 34.2. India's Balance of Payments on Capital Account ***(in Billion US $)***

	2005-06	2006-07	2007-08	2008-09	2009-10	2010-11	2011-12
External Assistance (Net)	1.7	1.8	2.1	2.6	2.9	4.94	2.3
Commercial Borrowing (Net)	2.5	16.1	22.6	7.0	2.8	12.16	10.3
Non-Resident Deposits (Net)	2.8	4.3	0.2	– 4.3	2.9	3.14	11.9
Foreign Investment (Net)	15.5	14.8	43.3	3.5	50.4	42.13	39.2
of which							
(*i*) FDI net	3.0	7.7	15.9	17.5	18.0	11.83	22.1
(*ii*) Portfolio Investment (Net)	12.5	7.1	27.4	–15.0	32.4	30.3	17.2
(*iii*) Other capital flows (Net)	2.4	9.2	39.7	–9.7	–13.1	–10.48	–7.0
Capital Account Total (Net)	**24.9**	**46.1**	**107.9**	**8.6**	**51.6**	**63.74**	67.8
Use of Exchange Reserves*	–15.0	–36.6	–92.2	+20.1*	–13.4*	(–13.1)*	(+12.8)*

* *Also includes errors and omissions*

Source: RBI Annual Report 2012-13. Use of foreign exchange reserves (–indicates increase of reserves, and + indicates decrease of reserves on BOP basis.

Capital inflows in the capital account can be classified into ***debt creating*** and ***non-debt creating.*** Foreign investment (both direct and portfolio) represents non-debt creating capital inflows, whereas external assistance (i.e. concessional loans taken from abroad), external commercial borrowing (ECB) and nonresident deposits are debt-creating capital inflows.

It will be seen from Table 34.2, during 2007-08, there was net capital inflow of 43.3 billion US dollars on account of *foreign investment (both direct and portfolio)*. The Table 34.2 gives the position of India's balance of payments in capital account for seven years, 2005-06, 2006-07, 2007-08, 2008-09 and 2009-10, 2010-11 and 2011-12. When all items of balance of payments on capital account are taken into account we had *a surplus* of 107.9 billion US dollars in 2007-08. Taking into current account deficit of $ 15.7 billion on current account in year 2007-08 there was accretion to our foreign exchange reserves by $ 92.2 billion in 2007-08. Global financial crisis affected our capital account balance as there was ***reversal of capital flows after Sept. 2008*** with the result that ***we used*** $ 20.1 billion of our foreign exchange reserves in 2008-09 resulting in *decrease* of our foreign exchange reserves. That is, because we used our foreign exchange reserves equal to $ 20.1 billion, there was decline in our foreign exchange reserves by $ 20 billion in 2008-09. The situation improved in 2009-10 as foreign direct investment (FDI) and portfolio investment by FIIs picked up. As a result there was net capital account surplus of $ 51.6 billion in 2009-10 and after meeting the current account deficit of $ 38 billion there was addition to our foreign exchange reserves by $ 13.4 billion in 2009-10. In 2010-11 also there was surplus on capital account of $ 63.74 billion and after meeting current deficit we added $ 13.1 billion in our foreign exchange reserves in 2010.11.

However, in 2011-2012 and 2012-13 the situation regarding capital flows changed significantly and capital flows were not sufficient to meet the large current account deficit (CAD). Consequently, in 2011-12 withdrawal from foreign exchange reserves of 12.8 billion US dollars was made. In 2012-13 also due to large deficit on current account the withdrawal of some foreign exchange reserves is likely to be made.

Capital flows are driven by pull factors such as economic fundamentals of recipient countries and push factors such as policy stance of source countries. The capital flows have implications for exchange rate management, overall macroeconomic and financial stability including liquidity conditions. Capital account management therefore needs to emphasize promoting foreign direct investment (FDI) and reducing dependance on volatile portfolio capital. This would ensure that to the extent current account defect is bridged through capital surplus it would be better if it is done through stable and growth enhancing foreign direct investment flows. In the present international financial situation, reserves are the first line of defence against the volatile capital flows. However, the decline in reserves as a percentage of GDP is a source of concern.

Large Invisible Surpluses. At a micro-level the balance of payments profile reveals important trends. In the recent years deficits in the trade account have been made up by the large invisible surpluses resulting in a small deficit in current account balance. *The robust growth in invisibles is due to large inflows of private transfers and non-factors services.* Buoyant inflows of private transfers have been one of the main factors contributing to remarkable growth in invisibles. The current high level of private transfers which comprise largely inflows of remittances from Indians working abroad have made India the highest global recipient of remittances. The bulk of these remittances come in from expatriates in the USA and the Middle East.

In addition to private transfers, the contribution of *non-factor services* to the invisible account has been increasing steadily since 2001-02. This contribution increased further in 2006-07, 2007-08, 2008-09, 2009-10 and 2010-11. Among the non-factor services enhancing the invisible surplus is the *buoyant earnings from software services*. Net inflows from software services increased from US $ 6.9 billion in 2001-02 to US $ 10 billion in 2003-04. The software services (net) recorded a rise of 31.7 per cent during 2005-06, 30.4 per cent in 2006-07 and 28.3 per cent in 2007-08.

The high skill intensity of the Indian work force has given a decisive comparative advantage to Indian software services exports and has helped the country in carving out a niche in the global market for software services and IT-enabled services. Besides, in recent years, India has emerged as one of most preferred destination of outsourcing IT services from advanced economies. While software services exports more than trebled between 1998-99 and 2003-04, exports of IT -enabled and business process outsourcing (BPO) services have increased significantly in recent years.

On the other hand, the capital account surplus has not been growing strongly due to unsteady growth in *non-debt creating foreign investment flows*. Though *debt-creating capital inflows* through external commercial borrowing and external assistance have been significantly brought down and in fact in many years there were *net capital outflows* on these counts. However it is matter of serious concern that in recent years our dependence on volatile capital inflows through portfolio investment by FIIs has largely increased.

It is evident from above that trends indicate that the *fast growing invisibles and non-debt creating foreign investment flows* are the main factors behind large accumulation of foreign exchange reserves.

Does Balance of Payments must always balance ?

It is often said that balance of payments must always balance. What does it mean ? The individuals and business firms of an economy have to pay for the imports from abroad. If exports are not sufficient to pay for the imports, then how the balance of payments will be in balance. For example, the balance of payments on current account of India had been in deficit for most of the years till 2000-01. Deficit on current account implies that the residents of a country are spending more on imports of goods and services than the incomes they are earning from exports of goods and services. For the overall balance of payments to be in balance, this deficit in the current account of the balance of payments must by financed by selling capital assets such as shares and bonds of companies or other assets such as gold or foreign exchange reserves of a country or by borrowing from abroad. Both by selling assets or by borrowing from abroad, foreign capital flows into the country as has been happening in the last several years in India. These foreign capital inflows are shown in the capital account of the balance of payments which must be in surplus to finance the deficit in the current account. Thus

$$\text{current account deficit} + \text{capital account surplus} = 0.$$

However, it is worthwhile to note that this "balance" is in the accounting sense only. Surplus on current account can lead to the grant of loans to the other countries by the Government or it can lead to the increase in the reserves of foreign exchange which show up themselves in the capital account.

On the other hand, a deficit on current account can be met by capital inflows from abroad, that is, by obtaining foreign investment or getting foreign aid or by drawing from IMF or by running down country's foreign exchange reserves. Thus the surplus or deficit in the current account of a country's balance of payments gives rise to further financial transactions which show up themselves in capital account. In other words, if the balance of payments is used in the wider sense so as to include external assistance, drawing from IMF, drawing upon the country's reserves also as distinguished from its narrower sense, the balance of payments of a country must always balance—all the receipts taken together must be equal to all the payments taken together.

The above fact has an important lesson that must be borne in mind. If a country has no foreign currency reserves or it has no assets to sell to pay for the imports and if no body is willing to lend to it, it will have to cut down its imports which will reduce productive activity in the economy and adversely affect economic growth of the country. Such a crisis situation arose in India in 1991 when our foreign exchange reserves had fallen to a very low level and no one was willing to lend to us or give us aid. In fact, due to loss of confidence of foreign investors, *capital outflows* were taking place.

Therefore, in 1991 India had to mortgage its gold to Bank of England and Central Bank of Japan to get the necessary foreign exchange to pay for the needed imports. We had to accept the pre-conditions of IMF for providing us assistance to tide over the crisis. It is interesting to note this was done under the guidance of Dr. Manmohan Singh, the present Prime Minister of India, who was then the Finance Minister.

GLOBALISATION, CAPITAL FLOWS AND BALANCE OF PAYMENTS

The globalization of the Indian economy has an important consequence with regard to capital flows into the economy. Suppose India faces given prices of its imports and a given demand for its exports of goods and services. Under these circumstances, if domestic rate of interest (or rate of return on investment) is higher as compared to what exists abroad, then, given the mobility of capital, foreign capital will flow into the Indian economy to a very large extent. This principle can be expressed as follows.

$$BP = NX(Y_d, Y_f, R) + CF\,(i_f - i_d)$$

where BP = balance of payments, NX is net exports (*i.e.* exports–imports which is also called trade balance), CF stands for surplus in the capital account of the balance of payments, that is, capital flows. i_f represents rate of interest in foreign market and i_d represents rate of interest in the domestic economy.

The above equation reveals that trade balance (NX) is a function of level of domestic income (Y_d) and foreign income (Y_f) and real rate of exchange (R). An increase in the domestic income due to higher industrial growth or fall in real exchange rate of rupee will adversely affect the trade balance (NX) by increasing imports. $i_f - i_d$ in equation (*ii*) measures interest rate differential between the foreign country and domestic economy on which *i.e.* net capital flows depend. Further, the above equation (*ii*) shows that higher interest rate or rate of return in India as compared to that in the foreign country such as the United States will cause large capital inflows into India. Such capital inflows have actually taken place in India since 2003. Due to large capital inflows into the Indian economy our foreign exchange reserves crossed 100 billions US dollars in December 2003, reached 170 billion US $ in December 2006 and further increased to 247 billion US $ dollars in September 2007, and to 300 billion US $ in Sept. 2008. Due to reversal of capital flows, there was decline in our reserves in 2008-09 and in March 2009, they stood at US $252 billion. In the second half of 2009-10 there had been reversal of capital flows and capital inflows into Indian economy occurred on a large scale in 2009-10 and 2010-11 resulting in increase of foreign exchange reserves to $ 304 billion at end-March 2011. However, there was decline in our foreign exchange reserves in 2011-12 and our foreign exchange reserves stood at $ 294 billion in end-February 2013.

Globalisation has both advantages and disadvantages. It is through globalisation and openness of an economy that foreign trade of a country increases which promotes economic growth. Trade between countries help them to specialise in the production of goods and services according to their factor endowments and comparative efficiency. Besides, globalisation helps in the transfer of technology from the developed countries to the developing countries. Globalisation also promotes capital flows between countries which in general are welcome. Capital inflow in the form of foreign direct investment (FDI) adds to the productive capacity of a country by increasing capital accumulation. Capital inflows in the form of portfolio investment by FIIs (Foreign Institutional Investors), which are invested in buying equity shares and corporate and Government bonds lead to the development of financial markets. Besides, capital flows provide foreign exchange which can be used to meet the current account deficit which generally emerges in a developing country such as India due to large imports of fuel, machines and industrial raw materials required for industrial growth of the economy.

However, the global financial crisis of 2007-09 which originated in the sub-prime housing loan market in the US and enveloped the entire world has clearly brought out the adverse impact of globalisation. It adversely affected growth of exports of developing countries such as India which brought about large current account deficit. It also caused capital outflows from them which led to the stock market crash. When capital flows are large and volatile they hurt macroeconomic stability. Large capital inflows as they occurred in India in 2010 lead to appreciation of exchange rate of the national currency (Rupee in case of India) which adversely affects growth of our exports and encourage imports. As a result they widen current account deficit.

Owing to these adverse effects of globalisation each country decides about the extent of openness of its economy with which it is quite comfortable by imposing some restrictions on their foreign trade, especially in financial services. Besides, because of the adverse effects of large capital inflows, some countries are trying to control them by imposing taxes on capital inflows. However, in case of India size of capital inflows were till 2010-11 within our absorptive capacity. In 2011-12 and 2012-13 there were not sufficient capital inflows to meet our current account deficit (CAD)Therefore, we need larger capital inflows rather than putting any restrictions on them.

Although in 2008-09 due to inadequate capital inflows current account deficit of India was financed by withdrawing from foreign exchange reserves but in 2009-10 and 2010-11 it was financed by surplus in capital account and thus there was gainful absorption of foreign capital inflows. If India wants to continue to grow at a high rate of 9% there will deficit on current account of BOP since growth in our exports cannot keep face with our higher growth in imports due to rapid increase in our industrial activity. Current account deficit is a matter of concern only if growth is not high or if stable capital inflows are not adequate to finance the current account deficit.

It will be seen from Table 34.1 and 34.2 that from 2005-06 to 2011-12 that capital surplus [*i.e.*, capital account (net)] exceeded our current account deficit, *except for the year 2008-09 and 2011-12* with the result that *there was addition to our foreign exchange reserves* (see last row of Table 34.2). Note that minus (–) sign in the use of reserves for various years implies that instead of using foreign exchange reserves in these years we added to our foreign exchange reserves. In the year 2008-09 when there was global financial crisis which caused not only negative growth in our exports but also large capital outflows from the Indian economy with the result that capital surplus in 2008-09 was quite small and fell short of our current account deficit which was quite large in this year. As a result we withdrew $20 billion from our foreign exchange reserves to meet the current account deficit in 2008-09. Hence the plus sign before US $ 20 in 2008-09. However, in 2009-10 there was revival of large capital inflows with capital account (net) equal to US $ 51.6 billion. With $ 38.4 billion deficit in current account we instead of withdrawing from our foreign exchange reserves we added to them in 2009-10. This means India successfully tackled global financial crisis and its consequences. However, in 2011-12 again capital inflows in India were not sufficient to meet fully our current account deficit and as a result we had to withdraw $ 12.8 billion from our foreign exchange reserves. However in 2012-13 capital inflows into India through foreign direct investment has declined and our current account deficit which is estimated to be quite high has been financed more by *volatile capital flows by FIIs which is a matter of serious concern.* This is because these volatile capital flows affect our foreign exchange rate stability, stock market prices, price stability, and thus create macroeconomic instability.

EQUILIBRIUM AND DISEQUILIBRIUM IN THE BALANCE OF PAYMENTS

Before we analyse the causes of disequilibrium in the balance of payments, we would like to explain what is meant by equilibrium in the balance of payments. We have noted above that when we add up all the demand for foreign currency and all the sources from which it comes, these two amounts are *necessarily equal* and thus the overall account of the balance of payments necessarily balance or must always be in *equilibrium.*

What then do we mean by when we say that the balance of payments of a country is 'in equilibrium or disequilibrium'. As a matter of fact, when we speak of equilibrium or disequilibrium in the balance of payments we refer to the balance on those parts of the account which do not include the accommodating items such as borrowing from the IMF, use of SDRs, drawing from the reserves of foreign currencies held by the Central Bank, etc. *When excluding these accommodating items there is neither deficit nor surplus in the overall balance of payments, it is said to be in equilibrium. When in this sense, there is either deficit or surplus, the balance of payments is said to be in disequilibrium.* The deficit in balance of payments can be financed by drawings from the IMF, use of SDRs, drawings from the reserves of foreign currencies and loan and aid received from abroad. For example in 2001-02, we added to our foreign exchange reserves to the tune of 11757 million US dollars. However for previous several years India's balance of payment on current account was in deficit. To finance the dificits India borrowed from IMF or from other countries or even resorted to commercial borrowing from abroad. But India's balance of payments for the year 2001-02 was favourable.

Basic Balance of Payments, Autonomous Items and Accommodating Items

However, a more important and popular concept of balance of payments equilibrium has been of *basic balance.* The concept of basic balance is based upon the idea of *autonomous items* in the balance of payments. The autonomous items in the balance of payments are those items which cannot be influenced or changed so easily or quickly by the Government and they are determined by some long-term factors. In this concept of basic balance, besides the items in the current account, *the long-term capital movements* both on private or Government account contained in the capital-account balance of payments are regarded as autonomous. On the other hand, in the capital account *short-term capital movements* such as borrowing from IMF or Central Banks of other countries, drawings from SDR, change in foreign exchange reserves are transitory and of *accommodating nature* and are therefore excluded from the concept of basic balance or of dequilibrium. The recourse has to be made to these accommodating items (also called *compensatory items*) so as to ensure equality between payments and receipts of foreign exchange. Changes in the compensatory items are made so as to offset the surplus or deficit in the autonomous items. Thus," *when autonomous movements cancel out over some appropriate time period and there is no need for compensatory movements, the balance of payments is in equilibrium.*[1] *Note that the equilibrium is a state of balance which can be sustained without intervention by the Government.*

The concept of balance of payments in the sense of basic balance can be represented by the following equation:

$$(X - M) + LTC = 0$$

where X stands for exports including invisible items.

M stands for imports including invisible items.

LTC stands for long-term capital movements.

1. C.P. Kindleberger, *op. cit.*, p. 311.

If $(X - M)$ is positive (*i.e.*, $X > M$), then for balance of payments to be in equilibrium, *LTC* will be negative and equal to $(X - M)$. This implies that there will be *net capital outflow*. On the other hand, if $M > X$, then for the balance of payments to be in equilibrium *LTC* must be positive (that is, there will be *net capital inflow* to offset the deficit in the current account).

When the balance of payments of a country is in equilibrium, the demand for the domestic currency is equal to its supply. The demand and supply situation is thus neither favourable nor unfavourable. If the balance of payments moves against a country, adjustments must be made by encouraging exports of goods, services or other forms of exports, or by discouraging imports of all kinds. No country can have a permanently unfavourable balance of payments. Total liabilities and total assets of nations, as of individuals, must balance in the long run.

This does not mean that the balance of payments of a country should be in equilibrium individually with every other country with which she has trade relations. This is not necessary, nor is it the case in the real world. Trade relations are multilateral. India, for instance, may have balance of payments deficit with the United States and surplus with the United Kingdom and/or other countries, but each country, in the long run, cannot receive more value than she has exported to other countries taken together.

Equilibrium in the balance of payments, therefore, is a sign of the soundness of a country's economy. But disequilibrium may arise either for short or for long periods. A continued disequilibrium indicates that the country is heading towards economic and financial bankruptcy. Every country, therefore, must try to maintain balance of payments in equilibrium. To know how this can be done involves the study of the causes of disequilibrium.

CAUSES OF DISEQUILIBRIUM IN THE BALANCE PAYMENTS

There are several variables which join together to constitute equilibrium in the balance of payments position of a country, *viz*., national income at home and abroad, the prices of goods and factors, the supply of money, the rate of interest, etc., all of which determine the exports, imports and demand and supply of foreign currency. At the back of these variables lie the supply factors, production functions, the state of technology, tastes, the distribution of income, the state of anticipations, etc. If there is a change in any of these variables and there are no appropriate changes in other variables, disequilibrium will be the result.

The main cause of the disequilibrium in the balance of payments arises from imbalance between exports and imports of goods and services. When for one reason or another exports of goods and services of a country are smaller than their imports, disequilibrium in the balance of payments is the likely result. Exports may be small due to the lack of exportable surplus which in turn result from low production or the exports may be small because of the high costs and prices of exportable goods and severe competition in the world markets. An important cause of small exports is the inflation or rising prices in the country. When the prices of goods are high in the country, its exports are discouraged and imports encouraged. If it is not matched by other items in the balance of payments, disequilibrium emerges.

Cyclical Disequilibrium

Cyclical disequilibrium is caused by the fluctuations in the economic activity or what are known as trade cycles. During the periods of prosperity, prices of goods fall and incomes of the people go down. These changes in incomes of the people and prices of goods affect exports and imports of goods and thereby influence the balance of payments."If prices rise in prosperity and decline in depression, a country with a price elasticity for imports greater than unity will experience a tendency for a decline in the value of imports in prosperity, while those for which imports price elasticity is less than one will experience a tendency for increase. These tendencies may be overshadowed by the effects of income changes, of course. Conversely, as prices decline in depression, the elastic demand will bring about an increase in imports, the inelastic demand a decrease."[2]

Secular or Long-Run Disequilibrium

Secular (long-run) disequilibrium in balance of payments occur because of long-run and deep-seated changes in an economy as it develops from one stage of growth to another. The current account in the balance of payments follows a varying pattern from one stage to another. In the initial stages of development, domestic investment exceeds domestic savings and imports exceed exports. Disequilibrium arises due to lack of sufficient funds available to finance the import surplus, or the import surplus is not covered by available capital from abroad. Then comes a stage of growth when domestic savings tend to exceed domestic investment and export outrun imports. Disequilibrium may result because the long-term capital outflow falls short of the surplus savings or because surplus savings exceed the amount of investment opportunities abroad. At a still later stage of growth domestic savings tend to equal domestic investment and long-term capital movements are , on balance, zero.

Thus we see that a secular disequilibrium will occur when either the long-term capital movements get out of adjustment with deep-seated factors affecting savings and investment, or planned savings and investment change without an offsetting change in the movement of long-term capital. If investment adjusted itself readily to the amount of domestic savings plus foreign capital there could be no tendency for secular disequilibrium.

The balance-of-payments position will be in equilibrium, if the international capital flow falls into line with the requirements of domestic investment minus domestic savings. There is a tendency to secular disequilibrium, because of domestic savings and domestic investment are independent of the foreign capital flow and are of different magnitudes. There is a strong tendency for underdeveloped countries to over-invest and/or undersave. The underdeveloped countries are investing larger than their domestic savings and exports allow them because they are eager to acclerate the rate of economic growth. This tendency to over-invest causes a secular disequilibrium in the balance of payments.

Technological Disequilibrium

Technological disequilibrium in the balance of payments is caused by various technological changes. Technological changes involve inventions or innovations of new goods or new techniques of production. These technological changes affect the demand for goods and productive factors which in turn influence the various items in the balance of payments. Each technological change implies a new comparative advantage to which a country adjusts to. The innovation leads to increased exports if it is a new good and export-biased innovation. The innovation may lead to decline in imports if it is import-biased. This will create a disequilibrium. A new equilibrium will require either increased imports or reduced exports.

Structural Disequilibrium

Let us see how the structural type of disequilibrium is caused." *Structural disequilibrium at the goods level* occurs, when a change in demand or supply of exports alters a previously existing equilibrium, or when a change occurs in the basic circumstances under which income is earned or spent abroad, in both cases without the requisite parallel changes elsewhere in the economy."[3]

Suppose demand in foreign countries for Indian handicrafts falls. The resources engaged in the production of these handicrafts must shift to some other line or the country must restrict imports, otherwise the country will experience a structural disequilibrium. A change in supply may also cause a structural disequilibrium. Suppose Indian jute crop falls because of the change in the shift in the crop-pattern, Indian jute exports will fall and a disequilibrium will be created. Apart from goods, a

2. C.P. Kindleberger, *op. cit.*, p. 526.
3. C.P. Kindleberger, *op. cit.*, p. 526.

loss of service income may also upset the balance-of-payments position on current account. Besides, the loss of income may arise because foreign investment has proved a failure or it has been confiscated or nationalised, *e.g.* nationalisation of Anglo-Iranian Company in Iran. A war also produces structural changes which may affect not only goods but also factors of production.

A deficit arising from a structural change can be filled by increased production or decreased expenditure, which in turn affect international transactions in increased exports or decreased imports. Actually, it is not so easy because the resources are relatively immobile and expenditure not readily compressible. Under such circumstances, more drastic steps are called for to correct a serious disequilibrium.

"Structural disequilibrium *at the factor level* results from factor prices which fail to reflect accurately factor endowments ... *i.e.*, when factor prices, out or line with factor endowments, distort the structure of production from the allocation of resources which appropriate factor prices would have indicated"[4] If, for instance, the price of labour is too high, it will be used more sparingly and the country will import highly capital-intensive equipment and machinerry. This will lead to disequilibrium in the balance of payments on the one hand and unemployment of labour on the other.

Conclusion

We have explained above four types of disequilibria-cyclical, secular and two kinds of structural disequilibria and how they are caused. In each case, the causes manifest themselves through changes in export of goods and services, making one exceed the other.

We have already detailed the various items that enter into the balance of payments. Any cause that leads to a persistently one-sided movement in those items may cause a disequilibrium. For instance, certain causes may lead to falling off in the export of merchandise, imports remaining unaffected or moving in the opposite direction. Falling off in exports may be due to all sorts of causes. Take, for example, the case of exports and imports of goods. Our exports may fall because of decreased production due to seasonal factors or other causes. The demand for our goods in the international market may fall off because of a fall in the purchasing power of consumers of such goods or because of a comparatively high cost of production in India which reduces our competitive strength in the international market. Our exports may become dear to foreigners because of an appreciation of our exchange rate, that is, a rise in the value of the rupee, say from ₹ 42.50 per US dollar to ₹ 40 per US dollar. If we persist in artificially keeping the value of the rupee at a higher level than justified by economic forces, unfavourable balance of trade and payments will tend to persist.

In the same way, disequilibrium may arise due to excessive imports or services neither balanced by exports nor import of capital, etc. Compulsory exports in the form of reparations or indemnities also cause international disequilibrium and obstruct the harmonious trade relations between the countries concerned.

HOW DISEQUILIBRIUM CAN BE CORRECTED

When serious disequilibrium arises in a country's balance of payments, steps must be taken to correct it, if the country's economy is to be kept in a sound condition. Obviously, the causes which are responsible for such a state of affairs must be removed. The 'classical' view of the adjustment mechanism is: "An active or passive balance, accompanied by an inflow or outflow of gold, was formally supposed to result in an expansion or contraction of the domestic money supply; and this expansion or contraction was expected to bring about a rise or fall in the level of domestic costs and prices tending, in the former case, to stimulate imports and discourage exports or, in the latter to discourage imports and stimulate exports. Gold flows, changes in the quantity of money and changes in relative levels thus appeared as the principal factors in the mechanism of adjustments"[5]

4. See. C.P. Kindleberger, *International Economics*, 1978.
5. See C.P. Kindleberger, *International Economics*, 1978.

But gold standard has been abandoned long ago. These days different countries of the world are under managed currency standard. Therefore gold flows no longer occur to bring the balance of payments into equilibrium. Recent currency experience has, however, led to certain modifications in the classical theory. It is now thought that changes in the flow of income induced by balance of payments serve as an equilibrating factor."The main point is that any active or passive balance of current transaction....tends directly to expand or contract the total flow of money income within a given country... The changes induced by the balance of payments in the flows of income and expenditure affect, in turn, the demand for imported as well as home-produced goods and so react on the balance of payments to bring it into equilibrium".[6]

However, these automatic adjustments or corrections in the balance of payments through either changes in prices of goods and factors or through changes in the incomes do not always work due to the presence of various rigidities and immobilities in the system. When the causes of disequilibrium in the balance of payments are deeper and serious, then the automatic correction via price and income changes does not work at all. Under such circumstance, some concrete measures are required to be taken to restore the equilibrium in the balance of payments. Disequilibrium in the balance of payments may be corrected by the following methods by the Government.

There are four well-known methods of correcting in adverse balance of payments:

1. Trade Policy Measures : Expanding, Exports and Restraining Imports

Trade policy measures to improve the balance of payments refer to the measures adopted to promote exports and reduce imports. Exports may be encouraged by reducing or abolishing export duties and lowering the interest rate on credit used for financing exports. Exports are also encouraged by grainting subsidies to manufacturers and exporters. Besides, on export earnings lower income tax can be levied to provide incentives to the exporters to produce and export more goods and services. By imposing lower excise duties, prices of exports can be reduced to make then competitive in the world markets.

On the other hand, imports may be reduced by imposing or raising tariffs (*i.e.*, import duties) on imports of goods. Imports may also be restricted through imposing import quotas, introducing licenses for imports. Imports of some inessential items may be totally prohibited.

Before the economic reforms carried out since 1991 India had been following all the above policy measures to promote exports and restrict imports so as to improve its balance of payments position. But they had not achieved nuch success in their aim to correct balance of payments disequilibrium. Therefore, India had to face great difficulties with regard to balance of payments. At several occasions it approached IMF to bail it out of the foreign exchange crisis that emerged as a result of huge deficits in the balance of payments. At long last, economic crisis caused by persistent deficits in balance of payments forced India to introduce structural reforms to achieve a long-lasting solution of balance of payments problem.

2. Expenditure-Reducing Policies

The important way to reduce imports and thereby reduce deficit in balance of payments is *to adopt monetary and fiscal policies that aim at reducing aggregate expenditure* in the economy. The fall in aggregate expenditure or aggregate demand in the economy works to reduce imports and help in solving the balance of payments problem. The two important tools of reducing aggregate expenditure are the use of (1) tight monetary policy and (2) contrationary fiscal policy. We explain them below.

Tight Monetary Policy. Tight monetary is often used to check aggregate expenditure or demand by raising the cost of bank credit and restricting the availability of credit. For this bank rate

6. *Ibid.*

is raised by the Central Bank of the coutnry which leads to higher lending rates charged by the commercial banks. This discoruages businessmen to borrow for investment and consumers to borrow for buying durable cosnumers goods. This therefore leads to the reduction in investment and consumption expenditure. Besides, availability of credit to lend for investment and consumption purposes is reduced by raising the cash reserve ratio (CRR) of the banks and also undertaking of open market operations (selling Government securities in the open market) by the Central Bank of the country. This also tends to lower aggregate expenditure or demand which will helps in reducing imports. But there are limitations of the successful use of monetary policy to check imports, especially in a developing country like India.This is because tight monetary policy adversely affects investment increase in which is necessary for accelerating economic grwoth. If a developing country is experiencing inflation, tight monetary policy is quite effective in curbing inflation by reducing aggregate demnad. This will help in reducing aggregate expenditure and, depending on the income propensity to import, will curtail imports. Besides, tight monetary policy helps to reduce prices or lower the rate of inflation. Lower price level or lower inflation rate will curb the tendency to import, both on the part of businessmen and consumers.

But when a developing country like India is experiencing recession or slowdown in economic growth along with deficits in balance of payments, use of tight monetary policy that reduces aggregate expenditure or demand will not help much as it will adversely affect economic growth and deepen economic recession. Therefore, in a developing country, monetary policy has to be used along with other policies such as a appropriate fiscal policy and trade policy to tackle the problem of disequilibrium in the balance of payments.

Contractionary Fiscal Policy. Appropriate fiscal policy is also an important means of reducing aggregate expenditure. An increase in direct taxes such as income tax will reduce aggregate expenditure. A part of reduction in expenditure may lead to decrease in imports. Increase in indirect taxes such as excise duties and sales tax will also cause reduction in expenditure. The other fiscal policy measure is to reduce Government expenditure, especially unproductive or non-developmental expenditure. The cut in Government expenditure will not only reduce expenditure directly but also indirectly through the operation of multiplier.

It may be noted that if tight monetary and contractionary fiscal policies succeed in lowring aggregate expenditure which causes reduction in prices or lowering the rate of inflation, they will work in two ways to improve the balance of payments. First, fall in doemstic prices or lower rate of inflation will induce people to buy doemstic products rather than imported goods. Second, lower doemstic prices or lower rate of inflation will stimulate exports. Fall in imports and rise in exports will help in reducing deficit in balance of payments.

However, it may be emphasised again that the method of reducing expenditure through contractionary monetary and fiscal policies is not without limitations. If reduction in aggregate demand lowers investment, this will adversely affect economic growth. Thus, correction in balance of payments may be achieved at the expense of economic growth. Further, it is not easy to reduce substantially government expenditure and impose heavy taxes as they are likely to affect incentives to work and invest and invite public protest and opposition. We thus see that correcting the balance of payments through contractionary fiscal policy is not an easy matter.

3. Expenditure - Switching Policies : Devaluation

A significant method which is quite often used to correct fundamental disequilibrium in balance of payments is the use of expenditure-switching policies. Expenditure switching policies work through changes in relative prices. Prices of imports are increased by making domestically produced goods relatively cheaper. Expenditure switching policies may lower the prices of exports which will encourage exports of a country. In this way by changing relative prices, expenditure-switching policies help in correcting disequilibrium in balance of payments.

The important form of expenditure switching policy is the reduction in foreign exchange rate of the national currency, namely, devalaution. By devaluation we mean reducing the value or exchange rate of a national currency with respect to other foreign currencies. It should be remembered that devaluation is made when a country is under fixed exchange rate system and occasionally decides to lower the exchange rate of its currency to improve its balance of payments.

Under the Bretton Woods System adopted in 1946, fixed exchange rate system was adopted, but to correct fundamental disequilibrium in the balance of payments, the countries were allowed to make devaluation of their currencies with the permission of IMF. Now, Bretton Woods System has been abandoned and most of the countries of the world have floated their currencies and have thus adopted flexible exchange rate as determined by market forces of demand for and supply of them. However, even in the present flexible exchange rate system, the value of a currency or its exchange rate as determined by demand for and supply of it can fall. Fall in the value of a currency with respect to foreign currencies is described as depreciation. If a country permits its currency to *depreciate* without taking effective steps to check it, it will have the same effects as devaluation. Thus, in our analysis we will discuss effects of fall in value of a currency whether it is brought about through devaluation or depreciation. In July 1991, when India was under Bretton-Woods fixed exchange rate system devalued its rupee to the extent of about 20%. (From ₹ 20 per dollar to ₹ 25 per dollar) to correct disequilibrium in the balance of payments.

Now the question is how devaluation of a currency works to improve balance of payments. As a result of reduction in the exchange rate of a currency with respect to foreign currencies, the prices of goods to be exported fall, whereas prices of imports go up. This encourages exports and discourages imports. With exports so stimulated and imports discouraged, the deficit in the balance of payments will tend to be reduced. Thus policy of devaluation is also refered to as *expenditure switching policy* since as a result of reduction of imports, people of a country switches their expenditure on imports to the domestically produced goods. It may be noted that as a result of the lowering of prices of exports, export earnings will increase if the demand for a country's exports is price elastic (*i.e.*, ep > 1). And also with the rise in prices of imports the value of imports will fall if a country's demand for imports is elastic. If demand of a country for imports is inelastic, its expenditure on imports will rise instead of falling due to higher prices of imports.

Devaluation: Marshall Lerner Condition. It is clear from above that whether devaluation or depreciation will lead to the rise in export earnings and reduction in import expenditure depends on the price elasticity of foreign demand for exports and domestic demand for imports. Marshall and Lerner have developed a condition which states that devaluation will succeed in improving the balance of payments if sum of price elasticity of exports and price elasticity of imports is greater than one. Thus, according to Marshall-Lerner Condition, devaluation improves balance of payments if

$$e_x + e_m > 1$$

where e_x stands for price elasticity of exports

e_m stands for price elasticity of imports

If in case of a country $e_x + e_m < 1$, the devaluation will adversely affect balance of payments position instead of improving it. If $e_x + e_m = 1$, devaluation will leave the disequilibrium in the balance of payments unchanged.

Income Absorption Approach to Devaluation. Further, for devaluation to be successful in correcting disequilibrium in the balance of payments a country should have sufficient exportable surplus. If a country does not have adequate amount of goods and services to be exported, fall in their prices due to devaluation or depreciation will be of no avail. This can be explained through income-absorption approach put forward by Sidney S Alexander[7]. According to this approach, trade balance is the difference between the total output of goods and services produced in a country and its absorption by it. By absorption of output of goods and services we mean how much of them is used up for consumption and investment in that country. That is, absorption means the sum of consumption and investment expenditure on domestically produced goods and services. Expressing algebraically we have

$$B = Y - A$$

where B = trade balance or exportable surplus

Y = national income or value of output of goods and services produced

A = Absorption or sum of consumption and investment expenditure

It follows from above that if expenditure or absorption is less than national product, it will have positive trade balance or exportable surplus. To create this exportable surplus, expenditure on domestically produced consumer and investment goods should be reduced or national product must be raised sufficiently.

To sum up, it follows from above that *for devaluation or depreciation to be successful in correcting disequilibrium in the balance of payments, the sum of price elasticities of demand for a country's exports and imports should be high (that is, greater than one) and secondly it should have sufficient exportable surplus.* The devaluation will also not be successful in the achievement of its aim if other countries relaliate and make similar devaluation in their currencies and thus competitive devaluation of the exchange rate may start.

After Independence India devalued its currency three times, first in 1949, the second in June 1966 and third in July 1991 to correct the disequilibrium in the balance of payments. The devaluation of June 1966 was not successful for some time to reduce deficit in the balance of payments. This is because the demand for bulk of our traditional exports was not very elastic and also we could not reduce our imports despite their higher prices. However devaluation of July 1991 proved quite successful as after it our exports grew at a rapid rate for some years and growth of imports remained within safe limits.

4. Exchange Control

Finally, there is the method of exchange control. We know that deflation is dangerous; devaluation has a temporary effect and may provoke others also to devalue. Devaluation also hits the prestige of a country. These methods are, therefore, avoided and instead foreign exchange is controlled by the government. Under it, all the exporters are ordered to surrender their foregin exchange to the Central Bank of a country and it is then rationed out among the licensed importers. None else is allowed to import goods without a licence. The balance of payments is thus rectified by keeping the imports within limits.

After the Second War World a new international institution 'International Monetary Fund (IMF)' was set up for maintaining equilibrium in the balance of payments of member countries for a short term. Member countries borrow from it for a short period to maintain equilibrium in the balance of payments. IMF also advises member countries how to correct fundamental disequilibrium in the balance of Payments when it does arise. It may, however, be mentioned here that no country now needs to be forced into deflation (and so depression) to root out the causes underlying disequilibrium as had to be done under the gold standard. On the contrary, the IMF provides a mechanism by which changes in the rates of foreign exchange can be made in an orderly fashion.

Conclusion. In short, correction of disequilibrium calls for a judicious combination of the following methods:

(*i*) Monetary and fiscal changes affecting income and prices in the country;

(*ii*) Exchange rate adjustment, *i.e.*, depreciation or appreciation of the home currency;

---

7. Sidney S. Alexander, "Effects of Devaluation on Trade Balance", *IMF Staff Papers*, Vol. 11 (April, 1952).

(*iii*) Trade restrictions, *i.e.*, tariffs, quotas, etc.;
(*iv*) Capital movement, *i.e.*, borrowing or lending aborad; and
(*v*) Exchange control.

No reliance can be placed on any single tool. There is room for more than one approach and for more than one device. But the application of the tools depends on the nature of the disequilibrium. There are, we have said, three types of disequilibrium: (1) cyclical disequilibrium, (2) secular disequilibrium, (3) structural disequilibrium (at the goods and the factor level). It is more appropriate that fiscal measures should be used to correct cyclical disequilibrium in the balance of payments. To correct structural disequilibrium adjustment in exchange rate should be avoided. Capital movements are needed to offset deep-seated forces in secular disequilibrium.

The main methods of desirable adjustment are, therefore, monetary and fiscal policies which directly affect income, and exchange depreciation (that is, devaluation) which affects prices in the first instance. Devaluation or depreciation of exchange rate can also have income effect through price effects. Monetary and fiscal policies affect relative prices also.

QUESTIONS FOR REVIEW

1. Distinguish between balance of trade and balance of payments.
2. What is meant by balance of payments on current account? Explain the visible and invisible items on the current account.
3. Distinguish between current account and capital account of the balance of payments. Mention the various items on both these accounts of the balance of payments.
4. When is country's balance of payments said to be in equilibrium ? Explain the factors that cause disequilibrium in the balance of payments.
5. Balance of payments must always balance. Is it true? Explain.
6. What is devaluation ? Is it an effective way of correcting disequilibrium in the balance of payments.
7. Explain the various measures that can be adopted to correct disequilibrium.
8. What is expenditure reducing fiscal policy ? How does it help to maintain the current account of the balance of payments in equilibrium?
9. What is meant by devaluation ? Under what conditions is it expected to improve the balance of payments position of an economy ?
10. Discuss the absorption approach to devaluation as a measure of correcting balance of payments deficit.
11. Distinguish between Expenditure Reducing and Expenditure Switching policies to correct the balance of payments disequilibrium.
12. What is globalisation ? Explain its advantages and disadvantages with special reference to India.

CHAPTER 34A

The Monetary Approach to the Balance of Payments

Introduction

Monetary approach regards balance of payments as a purely monetary phenomenon. Advocates of monetary approach argue that disequilibrium in the balance of payments affects the supply and demand for money. According to them, disequilibrium in the balance of payments is reflection of monetary disequilibrium and therefore can always be corrected by adjustment in money stock. In an open economy decrease or increase in foreign exchange reserves form the basis of expansion in money supply. We state below a basic equation of monetary approach.

$$\Delta M = \Delta D + \Delta R \qquad \ldots (1)$$

where ΔM is change in money stock, ΔD is change in domestic credit or assets of the Central Bank of the country and ΔR is change in foreign exchange reserves.

The above equation can be written as

$$\Delta R = \Delta M - \Delta D \qquad \ldots (2)$$

The above equation (2) shows that the change in the Central Bank's foreign exchange reserves (assets) is equal to the change in the stock of high powered money (ΔM) minus the domestic credit (ΔD) extended by the Central Bank. The important thing to note in the above equation (2) is that ΔR, that is, change in foreign exchange reserves (assets) of the Central Bank indicates the balance of payments of a country in a year. According to the monetary approach, a deficit in balance of payments of an economy with a fixed exchange rate regime, implies a decline in the foreign exchange reserves (assets) of the Central Bank which leads to the contraction of money supply (M). On the other hand, an increase in the foreign exchange reserves (assets) implies a surplus in balance of payments which causes expansion in money supply (M) in an open economy with a fixed exchange rate system.

Monetary approach explains the changes in price level in the economy in terms of demand for money relative to the money supply in whose determination the changes in foreign exchange reserves play an important rate. According to the approach,

$$M^d = kPY$$

where M^d stands for demand for money to hold, k is the fraction of nominal income which people want to hold in terms of money, P is the price level and Y is real national income.

Monetary equilibrium is achieved when

$$M^d = M^S$$

or

$$kPY = M^S$$

When money supply M^S exceeds the demand for money (kPY), this excess of money will cause price level to rise, real national income (output) remaining the same.

Monetary Approach : Automatic Adjustments

When balance of payments is thrown into disequilibrium, adjustments take place to restore equilibrium in the balance of payments. The Classical economists believed in automatic mechanism of adjustment through which disequilibrium in balance of payments (that is, when there is either deficit or surplus in it) is self-correcting. They thought monetary contraction or monetary expansion will bring the balance of payments into equilibrium when there is deficit or surplus in it. Let us elaborate their viewpoint. Suppose a country has a deficit in its balance of payments. This means demand for foreign currency exceeds the amount of it being supplied by the private market. This will tend to raise the exchange rate (i.e., domestic currency will tend to depreciate). When the Central Bank is committed to keep the exchange rate fixed at a particular level, it will have meet the excess demand for foreign currency by selling the foreign exchange reserves from its stock. The this sale of foreign exchange reserves by the Central Bank leads to the contraction in domestic high powered money. The reduction in domestic high powered money will lead to the decrease in money supply in the economy. It is assumed that Central bank *will not sterlise* the impact of sale of foreign exchange reserves on the money supply in the domestic economy. As a result of the contraction of money supply in the domestic economy through sale of foreign exchange reserves in situation of deficit in balance of payments, aggregate demand curve AD_0 (which is drawn with a fixed money stock) will over time shift downward to the left. With the downward shift in the aggregated demand curve, price level in the economy will fall which will increase competitiveness of the domestic economy. This will tend to raise our exports and reduce our imports and in this way over time external balance will be restored once this external balance is achieved, there will be no pressure on foreign exchange rate to change.

On the other hand, when there is surplus in balance of payments, it implies that supply of foreign exchange in the private market will be larger than the demand for it. As a result, the domestic currency will tend to appreciate. The Central Bank which, under fixed exchange rate system, in committed to keep the exchange rate pegged at a certain level will be buying the foreign exchange from the market which will lead to the increase in its foreign exchange reserves. In the absence of any sterlisation measure, the increase in foreign exchange reserves of the Central Bank will lead to the expansion in money supply in the economy. The expansion in money supply will cause our prices to rise which will tend to reduce our exports and increase our imports and in this way over time trade surplus will be eliminated and equilibrium in the balance of payments restored.

From above it is clear from above that monetary approach relies on adjustments in money supply and prices to restore external balance if it is disturbed by certain shocks to the economy. Monetary approach to balance of payments is explained in a variety of ways. It can be explained using *IS–LM* model or *AD–AS* model or using money demand function. In what follows we use *AD–AS* model to explain the monetary approach to adjustment to the balance of payments disequilibrium and are illustrated in Fig. 34A.1 where aggregate demand curve *AD* and aggregate supply curve *AS* are drawn. Aggregate demand curve *AD* is sloping downward. As explained in an earlier chapter, in a closed economy the *AD* curve slopes downward for three reasons. First, when the price level falls, the purchasing power of consumers' money balances increases. This induces the consumers to buy more at lower price levels. This is called *real balance effect.* Second, as price level falls, people's transactions demand for money decreases which, given the money supply, lowers the rate of interest. At lower rate of interest, investment spending increases. This is called *interest effect.* In an open economy will a fided exchange rate there is an additional factor responsible for downwards-sloping aggregate demand curve. A fall in the price level of a country relative to that of others, makes its exports cheaper and imports more expensive. As a result, its exports increase and imports decrease so that there is increase in net exports. So this reason for downward sloping of aggregate demand curve is called *trade effect.* The, aggregate demand of an open economy is therefore aggregate expenditure by domestic residents which we name as *AE* plus net exports (*NX*). That is,

$$AD = AE + NX$$

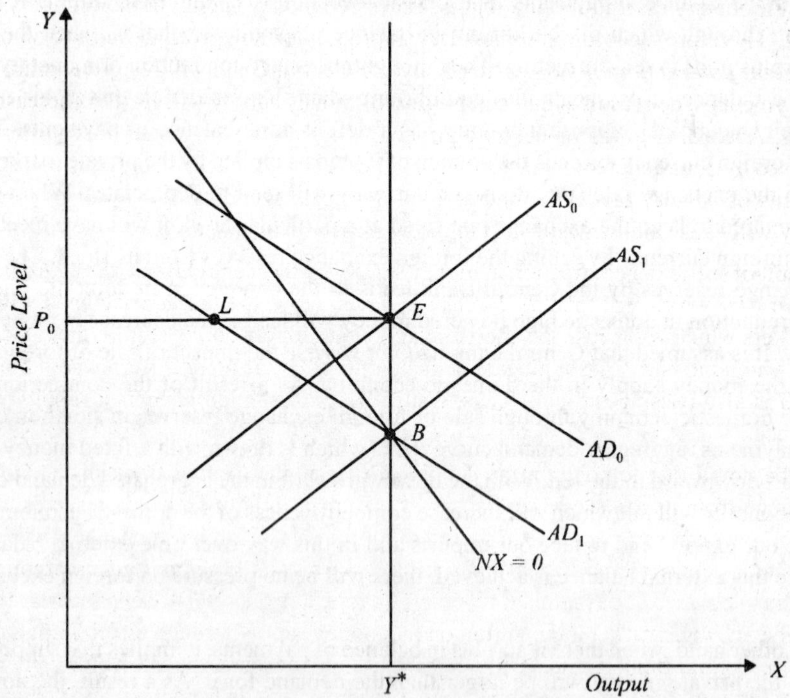

Fig. 34A.1. *Monetary Approach : Balance of Payments Adjustment with a Fixed Exchange Rate*

It is worthwhile to note that aggregate demand curve is drawn *for a given foreign price level* and a *given nominal money supply in the economy*. An increase in money supply causes an upward shift in the aggregate demand curve. In Figure 34A.1 the short-run aggregate supply curve AS_0 is also drawn assuming given wages and costs. It will be seen that the given aggregate demand curve AD_0 and aggregate supply curve AS_0 are in equilibrium at point *E* corresponding to *Y** level of 34A.1 income which is a full-employment level of income *Y**. In Figure 34A.1 trade balance equilibrium curve $NX = 0$ has also been drawn which is sloping downward. The reason for its downward sloping is that as income increases, there will be more imports and for trade balance to remain in equilibrium, price level has to fall to ensure more exports so that trade balance remains in equilibrium ($NX = 0$) with the increase in income.[1] Further, trade balance equilibrium $NX = 0$ curve is steeper than the aggregate demand curve AD_0.

Monetary Approach : Adjustment with a Fixed Exchange Rate

Initially, macroequilibrium is at point *E* where aggregate demand curve AD_0 interesects the short run aggregate supply AS_0 at full-employment level of income *Y**. It will be seen that at point *E*, aggregate demand which incorporates net exports (*NX* or *X–M*) exceeds the trade balance ($NX = 0$) by the amount *LE*. That is, the country is running a deficit in its trade balance. According to monetary approach, this deficit in trade balance is due to aggregate demand curve lying at a higher level. This higher aggregate demand i.e. higher spending by the people of a country arises, according to this approach, as a result of excessive expansion in money supply. A large expansion in money supply leads to more spending which causes more imports and less exports. It causes less exports because a part of the increase in money supply is spent on domestically produced goods which leads to the decline in exports of the country. With higher imports and lower exports deficit in balance of payments occurs. Thus the proponents of monetary approach believes that balance of payments deficit is

1. It is assumed here that both exports and imports are sufficiently price elastic.

a reflection of monetary disequilibrium, that is, excessive money supply in the economy relative to demand for it. Therefore, according to monetary approach for any given deficit in balance of payments a *sufficient contraction of money* supply by the Central Bank will restore equilibrium in the balance of payments. The reason is that contraction of money supply will lead to decrease in aggregate spending. According to the monetary approach, when there is monetary disequilibrium in the economy caused by contraction of money supply by the Central Bank $M^S < kpY$, this will cause prices to fall. In terms of AS-AD model the decrease in aggregate spending as a result of contraction in money supply will cause a downward shift in the aggregate demand curve.

As a result of sufficient contraction in money supply by the Central Bank, the aggregate demand curve shafts to AD_1 which will tend to lower price level. Now, the fall in price level will raise real wages of workers which will cause the short-run aggregate supply curve, shift to the right, say to the position AS_1 which intersects the aggregate demand curve AD_1 at point B from where trade-balance curve $NX = 0$ is also passing through. Thus, a sufficient contraction of money supply restores the external balance.

It may be noted that to contract the supply of money the Central Bank of the Country sells foreign exchange from its reserves. If there are no sufficient foreign exchange reserves, the country can borrow foreign currency from abroad. In return for the sale of foreign exchange it will get domestic currency and as a result domestic currency in circulation falls. An important assumption of monetary approach to balance of payments is that the Central Bank does not offset or *sterlise* the effect of sale of foreign exchange market intervention on the money supply through undertaking open market operations. The Central Bank if it so desires can sterlise the impact of the sale of foreign exchange on money supply through its open market operations by buying bonds from the market. Thus monetary approach assumes that no such sterlisation operations are undertaken by the Central Bank.

On the other hand, if a country has a *surplus in balance of payments*, to restore external balance, it will increase the supply of high powered money by buying foreign exchange from the market. With this money supply in the economy will increase. The excess of money supply (M) relative to the demand for it (kPY_0) will lead to the increase in aggregate spending or aggregate demand. The adjustment in this way will help in eliminating the surplus and restoring equilibrium in the balance of payments.

When balance of payments is not in equilibrium, it requires an adjustment in policy to restore equilibrium. As explained above, the classical economists believe in automatic mechanism of adjustment through which disequilibrium in the balance of payments (that is, when there is either deficit or surplus in it) is self correcting. They thought through changes in money stock and relative price level equilibrium would be restored in the balance of payments. However, this automatic process of adjustment to restore balance-of-payments equilibrium is quite slow and takes a very long time to achieve equilibrium in the external sector and in the mean time the economy has to pass through a long period of recession and its associated unemployment of workers. It therefore requires explict policy changes so that the economy moves rapidly to the external balance. These policies are *of expenditure switch-*

---

2. Some economists while discussing the monetary approach with fixed exchange rate system also assume pruchasing-power parity according to which $P = eP_f$ where P is the domestic price level and P_f is the foreign price level and e is the exchange rate. With a fixed exchange rate (e) and the given fixed foreign price level (P_f),. then from the purchasing power parity it follows that domestic price level (P) will also be given and fixed. However, in our analysis we do not assume purchasing power parity and therefore in our analysis domestic price level is flexible even with the assumptions of fixed exchange rate and the given fixed foreign price level. It may also be noted that empirical evidence also does not support the purchasing power parity hypothesis.
3. It is important to note that in the Keynesian analysis, the impact of monetary contraction on spending is explained in a different way. According to the Keynesian analysis, contraction of money supply causes interest rate to rise. At higher interest rate investment spending falls which reduces aggregate demand.

ing type or *of expenditure-reducing type*. The adjustment process to achieve the external balance also depends on whether the economy is working in a fixed exchange regime or in a flexible exchange rate system.

Evaluation

Monetary approach has been extensively used by IMF while suggesting measures to correct disequilibrium in the balance of payments. For instance, following the monetary approach in 1991, iMF suggested devaluation as a short-term measure to correct disequilibrium in India's balance of payments and as a long-term measure it suggested the adoption of tight money policy to check inflation so as to achieve economic growth with stability.

A significant implication of monetary approach is that devaluation/depreciation can improve balance of payments only in short run its effect in the long run is quite uncertain. As devaluation of domestic currency is made, in the short run; it encourages exports and discourages imports by increasing competitiveness of the economy. With the increase in exports and decrease in imports after a time period trade surplus emerges which leads to the increase in foreign exchange reserves. As a result, over time money stock in the domestic economy increases causing increase in aggregate demand and in price level. The higher aggregate demand and price level bring back the economy into full employment equilibrium and external balance.

Commenting on the monetary approach to balance of payments, Dornbusch and Fischer write, "in the short run the depreciation does improve country's competitive position and this very fact gives rise to trade surplus and therefore increase in the money stock. Over the course of time the rising money supply raises aggregate demand and therefore prices until the economy returns to full-employment and external balance. Devaluation thus exerts only a transitory effect on the economy which lasts as long as price and money supply have not increased to match fully the higher import prices".[4]

The Monetary Approach Under Flexible Exchange Rate

In monetary approach to balance of payments under flexible exchange rate regime, it is assumed that *capital is perfectly mobile between countries*. Besides, both exchange rate and prices are allowed to vary in response to the monetary shocks. To begin with, it is important to explain how prices and exchange rate adjust to the state of the economy. *While under the fixed exchange, the balance of payments equation is used to predict how foreign exchange reserves will change, in case of flexible exchange rate regime, balance of payments equation is used to prodict the changes in exchange rate.*

Figure 34A.2 depicts different situations regarding interest rate and their impact on changes in exchange rate, price levels and on balance of payments. In Figure 34A.2, *BP* is the balance of pay

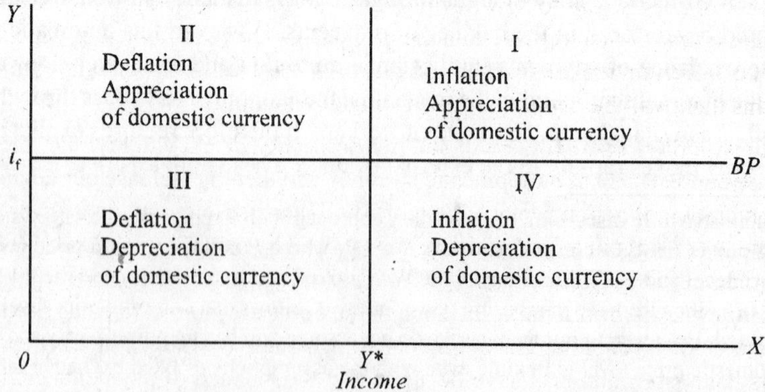

Fig.34A.2. *Adjustment in Prices and Exchange Rate*

4. Dornbusch, Fischer and Startz, op. cit. p.473

ments line at which domestic interest rate equals foreign interest rate ($i = i_f$). Along the *BP* line, balance of payments is in equilibrium. If the domestic interest rate (i) is higher than the foreign interest rate, there will be *net inflows of capital* which will cause appreciation of domestic currency. As a result, our exports decline and imports increase and balance of payments will be in deficit situation.

On the the other hand, if domestic interest rate is lower than the foreign interest rate, there will be *net capital outflows*, which will cause the domestic currency to depreciate. The depreciation of domestic currency will raise exports and lower imports and as a result the economy will move towards the equilibrium balance of payments line *BP*. Two assumptions are made in explaining the adjustment under flexible exchange rate. First, the prices would be rising when output expands beyond built employment level of output Y^* and price level will fall if output falls below the full-employment level of income Y^*. That is, on the right side of potential income Y^*, prices will be rising (i.e. inflation will occur) and an the left side of Y^*, prices would be falling i.e. deflation will occur. Second, capital is assumed to be perfectly mobile so that if domestic interest rate differes from foreign interest rate, appropriate capital movements will take place to cause the interest rate to change so that it becomes equal to the foreign interest rate and as a result the economy moves towards the equilibrium balance of payments line *BP* along which domestic interest rate equals foreign interest rate.

How the economy moves towards the balance of payments equilibrium line *BP* when domestic interest rate diverges from the foreign interest rate is the result of complicated set of adjustments involving changes in exchange rate, prices, exports and imports of a country. Given the perfect capital mobility of capital, the exchange rate adjusts very *rapidly* so that we are always close to or on the balance of payments equilibrium line *BP*. We explain below these adjustments when in a country working at full-employment level of output Y^*, there is expansion in money supply.

Adjustment with a Flexible Exchange Rate : Effect of a Monetary Expansion

Under a flexible exchange rate system and perfect capital mobility, how a monetary expansion will affect exchange rate, price level, aggregate income, money supply and balance of payments is illustrated in Figure 34A.3. Suppose initially the economy is in equilibrium at point *E* at balance of payments line *BP* corresponding to full-employment level of income Y^*. Since at point *E*, IS_0 and LM_0 curves intersect, it implies that there is equilibrium in the goods market as will as in money market and therefore at point *E* demand for and supply of money are equal. Now suppose that the Central Bank of the country expands the money supply in the economy. This monetary expansion will shift the LM curve to the right, say to new position LM_1. It will be seen from Figure 34A.3 that *IS* curve being given, the new *LM* curve LM_1 cuts the original IS_0 curve at point *L* at which new goods and money market equilibrium will be reached and rate of interest falls below the foreign interest rate i_f. As a result of this there will be *capital outflow* from our economy.

Capital outflow implies that people will sell our domestic currency to buy the foreign currencies. This will cause depreciation of our domestic currency and thereby increase our competitiveness. Thus with the depreciation of our currency our exports will increase and imports decrease which will shift the to *IS* curve to the right to a new position, say to IS_1. The new IS_1 curve intersect LM_1 curve at the new equilibrium point *H*. Thus economy has quickly moved from the original equilibrium point *E* via point *L* to the new equilibrium point *H*. Though the domestic interest rate has risen to the level of foreign interest rate, the level of income or output has increased, exchange rate has depreciated and as a result exports have risen, imports have declined and the balance of payments equilibrium has been restored. But this is still not the end of adjustments to monetary expansion. This is because at point *H* output or income is larger than full- employment level Y^*. As a result, price level will rise

5. Milton Friedman, "A Theoretical Framework for Monetary Analysis" in Robert Gordon, ed., *Milton Friedman's Monetary Framework*, University of Chicago Press, 1974, p. 27

which implies that real monetary balances $\left(\frac{M}{P}\right)$ will decrease. With this decrease in real money

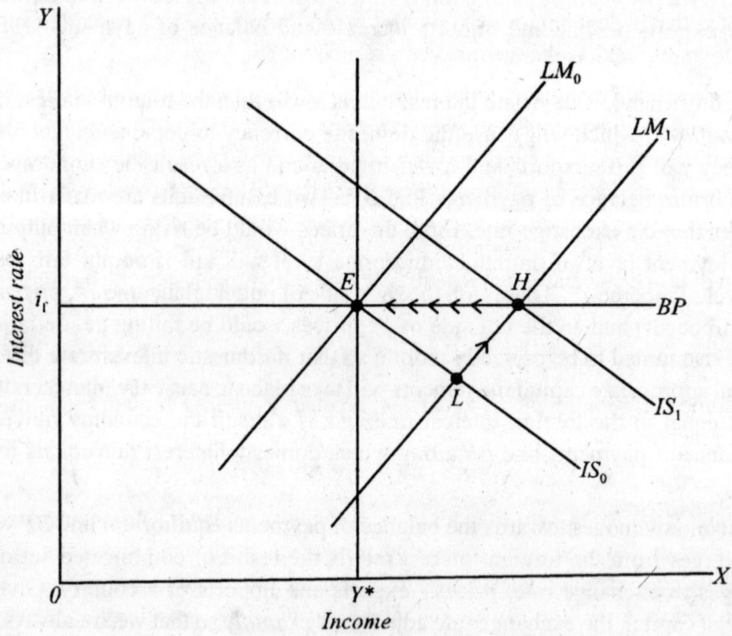

Fig. 34A.3. *Adjustment Process with Flexible Exchange Following the Expansion in Money*

balances, *LM* curve will start shifting to the left, interest rate will be tending to rise and capital inflows will tend to occur which will result in appreciation of domestic currency. The appreciation of domestic currency will cause exports to decline and imports to increase. That is, ultimately net exports will decline causing a leftward shift in the *IS* curve back *toward* the initial equilibrium point *E*. This adjustment point will continue until point *E* is reached once again.

Let us sum up the adjustments that have occurred when the economy has returned to the original point *E* after the monetary expansion. At point *E* reached again after monetary expansion, domestic interest rate has once again risen to the level of foreign interest rate, and relative prices have returned to their initial level, $\frac{eP_f}{l}$ where P_f is the foreign price level and *P* is the domestic price level and *e* is the exchange rate, (*e.g.* number of rupees per US dollar). The domestic price level in the domestic economy has risen to the extent of depreciation in exchange rate of rupee with US dollar which will keep relative prices, namely, $\frac{eP_f}{P}$, constant.[6] In moving from initial point *E* to *L* as a result of monetary expansion, exchange rate of rupee depreciated immediately before the rise in price level in the domestic economy. But when the prices in India started rising, real money balances declined causing a shift in *LM* curve toward point *E*, some of the depreciation of rupee was reversed. Over the whole process, given the flexibility of exchange rate and prices, exchange rate of dollars in terms of rupees is likely to change in the same proportion as the rise in price level in India, leaving the relative

6. Note that the depreciation of rupee imples that US dollar will apprecaite.In other words, rate of exchange of US dollar for rupees will rise. Thus, the depreciation of domestic currency (rupee) means the rise in exchange rate of US dollar in terms of rupees. For example,when foreign exchange rate of rupee per dollar rises from Rs. 45 per dollar to Rs. 47 per US dollar, the rupee depreciates and US dollar appreciates.

prices $\left(e\frac{P_f}{P}\right)$ and therefore aggregate demand unchanged. In the monetary approach in the long run *money is therefore considered as entirely neutral.* That is, in the long run, money changes only the nominal variables, that is, exchange rate, money prices, while the real variables such as level of output and employment, real exchange rate remain unaffected.

It follows from above that ultimately in the long run the adjustment process after the expansion in money supply leads to the *increase in nominal money, price level and exchange rate (number of rupees per US dollar) in the same proportions and therefore real monetary balances, relative prices* (between the home country and the foreign country) and the real exchange rate remain the same. Only in the short run monetary expansion causes increase in national income, rise in nominal exchange rate (i.e. depreciation of home currency) increase in real monetary balances $\left(\frac{M}{P}\right)$ through rise in nominal money (M), and rise in real exchange rate $\left(\frac{e.P_f}{P}\right)$. In the short run real exchange rate $\left(\frac{e.P_f}{P}\right)$ rises because while domestic price level (P) and foreign price level (P_f) remain the same, the nominal exchange rate (e) increases.

EXCHANGE RATE OVER SHOOTING

Overshooting of exchange rate means that as a result of changes in monetary policy exchange rate changes more than its target in the short run or medium term. The adjustment of exchange rate towards its long-run equilibrium level is frequently accompanied by a *larger change in the short run or medium term* than its final long-run equilibrium position. Thus, *exchange rate overshooting implies a large volatility of exchange rate.* This hypothesis of exchange rate overshooting was first of all propounded by R. Dornbusch, it is therefore also known as *Dornbusch overshooting* of exchange rate.

The overshooting of exchange rate in the short run or medium term also follows from our above analysis of the effects of monetary expansion. We saw in our above analysis that during the adjustment process following the expansion in money supply the *nominal exchange rate and prices do not move at the same rate.* When interest rate falls due to expansion in money supply, the nominal exchange rate rises immediately (i.e. domestic currency depreciates quickly) but prices rise only gradually. Therefore, in the short run relative prices of the home country fall resulting in more exports and less imports. But in the long run when prices rise, change in nominal exchange rate is somewhat reversed so that ultimately it reaches its new long-run equilibrium level which is less than it reached in the shrot or medium term but is higher than the initial level before the expansion in money supply.

The time paths of the nominal money supply, exchange rate and price level following the expansion in money supply are shown in Figure 34A.4 where along the X-axis time is measured and along the Y-axis money, exchange rate and price level are measured. For all these variables, we take an index which is equal to 100 before the monetary expansion. To start with, the economy is in long-run equilibrium at point E_1 where the index of each of the variable (money supply, exchange rate and price level) considered here is equal to 100. Now suppose at time T_1, money supply is increased by 40 per cent and remain at that higher level as shown by the dotted horizontal line at 140. As a result of 40 per cent expansion in money supply, exchange rate of home currency immediately depreciates and in fact exchange rate (say number of rupees per US dollar) increases more than the expansion in money supply and in Figure 34A.4 this has been shown to have risen to 160 or to point E_2, that is, 60 per cent rise as compared to 40 per cent increase in money supply. However, prices do not rise in the short run.

Following the expansion in money supply at time T_1 more adjustments take place. With the rise in exchange rate, that is, depreciation in the value of the domestic currency, exports of the home country increases and imports decrease and therefore national output increases beyond the full-employment level. As a result, price level rises in the home country that results in the decrease in *real*

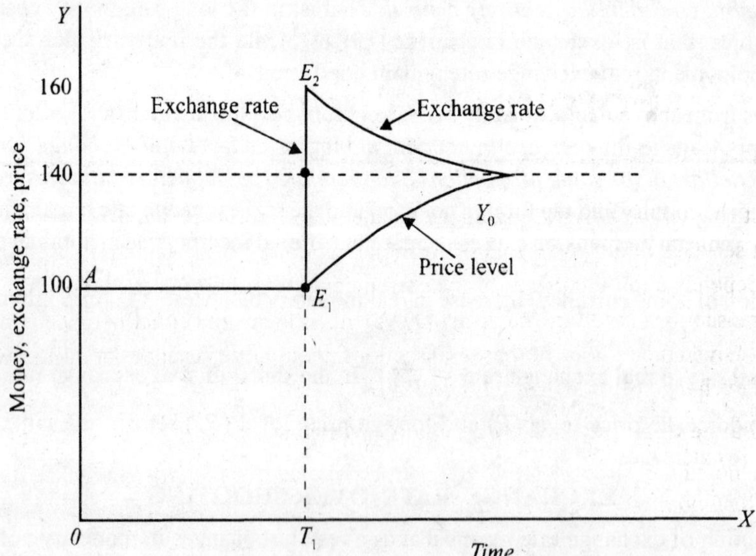

Fig. 34A.4. *Exchange Rate Overshooting*

money balances. With the rise in price level and decrease in real money balances, exchange rate of the home currency appreciates which offsets a part of the initial fast depreciation of the home currency. Over time price level rises corresponding to the higher money supply and exchange rate adjusts to the higher money supply and higher price level in the long run. In Figure 34A.4 the exchange rate falls from the high level of 160 to the new long-run equilibrium level of 140. The real variables such as national income and also real exchange rate $\left(\frac{e.P_b}{P}\right)$ remain unchanged in the long run. It is thus clear from Fig. 34A.4 that in the adjustment process, following the expansion in money supply, the exchange rate first overshoots from 100 to 160 and then in the long run reaches the new long-run equilibrium level of 140. To quote Dornbusch and Fischer, "The exchange rate overshoots its new equilibrium level when, in response to a dusturbance, it first moves beyond the equilibrium it ultimately will reach and then gradually returns to the new long-run equilibrium position."[7]

It follows from above that exchange rate is highly volatile.

7. R. Dornbusch, S. Fischer, & R. Startz, *Macroeconomics*, Tata McGraw Hill, 8th edition, P.476.

CHAPTER 35

Foreign Exchange Rate

In the last chapter we have discussed the balance of payments which describes the transactions of goods and services and movements of financial capital between countries. The value of these transactions depends upon the prices of the currencies of various countries. For example, in India the value of transactions involving balance of payments is measured either in rupee terms or in terms of US dollars. Given the volume of these transactions, their value in rupees or dollars would depend on the rate of exchange of rupee with US dollar.

Foreign Exchange Rate and Foreign Exchange Market

It may be noted that the *foreign exchange is the name given to any foreign currency. Thus US dollars* or *British pounds* are *foreign exchange for India*. Further, the exchange rate is the *price of*

Table 35.1 Foreign Exchange Rates of Indian Rupee

(Market Rate in Rs. Per Unit of Foreign Currency)

Foreign Currency	*Exchange Rate (on Dec. 11, 2007)*	*Exchange rate (on Nov. 27, 2008)*	*Dec. 29, 2011*	*March 2012 2013*
US Dollar	39.34	49.44	52.71	54.7
British Pound	80.63	75.96	82.41	83.26
Canadian Dollar	38.54	40.35	51.75	53.56
Euro*	57.77	64.24	68.91	71.5
UAE (*Dhiran*)	10.71	13.57	14.35	14.39
Swedish Kroner	6.10	–	7.57	8.21
Swiss Francs	34.68	–	56.10	57.8
Japanese 100 Yen	33.16	52.89	67.63	58.5
Australian Dollar	34.84	32.09	53.57	56.2
Singapore Dollar	27.28	32.81	40.78	44.0
New Zeland Dollar	30.58	–	40.62	44.6

*Euro is the Common Currency of European Union consisting of a number of European countries.

a country's currency in terms of another country's currency. Thus, at present (Dec. 29, 2011) one US dollar is exchanged for about 52.7 rupees of India (the spot exchange rate). Thus 52.7 Indian rupees for one US dollar is the exchange rate of a dollar in terms of rupees. In the accompanying table we give the exchange rates of Indian rupee in terms of currencies of some important countries of the world. There had been 15 per cent appreciation of Indian rupee vis-a-vis US Dollar between Oct. 2006 and Dec. 2007. Beyond Jan.2008, rupee started depreciating under pressure of capital outflows by FIIs and it fell ₹ 49.44 to a US dollar on Nov. 27, 2008. From later half of 2009-10 to Aug. 2011, as a result of return of capital flows to India rupee started depreciating and its value rose to around ₹ 45 to a US dollar at end-Aug. 2011. However, again from Sept. 2011 due to Eurozone sovereign debt crisis there has been large capital outflows by FIIs from India (and other emerging economies) resulting in drastic depreciation of Indian rupee which fell to even ₹ 54 a US dollar on Dec. 15, 2011. But due to intervention of RBI by way of selling dollars in the foreign exchange market from its foreign exchange reserves, the value of rupee fluctuated within range of ₹ 52 to ₹ 53 to a US dollar from December 16, 2011 and January 13, 2012. It will be seen that Indian rupee has depreciated against currencies of all countries in March 5, 2013 except Japan. On March 5, 2013, value of rupee was 54.9 rupees per US dollar.

The exchange rate of rupee is now market determined and has shown great volatility in the last seven years (2004-11).

Floating (Flexible) and Fixed Exchange Rate System

Since exchange rate is a price, its determination can be explained through demand for and supply of currencies. Suppose we consider the transactions between two countries, India and USA. In this case therefore the demand for and supply of dollar is the demand for and supply of foreign exchange from the Indian perspective and the price of a US dollar in terms of Indian rupees or a number of dollars per Indian rupee is the exchange rate. *The system of exchange rate in which the value of a currency is allowed to adjust freely or to float as determined by demand for and supply of foreign exchange is called a flexible exchange system which is also known as floating exchange system.*

On the other hand, if the exchange rate instead of *being determined by demand for and supply of foreign exchange is fixed by the Government, it is called the fixed exchange rate system* which prevailed in the world under an agreement reached at Bretton Woods in New Hampshire in July 1944. It may be noted that under the fixed exchange rate system, exchange rate is not determined by demand for and supply of foreign exchange but is pegged at a certain rate. At the fixed exchange rate, if there is disequilibrium in the balance of payments giving rise to either excess demand or excess supply of foreign exchange, the Central Bank of the country has to buy and sell the required quantities of foreign exchange to eliminate the excess demand or supply.

In 1977 USA decided to float its dollar and switched over to the flexible exchange system resulting in the collapse of Bretton Woods System of fixed exchange rate. Both the floating (flexible) and fixed exchange rate system have ther merits and demerits which will be discussed in a later section.

Appreciation and Depreciation of Currencies

It is important to explain the meanings of the terms, appreciation and depreciation, of currencies which are often mentioned in the discussion of foreign exchange rate. Let us consider the exchange rate of rupee for dollar. Appreciation of a currency is the increase in its value in terms of another foreign currency. Thus, if the value of a rupee in terms of US dollar increases from ₹ 45.50 to ₹ 44 to a dollar, Indian rupee is said to appreciate. This indicates strengthening of the Indian rupee. Note that when Indian rupee in dollar terms appreciates, the dollar would depreciate. On the other hand, if the value of Indian rupee in terms of US dollars falls, say from ₹ 45.5 to ₹ 46 to a dollar, the Indian rupee is said to depreciate which shows the weakening of Indian rupee. Thus, under a flexible exchange system, the exchange value of a currency frequently appreciates or depreciates depending upon the demand for and supply of a currency.

In a fixed exchange rate system the government has to buy or sell foreign exchange in order to maintain the rate at the controlled level. However, even under the fixed exchange rate system, the value of one's currency can be changed only occasionally. For instance, in June 1966, the value of rupee in terms of US dollar and U.K's, pound sterling was lowered. Again in July 1991 India reduced its value of rupee in terms of dollar by about 20 per cent. Such a one-time lowering of value of its currency in terms of foreign exchange occasionally by a country is called *devaluation* as distinguished from depreciation which can often take place under the influence of changes in demand for and supply of a currency. On the other hand, with a fixed rate exchange system if a country raises the value of its currency in terms of foreign currency, it is called *revaluation*. It should be noted that since March 1993 India has also now made its rupee convertible into a foreign currency and allowed its value to adjust freely depending upon demand and supply forces.

Managed Float System in India

It is important to note that India as most of other countries including USA, Great Britain, France, there is at present flexible or floating exchange rate system. Besides, like other countries India has not adopted a perfectly flexible or floating exchange rate system. The changes in exports and imports, capital outflows and capital inflows bring about a large fluctuations in foreign exchange rate of rupee. It may be noted that large depreciation or appreciation of exchange rate adversely affects the economy, especially its exports and imports. In order to prevent large appreciation and depreciation of Indian rupee, Reserve Bank of India often invervenes to ensure that exchange rate should remain within reasonable limits. When the rupee is depreciating too much, Reserve Bank of India intervenes and sells dollars from its reserves of foreign exchange. This increases the supply of dollars in the market and prevents the depreciation of the rupee.

On the other hand, when rupee is appreciating too much, Reserve Bank of India intervenes and buys dollars from the market. This redcues the supply of dollars in foreign exchange market which prevents the appreciation of exchange rate of rupee. Therefore, through the intervention by Reserve Bank of India, exchange rate of rupee is not allowed to change beyond certain limits. Therefore, such a system that has been adopted by India under which the Central Bank of a country intervenes in foreign exchange market to prevent large functions in exchange rate is not completely flexible or floating exchange rate system but is managed by the Central Bank. Therefore, it is called *managed float system.*

Managed Float System in India and RBI Intervention

It is important to note that even with the present flexible exchange rate system in India there is a managed float system because RBI intervenes in foreign exchange market to influence the exchange rate of rupee and keep fluctuations in it within reasonable limits. Thus when rupee in the free market depreciates much and RBI does not want much depreciation, it will sell foreign exchange from its reserves in the foreign exchange market to prevent it from depreciating. On the other hand, when rupee appreciates much against foreign currencies RBI intervenes and buys foreign exchange. This move of RBI prevents rupee from appreciating.

Note that appreciation of rupee as compared to other currencies makes the Indian exports expensive and therefore discourages them. Although RBI does not follow any fixed exchange rate target through sale and purchase of foreign exchange, it aims at preventing large volatility in foreign exchange rate of rupee.

However through sale and purchase of foreign exchange by RBI has implications for maintaining price stability. This is because when RBI buys foreign exchange from the market it issues new money (i.e. rupee currency) to pay for it. This new money comes into circulation in the Indian economy and thus leads to the expansion in money supply. If aggregate supply of goods remains the same or does not increase much, this expansion in money will cause rise in general price level (i.e. inflation) in the economy. To check inflation, RBI can *sterlise* the impact of increase in foreign exchange inflows by selling government securities to the banks. The banks will give cash to RBI against the purchase of these securities. In this way RBI mops up excess liquidity (i.e. cash reserves) of the banks caused by the inflows of foreign exchange. The proceeds of the government securities sold to the banks can be kept by RBI in a separate account which cannot be used by the Government and therefore cannot affect prices. However, there is limit to which the sterlisation can take place.

SOME IMPORTANT EXCHANGE RATE CONCEPTS

As the Indian economy gets more integrated with the world economy (that is, has extensive trade and capital flows with the rest of the world), exchange rate of rupee with foreign currencies will play a very important role as it will determine competitiveness of Indian goods and services in the international markets. The rupee has different exchange rates with foreign currencies of its various trade partners. A bilateral exchange rate with a foreign currency, say the US dollar, in nominal terms is not a good exchange rate with which to measure the competitiveness of the rupee. Further, the exchange rate of rupee with a single currency in nominal terms would not measure the differences in changes in prices and costs in the domestic economy as compared to the changes in prices in all the trade partners. To deal with this issue the effective exchange rate (EER) concept is used.

Nominal Exchange Rate (NER). Foreign exchange rate is generally quoted as the number of units of a domestic currency required to purchase one unit of a foreign currency. For example, rupees 40 per US dollar refers to foreign exchange rate of the Indian rupee in terms of US dollar and means that Rs. 40 can buy one US dollar in foreign exchange market. Likewise, there is foreign exchange rate between rupee and the pound sterling, between rupee and the Yen, between rupee and Mark and so on. This exchange rate of rupees per US dollar, or per pound sterling is called *nominal exchange rate* (NER).

Nominal Effective Exchange Rate (NEER). In addition to the nominal exchange rate, the economists often use the concept of nominal effective exchange rate. The nominal *effective exchange rate is the weighted average of nominal exchange rates* where the weights used are the shares of the trading partners in the foreign trade of a country. Suppose the US accounts for 60 per cent of total trade with India, and the United Kingdom accounts for 40 per cent of trade with India, then the nominal effective exchange rate is given by

Nominal Effective exchange rate (NEER) = $(NER_{US}\ W_{US}) + (NER_{UK} \times W_{UK})$

where NER_{US} and NER_{UK} are the nominal exchange rates of the US and UK respectively for the India rupee and W_{US} and W_{UK} are trade shares of the US and UK respectively with India. Suppose the US accounts for 60 per cent in India's trade and NER of the Indian rupee with the US dollar is Rs. 44 while UK accounts for 40 per cent in India's trade and nominal exchange rate of rupee with pound sterling is Rs. 85, the nominal effective exchange rate is

$$\begin{aligned} NEER &= 44 \times 0.6 + 85 \times 0.4 \\ &= 26.4 + 34.0 = 60.4 \end{aligned}$$

Real Exchange Rate. Real exchange rate measures the relative price of the two currencies after adjusting for price levels prevailing within two countries. For example, *real exchange rate between rupee and US dollar is defined as the rupee price of a basket of goods in India relative to a dollar price of the same basket of goods in the USA.* Thus real exchange rate is given by

$$RER = NER\left(\frac{P_{US}}{P_{In}}\right)$$

where NER is the nominal exchange rate between the two currencies and P_{US} is the price level in the USA and P_{In} is the price level in India. While the nominal exchange rate measures the rate at which currencies of the two countries are exchanged, real exchange rate measures the rate at which domestic goods can be exchanged for foreign goods. An example will clarify the meaning of real exchange rate. Suppose Rs. 44 are required to buy one US dollar, that is Rs. 44 per US dollar is the nominal exchange rate (NER) between the Indian rupee and the US dollar. If a basket of goods costs Rs. 200 in India and the same basket of goods costs 20 dollars, then real exchange rate (RER) will be

$$RER = (NER)\frac{P_{US}}{P_{In}} = 44 \times \frac{20}{200} = 4.4$$

Thus 4.4 is the real exchange rate of the Indian rupee. This means 4.4 units of Indian goods are needed to buy one unit of US goods. Real exchange rate is used as a measure of *international competitiveness*. A rise in real exchange rate indicates foreign goods (in our example the US goods) have become more expensive relative to domestic goods of a country. This means competitiveness of our goods has increased relative to that of the USA.

Real Effective Exchange Rate (REER). *Real effective exchange rate is the weighted average of real exchange rates with all its trade partners, the shares of different countries in its total trade are used as weights.* Thus, in India 5 countries real effective exchange rate (REER) is prepared and the shares of major trade partners such as the USA, UK, other European countries, Japan with India are used as weights for calculating real effective exchange rate.

DETERMINATION OF EXCHANGE RATE

We are now in a position to explain how in a flexible exchange system the exchange of a currency is determined by demand for and supply of foreign exchange. We assume that there are two countries, India and USA, the exchange rate of their currencies (namely, rupee and dollar) is to be determined. Thus, we explain below how the value of a dollar in terms of rupees (which will conversely indicate the value of a rupee in terms of dollars) is determined.

At present in both USA and India there is floating or flexible exchange regime. Therefore, the value of currency of each country in terms of the other depends upon the demand for and supply of their currencies.

It is in the foreign exchange market that the exchange rate among different currencies is determined. The foreign exchange market is the market in which the currencies of various countries are converted into each other or exchanged for each other. In our case of the determination of exchange rate between US dollar and Indian rupee, the Indians sell rupees to buy US dollars (which is a foreign currency) and the Americans or others holding US dollars will sell dollars in exchange for rupees. It is the demand for and supply of a foreign currency or exchange that will determine the exchange rate between the two.

Demand for Foreign Exchange (US Dollars)

The demand for US dollars comes from the Indian people and firms who need US dollars to pay for the goods and services they want to import from the USA. The greater the imports of goods and services from the USA, the greater the demand for the US dollars by the Indians. Further, the demand for dollars also arises from Indian individuals and firms wanting to purchase assets in the USA, that is, desire to invest in US bonds and equity shares of the American companies or build factories, sales facilities or houses in the USA. The demand for dollars also arises from those who want to give loans or send gifts to some people in the USA. Thus, for whatever reasons the Indian residents need dollars they have to buy them in the foreign exchange market and pay for them with the Indian currency, the rupees. All of these constitute demand for dollars, the foreign exchange.

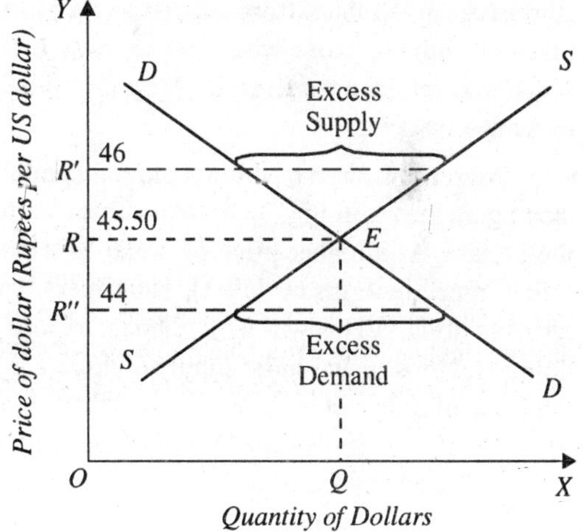

Fig. 35.1. *Determination of Exchange Rate of a US Dollar in Terms of Rupess*

To sum up, the demand for dollars by the Indians arises due to the following factors:

1. The Indian individuals, firms or Government who import goods from the USA into India.

2. The Indians travelling and studying in the USA would require dollars to meet their travelling and education expenses.

3. The Indians who want to invest in equity shares and bonds of the US companies and other financial instruments.

4. The Indian firms who want to invest directly in building factories, sales facilities, shops in the USA.

An important thing to understand is how the demand curve for a foreign exchange would look like. *When there is a fall in the price of dollar in terms of rupees, that is, when the dollar depreciates, fewer rupees than before would be required to get a dollar.* With this, therefore, a dollar's

worth of US goods could be purchased with fewer rupees, that is, the US goods would become cheaper in terms of rupees for Indians. This will induce the Indian individuals and firms to import more from the USA resulting in the increase in quantity demanded of dollars by the Indians. On the other hand, *if the price of US dollar rises, (that is US dollar appreciates) a dollar's worth of US goods would now cost more in terms of rupees making American goods relatively expensive than before*. This will discourage the imports of US goods to India causing a decrease in quantity demanded of dollars for imports.

It therefore follows from above that at a lower price of dollars, the greater quantity of dollars is demanded for imports from the USA and at a higher price of dollar, the smaller quantity of dollars is demanded for imports from the USA by the Indians. This makes the demand curve for dollars downward sloping as shown by the *DD* curve in Fig. 35.1.

Supply of US Dollars (i.e., Foreign Exchange)

What determines the supply of dollars in the foreign exchange market. The individual firms and Government *which export Indian goods to the USA will earn dollars from the American residents who would buy the Indian goods imported into the USA and pay their price in dollars*. Further, the Americans who travel in India and use the services of Indian transport, hotels etc., will also supply dollars to be converted into rupees for meeting these expenses.

Besides, the *American firms and individuals who want to buy assets in India, such as bonds and equity shares of Indian companies or wish to make loans to the Indian individuals and firms will also supply dollars*. There are Indians who are working in the USA and send their earnings in dollars to their relatives and friends. The supply of these dollars by the Indians working in the USA popularly called *remittances from the USA* also add to the supply of dollars. Those holding dollars who have earned them from exports to the USA and the foreign firms and individuals who want to invest in India or those who want to make loans to Indians or the American tourists travelling in India, and remittances from USA by the Indians working there will supply dollars in the foreign exchange market.

The supply curve of dollars plotted against the price of dollar in terms of rupees is positively sloping as shown in Fig. 35.1. What accounts for the upward sloping nature of the supply curve of the dollars. At a higher price of dollar in terms of rupees (or, in other words, lower value of the Indian rupee in terms of dollar), 100 rupees worth of Indian goods would be relatively cheaper in terms of dollars. This will tend to boost exports of the Indian goods to the USA at a higher price of dollar and thus ensure more supply of dollars in the foreign exchange markets. On the other hand, if the price of dollar in terms of rupees falls (i.e. its exchange rate for Indian rupee declines) the 100 rupees worth of Indian goods would become relatively expensive in terms of dollars. This will discourage the exports of Indian goods to the USA and reduce the quantity supplied of dollars in the foreign exchange market.

The Equilibrium Exchange Rate

It will be seen from Figure 35.1 that the equilibrium exchange rate, that is, the equilibrium price of dollar in terms of rupees is equal to *OR* or Rs. 45.50 per dollar at which demand for and supply curve of dollars intersect and therefore the market for dollars is cleared at this rate. At a higher price of dollars *OR'* or Rs. 46 the quantity supplied of dollars exceeds the quantity demanded. With the emergence of excess supply of dollars, its price, that is, the exchange rate will again fall to *OR* or Rs. 45.50. On the other hand, if the rate of exchange is lower than *OR*, say it is *OR''* or Rs. 44 per dollar, there will emerge the excess demand for dollars. This excess demand of dollars would push up the price of dollars to the level of *OR* or Rs. 45.50 per dollar.

CHANGES IN EXCHANGE RATE

In our analysis of determination of exchange rate through demand and supply of foreign exchange we have assumed that the underlying forces which determine demand for and supply of foreign exchange remain constant. In our foregoing analysis it is only changes in the exchange rate that cause the quantity supplied and demanded of foreign exchange to change and bring about the equilibrium between demand for and supply of foreign exchange.

The equilibrium in the foreign exchange market will be disturbed if some changes occur in the underlying factors that determine the demand for and supply of foreign exchange. For example, if there is increase in incomes of the American people due to the boom conditions in the US economy, it will affect the equilibrium rate of exchange. The increase in incomes of the people of USA will lead to the increase in demand for imported goods including those of India. Now, with this increase in demand for imported Indian goods, they will spend more dollars on the Indian goods. This will increase the supply of dollars to buy Indian goods in the foreign exchange market causing a rightward shift in the supply curve from *SS* to *S'S'* , as shown in Fig. 35.2. This increase in the supply of dollars in foreign exchange market will lower the price of dollar in terms of rupees from *OR* (Rs. 45.50 per dollar) to *OR'* (Rs. 45 per dollar). This implies that increase in imports by USA from India leading to more exports from India will cause the dollar to depreciate and the Indian rupee to appreciate. It will be seen from Figure 35.2 that with the increase in supply of dollars and supply curve shifting to the right to *S'S'* position, at the original price *OR* (or Rs. 45.50 per dollar) there is excess supply of dollars by *EN* amount which will result in lowering the price of dollar to the level of *OR'* or Rs. 45 per dollar. This means increase in supply of dollars has led to the appreciation of rupee from Rs. 45.50 per dollar to Rs. 45 per dollar.

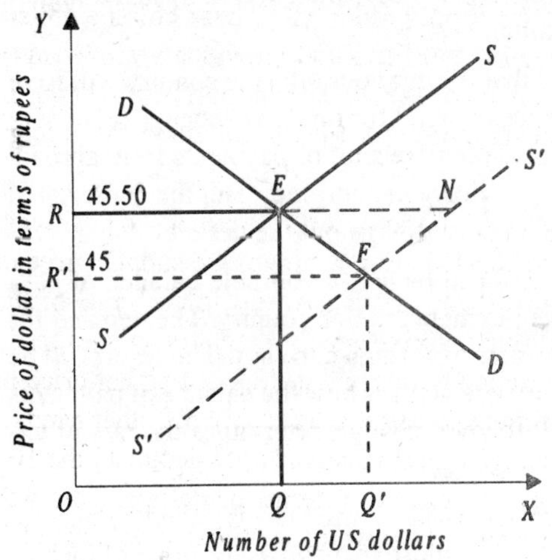

Fig. 35.2. *Increase in Incomes of US people leading to more exports from India will lower the price of dollar and increase Indian exports*

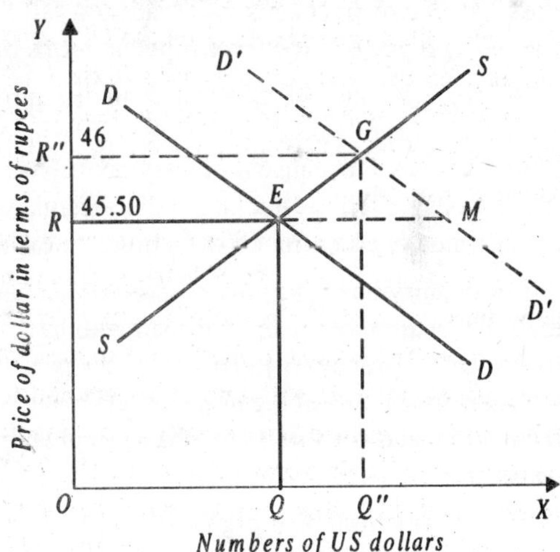

Fig. 35.3. *Increase in the imports from USA by the Indian causes increase in demand for dollars and lowers the price of ru pee (i.e. raise the price of US $).*

On the other hand, if due to the increase in incomes of the Indian people causing a rise in demand for American consumer goods or there is picking up of industrial activity in India requiring more imports of materials, machines, equipments and other capital goods from the USA the Indian imports from USA will increase. The increase in imports from USA by India will have to be paid in dollars causing the demand for dollars to increase and as a result demand curve for dollar shifts to the right from *DD* curve to *D'D'* curve (see Fig. 35.3). This will upset the initial equilibrium at price *OR* (Rs. 45.50 per dollar) as with the increase in demand for dollars following the increase in imports from USA there will emerge excess demand for dollar which will push up the price of dollar to

OR′ ′ (Rs. 46 per dollar) so as to bring balance between demand for and supply of dollars (*i.e.*, foreign exchange). Note that rise in price of dollar in terms of rupees implies depreciation of the value of rupee from Rs. 45.50 to Rs. 46 per dollar.

It will be observed in Fig. 35.3 that as a result of adjustments following the increase in demand for dollars, the price of dollar has risen to *OR*″ (Rs 46 per dollar) and the amount of dollars spent by Indians on imports from the USA increases to *Q*″

FOREIGN EXCHANGE RATE AND BALANCE OF PAYMENTS

It will be understood from above that the various items in the country's balance of payments lie at the back of demand for and supply of a foreign currency. That is why the explanation of determinantion of foreign exchange rate through demand and supply is also called the *Balance of Payments Theory of Foreign Exchange*. The demand for foreign exchange arises from the debit items in the balance of payments, whereas the supply of foreign exchange arises from credit items. The debit items relate to all payments made during a given period by residents of a country to foreigners, and credit items include all payments received during the given period from foreigners by the residents. These payments may be on any account, *e.g.* goods bought and sold, services rendered and received, capital borrowed or lent, and so on.

By way of illustration, if India has a net debit in its balance of payments, its demand for foreign exchange, say, U.S. dollar, must exceed its supply of U.S. dollar with the result that the rupee price of U.S. dollar will go up or, what comes to the same thing, the external value of the rupee must go down in terms of dollar. The rupee becomes cheap in terms of dollar. Conversely, a net credit in India's balance of payments will lead to a fall in the rupee-price of dollar, which means a higher value of the rupee or expensive rupee in terms of US dollar.

When the balance of payments is in disequilibrium, that is, unfavourable, the country will have a weak exchange rate position. There will be increase in the demand for foreign exchange relative to the supply thereof, because more payments have to be made than receipt of payments from abroad. In this case there will be decline in the external value of the domestic currency. But the depreciated external value of its currency will stimulate exports and help it to wipe out the deficit.

If a country has a surplus on current account, it is said to have a favourable balance of payments. There are more people abroad who have to make payments to this country. The demand for this country's currency will increase on the part of the holders of foreign currency. The result will be that the external value of the domestic currency will appreciate. This is how the balance of payments affecting demand for foreign exchange and supply of foreign exchange determines the rate of exchange.

The explanation of foreign exchange through demand or what sometimes is called balance of payments theory of exchange rates is superior because (*a*) it is more realistic as the price of foreign currency is seen here as a function of many significant variables and not merely purchasing power expressed in general price level, and (*b*) it clearly shows the possibility of correcting balance of payments disequilibrium through exchange rate adjustment rather than through domestic price deflation as implied by the purchasing power parity.

The chief merit of demand-supply approach to the determination of exchange rate or what is sometimes called balance of payments theory of foreign exchange is that it explains the determination of foreign exchange rate through general demand and supply analysis. Further, important fact brought out by the theory is that not only exports and imports of goods but also other items in the balance of payments such as invisible items, long-term capital movements also play a significant part in determining demand for and supply of foreign exchange and the equilibrium rate of exchange. Thus, this theory puts forward more correct explanation of the determination of foreign exchange rate by visualising foreign exchange as a function of several variables and not just purchasing power representing the general price level. This theory also highlights an important fact that disequilibrium in the balance of payments, if left to the market forces, can be corrected through depreciation or appreciation in exchange rate.

FACTORS AFFECTING EXCHANGE RATE

Having now explained how the exchange rate between different currencies of various countries is determined, we can now explain the factors that are likely to affect the exchange rate between currencies. Changes in all those factors mentioned above which determine the demand for and supply of currencies can influence the exchange rate which will adjust according to the changes that have occurred.

Purchasing Power Parity: The Relative Price Levels

If there are no restrictions imposed on trade by the countries the exchange rate between two national currencies is allowed to adjust freely and with the further assumption that costs of transport of goods between the countries is nil, then the exchange rate between the two currencies will reflect the differences in the price levels in the two countries. This is because with the above-mentioned assumptions if the price of the same good BPL TV set is lower in Britain than in India, then it will pay traders to buy the BPL TV sets in Britain and sell them in India. This will reduce the supply of TV set in Britain pushing up its price there and increase the supply of TV sets in India and thus causing a decline in its price in India. This process would continue till the price differential of the same quality of T.V. sets is eliminated and the same price of TV set prevails in the two countries. Thus, if law of same price holds and each country consumes the same market basket of goods, the exchange rate between the two currencies would be determined by the relative price levels in the two countries. For example, if prices in Britain and India are such that a pair of same quality of shoes costs 5 pound in England and 350 rupees in India, then the exchange rate between rupees and pound would be 1 pound for 70 rupees. If the exchange rate between the two is different from this, it will be possible for the businessmen to make profits in sending pairs of shoes from a country to the other depending on the price levels in the two countries. We therefore conclude that price levels of commodities in the different countries influence the exchange rate between their currencies.

It may however be noted that it is only in the long run and with no restrictions on the trade between the two countries that relative price level in the two countries will be reflected in the exchanges rate.

Rate of Inflation and Exchange Rate

Having shown the effect of relative price levels in the countires on the exchange rate between their currencies, we can now explain how a relatively higher rate of inflation in a country can affect the exchange rate of its currency. Suppose in India a relatively higher rate of inflation prevails than in the USA, how will it affect the exchange rate between the rupee and dollar?

A relatively higher rate of inflation causing rise in prices of the goods in India as compared to those in the USA will make US goods relatively cheapter and the Indian goods expensive. This will serve as incentive for the Indian individuals and firms to increase their imports of goods from USA. This will raise the demand for US dollars shifting the demand curve for dollars in the foreign exchange market to the right, as shown in Fig. 35.4 where the demand curve is shown to have shifted from *DD* to *D'D'* under the influence of higher rate of inflation in India.

However, at the same time due to higher price level American people will find Indian goods more expensive and as a result will reduce their imports of Indian goods. This will cause a decline in exports of goods from India to the USA, shifting the supply curve of dollars to the left to $S'S'$. Both

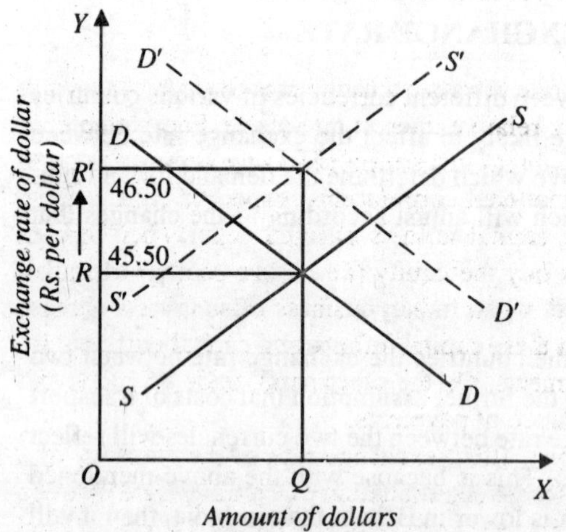

Fig. 35.4. *Effect of a Relatively Higher rate of Inflation on the Exchange Rate of a country*

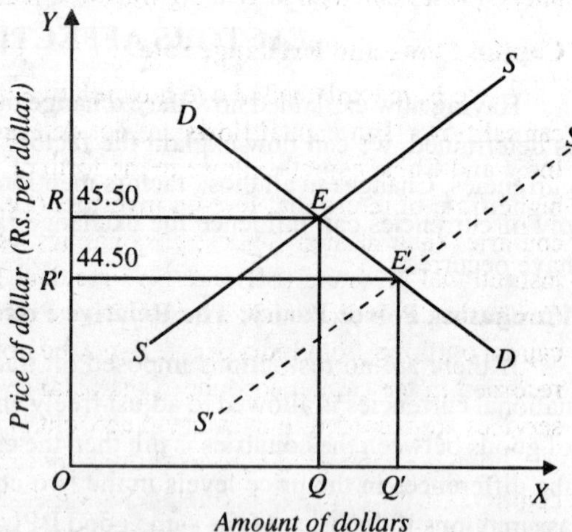

Fig. 35.5. *Effect of a Relatively Higher Rate of Interest in India on the Exchange Rate*

these effects of a higher price level due to higher rate of inflation in a country, namely, rise in imports of US goods into India and the reduction in Indian exports to the USA will cause the foreign exchange rate of dollar in terms of rupees to rise and the price of Indian rupee in terms of dollar will fall. *Thus, as a result of higher rate of inflation in India, the US dollar will appreciate and the Indian rupee will depreciate* (See Figure 35.4).

Interest Rates and Exchange Rate

Another important factor influencing the exchange rate is the interest rate in a country relative to interest rate of other countries with which it trades its goods. Suppose there are no restrictions imposed by the Governments on the flow of funds between the countries. Assume that interest on securities or bonds in USA is 5 per cent whereas it is 8 per cent in India. Thus businessmen, firms, banks etc., with funds to invest would obviously have incentive to buy securities and bonds of the Indian companies. That is, there will be *flight of capital* from the USA or capital inflows into India the American business corporations, firms, banks etc. will use their funds to purchase high-yielding Indian securities. In order to buy the Indian securities, they will have to convert dollars into rupees, and thus increasing the demand for dollars. Consequently, the supply of dollar curve will shift to the right. This will pull down the foreign exchange rate of dollar in terms of rupees (Conversely, the exchange rate of rupee in terms of dollar will appreciate). Thus, *a relatively higher interest rate in India as compared to India would lead to the depreciation of dollar and appreciation of rupee.* This is what the actually happened in India in the year 2003 and 2004.

Figure 35.5 illustrates the effect of higher interest rates in the USA on the dollar-rupee exchange rate. Initially, the demand for and the supply of US dollar are given by the curves *DD* and *SS* respectively. The balance between the two determines *OR* (or Rs. 45.50 per dollar) as the exchange rate between the two. With the flow of United States funds in the India to buy the Indian securities and shares and stocks, the supply curve for dollars shifts to the right to the new position *S'S'* (dotted) and lower the equilibrium exchange rate to *OR'* (Rs. 44.50 per dollar) is determined.

It may be noted that during the early eighties, the Federal Reserve Bank of USA adopted a tight money policy to fight inflation which caused very high interest rates in USA. These high interest rates attracted a lot of foreign capital, particularly from Japanese firms which due to high saving rate in Japan had a large amount of funds to make investment in American bonds. To purchase American bonds Japanese had to convert Yens into dollars. This caused the increase in demand for dollars and caused a sharp rise in the price of dollar. It is thus clear that *like the relative price levels, relative interest rates can also have a significant effect on the exchange rate.*

Capital Flows and Exchange rate

We have explained above how relative interest rate affects exchange rate through changes in capital flows. But capital flows are not determined by relative interest rate alone. For example, in India and China capital inflows in the form of foreign direct investment (FDI) are occurring due to higher rate of return that foreign investors (*i.e.*, multinational corporations) expect to earn in these countries than in their domestic economies. Besides, capital inflows in India occur when foreign institutional investors (FII) and Non-resident Indians buy the equity (*i.e.*, share capital) of Indian Companies in Indian stock market. On the other hand, when Indian business class invests abroad, capital outflows from India occur. It may be noted that these capital inflows and capital outflows are recorded in the capital account of the balance of payments. On the other hand, trade of goods and services are recorded in the current account of the balance of payments.

We are interested here to show how capital flows affect exchange rate of the currency of a country. This is shown in Figure 35.5 (a) and 35.5 (b) where determination of exchange rate between rupee and US dollar is shown. To begin with in Fig. 35.5 (a), we have drawn demand curve *DD* and supply curve *SS* of US dollar as determined by flows of trade of goods (that is, imports and exports) between the two countries, without any capital flows taking place between the two countries. These demand and supply curves, *DD* and *SS*, determine equilibrium exchange rate *OR* (or Rs. 45 per US doller). Note that at this equilibrium exchange rate, there is equilibrium in the current account

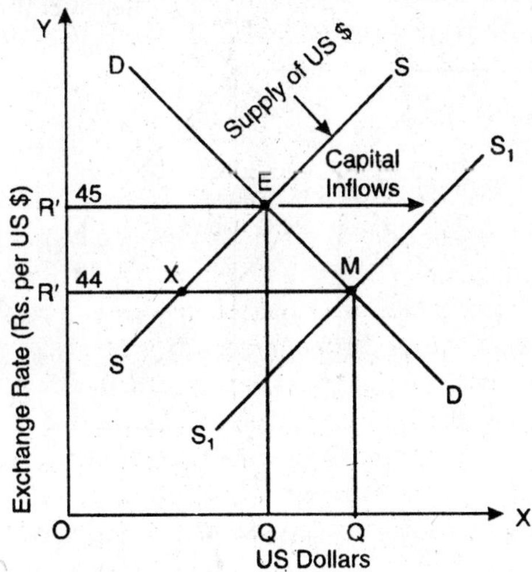

Fig. 35.5(a) *Effect of Capital Inflows on Excange rate*

balance of payments since we are so far assuming that no capital flows occur. Now suppose foreign institutional investors (FII) and Non-Resident Indians buy shares of the Indian companies. They will therefore bring dollars and convent them into rupees for buying shares of the Indian companies. These capital inflows will increase the supply of US dollars causing a shift in the supply curve to the right, say to the new position S_1S_1. The new supply curve of dollars S_1S_1 intersects the demand curve

1. We consider invisibles which mainly consist of services as a part of trade balance. Therefore, in our case here, no distinction is drawn between trade balance and current account balance.

DD of dollars at point *M* and determine the new exchange rate *OR*' (or Rs. 44 for a dollar). Thus, as a result of capital inflows, the Indian rupee has appreciated (and dollar depreciated). It may be noted that at the new equilibrium exchange rate *OR*' (or Rs. 44 for a dollar), the overall balance of payments (that is, total inflows and outflows of US dollars on account of both trade and capital flows) will be in equilibrium. However, in this situation due to capital inflows as depicted in Fig. 35.5 (*a*), *current account must be in deficit* while the overall balance of payments is in equilibrium. Since as a result of capital inflows the exchange rate of rupee has appreciated, this will cause the total Indian exports of goods and services to decline. Total exports of goods and services at the new exchange rate *OR*' (or Rs. 44 for a dollar) is given by the point on the *original* supply curve of dollars *SS* corresponding to this new exchange rate *OR*'. From Figure 35.5(*a*), it is clear that total exports of goods and services *R'X* are less than the imports of goods and resources *R'M*. Thus there is deficit of *XM* on current account. This deficit on current account is met by surplus in capital inflows of capital account since overall balance of payments balances at the new equilibrium exchange rate. We thus reach an important conclusion that the *deficit in current account implies capital inflows (i.e., foreign investment) of that order occur in the economy in that year.*

Capital Outflows. Let us take the opposite case when instead of net capital inflows, there are net apital outflows. For example, the rate of return on investment rises in the USA or interest rate falls in India as compared to that in USA. This will cause capital outflows from India and result in shifting the demand curve of US dollars in foreign exchange market. This is illustrated in Figure 35.5 (b).

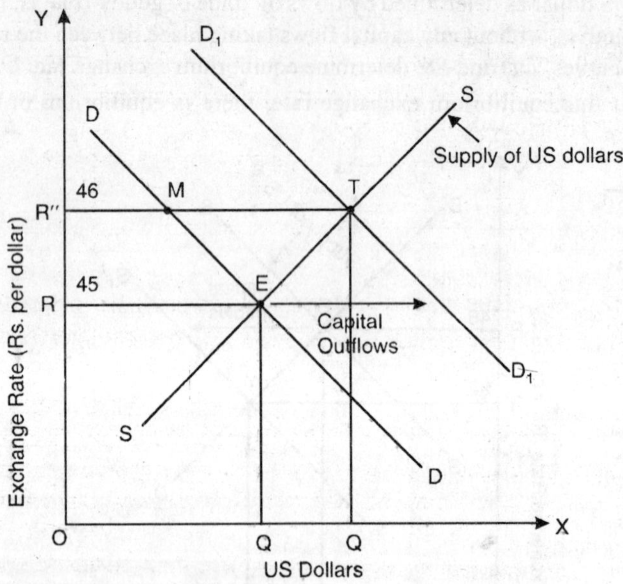

Figure 35.5 (b) *Foreign Exchange Market with Capital outflows*

where demand curve of US dollars *DD* and supply curve *SS* of US dollars determine equilibrium exchange rate *OR* (or Rs. 45 for a dollar) when there are no capital flows. Now suppose that net capital outflows occur due to the factors mentioned above. Capital outflows require that those who want to invest abroad will convert Indian rupees into US dollars to invest in the USA. This will cause an increase in demand for US dollars resulting in a shift of the demand curve for US dollars to the right, say to D_1D_1. The new demand curve for US dollars intersects the given supply curve *SS* of dollers at the new point *T* and determines the exchange rate *OR*" (or Rs. 46 for a dollar), that is, US dollar appreciates and the Indian rupee depreciates. Since the Indian rupee depreciates, the Indian exports of goods and services will increase because depreciation of Indian rupee will make the Indian goods and services cheaper. In Figure 35.5 (*b*), at the new exchange rate *OR*" (Rs. 46 for a dollar) exports of Indian goods and services increase to *R"T*. On the other hand, depreciation of Indian rupee will make the Indian imports costlier than before and will therefore lead to the decrease in imports to *R"M* at the new exchange rate *OR*". With this the Indian exports of goods and services exceed its imports by the amount *MT*. Thus, there will be surplus in balance of payments on current account of India which will be equal to the capital outflows. We thus reach an important conclusion that *surplus on current account of the balance of payments implies that there will be capital outflows of that order*.

PURCHASING POWER PARITY THEORY

No country today is rich enough to have a free gold standard, not even the U.S.A. All countries have now paper currencies and these paper currencies of the various countries are not convertible into gold or other valuable things. Therefore, these days various countries have paper currency standards. The exchange situation is difficult in such cases. In such circumstances the ratio of exchange between the two currencies is determined by their respective purchasing powers.

The purchasing power parity theory was propounded by Professor Gustav Cassel of Sweden. According to this theory, rate of exchange between two countries depends upon the relative purchasing power of their respective currencies. Such will be the rate which equates the two purchasing powers. For example, if a certain assortment of goods can be had for £1 in Britain and a similar assortment with Rs. 80 in India, then it is clear that the purchasing power of £1 is equal to the purchasing power of Rs. 80. Thus, the rate of exchange, according to purchasing power parity theory, will be £1 = Rs. 80.

Let us take another example. Suppose in the USA one $ purchases a given collection of commodities. In India, same collection of goods costs 45 rupees. Then rate of exchange will tend to be

$1 = 45 rupees.

Now, suppose the price levels in the two countries remain the same but somehow market exchange rate moves to

$1 = 46 rupees.

This means that in USA one US$ can purchase commodities worth 45 rupees. It will pay people to convert dollars into rupees at the exchange rate, ($1 = Rs. 46), purchase the given collection of commodities in India for 45 rupees and sell them in U.S.A. for one dollar again, making a profit of 1 rupee per dollar worth of transactions. This will create a large demand for rupees in the USA while supply thereof will be less because very few people would export commodities from USA to India. The value of the rupee in terms of the dollar will move up until it will reach $1 = 45 rupees. At that point, imports from India will not give abnormal profits. $1 = 45 rupees is called the purchasing power parity between the two countries.

Thus while the value of the unit of one currency in terms of another currency is determined at any particular time by the market conditions of demand and supply, in the long run the exchange rate is determined by the relative values of the two currencies as indicated by their respective purchasing powers over goods and services. In other words, the rate of exchange tends to rest at the point which expresses equality between the respective purchasing powers of the two currencies. This point is called the purchasing power parity. Thus, under a system of autonomous paper standards the external value of a currency is said to depend ultimately on the domestic purchasing power of that currency relative to that of another currency. In other words, exchange rates, under such a system, tend to be determined by the relative purchasing power parities of different currencies in different countries.

In the above example, if prices in India get doubled, the value of the rupee will be exactly halved. The new parity will be $1 = 90 rupees. This is because now 90 rupees will buy the same collection of commodities in India which 45 rupees did before. We suppose that prices in USA remain as before. But if prices in both countries get doubled, there will be no change in the parity.

In actual practice, however, the parity will be modified by the cost of transporting goods (including duties etc.) from one country to another.

Criticism of Purchasing Power Parity Theory

The purchasing power parity theory has been subject to the following criticisms:

The actual rates of exchange between the two countries very seldom reflect the relative purchasing powers of the two currencies. This may be due to the fact that governments have either controlled prices or controlled exchange rates or imposed restrictions on import and export of goods. Moreover, the theory is true if we consider the purchasing power of the respective currencies in terms of goods which enter into international trade and not the purchasing power of goods in general. But we know that all articles produced in a country do not figure in international trade. Therefore, the rate of exchange cannot reflect the purchasing power of goods in general. For example, in India we may be able to get a dozen shirts washed with Rs. 40, but only 2 shirts with one dollar in the USA. Obviously, the purchasing power of one dollar in the USA is much less than the purchasing power of Rs. 40 in India. This is due to the fact that *dhobis* do not form an article of international trade. If dhobis entered into international trade and freely moved into the U.S.A., then in terms of clothes washed, the purchasing power of Rs. 40 may be equalised with the purchasing power of a dollar.

Further, it is very difficult to measure purchasing power of a currency. It is usually done with the help of index numbers. But we know that the index numbers are not infallible. Among the difficulties connected with index numbers are the following important ones: (*i*) Different types of goods that enter into the calculation of index numbers; (*ii*) Many goods which may enter into domestic trade may not figure in international trade; (*iii*) Internationally traded goods also may not have the same prices in all the markets because of differences in transport costs.

Besides, the theory of purchasing power applies to a stationary world. Actually the world is not static but dynamic. Conditions relating to money and prices, tariffs, etc., constantly go on changing and prevent us from arriving at any stable conclusion about the rates of exchange. The internal prices and the cost of production are constantly changing. Therefore, a new equilibrium between the two currencies is almost daily called for. As Cassel observes, "differences in two countries' economic situation, particularly in regard to transport and customs, may cause the normal exchange rate to deviate to a certain extent from the quotient of the currencies intrinsic purchasing powers." If a country raises its tariffs, the exchange value of its currency will rise but its price level will remain the same.

Besides, many items of balance of payments like insurance and banking transactions and capital movements are very little affected by changes in general price levels. But these items do influence exchange rates by acting upon the supply of and the demand for foreign currencies. The Purchasing Power Parity Theory ignores these influences altogether. Further, the theory, as propounded by Cassel, says that changes in price level bring about changes in exchange rates but changes in exchange rates do not cause any change in prices. This latter part is not true, for exchange movements do exercise some influence on internal prices.

The purchasing power parity theory compares the general price levels in two countries without making any provision for distinction being drawn between the price level of domestic goods and that of the internationally traded goods. The prices of internationally-traded goods will tend to be the same in all countries (transport costs are, of course omitted). Domestic prices on the other hand, will be different in the two countries, even between two areas of the same country.

The purchasing power parity theory assumes that there is a direct link between the purchasing power of currencies and the rate of exchange. But in fact there is no direct relation between the two.

Exchange rate can be influenced by many other considerations such as tariffs, speculation and capital movements.

According to Keynes, there are two basic defects in the purchasing power parity theory, *viz.* (*i*) it does not take into consideration the elasticities of reciprocal demand, and (*ii*) it ignores the influences of capital movements. In Keynes's view, foreign exchange rates are determined not only by the price movements but also by capital movements, the elasticities of reciprocal demand and many other forces affecting the demand for and supply of foreign exchange. "By elasticity of reciprocal demand is meant the responsiveness of one country's demand for another country's exports with respect to price or income." As for price elasticity, generally speaking, greater the proportion of luxuries and semi-luxuries in the exports demanded, the more elastic will be the country's demand for another country's exports. It will also be more elastic, when there is a greater number of alternative markets in which to buy and greater the capacity to produce the effective substitutes for goods imported. As for the income elasticity of demand for imports, changes in demand for goods and services and in the derived demand for foreign exchange is functionally related to the changes in national income. How far is a country's demand for another's exports responsive to a change in national income, will influence the rate of exchange. In other words, it is the character of the propensity to import out of a given income, that is, supposed to affect the exchange rate independently of international price movements. Technological improvement adding to the productivity of the country and making its goods cheaper and better, tariff changes and exports subsidies affect exchange rates via their influence upon reciprocal demand quite independently of international price movements.

Capital movements, both short-term and long-term, are the other important influences. There is hot money flying from a country trying to make profits or avoid loss on exchange fluctuations and there is a 'refugee capital' seeking safely and security abroad. An actual or expected change in the domestic price of a foreign currency may lead to inflow or outflow of 'hot money' causing a further change in the exchange rate without there being price changes in either country. The inflow tends to raise the exchange value of the currency of the capital receiving country and outflow will lower it. Long-term movement of capital also has a similar effect.

In view of the defects pointed out above the purchasing power parity theory does not offer an adequate or satisfactory explanation of fluctuations in the rates of exchange. The determination of the exchange rate depends not only on international price relations but on many other factors as mentioned above. This leads to a more adequate explanation of the determination of foreign exchange rates through demand for and supply of foreign exchange viz. balance of payments theory. This theory has been explained above.

EFFECTS OF CHANGES IN EXCHANGE RATE (DEPRECIATION OR DEVALUATION) ON THE ECONOMY

Under the recent economic reforms in India, not only have we liberalised the Industrial sector but have also opened up the economy, made our currency convertible and allowed exchange rate to adjust freely. It is important to understand the full implications of opening up the economy and allowing our currency to 'float'.

It is worthwhile to note that under a fixed exchange rate system when citizens of a country spend some of their income on imports, it reduces the value of multiplier because imports, like savings and taxes, serve as a leakage from the circular flow of income. On the other hand, exports, like investment and Government expenditure, raise the aggregate demand for domestically produced goods and services and thereby cause an expansion in output through a multiplier process.

However, under a variable or floating exchange rate system, the effect of imports and exports on real output is highly complicated. First, the volume of imports and exports depends not only on income, price level, interest rate but also on the exchange rates themselves. Thus when due to some factors, foreign exchange rate changes, it will have an effect on the level of GNP and the price level. Further, exchange rates themselves will adjust to the changes in the economy. We discuss below the effects of changes in the exchange rate, especially of depreciations and devaluation of the exchange rate, on exports, imports, national income, balance of payments and the price level in the economy.

Effects of Depreciation (or Devaluation) on Imports, Exports and Real National Income

From our foregoing discussion of determination of exchange rate through demand and supply curves of foreign exchange it follows that when a currency of a country, say Indian rupee, depreciates as a result of demand and supply conditions or is devalued by the Government, the prices of Indian exports in terms of foreign currency (say dollar) will fall. This will cause the increase in quantity demanded of Indian exports. As a result, Indian exports will increase. On the other hand, depreciation or devaluation of Indian rupee will make the imports from foreign countries more expensive in terms of rupees (for example, a dollar's worth of US goods will cost more in terms of the Indian rupee) when the Indian rupee depreciates or is devalued. Thus, higher prices of imports will induce individuals and firms in India to import less and they will make an attempt to substitute domestically produced goods for imports from abroad. Thus, *as a result of depreciation or devaluation and consequently increase in exports and decline in imports, the net aggregate demand for domestically produced goods will increase.* And if level of output, especially industrial output is lower because of demand recession, the increase in net aggregate demand or increase in expenditure on domestic output will cause expansion in output and is therefore likely to increase GNP or real national income. A *devaluation or depreciation can therefore serve as a stimulus to the economy.*

This is illustrated in Fig. 35.5(c) where increase in net exports as a result of depreciation causes aggregate demand curve to shift from AD_0 to AD_1. It will be seen from figure 35.5(c) that given the short-run aggregate supply curve *SAS*, this leads to the increase in real GDP to by Y_0Y_1 and price level rises from P_0 to P_1.

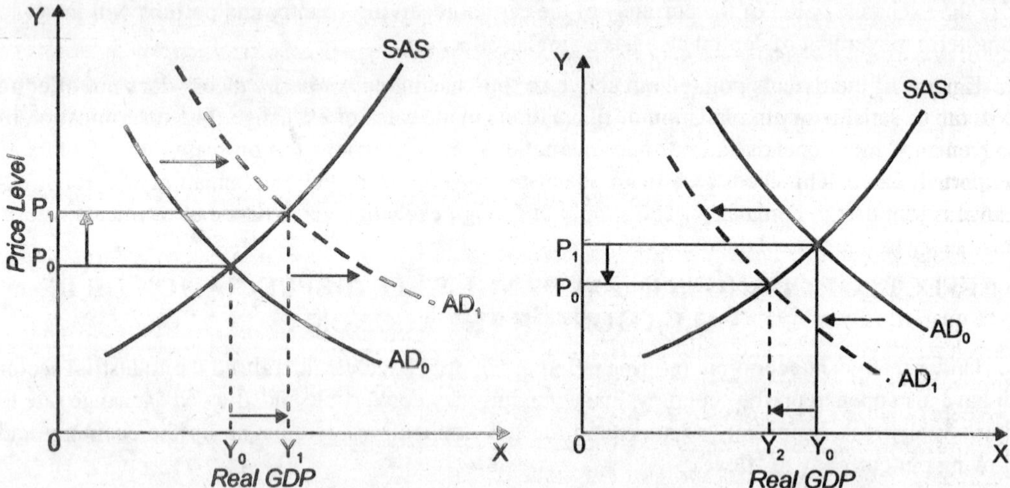

Fig. 35.5(c). *Depreciation causes net exports to rise which leads to the increase in both GDP and price level.*

Fig. 35.5(d). *Appreciation of national currency causes fall in net exports and leads to decline in both GDP and price level.*

It will be recalled that in the Keynesian model of determination of real national income (GNP), the effect of net exports, that is, *X–M*, where *X* denotes value of exports and *M* denotes value of imports, is similar to investment in its effect on national income. Both raise national income through a multiplier process. It may be noted here that because of the favourable effect of depreciation or

devaluation of currency on exports, imports and real GNP, the countries are tempted at times to intervene in the foreign exchange market, devalue their currency to provide stimulus to their economies. However, if one country devalues its currency to stimulate its economy, the other countries can also do so. Now, when all countries attempt to devalue their currencies, there will be no gain in real income for any of them. Such a situation actually occurred during the early years of Great Depression (1929-33). In their attempt to maintain their exports and protect their level of income and employment, many countries devalued their currencies without bothering about its adverse effects on the economies of the other countries. Such policies of competitive devaluation are generally called **"beggar thy-neighbour"** policies. Since all followed this beggar thy-neighbour policy, no one could maintain their export sales and protect domestic employment and level of economic activity which were badly hurt by the severe depression that gripped their economies.

On the contrary, the appreciation of a national currency will have opposite effect. When the currency of a country appreciates, its exports will become costlier causing a decline in them, whereas its imports will become cheaper resulting in increase in them. As a result, net exports of the country will decline leading to the decrease in net exports and will therefore cause leftward shift in the aggregate demand curve *AD* as is shown in Fig. 35.(*d*). This will cause fall in both real GDP and price level.

Devaluation and the Balance of Trade: The J Curve

As explained above, lowering of the value of a currency of a country tends to raise its exports by making its goods cheaper for foreigners. On the other hand, devaluation or depreciation makes the imports from abroad expensive in terms of domestic currency (rupees in case of India) and therefore the imports tend to fall. *With exports increasing and imports declining, it is expected that devaluation (depreciation) will reduce a country's trade deficit.* As a matter of fact, in recent years when a country experienced a severe disequilibrium in the balance of trade or balance of payments, it devaluated its currency to raise exports and reduce imports and thus to restore equilibrium in the balance of payments. However, it may be noted that the effect of devaluation or depreciation on balance of trade is ambiguous and quite uncertain because a good deal depends on the price elasticity of exports and imports of a country. For example, if the *price-elasticity of exports* in terms of a foreign currency of a country is less than unity, the value of exports in terms of a forcign currency will fall as increase in physical volume of exports will be more than offset by the depreciation of the currency. On the other hand, if the demand for imports is inelastic, they will not decrease despite devaluation.

Many economists are of the view that devaluation is likely to worsen the balance of trade for the few quarters (probably three to six) after the initial devaluation. However, they think after a time lag, the balance of trade may improve. In fact, a concept called *J. Curve effect* has been put forward. According to this, after the initial depreciation the balance of trade moves according to the shape of the letter *J*. This means that in the first few quarters following devaluation the balance of trade becomes worse and after that it becomes positive and starts improving. This *J*-curve effect is shown in Fig. 35.6 where along the X-axis we measure time, that is, quarters after devaluation and on the Y-axis we measure the balance of trade. If the value of

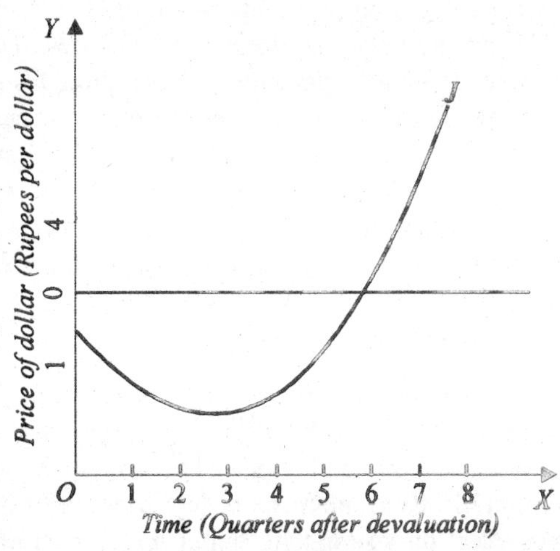

Fig. 35.6. *The Effect of Devaluation on the Balance of Trade : The J Curve*

balance of trade is positive, that is, if the balance of trade lies above the zero line and the curve rises the balance of trade improves. If the balance of trade is negative, it will be below the zero line and if the curve slopes down, it implies that balance of trade worsens. It will be seen from Fig. 35.6 that in the first few quarters, the balance of trade remains negative and also deteriorating and then starts improving and ultimately in the long run turns positive.

Now, pertinent question arises how the *J*-curve comes about. We will explain this with reference to devaluation (depreciation) of rupee. It may be recalled here that balance of trade is equal to the value of exports minus value of imports. Thus;

Balance of Trade = Value of Exports in Rupees – Value of Imports in Rupees

It may be noted that value of both exports and imports is equal to the volume of exports or imports multiplied by the rupee price of exports and imports respectively. The depreciation (devaluation) of the currency affects both the volume and rupee price of exports and imports. First, depreciation (devaluation) of currency increases the volume of exports and reduces the volume of imports, both of which have a favourable effect on the balance of trade, that is, they will lower the trade deficit or increase the trade surplus. This has been explained above. Secondly, as a result of devaluation, rupee-price of exports is not likely to change much in the short run. The rupee-price of exports depends on the domestic price level and, in the short run, the devaluation (depreciation) of rupee will have only a very small effect on the domestic price level. On the other hand, the rupee-price of imports increases immediately after devaluation. Imports into India from abroad would be more costly because as a result of devaluation a hundred rupee note will buy fewer US dollars and pound sterlings than before. Thus, *a rise in the rupee-price of imports has a negative effect on the balance of trade*, that is, it will tend to increase the trade deficit or reduce the trade surplus.

Price effect and Quantity Effect of devaluation. An example will make clear the negative effect of depreciation or devaluation on the balance of trade as a result of devaluation or depreciation. Suppose the rupee cost of a particular US machine goes up from Rs. 50,000 to 60,000 following the devaluation of rupee from Rs. 46 per dollar to Rs. 44 per dollar. Thus with the rise in price of a US machine, Indians *will spend more* on a US machine than before. This is a *price effect*. But increase in the price of the US machine will lead to *the decrease in the quantity demanded* of US machines by the Indians. This is the *quantity effect*. Now, the net effect of devaluation on the *value of imports* depends on whether quantity effect is larger than price effect or vice versa. And this depends on the price elasticity of imports. It therefore follows that net effect of devaluation (depreciation) on the balance of trade could go either way. The historical experience shows that initially the negative effect predominates. This is because whereas the effect of devaluation/depreciation on the price of imports is quite fast, it takes some time for quantity of imports to decline in response to the rise in rupee-price of imports and the value of exports to increase in response to the fall in price of exports in terms of foreign currency. According to the *J-Curve Effect*, the initial effect of devaluation/depreciation on the balance of trade is negative and when in the long run imports and exports adjust to the changes in prices, the net effect on the balance of trade becomes positive. The more price elastic is the demand for exports and imports, the greater the improvement in the balance of trade in the long run.

Devaluation and Inflation

The devaluation or depreciation of currency tends to raise the price level in the country and thus increase the rate of inflation. This happens because of two reasons. As a result of depreciation/devaluation, prices of imported goods rise. In case of imports of consumer goods rise in their prices directly leads to the increase in the rate of inflation. In case of imports of capital goods and raw materials, the rise in their import prices will not only directly raise the price level but as they are used as inputs in the production of other goods, rise in their imports prices will also push up the cost of production of these other goods and thus will bring about cost-push inflation.

Second, as explained above, depreciation makes the exports cheaper and therefore more competitive in the world markets. This causes the exports of goods to increase and reduces the supply and availability of goods in the domestic market which tends to raise the domestic price level. Besides, due to higher prices of imported goods, people of a country tend to substitute domestically produced goods for the now more expensive imports. As a result, the aggregate demand or expenditure on domestically produced goods and services will increase causing either expansion in output of goods or rise in their prices or both. However, if the economy is working close to the capacity output, the effect will be more on raising prices of goods.

FIXED EXCHANGE RATE AND THE BRETTON WOODS SYSTEM

Until a few years ago, there was fixed exchange rate system introduced during the last year of the Second World War. This fixed exchange rates system under Bretton Woods System of foreign exchange is known as the Bretton Woods System as a group of economists from the United States and Europe met at the Bretton Woods, a town in New Hampshire to devise this system. According to the agreement made there, an international organisation, called *International Monetary Fund* (IMF) was set up to administer the new fixed exchange rates system. According to the rules framed under the agreement, the USA was to fix a parity or par value for its dollar *in terms of gold,* whereas other countries were required to fix parities for their currencies *in terms of dollars*. Since US dollar was tied to gold, the currencies of other countries with fixed exchange rate with US dollar automatically got pegged (that is, fixed) with a certain gold value. The Government of the USA made a commitment to maintain the convertibility between dollar and gold at a fixed rate, whereas other countries agreed to maintain the convertibility of their currencies with US dollar. The USA fixed $35 per ounce of gold as the convertible rate. The change in these fixed exchange rates (devaluation or revaluation) was to be made with the consent of IMF in case of *fundamental disequilibrium* in the balance of payments. The Bretton Woods agreement did not define the fundamental disequilibrium but in practice it came to mean *chronic and large* deficit in the balance of payments. Therefore, when a country was experiencing a *large and persistent* deficit in balance of payments it was allowed by IMF to devalue its currency to the extent required to improve the balance of payments position. Thus, faced with the serious problem of balance of payments India devalued its rupee by 36.5 per cent in 1966. Again in July 1991, India devalued its rupee by about 20 per cent to tide over the serious foreign exchange crisis which arose due to deficit in balance of payments.

IMF maintains funds or reserves with itself which are contributed by member countries. IMF was given power to give loans to the member countries when they had short-term or temporary deficit in the balance of payments from its reserves. In case of fundamental disequilibrium its function was to advise the countries to devalue their currency to tide over the problem of deficit in balance of payments. The purpose was to achieve a relatively fixed or stable exchange rate system which was required for promotion of world trade.

It may be noted that, under Bretton Woods System, *to maintain the exchange rate at the specified level, the Governments (or their Central Banks) were to keep with themselves reserves of internationally accepted foreign currencies*. Thus gold, which in the previous years served as an international currency was substituted by reserves of foreign currencies that were widely used in international dealings. The US dollar became the important currency in which the reserves were to be kept by the other countries to maintain the exchange rate of their currency. Pound Sterlings, German Marks, Japanese Yen were also kept for this purpose.

To maintain the fixed exchange rate Bretton Woods System required the intervention by the Governments or their Central Banks. How they maintained the exchange value of their currency by using the reserves of foreign currencies is illustrated in Fig. 35.7 where the *demand and supply curves DD and SS* of US dollars are drawn. Along the *X*-axis the quantity of US dollars and on the *Y*-axis, the value of US dollar in terms of Indian rupees is measured.

Suppose the Government of India is committed to maintain the exchange rate of its currency with US $ at *OR* level which is also assumed to be the equilibrium exchange rate as determined by demand for and supply of dollars. Now, suppose due to the recessionary conditiones in the USA the demand of the USA for Indian exports greatly declines. This will reduce the supply of US dollars causing a shift to the left in the supply curve of US dollars to $S'S'$. Now, given the demand curve *DD* of dollars remaining unchanged, at the exchange rate *OR* the quantity supplied of US dollars falls to *RL* whereas the quantity demanded of dollars continues to be *RE*. As a result, the excess demand of US dollars emerges at the fixed exchange rate *OR* and if left free to the market forces, the equilibrium exchange rate *will rise to OR′ level.* That is, price of *US* dollar in terms of rupees will appreciate or in other words the Indian rupee will depreciate. *In order to maintain the exchange rate of rupee in terms of dollar, and to prevent it from depreciating, the Government or RBI must sell US dollars from its foreign exchange reserves to increase the supply of US dollars in the masket.* This is how the exchange rates of different countries remained fixed despite the frequent changes in demand for and supply of their currencies.

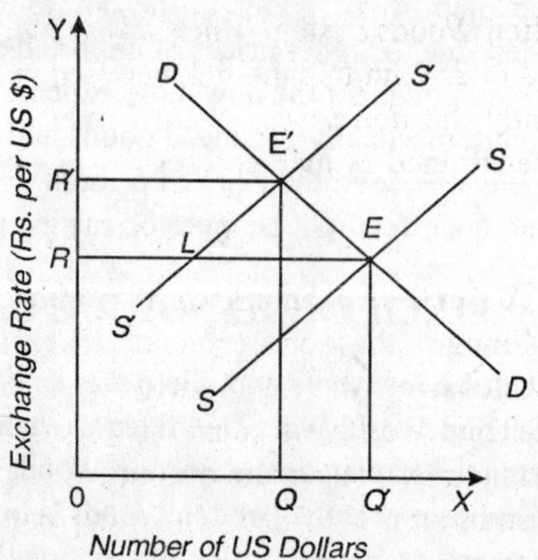

Fig. 35.7. *Government Intervention to Maintain the Exchange Rate at the Fixed Level*

Collapse of the Bretton Woods System

Fixed exchange rate system under the Bretton Woods arrangement came under heavy pressure during the sixities and it ultimately collapsed in the early seventies. As seen above, under the Bretton Woods System the US dollar became internationally accepted currency in which reserves of the countries were kept for international transactions. Before the Bretton Woods System gold was accepted as international medium of exchange. Under the Bretton Woods System, the US dollar also assumed the role of international currency for three reasons. First, after World War II, the United States emerged as the strongest economy. Secondly, the United States had accumulated a large stock of gold. Thirdly, during 1934 and 1971, the United States had been following the policy of selling and buying gold to other countries at a fixed exchange rate of $35 per ounce. As under the Bretton Woods System, the dollar was converted into gold at a fixed rate (that is, $35 per ounce), it was considered '*as good as gold*'.

Since the World's supply of gold did not increase adequately to meet the requirements of rapidly expanding international trade and finance, the dollar increasingly became the world currency in which international reserves were kept by various countries. But a serious problem arose which caused the demise of Bretton Woods system. The United States had a large and persistent deficit in balance of payments during the fifties and sixities. To meet these deficits, the US used its gold reserves for making payments to other countries, especially Germany and Japan. Obviously, this could not go on for ever because its gold reserves would have eventually run out. In fact, this was the big flaw in the fixed exchange rate system adopted under the Bretton Woods arrangement. Further, as a result of surplus balance of payments with the United States, other countries, especially Germany and Japan, acquired not only gold but also a large quantity of the dollars from the US which were kept as reserves.

With the passage of time reserves of dollars and gold held by other countries increased very much while the reserves of gold with USA declined a great deal, the doubts arose about the ability of the USA to fulfil its commitments of converting dollars into gold at the agreed exchange rate of $35 per ounce. Widespread fears emerged that there would be run on the dollar, that is, countries holding dollars would *en masse* try to exchange dollars for gold. If it had actually happened it would have greatly hurt the international trade and finance. Therefore, in view of the large and persistent deficit in balance of payments, it was decided by the US Government to withdraw convertibility of dollar into gold at the rate of $35 per ounce on August 15, 1971. This brought about the collapse of the Bretton Woods System which was supported by the US commitment to convert dollar into gold at a fixed rate. With this the link between gold and international value of the dollar ended and consequently the *dollar was floated*, that is, permitted its exchanged rate with other currencies to be determined by market forces.

FIXED AND FLEXIBLE EXCHANGE RATES

A study of economic history shows that three different exchange rate systems have been prevailing in the world economy. The first exchange rate system, popularly called *Gold Standard* prevailed over 1879-1934 period with the exception of World War I years. Under the gold standard, currencies of different countries were tied to gold (that is, the value of currency of each country was fixed in terms of a certain quantity of gold). With this the exchange rate between different countries got automatically fixed. Thus, the gold standard represented fixed exchange rate system. As explained above, from the end of World War II to 1971, another fixed exchange rate system, generally known as Bretton Woods System prevailed. Under this the US dollar was tied to a certain quantity of gold and the currencies of other countries were tied to dollar or in some countries directly to gold. However, as seen above, in 1971 due to large and persist deficit in balance of payments of the United States. Bretton Woods system also broke down. Since then, the *flexible* or what is also called *floating exchange rate system* has been existing. But even in this flexible or floating exchange rates the Government (or the Central Bank) of the countries intervenes to keep the international value of their currencies (i.e., exchanges rate) within certain limits. Therefore, even in the post 1971 period, the exchange rate system is not *purely* flexible and has therefore been called **Managed Float System**. We discuss below the merits and demerits of the fixed and flexible exchange rate system.

Merits of Fixed Exchange Rate System

Exchange Rate Stability. In defence of fixed exchange rate system, it has been pointed out that it ensures stability in exchange rate. Exchange rate stability, it is said, is necessary for orderly development of the international economy and rapid growth of world trade. If the exchange rate is unstable or variable, the exporters will not be certain about the price they would receive for the goods to be exported by them; the importers will not be certain about the price and the payments they have to make for their imports. These uncertainties involve risks for exporters and importers. This greatly harms the growth of world trade. Thus, the chief merit of fixed exchange rate system is that it eliminates the possibilities of such uncertainties and associated risks and thereby promotes foreign trade.

It is important to note that for the developing countries a stable or fixed exchange rate system has a special advantage. This is because the developing countries have a large and persistent balance of payment deficits. As a consequence, if the exchange rate is flexible and not fixed, due to these large persistent deficits, the exchange rate or international value of their currencies will be continuously falling. Thus fixed exchange rate system prevents this continuous tendency for the depreciation of their currencies.

Promotes Capital Movements. Another advantage of fixed exchange rate is that it facilitates capital movement by private firms. A stable currency does not involve any uncertainties about capital loss on account of changes in exchange rate. Therefore, fixed exchange rate system would attract foreign capital investments. Foreign private firms would not be interested in making investment in those countries whose currency is not stable. Since foreign investment is an important source of economic growth, the fixed exchange rate system would promote rapid economic growth of the developing countries.

Prevents Capital Outflow. Further, flexible and unstable exchange rates may at times of difficult economic situation may encourage *flight of capital*, as happened in case of Mexico a few years ago causing a serious balance of payments problem. On the other hand, a stable exchange rate ensures that such capital outflow would not occur.

Prevents Speculation in Foreign Exchange Market. Another important merit of fixed exchange rate system is that it does away with speculation in foreign exchange markets. The advocates of fixed exchange rate system points out that the flexible and unstable exchange rate encourages speculation in foreign exchange market. The operators in foreign exchange market try to take advantage of the fluctuations in exchange rate as freely determined by demand and supply forces. They try to manipulate the exchange rate through their actions of buying and selling foreign exchange and try to obtain speculative gain in this way. Ragnar Nurkse in his study of *International Currency Experience* which he conducted for the period of twenties found that because of speculative activities, flexible exchange rate had a destabilising influence. It caused greater fluctuations than would have been the case otherwise. By eliminating speculation fixed exchange rate system ensures stability in the exchange rate.

Serves as an anchor against inflation. Another important advantage of fixed exchange rate system is that it prevents the Government of the countries from adopting inflationary policies. Generally, Governments have often been tempted to pursue undue expansionary fiscal and monetary policies to lower unemployment and create boom conditions. However, inflation has several bad effects for the economies. It increases inequalities of income and wealth and hurts the poor most. Further, inflation hampers economic growth in the long run. Fixed exchange rate system forces the Governments to achieve price stability by taking effective anti-inflationary measures. This is because in the case of fixed exchange rate, inflation will cause balance of payments deficits and result in loss of international reserves. Therefore, this forces the Government to adopt measures to check inflationary pressures in the economy. To quote B. Soderston, "Fixed exchange rates can serve as an anchor. Inflation will cause balance of payments deficits and losses in reserves. Hence the authorities will have to take counter measures to stop inflation. Fixed exchange rates should therefore impose a discipline on governments and stop them from pursuing inflationary policies which are out of tune with the rest of the world."[1]

Promotes economic integration of the world. It has also been argued in favour of fixed exchange rate system that it is necessary for achieving economic integration of the world community. This is similar to a single common currency in a country which promotes economic integration of a nation in the sense that it facilitates communication, trade and free movement of finance between different regions of a country. It ensures free competition among all producers and consumers of various countries. Similarly, a common currency would promote economic integration of the world. Fixed exchange rate between the currencies of the various countries approximately serves the purpose of a single currency between diferent countries. Thus, fixed exchange rates among different currencies is a necessary condition for the purpose of *forming economic union* between various countries, that is, forming a regional grouping. To enjoy the advantages of economic unity in recent years, there is a proposal for issuing a single currency for European countries to strengthen the economic integration of European countries.

Promotes growth of internal money and capital markets. Another big advantage of the fixed exchange rate system is that it promotes growth of internal money and capital markets. Since flexible exchange rates cause uncertainties about the future exchange rates, individuals, companies and institutions are reluctant to lend to and borrow from the internal money and capital markets.

In view of the above advantages, a fixed exchange rate system prevailed for a long time from 1944 to 1971. As we have seen above that the Bretton Woods aggreement adopted a fixed exchange

1. B.Soderston, *International Economics*, 2nd edition, Macmillan, 1980, p. 402.

rate system because of the above mentioned merits, IMF permitted a change in the exchange rate only in case of fundamental disequlibrium in the balance of payments.

Demerits and Problems of Fixed Exchange Rates

Fixed exchange rate had however a great flaw in that the countries with a large and persistent balance of payments deficits were losing gold and other foreign assets. This could not go on forever as evidently stock of gold and foreign currencies would have run out. That is why the USA abandoned Bretton Woods System which represented fixed exchange rate system. The other countries facing problem of balance of payment deficit found their international reserves dwindling which forced them to devalue their currency. The devaluation has an inflationary potential.

On the other hand, under the fixed exchange rates, the countries with a balance of payments surplus will be providing its national currency and in return it will receive foreign currencies and assets such as US dollar, pounds, gold. The increase in foreign assets would lead to the expansion in money supply which is likely to create inflationary pressures in the economy. But remember an important difference between the countries with balance of payments deficits and the countries having balance of payment surplus. Whereas due to depletion of reserves of gold and foreign currencies, the countries with deficit balance of payments are forced to *devalue* their currency to overcome the deficit, the countries with a balance of payments surplus generally do not *revalue* their currency for the fear that it would discourage exports. Instead, the countries with surplus BoP face the problem of inflation and try to tackle it with other policies.

Another problem with the fixed exchange rate system is that *at what level exchange rate should be fixed.* If the exchange rate of a foreign currency with a national currency is fixed or pegged at the equilibrium level, that is, at the rate at which its quantity demanded equals quantity supplied, no problem arises. However, for the Government it is difficult to find such an equilibrium exchange rate of a foreign currency in terms of the national currency. Further, as underlying conditions change as they do so frequently, the equilibrium exchange rate will also change giving rise to the problems. If the exchange rate of a foreign currency in terms of the national currency is fixed at a lower level, there will be deficit in the balance of payments (BoP). On the other hand, if the exchange rate of a foreign currency in terms of the national currency is fixed at a higher than the equilibrium level, there will be surplus in balance of payments (BoP). Consider Fig. 35.8, where demand and supply curves of dollars respectively for India at various prices of a dollar in terms of rupees are drawn ₹ 45.50 to a dollar is the equilibrium

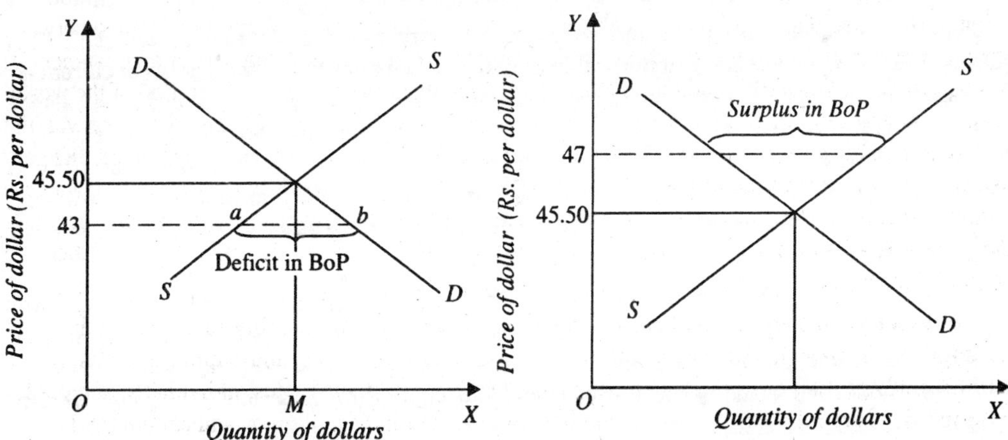

Fig. 35.8. *Overvaluation of a Currency Cuasing Deficit in BoP.*

Fig. 35.9. *Undervaluation of a Currency Leading to the Problem of surplus in BoP.*

exchange rate. If the Government or Reserve Bank of India fixes the exchange rate at ₹ 43 to a dollar as the exchange rate, the quantity demanded of dollars by Indians would exceed the quantity supplied so that there would be deficit in India's balance of payments. This means that at ₹ 43 to a dollar *Indian rupee is overvalued.* As a result, India's stock of foreign exchange (*i.e.*, dollars) and other foreign assets will decline. Sooner or later India will be forced to take policy measures to correct this deficit in BoP. India will have to adopt contractionary fiscal and monetary policies to reduce the aggregate expenditure in the economy so that imports decrease or it will impose various restrictions on imports to reduce them. To reduce persistent deficit in BoP, it may even resort to devaluation.

Now, consider Fig. 35.9 if the Government fixes the exchange rate of ₹ 47 to a dollar, the quantity supplied of dollars by other countries would exceed the quantity demanded by the Indians. As will be seen from Fig. 35.9, this causes *surplus in balance of payments* (BoP). This implies that at ₹ 47 to a dollar, the *Indian rupee is under-valued* (or, which is the same thing, *dollar is overvalued* in terms of rupees). Historical experience shows that countries with surplus in BoP have been reluctant to *revalue* their currency (that is, to raise the international value of their currency). Thus, a *surplus in balance of payments also gives rise to a problem.* As a result of this surplus India will accumulate dollars (*i.e.*, foreign exchange) for which it would pay rupees, the national currency. The new rupee notes would be printed to pay for dollars. Thus, surplus in BoP leads to the expansion in money supply generating inflationary pressures in the Indian economy. To check inflation, the Indian Government might therefore take steps to eliminate the surplus in BoP by encouraging imports or restricting exports. Further, it may try to take steps to neutralise the impact of surplus in BoP on expansion in money supply. For this purpose, it might encourage *capital outflow* (*i.e.*, investment abroad) by private firms or provide financial assistance to other countries on a scale which is considered undesirable by its people.

In view of the above drawbacks and problems the fixed exchange rate has been given up despite its various advantages explained above.

Merits of Flexible Exchange Rates

Under the flexible exchange rate system, exchange rate between different currencies, like the prices of commodities are freely determined by market forces, that is, by demand and supply forces. With the change in economic conditions underlying demand and supply, the exchange rate will automatically change without any intervention by the Government. That is why, it is called flexible or variable exchange rate system. It has the following merits.

Problems of undervaluation and overvaluation are avoided. The advocates of flexible exchange rates contend that under it the problems of undervaluation and overvaluation of currencies which are found in the fixed exchange rate system are avoided. Whenever there is deficit in balance of payments implying overvaluation of the national currency under the flexible exchange rates, it will depreciate (that is, its value will fall) which on the one hand will make exports cheaper and thereby encourage them and on the other will make the imports costlier than before which will tend to discourage them. Thus, increase in exports and decline in imports as a result of depreciation will lead to the automatic correction in the balance of payments.

On the other hand, whenever there is surplus in the balance of payments, the exchange rate will appreciate which will tend to reduce exports and raise imports. This again will tend to automatically restore the balance of payments equilibrium. This is how the flexible exchange system works to ensure the equilibrium in the balance of payments. To quote Prof. Soderston, "The same factors

2. See Miltion Friedman, 'The Case for flexible Exchange Rate', AEA, *Readings in International Economics*, Vol. XI.
3. *Ibid.*

which under the fixed rates give rise to deficits and surpluses in the balance of payments would under floating rates make the exchange rate depreciate or appreciate. Thereby equilibrium would be preserved and the Government could be freed from consideration regarding external balance".

Promotes growth of multilateral Trade. The advocates of flexible exchange rates system are strongly of the view that as unlike fixed exchange rates system, this does not create serious and difficult problems, it will ensure rapid growth of multilateral world trade.[2] Further, they point out that promotion of world trade under the flexible exchange rates would not interfere in any way the adoption of policies to achieve domestic economic stability.[3]

Flexible exchange rates does not necessarily show large fluctuations. It has been pointed out in defence of the flexible exchange rates that the problems of undervalued or overvalued currency found under the fixed exchange rate regime are not found in the flexible exchange rate system. Further, it is contended that exchange rates being flexible does not necessarily mean there will be large fluctuations in them. Even under flexible exchange system there need not be large fluctuations in exchange rates. According to them, changes in exchange rates will occur only when economic conditions underlying demand for and supply of foreign currencies change. Further, according to them, random fluctuations around the normal exchange rates would be smoothened out through operations by private speculators. Thus, according to Soderston "if the currency appreciated above its equilibrium value, if its price fell in terms of foreign currency, speculators would buy the currency; and if it depreciated, speculators would sell the currency. Thereby they would smooth out fluctuations and help to keep the exchange rate stable. If the underlying conditions changed, however the price of foreign exchange would also change."

It ensures individual freedom. The system of floating exchange rate is advocated on the basis of philosophy that Government should intervene in the economy as little as possible and the individuals should be left free to pursue their economic interests. It has been noted above, the alternative to floating exchange rates system is the fixed exchange rates which require controls and restrictions which are implemented by experts who generally do not work under effective democratic controls. Generally, they fix the exchange rate out of consideration for other than economic objectives, for example for the purpose of retaining a certain market structure or influencing income distribution.

It frees government from problems of balance of payments. A great merit of flexible exchange rates is that it frees the Government from problems of balance of payments. As has been seen above, the fixed exchange rates system leads either to deficit or surplus in balance of payments. Under this system the Government remains preoccupied with the questions of devaluation or revaluation of their currencies. Since floating exchange rates work automatically to restore balance of payments equilibrium, the Government need not pay any attention to the balance of payments. Instead, the Governments can concentrate on solving their domestic problems of economic stability, inflation and unemployment. "Flexible exchange rates should therefore give an increased freedom both to individuals and countries to pursue whatever aims they have for their economic policies."[4]

Demerits of Flexible Exchange Rates System

Flexible exchange rates system is also not without shortcomings. It has been opposed on some important grounds. We briefly explain below some important arguments given against flexible exchange rates.

1. Flexible Exchange Rates Create a Situation of Instability and Uncertainty. An important argument against flexible exchange rates is that too frequent fluctuations in exchange rate under it create uncertainty about the exact amount of receipts and payments in foreign exchange transac-

---

4. B. Soderston, *op. cit.*
5. Milton Friedman, *op. cit*

tions. *This instability hampers foreign trade and capital movements between the countries.* However, Friedman does not accept this charge against flexible exchange rates. He argues that flexible exchange rate is not necessarily an unstable exchange rate. According to him, it is the underlying economic conditions determining foreign trade that often change causing changes in the foreign exchange rate and for this the flexible exchange rates should not be blamed.

2. Dampening Effect on Foreign Trade. Under the flexible exchange rates, the price of foreign exchange or international value of the national currency is quite uncertain. As a result, they are unable to take proper decisions regarding exports and imports of goods. Obviously, this has a dampening effect on the volume and growth of foreign trade. However, Friedman does not agree with this and points out that traders can always protect themselves against risks arising out of the changes in the exchange rate by hedging in the future market.[5] However, Soderston has challenged this view of Friedman and points out that no markets exist today that can protect traders against risks arising out of flexible exchange rates.[6]

It may however be noted that from the empirical evidence since 1971 when exchange rates have been flexible, it does not appear that flexible exchange rates have a dampening effect on the growth of foreign trade. In fact, the growth of world trade since 1971 has been fairly good.

3. Widespread Speculation with a Destabilising Effect. The system of flexible exchange rates has been opposed on the ground that under it there is widespread speculation regarding exchange rates of currencies which has a large destabilising effect on these rates. Friedman, on the other hand, contend that *speculation has a stabilising influence on exchange rates*. However, whether or not speculation has a destablising or stabilising effect is a highly controversial issue in economics which has so far remained unresolved.

4. Provides an Inflationary Bias to an Economy. Another shortcoming of the flexible, exchange rates is that they have an inflationary impact on the economy. It has been pointed out that whenever due to deficit in balance of payments, the currency depreciates, the prices of imports go up. The higher prices of imported materials raise the prices of industrial products and thus generate cost-push inflation. However, in defence of flexible exchange rates, it has been pointed out that when demand for imports decline due to appreciation of national currency, the *foreign suppliers are compelled to reduce their prices* to protect markets. Through this reduction in prices in the face of declining demand is theoretically possible, it may not happen in actual practice.

To sum up, there are merits and demerits of flexible exchange rate system. Whether a flexible exchange rate systems suits an economy depends on circumstances. It depends on characteristics of the economy which adopts flexible exchange rate system. Further, it may be noted that since 1971 when Bretton Woods System representing the fixed exchange rate system was abandoned, it is not perfectly free flexible exchange rate system that has been adopted. Instead, it is what is called *Managed Float System* that has been prevailing. Under the managed float system, the exchange rates are flexible, that is, they change as a result of changes in demand and supply of currencies, but the Government or Central Bank intervenes through demand and supply to keep the variations in exchange rate within certain limits so as to ensure stability and certainty of the foreign exchange rates.

CURRENCY CONVERTIBILITY

For the rapid growth of world trade and capital flows between countries convertibility of a currency is desirable. Without free and unrestricted convertibility of currencies into foreign exchange trade and capital flows between countries cannot take place smoothly. Therefore, to achieve higher rate of economic growth and thereby to improve living standards through greater trade and capital flows, the need for convertibility of currencies of different nations has been greatly felt. Under Bretton Woods system fixed exchange rate system was adopted by various countries. In order to maintain the exchange rate of their currencies in terms of dollar or gold various countries imposed

6. B. Soderston, *op. cit.*, p. 303.

several controls over the use of foreign exchange. This required some restrictions on the use of foreign exchange and its allocation among different uses, the currency of a nation was converted into foreign exchange on the basis of officially fixed exchange rate.

When Bretton Woods system collapsed in 1971, the various countries switched over to the floating foreign exchange rate system. Under the floating or flexible exchange rate system, exchange rates between different national currencies are allowed to the determined through market demand for and supply of them. However, various countries still imposed restrictions on the free convertibility of their currencies in view of their difficult balance of payment situation.

Meaning of Currency Covertibility

Let us first explain what is exactly meant by currency convertibility. By convertibility of a currency we mean currency of a country can be freely converted into foreign exchange at *market determined rate of exchange*, that is, exchange rate as determined by demand for and supply of a currency. For example, convertibility of rupee means that those who have foreign exchange (*e.g.* US dollars, Pound Sterlings etc.) can get them converted into rupees and vice-versa at the market determined rate of exchange. Under convertibility of a currency there are authorised dealers of foreign exchange which constitute foreign exchange market. The exporters and others who recieve US dollars, Pound Sterlings etc. can go to these dealers which are generally banks and get their dollars exchanged for rupees at the market determined rates of exchange. Similarly, under currency covertibility, importers and other who require foreign exchange can go to these banks dealing in foreign exchange and get rupees converted into foreign exchange.

Current Account and Capital Account Convertibility of Currency

A currency may be convertible on current account (that is, exports and imports of merchandise and invisibles) only. A currency may be convertible on both current and capital accounts. We have explained above the convertibility of a currency on current account only.

By capital account convertibility we mean that in respect of capital flows, that is, flows of portfolio capital, direct investment flows, flows of borrowed funds and dividends and interest payable on them, a currency is freely convertible into foreign exchange and vice-versa at market determined exchange rate. Thus, by convertibility of rupee on capital account means those who bring in foreign exchange for purchasing stocks, bonds in Indian stock markets or for direct investment in power projects, highways steel plants etc. can get them freely converted into rupees without taking any permission from the government. Likewise, the dividends, capital gains, interest received on purchased stock, equity etc. profits earned on direct investment get the rupees converted into US dollars, Pound Sterlings at market determined exchange rate between these currencies and repatriate them. Since capital convertibility is risky and makes foreign exchange rate more volatile, is introduced only some time after the introduction of convertibility on current account when exchange rate of currency of a country is relatively stable, deficit in balance of payments is well under control and enough foreign exchange reserves are available with the Central Bank.

Convertibility of Indian Rupee

In the seventies and eighties many countries switched over to the free convertibility of their currencies into foreign exchange. By 1990,70 countries of the world had introduced currency convertibility on current account, another 10 countries joined them in 1991.

As a part of new economic reforms initiated in 1991 rupee was made partly convertible from March 1992 under the "*Liberalised Exchange Rate Management*" scheme in which 60 per cent of all receipts on current account (*i.e.* merchandise exports and invisible receipts) could be converted freely into rupees at market determined exchange rate quoted by authorised dealers, while 40 per cent of them was to be surrendered to Reserve Bank of India at the officially fixed exchange rate. These 40 per cent exchange receipts on current account was meant for meeting Government needs for foreign exchange and for financing imports of essential commodities. Thus, partial convertibility of rupee on current account meant a *dual exchange rate system*. This partial convertibility of rupee on current account was adopted so that essential imports could be made available at lower exchange rate to ensure that their prices do not rise much. Further, full convertibility of rupees at that stage was considered to be risky in view of large deficit in balance of payments on current account.

As even after partial convertibility of rupee foreign exchange value of rupee remained stable, *full convertibility on current account* was announced in the budget for 1993-94. From March 1993, rupee was made convertible for *all trade in merchandise*. In March 1994, even indivisibles and remittances from abroad were allowed to be freely convertible into rupees at market determined exchange rate. However, on capital account rupee remained nonconvertible.

Advantages of Currency Convertibility

Convertibility of a currency has several advantages which we discuss briefly :

1. **Encouragement to exports.** An important advantage of currency convertibility is that it encourages exports by increasing their profitability. With convertibility profitablility of exports increases because market foreign exchange rate is higher than the previous officially fixed exchange rate. This implies that from given exports, exporters can get more rupees against foreign exchange (*e.g.* US dollars) earned from exports. Currency convertibility especially encourages those exports which have low import-intensity.

2. **Encouragement to import substitution**. Since free or market determined exchange rate is higher than the previous officially fixed exchange rate, imports become more expensive after convertibility of a currency. This discourages imports and give boost to import substitution.

3. **Incentive to send remittances from abroad.** Thirdly, rupee convertibility provided greater incentives to send remittances of foreign exchange by Indian workers living abroad and by NRI. further, it makes illegal remittance such '*hawala money*' and smuggling of gold less attractive.

4. **A self-balancing mechanism.** Another important merit of currency convertibility lies in its self-balancing mechanism. When balance of payments is in deficit due to over-valued exchange rate, under currency convertibility, the currency of the country depreciates which gives boost to exports by lowering their prices on the one hand and discourages imports by raising their prices on the other. In this way, deficit in balance of payments get automatically corrected without intervention by the Government or its Central bank. The opposite happens when balance of payments is in surplus due to the under-valued exchange rate.

5. **Specialisation in accordance with comparative advantage.** Another merit of currency convertibility ensures production pattern of different traditng countries in accordance with their comparative advantage and resource endowment. It is only when there is currency convertibility that market exchange rate truly reflects the purchasing powers of their currencies which is based on the prices and costs of goods found in different countries. Since prices in comeptitive environment reflect that prices of those goods are lower in which the country has a comaparative advantage, this will encourages exports. On the other hand, a country will tend to import those goods in the production of which it has a comparative disadvantage. Thus, currency convertibility ensures specialisation and international trade on the basis of comparative advantage from which all countries derive benefit.

6. **Integration of World Economy.** Finally, currency convertibility gives boost to the integration of the world economy. As under currency convertibility there is *easy access to foreign exchange*, it greatly helps the growth of trade and capital flows between the countries. The expansion in trade and capital flows between countries will ensure rapid economic growth in the economies of the world. In fact, currency convertibility is said to be a prerequisite for the success of gloabilisation.

Capital Account Convertibility of Rupee

As explained above, under Capital Account Convertibility any Indian or Indian company is entitled to move freely from the Rupee to another currency to convert Indian financial assets into foreign financial assets and back, *at an exchange rate fixed by the foreign exchange market and not by RBI.* In a way, capital account convertibility removes all the restrains on international flows on India's capital account. There is a basic difference between current account convertibility and capital account convertibility. In the case of current account convertibility, it is important to have a transaction – importing and exporting of goods,buying and selling of services, inward or outward remittances, etc. involving payment or receipt of one currency against another currency. *In the case of capital account convertibility, a currency can be converted into any other currency without any transaction.*

The Reserve Bank of India appointed in 1997 the Committee on Capital Account Convertibility with Mr. S.S. Tarapore, former Deputy Governor of RBI as its chairman. Tarapore Committee defined capital account convertibility as the freedom to convert local financial assets with foriegn financial assets and vice-versa at market determined rate of exchange. In simple language, capital account convertibility allows any one to freely move from local currency into foreign currency and back. *The purpose of capital convertibility is to give foreign investors an easy marekt to move in and* move out and to send a strong message that Indian economy was strong enough and that India had sufficient forex reserves to meet any flight of capital from the country to any extent.

The Benefits of Capital Account Convertibility

The Tarapore Committee mentioned the following benefits of capital account convertibility to India.

1.availibility of large funds to supplement domestic resources and thereby promote economic growth.

2. improved access to international financial markets and reduction in cost of capital.

3. incentive for Indians to acquire and hold international securities and assets, and

4. improvement of the financial system in the context of global competition.

Accordingly, the Tarapore Committee recommended the adoption of capital account convertibility. Under the system of capital account convertibility proposed by this committee the following features are worth mentioning :

(a) Indian companies would be allowed to issue foreign currency denominated bonds to local investors to invest in such bonds and deposits, to issue Global Deposit Receipts (GDRs) without approval of the RBI or Government to go in for external commercial borrowings within certain limits, etc.

(b) Indian residents would be permitted to have foreign currency denominated deposits with banks in India, to make financial capital transfers to other countries within certain limits, to take loans from non-relatives and others upto a ceiling of $ 1 million, etc.

(c) Indian banks would be allowed to borrow from overseas markets for short-term and long-term upto certain limits, to invest in overseas money markets, to accept deposits and extend loans denominated in foreign currency. Such facilities would be available to financial institutions and financial intermediaries also.

(d) All-India financial institutions which fulfil certain regulatory and prudential requirements would be allowed to participate in foreign exchange market along with authorised dealers (ADs) who are, at present, banks.In a later stage, certain select NBFCs would also be permitted to act as authorised dealers in foreign exchange market.

(e) Banks and financial institutions would be allowed to operate in domestic and international markets and they would also be allowed to buy and sell gold freely and offer gold denominated deposits and loans.

Preconditions for Capital Account Convertibility

The Tarapore Committee recommended that, before adopting capital account convertibility (CAC), India should fulfil three crucial pre-conditions :

(i) **Fiscal deficit** should be reduced to 3.5 per cent. The Government should also set up a Consolidated Sinking Fund (CSF) to reduce Government debt.

(ii) The Governments should fix the annual inflation target between 3 to 5 per cent. This was called *mandated inflation target* — and give full freedom to RBI to use monetary weapons to achieve the inflation target.

(iii) The Indian financial sector should be strengthened. For this, interest rates should be fully deregulated, gross non-performing assets (NPAs) should be reduced to 5 per cent, the average effective cash reserve ratio (CRR) should be reduced to 3 per cent and weak banks should either be liquidated or be merged with other strong banks.

Apart from these thee essential pre-conditions, the Tarapore Committee also recommended that :

(a) RBI should have a monitoring exchange rate band of 5 per cent around Real Effective Exchange Rate (REER) and should intereven only when the real exchange rate (RER) is outside the band :

(b) The size of the current account deficit should be within manageable limits and the debt service ratio should be gradually reduced from the present 25 per cent to 20 per cent of the export earnings :

(c) To meet import and debt service payments, forex reserves should be adequate and range between $ 22 billion and $ 32 billion; and

(d) The Government should remove all restrictions on the movement of gold.

It was generally agreed that full convertibility of the rupee, both on current account and capital account was a welcome measure and ***is necessary for closer integration of the Indian economy with the global economy***.

The major difficulty with the Tarapore Committee recommendation was that it would like the capital account convertibility to be achieved in a 3 year period – 1998 to 2000. The period was too short and the pre-conditions and the macroeconomic indicators could not be achieved in such short period. Basically, the Committee failed to appreciate the political instability in the country at that time, and the complete absence of political will and vision to carry forward the process of economic reforms and economic liberalisation. The outbreak of Asian financial crisis at this time was also responsobile for shelving the recommendation of Tarapore Committee.

Conclusion

In a speech at RBI on March 18, 2006, Prime Minister Dr. Manmohan Singh stated: "Given the changes that have taken place during the last two decades, there is merit in moving towards fuller capital account convertibility with a transparent framework... I will, therefore, request the Finance Minister and RBI to revisit the subject and come out with a roadmap based on current realities." Promptly, within two days RBI constituted the **"Comittee on Fuller Capital Account Convertibility"** with S.S. Tarapore again as chairman. This Tarapore Committee submitted its report in September 2006 (more commonly called the Second Tarapore Report).

The second Tarapore Committee had drawn up a roadmap for 2011 as the target date for fuller capital convertibility of rupee and mentioned that the conditions were quite favourable. These conditions were

1. Strong fundamentals of the Indian economy
2. A good amount of foreign exchange reserves of $ 165 million that existed in 2006.
3. More liberalised use of foreign exchange already in place.
4. A financial system better geared to deal with external capital flows

The fuller capital convertibility of rupee seemed to be desirable at the end of 2006 when the committee submitted its report. However, economic events, especially global financial crisis of 2007-09, broughly about a sea change in the economic situation. The Indian economy would have been greatly affected by the global financial crisis if we had implemented the recommendations of Tarapore Committee recommendations. We could not have coped with the extent of capital outflows that took place during 2008-09.

Problems

But convertibility of currency can give rise to some problems. Firstly, since changes in market determined exchange rate is generally higher than the previous officially fixed exchange rate, prices of essential imports rise which may generate cost-push inflation in the economy. Secondly, if currency convertibility is not properly managed and monitored, market exchange rate may lead to the *depreciation of domestic currency*. If a currency depreciates heavily, the confidence in it is shaken and no one will accept it in its transactions. As a result, trade and capital flows in the country are adversely affected.

Thirdly, convertibility of a currency sometimes makes it highly volatile. Further, operations by speculators make it more volatile. Further, operations by speculators make it more volatile and unstable. When due to speculative activity, a currency depreciates and confidence in it is shaken there is capital fight from the country as it happened in 1997-98 in case of South East Asian economies such as Thailand, Malaysia, Indonesia, Singapore and South Korea. This adversely affects economic growth of the economy. In the context of heavy depreciation of the currency not only there is capital flight but inflow of capital in the economy is discouraged as due to depreciation of the currency profitability of investment in an economy is adversely affected.

FOREIGN EXCHANGE RATE, BALANCE OF PAYMENTS AND INFLATION

Changes in foreign exchange rate have an important effect on the balance of payments of a country. When there is depreciation or devaluation in the currency of a country, its exports become cheaper and imports dearer than before. This causes exports to increase and imports to decrease causing reduction in deficit in balance of payments. Thus in order to check increase in deficit in balance of payment and to restore equilibrium in it, devaluation or depreciation of the domestic currency against foreign currencies is often undertaken.

Besides, the foreign exchange inflows in various forms such as those resulting from rising exports, portfolio investment by FIIs (Foreign Institutional Investors), foreign direct investment (FDI) not only affect foreign exchange rate of the domestic currency but also affect money supply in the economy and therefore inflationary situation in the country.

Thus higher appreciation in the value of rupee against US dollar in recent years in India has been the direct result of large capital inflows in India. The price of Indian rupee against US dollar has risen from around ₹ 45 in January 2007 to 39.2 in mid Nov. 2007, that is, over 11 per cent appreciation in the year 2007 alone. This appreciation of rupee has been driven by foreign exchange inflows partly by rising software exports but more importantly inflows by FIIs coming in large quantity to take advantage of the stock market boom in India. Besides foreign exchange inflows through NRI deposits lured by higher interest rates in India than those prevailing in their country of residence. Further, large capital inflows through foreign direct investment (FDI) in India have occurred in recent years.

These large inflows of foreign exchange in India through its effect on the supply of dollars in foreign exchange market would have caused a very high appreciation of rupee vis-a-vis US dollar but RBI did buy some dollars from market from time to time to prevent it and built up reserves of foreign exchange. But RBI could not buy dollars as fast as the large inflows came in. This resulted in appreciation of rupee. RBI could not ensure foreign exchange rate stability in situation of large capital inflows by buying sufficient amount of dollars from the market. This is because when RBI buy dollars from the market, it gives the Indian rupees in exchange for the dollars. In this way more rupee currency is pumped into the Indian economy resulting in a large increase in money supply which causes higher rate of inflation. Therefore only modest efforts were made by RBI to buy dollars from the market to prevent very high appreciation of rupee on the one hand and ensure that money supply or liquidity in the economy does not rise much and inflation is kept under control, RBI *sterilized* to some extent the increase in money supply or liquidity by selling to banks Government securities and keeping the money so received from them in a special account not to be used by Government or others. This has been called *market stabilisation scheme* (MSS). Besides, buying of dollars from the market has caused large increase in foreign exchange reserves with RBI which now (Dec. 2007) stands at US $ 270 billion. The use of some of these foreign exchange reserves for investment in building up infrastructure is now being planned. Since, as mentioned above, RBI could not buy dollars as fast as they came resulting in appreciation of rupee whose value now is ₹ 39.32 for a US dollar (Mid. Dec. 2007) up from the level of around ₹ 45 for a dollar in Jan. 2007.

An important conclusion which follows from above is that there is a **clash between foreign exchange rate stability and domestic price stability** and RBI has been attempting to strike a balance between foreign exchange rate stability and domestic price stability. If in order to ensure foreign exchange rate stability RBI mops up sufficient dollars, it will result in pumping large sum of Indian rupees into the economy which will lead to the large increase in money supply causing a high rate of inflation. If to check inflation and ensure price stability, it does not mop up dollars from the market and let dollar inflows come. this will result in appreciation of rupee. Thus it has to strike a balance and follow a mix of policies. It will undertake to buy *some* dollars or foreign exchange inflows to check too much appreciation of Indian rupee and will also attempt to control inflation by *not buying* large amount of dollar inflows and let appreciation of rupee to take place to some degree. It is this mix of policies that RBI is following. It is important to note that appreciation of rupee adversely affects India's exports and leads to loss of jobs.

Appreciation of rupee also makes imports cheaper causing increase in them. Fall in exports and rise in imports will adversely affect balance of payments on current account. However, more imports brought in through appreciation of rupee adds to aggregate supply of output and help in controlling inflation. Besides, cheaper imports of raw materials and capital goods will reduce unit cost of production and therefore profit margin of exporters may not decline much.

QUESTIONS FOR REVIEW

1. What is meant by foreign exchange rate ? How is it determined ?
2. Distinguish between floating exchange rate and fixed exchange rate. What type of exchange rate system has been currently adopted by India?
3. Explain the factors that cause changes on the exchange rate of a currency. How the exchange rate of rupee in terms of US dollar will be affected if India has a deficit on current account of the balance of payments?
4. Explain the factors which determine demand for foreign exchange, say US dollars.
5. Explain the factors which determine supply of foreign exchange, say US dollar, for India.

6. **Explain the fixed exchange rate system adopted under the Brelton Woods system. Why did it collapse?**
7. **Explain how a foreign exchange rate is determined. How will the following factors affect foreign exchange rate of rupee?**
   (*a*) **Higher rate of inflation in India**
   (*b*) **Higher rates of interest in India**
8. **Critically examine purchasing power parity theory of foreign exchange. What shortcomings of this theory was pointed out by Keynes.**
9. **What is meant appreciation of Indian rupee? How will it affect exports, imports and level of national income of India.**
10. **Distinguish betwen depreciation and devaluation. How will devaluation or depreciation will affect balance of trade and the national economy. Explain in this connection the concept of *J-Curve*.**
11. **What is meant by appreciation of a currency? What will be the effect of appreciation of rupee against dollar on our balance of trade, foreign exchange reserves and price level in the Indian economy.**
12. **How is exchange rate determined in open market? What factors make exchange rate fluctuate?**
13. **Explain the merits of a flexible exchange rate system. Discuss why Bretton Woods system had favoured relatively fixed exchange rates.**
14. **A real depreciation will worsen the trade balance in the short run, but will gradually improve in the long run.**
15. **How do exchange rate changes help in the trade adjustment process? Discuss the role of monetary or domestic credit factors.**
16. **How far under flexible exchange rates can countries pursue their own national montary and fiscal policies without having to worry about the balance of payments ? Is there a need for policy synchronization?**
17. (*a*) **What is meant by *Currency Convertibility*? Distinguish between current account and capital count convertibility of a currency.**
    (*b*) **What are the advantages of currency convertibility and what problems are faced by making convertibility of a currency.**
18. **Explain the impact of Capital inflows on foreign exchange rate and inflation in the economy. Explain in this connection clash between foreign exchange rate stability and domestic price stability.**

CHAPTER 36

National Income and Foreign Trade Multiplier : Saving-Investment Approach

Introduction

Keynes explained his investment multiplier in the context of a closed economy where neither exports nor imports of goods occur. Keynesian theory of multiplier has been extended to the open economy where there are flows of goods and capital between a country and others. We have seen in the saving-investment approach that in a closed economy equilibrium level of national income is determined by the equality between intended saving and investment ($S = I$). Now, in the open economy foreign trade, that is, exports and imports of an economy are also to be taken into account as these also influence the determination of national income. Further, like investment expenditure, exports have also a multiplier effect on changes in the national income of a country. The value of *foreign trade multiplier* or what is also called *export multiplier* depends not only on the marginal propensity to save but also on the marginal propensity to import. Therefore, in what follows we shall first explain the concept of the import function and how marginal propensity to import is derived from it. After explaining this we shall proceed to explain how foreign trade multiplier depends on marginal propensity to import and how changes in exports and imports create multiplier effect on changes in the equilibrium level of national income.

The Import Function

In an open economy consumers of a country also spend some income on imported goods. The imports of a country depend on its level of income. The higher the level of income, the prices of imported goods and tastes of consumers remaining the same, the greater will be its imports. *The relationship between imports and level of income of a country is called the import function* and is written as

$$M = f(Y)$$

where M stands for imports and Y for income of a country.

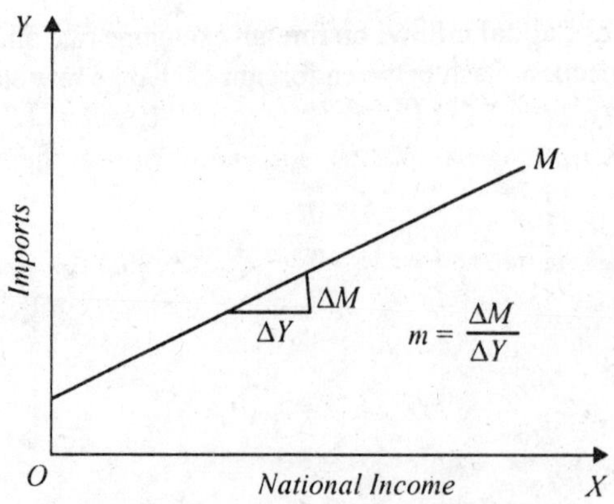

Fig. 36.1. *The Import Function.*

We have shown the import function in Fig. 36.1 where on the X-axis the level of national income and on the Y-axis imports of a country are measured. It will be seen that even at zero national income some imports are undertaken by exporting some capital accumulated in the past or by borrowing from abroad. There are two concepts of propensity to import which should be understood. First, *average propensity to import* is defined as the *proportion or percentage of national income spent on imports*, that is, it is rupee value of imports divided by national income or $\frac{M}{Y}$. Large countries such as the U.S.A., Russia and India have low average propensity to import and small countries such as Great Britain and Holland have high average propensity to import. The average propensity to import in India is between 0.02 and 0.03.

More important concept is the marginal propensity to import. *The marginal propensity to import measures the change in import as a result of increase in national incomes* and is algebraically expressed as $\frac{\Delta M}{\Delta Y}$ where ΔM is the change in value of imports and ΔY is the increase in national income. If imports increase by Rs. 3 when national income rises by Rs. 100, the marginal propensity to import $\left(\frac{\Delta M}{\Delta I}\right)$ will be equal to $3/100 = 0.03$ or 3 per cent. If increase in income by Rs. 100 leads to the increase in imports by Rs. 10, the marginal propensity to imports is $10/100 = 0.1$ or 10 per cent.

The Foreign Trade Multiplier in an Open Economy

In a closed economy equilibrium level of national income is determined at the level where intended saving equals intended investment ($S = I$). Saving represents leakage or *withdrawal* of some money from the income flow, while investment is the *injection* of some money into the income stream. The level of national income is in equilibrium (that is, circular flow of income is constant) when leakage from the income stream in the form of savings is equal to the injection of investment expenditure. In an open economy, the role of foreign trade, that is, exports and imports of a country are also to be considered. Imports by consumers of a country represent the expenditure on imported goods by the residents of the country and leads to the leakage of some income from domestic economy. Therefore, in addition to saving, imports are other from of leakage that occur in an open economy. On the other hand, exports represent expenditure by the people of foreign countries on the goods produced in the domestic economy and are, like domestic investment, injection into the income stream of an open economy. Therefore, *equilibrium level of national income in an open economy is determined at the level at which total leakage, that is, savings plus imports ($S + M$) equal total injection, that is, domestic investment plus exports ($I + X$) into the income stream.*

Thus, in an open economy, national income is in equilibrium at the level at which

$$S + M = I + X$$

When a change in any of the above four variables occurs, then the change on the left side of the above equation must equal the change on the right side if the new equilibrium is to be achieved.

Hence

$$\Delta S + \Delta M = \Delta I + \Delta X \qquad \ldots (1)$$

Now, change in saving, $\Delta S = s. \Delta Y$

Where s = marginal propensity to save and

ΔY = change in national income.

Likewise, change in imports, $\Delta M = m. \Delta Y$

where m = marginal propensity to import.

Thus, rewriting equation (1) we have

$$s\,\Delta Y + m.\Delta Y = \Delta I + \Delta X$$

or

$$\Delta Y\,(s + m) = \Delta I + \Delta X$$

$$\Delta Y = \frac{1}{s+m}(\Delta I + \Delta X) \qquad \text{...(2)}$$

It will be known from equation (2) that change in either investment or exports will cause income to increase by the multiple, $\frac{1}{s+m}$. Thus $\frac{1}{s+m}$ is the foreign trade multiplier which is generally denoted by K_f. Thus, if exports increase by ΔX, the national income will rise by $\Delta X \cdot \frac{1}{s+m}$.

Hence, $K_f = \frac{1}{s+m}$

Thus, *foreign trade multiplier is equal to the reciprocal of marginal propensity to save (s) plus marginal propensity to import* (*m*). It is evident that smaller the leaks, that is, smaller the values of marginal propensity to save (*s*) and marginal propensity to import, the greater the value of foreign trade multiplier. Let us given an example. If $s = 0.2$ and $m = 0.2$, then

Foreign trade mutiplier, $K_f = \frac{1}{0.2+0.2}$

$= \frac{1}{0.4}$ or 2.5

Again, if s = 0.3 and m = 0.2, then

Foreign trade multiplier $= \frac{1}{0.3+0.2} = \frac{1}{0.5}$

$= 2$

Graphic Representation of Foreign Trade Multiplier

The foreign trade multiplier has been graphically illustrated in Fig. 36.2 where $S + M$ is the saving plus import function curve and X_0 is the export curve which is constant as it has been assumed to be an autonomous variable, that is, independent of the level of income. To simplify our analysis we assume that there is no investment, equilibrium level of national income will therefore be determined by consumption (saving) and exports. Initially, the economy is in equilibrium at level of income Y_0 where $S + M = X_0$, investment being zero. Suppose there is autonomous increase in

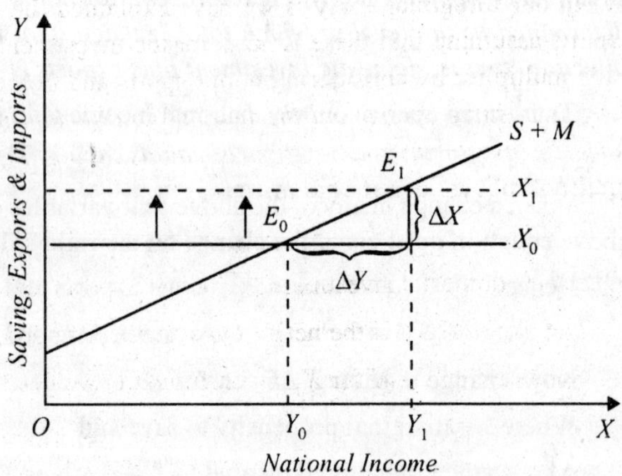

Fig. 36.2. *Foreign Trade Multiplier with No Investment*

exports so that export curve shifts upward from X_0 to X_1, It will be seen from Fig. 36.2 that equilibrium income increases to Y_1.

Thus increase in exports (ΔX) has led to the increase in income (ΔY) equal to $Y_1 - Y_0$ which is much greater than change in exports (ΔX). $\frac{\Delta Y}{\Delta X}$ is the foreign trade multiplier whose value depends on the slope of saving-import function curve $S + M$ which is equal to the reciprocal of the sum of marginal propensity to save and marginal propensity to import $\left(\frac{1}{s+m}\right)$

How the Foreign Trade Multiplier Works ?

The foreign trade multiplier works in the same way as Keynes' investment multiplier. When there is increase in exports, it will cause the increase in income of the exporters and those employed in the export industries. They will save some of the increase in their incomes and will spend a good part of the increases in their incomes on consumer goods, both domestic and imported ones. While savings do not generate further income and represent leakage from the income stream, expenditure on imports leads to the increase in the incomes of the foreign countries from which goods are imported. Thus expenditure on imports also represents a leakage from the income stream as far as domestic economy is concerned. But the increased expenditure on domestic goods as a result of increase in exports will go on increasing incomes in various successive rounds of spending till the multiplier fully works itself out.

It may be noted that increase in exports of a country can occur due to several reasons. There may be change in tastes or demand of the people of foreign countries for goods of a country. To begin with, the exporters may meet the demand for exported goods by selling their inventories and enjoy higher incomes. But in the next periods, they will make efforts to increase the production of exported goods and employ more workers. This will generate new income and employment in the export industries. But the working of multiplier does not stop here. Those employed in export industries will spend a good part of their increased incomes on goods produced by other industries and in this way increases in income, production and employment will spread in the whole of the domestic economy.

The Foreign Trade Multiplier : With Both Exports and Domestic Investment

In our foregoing analysis we have explained the multiplier effect of autonomous increase in exports assuming that there is no domestic investment. We will now further elaborate the foreign trade multiplier by considering both exports and domestic investment. *In an open economy when there is positive investment the level of equilibrium in national income is reached when sum of domestic investment and net exports equals saving.* Thus, in an open economy the condition for the equilibrium level of national income is

$$I_d + X_n = S \qquad ...(1)$$

where I_d is domestic investment, X_n is net exports and S is the saving

Net exports (X_n) is the net of exports over imports, that is, $X_n = X - M$

Substituting $X - M$ for X_n in equation (1) we get

$$I_d + (X - M) = S$$

or

$$I_d + X = S + M$$

In the case when there is positive domestic investment the determination of the equilibrium level of national income is graphically shown in Fig. 36.3. The curve I_d represents autonomous domestic investment which remains constant. S is the saving function curve showing that saving is the increasing function of income. Over the domestic investment curve (I_d) we have added the exports (X) of the economy to get $I_d + X$ curve. To the saving function curve we have added the import function curve to obtain the aggregate of saving and import functions curve ($S + M$). It will be observed from Fig. 36.3. That $I_d + X$ equals $S + M$ at point E and thus the equilibrium level of national income Y_0 is determined. Note that at Y_0 level of income saving (S) and domestic investment (I_d) are also equal. Thus, at equilibrium income Y_0 :

$$I_d + X = S + M$$

$$I_d = S$$

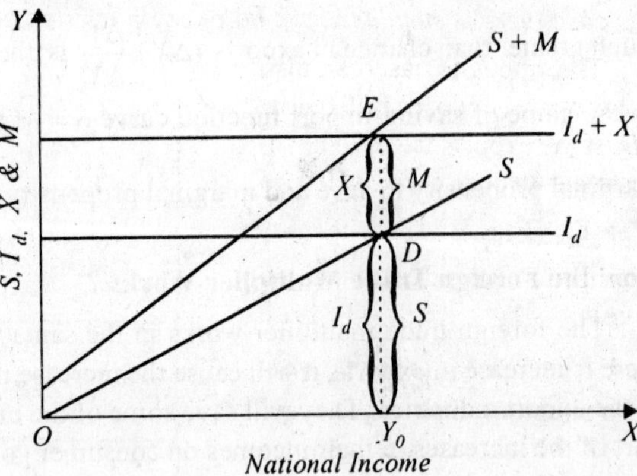

Fig. 36.3. *Foreign Trade Multiplier with Both Exports and Investment*

Therefore, at Y_0 equilibrium income :

$$X = M$$

The equality of exports (X) with imports (M) implies that there is equilibrium in the *balance on the current account.* However, it is important to note that it is *not necessary* that at equilibrium level of income exports (X) equal imports (M). This *equilibrium in the current account balance along with equilibrium of saving and domestic investment only when exports are equal to imports at the equilibrium level of income determined by the equality of saving and domestic investment.* In Fig. 36.3. at equilibrium income Y_0 at which saving equals domestic investment, imports are equal to DE. If exports happen to be equal to DE, the equilibrium in the current account balance will also occur. However, this is not necessary because exports may be greater or less than the imports DE.

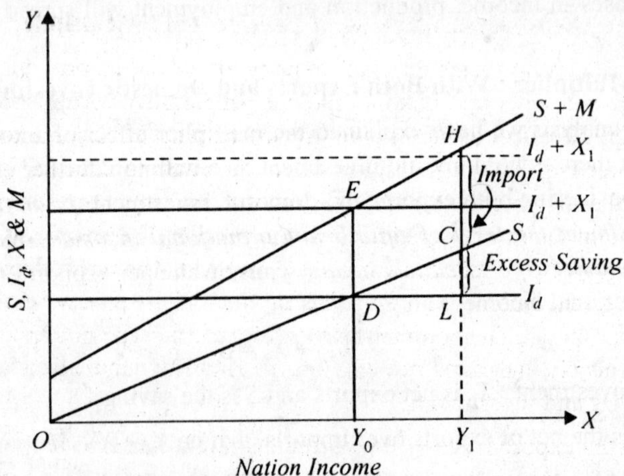

Fig. 36.4. *Equilibrium with Export Surplus*

Suppose autonomous exports increase so that the investment - exports curve shifts above to $I_d + X_1$ as shown in Figure 36.4. This new $I_d + X_1$ curve intersects $S + M$ curve at point H and as a result equilibrium national income Y_1 is determined. It will be seen from Fig. 36.4 that at national income Y_1 the volume of exports is *LH* which exceeds the imports *CH* by *LC* amount. Note that *LC* is the amount by which saving exceeds domestic investment. It is this excess of saving over domestic investment that maintain the equation $I_d + X = S + M$ despite exports (*X*) being not equal to imports (*M*). Thus, *in this case there is surplus in the balance on current account.*

The opposite case can also occur when exports fall below *ED*. If the exports fall and the investment-export curve shifts to $I_d + X_2$, (Fig. 36.5), the new equilibrium is reached at income level Y_2 at which $I_d + X_2 = S + M$. In this equilibrium situation imports are equal to *VT* which exceeds exports (X_2) which are equal to *KT*. Thus, though the open economy is in equilibrium as $I_d + X_2 = S + M$ at income level Y_2, there exists *import surplus* which again implies that there is disequilibrium in the balance of payment on the current count.

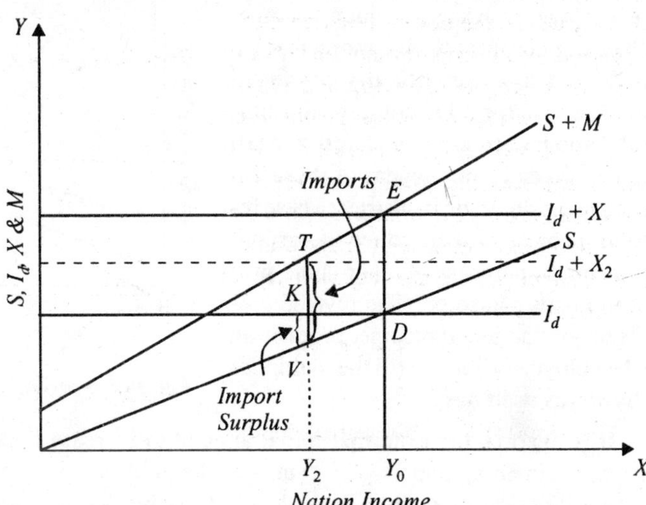

Fig. 36.5. *Equilibrium with Import Surplus*

However, in this case of import surplus, domestic investment must exceed domestic saving by an equal amount so as to maintain the equality of $I_d + X$ with $S + M$. This is possible only if a country borrows from abroad to keep investment greater than domestic savings.

The above analysis shows that while the open economy as a whole may be in equilibrium, it is not necessary that balance of payment (on current account) will also be in equilibrium.

Increase in Imports : The Reverse Working of Foreign Trade Multiplier

Whereas increase in exports has an expansionary effect on national income, the increase in imports will have opposite effect on national income. Imports will bring about contraction in national income. Further, the effect of increase in imports on national income will not be equal to the increase in imports but will have a multiplier effect in reducing national income. There can be several reasons for the increase in imports of a country. An important reason for the increase in imports is the change in tastes or preferences of the people. The people of a country may have started preferring the imported goods as compared to *Swadeshi* (home produced) goods. The reduction in import duties on the imports and thus making them cheaper may be another reason for the increase in imports a country. The contractionary effect of increase in imports on the income and employment in a country is illustrated in Fig. 36.6. To simplify our analysis we have assumed that there are no net savings and investment.

In this Fig. 36.6 the export curve is a horizontal straight line since exports are assumed to be authonomous of changes in national income. The curve *M* represents the import function curve which slopes upward showing that it changes with national income. The two curves *X* and *M* intersect at point *E* and determine Y_0 equilibrium level of national income. Now suppose that there is increase in imports ($\Delta M = ET$), say due to the change in preferences for foreign goods, and as a result import function curve shifts above to the position M_1, the export curve *X* remaining unchanged.

It will seen from Fig. 36.6 that new import function curve M_1 and export curve X intersect at point E_1 and as result the equilibrium level of income falls to Y_1. Note that reduction in income is greater than the increase in imports; ΔY is much greater than ΔM. This is due to the working of foreign trade multiplier which in the present case works to reduce income. When the consumers buy more foreign goods and less domestically produced goods, the demand for domestically produced goods decreases which result in fall in incomes and employment of those engaged in the domestic industries. These reduced incomes further reduce the expenditure on the purchase of other home-produced goods and so on. The reverse process of contraction of income, production and employment goes on till the multiplier fully works itself out.

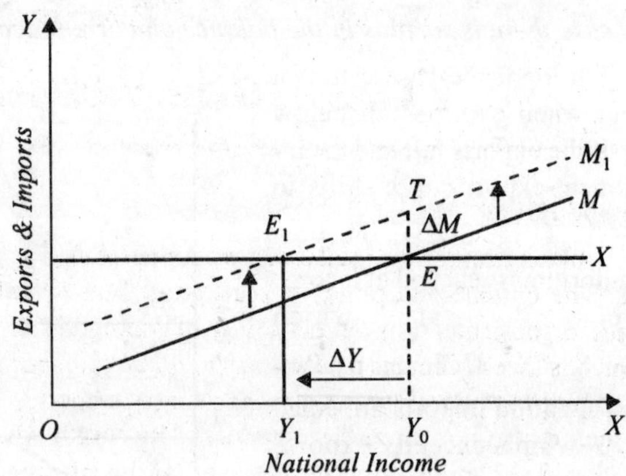

Fig. 36.6. *Reverse Working of Foreign Trade Multiplier*

It is important to note that initial attempt to increase imports has not finally resulted in any increase in imports. Imports Y_0E at the initial equilibrium income Y_0 are equal to imports Y_1E_1 in the new equilibrium at the much lower level of income. This is another paradox which is described as *import paradox*. What has actually happened is that the increase in imports and consequent upward shift in the import function leads to a large contraction in income through the reverse working of foreign trade multiplier so that in the new equilibrium at a much lower income, less is imported. This is generally referred to as income effect. Thus, this *import paradox* is of the same nature as paradox of thrift explained earlier.

QUESTIONS FOR REVIEW

1. What are import function and marginal propensity to import ? How does marginal propensity to import determine the value of foreign trade multiplier ?
2. What do you understand by foreign trade multiplier ? How is it related to marginal propensity to save and import ?
3. In an open economy national income is in equilibrium when the sum of saving and imports equals the sum of domestic investment and exports. Explain and illustrate diagrammatically.
4. What is foreign trade multiplier ? Explain how it works.
5. Explain that in an open economy the equilibrium in the current account balance occurs only when exports are equal to imports at the equilibrium level of national income determined by the equality of planned saving and domestic investment.
6. Suppose in an open economy, imports increase. How will it affect national income ? In this context explain the reverse working of foreign trade multiplier.

CHAPTER 37
Free Trade Versus Protection

Introduction

In this chapter we shall discuss commercial policy which is a highly important issue in economics. The commercial policy is concerned with whether a country should adopt the policy of free trade or of protection. If the policy of protection of domestic industries is adopted, the question which is faced whether protection should be granted through imposing tariffs on imports or through the fixation of quota or through licensing of imports. The commercial policy has been the subject of heated discussion since the time of Adam Smith who advocated for free trade and recommended that tariffs should be removed to avail of the advantages of free trade[1]. Even today, economists are divided over this question of commercial policy. Various arguments have been given for and against free trade. If the policy of protection of domestic industries is adopted, the question is whether for this purpose tariffs should be imposed on imports or quantitative restrictions through quota and licensing be applied. The readers should be knowing that a Bharatiya Janata Party in India has been demanding a policy of '*Swadeshi*' which in essence means that domestic industries should be protected against low-priced imports of goods from abroad, that is, free trade should not be allowed.

Besides Adam Smith, the other famous classical economist David Ricardo in his famous work "*On the Principles of Political Economy and Taxation*" also defended free trade to promote efficiency and productivity in the economy. We have seen in a previous chapter that Adam Smith and the other earlier economists thought that it pays a country to specialise in the production of those goods it can produce more cheaply than any other country and import those goods it can obtain at less cost or price than it would cost to produce them at home. This means they should specialise according to absolute cost advantage. However, Ricardo put forward the 'Theory of Comparative Cost' where he demonstrated that to obtain benefits from trade it is not necessary that countries should produce these goods for which their absolute cost of production is the lowest. He proved that it could pay a country to import a good even though it could produce that good at a lower cost, if its cost is relatively lower in the production of some other good. Ricardo's theory of trade rests on the idea of relative efficiency or comparative cost.

Despite the classical arguments for free trade to promote efficiency and well-being of the people, various countries have been following the protectionist policies which militate against free trade. By imposing heavy tariff duties on imports of goods or fixing quotas of imports they have prevented free trade to take place between countries. Several arguments have been given in favour of protection. In what follows we spell out this free trade vs. protection controversy.

CASE FOR FREE TRADE

The following arguments have been given in defence of free trade.

1. Gains in Output and Well-being from Specialisation

The case for free trade is fundamentally based on the gain in output and well-being a country obtains from specialising in the production of those goods in which it is relatively more efficient and therefore export a part of them and in exchange gets those goods from other countries in production

1. See Adam Smith, *The Wealth of Nations*, Modern Library Edition.

of which they are comparatively more efficient. Specialisation and trading in this way would achieve a more efficient allocation of resources and a higher level of output and well-being. To quote Prof. Haberler, "International division of labour and international trade which enable every country to specialise and to export those things which it can produce cheaper in exchange for what others can provide at a lower cost, have been and still are one of the basic factors promoting well-being and increasing national income of every participating country"[2]

2. Gains from Economies of Scale

An important gain from trade is that it enables the trading countries to benefit from the economies of scale. If a country does not trade with others, its firms will produce goods to meet the domestic demand for a product. If domestic demand for a product is small, each of them will produce at a higher cost since they would not be able to enjoy the benefits of the economies of large scale production. Accordingly, the production of goods will be inefficient. Trade allows a country to export goods with the result that level of output of goods in a country will exceed domestic demand within a country. Thus trade expands the market for goods and enables the producers to take advantage of the economies of scale. Adam Smith was the first economist who pointed out that specialisation was limited by the size of the market. Trade makes it possible for the producers to move beyond domestic market into international market and therefore makes it worthwhile to specialise and produce on a large scale and thereby to lower cost per unit.

For example, in a small country such as Ceylon domestic demand would not be sufficient to produce efficiently large luxury cars on a large scale at a lower cost. Their production on a large scale at lower cost requires wider international market for sale of luxury cars.

3. Long-Run Dynamic Gains

Free trade also leads to dynamic gains being obtained from trade. Dynamic gains from trade refer to its stimulation of economic growth. Dennis Robertson described foreign trade as '*an engine of growth*'. The stimulation of growth through foreign trade are apparent from the rapid growth of such economies such as Japan, Taiwan, South Koria, Singapur, Hongkong and China. Free trade promotes economic growth through: (1) raising the rate of saving and investment; (2) import of capital goods, and (3) transfer of technology.

(*i*) *Raising rate of saving and investment*. As mentioned above, increase in national product or real national income of a country obtained through trade above the level that prevails in autarky leads to a higher level of saving. The higher level of saving ensures a higher rate of investment and capital formation which stimulates growth. Hence if trade raises the rate of saving, it also promotes economic growth. The higher rate of saving makes it easier for the developing countries to break 'the vicious circle of proverty' and to "take off into self-sustained growth"[3]

(*ii*) *Import of capital goods*. Besides trade permits a country to import capital goods in exchange for exports of consumer goods or surplus raw materials. and thereby accelerates industrial growth. Imports of capital goods adds to the capital stock in a country and raises its productive capacity more than it would have been possible without trade. Free trade also often enables a country to borrow from other countries to finance import of capital goods.

(*iii*) *Transfer of technology*. If different countries worked in isolation the new technology developed in one country would remain confined locally. Through trade technological progress tends to feed on each other. A technology discovered by one is improved by another and so technology goes on being improved successively. Imagine if every country had to invent a wheel, a steam engine, electricity operating in an isolated manner, how slow would have been the progress in technology.

---

2. G. Haberler, *International Trade and Economic Growth*.
3. *Ibid*.

The trade increases international diffusion of technology and in this way transfer of technology from the developed countries to the developing countries have been possible. In the modern times technology developed in one country by a firm is licensed to firms in other countries. Through this process, technology is transferred from country to country. In the absence of trade between countries such transfer of technology would not take place and as a result economic growth would be slower.

4. Promotes Competition and Prevents Monopoly

The case for free trade also rests on the fact that it promotes competition and prevents the emergence of monopolies in the domestic economy. In the absence of trade and therefore without facing any competition from foreign firms, domestic firms tend to become inefficient which causes rise in cost per unit of output and therefore higher prices of goods.

When trade is free, increased competition by foreign firms forces domestic firms to adopt measures to increase their efficiency and make efforts to reduce cost by employing lowest-cost production techniques. Free trade also compels them to be innovative and to improve the quality of their products. Further, free trade provides consumers a wide range of products from which to choose. The increase in efficiency and the adoption of improved technology not only lowers prices of products but also contributes to economic growth.

5. Political Gains from Free Trade

Free trade, as explained above, increases well-being or standared of living of the trading countries and this mutual welfare gains from trade make different nations economically dependent on each other. The economic interdependence raises the likelihood of reduced hostility between countries. Economic interdependence provides powerful incentives for peaceful solution of disputes. Trade between economically interdependent countries increases the potential losses from war and thus reduces the likelihood of armed conflict.

Despite the above gains from free trade, countries have put up various barriers to free trade flows. The important barriers to free trade are (1) the imposition of tariffs (i.e., duties on imports of goods), (2) the fixation of import quotas, (3) the licensing of imports. *The reasons for these trade barriers are that different nations want to protect their domestic industries, to increase employment opportunities, to improve their balance of payments and to achieve* other goals. We therefore discuss below the case for protection and then in a later section will examine the impact of trade barriers, especially tariffs on welfare and growth.

CASE FOR PROTECTION

Despite gains from free trade, many arguments have been given against free trade and in favour of protection. By protection we mean in order to safeguard the domestic industries from low-priced imports some barriers against import of foreign goods are imposed. Some arguments given in defence of protection are irrational and invalid, whereas some are valid. We critically examine below various arguments given in favour of protection (*i.e.*, against free foreign trade).

Nationalism

First argument for protection has been that nationalistic feeling or patriotism requires that people of a country should buy products of their domestic industries rather than foreign products. In the USA there has been a campaign '*Be American, buy American*' appealing people to buy American goods instead of imported foreign products. Similarly, in India recent campaign of '*Swadeshi*' appeals to the patriotic feeling of the Indian people that we should protect our indigenous industries and impose barriers on imports of foreign goods or provide subsidies to our industries. However, this argument is misplaced and invalid. Those policy makers who yield to such arguments deny the people of a country the gains from trade such as rise in productive efficiency and greater well-being, stimulus to growth through higher capital formation and spread of superior technology. Thus restrictions imposed on trade in the name of nationalism or *swadeshi* are actually contrary to our national interests because they promote inefficiency and prevents rapid economic growth.

Employment Argument

An important argument for protection is that it will lead to increase in domestic employment or at least preserves present domestic employment. It is often believed that imports of goods from abroad reduce domestic employment. Therefore, if instead of imports we produce those goods at home, employment in the country will increase. Besides, as prices of imported goods are lower, the domestic producers would not be able to compete with them and may be competed out of the market. This will destroy even present jobs in the domestic industries. It is therefore concluded that protection of domestic industries will lead to their expansion and therefore employment in them will increase.

In our view employment argument for protection is not logical and valid. This argument ignores the adverse effects of protection on our industries. An important economic principle is that exports must pay for imports. If imports are restricted by imposing barriers, the exports cannot remain unaffected. For example, many raw materials and capital goods are imported to be used in industries which export goods. If imports are restricted, exports will therefore fall. This will lead to the decline in employment in export industries which will offset the increase in employment in the import-substituting industries.

Further, when you restrict imports to protect domestic industries so that they should expand, other countries are likely to retaliate and will impose restrictions on our exports which are imported by them. This too will reduce exports and cause reduction in employment in export industries. Thus net effect on employment of restricting imports for providing protection to domestic industries may not be positive.

Infant Industries Argument

A powerful argument given in support of protection, especially in the context of developing countries is infant industries should be provided protection from the competition of low-priced imports of the mature and well-established industries of the developed industrialised countries. Shortly after American Revolution, Alexander Hamilton argued that British industrial supremacy was due to its early start over American infant industries. He pointed out that these infant American industries required temporary protection for some time so that they should grow and achieve production efficiency and economies of scale before they could successfully compete with low-cost British goods. He thus argued that temporary protection of infant American industries was necessary for industrial development of America.

Similarly, the infant industry argument has been advanced for protecting infant industries of the developing countries from competition of the low-cost firms of the industrialised developed countries. Given some time, these infant industries will grow and will be able to benefit from the economies of scale and learn the techniques necessary to lower their cost of production. As a result, over a period of time their cost per unit will go down and will therefore be in a position to compete with the foreign imports. Therefore, for some time they should be protected otherwise they would be destroyed by foreign competition.

However, there are some lacuna in infant industry argument. First, it is assumed that protected infant industries will make efforts to lower cost when provided protection. However, actual experience shows that it is more likely that protected industries lose incentives to become efficient and lower cost. It is said "once an infant, always an infant." Secondly, even if an industry makes efforts to improve productivity and lower cost per unit when it is provided protection, it has been assumed in the argument that the Government is the best judge as to which industries will prove to be capable of competing low-priced foreign goods. It has been asserted in defence of free trade that selection of industries which will acquire competitive strength can be done better by private market mechanism. It is pointed out that when opening up the economy to foreign competition the domestic industries would try to increase their efficiency. As a result, only those industries will survive which are efficient and produce at a lower cost. Therefore, it is argued that it is better if the domestic industries are left to foreign competition and in this way they will have incentives to improve productivity to escape from losses. Only those domestic industries will survive and operate which are efficient and produce at a low cost per unit.

Indian Automobile industry is a shining example of an industry not making any efforts to become efficient even after given protection for more than three decades. Before the setting-up of Maruti Udyog with Japanese collaboration, Indian car industry was fully protected by heavy duties on imports of cars. The two domestic firms producing Ambassador and Fiat cars did not make any efforts to improve their efficiency, nor did they bring out any better models of their cars. It is only after 1991 that following the policy of liberalisation that new foreign firms such as Daewoo of South Korea, General Motors have come in India and producing new models and at relatively low prices. Even Maruti is now trrying to improve its efficiency further and brought out new models of Maruti such as Zen, Esteem.

However, it may be noted that in developing countries the Government is in a better position to protect certain industries such as steel, cement *which lead to an expansion of the infrastructure of the developing economies*. This is because these industries create external economies and the private firms will not be compensated for creating these external benefits.

Anti-dumping Argument

The other important argument for protection is that foreign producers compete unfairly by dumping the goods in another country. Dumping is a form of price discrimination when producers of a country sells goods in another country at lower prices than those charged at home. Of course, consumers in a country in which foreign goods are dumped are beneficiaries, the industries of that country suffer as they are unable to compete with the '*dumped goods*'. Besides, there is more harmful '*predatory dumping*' which implies that foreign firms try to sell goods in other countries even below cost to establish a worldwide monopoly by driving competitors out of the market. Once the local industries are competed out, they raise prices to obtain monopoly profits.

There is a lot of evidence that firms of USA and Japan often indulge in dumping of their goods in other countries to eliminate competition. But, in our view, instead of providing protection to domestic industries through tariffs or non-tariffs barriers, it will be a better policy to enact laws against dumping. Dumping should be prohibited by law declaring it illegal. In India such a law has been enacted but is not being properly implemented.

Correcting Balance of Payment Deficit

Correcting deficit in balance of payments is also mentioned as justification for imposing tariffs to restrict imports or fixing of quotas of imports. This appears to be a valid argument for providing protection. However, in our view the solution for fundamental disequilibrium in the balance of payments lies in the adoption of suitable adjustment in exchange rate, appropriate fiscal and monetary policies to lower domestic prices so as to encourage exports. The deficit in balance of payments can be reduced by ensuring rapid growth in exports of a country.

Redistribution of Income

Case for protection has also been built up on the ground that it can be used for making desirable redistribution of income from one section of society to another. Protection makes some people better off, while others worse off. By providing protection to domestic producers their profits can be raised at the expense of consumers who suffer a loss in consumer surplus as protection denies them consumption of low-priced imported goods. That is, protection redistributes income in favour of domestic producers.

Sometimes protection causes transfer of income from some factors to the others. For example, Heckscher-Ohlin Model of international trade shows that trade benefits the abundant factor and harms the scarce factor. It is therefore scarce factor that demands protection by the Government against imports so that its income may not decrease. This implies that the workers, the owners of labour, and capitalists tend to take opposite views with regard to protection. This is however not confirmed by empirical evidence.

In some countries one of the objectives of economic policy is to redistribute income from the rich to the poor. This can be done by imposing high tariffs on imports of goods considered to be luxury items and levying tariffs on exports of those goods which are considered as necessities. Higher import tariffs on luxuries will reduce the incomes of the rich as they would pay taxes to the Government. Similarly, higher taxes on exports of necessities ensure greater supplies of them in the domestic market which would lower their domestic prices and benefit the poor.

It may however be noted that direct taxes such as income tax are considered better methods of redistributing income among various sections of a society than the commercial policy. This is because as we shall see below import tariffs levied for protecting industries cause downweight loss of welfare which are avoided under the direct tax system.

Conclusion

We have critically examined the various arguments in favour of protection. Some of them are valid, other appears to be misplaced. Some people consider trade as a '*zero sum game*', that is, in trading if one gains, the other loses. This has given rise to the doctrine of exploitation. For example, it is believed by some that the developing countries like India are exploited by the developed countries such as the USA, Japan, Britain. That is, the developing countries are net losers in trading with the developed countries. However, in our view, this is wrong thinking. No trade can occur without expectations of gain. India would not have entered into trade relations with USA if it did not expect to gain from it. Trade occurs between two countries if it benefits both the trading partners, the developed and the developing countries. Therefore, in our view world trade should be promoted by lifting barriers put up by various countries based on wrong notions about effects of free trade. Some countries such as USA and Japan have resorted to protectionist measures as a retaliation against foreign countries who restrict imports into their countries. The retaliatory actions of imposing trade barriers have done great harm to the expansion of world trade. New international organisation WTO (World Trade Organisation) which has replaced earlier GATT has been set up. WTO has framed rules which every country should observe so that barriers to trade be removed and world trade be promoted without doing any injustice to the member countries. It may be noted that retaliatory activities of restricting imports from foreign countries generally lead to the depression in the economies of the world as it happened during the worldwide depression of 1930s. The retaliatory activities may cause another global depression.

TRADE BARRIERS

Despite many benefits of free trade, the various countries have put up barriers to trade. A number of instruments are used as barriers to free trade but most important are tariffs and quotas. Both tariffs and quotas can be imposed either an imports or exports but they are mostly imposed on imports. Barriers to exports are quite uncommon. We briefly explain below these tariff barriers.

1. Tariffs. Tariffs are excise duties imposed on imported goods. The objective of imposing tariffs may be either raising revenue for the Government or providing protection to the domestic industries. Therefore, two types of tariffs are distinguished: (1) revenue tariffs, and (2) protective tariffs. *Revenue tariffs* are usually imposed on the imports of those products which are not produced

domestically. Rates of revenue tariffs are generally small but yields a good revenue for the Government. For example in USA, tariffs are imposed on tin, coffee and bananas which are not produced in that country. Their obvious purpose is to provide revenue to the Government.

Protective tariff, on the other hand, are imposed to provide protection to the domestic producers from foreign competition. The rates of these tariffs are not so high as to completly prohibit their imports into a country. Rise in prices of their products as a result of imposition of tariffs, foreign producers lose their superior competitive power.

Import Quotas

Import quotas are another instrument used to check free trade. Import quotas refer to the maximum quantities of goods which may be permitted to be imported during any period of time. They are also referred to as *quantitative restrictions* on imports. Quotas are more effective method of reducing trade than tariffs. A given commodity may be imported in a relatively large quantity despite high tariffs but low quotas totally stop the imports of a commodity beyond the fixed quota of the commodity. Since international negotiations to reduce trade barriers have tended to focus on tariffs, the various countries have resorted to non-tariff barriers to free trade. We discuss below the effects of tariffs and quotas.

EFFECTS OF A TARIFF

Let us now examine the economic effects of tariffs used as a trade barrier to protect domestic industries. We use partial equilibrium approach represented by supply and demand analysis to examine the effects of tariffs. Let us take a product, say computer, in which India has a comparative disadvantage. In Fig. 37.1 we have drawn domestic demand and supply curve D_d and S_d respectively of computers in India. In the absence of foreign trade, domestic price OP_d is determined at which OQ quantity of computers is demanded and sold. Assume now that the Indian economy is now opened to trade with USA which has a comparative advantage in the production of computers. Suppose OP_w represents the world price at which USA sells computers. We assume that when the Indian economy is opened to trade, it can import computers from the USA at this world price OP_w. In other words, free trade price is OP_w. It will be seen from Fig. 37.1 that at free trade OP_w, the domestic demand (or consumption) for computers is OH and the domestic producers are supplying ON quantity. Thus, with free trade out of OH quantity of consumption of computers, domestic production is ON. The quantity NH of computers is being imported.

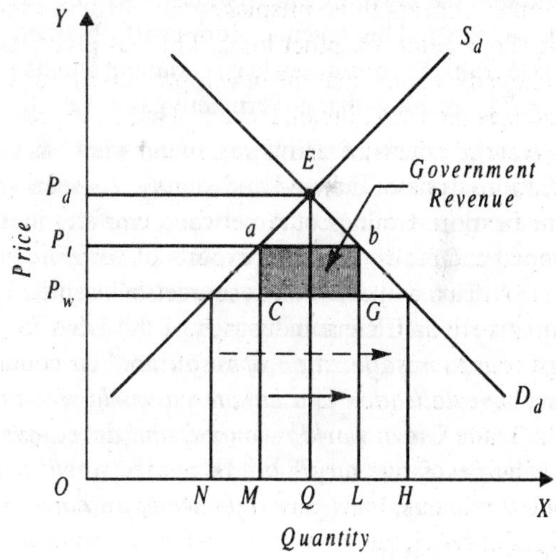

Fig. 37.1. *Economic Effects of a Tariff.*

Consumption Effect. Now suppose that in order to protect domestic computer industry India imposes a tariff of $P_w P_t$ per computer. As a result price of computer in India will rise to OP_t. The imposition of tariff and consequently rise in the price of computers in India will have a variety of effects. First, as shall be seen from Fig. 37.1 that at a higher price OP_t, the consumption of computers in India will decline to OL computers as the higher price causes buyers of computers to move up the demand curve D_d. This is a *consumption effect* of the tariff. It follows that the Indian consumers of computers have been badly hurt by the imposition of tariff on computers. As a result of tariff, they pay $P_w P_t$ more per computer which they now buy at the higher price. Besides, tariff induces them to buy fewer computers with the result that they reallocate a part of their expenditure to less desired substitute products.

Production Effect. Second, tariff benefits Indian producers of computers as they will now be able to sell their computers at a higher price OP_t instead of free trade price OP_w. Further, at a higher price OP_t, they will produce and supply more computers by moving up the domestic supply curve S_d. It will be seen from Fig. 37.1 that at price OP_t, domestic producers of computers raises domestic production and quantity supplied from *ON* to *OM*. This is the *production effect* of tariff. It should be further noted that the increase in domestic production of computers by *NM* implies that some scarce resources will be bid away from other presumably more efficient industries.

Trade Effect. Third, as a result of imposition of tariff by India, American producers will be hurt. It may be noted that American producers would not get the higher price OP_t as the higher price is due to tariff which will be obtained by the Indian Government. For American producers price of computers will remain at OP_w. Since due to rise in price to OP_t, domestic production increases to *OM* and domestic consumption falls to *OL*, the imports of computers fall from *NH* to *ML*. This is trade effect of tariff.

Revenue Effect. Now, the important effect which is to be examined is whether economic well-being of the nation will increase as a result of imposition of tariff. The answer is in the negative. Of course, the Indian Government will gain from tariff equal to the revenue it collects from tariff. With rise in price by $P_w P_t$ per computer and the import of computers reduced to *ML*, (or *ab*) the total revenue of the Government from tariff will be equal to the shaded area *abGC*. This is the revenue effect of tariff. This revenue from tariff obtained by the Government is "essentially a transfer of income from the consumers to government and does not represent any net change in the nation's well being. The result is that government gains a portion of what consumers lose."[4]

But the effects of tariffs go beyond what has been explained above on the basis of partial equilibrium analysis of demand and supply. As seen above, the imposition of tariff on computers will reduce export earnings of American computer industry–the industry in which it has a comparative advantage. Because of 'ower exports of computers, the production of computers will be reduced in the USA. This will cause the resources to be shifted from relatively more efficient computer industry to relatively inefficient industries of the USA in which it has a comparative disadvantage. Thus *tariffs cause misallocation of resources*. To conclude in the words of Professors McConnel and Brue, "*specialisation and unfettered world trade based on comparative advantage would lead to the efficient use of world resources and an expansion of the world's real output. The purpose and effect of protective tariffs are to reduce world trade. Therefore, aside from their specific effects upon consumers, foreign and domestic producers, tariffs diminish the world's real output.*[5]

Effects of Quotas

Quotas are quantitative restrictions on the quantity or value of a commodity to be imported in a country during a period. Since quota limits the imports of a commodity, it reduces supply of a commodity in a country as compared to the case with a free trade. Like tariffs, quotas raise the prices of imported goods and encourage domestic production of those goods. But in case of quotas, the government does not collect any revenue. Quotas may be imposed against imports from all countries or used against the imports of only a few countries.

Economic effects of quota are graphically shown in Fig. 37.2 where *DM* and *SM* are domestic demand and supply curves of a commodity respectively. In the absence of trade price of the com-

4. Campbell R. McConnell and Stanley L. Brue, *Economics: Principles, Problems and Policies*, 11th edition, McGraw-Hill, New York, 990, p. 784.
5. *Ibid.*, p. 784.

modity in the country is P_A. Suppose the world price of the product is P_w. Under free trade, at price P_w of the commodity the domestic producers of country will produce OQ_1 quantity but as domestic demand of the product at price Pw is OQ_3, the quantity $Q_1 Q_3$ represents the imports at the world price Pw. Now assume that the Government imposes a quota that fixes the quantity of the product equal to Q_1Q_2 to be imported. With this the total supply of the product in the domestic market will be away from the domestic supply S_M equal to the distance $Q_1 Q_2$. Incorporating the quota equal to $Q_1 Q_2$, we draw a new supply curve S_M + Quota, which is to the left of the free-trade supply curve S_M. It will be seen from Fig. that interaction of the supply curve (S_M + Quota) with the domestic demand curve D_M determine higher price P_Q than the world price P_w. It will be seen from Fig. 37.2 that difference AB between demand and domestic supply at price P_d is exactly equal to the fixed quota of Q_1Q_2 quantity of imports. It is thus dear that like tariffs fixation of quota has served to limit trade and raise price. It will therefore have same effects as we have explained in case of tariff. It may however be noted that unlike tariff in case of quota Government would not collect any revenue.

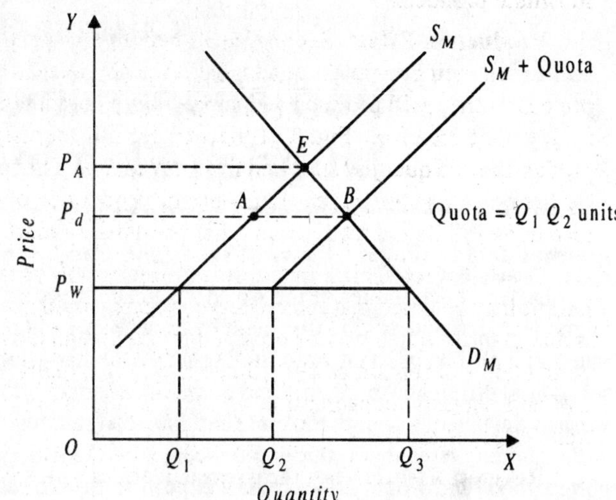

Fig. 37.2. *Effects of Quota*

QUESTIONS FOR REVIEW

1. Explain the gains from free trade for a developing country like India. In view of these gains from free trade, explain why the various countries put up various barriers to trade.
2. Critically examine the case for free trade in respect of developing countries like India.
3. What arguments are given in favour of protection? Do you think protection is right trade strategy for India in the emerging international economic environment ?
4. Critically examine the following arguments in support of protection.
   1. Infant industry argument
   2. Employment argument
   3. Balance of payment argument
   4. Promotion of *Swadeshi*
5. Explain the economic effects of tariffs. Compare them with effects of quota.
6. Tariffs cause misallocation of resources. Discuss.
7. The purpose and effect of protective tariffs is to reduce world trade. Discuss.
8. Explain the effects of quota. The fixation of quota for imports of goods reduces trade and raise prices. Examine critically.

CHAPTER 38

International linkages and Mundell-Fleming Model

International Linkages : Flows of Trade and Capital in an Open Economy

Different economies of the world are linked together through two channels: (1) through trade in goods and services; (2) movement of finance or capital across countries. It is because of these international linkages that both the higher economic growth and recession in the U.S.A. make a substantial difference to income and output in other countries such as India, Mexico, Japan and vice versa as the latter have both the trade and financial relations with the former. For example, recession in the United States that reduces the incomes of the American people affects their demand for imported goods and would affect India's exports to the United States. Besides, if the Central Bank of America lowers interest rate below that prevailing in India, this will increase capital outflows from the United States to India as was witnessed during in 2002-03 and 2003-04. Dollar inflows into India will affect the foreign exchange rate of rupee and also the reserves of foreign exchange with Reserve Bank of India. It will be recalled that reserves of foreign exchange with RBI determine the money supply in India.

It is quite evident from above that in this age of globalisation when the economies of the world have been integrated through flows of trade and capital, growth and recession in one economy have world-wide repercussions. International linkages in the area of financial and capital movements have acquired crucial importance in modern times. The households, banks or corporate firms, say of the USA, can hold assets such as government bonds, corporate bonds, equity (i.e. share capital) of companies not only of their own country but also those of foreign countries. In most countries of the world today (India included) there are no restrictions on holding of financial assets such as corporate bonds, equity capital (i.e. corporate shares) and physical assets abroad. As a matter of fact, portfolio managers of the banks or large corporations shop around the world for parking their funds in the assets of the countries which offer them most attractive yields. It is through shifting of their assets by rich households, banks or corporate firms that link financial markets around the world. This mobility of capital or finance to search for better yield around the world affects income and employment, exchange rates and interest rates at home and abroad.

As mentioned above, households, institutional investors, banks and corporate firms search around the world for the highest return (of course, adjusted for risk). As a result, returns or yields in capital markets in various open economies get linked together. For example, if rates of interest or return on equity capital in India rise relatively to those in the USA, the US investors would try to lend or invest their capital in India to take advantage of higher returns. On the other hand, the borrowers would turn to the USA to borrow funds from the US financial markets to take advantage of lower rates of interest.

National Income and Trade Balance in the Open Economy

An important difference between the open economy and the closed economy is that in an open economy, the aggregate expenditure in any year need not be equal to its output of goods and services. This is because a country can spend more than the income it earns from production of goods and services. It can do so by borrowing from abroad. On the contrary, a country can spend less than the value of goods and services it produces because it can lend the difference to foreigners. To understand it fully recall the national income accounting explained in an earlier chapter.

It will be recalled that the economy's gross domestic output (GDP) can be divided into the four components :

$$Y = C + I + G + NX \quad ...(1)$$

where C stands for consumption expenditure, I for investment, G for government purchases of domestic goods and services and NX for net exports. NX is the difference between expenditure on exports (EX) and expenditure on imports (IM). Thus, net exports (NX) = $EX - IM$. The net exports is also known as belance of trade.

From the national income accounts identity given in equation (1) above we can know the relationship between net exports, gross national product and aggregate domestic expenditure. To do so we rearrange the equation (1) above as under :

$$NX = Y - (C + I + G) \quad ...(2)$$

where $(C + I + G)$ represents aggregate domestic expenditure and Y represents Gross Domestic Product (GDP). The equation (2) shows that if Gross Domestic Product (Y) exceeds aggregate domestic expenditure $(C + I + G)$, net exports (NX) are positive, that is, we are exporting more than we are importing. On the other hand, if a country's Gross Domestic Product is less than aggregate domestic expenditure, it will be importing more than it is exporting and therefore its net exports will be negative.

SAVING, INVESTMENT AND INTERNATIONAL FLOWS OF GOODS AND CAPITAL IN AN OPEN ECONOMY

We have seen that saving and investment play an important role in determining the level of national income and employment in an economy in the short run. Besides, saving and investment are crucial to the long-run economic growth of a country. It is therefore important to know how saving and investment are related to the international flows of goods and capital. This can be shown by rearranging the national income accounts identity. Let us first rewrite the national income identity.

$$Y = C + I + G + NX \quad ...(1)$$

Rearranging we have

$$Y - C - G = I + NX \quad ...(2)$$

Since saving is the part of national income (Y) that is left after expenditure on consumption by households and Government purchases of goods and services[1], $Y - C - G$ in (2) above represents saving (S) of the economy. Note that national saving $Y - C - G$ is the sum of private saving which is equal to $Y - T - C$ (where T represents taxes) and public saving which is equal to $T - G$. Thus National Saving = Private Saving + Public Saving

or

$$S = (Y - T - C) + (T - G)$$
$$= Y - C - G$$

writing S for $Y - C - G$ in national income identity in (2) above we have

$$S = I + NX \quad ...(3)$$

Subtracting I from both sides of equation (3) we have

$$S - I = NX \quad ...(4)$$

1. All Government expenditure on goods and services is treated as consumption expenditure. Though this is strictly true of the capitalist developed economies, it is not true of developing countries like India where Government undertakes a lot of investment expenditure.

The national income accounts identity of the open economy presented in (4) above shows that economy's net exports (*NX*) must always be equal to the difference between domestic saving and investment ($S - I$). This difference between domestic saving and investment represents net capital flows. The equation (4) above shows that net capital outflow equals net exports. Note that the net exports (*NX*) in the present context includes not only exports and imports of *merchandise* but also of invisibles (i.e. services). Therefore, the concept of net exports (*NX*) used here is what is generally called *current account balance.* Net capital inflow is also called *net foreign investment* by some economists. Thus the equation (4) indicates that if domestic saving (*S*) exceeds investment (*I*), that is, if there are *net capital outflow*, the economy will be lending or investing the excess saving abroad. If, on the other hand, investment in the economy is greater than its domestic saving, that is, if there are *net capital inflows* it means it will be receiving net investment funds from abroad. Thus net capital inflow, that is, the difference between investment and domestic saving of the economy ($S - I$) equals the difference between the amounts the residents of country will be lending or investing abroad and the amount that the foreigners will be lending or investing in that country.

Thus the net capital inflow represents the international flow of funds to finance investment in a country. It follows from above that the difference between domestic saving and investment, that is, net capital flows always equal the net exports. It may be noted that *net exports is also called trade balance.* If services are included in it, net exports are called *current account balance* because it represents to what extent trade in *both goods and services* of a country departs from the equality of their imports and exports. Thus

Net capital flow ($S - I$) = Current Account Balance

For sake of simplicity we use the term trade balance in the sense of current account balance. From our above analysis we arrive at the following conclusions :

(1) If domestic saving exceeds investment ($S > I$) for an economy it follows from above that net exports (*NX*) or trade balance will be positive. In other words, in this case the country will be running a *trade surplus*. This case implies that the residents of the country would be lending or investing abroad. That is, there will be *capital outflow* from the economy.

(2) If domestic saving is less than investment ($S < I$ *or* $S - I < 0$) of a country, its net exports will be negative, that is, the country's will be running a *trade deficit.* In this case there will be *capital inflows* in a country to finance the extra imports.

(3) Thirdly, if saving equals investment ($S = I$ *or* $S - I = 0$), the net exports (*NX*) or capital flows will be zero, that is, the country's current account will be in balance or the country will have balanced trade.

It follows from above that the identity of national income accounts of an open economy ($S - I = NX$) that the ***international flows of capital and international flows of goods and services are the two sides of the same coin.*** It may however be noted that international flows of capital can take many forms. First, foreigners can lend to a country when it has excess of imports over exports. Secondly, the foreigners can buy domestic assets such as the American firms buying shares in the Indian Stock Exchange or buying physical assets in India. By buying assets of another country, the foreigners make investment and provide financial funds to the country.

THE GOODS MARKET AND *IS* CURVE IN THE OPEN ECONOMY

The analysis of determination of national income, employment and rate of interest in open economies is also made in the framework of *IS –LM* model with a few changes. In particular, *IS* curve in the open economy contains a new term of net *exports (NX)*.

An important change in the *IS-LM* model applicable to an open economy is that in it *domestic spending* does not determine level of national income and output. Instead, it is *spending on domestic goods* that determines level of national income and employment in an open economy. A part of spending by domestic residents is done on imports from foreign countries and the rest on domestically produced goods and services. Besides, a part of spending on domestic goods is by foreigners to whom we export goods. Thus, net exports which means exports minus imports together with spending by domestic residents on domestic goods constitute aggregate demand for or spending on domestic goods. Thus, goods market equilibrium in an open economy is represented by the following equation:

$$Y = C + I + G + NX$$

or $$Y = C + I + G + (X–M)$$

Where NX or $(X–M)$ represents next exports. The above equation states that equilibrium level of national income is equal to the sum of consumption demand (C), investment demand (I), government purchases of goods and services (G) and net exports (NX). Consumption expenditure (C) depends on disposable income or Y-T, investment depends negatively on interest rate, G is autonomous government expenditure and net exports, among others, depends on exchange rate (e).

Incorporating the above in the *IS* equation we have the following *IS* curve for an open economy :

$$IS \text{ curve} : Y = C\,(Y–T) + I\,(r) + G + NX\,(e)$$

Net Exports (*NX*). The term net exports (NX) needs further elaboration. Net exports, as menioned above, represents the excess of exports over imports, depend on domestic income (Y) which affects spending on imports and therefore net exports. Besides, net exports depend on (1) foreign income (Y_f) which affects foreign demand for our exports and (2) the real exchange rate which we denote by R. Depreciation in real exchange rate will increase our exports and reduce our imports and as a result improves our trade balance as demand shifts from foreign goods to the domestically produced goods. It may be noted that real exchange rate is the ratio of price of foreign goods (P_f) to price of goods at home (P_h). That is $R = \frac{P_f}{P_h}$ • If e is the nominal exchange rate (that is, ratio of prices of domestic and foreign currencies), then the real exchange rate R equals $e.\frac{P_f}{P_h}$. Now, depreciation of national currency will lower the prices of its exports and raise the prices of its imports. This will tend to increase exports and reduce imports and thereby tend to improve trade balance. The net exports or trade balance can be represented as under:

$$NX = X - M$$

$$NX = X\,(Y_f, R) - M(Y,R)$$

$$NX = NX\,(Y,Y_f, R)$$

It follows from the last equation that net exports depend on (1) domestic income or output (Y), which determines imports; (2) foreign income (Y_f) which determines demand for our exports; and (3) real exchange rate (R) which determines prices of our exports and imports. Three important results follow from the equation for net exports.

1. *A rise in our domestic income, other things remaining the same, will raise our spending on imports and hence adversely affect trade deficit.*

2. *A rise in foreign income, say of the USA, other things remaining the same, will increase our exports and improve our trade balance. As a result, aggregate demand will increase in our country with a favourable effect on our national income, output and employment..*

3. *A depreciation in real exchange rate of our currency will increase our exports and reduce our imports with a favourable effect on national output and employment.*

MACRO-ECONOMIC EQUILIBRIUM IN AN OPEN ECONOMY: WITHOUT CAPITAL FLOWS: IS-LM MODEL

IS – LM curve model involves the determination of national income and rate of interst through joint equilibrium of goods market and money market. Since in an open economy a part of increase in income is spent on imports rather than on domestically produced goods, *IS* curve of an open economy is steeper than that of a closed economy. This means that for a given reduction in interest rate, a smaller increase in output and income is required to restore equilibrium in the goods market.

Besides, as explained above, *IS* curve of the open economy also includes net exports (*NX*) as a component of aggregate demand for goods. The real exchange rate of the national currency, which determines the prices of exports and imports and thereby determine net exports also affects the open economy *IS* curve. Fore example, depreciation of real exchange rate of the national currency which raise exports and lowers imports results in increase in net exports and will therefore cause an outward shift in the *IS* curve to the right. Similarly, increase in foreign income which will raise foreign spending on our goods will lead to the increase in net exports, which is a component of aggregate demand, will also cause a shift in the IS curve to the right.

LM curve which represents money market equilibrium at various rates of interest and level of income is represented by the following equation:

$$\frac{M}{P} = L(r, Y)$$

where $\frac{M}{P}$ stands for supply of real money balances, and $L(r, Y)$ for demand for money which is determined by rate of interest (r) and level of income (Y).

The intersection of open-economy *IS* and *LM* curves determine jointly the income and rate of interest in the open economy. This is shown in Figure 38.1. It will be seen that open economy *IS* and *LM* curves interest at joint *E* and determine Y_0 equilibrium level of income and r equilibrium rate of interest.

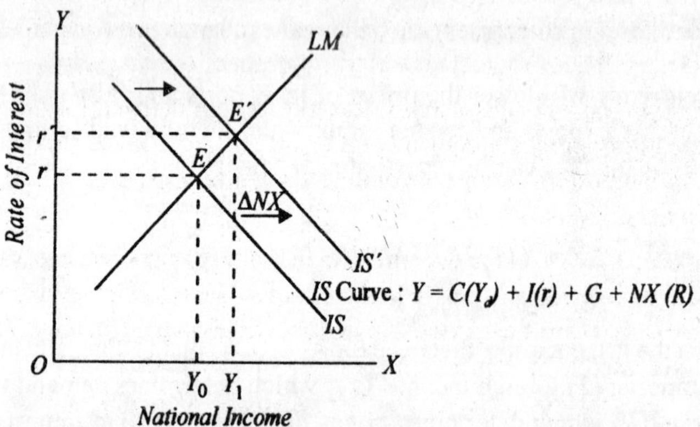

Fig. 38.1. *Determination of Income in the Open Economy through IS and LM Curves*

Impact of Increase in Net Exports (NX).

Since equilibrium level of income in the open economy depends on foreign income (Y_f) and real exchange rate (R), changes in foreign income or real exchange rate will affect equilibrium level of income. For example, if foreign income increases, it will raise the foreign spending on domestic goods or, in other words, it will increase our net exports. The increase in net exports (*NX*) will cause a shift of *IS* curve to the right. This is shown in Figure 38.1 where as a result of increase in foreign income, say of the United States, which is our important trade partner. *IS* curve shifts from *IS* to *IS′* With this it will be seen that equilibrium level

of income has risen to Y_1 and rate of interest to r'. It should be noted that increase in income also implies increase in output and employment.

On the other hand, if there is recession in foreign economies, as was the case of American economy during 2001-03 and again in 2007-09, it will reduce their imports and thereby reduce foreign demand for our exports. This will cause a leftward shift in the *IS* curve. As a result, our level of income and output will fall. Besides, rate of interest will also decline.

Effect of Depreciation on Exchange Rate

Let us now see how depreciation in real exchange rate of the national currency, say Indian rupee, affects our national income. This can also be explained with the help of Figure 38.1 As explained above, depreciation in exchange rate encourages exports and discourages imports and thereby leads to increase in net exports. Since net exports increasese at each level of income, *IS* curve shifts to the right, say to *IS′* in Figure 38.1. Thus, as a result of depreciation in real exchange rate, equilibrium level of domestic income will increase.

Conclusion: In the Table 38.1 given below, we summarise the effects of changes in domestic spending, foreign income and depreciation in real exchange rate on domestic income and net exports. It may be noted that + sign indicates increase and – sign indicates decrease. It will be seen from this table that increase in domestic spending leads to *increase in domestic income and to decrease in net exports.* Increase in domestic spending leads to greater aggregate demand for

Table 38.1. Effects of changes in domestic spending, foreign income and real depreciation on domestic income and net exports

Increase in	Increase in Domestic Spending	Increase in Foreign Income	Depreciation in Real Exchange Rate
Domestic Income	+	+	+
Net Exports	–	+	+

goods and services and have therefore favourable effect on the level of domestic income. Since a part of increase in domestic spending is made on imports of goods from abroad, it increases imports and, given the exports, will cause a decrease in net exports of the economy.

Increase in foreign income causes an increase in foreign demand for our goods (i.e. exports) which are a component of aggregate demand and has therefore a favourbale effect on the level of domestic income. As increase in foreign income leads to more exports, it will, given the imports, cause an increase in net exports.

Lastly, as explained above, since depreciation in real exchange rate causes increase in exports and decrease in imports, it leads to increase in net exports. Increase in net exports raises aggregate demand for goods and has, therefore, a favourable effect on domestic income. Thus, depreciation of real exchange rate increases both domestic income and net exports.

THE MUNDELL - FLEMING MODEL

One of the important fact about the world economy today is the high degree of integration or linkage among financial or capital markets. As mentioned above, households, banks or corporations of different countries search around the world for the highest return (of course, adjusted for risk). As a result, returns or yields in capital markets in different countries get linked together. For example, if rates of interest or return on equity capital in India rise relative to those in the USA, the US investors would try to lend or invest their capital in India to take advantage of higher returns. On the other hand, the borrowers would turn to the USA to borrow funds from the US financial markets to take advantage of lower rates of return.

The tendency for the rates of return on capital to become equal in financial markets of different countries as a result of perfect mobility of capital was formalised in a model in the **1960s** by Robert Mundell, now a professor at Columbia University and the Late Marcus Fleming, an economist at the IMF. They assume (1) **a small open economy** (2) ***tax rates are the same everywhere***, (3) *foreign investors do not face political risk (i.e. the fear of nationalism of foreign assets, restrictions of transfer of assets, risk of default by foreign governments)*. Under these conditions and with perfect mobility of capital investors or foreign asset holders would try to invest in the asset in any country that yields the highest return. This would force rates of return on assets to become equal everywhere in the international capital markets because no one would invest at a lower return. It may however be noted that perfect equlisation of returns in different countries is crucially dependent on the twin assumptions of perfect mobility of capital and fixed foreign or world interest rate for an economy. In fact, as mentioned above, Mundell-Fleming model assumes a small open economy which is incapable of influencing world interest rate. Besides, it assumes perfect capital mobility.. "*Capital is perfectly mobile internationally when investors can purchase assets in any country they choose, quickly with low transaction costs, and in unlimited amounts*. When capital is perfectly mobile, asset holders are willing and able to move large amounts of funds across borders in search of the highest return or lowest borrowing costs"[1] The assumption of a small open economy with perfect capital mobility plays an important role in Mundell-Fleming model. The assumption of a small open economy implies that the economy can borrow or lend as much as it likes in world financial markets without affecting rate of interest. Thus, for a small open economy, rate of interest is determined by the world interest rate. Mathematically, we can state this assumption as

$$r = r_f$$

where r stands for domestic interest rate in the economy and r_f is the world rate of interest. It is the perfect mobility of capital that makes domestic interest rate (r) equal to the world interest rate. If due to some event or economic policy domestic interest rate happens to be lower than the world interest rate, the capital outflows would drive the domestic interest rate back to the world interest rate. On the other hand, if some event or policy causes domestic interest to exceed world interest rate, then the capital inflows would bring down the domestic interest rate to the level of world interest rate. Hence the equation $r = r_f$ represents that internationd flow of capital quickly brings the domestic interest rate equal to the world interest rate.

The Mundell-Fleming model, with domestic interest rate determined by the world interest rate, focuses on the role of exchange rate in the determination of national income in the short run. Another important aspect of Mundell-Fleming model is that behaviour of the economy depends on whether it adopts the fixed exchange rate system or flexible exchange rate system. In what follows we first explain below Mundell-Fleming model when the economy operate under the fixed exchange rate system and then analyse the model when the economy has adopted the flexible exchange rate system.

The Mundell-Fleming model of a small open economy with perfect capital mobility can be described by the following equations for *IS* and *IM* curves

IS equation : $Y = C(Y - T) + I(r_t) + G + NX(R)$

LM equation : $\dfrac{M}{P} = L(r_f,\ Y)$

The *IS* equation describes the goods marks equilibrium and the second *LM* equation describes money market equilibrium. G and T are the variables determined by fiscal policy, M is the monetary policy variable and they are important exogenous variables. The price P and world interest rate (r_4)

1. R. Dornbusch, S Fischer, R. Startz, *Macroeconomics*, TATA McGrawhill, 2002, P.282.

are the other exogenously given variables. The interest rate being given, the intersection of *IS* and *LM* curves determine the level of national income at which both the goods market and money market are in equilibrium. Besides, in case of the variable exchange rate system, the equilibrium of the two markets also determine the exchange rate.

However, Mundell – Fleming Model is based on same conditions which do not prevail in the real world. First, there are tax differences among countries which hinder the mobility of capital in response to interest-rate differentials among countries. Secondly, exchange rates between different currencies can change, sometimes considerably, which affect return in dollars on foreign investment. Finally, countries adopt measures to restrict capital outflows or simply default in making payments. These are some of the reasons due to which interest rates in different countries are not equal.

Mundell-Fleming Model of the Small Open Economy with a Fixed Exchange Rate Regime : Impact of Monetary Policy

An important result of the Mundell–Fleming linkage model under fixed exchange rate regime is that a central bank of a country cannot pursue an independent monetary policy. Under perfect mobility, a very small difference in interest rates in different countries would cause infinite capital flows that would bring about changes in balance of payments. These changes in balance of payments will affect exchange rate between different national currencies which would eliminate interest rate differential. Take an example. Suppose Central Bank of a country tightens its monetary policy so as to raise interest rate in the economy. When with the adoption of this policy interst rate rises in the economy, foreigners will shift their investible funds to this country so as to take advantage of the higher interest rate. With a huge inflow of capital, foreign exchange rate of the domestic currency will rise, that is, the currency of the country that adopts a higher interest rate monetary policy will appreciate. This appreciation of the currency will discourage exports and encourage imports which would have an adverse effect on balance of payments. This will force the Central Bank of the country which is committed to maintain the exchange rate at the fixed level to intervene to prevent the appreciation of exchange rate of the national currency.

To prevent the currency from appreciation, the Central Bank will buy the foreign currency, say US dollar. This will lead to the increase in foreign exchange reserves with the Central Bank which will issue more national currency against the increase in foreign exchange reserves. As a result, money supply in the economy will expand causing the rate of interest to fall. Thus, with the perfect mobility of capital and given a fixed exchange rate, domestic interest rate has been pushed back to the initial level. To quote Dornbusch and Fischer again, *"Under fixed exchange rates and perfect capital mobility, a country cannot move out of line with those prevailing in the world market. Any attempt at independent monetary policy leads to capital flows and need to intervene until interest rates are back in line with those in the world market"*[2].

It follows from above that, given a higher degree of capital mobility across countries, interest rates cannot be very much different. The differences in interest rates beyond a point will bring about capital flows across countries that will tend to provide world level yield in all of them.

Expansionary Monetary Policy Under Fixed Exchange Rate and Perfect Capital Mobility. Let us now analyse the effect of monetary expansion under the fixed exchange rate regime using *IS-LM* model. Consider Figure 38.2 where in panel (a) we have drawn the *IS* and *LM* curves as well as the

---

2. Dornbusch and Fischer, *op. cit.* p.285

horizontal straight line *BP*. The horizontal line *BL*= 0 at domestic interest rate i equal to foreign interest rate i_f ($i=i_f$) shows that the country has neither deficit nor surplus in its balance of payments, that is, its balance of payments is in equilibrium. At any other interest rate

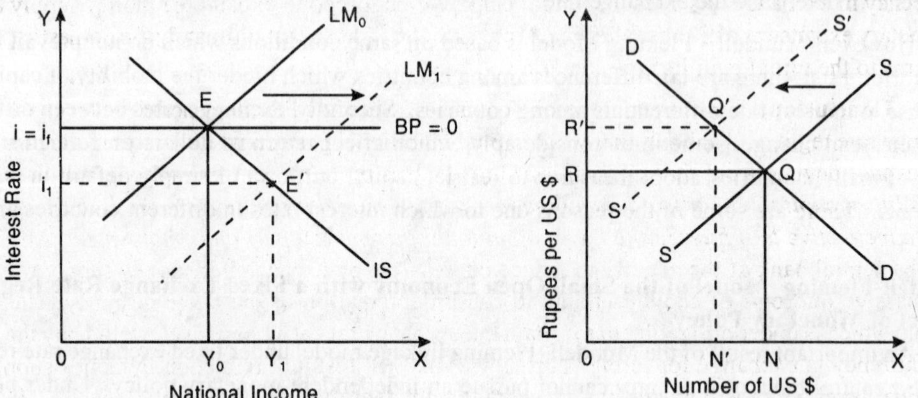

Panel (*a*) IS-LM Model of the Open Economy Panel (*b*) Determination of Foreign Exchange Rate

Fig. 38.2. *Effect of Monetary Expansion Under the Fixed Exchange Regime and Perfect Capital Mobility*

massive capital flows will occur which will cause disequilibrium in the balance of payments and will force the Central Bank to intervene to maintain the exchange rate.

To illustrate this we consider that Government adopts a policy of monetary expansion. Let the economy in panel (a) of Fig. 38.2 is initially at point *E* where the given *IS-LM* curves intersect at *E* which determines domestic rate of interest i which is equal to foreign rate of interest i_f. With monetary expansion, *LM* curve shifts to the right and as a result the economy moves to the new equilibrium position *E′* where domestic rate of interest has fallen to i_1. At the new position *E′* economy will have a large deficit in balance of payments which will exert a pressure on the exchange rate of domestic currency to *depreciate*. Determination of foreign exchange rate is shown in panel (*b*) of Fig. 38.2 where initially demand curve *DD* and supply curve *SS* of US dollars determine exchange rate equal to *OR* (*i.e.* number of rupees per US dollar). When as a result of expansion in money supply, LM_1 curve shifts to the right to the new position *LM* and consequently domestic rate of interest falls to i_1 (panel (*a*) of Figure 38.2), there will be large capital outflows. These capital outflows will reduce the supply of US dollars in foreign exchange market and as a result supply curve of US dollars shifts to the left to $S'S'$ (panel (*b*) of figure 38.2) resulting in the new exchange rate R' (that is, more rupees per US dollar). This means Indian rupee will depreciate. To maintain the exchange rate, the Central Bank of the country will intervene; it will sell foreign currency reserves in the foreign exchange market. The supply of domestic money supply in the economy will therefore decrease. As a result of this reduction in domestic money supply, *LM* curve will shift back to the left [see panel (a) of Fig. 38.2]. This process of contraction in money supply and consequent shifting back of *LM* curve to the left will continue until the initial equilibrium at *E* is reached again. As a matter of fact, with perfect capital mobility, the economy is not likely to reach at the new equilibrium joint *E′*. This is because the response of capital flows is so large and quick that the Central Bank will be forced to reverse quickly the initial expansion in money supply before the new equilibrium at *E′* is reached.

Contraction in Money Supply Under fixed Exchange Rate System. Conversely, if the Central Bank adopts the policy of contraction in money supply, *LM* curve will shift to the left of the initial equilibrium point *E*. Given the *IS* curve the new equilibrium will be reached at a higher domestic rate of interest as compared to foreign interest rate. This will induce massive capital inflows which will increase the demand for domestic currency and as a result domestic currency will appreciate. To maintain the exchange rate, the Central Bank will buy the foreign currency and give the domestic currency in exchange. As a result, central bank will be forced to expand the money supply and this monetary expansion will cause shift in *LM* curve to the right so that ultimately the domestic economy returns to the initial equilibrium situation .

Conclusion. From the foregoing analysis of Mundell-Fleming model under the fixed exchange rate regime, it follows that when capital mobility is perfect, interest rates in the home country cannot deviate from those prevailing abroad. It is quite evident from above that *with perfect mobility of capital, under fixed exchange rate regime, monetary policy in a small open economy is quite ineffective to influence the levels of national income (output) and employment.* Any attempt by the central bank of the country to reduce interest rate by expansion in money supply would lead to massive outflows of capital tending to cause depreciation of the home currency. The Central Bank, which is under obligation to maintain the exchange rate at a fixed level, would buy the domestic currency in exchange for foreign currency. This will result in reduction in money supply to its original level with the home economy again attaining equilibrium at the initial level. This shows under fixed exchange rate regime, the *Central bank of a country cannot undertake an independent monetary policy.*

Mundell-Fleming Model : Role of Expansionary Fiscal Policy under Fixed Exchange Rate System

While expansionary monetary policy under fixed rate regime is quite ineffective to affect national income and output, fiscal policy is highly effective, given the perfect mobility of capital. To show this through open economy *IS-LM* model, consider Figure 38.3. Suppose adopting expansionary fiscal policy Government increases its expenditure with money supply remaining unchanged. It will be seen from panel (a) that increase in government expenditure causes shift in the *IS* curve to the right to the new position *IS'*. As will be seen from panell (a) this raises both the interest rate and level of national income (output). The higher domestic rate of interest *as compared to the world*

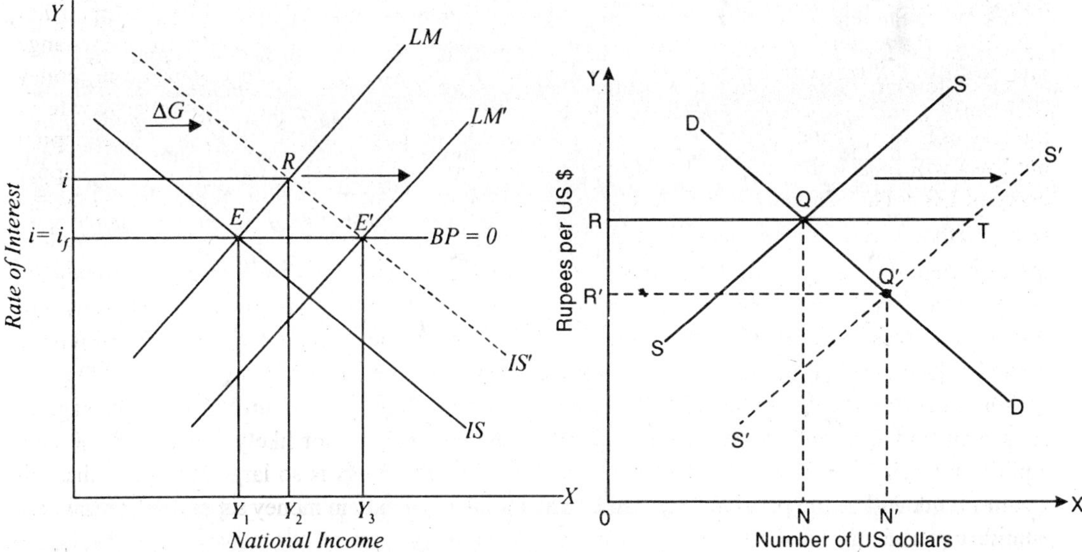

Panel (*a*) : *Determination of National Income and Rate of Interest* Panel (*b*) : *Determination of Foreign Exchange Rate*

Fig. 38.3 *Effect of Expansionery Fiscal Policy in a Small Open Economy under Fixed Exchange Rate* *interest rate* (i_f) *will cause capital inflows into the economy*. These capital inflows will **bring about** appreciation in exchange rate of national currency. The determination of foreign **exchange rate is** illustrated in panel (*b*) of Figure 38.3. It will be observed from panel (*b*) that as a result of capital inflows, supply curve of foreign exchange (*i.e.* US dollars) shifts to the right from *SS* to *S'S'*. The new supply curve *S'S'* of foreign exchange rate intersects the demand curve for foreign exchange at point *Q'* and determines the lower new foreign exchange rate *R'* (rupees per US dollar). This implies that there is appreciation of rupee. To maintain the exchange rate at *R* the Central Bank will have to expand money supply which will cause a shift in *LM* curve to the right and increase national income further. It will be seen from panel (*a*) of Figure 38.3 that money supply is increased so much that *LM* curve shifts to the new position *LM'* and domestic rate of interest falls back to the original level so that it is again equal to the world interest rate ($i=i_f$). Thus, in this case, with endogenous expansion in money supply to maintain the exchange rate, interest rate effectively remains fixed at a given level. Fiscal expansion leads to increase in national income by Y_1Y_3, equal to the Keynesian multiplier effect.

Conclussion

The upshot of the above analysis is that the *commitment to maintain a fixed exchange rate makes the changes in money supply endogenous*. This is because the Central Bank through its intervention has to sell or buy the foreign exchange as the case may be to maintain the exchange rate system at the fixed level. The Central Bank under the fixed exchange rate system with perfect capital mobility *cannot conduct an independent monetary policy* to achieve domestic economic stability. However, *government can use expansionary fiscal policy to raise the level of national income and employment.*

MUNDELL-FLEMING MODEL FOR A SMALL OPEN ECONOMY UNDER FLEXIBLE EXCHANGE RATES

We now use Mundell-Fleming Model to explain how monetary and fiscal policies in a small open economy work when there is completely flexible exchange rate regime and perfect capital mobility. It is assumed that domestic prices remain fixed while exchange rate is fully flexible. It is important to note that under flexible exchange rate regime, the Central Bank does not intervene in the market for foreign exchange. The exchange rate adjusts itself to bring the demand for and supply of foreign exchange in equilibrium. Therefore, *under flexible exchange rate system and without the intervention of the Central Bank, balance of payments must always be in equilibrium*, that is, there is neither any deficit nor any surplus. This implies that any current account deficit must be financed by private capital inflows. On the contrary, any current account surplus must be balanced by capital outflows. It is worth noting again that it is adjustments in foreign exchange rate under flexible exchange rate system that guarantees that sum of current and capital accounts of blance of payments is zero

A second *important consequence of fully flexible exchange rate regime is that under it the Central Bank can pursue its independent monetary policy*, that is, it can expand or contract the money supply at will according to its assessment of the needs of the domestic economy. Since under flexible exchange rates, there is no obligation for the Central Bank to intervene there is no any link between the balance of payments and the money supply in the economy.

In Mundell-Fleming model the assumption of perfect capital mobility ensures that at only one interest rate which is equal to world interest rate ($i = i_f$) the balance of payments is zero, that is, in equilibrium ($BP = 0$). At any rate of interest other than this causes a change in the real exchange rate through its effect on capital flows for the domestic economy. Assuming that domestic and foreign prices of goods (p and p_f) remain constant, decline in the domestic interest rate below the world

interest rate (*i.e.* i_f) will cause unlimited capital outflows and bring about depreciation in the exchange rate. As explained above, exchange rate is a determinant of net exports (*NX*) which in the open economy affects aggregate demand and therefore determines level of open economy *IS* curve (*IS* curve : $Y = (Y, i) + NX(Y, Y_f, R)$ where *R* stands for the exchange rate and *NX* for net exports). Now, depreciation in the exchange rate following capital outflows when $i < i_f$ will raises exports and reduce imports and will cause increase in net exports (*NX*). The increase in net exports will shift the *IS* curve to the right and thereby affect national income and output.

On the contrary, if $i > i_f$, there will be unlimited capital inflows causing appreciation in the exchange rate which will reduce exports and increase imports and will thus lead to the reduction in net exports (*NX*). The reduction in net exports (*NX*) as a result of appreciation in the exchange rate causes a shift in the *IS* curve to the left and will therefore affect national income and output.

In the small open economy with international linkages in terms of trade of goods and capital flows, our open economy model under flexible exchange rate regime consists of the following three equations.

$$IS \text{ curve} : Y = A(Y, i) + NX(Y, Y_f, R) \quad \ldots(i)$$

$$BP = NX(Y, Y_f, R) + CF(i - i_f) \quad \ldots(ii)$$

$$i = i_f \quad \ldots(iii)$$

where *CF* stands for capital flows.

With this Mundell-Fleming linkage model of a small open economy under flexible exchange rate regime we explain below the effect on national income (output), interest rate and exchange rate of the following factors and policies.

1. Exogenous increase in exports
2. Fiscal policy
3. Monetary policy

Exogenous Increase in Exports under Flexible Exchange Rate

The effect of exogenous increase in exports, say due to the increase in world demand for our goods, is shown in Figure 38.4 Initially, the economy is in equilibrium at point *E* with national output equal to Y_0 and interest rate *i* which is equal to world interest rate i_f $(i=i_f)$. When there is exogenous increase in our exports, *IS* curve shifts to the right to *IS*′.

Now, new *IS*′ curve interests *LM* curve at point *E*′ where both goods and money markets clear. It may be noted that at this new equilibrium point, *E*′, national income increases. The increase in national income also induces the rise in equilibrium interest rate above the world interest rate i_f. This higher domestic interest rate will lead to the capital inflows which will exert pressure on the exchange rate. These capitals inflows, as seen above, will cause the domestic currency to appreciate. The appreciation in exchange rate will make our exports relatively expensive and imports cheaper than before. As a result, demand shifts away from domestic goods and as a result net exports (*NX*) to decline.

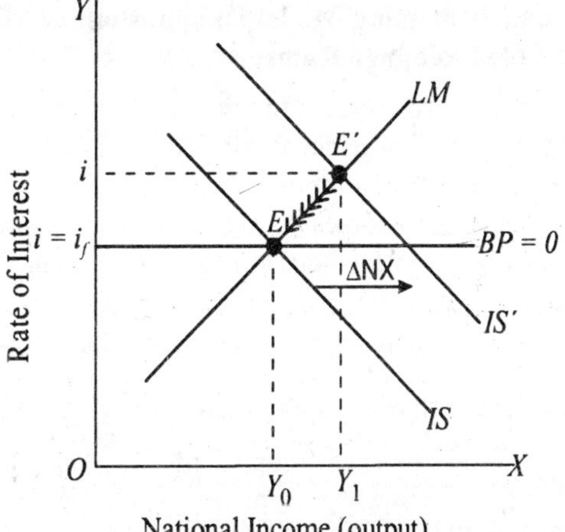

Fig. 38.4. *Effect of Exogenous Increase in Exports*

In Figure 38.4, the appreciation of exchange rate and consequently decline in net exports will cause a shift in the *IS* curve back to the left. The capital inflows will continue and net exports will go on declining as a result of appreciation of domestic currency until *IS* curve shifts back to the original level *IS* and equilibrium level of national income and output is restored at OY_0 level which is consistent with monetary equilibrium at the world rate of interest.

Conclusion. It follows from above that under conditions of perfect capital mobility, increase in exports of a small open economy has no lasting effect on the equilibrium level of national income and output. Increase in net exports (NX) causes interest rate to rise through increase in level of national income. This induces capital inflows which result in appreciation of the exchange rate and reduces net exports. This cancels out the effect on national income of the initial exogenous increase in exports of a country.

Effect of Expansionary Fiscal Policy in a Small Open Economy under Flexible Exchange Rate

We can use the Mundell-Fleming linkage model to analyse the effect of expansionary fiscal policy in a small open economy under flexible exchange rate system. Expansionary fiscal policy has the same effect as that of exogenous increase in exports explained above. Under expansionary fiscal policy either government expenditure is increased or taxes are reduced. This fiscal expansion leads to the increase in aggregate demand and causes a shift in the *IS* curve to the right. This, given the *LM* curve, induces the interest rate to rise and invites capital inflows into the economy. These capital inflows result in appreciation of the exchange rate. This appreciation of the exchange rate induced by higher interest rate leads to reduction in exports and increase in imports. As a result, there is the reduction in net exports which completely offsets the impact of fiscal expansion on national income and output.

We arrive at an important conclusion from our above analysis. *Real disturbances such as exogenous increase in exports or expansion in government expenditure or a tax cut does not affect equilibrium level of income in a small open economy under flexible exchange rate system with perfect capital mobility.* We have seen above that under the fixed exchange rate regime, expansionary fiscal policy in a small open economy is highly effective in increasing the level of national income. However, under flexible exchange rate system with conditions of perfect capital mobility, equilibrium level of aggregate income or output remains unaffected as a result of expansionary fiscal policy. Under flexible exchange rate fiscal expansion causes appreciation of exchange rate which causes exports to decrease and imports to increase and thus leads to a shift in the composition of domestic demand towards foreign goods and away from domestic goods.

Mundell-Fleming Model : Expansionary Monetary Policy in a Small Open Economy under Flexble Exchange Rates

In sharp contrast to the expansionary fiscal policy, in Mundell-Fleming model expansionary monetary policy under flexible exchange rate regime is highly effective in raising the level of national income or output. This favourable affect of expansion in money supply on the level of national output comes through its causing depreciation in exchange rate of domestic currency. Consider Figure 38.5 where to begin with *IS* and *LM* curves interest at point *E* and determine level of national income Y_0 and rate of interest i, $(i = i_f)$. Now, suppose there is increase in the nominal quantity of money supply *M*. Since we are assuming that prices of goods remain constant, increase in money will bring about increase in real money balances, $\frac{M}{P}$. With this at the equilibrium point *E*, there will be excess supply of real money balances. To restore equilibrium, rate of interest will have to fall or aggregate income will have to rise. As a result *LM* curve shifts to the right to the new position *LM′*. The new *LM′* curve interesects the original *IS* curve at new point *E′*. At the new point *E′*, whereas goods and money markets are in equilibrium (at the initial exchange rate), rate of interest has fallen below the world interest rate i_f. This will cause capital outflows from the country.

These capital outflows will reduce the supply of foreign exchange (say *US* dollars) and lead to the depreciation of the domestic currency. The depreciation of domestic currency will make exports of the country relatively cheaper and its imports relatively expensive than before. This will lead to increase in exports and reduction in imports of the country resulting in larger net exports (*NX*). Increase in net exports (*NX*), which is a component of aggregate demand, will cause *IS* curve to shift to the right. The point *E′* is really not a final equilibrium point as adjustment process is not complete at point *E*. *IS* curve will continue shifting to the right until the joint equilibrium of goods market and money market is established at the rate of interest which is equal to the world interest rate. In Figure 38.5. such equilibrium is reached at point *E′′* at which new *LM* and *IS* curves interesect and determine rate of interest $i = i_f$. It will be seen from Figure 38.5 that at the new final equilibrium point *E′′*, level of national income (or aggregate output) Y_1 is greater than the initial income Y_0.

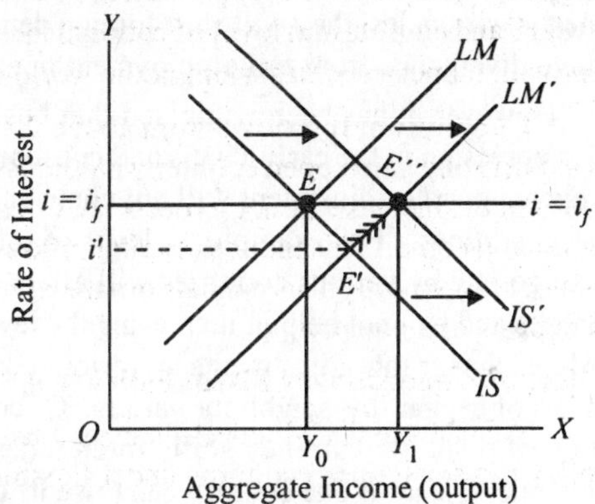

Fig. 38.5. *Mundell Fleming Model : Effect of Expansion in Money Supply on Level of Income or Output in a Small Open Economy under Flexible Exchange Rate System*

Comparison. It is interesting to compare in case of a small open economy the impact of expansion in money supply under flexible rate system with that under fixed exchange rate regine. Under the fixed exchange rate regime the expansionary monetary policy is quite ineffective in raising national income or aggregate output. Any attempt to increase money supply lowers rate of interest below the world interest rate which causes unlimited capital outflows. These capital outflows lead to the reversal of increase in money supply so that finally the equilibrium of the economy is restored at the initial level of income or output.

On the other hand, under flexible exchange rate system where Central Bank does not intervene, increase in money supply, as seen above, is not *reversed* in the foreign exchange market. Capital outflows that take place in the foreign exchange market following the fall in the rate of interest below the world rate of interest leads to depreciation of domestic currency. This depreciation causes exports to increase and imports to decline resulting in increase in net exports (*NX*). Consequently, expansion in income or output actually occurs assuming fixed prices. Thus, ability of the Central Bank to control money supply under flexible exchange rate is an important effect of the flexible exchange rate system.

Beggar thy neighbour Policy and Competitive Depreciation

We have seen above expansionary monetary policy causes depreciation of domestic currency and thereby leads to increase is net exports and therefore an increase in income and employment in the economy. Depreciation of domestic currency causes a shift in demand from foreign goods towards domestic goods. As a result, income (or output) and employment abroad decline. That is, one country gains at the expense of the other country. Therefore, expansion in net exports and therefore in income and employment as a result of depreciation has been called *beggar thy-neighbour policy*. That is, increase in output and employment in one country takes place by creating unemployment and loss of output in other countries.

It follows from above that *depreciation in exchange rate is mainly a way of shifting demand from foreign goods towards domestic goods rather than increasing the level of world demand.* Exchange rate adjustment can play an important role in promoting economic stability at full employment level when different countries find themselves in different phases of business cycles. That is, some are in boom phases and experiencing over full employment while others are in recession phase of business cycles. In this case, if the countries experiencing recession depreciate their domestic currencies, they will shift foreign demand to their domestic products. In this way this will remove divergence from full employment in each country.

However, it has been witnessed that business cycles are highly synchronised such as world-wide depression in the early 1930s and consequence of oil shack of 1973 and also recently in 2001-03, exchange rate adjustment will not contribute much towards achieving world-wide full employment conditions. For example, if level of total world demand is deficient, then depreciation in exchange rate by various countries will affect only the distribution of given world demand among countries and will not help in increasing the level of world demand for goods and services. In other words, exchange rate adjustments by various countries experience recessionary conditions are merely policies of beggar thy-neighbour variety. Of course, from the angle of an individual country depreciation of domestic currency shifts foreign demand to itself and is able to increase its output and employment. But, if one country can raise its output and employment by depreciating its currency, others can also do so. This leads to *competitive depreciation by different countries* for attracting world demand for their goods at the expense of others.

ASSET MARKETS AND EXCHANGE RATE EXPECTATIONS

A fundamental feature of models of exchange rate determination is the assumption of international capital mobility. In this connection with capital mobility the asset markets and asset prices play an important role because capital between countries flow in response to the return on assets. Two important asset markets of a country are bond market and stock market where bonds and equity shares are sold and bought. Given the well-integrated asset markets of various countries, it is expected that interest rates will be equated across countries due to perfect mobility of capital among them. Interest is return on bonds which are important financial assets. In addition to bonds, stocks of corporate firms are other important financial assets in which people make investment. It is important to note that *price of a stock is the net present value of expected future returns/dividends.* Changes in expectations of future dividends and capital gains affect the price of a stock of a company.

On bonds periodic fixed payments (generally called coupens) are paid and then at the end of maturity period, face value of the bond is paid. Price of a bond is the present value of future periodic payments and the maturity amount paid at the end. Bond prices are inversely related to interest rates. For example, if a bond carries a payment of Rs 100 from a year now and the prevailing market interest rate is i, then the price of the bond is given by

$$P = \frac{100}{1+i}$$

where P stands for the price of a bond and i is the market interest rate.

It will be seen from above that higher is the interest rate, the lower will be the price of bond because Rs 100 will now be discounted at a higher interest rate. Therefore, due to changes in market interest rate, bond prices will change. Fall in the interest rate will raise bond prices, and rise in market interest rate will lower bond prices. Therefore, due to changes in market rate of interest prices of long-term bonds are subject to considerable price fluctuations. Since price of a stock of a corporate company is the present value of expected dividends and capital gains in future it is also influenced by long-term interest rates. Therefore, stock prices fall when interest rates rise and vice versa.

Our purpose of foregoing analysis of prices of financial assets (bonds and stocks) is that they are intimately related to market rate of interest. In fact, rate of interest is generally regarded as a return on capital. In our analysis that follows we will also take market interest rate prevailing in a country as a proxy for the return on capital.

As mentioned above in the analysis of exchange rate determination, with perfect mobility of capital internationally we expect interest rate or return on capital assets (*i.e.* bonds and stocks) to be equated across countries. Capital moves internationally across countries due to differentials in yields or returns on assets. However, this general rule does not seem to apply to actual world situation. For example, interest rates generally do not correspond to actual world situation. The interest rates in the USA and European countries whose capital markets are well integrated are not equal. How do we explain this fact? In what follows we shall explain it is *expected changes in foreign exchange rate* that explain the yield or interest rate differentials between countries despite the existence of international capital mobility. *Interest rates in a country with a depreciating currency should be sufficiently higher to compensate for the asset holders for lowering of yields on assets due to depreciation of a currency.* For example, suppose domestic real interest rate in India is 6% and in the USA it is 8%, then if US dollar is expected to depreciate over the next year by 5 per cent as against the Indian rupee is then in this case with 5 per cent depreciation of US dollar, the return on investment on a US asset will be 8 – 5 = 3 per cent which is less than the return of 6 per cent on the asset in India. As a result, investment in India becomes more attractive as compared to that in the US and therefore capital flows from the US to India will occur.

It is evident from above that in the analysis of interest rate equalisation through international mobility of capital *we must incorporate in our analysis expected changes in exchange rates of currencies of various countries.* Let us express it in motational terms. Let investment in domestic bonds earns the interest rate i. If interest rate or return on the bonds of a country, say of the US, is i_f plus the earning made on the change in the value of the US dollar is given by

$$i = i_f + \frac{\Delta e}{e}$$

where, i is the domestic interest rate, i_f is the interest rate on foreign bonds and $\frac{\Delta e}{e}$ is the expected change in the exchange rate.

With the incorporation of exchange rate expectations in determination of rate of return on bond, the equation for the balance of payments which shows the direction of capital flows will now be different because now capital flows are affected by the difference between the domestic interest rate and foreign interest after making adjustments for expected changes in the exchange rate of currencies.

The equation for balance of payments without introducing the expected changes in foreign exchange rate is given by

$$BP = NX(Y, Y_F, \frac{e\,P_f}{P} + CF\,(i - i_f) \qquad \text{... (1)}$$

where e is the nominal exchange rate between the currencies, p_f is the foreign price level and p is the domestic price level.

According to the above equation, balance of payments is equal to trade balance (NX) which depends on domestic income (Y), foreign income (Y_f) and real exchange rate $(\frac{ep_f}{p})$ plus capital account surplus (CF) which depends on the difference between the domestic interest rate (i) and foreign interest rate (i_f)

Incorporating the expected change in the exchange rate of currencies, the balance of payments equation can be written as

$$B_p = NX\left(Y, Y_F, \frac{ep_f}{p}\right) + CF\ (i - i_f + \frac{\Delta e}{e}) \quad ...\ (2)$$

where $\frac{\Delta e}{e}$ can be positive or negative depending on the expectations about the change in exchange rate.

The above equation (2) for equilibrium balance of payments reveals that even when capital is freely mobile internationally, interest rates (i and i_f) of the countries will differ because in equilibrium $i = i_f - \frac{\Delta e}{e}$, that is , i will not be qual to i_f. The difference in the interest rates is due to the expected change in the exchange rate between the currencies which affect the earnings from bonds of the countries. The capital flows are governed by the differences between domestic interest rate and foreign interest rate adjusted for the expected changes in foreign exchange rate. Given the domestic interest rate, decrease in foreign interest rate or expectations of depreciation of the foreign currency would cause capital outflows from the foreign country. On the other hand, increase in domestic interest rate and expectations of appreciation of domestic currency would encourage capital inflows in the domestic economy.

It follows from above that when we incorporate the expectations about changes in exchange rate between currencies, the differences in interest rates (or rates of return on assets) will persist even when capital is freely mobile. To quote Dornbusch, Fischer and Startz, "*The adjustment for exchange rate expectations accounts for international differences in interest rates*"[3]

Speculative Capital Flows and their Impact on the Economy

Change in expectations about exchange rate of currencies give rise to speculative capital flows that affect not only the *actual* exchange rate but also domestic interest rate and national output of the domestic economy,. This is illustrated in Fig. 38.6. Initially the equilibrium is at point

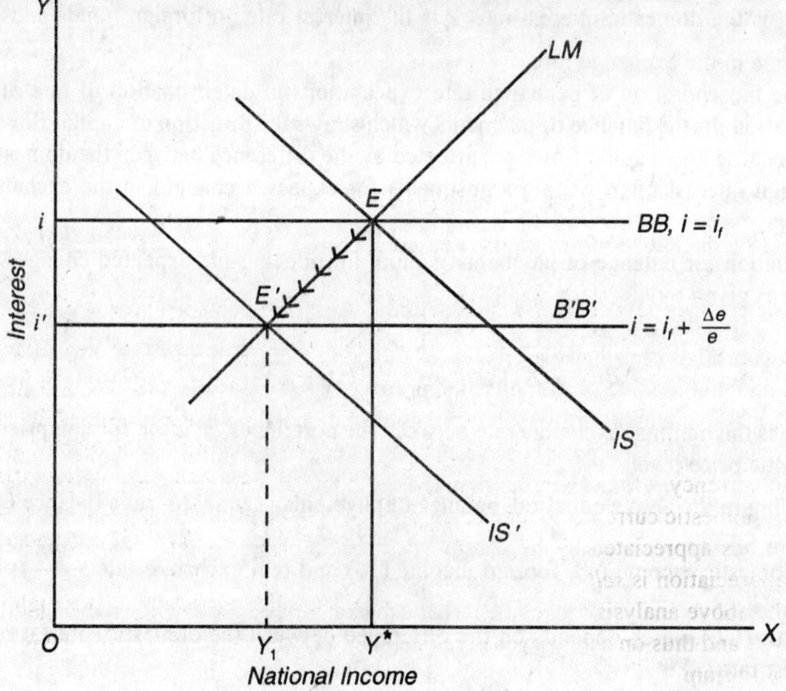

Fig. 38.6. *Impact of Expected Appreciation of Domestic Currency*

3. Dornbusch, Fischer and Startz, *Macroeconomics*, 9th edition, p.317

E where *IS* and *LM* curves intersect and determine y^* as the equilibrium national output. Besides, at point *E* the balance of payments is in equilibrium as the domestic interest rate (i) is equal to the foreign interest rate ($i = i_f$). With this equilibrium there is no tendency for capital flows to occur and economy's equilibrium national income or output is y^*. It is important to note that we have assumed perfect international capital mobility, that is, capital will move massively into and out of the economy when domestic interest rate differs from foreign interest rate. It is further assumed that nominal foreign interest rate i_f is also given.

Now suppose that due to change in exchange rate expectations, domestic currency is expected to appreciate to a certain extent. This will induce capital inflows into the domestic economy as long as the domestic interest rate (i) exceeds the foreign interest rate (i_f) after making adjustment for changes in foreign exchange rates of currencies. Note that appreciation of a domestic currency implies depreciation of foreign currency. For example, appreciation of rupee against US dollar means the depreciation of US dollar. The *large inflows of capital will take place until* $i = i_f + \frac{\Delta e}{e}$. Let us explain how it occurs. With expected appreciation of home currency, *BB* line in Fig. 38.6 will shift below to *B'B'* by the *extent of appreciation of domestic currency*. The expected appreciation of domestic currency implies that exports of the domestic economy will become more expensive and imports relatively cheaper. As a result, exports of domestic economy will decline and its imports will rise. The fall in exports and rise in imports implies that domestic output will decline. This will cause *IS* curve to shift below. The reduction in aggregate income and output of the economy will induce reduction in demand for money causing domestic interest rate to fall and as a result we move downward along the given *LM* curve. The new monetary equilibrium will be reached when the domestic interest rate falls to a level equal to $e_f + \frac{\Delta e}{e}$. Thus the new equilibrium will be reached as a result of massive capital inflows. It follows therefore that in equilibrium

$$i - \frac{\Delta e}{e} = i_f$$

or

$$i = i_f + \frac{\Delta e}{e}$$

where $\frac{\Delta e}{e}$ is the expected appreciation of domestic currency.

In Fig. 38.6 the new equilibrium is reached at point *E'* where *IS'* curve cuts the *LM* curve at point *E'* and determines new domestic interest rate *i'* which has become equal to $i_f + \frac{\Delta e}{e}$. It will be further seen from Fig. 38.6 that the change in expected exchange rate not only affects domestic interest rate, national income or output but also *actual* exchange rate. When at the initial equilibrium point *E*, massive capital inflows into the domestic economy occur, the demand for domestic currency increases in the foreign exchange market because foreign currency has to be converted into domestic currency. This raises the demand for domestic currency and causes the *actual* exchange rate of domestic currency to appreciate and the new equilibrium is reached when the actual exchange rate has appreciated to the extent of expected change. Thus, "the expectations of exchange rate appreciation is *self-fulling expectations*" [4].

From the above analysis it is evident that "exchange rate expectations, through their impact on capital flows and thus on actual exchange rates, are a potential source of disturbance to macroeconomic equilibrium."[5]

4. Dornbusch, Fischer and Startz, *op.cit*, p.524 .
5. *Ibid*

Chapter 38A
Globalisation, Commercial Policy and WTO

Introduction : Meaning of Globalisation

In this chapter we will discuss the integration of the Indian economy with global economy. Globalisation is one of the most frequently used word which means different things to different people. In true economic meaning, globalisation refers to the increased openness of an economy to the international trade, capital flows (both portfolio and foreign direct investment, FDI), transfer of technology and free movement of labor or people. Thus **globalisation means the integration of economies of the world resulting from free flows of trade, capital, labor (or people) and technology.** The term globalisation signifies new international economic order which envisages the following:

(*a*) free flow of trade of goods and services between different countries of the world.

(*b*) free flow of capital among countries.

(*c*) free flow of technology among different countries of the world.

(*d*) free movement of labor or people internationally.

The growing interaction between different countries of the world has made the idea of globalisation increasingly popular in recent years. In the past there has been a movement to form regional groupings such as European Union (EU) formed by European countries and NAFTA (North American Free Trade Association) set up by North American countries to promote their regional interests by removing trade barriers among them. However, these regional groupings (also called *custom unions*) were found to be inadequate as they did not enable the countries forming these unions to produce on a global scale and enjoy all economies of scale and take full advantages from the modern technologies. Therefore, the developed countries pleaded for globalization to get benefits from widening of the size of the market for their products, locating and spreading optimally capital investment across different countries.

For developing countries like India globalisation carries benefits and opportunities as well as costs and risks. Both India and China have been recently using globalisation as an opportunity to accelerate rate of economic growth so as to catch up with the developed countries.

CASE FOR GLOBALISATION OF INDIAN ECONOMY

Several arguments have been given for integrating Indian economy with the global economy since 1991 when structural reforms were initiated in India. Tariffs and non-tariff barriers have been removed to promote free trade, the Indian economy has been opened up to foreign investment and import of technology from the developed countries. The following benefits of liberalisation and globalisation of Indian economy have been emphasised.

1. **Shift from Import-Substitution to Export-Led Growth Strategy.** The failure of import substitution strategy of industrial growth to achieve sustained growth forced India and other developing countries to pursue export-led growth strategy (which is also called outward looking strategy of development). It has been argued that by expanding exports to the other countries and getting required imports from them based on their respective *comparative costs*, developing countries will be able to achieve faster rate of economic growth. An important argument for trade liberalisation from the viewpoint of the developing countries is that they will gain from it as they have a comparative advantage in abundant, low-cost unskilled labor. If they specialise in the production of those

goods which are labour-intensive, greater integration into global markets would increase their exports and production. This will help in generating more employment opportunities for the poor.

The strategy of development focussed on export promotion requires that other countries, especially developed countries should not prevent the imports to their countries through imposition of tariffs and non-tariff barriers. This is possible in the framework of a global economy with free movements of trade, capital and technology among countries. The setting up of WTO on Jan 1, 1995 was a step towards that direction. Accordingly, the entry of India in WTO in 1995 was a step to further globalise its economy.

2. **Foreign Capital Inflows**. The globalisation or integration of the Indian economy with the world economy is also beneficial because it would give a boost to foreign capital inflows in the form of portfolio investment and foreign direct investment (FDI). Portfolio investment will bring valuable foreign exchange currencies in India and free us of balance of payments difficulties. With sufficient foreign exchange reserves, balance of payments constraint on accelerating the growth process will be removed.

In the eighties due to shrinkage of foreign assistance, India had to resort to external commercial borrowings (ECB) which carried relatively higher rates of interest and increased the burden of external public debt. It may be noted that small foreign exchange reserves led to the economic crisis of 1991. As shall be explained later, the role of foreign direct investment is more important than portfolio foreign investmenet as it raises the rate of real investment in the economy and helps us to achieve a faster rate of economic growth. Foreign direct investment (FDI), like domestic investmenet, has a multiplier effect on output and employment.

3. **Globalisation and Transfer of Technology**. Another benefit flowing from globalisation of the Indian economy is that it acts as a mechanism for the transfer of technology from the developed countries. Due to financial constraints, Indian companies are in a position to invest only a small amount of funds on R & D. Therefore, it is through globalisation of its economy that we will be able to get advanced technology from the developed countries. The technological upgradation of the Indian industries will lead to higher productivity and help us to achieve a higher rate of industrial growth. It is worth noting that it is the multinational corporations (MNCs) that are carriers of technolgy to the developing countries through technological and financial collaboration with doemstic enterprises.

Globalisation makes faster diffusion of new ideas and advanced technologies in the world. This will make possible for the developing countries like India to catch up the developed countries more quickly.

4. **Increased Market Access**. An important benefit of globalisation is increased market access. Long ago Adam Smith wrote in 1776 that division of labor is limited by the size of market. Free trade accompanying globalisation widens the markets for products of industries. The larger the market in which products can be sold, the greater the benefit that will accrue as a result of economies of scale and specialisation. This will lower unit cost of production and increase the competitiveness of manufactured products. Thus globalisation will ensure greater gain from trade. In addition, the wider market increases the incentives for investing in new innovations as the potential return on investment in them will increase.

5. **Faster Economic Growth and Poverty Reduction**. Above all, it has been argued by some prominent economists such as Jagdish Bhagwati, T.N. Srinivasan, Arvind Panagariya, that globalisation will help in faster rate of reduction in poverty through acceleration of economic growth. To quote professor Arvind Panagariya, "Countries that have achieved significant poverty reduction are generally those that have grown rapidly and have, in turn, been open to trade. The most obvious example are the Newly Industrialized Economies (NIEs) including Hong Kong, Singapore, Republic of Korea and Taiwan that have entirely eliminated poverty according to the *dollar-a-day poverty line*. On the

other hand, countries such as India that remained autarkic[1] and grew at less than 1.5% in per capita terms until late seventies experienced little reduction in the trend poverty ratio. Both India and China achieved poverty reduction after they began to dismantle *autarkic policies* and began to grow rapidly".[2]

6. **Employment Arguement**. An important arguement for libaration of trade and capital flows is that it will generate more employment oportunities. Employment increases on two counts. First, the growth in exports based on comparative cost advantage will lead to the creation of more employment opportunities. Secondly, employement opportunities also increase following the removal of restrictions on capital flows. The greater capital inflows, especially in the form of foreign direct investment (FDI), create not only more direct employment for labour but they have also a multiplier effect on the growth of employment and output.

MEASURES ADOPTED IN INDIA TO PROMOTE GLOBALISATION

The first Iraq war in 1991 involving gulf countries resulted in sharp rise in oil prices which landed India in acute balance of payments. To overcome this crisis and restore economic health of Indian economy many far-reaching changes in economic policy were made to promote globalisation of the Indian economy. The following measures are worth mentioning in this regard.

1. Import Liberalization. For liberalising foreign trade, *import controls through licesing was* abolished. With this almost all items of capital goods, raw materials, intermediate goods can be freely imported subject only to payment of customs duties. For some time quantitative quantitative restrictions on consumer goods remained but with effect from 1995 all quantitative restrctions, even on imports of consumer goods, have been lifted.

To liberalise imports peak customs duties which in some cases were as high as over 300 per cent were lowered in stages to 150 per cent in July 1991, to 85 per cent in Feb. 1993, 50 per cent in 2002. The average import duty was further reduced to 31 per cent in 2003 and to 20 percent in Jan. 2004, to 15 per cent in 2005 and further to 12.5% in 2006. Import duties on capital goods have been reduced even below 20 per cent for certain categories. This phased reduction in exceptionally high custms duties and a phased removal of quantitative restrictions on imports has substantially reduced anti-export bias in the earlier trade and balance of payment policies.

2. Imports of Gold and Silver have been considerably liberalised. This reduced the incentive for smuggling. In Jan. 2004 imports of gold were made free from any commission charged for it.

3. Market-Determined Exchange Rate. An important measure in external sector was to devalue the rupee in July 1991 and after about 2 years in 1993 exchange rate was changed from basket based pegged exchange rate system to *market-determined exchange rate*. With this the exchange rate of the rupee today is determined by demand and supply conditions in the foreign exchange markets.

4. Convertibility of Rupee. Another important reform for globalising the Indian economy was the convertibility of rupee on balance of payments on current account. This implies the importers can get their required quantity of foreign exchange by converting their rupee resources into dollars from the foreign exchange market. The exporters do not have to surrender their foreign exchange (US dollar or EU Euro) earned abroad to RBI but can now sell them in the foreign exhcnage markets.

5. Liberalisation of Foreign Investmenet. The new economic policy adopted since 1991 considerably liberalised the scope of foreign investment, both direct and portfolio. Earlier investmenet by foreign companies required prior approval of the government and was restricted to 40 per cent equity participation and was also subjected to the conditions of technology transfer to India. Besides, foreign investmenet was permitted in priority areas only. Foreign portfolio investmenet was allowed mainly into a limited number of public sectors bond issues. The new economic policy of 1991

1. Autarkic means the closed nature of the economy having not much trade transactions with other country and which aims at achieving self-sufficiency.
2. Arvind Panagariya, Open up trade, get rich, *The Economic Times*, April 25, 2003.

plrovided for automatic approval of foreign direct investment, that is, no prior permission from the government is required upto 51 per cent of the total equity capital of the firms in 34 priority industries. In 1996, the government raised this ceiling limit for auotmatic approval from 51 per cent to 74 per cent for foreign equity participation.

Criteria for approval of foreign investment greater than 51 per cent equity participation prior to 1996 (and greater than 74 per cent after 1996) in priority industries and foreign equity participation in non priority industries which was approved on case to case basis was quite liberalised to attract more foreign investmenet. Besides, it is worth mentioning that elimination of industrial licensing restrictions, openning up to the private sector of a number of industries previously reserved for the public sector which increased the growht of domestic corporate sector also served to promote foreign private investment.

Portfolio Foreign Investment. An important feature of new economic policy adopted since 1991 is that it has laid stress on *non-debt creating capital inflows*, such as direct foreign investment and foreign portfolio investment for reducing reliance on *debt flows* as the chief source of external resources. Accordingly, in addition to foreign direct investment, foreign portfolio investment has also been liberalised. Portfolio foreign investment refers to the foreign firms, foreign institutional investors and NRI who invest in the equity bonds and securities of Indian firms. In case of foreign portfolio investment foreign investors get returns in the form of yearly payable dividents/interest and capital gains accrued but do not excercise any direct control in running these companies. Foreign private portfolio capital inflows are welcome as they provide needed finance to the Indian firms and also bring the much needed foreign exchange. But it is important to mention that they are prone to greater volatility. The currency crisis of East Asian countries in 1997-78 was mainly precipitated by the sudden flight of portfolio foreign capital. Therefore, sufficient foreign exchange reserves must be maintained to save the domestic currency from such sudden capital flight. In the new economic policy of 1991, foreign portfolio investment was also liberalised. In Feb. 1992 the Indian firms of good standing were allowed to raise funds through equity and convertible bond issues in Euromarkets and in September 1992 registered Foreign Institutional Investors (FII) were allowed to purchase both equity and debt securities directly in the Indian markets.

The Foreign Exchange Regulation Act (FERA) has been replaced by Foreign Exchange Managment Act (FEMA) to remove a number of constraints earlier applicable to firms with foreign equity operating in India. Besides, FEMA makes it easier for Indian companies to operate abroad. Further, procedure for Indian companies to invest abroad and also raise funds abroad through ECB (*External Commercial Borrowing*), that is, through ADR (American Depository Receipts) and GDR (General Depository Receipts have been simplified.

Foreign institutional investors (FII) found Indian stocks particularly attractive for the purpose of risk diversification. Both 'pull' factors and 'push' factors worked to attract foreign portfolio investment into India. The pull factors include the improvement in Indian macroeconomic environment following the abolition of licensing system and banking and financial sector reforms. On the other hand, 'push' factors included the fall in interest rates and yields and slowdown in economic growth in USA and other developed countries. These prompted foreign investors to invest in India and other developing countries, especially China, to get higher yields on their investment.

DANGERS AND RISKS OF GLOBALISATION

Globalisation is not without dangers and risks. Stakes of poor countries like India are much higher for pursuing pro-globalisation policies. The historical experience of the colonial period shows that free tradc and capital inflows helped imperialist countries more than the poor under-developed countries. With help of free trade and capital investment in some particular spheres, the developed countries exploited the poor countries which happened to be their colonies and drew away resources from them. With achievement of independence by the developing countries, though the situation today is vastly different but the developed countries has not shed their behaviour of promoting their own interests at the cost of developing countries. In fact, as has been stressed by Joseph Stiglitz, a Nobel Laurate in economics, that while US and European countries preach free trade and globalisation, they actually practice protectionist polices to safeguard their domestic industries. Imposition of tariffs on imports of steel and grant of subsidies on farm products and cotton textiles by the developed countries such as the USA to protect their domestic industries which caused widespread protests around the world is a shining example of such double standards.[3] To quote Stiglitz, "*I have always been struck by the divergence between the policies that America pushes on developing countries and those practiced in the US itself*".[4] Therefore, he advises that the developing countries should look carefully not what America says but at what it did in the years when America emerged as the industrial power, and what it does today.

Even Dr. Manmohan singh who has been the votary of free trade and free capital flows between countries in his address to the United Nations General Assembly in September 2011 said that recent events had called into question that globalisation would always do social good. He lamented the tendency on the part of developed countries to adopt protectionist policies to protect their own interest at the cost of the developing countries. To quite him, "*Till a few years ago, the world had taken for granted the benefits of globalization and global interdependence. Today we are being called upon to cope with the negative dimensions of those very phenomena.*"

An important disadvantage of globalisation is the danger posed by free flows of capital, especially portfolio capital, which are highly volatile and are a source of great macroeconomic instability. When there are large capital inflows into a country, the currency of a currency appreciates which makes its exports costlier and therefore cause reduction in them which not only adversely affects its current account balance of payments but also adversely affects its levels of GPP and employment. Besides, excess capital inflows in an economy lead to the expansion on money supply and if not sterlised by the RBI will add to the inflationary pressures in the economy.

On the other hand, when there are large capital outflows from an economy, they cause depreciation of the national currency which though tend to increase its exports but carry some risks. First, depreciation makes the imports more expensive and therefore leads to the rise in prices of commodities and raw materials imported from abroad and causes cost-push inflation in the economy. Further, depreciation of a national currency, say the Indian rupee, will raise the burden of external debt as more rupees are required to pay for a US dollar. Further, countries like India badly need foreign capital flows to finance its current deficit. In the absence of adequate capital flows, some US dollars will have to withdrawn from foreign exchange reserves resulting in the decline in our foreign exchange reserves. As foreign exchange reserves are available in limited quantity, in the absence of adequate capital flows to India year after year deficit in current account cannot be easily financed.

Therefore, in view of the present author, though the case for globalisation is theoretically quite sound , but it carries with it many risks and dangers. If promoted in its true spirit by all countries, it would lead to rapid economic growth in both the developed and developing countries. But, the developed countries are interested in promoting their own interests even at the cost of the poor developing countries on whom they impose policies of liberalisation and globalisation through their greater say in World Bank and IMF. Therefore, globalisation and reduction of tariffs and removal of quantitative restrictions on imports from US, Japan and European countries, carry a good deal of risk for them. This is quite evident from the recent failure of talks held under the auspices of WTO at Doha, Seatle, Singapore and Cancun. These talks to liberalise trade between the developed and developed countries failed because US and EU (European Union) were not willing to reduce huge subsidies they are providing to their farmers on agricultural products and also subsidies on exports of

3. Joseph Stiglitz, Protectionism : US Style, *Economic Times*, May 8, 2002.
4. Joseph Stiglitz, "Do what we did, not what we say" *The Economic Times*, Nov. 3, 2003.

these products. This support by the developed countries to their farmers prevent agricultural exports from the developing countries. In this way exports from developing countries are prevented even when they enjoy comparative advantage in their production. That is why the people of the developing countries of Asia, Africa and Latin America are protesting against them during the multilateral talks being held under the auspices of WTO.

Protectionist Policies of US and European Countries

An important example of protectionist's policy of US is its imposition of the higher tariffs on imports of steel and subsidies on cotton testiles which prevent exports of these commodities from the developing countries, especially African countries and India. USA tried to use some provisions of WTO agreements regarding use of "safeguards for protecting employment" to defend these import tariffs and subsidies on cottons textiles. Recently, in Nov. 2003, WTO dispute settlement body has given its verdict against the imposition of higher tariffs on steel by the USA and has asked it to scrap them. The reluctance of USA to remove tariffs on imports of steel and subsidies on cotton textiles is against the spirit of globalisation.

Recent Protectionist Measures by the US: Through business process outsourcing (BPO), American firms and businesses are outsourcing various types of services such as medical transcription, insurance connected work, various types of office jobs done through telecommunication and computer internet in call-centres from India. This BPOs have created good deal of employment opportunities for Indian educated youth. But recently there is anti-outsourcing campaign in the USA and UK. The new US President Obama has withdrawn tax-breaks (i.e. tax concession) from those corporate enterprises which outsource their jobs, that is, get some services done from abroad (e.g. India and China). Besides, he has imposed visa restrictions for foreign skilled workers (e.g., software professionals) to protect jobs in the US. These protectionist measures will harm the Indians. Some US states are even trying to enact laws to prvent outsourcing and thereby use of foreign (Indian) cheap skilled labour. This is against the spirit of free trade as India has a comparative advantage in these business processing services because its educated skilled labor is available at comparatively much lower wages. Some Americans have argued "*our resources should not be used to create jobs overseas when we have skilled workers and unemployment at home*". But business processing services for American business firms are like exports from India based on comparative costs advantage and therefore to prevent them to protect employment of American labor is an argument in favour of protection.

Volatility in Exchange Rate and Economic Instability

Another adverse consequence of liberalisation and globalisation is the creation of volatility in foreign exchange rate of rupee which has adversely affected the Indian economy. Under the policy of economic reforms we allowed free movements of capital flows into and out of India and switched over to the market-determined exchange rate and made the rupee convertible. From 2003-04 to 2007-08 there were large capital inflows into the Indian economy, mainly through portfolio investment by FIIs which caused appreciation of Indian rupee whose value rose from above ₹ 46 to a US dollar in 2002-03 to ₹ 44.27 at the end of March 2006 and further to ₹ 39.4 to a US dollar in mid-Nov. 2007. This appreciation of rupee adversely affected our exports. Besides, large inflows of US dollars got converted into rupees which caued rapid increase in money supply generating inflationary pressures in the Indian economy. Further, large capital inflows, especially through portfolio investment by FIIs in the Indian stock market, artificially caused high rise in price of shares of Indian companies.

However, in 2008-09 the opposite happened when due to liquidity crunch in the banking system in the US caused by large-scale defaults on sub-prime housing loans and mortgage failures, FIIs started *net capital outflows* from India by selling shares of Indian companies there was heavy depreciation of rupee. The rupee which was around ₹ 39.4 to a US dollar in Nov. 2007 fell to around ₹ 50 to a dollar in the second week of Nov. 2008. After remaining stable in the range of ₹ 48 – 49 to a dollar for some months it again fell to around ₹ 52 to a US dollar in the first week of March 2009. Though this depreciation of Indian rupee will promote exports which at present (March 2009) have been slowing down for the last six months in succession, the imports will become costlier. Besides, weakening of rupee will further induce capital outflows which in turn will cause more depreciation of rupee. This increased pressure on rupee will compell RBI to intervene and supply US dollars from its reserves (which at present are of sizable size of $ 250 billion) to prevent further fall in the exchange rate of rupee against US dollar.

It may be noted that it is highly important for RBI to check further depreciation of rupee as the value of a currency is a reflection of the underlying strength of the economy whose rating outlook is downgraded when value of its currency falls drastically. Therefore, RBI must intervene in the economy to prevent sharp fall in the foreign exchange rate of rupee and to ensure exchange rate stability.

Besides, the large capital outflows from India by FIIs caused liquidity crunch in the Indian banking system of the second half of 2008-09 which adversely affected investment in the Indian economy whose growth rate is estimated to fall to less than 7 per cent in 2008-09 as compared to 9 per cent growth rate achieved in the previous four years (2004-08). It follows from above that globalisation of Indian economy with liberalisation of capital flows and market-determined exchange rate and convertibility of rupee has caused a lot of volatility in exchange rate of rupee and economic instability and is therefore not without risks and dangers.

GLOBAL COMMERCIAL POLICY

Commercial policy rates to policies regarding exports and imports of a country. Since trade between countries now plays a vital role in promoting growth and well-being of the people of a country, commercial policy has acquired great importance today. Before 1947, the countries were free to impose tariffs on the imports. But when one country raised tariffs to protect domestic industries and to promote employment at home, other countries retaliated and raised their tariffs too. This tariff wars resulted in reduction in world trade and output and lowered efficiency in production. It was therefore realised that to improve productivity and national income of all countries free trade between countries should be promoted and for that purpose tariffs imposed by different countries must be reduced.

Types of Regional Agreements

The first step in liberalisation of trade among countries has been the regional agreements between a small number of countries. A smaller number of countries agree to reduce or eliminate tariffs on each other's imports and thus liberalise trade among them. North American Free Trade Agreement (NAFTA) was the trade agreement reached between some countries of North America which agreed to reduce and ultimately eliminate tariffs on the imports of member countries. Another important regional agreement has been the agreement among a number of European countries, European Economic Community (EEC) which is now called European Union (EU). In order to obtain gain from trade, they removed tariffs on the imports of member countries. European Union is a highly successful common market. Through it, member European countries have achieved a high degree of economic integration. They have not only eliminated tariffs on imports of member countries but have also allowed free movement of capital and labour among the member countries. The European Union (EU) is a powerful economic block whose chief objective has been to compete with Japan and the USA. They pursue a common agricultural policy which subsidise their agricultural products and guarantee farm prices to protect the interest of their farmers. Since January 1999, through an agreement, a common currency, called '*Euro*' has been introduced.

It will be useful to describe the standard forms of regional trade agreements aimed at liberalising trade among them. They are (1) Free Trade Area (FTA), (2) Custom Union (CU) (3) Common market, and (4) *Economic Union* we explain them below briefly.

Free Trade Area (FTA). Under it, member countries reach an agreement to remove tariffs on the imports from member countries. But member countries are free to impose tariffs and other restrictions on imports from the other countries under it.

Customs Union. A customs union is a free trade area *plus* an agreement about *common tariff and non-tariff restrictions* on the imports of non-member countries. Because they impose a common tariffs on the imports of the rest of the world they do not keep any custom controls on the goods moving among the member countries. An important example of customs union has been European Union (EU), though in recent years it has moved towards a greater degree of integration, namely, common market as explained below. A customs union differs from free trade agreement in two ways. First important difference is that a customs union has a common external tariff. A common external tariff means that each member country of a customs union replaces its own tariff schedule by the same external tariff schedule agreed to by the members of a customs union. For example an Indian firm exporting to UK, West Germany, Portugal (who are the members of EU) faces same tariff rates on its exports to whichever of these countries it exports goods. The second important difference between free trade area (FTA) and customs union is that free trade area does not include trade in agricultural products, services and financial flows, while most of the customs unions cover a wide range of international trade that includes trade in agricultural products, services and capital flows.

Common market. A common market type of regional trade agreement represents a great degree of economic integration among a number of countries. A common market is a customs union that not only impose a common tariff barriers on the imports from the rest of the world but also allow free movement of labour and capital among its members. The European Union (EU) in its current form comes near to the idea of a common market.

It is worth noting that free mobility of capital in common market ensures more efficient allocation of capital within the member countries of a common market which has a favourable effect on their output of goods and services. Besides, in a common market, labour is free to move within the member countries of a common market and this allows for more efficient allocation of human capital which also adds to output in the member countries of a common market. But it is worth noting that free mobility of labour between member countries of a common market is not without problems. This is because large wage differenticals among the member countries may result in a large migration of labour from one country to another which will affect their national wage levels.

Economic Union. Another form of regional agreement is economic union. Economic union is an agreement between countries that involve not only free trade of goods and services, free mobility of capital and labour within member countries and common external tariffs but also some degree of unification is monetary and other government policies.

An essential requirement of the formation of economic union is the creation of common currency which facilitates the transactions between member countries of economic union and adoption of uniform monetary policy. Thus an economic union represents a deeper form of economic integration. In order to move towards the ultimate goal of formation of an economic union, European Union adopted a common currency called *Euro* in 1995. Euro is thus currency of several European countries. However, the U.K has still its own currency, 'Pound Sterling'. Besides, European countries which constitute European Union (EU) has also adopted a uniform policies of providing agricultural subsidies to their farmers to protect them from cheaper imports from developing countries and the United States.

However the world economy has no full-fledged economic union containing all its features. However, European union is strongly moving in the direction of formation of fully integrated economic union.

Some Trade Agreements : NAFTA, European Union and ASEAN

Let us explain in brief some important free trade agreements in the world today. It is through these agreements that there is greater economic integration of various countries.

NAFTA (North American Free Trade Area). In 1988 a comprehensive agreement was signed between the US and Canada covering elimination of tariffs on all goods and most non-government services to promote trade between them. In 1993, Mexico joined this free trade agreement and this agreement between these three countries, namely, US Canada and Mexico has been called NAFTA which envisaged removal of all trade barriers between them after a 15 years phasing in period.

European Union (UE). The world's largest and most successful customs union is the European union which has increasingly moved in the direction of common market. European Union is the association of European countries that have agreed to free trade area by eliminating tariffs between them and also impose a common external tariff. Presently, European Union (EU) includes 15 countries, prominent among them are France, Belgium, West Germany, Luxembourg, Italy, the United Kingdom, Denmark, Ireland, Greece, Spain, Portugal, Austria, Sweden joined the European Union in 1986.

European started its growth in 1951 when the European *Coal and Steel Community* (ECSC) was formed to eliminate trade barriers (i.e. tariffs and quotas) to promote free trade in coal and steel between them. This association was later merged into European Union. Recently, member countries of European Union (EU) have agreed to issue a common currency called Euro.

ASEAN (Association of South East Asian Countries). A group of countries of South East Asia, namely, Indonesia, Malaysia, Philippines, Singapore, Thailand have formed a free trade group within which member countries have removed tariffs and also fixed a common external tariff for other countries. This has significantly promoted trade between them and also because common external tariff in low, it has no large trade diversion effect.

EFFECTS OF REGIONAL TRADE AGGREMENTS : TRADE CREATION AND TRADE DIVERSION

Liberalisation of trade by eliminating tariffs within a free trade area or customs union has both benefits and costs as it affects resource reallocation within countries. The effects of economic integration through regional trade agreements have been divided into two categories : trade creation and trade diversion. In what follows we explain these effects.

Trade Creation

When through free trade agreements, the two countries mutually eliminate tariffs, trade between the two countries. This favourable effect on world trade is called *trade creation.* This trade creation occurs because producers in one member country to a free trade agreement are able to sell some products in another member country at cheaper prices than those by the domestic producers as the latter lose tariff protection as a result of free trade agreements. For example when North American Free Trade Agreement (NAFTA) eliminating tariffs between the member countries came into effect with both USA and Mexico as members some Mexican firms found that they could sell their some products in the USA cheaper than the domestic American firms, while some American firms found that they could sell some of their other products in Mexico at cheapter prices than the Mexican firms. This led to more trade between Mexico and the United States. This happens because elimination of previous differential tariffs between the member countries of free trade area will cause prices of goods to change in the member countries after the trade agreement eliminating tariffs. Suppose before NAFTA, Mexico was imposing 20 per cent tariff on imports of cars. Now, with the elimination of tariffs American cars became cheaper in Mexico than the prices of domestic producers of cars in Mexico. This led to more exports of American cars in Mexico after the implementation of NAFTA. Similarly, some Mexican firms found that when agreement came into effect they could sell some of their products in the USA at cheaper rates than the domestic American Competitors. Thus NAFTA led to more trade between the member countries with beneficial effects on resource allocation. This trade creation leads to the gain in efficiency in the use and allocation of resources as more efficient member countries of free trade area displaced less efficient countries for production of various goods.

Trade Diversion

Apart from trade creation, regional free trade esuch as FTA, customs union has also bad effect of trade diversion. When as a result of elmination of tariffs trade between member countries of a free trade area (for example, between the US and Mexico) increases, it causes export losses to the non-member countries. These export losses to other (*i.e.* non-member) countries are known as trade diversion.Trade diversion causes loss of efficiency in resource use because less efficient member countries of a free trade area displace more efficient non-member countries. Thus, "*from global perspective trade diversion represents an inefficient use of resource.*"[5]

Whether or not regional trade agreement between some countries increases world trade depends on as to whether trade creation effect is larger than trade diversion. However, from the narrow national point of view of members of free trade agreement, it causes some gain as well as some loss. In so far as there is common desire to increae domestic production in the member countries of free trade area, it brings mutual benefits to the member countries. It gives producers of the member countries of free trade agreement an advantage over producers of the rest of the world. This causes increase in production of goods and services in the member countries of free trade area or customs union and also trade between them. However, as explained above, it leads to reduction of trade of members of a union with non-member countries.

GATT AND WTO

GATT (General Agreement on Tariffs and Trade)

During the period of Great Depression (1929-33) and the Second World War various countries imposed high tariffs on the imports to protect domestic industries. They followed what is called '*Beggar Thy Neighbour*' policy. The high tariffs resulted in large shrinking of world trade bringing about loss of efficiency in resource use in the world economy. As a reaction against the devastation caused by high tariffs during the thirties and Second World War period, the General Agreement on Tariffs and Trade (GATT) was established in 1947 after the Second World War. GATT aimed at liberalisation of trade between countries by visualised ***multilateral trading system*** and to promote trade between various countries sought to reduce tariffs significantly. GATT organised various rounds of negotiations between member countries that led to reduction of tariffs. As a result not only trade between countries increased but world GNP also significantly rose after 1947.

In one of the negotiations carried out by GATT, Kenedy Round which began in early 1960s member countries agreed to make large reduction in tariffs starting from 1967s. Another Round Tokyo Round resulted in further cuts in tariffs in 1979.

In the latest round under GATT, Uruguay Round negotiations started in 1986 and concluded in 1994, a comprehensive agreement of 40 per cent reduction in tariffs was reached. This sought to promote world trade significantly. Besides, Uruguay Round of talks established a world body called WTO (World Trade organisation) to achieve further liberalisation of free trade among countries. WTO came into existence in January 1995. The objective of WTO is to ensure efficiency in use of world resources and specialisation of various countries in accordance with their comparative advantage. We explain below WTO at same length.

World Trade Organisation (WTO)

An important step in global commercial policy in setting up of World Trade Organisation (WTO) is a very important trade organisation to promote free trade among different countries. Protection has harmful effects on economic growth and consumer welfare. Bretton Woods Conference held in 1944 which recommended the setting up of International Monetary Fund (IMF) and World Bank (WB) also recommended the establishment of an International trade organisation to promote free trade among nations. However, while IMF and World Bank were established in 1946, agreement

5. Lipsey and Chrystal, 9th edition, p. 591

to set up International Trade Organisation could not be finally reached. Instead, a less formal organisation called GATT (General Agreement on Tariffs and Trade) was set up to guide the international trading system based on rules and principles agreed between the member countries. However, it was found to be weak and ineffective although it succeeded in achieving its objective of promoting world trade to some extent by bringing down the level of tariffs on manufactured products imposed by the developed countries. The process of liberalisation of trade, however, suffered a set back since 1974. Although the process of reducing tariff barriers continued, Non-Tariff Barriers (NTB's) were substantially increased by various countries including the developed countries. Strangly enough, it was found that while the developed countries were adopting Non-Tariff Barriers such as quantitative restrictions to protect their industries, the developing countries were liberalising their trade by reducing tariff on the imports from the developed countries.

Unlike GATT, the WTO is a permanent organisation created by international treaty ratified by the governments and legislatures of member states. As the principal international body concerned with solving trade problems between countries and providing a forum for multilateral trade negotiations, it has global status similar to that of the International Monetary Fund and the World Bank.

Object of WTO

The objective of WTO agreements is *to establish **a multilateral trading system*** in order to promote free and fair trade among nations. Dunkel Act on which WTO has been founded is wedded to liberalisation of trade based on comparative costs. Accordingly, this provides for a multilateral framework for trade not only in industrial and agricultural goods but also in services. It also seeks to protect ***trade related intellectual property rights* (TRIPS).** By committing the member countries to give Most Favoured Nation (MFN) treatment to all trading partners, it has sought to discourage bilateral trading so as to encourage multilateral trading system.

At present there are 148 member countries of WTO and includes both developed and developing countries of the world.

Functions of WTO

WTO has the following five functions to perform :

(1) The WTO provides the framework for implementation, administration and operation of multilateral trade agreements reached at Uruguay Round.

(2) The WTO provides the forum for further negotiations among its member states concerning their multilateral trade relations with regard to the matters included in the agreements reached at Uruguay Round.

(3) The WTO undertakes the task of *settlement of disputes* among the member states, which arise from their different understandings of the rules and procedure agreed upon.

(4) The WTO administers the '*Trade Review Mechanism.*'

(5) In order to evolve a coherrent global economic policy to promote free and fair trade among the different countries, WTO cooperates in an appropriate manner with the IMF; World Bank and its affiliated agencies.

WTO Bodies for Administration

The two important bodies in WTO have been set up to perform its various functions.

1. Dispute Settlement Body (DSB). The DSB, on which all member countries can sit, usually meets twice a month to hear complaints of violations of WTO rules and agreements. It sets up expert panels to study disputes and decide if the rules are being broken. The DSB's final decisions, unlike those of a similar but less powerful body in the old GATT, cannot be challenged.

2. Trade Policy Review Body (TPRB). The TPRB is a forum for the entire membership to review the trade policies of all WTO member countries. Major trading policies are reviewed every two years, others every four years.

Other major bodies are the Council for Trade in Goods, the Council for Trade in Services and the Council for *Trade-Related Aspects of Intellectual Property Rights* (TRIPS).

The Guiding Fundamental Principles and Features of WTO

The following fundamental principles have been provided for the functioning of WTO as a multiple trading system. These principles represent the salient features of WTO.

(*a*) **Non-Discrimination.** This is the most important principle on which WTO has been founded. The principle of non-discrimination means two things. (1) All trading partners will be granted the most favoured nation (MFN) status, that is, each member state of WTO will treat every other member state equally as the most favoured nation doing trade. No discrimination will be done by a member of state between different trading states who are also members of WTO. Foreign goods, services, trade marks, patents and copyrights shall be given the same treatment as is given to nationals of a country.

(b) Free Trade. The objective of WTO, as in case of GATT, is to promote free trade among nations through negotiations. For this purpose WTO has to work for progressive liberalisation of trade through reduction in tariffs and removal of quantitative restrictions on imports by member countries.

(*c*) **Stability in the Trading System.** Under WTO agreements member states are committed not to raise tariff and non-tariff trade barriers arbitrarily. This provides stability and predictability to the trading system.

(*d*) **Promotion of Fair Competition.** WTO system of multilateral trading system provides for transparent, fair and undistorted competition among the various countries. Rules such as Most Favoured Nation (MFN) treatment to all trading parties, equal treatment to foreign goods, patents and copyrights as with nationals ensure fair competition among trading countries. Besides, WTO agreement provides for discouraging unfair competitive practices such as export subsidies and dumping (that is, selling products abroad below domestic prices to gain market access).

(*e*) **Market Access Commitment.** WTO agreements which seek to establish multilateral trading system require the member countries to undertake market access commitment on reciprocity basis. In fact, market access is ensured by abolsihing non-tariff barriers as well as by reducing tariffs. The undertaking on market access requires that member countries will cut tariffs on industrial goods and agricultural products by about 37 per cent. In order to provide market access for the products of developing countries to the USA, USA agreed to cut down farm subsidies. The developing countries are also required to reduce agricultural subsidies to the level of 10 per cent of the value of agricultural produce.

In the area of trade in services, market access has been ensured by giving foreign service suppliers the same treatment as demestic service suppliers.

WTO Agreements. To ensure liberalisation of trade among nations to promote economic growth in the world various agreements have been made. They are

1. *Tariff reduction* for growth of trade in manufactures.
2. *Removal of quantitative restrictions* on trade imposed by various countries.
3. *Liberalisation of agricultural trade* through reduction in tariffs and reduction in agricultural and export subsidies.
4. Liberalisation of trade in services through **General Agreement on Trade in Services (GATS).**
5. ***Trade Related Intellectual Property Rights*** **(TRIPS)** to provide patent protection to products and processes in all fields of technology.

India' and other developing countries which have formed a group of 20 called G-20, demand that the industrialised countries should reduce agricultural subsidies and allow free

movement of skilled and specialised labour. In its negotiating proposal, India has demanded substantial reduction in tariffs, elimination of trade-distorting domestic support and export subsidies to agriculture by developed countries. The movement of professionals (*i.e.*, skilled labour) from developing countries to developed countries is constrained by a number of factors such as lack of specific sectorial commitments, lack of mutual recognition of qualifications, lack of transparency in administration of *visa* regimes, discriminatory practices in use of Economic Needs Test and social security contributions. India and group of G-20 of developing countries have therefore, sought liberalisation of movement of professionals through removal of these constraints.

Failure of WTO Development Round Talks at Cancun.

From Sept. 10 to 14,2003 trade ministers of developed and developing countries met for the next stage of talks on multilateral trading system. In an earlier meeting at Doha in Nov. 2001 ministers recognised the inequities of Uruguay Round of negotiations. It was expected that the developing countries would get a just and fair global trading system at the conclusion of Cancun meeting. But these hopes were not fulfilled and Cancun meeting ended in a failure. At Cancun, a group of 20 developing countries led by India, Brazil and China frustrated the attempts of US-European Union Cambine to pressurise the developing countries to accept the agenda that suited them most and was against the interests of the developing countries. *Draft declaration prepared by WTO allowed the developed countries to maintain or keep domestic subsidies and support for their agriculture and farmers but avoided eliminating export subsidies and credit concessions on their exports, especially on farm products and textiles.* On the other hand, draft declaration sought even stiffer tariff cuts by developing countries. In this way, developing countries were badly treated with regard to market access of their products to the developed countries. All these were not acceptable to the developing countries including India. African countries who are badly hit by the subsidies and domestic support on the farm products by the developed countries walked out of the meeting. As a result, Cancun meeting ended without adopting any declaration. The lesson from the failure of Cancun meeting is that unless the developed countries look beyond their own interests and try to evolve multilateral trading system which is just and fair to the developing countries talks cannot succeed. However, talks in this regard to arrive at an agreement acceptable to all are still continuing.

Agreement on TRIPS. On December 6, 2005, the General Council of WTO adopted the amendment to the TRIPS to address public health concerns of developing countries which was reaffirmed by Hong Kong Declaration. This amendment enables manufacturing and export of pharmaceutical products under compulsory license to countries with limited or no manufacturing capacities in the pharmaceutical sectors. On Trips, CBD (Convention of Bio-Diversity) on relationship and protection of traditional knowledge, India along with a number of other developing countries which are rich in bio-diversity proposed that the Trips Agreement of WTO should be amended to provide for : (*i*) disclosure of source of the traditional knowledge used in the invention; (*ii*) disclosure of evidence of prior informed consent under the relevant national regime; and (*iii*) disclosure of evidence of benefit sharing under the relevant national regime. With this amendment the use of India's natural herbs such as Neem, Arjuna, Ashavgandha and others for preparing medicines and also certain plant varieties such as Basmati rice will get protection from the use by multinational companies.

DOHA ROUND OF DEVELOPMENT NEGOTIATION UNDER WTO

In Hong Kong India made some modest gains in the field of agriculture, industrial products and TRIPS. A good number of issues concerning liberalisation of global trade are yet to be resolved. However, much depends on future negotiations during which several issues particularly regarding market access for manufactured goods (NAMA) and services are to be resolved. Whether in these future negotiations, developed countries will adopt an attitude which ensure fair and free trade from the viewpoint of LDCs and developing countries. The developed countries proposed to link lower

farm subsidies by them to gain greater market access for non-agricultural goods in the developing countries. This is against the letter and spirit of Hong Kong Declaration. And it is these kinds of tactics of the developed countries that Juseph Stiglitz predicted and thought that due to this Doha Round Negotiations for Development will collapse.

In our view it must be made clear to the developed countries that the artificiality of prices arising out of the substantial domestic agricultural subsidies provided by the developed countries them must be dealt with firmly if we are to make any headway towards fair trade in agriculture. Developing countries have a right to use the flexiblities provided in Hong Kong declaration to protect their small and medium enterprises and their infant industries like automobiles. Therefore, in future trade negotiations no compromise be made on flexibilities in conection with agriculture and industrial products granted to the developing countries in Hong Kong declaration. We agree with Muchkund Dubey who have been associated with earlier Uruguay Round negotiations when he writes "The initiatives of India, Brazil and other major developing countries have indeed brightened up the prospects of concluding the Doha Round by the end of 2006 or thereafter. However, the magnitude of the problems still remaining unresolved should not be underestimated. There are still seemingly irreconcilable differences on some of major elements of modalities. The time available is too short. Therefore, one cannot rule out the possibility of the agreement reached in Hong Kong falling apart and the Doha Round being delayed indefinitely posing new threats to the multilateral trading system.[6]

The Doha Round of trade negotiations are under way for the last ten years (since 2001). Negotiations pasued in December 2008 but again resumed but so far talks have not been concluded and also there has not been much progress in this regard too. It may recalled that main purpose of setting up WTO was to usher in era of trade liberalisation. Thus, if Doha Round which focuses on the *developmental dimension* fails, it would affect free trade and the countries would enter into bilateral trade agreements providing for trade preference to the parties to the agreements. To promote multilateral trade mechanism India is working with coalition groups in the WTO towards an early conclusion of the Doha Round. *Its stands has been made quite clear that it favours the protection of poor, substance farmers of developing countries and gives priority to vulnerable industries of the developing countries.*

Doha Round Talks in the Area of Agriculture. In the area of agriculture discussions are still taking place on the basis of revised Draft of *agriculture modalities* of December 2008. According to this draft, developed countries would have to reduce their bound tariffs in equal annual instalments over 5 years with an overall minimum average cut of 54 per cent. And developing countries have to reduce their bound tariff with a maximum overall average cut of 36% per cent over a larger implementation period of 10 years. Developing countries would have a special products (SP) entitlement of 12 per cent of agricultural tariff lines. An average tariff cut of 11 per cent is proposed on SPs including 5 per cent of total tariff lines at zero cuts. There are also reductions proposed for various categories of domestic and export subsidies.

Non-Agricultural Market Access (NAHA) Negotiations.

In the case of Non-Agricultural Market Access (NAMA) negotiations, the tariff reductions are proposed through a non-linear swift formula with three coefficients of 20, 22 and 25 for formula reductions linked to specific flexibilities for protecting sensitive NAMA tariff lines of developing countries.

India has said any attempt to dilute the development agenda of the Doha round of the WTO talks will not be acceptable and demands for more market access from developing countries by developed countries cannot be entertained. The US has asked large developing countries including India, Brazil and China to remove duties on some industrial goods but has been refused as these

6. Much kund Dubey, WTO Hong Kong Declaration: An Appraisal, EPW, Jan. 7., 2006

countries claim that it goes beyond the commitments that they have to undertake in the on-going round. This is now the primary issue holding up the Doha negotiations which is into its tenth year. According to WTO Director General Pascal Lamy, while the Doha round is stuck in a deadlock, the relevance of the multilateral institute has not yet waned. WTO is a member driven organization and its negotiations are a collective enterprise, India is a good example of how trade can be leveraged to achieve growth and reduce poverty," he added. As per WTO estimates, the Doha round that seeks to open up trade further in goods and services, is expected to result in gains worth $282 billion.

Another important aspect of NAMA negotiations pertain to *Non-Tariff Barriers* (NTBs). With regard to this, India is one of the initial proponents of the Horizontal Mechanism (HM) proposal. It aims to bring in a ministerial decision on "Procedures for the facilitation of NTBs.. This proposal has received the support of more than 100 WTO Member countries. Though the Doha mandate refers to NTBs in the context of 'products of export interest to developing countries', there have been some moves to utilise this increasing market access of remanufactured goods by some countries, led by United States of America.

The Services Negotiations at the WTO

In services India has been a demandeur. It has also offered substantial sectoral and modal coverage in its initial and revised offers which are subject to the conditions of receiving satisfaction in respect of its Mode 1 and Mode 4 requests. India is the coordinator of the plurilateral requests in Model (cross-border supply) and Mode 4 (Movement of Natural Persons) - the crore areas of its interest in the services negotiations. India is also co-sponsor of plurilateral requests in computer and related services (CRS) and architectural, engineering and integrated engineering services.

India has shown considerable movement from Uruguay Round commitments to revised offers; however its primary requests in Modes 1 and 4 have not been addressed by key developed countries. Some of the major developed country members have shown little or no movement in their Mode 4 offers which is a major cause of concern to India. The US and other developed countries such as Australia are trying to introduce a new approach to services negotiations by way of the clustering initiative. India has opposed this cluster approach on procedural as well as substantive grounds. The lack of progress in services under the Doha Round is not due to problems with the approach of negotiations but because of lack of political will, inadequate response from developed countries in sectors and areas of export interest to developing countries, and little movement in agriculture and NAMA.

Rules Negotiations at Doha Round Talks

Negotiations are taking place in the Negotiating Group of Rules (NGR) aimed at clarifying and improving disciplines under the Anti-Dumping Agreement and the Agreement on Subsidies and Countervailing Measures (ASCM), while preserving the basic concepts, principles, and effectiveness of these agreements and their instruments and objectives. Members are also discussing new disciplines for fisheries subsidies.

Consensus eludes on the bigger issues in anti-dumping such as zeroing, sunset reviews, lesser duty rule, public interest, causation, and anti-circumvention. In Subsidies Agreement, considerable divergence remains in the proposals on specific subsidies in the case of inputs provided at regulated prices, and benchmarks for export finance. India has been seeking strengthened anti-dumping rules so as to prohibit the use of zeroing in dumping margin calculation, strengthening of the rules for conduct of sunset reviews, and mandatory application of lesser duty. In the Subsidies Agreement, India is opposed to the enlargement of the scope of prohibited subsidies in the ASCM and /or limiting of the existing flexibilities for the developing countries. In the negotiations on the new disciplines on fisheries subsidies, India is seeking effective special and differential (S&D) treatment for the developoing countries, particularly in the light of employment and livelihood concerns for

small, artisanal fishing communities and for retaining sufficient 'policy space' so as to enable it to develop its infrastructure.

Trade Facilitation at Doha Round Negotiations

Another important area of the Doha round is the negotiations on trade facilitation. Simplification of trade procedures by reducing trading costs is in the interest of all WTO members. A Draft Consolidated Negotiation Text on Trade Facilitation was worked out by the WTO members on 14 December 2009. The draft text has since been revised six times in 2010 through discussions in the meetings of the Negotiating Group on Trade Facilitation. India has been actively participating in these meetings and has also tabled a few proposals on 'Customs Cooperation', Rapid Alerts System of Customs Union', and 'Appeal Mechanism', Developed countries do not want to change their trade procedures but expect others to do so. Developing countries have, by and large, adopted an extra defensive approach to negotiations. Least developed countries, in general, do not want to undertake any binding commitment. Capacity constraints and lack of resources are two major factors that prevent developing countries (and least developed countries) from taking on binding commitments in trade facilitation. The current scenario indicates that developed countries and other donors may not invest in building physical infrastructure in these countries, although the July 2004 Framework Agreement clearly links commitments to support and assistance for infrastructure development. It is important that this linkage is respected by the entire WTO membership particularly the developed countries and that of adequate assistance is provided for implementation of commitments so that a high standard agreement on trade facilitation can be reached.

APPENDIX TO CHAPTER 38A

Foreign Capital Flows and their Impact on Macroeconomic Stability

VOLATILITY OF CAPITAL FLOWS INTO INDIA : ITS IMPACT

As explained in the previous chapter capital flows in the form of foreign direct investment (FDI) and portfolio investment by FII play not only an important role in economic growth of the country but also are badly needed to finance the deficit in current account of our balance of payments. However, volatility of capital flows creates a last of macroeconomic instability in the Indian economy. This volatility creates sometimes boom in stock market and some times crash in it; capital inflows cause appreciation of exchange rate of rupee and thereby adversely affect our exports and through creating excess liquidity they add to inflationary pressures in the economy. On the other hand, capital outflows cause depreciation of rupee and thereby encourage exports but make our imports costlier.

Volatile capital movements have influenced the domestic stock price movements, exchange rate and domestic liquidity conditions significantly in the past. In 2009-10, the current account deficit widened to 2.8 per cent of GDP and, in 2010-11 it was estimated at 2.6 percent of GDP. Volatile capital flows have been a potential source of instability for emerging market economies (EMEs). Costs of volatility of the capital flows could magnify for an economy during periods of both too little and too much of capital flows, unless they are managed judiciously. India, in recent years, had to manage phases of capital flows characterised by large net inflows as well as sudden outflows in the midst of a global crisis. *A judicious mix of flexible exchange rate, sterilisation of the impact of inflows on domestic liquidity, cautious approach to liberalisation of the capital account and the cushion of foreign exchange reserves has been used to deal with the adverse ramifications of capital flows.*

Volatility of capital flows is caused mainly by investment by FIIs. In India it is the inflows and outflows of portfolio capital by FIIs that have caused a lot of macroeconomic instability in the Indian economy. The total *net* FII flows to India in 2009 stood at US $ 18.51 billion. These flows grew remarkably in 2011 and India received FII investment worth US $ 39.71 billion in 2010 which has been the highest in the last decade. These inflows were largely driven by equity inflows which remained buoyant on the back of strong domestic macroeconomic fundamentals and high GDP growth. FIIs have been quite active in the debt segment as well in 2010. However, against the high net FII inflows of 2010, the flows during the year 2011 were quite low. During the first ten months (Jan.-Oct.) of the calender year 2011 India received only $ 4.68 billion against US $ 39.47 billion during 2010. FII investment in India during 2007-11 is given below in Table 38A.1.

Table 38A.1. FII Investment in India

Segment	2007	2008	2009	2010	2011*
Equity	17.65	–11.97	16.87	29.36	0.39
Debt	2.34	2.63	1.64	10.11	4.27
Total	19.99	–9.34	18.51	39.47	4.66

Source: MOF *Mid-year review* 2011-12

* Investment upto Oct. 31, 2011

Capital Inflows and Economic Instability

While capital inflows during 2009-10 remained moderate, in 2010-11 there was a return of another phase of surge in capital flows to India in response to global search for higher yields in an environment of easy liquidity conditions in advanced economies and the prospect of relatively higher return on investment in India in view of its superior growth outlook. The Indian economy grew at 8.5 per cent during 2010-11 which is the second highest growth rate in the world, next only to China. While stronger growth could help in absorbing higher magnitude of foreign capital within the limits of sustainable current account deficit, excess capital inflows would entail the risk of exerting *appreciation pressure on the exchange rate of the rupee*, which in turn could weaken the competitive advantage of Indian exports. Sterilised intervention by RBI could limit the pressure on appreciation of the rupee on account of capital inflows, but may lead to a higher interest rate environment. *Unsterilised intervention* by the RBI that could relieve the pressure on both exchange rate and interest rate, however would involve excess liquidity creation. In an environment of high inflation, this could only increase the inflationary situation further.

High inflation would also adversely impact export competitiveness through appreciation of the real effective exchange rate (REER), which would further widen the current account deficit. Excess capital inflows, thus, would continue to pose challenges for the country's exchange rate, interest rate and inflation environment and through these channels, may at times also weaken the beneficial impact of capital flows on economic growth. Unlike the pre-global crisis period, international perception seems to have changed significantly *in terms of support for use of soft capital controls to deal with excessive capital flows*. In the case of emerging market economies (EMEs), surges in capital flows into them have contributed to asset price build up, along with exchange rate appreciation. Given the complications, asset price build-up could pose problem for monetary policy and the potential risks to financial stability. Therefore, anagement of capital flows into India would need to strike a balance between the objectives of growth and financial stability.

Stronger recovery in India in 2009-10 and 2010-11, ahead of the global recovery along with positive sentiments of global investors about India's growth prospects, encouraged a revival in capital flows into India during 2009-10. The turnaround was mainly driven by large capital inflows under profitfolio investment by FIIs and short-term trade credits. As a result *net* capital flows into India at US $53.4 billion (3.8% of GDP were much higher during 2009-10 as compared to US $6.8 billion (0.5 per cent of GDP) in 2008-09. The strong domestic demand for goods in India, unlike many other emerging markets which depend on exports to the West where consumer confidence is waning, was an added attraction. Net equity inflows hit $ 23-25 billion in 2010-11, while net debt flows will also be significantly higher. Globally, with debt investment yields so low, money continues to be allocated to equities and gold. And within the equity universe, emerging markets, especially India, witnessed increased capital inflows and many new investors in 2009-10 and 2010-11.

The fact that when a country witnesses a volatile capital flow comprising short-term capital flows while stable capital flows represented by FDI slows down, country faces an acute problem of economic instability. This forced Brazil with an emerging economy to go in for capital controls in April 2011 to ensure economic stability. The too much inflows of volatile capital in Brazil threatened to fuel an *asset bubble*. Surprisingly enough, the champion of free flow of capital, International Monetary Fund conceded in April 2011 that governments can resort to capital controls when they have to prevent economic destabilisation.

Now the pertinent question where does India, a prominent emerging market economy, stand ? It is a very difficult situation. The emerging economies of Brazil, Russia, India and China – normally known as BRICs for their uniform opportunities in the past – are beginning to diverge. Inflation is a common theme running across these countries. So are slowing domestic growth and investment

opportunities, but not the current account deficit. That throws up a peculiar problem for Indian policy makers who need the foreign capital flows to keep the economy growing by financing its current account deficit. But we also need to prevent rise in inflation due to large capital inflows. This requires fine-tuning *capital flows management*. We cannot resort to controlling capital inflows whether through FDI or FII for we need them to finance our current account deficit which is now of a significant size. For India it is a big problem to rely on volatile capital inflows by FIIs for financing our current account deficit. What we need are *stable and long term* capital flows of foreign direct investment.

Capital Outflows and Economic Instability

There was capital flight from the Indian markets in Feb, 2011 but it returned to India in April and there was *net inflow of capital* of US $3.1 billion by FIIs in April-July 15, 2011 bringing boom in the Indian stock and bond market and also led to appreciation of rupee to some extent. However, from Aug. 2011 there has again been outlow of capital due to worsening of sovereign debt crisis of European countries and slowdown of the US economy. This caused Bombay Stock Exchange Index (SENSEX) to fall heavily from over 18000 to 16200 on September 24, 2011 and further to 15500 in Mid-December 2011, Besides, this capital outflow has led to a large depreciation of rupee from September 2011. The Indian Rupee which was around ₹ 44 to a US dollar fell to nearly ₹ 52 to a US dollar on Nov. 22, 2011 and further to ₹ 53 to a US dollar in mid-December 2011. The sharp-depreciation of the Indian rupee caused by capital outflows from Sept. 2011 is proving to be highly harmful for the Indian economy. To prevent excessive depreciation of the Indian rupee the RBI is using its foreign exchange reserves to sell US dollars in foreign exchange market. This will cause decline in foreign exchange reserves which are needed to cover imports of goods and services needed for industrial growth. Further, lack of adequate foreign exchange reserves with the RBI will lead to the loss of confidence among foreign investors about the ability of the country to pay back the loans from foreign financial institutions. Besides, weakening of the rupee is likely to cause losses to the foreign investors who repatriate their profits to their home countries. This will discourage inflows of foreign direct investment needed for economic growth of the country. It is evident from above the that capital flows create a lot of macroeconomic instability and therefore they need to be prudently managed. As mentioned above, India faces a different problem from other emerging economies as it has to contend with a large deficit on current account balance that during the year 2011-12 may go up to 3 % of GDP for which we need foreign exchange. In this context it is not advisable for India to impose any control on foreign capital inflows. Our foreign exchange reserves stood at around US $304 billion at end-March 2011 and if monthly deficit on current account goes on occurring at the present rate and given the capital outflows (in Sept.-Dec. 2011) we may find it difficult to meet our current account deficit unless capital flows are reversed.

Further, of late there is another adverse situation that is developing is the falling cover of our exchange which means the number of months of imports that our foreign exchange reserves can finance. After touching a peak of being able to Finance 16.5 months imports in February 2010, it fell to 9.5 months in Feb. 2011.

However, things go on changing dramatically depending on the global economic and financial situation. When there are large capital outflows causing depreciation of rupee as it is occurring now in Sept.-Dec. 2011, there is need for intervention by RBI to sell US dollars from its foreign exchange resourves to check excess depreciation of rupee. On the other hand, when there is excess capital inflows causing appreciation of exchange rate of rupee, the RBI can intervene and buy or absorb some foreign exchange (*i.e.* dollars) coming into the country.

Composition of Capital Flows : A Problem

But the problem for India is more of the adverse nature is composition of capital flows. In the recent past *capital flows are more of portfolio route by FIIs* which was the largest component of total capital flow in FY 2010-11 (see Figure -38A.1). The difficult problem posed by these volatile capital

flows, as mentioned above, is that they are being used to finance widening deficit in current account balance. Foreign direct investment (FDI) which prior to 2010 was the largest component of capital inflows has declined in 2010-11 (see Fig. 38A.1). As will be seen from Fig. 30A.1 the NRI deposits also have slowed down in 2010-11. Even the external commercial borrowing (ECB) has also not risen much in 2010-11 as compared to 2009-10. Because of these the Reserve Bank has to use its policy regarding management of capital flows and foreign exchange rate more proactively than adopt a mere reactive policy in this regard. Even though with the use of proper foreign exchange rate policy the RBI can encourage imports to fight inflation. But it has refrained from doing so. The extent of the RBI intervention in the foreign exchange market has been much less in the last two years. Exchange rate policy has not been used to promote exports or to encourage imports to fight inflation.

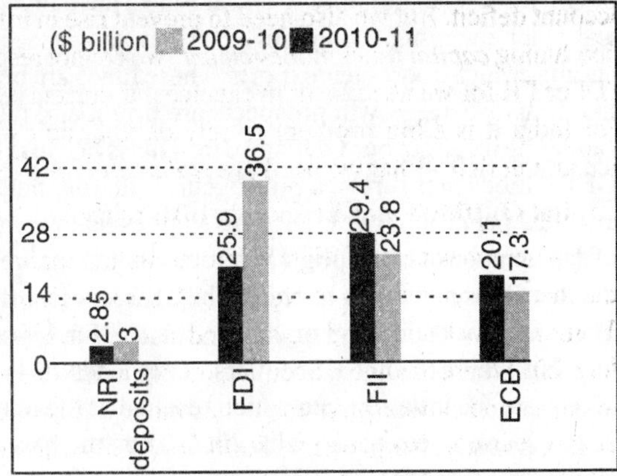

Fig. 38A.1. *Compostion of Capital flows in 2009-10 and 2010-11*

It is due to the lack proactive policy of management of capital flows and foreign exchange rate that there is a lot of macroeconomic instability in the Indian economy. When capital outflow by FIIs occur we face a problem of crash in Indian stock market and depreciation of exchange rate of rupee as it is occurring at present (Sept.-Dec. 2011). By increasing the costs of imports (including crude oil) this results in rise in inflation which adds to the problem of ongoing inflation unless they are offset by fall in international commodity prices.

On the other hand, when there is excess capital inflows beyond our absorptive capacity as occurred during April-July 2011 this leads to the appreciation of rupee which makes our exports less competitive and increases excess liquidity in the economy. Intervention by the RBI in such a situation is called for but it has been hesitant to intervene. Explaining this non-intervention Dr. D. Subba Rao, the present Governor of the RBI, states, "*If this resultant liquidity is left unsterilised, it fuels inflationary pressures. If the resultant liquidity is sterilized, it puts upward pressure on interest rates which, apart from hurting competitiveness, also encourages further flows*". This is arguing for unfettered free market in foreign exchange and no controls over the capital flows.

This indicates the RBI should be more watchfal of the movement of capital flows and foreign exchange rate of rupee and should actively intervene in forex market to ensure exchange rate stability and to encourage stable long-run capital flows into the Indian economy.

Macroeconomic Instability. It follows from above that the capital flows, if not regulated properly, can lead to macroeconomic instability. They cause changes in foreign exchange rate which affect exports and imports and therefore the balance of payments of a country. They also lead to the changes in foreign currency assets of Reserve Bank of India bringing about changes in money supply and thus causing price instability. Thus large capital inflows, if not regulated properly, cause inflation in the economy by bringing about expansion in money supply. Besides, as seen above, the large capital inflows of portfolio type affect stock market prices; when they come into the country, they generate boom in the stock market but when there is reversal of these flows, they cause crash in the stock market.

Controlling Capital Inflows

It may be noted that the central banks of the US and Japan have reduced their interest rate to almost zero and bought government securities from the market to pump more money into the market.

From Nov. 2010, to June 2011 the US Federal Reserve pumped in $ 600 billion in the US economy which led to capital outflow from the US economy to the emerging economies and cause depreciation of US dollar. Besides, their Central Banks have given loans to their FIIs which are investing in India, and other emerging economies. Besides, the depreciation of the US dollar will make their products cheaper which boost their exports. These funds are being brought by FIIs into the emerging economies like India where growth prospects are bright and rates of return on capital are quite high. Besides, capital flows affect our GDP growth. This is because exports at present are not a negligible part of our GDP. Goods and services put together (that is, both merchandise and invisible exports) add up to about 22 per cent of our GDP. This implies that we cannot afford to let our exports decline on account of appreciation of our rupee. Therefore, when there are large capital inflows there is absolutely necessary that the RBI intervenes to check the appreciation of rupee rather than go on waiting and watching. There are two main ways of capital control. First, the RBI intervenes in the foreign exchange market in a big way and buy US dollars. This leads to the expansion in money supply that will further accelerate the inflation rate which reached at the uncomfortable level of 8.53 per cent in December 2010 (year-on-year basis) with 2004-05 as the base. But this inflation was checked by *sterilization measure* adopted by the RBI.

It may however be noted that *at present adequate capital flows into India are necessary for meeting its current account deficit which is estimated at 4.2% per cent of GDP in 2011-12 and around 4.8% of GDP in 2012-13*. The matter of concern for us is that in view of decline in capital inflows through foreign direct investment (FDI) we are meeting our large current deficit with portfolio capital inflows which are quite volatile and when there is reversal of these inflows it creates problems for the Indian economy. For instance after a surge of these portfolio capital inflows prior to August 2011, there had been reversal of these inflows from September 2011 onwards which put pressure on stock market prices and exchange rate of rupee. Therefore, what is needed is to encourage capital inflows through foreign direct investment to build infrastructure facilities and to meet to a large extent the country's current account deficit through these stable FDI inflows. Besides, at present in view of large current account deficit there is no need for imposing any tax on inflows of portfolio capital, but Reserve Bank of India should prevent the adverse consequences of its volatility through its timely intervention in foreign exchange market.

PART VIII
THEORIES OF ECONOMIC GROWTH

- Economic Growth and its Determinants.
- Harrod-Domar Model of Growth
- Neoclassical Theory of Growth
- New Theory of Growth (Endogenous Growth Model)
- Theory of Economic Development with Surplus Labour : Lewis Model
- Limitations and Relevance of Keynesian Economics to Developing Countries
- Nature of Unemployment and Development Strategy in Labour-Surplus in Developing Countries
- Global Financial Crisis and Eurozone Crisis its Impact on World Economy

CHAPTER 39

Economic Growth and its Determinants

Before explaining the factors which determine economic growth and development and the common characteristics of the developing countries it is useful to describe how the terms economic growth and development are interpreted by the economists. In the fifties and sixties when the economics of growth and development were evolved, economic growth and development were considered to have the same meaning and therefore these two terms were used interchangeably. Today, however, an important distinction is drawn between economic growth and economic development. In what follows we first explain the meaning of these terms and the distinction between them.

Meaning of Economic Growth

Economic growth has been defined in two ways. In the first place, *economic growth is defined as a sustained annual increases in an economy's real national income over a long period of time.* In other words, economic growth means *rising trend of net national product at constant prices*. This definition has been criticized by some economists as inadequate and unsatisfactory. They argue that total national income may be increasing and yet the standard of living of the people may be falling. This can happen when the population is increasing at a faster rate than total national income. For instance, if national income is rising by 1% per year and population is increasing at 2% per year, the standard of living of the people will tend to fall. This is so because when population is increasing more rapidly than national income, per capita income will go on falling. Per capita income will rise when the national income increases faster than population.Therefore, the second and better way of defining economic growth is to do so in terms of per capita income. According to the second view, *"economic growth means the annual increase in real per capita income of a country over the long period.* Thus Professor Arthur Lewis says that *"economic growth means the growth of output per head of population"* Since the main aim of economic growth is to raise the standards of living of the people, therefore the second way of defining economic growth which runs in terms of per capita income or output is better.

Another point which is worth mentioning in regard to the definition of economic growth is that the increase in national income or more correctly increase in per capita income or output, must be a 'sustained increase' if it is to be called economic growth. By sustained increase in per capita income we mean the upward or rising trend in per capita income over a long period of time. A mere short-period rise in per capita income, such as that occurs over a business cycle, cannot be validly called economic growth.

Now, almost universally, rates of economic growth are measured both in terms of increase in overall Gross National Product (GNP) or Net National Product (NNP) and increase in per capita income. While Gross National Product (GNP) measures the total output of goods and services which an economy is capable of producing, per capita income measures how much of real goods and services which an average person of the community will have for consumption and investment, that is, average level of living of a citizen of a country.

Thus, world organizations such as World Bank, and IMF have been employing both these measures of economic growth in their annual World Development Reports for comparing growth and levels of living of the developed and the developing countries. In India also our Planning Commission, Central Statistical Organization (CSO), and Reserve Bank of India have been measuring economic growth on the basis of both overall GNP or NNP and per capita income. The recent estimates of annual growth in GNP and per capita income is given in Table 39.1. This table reveals an interesting feature *that economic growth achieved in recent years is higher in the developing countries than in the developed countries*. However, it should be noted that in the past several decades the present-day developed countries recorded much higher growth rates than the developing countries which remained static for a long period. As a result, per capita income and levels of living of the people of the developed countries are now much higher as compared to those of the developing countries. The problem of the developing countries is to catch up with the developed countries through attaining rapid economic growth so as to enjoy higher levels of living.

Table 39.1.GNP Per Capita, Growth Rate and Population in Some Developed and Developing Countries.

Country	Population (millions) 2009	GNP per Capita in 2009 (US Dollars)	Growth Rate of GNP 1980-90	1990-2000	2000-09
Developed Countries					
U.S.A.,	307	46,360	3.0,	3.5	2.0
Australia,	22	43,770	3.5	3.9	3.3
U.K.	62	41,378	3.2	3.7	2.0
Canada	34	41,980	3.4	3.1	2.0
Japan	128	38,080	4.1	1.3	1.1
Developing Countries					
India	1155	1,230	5.8	6.0	7.9
China	1331	3,650	10.2	10.6	10.9
Pakistan	170	1,000	6.3	3.8	5.2
Bangladesh	162	580	4.3	4.8	5.9
Sri Lanka	20	1,990	4.2	5.3	5.8

Source: World Bank, *World Development Report*, 2011

Meaning of Economic Development : Traditional View

As mentioned above no distinction was drawn between economic growth and development in the beginning of the evolution of economics of development. However, since the seventies it has been thought necessary to distinguish between economic growth and economic development. There are two views even about the concept of economic development. The traditional view has been to interpret it in terms of planned changes in the structure of national product and the occupational pattern of labour force and also the institutional and technological changes that bring about such changes or accompany such changes. It may be noted that Kuznets in his study of *Modern Economic* Growth interpreted the process of modern economic growth which involves these structural changes[1]. In this view during the process of economic growth share of agriculture in both national product and employment of labour force declines and that of industries and services increases. Various strategies of development which were suggested until 'seventies' generally focussed on rapid industrialization so that structural ansformation could be achieved. For this purpose appropriate institutional and technological changes were recommended to bring about such structural changes. Thus C.P. Kindleberger

1. It may be noted that Kuznets in his study of "*Modern Economic Growth*" interpreted the process of modern economic growth which involves these structural changes.

writes, *economic growth means more output and economic development implies both more output and changes in the technical and institutional arrangements by which it is produced.* [2]

Thus, according to traditional view, economic development implies growth plus structural change. Structural change refers to changes in technological and institutional factors which cause shift of labour from agriculture to modern manufacturing and services sectors and also generate self-sustaining growth of output. An aspect of structural change which is of special mention is that during the process of economic development there occurs a shift of working population from low productivity employment in agriculture to the modern industrial and services sectors having higher levels of productivity of labour. That is, during the process of economic development percentage share of working population in agriculture sharply falls whereas percentage shares of working population employed in modern industrial and services sectors substantially increase. Along with this change in sectoral distribution of labour force there occurs a change in sectoral composition of national income in which percentage contribution of agriculture to national income declines, percentage contributions to national income of industrial and services sectors increase. This occurs due to the change in pattern of consumption of the people as economy grows and people's income increases as well as due to the changes in levels of productivity in the different sectors of the economy.

It is worth mentioning that in this view causal references were made to the role of some social factors such as growth of literacy, education and good health in economic development but they were considered to be of secondary importance. On the whole, in this view of economic development which generally prevailed till seventies, development was considered to be an economic phenomenon in which benefits from growth in overall GNP or per capita GNP and the structural changes accompanying it would trickle down to the poor and unemployed. No separate or special attention was paid to eliminate mass poverty and unemployment and to reduce inequalities in income distribution.

The Concept of Economic Development : The Modern View

The experience of the developing countries during the sixties and seventies showed that whereas target rates of economic growth were in fact achieved trickle-down effect in the form of creation of more employment opportunities, rise in wages and improvement in income distribution did not operate. The problems of poverty, unemployment and income inequality further worsened instead of getting reduced during the process of growth in the Fifties and Sixties in the developing countries. For instance, in India Dandekar and Rath[3] found that 40 per cent of rural population in India lived below the poverty line in 1968-69. Using some what different approach, B.S. Mimhas[4] estimated that 37 per cent of rural population in India lived below the poverty line in 1967-68. Similarly, the magnitude of poverty and unemployment and the extent of income inequalities also increased in many other developing countries.

Thus, due to the failure of traditional strategies of development in solving the problems of poverty, unemployment and inequality, it was realised in the seventies that the concept of development should be broadened so that it should signify that well-being of the people has increased. This led to the view that economic development should not be judged on the basis of growth in GNP alone. Therefore, when we regard the well-being of the masses as the ultimate objective of development, we have to see whether poverty and unemployment are decreasing and how the increases in gross national product or national income are being distributed among the population. Economic development will take place in true terms only if the poor people are raised above the poverty line. Late Prof. Sukhamoy Chakravarty rightly writes, "*The rate of growth strategy is by itself an inadequate device to deal with the problems of generating employment opportunities and for reducing*

2. C.P. Kindleberger, *Economic Development*
3. Dandekar and Rath, *Poverty in India*, 1971.
4. B.S. Minhas, Poverty, Land Redistribution and Development Strategy, *Indian Economic Review*, 1971

economic disparities. Much depends on the composition of the growth process and how growth is financed and how benefits from growth process are distributed.[5]

It is worth mentioning that there is no guarantee that when there is increase in GNP, employment will also increase. It can happen that with the use of more capital-intensive technique while production may be increasing at a rapid rate, employment may be falling instead of rising. According to the modern perception of economic development, rapid increase in GNP secured through displacing labour by machines and thus causing rise in unemployment and under-employment cannot be called true economic development. Professor Dudley Seers makes the meaning of economic development according to the new perception in the following words:

"*The questions to ask about a country's development are therefore: What has been happening to poverty? What has been happening to unemployment? What has been happening to inequality? If all three of these have declined from high levels, then beyond doubt this has been a period of development for the country concerned. If one or two of these central problems have been growing worse, especially if all three have, it would be strange to call the result development even if per capita income doubled.* "[6]

Recently, the concept of economic development has been further widened so that it now involves not only reduction in poverty, inequality and unemployment but also requires improvement in *quality of life which includes cleaner environment, better education, good health and nutrition*. Thus World Development Report 1991, published by World Bank asserts: "*the challenge of development is to improve the quality of life. Especially in the World's poor countries, a better quality of life generally calls for higher incomes but it involves much more. It encompasses as ends in themselves better education, higher standards of health and nutrition, less proverty, a cleaner environment, more equality of opportunity* "[7] Thus the concept of economic development has been greatly broadened. Today economic development is interpreted as not only in more growth in economic well-being but also in terms of good quality of life which, according to Prof. Amartya Sen, consists in 'enlargement of opportunities for people and freedom of human choices'. This new concept of development includes achievement of freedom from servitude to ignorance and illiteracy. It also includes enjoyment of human rights. Thus United Nations '*Human Development Report*' of 1994 in the writting of which Prof. Amartya Sen made a significant contribution, asserts, "Human beings are born with certain potential capabilities. The purpose of development is *to create an environment in which all people can expand their capabilities, and opportunities can be enlarged* for both present and future generations..... .Wealth is important for human life. but to concentrate on it exclusively is wrong for two reasons. First, accumulating wealth is not necessary for the fulfilment of some important human choices .... Second, human choices extend far beyond economic well-being. In his recent book, Amartya Sen writes "Economic growth cannot be sensibly treated as an end in itself. Development has to be more concerned with enhancing the *lifes we lead and the freedoms we enjoy*."[8]

On the basis of various ingredients of good quality of life and other criteria such as enlargement of human choices and freedom a human development index is prepared by United Nations Development Programme (UNDP). This human development index is considered as a better indicator of economic development.

---

5. Sukhamony Charkravarty, Some Observations on Growth Process, *Seminar*, 1971
6. Dudley Seers, "The Meaning of Development" presented at the Eleventh World Conference of the Society for International Development. (New Delhi), 1969.
7. United Nations, *Measures for Economic Develpment of Under-developed Countries*, 1951
8. See Amartya Sen, *Development as Freedom*, Oxford University Press, 2001, 175

FACTORS DETERMINING ECONOMIC GROWTH

The process of economic growth is a highly complex phenomenon and is influenced by numerous and varied factors such as economic, political, social and cultural factors. It is believed by some economists that the capital is the only requirement for growth and therefore the greatest emphasis be laid on capital formation to bring about economic development. But this is wrong. As Professor Nurkse r.ghtly remarks, *"Economic development has much to do with human endowments. social attitudes, political conditions and historical accidents, Capital is a necessary but not a sufficient condition of progress"*.[2] The following are various factors which determine economic growth and development:

(i) Supply of *Natural* Resources;
(ii) Capital formation which depends upon the rate of domestic saving and investment and inflow of foreign capital";
(iii) Growth of population;
(iv) Technological Progress; and

We examine below each of these factors in turn,

Supply of Natural Resources

The quantity and quality of natural resources play a vital role in the economic development of a country, Important natural resources are land, minerals and oil resources, water, forests, climate, etc. The quantity and quality of natural resources available in a country puts a limit on the level of output of goods which can be attained. Without a minimum of natural resources there is not much hope for economic development. It should, however, be noted that *resource availability is not a necessary condition for economic growth,* For instance, India though rich in natural resources, has remained poor and under-developed. This is because resources have not been fully utilised for productive purposes, Thus it is not only the availability of natural resources but also the ability to bring them into use which determine the growth of an economy. On the other hand, Japan has a relatively few natural resources but has shown a very high rate of economic growth and as a result has become one of the richest countries in the world. 'How has Japan done this miracle? It is international trade that has made possible for Japan to 'achieve higher growth rate. Japan imports many of natural resources such as mineral oil it requires for production of manufactured goods. It then exports manufactured goods to the countries that are rich in natural resources. Thus experience of Japan shows that abundant natural resources are not a necessary condition for economic growth.

Supplies of natural resources can be increased as a result of new discoveries of resources within a country or technological changes which facilitate discoveries or transform certain previously useless materials into highly useful ones. It should also be noted that the scarcity of certain natural resources can be overcome by *synthetic substitutes.* For example, the synthetic rubber is being increasingly used in the place of natural rubber in advanced countries. Further, nylon which is a synthetic substance is being largely used in place of silk which is a natural substance.

The use of natural resources and the role they play in economic growth depend, among other things, on the type of technology. The relationship of resources to the kind and level of technology is very intimate. One does not have to go back very far in history to find when an item currently as valuable as petroleum was of little or no significance. It is only recently that the various radioactive elements have come to be regarded as valuable. In many developing economies there are, no doubt, deposits of many minerals that are not being used because of technological deficiencies.

Capital Formation

Labour is combined with capital to produce goods and services. Workers need machines, tools and factories to work. In fact the use of capital makes workers more productive. Setting up of more factories equipped with machines and tools which raise the productive capacity of the economy. Therefore, in the opinion of many economists, capital formation is the very core of economic development. Whatever the type of economic system, without capital accumulation the process of economic growth cannot be accelerated. Levels of productivity in the United States of America are very high mainly because American people ork with more and better type of capital goods built up over the last several years. Low productivity and poverty of developing countries is largely due to the scarcity or shortage of real physical capital in these countries. Economic growth cannot be speeded up without accumulating various types of capital goods, that is, without building factories, machines, tools, dams, bridges, roads, railways, ports, ships, irrigation works, fertilizers, etc., much economic development is not possible.

But capital formation requires saving, that is, the sacrifice of some current consumption. An increase in supplies of capital goods can only result from investment, and investment in turn is only possible if a portion of current income is saved. Thus saving is essential to economic growth. According to Professor Arthur Lewis, *"The central problem in the theory of economic growth is to understand the process by which a community is coltverted from being a 5 per cent saver to a 12 per cent saver with all the changes in attitudes, in institutions and in techniques which accompany this conversion".*[4] Underdeveloped economies generally save very little. For instance, saving in India on the eve of independence was about 6 per cent of the national income. On the other hand, rich countries save from 15 to 30 per cent of their national income. In order to bring about economic growth, rate of savings must be stepped up to over 15 per cent of national income. But in developing countries, the rate of saving has been low because income of the people has been low and that they are living at the level of subsistence. Thus, the lower the per capita income, the more difficult it is to forgo current consumption. It is difficult for people living at or near subsistence level to curtail current consumption. This in large part explains the low of saving in the poor, underdeveloped countries.

It may be noted that gross saving rate in India has now risen to 34 per cent of national income in 2009-10. However, for achieving 9 per cent rate of growth in GNP which is now the target of planning in India it is estimated that 36 per cent rate of saving is needed if capital-output ratio remains constant at 4 which was actually obtained in the 9th plan period.

It must be emphasized, however, that savings in itself do not contribute to economic growth. It is only when savings are invested and used productively that they contribute to economic growth. If savings are hoarded in the form of gold or precious jewels, or if they are used for buying land, they do not result in an increase in supplies of capital goods and thus make no contribution to economic growth. Studies conducted to examine the relationship between investment and growth in terms of increase in GDP have found that there exist a *strong correlation between the two* though it is not perfect. Countries that allocate a larger fraction of their GDP to investment such as Japan and Singapore achieved high growth rates, and countries that allocate a small share of GDP to investment such as Bangladesh and Nepal have low growth rates.

Foreign Capital: Foreign Aid and Foreign Investment

As domestic savings are not sufficient to make possible the necessary or desired accumulation of capital goods, borrowing from abroad may play an important role. Professor AJ. Brown rightly says that *"Development demands that people somewhere should refrain from spending a part of their incomes, thus allowing a part of the world's productive resources to be used for accumulation of capital goods. The people who can best afford to do this are generally those who live in countries of high average income. On the other hand, the countries where development is likely to alleviate suffering and promote welfare to the greatest extent are those where average incomes are low. There*

4. Arthur Lewis, Economic Development with Unlimited Supplies of Labour, *Manchester School,* 1954.

is a strong general case for the rich countries lending to the poor ones."[5] Nearly every developed state obtained the foreign assistance to supplement its own small saving during the early stages of its development. England borrowed from Holland in the seventeenth and eighteenth centuries, and in turn came to lend to almost every other country in the world in the nineteenth and twentieth centuries. The United States of America, now the richest country in the world, borrowed heavily in the nineteenth century, and has now emerged as the major lender country of the twentieth century which is assisting the poor countries in their attempts to bring about economic growth. .

It should be noted that foreign capital does not flow into the developing countries in the form of *aid* alone (that is, loans at concessional rates of interest) but also through *direct investment* by foreign companies. Foreign direct investment (FDI) is an important way for a country to accelerate its economic growth. Though the foreign companies send back profits earned, their investments in factories *increase the rate of capital accumulation* in the developing countries leading to a higher rate of economic growth and higher productivity of labour. Besides, foreign direct investment enables the developing countries *to learn the new advanced technologies* developed and used in the rich developed countries.

The importance of foreign capital is reinforced by *the need of a developing country for foreign exchange to buy imports.* A developing country has to import huge quantities of capital goods, technical know-how and essential raw-materials which are required for industrial growth and building up of infrastructure such as power projects, roads, irrigation facilities, ports and telecommunication. For all these, foreign exchange is needed which can be obtained if foreign rich countries lend it to developing economies or if foreign companies make direct investment in the developing countries. If foreign assistance is not forthcoming in adequate quantity, then the developing countries will experience serious difficulties of balance of payments. In the absence of sufficient borrowing from abroad, or direct foreign investment, rapid economic development of the developing countries will turn their balance of payments seriously adverse.

Furthermore, developing countries suffer not only from a shortage of savings but also from a *lack of technical know-how, managerial ability,* etc. Foreign capital when it comes in the form of private investment in developing countries by foreign companies, especially the multinational corporations (MNCs) bring with it these complementary factors which are very essential for development..

Due to bad experience of the colonial rule in the past, the developing countries were generally against the foreign capital, especially against private foreign investment. However the fears of foreign investment and aid are now no longer there. Further, now *multilateral foreign aid* is available through World Bank and International Monetary Fund (IMF) which provide loans at concessional rates to the developing countries for accelerating growth. As far as private, foreign investment is concerned, the developing countries (induding China and India) are competing with each other to attract private foreign investors. In India, the Government has set the target of achieving annual inflow of $10 billion of foreign direct investment. It has now been realised that foreign investment will not only supplement domestic saving and thereby raise the rate of investment, bring better technology and managerial know-how but will also ease the problem of foreign exchange. Through raising the rate of investment and providing foreign exchange resources, it will not only increase output but will also generate employment opportunities: Besides, like the domestic investment, *foreign investment also produces a multiplier effect on output, income and employment* in the developing countries.

In the last fifteen years, China's very high rate of economic growth which is generally described as *"Chinese growth miracle"* is due to higher inflow of foreign direct investment (FDI) as compared to India. Foreign direct investment flows to China grew from $3.5 billions from 1990 to $53 billion in

5. AJ. Brown, *Introduction to the World &onomy.*

2002. On the other hand, FDI flow to India was a low $0.4 billion in 1990 and rose to $5.5 billion in 2002. Further, FDI has contributed significantly to the rapid growth of China's manufacturing exports. In India by contrast FDI has been much less important in driving India's export growth, except in information technology. For higher foreign direct investment flows to China World Investment Report 2003 mentions among other things that China has more business-oriented and FDI-friendly attitudes, its FDI procedures are easier and decisions are taken rapidly. Besides, China has more flexible labour laws, a better labour climate and better entry and exit procedures for business. It is therefore not unexpected that China has emerged at the top in attracting FDI flows. Against this, at present (i.e. in 2002) India is 15th in the World's FDI destination..

Human Capital: Education And Health

Till recently economists have been considering physical capital as the most important factor determining economic growth and have been recommending that rate of physical capital formation in developing countries must be increased to accelerate the process of economic growth and raise the living standards of the pople. But in the last three decades of economic research has revealed the importance of education as a crucial factor in economic development, Education refers to the development of human skills and knolwedge of the labour force. It is not only the quantitative expansion of educational opportunities but also the qualitative improvement of the education which is imparted to the labour force that holds the key to economic development. Because of its significant contribution to economic development, education has been called as *human capital* and expenditure on education of the people as *investment in man or human capital.* Speaking of the importance of education or human capital. Prof. Harbison writes: "human resources constitute the ultimate basis of production, human beings are the active agents who accumulate capital, exploit natural resources, build social, economic and political organisations; and carry forward national development. Clearly, a country which is unable to develop the skills and knowledge of its people and to utilise them effectively in the national economy will be unable to develop anything else."[6]

TABLE -39.1 : **Sources of US Economic Growth**, 1929-1982 (per cent)

Annual growth of output (per cent)	2.9
(a) Growth in labour input	32
(b) Growth in labour productivity :	
(1) Education per worker	14
(2) Capital formation	19
(3) Technological change	28
(4) Economies of scale	9
(5) other factors	–2

Source: Edward E. Denison, *Trends in American Economic Growth* (1929-82) The Brookings Institution 1983, p. 30.

Several empirical studies made in developed countries, especially the U.S.A. regarding the sources of growth or, in other words, contributions made by various factors such as physical capital, man-hours, (i.e., physical labour), education etc. have shown that education or the development of human capital is a significant source of economic growth. Professor Solow[7] who was one of the first economists to measure the contribution of human capital to economic growth estimated that for United States between 1909 and 1949, 57.5 per cent of growth in output per man hour could be attributed to the *residual factor* which represents the effect of technological change and of the improvements in the quality of labour mainly as a consequence of education.

6. Frederick Harbison, *Human Resources as the Wealth of Nations.* Oxford University Press, 1973, p.
7. Robert M. Solow, Technical Change and Aggregate Production Function, *Review of Economics andStatistics,* Aug. 1957.

Denision, another American economist made further refinement in estimating the contribution to economic growth of various factors. Denision tried to separate and measure the contributions of various elements of 'residual factor'. Denson's estimates for various sources of US growth during 1929-82 are given in Table 39.1 As will be seen from the Table 39.1 Gross Domestic Product in the USA grew at the rate of 2.9 per cent per annum over this period. The factors determining growth in this period have been divided into two groups. It will be seen from the table that the *growth in the quantity of labour* accounted for 32 per cent of growth in GDP of the USA over this period. The other group consists of *various variables determining growth in labour productivity has-been* divided into five factors. It is noteworthy that education per worker contributed 14 per cent to growth in output during this period, technological change contributed 28 per cent to the growth in output. Thus, growth in education per worker and technological change togehter accounted for 42 per cent of growth in the output in the USA over this period whereas capital formation contributed 19 per cent to the growth rate. This shows the great importance of education and technological change as determinants of economic growth.[8]

Another approach to measure the contribution of education is based upon the analysis of the relationship between expenditure on education and income. Using this approach Schultz studied the relationship between expenditure on education and individual income and also the relationship between expenditure on education and physical capital formation for the United States during the period 1900 to 1956. He found that when measured in constant dollars, "the resources allocated to education rose about three and a half times (a) relative to consumer income in dollars, (b) relative to the gross formation of physical capital in dollars.[9] This implies that the "income elasticity" of the demand for education was about 3.5. over the period or, in other words, education considered as an investment could be regarded as 3.5 times more attractive than investment in physical capital. It may, however, be noted that these estimates of Schultz only indirectly reflect the contribution of education to economic growth.

In our above analysis we have explained that education is regarded as investment and like investment in physical capital, it raises productivity of labour and thus contributes to growth of national income. Some economists have argued that education is of crucial importance not only because education raises the productivity and therefore earnings of individual workers, but it creates *positive externalities, that is, beneficial external effects*. A positive *externality* occurs when the activity of a person provides benefits to *others*. For example, an educated person might generate new ideas which may lead to the improvement in methods of producing goods. When these ideas become a part of society's pool of knowledge *(i.e.* stock of human capital), everyone can use them and derive benefits from them. These ideas are therefore external benefits of education. One problem facing the developing countries, especially India is of *brain drain,* that is, migration of a large number of highly educated persons (such as those trained by IIT, 11M and medical colleges) to the developed countries such as the USA to make higher earnings there. If education has positive external effects, then this brain drain will deprive the Indian economy of the beneficial effects which these educated people would have created here.

Technological Progress and Economic Growth

Another important factor in economic growth is progress in technology, Use of advanced techniques in production or *progress in technology brings about a significant increase in per capita output.* Technological advance refers to the discovery of new and better ways of doing things or an

8. B.F. Denison, *Trends in American Growth* (1929.82) The Brookings Institution, 1983, p. 30.
9. Schultz, Education and Economic Growth, in Nelson B. Henry (ed.). *The Sixtieth Year book of the National Society for the Study of Education.* University of Chicago Press, 1961.

improvement in the old ways. Sometimes technological advances result in an increase in available supplies of natural resources. *But more generally technological advance results in increasing the productivity or effectiveness* with which natural resources, capital and labour are used and worked to produce goods. As a result of technological advance it becomes possible to produce more output with same resources or the same amount of product with less resources.

But the question arises as to how does the technological progress take place. The technological progress takes place through *inventions* and *innovations.* The word invention is used for the new scientific discoveries, whereas the innovations are said to take place only when the new scientific discoveries are used for actual production processes or commercial purposes. Some inventions may not be economically profitable to be used for actual production.

It is quite well known that improvements in technology greatly increase the effectiveness with which natural resources are used. In United States, for instance, increased used of mechanized power-driven farm equipment on land has greatly raised the agricultural productivity of land per hactare. It may also be noted that some technological improvements have resulted in the increased effectiveness with which capital goods are used. But, as stated above, technological change more generally results in higher productivity of resources. Technological change raises the productivity of workers through the provision of better machines, better methods and superior skills. By bringing about increase in productivity of resources the progress in technology makes it possible to produce more output with the same resources or the same amount of output with less resources.

Technical progress manifests itself in the change in production function. So a simple measure of the technical progress would be the comparison of the position of production function at two points of time. The technological change may operate upon the production function through improvements of various sorts such as a superior equipment, an improved material, and superior organisational efficiency. Also, the technological progress may express itself in making available new products. It is now widely accepted that technological change raises productivity and that a *continuous technological change will enable the economy to escape from being driven to the stationary state or economic stagnation.* Clatsical econorqists like Ricardo and J.S. Mill expressed fear that the increase in the stock of capital will sooner or later, because of the operation of diminishing returns, land the economy into stationary state beyond which economic growth will come to an end. *Classical economists remained occupied with the idea of a stationary state because they did not take into account technological progress that could postpone the occurrence of a stationary state and ensure continued economic growth.* Indeed, if technological progress continuously takes place, demon of stationary state can be put off indefinitely.

It may be noted that Adam Smith viewed technological progress as a rise in productivity of workers as a result of increase in division of labour and specialisation. "'The rise in productivity leads to the growth in national income. But it was J.A. Schumpeter who laid great stress on the role of technological innovations in bringing about economic growth. He laid stress on the introduction of technical innovations in bringing about economic progress. It is the entrepreneur who carries out the innovations and organises the production structure more efficiently. As, according to Schumpeter, innovations occur in spurts rather than in a smooth flow, economic progress is not a smooth and an uninterrupted process. The pace of economic progress is punctuated by the pace of innovations.

Prof. Rostow proposed five stages in the development of an econo stages are : (i) traditional society; (ii) preconditions for take off; (iii) take-off into self-sustaining growth; (iv) drive to maturity and (iv) stage of high mass consumption. It may be noted that the economic transformation of the society from one stage to another involves, along with other things, a change in the level and character of technology. In the present age of greater specialisation it is the technology factor: that und rlies all major aspects of the modern productive apparatus such as decision making, production programming, skill requirements and market strategy.

Productivity of worker depends upon the quantity and quality of capital tools with which the labourers work. For higher productivity the instruments of. production have to be technologically more efficient and superior. The technological options open to an economy determine the input-mix of production. A commodity can be produced by various technologies. The quantity and quality of capital, skills and other factors required for production is directly dependent on the efficiency of the technique of production being used. Also, the managerial and organisational expertise has to be in tune with the technological requirements of production. Viewed thus, technology in the present stage of economic development is an indispensable factor of production.

This is the age of technology. The developing countries are obsessed by the desire to make rapid progress in technology so as to catch up with the present-day developed countries. Strenuous efforts are being made to use improved technology in agriculture, industries, health, sanitation, education and, in fact, in all walks of human life. Indeed, the newly emerging nations have come to regard technology as a bastion of national autonomy and as a status symbol in the international community.

The process of technological progress is inseparably linked with the process of capital formation. In fact, both go hand in hand. Technological progress is virtually impossible without capital formation. It is because the introduction of superior or more efficient techniques require building up of new capital equipment which incorporates new technology. In other words, new and superior technology can contribute to national product and its growth if it is first embodied in the new capital equipment. The new capital investment has,. therefore, been called the vehicle for the steady introduction of new technology into the economy.

The new inventions and innovations lead to new and more efficient techniques of production and new and better products. As is well known, it is the inventions and innovations in cotton textile industry that led to the industrial revolution in England. In the olden times inventions were the work of some individuals and innovations were introduced into the production process by the private entrepreneurs. Keeping in view the importance of technological progress in the economic growth of a country, the governments of various countries are spending a lot of money on *"research and development" (R & D),* which is carried on in various laboratories and institutes to promote technological progress.

Developing countries are using the technology imported from the developed countries because they have not yet made sufficient progress in technology, nor have they developed to an adequate extent capital goods industries which produce capital goods, embodying advanced technology. But imitation and use of the technology of the advanced countries by these under-developed countries has produced one unfavourable result. It is that the technology of the advanced countries is not in accordance with the factor endowments of these developing countries, since they have abundance of capital while the developing countries have surplus labour. As a result of the use of the capital-intensive technology, enough employment opportunities have not been created by the large-scale industries using imported technology. As a result, unemployment in developing countries like India has been increasing despite the progress in industrialisation of the economy. In view of this not so happy experience in regard to the creation of employment opportunities by industrial growth, an eminent English economist, Prof. Schumacher has recommended the use of *intermediate technology* or what is also known as *appropriate tecllnology* by the developing countries like India. *By intermediate or appropriate technology we mean the technology which is labour-intensive and yet highly productive so that with its use enough employment opportunities are created along with more production.* But in order to find out this appropriate technology for several industries, a good deal of research and development *(R & D)* activity is required to be carried out.

The Growth of Population

The growth of population is another factor which determines the rate of economic growth. The growing population increases the level of output by increasing the number of working population or labour force provided all are absorbed in productive employment. We saw above that according to estimates of Denison, increase in the quantity of labour contributed to the extent of 32 per cent to economic growth of output in the USA during 1929-1982. Moreover, the increase in population leads to the increase in demand for goods. Thus, growing population means growing market for goods which facilitates the process of growth. When market for goods is enlarged, they can be produced on a large scale and thus economies of large-scale production can be reaped. The economic history of U.S.A. and European countries shows that population growth contributed greatly to the increase in their national output.

But what has been true of U.S.A. and European countries may not be true in case of the present-day developing countries. Whether or not the growth of population contributes to economic growth depends on the existing size of population; the available supplies of natural and capital resources, and the prevailing technology. In the United States, where supplies of natural and capital resources are comparatively abundant, the growth in population raises national output by increasing the quantity of labour. In India where supplies of other economic resources especially capital equipment, are relatively scarce, increase in population hinders economic growth instead of promoting it.

Labour is combined with capital to produce goods and services. Therefore, increase in the quantity of labour force will contribute to economic growth when the cooperating factor capital is also increasing. In the modem times workers need machines, tools and factories to work. Since a developing country such as India has a lot of surplus labour but a small stock of capital, the workers cannot be productive unless they are employed in some activities. We thus see that a rapidly growing labour force by itself is no guarantee of economic growth. Increase in national output, that is, economic growth is pqssible only when the supplies of capital and other resources are increasing adequately along with the growth of labour force. If, on the other hand, when the supplies of capital and the other resources are meagre, the increase in the labour force (or population) will merely add to unemployment and will not bring about increase in national output.

As stated above, economic growth requires increasing supplies of capital goods. Increasing supplies of capital goods become possible only with higher rate of investment. And a higher rate of investment, in turn, is possible if rate of saving is high. Now, *increase in population by adding to number of mouths to be fed tends to raise consumption and, therefore, lowers both saving and investment.* Thus rapid growth of population by causing lower rate of saving and investment tends to hold down the rate of economic growth in developing countries. Thus, under conditions like those in India population growth actually impedes economic development rather than facilitates it

It is worth noting here that *changes in total* GDP which are used to measure rate of economic growth are not a good measure of economic well-being. For the purpose of evaluating changes in economic well being or living standards of the people of a country GDP *per capita* is more important for it tells us the amount of goods and services that is available for an individual in the economy. But how does growth in population or labour force affect GDP per capita? The reason is that rapidly increasing labour forces forces the economy *to spread more thinly* the other cooperating factors, esp ially capital and land. As a result, capital or land per worker declines causing decline in productivity or GDP per worker.

Further, rapid population growth nullifies out efforts to raise the living standards of our people. In other words, *a high rate of increase in population swallows up a large part of the increase in national income so that per capita income or living standard of the people does not rise much.* This is precisely what has happened during the planning era in India. Thus while the aggregate national income of India went up by 17.5 per cent in the first plan period and 20 per cent in the second plan period, per capita income rose by only 8 per cent and 9 per cent respectively. Over the period of the third plan, as against an increase of 11.5 per cent in national income, per capita income improved by only 0.5 per cent. The relatively slow rate of rise in per capita income has been due to rapid population growth. The annual rate of population growth which was no more than 1.86 per cent in the First Plan period went up to 2.15 per cent in the second plan period.and further to 2.25 per cent in the third and fourth Plans.

CAPITAL-OUTPUT RATIO

Capital-output ratio is the amount of capital required to produce output worth Re. 1. If Y stands for output or income and K for the stock of capital used to produce that output, then $\frac{K}{Y}$ represents capital-output ratio. It is useful to distinguish between marginal capital-output ratio and average capital-output ratio. Whereas average capital-output ratio describes the ratio of total capital to total output or income of the economy, marginal capital-output ratio is ratio of *increment* in the stock of capital to the *increment* in output. Therefore, marginal capital-output ratio can be written as $\frac{\Delta K}{\Delta Y}$ where ΔK is the increment in capital and ΔY is the resultant increase in income. or output. Therefore, marginal capital-output ratio is also called *incremental capital-output ratio* (ICOR).

The rate of economic growth of a country depends upon the rate of capital formation and capital-output ratio. Capital-output ratio determines the rate at which output grows as a result of a given volume of capital investment. For example, a capital-output ratio of 4 would mean, in Indian rupees, that a capital investment of Rs. 4 results in the addition of output worth Re. 1. Hence, in order to produce a given level of output, smaller capital investment would be needed if the capital-output ratio is lower than when it is higher.

Factors Determining Capital-Output Ratio

It is difficult to estimate the capital-output ratio of an economy. The productivity of capital depends upon many factors such as the degree of technological development associated with capital investment, the efficiency of handling new types of equipment, the quality of managerial and organi ational skill, the existence and the extent of the utilisation of economic overheads and the pattern and rate of investment. For instance, the higher the proportion of investment devoted to the production of light consumer goods, the lower the capital-output ratio; and higher the proportion of investment devoted to public utilities, *i.e.,* economic and social overheads, the higher will be the capital-output ratio, and vice versa. Likewise, the greater the investment devoted to basic heavy industries, the higher will be the capital-output ratio, and vice versa. The superior organising ability and the use of better technolgy will lower the capital-output ratio. The capital-output ratio also varies with the prices of inputs.

It is agreed that capital-output ratio in developing countries is generally higher, *i.e.,* the capital is less productive in them than in developed countries. This is so because there is a relative inefficiency of the industries which produce capital goods. There is the greater wastage of capital in the process of production due to low level of technical knowledge. Besides, owing to indivisibilities, certain kinds of investment are bound to be initially underutilised. As development proceeds in the developing countries the pattern of demand shifts towards the more capital-intensive industries.

In order to gain the most from capital formation, a country must also undergo technological and organizational progress, so that the capital-output ratio be reduced. Thus, the grwoth of the rate fo output depends not only on the amount of capital accumulated but also on how much capital is required per unit increase in output (*i.e.,* incremental capital-output ratio). The lower the incremental capital-output ratio, the more accelerated is economic growth. A low capital-ratio is, thus, as significant as large capital accumulation. But it must also be pointed out that a low increament capital-output ratio requires technological and organisation progress so that capital becomes more productive.

Limitations of Capital-Output Ratio

It may, however, be pointed out that the concept of capital-output ratio suffers from certain limitations. Its precise calculation presents some formidable difficulties. Hence, the quantitive relationship between capital investment and output, which the capital-output ratio suggests, may prove to be misleading. It would, therefore, be hazardous to base the estimates of capital requirements of an industry or economy on such ratios. Neither can the capital stock be assumed with any exactitude; nor is the other side of the ratio, *i.e.,* output capable of any precise measurement. Besides the index number problems, a clear distinction cannot be often made between capital goods and non-capital goods. Returns to social overheads, in particular, cannot be calculated accurately. Further, capital-output ratio is influenced by several variables, *e.g.,* technological improvements, better utilisation of equipment, organisational improvements, labour efficiency, and these factors elude quantitative measurement.

Hence, the concept of capital-output ratio has only a limited practical significance, because it cannot indicate the actual contribution of capital alone in a given scheme of investment. Great caution is, therefore, necessary in making use of a particular capital-output ratio in the adoption of actual investment policy.

APPENDIX TO CHAPTER 39

Saving, Investment and India's Growth Performance

Introduction

In the foregoing chapter we have explained the various factors that determine economic growth of a country. A crucial determinant of economic growth is the rate of domestic capital formation which depends on rates of saving and investment. It is mainly because of large increase in rates of saving and investment (*i.e.,* capital formation) that India has achieved a very high rate economic growth (9 per cent per annum during the period 2003-04 to 2007-08) in terms of gross domestic product (GDP). In fact, *India's growth story is one of growth miracle*, like that of China, in recent years. Before that we talked about Japanese growth miracle and East Asia's growth miracle. Even in the years 2008-09 and 2009-10 when the developed countries were experiencing worst ever recession after the Great Depression of 1930s due to global financial crisis (2007-09), India achieved 6.8 per cent and 8.0 per cent growth rate respectively. From 2010-11 onwards it is estimated that India again will return to high growth rate trajectory of 9 per cent per annum. Indeed, India has been the second highest growing country of the world next only to China and has been called an *emerging economy*. However India's growth story has taken a severe blow as rate of GDP growth has sharply fallen to 5.9 per cent in 2011-12 and to 5.0 per cent in 2012-13. The crucial question is what explains the earlier high rate of GDP growth rate of India and slowdown in growth rate in the last two years. As we will see below it is mainly high rates of gross domestic saving (GDS) and gross domestic capital formation (GDCF) that accounts for high growth rate achieved by India till 2010-11.

Gross Domestic Capital Formation (GDCF)

As explained above, gross domestic capital formation is an important factor that determines economic growth of a country. Gross domestic capital formation (GDCF) is also referred to as *aggregate investment* and represents the addition to the stock of physical capital goods such as factories, physical equipment and machines which are meant for use in future production of goods and services. The Indian nationals also make investment abroad by purchasing fixed assets in foreign countries. The foreign investment by the Indians are excluded to arrive at the estimate of gross domestic capital formation. However, some foreign companies make investment in India and this foreign direct investment (FDI) also contributes to the gross domestic capital formation (GDCF). Besides, some capital goods such as machinery and equipment are imported from abroad to build the domestic stock of capital. Thus domestic capital formation has some imported components. Gross domestic capital formation is divided into two categories.

(1) Gross fixed capital formation (GFCF) which consists of (a) addition to machinery and equipment in both the public and private sectors. (This is generally referred to as *business fixed investment*) and (b) construction of new houses (*i.e.* residential houses), new buildings and offices.

(2) Inventory investment which represents *addition to the stocks of goods* in a year. When inventories of goods decline, there is a negative inventory investment.

(3) Investment in valuables. In a year people make investment in precious metals such as gold, diamond, platinum and jewellery. Investment in these valuables is unproductive from social point of view. In recent years in India demand for gold by the people has increased substantially and a large quantity of gold has been imported from abroad. The large quantity of imports from abroad is an important factor responsible for deficit in our current account in the years 2011-12 and 2012-13.

By summing up the data of the above two items we get gross domestic capital formation (GDCF) of a year. Changes in **real gross domestic capital formation in India at market prices** are shown in Table 39A.1. It will be seen from this table that real gross domestic capital formation (GDCF) has shown a rising trend since 2001-02. The real GDCF as per cent of GDP at current market prices rose from 23.6 per cent in 2001-02 to 32.7 per cent in 2004-05 and further to 37.7 per cent in 2007-08.

Table 39A.1: Gross Domestic Savings and Capital Formation in India.

(*as per cent of GDP at current market prices*)

	2001-02	02-03	03-04	04-05	05-06	06-07	07-08	08-09	09-10	10-11*	11-12*
Gross Domestic Savings	**23.6**	**26.5**	**29.7**	**32.2**	**33.1**	**34.4**	**36.4**	**32.2**	**33.7**	**34.0**	**30.8**
(a) Public	-2.0	-0.7	1.2	2.3	2.4	3.6	5.0	0.5	2.1	2.6	1.3
(b) Private	25.6	27.2	28.5	29.9	30.7	30.9	31.4	31.7	31.6	31.4	29.5
(i) Household	22.0	23.1	23.8	23.3	23.2	22.9	22.6	23.8	23.5	23.5	22.3
Financial	10.8	10.3	11.3	9.8	11.4	10.9	11.2	10.8	11.8	10.4	8.0
Physical	11.2	12.7	12.4	13.5	11.8	11.9	11.5	13.1	11.7	13.1	14.0
(ii) Private Corporate	3.6	4.1	4.7	6.6	7.5	8.0	8.7	7.9	8.1	7.9	7.3
Gross Domestic Capital Formation (GDCF)	**23.6**	**25.3**	**28.0**	**32.7**	**34.3**	**35.5**	**37.7**	**34.5**	**36.5**	**36.8**	**35.0**
Public	6.9	6.2	6.3	7.4	7.9	8.4	8.9	9.5	9.2	8.4	7.9
Private	16.8	18.5	19.4	23.8	26.3	26.4	27.6	24.6	24.9	26.5	24.9
Gross Fixed Capital Formation (GFCF)	**23.1**	**24.1**	**24.8**	**28.8**	**30.4**	**31.4**	**33.0**	**32.0**	**30.8**	**31.7**	**30.6**
Change in stocks	0.6	0.6	0.8	2.5	2.8	3.4	3.5	2.0	3.3	3.1	2.1
Valuables	0.6	0.6	0.9	1.3	1.1	1.2	1.1	1.3	1.7	2.1	2.7
Saving-investment GAP@	**0.6**	**1.2**	**1.6**	**–0.5**	**–1.2**	**–1.1**	**–1.3**	**– 2.4**	**–2.8**	**–2.8**	**–4.2**

Note : (i) Figures may not add up due to rounding off.

* Revised Estimates.

@ : refers to the difference between the rates of saving and investment.

Source : GOI, *Economic Survey*, 2008-09, p.6., 2009-10, 2010-11, 2011-12 and 2012-13.

In line with the GDCF, the Gross Fixed Capital Formation (GFCF) as per cent of GDP rose from 23.1 per cent in 2001-02 to 33 per cent in 2007-08 and fell to 32 per cent in 2008-09 and 30.8 per cent in 2009-10 due to global financial crisis (2008-09). It should be noted that in the revised series with 1999-2000 as the base year, a new item '*valuables*' covering expenditure on *acquisition of precious metals and stones* as a store of value has been included in Gross Domestic Capital Formation on the basis of 1993 System of National Accounts of United Nations.

Gross domestic capital formation (GDCF) at current market prices (adjusted for errors and omissions) increased from Rs. 18,65,899 crore in 2007-08 to Rs. 19,44,328 crore in 2008-09 and at constant (2004-05) prices, it decreased from Rs. 16,22,226 crore in 2007-08 to Rs. 15,57,757 crore in 2008-09. The rate of gross capital formation at current market prices rose from 32.7 per cent in 2004-05 to 37.7 per cent in 2007-08 but under the impact of global financial crisis declined to 34.9 per cent in 2008-09. As a result of stimulus measures adopted by the government gross domestic capital formation rose to 36.5% in 2009-10 and 36.8% of GDP in 2010-11 (see Table 39A.1).

The rate of gross capital formation or simply the investment rate has increased in both the public and private sectors. In the public sector, it rose continuously from 7.4 per cent in 2004-05 to 9.5 per cent in 2008-09, whereas in the *private sector*, it increased from 23.8 per cent in 2004-05 to 27.6 per cent in 2007-08 before falling to 24.6 per cent in 2008-09. Between 2007-08 and 2008-09, the investment rate for the *private corporate sector* declined significantly from 16.1 per cent to 12.7 per cent, whereas that of the household sector increased from 11.5 to 12.2 per cent.

The savings-investment gap, reflecting the gap between gross domestic savings and investment which was –2.4% in 2008-09 and –2.8% in 2009-10 rose sharply to –4.2% in 2010-11 and is estimated at around 5% of GDP in 2012-13. This saving-investment gap implies current account deficit in our balance of payments, and requires capital inflows to finance it. If these capital inflows are of portfolio capital by FIIs, they are quite volatile and poses a problem for macroeconomic stability of the economy.

A significant aspect of gross capital formation is the rate of **gross fixed capital formation** compared to the change in stock and valuables. *It is gross fixed capital that leads to the increase in productive capacity* of the economy and therefore its growth potential. It will be seen from Table 39A-1 that gross fixed capital formation rose from 23.1 percent of GDP in 2001-2002 to 33.0 per cent of GDP in 2007-08 after which it started falling and declined to 30.6% of GDP in 2011-12. To accelerate economic growth in future, rate of gross fixed capital formation has to he raised. Further, it will be seen from Table 39.A-1 that it is the proportion of 'valuables' in gross domestic capital formation that has risen in recent years. It is due to greater preference of the people to invest in gold and jewellery as hedge against inflation. But this is unproductive investment as this does not add to productive capacity.

Gross Domestic Saving (GDS)

We now turn to explain how gross domestic capital formation is financed. The chief source of financing domestic capital formation is gross domestic saving. Apart from the funds kept on account of consumption of fixed capital to acquire new capital goods, the savings by households, corporate firms and government are used to finance domestic capital formation. Besides, *net capital transfers* from the rest of the world are also used to finance domestic capital formation.

Central Statistical Organisation (CSO) of India, which is entrusted with the task of estimating national income accounts, classifies domestic savings into three categories: (1) Domestic savings by private sector which is further divided into (a) household savings and (b) corporate sector savings and (2) Public sector savings. The gross domestic saving and its components at *current market prices* as a percentage of GDP in case of India are shown in Table 39A-1.

It will be seen from this table that gross domestic saving (GDS) of India as a proportion of GDP at current market prices has shown an increasing trend since 2001-02. Thus Gross Domestic Saving as proportion of GDP at *current* market prices rose from 23.6 per cent in 2001-02 to 29.7 per cent in 2003-04 and further to 36.4 per cent in 2007-08. The rate of gross domestic saving (GDS) at current market prices was estimated at 32.2% and 33.7% of GDP in 2008-09 and 2009-10 respectively. The objective of Eleventh Five Year Plan (2007–2012) was to raise it to 35 per cent which had been achieved earlier in 2006-07. It will be further observed that the rise in saving rate since 2001-02 has been contributed mainly by its two components–public sector saving and private corporate sector savings. The higher public sector saving in the years 2003-04 to 2007-08 was due to the *decline in revenue deficit* of the general government, perhaps due to the progress in the implementation of FRBMA (Fiscal Responsibility Budget Management Act) and higher savings of non-departmental enterprises. Higher savings by the corporate sector from 2001-02 to 2009-10 reflect the *higher retained earnings* from their higher profits made by them.

Sectoral Shares in Gross Domestic Saving

Gross domestic savings (GDS) at current market prices in 2008-09 were estimated at Rs. 18,11,585 crore, amounting to 32.2 per cent of GDP at market prices as against 36.4 per cent in the previous year. The fall in the rate of GDS was mainly due to the fall in the rates of savings of the public sector (from 5.0 per cent in 2007-08 to 0.5 per cent in 2008-09) and private corporate sector (from 8.7 per cent in 2007-08 to about 8 per cent in 2008-09 and 2009-10). However, in 2010-11 public sector saving rose to 2.6 per cent of GDP at market prices. In respect of the household sector, the rate of saving was estimated to be 22.6 per cent in 2007-08, 23.8% in 2008-09 and 23.5% of GDP in 2009-10 and 2010-11 and declined to 22.3% of GDP in 2011-12.

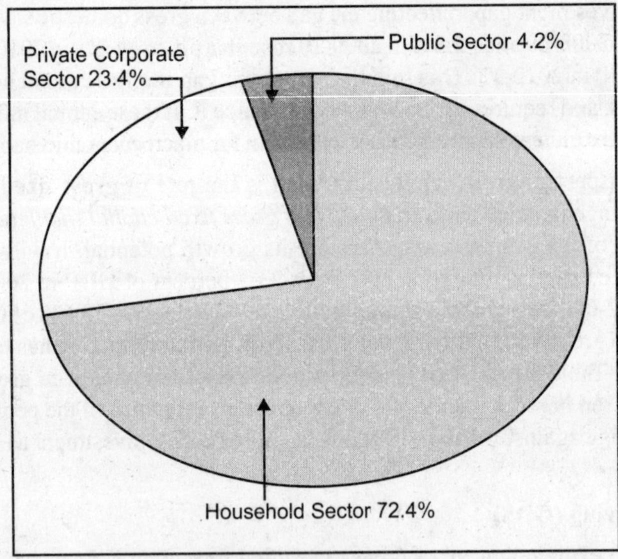

Fig. 39A.1. *Sectoral Shares as Percentage of Total Gross Domestic Saving,* 2011-12

EXPLAINING INDIA'S GROWTH PERFORMANCE

In the last seven years or so (*i.e.,* since 2003) India has emerged as one of the fastest growing economies of the world. In fact, next to China, India's growth rate since 2004 is the highest in the world. This is often referred to as **India's growth miracle.** Before Eighties of the last century India's average growth rate stuck around 3.6 per cent per annum which Late Prof. Raj Krishna called Hindu rate of growth. In the eighties India[1]s average rate of economic growth rose to 5.6 per cent per annum and further in the nineteenth and up till 2002-03 (*i.e.,* in 12 years period). India's average growth rate went up to 6.2% per annum under liberalisation and globalisation of the Indian economy. But since 2004 to FY 2007-08 India's average annual growth rate of GDP rose to around 9 per cent per annum. In 2008-09 while the advanced developed countries were experiencing recession (*i.e.,* negative growth), India succeeded in achieving 6.7 per cent growth in 2008-09 which further rose to 8.0 per cent in 2009-10. It is now estimated that rate of growth of GDP rose to 8.6 per cent in 2010-11 and to 9.3% in 2011-12.

Table 39A.2 : Rate of Gross Domestic Saving and Fixed Capital Formation

as % of GDP

	2001-02	02-03	03-04	04-05	05-06	06-07	07-08	08-09*	09-10*	10-11*	11-12*
Gross Domestic Saving (GDS)	23.6	26.6	29.7	32.2	33.1	34.4	36.4*	32.0	33.7	34.0	30.8
Household Saving	22.0	23.1	23.8	23.3	23.2	22.9	22.6	23.6	25.2	23.5	22.3
Private Corporate Sector	3.6	4.1	4.7	6.5	7.5	6.0	8.87	7.4	8.4	7.9	7.2
Public saving	–2.0	–0.7	1.2	2.3	2.4	3.6	5.0	1.0	0.2	2.6	1.3
Fixed Capital formation (FCF)	23.1	24.1	24.8	28.8	30.4	31.4	33.0	32.3	31.7	31.7	30.6
GDP_{mp}	–	–	8.4	8.3	9.3	9.4	9.6	6.7	8.6	9.3	6.2

Source : *CSO. Data after 2004-05 are based on new national income series with 2004-05 as base.*

* Revised Estimates

Now the question is, how do we account for such a high growth in GDP since 2004 in India? Growth depends mainly on rate of saving and investment (or, in other words, on rate of capital formation) and improvement in technology or capital-output ratio. In India such as other emerging economies, China, Indonesia and South Korea, it is increase in rate of saving and investment (*i.e.*, rate of capital formation) that brought about a sharp growth in GDP since 2004. Rates of saving and capital formation and GDP growth are given in Table 39A.2 Prior to 2003-04 rate of saving in India was around 24 to 26% of GDP. But, as will be seen from Table 39A.2, from 2003-04 to 2007-08 (that is, prior to global financial crisis) average rate of saving rose to 36.4 per cent of GDP which pulled up the rate of investment or capital formation. As a result, *average* growth rate of GDP for the five years period (2003-08) rose to 9 per cent. With this India became the second fastest growing economy of the world next only to China.

In keeping with the higher saving rate from 2004-05 onwards, *average rate of fixed capital formation* (FCF) rose to 33 per cent of GDP in 2007-08 (see 5th row in the Table). This higher growth rate of fixed capital formation caused 9 per cent average growth in GDP during 2004-05 to 2007-08. In 2008-09 global financial crisis (2007-09) and consequently global meltdown caused fall in saving rate to 32.0% of GDP in 2008-09, rose again to 33.7% in 2009-10 and 34.0% in 2010-11 before falling to 30.8 per cent of GDP in 2011-12. This was due to the substantial increase in consumption expenditure under the fiscal stimulus measures to keep the growth momentum which caused drop in public saving rate to 0.5 per cent of GDP as compared to 5.0 per cent in 2007-08. This financial crisis which caused negative growth of India's exports in 2008-09 slowed down rate of economic growth in 2008-09 to 6.7 per cent. However, while advanced developed countries of the US, Japan, European countries experienced worst ever recession since the Great Depression of 1930s. India was successful in attaining the growth rate of 6.7 per cent in 2008-09. With the saving rate going up to 33.7% of GDP and gross fixed capital formation going up to 32.3 per cent of GDP in 2009-10, GDP growth rate rose to 8.6 per cent. Saving rate further rose to 34.0 per cent of GDP in 2010-11 and with gross capital formation of 31.7 per cent GDP growth rate went up to 9.3 per cent in 2010-11. However, in 2011-12 saving rate fell to 30.8 per cent and gross fixed capital formation to 30.6 per cent, GDP growth rate declined to 6.2 per cent. In 2012-13 for various reasons explained below GDP growth rate further dipped to 5 per cent—lowest in 10 years.

Reasons for Substantial Rise in Saving Rate Since 2003-04

Now, what has caused saving rate in India to rise substantially since 2004. Components of saving rate are : (1) household savings, (2) private corporate sector saving and (3) public saving. It will be seen from Table 39A.2 that while household savings stuck to around 23.5 per cent of GDP and therefore it cannot explain remarkable rise in overall saving rate in the Indian economy since 2004. It is the private corporate sector which registered a substantial rise in saving rate from 4.7 per cent of GDP in 2003-04 to 8.87 per cent of GDP in 2007-08, that is, the private corporate sector saving doubled in the four-year period. After dipping to 7.4 per cent of GDP in 2008-09, the year of global crisis, the private corporate sector again rose to 8.4% in 2009-10 and about 8 per cent of GDP in 2010-11. Even in the crisis years of 2008-09 and 2009-10, the saving of private corporate sector was around 8 per cent of GDP. It is this significant increase in corporate sector saving that resulted in higher rate of fixed capital formation which contributed to a big jump in growth rate to around 9 per cent in these years.

Besides, large increase in public saving since 2004 also contributed a lot to the increase in the overall saving rate and capital formation from 2003-04 to 2007-08. After 2007-08 due to fiscal stimulus, public saving and its contribution to capital formation declined. The public sector saving which was negative prior to 2003-04 turned positive and rose to 5 per cent of GDP in 2007-08. (See 4th row in Table 39A.2). Thus private corporate sector and public savings together increased by around 10 per cent from 2003-04 to 2007-08, which brought about higher rate of overall saving and capital formation and ensured higher rate of economic growth. It will be seen from Table 39A.2 that fixed capital formation which was 24.8 % of GDP in 2003-04 rose to 33% of GDP in 2007-08 and 2008-09. No wonder that with such a high rise in fixed capital formation that the average growth rate in GDP in 2004-08 rose to over 9%.

How do we explain the large increase in saving of the private corporate sector ? It is primarily due to the increase in profitability of private corporate sector as measured by the ratio of *profit after tax (PAT) to sales*, which rose from 3.6% to 8% in the six years period, 2003-09[1]. Besides the rise in profitability of the corporate sector, the companies also *reduced dividend rate* from half of profits to 1/4th of them[2]. That is, the corporate companies retained (*i.e.,* saved) a greater amount of profits for their expansion or capital formation. Thus, the profits of the corporate sector not only increased faster on account of higher economic growth but also distributed less of them as dividends that resulted in substantial increase in corporate sector saving.

As regards the public sector savings, they rose from negative rate in 2003-04 to 5 per cent of GDP in 2007-08. It occurred due to increase in tax revenue, especially from the corporate sector. Thus, revenue from corporate tax rose from 1.9 per cent of GDP to 3.6 per cent during this period. Indeed, as a result of it since 2004 *overall tax–GDP* ratio rose from 8.9 per cent in 2003-04 to 10.7 per cent in 2007-08. This better tax performance along with Government control of its public expenditure under the Fiscal Responsibility Budget Management (FRBM) Act resulted in the fall in Central government's fiscal deficit to 2.8 per cent of GDP in 2007-08. Thus, the improved performance of both the private corporate sector and the public sector in the liberalisation era has become the significant driver of faster economic growth of the Indian economy.

It may be further noted that the rapid growth of some new sectors such as Telecome and IT which hardly existed before 2000 contributed a good deal to rapid economic growth since 2004. Besides, low interest rate policy of the Reserve Bank of India made borrowing from the banks cheaper which created large demand for *consumer durables* such as cars and housing. This ensured relatively higher growth of consumer durables since 2003-04.

Lastly, it is important to note that despite opening up of the Indian economy since 1991, from the demand side, India's growth has been driven mainly by *increase in domestic demand.* Both the increase in households' consumption expenditure and Government's consumption expenditure have contributed to the higher rate of economic growth since 2004.

SLOWDOWN IN INDIA'S ECONOMIC GROWTH IN 2011-12 AND 2012-13

It may be noted that rate of economic growth slowed down in 2011-12 and 2012-13. Several factors are responsible for it. Because at times of global slowdown in 2008-09 in India there was fiscal and monetary space, timely stimulus measures allowed the economy to recover fairly quickly to a growth of 8.6 per cent in 2009-10 and 9.3 per cent in 2010-11. Since then a number of factors, both global and domestic, have led to a slowdown of the Indian economy. The slowdown in the Indian economy began in the second quarter of 2011-12 when the growth rate fell to 6.7 per cent from a level of 8.0 per cent in the first quarter, continued in the subsequent quarters. From the quarter 4 of 2011-12 and quarters 1 and 2 of 2012-13, growth has been in the range of 5.3 to 5.5 per cent. In the whole year 2011-12 the growth rate of GDP at factor cost was 6.2 per cent as against 8.6 per cent in 2009-10 and 9.3% in 2010-11 (Revised Estimates) and is now estimated by CSO to be 5 per cent in 2012-13, the lowest in the ten years.

It may however be noted that slowdown in economic growth is not just confined to India. There has been a general slowdown in the global economy which has been passing through a rather prolonged phase of uncertainty. The recovery from the global crisis of 2008-09 in the advanced economies has been slow and uneven, with a decisive resolution of sovereign debt problem of the Eurozone area has yet to be achieved. Having achieved a GDP growth of 5.1 per cent in 2010, the rate of growth in the global economy declined to 3.8 per cent in 2011 and is expected to decline further to 3.3 per cent in 2012, as per the World Economic Outlook released

1. Sumant Sinha, Decoding the saving rate miracle, *The Economic Times*, Oct. 22, 2010
2. *Ibid.*

by the IMF in October 2012. The rate of growth of advanced economies declined from 3.0 per cent in 2010 to 1.6 per cent in 2011 and is expected to decline further to 1.3 per cent in 2012. Even the emerging economies have slowed down during this period, partly as a result of the slowdown in their export markets. China's growth declined from 10.4 per cent in 2010 to 9.3 per cent in 2011 and is expected to be 7.8 per cent in 2012. Brazil's growth dipped from 7.5 per cent in 2010 to 2.8 per cent in 2011 and is expected to be 0.7 per cent in 2012.

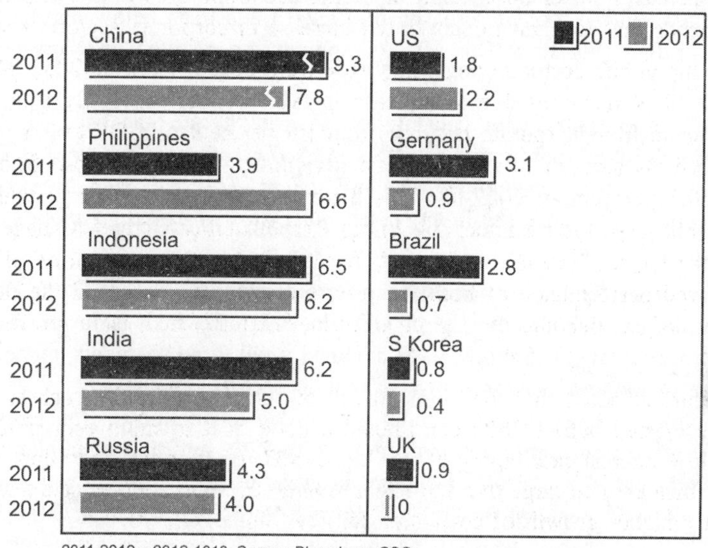

Fig. 39A.2. Growth Rates in Major Countries of the World in 2011 and 2012.

As stated above, slowdown in India's economic growth began in the second quarter of 2011-12 but the slowdown has been sharper in 2012-13. Whereas, growth rate in the whole year 2011-12 fell to 6.2 per cent as against 8.6 per cent in 2009-10 and 9.3% in 2010-11, the growth rate in the first half of 2012-13 fell to 5.4 per cent and for whole year it is estimated to be 5.0 to 5.5 per cent. What accounts for this recent slowdown in India's economic growth rate?

The slowdown in growth rate in India in 2011-12 and 2012-13 can be explained in terms of both global factors and domestic factors. First, the slowdown in growth in advanced economies and near recessionary conditions in Europe resulted not only in *lower growth of international trade but also lower capital flows*. As a result, the growth rate of India's exports declined which contributed to decline in overall growth rate and also caused problem of current account deficit (CAD). Besides, fall in capital flows not only resulted in lower investment in the Indian economy but also made the problem of financing current account deficit (CAD) difficult.

Further, international price of crude oil remained high which led to the increase in fuel subsidy bill of the Indian government and drained away resources from public investment. This also adversely affected economic growth. Besides, high crude oil prices led to the widening of India's trade and current account deficits which caused sharp depreciation of rupee which adversely affected the sentiments of foreign investors.

Turning to the domestic factors, higher borrowing costs for the corporate sector due to high RBI's repo rate, the rate at which Reserve Bank lends to the commercial banks, discouraged investment by the corporate sector harming economic growth. The Reserve Bank of India continued to follow a relatively tight monetary policy to control inflation although there was some relaxation in it by lowering cash reserve ratio (CRR) and by reducing repo rate by 0.50 per cent in April 2012 and 0.25 per cent in the end of January, 2013. As a result of this tight monetary policy of RBI, the cost of borrowing remained at an elevated level and this had an impact on investment and growth in the Indian economy, particularly that of the industrial sector. The erratic power supply due to coal shortage caused delays in implementation of investment projects. made financing more difficult and investors more cautious. Clearances from environment ministry of various investment projects also resulted in lower investment. Further due to various scams and corruption charges against several ministers and bureaucrats caused **policy paralysis** which made investors hesitant to make investment.

Besides, rainfall in the monsoon season of 2012-13 had been below normal, particularly in the key months of June and July. This affected sowing and resulted in a lower growth rate of agriculture and allied sectors.

But the most important factor causing fall in growth rate has been fall in saving and investment rates both by the public and private sectors. *Therefore in our view, what the economy needs most of all and most urgently is new investment. This will step up currently flagging aggregate demand and also ease the supply constraints, so that existing capacity is fully utilized and new capacity is built up.*

A more worrisome for the economy's long-term growth rate is that Gross Domestic saving (GDS) rate fell sharply to 30.8 per cent of GDP in 2011-12 which is lower since 2005-06 as against 34 per cent in 2010-11. Savings have declined in all three segments, namely, households, private corporate sector and Government (*i.e.,* public sector). The slower growth rate in GDS in 2011-12 as compared to 2010-11 has mainly been due to **decline in household** saving from 23.5% to 22.3%, private corporate sector from 7.9% to 7.2% and that of public sector from 2.6 per cent to 1.3 per cent. As a result of decline in gross domestic saving gross investment rate (as % of GDP) fell to 35 per cent in 2011-12, down from 36.8 per cent in 2010-11. No wonder that growth in GDP fell sharply to 6.2 per cent in 2011-12 (lowest in nine years) from 9.3 per cent in 2010-11 (as per revised estimates).

Table 29A.3 Growth in GDP, Saving and Investment in Recent Years

	2008-09	2009-10	2010-11	2011-12
Real GDP growth (%)	6.7	8.6	9.3	6.2
Gross Savings Rate (% of GDP)	32	33.7	34.0	30.8
Gross Investment Rate (% of GDP)	34.3	36.5	36.8	35.0

Source: CSO, Revised Estimate (Jan. 31 2013)

A high domestic saving and investment rate has always been the strong point of the Indian economy and, as explained above, it is due to them that India achieved a high rate of GDP growth (near 9 per cent) from 2003-04 to 2010-11 with a break of the year 2008-09 only when there was 6.7 per cent of growth due to global financial crisis. It is due to this high 8 per cent plus GDP growth as a result of high rates of saving and investment that India became the second fastest growing country of the world, next only to China. In the years 2011-12 and 2012-13, the fall in saving and investment rates is responsible for slower growth in GDP, apart from other factors impeding growth explained above.

Therefore, in our view what the country needs most of all and most urgently is the increase in investment, especially in infrastructure. This will step up currently flagging aggregate demand and also ease the supply constraints so that existing capacity is fully utilized and new capacity is built up.

CHAPTER 40
Harrod-Domar Model of Growth

Dual Effect of Investment: Income Effect and Capacity Effect

Keynes in his General Theory was concerned with the determination of income and employment in the short run. He explained that since in the short-run situation of developed capitalist economies aggregate demand was deficient in relation to the aggregate supply of output, the equilibrium will be established at less than full employment level. Since the propensity to consume (and therefore saving propensity) is given and remains constant in the short run, if the amount of investment as determined by expected rate of profit and the market rate of interest is not equal to the amount of saving at the full-employment level of income, the economy will be in equilibrium at less than full capacity level (*i.e.* less than employment level) of output. He did not go into the question of the long-run growth of the economy. In fact, he overlooked the effect of investment in a given period on the increase in productive capacity. However, *investment has a dual effect.* Firstly, investment increases aggregate demand and income of the people through the multiplier process, and secondly, it raises the productive capacity of the economy through the addition it makes to the stock of capital. Indeed, investment by very definition means the addition to the stock of capital. While Keynes took into account the demand effect of investment, he ignored the capacity effect of investment.

Harrod[1] and Domar[2] extended the Keynesian analysis of income and employment to long-run setting and therefore considered both the income and capacity effects of investment. Harrod and Domar models of economic growth explained at what rate investment should increase so that steady growth is possible in an advanced capitalist economy. In the growth models of Harrod and Domar, the rate of capital accumulation plays a crucial role in the determination of economic growth. The problem of present-day mature economies lies in averting both secular stagnation and secular inflation. It were the pioneer works of Harrod and Domar that set the ball rolling in regard to this issue, i.e., the maintenance of steady growth in advanced industrialised countries. The *Harrod and Domar models seek to determine that unique rate at which investment and income must grow so that full employment level is maintained over a long period of time, i.e., equilibrium growth is achieved.*

Harrod and Domar developed their models of steady growth quite separately, though Harrod published his theory earlier than Domar. Although their models of steady growth differ in details, yet the underlying basic idea is the same. Both of them assigned to capital accumulation a crucial role in the development process. But they emphasised the double role of the investment process, viz., generating income (increasing demand) and adding to the productive capacity of the economy. The classical economists confined their attention to the capacity side only, whereas the earlier Keynesian economists studied the problem of demand only whereas Harrod and Domar considers both sides.

They start with full employment equilibrium level of income. According to them, to maintain full employment equilibrium, demand (total spending) generated by investment must be sufficient to be the additional output caused by this investment. To ensure steady growth with full employment

1. R.F. Harrod, *Towards a Dynamic Economics*, Macmillan & Co. London, 1948.
2. E. Domar, Capital Expansion, Rate of Growth and Employment, *Economica* Vo;. 14, 1946

the absolute amount of net investment must keep increasing and there must also be continuous growth of real national income. Because if demand and income did not increase while annual investment went on occurring, the additions made to the capital stock would remain unutilised and also employment could not be provided to the growing labour force which would result in unemployment of these two major resources. Obviously, such a situation is not conducive to steady economic growth.

DOMAR'S GROWTH MODEL

Capacity Effect of Investment

Let us first consider the supply side, that is, the capacity effect of investment. Increase in national output or national income of an economy during a period depends upon the increase in the stock of capital (which is represented by ΔK) during a period and the output-capital ratio or the productivity of capital. Assuming that both national income and the capital stock are measured in money, output-capital ratio can be written as $\Delta Y/ \Delta K$, where ΔY stands for the increase in the national income and ΔK for the increase in the stock of capital. Thus if Rs. 4 worth of capital goods is required to produce one rupee worth of real output, marginal output-capital ratio $\left(\frac{\Delta Y}{\Delta K}\right)$ is equal to 1/4 or 0.25. Thus, the absolute increase in national income during a period (ΔY) can be obtained from increment in stock of capital ΔK multiplied by the output produced by a unit of capital $\left(i.e.\ \frac{\Delta Y}{\Delta K}\right)$. In symbolic terms we may express this as follows:-

$$\Delta Y = \Delta K . \frac{\Delta Y}{\Delta K} \qquad ...(i)$$

Now, change in capital stock (ΔK) is nothing else but investment. Therefore, following Domar in place of ΔK we can write I. The marginal output-capital ratio $\Delta Y/\Delta K$ which is assumed to be constant as well as equal to average output-capital ratio $\left(\frac{Y}{K}\right)$ by Domar and Harrod, can be denoted by σ. Thus, as Domar puts it, growth in capacity-output can be written as under:

$$\Delta Y = I\sigma \qquad ... (ii)$$

It may be noted that output-capital ratio (σ) is reciprocal of capital-output ratio *i.e.* $\left(\frac{\Delta K}{\Delta Y} \text{ or } \frac{K}{Y}\right)$. Let us give an example. If Rs. 500 crores are invested in a year and capital-output ratio is 4 (i.e. output-capital ratio will be 1/4), then growth in output in a year will be.

$$\Delta Y = 500 \times {}^{1}\!/_{4}$$

$$= 125 \text{ crores}$$

Demand or Income Effect of Investment

Now, according to Domar, growth in capacity output will be realised only if aggregate demand or income of the people increases by a sufficient amount. The increase in aggregate demand or income is explained by the Keynesian theory of multiplier. Domar has based his analysis of demand or income effect of investment on the Keynesian theory of multiplier and income determination. According to this, *increase in income (or aggregate demand) is given by the increase in investment (ΔI) and the size of multiplier, i.e.* $1/s$ where s is the marginal propensity to save (assumed by Domar to be equal to the average propensity to save). Thus, according to income effect of investment,

$$\Delta Y = \frac{1}{s} . \Delta I \qquad ... (iii)$$

Note. that $\frac{1}{s}$ represents the size of investment multiplier.

The growth in income (ΔY) must be large enough to generate demand equal to capacity growth in output as explained above.

Domar's Growth Equation in Terms of Rates of Growth

It is greatly helpful to express the above growth equation in terms of *rates of growth of income and capital*. That is, growth in income and capital should be expressed as ratios of total income. For doing so we divide both sides of equation (*i*) above by Y and obtain :

$$\frac{\Delta Y}{Y} = \frac{\Delta K}{Y} \cdot \frac{\Delta Y}{\Delta K} \quad ...(iv)$$

$\frac{\Delta Y}{Y}$ represents the rate of growth of income and is therefore written as simply G_y. Besides, ΔK stands for increment in capital during a given time period and is nothing else but investment. Therefore, for ΔK in the equation (*ii*) we can write I which represents investment. With these changes, we get the following equation :

$$G_y = \frac{I}{Y} \cdot \frac{\Delta Y}{\Delta K}$$

If it is further assumed that output-capital ratio remains constant, then the marginal output-capital ratio $\left(\frac{\Delta Y}{\Delta K}\right)$ will be equal to average output-capital ratio $\left(\frac{Y}{K}\right)$. With this assumption and also expressing output-capital ratio by σ we can write the above equation as follows

$$G_y = \frac{I}{Y} . \sigma \quad ...(v)$$

Where G_y = Growth rate of output or income

$\frac{I}{Y}$ = Rate of investment as ratio of national income

σ = Output-capital ratio

From the growth equation (v) above, it is clear that, given the output-capital ratio, rate of growth of output depends upon the rate of investment; the greater the rate of investment, the greater the rate of growth of output or income. To maintain full-employment equilibrium as the economy grows at a steady rate, savings (S) must remain equal to investment (I). Therefore, in equation (v) we can write $\frac{S}{Y}$ for $\frac{I}{Y}$. By doing so and rewriting equation (v) we have

$$G_Y = \frac{S}{Y} . \sigma$$

Since $\frac{S}{Y}$ represents ratio of savings to national income, we can write it as s. With rewriting the above equation we have,

$$G_Y = s.\sigma \quad ... (vi)$$

The above equation (*vi*) represents the productive capacity effect of investment and saving and therefore represents the supply side of the growth problem.

The Condition for Equilibrium Growth

To achieve and maintain equilibrium or balanced growth, aggregate demand (*i.e.* aggregate expenditure) must increase at the rate which is large enough to absorb the increase in capacity-output. We have explained above (equation, *iii*) that aggregate demand or income increases at the rate $\frac{1}{s} . \Delta I$ where s is propensity to save and ΔI is the absolute increase in investment. On the other hand, as shown by equation(*ii*) above, the increase in capacity output occurs at the rate of $I\sigma$ where I is the absolute rate of investment and σ is the output-capital ratio. Thus, *steady equilibrium growth rate will be achieved only if rate of growth of aggregate expenditure (demand or income) equals the rate of growth in capacity output.*

Thus, it follows that to *maintain full-employment equilibrium growth of output* the following condition must hold.

$$\frac{1}{s}.\Delta I = I\sigma$$

$$\frac{\Delta I}{I} = s\sigma$$

where $\frac{\Delta I}{I}$ represents the rate of growth of investment.

As seen above in equation (*vi*), rate of growth of income $\left(\frac{\Delta Y}{Y} \text{ or } G_Y\right)$ is also equal to $s\sigma$, it follows that for equilibrium growth $G_y = \frac{\Delta Y}{Y} = \frac{\Delta I}{I} = s\sigma$

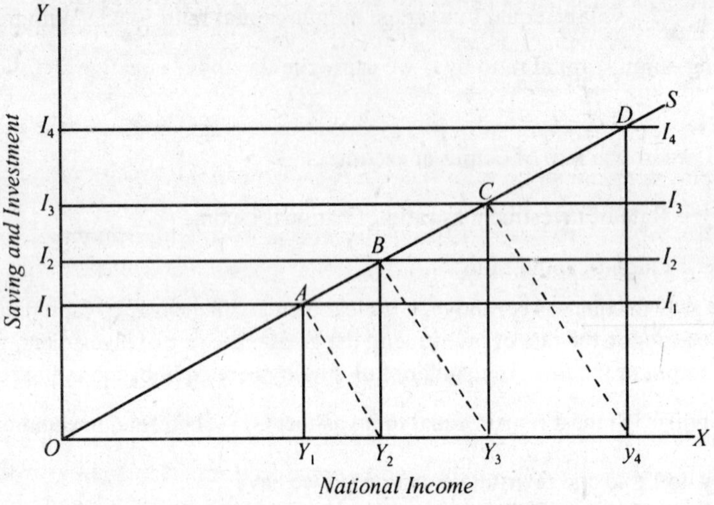

Fig. 40.1. *Harrod-Domar Model of Equilibrium Growth*

Thus, the essential condition for maintaining a continuous equilibrium state of full employment is that investment and real income must both grow at a constant annual rate. This rate should be equal to the propensity to save (s) multiplied by output-capital ratio, (σ) *i.e.*, $s\sigma$.

We can explain the model in geometrical terms with the help of the Fig. 40.1 given above. Here real income is measured along the horizontal axis, while saving and investment (in real terms) are measured along the vertical axis. The saving function is represented by the line OS starting from the origin. Its slope is given by the marginal propensity to save (s) which is assumed to remain constant for a considerable period of time. The initial investment demand is represented by curve I_1I_1. This intersects the saving function OS at the point A so that the corresponding equilibrium level of income is Y_1. We assume that it corresponds to the full-employment level of national inocme.

Now, the new capital so created (represented by OI_1) will lead to the increase in productive capacity as determined by output-capital ratio. Given the output-capital ratio, investment OI_1 leads to Y_1Y_2 increase in output or income. As a result, national income will increase to Y_2. The ratio between the increase in income (ΔY or Y_1Y_2) and the increase in investment (OI_1) is given by the 'output-capital' ratio σ. But the new equilibrium level of income Y_2 will be relalised or maintained only if the investment demand function shifts upward to I_2I_2 and intersects the saving function OS at the point B, which is vertically above Y_2.

However, as soon as the new capital equipment represented by the higher level OI_2 starts producing goods, capacity output or income will rise to Y_3 (indicating an increase by an amount σ times OI_2 over the previous level of income (Y_2). But the new level of income Y_3 will be maintained only if investment increases so much that the new investment demand curve I_3I_3 intersects the saving function OS at C. In this way, the process will continue so long as the investment increases by the appropriate amount in each period. The income would successively go on rising by an amount σ times the previous period's investment. And the investment in each period would rise by s times the output-capital ratio. Thus, income would continue to grow at the steady rate of $s\sigma$.

It is evident from the basic equation $\frac{\Delta I}{I} = s\sigma$ that greater the saving rate(s), the greater will be the growth of investment needed to maintain the steady growth with full employment. Similarly, greater the value of σ (*i.e.* the output-capital ratio), the greater should be the increase in income to avoid emergence of excess capacity. But greater income is possibly only through greater investment. Hence, if income is to grow at a steady rate, investment must also grow at the annual steady rate given by $s\sigma$.

If $\frac{\Delta I}{I} < s\sigma$, *i.e.*, that is, if sufficient growth in investment does not take place, steady growth with full employment cannot be achieved. On the other hand, if today's investment is sufficient to achieve equilibrium growth with full employment, investment will have to be much more in the next period for generating sufficient increase in demand so as to utilise fully the expanded production capacity and to avoid the under-utilisation of capital stock which will result in a fall in investment, and so cause depression. In other words, "*the economy must, so to speak, run faster and faster to stay in the same place, otherwise, it will slip downwards.*"[3]

HARROD'S GROWTH MODEL

Though Harrod's model of growth is similar to that of Domar, but it differs from the latter in details. Therefore we will explain below the essential features of Harrod's growth theory separately. In his essay "*Towards a Dynamic Economics*", Harrod put forward a theory which can be considered as truly dynamic. Explanation of secular trends is his main theme. He seeks to explain the secular causes of unemployment and inflation and the factors which determine the equilibrium and the actual rate of capital accumulation.

The classical economists considered economic development as a race between technological progress and capital accumulation on the one hand, and growing population and diminishing returns from land on the other. Harrod drops diminishing returns, regards technological progress and population growth as independent factors. In Harrod's analysis of economic growth there are three basic elements: (a) population growth, (b) output per head as determined by level of technique or inventions and (c) capital accumulation. Inventions may be neutral, i.e., leave the capital coefficient unchanged, or capital-saving, *i.e.*, reducing the capital coefficient, or 'labour-saving' which will increase the capital-output ratio. It may be noted that capital-output ratio is the reciprocal of output-

3. Meir and Baldwin, *Economic Development*, 1966, p. 107.

capital ratio (σ), the concept used by Domar. It is important to mention that Harrod uses the concept of incremental capital-output ratio, which is the reciprocal of marginal output-capital ratio (σ) of Domar's model.

While arriving at the behaviour of income as a response to entrepreneurial decisions regarding investment, Harrod makes two assumptions: (i) Saving in any period of time is a constant proportion s of the income received during that period, and (ii) the investment is proportional to the rate of increase of income. The second assumption *is in fact the acceleration principle which states that the increase in output or income that occurs induces an increase in the stock of capital.*

Harrod begins his analysis of growth by marrying together acceleration principle and the theory of investment multiplier. As in Domar's model, Harrod explains that growth rate $\left(G_y \text{ or } \frac{\Delta Y}{Y}\right)$ depends on the rate of capital formation (or investment) and capital-output ratio which he defines as " the value of the capital goods required for the production of a unit increment of output". He put forward, three growth equations. He takes saving as a fixed proportion of national output or income. Presenting a more elaborative analysis of growth than Domar, Harrod advanced three growth equations.

Harrod writes his first growth equation as follows:

$$G_y = \frac{s}{v} \qquad ...(i)$$

Where G_y is the rate of growth in a period $\left(\frac{\Delta Y}{Y}\right)$, s is the rate of saving (*i.e.* proportion of saving to national income $\left(\frac{S}{Y}\right)$, and v is the capital-output ratio. It is important to note that capital-output ratio v in Harrod's growth equation (*i*) above is the one that is *actually obtained* from the extra capital accumulation (ΔK) and increase in production of goods and services in a year (ΔY) Harrod derives this growth equation as follows.

Following the Keynesian framework, Harrod takes that actual saving must be equal to actual investment. Further, since Harrod takes saving (S) as a constant proportion of national income (Y) in a period we have

$$S = sY_t$$

where s is propensity to save.

Investment (I or ΔK) in a period t depends on the rate of increase in production (or income) that is, ΔY ($or\ Y_t - Y_{t-1}$) and the actual capital-out put ratio (v). Thus we have

$$\Delta K \text{ or } I = v(Y_t - Y_{t-1})$$

Since in a period *actual* saving must be equal to *actual* investment we have

$$v(Y_t - Y_{t-1}) = sY_t$$

Dividing both sides by Y we have

$$\frac{v(Y_t - Y_{t-1})}{Y_t} = s$$

or

$$\frac{(Y_t - Y_{t-1})}{Y_t} = \frac{s}{v}$$

Since $\frac{(Y_t - Y_{t-1})}{Y_t}$ represents actual growth of output or income we can denote it by G_y. Thus

$$G_y = \frac{s}{v}$$

G_y is the growth of output or income which *actually* occurs in a period. The above growth equation is in fact a truism as it is always true by definition depending as it is on the accounting identity that actual investment equals actual savings of a period.

Warranted Rate of Growth

Harrod proposes a second growth equation which he calls a fundamental growth equation to describe the *equilibrium geowth at a steady rate.* The warranted rate of growth is taken to be that rate of growth *which if it occurs will keep the entrepreneurs satisfied that* they have produced neither more nor less than the right amount. Being satisfied with the achievement of this growth rate, the entrepreneurs will maintain or perpetuate the same rate of growth. Warranted rate of growth is thus equilibrium rate of growth in the sense that producers, if they achieve it, will be induced to maintain it. The condition for warranted rate of growth is stated as under :

$$G_w = \frac{s}{v_r} \qquad ...(ii)$$

Harrod denotes capital-output ratio by the letter *C*, but following the modern practice we are using *v* for it.

G_w= "Warranted rate of growth", which is that rate of income growth of output or income. ($\Delta Y/Y$), which will keep entrepreneurs satisfied with the amount of investment they have actually made, i.e., it is in fact the full capacity rate of growth.

v_r = required incremental capital-output ratio to sustain the warranted rate of growth and is determined by the state of technology and the nature of goods constituting the increment in output.

s = average propensity to save.

The sort of entrepreneurial behaviour envisaged by Harrod means that *to maintain full employment, the desired (ex-ante) saving out of the full-employment income must be offset by an equal amount of desired investment.* But to induce this much investment, income must be growing.

In both the above equations *(i) and (ii) above s* is the same because Harrod assumes that the saving intentions are always realised so that ex-ante savings are always equal to ex-post savings.

Thus, Harrod is able to show that for dynamic equilibrium $G_w = \frac{s}{v_r}$

It is important to note that v_r in growth equation (*ii*) is different from *v* of the growth equation (*i*), As noted above, *v* in Harrod's growth equation (*i*) shows the increment in the amount of new capital installed during a period divided by the *increase in output actually obtained* from it during that period. It shows what has been *actually* produced with the addition to the capital stock in a period and *not whether producers are satisfied with the increase in output actually realised.* For example, if there are boom conditions in the economy and as a result the increase in capital installed during the period is fully utilised, actual capital-output ratio (*v*) will be lower. On the other hand, if there is a demand recession in the economy, good amount of extra capital installed will not be utilised for production and consequently incremental capital-output ratio (*v*) will be higher.

But what determines the size of the required incremental capital-output ratio (v_r) which keeps entrepreneurs to perpetuate thangrund. The size of the v_r is determined by technological conditions and the nature of goods comprising the increment of output. *This warranted rate of growth will be achieved if sufficient increase in income takes place during the growth process.*

The proportion of investment to income being fixed, an increase in income would mean that in the next period both income and investment must be higher. In such a situation the producers would like to perpetuate the rate of growth which they have already realised. Under such circumstances the producers invest in the hope that they will be able to sell what they have planned to produce. In other words, the producers will desire to invest an amount required by $G_w v_r$, which will be equal in magnitude to *s*, *i.e.*, the given proportional investment rate.

Condition for Equilibrium Growth Rate

Now, what is the condition for equilibrium growth rate? *In Harrod's model, if incremental capital-output (v) actually relalised happens to be equal to required capital-output ratio (v_r), warranted by technological and other conditions, then the actual rate of growth, G_Y is equal to the warranted rate of growth (G_w), the rate which the circumstances of the economy warrants, the economy will be growing at the equilibrium rate ($G_y = G_w$).* It may be noted that actual rate of growth will be equal to warranted rate of growth when investment is increasing at the rate high enough to generate adequate demand to ensure capacity growth rate (G_w).

Harrod lays down a condition for steady growth by saying that the actual rate of growth must be equal to the warranted rate of growth, i.e., the rate of increase in output or income should be just so much as to keep the entrepreneurs satisfied with the actual investment they have made.

Thus, so long $v_r = v$, the producers would like to perpetuate a growth rate that is equal to the actual or realised rate. In other words, G_y (the actual growth rate) will be the same as that which the producers want to perpetuate, i.e., G_w. But we have seen above that G_w stands for the rate of growth which when realised leaves the entrepreneurs in a state of mind that they shall be prepared to undertake a similar advance in the future. Furthermore, if the income increases at this rate it will continue to increase at this rate. This is how a steady growth rate is assured. Income will have to grow faster and faster, if the entrepreneurs are to be convinced that the higher investment was desirable. In this way, both income and investment will go on increasing from one period to the next. There is thus a cumulative equilibrium growth of income and investment.

Graphic Illustration of Harrod's

We can geometrically illustrate Harrod's model with the help of Fig. 40.2 given below. Here income is measured along the horizontal axis, while saving and investment are measured along the verical axis. The line *OR* is drawn with a slope *s* (of the fundamental equation $G_w = \frac{s}{v_r}$) where/s represents the saving function. The line *KA* represents the Harrodian investment function $I = v_r \; \Delta Y$ *i.e.*, $v_r = \frac{I}{\Delta Y}$). For the sake of convenience we may write this function as $I_t = v_r(Y_t - Y_{t-1})$. This means that the investment will be zero if the current income (Y_t) is the same as the previous income (Y_{t-1}). As such the line *KA* cuts the income-axis at *K* which corresponds to the previous period's income (Y_{t-1}). Further, the slope of the investment function *KA* is equal to v_r and this is greater than 45° on the assumption that $v_r > 1$

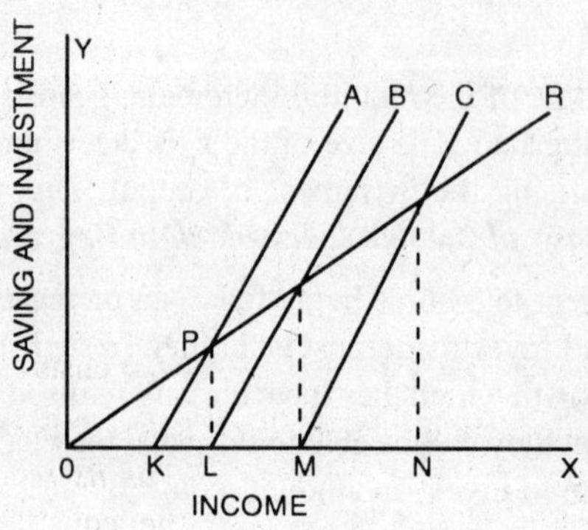

Fig. 40.2. *Graphical Representation of Warranted Growth Rate of Harrod's Model*

From the Fig. 40.2 given above, it can be seen that the saving-investment equilibrium in the current period is attained when the level of income is *OL*. And this level of income in the current period is more than the previous period's income level by an amount *KL*. Thus, the warranted rate of growth $G_w = \left(\frac{\Delta Y}{Y} = \frac{Y_t - Y_{t-1}}{Y_t}\right)$ is given by $\frac{KL}{OL}$.

In the succeeding period $(t + 1)$, *OL* becomes the previous period's income and the investment function shifts to *LB*. So if v_r remains unchanged, *LB* will be parallel to *KA*. The new saving-investment equilibrium will be established where *LB* intersects *OR*. And this occurs at the income level of *OM*. As such the warranted rate of growth in the period $(t + 1)$ would be $\frac{LM}{OM}$ In the same way, the investment function of the period $(t + 2)$ will be given by the line *MC*, generating an equilibrium level of income *ON* and the corresponding warranted rate of growth of $\frac{MN}{ON}$.

Now, it may be observed that due to the properties of similar triangles, $\frac{KL}{OL}, \frac{LM}{OM}, \frac{MN}{ON}$ are equal to each other. This implies that so long as the values of s and v_r remain unchanged, the warranted rate of growth takes place at an unchanged proportionate rate. However, with the passage of time, the investment function goes on shifting successively to the right and the income would go on increasing at the warranted rate if the saving-investment equilibrium continues to be maintained in the successive periods.

Natural Rate of Growth.

Expansion, however, cannot go on indefinitely. The availability of labour and natural resources would put the limit. In other words, it is not necessary that the warranted rate of growth G_w (which is also equal to the actual rate of growth G_y) is the maximum attainable rate of growth. With this view in mind. Harrod introduces yet another rate of growth called the '*natural rate of growth*'., G_n which is the maximum rate of growth allowed by the increases of macro variables like population growth, technological improvements, and growth in natural resources. In fact, *G_n is the highest attainable growth rate which would bring about the fullest possible employment of the resources existing in the economy*. This may be considered as the ceiling rate of growth. Joan Robiuson calls it the maximum feasible rate of growth. If l stands for growth rate of population (or labour force) and t for technological progress (*i.e.* rate of increase of productivity), then natural rate of growth can be written as

$$G_n = l + t$$

Hence for the equilibrium growth rate at full employment of all existing resources, the following condition must be satisfied:

$$G_n = G_w = G_y$$

Any deviation from this path would bring about instability in the economy.

The Golden Age

The equality of three growth rates ($G_y = G_w = G_n$) ensures that economy is in moving or dynamic equilibrium. This is also called *balanced growth equilirbrium*. Joan *Robinson describes the equality of these three growth rate as a golden age as its represents a very satisfactory and happy situation*. This is a happy situation because the equality of these three growth rates ($G_y = G_w = G_n$), will ensure steady equilibrium growth rate along with full unemployment of labour and without creating excess productive capacity. However, Joan Robinson has emphasised that the gold age, namely, the equality of three growth rates "*represents a mythical state of affairs not likely to obtain in any actual economy*"[4]. This is because the four key variables, namely, propensity to save (s), required capital-output ratio (v_r) of the warranted rate of growth, the rate of growth of population (l) and and rate of technological change (t) are determined quite independetely of each other. While the warranted rate of growth (G_w) is determined by the value of s and v_r, the natural rate of growth is determined by rate of population growth (l) and the rate of technological progress (t). The gold age or balanced growth equilibrium of $G_y = G_w = G_n$ will occur only when the four variables, s, v, l and t have appropriate values. But this seems to be very unlikely to occur. It is only by chance that these four variables will have right or appropriate values to guarantee the golden age equilibrium.

Relevance of Harrod-Domar Growth Model for Developing Countries

Harrod and Domar models are closely similar to each other. As pointed out earlier both these economists have sought to utilise the Keynesian framework, which was originally designed to tackle the short-term problems of a static economy to the dynamic problems associated with long-term sustained growth. Starting with an economy at full employment level, these economists have sought to provide answer to the following questions:

(a) How can a steady rate of growth be maintained at full employment level without inflation or deflation?

(b) Under what circumstances the rate of increase of income would be such as to save the economy from being entrapped in secular stagnation or secular inflation?

However there are some limitations of applying Harrod-Domar models to the conditions of developing countries. First, to assume away the role of government is to disown the realities completely. In fact, due to the vast structural changes to be effected government in these economies must step in a big way to initiate and accelerate economic development as an efficient manager of the whole economy, lest we may slip down the slope. Besides, the assumption of an initial full-employment level of income is not valid for the developing countries; disguised unemployment pervades these underdeveloped economies, especially the labour-surplus economies. It is a case of structural disequilibrium arising basically from the imbalance between labour and capital. Even if we make allowance for the entire savings to be invested, the growth of capital stock fails to match with the growth of labour force. Being based on fixed capital-output and capital-labour ratio, the Harrod and Domar models have only limited applicability the developing world. Their peculiar problems demand a different solution from the one suggested by these models. *To absorb the surplus labour force, there is a need to bring down both the capital-output and capital-labour ratios through reducing capital intensity*. The Harrod-Domar models by assuming a constant capital coefficients rule out such a possibility.

Secondly, the usefulness of models based on the concept of capital-output ratio is of little operational significance in developing economies. Depending on the nature and degree of various shortages, bottlenecks and market imperfections, the productivity of invested capital is amenable to considerable fluctuations. It is indeed very difficult to have an accurate and valid estimate of a concept like capital-output ratio under such fluid conditions. Commenting in this regard, Prof. Hirschman[5] remarks that the predictive and operational significance of a model based on the concept of *capital-output* ratio is far less for an underdeveloped economy than for advanced econo-

4. Joan Robinson, *The Accumulation of Capital*, London, 1956,
5. Hirschman, *Strategy of Economic Development*, 1957.
6. Sukhamoy Chakravarty, *The Logic of Investment Planning*, p.43.

mies. Models such as these, therefore, cannot explain the mechanism through which economic growth can get under way and could be carried forward in the present-day developing economies.

Thirdly the Harrod-Domar growth variables are aggregative in nature and, therefore, fail to show the sectorial interrelationship. The processes of development of the developing economies are, as is being increasingly acknowledged, fundamentally linked with structural and institutional changes. Their highly aggregative nature, comments Prof S. Chakravarty[6], 'prevents them from being used as a tool in detailed quantitative policy making and conceals many structural aspects of the problem of a steady rate of growth.

Fourthly and very importantly, these models can at best offer counter-cyclical and counter-stagnation policy formulation. They are in no way any guide to industrialisation programming for growth which is the dire necessity of developing countries. For instance, in Harrod's model, the deviations between the actual, warranted and natural rates of growth indicate that the advanced economies are subject to cyclical fluctuations and secular stagnation. Harrod is of the view that chronic deflation is a far greater possibility in advanced countries on account of the fact that these countries save more than the investment can absorb. Domar has also presented a similar reasoning. He similarly maintains that the likelihood of effective demand falling short of productive capacity is more pronounced. Of course, even in developing countries, the problems of growth of effective demand falling short of growth in capacity output cannot be denied but the developing countries face more severe problems of low savings and low productivity of investment.

Further, Harrod excludes autonomous investment as an explicit variable in his formulation of *'warranted'* saving-investment equality. But the exclusion of autonomous investment as an important factor in determining growth in developing countries by Harrod in his growth model renders Harrod's concept of 'warranted' growth rate analytically inadequate for the purpose of developing countries. The apparent reason for this exclusion is to be partly found in Harrod's desire to make place for the acceleration principle in his growth model. He also ignored the role of public investment to which Keynes assigned a crucial role. But, autonomous investments, whether public or private, are of pivotal importance to the developing countries. Besides, Harrod-Domar growth models assume that propensity to save and the capital-output ratio are constant. But actually they are likely to change over the long-run. Further, if the proportion of factors can be changed as labour may be substituted for capital, then adjustment within the economy can be easily made and steady growth made possible without any rigid conditions.

In spite of the fact that these models are of limited applicability to the developing countries and fail to highlight the crucial issues involved in the development process of these economies they nevertheless *are useful in fixing the overall targets of income, investment and savings* and in checking the consistency of such targets. Prof. Kurihara states that "Harrod and Domar have made the essential nature of the growth mechanism operationally significant, for they stress saving ratio and the capital-output ratio (or its reciprocal) as measurable strategic variables to investigate and possibly to manipulate for a desired rate of growth. Because of the universal character of these strategic variables, the growth mechanism discussed by Harrod and Domar is applicable to all economic systems, albeit with the modification".[7]

An indirect use of these models has actually been made in some countries. For instance, in the First Five Year Plan of India, the rate of saving was planned to be raised through keeping the marginal rate of saving above the average rate of saving. And the current rate of capital formation and therefore growth of the economy was sought to be maximised through raising the marginal rate of saving. Thus, these models served to guide the planners in determining the growth rate of the Indian economy. Commenting on these models, Prof. S. Chakravarty remarks that "*The great service that*

6. *Ibid.*, p.185
7. K.K. Kurihara, *The Keynesian Theory of Development*, 1959. Ch. 9. pp.153-154

these models perform is to indicate very roughly the dimensions of the problem involved in raising the per capita income level in an underdeveloped country".[8] As noted above, Harrod-Domar model brings out the crucial role for the continuous growth of investment to ensure sustained growth at a steady rate. If investment is not growing sufficiently, the problem of deficient demand will emerge which will bring about recesionary condition even in a developing country. The demand recession will result in rise in capital-output ratio due to the underutilisation of productive capacity. The Indian growth experience clearly brings out this fact. From the mide-sixties to the late seventies the Indian economy witnessed the problem of demand deficiency due to the fall in public investment resulting in lower industrial grwoth and increase in capital output-ratio. Again during 1997-2003 low industrial growth rate was achieved due to deficiency in demand resulting from stagnation is investment.

Further, Prof. Kurihara contends that though these models are "designed to indicate the conditions of progressive equilibrium for an advanced economy", yet he says these models are "important not only because they represent a stimulating attempt to dynamise and secularise Keynes's static short-run saving-investment theory, but also because they are capable of being modified so as to *introduce fiscal policy parameters as explicit variables* in the economic growth of an under-developed country".[9] He further writes, these growth models have this positive lesson for under-developed economies, that state should be allowed to play not only a stabilizing role but also a developmental role, if these economies are to industrialise more effectively and rapidly than the now industrialised economies did in conditions of *laissez faire.*[10]

8. S. Chakravarty, *Op. cit.*
9. K.K. Kurihara, *The Keynesian Theory of Development, 1959.* Ch.9. pp.153-154.
10. *Ibid.*, p.185.

CHAPTER 41

Neoclassical Theory of Growth

Introduction

Having discussed Harrod-Domar growth model in the last chapter we will discuss neoclassical growth theory in the present chapter. The neoclassical growth theory was developed in the late 1950s and 1960s of the twentieth century as a result of intensive research in the field of growth economics. The American economist Robert Solow, who won a Noble Prize in Economics and the British economist, J. E. Meade are the two well known contributors to the neo-classical theory of growth. This neoclassical growth theory lays stress on capital accumulation and its related decesion of saving as an important determinant of economic growth. Neoclassical growth model considered two factor production function with capital and labour as determinants of output. Besides, it added *exogenously determined factor, technology*, to the production function. Thus neoclassical growth model uses the following production function :

$$Y = AF(K, L) \qquad \text{... } (i)$$

Where Y is Gross Domestic Product (GDP), K is the stock of capital, L is the amount of unskilled labour and A is exogenously determined level of technology. Note that change in this exogenous variable, technology, will cause a shift in the production function.

There are two ways in which technology parameter A is incorporated in the production function. One popular way of incorporating the technology parameter in the production function is to assume that technology is *labour augmenting* and accordingly the production function is written as

$$Y = F(K, AL) \qquad \text{... } (ii)$$

Note that labour-augmenting technological change implies that it increases productivity of labour.

The second important way of incorporating the technology factor in the production function is to assume that technological progress *augments all factors* (both capital and labour in our production function) and not just augmenting labour. It is in this way that we have written the production function equation (i) above. To repeat, in this approach production function is written as

$$Y = AF(K, L)$$

Considering in this way A represents *total factor productivity* (that is, productivity of both factor inputs). When we empirically estimate production function specified in this way, then contribution of A to the growth in total output is called *Solow residual* which means that total factor productivity really measures the increase in output *which is not accounted for by changes in factors, capital and labour.*

Unlike the fixed proportion production function of Harrod-Domar model of economic growth, neoclassical growth model uses *variable proportion production function,* that is, it considers unlimited *possibilities of substitution between capital and labour* in the production process. That is why it is called neoclassical growth model as the earlier neoclassicals considered such a variable proportion production function. The second important departure made by neoclassical growth theory from Harrod-Domar growth model is that it assumes that *planned investment and saving are always*

1. Robert Solow, "A Contribution to the Theory of Economic Growth", *Quarterly Journal of Economics,* February 1956.

2. J. E. Meade, *Theory of Economic Growth.*

equal because of immediate adjustments in price (including interest). With these assumptions, neoclassical growth theory focuses its attention on supply side factors such as capital and technology for determining rate of economic growth of a country. Therefore, unlike Harrod-Domar growth model, it does not consider aggregate demand for goods limiting economic growth. Therefore, it is called '*classical*' along with '*neo*'. The growth of output in this model is achieved at least in the short run through higher rate of saving and therefore higher rate of capital formation, However, diminishing returns to capital limit economic growth in this model. Though the neoclassical growth model assumes *constant returns to scale* which exhibits *diminishing returns to capital and labour separately.*

We explain below how neoclassical growth model explains economic growth through capital accumulation (*i.e.*, saving and investment) and how this growth process ends in *steady state equilibrium. By steady state equilibrium for the economy we mean that growth rate of output equals growth rate of labour force and growth rate of capital* $\left(i.e. \frac{\Delta Y}{Y} = \frac{\Delta L}{L} = \frac{\Delta K}{K}\right)$ *so that per capita income and per capita capital are no longer changing.* Note that for income per capita and capital per worker to remain constant in this steady state equilibrium when labour force is growing implies that *income and capital must be growing at the same rate as labour force.* Since growth in labour force (or population) is generally denoted by letter 'n', in this steady state equilibrium, therefore, $\frac{\Delta Y}{Y} = \frac{\Delta K}{K} = \frac{\Delta N}{N} = n$. Neoclassic growth theory explains the process of growth from any initial portion to this steady state equilibrium.

Neoclassical Growth Theory : Production Function and Saving

As stated above, neoclassical growth theory uses following production function :

$$Y = AF(K, L)$$

However, the neoclassical theory explains the growth process using the above production function in its intensive form, that is, in per capita terms. To obtain the above production function in per capita terms we divide both sides of the given production function by L, the number of labour force. Thus

$$\frac{Y}{L} = AF\left(\frac{K}{L}, \frac{L}{L}\right)$$

$$= AF\left(\frac{K}{L}, 1\right) = AF\left(\frac{K}{L}\right) \quad \text{... (2)}$$

To begin with we assume that there is no technological progress. With this assumption then equation (2) is reduced to

$$\frac{Y}{L} = F\left(\frac{K}{L}\right) \quad \text{... (3)}$$

The equation (3) states that output per head $\left(\frac{Y}{L}\right)$ is a function of capital per head $\frac{K}{L}$. Writing y for $\frac{Y}{L}$ and k for $\frac{K}{L}$, equation (3) can be written as

$$y = f(k) \quad \text{... (4)}$$

Now, in Figure 41.1 we represent the production function (4) in per capita terms. It will be noticed from Figure 41.1 that as capital per capita (k) increases output per head increases, that is, marginal product of labour is positive. But, as will be seen from Figure 45.1, the slope of the production function curve decreases as capital per head increases. This implies that marginal product of capital diminishes.

That is, the increase in capital per head causes output per head to increase but at a diminishing rate.

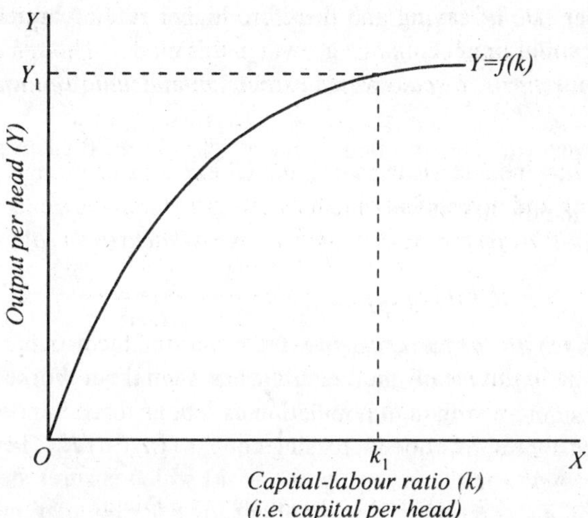

Fig. 41.1. *Production function relating output per head to output per head*

It will be seen from the Figure 41.1 that at capital-labour ratio (*i. e.* capital per worker) equal to k_1, output per head is y_1. Similarly we can read from the production function curve: $y = f(k)$ the output per head corresponding to any other capital per head.

Neoclassical Growth Theory : Fundamental Growth Equation

According to neoclassical theory, rate of saving plays an important role in the growth process of an economy. Like the Harrod-Domar model, neoclassical theory considers saving as a *constant fraction of income*. Thus,

$$S = sY \quad \ldots (5)$$

Where S = saving

Y = income

s = propensity to save

Since s is a constant fraction of income, average propensity to save is equal to marginal propensity to save. Further, since national income equals national product, we can also write equation(5) as

$$sY = sF(K, L)$$

As in neoclassical theory planned investment is always equal to planned saving, *net addition to the stock of capital* is (ΔK), which is the same thing as investment (I), can be obtained by deducting *depreciation* of capital stock during a period from the planned saving. Thus,

$$\Delta K = I = sY - D \quad \ldots (6)$$

Where ΔK = net addition to the stock of capital, I stands for investment and D for depreciation. Depreciation occurs at a certain percentage of the existing capital stock. The total depreciation (D) can be written as

$$D = dK$$

Substituting dK for D in equation (6) we have

$$\Delta K = sY - dK$$

or $$sY = \Delta K + dK \qquad \text{... (7)}$$

Now dividing and multiplying the first term of the left hand side of equation (7) by K we have

$$sY = K \cdot \frac{\Delta K}{K} + dK \qquad \text{... (8)}$$

We have seen above, *for the steady state equilibrium,* growth of capital $\left(\frac{\Delta K}{K}\right)$ must be equal to growth of labour force $\left(\frac{\Delta L}{L}\right)$, so that capital per worker and therefore income per head remains constant. If we denote growth rate of labour force $\left(\frac{\Delta L}{L}\right)$ by n, then in steady state $\frac{\Delta K}{K} = n$.

Substituting n for $\frac{\Delta K}{K}$ in equation (8) we have

$$sY = K.\, n + dK$$

or $$sY = (n + d)\, K \qquad \text{... (9)}$$

The above equation (9) is a fundamental growth equation of the neoclassical growth model and states the condition for the steady state equilibrium when capital per worker and therefore income per capita remains constant even though population or labour force is growing. Thus, for steady state growth equilibrium capital must be increasing equal to $(n + d)\,K$. Therefore $(n + d)\,K$ represents the *required investment* (or change in capital stock) which ensures steady state when capital and income must be growing at the same rate as labour force (or population)

The Growth Process

From the growth equation (9) it is evident that if planned *saving sY is greater than the required investment* (*i.e.* $(n + d)\,K$) *to keep per capita income constant, capital for worker will increase.* This increase in capital per worker will cause increase in productivity of worker. As a result, the economy will grow at higher rate than the steady-state equilibrium growth rate. However, this higher growth rate will not occur endlessly because diminishing returns to capital will bring it down to the steady rate of growth, though at a higher levels of per capita income and capital per worker.

In order to graphically show the growth process the growth equation is conventionally used in *intensive form*, that is, in per capita terms. In order to do so we divide both sides of equation (9) by L and have

$$\frac{sY}{L} = (n + d)\frac{K}{L}$$

where $\frac{Y}{L}$ represents income per capita and $\frac{K}{L}$ represents capital per worker (*i.e.* capital-labour ratio)

Writting y for $\frac{Y}{L}$ and k for $\frac{K}{L}$ we have

$$sy = (n + d)\, k \qquad \text{...(10)}$$

The equation (10) represents fundamental neoclassical growth equation in per capita terms.

Growth Process and Steady Growth Rate. Figure 41.2 shows the growth process that moves the economy over time from an initial position to the steady state equilibrium growth rate. In this Figure 41.2 along with per capita production function ($y = f(k)$) we have also drawn per capita saving function curve sy. Besides, we have drawn $(n + d)k$ curve which depicts required investment per worker to keep constant the level of capital per capita when population or labour force is growing at a given rate n.

In Figure 41.2 $y = f(k)$ is per capita production function curve as in Figure 41.1. Since per capita saving is a constant fraction of per capita output (*i.e.* income), the curve *sy* depicting per capita saving function is drawn below the per capita output function curve ($y = f(k)$) with

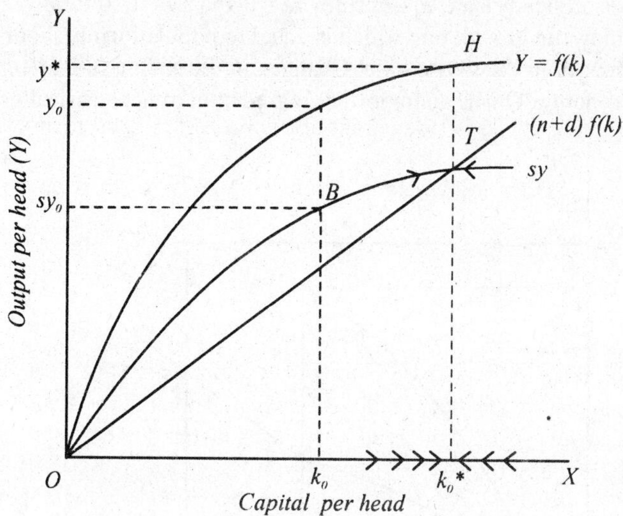

Fig. 41.2. *Neoclassical Model : Growth Process and Steady State Equilibrium*

the same shape. Another straight line curve labelled as $(n + d)k$, is drawn which depicts the *required investment* to keep capital per head (*i.e* capital-labour ratio) constant at various levels of capital per head.

Now, let us assume the current capital per head is k_o at which per capita income (or output) is y_0 and per capita saving is sy_0. It will be seen from Figure 41.2 that at capital per head k_0, per capita saving *sy* exceeds investment required to maintain capital per head equal to k_0 ($sy_0 > (n + d)k$). As a result, capital per head (k) will rise (as indicated by horizontal arrows) which will lead to increase in per capita income and the economy, moves to the right. This adjustment process will continue so long as $sy > (n + d)\ k$. It will, seen when the economy reaches at capital per head equal to k^* and per capita income equal to y^* corresponding to which saving curve *sy* interseets the $(n + d)\ k$ curve at point *T*.

It will be noticed from Figure 41.2 that the adjustment process comes to rest at capital per head equal to k^* because saving and investment corresponding to this state is equal to the investment required to maintain capital per head at k^*. Thus point *T* and its associated capital per head equal to k^* and income or output per head equal to y^* represent the steady state equilibrium. It is worth noting that whether the economy is initially at the left or right of k^*, the adjustment process leads to the steady state at point *T*. It may however be noted that in steady-state equilibrium, the economy is growing at the same rate as labour force (that is, equal to n or $\Delta L/L$).

It will be seen from Figure 41.2 that although growth of economy comes down to the steady growth rate, its levels of per capita capital and per capita income at point *T* are greater as compared to the initial state at point *B*.

An important economic implication of the above growth process visualised in neoclassical growth model is that *different countries having same saving rate and population growth rate and access to the same technology will ultimately converge to same per capita income although this convergence process* may take different time in different countries.

Impact of Increase in the Saving Rate

As has been explained above that in steady state, both capital per head (k) and income per head (y) remain constant when economy is growing at the rate of growth of population or labour force (*i.e.* n). In other words, in steady state equilibrium $\Delta k = 0$ and $\Delta Y = 0$. It follows from this that steady state growth rate or long-run growth rate which is equal to population or labour force growth rate n is not affected by changes in the saving rate. Changes in the saving rate affect only the *short-run growth rate* of the economy. This is an important implication of neoclassical growth model.

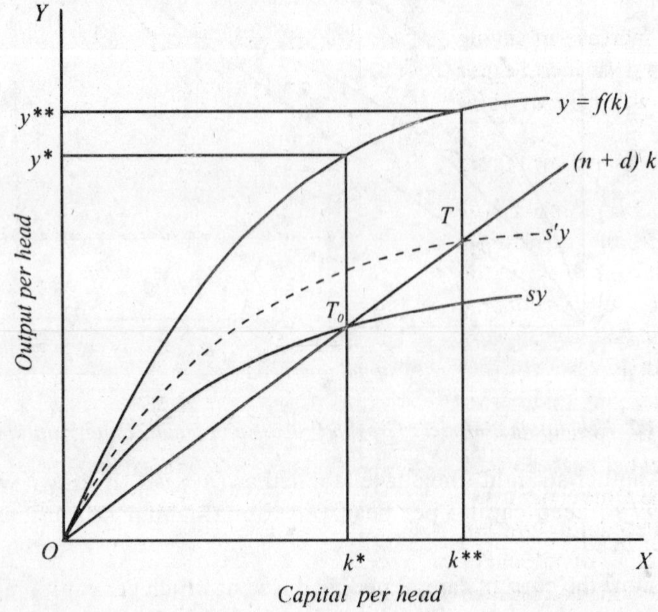

Fig. 41.3. *Impact of Increase in Saving Rate*

Now an important question is why do we get this apparently incredible result from the neoclassical growth theory. Impact of increase in the saving is illustrated in Figure 41.3. It will be seen from this figure that initially with the saving curve *sy*, the economy is in steady state at point T_0 where the saving curve *sy* intersects required investment curve $(n + d)\ k$ with k^* as capital per head and y^* as income (output) per capita. Now suppose that saving rate increases, that is, individuals in the society decide to save a higher fraction of their income. As a result, saving curve shifts to the new higher position s'y (dotted). This higher saving curve $s'y$ intersects the $(n + d)k$ curve at point T_1 which therefore represents the new steady state. We thus see that increase in saving rate moves the steady state equilibrium to the right and causes both capital per head and income per head to rise to k^{**} and y^{**} respectively Note that in the new steady state the economy grows at the same rate as the growth rate of labour force (or population) which is denoted by n. It therefore follows that long-run growth rate of the economy remains unaffected by the increase in the saving rate though the steady state position has moved to the right.

Two points are worth noting here. First, though long-run growth rate of the economy remains the same as a result of increase in the saving rate, capital per head (k) and income per capita (y) have risen with the upward shift in the saving curve to $s'y$ and consequently the change in steady state from T_0 to T_1, capital per head has increased from k^* to k^{**} and income per head has risen from y^* to y^{**}.

However, it is important to note that in the transition period or in the short run when the adjustment process is taking place from an initial steady state, to a new steady state a higher growth rate in per capita income is achieved. Thus, in Figure 41.3 when with the initial steady state point T_0, saving rate increases and saving curve shifts upward from sy to $s'y$, at the initial point T_0, planned saving or investment exceeds $(n + d)\ k$ which causes capital per head to rise resulting in a higher growth in per capita income than the growth rate in labour force (n) in the short run till the new steady state is reached.

The effect of increase in saving on growth in output or income per head (y) and growth rate of total output $\left(i.e. \frac{\Delta Y}{Y}\right)$ is shown in Figure 41.4(a) and 41.4(b). Figure 41.4(a) shows the growth in output (income) per head as a result of increase in the saving rate. To begin with, the economy is initially in steady state equilibrium at time t_0 with output per head equal to y^*. The increase in saving rate causes capital per head to rise which leads to the growth in output per head till time t_1 is reached. At time t_1 the economy is again in steady state equilibrium but now at a higher level y^{**} of output per head. Note that in the transition persued from t_0 to t_1, output per head increases but at a diminishing rate

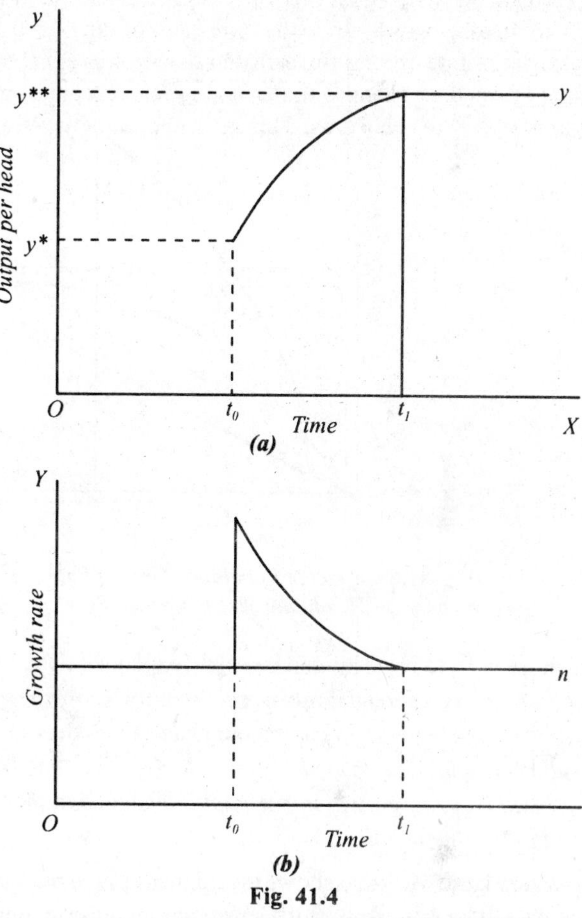

Fig. 41.4

Figure 41.4 (b) illustrates the adjustment in growth rate in total output $\left(i.e. \frac{\Delta Y}{Y}\right)$. It will be seen from Figure 41.4 (b) that starting from initial steady state at time t_0 the increase in saving rate and capital formation leads to growth rate in total output higher than the steady growth rate n in the period from t_0 to t_1 but in period t_1 it returns to the steady growth rate path n. It is thus evident that the higher saving rate leads to a higher growth rate in the short run only, while *long-run growth rate* in output remains unaffected. *The increase in the saving rate raises the growth rate of output in the short run due to faster growth in capital and therefore in output.* As more capital is accumulated, the growth rate decreases due to the diminishing returns to capital and eventually falls back to the population or labour force growth rate (n).

Effect of Population Growth

For developing countries like India it is important to discuss the effect of increase in population growth rate on steady levels of capital per head (k) and output per head (y) and also on the steady-state rate of growth of aggregate output. Figure 41.5. illustrates these effects of population growth. An increase in population growth rate causes an upward shift in $(n + d)\ k$ line. Thus in Figure 41.5, the increase in population growth rate from n to n' causes upward shifts of $(n + d)\ k$ to $(n' + d)\ k$

curve dotted. It will be seen from the Figure 41.5 that the new $(n' + d)\,k$ curve cuts the given saving curve sy at point T' at which capital per head has decreased from k^*_1 to k^*_2 and output per capita has

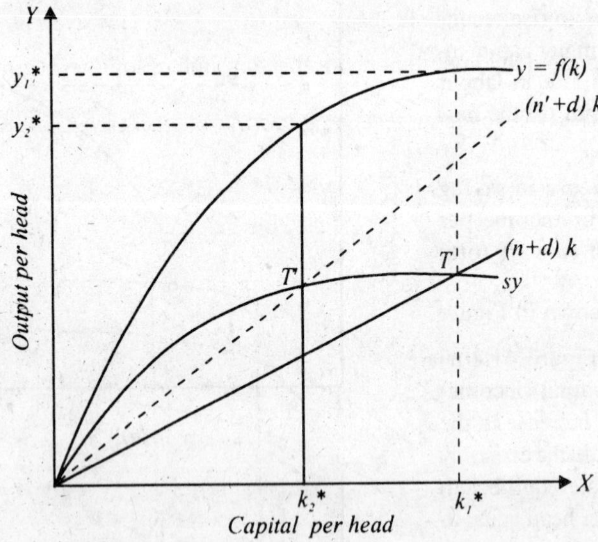

Fig. 41.5 *Effect of Population Growth Rate on Capital Per Head, Output Per Head, and Steady Growth Rate*

fallen from y^*_1 to y^*_2. This can be easily explained. Due to higher growth rate of population a given stock of capital is spread thinly over labour force which results in lower capital per head (*i.e.* capital-labour ratio). Decrease in capital per head causes decline in per capita output. *This is an important result of neoclassical growth theory which shows that population growth in developing countries like India impedes growth in per capita income and therefore multiplies our efforts to raise living standards of the people.*

The Figure 41.5 also shows that higher growth rate of population raises the steady-state growth rate. It will be seen from this figure that increase in population growth rate from n to n' causes $(n + d)\,k$ curve to shift upward to the new position $(n' + d)\,k$ (dotted) which intersects the saving curve at new steady-state equilibrium point T'. The steady state growth rate has therefore risen to n', that is, equal to the new growth rate of population. It may however be noted that *higher steady rate of growth* is not a desirable thing. As a matter of fact, a *higher steady growth means that to maintain a certain given capital-labour ratio and per capita income the economy has to save and invest more.* This implies that a higher rate of population acts as an obstacle to raise per capita income and therefore living standards of the people. Thus, this result provides a significant lesson for the developing countries like India, that is, if they want to achieve higher living standards for its people they should make efforts to control population growth rate.

Long-run Growth and Technological Change

Let us now analyse the effect of technological change on long-run growth of an economy. It is important to note that neoclassical growth theory considers technological change as an *exogenous variable*. By exogenous technological change we mean it is determined outside the model, that is, it is independent of the values of other factors, capital and labour. That is why neoclassical production function is written as

$$Y = AF(K,L)$$

where A represents exogenous technological change and appears outside the bracket.

In the foregoing analysis of neoclassical growth theory for the sake of simplification we have assumed that the technological change is absent, that is, $\frac{\Delta A}{A} = 0$. However, by assuming zero technological change we ignored the important factor that determines long-term growth of the economy. We now consider the effect of exogenous technological imnrovement over time, that is, when $\frac{\Delta A}{A} > 0$ over time.

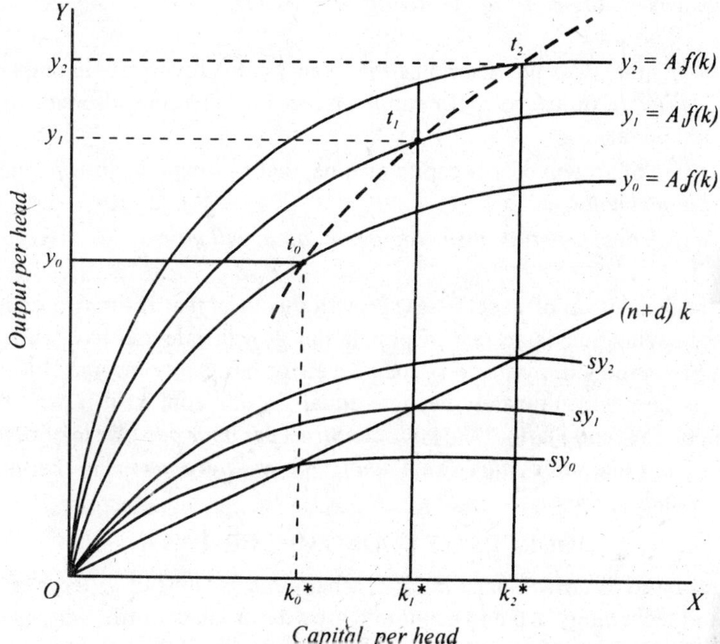

Fig. 41.6. *Growth in Capital Per Head and Output Per Head with Exogenous Technological Change*

The production function (in per capita terms), namely, $y = Af(k)$ considered so far can be taken as a snapshot in a year in which A is treated to be equal to 1. Viewed in this way, if technology improves at the rate of 1 per cent per year a snapshot taken in a year later will be $y = 1.01 f(k)$, 2 years later, $y = (1.01)^2 f(k)$ and so forth. As a result of this technological change production function will shift upward. In general, if technological improvement $\frac{\Delta A}{A}$ per year is taken to be equal to g per cent per year, then production function shifts upward at g per cent per year as shown in Figure 41.6 where to begin with production function curve in period t_0 is $y_0 = A_0 f(k)$ corresponding to which saving curve is sy_0. With this, in steady state equilibrium, capital per head is equal to k^*_0 and output (income) per head is y_0. With g per cent rate of technological progress in period t_1, production function shifts to $y_1 = A_1 f(k)$ and correspondingly saving curve shifts upward to sy_1. As a result in period t_1, in new steady state equilibrium capital per head rises to k^*_1 and per capita output to y_1. With a further g per cent rate of technological progress in period t_2, production function curve shifts to a higher level, $y_2 = A_2 f(k)$ and associated saving curve shifts to sy_2. As a result, capital per head rises to k^*_2 and per capita output to y_2 in period t_2. We thus see that progress in technology over time causes growth of per capita output (income). With this aggregate output will also increase over time as a result of technological progress.

The neoclassical growth theory has been successfully used to explain increase in per capita output and standard of living in the long term as a result technological progress and capital accumulation.

Conclusion : Key Results of Solow Neoclassical Model

Let us sum up the various key results of Solow's neoclassical growth model.

1. Neoclassical growth theory explains that output is a function of growth in factor inputs, especially capital and labour, and technological progress.
2. Contribution of increase in labour to the growth in output is the most important.
3. Growth rate of output in steady-state equilibrium is equal to the growth rate of population or labour force and *is exogenous of the saving rate, that is, it does not depend upon the rate of saving.*
4. Although saving rate does not determine the steady-state growth rate in output, it does cause *an increase in steady-state level of per capita income* (and therefore also total income) through raising capital per head.
5. Steady state rate of growth of per capita income, that is, *long-run growth rate is determined by progress in technology.*
6. *If there is no technical progress, then output per capita will ultimately converge to steady state level.*
7. A significant conclusion of neoclassical growth theory is that if the two countries have the same rate of saving and same rate of population growth rate and have access to the same technology (*i.e.* production function), their levels of per capita income *will eventually converge,* that is they will ultimately become equal. In this context it is worthwhile to quote Dornbusch, Fischer and Startz. "*The poor countries are poor because they have a less capital but if they save at the same rate as rich countries, and have access to the same technology, they will eventually catch up.*[3]

SOURCES OF ECONOMIC GROWTH

An important issue in growth economics is what contributions of different factors, namely, capital, labour and technology make to economic growth. In other words, what is relative importance of these different factors as sources of economic growth. Robert Solow and Denison have attempted to study the relative importance of the various sources of economic growth by using the concept of production function. The rate of economic growth in an economy and differences in income levels of different countries and also their growth performance during a period can be explained in terms of the increase in these sources of economic growth.

It wll be recalled that the production function describes the amount of total output produced depends on the amount of different factors used and the state of technology.

The following production function has been used to measure the various sources of economic growth

$$Y = AF(K, L) \quad \ldots (1)$$

where Y = total national product
K = the quantity of physical capital used
L = the quantity of labour used
A = the state of technology

The production function equation (1) shows that increase in capital and labour and improvement in technology will lead to growth in national output.

Note that improvement in technology causes output increases with the given factor supplies. In other words, advancement in technology leads to the increase in productivity of factors used. There-

3. Dornbusch, Fischer, Startz, *op. cit.* p.61

fore, improvement in technology is generally measured by growth in **total factor productivity (TFP).**

It will also be noticed from the production function equation (1) that technology (A) has been taken to be a multiplicative factor. This implies that progress in technology increases the marginal productivity of both capital and labour uniformly. Such technological change is generally referred to as **neutral technological change**. Besides, we measure the sources of economic growth with the above production function by assuming *constant returns to scale.* Constant returns to scale implies that increase in inputs, that is, labour and capital, by a given percentage will lead to the same percentage increase in output. Further, the increase in improvement in technology (A) or what is also referred to as increase in total factor productivity causes a shift in the production function.

With the above assumptions it can be proved that the following factors represent the sources of economic growth.

or $$\frac{\Delta Y}{Y} = \left(\theta \times \frac{\Delta K}{K}\right) + \left(1-\theta\right) \times \frac{\Delta L}{L}\Bigg) + \frac{\Delta A}{A} \qquad \ldots (2)$$

or $$\text{Growth of Output} = \begin{pmatrix} \text{Share} & & \text{Growth} \\ \text{of} & \times & \text{in} \\ \text{Capital} & & \text{Capital} \end{pmatrix} + \begin{pmatrix} \text{Shar} & & \text{Growth} \\ \text{of} & \times & \text{in} \\ \text{Labour} & & \text{Labour} \end{pmatrix} + \text{Technical Progress}$$

where θ denotes share of capital in national product, $1 - \theta$ denotes share of labour in national product.

The above equation, which is generally referred to as *growth accounting equation* shows the various sources of growth which are summarised below :

1. The contribution of increase in capital to the growth in output (G or $\frac{\Delta Y}{Y}$) is given by increase in $\left(\frac{\Delta K}{K}\right)$ capital multiplied by the share (θ) of capital in national product;
2. The increase in labour force contributes to rate of economic growth equal to the labour share ($1 - \theta$) in national product multiplied by the growth in labour in force $\left(\frac{\Delta L}{L}\right)$; and
3. The technological improvement $\frac{\Delta A}{A}$ which is measured by the increase in total factor productivity also makes an important contribution to economic growth. As mentioned above, technological progress leads to the increase in total factor productivity (*TFP*) which implies that with the given resources (*i.e.* capital and labour) more output can be produced.

Proof

We can formally prove the growth accounting equation mentioned above. In the production function equation (1) the change in output (ΔY) depends on changes in various inputs or factors — capital and labour ΔK and ΔL and change in technology. This can written as under :

$$\Delta Y = F(KL)\,\Delta A + MP_k \times \Delta K + MP_L \times \Delta L \qquad \ldots (3)$$

Where MP_k and MP_L represent marginal products of labour and capital respectively.

Dividing both sides of equation (3) by Y we have

$$\frac{\Delta Y}{Y} = \frac{F(K,L)\,\Delta A}{Y} + \frac{MP_K \cdot \Delta K}{Y} + \frac{MP_L \cdot \Delta L}{Y}$$

Since $Y = AF(K, L)$ we have

$$\frac{\Delta Y}{Y} = \frac{F(K,L)\Delta A}{AF(K,L)} + \frac{MP_K \cdot \Delta K}{Y} + \frac{MP_L \cdot \Delta L}{Y}$$

or
$$\frac{\Delta Y}{Y} = \frac{\Delta A}{A} + \frac{MP_K}{Y} \cdot \Delta K + \frac{MP_L}{Y} \cdot \Delta L \quad \text{... (4)}$$

Now multiplying and dividing the second term of the left-hand side of equation (4) by K and also multiplying and dividing the third term of left-hand side of the equation by L we have

$$\frac{\Delta Y}{Y} = \frac{\Delta A}{A} + \frac{K.MP_K}{Y} \cdot \frac{\Delta K}{K} + \frac{L.MP_L}{Y} \cdot \frac{\Delta L}{L} \quad \text{... (5)}$$

Now, if rewards of factors of production are determined by marginal products of factors as actually is the case under perfect competition in neoclassical theory, then $\frac{K.MP_K}{Y}$ represents the share of capital in national product which we denote by θ and $\frac{L.MP_L}{Y}$ repersents the share of labour in national product (Y) which we denote by 1 – θ, then substituting these in equation (5) we have :

$$\frac{\Delta Y}{Y} = \frac{\Delta A}{A} + \theta \frac{\Delta K}{K} + (1-\theta) \frac{\Delta L}{L}$$

The above is the same as growth accounting equation (2) which indicates the sources of growth of output.

TABLE 41.1

SOURCES OF ECONOMIC GROWTH

	Output	Capital	Labour	Total Factor Productivity
United States				
1960–73	4.0	4.0	1.7	1.6
1973–90	2.5	3.4	2.1	0.0
Japan				
1960–73	10.0	10.6	1.3	5.9
1973–90	4.0	5.80	1.0	1.8
Europe				
1960–73	4.9	5.7	(–)10.1	3.2
1973–90	2.3	3.1	0.1	1.3

Source : Kumiharu, Shigehra, "*Causes of Declining Growth in Industrialised Countries in Policies For Long-run Economic Growth*". 1992.

In Table 41.1 we present the contributions made by capital, labour and total factor productivity (*i.e* technical improvement) in growth of output in the United States, Japan and the major countries of Europe in the two periods 1960-73 and 1973-90. It will be seen from the table that growth of capital and improvement in total factor productivity (*i.e.* technological progress) have been the important sources of economic growth, especially in case of economic growth in Japan and European countries. Table 41.1 further reveals that it is decline in total factor productivity (*i.e.* technological improvement) and in growth of capital that is responsible for slowdown of economic growth in the USA, Japan and European countries during the period 1973-90.

1. See Dornbusch and Fischer, *Macroeconomics,* 6th edition McGraw Hill, pp. 265–266.

Knowledge or Education : the Missing Factor

In the above growth accounting equation one factor, namely knowledge or education is missing which has been stressed among others by Nobel Laurette Prof. Amartya Sen as an important factor contributing to economic growth. It may be noted that increase in knowledge or education increases the productivity of workers by improving their productive skills and abilities. Besides, increased knowledge raises the productivity of capital and raises the return to investment in capital goods. Since investment in promotion of knowledge or education makes workers and machine more productive, the workforce equipped with knowledge and education is often called *human capital* which is regarded by modern economists as an important source of economic growth. Thus human capital or knowledge and education is the important missing factor in the growth equation of neoclassical economists, Solow and Denison. On including human capital as a separate factor which contributes to growth of output, the production function can be written as under.

$$Y = A\,F\,(K, L, H)$$

where H represents human capital which was omitted by Robert Solow in his growth accounting equation.

Economies of Scale and Economic Growth

Robert Solow in his study of sources of growth in real income did not consider economies of scale as a factor contributing to growth. Solow assumed constrant returns to scale which implies if each factor in the production function increases by one per cent, output also increases by one per cent. However, some economists such as Denison and those associated with World Bank emphasise *economies of scale* or what is also called increasing returns to scale as a separate factor determining the rate of economic growth. In case of the United States Denison estimated that of 2.92 per cent annual growth in national income recorded during the period 1929–1982, 0.26 per cent was due to economies of scale. However, whether there are increasing returns to scale or constant returns to scale is an empirical matter for investigation.

CHAPTER 42

New Theory Of Growth (*Endogenous Growth Model*)

Introduction

Neoclassical growth theory dominated the economic thinking for three decades (1955–1985), though it could not explain important facts about economic growth in various countries. By the late 1980s, the dissatisfaction with neoclassical growth theory to explain the real growth phenomenon increased so much that a need was greatly felt to propound a new theory of growth. There are three basic difficulties with the neoclassical growth model. First, it implies that increase in saving rate has only a temporary or short-run effect on rate of growth and it *does not affect the long-run rate of economic growth.*

Secondly, neoclassical growth theory implies *convergence of growth rates*. That is, growth rates of countries whether having high or low saving rates will converge over time, though this convergence may be slow. This convergence implies that different countries with high and low saving rates but having same rate of population growth rate would over time achieve the same rate of growth in their national income in the long run $\left(i.e., \frac{\Delta Y}{Y} = \frac{\Delta N}{N}\right)$ while *growth rates in per capita income* $\left(\frac{\Delta y}{y}\right)$ *of these countries will tend to be equal to zero in long-run steady state equilibrium.*

More importantly, neoclassical growth theory explained that long-run rate of economic growth depended on *technological change which was considered as exogenous*. By treating technological change as exogenous, neoclassical growth theory could not focus on the fundamental forces which determine long-run growth of nations. Furthermore, if there is free flow of technological knowledge between nations we should expect the rate of technological progress to converge and therefore cause long-run growth rates of different countries to converge. However, it was found in the real world that such convergence of long-run growth rates were not taking place or were occurring in case of only limited number of countries. Thus neoclassical theory could not explain differences in growth rates of different countries nor it could explain greater proportion of economic growth observed in different countries.

A basic concern of development economics is to explain why per capita incomes and growth rates differ among countries. Thus the main motive of new growth theory is to explain differences in growth rates among countries and what are contributions of different factors to rates of growth observed in them.

Endogenous Growth Models

The new growth theory extends the neoclassical theory by making the rate of technological progress or rate of population growth or both as *endogenous* factors. The new growth theory goes more deeply into ultimate sources of growth. Three different approaches have been adopted to make technological change as endogenous factor in determining economic growth.

First, to incorporate endogenous technological change, the production function is modified as under:

$$Y_t = F(K_t, N_t, A_t) \qquad \dots (1)$$

It will be seen from the equation (1) that the level of aggregate output depends on the quantities of capital (K_t), and labour (N_t) used in the production as well as on technology (A_t) which is treated as endogenous factor and therefore appears inside the production function as an input. However, the relationship between output and technology is not the same as between output and other inputs, capital and labour. This is because while the output of an individual firm depends on its own level of capital and labour but also on the *technology used by other firms whose benefits also accrues* to it. Looking at the relationship between output and technology in this way we can write production function of an individual firm denoted by the subscript *i* as under :

$$Y_{it} = F(K_{it}, N_{it}, A_t)$$

Note that in the technology input subscript *i* does not appear because this technology may not be its exclusive input, but may be copied or imitated from others. The technology is not assumed to progress exogenously but to grow endogenously when more investment by firms takes place or may be the result of the efforts of labour. But some of the benefits of the new technology discovered and used by a firm will spill over to other firms in the economy. Paul Romer,[1] one of the pioneers of endogenous growth theory has put forward the view that *investment is a source of technological progress*. He distinguishes between *private returns* to capital and *social returns* to capital. According to Romer, an individual firm does not capture all the benefits of increase in its stock of capital, as it also creates benefits which are *external to the firm*. Capital accumulation by a firm, that is, investment by a firm causes not only increase in new *machines* but also *new ways of doing things*. These new better methods of doing things result either from deliberate investment in research and development and sometimes as accidental byproducts of investment activity by a firm. These new methods and ideas of doing things can be easily copied try others who also get benefits from these new methods.

This endogenous growth theory considers that whereas production function of a firm exhibits constant returns to scale *(i.e.,* constant returns as to all factors) but there occur *external increasing returns to scale.* These external increasing returns are due to the technological improvements which result from (1) rate of investment, (2) size of the capital stock, and (3) the stock of human capital.

This approach to endogenous technological change can be incorporated into neoclassical growth model. Let λ stand for rate of technological change, then the view that technological change is the result of investment[2] can be written as

$$\lambda = a + b\left(\frac{\Delta k}{y}\right) \qquad \dots (3)$$

Where a is exogenous component of technological progress, $b\left(\frac{\Delta k}{y}\right)$ is the endogenous component, $\frac{\Delta k}{y}$ being the rate of investment (*i.e.,* change in stock of capital expressed as a proportion of income growth). Since saving rate is exogenous and is equal to $\frac{\Delta k}{y}$, substituting s for $\frac{\Delta k}{y}$ in (3) we have

$$\lambda = a + bs \qquad \dots (4)$$

Now recall that in the neoclassical growth model,

1. Paul Romer, *Increasing Returns and Long-Run Growth*
2. For investment as a source of technical progress See M. Scott, A New Theory of Endogenous Economic Growth, *Oxford Review of Economic Policy,* Winter 1992 and M. King and M Robson, Investment and Technical progress *Oxford Review of Economic policy*, 1992.

$$\Delta k = sf(k) - (n + d)\, k \qquad \text{... (5)}$$

where n is rate of popultion growth and d is depreciation

To simplify our analysis we ignore depreciation (d). Therefore, equation (5) can be rewritten as

$$\Delta k = s\, f(k) - nk \qquad \text{... (6)}$$

Now, if in neoclassical model we consider labour-augmenting type of exogenous technological change which is of the type of Harrod neutral technological change, then $\lambda + n$ would represent the growth rate of augmented labour force (L), λ being the rate of technological change and n being the growth rate of simple labour. Therefore, substituting labour-augmenting labour force $\lambda + n$ for n in equation (6) we have

$$\Delta k = sf(k) - (\lambda + n)k \qquad \text{... (7)}$$

For steady state equilibrium we have

$$Sf(k)^* = (\lambda + n)k^* \qquad \text{... (8)}$$

From equation (4), we know that rate of technological progress (λ) is composed of exogenous and endogenous parts ($\lambda = a + bs$). Substituting $a + bs$ for λ in steady –state in equilibrium equation (8) we have

$$Sf(\overset{*}{k}) = (a + bs + n)\overset{*}{k} \qquad \text{...(9)}$$

The above equation (9) represents the steady growth rate equation of endogenous growth theory. *According to this, output (income) per worker will grow at the rate $\lambda = a + bs$. From this it follows that the increase in the saving rate and therefore rise in the investment rate will cause a permanently higher growth rate.* Therefore, there will be no tendency for convergence of the growth rate.

We can consider investment as a source of technical progress for various reasons. If investment simply consists of duplication of existing capital, then that investment does not lead to innovation or technological change. However, investment may lead to innovation as firms attempt to solve their problem, especially to raise their productivity. They will try to discover new methods or designs of machines which can raise productivity and for this purpose they will make investment. Such investment will lead to innovation or technical progress. For example, investment by car manufacturers in India has led to new designs and models of cars which are fuel efficient and pollution-free. Thus their investment in research and development has led to new innovations or technical progress.

Furthermore, if investment by a firm is successful, the other firms will also try to adopt them with some modifications which suit their needs. Thus expansion in investment may represent a sequence of innovations with each innovation improving upon the previous innovation. Such a type of technological progress has been called **learning by watching**. Beneficial external effects resulting from learning by watching are key determinants of economic growth. Therefore, policies to increase investment should be adopted. Because of the externalities *social returns* to investment exceed private returns. The rapid and quicker increase in overall growth can be achieved through Government adopting proper policies to promote investment in research and development.

Investment in Human Capital and Learning by Doing

In the above approach to endogenous technology the progress in technology is assumed to depend on growth of capital, that is, investment. New investment fosters innovations and improvements in machines and tools that also creates external benefits and lead to increasing returns for the economy as a whole. In an other important model of endogenous growth theory, *investment in human capital*, (that is, labour input) is also assumed to be the source of technological progress. Arrow introduced the concept of *learning by doing*. According to this, the greater the level of labour input, the greater is the scope for learning and acquiring of new skills. An endogenous growth model which lays stress on the accumulation of human capital has been developed by Lucas[3]. According to this model, labour can be devoted either to production or to the accumulation of human capital, that is, acquiring of new skills and knowledge. Acquiring of new skills and knowledge will not only make a worker more productive but also increase the productivity of capital and other workers in the economy. Each new knowledge or skill makes the next idea possible and so the knowledge can grow indefinitely. Let e be the proportion of labour input directly devoted to production and H be the human capital, then the Cobb-Douglas type production function can be stated as under:

$$Y = AK^{a}(HeL)^{1-a}$$

where the technology coefficient $A = H^b$ represents the external effect of human capital (H) on productivity of capital (K) and labour (eL). Since human capital (H) is a function of labour input, output per worker can be obtained as a function of capital and labour according to this approach, as with the earlier one of investment in physical capital. Though each firm faces constant returns to scale, there are increasing returns to the economy as a whole.

Policy Implications of New Growth Theory

New growth theory with its emphasis on endogenous technological change has important policy implications which in some important respects differ from the neoclassical growth theory. First. whereas neoclassical theory predicts that growth rates of different countries with same rates of saving and population growth and with access to the same technology will converge, in the endogenous growth theory there is no force leading to the convergence of growth rates of different countries with closed economies.[4] This is because of *the possibility of sustained long-term growth resulting from increasing returns to scale* which was not accounted for in the neoclassical theory. Growth rates of different countries in new endogenous growth theory will remain constant or differ depending on their saving rates and technological levels. This is because of large differences in investment in human capital, research and development and increasing returns or external benefits accruing from them. Furthermore, new growth theory emphasises that higher saving rate will ensure a higher long-run economic growth but not there is no any mechanism working which ensures that per capita income in poor countries will catch up with those of the rich countries with similar saving rates.[5] The external increasing returns to the accumulation of capital, both physical and human, implies that rate of return on capital in capital-abundant rich countries will not fall in the developed rich countries relative to the poor less-developed countries. As a matter of fact, it is possible that due to endogenous technological improvement, rate of return to capital in capital– abundant rich countries exceeds that of capital-scarce countries and as a result capital may not flow from rich to poor countries. It is noteworthy that "potentially high rates of return on investment offered by developing countries with low capital ratios are greatly eroded by lower levels of complementary investments in human capital (education), infrastructure or research and development (R & D)[6].

In sharp, contrast to the policy implication derived by some from neoclassical theory, important implication of endogenous growth theory is that because individual firms do not capture full benefits from the positive externalities created by their own investments, the free market will lead to the accumulation of less than optimal level of complementary capital[7]. This will cause lower rate of economic growth in them. Lastly, because of the externalities created by investment, the new endogenous theory of growth envisages greater role of Government in improving the efficiency of resource allocation and promoting investment to raise rate of economic growth in the developing

3. R. Lucas. "On the Mechanics of Economic Development", *Journal of Monetary Economics*, 22 (1988). pp. 3–42.
4. An important emperical study by Robert Barrow "*Determinants of Economic Growth : A Cross Country emperical Study*", find no evidence of convergence of growth rates.
5. Michael Tadaro, *Economic Development*, Addisen-Wesley, 6th' edition, 1997, p.p 92–93
6. *Ibid*, p. 93.
7. Todaro, *op. cit*. p. 93.

countries. The Government can directly make adequate investment in economic infrastructure such as power, communication, roads and highways and in human capital (*i.e.*, education and health care) which promote private investment and generate increasing returns to scale. Though in many respects endogenous growth theory is a mere extension of neoclassical theory of growth, it however, makes a departure from the neoclassical policy of free market and passive role of Government, To quote Todaro, "*in contrast to neoclassical counter revolution theories models of endogenous growth suggest an active role for public policy in promoting economic development through direct and indirect investment in human capital formation and the encouragement of foreign private investment in knowledge intensive industries such as computer software and tele-communications.*"[8]

Lastly, it may be noted that endogenous growth theory, like the neoclassical theory, focuses on supply–side factors determining economic growth and *totally neglects role of adequate growth in effective demand* for sustained long-run growth of the economy. As has been recently seen that in both the developed and the developing countries lack of effective demand due to sluggish investment, decline in exports and, in countries like India due to monsoon dependent decline in agricultural growth rate may come about. As result of lack of effective demand recession occur in the economy which slows down the short-run economic growth which may ultimately affect long-term growth rate. For instance, for the first time after the second world war, the Japanese economy which achieved very high growth states in the past has been experienced recessionary conditions and a very slow growth rate for almost a full decade now. This growth experience of the Japanese economy cannot be explained by new endogenous growth theory.

8. Todaro, *Economic Development*, Pearson Education (Singapore), 8th edition, p. 148.

CHAPTER 43

Theory of Economic Development With Surplus Labour : Lewis Model

An eminent development economist Arthur Lewis put forward his model of "*Economic Development with Unlimited Supplies of Labour*"[1] which envisages the capital accumulation in the modern industrial sector so as to draw labour from the subsistence agricultural sector. Lewis model has been somewhat modified and extended by Fei and Rains[2] but the essence of the two models is the same. Both the models (that is, one by Lewis and the other modified one by Fei-Ranis) assume the existence of surplus labour in the economy, the main component of which is the enormous disguised unemployment in agriculture. Further, they visualise 'dual economic structure' with manufacturing, mines and plantations representing the modern sector, the salient features of which are the use of reproducible capital, production for market and for profit, employing labour on wage-payment basis and modern methods of industrial organisation. On the other hand, agriculture represents the subsistence or traditional sector using non-reproducible land on self-employment basis and producing mainly for self-consumption with inferior techniques of production and containing surplus labour in the form of disguised unemployment. As a result, the productivity or output per head in the modern sector is much higher than that in agriculture. Though the marginal productivity in agriculture over a wide range is taken to be zero, the average productivity is assumed to be positive and equal to the bare subsistence level.

Lewis' Model of Development with Surplus Labour

In the labour-surplus models of Lewis and Fri-Ranis, the wage rate in the modern industrial sector is determined by the average productivity to which is added a margin (Lewis fixes this margin at 30%) which is required for furnishing an incentive for labourers to transfer themselves from the countryside to the urban industries as well as for meeting the higher cost of urban living. In this setting, the model shows how the expansion in the industrial investment and production or, in other words, capital accumulation outside agriculture will generate sufficient employment opportunities so as to absorb all the surplus labour from agriculture and elsewhere.

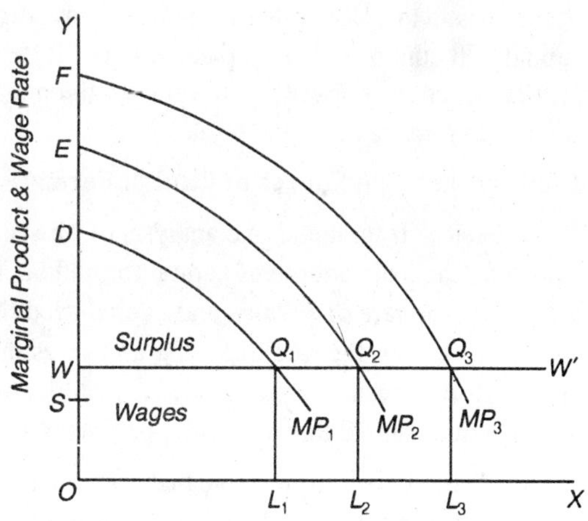

Fig. 43.1. *Capital Expansion and Growth in Labour Employment*

1. Authur Lewis, "Economic Development with Unlimited Supplies of Labour", *Machester School*, 22, May 1954.
2. C.H. Fei and Gustav Ranis, *Development of the Labour Surplus Economy*, Irwin, 1964.

The process of expansion and capital accumulation in the modern sector and the absorption of labour by it is explained by the accompanying Fig. 43.1 where *OS* represents the real wages which a worker would be getting in the subsistence sector, that is, *OS* is the average product per worker in the subsistence sector. *OW* is the wage rate fixed in the modern sector which is greater than *OS* (*i.e* average product in agriculture) by 30%. So long as surplus labour exists in the economy any amount of labour will be available to the modern sector at the given wage rate *OW*, which will remain constant. With a given initial amount of industrial capital, the demand for labour is given by the marginal productivity curve MP_1. On the basis of the principle of profit maximisation, at the wage rate *OW*, the modern sector will employ OL_1 labour at which marginal product of labour equals the given wage rate *OW*. With this the total share of labour *i.e.* total wages in the modern sector will be OWQ_1L_1 and WQ_1D will be the capitalists' surplus. Now, *Lewis assumes that all wages are consumed and all profits saved and invested.* When the capitalists will reinvest their profits for setting up new factories or expanding the old ones, the stock of capital assets in the modern sector will increase. As a result of the increase in the stock of industrial capital, the demand for labour or marginal productivity curve of labour will shift outward, for instance, from MP_1 to MP_2 in our diagram. With MP_2 as the new demand curve for labour and wage rate remaining constant at *OW*, OL_2 amount of labour will be employed in the modern sector. In this new equilibrium situation profit or surplus accruing to the capitalist class will be equal to WQ_2E which is larger than the previous $WQ_1 D$. The new surplus or profits of WQ_2E will be further invested with the result that capital stock will increase and the demand or marginal productivity curve for labour will further shift upward, say to MP_3 position. When the demand curve for labour is MP_3, employment of labour will rise to OL_3. In this way, the profits earned will go on being reinvested and expansion of the modern sector will go on absorbing surplus labour from the subsistence sector until all the labour surplus is fully absorbed in productive employment.

It is worth mentioning that in Lewis Model, the rate of accumulation of industrial capital and, therefore, the absorption of surplus labour depends upon the distribution of income. In this the share of profits and therefore rate of saving and investment will rise continuously in the modern sector and capital will continue to be expanded until all the surplus labour has been absorbed. Rising share of profits serves as an inventive to reinvest them in building industrial *capacity as well as a source of savings to finance it.*

Profit as the Main Source of Capital Formation

It is clear from the above analysis of Lewis model with unlimited supply of labour that profits constitute the main source of capital formation. The greater the share of profits in national income, the greater the rate of savings and capital accumulation. Thus with the expansion of the modern or capitalist's sector, the rate of saving and investment as percentage of national income will continuously rise. As a result, rate of capital accumulation will also increase relatively to national income. It is of course assumed that all profits or a greater part of profits is saved and automatically invested.

It is also evident from above that share of capitalist's profits depends on the share of the capitalist sector in the national product. As the capitalist or modern sector expands, the share of profits in national product will rise. This rise in the share of profits in national product is due to the assumptions of the model that wage rate remains constant and prices of the products produced by the capitalist sector do not fall with the expansion in output. To quote Lewis himself, "*If unlimited supplied of labour are available at constant real wage rate, and if any part of the profits is reinvested in productive capacity, profits will grow continuously relatively to the national income*".[3]

3. Arthur Lewis, *op.cit.*

A Critical Appraisal of Lewis Model

The validity and usefulness of the labour-surplus model of Lewis for developing countries like India depend of course on the extent of which their underlying assumption are valid for the economies in question. We are here not interested in validity of all the assumptions, explicitly or implicitly, made in this model. In our view the basic premise of this model is wrong and that makes it unrealistic and irrelevant for framing a suitable development strategy to solve the problem of surplus labour and unemployment. The basic premise of the model is that industrial growth can generate adequate employment opportunities so as to draw away all the surplus labour from agriculture in an over-populated developing country like India where population is currently increasing at the annual rate of around 2 per cent from 1951 to 2001. This premise has been proved to be a myth in the light of generation of little employment opportunities in the organised industrial sector during over fifty five years of economic development in India, Latin American and African countries.

For instance, in the 14 years (1991-2005) of industrial development in India during which fairly good rates of industrial production had been achieved, the *organised industrial employment* registered a negative growth rather than making any significant impact on the urban unemployment situation, and providing a solution to the labour-surplus problem in agriculture. Thus, the generation of adequate employment opportunities and as a result the absorption of surplus labour from agriculture in the expanding industrial sector has not found as predicted by Lewis model.

In may be pointed out here that migration of some workers from the rural to the urban areas in India has occurred as shown by the slight increase in the degree of urbanisation noticed in the various censuses but these immigrants to the urban areas have not been absorbed in the modern high-productivity employment, as envisaged by Lewis and Fei-Ranis. This is evident from the statistical data about meagre increase in employment in the organised sector. These immigrants to the urban areas have been mainly employed in petty trade, domestic service and casual work in which the disguised unemployment and poverty exist as acutely as in agriculture. Thus, as things are stand, the traditional sector of the economy is simply moving from the countryside into the cities in apparent contrast to the Lewis model.

Lewis Model Neglects the Importance of Labour Absorption in Agriculture

A grave weakness of the models of Lewis and Fei-Ranis is that they have ignored the generation of productive employment in agriculture. No doubt, Lewis in his later writings and Fei-Ranis in their modified and extended version of Lewis model have envisaged an important role for agricultural development so as to sustain industrial growth and capital accumulation. But they visualise such an agricultural development strategy that will *release labour force from agriculture* rather than absorbing them in agriculture. Thus to quote Fei and Ranis :

"In such a dualistic setting the heart of the development problem lies in the gradual shifting of the economy's centre of gravity from the agricultural to the industrial sector through *labour reallocation.* In this process each sector is called upon to perform a special role: productivity in the agricultural sector must rise sufficiently so that *smaller fraction of the total population can support the entire economy* with food and raw materials, thus enabling agricultural workers to be released; simultaneously, the industrial sector must expand sufficiently to provide employment opportunities for the released workers .... *labour reallocation must be rapid enough to swamp massive population increases if the economy's centre of gravity is to be shifted over time.*"[4]

4. Fei and Ranis, *op. cit.*

We have shown above that employment potential of organised industrial sector, given the capital intensive techniques used in it, is so little that labour reallocation between agriculture and industry and "smaller fraction of the total population being employed in agriculture" is just not possible in labour-surplus developing countries like India. Indeed, a good amount of employment opportunities can be generated in agriculture itself by capital accumulation in agriculture, adopting proper agricultural technologies and making appropriate institutional reforms in the pattern of land ownership.

Even about the African countries most of which do not suffer from the Malthusian problem of over-population but are currently faced with acute urban unemployment (especially of what is known as "*Unemployment of School Leavers*" majority of which have migrated from the villages to the urban areas) the expert opinion has veered round to the view of seeking solution of labour-surplus problem within agriculture. Thus Sara S. Berry remarks about the African experience : "Most students of the problem of rising African urban unemployment agree that the solution to the problem lies in raising incomes and employment opportunities in agriculture so as to ensure a new market equilibrium with more people productively employed in agriculture."[5]

Assumptions of Adequate labour-Absorptive Capacity of the Modern Industrial Sector. Another related shortcoming of development models of Lewis. Fei and Ranis is their assumption that the growth of industrial employment (in absolute amount) will be greater than the growth in labour force (which in India at present is of the order of about 12 million people per year). Because only then the organised industrial sector can absorb surplus labour from agriculture. The employment potential of industrial sector is so little that far from withdrawing labour currently employed in agriculture, it does not seem to be possible for organised industries and services, on the basis of existing capital-intensive technologies, even to absorb the new entrants to the labour force.

An important drawback of Lewis model is that it has neglected the importance of agricultural growth in sustaining capital formation in the modern industrial sector. When as a result of the expansion of capitalist modern sector, transfer of labour from agriculture to industry takes place, the demand for foodgrains will rise. If the output of foodgrains does not increase through agricultural development to meet the additional demand for foodgrains, prices of foodgrains will rise. With the rise in prices of foodgrains wages of industrial labour will increase. Rise in wages will lower the share of profits in the industrial product which in turn will slow down or even choke off the process of capital accumulation and economic development. Thus, if no allowance is made for agricultural growth, the expansion of modern sector and capital accumulation in it is bound to halted. Thus, neglect of agriculture in the development strategy pursued in India from the Second Plan to the Fourth Plan virtually resulted in stagnation in the industrial sector, during the period 1966-1979.

The Assumption of Constant Real Wage Rate in the Modern Sector. The assumption of constant real wages to be paid by the urban industrial sector until the entire labour surplus in agriculture has been drawn away by the expanding industrial sector is quite unrealistic. The actual experience has revealed a striking feature that in the urban labour markets where trade unions play a crucial role in wage determination there has been a tendency for the urban wages to rise substantially over time, both in absolute terms and relative to average real wages, even in the presence of rising levels of urban open unemployment . The rise in wages, as explained above, seriously impairs the development process of the modern sector in Lewis model.

5. Sara S. Berry, Economic Development with Surplus Labour : Further Complications Suggested by Contemporary African Experiences, *Oxford-Economic Papers*, June 1970.

It Neglects the Labour-Saving Nature of Technological Progress. A serious lacuna of the Lewis model from the viewpoint of employment creation is its neglect of the labour-saving nature of technological progress. It is assumed in the model, though implicity, that rate of employment creation and therefore labour transfer from agriculture to the modern urban sector will be proportional to the rate of capital accumulation in the industrial sector. Accordingly, the greater the rate of growth of capital formation in the modern sector, the greater the creation of employment opportunities in it. But if capital accumulation is accomplished by labour-saving technological change, that is, if the profits made by the capitalists are reinvested in more mechanised labour-saving capital equipment rather than in existing types of capital, then employment in the industrial sector may not increase at all. This is corraborated by the Indian experience where even with a very rate of industrial growth during 1991-2008 employment in the organised sector of the Indian economy has remained stagnant.

Lewis model has been reproduced in Fig. 43.2 with a modification that profits made are reinvested in labour-saving capital equipment due to the technoloical change that has taken place. As a result of this, marginal productivity curve does not shift uniformly outward but crosses the original marginal productivity curve from above. It is evident from Fig. 43.2 that with the constant wage rate *OW*, the employment of labour does not increase even though marginal productivity curve has shifted.

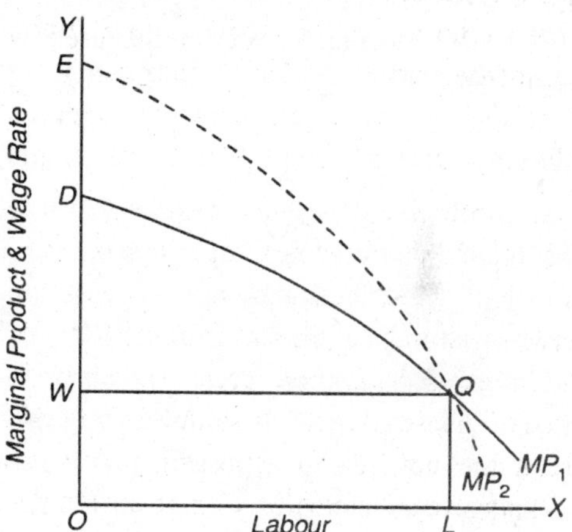

Fig. 43.2. *Capital Expansion with Labour-Saving Technological Change*

It will be observed from Fig. 43.2 that though employment of labour and total wage (*OWQL*) have remained the same, the total output has increased substantially, the area *OEOL*is much greater than the area *ODQL*. This illustration points to the fact that while the industrial output and profits of the capitalist class can increase, the employment and incomes of labour class remain unchanged. Although *GNP* has increased, labouring class has not received any benefit from it. It is not just theoretical illustration but has been actually borne out by the experience of industrial development of several developing countries. This experience shows that while industrial output has significantly increased, employment has lagged far behind.

Lewis Model Ignores the Problem of Aggregate Demand.

A serious factor which can slow down or even halt the expansionary process in Lewis model is the problem of deficiency of aggregate demand. Lewis assumes, though implicity, that no matter how much is produced by the capitalist or modern sector, it will find a market. Either the whole increment in output will be demanded by the people in the modern sector itself or it will be exported. But to think that entire expansion in output will be disposed of in this manner is not valid. This is because a good part of the demand for industrial products comes from the agricultural sector. If agricultural productivity and therefore incomes of the farming population do not increase, the problem of shortage of aggregate demand will emerge which will choke off the growth process in the capitalist industrial sector. However, once an allowance is made for the increase in agricultural productivity through a priority to agricultural development, the basic foundations of Lewis model crumble down. This is because a rise in agricultural productivity in Lewis model will mean a rise in wage rate in the modern capitalist sector. The rise in the wage rate will reduce the capitalist's profits which in turn will bring about a premature halting of the expansionary process.

Conclusion

Despite several limitations and drawbacks Lewis model retains a high degree of analytical value. It clearly points out the role of capital accumulation in raising the level of output and employment in labour-surplus developing countries. The model makes a systematic and penetrating analysis of the growth problem of dual economies and brings out some of crucial importance of such factors as profits and wages rates in the modern sector for determinating the rate of capital accumulation, economic growth and employment generation. It underlines the importance of intersectoral relationship (*i.e.* the relationship between agriculture and the modern industrial sector) in the growth process of a dual economy.

CHAPTER 44

Limitations and Relevance of Keynesian Economics for Developing Countries

Introduction

In the previous chapters we have explained the various elements of Keynesian macroeconomics. As studied before, Keynesian theory was mainly concerned with cyclical unemployment which arose in industrialised capitalist countries especially in times of depression. During the period of Greet Depression (1929–33), the developed capitalist countries faced a drastic fall in GNP resulting in severe unemployment. J.M. Keynes explained that it was fall in aggregate effective demand for goods and services that was responsible for depression and huge unemployment that arose during the period of depression. Keynes put forward a theory of income and employment which explained the determination of income and employment through aggregate demand and aggregate supply. In the early fifties although few economists caused doubts on the validity of the Keynesian theory as applied to the advanced developed countries of the West, a number of eminent Indian economists cast doubts on the applicability of Keynesian economics to the developing countries like India. Prominent among those who held that Keynesian theory was not relevant in the context of the under-developed economies, mention may be made of Dr. V.K.R.V. Rao[1] and Dr. A.K. Dass Gupta[2] who pointed out that the nature of the economic problems of the developing countries was quite different from the problems that arose during the Great Depression in the developed countries of the West and therefore the Keynesian theory of income and employment and the policy recommendations were not very helpful in the context of the then under-developed countries. In what follows we first explain this traditional view regarding the inapplicability and irrelevance of Keynesian economics to the developing countries like India. However, in recent years, in my view, after five decades of economic growth and development in the developing economies like the Indian many principles and postulates of Keynesian theory have become quite relevant to the problems of the present day developing countries. We discuss below these traditional and modern views about the relevance of Keynesian economics to the developing countries.

TRADITIONAL VIEW: LIMITATIONS IRRELEVANCE OF KEYNESIAN ECONOMICS FOR DEVELOPING COUNTRIES

The Demand-Deficiency Problem

The principle of deficiency of effective demand is perhaps the most important proposition put forward by J.M. Keynes. It was pointed out that Keynes explained that drastic decline in GNP and increase in involuntary unemployment that occurred during the period of depression was due to deficiency of aggregate demand caused by decrease in investment demand, but the problems of lack of economic growth, poverty and unemployment were due to entirely different reasons. Poverty and unemployment in developing countries, it was pointed out, was caused by more fundamental and

1. J.M. Keynes, *The General Theory of Employment Interest and Money*, Macmillan, 1936.
2. V.K.R.V. Rao Investment, Income and the Multiplier in an Underdeveloped Economy, *Indian Economic Review*, 1952.
3. A.K. Das Gupta Keynesian Economics and Underdeveloped countries, published in V.B. Singh (ed.), *Keynesian Economics — A Symposium*.

structural factors such as lack of capital stock relative to labour force of these economies. Thus, Dr. A.K. Das Gupta wrote, "Indeed whatever be the generality of the General Theory may be in the sense in which the term 'general' was used by Keynes the applicability of the propositions of the General theory to conditions of an underdeveloped economy is at best limited"[3].

Therefore, it was explained that Keynesian policy prescriptions to raise aggregate demand such as increase in Government expenditure by deficit financing cannot be adopted to accelerate the growth of income and employment. It was emphasised that the nature of unemployment prevailing in the developing countries was different in that it was of the type of chronic disguised unemployment caused by deficiency of physical capital and lack of wage goods[4] rather than decline in effective demand which was stressed by Keynes to be responsible for the rise in cyclical, involuntary and open unemployment.

Keynes' Policy Prescriptions are not Relevant

It was emphasised by Dr. V.K.R.V. Rao that Keynesian policy prescription of deficit financing to overcome depression, if adopted in the developing countries to finance increase in investment expenditure by the Government was likely to generate inflationary pressures in the developing countries rather than increasing real income, output and employment. In fact, Dr. V.K.R.V. Rao, among others, contended that in the developing countries it was classical economics which laid stress on increasing the rate of saving for accelerating rate of growth of income and employment was applicable and relevant rather than Keynesian economics which emphasised deficiency of effective demand. Thus, Dr. Rao ends his article, already quoted, "*It is the classical thesis which is operative for the other category (meaning, the underdeveloped countries) where you move from one level of development to a higher level of development.*"[5] He adds further, "old-fashioned prescription of '*work harder and save more*' still holds good as the medicine for economic progress, at any rate as far as the underdeveloped countries are concerned." [6] While Dr. V.K.R.V. Rao, Dr. A.K. Das Gupta and their followers laid stress on classical policy prescription of rapid accumulation of physical capital to accelerate economic growth and generate employment opportunities, Professor, Vakil and Brahmananda emphasised the rapid expansion of wage goods (i.e. essential consumer goods of which most important are foodgrains) as the remedy for accelerating growth and removing poverty and unemployment.

Keynesian Multiplier is Inapplicable to Underdeveloped Countries

In his well known paper quoted above, Dr. V.K.R.V. Rao emphasised that Keynesian investment multiplier is not applicable to underdeveloped economies. He showed that in underdeveloped countries the operation of multiplier leads to the increase in prices rather than output and employment. Therefore, according to him, in under-developed countries multiplier works in money terms and not in real terms. The reason is that there are essential conditions for the operation of *Keynesian multiplier* in real terms. One important condition is that the supply curve of output should be elastic so that when aggregate demand for goods increases as a result of the working of multiplier process, output should be adequately increased without bringing about rise in the price level. But it was asserted that since in underdeveloped countries there was little excess production capacity in consumer goods industries, the supply of goods could not be increased due to the desired extent.

The second condition for the working of multiplier in real terms without causing inflation is that the supply of working capital, raw materials, power can be easily increased to meet the increases in their demand as a result of the working of multiplier. This condition too was also not fulfilled in case of the underdeveloped countries like India.

3. A.K. Das Gupta, *op.cit.* p. 159
4. See A.K. Dass Gupta *op.cit.* and also P.R. Brahmananda, "The General Theory and the Problems of Development of Backward Areas " *Journal of the University of Bombay*, July 1952.
5. *Op. cit.* p. 218.
6. *Ibid*, p. 288

The third condition for the working of multiplier in real terms was that there should be involuntary open unemployment. That is, there are a large number of workers who are without work and would like to work if they find employment at the prevailing wage rates. However, as mentioned above, the nature of unemployment in developing countries is different. *Instead of open involuntary unemployment there is disguised unemployment.* These disguisedly unemployed workers do not realise that they are unemployed. They are supported by joint family system and they would like to remain in agriculture though their services are not actually required and in fact their marginal productivity in agriculture is zero or negligible. It was argued that they are not really involuntarily unemployed in the Keynesian sense and would not be readily coming to supply their labour services in expanding industries as a result of the operation of investment multiplier.[1] Thus, Dr. V.K.R.V. Rao argued that the particular form which unemployment in an underdeveloped country like India takes are for Keynesian purposes practically analogous with one of full employment and to that extent prevents the working of multiplier for increasing employment and output.[7]

It was further asserted by the economists in the fifties that in underdeveloped countries the principal occupation of the people was agriculture and the greater proportion of their income was spent on foodgrains as income elasticity of foodgrains was very high. On the other hand, when during the fifties, it was pointed out that supply of agricultural products was inelastic in the underdeveloped countries like India. This is because they thought production in agriculture was subject to uncertain natural factors like climate and rainfall. The farmers also lack other inputs like fertilisers, high quality seeds, irrigation facilities. In view of these constraints of the farmers, it was difficult for them to increase agricultural production, especially of foodgrains, adequately in response to the increase in aggregate demand resulting from the operation of investment multiplier. Thus, the result was the rise in prices of foodgrains which through wage-price spiral would result in inflation in the underdeveloped countries.

MODERN VIEW : RELEVANCE OF KEYNESIAN ECONOMICS IN SOME IMPORTANT RESPECTS

Much of the above arguments for irrelevance of Keynesian economics and instead the applicability of classical economics were advanced in the early fifties when the developing countries were industrially backward and there was a paramount need for underscoring the importance of capital accumulation through raising the rate of saving. That the inadequate growth in aggregate demand could serve as a constraint on the process of industrial growth was totally neglected. Thus, the fashion among economists in the fifties and sixties was to lay stress on the importance of supply-side factors with which classical economics was concerned to the total neglect of the demand-side of the problem of economic growth.

However, in the begining of the current millennium, the situation in the developing countries has vastly changed as a result of 50 years of economic development and structural transformation that has taken place in their economies. With this change in the economic conditions of the developing countries, a number of modern economists think that several crucial elements of Keynesian economics have become relevant to the present-day developing countries. The following elements of Keynesian economics has become relevant to the present-day developing countries:

1. The Problem of Demand Deficiency
2. Investment Behaviour of Entrepreneurs
3. Portfolio Choice
4. Theory of Consumption Function
5. Principle of Income Multiplier
6. Government Intervention to achieve economic stability and promote economic growth.

---

7. See Dr. V.K.R.V. Rao, *op.cit.* p. 159.
8. *Ibid.*

We discuss below how the above principles of Keynesian economics have become applicable to the present-day developing countries.

Problem of Deficiency of Effective Demand

Development experience of the last half a century has revealed that even in the developing countries the role of adequate growth in effective demand for achievement of sustained economic growth on which Keynes laid a great emphasis cannot be ignored. Late Prof. Sukhamoy Chakravarty rightly remarks, "*So far the demand has been disregaded on the ground that we always have full utilization of capacity as capital goods will necessarily earn positive return. Empirical evidence suggests that this is not a safe assumption to make even in a developing country i.e., capital can remain under-utilised when the capital services earn a positive price*".[9]

Even in the early fifties Ragnar Nurkse in his now well-known work, "*Problems of Capital Formation in Underdeveloped Countries*" had emphasised that investment in the developing countries was low because of narrow size of the market. According to him, inducement to invest in modern capital equipment in the developing countries is low because the size of the market, which is needed to ensure their optimum or full use is limited. By size of the market, he means the level of aggregate demand for goods. Of course, the demand deficiency problem to accelerate investment in the developing countries is of different nature than that mentioned by Keynes. The narrow size of the market in the developing countries is primarily due to the mass poverty prevailing in these countries. This mass poverty has been caused by lack of adequate economic growth, the existence of huge unemployment and underemployment and a highly skewed distribution of income. Poverty of the people means that they have small purchasing power so that the level of effective demand is low which adversely affect inducement to invest in consumer goods industries. As a result, sustained rapid growth of consumer goods industries is not possible. As a matter of fact, in certain periods of industrial development in these economies lack of effective demand has caused slowdown and deceleration of industrial growth and smaller utilisation of established capital stock. For example, in the period from mid-sixties to the late seventies (1966–1977) the Indian industrial sector witnessed a deceleration in its growth rate. Various explanations for it have been offered but the widely accepted view has been that of decline in effective demand caused by decrease in public investment during this period.[10] Besides, slowdown in industrial growth has also been attributed to the fall in growth of agricultural production resulting in lower incomes and demand of the rural people for the industrial products[11].

Apart form the above explanation of the actual slackening of demand for industrial products in certain specific periods of industrial growth, even theoretically, the emergence of slackening of effective demand causing under-utilisation of the existing capital stock in the industrial sector of the developing countries has been brought out. Thus Prof. Sukhamoy Chakravarty argues "industrial prices are usually quite sticky while agricultural prices are liable to fluctuate. As a result when agricultural prices go up, notably the prices of food, money wage rates remaining constant, the proportion of wage income spent on food rises, leading to the erosion in the residual purchasing power." This implies the slackness of demand for the industrial products, which will cause "the emergence of excess capacity in the industrial sector."[12] He further adds. "If, on the other hand, money wages go up, the general price level tends to rise with a concomitant *reduction in the real*

---

9. Sukhamoy Chakravarty, Keynes, Classics and the Developing Economies, printed in his *Selected Economic Writings*, Oxford University Press, 1993, p. 23.
10. See C. Rangarajan; Agricultural Growth and Industrial Performance India, 1982.
11. See K.N. Raj, Growth and Stagnation of Indian Industrial Development, *Economic and Political Weekly*, Annual Number 1997 and Sukhamoy Chakravarty. On the Question of Home Market and Prospects of Industrial Growth, *Economic and Political Weekly*, Special Number, April 1979. See also C. Rangarajan, *op. cit.*
12. Sukhamoy Chakravarty, Keynes, Classics and Developing Countries, *op.cit.*

purchasing power of 'relatively fixed income recipients' a category which for this purpose should include even workers in the unorganised sector, beneficiaries of government transfer payments etc."[13] This adversely affects demand for industrial products.

Prof. Chakravarty also explains that the use of imported capital-intensive technology in various sectors of the economy results in highly skewed distribution of income. which causes slackening of demand and emergence of excess capacity in the industrial sector. He thus writes, "the importation of modern capital intensive technology frequently accentuates the problem by generating a highly skewed income distribution which restricts the market size further, making it more profitable to sell lower volumes at a higher profit margin."[14]

Recent Demand Deficiency Problem in the Indian Economy : It may be noted that since mid 1996 till date (April 2003), that is, in the last six years the Indian economy has again witnessed a slowdown in industrial growth. There is a general consensus that this slowdown in industrial growth has been mainly caused by decline in effective demand. The demand from all important sources namely, agriculture, investment and exports have decreased. Thus, authors of Economic Survey (1998–99) write, "*The slowdown in industrial growth may be attributed primarily to slacking in aggregate demand.*[15] Among the factors causing this slackening of aggregate demand three factors have been mentioned : (i) fall in demand for Indian exports, (2) decline in consumption demand by the rural people due to negative growth in agriculture, for example in 1997–98, 1999–2000, 2000–01, and 2002-03 and (3) slow growth of investment, both by the public and private sector.

From our above analysis of the relevance of demand deficiency as a constraint on industrial growth, it should not be understood that supply-side factors such as raising the rate of saving and capital formation to accelerate economic growth are unimportant. *What is being emphasised here is that it is not adequate to rely merely on supply-oriented growth models such as the one used by IMF and World Bank whose structural adjustment reforms seek to tackle only supply-side factors determining economic growth to the utter neglect of the fact that economic growth may also be demand-constrained.*[16]

It is clear from above that the industrial growth in the developing countries may also be demand-constrained, apart from constraints of resources such as rate of saving, stock of capital, infrastructure facilities, and raw materials availability.

Investment Behaviour in Developing Countries

Keynesian economics is also relevant to the developing countries with regard to its analysis of investment behaviour as distinct from the classical analysis. Classical economists did not distinguish between decision to save and decision to invest. According to them, decisions regarding saving and investment were coterminus. *Keynes distinguished between decision to invest and save and argued that it was investment that determined saving and not the other way around.* According to him, when investment goes up, income will increase through the operation of multiplier and at a higher level of income more will be saved.

An important contribution made by Keynes to the theory of investment refers to the role of *business expectations* in determining investment. According to him, the rate of investment is determined by rate of interest on the one hand and marginal efficiency of capital on the other. Marginal efficiency of capital refers to the expected rate of return on investment. The marginal efficiency of capital depends on the state of business expectations regarding future prospective yields from the investment currently made.

13. *Op. cit.* pp. 23-24.
14. *Op. cit.* p. 27.
15. For similar view see V.N. Pandit, Macroeconomic Characteristics of the Indian Economy: Theories, Facts and Fancies, in Prabhat Patanaik (ed.) *Macroeconomics*, Oxford University Press, 1997.
16. For similar views, See Sukhamoy Chakravarty, *op. cit.* p. 24.

When businessmen become pessimistic about future prospective yields, the marginal efficiency of capital declines which adversely affects investment.This investment behaviour as visualised by Keynes is as much relevant to the investment in the modern sector of the developing countries as to the industrialised developed economies. Given this investment behaviour, "*It is then no longer sufficient that the community's propensity to save should be stimulated. We also need to ensure that investment climate is suitably improved*".[11] In building up favourable investment climate business expectations have to be influenced through appropriate fiscal and monetary measures adopted by the Government. Writing about investment behaviour in the contemporary countries, Prof. Chakravarty further writes, "given the present state of technical knowledge, there is much greater use of fixed capital in industrial processes. Since decisions to invest in fixed capital imply commitment of resources to a prolonged and uncertain future, the question of time and uncertainty becomes crucial. At this stage we have to introduce the problem of expectations which bring us into the domain of Keynes' theory."[12]

It may be noted that the periodic decline in private investment in India which is an important factor causing slowdown in industrial growth, can be explained in terms of '*animal spirits*', a term used by Keynes to refer to the waves of pessimistic and optimistic expectations of investors. Thus, due to political and economic uncertainty as well as due the uncertainty about the ability of the Government to pursue certain crucial economic reforms, there is lack of investors' confidence which has prevented them from investing in new shares and physical capital assets.

The above analysis clearly brings out the relevance of Keynes' investment analysis to the developing countries.

Portfolio Choice by Investors

Another important element of Keynesian analysis which is relevant to the developing countries is related to portfolio choice. Since classical economists were concerned with the economy where there existed a commodity money and credit played no role in it, they were not concerned with portfolio choice. In the modern exchange economy even in developing countries like India credit plays a crucial role and portfolio choice by the investors, at least among three types of assets, namely, bonds and shares, physical capital assets and money balances (for example, in the form of bank deposits) must be made. In the developing countries the situation may arise when due to high capital costs and low prospective yields expected from them the investors may not be induced to invest in physical assets and new bonds or shares of companies and instead opt for keeping their savings in the form of money balances (for example, in time deposits of banks).

It is important to note that in recent years (1997-2003) such a Keynesian type situation is prevailing in the Indian economy where investment in shares and physical capital assets by households have declined and instead investment in bank deposits greatly increased.[13] *Economic Survey* of Government of India for the year 1998-99 makes a special mention of such a change in the portfolio choice by the households. Thus, it writes, "*The uncertainty combined with performance of stock markets since the boom of 1994 and lack of trust in issuing companies and market intermediaries has also led to a shift of retail investors from riskier investment into safe heavens like bank deposits and post-office savings.*"[14] The same behaviour has been witnessed in 2008-09 in India when following the global financial crisis, the sharp decline in prices of corporate shares and mutual fund occurred, the people in large number switched over to investment in fixed deposits of banks.

The portfolio choice has also caused stagnation of investment in the years 1996-2002, which, as seen above, can not be explained in terms of classical economics. In fact, the followers of classical

---

11. Sukhamoy, Chakravarty, *op. cit.*
12. *Ibid.*
13. See Annual Reports of RBI for Years 1996, 1997 1998, 1999, 2000, 2001.
14. Government of India, *Economic Survey*, 1998-99, p. 6.

economists think that due to relative shortage of physical capital in the developing countries, rate of return on investment must be high, which, as seen above, is contrary to what has been actually observed. This clearly brings out the correctness of Keynes's fundamental insight into the determination of investment and portfolio choice. To quote Prof. Chakravarty again, "We can easily imagine situations where people try to shy away from investing in physical assets, the rate of return and the rate of interest is such as to give an edge to holding savings in the form of cash balances. The *resulting situation will be of Keynesian type.*"[21] Elaborating further he writes that "Uncertainties surrounding physical investment decisions are often much larger in developing countries and the cost of making a wrong decision is often quite high in a market which is very often quite small and slowly growing".[22]

It is clear from above that with regard to portfolio choice Keynes's insight was quite significant and is relevant to the behaviour of investors both in the developed and developing countries.

Keynes's Consumption Function

An important contribution of Keynes was his consumption function. Classical economists thought that rate of interest was the dominant influence on decision to consume and save. However, Keynes argued that consumption is a function of current level of absolute income ($C = a + bY$) where C is the amount of consumption and Y is the current level of absolute income. Using consumption expenditure data of the Indian economy researchers have found that in accordance with Keynes' consumption function, disposable income is the dominant determinant of private consumption expenditure in the Indian economy and further that rate of interest does not play any significant role in determining consumption.[23] Besides current income, income distribution and the amount of wealth which were considered by Keynes as objective factors determining consumption have also been found to be important factors determining consumption expenditure. It is interesting to note that no empirical evidence in favour of post-Keynesian theories of consumption, namely, Modigliani's Life Cycle theory of consumption and Friedman's Permanent Income hypothesis of consumption have been found applicable to India.[24] Thus, Keynes's principle of consumption function is very relevant to the developing countries like India and accordingly it has been extensively used in various econometric models of the Indian economy.[25]

Keynesian Multiplier and the Present-Day Developing Countries

As shown above, it was explained by V.K.R.V. Rao and others that in the developing countries Keynesian multiplier does not work in raising real income or output and employment but instead it works only in money terms which gives rise to inflationary pressures in the economy. The inapplicability of the Keynesian multiplier was based on the assumption that in the developing economies capital stock (or production capacity) tended to be fully utilised and there existed no excess capacity in consumer goods industries. Further, irrelevance of multiplier to the developing countries was based on the premise that most of the demand generated by increase in investment was directed towards foodgrains whose supply could not be easily increased.

But the situation in the present-day developing countries has substantially changed. For example, in the Indian economy today (*i.e.*, in the year 2003) there exists a good deal of excess capacity in consumer goods industries and also during the periods of deceleration in industrial growth of 1966-1977 and 1997-2003 a lot of excess capacity existed in the consumer goods industries. Further, thanks to the green revolution even foodgrains production can be increased in response to the rise in demand for them. Thus, in the present prevailing situation of unutilised capital stock in consumer goods industries, the increase in investment will produce a real multiplier effect on increase in output and employment, though due to some supply-side bottlenecks such as lack of infra-

---

21. *Op. cit.*, pp. 26-27.
22. *Ibid.*, p. 27.
23. See V.N. Pandit, *op.cit.*, p. 204.
24. *Ibid.*
25. *Ibid.*

structure such as power, good roads, highways and ports and imperfections in the Indian economy the size of multiplier is not as high as warranted by the high marginal propensity to consume. Even where there is no excess capacity, demand generated by stepping up of investment, private or public, leads to more investment for expansion of productive capacity which is usually termed as the acceleration effect.[26] Indeed, the combined working of multiplier and accelerator, which is called *super-multiplier*, can take place as a result of increase in investment, private or public, in the present context of the developing countries.

Role of Government Intervention

A fundamental departure from classical economics made by Keynes related to the intervention by the Government for regulating the economy if full employment is to be re-established. Keynes showed that if left free the market mechanism would not work to restore automatically full employment if the economy finds itself in the grip of depression caused by deficiency of effective demand arisen due to the fall in marginal efficiency of capital. The same applies to the problem of sustained economic growth in the developing countries. If left completely free to the market mechanism there is no guarantee that sustained economic growth will be achieved in the developing countries. In the developing countries, the Government has to intervene by way of adoption of suitable fiscal and monetary policies to stimulate not only private investment to achieve rapid growth but also to ensure growth with price stability. Besides, for achieving sustained economic growth it requires that Government should step up public investment in building up economic infrastructure such as power, telecom, irrigation, ports, roads and highways to tackle supply-side bottlenecks to economic growth but also to invest in social capital such as education, public health. In the context of developing countries, stepping up public investment is likely to stimulate private investment rather than reducing it. Contrary to the popular perception, the analysis of empirical data of the Indian economy by Professors Pandit, Krishnamurthy, and Sharma find clear evidence for **crowding-in-effect** of public investment.[27] Public investment not only generates demand for the private sector but also improves infrastructural facilities such as power, transport, communication, which help private sector investment and stimulates overall growth of the economy. All this is contrary to classical economics which believes in *Laissez Faire* policies.

From the foregoing analysis we conclude that certain crucial elements of Keynesian analysis have become relevant to the present-day developing countries.

QUESTIONS FOR REVIEW

1. Discuss the nature of unemployment in an under-developed country. Explain the limitations of Keynesian tools and remedies in reducing unemployment in the under-developed countries.
2. How far is the Keynesian theory of income and employment applicable to developing countries?
3. Discuss the nature of unemployment in developing countries like India. How far can Keynesian theory of income and employment be used to remove unemployment in developing countries?
4. What is the Keynesian prescription for raising the level of employment in an advanced capitalist economy ? Can this prescription help in solving the unemployment problem of a developing country like India ?
5. Explain in what respects Keynesian macro-economic analysis is relevent to the present-day Indian economy.

---

26. In case of investment in Indian industries Prof. V.N. Pandit finds some evidence in favour of the acceleration hypothesis. See his "Macroeconomic Characteristics of the Indian Economy", in Prabhat Patnaik (ed.) *Macroeconomics*, Oxford University Press, p. 205.
27. See, K. Krishnamurthy, V.N. Pandit and P.D. Sharma, Parameters of Growth in a Developing Economy: The Indian Experience, *Journal of Quantitative Economics*, 1989.

CHAPTER 45

Nature of Unemployment and Development Strategies in Labour-Surplus Developing Countries

As explained in the previous chapter, Keynesian theory is mainly concerned with cyclical unemployment which emerges in the developed capitalist countries, specially in times of depression. During the period 1929-33, the developed capitalist economies suffered from serve depression which caused huge magnitude of unemployment. Keynes analysed this cyclical type of unemployment and asserted that it was caused by deficiency of aggregate demand. That is, unemployed in advanced developed countries generally arises in a short period, say two to three years in *recessionary* phase of business cycle due to deficiency of aggregate demand. When the economy recovers from recession in these advanced countries, the cyclical unemployment disappears and as a result full-employment comes to prevail. Thus, unemployment in developed countries is a short-run phenomenon. On the other hand, the nature of unemployment in under-developed countries is quite different; *it is of chronic and long-term nature*. It is now recognised that the chronic unemployment and under-employment in less developed countries are not due to the lack of aggregate effective demand which, according to J.M. Keynes, was responsible for unemployment in developed countries in times of depression. Rather it is caused by the operation of basic strucutral factors and stated to be due to the lack of land, capital and other complementary resources in relation to the total population and labour force. In the pehnomenon examined by Keynes, not only labour force but also capital equipment was unemployed due to the deficiency of aggregate effective demand. In other words, in the Keynesian scheme, both the labour force and capital equipment were crying out for full employment which could be achieved by raising the level of aggregate monetary expenditure. Thus, according to Joan Robinson : "*Keynes' theory has little to say, directly, to the under-developed countries, for it was framed entirely in the context of an advanced industrial economy, with highly developed financial institutions and a sophisticated business class. The unemployment that concerned Keynes was accompanied by under-utilisation of capacity already in existence. It had resulted from a fall in effective demand. The unemployment of under-developed economies arises because capacity and effective demand never have been great enough*"[1].

Lack of Capital as the Cause of Unemployment in Developing Countries

In sharp contrast to deficiency aggregate demand which is responsible for cyclical unemployment in the developed countries, lack of capital stock with which to employ labour is said to be the basic cause of unemployment in labour-surplus developing countries such as ours. In the modern world, man by himself can hardly produce anything. Even the primitive man needed some elementary tools like the bow and arrow to engage in hunting for the earning of his livelihood. With the growth of technology and specialisation, he needs much more capital with which to engage in the productive activity. If he is an agriculturist, he needs a piece of land and also a plough, a pair of oxen, seeds and some foodgrains and other necessities of life to sustain himself during the period of sowing to the reaping of the harvest. In the industrial sector, he needs factories to work in and machines to work with. All these aids to production belong to the community's stock of capital. *Now, if the working force grows faster than the stock of capital of a country, the entire addition of labour force cannot be absorbed in productive employment because not enough instruments of production would be there to employ them. The resulting unemployment is known as the long-term or chronic unemployment.*

1. Joan Robinson, *Economic Philosphy*, p. 119

A nation's stock of capital can be enlarged by increased investment which in the absence of any unutilised resources, requires additional saving on the part of the community. The concern of the classical economists was to ensure that the rate of capital formation was kept sufficiently high so that employment opportunities were successively enlarged to absorb the additions to the working force of a country as a result of population growth. This is also the problem that the developing countries like India are facing today. In recent times, the labour force in India has been growing at more than 2 per cent per year, yet our rate of investment expressed as a percentage of our stock of capital has not been growing at a fast enough rate so as to keep pace with the growth of population. As a result, the country's ability to offer productive employment to the new entrants in the labour market has been severely limited. This manifests itself in two things: first, the prevalence of large-scale open unemployment in the urban areas as evidenced by the statistics of employment exchanges; second, it manifests itself in the form of under-unemployment as well as disguised unemployment in agriculture in the rural areas.

The existence of unemployment due to lack of capital or other co-operating factors was an important question which was discussed by Marx in the context of advanced industrialised countries. Therefore, such unemployment has sometimes been called *Maxian unempoyment*[2] as distinguished from Keynesian unemployment which is caused by the deficiency agregaed demand. According to Marx, the number of workers employed by the modern industries depends upon the amount of capital in existence, and there is what he called, "*reserve army of unemployed labour*" because there is inadequate capital to employ all the available labour.[3] However, in our view, Maxian unemployment (or reserve army of unemployed labour is more of the nature of *technological unemployment* caused by the use of highly capital intensive or mechanised techniques of production rather than the deficiency of capital stock as such.

Thus, the standard explantation for the existence of labour surplus or unemployment and under-employment in less developing countries like India is that as compared with the magnitude of population and labour force there is limited availability of capital or complementary resources which include land, factories, machines, tools and implements–the means with which labour produces. Now, if the population grows faster than the stock of capital of a country, the entire addition to the labour force cannot be absorbed in productive employment.

Capital as the major bottleneck to growth of employment was emphasised by Harrod-Domar model[4] of economic growth in which capital accumulation plays a pivotal role and according to which rate of growth of output depends upon the proportion of national income saved. Thus, according to this model the rate of growth of output depends upon the proportion of total investment to national income divided by the capital-output ratio, *i.e.*,

$$g = \frac{I}{v}$$

where

g = rate of growth of output,

I = rate of investment (defined as proportion of national income),

v = capital-output ratio.

2. See Joan Robinson, *An Essay on Marxian Economics.*
3. It may also be noted that, according to Marx, accumulation of industrial capital, that is, establishment of large-scale factories and machines displaces labour engaged in handicrafts or artisan activities because the latter would not be able to withstand the competiton from the former. Marx believed that the accumulation of industrial capital could never proceed fast enough to create employment for all who were displaced by the new machines. Therefore, *Marxian unemployment* has been referred to as *"technological unemployment"*.
4. Harrod-Domar Model was originally developed to explain the conditions for steady growth in developed industrialised countries but with slight extension this model has been extensively used in economic planning of less developed countries to explain the problem of growth of both output and employment

Harrod-Domar model assumes capital-coefficients (i.e., capital-output ratio and capital-labour ratios) to remain constant. With constant capital-output and capital-labour ratios, the more the capital, the more will be both output and employment. Therefore, when adapted to the less developed countries, this model suggests that the *rate of growth of output and therefore of employment is determined by the growth of capital stock.* Thus, according to the Harrod-Domar model, the solution to the problem of unemployment in labour-surplus developing countries lies in sufficient increase in the rate of investment or capital accumulation. It is important to note that *in this model and the various strategies of growth based on it considers stepping up investment and capital accumulation in the modern industrial sector*. The increase in capital formulation in agriculture to promote growth of employment opportunities was not generally considered in these industrialisation, led development strategies.

Lack of Wage Goods and Unemployment in Developing Countries

It is worth mentioning a dissenting view regarding the cause of unemployment and under-employment in developing countries. This dissenting view had been put forward by Prof. P.R. Brahmananda and C.N. Vakil of Bombay University. According to them, the basic cause of unemployment in developing countries is the deficiency of the availability of essential consumer goods such as foodgrains, often called *wage goods*. They point out that when the unemployed people or disguisedly unemployed people who are withdrawn from agriculture are engaged in some public works, they will have to be supplied with wage-goods so that employed labourers can subsist. If the wage-goods are not sufficiently available, their employment in capital-creation works cannot be sustained. Given the real wage rate, a particular number of people can be employed in the economy, depending upon the supply of wage-goods in the economy. Now, the total quantity of wage-goods required to employ all the disguised unemployed workers in agriculture, according to them, would exceed the actual available supply of wage-goods even when the release of wage goods by the withdrawal of disguised unemployed is taken into account. Thus, according to Prof. Brahmananda and Vakil,[5] there exists a *wage-goods* gap which is the fundamental cause of unemployment in labour-surplus developing countries

A prominent Indian economist Prof. A.K. Sen in his study for ILO has also emphasised the supply of wage-goods in determining employment in developing countries. According to Prof. Sen, the quantum of wage employment in the economy depends on the total supply of wage-goods on the one hand and thc real wage-rate on the other. If E represents the quantum of employment, M represents the supply of wage-goods and W, the real wage-rate, then the employment which can be provided will be given by the following equation.[6]

$$E = \frac{M}{W}$$

It is thus evident from Sen's above equation that if the supply of wage-goods (M) is less than the required supply to provide all labour force, then all workers cannot be fully employed, which will result in the emergence of unemployment. Thus, to generate enough employment and solve the problem of unemployment and under-employment, the wage-goods industries, especially agriculture, should be accorded a high priority in the startegy of economic development.

Most of the unemployment in underdeveloped countries is of a different nature from that in advanced and developed countries. A major part of unemployment in the present-day developed countries is of cyclical nature which is due to *deficiency of aggregate effective demand.* But

---

5. C.N. Vakil and P.R. Brahmananda, "*Planning for an Expanding Economy*". Vora and Co., 1956, pp. 111-112.
6. Amartya Sen, *Technology and Employment*, Oxford University Press.

most of the unemployment in developing countries is not cyclical. Thus, in developing countries, there is not much Keynesion type short-term unemployment. Instead, it is a chronic problem.

Use of Capital Intensive Techniques and Unemployment

An important factor responsible for slow growth of employment has been the use of capital-intensive techniques of production, even in consumer goods industries where alternative labour-intensive techniques are available. Even before 1991, under the industrial policy resolution 1956, the development of consumer goods industries were left open for the private sector. However, private sector prefers to invest in highly capital-intensive plants and equipment on the basis of technology developed in labour-scarce western countries. It is argued by them the alternative labour-intensive techniques have low productivity and small surplus-generating capacity. However, the important reason for the use of capital-intensive techniques has been the availability of cheap capital. Even firms in modern small industry sector which were expected to generate large employment opportunities have also tended to use capital-intensive techniques of production. Thus, Prof. J.C. Sandesara states, "*the availability of cheap capital has tended to encourage the modern small-scale industries sector to over-capitalise and use more capital-intensive methods of production and thus reduce employment potential*"[7].

In agriculture, reckless mechanisation of various agricultural operations despite the existence of surplus labour has reduced the employment-augmenting effect of new high-yielding technology involving the use of HYV seeds, fertilisers and pesticides. This has prevented the generation of enough employment opportunities in rural areas.

Now, a pertinent question is why capital-intensive techniques are used in industries despite the condition of labour-abundance in the economy. First reason is the *relatively low price of capital*. Relatively low price of capital has caused by (*a*) lower rate of interest, (*b*) liberal depreciation allowance on capital investment permitted in the taxation system of the country, (*c*) relatively cheap capital equipment imported from abroad. Second, higher wages of labour in the organised sector relative to their productivity under pressure from trade unions. Thirdly, rigid labour laws also discourage the employment of labour. It is difficult to retrench labour even when it is not required in case an industrial unit becomes sick and proposes to close down or exit.

Fourthly, Research and Development (R & D) activity has not been adequately directed to discover and identify labour-intensive appropriate techniques to be used in industries which, though labour-intensive, have also reasonably good productivity.

Neglect of the Role of Agriculture in Employment Generation

An important factor responsible for slow growth of employment opportunities is the neglect of agriculture for generating employment opportunities. The general perception, as existed in the first three five year plans in India (1951-65) as well as in the theoretical models of growth for dualistic economies such as Lewis "*Economic Development with Unlimited Supplies of Labour*" was that agriculture already contained surplus labour and it was required to withdraw this surplus labour from agriculture and employ them in the modern industrial sector. By the mid-sixties it was realised that not to speak of employing new entraints to the labour force year after year, the modern industrial sector could not absorb productivily even a fraction of the then existing unemployed persons in the forcible feature.

Besides, an important cause of unemployment prevailing in the rural areas of developing countries like India is inequitable distribution of land so that many agricultural households have *no adequate access to land* which is an important asset for agricultural production and

7. J.C. Sandesara, *Small-scale Enterprises in Industrial Development. The Indian Experience* (*1998*), Sage Publications, Delhi.

employment. Sub-division of land holdings under the pressure of rapid population growth since 1951 has further reduced access to land for several agricultural households. As a result, many persons who were self-employed in agriculture have become landless agricultural labourers who suffer from acute unemployment and under-employment.

Agriculture though containing surplus labour can generate employment opportunities if proper strategy for its development is adopted. For instance, the emperical evidence shows that on an irrigated hectare of land the number of man-hours employed is almost twice that on the unirrigated land per hectare. Irrigation requires more labour input for watering the fields, but also since output per hectare on irrigated land is much higher, more labour is used for harvesting and threshing the crop. Besides, irrigation makes the adoption of double cropping possible which greatly raises the employment potential of agriculture.

It is worth noting that new agricultural technology, commonly called green revolution technology, involving the use of HYV (High Yielding Varieties) seeds, greater use of fertilisers and pesticides along with water is highty labour absorptive. What is equally important, this new green revolution technology is *size-neutal*, that is, it can be equally well adopted by small farmers. Further, HYV seeds are of short-duration type, that is, they mature in a short time so that they make multiple cropping more feasible. The use of double or multiple cropping greatly enhances the opportunities of employment generation in agriculture. The experience of Punjab, Haryana and Western UP is a shining example of large employment generation in agriculture. What is needed for the generation of large employment opportunities in agriculture is that the new green revolution technology should be widely diffused and adopted in the backward and lagging agricultural regions in India.

Lack of Infrastructure

We have explained above lack of physical capital with which labour is equipped for productive employment as the cause of unemployment prevailing in the developing countries like India. By capital we generally mean machines, plant & equipment, factory buildings etc. But a similar factor responsible for huge unemployment prevailing in these countries is lack of infrastructure such as roads, power, telecommunications, highways, irrigation facilities in agriculture. Inadequate availability of infrastructure is a great obstacle for the generation of opportunities for productive employment.

It follows from above that unemployment and under-employment prevailing in India and other developing countries is *not cyclical Keynesian type of unemployment caused by decline in aggregate demand.* Unemployment, and under-employment in India are caused by more basic structural factors such as lack of capital, use of capital-intensive technologies, lack of access to land for agricultural household, lack of infrastructure, rapial growth of population resulting in large annual increments in labour force year after year.

THE CONCEPT OF DISGUISED UNEMPLOYMENT

At the theoretical level, the existence of disguised unemployment in the case of overpopulated countries such as India has been hotly debated. However, Professor Ragnar Nurkse, Arthur Lewis, Gustav Ranis and John C.H. Fei, P.N. Rosenstein Rodan, Vakil-Brahmananda, Amartya Sen and many others are firmly of the view that in the densely populated countries such as India, Pakistan, Egypt and Bangladesh, disguised unemployment in agriculture exists on a large scale. Some definitions of disguised unemployment are worth mentioning. Ragnar Nurkse defines the disguised unemployment in the following way : "These countries suffer from large-scale disguised unemployment in the sense that even *with the unchanged techniques* of agriculture, a large part of the population engaged in agriculture could be removed without reducing agricultural output. That is the definition of the concept of disguised unemployment as applied to *the situation with which we are concerned.* The same farm output could be obtained with a smaller labour force... In technical terms, the marginal productivity of labour is zero."[8] Professor Rosenstein Rodan describing the disguised unemployment as the "basic concept which has a clear and unequivocal m aning" defines it as "*that amount of population in agriculture which can be removed from it without any change in the method of cultivation, without leading to any reduction in output*".

From the above definitions of disguised unemployment, it is clear that its removal or withdrawl involves *ceteris paribus* condition. Thus, changes in the production techniques are especially rules out. In estimating disguised unemployment, to quote Nurkse again, "We exclude technological advance, more equipment, mechanisation, better seeds, improvements in drainage, irrigation and other such conditions". It may, however, be noted that the concept of disguised unemployment does admit *changes in organisation* or production and work (as distinguished from the *changes in technology and the amount of capital equipment and other cooperating factors*) when some workers are withdrawn from agriculture. To quote Nurkse again, "One thing, however, one needs not and probably cannot exclude and that is better organisation. If surplus labour is withdrawn from the land, the remaining people will not go on working in quite the same way. We may have to allow for changes in the manner and organisation of work including possibly a consolidation of scattered strips and plots of land.[9]

Another worth-noting point about disguised unemployment is that it is applicable to self-employed farmers of extended family system and does not apply to the wage employment which usually takes place on the large sized capitalist farms. Thus, the U.N. group of experts writes "the significance of the term 'disguised' is that it is applied only to persons who are not normally engaged in wage employment, but are self-employed". They further say : "The term is not applied to wage labour; presumably employers will not employ a labourer for wages unless his labour increases the product."

Prof. Amartya Sen's Analysis of Disguised Unemployment

Though the concept of disguised unemployment visualises production aspect of unemployment, it mainly manifests itself in idleness, that is, time not worked. In other words, disguised unemployment appears in the form of reduction in the hours worked in a day or a week and days in a week, or a month or year. As long as more work opportunities are available on the family farms, the additional labour is employed for that and as a result total output increases, though at a dimisnishing rate. When all the work opportunities on the farm are exhausted, no more addition to labour input will bring about increase in output. When the size of the families continues to increase due to the rapid growth of population and when alternative employment opportunities outside their families are not available, the additional members have to be absorbed on the family farms. Since on the family farms a point reaches beyond which no increase in labour input leads to the rise in total output, additional workers are absorbed by sharing of the work among more workers rather than by increasing the quantum of labour input employed on the farms. In other words, the same quantity of labour is now applied by more workers. As a result, the number of working hours performed by all labourers in a day, or week and days in a month or year are reduced.

Distinction between marginal productivity of labourers and marginal productivity of labour. In explaining the concept of disguised unemployment, Amartya Sen has drawn the distinction between marginal product of *labourers* and marginal product of *labour*. He explain that it is the *marginal productivity of labourers over a wide range* which is zero and not the *marginal productivity of labour* (*i.e.*, labour input) over a wide range of labour used. In fact *marginal productivity of labour* is just equal to zero at the margin. Therefore, the distinction drawn between *labour and labourers* by Prof. Amartya Sen is significant since it helps in understanding the nature of disguised unemployment and the form in which it appears as well as in removing the apparent contradiction between the disguised unemployment and rational behaviour. Thus, Prof. Amartya Sen writes :

---

8. R. Nurkse, *Problems of Capital Formation in Under-developed Countries*, p. 32.
9. *Op. cit.*, p. 33.

"This confusion arises because of not distinguishing between *labour* and *labourer*. It is not that too much labour is being spent in the production process, but that too many labourers are spending it. Disguised unemployment thus normally takes the form of a smaller number of working hours per head per year; for example, each of three brother shepherding the sheep every third day. It is thus, the marginal productivity of the labourer, so to say that is nil *over a wide range* and the productivity of labour may be just equal to zero at the margin. It may also take the form of lower intensity of work with people 'taking it easy', *e.g.* the peasant having time to watch the birds while working. If a number of labourers went away, the others would be able to produce about the same output working *langer and harder*. There is not contradiction between disguised unemployment will naturally put on this disguise. A piece of land that can be cultivated fully by two, may actually be looked after by four, if a family of four working men having no other employment opportunity happens to own it."[10]

As is evident Professor Sen's quotations given above, the disguised unemployment appears not only in the form of the idle man hours (that is, all workers work for lesser hours of work than those considered standard or normal and remain idle for the rest) but also in the reduced intensity of work-hours performed. In other words, the disguised unemployment also creeps into work hours performed by labourers. This happens through what has been called work-spreading or work-stretching devices.

It is worth noting that not all sizes of farms suffer from disguised unemployment. As said above, large-sized farms generally use hired labour (or are cultivated through tenancy system) and granting that landlords of those farms operate on the principle of profit maximisation, no disguised unemployment will exist on those farms. As the size of the farms goes on declining, man-land ratio on them will be increasing. As the man-land ratio rises with the decrease in the size of farms, the average and marginal products of the labourers will diminish due to the operation of diminishing returns. Since a certain minimum ratio of land to labour is required even in the most labour-intensive agricultural processes, a point will reach when the further reduction in the size of the farm and consequently further increase in the man-land ratio will result in zero marginal product of labour.

Graphic Illustration of Sen's Concept of Disguised Unemployment. Let us graphically explain the concept of disguised unemployments as has been clarified by Prof. Amartya Sen. Consider Fig. 45.1 where along the *Y*-axis total output is measured and along the *X*-axis, labour (say labour hours) is measured. *TP* represents total product curve which in the beginning rises and after a point it becomes horizontal indicating thereby that total output remains constant after OL_1 amount of labour is spent. Now, according to Amartya Sen, it will be irrational on the part of the family to put in more labour on the farm beyond OL_1 since extra labour spent beyond OL_1 does not add to total output. Thus if the family goes beyond OL_1 and devotes OL_2 labour, then L_1L_2 labour input has been unnecessarily spent, for it has not brought any increment in output. *Marginal product of labour* is zero when OL_1 amount of labour is put in. Therefore, a rational family will put in OL_1 amount of labour.

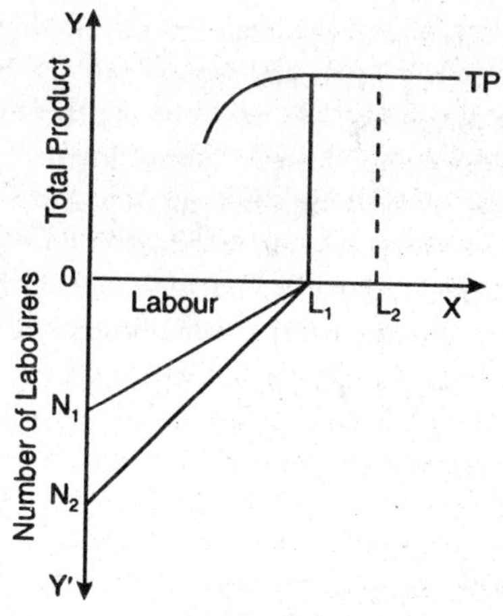

Fig. 45.1. *The Emergence of Disguised Unemployment*

But, according to Prof. Amartya Sen, the disguised unemployment occurs due to the fact that a *given amount of labour is spent by too many labourers*. Consider Fig. 11A.1. again. Along the south, number of labourers are measured. Suppose in the beginning OL_1 amount of labour is being put in by ON_1 labourers who are working normal hours in a week. If

10. Amartya Sen, *Choice of Techniques*, Basil Blackwell, 1957.

now the size of the family expands and the number of labourers increases from ON_1 to ON_2, the amount of land, other factors and technique of production remaining the same. As stated above, it will be futile and irrational to put in more labour beyond OL_1 even though the number of labourers in the family has increased. If the additional labourers do not get employment outside the family farm, the reaction of the family will be that the same amount of labour input OL_1 be shared by ON_2 labourers. As a result, the number of work hours devoted by each labourer will be reduced. The total output will not increase since the same amount of labour input OL_1 is being put in. It follows therefore that the increase in the number of labourers from ON_1 to ON_2 has not resulted in any increment in total output: only the same amount of labour is being shared by ON_2 labourers instead of ON_1. Thus *number of labouers N_1N_2 represents disguised unemployment since marginal productivity of a labourer over this range is zero.* Now if N_1N_2 labourers are withdrawn from the agricultural family, total output will not decline. With the withdrawal of N_1N_2 workers, the remaining workers will put in OL_1 labour so that each of them will work for normal hours.

The magnitude of disguised unemployment has been increasing in under-developed countries since the rate of capital accumulation has not kept pace with the rapid growth of population. It has been estimated that 15 to 30 per cent of agricultural labour force is disguisedly unemployed in various under-developed countries. This type of unemployment can be relieved by the development of non-agricultural sectors and by increasing the rate of capital formation that will open new avenues of employment. But the economies of such over-populated agricultural countries are generally stagnant and economic development has been slow to generate sufficient employment opportunities to absorb surplus farm labour. All this leads to the emergence of the phenomenon of continuously mounting pressure of disguised unemployment. The increasing pressure of population leads to subdivision and fragmentation of holdings with all their attendant evils. The farm income goes down with every generation. Low consumption of the unemployed presses down level of economic activity. Surplus available for investment is meagre. Thus mass disguised unemployment is a drag on economic progress. The problem can be solved only by stepping up the rate of investment above the rate of population growth. The central problem of economic growth in such countries is thus to create conditions under which rate of investment can be increased above that of growth of population.

MEASUREMENT OF UNEMPLOYMENT AND UNDEREMPLOYMENT IN INDIA

The surplus labour in a developing economy such as ours manifests itself in (*a*) open unemployment, (*b*) underemployment and (*c*) disguised unemployment. Therefore, a realistic assessment of the magnitude of surplus labour that exists in the Indian economy should contain information about all these three forms of unemployment. However, the measurement of unemployment in an economy such as ours where self-employment is predominant and the bulk of productive activity is carried on within household enterprises is a difficult task. A slight difference in the definitions and criteria adopted to measure unemployment often makes enormous change in its magnitude. For example, Late Professor Raj Krishna suggested the following four criteria to measure unemployment :

(*a*) *Time Criterion* : This refers to identifying those persons as unemployed who have no gainful work for less than some normal standard hours in a week or less than a certain normal standard days in a month or a year.

(*b*) *Willingness Criterion*: This calls a person unemployed when a person is either seeking or is available for work at the prevailing wage rate.

(*c*) *Income Criterion* : This considers those persons unemployed or underemployed who have income (or expenditure) less than a certain '*poverty norm*' generally fixed on the basis of minimum calories required for subsistence.

(*d*) *Productivity Criterion* : This considered those persons as unemployed or underemployed who may be working but they have less than some normal standard of productivity.[11]

Thus, a change from time and willingness criteria to productivity criterion changes the estimate of rural unemployment for the year 1972-73 from 8.21 per cent of rural labour force (on daily status basis) to 33.7 per cent.[12]

Note that both willingness and time criteria have been used in India in the various rounds of National Sample Survey, to measure unemployment in the economy. Productivity criterion has been used by Ashok Mathur, Shakuntala Mehra, Ashok Rudra and Amartya Sen to measure the extent of disguised unemployment in the Indian agriculture. Further, using household expenditure data from earlier rounds of NSS, Dandekar-Rath in their study of "*Poverty in India*" adopted income criterion to measure the magnitude of unemployment in the Indian economy.

Measurement of Unemployment in India : Usual Status Weekly Status and Daily Status Unemployment

We now discuss the approaches to measure open unemployment and underemployment in India adopted since 1972-73. On the basis of time and willingness criteria open unemployment and underemployment have been estimated using the following three approaches which were recommended by an expert committee headed by Prof. M.L. Dantwala.

(*i*) **Usual Status Approach.** This approach records only those persons as unemployed who had no gainful work for a *major time* during the 365 days preceding the date of survey and are seeking or are available for work. Thus, the estimates of unemployment obtained on the basis of usual status approach are expected to capture long-term open unemployment.

(*ii*) **Weekly Status Approach.** In this approach current activity status relating to the week preceding the date of survey is recorded and those persons are classified as unemployed who did not *have gainful work even for an hour on any day in the preceding week* and were seeking or were available for work. The persons who may be employed on usual status approach may however become intermittently unemployed during some seasons or parts of the year. Thus, unlike the usual status approach, *weekly status approach would capture not only open chronic unemployment but also seasonal unemployment*. Besides, this approach provides weekly average rate of unemployment

(*iii*) **Daily Status Approach.** As noted above, the weekly status approach records a person employed *even if he works only for an hour on any day of the whole week*. It is thus clear that the weakly status approach would tend to underestimate unemployment in the economy because it does not appear to be proper to treat all those who have been unemployed for the whole week except an hour as employed. Indeed, the demand for labour in farming and non-farming households often fluctuates over a small period within a week. Hence the need for the use of daily status approach to measure the magnitude of unemployment and underemployment in India.

In the daily status approach current activity status of a person with regard to whether employed or unemployed or outside labour force is recorded *for each day in reference week*. Further, for

11. Likewise, Prof. Amartya Sen has distinguished between *income aspect, production aspect* and *recognition aspect* of employment and defined unemployment accordingly. While his concept of unemployment based on 'production aspect' is the same as productivity criterion, his recognition concept of unemployment differs from "willingness criterion" only in that he calls all those persons as unemployed who are seeking work regardless of whether or not they already have some job. His income concept of unemployment, however, conceptually differs from Raj Krishna's 'income criterion' in that it is "*concerned with that part of one's income which is received on condition that one works*"' rather than earning of minimum income required for subsistance.
12. 33.7 per cent of labour force was Sen's estimate of rural unemployment for the year 1972-73 on the basis of his productivity criterion.

estimating employment and unemployment, *half-day has been adopted as a unit of measurement*. A person who works for 4 hours or more upto 8 hours on a day is recorded as employed for the full day and one who works for an hour or more but less than 4 hours on a day is recorded as employed for half-day. Accordingly, persons having no gainful work even for one hour on a day are described as unemployed for full day provided that they are either seeking or are available for work.

Thus, the daily status approach would capture not only the unemployed days of those persons who are usually unemployed but also the unemployed days of those who are recorded as employed on weekly status basis. Hence daily status concept of unemployment is more inclusive than those of usual status and weekly status approaches and would yield an average number of unemployed person days per day in the year indicating the magnitude of both open unemployment and underemployment. They are also referred to as *person-years unemployed* so as to distinguish them from persons unemployed.

The estimates of unemployment on the basis of above three approaches are presented in Table 45.1. It may be observed from this table that according to NSS 2004-05 round, 3.1 per cent of labour force was unemployed on usual principal status basis, 4.4 per cent on weekly status basis and 8.3 per cent of labour force was unemployed on current daily status basis. Assuming the same unemployment rates, Planning commission estimated current daily status unemployment to be of the order of 34.7 million persons in 2004-05 and 36.7 million persons in 2006-07.

Table 45.1. Magnitude of Unemployment in the Indian Economy (% of Labour Force).

Approach	1977-78	1983	1987-88	1993-94	1999-2000	2004-05	2009-10
Usual Principal Status	4.23	2.77	3.77	2.58	2.8	3.06	2.5
Current Weekly Status	4.48	4.51	4.80	3.6	4.4	4.4	3.6
Current Daily Status	8.18	8.28	6.01	5.95	7.3	8.3	6.6

Source: Planning Commission, and *Tenth Five Year Plan, and Eleventh Five Year Plan Document*

It will be observed from Table 45.1 that as compared to 1993-94, *all rates of Unemployment* (*usual status, weekly status and daily status*) increased in 1999-2000 and 2004-05. This clearly shows that economic reforms initiated since 1991 have led to the worsening of unemployment situation in the Indian economy. However, unemployment of all these types declined in 2009-10 as will be seen from Table 45.1. This is probably due to starting of Mahatma Gandhi Rural -Unemployment Gurantee Scheme (MGNREGS). In our view employment generated under this scheme is neither geniune nor stable.

Note that, contrary to what could be expected, usual status unemployment is very low. This is for two reasons. First, a person to be identified as unemployed on usual status approach has to pass through a severe test, namely, he did not work for a *major time* during the 365 days preceding the date of survey. Now, in an economy where there is predominance of self-employed households engaged in family-based enterprises, it is quite easy for a person to have worked for some days even during the lean periods of the year and therefore get registered as employed rather than unemployed. Secondly, during the slack seasons of the year some persons, mainly women, withdraw themselves from the work force. Therefore, instead of being counted as unemployed, they are treated as 'outside labour force', for they generally report as 'not available for work'. As a result, usual status unemployment estimates are relatively very low.

Further, it is noteworthy that both the usual and weekly status approaches reveal a rather small magnitude of surplus labour. This is because, as mentioned above, *both these approaches measure open unemployment in the country*. However, in India with predominance of self-employed households and absence of social security system to support the people, they can hardly afford to remain absolutely unemployed. The new hands that are added to the labour force every year as a result of

13. See CSO, *National Sample Survey, 32nd round* (1977-78), Report No. 298, p. 20

increasing population do not remain openly unemployed; they share employment and work with others so that there is more of underemployment and disguised unemployment rather than open unemployment.

Thus, quite expectedly, the daily status approach which seeks to capture both open unemployment and underemployment reveals that quite a large magnitude of surplus labour exists in India. It will be seen from Table 45.1 that 8.3 per cent of labour force was found unemployed in 2004-05 on daily status basis. Assuming the same rate, Planning Commission estimated that the magnitude of daily-status unemployment increased from 20 million persons in 1993-94 to 36.7 million persons in 2006-07.

However, even the daily status approach, does not fully measure the magnitude of surplus labour in the Indian economy. Evidently, this also would have a tendency to under-record unemployment as it considered a person working for only 4 hours (1/2 of the standard day) as fully employed and a person who worked for an hour (1/8th of the standard day) as employed for half-day. In fact, as an alternative, hourly status approach measuring employment and unemployment in terms of man-hours is more appropriate.

Further, even the *daily status approach like the usual and weekly status approach, cannot fully capture disguised unemployment of those persons whose intensity of work and consequently productivity is very low even though they are employed for a long time.* In India, as in other labour-surplus developing countries, people are generally found to be working longer hours and larger number of days than one is really required to do the given work by stretching or spreading the work. Therefore, *for the proper assessment of the magnitude of surplus labour that exists in the Indian economy, unemployment on the basis of daily/hourly status ought to be supplemented by a measure of disguised unemployment based on a norm of productivity or work-intensity.* Despite the above limitations it is clear that daily status unemployment is a relatively better measure of the magnitude of surplus labour as it covers open unemployment as well as a good amount of underemployment.

VARIOUS DEVELOPMENT STRATEGIES FOR LABOUR-SURPLUS DEVELOPING COUNTRIES

In what follows we shall critically examinc some well-known strategies of development especially from the point of view of whether they provide an adequate answer to the problem of surplus labour in India. This critical evaluation will enable us to bring out the various policy measures which need to be adopted for designing an appropriate development strategy to ameliorate the problem of unemployment and underemployment in India. It is important to note that a development strategy for promoting growth of employment is based on a particular diagnosis and explanation of the problem of surplus labour. As an explanation of unemployment and from the viewpoint of generation of new employment opportunities, the various employment strategies and aproaches have been proposed from time to time by different economists The important approach to unemployment and employment is what can be called industrialisation-led strategy of development. Some economists, prominent among whom are R Nurkse, Aurther Lewis, Eckaus, Joan Robinson, P.C. Mahalanobis, Hirschman, Fie-Rains and Jorgenson attribute unemployment in the developing countries to the lack of industrialisation and therefore suggest stepping up the rate of investment or capital formation for the expansion of modern industrial sector in which to absorb labour.

Vakil and Brahmananda laid stress on wage-goods gap as a cause of unemployment and put forward a development strategy which assigned a high priority to wage-goods industries in thc allocation of investment resources so as to increase the supply of wage goods. Another group of economists led by Schumacher[14], Myrdal[15] and Singer hold the use of capita-intensive technology

14. E.F. Schumacher, "*Small is Beautiful*" Bord Briggs, London.
15. Gunnar Myrdal, *Asian Drama; An Enquiry into the Poverty of Nations*, Penguin Books, New York, 1968.

in the large-scale industries responsible for the mounting unemployment problem in developing countries. This approach leads to the adoption of labour-intensive techniques as an essential part of the development strategy. Finally, some economists, more prominently, Dandekar and Rath, J.P. Lewis, B.S. Minhas have proposed undertaking of rural public works on a large scale as a solution to the problem of unemployment and poverty. According to them, adequate employment opportunities cannot be generated, at least in the short run, through any emphasis on accelerating investment or capital formation in the modern industrial sector and on choice of any particular pattern of investment within industrial sectors. Hence the argument for undertakinig rural public works to generate employment opportunities. In what follows, we shall examine these various strategies of development for productive absorption of surplus labour.

Industrialisation-led Strategy of Development : Lewis Model of Growth

Influenced by the growth experience of the western developed countries and based on Lewis model of growth[16], the several developing countries adopted industrialisation-led strategy of development for absorbing surplus labour in the modern industrial sector.

An essential feature of this approach is that it seeks to generate more employment opportunities by *achieving higher rate of industrial grwoth through accelerating investment* or capital accumulation. Besides, it regards labour and capital as complementary inputs. In less developed countries the accumulation of stock of capital and modern industries had not been growing at a rate fast enough to keep pace with the growth of population. As a result, surplus labour in the form of disguised unemployment on large scale in agriculture came to prevail in the developing countries. Lewis model and industrialisation-led strategy of development based on it visualised shift of their surplus labour from agriculture where labour-productivity was very low to be employed in the industrial sector at a higher level of productivity. In this way economic growth will also take place due to increase in labour productivity.

In their growth models for a dualistic economy with surplus labour, Lewis and Fei-Ranis[17] also regard capital as the crucial factor for the expansion of employment in the modern industrial sector. While their models suggest that rate of growth of employment depends upon the rate of capital accumulation and economic growth, it differs from Harrod-Domar model in the sense that they draw distinction between the two sectors of a less developed economy: (1) the subsistence agricultural sector which is characterised by surplus labour, low producitivity and self-employment; and (2) the modern industrial sector which is characterised by wage employment and high productivity.

These growth models emphasize transfer of surplus labour from the subsistence agricultural sector to the modern industrial sector. And this *transfer of labour and expansion of employment opportunities in the modern industrial sector is determined by the rate of capital accumulation.* Therefore, in this strategy increase in rate of capital accumulation and economic growth in the modern industrial sector would generate enough employment opportunities to withdraw over a number of years all the disguised unemployed labour from agriculture.

It was assumed in this industrialisation-led development strategy that agriculture would adjust itself endogenously to the requirements of industrial growth. The assumption of unlimited supply of labour at a *given wage rate* implied that agriculture will adjust endogenously without lowering of agricultural production. Lewis realised that if on withdrawal of labour from agriculture productivity of labour in agriculture falls, it will cause prices of agricultural output, especially, food to rise. The rise in food prices will lead to the rise in wage rates of labour in the industrial sector. The rise in

16. Arthur Lewis, Economic Development with Unlimited Supply of Labour, *Manchester School*, Vol. 22, 1954.
17. J.C.H. Fei, and G. Ranis, *Development of the Labour Surplus Economy, Theory and Policy*, Irwin, Homesood, 1964.

wages would lower profits in the industrial sector and bring about stoppage of further industrial growth.

A Critical Appraisal of Industrialisation-led Strategy of Development

The industrialisation-led strategy of development rightly lays stress on the importance of capital goods for generating employment. Without some capital goods such as tools, implements, machinery and equipment, it is hard to generate productive employment in both the large-scale and small-scale industries. Above all, shortage of infrastructure such as steel, power, cement and transport facilities serves as an important bottleneck for the expansion of output and employment in both industry and agriculture. Therefore, expansion in their supply would promote the growth of output and employment in the economy.

However, *industrialisation-led startegy did not sufficiently recognize the importance of wage-goods constraint for generation of employment opportunities*. Thus, at a time when fixed capital alone was thought to be necessary for industrial growth Vakil and Brahmananda[18] made a valuable contribution by highlighting the importance of wage goods for expansion of both industrial output and employment. But the assertion that the increase in the supply of wage goods alone is both a necessary and sufficient condition for generation of output and employment sounds quite unrealistic.[19] It is not a right approach to think of capital goods versus wage goods. Indeed, increase in the supply of both is needed to solve the problem of unemployment. The availability of wage goods serves as a constraint for generating wage-employment for without them the demand of the newly employed persons for wage goods would not be met. But if opportunities for productive employment are to be generated in the very first instance either in industry or in agriculture, labour needs to be provided with some capital goods.

It is worthwhile to note that growth of the modern industrial sector was expected to absorb not only the openly unemployed but also the disguised unemployed persons from agriculture. However, the actual experience belies the hopes of generating sufficient employment opportunities through industrial growth. For instance, an annual average rate of growth of around 6 per cent achieved by the industrial sector in India during the four decades (1956-96) and over 7 per cent during 1996-2008 and a very high increase in the rate of net capial formation (from 5.5 per cent in 1950-51 to 25 per cent of national income in 1995-96 has not been able to generate enough employment opportunities in India. It is thus clear that not much employment opportunities can be generated directly through growth of modern industrial sector even with high rate of increase in its output.[20]

Industrialisation-led strategy based on Lewis model underplayed the importance of growth of agricultural output. Without the growth of marketable surplus of agricultural output, especially food, the sustained growth in the industrial sector could not be achieved. In the case of Soviet Russia, the required food surplus was procured *through forcible collection* from the farmers. In democratic countries like India, such forcible collection was ruled out. The neglect of agriculture in India in the Second Five Year Plan led to the food shortage in the early sixties. This caused not only inflation in the economy but we had to import foodgrains under PL 480 from the USA to feed our growing population.

---

18. C.N. Vakil and P.R. Brahmananda, *Planning in an Expanding Economy*, Vohra & Co., Bombay, 1986.
19. It may be noted that Brahmananda later modified his wage-woods strategy by incorporating in what he calls "*Integrated Wage-goods Complex*" which includes not only the wage-goods but also the capital goods required for the production of wage-goods. But the role of intermediate capital goods such as seel, cement, coal and power required for the production of wage-goods and also for investment sector has not been fully recognised by him even in his '*Extended Wage-goods Strategy*'.
20. Note that the growth of modern industrial sector generates few employment opportunities is also corroborated by the experience of Latin American countries such as Brazil, Argentina, Mexico, Columbia, Peru, Venezuela which have achieved annual rate of industrial growth ranging from 7.6 per cent to 10 per cent during the last few decades and still they face the mounting problem of surplus labour.

A serious drawback of strategies of employment generation through industrial growth is that *they have ignored the possibilities of absorbing labour productively in agriculture*. These strategies regarded agriculture merely as the source of labour supply to the expanding industries. Even in growth models of Lewis and Fei-Ranis of a labour-surplus dual economy, both surplus labour and dualism have been sought to be eliminated by way of shifting labour from agriculture to the modern industrial sector.[21] But there is ample scope for absorbing labour in the Indian agriculture provided proper agricultural policies are adopted. India employs much less labour per hectare than other countries like Japan.[22] A good amount of labour can be productively absorbed in the Indian agriculture through rapid growth of its output by increasing cropping intensity and irrigation facilities and through the adoption of new high yielding technology. Reckless mechanisation, that is, use of labour-displacing agricultural machines such as tractors, combine harvestors is to be avoided if more employment opportunities are to be created in agriculture.

Finally, industrialisation-led growth strategies focussed on industrial growth for employment generation and *ignored the importance of institutional reforms, especially in agriculture, for promoting the expansion of employment opportunities*. Land reforms in agriculture such as redistribution of land and changes in the tenancy system can play an important role in increasing employment opportunities for landless labourers, small and marginal farmers and share-croppers. There exist large inequalities in land-ownership in India with the result that whereas a large number of rural households have either insufficient or no land to provide them adequate employment and income, a few families, on the other, own such a large amount of land that they cannot manage it efficiently. Consequently, there is underutilization of land and irrigation potential. Further, it is generally believed that employment per hectare and cropping intensity are higher on small farms as compared to those on large farms. This may be taken to imply that redistribution of land through imposition and effective implementation of ceiling on land holdings will bring about increase in employment opportunities in agriculture.

To sum up, agriculture contains immense employment potential provided proper strategy for its development involving technological and institutional changes is adopted. This has however, been ignored by the maintsteam of the industrialisation-oriented strategies of development.

Mahalanobis' Heavy-Industry Strategy of Development

It will be useful to explain first Mahalanobis model of growth which provided a rationale for the heavy industry biased development strategy. An important point to note is that Mahalanobis identifies the rate of growth of investment in the economy not with rate of growth of savings as is usually considered by the economists but with rate of growth of output in the capital goods sector within the economy. The growth of capital goods sector in turn depends upon the proportions of total investment allocated to the capital goods sector and output-capital ratio in the capital goods sector. Given the output-capital ratio in capital goods sector *(i.e.* heavy industries), he proves that if the proportion of total investment allocated to the capital goods is relatively greater, the rate of growth of output of capital goods will be greater and hence, given the Mahalanobis assumption, the future rate of growth of investment in the economy will be greater. Now, the greater the rate of investment, the greater will be the long-term rate of growth. We thus see that Mahalanobis shows that the proportion of total investment resources allocated to the capital goods industries for each year is the most important factor determining the long-term rate of growth of national income. Let us represent his two-sector growth model.

---

21. It is important to note that Fei-Ranis have emphasised the importance of agricultural development in the growth process of a labour-surplus economy, but they have envisaged such a pattern of agricultural development which ensures more and more at agricultural output for less and less use of labour input.
22. In the middle 1950s, labour input per hectare of net sown area was 530 working mandays in Japan, as against only 137 in West Bengal.

It is worth noting that Mahalanobis recognises that output-capital ratio in the consumer goods sector is greater than the output-capital ratio in the capital goods sector. If this is the case, then It apparently implies that growth of output or income will be greater if more investment is made in the consumer goods sector. But in this case the higher rate of growth of income will be only in the short run. Mahalanobis model shows that after a critical range of time, the larger the investment allocated to capital goods industries, (λ_k) *i.e.*, the higher will be growth in output or income. Elaborating this point Prof. Raj states, "*The logic here is the same as the more common proposition that a higher rate of investment (i.e., a larger proportion of the productive factors used for accumulation) would result in a smaller volume of output being available for consumption in the short run but that over a longer period, it would result in higher rate of growth of consumption; the difference is that the choice is here stated as between investment in capital goods and investment in consumer goods industries.*[23]

The rationale of Mahalanobis growth model and development strategy can be expressed in simple words without mathematical language. According to Mahalanobis, rate of economic growth depends upon the capital formation or real investment. The greater the rate of capital formation, the greater the rate of economic growth. The rate of capital formation in an economy, according to Mahalanobis, depends upon the capacity of the economy to produce capital goods. Thus, according to him, given a closed economy, the rate of real capital formation depends not upon the savings of the economy but on the capacity to produce capital goods. Even if the rate of savings is substantial raised in order to accelerate the rate of capital formation, it would be futile, for required capital goods would not be there if there is a lack of capacity to produce capital goods. Of course, this is based on the *closed economy* assumption.

Thus, according to him, if large investment is not made in the basic heavy industries producing capital goods, the country will for ever remain dependent on foreign countries for the imports of steel and capital goods like machinery for real capital formation. Since it is not possible for India to earn sufficient foreign exchange by increasing exports, the capital goods cannot be imported in sufficient quantities owing to foreign exchange constraint. The result will be that the rate of real capital formation and the rate of economic growth in the country will remain low. Thus, Mahalanobis was of the opinion that without adequate investment in basic heavy industries, it would not be possible to achieve rapid self-reliant economic growth. Therefore according to him, to achieve rapid economic growth and self-reliance, it would be necessary to give the highest priority to basic capital goods industries in the development strategy of a plan.

Employment Generation in Mahalanobis Model. It is necessary in this connection to mention Prof. Mahalanobis' views on increasing employment opportunities and to achieve a stage of full employment. According to him, productive employment can be increased only by increasing the production of capital goods like steel, electricity, machinery, fertilizers, etc. Whether it is increase in employment in the industrial sector or in the agricultural sector it cannot be achieved without increasing the output of capital goods. To quote him, "*The only way of eliminating unemployment in India is to build up a sufficiently large stock of capital which will enable all unemployed persons being absorbed into productive capacity. Increasing the rate of investment is, therefore. the only fundamental remedy for unemployment in India.*"[24] Thus, in Prof. Mahalanobis' opinion, not only to achieve the objective of rapid economic growth but also to achieve the goal of full employment, it is necessary to accord high priority to capital goods industries in the development strategy.

Import-substituting Industrialisation. Mahalanobis' emphasis on basic heavy industries was also due to his objective of meeting the requirements of higher rate of capital accumulation from

23. K.N. Raj, Growth Models in Indian Planning, *The Indian Economic Review*, Feb. 1961. Reprinted in C.D. Wadhwa, "*Some Problems of India's Economic Policy*" Tata Publishing Co. Ltd., Bombay.
24. P.C. Mahalanobis, The Approach of Operational Research to Planning in India. *Sankya*, Vol. 16. December 1953

within the economy and therefore enabling the economy to stop imports of foreign capital equipment and machines. To quote him, "The proper strategy would be to bring about a rapid development of the industries producing investment goods in the beginning by increasing appreciably the proportion of investment in the basic heavy industries. As the capacity to manufacture both heavy and light machinery and other capital goods increases, the capacity to invest by using domestically produced capital goods would also increase steadily and India would become more and more independent of the imports of foreign machinery and capital."[25] In fact, Mahalanobis growth model advocates import-substitution type of industrial development strategy.

It is important to note that Mahalanobis assumed though implicitly that export earnings of India cannot be sufficiently increased. If this assumption is not valid, as has been pointed out by several critics, then he could not justifiably identify rate of investment in the economy with the domestic output of capital goods. If exports of a country can be adequately raised, the various capital goods can be imported in exchange for exports. In that case rate of investment or rate of capital accumulation in the economy can be stepped up without giving high priority to the basic heavy industries provided the exports.can be adequately increased. Thus the assumption of stagnant exports is crucial in the Mahalanobis growth model for providing the rationale for a general shift in the investment pattern to the domestic production of capital goods.

Mahalanobis Growth Model and Development Strategy in India's Five-Year Plans

As pointed out above, Mahalanobis heavy industry first strategy of development was put into actual practice in India's Five-Year Plans beginning from the Second Plan. India started its planned development of its economy in 1951 when First Five-Year Plan was started. However, the Five year Plan did not propose any explicit strategy of development; it took over several projects which had been worked out earlier and some of them were already in the process of being carried out. It laid emphasis on stepping up the rate of saving and therefore investment and growth by maintaining the marginal rate of saving at a substantially higher level than the average rate of saving. Although it did not present any explicit formulation of development strategy regarding the pattern of investment its emphasis was on agriculture, irrigation, power and transport aimed at creating the base for more rapid industrialisation of the economy in the future.

Second Five Year Plan, based as it was on Mahalanobis growth model, proposed an explicit strategy of development which gave top priority to basic heavy industries. Not only the objectives of rapid rate of economic growth and employment generation but also the aim of self-reliant and self-generating economy were sought to be achieved by *"the building up of economic and social overhead, exploration and development of minerals and the promotion of basic industries like steel, machine building, coal and heavy chemicals."*[26] Identifying under-development with dependence on agriculture and thinking industrial growth especially the development of heavy industries as the core of development underlaid the approach and strategy of the Second Five-Year Plan. To quote from Second Plan again. "low or static standards of living, underemployment and unemploy-ment, and to a certain extent even the gap between the average incomes and the highest incomes are all manifestations of the basic under-development which characterises an economy depending mainly on agriculture. Rapid industrialisation and diversification of the economy is thus the core of development. But *if industrialisation is to be rapid enough, the country must aim at developing basic industries and industries which make machines to make the machines needed for further development."*[27]

It is clear from above that in the Second Plan there was clear shift of priorities from agriculture to industries and within industries to basic heavy industries. As mentioned above, the logic of

25. *Ibid,* p.22
26. Government of Inida/ Planning Commission, *Second Five Year Plan,* 1956, p.24
27. *Ibid,* p.25

Mahalanobis in emphasizing heavy industries was that the growth of basic heavy industries will enable the economy to accelerate the rate of capital formation and therefore economic growth. In fact, he identified the rate of growth of investment in the economy with the rate of growth of output in the capital goods (sector) industries within the economy.

A Critical Evaluation of Heavy Industry Strategy of Development

A crucial weakness of Mahalanobis heavy industry strategy of development was pointed out by Professors Vakil and Brahmananda. They criticised heavy industry strategy in their now well knows joint work, "*Planning for an Expanding Economy.*" According to them, growth of national income and employment is determined by the supply of wage goods. According to them, the exists a wage-goods gap in under-developed countries like India and the basic cause of unemployment and disguised unemployment in them is the existence of this wage-goods gap. Wage goods act as a constraint on the growth of industrialisation and non-agricultural growth. Thus, in the determination of growth of income and employment, while Mahalanobis emphasised '*fixed capital*', Brahmananda and Vakil laid stress on the wage goods which are also called '*circulating capital*'.

There is no doubt that **Mahalanobis "heavy industry" strategy overlooked the importance of agriculture or wage goods in the growth process of the economy**. This manifested itself in the rapid rise of prices from the very beginning of the Second Plan. While a relatively large investment in the basic industries resulted in the creation of money incomes and consequently in a large increase in demand for wage goods, the supply of wage goods did not adequately increase due to the continued neglect of agriculture in India's planning strategy. This caused inbalance between demand for and supply of wage goods which has been responsible for inflationary situation in the India economy.

The view that there has been relative neglect of agriculture in Indian Plans has been forcefully and effectively expressed and provided by Professor Michael Lipton. He writes: "We have seen that neither allocations of public money, nor incentives to the movement of persons and other resources, have favoured agricultural development; that 70 per cent of the workers get less than 35 per cent of investment finance and a far smaller share of human skills. Several types of pressures on opinion and policy have combined to bias the allocation of cash, effort, personnel and research away from rural needs."[28]

A serious failure of Mahalanobis development strategy with its emphasis on basic heavy industries is that it **failed to generate adequate amount of employment opportunities.** Pattern of industrialization has been based on capital-intensive technology imported from abroad and has been oriented towards urban large-scale industries. If the emphasis were on rural-oriented industrialization promoting cottage and small-scale industries, using intermediate technologies, the problem of labour-surplus and unemployment would not have been as acute as it is now. Besides this, attention was not paid to absorb labour in the agricultural sector, and the agricultural development strategy that could absorb more labour in productive employment was not adopted.

From the foregoing analysis, it follows that if the mounting unemployment problem is to be tackled, the strategy of development adopted need to be revised and modified. In thelllew strategy, agriculture has to play a key role in generating enough employment opportunities for a long time to come. The fact that 58 per cent of the Indian labour force and majority of the unemployed and under-employed reside in the rural areas and further that the employment potential of the industries of large-scale type is very little, the promotion of agricultural and rural development must be made the springboard and the leading sector for generating productive employment for millions. Therefore, *the strategy for agricultural development should be such as will absorb productively the largest possible number of workers.*

---

28. M. Lipton, Strategy for Agriculture: Urban Bias and Rural Planning, Printed in P. Streeman and M. Lipton (ed.) *The Crisis of Indian Planning*, Oxford University press, 1960, p. 130

Another weakness of the "heavy industry first" strategy and development was that it chose pattern of investment with *higher capital-output ratio.* In basic heavy industries capital-output ratio was admittedly high and in agriculture and related activities, capital output ratio was low. Thus, the highest priority to basic heavy industries and low priority to agriculture in the pattern of investment meant the choice of high macro-value of incremental capital output ratio (ICOR). As has been made clear in earlier chapters that if a higher growth rate is desired, given little initial value of a rate of saving and annual increments therein over that projected period, then the criterion should be to choose a pattern of investment with a lower macro-value of capital-output ratio. In the case of India, this would have implied a high priority to be given to agricultural and related sectors over a long period of time. Therefore, the choice of the pattern of investment containing a high priority to basic heavy industries and low priority to agriculture meant a low rate of economic growth. As has been pointed out above, Mahalanobis and others supporting his strategy contended that their strategy would ensure high rate of growth in the long run. But in actual practice even 25 years (1956-80) Mahalanobis development strategy of 1955-56 failed to ensure more than 3.5 per cent average annual rate of growth. In the meantime people suffered a lot due to the inflation generated by the strategy and the non-availability of requisite amount of essential consumer goods.

Mahalanobis heavy industry strategy suffers from another weakness in that it heavily depends upon foreign exchange requirements. Though the strategy assumed that exports from the Indian economy could not be sufficiently increased it required a large amount of foreign exchange resources to establish a network of heavy capital goods industries which required the imports of capital equipment and machinery on a large scale from other countries. For a self-contained growth model, framed in the context of a closed economy or stagnant exports, this was an inner contradiction. This also had two evil effects. Becasue of the low priority to agriculture and consumer goods industries which had export potentials, export could not rise much, and secondly, due to the highest priority to heavy capital goods industries large imports of capital equipment and materials had to be made. Such was the large requirement of foreign exchange to import capital equipment that despite the liberal foreign aid received from countries especially the USA even then the country had to face a serious foreign exchange crisis.

However, far from moving the economy towards self-reliance the heavy industry strategy increased the dependence on foreign aid. Because of low priority to agriculture in the strategy, production of foodgrains did not increase adequately and as a result the imbalance between population and foodgrains further increased during the planning period. In order to correct this imbalance foodgrains had to be imported on a large scale from other countries. Whereas the imports of foodgrains into India during the First Plan period were of the order of 12 million tonnes, it rose to 17 million tonnes in the Second Plan period. The situation worsened in the Third Plan period as the implementation of heavy industry strategy further proceeded and 26 million tones of foodgrains were imported during the Third' Plan period. During the three years of plan-holiday period (1966-69), the imports of foodgrains jumped to 25 million *in three* years period. In the Fourth Plan period in which hangover of the heavy industry strategy persisted, foodgrains imports continued unabated with the exception of the Year 1972. During the six years period 1970-76,26.4 million tonnes of foodgrains were imported.[29]

It is thus clear that the imbalance between foodgrains and population was the direct result of the neglect of agriculture in India's heavy industry first strategy. Thus the most distressing effect of the strategy was that the country came to be dependent on even foodgrains. But for the imports of foodgrains under PL 480 and liberal foreign aid which was made available, India could not have been able to implement the Mahalanobis strategy for its inner contradictions and its inappropriateness to the Indian reality would have come to surface much earlier.

29. Government of India, Economic Survey, 1977-78, p.69

It may also be pointed out that in the Mahalanobis heavy industry strategy alternative policy of development of industries which had large export potential was not at all given any consideration. That supplies of some capital goods could be procured from abroad by development of export industries was ruled out. In this connection it was pointed out by the followers of Mahalanobis that the expansion of India's exports would mean the decline in its terms of trade. In our view, the contention that the increase in India's exports would necessarily mean decline in terms of trade was not justified. In fact, up to 1972 (*i.e.*, before the oil crisis) the terms of trade had been in India's favour. It may be pointed out that declining terms of trade argument was advanced by supporters of Mahalanobis strategy only after the Mahalanobis model had been accepted and put into actual practice.[30]

WAGE-GOODS STRATEGY OF EMPLOYMENT

The industrialisation-led strategy of development explained above neglects the constraint of wage goods availability on employment generation.[31] In their criticism of the development strategy of Second and Third Five Year Plans, Vakil and Brahmananda advanced what is known as wage-goods strategy of development. According to them, unemployment and disguised unemployment in less developed countries are due to the deficiency of the supply of wage goods. They have argued that the magnitude of employment in less developed countries is determined by the available amount of wage goods. This is because whenever employment for new men is created, say, in rural public works, it cannot be sustained unless adequate amount of wage goods, especially foodgrains, is available. Of course, when people are openly or disguised unemployed, they would be consuming some foodgrains. But in that situation their consumption would be very low because their budget would not allow them to consume more. Therefore, when they are given wage employment, their effective demand for wage goods will tend to increase. Hence, given the reasonable real wage rate (in terms of wage-goods) we can calculate the total amount of wage-goods required to obtain full employment. They call the difference between the required magnitude of wage-goods and the actually available supply of wage-goods as the '*wage-goods gap*'[32]. Open and disguised unemployment in less developed countries like India, according to them, is due to the existence of this wage-goods gap. The level of full employment can be attained only when this wage-goods gap is bridged by expanding the capacity to produce wage-goods.

We thus see that *whereas in Mahalanobis' approach to growth and employment "the entire emphasis was on the role of fixed capital, Vakil and Brahmanand's entire emphasis was on the role of wage goods as capital.*"[33] It may be noted that in his later works Brahmananda has modified his strategy in that he now assigns a high priority to what he calls '*Integrated Wage-goods Complex*' which includes not only wage-goods but also capital goods which are used for the production of wage-goods. Since they consider the supply of wage-goods as the most important determinant of

30. K.N. Raj and A.K. Sen, Alternative Patterns of Growth under Conditions of Export Earnings, *Oxford Economic Papers*, Feb. 1961,
31. Some models of industrial growth do take into account the wage-goods constraint and provide for it. Thus, Nurkse thought that withdrawal of disguised unemployed will leave behind enough foodgrains to be mopped up for feeding the transferred people. Likewise, Lewis Ranis also provides for the transfer of food from agriculture to feed the workers employed in expanding modern industrial sector. But the agricultural growth to make available sufficient quantities of foodgrains to feed the rising industrial labour force was not considered by them.
32. That the availability of wage goods is an important constraint on the growth of employment opportunities was first brought out by Ricardo (1815). In classical economics, wage-goods or wage funds have been treated as working capital as compared to fixed capital which consists of machines and equipment. Thus, importance given by Vakil and Brahmananda to wage-goods for the generation of employment opportunities is merely a revival of Ricardian thought.
33. Bhagwati and Chakravarty, *Indian Economic Analysis*, (1971), p. 14.

employment in less developed economies Vakil and Brahmananda proposed a development strategy which assigned the top priority to wage-goods industries, especially agriculture, in the pattern of investment. That is why they severely criticized the development strategy adopted in India's Second and Third Plans which gave high priority to basic heavy industries producing fixed capital goods.

It may be noted that like Nurkse, Vakil and Brahmananda believe that disguised unemployment in developing countries contains saving potential (in the form of wage-goods) for capital accumulation. By withdrawing the disguised unemployed from agriculture, some amount of wage- goods would be released for providing wage employment in the investment sector. But, unlike Nurkse, they think that the surplus of wage-goods so released will not be sufficient to provide employment to all the potentially available labour force. Therefore, they emphasised the expansion of the capacity to produce wage goods and for that purpose advanced a development strategy which envisaged greater allocation of investible resources to agriculture and other wage goods industries.

A Critical Evalution of Wage Goods Strategy

The assertion by Vakil and Brahmanada that the growth in employment solely and exclusively depends upon the supply of wage goods and that the capital goods (that is, heavy-industry products) play no important role in the creation of employment opportunities is open to question. Under adequate organisation and entrepreneurial ability as well as optimum-institutional forms, two important bottlenecks, namely, capital goods bottleneck and wage-goods bottleneck, are faced in creating opportunities for productive employment. For expansion in productive employment both these bottlenecks have to be overcome and to emphasise the breaking of one bottleneck, while making no attempt to tackle the other, is an unrealistic approach to the employment problem. Wage-goods are required, to meet the demands of the newly employed people, but if some people are to be employed in productive activities in the very first instance, they are required to be, equipped with some capital goods. Further, for the production of wage-goods themselves, capital goods are required. That is, labour is to be equipped with capital goods to produce wage goods. Professor Dantwala rightly points our that, "*it is a mistake to consider capital goods and wage goods as exclusive and unrelated categories. Anyone who studies the composition of inputs needed for transformation of traditional agriculture should be able to appreciate the inter-connection between the two.*"[34]

Thus, development strategy for rapid expansion of employment has to be such as will envisage the increase in production of both wage-goods and capital goods. Thus, to talk of wage-goods versus capital goods is a false issue and an unrealistic approach to the problem of employment since both are needed to generate employment; capital goods are required to make the employment productive and wage-goods are needed to feed the workers provided with new employment, that is, to sustain their employment. To say this, however, does not imply that all capital goods industries should be necessarily developed at home and given higher priority in the allocation of resources. Which specific capital goods should be produced at home and which imported from abroad should be decided on the basis of resource endowments and comparative advantage conceived in the dynamic context.

DEVELOPMENT STRATEGY: USING LABOUR-INTENSIVE TECHNOLOGY

An important school of thought led by Schumacher, Singer and Myrdal attribute the mounting problem of unemployment and underemployment in the developing countries to the use of capital-intensive technology. It has been observed that while industrial output in developing countries has increased at a reasonably good rate, growth of employment has lagged far behind. And this is said to be due to the use of capital-intensive technology. Thus, according to this school of thought, the

34. M.L. Dantwala, Approachs to Growth and Employment, *Economic and Political Weekly*, Dec. 1972, p. 2456

creation of meagre amount of employment opportunities due to the use of capital-intensive technology on the one hand and the growth of population at an alarming rate on the other has resulted in the huge magnitude of surplus labour.

It is worthwhile to note here that the modern industries using capital-intensive technology not only create few new opportunities of employment but also destroy employment in the traditional household industries. This unfavourable impact of modern sector on the traditional employment is what Myrdal calls *backwash effect*. According to this school of thought, modern manufacturing enterprises using capital-intensive technology produce goods on a mass scale which drive out the products of traditional household industries from the market. As a result, a good number of people engaged in these household industries are displaced.[35] They add to either open or disguised unemployment in agriculture.

In this context, **labour migration model of Todaro** has often been invoked, especially by Singer, to explain the mounting problem of urban unemployment in developing countries. According to Todaro[36], decision of rural workers to migrate to urban areas rests on the level of wage rate and the expectations of getting employment in the modern urban sector. A few employment opportunities at relatively higher wage levels created by capital-intensive technology in the modern urban sector attract many more rural workers than it is possible for this to absorb. This results in enormous increase in urban unemployment and underemployment.

Of course, Galenson-Leibenstein, M. Dobb, Amartya Sen have pointed out that *the use of capital-intensive techniques would generate more surplus resources which would be ploughed back into further investment and this would result in greater growth of employment than is possible through labour-intensive techniques*. But this has not been borne out by empirical evidence. For instance, estimates of saving and investment in India reveal that contributions of the public and the private corporate sectors to the domestic savings had not only been too small but also recorded slow growth in the four decades of planned development in India (1951-90). In spite of the fact the capital-intensive technology has been used in them. On the contrary, it is the savings of the household sector (consisting of households and unicorporated enterprises) which often use labour-intensive technology that had greatly increased. This raises doubts about the argument that capital-intensive techniques necessarily generate more surplus and therefore greater growth of employment.

There is another important aspect of the use of capital-intensive technology which is worth mentioning. The *use of capital-intensive techniques creates high profit-wage ratio and thereby accentuates inequalities of income*. These income inequalities create demand pattern oriented towards luxuries which are again produced by the use of capital-intensive techniques. This limits the size of market for labour-intensive goods consumed by the working classes and common man. Thus, the use of capital-intensive techniques gives rise to a vicious circle with causes slow growth not only of direct employment but also of indirect employment through its effects on the pattern of demand.

Why in Developing Countries Capital-Intensive Technology is Used ?

Now, a pertient question is why the developing countries have been using capital-intensive technology despite the fact that surplus labour prevails in them? There are two views about this. First, the alternative technology which though efficient but labour-intensive is generally not available. The available technology is the capital-intensive technology that was developed in the Western countries to suit their factor endowments. The Western technology is quite inappropriate for the developing countries which suffer from surplus of labour and shortage of capital. Now, given

35. In his famous study of the Industrial Evolution in India, D.R. Gadgil "*Industrial Evolution in Recent Times*" clearly brought out the decline of handicraft and displacement labour employed in them as a result of the growth of modern large-scale industries in India.
36. Michael, P. Todaro, "Income Expectations, Rural-Urban Migration and Employment in Africa", *International Labour Review*, Nov. 1971.

the technology imported from the Western countries, there is not much possibility of substitution of capital for labour. In view of this, J. Schumacher and Singer advocate for the development of what has been called *intermediate or appropriate technology*. Appropriate technology for the developing countries is that which though efficient should be labour intensive so that it conforms to their factor endowments.

According to Schumacher, the development of appropriate technologies does not imply the discovery of altogether new principles of science and technology. What is required is the application of basic principles of modern science and technology to evolove the appropriate production techniques. These appropriate production techniques may be obtained by scaling down the advanced techniques by adapting them so as to make them more labour intensive, or by scaling up handicrafts technique with the introduction of new tools and simple machines and thus improving economic efficiencies of these techniques while maintaining their labour-intensity.

On the other hand, several other scholars such as Ranis, Blaug, Layard and Woodhall, Little, Scott and Scitovsky are of the view that the slow growth of employment opportunities in the industrial sector is not due so much to the lack of flexibility in the production function but to the **distortions in factor prices.**[37] Due to the various concessions and subsidies provided in taxation structure by the Government such as liberal investment or development rebate, policy of low interest rate and over-valued foreign exchange rate have caused the price of capital to be very low relative to its scarcity. On the other hand, the prevailing wage rates are too high for a labour-surplus economy due to the strong bargaining power of the trade unions in the organised sector. According to them, these distortions in factor prices make capital relatively cheaper than labour induce the adoption of capital-intensive techniques in industries with the consequence that less labour is employed. In order to promote the use of more labour-intensive techniques, it is therefore imperative that all distorions in factor prices be corrected.

By emphasising the use of labour-intensive technology in developing countries, this strategy has brought into sharp focus the question of appropriate technological choices. In a labour-surplus economy the importance of the use of appropriate technology which is labour absorptive and at the same time quite efficient can hardly be denied. However, appropriate technologies for various manufacturing industries just do not exist and a good deal of more research and development (R & D) would have to be undertaken before appropriate techniques are evolved for several industries. Of course, to encourage the development and use of appropriate techniques the various factor price distortions ought to be removed. Whereas, in view of the prevailing price situation, wage rates of industrial workers do not seem to be high, the effective price of capital is low. Therefore, the various concessions and rebates in taxes on various types of capital investment should be drastically reduced and the lending rates of interest charged by banks and other financial institutions be raised so as to curb the tendency to substitute capital for labour.

As for technological choices in agriculture it may be noted that new high-yielding technology represented by a package of high-yielding varieties, fertilizers and pesticides is quite appripriate for a labour-surplus economy such as ours, for it not only raises yield per hectare substantially but is also labour absorptive.

RURAL PUBLIC WORKS FOR EMPLOYMENT GENERATION

This approach seeks solution to the unemployment problem not through emphasising any particular pattern of resource allocation or technological choice but through special employment schemes, especially rural public works. This approach regards the regular development process as

37. Eckaus in his famous work "*Factor-Proportions Problem in Underdeveloped Countries*" showed that either factor-price disequilibrium or limited possibilities of substituting labour for capital can result in unemployment in less developed economies. Blaug, Layard and Woodhall in their study on Educated Unemployment laid stress on distortion in factor prices being responsible for it.

being incapable of alleviating the problem of unemployment and underemployment in the foreseeable future. The launching of rural works programme on a large scale has been especially advanced by Dandekar and Rath[38] to solve the problem of mass poverty, which they maintain, is mainly caused by unemployment and underemployment. Rural public works also constituted the main thrust of the recommendations of Bhagwati Committee on unemployment in India to tackle the problem of mass rural poverty and unemployment. Further, the scheme of rural public works as a major source of employment generation in rural areas has also been strongly recommended by J.P. Lewis,[39] K.N. Raj, M.L. Dantwala, and Raj Krishna. Besides, B.S. Minhas[40] also suggested massive rural works programme in his "integrated programme of compulsory consolidation and land development."[41]

Employment generation through Rural Public Works started in 1977-78 on a regular basis under the '*Food for Work Programme*' during the regime of Janta Government and was later adopted as a part of the Sixth Five-Year Plan (1978-83). Under this scheme a major part of wages was paid in terms of foodgrains. The constraint of wage goods (*i.e.*, foodgrains) which stood in the way of implementation of earlier schemes of rural public works did not then exist. Since the Sixth Plan rural public works programme has continued under the various scheme called Jawahar Rozgar Yojana 'National Rural Employment Programme' (NREP), **Rural Employment Gurantee Scheme** (REGS). This programme intended to provide supplementary employment opportunities to the rural poor seeking work, especially during the leans periods. Projects relating to soil roads and water conservation, irrigation, flood protection and drainage, field channels in irrigation command areas, construction and improvement of village tanks and ponds, school and dispensary buildings, improvements of village environment, hygiene and sanitation have been undertaken under these programmes.

There can be hardly any two opinions about that rural public works can be helpful in providing employment to the rural poor, especially the landless labourers and marginal farmers who remain without gainful work for a large number of days in a year. At the same time the programme can be used to build **durable community assets** which would promote rural development. Further, by providing alternative avenues of wage employment the rural works programme can ensure reasonable wages to the agricultural workers. But the view that these rural public works should serve as a substitute for employment generation through a proper development strategy as was conceived by Dandekar and Rath and some others is open to question. For, *being construction activities, rural public works are, at best, an interim or short-run solution of the problem of unemployment* and leave the question unanswered as to how the growing number of work force will be productively employed in the long run. The lasting and long-term solution to the problem of unemployment and underemployment lies in designing a development strategy that involves laying greater stress on investment in labour-intensive industries and bringing about such technological and institutional changes that are appropriate for labour-surplus conditions of the Indian economy. However, the rural public works have an important role to play in an employment-oriented strategy. As stated above, with the scheme of rural public works we can build up durable assets or infrastructural facilities. Now, these assets or facilities will help in creating more employment opportunities in agriculture and rural industries in future. To fulfil this purpose, rural public works need to be integrated with the overall strategy of rural development rather than being formulated and implemented in isolation of it.

---

38. Dandekar, V.M. and Rath, N., *Poverty in India*, Indian School of Political Economy, Poona, 1971.
39. Lewis J.P., "The Public Works Approach to Low End Poverty Problem, *Journal of Development Planning*, Vol. 5.
40. Minhas B.S., Rural Poverty, Land Redistribution and Development Strategy, *Indian Economic Review*, Vol. 5, 1970.
41. In the strategy proposed by Minhas the scheme of rural public works was to be used for developing land and water resources after consolidation of land has been accomplished.

CHAPTER 46

Global Financial Crisis and Eurozone Crisis and their Impact on World Economy

Burst of Sub-prime Housing Bubble : The Origin of Crisis

From the second half of 2007 in the United States a financial crisis started with a burst of housing bubble which led to widespread mortgage defaults and hence large losses to banks and other financial institutions. This crisis occurred due to sub-prime housing loans given on a large scale by the American banks in the past several years. Why did this crisis occur ? But the foundations of this crisis were laid earlier. The IT bubble burst in 2000 throwing the American economy into recession. To get the economy out of recession the US Federal Reserve cut interest rates bringing about large increase in liquidity or money supply with the banks. With cheap availability of credit, the households even with poor credit worthiness borrowed funds from the banks to buy cars and houses. Americans went on a home buying spree. Prices of houses and real estate were rising rapidly. This rise in housing prices made both households and banks believe that their prices would continue rising. In view of low interest rates and excess liquidity with them lending for houses by banks was found to be quite attractive. As a results, banks provided housing finance even to sub-prime households, that is, households that had no capacity to pay back the loans on time.

One imprudent and irresponsible financial behaviour on the parts of banks was to provide *Ninja loans*, which stand for providing loans to households or persons which had no income and no assets. All this went on well as long as housing prices were rising. The building of houses in excess during the boom period led to their oversupply in the market which caused house prices to decline in 2006. But, like the IT bubble, housing bubble burst in the second half of 2007. With the fall in prices of houses which were held as mortgage the sub-prime households started defaulting on a large scale in making their installments. This caused heavy losses to the banks. With this the sub-prime housing market which had expanded on a large scale when there were soft interest rates and huge amount of liquidity with the banks tumbled. The size of this sub-prime housing market can be judged from the fact that as large as $1.4 trillion worth of sub-prime loans were given by the banks earlier.

Securitisation of Sub-prime Mortgage Housing Loans

But the above was not the end of the story of crisis. The banks that sold the sub-prime mortgage loans did not keep them with themselves. They sold them to other banks and investors through a financial innovation generally called CDO (collateralised debt obligations) securities which were backed by a host of mortgage assets. Therefore, CDO are also called '**Mortgage Based Securities** (MBS). Investment banks associated with Wall Street in the US repackaged the sub-prime housing mortgage loans into synthetic securities CDO that were quite complex. To make them quite safe for investment and thereby increase their marketability were given AAA, BBB rating by credit agencies. "A complex financial security that has been created by mixing hundreds of thousands of independent loans can fox even the smartest investor. Specialist agencies tell investors how safe a security really is. But these credit rating agencies did not do their job well enough. All sorts of rubbish were sold as good stuff."[1]

The American and European intermediaries such as banks, hedge funds, pension funds, mutual funds invested heavily in these complex securities (CDO) based on sub-prime mortgage loans

1. Niranjan Rajadhaksha, Meltdoion reconstructed, *Hindustan Times*, Delhi, Oct. 2008

being unaware of the risks involved. Further problem arose from leverage. Those who bought these mortgage-backed securities *borrowed heavily* from banks and other financial institutions to make investment in them. It has been reported that some Wall Street Investment Banks had borrowed 40 times more than they were worth. This was quite dangerous and risky adventure.

Huge Losses by American Investment Banks and Liquidity Crunch

The sub-prime mortgage loans burst in 2007 when housing prices fell at the fastest rates leading to defaults in payment schedules by borrowers. As a result, the value of underlying sub-prime housing securities declined along with the prices of special complex securities, CDOs based on them. As a result, the banks and investment funds that had bought billions of dollars worth of these complex securities based on sub-prime mortgages suffered heavy losses leading to the liquidity crunch. Many securities held by them could not the valued at all inflicting heavy losses on banks. As a results of huge losses a number of banks and investment institutions including Lehman Brothers went bankrupt. The other banks and financial intermediataries such as Citi Bank came to the brink of bankruptcy and lacked liquidity. They therefore stopped giving credit to consumers and corporate companies. This led to credit crunch which adversely affected consumption demand and investment and therefore caused slowdown in economic growth. In fact in the second and third quarters of 2008 in the United States there was drop in GDP and therefore the US economy slipped into recession. Paul Krugman the winner of 2008, Novel Prize for economics writes "The current crisis started with a burst of housing bubble which led to widespread mortgage defaults and hence to large losses at many financial institutions. The initial shock was compounded by secondary effects as lack of capital forced banks to pull back leading to further decline in the prices of assets leading to more losses and soon a vicious circle of "de-leveraging". Pervasive loss of trust in banks including on the part of other banks reinforced the vicious circle"[2].

Thus, top five US investment banks which had significantly increased their financial leverage during the 2004-2007 time period increased their vulnerability to the CDO related losses. As these institutions registered mounting Sub-prime losses, the financial markets panicked and liquidity was sucked out of the market, so much so that these institutions found it very difficult to raise capital to provide for the losses. The month of September eventually saw the "Top 5" of Wall Street succumbing to Sub-prime losses, with Lehman Brothers filing for chapter 11 bankruptcy, Merill Lynch being merged with Bank of America and Goldman Sachs and Morgan Stanley coverting into commercial banks, subjecting themselves to much tighter regulations. Bear Sterns had already been acquired by JP Morgan Chase in March 2008.

After the demise of the "Top 5", several other financial institutions who had large exposure to CDO faced closures or opted for hasty mergers to shore up capital. Investor confidence shrank significantly, and the credit markets around the world virtually dried up. The Federal Reserve and other central banks since then have injected substantial liquidity in the markets, either by means of lowering of interest rates or by bailing out distressed financial institutions, thus leading to nationalization of financial institutions on a large scale.

When in Aug. 2008, a very important American investment bank Lehman Brothers which had world-wide financial dealings and investment was allowed to go bankrupt by the US Treasury Department, it caused the world financial crisis, already severe, to get much more worse. This affected not only the confidence in the financial system of the US but also in the whole world financial structure. The redemption pressure on securities added to the liquidity problem of banks not only in the US but it spread to the banks and financial institutions of Europe, Brazil, Japan, China, India and others. The banks of other countries felt the pinch of the liquidity crisis and being risk-averse stopped providing credit to the companies which adversely affected economic growth in Europe, China and others. Recession emerged in Europe, Japan and growth in GDP in India

2. Paul Krugman, Moment of Truth, *New York Times*, Oct. 2008

and Japan slowed down. In September 2008, when the financial crisis gripped not only the US but also the whole world, Bush Government realised that rescue measures were needed to prevent the collapse of the financial system. It got $700 billion rescue plan passed by the American Congress to bail out the banks and other financial institutions to restore the confidence of the public. Delivering a note of warning Paul Krugman, Novel Laureate in economics wrote in early Sept. 2, 2008, "The consequences of Lehman's fall were appareat within days, yet the policy makers have largely wasted the past four weeks. *Now they have reached the moment of truth.* They would do better to do some thing soon –in fact they would better a coordinated rescue plan this weekend or the world economy may well experience its worst slump since the Great Depression".[3] In fact, the US Government delayed its rescue operations to salvage the US economy from slipping into recession by the end of 2008, GDP in the US had declined by 6.3 per cent. Not only the US but Europe and Japan also went into recession in the second and third quarters of the year 2008.

Rescue Measures Adopted in the US to Fight Crisis

It is evident from above that when there were defaults on payment of housing loans the prices of complex securities started falling. The erosion of the values of these securities dented banks' investment portfolio and led to the decline in the capital base of the banks. Many American banks lost heavily and called for rescue by the Government. Getting $700 billion rescue plan passed by the US Congress the US government purchased the complex and so called 'toxic' securities called CDO from the banks. This helped some banks from going bankrupt. Later the US Government also purchased the shares of some banks and financial institutions to bail them out.

Besides, the US Government cut direct taxes and sent refunds to the people to boost aggregate spending. However, it has been found that due to great uncertainty about future economic conditions a good part of increase in disposable income as a result of tax cut was saved by the American people and therefore tax reduction did not have the desired effect on stimulating expenditure and demand. Further, a fiscal stimulus package of $783 billion was provided by newly elected US President Barack Obama. This new package contains *increase in Government expenditure* as well as cut in taxes to boost consumption demand and investment by businesses. With the various fiscal measures of increase in public expenditure and tax cuts, fiscal deficit in the US is estimated to rise to 12.5% of GDP for the year 2009.

To overcome recession the US Federal Reserve (which is the Central Bank of the US) cut overnight interest rate to near zero so that credit becomes cheaper and more loans are provided by the US banks to businesses for investment and to consumers for buying durable consumer goods including houses. The Federal Reserve also took measures to increase money supply in the US economy so as increase the availability of credit. However, these monetary measures did not seen to work. Due to uncertain economic environment risk-averse banks were reluctant to give loans due to the risk of defaults by the borrowers. As a result, recession in the US further depend in the last quarter of 2008 and the earlier months of the year 2009. Therefore, in the fourth week of March 2009, a new plan of investing $ 1 trillion for buying *toxic assets* from banks that are blocking lending by banks. This plan involves public-private partnership to clean up the US banking sector to get credit flowing again. It is thought that it will clean up the banking of bad debts and restore provision of credit by them. Therefore, to end the crisis in the US, under this programme the government will provide the lion's share of the funding to purchase toxic assets to encourage private investors to participate.

Failure of Free Market System

It is evident from above that free market economy of the United States did not work well to automatically correct the crisis that *gripped* it following burst of housing loan bubble and therefore the intervention of the Government was called for to rescue the *sagging* financial system. In this regard it is worth noting that the role played by the Federal Reserve of America and policy of unregulated free market pursued by it earlier, especially under the Chairmanship of Greenspan. Since the seventies

3. Paul Krugman, *op. cit.*

when Reagan was the president of the United States, a policy of *complete deregulation* of market economy including its financial architecture has been followed. It is this lack of proper regulation of financial institutions, banks and stock market that led to the creation of complex and non-transparent securities (CDO).

Expressing his views about the cause of American financial crisis, Paul Krugman writes, "The real sin both of the Fed and Bush administration was the failure to exercise adult supervision over markets running wild. It was not just Alan Greenspan's unwillingness to admit that there was anything more than a lot of "froth" in housing markets or his refusal to do anything about sub-prime abuses. The fact is that as America's financial system has grown ever more complex *it has also outgrown the framework of banking regulation that used to protect us*-yet instead of an update that framework all we got were paeans to the wonders of free market."[4]

Crash in Stock Market

The problems of liquidity and credit crunch as a result of financial crisis led to the stock market crash in the United States and Europe. Share prices of many companies tumbled which caused heavy decline in the capital value of the companies and inflicted huge losses on the investors leading to the crisis of confidence for making more investment. The crash in Wall Street hit financial firms the hardest. Even cash-rich banks were scared of lending money to other banks and to the corporate companies following failure of Lahman Brothers. Some European banks suddenly went bust leading to severe credit crunch.

Adverse Effect on Flow of Credit, Investment and Growth

As a result of erosion of capital base of banks and other financial institutions, the liquidity problem faced by them adversely affected the flow of credit to the companies for financing working capital and fixed investment and to the consumers for buying durable goods such as cars, houses etc. This affected the real economy and adversely affected economic growth in the United States and Europe. As lines of credit to corporate dried up in the US and Europe even for meeting their needs of working capital, it affected payments to employees and suppliers. Lack of liquidity and credit crunch also stalled the ongoing investment projects. Fears of several banks and corporate companies going bankrupt arose as several companies and banks started laying off workers. As industrial output started falling the recessionery conditions *reminiscent* of Great Depression came to prevail in the developed economies of the US and Europe, Japan and Asian economies could not remain unaffected.

The loss of asset value of consuming households made them poorer and along with the credit crunch led to the decrease in demand for consumer durables such as cars, houses and a host of other goods. When a few years ago there was a boom in stock market prices of made them wealthier and the **wealth effect** brought about increase in consumption demand leading to consumption–led growth in the United States. Now, from the second half of 2007, when there was a drastic slide – down in share prices the *negative wealth effect* worked to lower the demand for consumer goods and through the working of accelerator dampened investment in the economies of the US and European Countries. This caused *first slowdown in their economies and ultimately recession in the second and third quarters of 2008.*

As mentioned above, the downward spiral accelerated after the failure of Lehman Brothers in September 2008. Money markets already badly affected stopped giving credit to consumers and corporate companies. The people and the banks in the United States and Europe started investing only in Government's treasury bills which were considered as quite safe.

As mentioned above, the financial crisis spilled over to the real economy. The failure of companies to get adequate credit for working capital and fixed investment brought the growth engine to a halt in the United States. The US economy went into recession in December 2007 and this downturn continued in 2008. It is estimated that GDP of the US declined by 6.3 per cent in the last quarter of

4. Paul Krugman "Dont't cry for me, America" *New York Times*, Ján., 2008

2008, the worst in the last 28 years (that is, since 1982). For a large number of industries, the growth rate year-on-year basis fell. Many companies cut jobs and started laying off workers. As a result of recession unemployment rate in the US rose to a high rate of 6.7 per cent in Nov. 2008 and further to 8.1 per cent in February 2009. Rate of unemployment in the US went on increasing further and cuts in jobs of several lakh persons in March to June 2009 drove the US unemployment rate to 26 years high level of 9.5 per cent in June 2009. Though in the last two quarters of 2009 the US economy recovered and registered a growth of around 3 per cent, unemployment rate still further rose to 10 per cent of labour force in Dec. 2009 worst after the depression of 1929-33. Latest report indicates that the US economy grew at 3.2 per cent year-on-year basis in the first quarter of the year 2010, while in the first quarter of the year 2009, the US economy shrank at a rate of 6.4%. In the whole year 2010, the growth of US economy has been estimated at 2.6 per cent.Thus the US economy recovered after a recession of around 3 years. However, despite the recovery of the US economy in terms of GDP growth, the rate of unemployment still remains high at 9.6% of labour force (Dec. 2010).

However, the US recovery has been short-lived. The rate of economic growth has slipped to 1.7 per cent in the first two quarters of the year 2011. This is despite the fact that the Federal Reserve went in for Quantity Easing 2 (QE2) under which it purchased bonds of the US Government to the extent of $600 billion in 2010-11 (upto June 2011). Besides, due to lower growth rate unemployment has stuck at 9.6 per cent of labour force. Further, in July 2011 due to **excessive *sovereign debt*** of the US S&P rating agency downgraded the US rating from AAA to AA+. This made the matters worse. Along with extremely low economic growth rate and high unemployment, this downgrading of the US rating due to excessive public debt of the US Government, has given rise to the fears of ***double-dip recession*** of the US economy which many economists predicted earlier. The emergence of the recession again, like the previous one in 2008, in the US economy would have adverse effects on the global economy.

How Crisis Spread to Europe and Other Countries

It is often said that "when America sneezes, the whole world catches cold" This has been found true in case of financial crisis too. Therefore, when all powerful US economy experienced severe financial crisis, the rest of the world could not escape from its fall-out. Due to the globalisation with its free flow of capital and goods between the US and other countries, especially the European countries which were closely integrated with the US economy, suffered a lot. In fact the surplus funds in the European countries and Japan were invested in the United States. Directly or indirectly capital flowing into America from global investors ended up financing the housing credit bubble that ultimately burst with painful consequences. Thus investors and banks of European countries and Japan suffered heavy losses and called for their being bailed out by their Governments or Central Banks. Following the cues from the crash in stock prices in Wall Street share prices in stock markets in European countries (and Asian countries including India) also crashed leading to heavy losses to the investors.

Besides, recession in the US economy affected exports of the European countries as well as of Japan and others Asian Countries (including India) to the United States leading to the decline in output of export goods in these countries with heavy job losses. This has caused recessionary conditions in these countries as well.

Summing up. In 2009, the global economy not only experienced a 'great contraction', but there was also significant uncertainty about the impact of the financial crisis in the advanced economies on the real economy. The successive and large revisions in the IMF's growth outlook for 2009 indicated the extent of uncertainty that resulted from the sub-prime financial crisis. In the first quarter of 2010, stronger evidence of recovery in the global economy started to emerge, though the speed of the recovery turned increasingly divergent as the emerging market economies remained ahead of the advanced economies in terms of both pace and strength of the recovery. The global recovery turned out to be fragile subsequently, following the concerns relating to sovereign debt in the Eurozone.

Persistence of high growth in India and China largely moderated the depth of the global recession in 2009, even though these countries also experienced slowdown in growth in relation to their high growth before the onset of global crisis. World trade contracted much sharper than the contraction in GDP in 2009, and is projected to stage a recovery in 2010. Reflecting the impact of weak global demand conditions as also the protectionist measures adopted by many countries, the decline in world merchandise trade volume was as high as 11.8 per cent in 2009. According to WTO, world exports of commercial services also declined for the first time after 1983 by 13.0 per cent during 2009. The impact of recession in the advanced economies was particularly strong on the employment situation in the USA and European countries.

As a result of the crisis, net capital flows to the emerging market economies declined. Unprecedented use of policy stimulus by countries around the world helped in averting another 'Great Depression' but the fiscal conditions of the advanced economies weakened significantly in that process. In managing the financial crisis, the costs of financial excesses in the private sector shifted to the public sector creating in turn the risk of potential sovereign debt crisis.

IMPACT OF GLOBAL FINANCIAL CRISIS ON INDIA

Since 1991 following the policy of globalisation, the Indian economy was also opened up to foreign capital and foreign trade of goods and services and thereby got integrated with the United States and European and other countries to a greater degree than before. Therefore, when financial crises gripped United States and European countries, India could not remain isolated. We explain below some important effects of global financial crisis on the Indian economy.

Stock-market Crash

Following the eruption of financial crisis when the Wall Street of the US and stock markets of the European countries crashed, its effect spilled over to India and our stock market (Dalal Street) was also badly hit. To meet the liquidity requirements or liabilities of their parent companies, Foreign Institutional Investors (FIIs) started selling the shares of the Indian companies held by them. The selling pressure by FIIs brought about a crash in Dalal Street (i.e., Bombay Stock Exchange). In the last few years FIIs had invested on a massive scale in the equity shares of several Indian companies operating in various industries from consumer goods to infrastructure industries. As a result of the buying spree of shares of Indian companies by FIIs, share prices rose to new heights. The Sensex which was around 6000 in 2004 rose to 8000 in Aug.-Sept. 2005 and went on rising further crossing 10,000 mark in 2006, 13000 mark in 2007 and reached the peak of around 21,000 mark in January 2008. At around this time, share prices in the US and European markets started falling sharply and the problems of liquidity and credit crunch assumed grave proportions. As mentioned above, this led FII to sell shares held by them in the Indian stock market to pull out capital from India. This was done to fulfil the needs of redemption pressures on their parent companies who were facing liquidity problem. As a result of this selling pressure, Sensex of Bombay Stock Market (which is called Dalal Street) started tumbling; it fell from around 21000 in Jan. 2008 to 11000 in Sept. 2008 and in its downward march it fell below 10,000 in Oct. 2008 and 9000 mark in Nov. 2008, that is, 60 per cent fall since Jan. 2008. This caused huge losses to the Indian companies and investors whose huge wealth was wiped out in a couple of months in 2008. Foreign institutional investors sold more than $ 13 billion worth of shares of Indian companies upto Nov. 2008 and repatriated them to their home countries. This also led to the decline in foreign exchange reserves held by RBI to $ 250 billion by the end of 2008.

Depreciation of Indian Rupee

But the effect of capital outflow by FIIs was not confined to drastic fall in share prices but was more deeper and devasting. When foreign institutional investors (FIIs) sold their shares in India they got rupees. They had to convert their rupees into dollars to send them abroad. This led to the increase in demand for dollars. Rupee-dollar exchange rate being determined by demand for and supply of currencies, the increase in demand for dollars caused appreciation of US dollar in terms of rupees, that is, rupee depreciated against US dollar. The Indian importers also demanded dollars to pay for the imports of goods. The Indian banks doing foreign exchange operations also bought US dollars at home to keep their foreign exchange operations afloat since due to credit crunch no one in foreign countries was willing to lend dollars to any Indian bank. This further raised the demand for dollars causing fast depreciation of rupee in the months of September, October and November 2008. The Indian rupee whose value had appreciated to ₹ 39.4 for a dollar in Dec. 2007 depreciated to ₹ 49.3 for a dollar in end-Oct. 2008 and further to all time low of ₹ 50.6 for a dollar in mid-Nov. 2008. This depreciation of Indiana rupee though made our exports cheaper, made our imports costlier. In Oct. and Nov. 2008, crude oil price declined from all time high of $ 147 per barrel to around 50 US dollar in Nov. 2008 and to $ 40 per barrel in Feb. 2009.

Liquidity Crunch in the Banking Sector

But the story of impact of capital outflow by FIIs did not end here. As a result of large outflow of dollars fast depreciation of rupee against dollar began. To prevent fast depreciation of rupee and maintain relative exchange rate stability, RBI intervened and supplied dollars from its foreign exchange reserves. With this too much depreciation of rupee was prevented but in this process of supplying more dollars in the foreign exchange market, it got rupees in return. As a result the quantity of rupees with the banking system declined causing liquidity problem in the Indian banking system which affected credit flow to the industry for financing of working capital and fixed investment projects. This problem became so severe that inter-bank credit market was mostly frozen; no bank was willing to lend to other banks as every bank needed liquidity to tide over contigencies and this restricted credit flow to the industries. Risk aversion by banks in India also played an important role in restricting credit flow to consumers for buying cars, houses etc. and companies for making investment.

Thus the cause of liquidity and credit crunch that arose in India was the sale of billions of dollars from its reserves by the RBI which withdrew rupees from the banking system in the process. It is estimated that each sale of a billion US dollars by RBI sucks around ₹ 5000 crores from the domestic market. The call rates, that is, rates at which banks lend to each other for a short period rose to all time high of 23 per cent.

Impact on Indian Economic Growth

When all powerful US economy witnessed slowdown in economic growth and ultimately experienced recessionary conditions as a result of financial crisis, its effect spilled over to Europe, Japan and other Asian countries. Britain, Germany, Italy and 15 nations sharing Euro slumped into recession for the first time after several years. In September 2008 IMF gave the bleak assessment of the global economy whose growth rate was expected to hit 3 per cent in 2008 and near zero in 2009. In September 2008. IMF also predicted lower growth of 7.7 per cent for India for the year 2008-09 which was later further lowered to 7 per cent as against over 9 per cent growth in the previous 4 years (2004-08). Our Finance Minister repeatedly assured that despite stock market crash, the fundamentals of the Indian economy are quite strong and Indian growth story is quite intact. Prime Minister Dr. Manmohan Singh also expressed the similar views and said that global meltdown would have minimal effect on India's economic growth. However, India's growth of GDP fell to 6.8 per cent in 2008-09 as against over 9 per cent per annum in the preceeding three years. In 2009-10 and 2011-11, the Indian economy recovered and its growth of GDP was 8 per cent and 8.6 per cent respectively.

However, as against the 11th plan target of 9 per cent annual growth, fall in India's growth to 6.7 per cent in 2008-09 and 8.0 per cent in 2009-10 will badly affect the targets of employment generation and poverty reduction. It is true that unlike that of China, India's economic growth depends more on domestic demand rather than external demand and is driven mostly by domestic saving and investment. However, at present after 18 years of globalisation, our exports constitute 14 per cent and imports 20 per cent of GDP (2006-07). Therefore, India could not escape from the adverse consequences of global meltdown. This is evident from industrial growth during the second half of the fiscal year 2008-09; India's industrial production (IIP) registered 4.8 per cent growth in September 2008 and a negative growth of 0.41 per cent in October 2008 for the first time in 15 years. For the whole year 2008-09 the growth in industrial production dipped to 3.7 per cent as compared to 10.3

per cent in 2007-08 and 14.9% in 2006-07. There was a fall in output of automobile, aviation and shipping industries. Besides, export-oriented industries such as textiles, leather, gems and jewellery have been badly hit by the global meltdown and registered a fall in production and employment opportunities. Agriculture registered 1.6 per cent growth rate in 2008-09 as compared to 4.7 per cent in 2007-08. There was a very slow growth of 0.4% in agriculture in 2009-10.

The most adverse consequence of global turmoil was that the growth rate of manufacturing in India fell to 3.2% in 2008-09 from 10.3 per cent in 2007-08. Not only did domestic demand come down even export orders fell substantially due to recession in the developed countries. The other important causes of slowdown in manufacturing are that banks were not willing to give credit and lack of adequate power supply and high input costs. It is worth mentioning that though growth rate of Indian economy slowed down under the impact of global financial crisis, its estimated growth rate of 6.8 per cent in 2008-09 and 8 per cent in 2009-10 was still quite high in view of the fact that other countries such as US, UK, Japan, Euro countries, Germany were experiencing severe recession (that is, contraction in GDP). In fact, growth rate of Indian economy is second highest in the world next only to China. However, a matter of serious concern is that employment situation worsend in the fiscal year 2008-09. There were large scale losses in jobs in the sectors like textiles, metals, leather and jewellery. With slowdown in economic growth in India unemployment in India also went up. Another matter of concern is that due to large increase in government expenditure to pull the economy out of recession and slow growth of agriculture, inflation rate as measured by CPI rose to more than 11 per cent in 2008-09. Besides there has been *severe food inflation* which in Feb. 2010 went up to around 20%. In 2009-10 and 2010-11 food inflation spilled over to manufactured products as well. Rate of infaltion based on CPI (for industrial workers) went upto 9.1% 2008-09, 12.4 in 2009-10 and 11% in 2010-11.

Exports and Balance of Payments

As a result of globalisation and the adoption of export-oriented strategy of growth in place of import substitution, the Indian economy now depends to a greater extent on external market to sell our goods and services. In 1990-91 we exported goods to the tune of 5.8 per cent of GDP whereas in 2006-07 our exports of goods rose to 14 per cent and our imports to 20 per cent of our GDP.[5]

Our foreign trade balance worsened during 2008-09. India's foreign trade balance registered a deficit of $60 billion in the first half of 2008-09 as against $ 30 billion in the first half of 2007-08. Actually, our exports in Oct. 2008 were not just down but declined 12.8% as compared to the same month of the previous year 2007. This negative trend continued in the remaining years of 2008-09. As a result, our target of exports of 200 billion US dollar for 2008-09 was revised downward to $ 175 billion. Actually, growth of Indian exports in 2008-09 was around $ 170 billion, much short of the original target. Due to global financial crisis the growth of our exports were bound to decline as a result of recessionary conditions in the US and the European countries. Besides, due to sharp depreciation of rupee during 2008-09, our imports also costed more despite the fall in international commodity prices and crude oil. Hitherto our export growth was bolstered by rising commodity prices and yet strong demand from emerging markets and oil producing countries. All such contributory factors are no longer there. In 2008-09 and 2009-10 deficit in our balance of payments on current account went up to 2.4% and 2.9% of GDP_{mp} respectively. However, beginning from Nov. 2009, there has been *positive* growth in our exports indicating recovery in the world economy, especially in the US. However, due to high growth in imports our current account deficit has gone up.

INDIAN RESPONSE TO THE FINANCIAL CRISIS

The major effects of global financial crisis were (1) stock market crash, (2) depreciation of Indian rupee due to capital outflows by FIIs and (3) credit crunch in the Indian economy following the drastic decline in the liquidity in the bank system.

5. GOI, *Economic Survey*, 2007-08, p.112

Monetary Policy Measures

Our response to the global financial turmoil has been both monetary and fiscal. The RBI which for several months before had been increasing cash reserve ratio and interest rates to fight against inflation reversed its monetary policy from Oct. 2008. The RBI took several steps to prevent fast depreciation of Indian rupee due to massive capital outflow by FIIs by selling billions of dollars in the foreign exchange market from its reserves. But for RBI intervention, the value of rupee would have gone much below Rs. 52 for a US dollar.

The problem raised by global financial crisis was diagnosed as the lack of liquidity in the money market which adversely affected the flow credit to industries. Therefore, to increase liquidity of the banking system, RBI cut cash reserve ratio (CRR) four times in Oct.2008 to January 2009 by 400 basis points (*i.e.* by 4 percentage points) from 9 per cent to 5 per cent. With this the RBI infused liquidity of ₹ 1,60,000 crores in the banking system. Besides, RBI reduced statutory liquidity ratio (SLR) from 25 per cent to 24 which enabled banks to get ₹ 20,000 crores from RBI against Government securities *for lending* to mutual funds. Besides, RBI released ₹ 25,000 crores to the banks in connection with the farm waiver scheme of the Central Government. It may be noted further that banks can also borrow from RBI through repo window of liquidity adjustment facility (LAF) scheme of RBI. Besides, unwinding of some *market stabilisation scheme* was also undertaken to increase liquidity with the banks. In this way about ₹ 2,00,000 crores had been infused into the domestic money market to alleviate the pressures brought on by deterioration in global financial environment. With infusion of this adequate liquidity in the system through various measures the banks could provide credit to the industries for financing working capital and fixed investment projects. This was expected to boost industrial growth which had slackened in the last few months.

However, it was felt that to fullfil the needs of credit of the companies, mere infusion of more liquidity was not enough unless the lending rates of banks were lowered to reduce the cost of borrowing. To achieve this, repo rate – the rate at which banks borrow from RBI for a short time and used as a policy signal – was cut five times by 4 percentage point from 9 per cent to 5 per cent in Oct. 2008. As a result of this various Indian banks (including SBI) reduced their prime lending rate (PLR) to around 12 to 12.5 per cent. With this banks lowerd their lending rates so that cost of borrowing from the banks fell and more credit was created for investment by the companies and there was more demand for durable consumer goods such as houses, cars etc. Besides, RBI cut *reverse repo rate*, which is the overnight rate of interest at which banks park their surplus funds with the RBI to 4 per cent. This was meant to encourage banks to give credit to business enterprises for investment and to consumers for buying houses, cars etc. rather than keeping surplus liquid funds with RBI.

However, reports from banks (in March 2009) revealed that though liquidity had eased in the system and banks had lowered their lending rates but credit to industries did not pick up to the extent it was expected to happen. As a result, most banks were sitting on surplus cash. This showed due to global meltdown and its adverse effects on various sectors of the Indian economy banks became risk averse and were not willing to lend for fear of defaults by the borrowers.

Fiscal Stimulus

Besides easy monetary policy it was emphasized that a fiscal stimulus to overcome recession and slowdown in economic growth was needed. This fiscal stimulus is in keeping with Keynesian macroeconomics as Keynes emphasized increase in government expenditure to get rid of depression in the nineteen thirties. To keep growth momentum and to ensure 7 per cent growth rate in 2008-09 the Indian Government came out with three fiscal stimulus packages which involved increase in Government expenditure and cut in indirect taxes to boost both consumption demand and investment demand. The first fiscal stimulus package announced on Dec. 6, 2008 involved ***increase in Government expenditure by ₹ 30,700 crore.*** This increase in Government expenditure was meant to help growth of infrastrucutre, textiles (which is a major employer of labour force) exports, housing, automobiles, and small and medium enterprises.

An important measure in the first fiscal stimulus package was **all-round cut in excise duty** (CENVAT) to raise the demand for goods and services. This 4% cut in excise duty was estimated to result in revenue loss of ₹8700 crore to the Government. Further, to *counter the slump in exports* due to global financial crisis, the first fiscal package provided for ***subsidising interest costs of exporters.*** It was hoped that lower interest costs of exporters would make the Indian exports more competitive. In order to give further boost to the exports, an additional fund of ₹1100 crore had also been provided to ensure full *refund of duties including service tax* paid on inputs.

In the first week of January 2009, it was felt that global recessionary conditions were still very strong which would adversely after growth of the Indian economy, the second fiscal stimulus packjage was announced on Jan. 2, 2009. While the first fiscal stimulus package focussed on direct increase in Goivernment expenditure the second fiscal stimulus package sought to improve or facilitate supply of finance to some organizations. For thus purpose in this second package to **increase expenditure on infrastructure** was sought by providing finance to non-banking finance Companies (NBFCs) *dealing exclusively with infrastructure finance.* For this purpose the public sector company Indian Infrastructure Finance Company (IIFC) was allowed to borrow ₹30,000 crore from the market by issuing tax-free bonds that would be used to assist in funding of projects worth ₹75000 crore.

Secondly, *a higher depreciation rate of 50 per cent for Commercial Vehicles (CVs)* like trucks, buses and vans bought in the period, January-March 2009 was allowed. Besides, an extra line of credit to non-banking financial companies (NBFCs) for purchase of CVs and assistance by it for purchase of buses for urban transport system under governmental urban renewal scheme. All these steps were expected to boost demand for CVs which had been badly hit by economic slowdown.

Further measures taken in this second stimulus package related to providing an indirect push to realty and infrastructure sectors by **removing exemption from countervailing duties** (CVDs) along with special CVDs for steel and cement, the two important inputs for real estate and infrastructure sectors. Besides, in order to ensure that Indian corporate sector get cheaper funds from abroad, in the second stimulus package the **government *increased the limit on investment* by foreign institutional investors (FIIs) in *rupee denominated* corporate bonds** issued by the Indian companies from $8 billion to $15 billion.

It was hoped that the above measures in the second fiscal stimulus package would result in additional credit supply of ₹56000 crore.

The Third Fiscal Stimulus Package. In *this third package* announced on Jan. 24, 2009 *the government sought to boost demand by cutting central excise duty, service tax and customs duty.* This was estimated to cost the exchequer ₹29,100 crores. The measures announced in this fiscal stimulus were :

1. Central excise duty was slashed further by 2 per cent from 10 per cent to 8 per cent. Along with this the earlier 4% cut in central excise duty announced in Dec. 2008 was extended beyond March 31, 2009. It was expected that if this cut in excise duty was actually passed on to the consumers by manufacturers, this would lead to the reduction in prices and therefore stimulate demand for goods.

2. As a further measure to boost demand, service tax was also cut across the board by 2 percentage point from 12 per cent to 10 per cent.

3. To provide relief to the power sector naptha imported for generation of electricity was fully exempted from basic customs duty beyond March 2009.

Summing up. The above fiscal stimulus packages were bound to increase domestic demand in the economy and helped in achieving 6.8 per cent rate of growth of the Indian economy in the fiscal year 2008-09 and 8 per cent in 2009-10 and 8.6 per cent in 2010-11. This was also expected to help in generating more employment opportunities and thereby prevent the problem of unemployment from getting more worse. Due to fiscal stimulus it was expected that fiscal deficit to rise to more than 6 per cent of GDP. However, in times of recessionary conditions, the higher fiscal deficit is an appropriate counter-cyclical policy. It is worth noting that increase in Government expenditure causes increase in aggregate income not only equal to the amount by which it is increased but has also a multiplier effect. The manifold increase in aggregate income or GDP, as a result of increase in Government expenditure is called *Government expenditure multiplier* which plays an important role in expansion in national income in an economy when productive capacity is not fully utilised due to deficiency of aggregate demand.

Recovery of the Indian Economy

From the slowdown caused by global financial crisis Indian economy recovered in the second-half of the year 2009-10 as a result of Government's fiscal stimulus measures and accomodative expansionary monetary policy of the RBI. The Indian economy recovered from the crisis first due to increase in Government expenditure under fiscal stimulus and later due to pick-up in private consumption and investment demand as a result of multiplier effect of increase in Government expenditure, especially incurred on infrastructre projects.

The growth of GDP which had reached over 9 per cent for three successive years prior to the crisis dipped to 6.7 per cent in 2008-09 but again rose to 8.6 per cent in the year 2009-10 and to 9.3% in 2010-11. However, due to slowdown in the US and other developed countries, lower growth of agriculture due to weak monsoon and European debt crisis India's growth will fell to 6.2 per cent or in 2011-12. The growth of industry which had fallen to 3.7 per cent in 2008-09 rose to 8 per cent in 2009-10 and 2010-11 but again fell to 7 per cent in 2011-12. Agriculture after registering a very low growth of 1.6% in 2008-09 and 0.4 per cent in 2009-10 achieved a high growth of 6.6 per cent in 2010-11. The lower growth of agriculture in 2008-09 and 2009-10 caused high food inflation in India in 2009-10 with which India is still struggling.

Exports and Foreign Investment

India's exports also revived in 2009-10. Exports which *slipped* into negative territory in Oct. 2008 due to global economic slowdown and a resulting fall in demand came out of the red after 13 months in November 2009. Since then every month the growth of our exports has been positive. Our exports during 2009-10 was around $ 182.2 billion as against exports worth $ 189 billion in the previous fiscal year. But for the recovery of our exports since Nov. 2009, decline in our exports during 2009-10 would have been much higher. During 2010-11 our exports recorded on an average 29.5 per cent growth (in US $) year-on-year basis which is quite impressive. This growth in our exports in 2010-11 was helped by global recovery real GDP growth rate in 2010.

Besides exports, foreign capital inflows (both portfolio investment and foreign direct investment, FDI) revived during 2009-10. It is because of portfolio capital inflows during 2009-10, that Indian rupee appreciated to around ₹44 per US $ and BSE Index shot up to around 20,000 mark in September 2010. Though in May 2010, due to Greek debt crisis FIIs got panicky and started selling their shares in the Indian stock market and repatriating dollars to the US. However, after a few months, Capital inflows by FII again started coming.

Global investors are getting better returns from India. Therefore, foreign direct investment inflows (FDI) into India in the year 2009-10 are estimated to be around $ 25.8 billion against $ 27.3 billion in the previous year 2008-09. In a globalised world, a congenial global economic environment and a sustainable balance of payments position are critical for achieving the policy goal of sustained growth of 9% per annum in India. The global recession in 2007-09 operated as a dampener on the prospects of a faster growth. Besides the conventional channels of trade and capital flows for transmission of external shocks to India's real economy, the uncertainty about global recovery continued to affect business confidence and market sentiments, which indirectly affected domestic private consumption and investment demand. India's high degree of resilience and capacity to manage a severe external shock was evident from the strength and pace of recovery in GDP growth during 2009-10. India achieved 8 per cent growth in GDP in 2009-10 and 8.6 per cent in 2010-11.

EUROZONE CRISIS AND ITS IMPACT

In 2010 the world again found itself in financial turmoil threatening another recession in the developed economies of the world, especially in European Euroland before the effects of global financial crisis (2007-09) had yet to fully wear off. The new crisis emerged not due to hitherto toxic assets as was the case of 2007-09 sub-prime crisis but due to the threat of defaulting on payment of its debt by governments of European countries especially by Greek government. Some economists have put forward the view that this new crisis is continuation of the previous crisis of 2007-09. This is because to overcome recession or slowdown following the financial crisis (2007-09) the governments of various European countries increased their public expenditure by heavily borrowing, especially from foreign sources and thereby increasing significantly their sovereign debt. The problem of Greece and other European Countries is of ***huge sovereign debt*** on which annual interest has to paid and the repayment of the principal sum borrowed. This has created the risk of default on paying debt by these countries.

The global financial system seems to be very fragile. Though Greece accounted for less than 2 per cent of the combined GDP of the European Union (EU), yet it set that entire region in turmoil and terrified investors throughout the world. Greek crisis created a good deal of uncertainty about the returns from their investment by investors in Greece and other Euroland countries bonds. As a result, during the Month of May 2010 stock market prices crashed not only in Europe but also in the USA and throughout Asia. Besides, the fears of *double-dip recession* and consequently large decline in stock market prices caused fall in world prices of commodities, crude oil and petroleum products. The price of crude oil went below $ 70 per barrel in May 2010.

Causes of Greek (Eurozone) Crisis

Governments of Greece and other Euro countries ran up record debts to pull their economies out of the deepest slump in 2007-09 since the Great Depression of 1930s and are new experiencing problem of defaulting on sovereign debt. Countries like India are suffering because of wrong-doings of the developed countries. While the US crisis of 2007-09 had broken out as most of the borrowers could not repay housing loans and therefore started defaulting on loan payments, in Greece and other European Countries, the problem has been created by governments which lived beyond their means and borrowed heavily thereby adding greatly to their debt burden which they are finding it difficult to repay now. Countries like Greece, Spain, Italy, Ireland and UK have been undertaking *double-digit fiscal deficit*. According to a report, the fiscal deficit of Greece in 2009 was 13.6 per cent of GDP, that of UK 11.6 per cent, of Spain 11.2 per cent and Ireland 11 per cent. According to Joseph Stiglitz, such a huge fiscal deficit is clearly unsustainable and was bound to cause problem of defaulting on payment of debt that increased due to heavy borrowing to meet the large deficits.

Debt of Greece and other European countries is very large. At present public debt of Greece stands at 115 per cent of GDP and is estimated to rise to 150 per cent of GDP in 2014. This is in part due to the fact that Greece, Ireland, Spain has been incurring large fiscal deficit in the past and has been adding 14 per cent annually to its sovereign debt and partly because Greece has been experiencing negative growth of 4 to 5 per cent annually. Greece faced dilemma. Getting back to sustainable fiscal path required cutting annual fiscal deficit by 10% by reducing public expenditure and increasing taxes. This was politically infeasible as it would have caused loss of a large number of jobs and therefore would have been resisted by the people who would protest vehemently as was actually revealed by widespread protests in 2010, 2011 and 2012. Besides, attempts to reduce fiscal deficit was likely to hamper economic growth which would lead to lower tax revenue in future. This is because withdrawing fiscal stimulus by cutting public expenditure and raising taxes will lower aggregate demand. These austerity measures in fact caused recession or lower GDP growth in European Countries.

It is worth mentioning that Greece had adopted Euro as its currency and no longer had its own currency. Therefore, because of its being locked into Euro, Greece *could not devalue the currency* so as to switch its aggregate expenditure from imports to exports.

In the absence of defaulting on debt, three possible options were available to Greece to overcome its debt crisis. First, Greece could withdraw from EU and revive its own currency and undertake its *devaluation* to expand exports and stimulate growth and thereby lower its debt burden. With its ending of membership of EU and revival of its currency Greece could print its own currency to pay off a part of its internal debt and thus easing its fiscal burden. This also applies to other countries. However, this scenario was unlikely to happen since no European country including Greece is prepared to see its dismemberment as EU comes to their rescue whenever required.

Secondly, Greece could remain in the EU and adopt harsh **austerity measures imposed by EU and IMF**. Accordingly, it could drastically cut its public expenditure on the one hand and increase its taxes to raise revenue on the other to reduce its annual fiscal deficits which will help in solving its debt problem over time. This, as pointed out above, was bound to be opposed and resisted strongly by the people and was therefore considered as politically infeasible. The third option to be adopted was to take only ***moderate and politically feasible austerity measures*** **along with** ***rescheduling*** **of its debt.** Note that austerity measures require ***fiscal compression***, that is, cutting of public expenditure and raising taxes.

It is not only Greece that is affected by heavy debt problem, similar debt crisis is also faced by Spain, Portugal, Ireland, Italy and even UK. If Greece defaulted on its debt, it was likely to cause similar situation in these other European countries. It was to prevent the fears of this **contagion effect** that EU in collaboration with IMF announced $ 1 trillion bail-out package for Greece and other Euro countries facing sovereign debt crisis so that these countries could repay their debt and interest on it. Besides, independent European Central Bank (ECB) was persuaded to announce that it would buy Greek government bonds to ease the pressure on redemption of Government bonds. It would help the Greek government for tackling its debt crisis. It is worth mentioning that EU while announcing its bail-out package put the condition that Greece and other Euro countries would adopt ***austerity measures,*** that is, cut their public expenditure and raise taxes to increase revenue so as to reduce fiscal deficit.

In 2011 again sovereign debt crisis in Greece arose in serious form putting financial markets all over the world in turmoil. European Central Bank (ECB) again came to its rescue and purchased its bonds but put strict conditions that Greece would adopt ***severe austerity measures*** (i.e. cut its expenditure and raise its resources through higher taxes) so that it is able to reduce its debt burden.

Spread of Sovereign Debt Crisis to other European Countries

In 2011 sovereign debt problem spread to other major economies of Eurozone such as Italy and Spain putting the whole Eurozone in the danger zone, that is, to the brink of default on their public debt. After some hesitation, in August 2011, European Central Bank (ECB) took emergency operations to bail them out. ECB purchased Italian and Spanish debt-bonds of the value of 22 billion Euro which was biggest bail-out operation undertaken by it so far. Besides, in Sept. 2011private banks which had given loans to Greece and other debt-ridden European countries agreed to write off 50 per cent of their debt to these countries and thus providing great relief to them.

However, investors realised that bail-out package for Greece and other Euro countries facing sovereign debt crisis would only postpone the date of their being declared insolvent. As a result, investors not willing to take risk started selling the Greek bonds and Government bonds of other Euro countries and sending dollars to the US to invest there which they considered as quite safe. As a result, US dollar greatly appreciated and Euro greatly depreciated.

It is worth mentioning that some economists were of the view that adoption of *harsh* austerity measures by Greece and other European countries and therefore cutting public expenditure and raising taxes as recommended by EU and IMF to solve their debt problem will not only hamper their recovery from the recession/slowdown following the global financial crisis (2002-07) but will also pose a risk to global economic recovery and growth and thus raising spectre of a ***double-dip recession***, especially when the US in 2011 also faced a sovereign debt problem. Barak Obama entered into a deal with the US Congress to raise the country's ***debt ceiling*** and thus managed to avoid the default but the US economy was moving from bad to worse in 2011 and 2012 despite the ***quantity easing*** policy pursued by the Federal Reserve.

In 2011 crisis seemed to be spreading to other European countries such as Spain, Ireland, Portugal, Italy, UK and even Hungary. The terrified investors exposed not only to Greek debt and its derivatives but also to the debts of other European countries. This resulted in great volatility in stock markets and foreign exchange markets throughout Europe, US and Asian countries. There was *flight of capital* from Greece and other European countries to the US in 2010 but in 2011, even the US was pushed into danger zone. This caused a great turmoil in financial markets in Europe, US and even in Asia. If this financial turmoil continues, the global economy may again slip into recession. Reports are already coming about the slow growth or near stagnation in not only large European countries but also of US. In France, the second-largest economy in the European Union after Germany, growth came to a standstill in 2010-11. The growth in the United States also slowed down in 2010-11 and

2011.12. The US is also slowing and could slip into recession. Another recession is already well under way in Greece and Portugal; growth in Spain, Italy and Britain is quite slow, domestic demand in Europe was weak and growth was dependent on sales from abroad, where signals are that they are shrinking. According to a recent report in the week-end of Aug. 2011 there was 0.7% fall in industrial production in 17 nations of European Union (EU) in June 2011 compared with May 2011. With less economic growth, governments will collect less tax revenue. They will have more trouble in paying their debts. That could make investors even more nervous and add to turmoil in the stock and bond markets, which will undercut business and consumer confidence, and will lead to yet slower growth, and ultimately recession. There is a real risk that there is a self-enforcing cycle under way here.

India did not escape from this new global crisis. The Indian exports to European countries and the US declined which adversely affected India's industrial growth. The decline in India's exports also brought about increase in current account deficit (CAD) to 4.2% of GDP in 2011-12 and further to around 5% GDP in 2012-13. Such a large current account deficit was unsustainable and was a matter of great concern. Besides, the large current account deficit in 2011-12 and 2012-13 put pressure in the Indian rupee which sharply depreciated.

Eurozone Treaty. Eurozone debt problem still remains unresolved threatening the breaking up of European union as well. In the first week of December 2011 European union summit was held in Berlin to make an attempt to solve Eurozone present debt crisis problem and to save Eurozone from splitting by preventing the future debt crisis. At this summit a Eurozone treaty was forged to bring about a deeper integration in Eurozone. However, Britain was not a party to this treaty. In this treaty EU leaders agreed to lend up to $200 billion to an emergency lending facility of the IMF to help it aid eurozone countries gripped by crises. This is in addition to the 440 billion Euro for European Financial Stability Fund (EFSF) already established by European governments, and a permanent € 500 billion facility called the European Stability Mechanism which was to be established by June 2012. This is in addition to the relief to Greece already provided by private banks in writing down and restructuring their loans up to 50%. Greek problem had not yet been solved that Spain, another important country of European Union was gripped with a crisis in middle of the year 2012. Spain posed a bigger wory than Greece. The Spanish government said that it would infuse 19 billion euros into distressed real estate lender Bankia SA whose troubles had led to a run on Spanish institutions. Also the Bank of Spain warned that the country might sink deeper into a recession. Dealers were worried about Spain because it was a much larger economy and might prove more difficult to bail out by the larger economies of northern Europe.

These arrangements for bailing out stressed economies were expected to go a long way in dealing with the existing debt problem. But they do not deal with the fiscal problem that underlies the debt problem, namely, that most EU governments spend much more than the revenues they raise, especially in a variety of generous entitlement programmes of the welfare state. Unless these governments conform to prudent fiscal rules that align their spending with their revenues, the sovereign debt problem will keep recurring. Hence the most significant achievement of the last EU summit was the agreement by all EU governments, except UK, to commit to a fiscal agreement. While this was a major step forward, details of how this will work are yet to be worked out. However, an adverse development (in Mid-January 2012) has been the downgrading the Standard and Poor of rating of 9 EU countries which is bound to affect the EFSE's credit worthiness and the available funds could will fall short of needs again. Standard and Poors downgraded the credit ratings of nine euro zone countries, while stripping France and Austria of their coveted triple-A status but not of EU paymaster Germany. Standard and Poor's rating actions were primarily driven by its assessment that the policy initiatives that have been taken by European policy makers in recent weeks might be insufficient to fully address onging systemic stresses in the eurozone. S&P cut the ratings of Italy, Spain, Portugal and Cyprus by two notches and the standing of France, Austria, Malta, Slovakia and Slovenia by one notch each. Thc move puts highly indebted. Italy on the same BBB + level as Kazakhstan and pushes Portugal into junk status.

In a potentially more ominous setback, negotiations of a debt swap by private creditors, seen as crucial to avert Greek default that would rock Europe and the world economy, broke up without agreement in Athens. If Greece cannot persuade banks and insurers to accept voluntary losses on their bond holdings, a second international rescue package for EU's most heavily indebted country will unravel, raising the prospect of bankruptcy in March, when it has to redeem $ 18.24 billion in debt.

Crisis in Cyprus

In March 2013, the important European country Cyprus faced with an acute debt burden problem. It may be noted that Cyprus has a large exposure to Greek debt and the second Greek bailout package in 2012 caused 56.9 billion hole in Cypriot budget. Now, because of its mounting debt burden it sought $ 13 billion from EU for its bail-out. The EU asked the Cyprus government to raise funds of $ 5.8 billion itself before it sanctions its bailout. In order to raise these funds Cyprus government proposed a tax on deposits in its banks. This created a turmoil in stock and foreign exchange markets in the world as two thirds of $ 88.4 billion total deposits in banks of Cyprus was in foreign currency. However, the Cypriot Government said that Cyprus had no choice but to accept the EU's bailout condition with levy on bank deposits or go bankrupt.

Cyprus is a routing centre for offshare investment due to its low tax regime. Before these investments were to be transferred to other countries these investment funds wre deposited in Cypriot banks. Imposition of tax on bank deposits, these investments wre to be affected. The proposed tax on bank deposits set a dangerous precedent for contries needing to be bailed out, especially in the Eurozone area. Depositors' savings were sacrosent and tax on deposits sent a shiver across the entire Eurozone causing Euro to tumble and stock markets to dive.

As a good part of bank deposits in Cyprus amounting to $ 38 billion was Russian, the Russian President Putin opposed the tax on bank deposits describing it quite unfair and setting a dangerous president.

Fortunately, the Cypriot parliament rejected its government proposal of imposing tax on bank deposits calling it as bank robbery. At the time of writing this piece Cyprus is pressing Russia to pump in funds to reduce its debt burden and to extend an existing 2.5 billion Russian loan.

It fellows from above that almost entire Eurozone is in crisis and in a state of stagnation and this Eurozone crisis has created uncertainty and risk which has prevented the investors from investing in bonds and shares of banks of this region. Besides, stagnation in European countries is responsible for slowdown in the Indian exports.

Cyprus Deal. After a good deal of negotiations. Cyprus clinched a deal with international lenders to shut down its second-largest bank and inflict heavy losses on uninsured depositors, including wealthy Russians, in return for a Euro 10-billion ($13 billion) bailout plan.

The deal came hours before a deadline to avert a collapse of the banking system between President Nicos Anastasiades and heads of the European Union, the European Central Bank and the International Monetary Fund. Without a deal, Cyprus banking system would have collapsed and the country could have become the first to crash out of the European single currency (Euro).

Swiftly backed by euro zone finance ministers, the deal will spare the Cyprus a financial meltdown by winding down the largely state-owned Popular Bank of Cyprus, also known as Laiki, and shifting deposits below €100,000 to the Bank of Cyprus to create a "good bank". Deposits above €100,000 in both banks, which are not guaranteed under EU law will be frozen and used to pay Laiki's debts and recapalise Bank of Cyprus through deposit/equity conversion. An EU spokesman said no tax on levy would be imposed on deposits in banks.

How did the Cyprus Crisis Come About ?

Cyprus, the smallest of the eurozone economies, was a robust economy till about two years ago, characterised by relatively high economic growth, low levels of unemployment and healthy state of government finances. Cyprus accounts for a very small fraction of the eurozone economy–about 0.2%. But its banking sector is strongly linked to Greece, which itself has been hit by sovereign debt worries. Cypriot banks had given out loans to top Greek borrowers that had accounted for nearly 160% of Cyprus's GDP. As the Greek economy ran into a crisis in 2010, it was the Cypriot banks that were among the hardest hit. A slowing economy also meant that the government did not have the adequate finances to bail out its banks.

Latest Change in Stance by EU and European Central Bank (ECB)

At long last there was a change in stance or thinking by EU and European Central Bank (ECB) in respect of solving the sovereign debt crisis. After the crises broke out in the late nineties in European countries such as Greece, Spain, Portugal, Italy, Ireland, EU and IMF joined together to bail them out of the crisis so as to keep the members within the union. For this purpose they imposed stringent austerity measures (cutting budget expenditure and raising taxes) so that they are able to pay back the loans taken. The many debt-ridden countries like Greece, Ireland, Portugal, Spain and Italy were forced to accept these conditions in return for bailout loans to reassure the jittery bond markets that they would be able to repay the loans. Accordingly, they slashed their budget expenditure and raised more tax revenue to achieve surplus in their budgets.

However, for austerity measures they had to pay a heavy price as their economies landed in recession or slowdown in economic growth. The evidence grew that cutting government expenditure drastically and raising taxes were less effective in reducing deficits than initially thought and perhaps counter-productive. This is because as growth of the economies slowed down due to austerity measures, it made it difficult to raise enough tax revenue to balance the budget.

EU stance regarding the solution of sovereign debt problem changed in its summit meeting on March 14, 2013 at Brussels where they reviewed the austerity measures regarding their effectiveness in solving the sovereign debt problem. It was found that the unemployment in Eurozone reached a record level of 11.9 per cent (Average of 17 member countries of EU) and slowdown in economic growth in some of them and recession in others. As a result, there was widespread discontent in European Countries such as Greece, Spain, Italy and Portugal which were forced to undertake austerity measures as a condition for their bailout by EU. In its submit at Brussels, leaders of EU agreed to relax the austerity conditions by postponing the budget cuts and higher deficit-cut targets by the debt-ridden European countries. That is, the European Union slowed its enforcement of deficit limit until the region economy turned around. Accordingly, the countries like Greece and Spain which had been bailed out were given more time to repay the loans to the countries such as Germany. This means there was ***rescheduling of debt*** and thereby easing the pressures on then to cut budget deficits sharply through reducing government expenditure and raising taxes.

Thus due to recession that overtook the debt-affilicted European Countries as a result of austerity measures financial leaders of EU and European Central Bank (ECB) realised their previous approach of strong austerity measures were wrong and now *more emphasis was placed on reviving growth.* This represents a clear shift from its earlier emphasis on stringent austerity measures to close budget deficits. However, the new EU stance does not mean that countries have not to follow austerity measures but instead they only need more time to follow austerity measures *that are needed to bring a country's balanced budget* in structural terms, that is, deficit excluding the effects of recession. And the EU commission has been asked to judge the performance of the debt-ridden countries in respect of their progress in reducing structural deficit. This provides the ailing countries more time to get their finances under control.

The change in recent stance of EU and European Central Bank implies that they have realised that their earlier stringent austerity measures imposed on their debt-ridden members did not deliver. As a result of these austerity measures Greece economy went into recession causing huge unemployment. In Greece as a result of this recession unemployment shot up 27 per cent of labour force in January 2013. Portugal's GDP dipped by 3.2 per cent in 2012 as its unemployment reached a record level of 17% of its labour force. Similarly, other European countries such as Spain, Ireland, Portugal, Italy experienced recessionary conditions as a result of adoption of austerity measures imposed by EU and IMF as a condition for their bailout. Prime Minister Mario Monty the supporter of austerity measures lost the elections in Italy held in February 2013.

Predictions by some economists, chiefly by Joseph Stiglitz that the austerity measures would harm growth and even bring about recession in the countries adopting them proved to be true. Austerity measures (cutting government expenditure) and raising taxes they argued would lower economic growth. Not only would they lead to decrease in aggregate demand that adversely affect economic growth but lower growth would also mean loss of revenue for government which will make harder to close the budget gaps. Greece and Spain are running deficit more than their official target limit. A growing number of European countries appear headed in the direction of less austerety no matter what the financial leaders EU decide because most people in their countries are opposed to the austerity policies of EU. Therefore, the new changed stance and rethinking about stringent austerity measures and therefore deciding in relaxing them would come as comfort to millions of Europeans, especially those living in countries that received bailouts, such as Greece, Ireland and Portugal. These countries remain under pressure to keep spending levels down and continue unpopular tax hikes even as they *battle recession.*

The Greek economy is in its sixth year of recession and the unemployment rate there has reached 27%. Portugal's economy contracted 3.2% last year–its severest annual downturn since 1975—and its unemployment rate is at record 17.2%.

The rethinking about strict austerity measures was prompted by recession in Eurozone region which was expected to end in the second half of year 2013. However, Germany which played an important role in bailout of the debt-afflicted countries like Greece and Spain expressed reservation about relaxing austerity measures and decision of about postponting of budget cutting and deficit targets. Germany's Chancellor Angela Merkel said after the EU sumbit meeting that it was necessary to trim the budget deficits to promote growth and investment. But despite Germany's reservations, EU in its sumit meeting at Brussels in March 2013 decided about relaxing of austerity measures to overcome recession and revive growth in the region.

However, it seems this Eurozone treaty has failed to boost sentiments. Analysts are sceptical about long-term steps taken to overcome current crisis. Markets have considered it as too little and too late.

Fall in capital inflows caused a crash in the Indian stock market and led to the sharp depreciation of the Indian rupee. EU's agreement to sign treaty to foster deeper economic integration is definitely the route to take for the longer term but it is unclear how this would unfold in the short term. However, if austerity measures become too stringent it could impact the global economy including India. A week Europe is a reality for at least the middle of the year 2014, though EU leaders have agreed on a treaty. That apart, a lot would depend on the manner of execution of this agreement.

Impact on India

European debt crisis and fragile US recovery have contributed to the growth slowdown of the Indian economy by hurting our exports and affecting capital inflows into India. The capital outflows have resulted in crash in our stock markets that have affected investment sentiments of the corporate world. The rupee's depreciation, while aggravated by domestic speculative activity, is primarily traceable to the ongoing sovereign debt crisis in Europe. The value of rupee which was around 44.50 rupees to a US dollar in August 2011 fell to as low as 54 rupees to a dollar on December 15, 2011 and was around ₹ 54.8 to a US dollar in the first week of April 2013. As observed during the crisis of 2008, the present crisis has again led to a large withdrawal of FII money from the Indian stock market, eroding its value. This large withdrawal of portfolio investments from India also led to the depreciation of the rupee.

The slowdown in GDP growth to 6.2 per cent in 2011-12 and 5 per cent in 2012-13 was partly due to Eurozone crisis. Eurozone debt crisis put a damper on India's exports to Europe, the biggest destination for Indian exports as well as capital inflows into the Indian equity and debt markets. The government blamed European crisis as important reason for India's slowdown in economic growth in recent years.

However, *we think that current slowdown in economic growth is partly a result* as pointed out above, of Eurozone debt crisis and overall global environment, especially slow recovery in the United States and stagnation in the European countries. Besides, increase in interest rates by RBI to fight inflation has led the corporate sector to defer investment has resulted in the drastic fall in output of capital goods. However, in our view, the Indian economy will soon recover once these short-run problems are resolved. Once inflation is brought under control RBI will cut its interest rates which will give a push to investment that will boost industrial growth. If investment in infrastructure increases, as is expected now, this will lead to the expansion in domestic demand for capital goods. This will ensure a higher growth rate of 6.5 per cent in the next year, 2013-14. Besides, we still have the ability to achieve 8% per cent growth rate even on the basis of our domestic market. This is because, *we still, on the supply side, have the fundamentals for higher growth rate. These are high saving and investment rates which even in the year (2011-12) are 30 per cent 35 per cent respectively. These will ensure higher growth in the next few years.*